THE
AUSTRO
LANGU

CW01501074

OF ASIA
AND MADAGASCAR

Some 800 Austronesian languages are spoken in the area extending from Madagascar to eastern Indonesia and to the north to Taiwan and the Philippines. They vary greatly in almost every possible respect, including the size and social make-up of the speech communities and their typological profiles. This book is designed to serve as a reference work and in-depth introduction to these languages, providing a source of basic information for linguists and other professionals concerned with this area. It highlights the cultural and linguistic diversity of this group of languages while at the same time keeping track of their common heritage.

Five introductory chapters on linguistic history, language politics, language endangerment, ritual speech and special registers, and major typological features have the entire area in their scope and provide a balanced and up-to-date discussion of the major issues. The core of the volume consists of grammatical sketches of twenty languages plus three chapters dealing with different aspects of Malay (Old Malay, *Malayic* varieties and Colloquial Indonesian), representing a good cross-section of the linguistic diversity found in the area.

Alexander Adelaar is Associate Professor and Reader in Indonesian at the University of Melbourne, Australia.

Nikolaus P. Himmelmann was previously Professor and Chair at the Westfalische Wilhelms-Universitat, Germany.

ROUTLEDGE LANGUAGE FAMILY SERIES

Each volume provides a detailed, reliable account of every member language, or representative languages of a particular family. Each account is a reliable source of data, arranged according to the natural system of classification: phonology, morphology, syntax, lexis, semantics, dialectology and socio-linguistics. Each volume is designed to be the essential source of reference for a particular linguistic community, as well as for linguists working on typology and syntax.

The Austronesian Languages of Asia
and Madagascar
*Edited by Alexander Adelaar &
Nikolaus P. Himmelmann*

The Bantu Languages
*Edited by Derek Nurse &
Gérard Philippson*

The Celtic Languages
Edited by Martin Ball & James Fife

The Dravidian Languages
Edited by Sanford B. Steever

The Germanic Languages
*Edited by Johan van der Auwera &
Ekkehard König*

The Indo-Aryan Languages
*Edited by George Cardona &
Dhanesh Jain*

The Indo-European Languages
*Edited by Paolo Ramat &
Anna Giacalone*

The Iranian Languages
Edited by Gernot Windfuhr

The Khoesan Languages
Edited by Rainer Vossen

The Manchu-Tungusic Languages
Edited by Alexander Vovin

The Mongolic Languages
Edited by Juha Janhunen

The Oceanic Languages
*Edited by John Lynch, Malcolm Ross &
Terry Crowley*

The Romance Languages
*Edited by Martin Harris &
Nigel Vincent*

The Semitic Languages
Edited by Robert Hetzron

The Sino-Tibetan Languages
*Edited by Graham Thurgood &
Randy LaPolla*

The Slavonic Languages
*Edited by Bernard Comrie &
Greville B. Corbett*

The Turkic Languages
*Edited by Lars Johanson &
Eva Csato*

The Uralic Languages
Edited by Daniel Abondolo

THE AUSTRONESIAN LANGUAGES

OF ASIA

AND MADAGASCAR

Edited by Alexander Adelaar and
Nikolaus P. Himmelmann

Routledge
Taylor & Francis Group

LONDON AND NEW YORK

First published 2005
by Routledge
First published in paperback 2011
by Routledge
2 Park Square, Milton Park, Abingdon, Oxon OX14 4RN

Simultaneously published in the USA and Canada
by Routledge
711 Third Avenue, New York, NY 10017

Routledge is an imprint of the Taylor & Francis Group, an informa business

© 2005, 2011 Selection and editorial matter, Alexander Adelaar and
Nikolaus P. Himmelmann; individual chapters, the contributors

Cartography by Chandra Jayasuriya, The University of Melbourne

Typeset in Times New Roman by
Newgen Imaging Systems (P) Ltd, Chennai, India
Printed and bound in Great Britain by
the MPG Books Group

British Library Cataloguing in Publication Data
A catalogue record for this book is available from the British Library

Library of Congress Cataloging in Publication Data
A catalog record for this book has been requested

ISBN 978–0–7007–1286–1 (hbk)
ISBN 978–0–415–68153–7 (pbk)
ISBN 978–0–203–82112–1 (ebk)

CONTENTS

ILLUSTRATIONS

CONTRIBUTORS

Alexander Adelaar, University of Melbourne, Australia
Jun Akamine, Nagoya City University, Japan
John Bowden, Australian National University, Canberra, Australia
Lea Brown, State University of New York, Buffalo, USA
Adrian Clynes, Universiti Brunei Darussalam, Brunei Darussalam
Aone van Engelenhoven, Leiden University, The Netherlands
Michael C. Ewing, University of Melbourne, Australia
Margaret Florey, Monash University, Australia
James J. Fox, The Australian National University, Canberra, Australia
Nikolaus P. Himmelmann, Ruhr-Universität Bochum, Germany
Anthony Jukes, University of Melbourne, Australia
Marian Klamer, Leiden University, The Netherlands
Paul R. Kroeger, Graduate Institute of Applied Linguistics, Dallas, USA
Michael D. Larish, Hawai'i Community College, Hilo, Hawai'i, USA
Waruno Mahdi, Fritz Haber Institute of the Max Planck Gesellschaft, Berlin, Germany
David Edwin Mead, SIL International, Davao City, Philippines
Alexander K. Ogloblin, University of St Petersburg, Russia
Janie Rasoloson, University of Sunderland, England
Carl Rubino, Linguistic consultant, Washington
Hein Steinhauer, Leiden University, The Netherlands
Graham Thurgood, California State University, Chico, USA
Naomi Tsukida, Aichi Prefectural University, Japan
Catharina Williams-van Klinken, University of Melbourne, Australia
Geoff Woollams, Queensland University of Technology, Brisbane, Australia
Elizabeth Zeitoun, Academia Sinica, Taipei, Taiwan
Erik Zobel, Johann Wolfgang Goethe-Universität, Frankfurt, Germany

PREFACE

The Austronesian language family is famous for its large number of languages and its enormous geographical spread, extending from Madagascar in the west to Easter Island off the shore of Chile in the east. The current volume covers the area from Madagascar to eastern Indonesia and, to the north, to Taiwan and the Philippines. It complements another volume in the same series, *The Oceanic Languages*, which is edited by John Lynch, Malcolm Ross and Terry Crowley. It is designed to serve as a reference work and in-depth introduction to the Austronesian languages found in this area, and it is meant to provide a source of basic information for linguists of all persuasions concerned with the cross-linguistically conspicuous features of these languages.

Some 800 Austronesian languages are spoken in Asia and Madagascar according to the fourteenth edition of the Ethnologue (see Table 2.1). They vary greatly in just about every possible respect. Numbers of speakers, for example, range from a dozen or two in some areas of Taiwan, Sulawesi or the Moluccas to about 80 million for Javanese. In terms of social setting and function, there are the languages of small groups of inner hill people practicing shifting agriculture in Mindanao, Borneo or Sulawesi, the languages of large, highly stratified societies such as Balinese or Javanese, widely used trade languages such as Malay and national languages such as Malay/Indonesian, Malagasy, Filipino and Tetun. All major European colonial powers have been present in the area for extended periods of time. This had far-reaching consequences, not only for the current political structure of the area, but also for the development of the local languages (see Chapter 3).

Linguistic structures are of course also extremely variegated, and they clearly do not adhere to a single typological profile. The Austronesian languages of Asia and Madagascar are most famous for their elaborate voice systems, but such systems are far from general, with some languages not having a single grammaticized voice alternation. Many languages in Taiwan, the northern Philippines and West Papua show intricate reduplication patterns, while other languages (including Standard Indonesian) allow little more than the simple doubling of the base. Chapter 5 provides many further examples of this structural variety. An instructive example of the kind of variation found even among closely related neighboring languages is provided by the combined sketch on Leti and Tetun by van Engelenhoven and van Klinken.

But there are also commonalities due to a common linguistic and cultural heritage. Linguistically the most important of these is the fact that Malay was the common trade language throughout the area for hundreds if not thousands of years. Its influence was weakest in the north (Taiwan, northern Philippines) and its current spread is somewhat more confined in that it is widely known and used only in Malaysia, Indonesia, and Brunei. Nevertheless, Malay influence is noticeable everywhere, and it is not only of a lexical nature but has also had an impact on grammar. Moreover, many different varieties of Malay are found almost throughout the area (see Chapter 7).

The volume highlights the cultural and linguistic diversity of this group of languages while at the same time keeping track of their common heritage. The five introductory articles on linguistic history, sociolinguistics and typology have the entire area in their scope and provide a balanced and up-to-date discussion of the major issues. The core of the volume consists of grammatical sketches of twenty languages plus three chapters dealing with different aspects of Malay, representing, we believe, a good cross-section of the linguistic diversity found in the area.

The selection of the twenty languages represented by grammatical sketches was guided primarily by the aim to provide a comprehensive and informative picture of the linguistic diversity characterizing the Austronesian Languages of Asia and Madagascar. But there were also various other considerations, of which space was naturally a major one. A further basic decision was to opt for longer, more in-depth sketches, thus allowing for the discussion of more intricate structures and analytic problems left out in less comprehensive sketches. This inevitably came at the price of having to cut down the number of languages under discussion. In some instances where there was a real choice, we opted for a language for which there is little descriptive material in English, rather than one for which good recent and up-to-date material is easily available (thus, for example, Javanese was given preference to Balinese, and Mori Bawah to Muna or Tukang Besi, etc.).

Another basic constraint was the availability of suitable authors. Inasmuch as other, more important considerations did not interfere, a conscious effort was made to represent a broad range of descriptive traditions. There are local research traditions, the oldest and strongest ones belonging to the Philippines and Madagascar, although the other countries are catching up fast. Dutch missionary and colonial government linguists have been a major force in Indonesian linguistics. Japanese researchers have had a strong and continuing impact on Formosan linguistics. French linguists have played a major role in Malagasy and, to a lesser extent, Chamic studies. A large part of the currently available work on East Timorese languages is by Portuguese scholars. There is a strong tradition of Russian research on mainland Austronesian languages and major languages in Indonesia. Most work on Philippine languages in the twentieth century was done in the American structuralist tradition initiated by Bloomfield's famous *Tagalog texts with grammatical analysis*. And last but not least, descriptive work has increased significantly in Australia, where resources traditionally focused on the Pacific have recently been redirected towards Southeast Asia.

In order to provide reasonably balanced coverage of the entire area, it was subdivided into a number of smaller regions, the linguistic profiles of which could be represented by one or two languages. Malagasy obviously represents Madagascar; Cham and Moken/Moklen represent mainland Southeast Asian Austronesian languages; Nias and Karo Batak, Sumatra; and so on. Obviously, the parameters underlying the selection as well as the actual selections themselves are potentially controversial in that quite a number of alternative choices are imaginable. With three languages, for example, Sulawesi may appear to be 'overrepresented'. But, in fact, Sulawesi seems structurally the most diverse region in the area, and one could well make a case for including even more Sulawesi languages. The Micronesian 'outliers' Chamorro and Palauan (Belau) do not belong geographically to the area covered here, but structurally and genetically they could, and perhaps should, have been included. These are certainly not the only instances where alternative choices are possible. However, given the constraints on space, available authors, etc. no selection would have been without shortcomings, and we can only hope that ours does not have more shortcomings than any alternative one.

Each sketch provides basic information on a language and highlights characteristics which distinguish it from the other languages represented in the volume. The general outline for a sketch is as follows:

1 *Introduction*: Notes on location, speaker number, subgrouping, dialects, language history, major sources.
2 *Phonology*: Segment inventories, practical orthography, syllable structure, stress, major phonological and morphonological alternations (including reduplication).
3 *Basic Morphosyntax*: Lexical and syntactic categories, basic clause structure, NP-structure, clause-level clitics, auxiliaries, etc.
4 *Deictics and directionals*: Paradigms and major uses of demonstratives and deictic adverbials, major uses and syntax of directionals.
5 *Major verbal alternations*: Voice, stative and potentive verbs, applicatives, causatives, etc.
6 *Nominalizations and nominal morphology*.

This is but a rough guideline to the structure of the sketches. A detailed fixed structure for each sketch would not have been feasible because the languages are so different that even this outline had to be adjusted to several of them. For example, the more isolating languages in mainland Southeast Asia and eastern Indonesia do not have much verbal morphology, and as a result, their sketches do not have a major section on verbal alternations. Similarly, some languages have fairly simple deictic systems. Their sketches consequently have no major section on deictics and directionals, the information on deictics being incorporated into the subsection on noun phrases.

Authors were encouraged to give particular attention to features of 'their' languages which distinguish them from other languages in the collection. This means that some chapters diverge quite significantly from the outline given above. The chapter on Javanese, for instance, has an extra section on Old Javanese tracking changes in the history of Javanese.

All articles are theoretically informed without orientation towards any particular theoretical model. Overly technical and framework-specific terminology is avoided. Common terms which have multiple meanings or are potentially controversial (e.g. *subject*) are given language-specific definitions. Authors were free to use the descriptive terminology they deemed most appropriate. However, this did not include the term *focus*, a term coined in Philippine linguistics to highlight the special characteristics of voice (or voice-like phenomena) in these languages. Its use was strongly discouraged because nowadays there is broad consensus that it is more misleading than helpful (see Chapter 5 for further discussion).

The volume is designed to complement rather than repeat information available in other recent sources on Austronesian languages, which are briefly listed in Chapter 1. Since these resources already include a superb set of maps for the area (the *Language Atlas of the Pacific Area*), a new edition of which is in preparation, we have kept the number of maps to a minimum. The principle of complementation rather than repetition also holds on the level of individual chapters. Colloquial Indonesian, for example, represents an aspect of a standardized, national variety of Malay which is usually ignored in the literature. The chapter by Ewing thus complements the widely available sources on written standard Malay.

N.P. Himmelmann, Bochum
A. Adelaar, Melbourne

ABBREVIATIONS

GLOSSING CONVENTIONS

Affix boundaries are indicated by a hyphen (-), clitic boundaries by an equals sign (=). Infixes in vernacular words are between angled brackets (<...>).

If morpheme boundaries are not indicated in the vernacular line, a colon is used in between grammatical category label and base meaning in the gloss (e.g. AV:get). If one formative represents two or more morphosyntactic categories, a period is used to separate the categories in the gloss (e.g. RLS.UG). Similarly, multiword glosses for single lexical bases are separated by periods (e.g. 'father.in.law').

Glosses for pronouns and pronominal clitics and affixes are as follows:

1s	1st person singular
2s	2nd person singular
3s	3rd person singular
1p	1st person plural
1pi	1st person plural inclusive
1pe	1st person plural exclusive
2p	2nd person plural
3p	3rd person plural

The letters *d* and *t* are used in analogous fashion to indicate respectively dual and trial (e.g. 1de = first person dual exclusive).

The pronominal glosses may be combined with the abbreviations for grammatical functions listed below, for example, 3s.SBJ, 1pi.NOM, 3d.ACC, 1pe.POSS, etc.

ABS	absolutive	AND	andative (directional particle or affix for movement towards speaker)
ACC	accusative		
ACL	accidental		
ACT	actor (pronoun), active (verbal prefix)	APASS	antipassive
		APP	applicative
ADJ	adjective marker	ART	article
ADV	adverb(ial)	ASSPL	associative plural
ADVS	adversative passive	ATD	attitude/attitudinal (deictic)
AGT	agent, agentive	AUX	auxiliary
AL	alienable	AV	actor voice
ALL	allative	BEN	benefactive
AN	animate	BV	benefactive voice
ANAPH	anaphoric (aforementioned)	CAU	causative
		CIRC	circumstantial

CLF	classifier	IMP	imperative
CMPR	comparative	IN	inclusive
CNJ	conjunction	INAL	inalienable
CNTP	contemplated	INAN	inanimate
COMP	complementizer	INCPL	incompletive
CONT	continuative	IND	indicative
COP	copula	INDEF	indefinite
CORE	core argument	INS	instrumental
CPL	completive	INTJ	interjection
CV	conveyance voice	INTR	intransitive
D.ADV	deictic adverbial	INTSF	intensifier
D.PTCL	discourse particle	INVIS	invisible
DAT	dative	INVOL	involuntary
DEF	definite	IPF	imperfective
DEM	demonstrative	IRR	irrealis
DET	determiner	ITER	iterative
DIR	directional	IV	instrumental voice
DIST	distal	JNT	joint action
DO	dynamic verb stem former ('do X')	LIM	limitative
		LK	linker, ligature
DTR	detransitivizer	LOC	locative
DU	dual	LV	locative voice
DUR	durative	MED	medial
DV	dative/directional voice	MIN	minimal (number of pronoun)
DYN	dynamic		
EMPH	emphatic	MOD	mood marker
ERG	ergative	MUT	mutated (see *Nias*)
ESS	essive	NEG	negation
EVD	evidential	NEWSIT	new situation
EVIT	evitative	NFIN	non-finite
EX/EXCL	exclusive	NMIN	non-minimal (number of pronoun)
EXIST	existential		
EXP	experiential (aspect)	NOLD	non-old information
FAM	familiar (term of address)	NOM	nominative
FOC	focus	NOW	now (deictic)
FRM	formal (politeness clitics)	NP	noun phrase
FUT	future	NR	nominalizer
GEN	genitive	NSBJ	non-subject
GER	gerund	OBJ	object
GV	goal voice	OBL	oblique
HAB	habitual	OLD	old information
HAVE	stativizing prefix on nouns (meaning 'have N')	OPT	optative
		OV	objective voice
HES	hesitation	PART	participle
HON	honorific	PASS	passive
HORT	hortative	PFV	perfective
HUM	human	PL	plural
IDX	indexer (see *Leti*)	PM	predicate marker
IMM	immediate (past)	PN	proper or personal name

POSS	possessive	ST	stative
POT	potentive (potential)	SUBJ	subjunctive
PP	prepositional phrase	TOP	topic
PRD	predicative (pronoun, deictic)	TR	transitive, transitivizer
		UG	undergoer
PRF	perfect(ive)	UV	undergoer voice
PRG	progressive	VEN	venitive
PRH	prohibitive	VIS	visible
PRPV	propositive	VOC	vocative
PRS	present tense		
PRX	proximal		
PST	past tense		
PTCL	particle	**LANGUAGE, SUBGROUP AND**	
PV	patient voice	**PROTOLANGUAGE**	
Q	question (particle)	**ABBREVIATIONS**	
QUA	'qualify as, become' (see *Biak*)	CEMP	Central-East-Malayo-Polynesian
QUOT	quotative	CM	Classical Malay
RCP	reciprocal	CMP	Central-Malayo-Polynesian
RCT	recent (deictic)	EMP	East-Malayo-Polynesian
RDP	reduplication	IM	Indonesian Malay
RECOG	recognitional (deictic)	Mkl	Moklen
REL	relative (particle/affix)	Mkn	Moken
REM	remote (deictic)	NJ	New Javanese
RES	resultative	OJ	Old Javanese
RFL	reflexive	OM	Old Malay
RLS	realis	PAn	Proto-Austronesian
RPRT	reportative	PC	Proto-Chamic
RQV	requestive	PDM	Pidgin-Derived Malay
RSN	reason, cause (preposition)	PM	Proto-Malayic
SBJ	subject	PMP	Proto-Malayo-Polynesian
SF	stem forming formative	PWMP	Proto-West-Malayo-Polynesian
SG	singular		
SOF	softening particle	SHWNG	South Halmahera-West New Guinea
SPEC	specific (article)		
SR	subordinator	WMP	West-Malayo-Polynesian

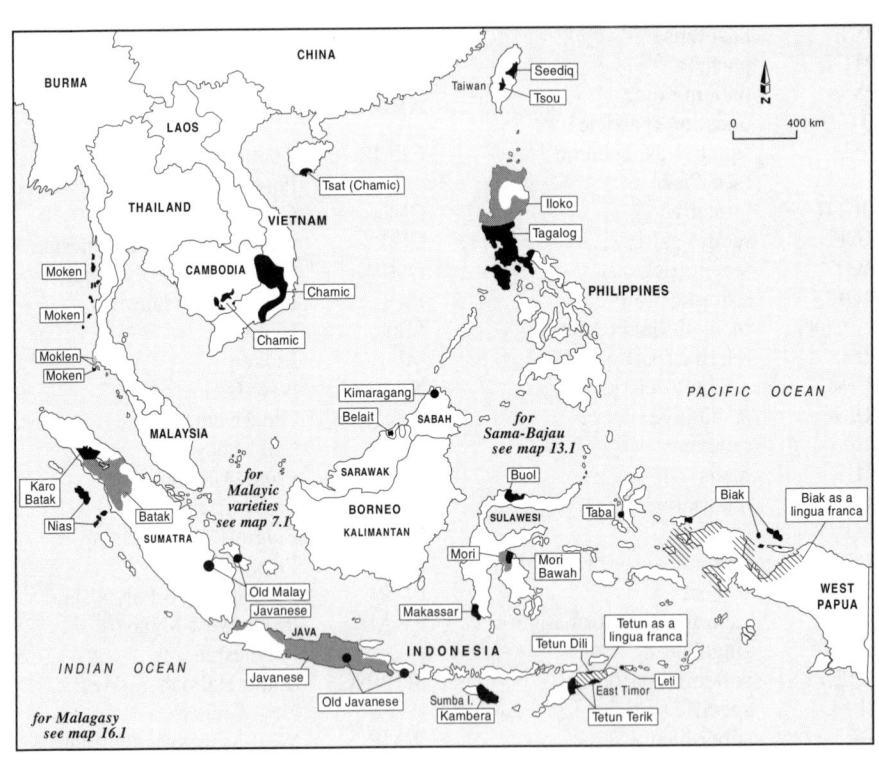

MAP I LANGUAGES DISCUSSED IN THE DESCRIPTIVE CHAPTERS OF THIS VOLUME

CHAPTER ONE

THE AUSTRONESIAN LANGUAGES OF ASIA AND MADAGASCAR: A HISTORICAL PERSPECTIVE

Alexander Adelaar

1 INTRODUCTION

The Austronesian language family has about 1,200 members, which together are spoken by some 270 million people. It is arguably the largest existing language family in terms of the number of its member languages (making up for 20% of the world's languages) and it is second in terms of its geographic spread (after the Indo-European language family). Austronesian languages range from Malagasy (in Madagascar and on the island of Mayotte) in the western part of the Indian Ocean to Rapanui or Easter Island in the southeastern part of the Pacific Ocean, and from the Formosan languages in Taiwan and Hawaiian in the northern reaches of the Pacific to Maori in New Zealand. The Philippines, Brunei, Polynesia, Micronesia, Melanesia and most of Indonesia and Malaysia are traditionally Austronesian-speaking, and there are pockets of Austronesian speakers on the Southeast Asian mainland in Thailand, Vietnam, Cambodia, Burma and Hainan (People's Republic of China). As a result of colonial administration and its aftermath there are also pockets of Austronesian speakers in Sri Lanka (Sri Lanka Malay), South Africa (Malay but now extinct), Netherlands (Moluccan Malay, Javanese and various Moluccan languages), Surinam (Javanese), Australia (Malay, various East Timorese languages) and Portugal (various East Timorese languages).

This chapter introduces the reader to various background aspects of the Austronesian languages of Asia and Madagascar which will not be individually discussed in the chapters that follow. It contains basic source literature on Austronesian linguistics (§2), a short explanation about writing systems (§3), basic information on Proto-Austronesian (PAn) and Proto-Malayo-Polynesian (PMP) grammar and how it might have evolved further into the present-day languages (§4), recent developments in the classification of the Austronesian languages in question (§5), Austronesian homeland and prehistory (§6), and language contact affecting the Austronesian languages west of the Pacific (§7).

Chamorro and Palauan (Belau) are spoken in Micronesia (in the Western Pacific area) and fall geographically outside the scope of this volume. However, they are included in the discussion on classification in this chapter because they are not Oceanic languages. They are both generally classified as West-Malayo-Polynesian (WMP; see Map 1.1).

1

2   IMPORTANT REFERENCE WORKS CONCERNING AUSTRONESIAN COMPARATIVE HISTORICAL LINGUISTICS

Modern Austronesian comparative historical linguistics begins with Dempwolff (1934, 1937 and 1938). This is a reconstruction of PMP phonology following the comparative method. It is based on a systematic comparison of eleven languages, and it includes a PMP lexicon. Although it is in many ways out of date, knowledge of this study is indispensable for a good understanding of the issues and further developments in the field that have emerged since, and it effectively incorporates the works of previous comparatists in the field of PAn phonology and lexicon.

Important expansions and refinements of Dempwolff's phonology are the works of Dyen (1947a, 1947b, 1951, 1953a, 1953b, 1962) and, later on, of Dahl (1976 and 1981). Dyen's merits lie particularly in the inclusion of Formosan languages in his comparisons (1963, 1965a), and in his study of the so-called Proto-Austronesian 'laryngeals' (which are in fact PAn *h, *? (glottals), *q (a uvular stop), and *S; Dyen 1953a). His lexicostatistical classification of Austronesian languages became the subject of much controversy but is nowadays outdated (Dyen 1965b). Dahl (1976) is a balanced criticism of Dyen's work; it focuses on phonological issues but it also discusses grammar and homeland theories and it gives a short historical overview of Austronesian studies. Dahl (1981) is a further elaboration on Proto-Austronesian phonology. Important refinements to PAn and PMP phonology are Blust (1990, 1993a, 1994a). Blust also made major contributions to the reconstruction of PAn lexicon; see his publications in *Oceanic Linguistics* (Blust 1970, 1980a, 1983–4, 1986, 1989). His unfinished *Comparative Austronesian Dictionary* is already partly available on request from the author (Blust to appear). Ross (1995) gives a clear summary detailing all major current issues and developments regarding Proto-Austronesian phonology, morphosyntax and classification.

In spite of comparative morphological studies of MP languages by various previous scholars (e.g. Humboldt 1836–9, Brandstetter 1893), Dempwolff did not venture into a grammatical comparison of MP languages, nor did other scholars for a long time after the publication of his reconstruction. It was not until 35 years later that such a reconstruction (for PAn) was undertaken, and Wolff's reconstruction (1973) was something of a *tour de force* considering the lack of previous systematic attempts based on a representative sample of Austronesian languages, He established a 'Philippine-type' morphology with verbs marked for aspect, mode and semantic role of subject. Several other studies of importance followed, most notably Starosta, Pawley and Reid (1982) and Ross (Ross 1995). The former claimed that the Austronesian verbal voice markers were originally nominalizing affixes which only developed into verbal voice markers after the break-up of PAn.

A recent book edited by Wouk and Ross (2002) contains several chapters dealing with PAn and PMP morphosyntax as well as with the changes that happened after the split-up of PMP. One major change appears to have been the development of an 'Indonesian-type' morphosyntactic model alongside the Philippine-type model inherited from PAn. Here again, the chapter by Ross provides the most comprehensive overview of changes that have taken place since PAn (a topic which will be dealt with in detail in Zobel to appear). Blust (in press) discusses the PAn affixes *ka- and *ka- -an, and various causative prefixes including *paka- (generic causative of stative verbs) which Zeitoun and Huang (2000) claim to be a concatenation of (causative) *pa- + (stative) *ka-. Blust has also written a monograph on Austronesian root theory (1988) and articles on reduplicated monosyllables (Blust 1976a), vocatives (Blust 1979) and Ca-reduplication (1998a).

Recent achievements in the fields of Austronesian language classification will be treated in §5.

In the area of culture history, there are a number of leading publications by Bellwood and by Blust. Bellwood (1997) is a comprehensive multidisciplinary study of the Austronesian past combining research data mainly from archaeology, linguistics and biological anthropology (for further discussion, see §6). Blust's publications cover Austronesian social organization (1976a, 1980b), PMP phratry dualism (1980c), the linguistic value of the Wallace line (1982), the settlement of mainland Southeast Asia (1994b), and the Austronesian homeland and subsequent spread of Austronesian speakers (1984–5, 1999). Other publications of interest are Mahdi (1988, 1994a and 1994b) and various papers in Pawley and Ross (1994).

A number of introductions to the anthropology of Austronesian societies have recently appeared or are about to appear: Fox (1993, 1997), Bellwood, Fox and Tryon (1995), Fox and Sather (1996), Vischer (in press) and Reuter (forthcoming).

Some atlases and wordlists have proven to be of great importance to the study of Austronesian linguistics. Wurm and Wilson's (1975) English–Austronesian finder-list is a very rudimentary tool for finding PAn, PMP and lower order etyma that had been reconstructed before 1975. The list has now become largely outdated. Wurm and Hattori's linguistic atlas of Southeast Asia and Oceania has detailed maps with explanatory notes on the back. Being the first linguistic atlas of such a wide scope, it contains various errors and drawbacks, as pointed out in Steinhauer (1986), but this does not prevent it from being an extremely useful tool in the study of Austronesian linguistics (an updated version is to appear). It is now supplemented by a linguistic atlas including a much larger part of the world and dealing specifically with language contact (Wurm, Mühlhäusler and Tryon 1996).

Tryon et al. (1995) is basically an 'annotated dictionary of synonyms for some 1200 lexical items in 80 different Austronesian languages' (Tryon 1995:1). It has for each language an introduction of varying length and depth providing a map, facts and figures, important bibliographical references and phonological and morpho-syntactical information. It also contains a listing of Austronesian languages which is excerpted from Grimes' Ethnologue and as such gives basic data on alternative names, dialects, classification and location, and general population figures for the area in which each language is spoken. No attempt has been made here to reproduce these data in detail as the same information is contained in the Ethnologue, where it is continually updated (Grimes 2000). Tryon's introductory chapter treats the language family in general and includes an overview of the history of Austronesian studies (a topic not covered here in any major way) (Tryon 1995). It also provides basic information on language distribution, ranking of languages according to numbers of speakers, classification, phonology and grammatical typology, settlement and migrations. And finally, it contains Ross's overview of important trends and issues in Austronesian comparative historical linguistics already mentioned above (Ross 1995).

3 WRITING

Except for Vietnamese, the major Southeast Asian languages have (or had) scripts that were derived from the Grantha- or Pallava-script from South India, which is indirectly related to the North Indian Devanagari script.

In Malaysia, Indonesia and the Philippines, these scripts have almost entirely been replaced by the Roman script. The oldest Austronesian written records are Cham stone inscriptions which date from the 4th century AD and were found in the former Champa empire (nowadays part of Vietnam, see Thurgood, this volume). The earliest Malay inscriptions date from the seventh century AD (see Mahdi, this volume); those in Javanese and Balinese date from the ninth century AD (see Ogloblin, this volume).

Pallava-derived scripts read from left to right, and are neither alphabets nor syllabaries. Each letter (or *aksara*) denotes a consonant followed by a default vowel *a* (some scripts use a default vowel other than *a*); if in a word a consonant is followed by a vowel other than this default vowel, this is indicated by small vowel signs on top, under or after the consonant (in some scripts vowel signs can even occur before – or before and after – the consonant). In some scripts, a dummy letter is used in order to write words beginning with a vowel. If a consonant occurs word-finally, this is indicated by a special following sign (sometimes called the 'vowel-killer'). Finally, clusters of consonants are indicated by writing the consonants under each other, as in Javanese, or by using the vowel-killer, as in the (North Sumatran) Batak script and the (South Sumatran) Rencong script, or they are not indicated at all. The last causes considerable phonological uncertainty and occurs in the Philippine and Buginese-Makassar scripts, which lack a vowel-killer. In Buginese texts, for instance, consonant gemination, final final velar nasals and final glottal stops are not indicated; furthermore, homorganic nasal + consonant clusters can be indicated but this is often not done (see also section 2.5 in Jukes, this volume). The Javanese and Batak scripts are very precise in contrast (although the Batak script does not indicate, (phonemic) stress in Toba Batak).

The Javanese script is also used for writing Madurese, Sundanese and (in a variant form) Balinese. Versions of the Buginese-Makassar script were (still are?) also in use in Southeast Sulawesi (for Wawonii), on Sumbawa (for Bimanese and Sumbawanese) and on Flores (Endenese) (Noorduyn 1993:535).

The different shapes of Pallava-derived scripts have probably developed through the use of various writing materials: for instance, the use of bamboo led to cuneiform letters in the Rencong script, whereas the use of palm-leaf allowed round-shaped letters in the Javanese script. Bataks and people in the Philippines used writing mainly (but not exclusively) for recording magico-religious and medicinal knowledge. The Javanese, Makassarese and Buginese used their scripts for more general purposes.

Pallava-derived scripts are hardly used any more nowadays, although there are still people practicing them in Java, Bali, the Batak regions, South Sulawesi, Mindoro and Palawan (Postma 1971:1). Among the Mangyan in Mindoro there have been initiatives to revive the local variant, which is now equipped with an (unauthentic) *pamudpod* (vowel-killer) to distinguish final consonants and consonant clusters (*A Primer* 1986: Introduction).

In Muslim areas (Malaysia, Southern Philippines, Indonesia), Arabic script came into use in the thirteenth century at the earliest. In East Madagascar it has been in use at least since the fourteenth century. It is often assumed that the Arabic script as used for Malay is originally an Indo-Persian adaptation, but this is not clear from a cursory inspection and remains to be investigated.

Originally designed for a Semitic language structure, the Arabic script (in its various adaptations) causes some inherent orthographic problems for Austronesian languages, where vowels are phonemically more salient and (usually) more variegated than in Arabic.

Some adaptations of the Arabic script are in reality adaptations of Jawi, the Malay version of the Arabic script, or (possibly) of Pégon, the Javanese version. For instance, the Tausug adaptation (used in the Sulu archipelago) follows Malay closely in the way it uses diacritics to indicate typically Austronesian sounds that do not occur in Arabic (such as *c*,*ɲ* and *ŋ*) and in the way it interprets Arabic sounds that do not occur in Tausug or Malay (e.g. the letter for Arabic *f*, which is pronounced [p]). Furthermore, some Tausug technical terms for the vowel diacritics used in Arabic script are derived from Malay, not from Arabic, e.g. *baris* is a general term denoting diacritic vowel signs (< Malay *baris* '1. line; 2. vowel sign'); *dapan* denotes the vowel sign for *u* (< Malay *dəpan* 'in front', cf. Arabic *dammah*) (cf. Cameron 1917). There are also various indications that the Sorabe (or *Volaŋ 'Onjatsy*) script reached Madagascar from Indonesia, and not from East Africa or the Arabian peninsula (Adelaar 1995a:332–339). For instance, the word *soratra* 'writing' is a Malay loanword (Adelaar 1989, 1995a). Metaphors like *reni soratri* 'mother of writing' for main letters and *zana 'tsoratri* 'child of writing' (Dahl 1983:71 fn.7) for diacritics are also found in the terminology for main letters and diacritics in Batak (cf. respectively *ina ni surat* and *anak ni surat*) and Buginese (cf. respectively *ina surə?* and *ana? surə?*). The use of the same metaphors here indicates that, even if the Malagasy did not have a Pallava-derived script, they seem to be an exponent of the writing traditions of the Malays and other Austronesian peoples who throughout the centuries have adapted Pallava-, Arabic- and European writing systems in a continuous tradition of literacy, sometimes carrying over writing conventions from one system into the next.

4 PAn AND PMP LINGUISTIC HISTORY: SOME BASIC INFORMATION

Blust (1999:34) proposes a PAn consonant system which is shown in Table 1.1 in main outline:

TABLE 1.1: PAn PHONOLOGY

	Labial	Dental	Palatal	Palato-velar	Velar	Glottal
Voiceless stops	p	t	c		k	ʔ
		C				
Voiced stops	b	d	z	j	g	
Nasals	m	n	ñ		ŋ	
		N				
Voiceless fricatives		S	s			h
Lateral		l				
Trills		r			R	
Semivowels	w		y			

PAn has moreover the following vowels: **a*, **ə*, **i*, **u*. It has the following diphthongs: *-iw*, *-uy*, *-ay*, and *-aw*.

Earlier interpretations of the PAn phoneme system often distinguish three **d*'s (Dahl 1981, Ross 1995). However, their evidence is based on Puyuma and Paiwan reflexes only. They occur in loanwords (usually borrowed from Puyuma into Paiwan) and should be discounted (Blust 1999:47–51).

The evidence for PAn **c*, **g* and **r* is weak (Wolff 1988; cf. also Mahdi 1988 regarding **r*). Ross (1995:58–59) accepts **c* for PMP only, but argues that there is sufficient evidence from Formosan languages for PAn **g* and **r*, even if they must have had a low functional load.

The nasal **N* is sometimes represented as a voiceless lateral **L*.

The phonology of PMP is somewhat simpler than that of PAn (except for the acquisition of a palatal nasal which in Ross' analysis is a post-PAn development). It generally

TABLE 1.2: PAn VERBAL MORPHOLOGY

	Actor	Patient	Location	Circumstantial
INDICATIVE				
Neutral	\<um\>V	V-ən	V-an	Si-V
Perfective	\<umin\>V	\<in\>V	\<in\>V-an	Si-\<in\>V
Durative	\<um\>-R-V	R-V-ən	R-V-an	Si-R-V
NON-INDICATIVE				
Atemporal	V	V-u	V-i	án-i + V
				(V-áni)
Projective	\<um\>V-a	V-aw	V-ay	án-ay + V
				(V-ánay)

underwent the following changes: PAn *C and *t > PMP *t; PAn *S > PMP *h (a glottal spirant which kept distinct from PAn *h); PAn *N and *n > PMP *n.

The grammars of PAn and of PMP are thought to have had a Philippine-type structure with verbs marked for actor-, patient-, local- and circumstantial voice. Their voice markers could be combined with various other affixes indicating tense, mode or aspect. The PAn verbal paradigm proposed by Ross (2002) distinguishes the voices mentioned above as well as neutral-, perfective- and durative aspect and atemporal and projective mode (Table 1.2).

Some further comments are in order for an accurate interpretation of this paradigm:

1 Although he is very uncertain about the reconstruction of PAn stress, Ross reconstructs oxytone roots (with stress on last syllable) and paroxytone roots (with stress on penultimate syllable). In both cases stress moved one syllable to the right if the root was suffixed.
2 There were four formal verb classes: (a) verbs which took the actor infix \<um\> (as indicated in Table 1.2); (b) verbs without \<um\> affix in actor voice; (c) verbs consisting of a derived stem beginning with (possibly causative) *pa-; and (d) verbs consisting of a derived stem beginning with (possibly stative) *ka-. Both *pa- and *ka- appeared as *ma- in actor voice after infixation of \<um\>.
3 Locative voice was also used as a Benefactive voice.
4 Ross is hesitant about the status of the circumstantial voice in PAn. *Si- (as well as another circumstantial prefix *Sa-) did occur in nominalizations at the break-up of PAn but may have developed into verbal pivot markers only later on, and in individual post-PAn branches. Also, it is probable that the non-indicative circumstantial suffixes developed from independent verbal modifiers and were not yet cliticized to the main verb in PAn.

Typologically, PMP must have been rather similar to PAn. The various differences between PAn and PMP grammar as discussed by Ross (2002) seem to have had little structural impact. In the pronominal system (among some other changes) the PAn polite and neutral series of free pronouns merged in one single free set. Furthermore, PMP seems to have had a somewhat more complex set of noun phrase markers.

However, what is more important for further developments in Malayo-Polynesian languages (and what does not appear from Table 1.3 below) is that, in contrast to PAn, PMP had acquired a variety of derivational prefixes including *paN- [+distributive] and *paR- [+durative], which became *maN- and *maR- respectively in active voice. (However, according to Zobel, fossilized forms of *paR- (and possibly also *paN-) are also attested in Formosan languages, Zobel to appear). These prefixes are widely reflected in WMP languages and (in fossilized form) in Oceanic languages.

TABLE 1.3: PMP VERBAL MORPHOLOGY

	Actor	Patient	Location	Circumstantial
Indicative				
Neutral	\<um>V	V-ən	V-an	i-V
Perfective	\<umin>V	\<in>V	\<in>V-an	i-\<in>V
Imperfective	\<um>-R-V	R-V-ən	R-V-an	i-R-V
Non-indicative				
Atemporal	V	V-a	V-i	V-àn
Projective	V-a	(V-aw)†	V-ay	

† Ross (2002a) is not certain about the PMP status of the patient projective ending *-aw*.

The verbal structure of PAn and PMP has been largely retained in the languages of Taiwan, the Philippines, Sabah, North Sulawesi and Madagascar, which are often referred to as Philippine-type languages (but see HIMMELMANN, TYPOLOGICAL CHARACTERISTICS for a somewhat different definition).

In Indonesian-type languages, i.e. many Austronesian languages spoken in Malaysia and western Indonesia, the PAn voice system is reduced to a simple opposition between actor and undergoer voice. However, different types of undergoers are often distinguished with the help of applicative suffixes, and these undergoers may also appear in subject position if the verb is in undergoer voice. Compare the various derivations of the Indonesian verbal root *tulis* 'to write', which combines with the prefixes *məN-* (actor voice) or *di-* (undergoer voice) and with the suffixes *-i* (locative-oriented) or *-kan* (more general applicative):

(1) a. *ia mənulis* /*məN-tulis*/ *nama-nya*
         3s   AV-write   name-3.GEN
         'She wrote her name.' (actor-voice)

     b. *nama-nya*   *di-tulis-nya*
         name-3.GEN   UV-write-3.GEN
         'She wrote her name.' (undergoer-voice)

     c. *aku mənulisi* /*məN-tulis-i*/ *amplop itu*
         1s   AV-write-LOC   envelope DIST
         'I scribbled on the envelope.' (actor-voice)

     d. *amplop*   *itu*   *ku-tulis-i*
         envelope DIST   1s.ACT-write-LOC
         'I scribbled on the envelope.' ('The envelope was scribbled on by me.')
         (undergoer-voice)

     e. *Ia mənuliskan* /*məN-tulis-kan*/ *saya* *bon*
         3s   AV-write-APPL   1s   receipt
         'He wrote me a receipt.' (actor-voice)

     f. *saya* *di-tulis-kan*   *bon*
         1s   UV-write-APPL   receipt
         'They wrote me a receipt.' (undergoer-voice)

However, note that in Indonesian many transitive verbs do not allow all six combinations, and that the derivations with -i and -kan sometimes have idiomatic meanings (see also EWING, COLLOQUIAL INDONESIAN).

Some languages (e.g. Batak languages, Old Javanese, Balinese, Sasak, several Sulawesi languages) in one way or another represent intermediate stages between the Philippine model and the Indonesian one. Hence it is not quite clear at this point whether it will be possible to establish a clear-cut boundary between the two types, and it is not obvious that their distinction would be a basis for subgrouping arguments (see below).

The historical transition towards the Indonesian model is explained by Starosta, Pawley and Reid (1982) and by Wolff (1996, 2002) through the fact that in Philippine-type (and some other Austronesian) languages, auxiliaries, negators and other preverbal markers can attract person-marking pronouns, while the lexical verb follows in the atemporal form. This is demonstrated with the following two sentences from Cebuano (Philippines), *Gi-tawg-an nako siya* (PST-call-LV 1s.GEN 3s.NOM) 'I called him' and *Wa nako siya tawg-i* (NEG 1s.GEN 3s.NOM call-LV) 'I didn't call him' (Zobel 2000:409). The first sentence is declarative, and is headed by the verb 'to call' which is also marked for tense. The second sentence is a negation; it has the negator as its head, which has the Actor pronoun cliticized to it. The (lexical) verb follows and is not marked for tense. At some point in time, these preverbal modifiers may have been lost, leaving the actor pronoun 'stranded' before the atemporal verb to which it eventually became cliticized or prefixed (Starosta, Pawley and Reid 1982). Or alternatively, the position of the actor pronoun before the atemporal verb may have become generalized to cases in which there was no preverbal modifier (Wolff 1996). There had now arisen an opposition between an actor-oriented neutral verb form and three non-actor-oriented forms of the atemporal verb, and in a last stage, the pattern of three non-actor-oriented forms became generalized over the actor-oriented forms (Wolff 1996). Compare the following schematic development based on Wolff (1996), where (1st person proclitic) ku= stands for any proclitic pronoun.

(2) ku=V   vs. maN-V   →   ku=V   vs. maN-V
    ku=V-i   ---   ku=V-i   vs. maN-V-i
    ku=V-an   ---   ku=V-an   vs. maN-V-an

Languages allowing this proclitic actor marking often do not have a full pronominal set to do so: Toba Batak has only first person proclitics (*hu-* '1s' and *ta* '1pi'), Indonesian has only 1s and 2s proclitics (*ku-* and *kau-* respectively), etc.

Although there are many languages showing some or all these Indonesian-type features, it is unlikely that they are inherited from a common (post-PAn) protolanguage. It is more likely that the relevant changes have happened independently or via contact in the various languages or language groups (Himmelmann 2002, Ross 2002, Wolff 2002).

5 THE INTERNAL CLASSIFICATION OF AUSTRONESIAN LANGUAGES

For a full picture of the main issues and developments in Austronesian classifications the reader is referred to Malcolm Ross (1995). His overview basically serves as a vantage point for the present section, which discusses various publications that have appeared since.

The classification of Austronesian languages proposed by Blust (1977 and later publications) is not without its problems (see below). Nevertheless, it is the one that is referred to most frequently in recent literature, including Ross (1995). It will therefore also serve as a point of reference in this section. Compare the following tree diagram:

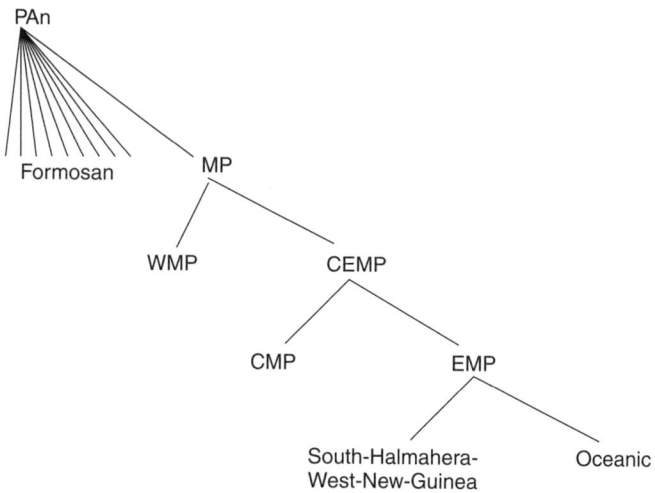

FIGURE 1.1 A TENTATIVE TREE DIAGRAM OF AUSTRONESIAN LANGUAGES (cf. BLUST 1980a AND 1999)

In this tree diagram, the Formosan languages (the Austronesian languages of Taiwan) belong to nine primary branches of the Austronesian family, whereas all non-Formosan languages belong to a tenth primary branch, Malayo-Polynesian (Blust 1999).

Furthermore, according to Blust (1980a), Malayo-Polynesian split into WMP and Central-East-Malayo-Polynesian (CEMP), whereas the latter in turn split into Central-Malayo-Polynesian (CMP) and East-Malayo-Polynesian (EMP).

Languages belonging to WMP are languages of the Philippines and West Indonesia as well as Chamorro, Palauan, Malagasy and Chamic; West Indonesia includes Bali, Lombok, West Sumbawa and Sulawesi, with the Banggai islands to the east and the Tukang Besi – and Muna-Buton islands to the southeast (see Map 1.1).

Languages belonging to CMP are languages of the Lesser Sunda Islands from East Sumbawa (with Bimanese) onwards to the east, and languages of the central and southern Moluccas (including the Aru Islands and the Sula archipelago, but not Obi, Misool or parts north; see Map 1.2).

The South-Halmahera-West-New-Guinea group consists of languages of Halmahera, Cenderawasih Bay as far as the Mamberamo River, and of the Raja Ampat Islands (Waigeo, Salawati, Batanta, Misool) together with their satellites (see Map 1.2).

Finally, Oceanic consists of Micronesian languages, Polynesian languages and the various language subgroups located in Melanesia (Blust 1980a:11–12).

The remainder of this section discusses the structure of some of the higher- and lower-order branches of the above family tree insofar as they have been the topic of recent investigation.

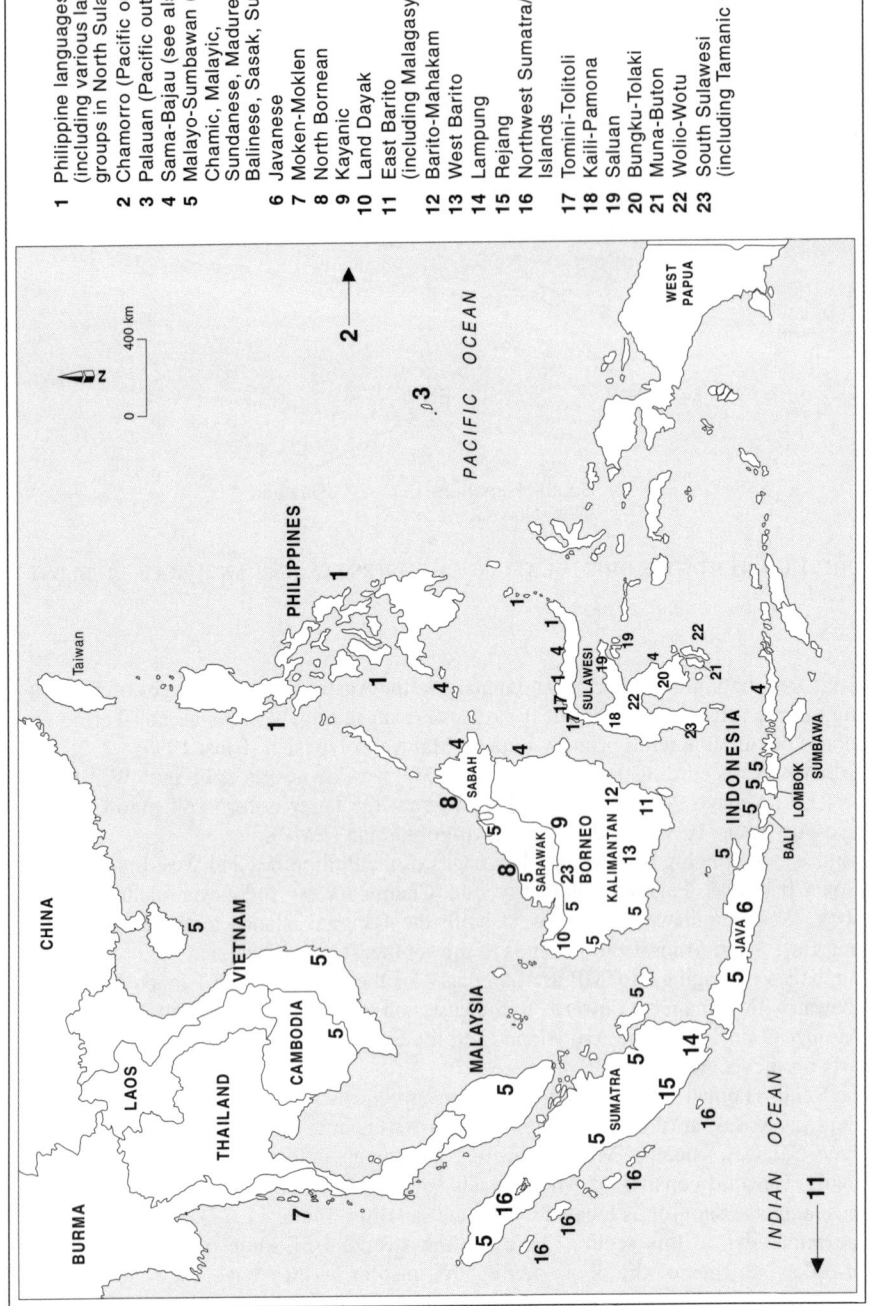

1 Philippine languages (including various language groups in North Sulawesi)
2 Chamorro (Pacific outlier)
3 Palauan (Pacific outlier)
4 Sama-Bajau (see also map 5)
5 Malayo-Sumbawan (including Chamic, Malayic, Sundanese, Madurese, Balinese, Sasak, Sumbawa)
6 Javanese
7 Moken-Moklen
8 North Bornean
9 Kayanic
10 Land Dayak
11 East Barito (including Malagasy)
12 Barito-Mahakam
13 West Barito
14 Lampung
15 Rejang
16 Northwest Sumatra/Barrier Islands
17 Tomini-Tolitoli
18 Kaili-Pamona
19 Saluan
20 Bungku-Tolaki
21 Muna-Buton
22 Wolio-Wotu
23 South Sulawesi (including Tamanic in Borneo)

MAP 1.1   WEST-MALAYO-POLYNESIAN LANGUAGE GROUPS

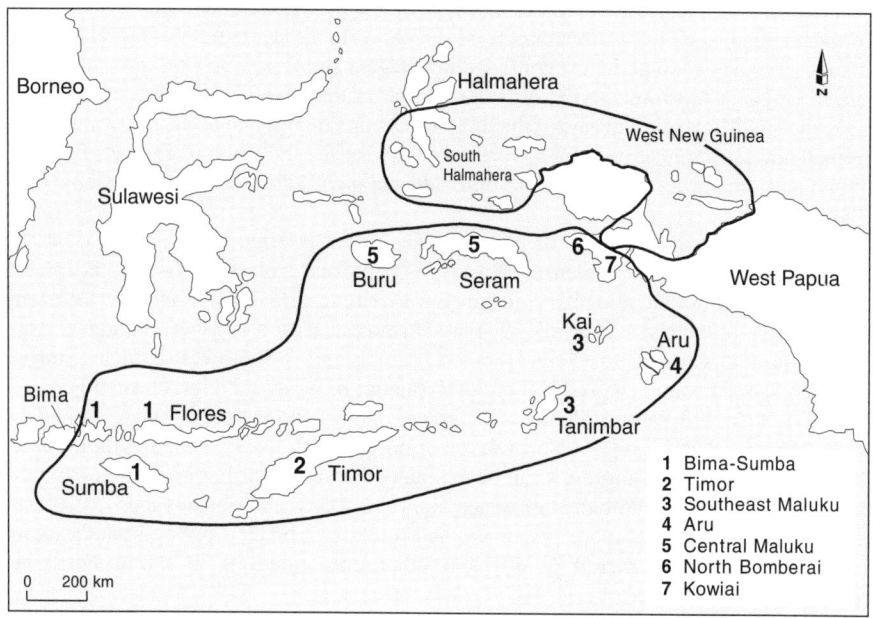

MAP 1.2 CENTRAL- AND EAST-MALAYO-POLYNESIAN LANGUAGE GROUPS

5.1 Formosan languages

There are about fifteen living Formosan languages. There are furthermore some extinct Formosan languages that are on record. As they represent several primary branches in the classification of Austronesian languages, they are of great importance for a comparative-historical study of the language family.

Most Austronesian linguists and archaeologists would agree that the Formosan languages take a special classificatory position within the Austronesian language family and that the original 'homeland' of Austronesian languages must be sought in Taiwan and, prior to Taiwan, in coastal South China (see section 6).

However, there is much more controversy about the internal classification of Formosan languages and about their exact position vis-à-vis the Malayo-Polynesian languages. The nineties have seen some important debates evolving around the following issues:

(1) How many Formosan subgroups are there?
(2) Do the Formosan subgroups together form one single primary branch of Austronesian, or does each of them constitute a primary branch directly continuing Proto-Austronesian?
(3) Do the Formosan languages form a primary branch (or several primary branches) with the Philippine languages, or are they a category on their own within the Austronesian language family?
(4) Are the Malayo-Polynesian languages a totally distinct primary branch within the Austronesian language family, or are they a subgroup within one of the Formosan subgroups?

(1) As far as the number of Formosan subgroups is concerned, until recently the Formosan languages were often classified into Atayalic (Atayal and closely related languages), Tsouic (Tsou and closely related languages) and Paiwanic (Paiwan and closely related languages), following Ferrell 1969. However, this classification has met increasing criticism. More particularly, of the three subgroups mentioned above, Paiwanic is ill-defined and far too heterogeneous. There is a case for the inclusion of Paiwan, Puyuma, Bunun and Amis, but the inclusion of other alleged members is much less evident (Ross 1995:69).

In an attempt to avoid some of the randomness that is often inherent in lexical and typological subgrouping evidence, Blust (1999) makes a classification of Formosan languages based on phonological evidence only. He reaches a division into the following nine primary branches: 1. Atayalic; 2. East Formosan, with a Northern branch (Basai-Trobiawan and Kavalan), a Central branch (Amis), and a Southwest branch (Siraya); 3. Puyuma; 4. Paiwan; 5. Rukai; 6. Tsouic; 7. Bunun; 8. Western Plains, consisting on the one hand of Central Western Plains with Taokas-Babuza and Papora-Hoanya, and on the other hand of Thao; and 9. Northwest Formosan, with Saisiyat and Kulon-Pazeh. Whether each of these subgroups can be maintained requires further investigation on the basis of more than phonological evidence alone. However, the obvious merit of Blust's classification is that it is more systematic and provides a better working hypothesis for further research than Ferrell (1969) and other classifications involving Formosan languages (see below).

(2) Dyen (1963) and Tsuchida (1976) suggested that the Formosan languages together form a primary branch of Austronesian. Blust's classification of Formosan languages into nine primary branches clearly precludes the existence of such a unitary branch. The idea of one primary branch reappears in the nineties in an expanded form (including Philippine languages, see below).

(3) There exist various scenarios involving the subgrouping of Formosan and Philippine languages. Already in 1982 Reid defined Malayo-Polynesian languages on the basis of whether or not they exhibit nasal infixation. This led to a tree diagram which is very different from Blust's, with only the Central Philippine languages belonging to Malayo-Polynesian, and Northern and Southern Philippine languages being placed at various levels higher up in the Austronesian tree. Dyen and Tsuchida (1991) conclude that Formosan and Philippine languages do form a single primary branch on account of the large amount of vocabulary that these languages share. Wolff (1995) reaches the same conclusion on the basis of shared vocabulary as well as of some striking typological similarities in verbal morphosyntax.

Others (Blust 1995, 1999, Ross 1995) reject a Philippine-Formosan branch. Blust is able to show that part of the lexical evidence amassed by Dyen, Tsuchida and Wolff is not exclusively shared between Formosan and Philippine languages and is therefore not critical for a subgrouping (Blust 1995:606–616), nor is there lexical evidence for a Formosan primary branch (Blust 1995:594–606). Another, more general, issue raised by Blust is the lack of directionality inherent in lexical evidence: if Formosan and Philippine languages share a word X and the remaining Malayo-Polynesian languages share a word Y, it cannot always be demonstrated that X is an innovation and Y is a retention, rather than the other way around. Phonological evidence, on the other hand, often provides that directionality: if one language shows *s* and a related language shows *h* in cognate vocabulary, it is phonologically highly probable that *h* is an innovation and not a retention. As to Wolff's argument of shared morphosyntactic typology, Blust points to the fact that other Malayo-Polynesian languages also share this typology (e.g. Malagasy) or at least show traces of it (e.g. Old Javanese, Chamorro or Toba Batak). It must therefore be a retention from Proto-Austronesian.

Blust's arguments are convincing. Nevertheless, the bulk of lexical and morphosyntactic similarities between Formosan and Philippine languages remains impressive and cannot be dismissed altogether as retentions. Some similarities may be due to contact. Contact did take place, not only between Formosan languages and Philippine languages (cf. Wolff 1995:573–574) but also between Formosan languages and other Austronesian languages (cf. §7), and among Formosan languages themselves, which remains an understudied phenomenon. The likelihood of contact cautions against the use of evidence from only a few Formosan sources in conjunction with evidence from (especially northern Philippine) Malayo-Polynesian languages in cases where the possibility of borrowing cannot be ruled out.

(4) It is possible that certain Formosan languages subgroup with PMP. Amis had already been singled out by Reid (1982) as being closer to Malayo-Polynesian than are other Formosan languages. He did so on account of two shared phonological mergers: PAn *C and *$t > t$, and PAn *N and *$n > n$.

As a general theoretical principle, Ross makes a distinction between a subgroup, which refers to a group of languages that have diverged because of a separation, and a linkage, which refers to a group of languages that have arisen by dialect differentiation (Ross 1995:45–47). 'A linkage is formed when a chain of diverse dialects persists for long enough for innovations to diffuse across parts of the chain, in overlapping or linking patterns, without spreading across the entire dialect chain' (Pawley 1999:130). Ross believes 'that Proto-Austronesian had already diversified into a linkage of dialects before the ancestors of Malayo-Polynesian speakers left Taiwan'. It is therefore important to ask from which part of the linkage this pre-PMP must have broken off. Ross thinks that the merger of PAn *C and *t shared by Amis, Bunun and PMP may be a lead: if Amis and/or Bunun also share other important innovations with PMP, they are probably the source of pre-PMP (Ross 1995:69).

Blust (1999:54), however, opposes attempts to subgroup Amis with PMP because phonological evidence clearly demonstrates that Amis belongs to the East Formosan branch (together with Siraya, Basai-Trobiawan and Kavalan). This branch is not only defined by the merger *C, *$t > t$, but also by the more significant change from *j to n, which never occurred in Bunun, nor anywhere else in the Austronesian language family.

This does not entirely exclude the possibility of a close kin relationship between Amis and PMP, but if there is such a relationship, it would involve the entire East Formosan branch, not just Amis. PMP and East Formosan would remain separate subgroups within a primary Austronesian branch, as they are both defined by a number of mutually exclusive phonological changes. The only evidence for such a branch would be the merger of PAn *C and *t to *t. On the other hand, if the phonological basis for an East Formosan–PMP branch is not immediately evident, there is some lexical evidence to support it. Blust himself (Blust 1999:46–47) points out that 'members of [the East Formosan] group have been in continuous contact with the sea since the break-up of PAn'. He gives evidence for the existence of maritime terms that are shared by MP and East Formosan languages but are not found in other Formosan languages.

In view of a possible close link between Malayo-Polynesian and East Formosan languages it is enlightening to have a further look at Siraya, a language which has not yet been fully exploited for its subgrouping evidence. As a member of the East Formosan branch, Siraya shares with Amis the changes *C, *$t > t$ and *$j > n$. The merger of PAn *N and *$n > n$ is reflected in some Siraya dialects, but not in others, which have l, e.g. *malituk* vs. *vanitok* (written 'vannitock') 'silver, money'; *sulat* vs. *sunat* ('sonnat') 'document' (Tsuchida and Yamada 1991:5). The last instance incidentally shows the directionality and relatively recent occurrence of this innovation: *sunat* must be borrowed from Tagalog (cf. *sulat* 'writing' which in turn derives from Malay *surat*, cf. Adelaar 1995a:332). It shows that the change (from a lateral to a nasal) was still in process at the time of borrowing, which must have been after the Malays had begun to extend their trade network to the Philippines.

Siraya shares a number of lexical features with Malayo-Polynesian that are not found in Amis or other Formosan languages, such as (PMP) **Ratus* 'hundred' and (Siraya) *ka-xatux-aŋ* id.; **laba* 'spider' and *rawa* id.; **kuliC* 'skin' and *k-m-urit* 'to peel'; **tuRut* 'follow' and *t-muxot* id.; **qaRus* 'stream' and *axu-aŋ* 'river'. It furthermore shares some irregular phonological changes that are not attested in other Formosan languages, and that are considered diagnostic for PMP by Blust (1995). These changes are syncope of **u* in PAn **paŋudaN* 'pandanus' > *pandal*, and reduction of the medial cluster in **biRbiR* 'lip' > (gospel dialect) *bibix* (but cf. *vixbix* in the Utrecht Manuscript dialect, Van der Vlis 1842). It appears, then, that various members of the East Formosan branch provide evidence for a closer link with Malayo-Polynesian. However, they do so each in their own way, and their evidence does not always seem to corroborate.

5.2 Malayo-Polynesian

Ross (1995:69) states that 'the unity of the Malayo-Polynesian languages is probably not open to serious question, and PMP is readily reconstructible'. However, if the existence of a Malayo-Polynesian subgroup has met relative acceptance among Austronesianists, its internal classification is much less established. Blust's subdivision is weak in several branches, and he himself accedes to the fact that West-Malayo-Polynesian is not a genetically attested subgroup (see below). However, as Ross points out, CEMP is also problematic, and so are its sub-branches CMP and EMP (Ross 1995:81, 82, 85).

5.3 West Malayo-Polynesian

In contrast to Malayo-Polynesian, WMP does not have a clear linguistic foundation. In the literature this category is often referred to as if it were an established subgroup, but the linguistic criteria for it have not been formulated and tested properly, and the genetic affiliations of its putative members remain to be investigated. This is acknowledged once again by Blust (1999:68), who says that this category has been used as a convenient 'catch-all' category for all MP languages other than the CEMP ones. 'No phonemic innovations characterize the WMP languages as a group, and a hypothetical PWMP is thus phonologically indistinguishable from PMP.'

Much more comparative research than has been done so far will be required to sort out the exact genetic relations between these languages. Many of them evidently do cluster in microgroups, but their exact genetic affiliations are very difficult to trace at the higher nodes, and scholars differ as to their classification. In some cases, existing lower-order subgroups and individual languages may be linked up together to form a major branch within WMP, but others, like Chamorro and Palauan (two WMP outliers in Micronesia), and also Rejang (Sumatra), are 'nuclear' members which do not seem to form a further subgroup at all with any particular language within WMP (see further below).

More or less in an attempt to create order in the chaos of subgrouping propositions regarding the languages that are allegedly included in the WMP 'fake' subgroup, Ross (1995:74ff.) distinguishes 24 groups that have been identified as WMP by previous scholars. His list does 'not entail a commitment to their genetic unity' but it is meant to highlight 'current issues' in the classification of languages labeled as WMP (Ross 1995: 74). Ross' 24 subgroups are only a working hypothesis to be used as a base for future adjustment into a more genetic classification. They are:

1 Batanic (south of Taiwan);
2 Northern Philippines;
3 Meso-Philippines;
4 Southern Philippines;
5 South Mindanao;
6 Chamorro and Palauan (outliers in Micronesia);
7 Sangiric (northern Sulawesi);
8 Minahasan (northern Sulawesi);
9 Gorontalo-Mongondic (northern Sulawesi);
10 Sama-Bajaw ('Sea Gypsies' living in Philippines, Sabah, Kalimantan, Sulawesi and East Indonesia);
11 Malayo-Chamic;
12 Moken and Moklen (Burma, Thailand);
13 Northwest Borneo;
14 Land Dayak (Borneo);
15 East Barito (including Malagasy; Borneo);
16 Barito-Mahakam (Borneo);
17 West Barito (Borneo);
18 Lampung (Sumatra);
19 Northwest Sumatra/Barrier Islands;
20 Java-Bali-Sasak (Lombok Island);
21 Central Sulawesi;
22 South Sulawesi;
23 Muna-Buton (Southeast Sulawesi); and
24 Tamanic (central Borneo).

Several publications have appeared since Ross (1995) was submitted to the publisher (which in fact happened several years before it was actually published). It is therefore necessary to adjust Ross' inventory of subgroups and to reduce it to some extent, as I will do in the remainder of this section. I will discuss the various new publications and present evidence for a rearrangement of his inventory in the following way:

1 Philippine languages (including the Sangiric, Minahasan and Gorontalo-Mongondic languages of North Sulawesi)
2 Chamorro (Pacific outlier)
3 Palauan (Pacific outlier)
4 Sama-Bajau (Philippines, Sabah, eastern Indonesia)
5 Malayo-Sumbawan (Malayic, Acehnese and Chamic, Balinese, Sasak, Sumbawanese, Madurese, Sundanese)
6 Javanese
7 Moken-Moklen (Mergui archipelago, Myanmar, insular and coastal West Thailand)
8 North Bornean

    9 Kayanic (central and eastern Borneo)
   10 Land Dayak (western Borneo)
   11 East Barito (southeastern Borneo, Madagascar)
   12 Barito-Mahakam (East Borneo)
   13 West Barito (central and southern Borneo)
   14 Lampung (South Sumatra)
   15 Rejang (Southwest Sumatra)
   16 Northwest Sumatra/Barrier Islands
   17 Tomini-Tolitoli (northwestern Sulawesi)
   18 Kaili-Pamona (western Sulawesi)
   19 Saluan (eastern Sulawesi)
   20 Bungku-Tolaki (southeastern Sulawesi)
   21 Muna-Buton (southeastern Sulawesi)
   22 Wolio-Wotu (southeastern Sulawesi)
   23 South Sulawesi.

5.4 Philippines

Some caution is in order regarding the term 'Philippine languages'. Although Philippine
languages seem to be closely related to each other (see below), in the literature the term
often refers to a typological category, usually including the languages of the Batan
Islands (South Taiwan) and of North Sulawesi (Sangiric, Minahasan and Gorontalo-
Mongondic) but excluding the Sama-Bajau languages (spoken in several spots along
the coasts of the southern Philippines, Sabah, eastern Borneo and eastern Indonesia,
see Akamine, this volume). This configuration of languages also underlies Zorc's
Philippine subgroup (Zorc 1986), although his subgrouping claim is based on lexical
evidence. Some authors also include the languages of North Borneo in this category
(Ross 1995:73).

   Blust (1991) agrees with Zorc's Proto-Philippine subgroup but he makes a different
internal classification. He identifies South Luzon and the Visayan islands as areas
with a low linguistic diversity, which, he asserts, is due to language leveling. He distinguishes a 'Greater Central Philippine subgroup', the members of which all have merged
PAn *R and *g to g and furthermore share some lexical and semantic innovations. These
members are South Mangyan, Tagalog, Bikol, the Visayan languages, Palawanic (but
not Kalamian), the Mindanao languages (but not South Mindanao) and the Gorontalo-
Mongondic languages. The Greater Central Philippine subgroup in turn belongs to
the Philippine subgroup together with all other Philippine languages and with
the Sangiric and Minahasan languages (but excluding the Sama-Bajau languages).
Around 500 BC speakers of Greater Central Philippine began to expand outward from
a center somewhere in northern Mindanao or the southern Visayas. This expansion
affected many other Philippine languages as well as the languages of Sabah but it did
not cause their disappearance. Nevertheless, the influx of lexical borrowings caused
by the Greater Central Philippine expansion makes it difficult to assess the genetic
affiliations of these other Philippine and Sabahan languages (Blust 1991, 1998b:42).

   In accordance with Blust's integration of all Philippine languages and various northern
Sulawesi groups into an encompassing Philippine subgroup, Ross' first five subgroups
together with his seventh, eighth and ninth ones can be reduced to one, the (greater)
Philippine subgroup (1).

5.5 Chamorro, Palauan, Sama Bajau

Various speculations exist as to the classification of Chamorro and Palauan. On the basis of their status as 'WMP outliers', or rather as non-Oceanic languages within Micronesia, they are usually mentioned together, which may unintentionally create the impression that they are closely related. The fact that Chamorro retains the PAn voice markers has sometimes created the impression that it is a Philippine language, or even a Formosan one. Using phonological and morphosyntactic arguments, Zobel shows that both languages are nuclear members within (West) Malayo-Polynesian. Their phonological histories do not link them up with any other Austronesian language or subgroup in particular, and they are both somewhat idiosyncratic representations of the Indonesian-type morphosyntactic model (Zobel 2002). However, see also Reid (2002) who argues that Chamorro is a Philippine language.

Chamorro (2) and Palauan (3) are classified as isolates. The position of Sama-Bajau as a nuclear group remains unchanged (4).

5.6 Malayic languages, Chamic languages and Bali-Sasak-Sumbawa

5.6.1 The Chamic subgroup and its affinity with Malayic

Thurgood (1999) studies the internal relationships and linguistic developments of Chamic languages. In the sixth century AD Cham became the lingua franca of the Champa kingdom in South Vietnam. It was spoken in a largely undifferentiated dialect chain extending along the coast of Vietnam and possibly even connecting with the east coast of Malaysia (see below). Vietnamese territorial expansion towards the South forced Cham speakers to spread over a wider area and the dialect chain developed into distinct Chamic languages including Tsat (Hainan), Rade, Jarai, Haroi, Chru, Roglai, Phan Rang Cham (or eastern Cham) (highlands of southern Vietnam) and Western Cham (Cambodia).

One form of Chamic, later to become Acehnese on Sumatra's north coast, must have split off at an earlier date but already after a dialect chain had begun to form. Remarkably, Thurgood considers Acehnese as a Chamic language directly subgrouping with Roglai. Earlier scholars tended to define Acehnese as an early branch-off within an Aceh-Chamic subgroup, giving it a status co-ordinate with the Chamic subgroup and assuming a breakaway from Acehnese before the Chamic languages had begun to diverge (Thurgood 1999).

Scholars had been speculating on a close relationship between Cham, Acehnese and Malay since Marrison (1975). Blust (1994b) argues for it on the basis of lexical evidence, also speculating that at one point in history (before Thai invasions) there might have been a more or less continuous dialect chain of Chamic and Malayic (see below) along the east coast of Southeast Asia. Although Thurgood (1999) does not directly aim at demonstrating a direct link between Chamic and Malayic, his reconstruction of Proto-Chamic confirms it beyond reasonable doubt.

5.6.2 Subgrouping attempts involving Malayic languages

Malayic is a genetic subgroup which includes Malay and all dialects and languages that are directly related to it, such as Kelantan-, Jakarta-, Kerinci-, Banjar- and Brunei-Malay, and furthermore Iban, Minangkabau and Kendayan. The homeland of Malayic is believed to be in West Borneo, although Malay (at least in its literary and standard forms) most likely originated in South Sumatra (Blust 1984–85, Adelaar 1985, 1992 and to appear). The internal classification of Malayic remains a much disputed topic. Adelaar (1985) divides the Malayic languages into one primary branch including Iban (West Borneo), and another including all other Malayic varieties. This is contested by Nothofer (1988), who proposes a wider Malayic subgroup also including Salako, Embaloh and Rejang. I present evidence against their inclusion (Adelaar 1993, 1994a and below), and I also refrain from an internal classification of the Malayic varieties on the basis of our present – insufficient – knowledge of them (Adelaar 1992).

In recent years, several other internal Malayic classifications have been made by Nothofer (1995, 1997a, 1997b), Collins (1994, 1996a) and Ross (in press).

Collins (1994) believes that the Malay varieties of Borneo form a single subgroup. His 'Proto-Malay' (the exact scope of which remains somewhat unclear, Adelaar 2004:14) existed as one or several closely related Austronesian languages some 2000 years ago. It split into a Sumatra/Malay peninsula branch and a Borneo branch; the Borneo branch developed into a northern branch (including Sambas and Brunei Malay) and a southeastern branch (with Banjar-, Kutai- and Berau Malay). A close historical link between Brunei Malay and Banjar Malay among others appears from their verb morphology, which includes a combination of the locative *-i* suffix with a following beneficiary-oriented suffix *-akan* (Collins 1996a:83–84). Bacan Malay (spoken on Bacan Island, North Moluccas) is an offshoot from Brunei Malay and also allows a concatenation of these suffixes (Collins 1996a).

Nothofer (1996, 1997a) proposes several branches which each correspond to a migration route from a Malayic homeland in Northwest Borneo. One route was in a northeastern direction and then further southwards and westwards along the Bornean coast, generating, among others, Brunei Malay and Banjar Malay. Another route was to the Tambelan and Riau archipelagos and the Malay peninsula. A third route was to the Bangka and Belitung Islands, South Sumatra and Java's north coast. Among the dialects established along the last route, Nothofer (1995) distinguishes some closely related varieties in the 'southwest corner' of the South China Sea, including Jakarta-, Seraway- and Bangka Malay. Nothofer (1997b) argues for a close relationship between these 'southwest corner' dialects and languages of Northwest Borneo (including Iban, Sarawak Malay and Kendayan), Tioman Malay (off the Malay peninsula's east coast) and Palembang Malay. He now classifies the Malayic varieties in West Borneo into West Borneo Malayic and Southwest Borneo Malayic.

As it stands, the data suggest a special genetic position for some of the Northwest Bornean varieties (primarily Kendayan and possibly Iban). Nevertheless, this remains to be demonstrated on the basis of linguistic data of a more critical nature than adduced so far. The evidence for some of the above classifications is too limited and in some cases even contradictory. In Adelaar (2004) I therefore maintain my earlier position that the Malayic subgroup is not capable of internal classification unless more linguistic data become available.

Ross' subgrouping argument is primarily based on morphosyntax (Ross in press). He divides the Malayic subgroup into Western Malayic Dayak (Kendayan) and 'nuclear Malayic' (all other Malayic varieties). Critical for this division is the application of the prefix *di-* as well as some other innovations. In nuclear Malayic varieties, *di-* became a verbal prefix occurring in passive constructions with a third person agent. In Kendayan, however, *di-* has not fully developed into a verbal prefix: the actor noun phrase is allowed to occur between it and the following verb, and it is prefixed directly to the latter only if the actor is not expressed. Compare *di-* in the following sample sentence (from the Salako subdialect): the first *di-* is directly followed by the actor and functions as an actor preposition, whereas the second *di-* functions as an undergoer voice marker which is prefixed to the verb in a clause without explicit actor:

(3) *Taŋkitn-e*   *dah*   *tabà* *di*   *daràh*   *kayo*
    sword-3POSS   already   thick   ACT   blood   enemy

    muŋkus   */N-buŋkus/,*   *anà?* *bisà* *di-buaŋ*
    CPL-wrap   NEG   can   UV-throw.away

'His sword had become thick, covered with the enemy's blood which could not be wiped off.'

Furthermore, nuclear Malay lost the PAn projective suffix *-a* (retained in Kendayan as *-a?*). Finally, according to Ross, nuclear Malayic uses the inflected verb form for atemporal aspect whereas Kendayan retained the original PMP atemporal verb marking, which is expressed by a bare stem (Ross in press).

Ross does not consider Old Malay (cf. Mahdi, this volume) to be a member of the Malayic subgroup, excluding it on the ground that it has not yet acquired the passive marker *di-* and that it still reflects the PMP transitive verbal prefix **maR-* as *mar-*. Contemporaneous Malayic varieties have *di-*, and they reflect **maR-* as *bər-* (or a related form with initial *b*).

As already mentioned, Kendayan may ultimately turn out to represent a separate primary branch. It is very different from other forms of Malayic and its aspectual distinction represents a substantial deviation from the consistent lack of aspect marking on verbs in other Malayic varieties. However, although Ross considers this distinction a PMP retention, it is far from identical with the way temporality and neutral aspect are marked in PMP (including most Malayic varieties), and it might just as well be an innovation. Furthermore, the other arguments adduced by Ross hinge on the assumption that Old Malay is not Malayic, but there are strong arguments favoring its inclusion in the Malayic subgroup. On the one hand, Old Malay shares its phonological history with other Malayic varieties, and on the other hand, both the absence of *di-* and the presence of a reflex of the projective marker **-a* are also observed in (nuclear) Malayic varieties. The prefix *di-* does occur in inscriptions of a somewhat later date, and it is also the only prefix not to have undergone the all-pervasive phenomenon of antepenultimate neutralization of vowels to schwa in most forms of Malayic, which shows that it is a late development. There is therefore little doubt that Old Malay and modern Malay are forms of the same language, in spite of some considerable differences between them. Once this is established, it follows that some critical features used to set off Kendayan against nuclear Malayic are not exclusive to it (Adelaar in press a).

5.6.3 A Malayo-Sumbawan subgroup

Mbete (1990) made a reconstruction of Proto-Bali-Sasak-Sumbawa, which gives ample evidence of the common phonological history of these languages and the lexical innovations they share. Ross (1995) refers to a Java-Bali-Sasak[-Sumbawa] subgroup, while admitting that it is a weak hypothesis.

Apparently Esser (unseen 1930 publication) included Bali-Sasak-Sumbawa as a separate branch in a Javanese-Madurese subgroup (cf. Mbete 1990:10), but he does not do so on his 1938 map which shows the Bali-Sasak-Sumbawa without affiliations to other

Austronesian languages in particular. Blust (1984–85) speculates on a subgroup including Javanese, Balinese, Sasak and Sumbawa, which together with Malayo-Chamic and the various Barito groups would have a common homeland in Southwest Borneo. The basis for this subgroup remains unclear. Its inclusion of Javanese is moreover at odds with an (equally problematic) Malayo-Javanic hypothesis, which in Nothofer's 1985 amendment posits Javanese as a primary branch coordinate with another branch including all other Malayo-Javanic members, including Malay, Madurese and Sundanese.

Similarities between Javanese and the Bali-Sasak-Sumbawa languages appear most clearly between Javanese and high register Balinese and Sasak. Sociolinguistically, however, there is no ground to use the high register vocabularies of these languages for the purpose of investigating their genetic affiliations because high register vocabularies are much more susceptible to borrowing than low register ones (cf. Clynes 1989, Nothofer 1975).

Adelaar (in press b) proposes a 'Malayo-Sumbawan' subgroup, which excludes Javanese and has a Madurese branch, a Sundanese branch, and one branch comprising the Malayic-, Chamic- and Bali-Sasak-Sumbawa languages. By using low Balinese lexicon only, he finds that Balinese, Sasak and Sumbawa share a significant part of their phonological history with Malayic and Chamic. Although some of the phonological developments are not forceful in themselves, or even unique to Balinese-Sasak-Sumbawa and Malayic, their configuration is striking. It includes PMP *w- > ø; PMP *q > *h; PMP *R, *r > *r; PMP *z > *j; PMP *j, *d > *d. In contrast, Madurese, Sundanese and particularly Javanese are phonologically more divergent from Malayic as well as from Chamic or Bali-Sasak-Sumbawa. Furthermore, Balinese, Sasak and Sumbawa have some basic vocabulary in common with Malayic as well as formal similarities in vocabulary such as the metathesis in *qudip 'to live' which is reflected in Malay hidup and in Balinese and Sasak idup (but not in Chamic *hudip). These common features should be seen against the histories of Lombok and especially Bali, where linguistic and cultural influence from Java has been overwhelming since the twelfth century, whereas Malay influence has been relatively weak.

This new subgrouping hypothesis requires a replacement of Ross' Malayo-Chamic and Java-Bali-Sasak groups with (5) Malayo-Sumbawan (including Chamic etc., as defined above) and (6) Javanese.

5.7 Moken and Moklen

Larish classifies the Moken-Moklen languages as a primary ('Moklenic') branch in a macrogroup together with Malay, Acehnese and Chamic (Larish 1999 and this volume).

However, Thurgood emphasizes that the phonological history of these languages sets them off rather sharply from Malayic and Chamic (including Acehnese). He points out that they do not share the change from PAn *q to h, but reflect k instead. Furthermore, both Chamic and Moken-Moklen have diphthongized PAn word-final high vowels, but they have done so each in very different ways (Thurgood 1999:58–59). One could add some other obvious differences in phonological history, such as PAn *w-, which became Moken and Moken b- whereas *w- was lost in Malayic and, after a following *a became colored to u, in Chamic; PAn *R, which became Moken and Moklen l but in Malayic and Chamic became r.

Moken-Moklen languages here will keep their status as a separate subgroup (7); more intensive research is required in the future to determine their position vis-à-vis Malayic and Chamic.

5.8 North Bornean

The Sabahan languages (Banggi, Dusunic, Murutic, Paitanic, Ida'an, Tidong) show various striking similarities with Philippine languages. They have a Philippine-type morphosyntax. They furthermore share some vocabulary, such as a reflex of *siam* for 'nine', and some phonological developments exhibiting, for instance, g for PAn *R. Blust (1998b) points out that the morphosyntactic patterns of Sabahan are also shared by non-Philippine languages such as the languages of Formosa, Malagasy, Chamorro and Toba Batak. They are very likely a retention from Proto-Austronesian and therefore not diagnostic for subgrouping. The g reflex for *R, although widely attested among Sabahan languages, is not attested in all of them and is not criterial for the Sabahan subgroup as a whole. Blust makes further investigations into the genetic affiliations of Sabah languages and finds that they have most of their critical phonological developments in common with the languages of North Sarawak (Kelabitic, Kenyah, Berawan-Lower Baram and Bintulu). These developments are: 1. Loss of *h; 2. Schwa epenthesis; 3. Consonant fortition; 4. Loss of initial *q; 5. reduction of consonant clusters; and 6. antepenultimate neutralization. Especially significant for a classification are schwa epenthesis and consonant fortition as well as the conditions under which these changes took place. Sabahan languages seem to share with Philippine languages the merger of an original palatal and dental series. However, on closer inspection it appears that the parts of this merger are either widely attested among Austronesian languages in general (i.e. the merger of *c and *s), or they are not clearly attested in Philippine languages (i.e. the merger of *z and *d and of *ñ and *n). Sabahan languages do share lexical innovations with both North Sarawakan languages and Philippine languages, but here again it appears that the number of shared innovations is higher with North Sarawak languages than with Philippine ones. Sabahan languages must have been affected by lexical diffusion coming from both other groups, as Blust (1998b) argues. All these facts taken together clearly show that Sabahan languages have more linguistic history in common with the languages of North Sarawak than with those of the Philippines, and Blust proposes a North Borneo subgroup. He points out that if Sabahan languages share lexicon with Philippine languages this is almost always with members of the Greater Central Philippines group. The reflex g for *R shown in many Sabahan languages is also a typical feature of Greater Central Philippines languages. Blust attributes these factors to contact-induced change as a result of the Greater Central Philippines expansion (see above). This expansion also had far-reaching contact effects in the peripheral parts of the Philippines and in North Sulawesi.

It is noteworthy that Blust's North Sarawak branch of North Borneo languages does not include the Kayanic languages (Kayan, Modang, Murik). In Hudson's (1978) classification of Bornean languages, Kayanic and Kenyahic languages belong together in the same lower-order subgroup (compare also Rousseau 1988:5), but this is rejected by Blust (Blust 2002:29–30). One of the developments that clearly set off Kayanic languages from Kenyahic ones is the fact that they often exhibit a final glottal stop where the latter have ø, and vice versa. Blust explains this as the result of an ordered set of phonological changes in Kayanic: 1. vowels were lengthened before a final glottal stop (< PAn glottal stop); 2. all words acquired a final glottal stop; 3. short vowels before a final glottal stop were lowered; and 4. final glottal stops were lost after long vowels. The genetic affiliations of Kayanic obviously need further study but for the time being it seems safe to give it a separate subgroup status. Ross' (1995) Northwest Borneo group is replaced by North Borneo (8) and Kayanic (9).

5.9 Other Bornean subgroups

Ross (1995) lists four other Bornean subgroups which are maintained here, to wit Land Dayak in western Borneo (10), East Barito in Southeast Borneo (including Malagasy in Madagascar) (11), Barito-Mahakam in eastern Borneo (12) and West Barito in central and southern Borneo (13).

With regard to East Barito, Dahl (1991) claimed that the Lom language on Bangka Island belongs to this group and is originally a form of Maanyan. However, it is clearly Malayic according to Nothofer (1994) and Adelaar (1995a).

5.10 Lampung, Northwest Sumatra/Barrier Islands, Rejang

Ross (1995) lists Nothofer's (1985) Northwest Sumatra/Barrier Islands group which includes the Batak languages and Gayo in Northwest Sumatra, and Nias, Mentawai, Sichule, Simalur and Enggano on the islands of the same name off Sumatra's west coast (14). He lists Lampung in South Sumatra as an isolate (15).

Rejang, another South Sumatran language (spoken in Bengkulu Province in southwest Sumatra) has a rather unique phonological history and should also be treated as an isolate (16) in the list of subgroups (cf. Blust 1984).

5.11 Sulawesi subgroups

Ross (1995) lists six independent Sulawesi subgroups: Sangiric (northern Sulawesi); Minahasan (northern Sulawesi); Gorontalo-Mongondic (northern Sulawesi); Central Sulawesi; South Sulawesi; Muna-Buton (Southeast Sulawesi). But other authors usually distinguish around ten subgroups. For instance, Sneddon (1993) lists the following ones: 1. Sangiric; 2. Minahasan; 3. Gorontalo-Mongondic; 4. Tomini (northern part of Central Sulawesi); 5. Bungku-Tolaki (eastern part of Central Sulawesi); 6. Kaili-Pamona (western part of Central Sulawesi); 7. Saluan (eastern tip of Central Sulawesi); 8. Banggai (id.); 9. Muna-Buton (Southeast Sulawesi); and 10. South Sulawesi. A slightly different constellation of nine subgroups is listed in Noorduyn's (1991) bibliography.

As mentioned above, Blust (1991) considers the Sangiric, Minahasan and Gorontalo-Mongondic languages as belonging to the Philippine group. The South Sulawesi languages will be discussed in the next subsection.

Van den Berg (1996) tries to combine the Kaili-Pamona, Bungku-Tolaki and Muna-Buton languages in a 'Celebic' group on the basis of various phonological changes: the loss of final consonants and of consonant clusters, the monophthongization of PMP final diphthongs and the shift of PMP to a back rounded vowel. However, the loss of final consonants appears to be due to an areal feature in most of the Sulawesi languages, and it postdates the emergence of the various Sulawesi subgroups (cf. Sneddon 1993). Sneddon concedes that this process may have begun in a stage ancestral to Kaili-Pamona, Bungku-Tolaki and Muna-Buton, but Mead (1996) demonstrates that this is not the case, which weakens Van den Berg's subgrouping claim.

On the basis of some sound developments in the Wolio-Wotu languages (consisting of Wolio, Wotu, Kamaru, Laiyolo and Kalao), Donohue (in press) gives them a separate subgrouping status from the Muna-Buton group. In Donohue's view, Wolio-Wotu may be closer to the Kaili-Pamona group, while Mead adduces evidence for macrogrouping Muna-Buton with Bungku-Tolaki languages (Mead 1998 and 2002).

In a recent paper presented at the 9th International Conference of Austronesian Linguistics in Canberra (2002), Van den Berg (in press) accepts the exclusion of Wolio-Wotu from the Muna-Buton group. He gives some phonological and grammatical arguments in support of the reduced Muna-Buton group, which in his analysis includes the Tukang Besi languages, albeit in a separate sub-branch.

In another paper presented at the same conference, Mead (in press a) has a closer look at the Saluan group, which is defined by eleven sound changes that its members have undergone since PMP. He includes Banggai in the group and argues that together with Balantak it forms a separate branch vis-à-vis the other Saluan languages, which together form another (western) branch. Mead (in press b) furthermore combines Bungku-Tolaki, Muna-Buton and Tukang Besi in a Southeastern Celebic group. This group shares the first eight sound changes that are diagnostic for Saluan-Banggai, and, according to Mead, forms Eastern Celebic with the latter. He speculates that the Tomini-Tolitoli, Kaili-Pamona and Wolio-Wotu groups may belong together in the western branch of an encompassing Celebic macrogroup. In so doing he in some way takes up Van den Berg's idea of a Celebic group (Van den Berg 1996), although he arrives at a different configuration of Sulawesi micro-groups.

Mead's inclusion of Banggai in a Saluan-Banggai group is convincing. Some of his eleven sound changes are of a general nature, but others are more diagnostic, such as (PMP) *awa > Saluan *oa. On the other hand, his evidence for a direct link between Banggai and Balantak is weak because it essentially depends on one change, the lowering of final *u to /o/ (the merger of *r and *R being of rather low diagnostic value). Except for the South Sulawesi, Gorontalo-Mongondic, Sangiric and Minahasan languages, languages of Sulawesi reflect PMP *j as either /y/ or ø. Mead reasonably assumes that in the case where *j became ø, it must first have changed to *y before it finally disappeared. Such a course of change strengthens the case for his Celebic macrogroup considerably. Other critical sound changes for it are PMP *ə > *o, PMP *d > *r, PMP *-aw, *-əw > *-o and PMP *-ay, *-əy > *-e (note that *-əw and *-əy are not distinguished from *-aw and *-ay respectively in Blust (1999)).

The various subgrouping hypotheses above are difficult to assess. There seems to be agreement on Donohue's claim that the Wolio-Wotu languages should be separated from the original Muna-Buton group. Progress has been made on the establishment of a possible Celebic subgroup, but it may still be too early to accept Mead's definition of it without additional evidence from various linguistic levels, especially regarding the inclusion of Tomini-Tolitoli, Kaili-Pamona and Wolio-Wotu. In the mean time, Ross' (1995) Central Sulawesi and Muna-Buton groups are too general. To remain on the cautious side, they are replaced by (17) Tomini-Tolitoli, (18) Kaili-Pamona, (19) Saluan, (20) Bungku-Tolaki, (21) Muna-Buton, and (22) Wolio-Wotu. While most of these are reasonably well established subgroups, the genetic unity of Tomini-Tolitoli has in fact never been proven, and it is not obvious that Tolitoli forms a low-level subgroup with the Tomini languages (see Himmelmann 2001:20).

5.12 A Tamanic-South Sulawesi subgroup

The Tamanic languages (Embaloh, Taman, Kalis) are spoken at the upper reaches of the Kapuas River in the northeastern part of West Kalimantan, Borneo. Ross (1995) lists them as an independent subgroup within WMP. However, there is substantial phonological, lexical, semantic and morphosyntactic evidence linking these languages directly to the South Sulawesi subgroup, and more particularly to Buginese (Adelaar 1994a). South Sulawesi languages are spoken in the southwestern peninsula of Sulawesi and comprise Makassar, Buginese, Seko and the northern subgroup (Sa'dan Toraja, Mandar, Massenrempulu, Mamuju, and Pitu Ulunna Salu) (Sneddon 1993:21).

Typical phonological innovations shared by Tamanic and Buginese are *$j > s$, loss of *p in various cognate forms, lenition or loss of *b, merger of *z and *d into d- and -r-, and monophthongization and heightening of final diphthongs. Exclusively shared lexical innovations include (Embaloh and Buginese) *sao* 'house', *si-ala* 'get married', *lino* '(the physical) world', Embaloh *liluʔ* and Buginese *lilu* 'forget', Embaloh *iŋar* 'nose' and Buginese *iŋəʔ*, Embaloh *sera* 'one' and Buginese *a-sera* [(ten) minus one=] 'nine' etc. An important grammatical innovation shared with South Sulawesi languages is the presence of four series of pronouns (free, absolutive, ergative and possessive). These series by and large reflect the Proto-South-Sulawesi pronominal system as reconstructed by Mills (1975). Similar pronoun systems are also found elsewhere in Sulawesi and the Philippines but in central Borneo there seems to be no system with the same formal and structural similarities.

Many of these innovations are idiosyncratic and regular enough to rule out chance resemblance as an explanation. Language contact is also an unlikely explanation considering that the Tamanic communities live deep in the almost impenetrable heart of Borneo. Furthermore, Tamanic languages as a rule maintained PAn root-final consonants whereas South Sulawesi languages (especially Buginese) have often lost them. Although some Buginese did migrate to Borneo, they have done so in fairly recent times (seventeenth century AD and later) and they are not to be confused with the Tamanic communities under discussion. Adelaar (1994a) concludes that Tamanic languages belong to the South Sulawesi language group and that they subgroup more directly with Buginese. Speakers of Proto-Tamanic must have left South Sulawesi in ancient times, long enough ago to wander (probably in stages) to the remote area where they have ended up today and to lose collective memory of the event. The inclusion of Tamanic in the South Sulawesi group brings the number of WMP subgroups to (23).

5.13 CEMP and CMP

Blust (1993b) endeavors to give a stronger foundation to his CEMP, CMP and EMP hypotheses put forward in Blust (1978). (This 1993b article was already referred to by Ross (1995) as 'Blust 1990a', an unpublished manuscript.) Blust collects a set of phonological, lexical, morphosyntactic and semantic innovations that are unique to CEMP languages. He also presents such evidence for the establishment of CMP, and he tries to make a clearer boundary between CMP and South-Halmahera-West-New-Guinea languages in the West Papua (West New Guinea) area by showing that the Northern Bomberai languages (Sekar, Onin and Uruangnirin, spoken on the Bomberai peninsula on the south coast of West Papua) are not South-Halmahera-West-New-Guinea but CMP. There is some strong evidence that they directly subgroup with Yamdena (spoken on the Tanimbar Islands, Southeast Moluccas) and must be the result of a migration from the Tanimbar Islands to West Papua. At a higher level, Yamdena and Northern Bomberai subgroup with Kei and Fordata (Southeast Moluccas), forming what could be defined as the 'Southeast Maluku' subgroup (not to be confused with 'Southeast Maluku' as defined by Mills (1991)).

Blust admits that the innovations that are critical for CMP do not always feature in each member of the proposed CMP group. For instance, the truncation of PMP word-final glides, (cf. PMP *-ay*, *-aw* > -a, and PAn *-uy* > -u) is reflected in many, but not all, alleged CMP languages. Their overlapping distribution shows that CMP languages must have developed from a linkage, and not from a (basically uniform) protolanguage. But, as implied in Ross (1995:82), the partly overlapping distribution of various innovations does weaken the argument for CMP.

According to Blust, CEMP is easier to demonstrate than CMP. Nevertheless, the morphosyntactic evidence for CEMP is also problematic. Blust adduces two innovations: (1) the use of proclitic subject markers on the verb; and (2) a morphologically marked distinction between alienable and inalienable possession. He points out that the proclitic subject markers in Moluccan languages have a different form than those in West Melanesian languages. It is therefore possible that the subject markers in these two areas are not commonly inherited but the result of a convergent development, which potentially weakens the evidence for CEMP. Moreover, proclitic subject markers are also found in many Sulawesi languages, as Blust admits, and in Barrier Island languages (see JUKES, MAKASSAR; MEAD, MORIBAWAH; BROWN, NIAS). These are WMP languages, and although, here also, the sets are formally different than the Moluccan and West Melanesian ones, their occurrence shows that the phenomenon of proclitic subject marking is not unique to CEMP.

Blust considers the distinction between alienable and inalienable possession as stronger evidence. Nevertheless, this distinction is not unique to CEMP either. It has also been observed in Puyuma (Tsuchida 1995), where, however, it is expressed in a formally different way. Historically, it can also be demonstrated to have happened in various Bidayuh (or Land Dayak) languages in West Borneo. These languages have a petrified suffix *-n* or *-tn* (both < *-n*), which can be explained as a historical inalienable noun suffix attached to terms for body-parts and kinship-relations ending in a vowel. Compare for instance the following evidence from Sungkung, which is spoken in six villages on the Sungkung mountain ridge in the Sambas and Sanggau regencies of West Kalimantan Province (Indonesia) along the Sarawak border (Adelaar personal fieldnotes):

PAn		> Sungkung	
maCa	'eye'		*batətn*
qaCəy	'heart'		*atitn*
qapəjuS	'bile'		*əmpudutn*
bulu	'body hair'		*burutn*
paqa	'thigh'		*pəʔətn*
bana	'husband'		*banən*
sawa	'wife'		*sawətn*
(ən)pu	'grandchild'		*sikutn*
su-aji	'younger sibling'		*siditn*

Note that Sungkung final nasals become preploded (*-n* > -tn) unless the preceding consonant is also a nasal. This inalienable suffix does not appear in body-part and kinship terms already ending in a consonant, which includes non-historical glottal stops as in *sinaʔ* 'mother' (< *si* + *ina*) and *samaʔ* 'father' (*si* + *ama*).

The suffix is also found in other Bidayuh languages such as Biatah (cf. Nais 1988) and Singhi (Reijffert 1956), which are both spoken in Sarawak. However, not all Land Dayak languages have the inalienable suffix, and those that have do not always show the same distribution as found in Sungkung. But then again, lack of uniformity in exhibiting an alienable/inalienable distinction – as well as in the extent to which it is exhibited – is also typical for CEMP languages. The innovation of a grammaticalized distinction between alienable and inalienable possession would be strong subgrouping evidence for CEMP if it were a single construction type involving the same basic marker(s) throughout the area where the alleged CEMP languages are spoken. What one finds instead, however, is quite a number of significant differences in possession constructions, as appears from a brief comparison of the relevant sections in STEINHAUER, BIAK; KLAMER, KAMBERA; WILLIAMS-VAN KLINKEN AND VAN ENGELENHOVEN, LETI AND TETUN; BOWDEN, TABA.

Ross (1995) also doubts the evidence for EMP: although the two putative branches within this subgroup, the South-Halmahera-West-New-Guinea group and Oceanic, are each phonologically well-attested, there is essentially no phonological evidence to support the claim that together they form an exclusive higher-level subgroup (Ross 1995:84–85).

Ross does not give a further division of the South-Halmahera-West-New-Guinea group. On the basis of the same practical criteria he used for establishing 24 WMP subgroups, he divides CMP into seven subgroups, as follows:

1 Bima-Sumba (eastern Sumbawa, Sumba, Flores);
2 Timor (Timor and Waimaha groups);
3 Southeast Maluku (Tanimbar and Kai Island groups);
4 Aru;
5 Central Maluku (Seram, Buru and their offshore islands);
6 North Bomberai (south coast of MacCluer Gulf, West Papua); and
7 Kowiai (south coast of Bird's Neck, West Papua).

Some further subgrouping has been done with regard to the Timor group. Van Engelenhoven puts Tetun and Waimaha together with the 'Luangic-Kisaric' languages in a South-East-Timor sub-branch of the Timor group. The Luangic-Kisaric languages are further divided into Kisaric (Roma and Kisar) and Luangic (Wetan, Leti and Nuclear Luangic, which in turn consists of Luang, Lakor and Moa) (Van Engelenhoven 1995:17). This classification also seems to be borne out by lexicostatistical percentages presented in Taber (1993).

In a rather unusual approach, Hull (1998) considers the Timor languages to be heavily creolized, linking them genetically with the 'Celebic' languages (primarily the Muna-Buton and Bungku-Mori languages) and relegating CMP features to a substratum.

To summarize, the classification of Austronesian languages remains uncertain. A systematic application of phonological criteria to Formosan languages has shown that their previous division into three primary branches does not hold and that there are probably many more primary branches. The Malayo-Polynesian subgroup seems well-defined, but its internal structure remains unclear. The South-Halmahera-West-New-Guinea and Oceanic subgroups are reasonably well-founded, and some progress has been made in lower-level subgrouping. However, a major branch such as WMP misses a linguistic foundation. Other major branches, such as CEMP, CMP and EMP, also remain contested and need further investigation.

6 THE AUSTRONESIAN HOMELAND AND AUSTRONESIAN MIGRATIONS

The homeland issue is much less controversial among scholars than is the issue of classification. The study of Austronesian prehistory is moreover remarkable for the successful multidisciplinary approach that has been taken by various linguists, archaeologists and anthropologists over the last two decades.

It is generally accepted among these scholars that Taiwan is the area from which Austronesian speakers dispersed, if it is not the Austronesian homeland itself. However, before the Neolithic Austronesians settled in Taiwan more than 6000 years ago they must have come from coastal South China (from present-day Fujian or Guangdong, Bellwood 1997:214).

Bellwood (1997) provides an updated and comprehensive multidisciplinary account of Austronesian prehistory based on combined research results from archaeology, linguistics, biological and social anthropology, and the paleoenvironmental sciences. It forms the basis of the present section.

Crucial for an appreciation of this prehistory is the development of agriculture in East Asia. Bellwood reminds us that agriculture originated autonomously in only a very few centers in the world. The areas around the Yellow River and Yangzi River seem to represent such a center (or possibly two independent centers) in East Asia. Millet was first cultivated along the Yellow River, and rice in the Yangzi River basin. These rivers run through much of central China, but 8000 years ago, when systematic agriculture began in this region, it was populated by a variety of ethnic groups. Some of these may have been among the ancestors of modern Chinese, but others must have been more Southeast Asian in cultural affiliation (Bellwood 1997:205).

From here agriculture must have spread to other parts of East Asia, including Southeast Asia. It must have spread to large parts of the present-day Austronesian world via Taiwan, where it was most prominent in the western part of the island. Neolithic sites representing the so-called Ta-pen-k'eng (Da-ben-keng) culture usually have radiocarbon dates going back to some 5000 years ago, although some sites are as old as 6300 years. The Ta-pen-k'eng culture is clearly linked to mainland Chinese culture complexes, and it is characterized by cord-marked and incised pottery and polished stone tools. It diversified later on in various other cultures in Taiwan, some of which are identified by Bellwood as Austronesian. These cultures include evidence for red-slipped and stamped pottery, and for 'stone net weights, hoes and possibly bones of domesticated pigs and dogs' (Bellwood 1997:219). Strangely enough, for a long time Ta-pen-k'eng and related sites did not provide evidence for cereal cultivation prior to 4500 years ago in Taiwan. However, Tsang (2001:11) recently found charred rice grains in a newly discovered Ta-pen-k'eng site, the Nan-kuan-li site near Tainan in south-western Taiwan.

The cultures that succeeded Ta-pen-k'eng in Taiwan have clear relatives in the Philippines and Indonesia (Bellwood 1997:ch. 7). Various Neolithic sites dating as far back as 2500 BC are found in the Philippines (cf. Dimolit, an open site in northern Luzon). Sites are found in Indonesia in the Talaud Islands north of Sulawesi (possibly 2500 BC but uncertain), in west Central Sulawesi (undated), on Kayoa Island to the west of Halmahera in the Moluccas (1200–300 BC), in Sabah (1500–500 BC), and on Timor (2500–2000 BC). These sites leave a fairly clear trail of red-slipped ceramics including decorated and (often) globular vessels, and furthermore of neolithic stone flake tools and bones of pigs and other animals.

After circa 1400 BC this chain of historically related archaeological sites continues eastward through Melanesia and (past the Solomons) into previously uninhabited territory. A clear series of sites ranges over a distance of 6500 km from the Admiralty Islands north of New Guinea to Samoa, representing the so-called Lapita culture which existed between 1400 and 800 BC. These thoroughly studied sites are well-dated and again contain red-slipped pottery as well as the bones of domesticated animals (including pigs, dogs and fowl).

The trail of sites becomes less clear towards western Indonesia. Java and Sumatra appear to be rather poor in Neolithic sites, which may be because 'Neolithic sites along former northern coastlines are now likely to be buried under many meters of alluvium and beneath the water table…and hence unavailable for archaeological research'

(Bellwood 1997:231). The Neolithic sites in peninsular Malaysia are unrelated to the Austronesian ones found in Sabah, Sulawesi and East Indonesia: they are linked to the immigration of Austro-Asiatic speakers. The origins of the latter, incidentally, also seem to be in present-day South China (Bellwood 1997:ch. 8).

The early Austronesians combined agriculture with maritime subsistence, animal husbandry (involving pigs, but also dogs and possibly other animals), and a technology that included canoes, wooden houses and pottery (possibly also weaving technology). Although generally agriculturalists, Austronesian peoples often continued to combine their agricultural skills with other economic resources such as hunting and fishing. Comparative linguistic evidence suggests that the Austronesians planted rice, sugarcane and gourds (Bellwood 1997:20). However, the rice that they must have brought along with them when they moved southward did not spread into Oceania and had difficulty at first adapting to large parts of insular Southeast Asia because equatorial climates were not favorable to its cultivation.

The peoples that lived in insular Southeast Asia before the arrival of Austronesians were evidently of an Australo-Melanesian or Negrito appearance (Bellwood 1997:ch. 7, cf. also Pawley 1999:105). Some of them had edge-ground stone axes and shell adzes but they did not use pottery, and they were not agriculturists. Some may have combined some form of plant management in their foraging economies (planting tubers or fruit trees) but this did not lead to the development of full-fledged agricultural societies. As a result, they were not equipped to resist the spread of Austronesian-speaking agriculturists, who were sedentary (and technologically more advanced). This led to their gradual assimilation, although some pre-Austronesian groups still survive in the (nowadays Austronesian-speaking) Negritos in the Philippines, the Orang Asli in Malaysia (some of whom are Mon-Khmer-speaking, and some of whom are hunter-gatherers), and Melanesian peoples in eastern Indonesia and Melanesia. One notable exception to this trend is New Guinea, which had an agricultural complex developed independently perhaps 10,000 years ago. Typically, the Austronesian influence only affected some coastal areas of the island and never penetrated it as thoroughly as it did elsewhere in Melanesia.

The Austronesian dispersal was slow given the fact that, after the Austronesians left Taiwan, it took them circa 4000 years to reach New Zealand (1200 AD) and Madagascar (possibly 700 AD). However, Bellwood points out that within this time span there was very much activity between 2000 BC and 1000 BC (roughly between the dates obtained from the sites in the northern Philippines and the period of colonization of Melanesia, western Micronesia and western Polynesia (Bellwood 1997:311)). It appears that the oldest dates for red-slipped and plain pottery anywhere south of Taiwan are not much older than 2000 BC, with the possible exception of Luzon. As Austronesians were already in Samoa (West Polynesia) by 1000 BC, Austronesian migrations must have taken place within a relatively short time within the second millennium BC (Bellwood 1997:232). Pawley suggests that there is a correlation between the long period of rest before the Austronesians moved from Taiwan to the Philippines (in the second millennium BC) and the development of an Austronesian linkage. A similar process must have occurred later on, when the (Polynesian) Austronesians paused for a thousand years in western Polynesia before they began to occupy eastern Polynesia, which happened between 300 and 1200 AD (Pawley 1999:112) or between 700 and 1200 AD (Bellwood 2001:12).

Blust speculates that the pause of at least a millennium between the settlement of Taiwan and that of the northern Philippines may be due to an initial lack of suitable boat technology. The first Austronesian settlers in Taiwan had bamboo sailing rafts, which did not enable them to move on to make the more difficult passage to the northern

Philippines. This passage would have been greatly facilitated by the invention of outriggers, which was apparently a late one. Blust is not sure whether outriggers were used prior to the break-up of PMP but he points out that many shipping terms can be reconstructed for PMP, but not for PAn. Outrigger canoes permitted a rapid settlement of Southeast Asia and Melanesia, where islands are 'relatively close-set' (Blust 1999:77). Blust relates the second long pause in Austronesian migrations, between the settlement of western Polynesia (and Fiji) and the settlement of East Polynesia, to the invention of the double canoe, which he believes occurred in the Fiji–Tonga–Samoa triangle.

There are presently no Austronesians living on the southern Chinese mainland. Blust points out that this area has been subject to a sinicization process throughout the last 2500 years of Chinese history. The gradual sinicization of Austronesian peoples in Taiwan is but a late rehearsal of this process. It has brought about an almost complete acculturation of earlier ethnic groups, and loss of their original languages. Therefore, Blust argues, even if there are no traces of an earlier Austronesian-speaking population on the mainland, it is not difficult to imagine that the Austronesian homeland was originally larger and included some mainland coastal areas, the P'eng-hu (Peng-hu, Pescadores) Islands and Taiwan. It is after all unlikely that the Austronesian migration to Taiwan from the outset would have left no trace in the earlier habitat on the mainland (Blust 1999:69).

7 LANGUAGE CONTACT

7.0 Introduction

This section gives only a very general and incomplete outline of language contact in Madagascar and the Asian part of the Austronesian world. It should be read in conjunction with Chapter 3 (this volume), and for further information and bibliographical references the reader is referred to Dutton and Tryon (1994) and to Wurm, Mühlhäusler and Tryon (1996; especially its sections on (insular) Southeast Asia, the Philippines and Taiwan).

In order to make the complicated issue of language contact more accessible to the reader, this section is further divided into three parts, dealing with influence from sources outside the Austronesian world (basically influence from languages from India, China, the Middle East and Europe, §7.1), language contact in areas bordering on the Austronesian world (contact between Austronesian and non-Austronesian languages in Austronesian border areas, §7.2), and contact among Austronesian languages (§7.3).

7.1 Influence from sources outside the Austronesian world (in chronological order)

The Malay peninsula and Indonesia are centrally located at a crossroads connecting three trade networks of global importance: the Indian Ocean, the China Sea, and the Spice Islands in East Indonesia. As a result, they became recipients of strong cultural and linguistic influences from India, China, the Middle East and Europe. Malay kingdoms along the Strait of Malacca and Javanese kingdoms became the main political forces in early insular Southeast Asian history, and it is largely through their languages (particularly Malay) that the linguistic influence from other civilizations found its way into other Malayo-Polynesian languages, including Malagasy and Philippine languages.

The Indian subcontinent was the first of these civilizations to have an impact. The first written evidence of this impact is some Sanskrit inscriptions from the fourth–fifth century AD. Linguistically, Indian influence is shown by the great number of Sanskrit loanwords in the languages under investigation, and by loanwords from contemporary languages in India (cf. Gonda 1973). Of these, the most important language was Tamil (which was also the vehicular language for the spread of part of the Sanskrit loanwords), although other languages from northern and southern India as well as Sinhalese also left their trace (Gonda 1973:80, Asmah Haji Omar 1975:303–335, Van Ronkel 1902). Influence from these other Indian languages remains a seriously under-studied area. A recent annotated list of Sanskrit loanwords in Malay is De Casparis (1997) which is reviewed thoroughly by Mahdi (2000).

Indian languages had a direct impact on Cham, Malay, Javanese, Balinese and (especially Tamil influence) Karo Batak (cf. Tideman 1936). Their influence affected other Austronesian languages indirectly, predominantly via Javanese (especially in the case of Sundanese, Madurese, (early) Balinese, Sasak and modern Indonesian) and Malay (in most other cases, including Philippine languages, cf. Wolff (1976), and Malagasy, cf. Adelaar (1989, 1994b, 1995a, 1995b)).

With the establishment of Persian rule in Northern India (thirteenth–seventeenth century AD), this area also became the center of the dispersal of Persian and early Arabic lexical influence on Indonesian and Philippine languages. It was only from the seventeenth century onwards that this role was taken over by Hadramaut and other trade and religious centers on the Arabian peninsula and (nowadays) also by Islamic centers elsewhere in the Middle East. The latter are currently having an enhanced effect on Malay/Indonesian and other languages of Muslim communities. Here again we see that particularly Malay (but in some cases also Javanese) became the main vehicles for the spread of Arabic and Persian lexicon in other parts of Southeast Asia.

Chinese influence in Southeast Asia is at least as old as the influence from Arabic and Persian, if not older. Chinese has exercised a lexical influence on various Malay dialects (especially Jakarta Malay, Bazaar Malay and Baba Malay, which is originally the language of a mixed Chinese-Malay community in Singapore, Malacca and Penang). There are also various speculations about the possible role of Chinese in the genesis of trade Malay (cf. Adelaar and Prentice 1996).

Chinese influence is strongest in Malaysia and Singapore, where the Chinese are a very large proportion of the population as a result of mass migrations especially from the late eigthteenth century onwards. Various dialects assume the role of contact language: Hokkien (in most places), Hakka (Sabah), Cantonese (in Kuala Lumpur, Seremban, Kuantan). Nowadays Mandarin is gaining ground at the cost of other Chinese varieties (especially in Singapore).

Other parts of Southeast Asia have been affected in different ways. In Indonesia, Chinese migrations date back to the thirteenth century but they increased in the 1860s. This resulted in two communities, an acculturated mixed Chinese-Indonesian (*Peranakan*) one that speaks a local Indonesian language, and a more authentic Chinese (*Totok*) one speaking usually Hokkien but also Hakka (Bangka Island, West Java, West Borneo), Teochew (West Borneo, East Sumatra and Riau) or even Cantonese (Bangka, Borneo). Bangka also developed a creolized Hakka dialect with many Malay loanwords (Skinner 1963:104). Chinese influence in Indonesia is limited in extent and scope in comparison with Indian, Arabic and European influence. Most of it is from the Hokkien (Fujian) dialect and belongs to the domains of food, building and places, shipping, numerals and measures, and concepts pertaining to Chinese subculture (Kong 1987:459). For Chinese influence in the Philippines, see Chan Yap (1980).

Borrowing from European languages began with the arrival of the Portuguese in Southeast Asia. They were soon followed by the Spaniards who, while initially also making efforts to get strongholds in Brunei and East Indonesia (especially Halmahera), assumed control over the Philippines and some islands in Micronesia (including Chamorro). The Portuguese and Spanish had a great impact on the linguistic geography of the areas under their respective administrations. They left many loanwords, which is probably due to the fact that they were the first Europeans to arrive in the area and therefore the first to introduce typically European objects and concepts (including Christianity). But they also left creole versions of their languages in the form of Portuguese-based creoles in Malacca (Baxter 1988), in Tugu near Jakarta (Schuchardt 1890) and in Bidau in East Timor (Baxter 1990), and in the form of Chavacano, which is a basically a cover term for various Spanish-based creoles (Lipski 1996:276–280). Portuguese remained the official language of East Timor until the Indonesian invasion in 1975 and has been re-established as such (along with Tetun) since its independence (Hajek 2000; STEINHAUER, LANGUAGE POLICY). It is becoming again a major source of borrowing into Tetun (Williams-Van Klinken, Hajek and Nordlinger 2002). The Dutch imprint on the languages of Indonesia and Malaysia was slight by comparison, considering that in most areas Dutch rule lasted much longer than Portuguese rule. The Dutch language nevertheless left many loanwords in Indonesian and in vernacular Indonesian languages, and also some in Malaysian Malay. After Indonesian independence there was a concerted effort by the Indonesian Language Center to replace Dutch loanwords with neologisms based on inherited Malay, Sanskrit, Arabic and Old Javanese lexicon. As a result, many Dutch loanwords disappeared from the Indonesian lexical inventory, although some of them persist in non-standard forms of Malay or in vernacular languages. Some Dutch creoles (such as Malay-based *Peco'* and Javanese-based *Javindo*) have become extinct or are on the verge of disappearance.

French influence played a major role in areas where the French were a colonial power, that is, in Madagascar and in Vietnam and Cambodia, where Chamic languages are spoken. It continues to play this role in Madagascar where it is in competition with Malagasy, the national language (cf. STEINHAUER, LANGUAGE POLICY). Malagasy has many French loanwords (and some English ones, see below). On the other hand, it seems that Malagasy has remained somewhat more resistant to European lexical influence than Malay and Tagalog. Finally, many French loanwords ended up in Malay and other Indonesian languages via Dutch in the colonial period.

Borrowing from English probably started in the seventeenth century (when the British had representations in Aceh and Bengkulu, in Sumatra) but it became a major lexical source in late eighteenth-century Malaysia and early twentieth-century Philippines. Malagasy also shows clear traces of borrowing from English, which stem from the nineteenth century when the British tried to get a foothold on the island and competed with the French to establish a colonial administration. In both Malaysia and the Philippines English influence continues in spite of the establishment of a native national language (see STEINHAUER, LANGUAGE POLICY). In this modern age of globalization, English has in general become the major source for lexical borrowing in the national languages of Southeast Asia (including Indonesian).

7.2 Language contact in areas bordering on the Austronesian world (in order from west to east)

Other manifestations of language contact are more local in their scope.

Malagasy has been in contact with Bantu languages in several stages of its post-migratory (African) history. Dahl (1988) identifies this influence as being from Comoran Swahili (Ngazije and Ndzuani).

Various Austronesian languages on the Southeast Asian mainland as well as Sumatra exhibit influence from Austro-Asiatic languages. This is clearly manifested in the phonology and lexicon of Chamic languages, including Acehnese (Thurgood 1999:47–59). Acehnese, in turn, affected the phonologies of Gayo (Eades in press) and Alas (a northern Batak variety). Austro-Asiatic influence also appears in Malayic: Malay words like *səmut* 'ant', *kətam* 'crab', *əlaŋ* 'kite', *mərak* 'peacock', *pərut* 'stomach' are not Austronesian and are shared with Austro-Asiatic languages (Shorto 1975, Thurgood 1999:360, cf. also Collins (1985) detailing features of a Malay dialect spoken by Orang Asli in Pahang). Like the Chamic languages, Malayic varieties such as Kerinci and Minangkabau as well as the WMP isolate language Rejang have undergone radical phonological changes in their last syllables. Some of these manifest areal features have also affected non-Austronesian languages on the mainland. In turn, Orang Asli languages exhibit influence from Malay.

Thai has been affecting the Malay dialects of southern Thailand and of the northern states of West Malaysia for a long time, although its influence is mainly lexical and hardly phonological (Tadmor 1995:14). Thai influence is also manifest in Moken and Moklen (see LARISH, MOKEN AND MOKLEN), and Burmese has influenced Moken (Naw Say Bay 1995). There has also been considerable lexical borrowing from Malay into Thai (Suthiwan 1992). Thurgood (1994) points to Austronesian influence on Tai-Kadai. Lexical borrowing probably took place in prehistorical times when the speakers of both language groups were still living in mainland China.

In the northernmost regions of the area under investigation, the Formosan languages have been in contact with local (Southern Min or Hokkien) Chinese for at least four centuries. For instance, the Siraya translation of the Gospel of St. Matthew (Gravius 1661) already contains several local Chinese loanwords. The Formosans have also been in contact with Japanese (during the occupation by the Japanese between 1895 and 1945) and with Mandarin, which have both served as linguae francae and have both left traces in Formosan languages (Li 1996:741). Tai-Kadai languages and Southern Min Chinese also influenced Tsat, a Chamic language spoken in Hainan (China) (Thurgood 1999:22).

Eastern Indonesia and East Timor form an interface area between Austronesian and various Papuan linguistic spheres. If basic vocabulary is used as an indicator, the languages in this area are overwhelmingly Austronesian, except in large parts of New Guinea and in North Halmahera, in a few limited areas in East Timor and on the islands of Alor, Pantar and Kisar in Indonesia. However, as far as grammatical typology is concerned, Austronesian languages in eastern Indonesia and East Timor have features that are quite different from those of the more conservative Austronesian languages of Taiwan, the Philippines and western Indonesia. These features differ to the extent that in a number of cases the classificatory labels have become almost insignificant, as pointed out by Capell (1982), Foley (1986, 1998), Hull (1998) and others who have worked in the area. CMP and SHWNG languages have in all likelihood left their traces on neighboring non-Austronesian languages. What is certain, however, is the (lexical) influence from Indonesian and regional (Ambonese, Ternatan) Malay as well as Tetun on neighboring non-Austronesian languages.

Austronesian languages exerted some influence on Australia. In North Australia (between Bathurst and Melville Islands to the west and Limmen Bight to the east), contact between Makassarese (collecting sea urchins) and Aboriginals caused the emergence of a Makassar-based pidgin language, 'Macassan' which is still testified to in a number of lexical items remembered by local Aboriginals or borrowed into their languages. However, some of the alleged Makassan loanwords seem to be of Malay rather than Makassar provenance (Urry and Walsh 1981:94–95). Makassar as well as Malay loanwords were also found in Yolngu-Matha (Northeast Arnhem Land; Walker and Zorc (1981)), and in languages of West Arnhem Land (Evans 1992, 1997).

7.3 Contact among Austronesian languages (contact languages in order from West to East)

Traditionally, the language area under investigation is by and large characterized by the presence of Austronesian regional contact languages that are used throughout a geographically delimited area (an archipelago, island, a river and its tributaries, a coast area, etc.). Since decolonization there has been a trend for these contact languages to be replaced by newly established national languages such as Indonesian, official Malaysian Malay, Pilipino, Thai, Vietnamese, etc.

Among these contact languages there are quite a few regional forms of Malay. The latter also occur in eastern Indonesia, where they include Ambon Malay (South Moluccas and in a subvariant in West Papua), Ternate Malay (North Moluccas) and Manado Malay (North Sulawesi). In the past, Malay was used as a contact language in the Philippines and, most likely, Madagascar. In Indonesia, one Malay contact language seems to have resisted the takeover by the national language rather well. Although Betawi, the original Malay dialect of Jakarta, is nowadays spoken by only a small minority, it has influenced official Indonesian to the extent that Jakartan Indonesian has emerged, a variant of Indonesian which is much more vibrant and popular than its formal counterpart. Another Malay contact language, Banjar Malay has had an expansion along the coast of East Kalimantan.

Malay has served various sociolinguistic purposes, including that of interethnic lingua franca, trade language, language for religious instruction, literary language, educational language, etc. An overview of Malay contact languages is Adelaar and Prentice (1996:676–688). See ADELAAR, MALAYIC for an insight into some of the linguistic variety of Malayic, Collins (1998) for a recent overview of the history of Malay, and Collins (1990, 1995a, 1995b, 1996b) for an annotated bibliography of Malay varieties.

Javanese is the Austronesian language with by far the highest number of mother-tongue speakers (see OGLOBLIN, JAVANESE and FLOREY, ENDANGERED LANGUAGES). It is also the most important regional language in Indonesia and has had an overwhelming impact on Indonesian lexicon. It has had an important role in the linguistic history of island Southeast Asia. In the fourteenth century AD, Java extended its political influence over many other areas in Indonesia and at one point even included parts of the Philippines and some of the coast of West Papua. However, in contrast to Malay, the influence of Javanese did not extend beyond the spread of loanwords, except for the languages in its vicinity. Of the latter, Sundanese, Madurese, Balinese and Sasak emulated the Javanese use of polite speech registers. The vocabulary of these registers is moreover largely borrowed from Javanese. Palembang Malay court jargon is largely based on Javanese lexicon. Banjar Malay adopted many Javanese loanwords (including much basic vocabulary) but it did not develop polite language registers. Javanese loanwords are occasionally also found in languages further away from Java (including languages as far away as Siraya (Taiwan) and Malagasy, cf. Adelaar 1994b).

In addition to Makassar influence on Australian languages (see above), lexical influence from South Sulawesi languages is found in various languages of Sulawesi, the Lesser Sunda Islands (Lombok, Sumbawa, and Flores), and Madagascar. South Sulawesi loanwords in Malagasy are most easily explained as having entered Malagasy and other members of the Southeast Barito language group before the early Malagasy left Borneo (Adelaar 1995a:350–351).

For the roles of Indonesian, Tagalog, Tetun, Malagasy and other national languages, see the sketches of these languages and Chapter 3 (this volume). For various other Austronesian contact languages in Asia, see the *Atlas of languages of intercultural communication* by Wurm, Mühlhäusler and Tryon (1996).

ACKNOWLEDGMENTS

I would like to express my gratitude to Peter Bellwood, John Hajek, Nikolaus Himmelmann, David Mead, Malcolm Ross and Elizabeth Zeitoun for their valuable comments on earlier versions of this chapter. They are in no way responsible for any errors in the present version.

REFERENCES

Adelaar, K.A. (1985) *Proto-Malayic: a reconstruction of its phonology and part of its morphology and lexicon*, PhD thesis, Leiden University.
——(1989) 'Malay influence on Malagasy: linguistic and culture-historical inferences', *Oceanic Linguistics*, 28/1:1–46.
——(1992) *Proto-Malayic: a reconstruction of its phonology and part of its morphology and lexicon*, Canberra: Pacific Linguistics (revised publication of Adelaar 1985).
——(1993) 'The internal classification of the Malayic subgroup', *Bulletin of the School of Oriental and African Studies*, 56/3:566–581.
——(1994a) 'The classification of the Tamanic languages (West Kalimantan)', in T.E. Dutton and D. Tryon (eds), 1–41.
——(1994b) 'Malay and Javanese loanwords in Malagasy, Tagalog and Siraya (Formosa)', *Bijdragen tot de Taal-, Land- en Volkenkunde*, 150/1:49–64.
——(1995a) 'Asian roots of the Malagasy: a linguistic perspective', *Bijdragen tot de Taal-, Land- en Volkenkunde*, 151/3:325–357.
——(1995b) 'Bentuk pinjaman bahasa Melayu dan Jawa di Malagasi', in Ismail Hussain, A. Aziz Deraman and Abd. Rahman Al Ahmadi (eds), *Tamadun Melayu. Jilid Pertama*, Kuala Lumpur: Dewan Bahasa dan Pustaka; 21–40.
——(in press a) 'On the classifiability of Malayic', in D. Gil (ed.), *Malay and Indonesian Linguistics*, London: Routledge-Curzon.
——(in press b) 'Malayo-Sumbawan', in P. Austin (ed.), *Working Papers in Bali, Lombok and Sumbawa*, London: School of Oriental and African Studies.
——(2004) 'Where does Malay come from? Twenty years of discussions about homeland, migrations and classifications', *Bijdragen tot de Taal-, Land- en Volkenkunde*, 160/1:1–30.
Adelaar, K.A. and Prentice, D.J. (1996) 'Malay: its history, role and spread', in S.A. Wurm, P. Mühlhäusler and D. Tryon (eds), 673–693.
A primer to Mangyan script. Surat Mangyan (1986), Panaytayan, Mansalay-4411, OR. Mindoro, Philippines.
Asmah Haji Omar, (1975) *Essays on Malaysian Linguistics*. Kuala Lumpur: Dewan Bahasa dan Pustaka.
Baxter, A.N. (1988) *A Grammar of Kristang (Malacca Creole Portuguese)*, Canberra: Pacific Linguistics.
——(1990) 'Notes on the Creole Portuguese of Bidau, East Timor', *Journal of Pidgin and Creole Languages* (Amsterdam/Philadelphia: Benjamins), 5:1/1–38.

Bellwood, P. (1997) *Prehistory of the Indo-Malaysian Archipelago* (revised edition) Honolulu: University of Hawai'i Press.

——(2001) Polynesian prehistory and the rest of mankind, in C.M. Stevenson, G. Lee and F.J. Morin (eds), *Pacific 2000. Proceedings of the Fifth International Conference on Easter Island and the Pacific*, The Easter Island Foundation, 11–25, Los Osos (CA): Bearsville Press.

Bellwood, P., Fox, J.J. and Tryon, D. (eds) (1995) *The Austronesians: history and comparative perspectives*, Canberra: Dept. of Anthropology, Australian National University, RSPAS.

Blust, R.A. (1970) 'Proto-Austronesian addenda', *Oceanic Linguistics* 9:104–162.

——(1976a) Dempwolff's reduplicated monosyllables, *Oceanic Linguistics*, 15:107–130.

——(1976b) Austronesian culture history: some linguistic inferences and their relation to the archaeological world, *World Archaeology*, 8/1:19–43.

——(1977) 'The Proto-Austronesian pronouns and Austronesian subgrouping: a preliminary report', *Working Papers in Linguistics of the University of Hawai'i*, 9/2:1–15.

——(1978) 'Eastern Malayo-Polynesian: a subgrouping argument', in S.A. Wurm and L. Carrington (eds), *Second International Conference on Austronesian Linguistics: proceedings, Fascicle I, Western Austronesian*, 181–234, Canberra: Pacific Linguistics.

——(1979) 'Proto-Western-Malayo-Polynesian vocatives', *Bijdragen tot de Taal-, Landen Volkenkunde*, 135:205–251.

——(1980a) 'Austronesian etymologies I', *Oceanic Linguistics*, 19:1–181.

——(1980b) 'Early Austronesian social organization: the evidence of language', *Current Anthropology*, 21/2. 205–47.

——(1980c) 'Notes on Proto-Malayo-Polynesian phratry dualism', *Bijdragen tot de Taal-, Land- en Volkenkunde*, 136:215–247.

——(1981) 'The reconstruction of Proto-Malayo-Javanic: an appreciation', *Bijdragen tot de Taal-, Land- en Volkenkunde*, 137:456–469.

——(1982) 'The linguistic value of the Wallace Line', *Bijdragen tot de Taal-, Land- en Volkenkunde*, 138:231–250.

——(1983–4) 'Austronesian etymologies II', *Oceanic Linguistics*, 22–23:29 149.

——(1984) 'On the history of Rejang vowels and diphthongs', *Bijdragen tot de Taal-, Land- en Volkenkunde*, 140/4:422–450.

——(1984–5) 'The Austronesian homeland: a linguistic perspective', *Asian Perspectives* (Honolulu), 26/1:45–67.

——(1986) 'Austronesian etymologies III', *Oceanic Linguistics*, 25:1–123.

——(1988) *Austronesian root theory. An essay on the limits of morphology*, Studies in Language Companion Series 19, Amsterdam/Philadelphia: John Benjamins.

——(1989) 'Austronesian etymologies IV', *Oceanic Linguistics*, 28:111–180.

——(1990) 'Patterns of sound change in the Austronesian languages', in Ph. Baldi (ed.), *Linguistic change and reconstruction methodology*, 231–267, Berlin: Mouton de Gruyter.

——(1991) 'The Great Central Philippines hypothesis', *Oceanic Linguistics*, 30:73–129.

——(1993a) '*S metathesis and the Formosan/Malayo-Polynesian language boundary', in Øyvind Dahl (ed.), *Language – a doorway between human cultures: tributes to Dr. Otto Christian Dahl on his ninetieth birthday*, 178–183, Oslo: Novus.

——(1993b) 'Central and Central-Eastern Malayo-Polynesian', *Oceanic Linguistics*, 32/2:241–293.

——(1994a) 'Obstruent epenthesis and the unity of phonological features', *Lingua*, 93:111–139.

——(1994b) 'The Austronesian settlement of mainland Southeast Asia', in K.L. Adams and T.J. Hudak (eds), *Papers from the Second Annual Meeting of the Southeast Asian Linguistics Society*, Tempe (Arizona): Program for Southeast Asian Studies, Arizona State University, 25–83.

Blust, R.A. (1995) 'The position of the Formosan languages: methods and theory in Austronesian comparative linguistics', in Li *et al.* (eds), 585–650.

——(1998a) 'Ca-reduplication and Proto-Austronesian grammar', *Oceanic Linguistics*, 37/1:29–64.

——(1998b) 'The position of the languages of Sabah', in Ma.L.S. Bautista (ed.), *Pagtanáw Essays on language in honor of Teodoro A. Llamzon*, 29–52, Manila: The Linguistic Society of the Philippines.

——(1999) 'Subgrouping, circularity and extinction: some issues in Austronesian comparative linguistics', in E. Zeitoun and P.J.-K. Li (eds), 31–94.

——(2002) 'Formalism or phoneyism? The history of Kayan final glottal stop', in K.A. Adelaar and R. Blust (eds), *Between worlds: Linguistic papers in memory of David John Prentice*, 29–37, Canberra: Pacific Linguistics.

——(in press) 'Three notes on early Austronesian morphology, to appear in *Language and Linguistics*', (Taipei: Academia Sinica).

——(to appear) *Austronesian Comparative Dictionary* (unpublished data on computer file).

Brandstetter, R. (1893) *Die Beziehungen des Malagasy zum Malaiischen*, Luzern.

Cameron, C.R. (1917) *Sulu writing*, Zamboanga (Philippines): Sulu Press.

Capell, A. (1982) 'Bezirkssprachen im UAN-Gebiet', in Reiner Carle *et al.* (eds), *Gava' Studies in Austronesian languages and cultures dedicated to Hans Kähler*, Veröffentlichungen des Seminars für Indonesische und Südseesprachen der Universität Hamburg Band 17, Berlin: Reimer Verlag.

Chan Yap, G. (1980) *Hokkien Chinese borrowings in Tagalog*, Canberra: Pacific Linguistics.

Clynes, A. (1989) *Speech styles in Balinese and Javanese*, unpublished MA thesis from the Australian National University.

Collins, J.T. (1985) 'Dialek Melayu di kampung Landai, Pahang: menuju penelitian tatabahasa Melayu di kalangan Orang Asli', *Dewan Bahasa* 29/7:476–493.

——(1990) *Bibliografi dialek Melayu di pulau Borneo*, Siri Monograf Bibliografi Sejarah Bahasa Melayu, Kuala Lumpur: Dewan Bahasa dan Pustaka.

——(1994) 'Sumbangan dialek Brunei dalam pengkajian sejarah Bahasa Melayu', in *Tinggal Landas ke Abad 21*, Bandar Seri Begawan: Dewan Bahasa dan Pustaka; 62–75.

——(1995a) *Bibliografi dialek Melayu di pulau Sumatera*. Siri Monograf Bibliografi Sejarah Bahasa Melayu. Kuala Lumpur: Dewan Bahasa dan Pustaka.

——(1995b) *Bibliografi dialek Melayu di pulau Jawa, Bali dan Sri Lanka*, Siri Monograf Bibliografi Sejarah Bahasa Melayu, Kuala Lumpur: Dewan Bahasa dan Pustaka.

——(1996a) 'Borneo and Maluku: the evidence from the language of Bacan', in P.W. Martin, C. Ozog and G. Poedjosoedarmo (eds), 73–88.

——(1996b) *Bibliografi dialek Melayu di Indonesia Timur*. Siri Monograf Bibliografi Sejarah Bahasa Melayu. Kuala Lumpur: Dewan Bahasa dan Pustaka.

——(1998) *Malay, World Language of the Ages. A sketch of its history*, Kuala Lumpur: Dewan Bahasa dan Pustaka.

——(2002) 'The study of Sarawak Malay in context', in K.A. Adelaar and R. Blust (eds), *Between worlds: Linguistic papers in memory of David John Prentice*, 65–76, Canberra: Pacific Linguistics.

Dahl, O.C. (1976) *Proto-Austronesian*, Scandinavian Institute of Asian Studies Monograph series No. 15 (2nd edition), Lund: Studentlitteratur – Curzon press.

——(1981) *Early Phonetic and Phonemic Changes in Austronesian*, Instituttet for sammenlignende kulturforskning, Oslo: Universitetsforlaget.

——(1983) *Sorabe révélant l'évolution du dialecte antemoro*, Antananarivo: Trano Printy Loterana.

——(1988) 'Bantu substratum in Malagasy' (special issue: Linguistique de Madagascar et des Comores), *Études Océan Indien*, 9:91–132.

——(1991) *Migration from Kalimantan to Madagascar*, The Institute for Comparative Research in Human Culture, Oslo: Norwegian University Press.

De Casparis, J.G. (1997) *Sanskrit loanwords in Indonesian. An annotated check-list of words in Indonesian and traditional Malay*, Jakarta: Badan Penyelenggara Seri Nusa (Universitas Katolik Atmajaya).

Dempwolff, O. (1934, 1937, 1938) *Vergleichende Lautlehre des Austronesischen Wortschatzes* (3 vols), Beihefte Zeitschrift für Eingeborenensprachen 15, 17, 19, Berlin: Dietrich Reimer Verlag.

Donohue, M. (in press) 'The pretenders to the Muna-Buton group' (to appear in *Pacific Linguistics*, Canberra).

Dutton, T.E. and Tryon, D.T. (eds) (1994) *Language Contact and Change in the Austronesian World*, Trends in Linguistics. Studies and Monographs. Berlin: Mouton – de Gruyter.

Dyen, I. (1947a) 'The Malayo-Polynesian word for "two"', *Language*, 23:50–55.

——(1947b) 'The Tagalog reflexes of Malayo-Polynesian D', *Language*, 23:227–238.

——(1951) 'PMP *Z', *Language*, 27:534–540.

——(1953a) *The Proto-Malayo-Polynesian laryngeals*, Baltimore: Linguistic Society of America.

——(1953b) 'Dempwolff's R', *Language*, 29:359–366.

——(1962) 'Some new Malayopolynesian initial phonemes', *Journal of the American Oriental Society* 82:214–215.

——(1963) 'The position of the Malayo-Polynesian languages of Formosa', *Asian Perspectives*, 7:261–271.

——(1965a) 'Formosan evidence for some Proto-Austronesian phonemes', *Lingua*, 14:285–305.

——(1965b) *A Lexicostatistical Classification of the Austronesian Languages*, International Journal of American Linguistics, Memoir 19, Baltimore: Waverly Press.

Dyen, I. and Tsuchida, S. (1991) Proto-Philippine as the nearest relative of Proto-Formosan, in Harlow, R. (ed.), *VICAL 2: Western Austronesian languages*, Auckland: Linguistic Society of NZ; 85–101.

Eades, D. (in press) *A grammar of Gayo, a language of Aceh, Indonesia*, Canberra: Pacific Linguistics.

Esser, S.J. (1938) 'Languages', in *Atlas van Tropisch Nederland*, Batavia: Koninklijk Nederlandsch Aardrijkskundig Genootschap.

Evans, N. (1992) 'Macassan loanwords in Top End languages', *Australian Journal of Linguistics*, 12:45–91.

——(1997) 'Macassan loans and linguistic stratification in western Arnhem Land', in P. McConvell and N. Evans (eds), *Archaeology and linguistics. Aboriginal languages in global perspective*, 237–260, Melbourne: Oxford University Press.

Ferrell, R. (1969) *Taiwan Aboriginal Groups:(…)*. Taipei: Academia Sinica, Institute of Ethnology.

Foley, W.A. (1986) *The Papuan Languages of New Guinea* (Cambridge Language Surveys), Cambridge: Cambridge University Press.

——(1998) 'Towards understanding Papuan languages', in J. Miedema, C. Odé and R.A.C. Dam (eds), *Perspectives on the Bird's Head in Irian Jaya, Indonesia. Proceedings of the Conference, Leiden, 13–17 October 1997*, 503–518, Amsterdam: Rodopi.

Fox, J.J. (ed.) (1993) *Inside Austronesian houses: perspectives on domestic designs for living*, Canberra: RSPAS, Dept. of Anthropology, Australian National University.

——(ed.) (1997) *The poetic power of place: comparative perspectives on Austronesian ideas of locality*, Canberra: RSPAS, Dept. of Anthropology, Australian National University.

Fox, J.J. and Sather, C. (eds) (1996) *Origins, ancestry and alliance*, Canberra: RSPAS, Dept. of Anthropology, Australian National University.

Gonda, J. (1973) *Sanskrit in Indonesia* (2nd edn), New Delhi: International Academy of Indian Culture.

Gravius, D. (1661) *Het heylige Euangelium Matthei en Johannis. Ofte Hagnau ka d'l-lig matiktik ka na sasoulat ti Mattheus ti Johannes appa*, Amsterdam: Michiel Hartogh.

Grimes, B.F. (2000) *Ethnologue: Languages of the world* (14th edition), Texas: Summer Institute of Linguistics.

Hajek, J. (2000) 'Language planning and the sociolinguistic environment in East Timor: colonial practice and changing language ecologies', *Current Issues in Language Planning*, 1:400–414.

Himmelmann, N.P. (2001) *Sourcebook on Tomini-Tolitoli languages. General information and wordlists*, Canberra: Pacific Linguistics.

——(2002) 'Voice in western Austronesian: an update', in F. Wouk and M. Ross (eds), 7–16.

Hudson, A.B. (1978) 'Linguistic relations among Bornean peoples with special reference to Sarawak: an interim report', in *Sarawak. Linguistics and development problems*, 1–45, Studies in Third World Societies (Williamsburg, VA) No. 3.

Hull, G. (1998) 'The basic lexical affinities of Timor's Austronesian languages. A preliminary investigation', *Studies in languages and cultures of East Timor* Volume 1 (Academy of East Timor Studies, University of Western Sydney):97–202.

Humboldt, Wilhelm von (1836–1839) *Über die Kawi-Sprache auf der Insel Java* (3 vols), Berlin.

Kong Yuan Zhi (1987) 'A study of Chinese loanwords (from South Fujian dialects) in the Malay and Indonesian languages', *Bijdragen tot de Taal-, Land- en Volkenkunde*, 143/4:452–467.

Larish, M.D. (1999) *The position of Moken and Moklen in the Austronesian language family*, PhD thesis, University of Hawai'i.

Li, P. Jen-kuei (1996) 'The lingue franche in Taiwan', in S.A. Wurm, P. Mühlhäusler and D.T. Tryon (eds), *Atlas of Languages of Intercultural Communication in the Pacific, Asia, and the Americas vol. II.1*, Trends in Linguistics Documentation 13, 741–743, Berlin: Mouton de Gruyter.

Li, P. Jen-kuei, Tsang, Cheng-hwa, Huang, Ying-kuei, Ho, Dah-an and Tseng, Chiu-yu (eds) (1995), *Austronesian Studies Relating to Taiwan*, Symposium Series of the Institute of History and Philology, Academia Sinica Number 3, Taipei: Academia Sinica.

Lipski, J.M. [with Mühlhäusler, P.; Duthin, F.] (1996) Spanish in the Pacific, in S.A. Wurm, P. Mühlhäusler and D. Tryon (eds), 271–298.

Lynch, J. (ed.) (in press) *Issues in Austronesian phonology*, Canberra: Pacific Linguistics.

Mahdi, W. (1988) *Morphonologische Besonderheiten und historische Phonologie des Malagasy*, Veröffentlichungen des Seminars für Indonesische und Südseesprachen der Universität Hamburg Band 20, Berlin-Hamburg: Dietrich Reimer Verlag.

——(1994a) 'Some Austronesian maverick protoforms with culture-historical implications I', *Oceanic Linguistics*, 33/1:167–229.

——(1994b) 'Some Austronesian maverick protoforms with culture-historical implications II', *Oceanic Linguistics*, 33/2:431–490.

——(2000) review of J.G. De Casparis (1997), *Bijdragen tot de Taal-, Land- en Volkenkunde*, 156/4:844–852.

Marrison, G.E. (1975) 'The early Cham language and its relation to Malay', *Journal of the Malayan Branch of the Royal Asiatic Society*, 48(2):52–59.

Martin, P.W., Poedjosoedarmo, G. and Ozog, C. (eds) (1996) *Language use and language change in Brunei Darussalam*, Athens: Ohio University Centre for International Studies.

Mbete, A.M. (1990) *Rekonstruksi protobahasa Bali-Sasak-Sumbawa*, PhD thesis, Universitas Indonesia (Jakarta).

Mead, D. (1996) 'The evidence for final consonants in Proto-Bungku-Tolaki', *Oceanic Linguistics*, 35:180–194.

——(1998) *Proto-Bungku-Tolaki: reconstruction of its phonology and aspects of its morphosyntax,* PhD dissertation, Rice University, Houston, Texas.

——(1999) *The Bungku-Tolaki languages of Southeastern Sulawesi,* Indonesia, Canberra: Pacific Linguistics, Australian National University.

——(2002) 'Proto-Celebic focus revisited', in F. Wouk and M. Ross (eds), 143–177.

——(in press a) 'The Saluan-Banggai microgroup of eastern Sulawesi', in John Lynch (ed.) (in press).

——(in press b) 'Evidence for a Celebic supergroup', in John Lynch (ed.) (in press).

Mills, R.F. (1975) *Proto-South-Sulawesi and Proto-Austronesian phonology,* PhD dissertation, University of Michigan, Ann Arbor.

——(1991) 'Tanimbar-Kei: an Eastern Indonesian subgroup', in R.A. Blust (ed.), *Currents in Pacific Linguistics. Papers in Austronesian languages and ethnolinguistics in honour of George W. Grace,* 241–263, Canberra: Pacific Linguistics.

Nais, W. (1988) *Bidayuh–English dictionary,* Kuching: Persatuaan Kesusasteraan Sarawak.

Naw Say Bay (1995) 'The phonology of the Dung dialect of Moken', in Bradley, D. (ed.), *Studies in Burmese languages,* 193–205, Papers in Southeast Asian Linguistics No.13, Canberra: Pacific Linguistics.

Noorduyn, J. (1991) *A critical survey of studies on the languages of Sulawesi.* KITLV Bibliographical Series. Leiden: Royal Institute of Linguistics and Anthropology.

——(1993) 'Variation in the Bugis/Makasarese script', *BKI* 149/3:533–570.

Nothofer, B. (1975) *The reconstruction of Proto-Malayo-Javanic* Verhandelingen van Koninklijk Instituut voor Taal-, Land-en Volkenkunde 73, The Hague: Martinus Nijhoff.

——(1985) 'The subgrouping of the languages of the Javo-Sumatran hesion: a reconsideration', *Bijdragen tot de Taal-, Land- en Volkenkunde,* 141/3–4:228–302.

——(1988) 'A discussion of two Austronesian subgroups: Proto-Malay and Proto-Malayic', in Mohd. Thani Ahmad and Zaini Mohamed Zain (eds), *Rekonstruksi dan cabang-cabang Bahasa Melayu Induk,* 34–58, Siri monograf sejarah bahasa Melayu, Kuala Lumpur: Dewan Bahasa dan Pustaka.

——(1994) ''Bahasa Lom' – Dari mana asalnya?' in L. Sihombing *et al.* (eds), *Bahasawan Cendekia: seuntai karangan untuk Anton M. Moeliono,* 193–208, Jakarta: P.T. Intermasa.

——(1995) 'The history of Jakarta Malay', *Oceanic Linguistics,* 34/1:86–97.

——(1996) 'Migrasi orang Melayu Purba: Kajian awal', *Sari,* 14:33–52.

——(1997a) *Dialek Melayu Bangka.* Bangi: Penerbit Universiti Kebangsaan Malaysia.

——(1997b) 'Klasifikasi varian Melayik di antara Sungai Semandung dan Sungai Pawan/ Sungai Keriau (Gerai, Tanjung Beringin, Randau Jeka')', Paper: Seminar Internasional Bahasa dan Budaya di Dunia Melayu (Asia Tenggara). Mataram, 21–23 Juli 1997.

Pawley, A.K. (1999) 'Chasing rainbows: implications for the rapid dispersal of Austronesian languages for subgrouping and reconstruction', in E. Zeitoun and P.J.-K. Li (eds), 95–138.

Pawley, A.K. and Ross, M.D. (1994) *Austronesian terminologies: continuity and change,* Canberra: Pacific Linguistics.

Postma, A. (1971) 'Contemporary Mangyan scripts', *Philippine Journal of Linguistics,* 2/1:1–12.

Reid, L. (1982) 'The demise of Proto-Philippines', in A. Halim, L. Carrington and S.A. Wurm (eds), *Papers from TICAL* vol.2, 201–216, Canberra: Pacific Linguistics.

——(2002) 'Morphosyntactic evidence for the position of Chamorro in the Austronesian family', in R.S. Bauer (ed.), *Collected papers on Southeast Asian and Pacific languages,* Canberra: Pacific Linguistics.

Reijffert, A. (1956) *Vocabulary of English and Sarawak Land Dyak (Singhi Tribe),* Kuching: Sarawak Government Printing Office.

Reuter, T.A. (forthcoming) *Sharing the earth, carving up the land*, Canberra: RSPAS, Dept. of Anthropology, Australian National University.

Ross, M.D. (1995) 'Some current issues in Austronesian linguistics', in D.T. Tryon *et al.* (eds), 45–120.

——(2002) 'The history and transitivity of western Austronesian voice and voice marking', in F. Wouk and M. Ross (eds), 17–62.

——(in press) 'Notes on the prehistory and subgrouping of Malayic', in J. Bowden and N.P. Himmelmann (eds) *Papers in Austronesian linguistics*, Canberra: Pacific Linguistics.

Rousseau, J. (1988) *Central Borneo: a bibliography*, Sarawak Museum Journal Special Monograph No. 5, Kuching (Sarawak): The Sarawak Museum.

Schuchardt, H. (1890) *Kreolische Studien IX. Über das Malaioportugiesische von Batavia und Tugu*, Wien: (Tempsky:) Kaiserliche Akademie der Wissenschaften.

Shorto, H.L. (1975) 'Achinese and Mainland Austronesian', *Bulletin of the School of Oriental and African Studies*, 38:81–102.

Skinner, G.W. (1963) 'The Chinese minority', in R.T. McVey (ed.), *Indonesia. Survey of World Cultures* (Southeast Asia Studies, Yale University), 97–117, New Haven (CT): Human Relations Area Files.

Sneddon, J.N. (1993) 'The drift towards final open syllables in Sulawesi languages', *Oceanic Linguistics*, 32:1–44.

Starosta, S., Pawley, A.K. and Reid, L. (1982) 'The evolution of focus in Austronesian', in A. Halim, L. Carrington and S.A. Wurm (eds), *Papers from TICAL* vol.2, 201–216, Canberra: Pacific Linguistics.

Steinhauer, H. (1986) 'Austronesian geographical prospects', *Bijdragen tot de Taal-, Land- en Volkenkunde*, 142:296–313.

Suthiwan, T. (1992) 'Kata pijaman Melayu dalam bahasa Thai', *Dewan Bahasa* 8/8:695 700.

Taber, M. (1993) 'Towards a better understanding of the indigenous languages of Southwestern Maluku', *Oceanic Linguistics*, 32:389–441.

Tadmor, U. (1995) *Language contact and systemic restructuring: the Malay dialect of Nonthaburi, Central Thailand*, PhD thesis, University of Hawaii.

Thurgood, G. (1994) 'Tai-Kadai and Austronesian: the nature of the historical relationship', *Oceanic Linguistics*, 33:345–368.

——(1999) *From ancient Chamic to modern dialects, 2000 years of language contact and change*, Oceanic Linguistics Special Series, Honolulu: University of Hawaii Press.

Tideman, J. (1936) *Hindoe-invloed in het noordelijk Batakland*, Uitgaven van het Bataksch Instituut nr. 23, Amsterdam.

Tryon, D.T. *et al.* (eds) (1995) *Comparative Austronesian dictionary. An introduction to Austronesian studies* (5 vols), Trends in Linguistics Documentation 10 (W. Winter and R.A. Rhodes (eds)), Berlin: Mouton de Gruyter.

Tryon, D.T. (1995) 'Introduction to the Austronesian comparative dictionary', in D.T. Tryon *et al.* (eds), 1–44.

Tsang, Cheng-hua (2001) 'Recent discoveries of the Tapengkeng culture in Taiwan: implications for the problem of Austronesian origins', paper: Seminar Perspectives on the phylogeny of East Asian Languages, Périgueux (France), 29–31 August 2001.

Tsuchida, Shigeru (1976) *Reconstruction of Proto-Tsouic phonology*, Study of languages and cultures of Asia and Africa monograph series No. 5, Institute for the study of Languages and Cultures of Asia and Africa, Tokyo.

——(1995) 'Alienable and inalienable distinction in Puyuma?' in P. J.-K. Li *et al.* (eds), *Austronesian studies relating to Taiwan*, 793–804, Taipei: Institute of History and Philology, Academia Sinica.

Tsuchida, S. and Yamada, Y. (1991) 'Ogawa's Siraya/Makatao/Taivoan (Comparative Vocabulary)', in S. Tsuchida, Y. Yamada and T. Moriguchi (eds), *Linguistic materials of the Formosan sinicized populations I: Siraya and Basai*, 1–94, Tokyo: The University of Tokyo, Department of Linguistics.

Urry, J. and Walsh, M. (1981) 'The lost "Macassar language" of Northern Australia', *Aboriginal History*, 5/2:90–108.

Van den Berg, R. (1996) 'The demise of focus and the spread of conjugated verbs in Sulawesi', in H. Steinhauer (ed.), *Papers in Austronesian Linguistics No.3*, 89 114, Canberra: Pacific Linguistics.

——(in press) 'The place of Tukang Besi and the Muna-Buton languages', in Lynch, J. (ed.).

Van der Vlis, C.J. (1842) *Formosaansche woorden-lijst, volgens een Utrechts Handschrift*, Verhandelingen van het Bataviaasch Genootschap 18:437–488.

Van Engelenhoven, A. (1995) *A description of the Leti language (as spoken in Tutukei)*, PhD thesis, Leiden University.

Van Ronkel, PH.S. (1902) 'Het Tamil-element in het Maleisch', *Tijdschrift voor Indische Taal- Land- en Volkenkunde* (Koninklijk Bataviaasch Genootschap voor Kunsten en Wetenschappen, Batavia) 45:97–119.

Vischer, M.P. (in press) *Precedence: processes of social differentiation in the Austronesian world*, Canberra: RSPAS, Dept. of Anthropology, Australian National University.

Walker, A. and Zorc, R.D. (1981) 'Austronesian loanwords in Yolngu-Matha of Northeast Arnhem Land', *Aboriginal History*, 5/2:109–134.

Williams-Van Klinken, C., Hajek, J. and Nordlinger, R. (2002) *Tetun Dili. A grammar of an East Timorese language*, Canberra: Pacific Linguistics.

Wolff, J.U. (1973), 'Verbal inflection in Proto-Austronesian', in A.B. Gonzalez (ed.), *Parangal Kay Cecilio Lopez*, 71–91, Quezon City: Philippine Journal of Linguistics (Special monograph 4).

——(1976) 'Malay borrowings in Tagalog', in C.D. Cowan and O.W. Wolters (eds), *Southeast-Asian history and historiography: Essays presented to D.G.H. Hall*, 345–367, Ithaca: Cornell University Press.

——(1988) 'The PAN consonant system', in R. McGinn (ed.), *Studies in Austronesian linguistics*, Ohio University Monographs in International Studies, 125–147, Athens: Ohio University.

——(1995) 'The position of the Austronesian languages of Taiwan within the Austronesian group', in P.J.-K. Li *et al.* (eds), 521–583.

——(1996) 'The development of the passive verb with pronominal prefix in Western Austronesian languages', in B. Nothofer (ed.), *Reconstruction, classification, description – festschrift in honor of Isidore Dyen*, 15–40, Hamburg: Abera Verlag.

——(1999) 'The monosyllabic roots of Proto-Austronesian', in E. Zeitoun and P.J.-K. Li (eds), 139–194.

——(2002) 'Final words: the development of the focus system', in F. Wouk and M. Ross (eds), 437–449.

Wouk, F. and Ross, M. (2002) *The history and typology of Western Austronesian voice systems*, Canberra: Pacific Linguistics.

Wurm, S.A. and Hattori, S. (eds) (1981–3) *Language atlas of the Pacific area*, Canberra: Pacific Linguistics.

Wurm, S.A. and Mühlhäusler, P.; Tryon, D.T. (eds) (1996) *Atlas of languages of inter-cultural communication in the Pacific, Asia and the Americas*, Berlin and New York: Mouton de Gruyter.

Wurm, S.A. and Wilson, B. (1975) *English finderlist of reconstructions in Austronesian languages (post-Brandstetter)*, Canberra: Pacific Linguistics.

Zeitoun, E. and Huang, L.M. (2000) 'Concerning ka-, an overlooked marker of verbal derivation in Formosan languages', *Oceanic Linguistics*, 39:391–414.

Zeitoun, E. and Li, P.J.-K. (eds) (1999) *Selected Papers from the Eighth International Conference on Austronesian Linguistics*, Symposium Series of the Institute of Linguistics (Preparatory Office), Taipei: Academia Sinica.

Zobel, E. (2002) 'The position of Chamorro and Palauan in the Austronesian family tree: evidence from verb morphosyntax', in F. Wouk and M. Ross (eds), 405–434.

——(to appear) *A diachronic study of Austronesian verb morphosyntax*, PhD thesis, Universität Frankfurt.

Zorc, R.D. (1986) 'The genetic relationships of Philippine languages', in P. Geraghty, L. Carrington and S.A. Wurm (eds), *Focal II: papers from the Fourth International Conference on Austronesian Linguistics*, Canberra: Pacific Linguistics.

CHAPTER TWO

LANGUAGE SHIFT AND ENDANGERMENT

Margaret Florey

1 INTRODUCTION

In recent years there has been a marked upsurge internationally in concern about the issue of language endangerment – by communities of speakers of endangered languages (ELs), the media, and among linguists. This increased attention has stemmed from a growing realization that the world's linguistic resources are rapidly shrinking. Estimates such as the widely quoted prediction that perhaps only 10% of the approximately 6000 languages in the world today could be classified as 'safe', while 10% are nearly extinct and 20% are moribund (Krauss 1992:6) highlight diminishing linguistic and cultural diversity and the loss of indigenous knowledge.

The various topics relating to language endangerment and language obsolescence have been the subject of much academic discourse through the past decade. Researchers have addressed issues from the perspectives of evaluating or describing programs aimed at reversing language shift or maintaining or renewing ELs (Fishman 1991, Hartman and Henderson 1994, Hinton 1994, Hinton and Hale 2001, Mugler and Lynch 1996), analyzing the issues facing a particular country or language family (Brenzinger 1992, Schmidt 1990, Robins and Uhlenbeck 1991), discussing community responses to language endangerment (Grenoble and Whaley 1998), offering suggested focus questions for the study of ELs (Dorian 1989), critiquing the role of specialists vis-à-vis language endangerment (Ostler 1998), producing tools for working with ELs (Thieberger 1995), placing language endangerment within the broader framework of the loss of biodiversity (Maffi 2001), and providing a survey accessible to non-specialists of the issues involved in language obsolescence (Crystal 2000).

Yet the concern and the initiatives which are emerging in other parts of the world have not been matched in the Austronesian region, which, despite its tremendous linguistic resources and the rapid pace at which minority languages are becoming endangered, remains remarkable for the lack of detailed information about many of the languages and their linguistic vitality. To date, there has been no comparable sense of urgency among linguists – or among speakers or community groups – to work towards the documentation and maintenance of endangered Austronesian languages. Indeed, Austronesian languages have received scanty attention in the volumes which purport to provide a regional overview of language endangerment. The *Atlas of the world's languages in danger of disappearing* (Wurm 1996) includes no maps or analysis of language endangerment for Austronesian languages – even for those languages for which this information has been reasonably well-documented, such as in Taiwan and Maluku (the Moluccas). Discussion of Austronesian languages in Robins and Uhlenbeck (1991) is limited to several pages focused largely on Indonesia. It is still too often the case that in many of the grammars and theses concerning specific Austronesian languages which are being written, comments on the vitality of languages are preliminary and fleeting, and such issues are usually not central to the research methodology.

The Austronesian region is home to perhaps 1200 languages, or 20% of the world's linguistic resources, and almost two thirds of all Austronesian languages are spoken within the countries covered by this volume. A quick survey of ethnolinguistic communities reveals very wide variation in the size of speaker populations, ranging from about 80 million for Javanese to just several hundred for the much smaller languages of eastern Indonesia, such as Huaulu. There are also great differences in linguistic vitality between regions, with documented levels of language endangerment highest among the Formosan languages of Taiwan, the languages of Negrito peoples in the Philippines, and the languages of the Moluccan islands in eastern Indonesia. Alongside language endangerment we are witnessing the growth in speaker numbers of encroaching languages (see section 3.2).

This chapter aims to survey language endangerment issues and ethnolinguistic vitality among the 800 or so Austronesian languages spoken in the fourteen countries represented within this volume. The second section reviews the key factors which are commonly drawn upon in assessments of the linguistic vitality of a language, discusses the terminology used to describe levels of fluency of speakers and the level of vitality of speech communities, and summarizes the symptoms and causes of language endangerment specific to Austronesian languages. Section 3 presents a country-by-country summary of the estimated ethnolinguistic vitality of Austronesian languages drawing on the most detailed sources available. The final section analyses more precisely what is being lost by focusing on languages, dialects, speech levels, and registers, and concludes by reviewing priorities for linguists working with Austronesian languages.

2 FACTORS IN ASSESSING LANGUAGE ENDANGERMENT

In the literature an array of factors is used to define language endangerment and to assess the vitality of languages, and language endangerment is attributed to a wide range of symptoms and causes. Such analyses have led to a profusion of terms used to characterize speech communities, including healthy, shifting, threatened, endangered, moribund, obsolescent, and extinct. This is a complex issue which reflects the concerns of linguists and members of speech communities. This section outlines both factors used to define language endangerment and the symptoms and causes of language endangerment which recur in the literature. Problems with applying particular factors are discussed throughout the chapter.

2.1 Domains of language use

Within a multilingual community, speakers select a language from among the linguistic resources available to them to talk with various members of their speech community about particular topics in a range of social contexts. The specific combination of speaker/s, interlocutor/s, topic, and context identifies domains of language use in a community, such as the home or family life, workplace, religion and/or ritual practices, and education. Himmelmann (forthcoming:20) takes as an 'essential symptom for the vitality of a language the number and quality of domains in which it is used' and proposes as a definition of endangerment 'languages whose usage domains are presently undergoing a rapid reduction'. For example, Mead (1999:58) reports language shift from Mori (Sulawesi) to Indonesian marked by a diglossic situation in which the domains in which Mori is spoken are decreasing.

2.2 Transmission and language acquisition

Language endangerment may be defined in terms of whether or not children are being linguistically socialized in an environment in which they are sufficiently exposed to the use of a language in a range of domains to be able to acquire full use of that language – that is, whether parents and older members of a community are speaking the language with and around children and young people. Steinhauer (forthcoming:1) proposes that 'a language...is probably irreversibly endangered when the original language is no longer passed on to new generations'. Wurm (1996:1) argues that a language is endangered when it is 'not learned any more by children, or at least by a large part of the children of that community (say at least 30 per cent)'. For example, Kershaw (1992:183) discusses language shift from Dusun to Brunei Malay and remarks that the older generation have 'failed to involve their children in all the domestic and economic activities in and through which alone the full range of Dusun vocabulary would have been acquired as a normal part of the process of maturation'.

2.3 Size of speaker community

Linguists and members of speech communities in which language shift is occurring frequently link the size of speaker population with levels of endangerment and suggest figures above which a language may be considered safe and below which the language is said to be endangered. This is a controversial issue and there is little consensus among linguists on what size constitutes a 'safe' or an 'endangered' speaker population. For example, Dixon (1991:231) suggests that 'Every language with fewer than 10,000 speakers is at risk of extinction in the medium term. Languages with up to 1000 speakers are severely at risk'. Crystal (2000:12–13) proposes a much smaller figure and contends that 'most people would accept that a language spoken by less than 100 is in a very dangerous situation' and that 'a total of 10,000 suggests safety in the short term, but not in the medium term'. Crystal provides a useful discussion of the issues involved in attempting to relate speaker population and endangerment. J.E. Grimes (1995) presents a mathematical model for the relationship between size of language group and its effect on language endangerment.

While it is plausible to surmise that languages which are numerically very small will struggle to survive alongside larger language communities, a comparison of case studies of language endangerment scenarios throughout the world indicates that there is no simple predictive relationship between the size of a speech community and the viability of a language. A language may survive in a small community in which it serves as an important marker of group identity, while conversely language maintenance may be of relatively little importance to a much larger ethnolinguistic community with social and political power. It is these contrasting cases which lead Dorian (1989:9) to suggest as one research focus question the issue of 'the phenomena of abrupt transmission failure or "tip," and of the persistence against seemingly high odds'.

The complexity of this issue is compounded by the fact that in the Austronesian language family there has always been great variation in the size of ethnolinguistic communities. As the data in Section 3 (below) indicate, the largest speech communities, which number hundreds of thousands or millions of speakers, are located in the western Austronesian region (e.g. Javanese, Tagalog, Minangkabau). These communities can be contrasted with those in the eastern Austronesian area, where languages which are comparatively large may have a population numbering only tens of thousands – for example, Keo (Flores Island, Nusa Tenggara) or Fordata (Tanimbar Islands, southeast Maluku), both with speaker populations estimated at 50,000. These languages coexist alongside others which, in recorded history, have always had a much smaller speaker base – for example, Batuley (Aru Islands, south Maluku), with a speaker population approaching 4000, or Huaulu (Seram Island, central Maluku), with a population of several hundred. Language use has been assessed as vigorous for some languages with relatively small speaker numbers: for example, Taloki (500 speakers) reportedly persists across domains despite the dominance of the Muna ethnolinguistic community (Mead 1999:42). Buru provides an interesting contrast. On this Central Moluccan island, C.E. Grimes (2000:98) found that use of the Li Enyorot dialect of Buru is 'not vigorous and a language shift to Malay is under way' despite a speaker population of almost 12,000, while use of the Rana dialect remains vigorous with a similar speaker population.

2.4 Linguistic resources

Language endangerment may be appraised through a perceived reduction in special registers, ritual languages, or speech levels. For example, the speech styles which were formerly used for ritual purposes in a community may have been replaced by the everyday or mundane variant of an indigenous language, or by an encroaching language. Similarly, some genres may be retained but the range of varieties within the genre may be reduced. For example, certain kinds of narratives such as origin stories and epic tales may be lost, while others such as folk stories are retained (see Florey 1993). That is, a shrinking of conceptual diversity is noted (Maffi 2001).

2.5 Language change

Where language shift progresses gradually through a community, the extent of language endangerment may be assessed through analysis of lexical and morphosyntactic change from one generation to the next. Linguists have noted the presence of 'reductive processes' (Dorian 1989), grammatical restructuring (Dorian 1981, Florey 1997, Schmidt 1985), and lexical innovation and loss (Gal 1989).

2.6 Speaker fluency

Related to the above issue, the magnitude of language endangerment may be determined by an assessment that levels of speaker fluency are diminishing. Such assessments may be made informally – through listening to people talking or through asking people to gauge their own fluency. More formal assessments may be made by testing language ability and plotting the results against age on a continuum of language proficiency (Dorian 1981, Florey 1997). There is a plethora of often poorly defined terms used to characterize speakers, including strong, fully competent, or fluent speaker (and this may be subcategorized to differentiate older fluent and younger fluent speakers), imperfect speaker, semi-speaker, rememberer, terminal speaker, word-inserter, and passive (and near-passive) bilingual. Evans (2001) provides a useful discussion about the pitfalls of working with labels such as these and the fluidity of speech communities and community perceptions of speaker ability.

2.7 Causes of language obsolescence

Himmelmann (forthcoming) draws a distinction between the symptoms and the actual causes of language obsolescence. Symptoms are directly observable indications that use of a given language is declining in a speech community. Some of these were reviewed in the preceding subsections. This section summarizes several of the major causes which have been implicated in the process of language shift within the Austronesian region, and these are further exemplified throughout the chapter.

Population dispersal and migration has been widespread in these countries, and includes unassisted (voluntary) migration, assisted resettlement programs such as the Indonesian government's *transmigrasi* program, and forced relocation such as the movement of the entire populations of Teun, Nila, and Serua islands in south Maluku to Seram island in central Maluku. Alongside the resettlement of migrants, the concomitant dispersal of aboriginal people from their homeland and extensive linguistic and cultural change is observed. This pattern has been documented, for example, in the Belait region of Brunei as a result of the oil industry (Martin 1996) and in Taiwan as a result of immigration of Chinese from the mainland. Himmelmann (forthcoming) points out that 'it does not take a large number of speakers of another language in order to change language usage' in such a setting.

Globalization and the introduction of languages of wider communication have impacted greatly on Austronesian languages. Colonization and the spread of non-indigenous religions has introduced Dutch, English, Spanish, Arabic and Portuguese to speakers of Austronesian languages. In the post-colonial era of nation building, national and official languages such as Indonesian, Malaysian, Tagalog, and various Chinese languages have continued to impact on minority languages, particularly through their widespread use in education (see also Steinhauer, Chapter 3 in this volume).

Intermarriage is often associated with sociopolitical change and increased contact between ethnolinguistic groups, and has been implicated in the process of language shift as it may lead to increased use of a lingua franca such as Brunei Malay (Martin 1996), Ambonese Malay (Florey 1991), or Sabah Malay (King 1992).

Religious conversion has had a wide-sweeping impact on language vitality. The influence of conversion to Islam on language shift has been noted for example in Brunei (Martin 1996) and Buru (C.E. Grimes 2000), while the influence of conversion to (Protestant) Christianity has been noted in Maluku (Florey 1991, 2001). In West Kalimantan, the Roman Catholic church is reported to have a policy to use Indonesian only with Dayaks because they consider the Dayaks have an advantage with their (usual) knowledge of Malay and this will further assist them in the wider society (Adelaar forthcoming).

3 ETHNOLINGUISTIC VITALITY OF AUSTRONESIAN LANGUAGES

This section provides a country-by-country survey of the estimated ethnolinguistic vitality of the Austronesian languages.

3.1 Sources

It is unfortunately still the case that the work of determining ethnolinguistic vitality is hampered by a paucity of detailed information for many languages. There are two principal resources which linguists commonly draw upon for general information about Austronesian languages – the *Ethnologue* (B.F. Grimes 2000) and the *Language atlas of the Pacific area* (Wurm and Hattori 1981, 1983; henceforth WH; a revised and updated version of this atlas is in preparation by Pacific Linguistics). Problems with these works mean that they do not provide a completely accurate perspective of the linguistic situation, and errors are too often replicated as authors and editors of each resource draw on the other for information.

The *Ethnologue* is compiled by staff at the Summer Institute of Linguistics (SIL), which is part of an international organization which includes the Wycliffe Bible Translators. In this region where far too many languages remain undocumented, SIL staff are often the only linguists documenting languages and publishing linguistic material. However, the ideological goals of the organization inform the linguistic training of staff, work undertaken in the field, and data collection practices, and these factors bear on the data presented in the *Ethnologue*.

Lexicostatistics is a method commonly used by SIL linguists to determine synchronic and diachronic relationships between languages. This method frequently yields a different estimation of the number of languages in a region, the number of dialects of a particular language, and the extent of mutual intelligibility between languages and dialects than the comparative method, which is more widely favoured in historical comparative linguistics.

A survey methodology is used by SIL field staff to provide a snapshot of ethnolinguistic vitality and determine research priorities. This method commonly depends on estimated speaker numbers from census or other administrative data and on self-reporting of speaker fluency, rather than drawing on more reliable methods such as language testing or long-term participant observation. These surveys generate imprecise data and, given the rapid pace of social and linguistic change, soon become outdated. However, it is again important to stress that the survey data are often the only information available and thus sometimes provide our only insight into language endangerment. An indication of the gaps in our knowledge is the number of languages listed in the *Ethnologue* as still requiring even basic survey work.

Given the issues outlined here, it is considered that the extent of language endangerment is underestimated in the *Ethnologue* and WH, and that the information in these resources is best regarded with caution.

3.2 Strong languages

Each situation involving language shift is characterized not only by a diminishing population of speakers of the threatened or endangered language, but also by a growing number of speakers of an encroaching language. Within the Austronesian region, languages which are growing in speaker population include languages of wider communication (such as English, Chinese, and Arabic), national languages (such as Tagalog and Indonesian), lingua francas (such as Malay throughout Indonesia, Malaysia, Brunei, and Singapore, Tetum in East Timor), and some smaller indigenous languages (such as Asilulu in Ambon Island and southwest Seram Island in eastern Indonesia).

Ten Austronesian languages appeared in the *Ethnologue*'s 'Top 100 languages in the world by population' (B.F. Grimes 1996) – Javanese, Sundanese, Indonesian, and Madurese in Indonesia, Tagalog, Cebuano, Ilokano, and Hiligaynon in the Philippines, Malay in Malaysia, and Malagasy in Madagascar. Speaker populations range from seven million for Hiligaynon to about 80 million for Javanese.

While Javanese and Sundanese have the greatest number of first language speakers, Malay is the most widely spoken Austronesian language. The influence of Malay may be ascribed not only to its political status, but also to its multiple roles as an indigenous language, a national language in Indonesia, Malaysia, Singapore and Brunei (Prentice 1990:913, Tryon 1995b:8), and a lingua franca – both as regional varieties of Malay and as the lexifier language for a number of pidgins and/or creoles (Prentice 1994). The varieties of Malay which are spoken as national languages in Indonesia and Malaysia are given different names – Indonesian (*bahasa Indonesia*) and Malaysian (*bahasa Malaysia*) – because of their status within separate countries. However, using the linguistic criteria of level of mutual intelligibility, these two 'languages' are linguistically dialects of one language. The combined figures for Indonesian and Malay(sian) would more accurately reflect the speaker population of Malay.

To the ten Austronesian languages in the *Ethnologue*'s 'Top 100 languages', Tryon (1995b:17) adds a further fifteen Austronesian languages which have a speaker population of more than one million speakers. Tryon points out that 'these twenty-five languages alone account for more than 240,000,000 speakers, or something like 87% of all Austronesian language speakers'. Eleven of these languages are located in Indonesia and the remaining four are spoken in the Philippines. Thus fifteen of the twenty-five largest Austronesian languages are found in Indonesia.

3.3 Endangered languages

A general picture of the degree of endangerment of Austronesian languages is given in Table 2.1 using data summarized from the *Ethnologue* (B.F. Grimes 2000). However, as noted in Section 3.1, the extent of language endangerment is underestimated in this source. Therefore in the country-by-country survey which follows, every attempt has been made to rely on more detailed published sources and information provided by linguists working in the field (including SIL linguists) to provide a more detailed and accurate picture of the number of endangered and moribund languages and the languages which are strong and gaining speakers to the detriment of ELs. Where possible, these works have been used to update or correct the information in the *Ethnologue* and WH.

The discussion below of linguistic vitality within each of the fourteen countries in this region focuses on the languages which have become extinct or are in danger of extinction, the languages which remain strong, and those languages which are encroaching or gaining speakers to the detriment of smaller languages.

3.3.1 Brunei

Seven languages are recognized as indigenous to Brunei – Dusun (Tutong₁ in WH), Tutong (Tutong₂ in WH), Bisaya, Belait (Balait Jati), and (Murat) Lun Bawang, and two Malay variants – Kedayan (Kadayan) and Brunei Malay (Martin 1992b). Nothofer (1991:155) treats Dusun and Bisaya as dialects of one language. None of these languages is listed as endangered in the *Ethnologue* or WH, but Sercombe (1999:596) asserts that 'a number of minority groups in Brunei appear to be undergoing a process of ethnolinguistic assimilation under the hegemony of the numerically and politically dominant Brunei Malays'. Two languages have become extinct – Dali (Daleh) and Lelak (Martin 1995:31). Speaker numbers are small for several languages – fewer than 500 for Murut (Martin 1992b:87) and fewer than a thousand for Bisaya and Belait, and relatively little is known about the latter (Martin 1996; see also CLYNES, BELAIT). Kershaw (1992) highlights the difficulties inherent in the community decisions implicated in the shift from

TABLE 2.1: NUMBER OF LANGUAGES AND ESTIMATED LEVEL OF ENDANGERMENT (B.F. GRIMES 2000)

Country and region	Number of Austronesian languages listed in the *Ethnologue*	Number of Austronesian languages listed as extinct or nearly extinct
Brunei	10	0
China (Hainan)	1	0
Comoros Islands	1	0
East Timor (Timor Lorosa'e)	13	0
Indonesia		
Java, Bali, Madura	9	0
Kalimantan	82	nearly extinct – 1
Maluku	114	extinct – 3 nearly extinct – 10 dialect extinction – 5
Nusa Tenggara	48	0
Sulawesi	114	nearly extinct – 1 endangered – 1
Sumatra	51	nearly extinct – 1
West Papua (Irian Jaya)	53	extinct – 1 nearly extinct – 3
Kampuchea	1	0
Madagascar	2	0
Malaysia		
Peninsular	7	nearly extinct – 1
Sabah	53	0
Sarawak	46	extinct – 1 endangered – 1
Myanmar (Burma)	1	0
Philippines	163	extinct – 3 nearly extinct – 3
Singapore	4	0
Taiwan	24	extinct – 7 nearly extinct – 6 dialect extinction – 2
Thailand	7	0
Vietnam	2	0
TOTAL	806	extinct – 15 nearly extinct – 26 endangered – 2 dialect extinction – 7

Dusun to Brunei Malay which, with perhaps 250,000 (first- and second-language) speakers, is the strongest Austronesian language in Brunei and is widely used as a lingua franca.

Three non-Malay, non-indigenous languages are also spoken by migrant populations in Brunei – Iban, Penan (Punan), and Mukah Melanau (Martin and Poedjosoedarmo 1996). While speaker numbers are fewer than fifty for Penan (Nothofer 1991, Martin and Sercombe 1992), each of these languages is represented by a much larger population in neighboring Sarawak. Standard Malay is also used in Brunei as a variant largely restricted to more formal domains such as education, ceremonial purposes and the media (Martin and Poedjosoedarmo 1996:6).

3.3.2 East Timor (Timor Lorosa'e)

Hajek (2002) discusses the complex linguistic and sociopolitical issues involved in determining the number and classification of indigenous languages in East Timor. The *Ethnologue* lists thirteen Austronesian languages for this country. Hajek (2002:182) proposes that 'the real number is likely to be in the range of 15–20' and points out that speaker numbers are far from certain given the extent of displacement of the population. To the list of Austronesian languages, Hajek (2002:185) adds Maku'a, listed in both WH and the *Ethnologue* as a Trans New Guinea language.

Himmelmann and Hajek (2001) provide recent evidence that Maku'a (Lóvaia) is moribund, with fewer than ten elderly speakers. Fataluku is the (non-Austronesian) encroaching language. The languages which have had the greatest impact on the vitality of smaller indigenous languages are Tetun and Indonesian. It is likely that the impact of Indonesian will diminish in the future, while the roles of Tetun and Portuguese will increase (Hull 1999). Hajek (2002) indicates that the future of Idate, Waima'a and Naueti is uncertain given both population displacement and the encroachment of Tetun.

3.3.3 Indonesia

The *Ethnologue* indicates that 467 Austronesian languages are spoken in Indonesia. This one country shows enormous linguistic diversity – in the number of languages, the size of ethnolinguistic groups, and the vitality of languages. As discussed above, the largest Austronesian language, Javanese, is indigenous to Indonesia, while the languages of eastern Indonesia are typically much smaller. The available data also indicate that the highest documented level of language (and dialect) endangerment in Indonesia is occurring in Maluku.

3.3.3.1 Indonesia – Java, Bali, Madura

Just four languages are indigenous to these three islands – Javanese and Sundanese in Java, Madurese in Madura, and Balinese in Bali (WH). The *Ethnologue* lists Osing as a separate language, but Clynes (1995a:469) notes that it is a dialect of Javanese which 'deviates significantly from others'. Kangean is also listed as a separate language, and Clynes (1995b:485) notes that it is a variety of Madurese which is 'barely understandable by East Madurese speakers' and has been recorded as a separate language in some publications. Badui and Tengger are listed in the *Ethnologue* as languages of this area, but are more accurately treated as dialects of Sundanese and Javanese respectively.

Javanese, Sundanese and Madurese are among the top one hundred languages in the world by population and Balinese is one of the twenty-five Austronesian languages with more than one million speakers (see Section 3.2). While none of these languages can yet be considered endangered, it should be noted that there is a shift towards Indonesian and regional Malay (Jakarta Malay) by young children, and that there is some impact on the use of the speech levels which are a feature of these languages.

3.3.3.2 Indonesia – Kalimantan

The *Ethnologue* lists 82 languages for Kalimantan of which only one, Lengilu, is recorded as nearly extinct. This language is estimated to have ten speakers. Figures from WH and the *Ethnologue* indicate that six languages are estimated to have fewer than 500 speakers – Bukat (400), Bukitan (WH estimate 550, *Ethnologue* estimates 410), Kereho-Uheng (Punan Keriau) (200), Punan Aput (Aput) (370), Punan Merah (137), and Punan Merap (200). In the context of the larger language groups in Kalimantan (many of which number in the tens of thousands), it is reasonable to suggest there may be some concern for the viability of these languages.

3.3.3.3 Indonesia – Maluku

The *Ethnologue* lists 114 languages for Maluku, and the highest documented degree of language endangerment in Indonesia is located here, with three languages estimated to be extinct, ten nearly extinct, and five dialects also verging on extinction. However, this figure underestimates the severity of the situation. Data from other sources for Maluku indicate that six languages are extinct, ten are nearly extinct, and a further nine languages are clearly endangered, while at least seven dialects are endangered or nearing extinction. As indicated in Section 2, language data from this region demonstrate that speaker numbers alone cannot be used as an accurate indicator of language vitality.

On Seram Island, a number of languages have been estimated to be moving rapidly towards obsolescence – Naka'ela, Loun, and Hulung on the north coast, and Piru, West Littoral (the label Collins 1983 uses for the language spoken in Eti, Kaibobo, Hatusua, and Waesamu), Kamarian-Rumakai, and Paulohi on the south coast of Seram (Collins and Voorhoeve 1983 (henceforth CV), Collins 1983). The *Ethnologue* erroneously suggests that Kaibobo is spoken in Rumahkay (*sic*). Amahai is moribund, with fewer than fifty speakers (Florey 2002, Florey and van Engelenhoven 2000, 2001, Collins 1983), although CV inaccurately suggest that it has approximately 500 speakers. The *Ethnologue* also lists as endangered Salas (Seram Island, Central Maluku), which is estimated to have only fifty speakers and it is noted that 'most use Masiwang as second language' (*sic*). Despite relatively large speaker numbers for Alune, language shift to Ambonese Malay has been noted (Florey 1991, 1993, 1997).

In examining the ethnolinguistic vitality of the languages of Buru Island, C.E. Grimes (1995, 2000) indicates that Hukumina is functionally extinct, with only one remaining elderly speaker, and Kayeli is moribund, with four remaining speakers. The Fogi dialect of Buru is endangered through the domination of Butonese migrants. Speakers of the Li Enyorot (Lisela) dialect of Buru are shifting to Ambonese Malay, a process which Grimes (2000:98) attributes to their participation in the 'greater Malay Islamic coastal culture'. The Kelang language of Kelang and Asaude Islands is endangered, and the Nusalaut language on Nusalaut Island is nearing extinction (Collins 1983, CV, *Ethnologue*).

In south (southeast and southwest) Maluku, the Imroing (Babar Islands) and Selwasa (Tanimbar Islands) languages may be endangered (Florey and van Engelenhoven 2000). The Teun, Nila and Serua ethnolinguistic groups were all displaced from their homeland in 1978 due to volcanic activity and relocated in transmigrant villages on south Seram Island. Each of these languages is considered endangered (ibid.).

Dialect extinction is documented for several languages in Maluku. However, such reports are not always accurate. CV suggest that the Southern Haruku dialect of Haruku (Haruku Island) and the Allang dialect of Larike-Wakasihu are extinct, but several elderly speakers of Southern Haruku and two elderly speakers of Allang have been located among the Moluccan migrant community in the Netherlands (Florey 2001b, Florey and van Engelenhoven 2001). Collins (1983) also includes as extinct Tenga-tenga on Ambon

Island, while the *Ethnologue* treats Tengah-tengah as a dialect of Tulehu, for which language use is recorded as vigorous. Although CV estimate that there are 4000 speakers for the southern dialect of Alune (formerly spoken in Kairatu village on Seram Island), this dialect is extinct (Collins 1983, Florey 1991). The Central Masela, East Masela and Tela dialects of Masela-South Babar (Babar Island) are estimated to have between 500 and 1000 speakers each and may be endangered (WH, Florey and van Engelenhoven 2000).

3.3.3.4 Indonesia – Nusa Tenggara

The *Ethnologue* lists 44 Austronesian languages for Nusa Tenggara. None of these languages is marked as extinct or nearly extinct, and the majority are documented as having a population of speakers numbering more than 10,000 and in some cases numbering upwards of 100,000 (for example, Sasak with 1.5 million, Manggarai with 400,000, Bima with 365,000). However, it appears that in this complex linguistic situation there are a number of smaller languages which are endangered through extensive contact with neighboring languages (both Papuan and Austronesian), lingua francas (such as Tetun (Tetun) and 'Timorese' (Dawan, Atoni) on Timor) and languages of wider communication. Hajek (2002) notes that the impact of colonization on languages in west Timor has been much greater than in East Timor. It has been observed that speakers of the Helong Darat dialect of Helong on Semau Island are beginning to shift to Kupang Malay as a result of contact with speakers from Roti and Savu (B.F. Grimes 2000). Despite large speaker numbers (approximately 150,000), some speakers of Lamaholot near Larantuka on the eastern tip of Flores are reported to have shifted to (Kupang) Malay.

3.3.3.5 Indonesia – Sulawesi

The *Ethnologue* lists 114 languages for Sulawesi and records only one of them, Dampal, as nearly extinct. Himmelmann (2001) surveyed eleven Tomini-Tolitoli languages and found that two of these languages are moribund. Dampal, a dialect of Dampelas, was found to have hardly any fluent speakers, and Himmelmann (2001:44) suggests that Taje 'may become extinct in the next decade or two'. He estimates that there are perhaps 200 speakers who are 'truly native Taje' with two Taje parents and who have reasonable fluency (2001:31). This situation is attributed to an endangerment scenario arising from immigration and intermarriage, and symptoms of endangerment are lack of intergenerational transmission and shrinking in domains of use. Himmelmann (forthcoming) notes that for all Tomini-Tolitoli languages there are some settings in which the language is endangered and two languages, Dampelas and Balaesang, are endangered in all communities despite numbers of speakers which appear strong (10,000 and 3200 respectively).

Similar observations hold for the two northernmost groups of Sulawesi languages, the Sangiric and the Minahasan languages. Himmelmann and Wolff (p. c.) report that two of the four Sangiric languages, Bantik and Ratahan (Toratán), appear to be no longer acquired by children. They estimate that 'only 500 good speakers of Toratán are left, mostly over 60 years of age, and a few thousand semi-speakers' (Himmelmann and Wolff 1999:3). They also suspect that all five Minahasan languages are in a similar state of endangernment. The whole Minahasan area – including the Bantik and Ratahan speaking areas – is characterized by a strong trend towards temporary outmigration. Since Dutch colonial times Minahasans have tended to study and work outside their native areas, often taking their families with them and only returning to their native villages for their retirement. Thus, for example, Minahasan policemen and teachers are found all over Sulawesi and adjoining parts of Indonesia. See Wolff (forthcoming) for further discussion.

Mead (1999:76) notes language shift for the Rahambuu language, which belongs to the Bungku-Mori-Tolaki group in Southeast Sulawesi, reporting that 'In some communities, Rahambuu is only used between members of the older generation, the children speaking exclusively Bugis or Indonesian'.

Languages which are not listed in the *Ethnologue* as nearing extinction yet which have very small speaker numbers include Budong-Budong, with seventy speakers or fewer, and the *Ethnologue* notes that 'speakers are becoming bilingual in Topoiyo through inter-marriage and geographical proximity' (B.F. Grimes 2000). Baras, with only 250 speakers, is considered endangered and it is noted that 'Some think the language will die out' (ibid.). Taloki has 500 speakers and there is a documented high level of bilingualism in Muna. Tomadino has 600 speakers and people are reported to use Bungku as their mother tongue. Very small speaker numbers are recorded for Kumberaha (250 speakers), Waru (350), and Busoa (500), although we have no accurate information on the status of these languages. As a further indication that speaker numbers are not an accurate measure of vitality, the *Ethnologue* notes that Sedoa has 600 speakers and yet that language use is reportedly vigorous.

Bugis and Makassarese are two of the twenty-five Austronesian languages with more than one million speakers. Manado Malay is also an encroaching language with speaker numbers estimated in the millions.

3.3.3.6 Indonesia – Sumatra

The *Ethnologue* lists 51 Austronesian languages for Sumatra, while Foley (1983) estimates that around twenty languages are spoken on Sumatra and surrounding islands. Overall, speaker numbers are very high and the *Ethnologue* and Tryon (1995b) include six Sumatran languages among the twenty-five Austronesian languages with more than one million speakers – Minangkabau, Acehnese, Toba Batak, Lampung, Dairi Batak and Rejang. Again, the accuracy of these figures should be treated with caution. McGinn (1982), who conducted fieldwork in South Sumatra, suggests a Rejang population closer to 200,000 speakers.

One language, Lom, is reported in the *Ethnologue* to have possibly fifty speakers and, if so, is moribund. The data source is Smedal, who produced a Lom wordlist (1987) which provides no information concerning number of speakers. Smedal himself reports that he is not a linguist and draws on data from WH and historical sources. Foley (1983) notes that 'Lom is a small language group reported in the 19th century in the north-east interior of Banka Island'. The language is marked as the Lom Group-Level Isolate and is surrounded by speakers of the Bangka dialect of Sumatra Malay. Smedal (1987:2) suggests that Bangka Malay speakers formerly could not understand Lom. However, Nothofer (1994) and Adelaar (1995:339–340) demonstrate that it is closely related to Malay, if not a dialect of it. The *Ethnologue* reports 850 Bangka Malay speakers of Lom, presumably as a second language (although this is not clear).

Enggano was considered endangered in the earlier part of the twentieth century due to population loss from disease and trauma. However, Foley (1983) notes that it now has a speaker population estimated at 1000 and its vitality may be improving.

3.3.3.7 Indonesia – West Papua (Irian Jaya)

Approximately fifty-three Austronesian languages are spoken in West Papua. We have very little accurate information for many of these languages. The *Ethnologue* lists just one language, Mapia, as extinct and reports that its speakers now speak Biak, and two languages are listed as nearly extinct. Two speakers are recorded in the *Ethnologue* for Tandia (in 1991), and it is noted that speakers have shifted to Wandamen. However, WH estimates that there are 350 speakers. The *Ethnologue* records six speakers for Dusner (in 1978) and this language may now be extinct.

3.3.4 Madagascar and Comoros Islands

The Austronesian language family is represented in Madagascar by dialects of Malagasy, of which there are perhaps ten million speakers. The Merina dialect is the strongest and forms the basis for the national language (Crystal 1997:320, WH). The *Ethnologue* estimates that 700 speakers of Malagasy are also located on the Comoros Islands, north-west of Madagascar. Literature concerning the history of Malagasy in the Comoros Islands and Madagascar was reviewed by Dahl (1951) and, for more recent publications, by Adelaar (1991, 1995). Given the small population on the Comoros Islands, it is expected that the local variant of Malagasy is threatened by contact with the much larger population of speakers of Comorian and by French and Arabic, which are languages of wider communication.

3.3.5 Malaysia

In Malaysia linguists are noting the impact on indigenous languages of the national language, Malaysian, which is ranked 54th in the top 100 languages in the world with an estimated first- and second-language speaker population of more than 17 million. Alongside standard Malay, major encroaching languages are the regional varieties which serve as lingua francas such as Sabah Malay.

3.3.5.1 Malaysia – Peninsular

Within Peninsular Malaysia one language – Kenaboi – is extinct (although the genetic affiliation of this language remains controversial) and one – Orang Kanaq – is documented as having only 34 speakers and thus near extinction (WH). Orang Seletar (541 speakers) and Duano' (1922 speakers) may reasonably be considered endangered given the small number of speakers relative to the strength and status of Malay.

3.3.5.2 Malaysia – Sabah

Fifty-three languages are listed in the *Ethnologue* for this state of Malaysia, and King (1992) provides an updated (lexicostatistical) classification of the languages of Sabah. The *Ethnologue* lists the Nabay dialect of Keningau Murut as nearing extinction. However, WH list 4000 speakers for this dialect. While no languages are listed in the *Ethnologue* as being close to extinction, it is noted that Sabah Malay and/or stronger indigenous languages are drawing speakers from some of the smaller language groups. Speakers of Abai Sungai (500 speakers) are switching to Sabah Malay, Dumpas (numbering 500–100 speakers) is threatened through high levels of intermarriage which encourages the use of a lingua franca, while speakers of Kota Maruda Talantang are said to be bilingual in Kimaragang. Second-language use of Sabah Malay is noted for Kuijau (alongside use of Central Dusun) and for Paluan (alongside use of Tagal). King notes that language shift is apparent among speakers of the Ambual dialect of Murut (1992:55) and Beaufort Murut (ibid.:57). King reports that a 1989 survey found that Lobu was moribund in Tampias (1992:60). Kopping (forthcoming) describes language shift over a thirty-year period in one east Sabah village from Kadazan to Sabah Malay.

3.3.5.3 Malaysia – Sarawak

Forty-six languages are listed for this Malaysian state and one, Seru, is recorded as extinct. Kanowit, with 170 speakers, is considered endangered as speakers are switching to Iban. Ghani and Ridzuan (1992) describe language shift from Miriek (Murik) to Sarawak Malay and indicate that Miriek is no longer the language of the home for speakers under thirty. Two languages with very small speaker populations may be considered endangered: Lelak (220) and Tanjong (100). The Punan Batu (50), Sian (70), and Ukit (120) dialects of Bukitan may also be endangered.

3.3.6 Philippines

The *Ethnologue* lists 163 Austronesian languages for the Philippines while McFarland (1996) estimates that there are 109 languages. Reid (1994a) observes that the Philippine population consists of two groups which are racially distinct. Historically the earliest inhabitants of the Philippines, the Negrito people are a racial minority who today comprise perhaps 32 ethnolinguistic groups and a population totaling approximately 31,000 located on seven Philippine islands, with the majority living on Luzon (Headland 2001a). Language endangerment in the Philippines is primarily affecting the languages of Negrito peoples and Headland (2001b:1) points out that 'All of these 33 Negrito groups speak endangered languages'. The nomenclature for these languages, including that used in WH and the *Ethnologue*, is rife with often baffling alternatives. Reid (1994a:448) provides a useful summary of the names and their etymologies, and indicates that the Negritos of Luzon refer to themselves as Agta, Atta, Arta, Alta, and Ayta, all of which mean 'Negrito person'. Negritos are vastly outnumbered by the non-Negrito populations (often referred to as 'lowlanders' or 'Christians'), with a population of almost 80 million. Using divergent methodologies, different versions of the historical linguistic relationships between the languages of northern Negritos and other languages in the Cordilleran subgroup of Austronesian are given in Reid (1994a) and McFarland (1996).

According to the *Ethnologue*, three of the languages spoken by Negrito peoples have become extinct (Dicamay Agta, Tayabas Ayta, and Katabaga) and three are listed as nearly extinct – Ata, Sorsogon Ayta, and Isarog Agta. Little information is available for Ata on Negros Oriental, which was estimated in a 1973 SIL survey to be spoken by approximately nine families (and is not included in McFarland 1983). This language is distinct from Ata Manobo of Mindanao, which is reportedly quite strong.

Reid (1994a) and Headland (2001a) locate six extant Ayta languages in western Luzon, and Reid (ibid.) also maps the extinct Tayabas Ayta of eastern Luzon. For western Luzon, McFarland (1983) does not mention Ayta but maps three languages within the Sambal subgroup (which are not spoken by Negrito peoples) and notes that they are very closely interrelated. The *Ethnologue* notes that Sorsogon Ayta (with only 40 speakers) is nearly extinct. Intermarriage is considered to be the factor impacting most heavily on Ayta.

Reid (1994a) maps eight Agta languages in eastern Luzon, including those subsumed under Dumagat ('sea-faring person') and Cagayan. Headland (2001a) provides population figures for thirteen extant Agta languages in eastern Luzon. His data also include Dicamay Agta, which was formerly spoken in eastern Luzon, and Villa Viciosa Agta, which was formerly spoken in northwestern Luzon and which appears likely to be extinct. The *Ethnologue* lists eleven named language variants for Agta, and suggests that Isarog Agta (with 1000 speakers) is nearly extinct. Figures given in Headland (ibid.) and the *Ethnologue* indicate that a number of other Agta languages which are not given this status are much closer to obsolescence, including Alabat Island Agta (fifty speakers), Camarines Norte Agta, and Mt Iraya Agta (both with 200 speakers). McFarland's (1983) data for the Agta languages appear very unreliable.

Reid reports that 'Sinauna Tagalog', a Sambalic language spoken by Negritos in a few mountain areas of Rizal and Quezon Provinces, is 'highly endangered, if not already extinct' (p. c.). The *Ethnologue* erroneously includes Sinauna as a named language variant of Agta.

Very small speaker numbers are recorded in the *Ethnologue* for two other languages of Negrito peoples not listed in WH. Reid (1989:47) reports that his language assistants claimed that only 25–30 households still spoke Arta, while the *Ethnologue* suggests that there were 16 or 17 speakers of Arta in 1992. Reid later (1994b:40) confirmed that 'there are only about 12 remaining speakers of this language living in Aglipay, Quirino'.

The speaker population of Northern Alta was estimated to be 240 speakers in 1992 (B.F. Grimes 2000 drawing on data provided by Reid). Reid (1994a) notes that Alta shows extensive lexical influence from (non-Negrito) Tagalog, while Arta has incorporated many loans from (non-Negrito) Ilokano and Gaddang. The *Ethnologue* indicates that Southern Alta is stronger, with approximately 1000 speakers. Reid (p. c., 1991) considers that the speaker population for this language, which is linguistically distinct from Northern Alta, may number at most 100 families, which Headland (p. c.) concludes on the basis of a demographic analysis of family size would mean approximately 400 people.

Batak, a language of Negrito people spoken in Palawan (Reid 1994a), may be endangered because of its small speaker population (WH estimates 1400) and because it is enclosed between immigrant speaker populations of Kagayanen to the north and south (see MacGregor 1995). Headland (p. c.), drawing on data collected by linguist James Eder, suggests a figure of no more than 400 Batak speakers. Inati (Ati), spoken on the islands of Panay and Negros Occidental (but not shown in WH), is undergoing language shift with a shrinking of domains and usage largely restricted to the home (B.F. Grimes 2000). Reid (p. c.) suggests that the Inati 'if not extinct are highly endangered groups'.

Molbog is a non-Negrito language which may be endangered. Although speaker numbers appear relatively healthy (approximately 6000), Zorc and Thiessen (1995) observe that the population is being displaced from its homeland on the islands south of Palawan by settlers from other areas in the Philippines. The *Ethnologue* notes that speakers also use Sama Mapun as a second language and some speak Tagalog.

3.3.7 Singapore

Austronesian languages indigenous to Singapore include Malay and Orang Seletar, an Aboriginal Malay language. A small population of speakers of Orang Seletar (numbering perhaps 500) survives on the north coast of Singapore. Although the *Ethnologue* notes that a survey is needed, this language is not listed as endangered despite the fact that its small population is greatly outnumbered by speakers of the majority languages which enjoy official status – Malay, Mandarin Chinese, Tamil, and English – and the other Chinese languages spoken by large populations.

3.3.8 Taiwan

The *Ethnologue* lists 24 aboriginal languages for Taiwan, including seventeen living languages, while WH list 23, removing the distinction between Amis and Nataoran Amis. Ten Formosan languages are officially recognized in Taiwan – Atayal, Bunun, Saisiyat, Tsou, Rukai, Paiwan, Puyuma, Amis, Yami and Thao (E. Zeitoun p. c.). In proportion to the number of languages, the greatest extent of language endangerment in the western Austronesian area occurs in Taiwan. The encroaching languages are primarily the Chinese languages – Minnan, Mandarin, and Hakka. The seven Formosan languages which are documented as extinct are Taokas, Hoanya, Papora, Siraya, Ketangalan, Basay, and Kulun. These ethnolinguistic groups are all located in western Taiwan, the area which has been subject to the greatest assimilationist processes of Chinese migration. A further four languages are moribund: Babuza, Kavalan, Thao (with fewer than ten remaining speakers), and Pazeh, for which Zeitoun (p. c.) estimates that there is now only one elderly speaker. WH note that Kanakanabu and Saaroa have speaker numbers of only 200–300, which suggests that these languages are seriously endangered, although not yet near extinction as stated in the *Ethnologue*. Several languages still have active speaker populations but have lost some dialect diversity. For example, Southern Amis is considered nearly extinct by WH, while Tsuchida (1995) reports that the Duhtu dialect of Tsou is endangered (with only 150 speakers) and the Iimutsu dialect is extinct, and the *Ethnologue* marks Nataoran (northern) Amis and the Taai dialect of Saisiyat as nearly extinct.

Formosan languages which reportedly remain relatively strong include Amis (*Ethnologue* estimates 130,000 speakers), Paiwan (WH estimates 53,000 speakers), Atayal (WH, *Ethnologue* estimate 66,000 speakers), Bunun (*Ethnologue* estimates 34,000 speakers), and Seediq (inaccurately listed in the *Ethnologue* as Taroko). WH estimates the number of Seediq speakers at 12,600, whereas the *Ethnologue* gives 28,000 as a figure. Tsukida (SEEDIQ) gives 25,000 and points out that 'those who are younger than twenty usually cannot speak Seediq'. One Formosan language – Bunun – is gaining speakers to the detriment of the two smaller ELs of Kanakanabu and Saaroa as speakers reportedly shift to Bunun.

3.3.9 China (Hainan), Kampuchea (Cambodia), Myanmar (Burma), Thailand, and Vietnam

Only twelve Austronesian languages are listed in the *Ethnologue* for these five countries. Larish (1999:106) reports that both Moken and Moklen are endangered Austronesian languages, although the Moken are retaining their language to a greater extent than the Moklen. Moken is predominantly spoken in Myanmar, while speakers of Moklen are located in Thailand. Larish draws on his own research and reviews previous estimates to suggest that the population of each language is approximately 2500, and considers that this may be too few to sustain ethnolinguistic vitality (1999:490). Larish noticed that 'numerous Moklen children do not converse in the Moklen language' (1999:103) and points to extensive structural convergence and lexical influence resulting from contact with Thai, Burmese, Mon-Khmer and Malay.

One Austronesian language, Tsat (Utsat), is spoken at the southern tip of Hainan. Maddieson and Pang (1993:75) observe that 'communal identity and language loyalty remain strong' despite the fact that almost all of the 4500 Utsat speak Southern Min, the local lingua franca. Thurgood (1999) concurs with this view but demonstrates that more than 1000 years of contact between the Utsat and Hainanese has led to widespread language change in Tsat with grammatical convergence and extensive use of Hainanese loanwords.

Strong languages include (western and eastern) Cham, represented by large numbers of speakers in Vietnam and Kampuchea and a relatively small refugee population in Thailand, Jarai, spoken in Vietnam, and two Malay variants spoken in Thailand.

4 REVIEWING RESEARCH PRIORITIES

The survey above has indicated that centers of comparatively high endangerment are found in Taiwan (where seven of the 24 aboriginal languages have become extinct, four are moribund and two are seriously endangered), Maluku in eastern Indonesia (where six languages have become extinct, ten are moribund, and a further nine are endangered), and among the languages of the Negrito peoples in the Philippines (where three languages have become extinct and the majority of the 25 other languages spoken by Negrito peoples are moribund or endangered). Conversely, centers of relative linguistic stability are reported among speakers of the larger Austronesian languages in other parts of Indonesia (Java, Bali, Nusa Tenggara), and in Vietnam, Kampuchea, and Thailand.

In discussions of language endangerment, concern often tends to focus on the obsolescence of entire languages and on language shift in everyday speech. However, this research focus touches on only one aspect of the wealth of knowledge affected by processes of language shift. Limiting the discussion to a count of the number of languages which have become extinct or which are moribund, or focusing only on the loss of entire languages and ignoring the loss of linguistic diversity obscures the complexity of the linguistic situation and of the issues which are being confronted by speakers and other concerned sections of the (academic and broader) community. Similarly, restricting the definition of 'endangered language' to those languages with small speaker populations disguises the extent of the problem.

Fox's survey (in this volume) of ritual languages, special registers and speech decorum in Austronesian languages indicates the richness of speech styles and linguistic practice found in these languages. It also provides a base against which we can assess what is being and might be lost if the processes of language shift and language obsolescence continue to impact on linguistic diversity among Austronesian languages. Some researchers documenting these languages have reported a reduction in linguistic diversity through the endangerment and loss of dialects, registers, and areas of specialized ethnolinguistic knowledge. For example, the overview above revealed loss of dialect diversity in several locations, including Maluku and Taiwan. Clynes (1995c) documents the loss of 'refined' speech levels of Balinese among young people speaking the Singaraja dialect, which is reflected both in vocabulary and in conversational practice. Bowden (2002) discusses the obsolescence of speech styles among the Taba of north Maluku. Van Engelenhoven (forthcoming) suggests that Lirasniara, a sung language formerly used in

speech communities in southwest Maluku, is not being transmitted to younger generations and is unlikely to survive twenty years. Kuipers (1998:xii) observed wide-sweeping
cultural changes alongside the transition from practice of the indigenous ancestral religion to the adoption of Christianity among the Weyewa, and reports 'the large-scale
rejection of feasting and ritual speech practices and the widespread adoption of
Indonesian in nearly all public gatherings'. Among the Alune of Central Maluku, the loss
of areas of specialized ethnolinguistic knowledge includes aspects of ethnomedicine
(Florey and Wolff 1998), personal names and avoidance vocabulary (Florey and Bolton
1997), and ethnobiological knowledge (Florey 2002). Headland (2001b) also reports the
loss of ethnobiological knowledge among the Casiguran Agta of the Philippines.

The preceding sections highlight the fact that the issue of language endangerment is
complex and multi-faceted. As Dixon (1991:230) points out, typically a community does
not realize its language is endangered until it is too late to reverse the process. Linguists
working throughout the Austronesian region are well placed to assist communities and
the profession in focusing attention on this issue. Among other tasks, they could provide
more complete information on speaker numbers, sound assessments of ethnolinguistic
vitality and speaker fluency, and topics of particular concern (including endangerment of
dialects, registers, and areas of specialized ethnolinguistic knowledge). In this way they
could contribute to an improved assessment of language endangerment. A related task is
to draw particular attention to linguistic situations which have been identified (by a community or a linguist) as critical and in urgent need of documentation. While his stand-
point remains controversial, Dixon (1997:144) strongly argues that the focus of linguistics
must revert to the task of describing languages: 'There is only one thing that really needs
to be done – *get out there and describe a language!*'

Confronted with the linguistic and sociocultural knowledge which is being lost, some
linguists are beginning to call for documentation of ELs which broadens beyond grammatical description. One linguist suggests as a guiding fieldwork principle, 'Assume
you'll be the last linguist ever to get there' (Dorian 1989:7). It is crucial that discussion
within our profession turns to a wider consideration of our involvement in the issues of
language endangerment and maintenance, including reviewing our fieldwork priorities,
the research-oriented and applied tasks we might undertake, the academic and applied
training we need to undertake them, and ways of working alongside community members.

ACKNOWLEDGMENTS

I wish to express my gratitude for the friendship and assistance I have received during
the past thirteen years in Indonesia (Maluku) and the Netherlands from the speakers of
the ELs of Alune, Amahai (Koako), Haruku, and Allang. Special thanks are due to those
people who read and commented on drafts of sections of this chapter. Suggestions were
kindly provided by Elizabeth Zeitoun (Academia Sinica) regarding the languages of
Taiwan and Peter Martin (University of Leicester) regarding the languages of Brunei.
Laurie Reid (University of Hawaii) and Tom Headland (SIL) contributed greatly to
updating our knowledge of the languages of Negrito peoples of the Philippines through
a lively email discussion on the subject and through their generosity in providing suggestions, references and unpublished data. I apologize for any remaining errors, which
are entirely my own. I would also like to thank Nikolaus Himmelmann and Sander
Adelaar for their insightful comments on several drafts, Michael Ewing for feedback and
support during the preparation of this chapter, and friends and colleagues in the academic

community who are closely involved in working with ELs for sharing their ideas, inspirations, and frustrations in conversations and writing over the years.

REFERENCES

Adelaar, K.A. (1991) 'New ideas on the early history of Malagasy', in *Papers in Austronesian linguistics, No.1*, (H. Steinhauer ed.), 1–22, Canberra: Pacific Linguistics.

——(1995) 'Asian roots of the Malagasy: a linguistic perspective', *Bijdragen tot de Taal-, Land- en Volkenkunde* 151/3:325–356.

——(forthcoming) 'Endangered Malayic isolects. The case of Salako, Cocos Malay and Sri Lanka Malay', in Collins and Steinhauer (eds).

Bowden, J. (2002) 'The Impact of Malay on Taba: a type of incipient language death or incipient death of a language type?', in Bradley and Bradley (eds), 114–143.

Bradley, D. and Bradley, M. (eds) (2002) *Language maintenance for endangered languages: an active approach*, London: Curzon Press.

Brenzinger, M. (ed.) (1992) *Language death: factual and theoretical explorations with special reference to East Africa*, Berlin: Mouton de Gruyter.

Clynes, A. (1995a) 'Javanese', in Tryon (ed.), 469–484.

——(1995b) 'Madurese', in Tryon (ed.), 485–494.

——(1995c) *Topics in the phonology and morphosyntax of Balinese based on the dialect of Singaraja, North Bali*, PhD thesis, Australian National University.

Collins, J.T. (1983) *The historical relationships of the languages of Central Maluku, Indonesia*, Canberra: Pacific Linguistics.

Collins, J.T. and Steinhauer, H. (eds) (forthcoming) *Endangered Languages and Literatures in South-East Asia*, Leiden: KITLV Press.

Collins, J.T. and Voorhoeve, C.L. (1983) 'Moluccas (Maluku)', in Wurm and Hattori (eds).

Crystal, D. (1997) *The Cambridge encyclopedia of language*, 2nd edition, Cambridge: Cambridge University Press.

——2000. *Language death*, Cambridge: Cambridge University Press.

Dahl, O. C. (1951) *Malgache et Maanyan: une comparaison linguistique*, Oslo: Egede Instituttet.

Dixon, R.M.W. (1991) 'The endangered languages of Australia, Indonesia and Oceania', in Robins and Uhlenbeck (eds), 229–255.

——(1997) *The rise and fall of languages*, Cambridge: Cambridge University Press.

Dorian, N. (1981) *Language death: the life cycle of a Scottish Gaelic dialect*, Philadelphia: University of Pennsylvania Press.

——(ed.) (1989) *Investigating obsolescence: studies in language contraction and death*, Cambridge: Cambridge University Press.

Dutton, T. and Tryon, D.T. (eds) *Language contact and change in the Austronesian world*, Berlin: Mouton de Gruyter.

Engelenhoven, A. van (forthcoming) 'Lirasniara, the sung language of Southwest Maluku (East-Indonesia)', in Collins and Steinhauer (eds).

Evans, N. (2001) 'The last speaker is dead – long live the last speaker!', in P. Newman and M. Ratcliff (eds), *Linguistic fieldwork*, 250–281, Cambridge: Cambridge University Press.

Fishman, J.A. (1991) *Reversing language shift*, Clevedon: Multilingual Matters Ltd.

Florey, M. (1991) 'Shifting patterns of language allegiance: a generational perspective from eastern Indonesia', in Steinhauer (ed.), 39–47.

——(1993) 'The reinterpretation of knowledge and its role in the process of language obsolescence', *Oceanic Linguistics* 32(2), 295–309.

Florey, M. (1997) 'Skewed performance and structural variation in the process of language obsolescence', in C. Ode and W. Stokhof (eds) *Proceedings of the Seventh International Conference on Austronesian Linguistics*, 639–660, Amsterdam: Editions Rodopi.

——(2001) 'Threats to indigenous knowledge: a case study from eastern Indonesia', in L. Maffi (ed.) *Language, Knowledge, and the Environment: the interdependence of biological and cultural diversity*, 402–426, Washington D.C.: Smithsonian Institution Press.

——(2002) 'Community aspirations towards language renewal among Moluccan migrants in the Netherlands', in Bradley and Bradley (eds), 257–271.

Florey, M. and Bolton, R.A. (1997) 'Personal names, lexical replacement, and language shift in eastern Indonesia', *Cakalele: Maluku Research Journal* 8, 27–58.

Florey, M. and Engelenhoven, A. van (2000) 'Moluccan languages in the Netherlands: documenting moribund languages in an immigrant setting', *Gesellschaft für bedrohte Sprachen, Bulletin No.* 4, 38–47.

——(2001) 'Language documentation and maintenance programs for Moluccan languages in the Netherlands', *International Journal of the Sociology of Language* 151, 195–219.

Florey, M. and Wolff, X.Y. (1998) 'Incantations and herbal medicines: Alune ethnomedical knowledge in a context of change', *Journal of Ethnobiology* 18, 39–67.

Foley, W.A. (1983) 'Sumatra', in Wurm and Hattori (eds).

Gal, S. (1989) 'Lexical innovation and loss: the use and value of restricted Hungarian', in Dorian (ed.), 313–331.

Ghani, Bibi Aminah Abdul and Ridzuan, Abang Ahmad (1992) 'Language shift among the Orang Miriek of Miri, Sarawak', in Martin (ed.), 131–145.

Grenoble, L.A. and Whaley. L.J. (eds) (1998) *Endangered languages: language loss and community response*, Cambridge: Cambridge University Press.

Grimes, B.F. (ed.) (1996) *Ethnologue: languages of the world*, 13th Edition, Dallas: Summer Institute of Linguistics.

——(2000) *Ethnologue: languages of the world*, 14th Edition, Dallas: Summer Institute of Linguistics.

Grimes, C.E. (1995) 'Buru (Masarete)', in Tryon (ed.), 623–636.

——(2000) 'Defining speech communities on Buru Island: a look at both linguistic and non-linguistic factors', in C.E. Grimes (ed.) *Spices from the east: papers in languages of eastern Indonesia*, 73–103, Canberra: Pacific Linguistics.

Grimes, J.E. (1995) 'Language endangerment in the Pacific', *Oceanic Linguistics* 34(1), 1–12.

Hajek, J. (2002) 'Language maintenance and survival in East Timor: all change now? Winners and losers', in Bradley and Bradley (eds), 182–202.

Hartman, D. and Henderson, J. (eds) (1994) *Aboriginal Languages in Education*. Alice Springs: IAD Press.

Headland, T.N. (2001a) 'Why Southeast Asian Negritos are a Disappearing People: A Case Study of the Agta of Eastern Luzon, Philippines', in T.N. Headland (ed.) *What Place for Hunter-Gatherers in Millennium Three?* [A special issue of the journal *Notes On Anthropology*, vol. 5, no. 2.], Dallas: Summer Institute of Linguistics.

——(2001b) 'Endangered Languages, Endangered Cultures: Why Should We Care?', Keynote lecture presented at The Eighth Annual UTA Student Conference in Linguistics, University of Texas at Arlington, February 22–23, 2001.

Himmelmann, N.P. (compiler) (2001) *Sourcebook on Tomini-Tolitoli languages: general information and wordlists*, Canberra: Pacific Linguistics.

——(forthcoming) 'Language endangerment scenarios in northern Central Sulawesi', in Collins and Steinhauer (eds).

Himmelmann, N.P. and Hajek, John (2001) 'A report on the current sociolinguistic situation in Lautém (East Timor)', *Studies in Languages and Cultures of East Timor* 4:88–97.

Himmelmann, N.P. and Wolff, J. (1999) *Toratán (Ratahan)*, München: Lincom.
Hinton, L. (1994) *Flutes of fire: essays on California Indian languages*, Berkeley: Heyday Books.
Hinton, L. and Hale, K. (eds) (2001) *The green book of language revitalization in practice*, New York: Academic Press.
Hull, G. (1999) *Mai Kolia Tetun: a course in Tetum-Praça, the lingua franca of East Timor*, 3rd edition, Sydney: Caritas Australia.
Kershaw, E.M. (1992) 'Final shifts. Some why's and how's of Brunei-Dusun convergence on Malay', in Martin (ed.), 179–194.
King, J.K. (1992) 'A preliminary update to the language situation in Sabah', in Martin (ed.), 41–68.
Kopping, E. (forthcoming) 'Kadazan language loss in an East Sabah village', in Collins and Steinhauer (eds).
Krauss, M. (1992) 'The world's languages in crisis', *Language* 68(1), 4–10.
Kuipers, J.C. (1998) *Language, identity, and marginality in Indonesia: the changing nature of ritual speech on the island of Sumba*, Cambridge: Cambridge University Press.
Larish, M. (1999) *The position of Moken and Moklen within the Austronesian language family*, Ann Arbor: UMI Dissertation Services.
MacGregor, L.A. (1995) 'Kagayanen', in Tryon (ed.), 363–368.
Maddieson, I. and Keng-Fong Pang (1993) 'Tone in Utsat', in J.A. Edmondson and K.J. Gregerson (eds), *Tonality in Austronesian languages*, 75–89, Honolulu: University of Hawaii Press.
Maffi, L. (ed.) (2001) *On biocultural diversity: linking language, knowledge, and the environment*, Washington: Smithsonian Institution Press.
Martin, P.W. (ed.) (1992a) *Shifting patterns of language use in Borneo*, Williamsburg: Borneo Research Council Inc.
——(1992b) 'Linguistic research in Brunei Darussalam: a review', in Martin (ed.), 81–105.
——(1995) 'Whither the indigenous languages of Brunei Darussalam?', *Oceanic Linguistics* 34(1), 27–43.
——(1996) 'Social change and language shift among the Belait', in Martin *et al.* (eds), 253–267.
Martin, P.W., Ozog, C. and Poedjosoedarmo, G. (eds) (1996) *Language use and language change in Brunei Darussalam*, Athens: Ohio University Center for International Studies.
Martin, P.W. and Poedjosoedarmo, G. (1996) 'Introduction: an overview of the language situation in Brunei Darussalam', in Martin *et al.* (eds), 1–23. Athens.
Martin, P.W. and Sercombe, P.G. (1992) 'The Penan of Brunei: patterns of linguistic interaction', in Martin (ed.), 165–178.
McFarland, C.D. (1983) 'Philippines', in Wurm and Hattori (eds).
——(1996) 'Subgrouping and number of the Philippine languages or How many Philippine languages are there?' in L.S. Bautista (ed.) *Readings in Philippine sociolinguistics*, 12–22. Manila: De La Salle University Press.
McGinn, R. (1982), 'Outline of Rejang syntax', *NUSA* 14.
Mead, D.E. (1999) *The Bungku-Tolaki languages of South-Eastern Sulawesi, Indonesia*, Canberra: Pacific Linguistics.
Mugler, F. and Lynch, J. (eds) (1996) *Pacific languages in education*, Suva: Institute of Pacific Studies.
Nothofer, B. (1991) 'The languages of Brunei Darussalam', in Steinhauer (ed.), 151–176.
——(1994) '"Bahasa Lom": dari mana asalnya?', in L.P. Sihombing *et al.* (eds), *Bahasa dan cendekiawan. Seuntai karangan untuk Anton M. Moeliono:* 193–208, Jakarta: Fakultas Sastra Universitas Indonesia.
Ostler, N. (ed.) (1998) *Endangered languages: what role for the specialist?*, Bath: The Foundation for Endangered Languages.

Prentice, D.J. (1990) 'Malay (Indonesian and Malaysian)', in B. Comrie (ed.), *The World's major languages*, 913–935, London: Routledge.

——(1994) 'Manado Malay: product and agent of language change', in Dutton and Tryon (eds), 411–441.

Reid, L.A. (1989) 'Arta, another Philippine Negrito language', *Oceanic Linguistics* 28(1), 47–74.

——(1991) 'The Alta languages of the Philippines', in R. Harlow (ed.), *VICAL 2, Western Austronesian and Contact Languages. Papers from the Fifth International Conference on Austronesian Linguistics*, 265–297, Linguistic Society of New Zealand: Te Reo Special Publication.

——(1994a) 'Unravelling the linguistic histories of Philippine Negritos', in Dutton and Tryon (eds), 443–475.

——(1994b) 'Possible non-Austronesian lexical elements in Philippine Negrito languages', *Oceanic Linguistics* 33(1), 37–72.

Robins, R.H. and Uhlenbeck, E.M. (eds) (1991) *Endangered languages*, Providence: Berg Publishers Limited.

Schmidt, A. (1985) *Young people's Dyirbal: an example of language death from Australia*, Cambridge: Cambridge University Press.

——(1990) *The loss of Australia's Aboriginal language heritage*, Canberra: Aboriginal Studies Press.

Sercombe, P.G. (1999) 'Adjacent cross-border Iban communities: a comparison with reference to language', *Bijdragen Tot de Taal-, Land- en Volkenkunde* 155(4), 596–616.

Smedal, O.H. (1987) *Lom-Indonesian–English & English–Lom wordlists. NUSA* 28/29.

Steinhauer, H. (ed.) *Papers in Austronesian Linguistics No.1*, Canberra: Pacific Linguistics.

——(forthcoming) 'Endangered languages in Southeast Asia', in Collins and Steinhauer (eds).

Thieberger, N. (ed.) (1995) *Paper and talk: a manual for reconstituting materials in Australian indigenous languages from historical sources*, Canberra: Aboriginal Studies Press.

Thurgood, G. (1999) *From ancient Cham to modern dialects: two thousand years of language contact and change*, Honolulu: University of Hawai'i Press.

Tryon, D.T. (ed.) (1995a) *Comparative Austronesian dictionary: an introduction to Austronesian studies*, Berlin: Mouton de Gruyter.

——(1995b) 'The Austronesian languages', in Tryon (ed.), 5–44.

Tsuchida, Shigeru (1995) 'Tsou', in Tryon (ed.), 293–296.

Wolff, J.U. (forthcoming) 'Causes of language attrition in Ratahan: a research agenda', in Collins and Steinhauer (eds).

Wurm, S.A. (ed.) (1996) *Atlas of the world's languages in danger of disappearing*, Paris/Canberra: UNESCO Publishing/Pacific Linguistics.

Wurm, S.A. and Hattori, S. (eds) (1981) *Language atlas of the Pacific area, Part 1: New Guinea area, Oceania, Australia*, The Australian Academy of the Humanities in collaboration with the Japan Academy: Pacific Linguistics.

——(1983) *Language atlas of the Pacific area, part II: Japan area, Taiwan (Formosa), Philippines, mainland and insular south-east Asia*. The Australian Academy of the Humanities in collaboration with the Japan Academy: Pacific Linguistics.

Zorc, R.D. and Thiessen, A. (1995) 'Molbog', in Tryon (ed.), 359–362.

CHAPTER THREE

COLONIAL HISTORY AND LANGUAGE POLICY IN INSULAR SOUTHEAST ASIA AND MADAGASCAR

Hein Steinhauer

1 INTRODUCTION

The present chapter discusses background and practice of language policy in those countries in which a majority of the population has a western Austronesian language as its mother tongue, i.e. in Malaysia, Indonesia, East Timor, Brunei Darussalam, the Philippines and Madagascar. In addition some notes will be presented with regard to western Austronesian languages which are spoken by a (sizable) minority in neighboring countries (Guam, Singapore, Taiwan, Thailand, and Vietnam).

The area under discussion is characterized by a wide variety of languages, totalling well over 10% of the estimated number of the languages of the world. Austronesian languages form the majority also in terms of their number of speakers, although more than 200 languages in this area belong to language groups other than Austronesian (Austro-Asiatic, Sinitic, Arabic, Dravidian, Indo-European and of course the non-Austronesian indigenous languages from East Indonesia).

The linguistic ecology of the area before the arrival of the first Europeans can only be reconstructed in vague terms. To what extent language policies existed in pre-colonial times must necessarily remain a matter of conjecture and circumstantial evidence. Languages such as Cham, Malay, Sundanese, Javanese, Buginese, Makassarese, Batak and various Philippine languages were used in script. The sultanates, kingdoms and empires which had existed before the arrival of the Europeans had in all likelihood not been monolingual states. Hinduism, Buddhism and Islam had been supra-ethnic religions long before the European expansion and the languages of their holy scriptures had to be accommodated within the existing language ecology. In many if not all language communities there existed and still exist language varieties for special purposes, such as charms, lawsuits, traditional ceremonies, interethnic contact, and situations requiring the exclusion of the uninitiated or possible evil powers (taboo languages; see FOX, RITUAL LANGUAGES).

The phenomenon of speech levels in languages such as Javanese, and especially the artificial character of many of the 'ceremonial' (*krama*) counterparts of 'common' (*ngoko*) words in that language, suggests conscious language engineering. What has since become a matter of communicative competence may once have been purposeful interference by some authority in the choice of a language variety or even in the shape of words and utterances.

'Some authority', because there is no policy without power. A language is a dialect with a navy, and power comes from the barrel of a gun. Whatever the situation in Southeast Asia may have been at the end of the European Middle Ages, it is obvious that its linguistic ecology changed dramatically with the arrival of the European mercantile convoys with their superior war potential.

At first, European control was geographically confined to shattered strongholds and their immediate hinterlands. In practice it was dependent on the vicissitudes of diplomacy and war, both with regional powers and rival Europeans. Their communicative needs were limited to the necessity to obtain commodities for trade and, to a lesser extent, to make converts.

Only when the Europeans in the course of the nineteenth century extended their interference by conquering the hinterlands of their earlier settlements and by active exploitation through large-scale plantation and mining projects did language become a matter of active political concern. The areas under discussion came under state control and started to develop into states, whose borders were defined by European armies and European politicians.

Hereafter I shall discuss the development and essentials of language policies for each of the countries involved. Not only governments had their language policies, but also other organizations, notably missionary societies. But I shall concentrate on the role of the state and discuss the role of the churches only in relation to the policies of the states.

2 INDONESIA

At the time of the arrival of the first Europeans Malay had become the major language of interethnic communication in Southeast Asia and beyond. Not only did it function as the language of interethnic trade, it had also become the language of Islam, presumably because Muslim merchants from India and the Middle East were the first to introduce Islam in the harbor towns of the archipelago. The arrival of the Portuguese put an end to the role of Malacca as the center of Islamic Malay culture. It did not change the role of Malay. For centuries the Portuguese had been fighting against the 'Moors' within and outside Portugal, and it lay in the nature of their *reconquista* that they did not confine themselves to trade after their conquest of Malacca in 1511. They vigorously started to spread Catholicism. And the language they used for this purpose was the language which was most widely understood: Malay. The Jesuit Francis Xavier, for instance, spent some months in Malacca in order to learn Malay before sailing on to East Indonesia to convert the Moluccans.

At the end of the sixteenth century under the reign of King Philip II, Portugal became united with Spain. The Netherlands, which had become part of the Spanish empire about a century earlier, were at war with Spain over high taxes and freedom of religion. With Spain being in charge of the Portuguese harbors, the Dutch had to sail to Southeast Asia themselves in order to acquire the goods they used to ship from Portugal to the rest of Europe. Being at war with Spain in Europe, they were also at war with the Portuguese in Southeast Asia. And since converts to Catholicism meant a safety risk for the Protestant Dutch, they had to fight them on the spiritual battlefield by converting them again, this time to Protestantism. Again it was Malay which became the main vehicle of their proselytizing activities. For a long time Protestant minds were divided over the variety of

Malay that should be used for a translation of the holy scriptures, but finally they chose a highly stilted form of Malay in Latin script which abounded with ill-adapted Arabic and Persian loanwords.

In their more secular dealings with the local population the Dutch also adapted to the local practice of using (varieties of) Malay in interethnic communication. Knowledge of Dutch among the local population was never stimulated.

After the first defeat of Napoleon, the Congress of Vienna (1814–15) decided that France should have a strong northern neighbor, and that therefore the Dutch 'possessions' in the East, which had been taken over by the English in 1811 after the annexation of the Netherlands by France, should be returned. At a subsequent conference in London it was agreed that by an exchange of territories in Sumatra and the Malay Peninsula the border between the Dutch and English spheres of influence would run through the Straits of Malacca. The result was that from 1824 onwards the Malay world was split, divided by the same sea route by which it was once united. And from that same time onwards Malay also became split, namely into a Dutch and a British variety.

Having regained their 'possessions' in the east, the Dutch started to exploit the colony more systematically, first for some decades by creating a forced plantation economy with commercial crops. They concentrated their activities on Java, which caused them to pay attention to the major language of Java, Javanese. Malay, however, remained the language of contact with most local rulers in and outside Java. The increasing exploitation forced the Dutch also to pay attention to education: they needed local people for all kinds of (lower) administrative jobs. In most schools Malay became the language of instruction. The general attitude of the Dutch was that Dutch, and the knowledge which came with it, was unfit for the local population and would endanger the colonial hierarchy of power. Only the nobility and children of local rulers were allowed to attend Dutch schools.

The intensification of Dutch colonialism also made it necessary to set up a special institute for the training of civil servants to be sent to the colony. Important in their training were Malay and Javanese. Training in Javanese, however, did not yield the expected results. In practice, Malay in various shades of corruption was used by Dutch civil servants and most other colonists in their contacts with the indigenous population. When in the course of the nineteenth century the Dutch extended their rule over the areas outside Java, the importance of Malay only increased, to an extent that standardization could no longer be postponed. This resulted in the spelling and grammar of Van Ophuijsen (Ophuijsen 1901 and 1910). Van Ophuijsen's grammar was based on classical Malay rather than on Malay as it was spoken in the shape of Bazaar Malay or one of the many indigenous varieties. It was this language which was spread all over Indonesia by pupils of the teachers training institute of Fort de Kocq (today Bukittinggi in West Sumatra). And it was this language which was used in the many books, both literary and educational, which were published by the governmental 'Committee for Popular Literature' (*Balai Pustaka*) in the final decades of Dutch colonial rule.

The same institution also published books in some of the major regional languages. At the same time the Dutch government employed a number of 'linguistic civil servants' whose task it was to study and describe lesser known regional languages.

Meanwhile, around World War I, the first national movements had begun to manifest themselves. For many of the nationalists Dutch was their first or first second language. However, it was not Dutch that was chosen as the incumbent national language. In 1928, the participants of the Second National Youth Congress proclaimed Malay (henceforth called Indonesian) as the unifying language of the unified peoples of Indonesia under the slogan 'one people: the Indonesians; one country: Indonesia; one language: Indonesian'.

Among the 500 Austronesian and non-Austronesian languages of Indonesia, Javanese was, and still is, by far the most important in terms of number of first-language speakers (more than one third of a population of well over 200 million people), but with its elaborate system of speech levels and long history of written and oral literature it was too much tied to Javanese culture and cultural expression to be suitable as a supra-ethnic language of a democratic, post-colonial society of free and equal citizens. Indonesian, on the other hand, did not have such an ethnic bias: Malay varieties had always had a supra-ethnic and supra-cultural function. Both the standardized form of the *Balai Pustaka* publications and the language of the indigenous press (often run by Chinese and Eurasians and in a language much closer to Bazaar Malay) had opened up visions of the world outside Indonesia, including events such as the Philippine revolution and the defeat of Russia by Japan. Yet the choice for Malay, and not Javanese or Dutch, to become 'Indonesian' was not the result of a reasoned debate, let alone some kind of referendum. The attitude of the Dutch police present at the meetings – by forbidding every discussion which they saw as 'political' – had caused enough anger and frustration that the aforementioned slogan proposed at the closing session by the congress' secretary, Mohamed Yamin, was immediately accepted. The point of no return came in World War II, when Japan forbade all use of Dutch in favor of Indonesian, which from then onwards effectively became the new national language. Already in the Japanese time corpus planning activities began. They were vigorously continued after independence (proclaimed on 17 August 1945). Under the aegis of Ministry of Education and Culture, a special language institute was set up to deal with all matters concerning the national language and other languages in use in Indonesia. This National Center for Language Development and Cultivation (*Pusat Pembinaan dan Pengembangan Bahasa*), as it was called from 1974, has the following major tasks: standardization and corpus planning of Indonesian; propagation of its (proper) use and language counselling; and coordination of linguistic research projects. Its official name was shortened to *Pusat Bahasa* ('Language Center') in 2001.

An important achievement in the field of standardization was the joint spelling reform of 1972 together with Malaysia, which united the Dutch and English based orthographies of both countries. The spelling reform was followed in 1975 by an agreement on terminology formation. The main standardization activities are the production of (standard) grammars and dictionaries (such as *Tata Bahasa Baku Bahasa Indonesia* 1988 and *Kamus Besar Bahasa Indonesia* 1988 and their subsequent revised editions).

Corpus planning mainly involves terminology development and, to a lesser extent, stylistics. Cooperation with Malaysia developed also in this field: since 1972 the *Majelis Bahasa Indonesia-Malaysia* (MBIM, Indonesian-Malaysian Language Council) has conducted joint meetings twice a year, in which the results of national terminology boards are compared. In 1985 Brunei Darussalam became an official member of the council, which was then renamed *Maj(e)lis Bahasa Brunei Darussalam-Indonesia-Malaysia* (MABBIM).

Propagation is done by weekly one-hour radio and television programs, courses (on request) for all layers of the civil and military service as well as for other sections of society, publication of books and pamphlets, and by the organization of a yearly 'language month' (consisting of congresses, seminars and various nationwide contests for schoolchildren on Indonesian language and literature). Linguistic research is carried out routinely by *Pusat Bahasa* staff and, on a project basis coordinated by the *Pusat Bahasa*, by teams all over Indonesia. Each year a number of these studies is published, dependent on the available budget and on relative quality. Some of these studies do deserve wider distribution, but as a measure against 'commercialization' of government functions the *Pusat Bahasa* is not allowed to market its publications.

After the fall of Suharto in 1999, the activities of the *Pusat Bahasa* have not remained unchallenged. Standardization is prescriptive and centralized per se. Moreover, spoken varieties of Malay/Indonesian were never standardized, and the differences between these and the official language are considerable. Consequently, the standardizing effors of the *Pusat Bahasa* were now associated by some critics with the dictatorial dirigism of the Suharto regime. Decentralization has become the solution to various problems with which Indonesia has been confronted since the economic crisis of 1998. A similar approach is being followed with respect to the tasks of the *Pusat Bahasa*. Until 1999 the Center had had only three regional branches; since 1999 that number has risen to seventeen. These regional branches are expected to take over the tasks of the central institute with regard to the local languages and the propagation of the national language in the provinces. To what extent this will result in more attention to the local languages has to be awaited.

It is very likely, however, that the ongoing decentralization of education will have such an effect. The constitution of 1945 already stipulated that the regional languages are an integral part of Indonesian culture and should be supported by the government if they were fostered by their speakers. In practice that meant that languages other than Indonesian were allowed as languages of instruction only in the lower grades of primary education, to be replaced completely by Indonesian in the fourth grade. Even this practice was forbidden for some years, to become reestablished since 1994. A new curriculum introduced in that year allowed for a few hours of 'local input'; for the rest the curriculum was the sole responsibility of Jakarta. After the fall of Suharto, as a measure to counteract break-away aspirations in regions outside Java, a new education policy was formulated which shifted the responsibility for education in the provinces from Jakarta to the local authorities. The implementation of this highly decentralized system of education started in 2001. It may be expected that now more attention will be paid to the local languages, which may result locally in problems and conflicts that on the national level had been avoided by the choice of Malay/Indonesian as the national language with a nation-building function: in most provinces there is no obvious local language which could be promoted to supra-ethnic status without being perceived by speakers of other local languages within the province as a takeover bid (see the sections on Tagalog and Malagasy below for comparable problems). The success of Malay for that matter as a language with a true nation-building function is illustrated by the fact that the independence movements at Indonesia's western and eastern extremes, i.e. in Aceh and Papua (West New Guinea), reject Indonesian as a possible national language once they are free. Instead they opt for 'Malay' alongside Arabic and Acehnese in Aceh and for regional Malay in Papua. The model of Malay for the Acehnese is probably the Malaysian standard variety. The latter differs considerably from Indonesian and is much more perceived as a vehicle of Islamic faith. In Papua varieties of East Indonesian spoken Malay similar to Ambonese Malay (see van Minde 1997 for a description) are widely used in everyday communication.

3 MALAYSIA

Compared to Indonesia the language ecology of Malaysia is in some respects more complicated. The number of languages currently spoken by its citizens may not exceed 50, but its colonial history has been more disruptive linguistically than the documented history of Indonesia. Before the arrival of the Europeans, the town of Malacca was the Malay window to the world. It had a mixed population of Malays, and expats and settlers from all over Southeast Asia and beyond, among them a community of Malaisized Chinese. The influence of the first Europeans (Portuguese 1511–1641, Dutch 1641–1824) did not reach very far beyond Malacca. Only around 1800 did the British appear on the scene, establishing themselves in Penang, founding Singapore, and taking over Malacca from the Dutch. In the course of the nineteenth century they expanded their influence to the sultanates in the interior, which had always been predominantly Malay, the Austro-Asiatic Aslian communities being marginal and marginalized.

East Malaysia (Sarawak and Sabah (formerly North Borneo)) had been under the suzerainty of the Brunei sultanate, which meant that the Malay spoken at the Brunei court had some status as the language of the state, whereas other varieties were used as a lingua franca among the multi-ethnic population. In the course of the nineteenth century the power of Brunei had weakened. As a result, Sarawak and Sabah became contested areas among European powers, and they were finally ceded by the Brunei sultan to become British protectorates (1888). Less than a decade later British power over the tin-rich states of mainland Malaysia was formalized by the establishment of the Federated Malay States, consisting of Selangor, Pahang, Negeri Sembilan, and Perak. Malay (in Arabic script) had been the language of the state in all mainland sultanates. It was almost entirely replaced by English in the Federated States, although Malay remained the language of the courts. In the unfederated states of Kelantan, Terengganu, Perlis, Kedah and Johor, which retained some autonomy in internal affairs, Malay maintained its position next to English. It was British policy therefore that all British officials serving in the Malayan civil service should know Malay.

British rule over mainland Malaysia caused major changes in the ethnic composition of the Malaysian population and in the country's linguistic ecology. The discovery of the tin mines led to large-scale immigration of Chinese miners, while for their rubber plantations the British contracted coolies from southern India. The present demographic constellation of the country (30% Chinese, 8% Indians, and 61% Malays and other 'indigenous' groups according to the census of 1990) is a direct consequence of its colonial economic exploitation.

Traditional education in the Malay sultanates as well as in Sarawak and Sabah was Islamic, with Malay as the language of instruction. Under British rule education was primarily private (Chinese, Muslim–Malay, Christian–English). British educational policy with regard to the Malays was inspired by the wish to teach them 'the dignity of manual labor' and to avoid 'the troubles which ha[d] arisen in India through over-education' (a colonial officer in 1915, quoted in Hassan Ahmad 1999:42), or as the Director of Education of the Federated Malay States put it in 1920: 'to make the son of the fisherman or peasant a more intelligent fisherman or farmer than his father had been' (ibid.). By the same token English education was deemed unfit for the Malays. However, English in education could be used for the newcomers from China and India.

Up until the independence of mainland Malaysia (1957), Malay vernacular state schools had been restricted to 4 or 6 years of primary education. The only Malay post-primary education was the teacher training schools, among which the Sultan Idris Training College at Tanjung Maling in Perak became the most influential. One of its teachers, Zainal Abidin bin Ahmad (Za'ba), became the founder of modern Malaysian Standard Malay (comparable to Van Ophuijsen in the Dutch Indies). Although based on the same classical Malay tradition as maintained in the Johor–Riau region, the standard varieties of Indonesian and Malaysian Malay are considerably different: European words were borrowed through English in Malaysia and through Dutch in Indonesia. Arabic loan-words are more frequent and less assimilated in Malaysia than in Indonesia. Original Malay vocabulary shows striking semantic differences. Derivational affixation is formally the same but is not parallel in distribution and/or meaning. Finally, Malaysian Malay had a later and English-based tradition of romanization.

Za'ba was also the director of the translation department of the *Pejabat Karang-Mengarang* (Book-Writing Bureau), which was modelled after *Balai Pustaka* in the Dutch Indies but had a smaller budget because 'the British [we]re more efficient than the Dutch'. In spite of that, the number of Malay school books published by the Bureau during its existence between 1924 and 1957 remained limited.

When mainland Malaysia was heading towards independence, the status of the original population and the Chinese and Indians became a hot issue, and so did the status of Malay and English. The compromise was that the 'immigrants' would acquire full citizenship of the new state, but that Malay would become the national language, which would replace English at all levels of education as well as in government within a period of ten years after independence. The governmental body to standardize, modernize, and propagate this Malay language, the *Dewan Bahasa dan Pustaka* (Council for Language and Literature), was the sister organization of the Indonesian *Pusat Bahasa*. It became operational in 1956. In contrast to the *Pusat Bahasa*, the Council does not have in-house research tasks. Its publishing activities are commercialized. In other fields their activities are similar: producing a standard dictionary and grammar, propagating the standard language and monitoring and advising on its use, organizing 'language month' activities, etc. As indicated in the previous section it cooperates with the Indonesian *Pusat Bahasa* in unifying spelling and in terminology development.

But in spite of these efforts, the transition towards Malay as the national language has been more difficult than in Indonesia. Sarawak and Sabah, which joined the Malaysian Federation in 1963, at first maintained English as the language of government. It was not until 1967 that Sabah adopted Malay as its official language, and Sarawak only decided to do so in 1985. Also in mainland Malaysia, the position of Malay as the sole national language was not unchallenged. Discussing the national language question, however, was made a punishable offense after the serious racial clashes between Malays and Chinese in Kuala Lumpur on 13 May 1969. Malay *was* the national language and its supra-ethnic function was emphasized by its new official name: *bahasa Malaysia*. However, for unclear reasons the old name *bahasa Melayu* was reintroduced in the 1990s.

The riots of May 1969 also meant the beginning of the implementation of the National Education System, that is, the gradual transition from education in English to education in the national language from kindergarten to university. Within this system the pre-independence private schools with Chinese or Tamil as a medium language continued to exist, albeit with the obligation to give thorough instruction in the national language. English remained a compulsory subject in all primary and secondary education. In the national schools with Malay as a medium language, the possibility exists to teach the 'mother tongue' (i.e. Chinese or Tamil) if this is the wish of a sufficient number of parents (and if teachers are available). Such facilities are not provided for the Aslian languages on the mainland or the various Austronesian languages in Sabah and Sarawak. Iban is given some attention in Sarawak, but efforts to give Kadazan-Dusun some status shattered on the failure to agree on a standard dialect (Prof. H. Asmah Haji Omar, p. c.).

Two developments hampered full implementation of the National Education System. In the 1990s Malaysia's economy began to attract international attention. The result was a mushrooming of private colleges providing education in English and leading to certificates for study at the British, Australian and American universities to which they were affiliated.

At the same time the Malaysian government started to issue ambiguous signals regarding the status of Malay. Government officials (including the Prime Minister) were criticized for using English in public speeches, even if no foreigners were in the audience. When they did speak Malay, they failed – with rare exceptions – to use the standardized pronunciation (which maintains a word-final [a] where the Johor has [ə]). Most confusing of all was the recurrent emphasis on the importance of English as the language of wider communication, essential for Malaysia's ambitious development policy to become a global high-tech and economic player by 2020. As a result, the efforts to make Malay the only language of instruction (including at tertiary level) were no longer wholeheartedly pursued. Especially in the fields of science and technology, English education has remained the norm at tertiary level, with the obvious effect that students who followed secondary education at Malay language schools are at a serious disadvantage.

So far, the status of Malay as a national symbol remains undisputed. However, as an official language to be used in official communication (including education and government) it has to compete with English, much more so than is the case in Indonesia.

4 BRUNEI DARUSSALAM

Since centuries before the European presence in the archipelago the Brunei sultanate had been an important centre in Southeast Asian trade. Its political power once reached as far as Manila and for a long time extended over the whole of northern Borneo. A variant of classical Malay was presumably the language of the court. The *puak Brunei* were numerically and politically the dominant group in this multi-ethnic country. Their mother tongue – Brunei Malay – is a distinct variety of Malay and considerably different from the court language and the current national language.

In the course of the nineteenth century Brunei lost control of Sabah and Sarawak and was reduced to its present size. It became a British protectorate from 1888 until its independence in 1984. However, Malay never ceased to be used in government (albeit alongside English), and in the constitution of 1959 it was declared the official language of the country.

After independence the Bruneian *Dewan Bahasa dan Pustaka* was established. It is the sister organization and a close copy of the Malaysian *Dewan Bahasa dan Pustaka* and the Indonesian *Pusat Bahasa*, with a similar task: the propagation and corpus planning of standard Malay. This standard Malay is very similar to the Malaysian standard, only differing from it in pronunciation and in its lexical influence from the local Brunei Malay. In developing a standard language Brunei cooperates with Malaysia and Indonesia. As mentioned in the section on Indonesia (above), Brunei joined its neighbours in forming the *Maj(e)lis Bahasa Brunei Darussalam-Indonesia-Malaysia* (MABBIM).

Meanwhile the role of the local Malay variety, Brunei Malay, is also growing within the linguistic ecology of the country – to the detriment of the six indigenous minority languages of the country, five of which are non-Malayic (Martin and Poedjosoedarmo 1996). Today it is generally accepted as the national lingua franca and it is increasingly used by Bruneians of other ethnic backgrounds. This is the Bruneian manifestation of the globally observable reduction of the domains in which minority languages are a proper vehicle of communication.

Until the end of the 1980s the minority languages were officially qualified as Malay dialects, which released the government from the obligation of paying special attention to them. Only since the last decade has the understanding gained ground that these languages are *not* Malay, and beginnings have been made to describe them (cf. CLYNES, BELAIT). Yet the undisputed state ideology remains *Melayu Islam Beraja* (to be Malay, Muslim, and governed by a King). The combined effects of the status of Malay (both Brunei Malay and the standard variety) and of educational policy are such that transmission of the minority languages to new generations is no longer guaranteed.

Before 1888 education had been identical with Islamic religious schooling, with an emphasis on Arabic and with Malay as the language of instruction. After 1888 this Malay education continued to expand and in 1914 the first secular Malay-medium school was established. Other schools followed. Only in 1952 was English introduced into the curriculum of these schools. Meanwhile English-medium schools had been established after the discovery of oil in 1929, which required increased communication with the outside world. These schools were private schools, organized by (non-sectarian) Christian missionaries. It was not until 1951 that the first government English school was opened.

Until 1985 both types of education coexisted, but in order to achieve equal opportunities for all citizens, both types of education were combined after independence (1984). Within this new system of bilingual education, Malay is the medium of instruction in the first three grades of primary education. In the next three grades of primary education and in the seven years of secondary education English is the medium of instruction for an increasing number of subjects, including science and mathematics (see Jones 1996 and Ożóg 1996 for details). The intended result of this system is that graduates of secondary education retain Malay as their 'first' language, while acquiring a high degree of proficiency in English as a second language.

The philosophy behind this model of additive bilingualism is that Malay, being the emblem of national culture and identity, *is* the first language of all citizens. However, the Malay which is supposed to be used at school as the medium of instruction and which is an obligatory subject at all levels of primary and secondary education is the standard variety, which is not the first language of any Bruneian. In practice, therefore, it is Brunei Malay which often replaces standard Malay as a medium of instruction, also in regions where a minority language is spoken.

5 EAST TIMOR

Among the 15–20 indigenous (Austronesian and non-Austronesian) languages currently spoken in East Timor, Austronesian Tetum is the most widespread. Presumably it was already the major language of inter-ethnic communication when the Portuguese made Dili their stronghold in the area. In any case the language was adopted by the Roman Catholic Church as the vehicle for the faith. Consequently it also became the language of contact between the Portuguese and the local population. In the capital, Dili, which was located in the Mambai-speaking area, a variety arose – known as Tetum-Praça – which, compared with the more western Tetum Terik dialects, contains some grammatical simplifications and above all a conspicuous number of Portuguese loanwords. Portuguese remained confined to the more formal domains. Yet the first four centuries of Portuguese presence in the area were not characterized by any consciously planned changes in the linguistic ecology. Only in the 1950s did Portugal change its policy: it now became the explicit objective to turn all East Timorese into Catholic, Portuguese-speaking citizens (cf. Hajek 2000). Education was the means to achieve this and many new (elementary) schools were built, resulting in some 75% of the schoolchildren obtaining Portuguese lessons in 1974, the year of the Portuguese revolution. Since the 1950s the use of Tetum and other regional languages had been forbidden in schools. Portuguese had to be the language of education, while also in church the role of Portuguese had become more important than before.

In 1975 the Portuguese withdrew from East Timor. And after a short interval in which the East Timorese nationalists tried to promote Tetum in education, Indonesian armed forces with the consent of the American government intervened and 'saved the country for the free world'. From then on Portuguese was repressed as the 'colonial language' the country had to be freed from. In order to smooth the integration of East Timor into the Indonesian Republic the use and knowledge of Indonesian had to be fostered as fast and as much as possible.

From 1976 to 1999 Indonesian was used throughout the educational system introduced by the Indonesians, which ranged from kindergarten to university. As a result several generations of students received their complete education in Indonesian, and although schooling may not have been successful everywhere because of the unstable political situation, the role and knowledge of Portuguese obviously lessened. However, refugees in Portugal and Australia and the guerrilla movement did not partake in this language shift, and continued to use Portuguese (and English) in their international public dealings, and Tetum and Portuguese internally. Not less importantly, the church did not shift to Indonesian either, in spite of Indonesian pressure. Instead, Tetum became the language of the Roman Catholic religion, with the grudging consent of the Indonesians: after all, a Tetum-speaking Catholic was less of a security risk than an Indonesian-speaking atheist (alias communist). One of the results of this church policy was the translation of the gospels into Tetum Terik.

After the destructive withdrawal of the Indonesian forces from East Timor in 1999 the linguistic ecology of the country changed again. For most East Timorese, Indonesian was no longer a neutral language – if it ever was. It was associated with military oppression and terror and is now officially the language of a foreign power. As such, Indonesian was disqualified as a possible national and official language for East Timor. On 30 August 2000 the *Conselho Nacional da Resistência Timorense* (CNRT) adopted the motion that Portuguese would be chosen as official language and Tetum as national language, and that Tetum had to be 'developed' within a period of five to ten years (Eccles 2000:23). On 11 December 2001 the new National Assembly adopted Portuguese and Tetum as the official languages of the new country. A proposal for Indonesian, known by some 70% of the population, was rejected.

The practical implementations of these decisions have to be awaited. Portuguese is ready for use: it is a standardized, modern language, in which teaching materials and other publications are – in principle – readily available. Most educated people older than 40–45 still know it quite well. Strong support is given from Portugal and Portuguese-speaking countries, financially and through expertise. The shift from Indonesian to Portuguese within the education system, however, can only be gradual.

As regards the status of Tetum much work still has to be done. The body responsible for the implementation of the national language policy is the *Instituto Nacional de Linguística* in Dili, the status of which can be compared with the Indonesian *Pusat Bahasa* and its sister organizations in Malaysia and Brunei Darussalam. A standard spelling (with some deviations from the most widespread practice until recently) has already been accepted. The next steps which have to be (or are being) taken are the production of a standard grammar, textbooks, teaching materials, and the 'modernization' of the lexicon in order to make the language suitable for use outside the domains of mostly informal spoken interchanges; finally, dictionaries will have to be produced. In any case, the future of the status of Tetum will depend on the progress and effectiveness of these corpus-planning activities.

During the United Nations interim government some pressure has been exerted to assign a (more) central place to English after independence. It is foreseen that English *will* have a place in education, but not too prominently: at the above-mentioned meeting of the CNRT it was stipulated that every hour devoted to English should be counterbalanced by two hours of Portuguese in order to avoid possible effects of 'linguistic imperialism' (Eccles 2000:24). To what extent Indonesian will continue to have a role in education (as a subject) is still uncertain.

East Timorese leaders realize that provisions have to be made for indigenous languages other than Tetum (Ramos Horta, p. c.). For the moment, however, priority will be given to the development and standardization of Tetum. Research with regard to all local languages is coordinated by the *Instituto Nacional de Linguística*.

6 THE PHILIPPINES

When the first Europeans arrived in the Philippines the majority of its estimated half million inhabitants lived in small territorial units, each originally belonging to a single kinship group. Only in the Sulu archipelago and in the adjacent areas of Mindanao had Islam made inroads and sultanates come into existence. From there Islam spread northward, to reach the Manila area by 1565. Malay influence must have been strong, starting in the tenth century or earlier (as suggested by the Laguna copper plate; see MAHDI, THIS VOLUME), and reaching as far north as southern Luzon.

The first reported interference in local affairs by Europeans was the arrival of Ferdinand Magellan at Cebu in 1521, who claimed the island for Spain. In 1565 the Spanish established themselves permanently on Cebu. They shifted their centre of administrative, military, commercial and religious activity to Manila in 1573. At the lower level of administration, Spanish colonial rule was indirect, thus creating a Filipino upper class of 'principales'. At the higher level, state and church were inseparable, so much so that the term 'friarocracy' was coined. Much executive and legislative power was assigned to the Jesuits and to the friars of the Augustinian, Dominican and Franciscan orders, all recruited from Spain or of Spanish descent. Most conspicuous among the lasting results of their activities were the conversion of the majority of the population to Catholicism and the establishment of a system of large land estates. From the very beginning the orders had the sole responsibility for education. Even after 1863, when the Spanish government established free public primary education, the friars kept the supervision of the educational system on all levels, whereas the Jesuits remained responsible for the teacher-training colleges. Although Spanish was the language of the government, the orders, with the exception of the Jesuits, opposed the teaching of Spanish to the 'indios'. An impressive number of publications in and on the major local languages had already appeared in the earliest decades of Spanish rule, most of them in or on Tagalog (Llamzon 1968:735).

Only a very few Filipinos had been allowed to enter Spanish schools. It was among these – mostly upper class – 'ilustrados' that the nationalist movement arose in the final decades of the nineteenth century. In its initial stages the emphasis was on assimilation and emancipation, one of its programs being the extension of Spanish teaching to a wider base of the population. Since most ilustrados were of Tagalog origin, like the famous author and national hero José Rizal, only Tagalog came to be considered as an alternative to Spanish. When the movement took a populist turn and its aims shifted towards independence, Tagalog became its first language. The geographical core of the movement was the Tagalog-speaking greater Manila area, and although the leaders of the revolution expressed notions of a national unit embracing all inhabitants of the Philippines, its actual scope remained limited.

In the provisional constitution of the First Republic (1897), it was proclaimed – in Spanish – that '[e]l tagálog será la lengua oficial de la República' (Tagalog shall be the official language of the republic) (Gonzalez 1980:12). With the outbreak of the Spanish–American war (April 1898) the revolt against Spain also spread to non-Tagalog areas, and on 12 June 1898 the Act of Independence was proclaimed, in Spanish. At the Constitutional Assembly (convening in Malolos, September 1898) representatives with non-Tagalog backgrounds were present. Among them were speakers of Ilokano, Bikolano, Kapampangan, Pangasinan and – notably – Bisayan. This linguistically mixed constellation of a largely Spanish-educated elite was the reason why Tagalog was rejected in favor of Spanish as the official language for the time being, to be used in 'acts of public authorities and judicial affairs' (Gonzalez 1980:20). Spanish also remained prominent in the educational program of the new republic, whereas no mention was made of any of the local languages.

However, the defeat of the Spanish meant the beginning of the Anglicization of the Philippines. In the Treaty of Paris of December 1898, Spain ceded the Philippines and some smaller former colonies to the United States in exchange for $20 million. From allies against the Spanish, the Philippine revolutionaries now became America's enemy: the revolution was crushed, and American institutions were established. Most important among these were the separation of church and state, representative bodies and mass education. Theoretically, the medium of instruction in schools and universities was supposed to be a local language. In practice it was English.

Meanwhile the old elite adjusted to the new situation: they kept their economic power and dominated political life. Since many of them were Spanish-educated, Spanish remained an official language alongside English. English soon became the most important if not the only language to be used in official domains, with the exception of the law, where Spanish could not be ousted so easily. In the 37 years of direct American rule the percentage of Filipinos able to speak English had risen to more than 25% (Gonzalez 1980:26), whereas the percentage of those with knowledge of Spanish towards the end of Spanish colonial rule had probably been less than 3%.

At the same time, the larger local languages were used in printing and in the press. Most of the publications were in Tagalog, however. And it was Tagalog which was proposed by some nationalists as the most suitable candidate for a national language. However, the question was sensitive from the start. Tagalog was spoken by some 20% of the Filipinos in and around the political, cultural and economic center of power. Bisayan, on the other hand, was the mother tongue of about twice as many speakers, and with its plantations and exports, the Bisayan homeland contributed significantly to the Philippine economy.

The discussion came to a temporary conclusion with the constitution of 1935, when the Philippines were granted independence within a commonwealth construction: according to the constitution it was stipulated that the National Assembly would 'take steps towards the development and adoption of a common national language based on one of the existing languages' (Gonzalez 1980:59). One year later the National Language Institute was established, which was responsible for the selection, standardization and elaboration of this common national language. Arguing that it was the best-studied Philippine language with the richest literature, the Institute recommended Tagalog as the most suitable base for the national language. On 30 December 1937 president Quezon proclaimed a national language based on the 'Tagalog dialect' to become effective two years later. In the meantime, a grammar, a Tagalog–English vocabulary and a teacher's manual were prepared. In 1940 Tagalog would be introduced as a subject in the fifth and sixth grades of elementary schools as well as in normal schools, if teachers were available. At the end of the Commonwealth period (July 1946) Tagalog would be an official language like English and Spanish, and it would gradually replace English as medium of instruction. The authority of president Quezon had saved Tagalog for the time being, but it was accepted with bitterness by the Bisayans, if indeed they accepted it at all.

Shortly after the Japanese conquest, however, Tagalog and Japanese were proclaimed official languages. For the time being the use of English was still allowed as a medium of instruction, to be replaced eventually by the local vernaculars. The production of schoolbooks in Tagalog was stimulated. At the same time the government of the 'Second Republic' (1942–44) conducted vigorous proficiency training campaigns in Tagalog among the non-Tagalog. Because of the war, however, the results outside the greater Manila area were limited.

After the war, Tagalog began to be taught as a subject at all levels of education. However, the efforts to disseminate the language were somewhat traditional: the accent shifted from proficiency training to training in grammatical knowledge, and the same teaching methods were applied to both Tagalogs and non-Tagalogs. In order to stress its national symbolic function, the language was called *wikang pambansa(ng Pilipino)* 'the (Philippine) national language'. After 1959 the official name became *Pilipino*. It was supposedly different from Tagalog and only 'Tagalog-based'. For speakers of other regional languages, however, and foremost the Bisayans, this epithet remained a thin disguise.

Meanwhile the continued standardization and elaboration efforts of the Institute of National Language (previously the National Language Institute) gave rise to fierce clashes between purists and liberals. In the early 1960s this even amounted to – unsuccessful – lawsuits against members of the Institute and high government officials in which the use of puristic Tagalog in the national language was challenged. In spite of these obstructions Pilipino gained ground. There was an increase in Pilipino publications, and the role of Pilipino in education, as a subject as well as a language of instruction, became more prominent (Bonifacio 1969). When towards the end of the 1960s the students revolted against American military and cultural imperialism, it was the common Manila variety of Tagalog which became the vehicle and symbol of their struggle.

Among the non-Tagalog elder generations, however, Pilipino continued to be felt as an implicit takeover bid by the Tagalogs. When in 1971 preparations were started for a convention to revise the American-based constitution, anti-Tagalog resentments flared up again and were vigorously voiced. As a result, Tagalog-based Pilipino was in fact rejected as the national language. In the constitution of 1973 it was stated that for the time being English and Pilipino would be the official languages, but steps would be taken to develop a new common national language based on all Philippine languages, to be known as *Filipino*.

The function of this new language was clear: a symbol of national unity. But it was less clear what it would look like, and how it should be propagated and disseminated. In the Aquino Constitution of 1986 the section on language asserts that

[t]he national language of the Philippines is Filipino. As it evolves, it shall be further developed and enriched on the basis of existing Philippine and other languages. Subject to provisions of law and as the Congress may deem appropriate, the Government shall take steps to initiate and sustain the use of Filipino as a medium of official communication and as language of instruction.

In 1988 President Aquino declared Filipino to be used as the medium of instruction at all levels of education and as the language of official communication in government. The decree itself was in English and had obviously bypassed the Congress. The latter had not yet passed the bill on the Commission on Filipino language, which was to be assigned the task of developing Filipino. This not yet existing Filipino now had to be used as medium of instruction, and as a consequence could only be Pilipino, or 'Tagalog in disguise' in the eyes of the non-Tagalog. The reaction was predictable: there was strong protest from the Congress because the decree 'kick[ed] the Constitution in the face [a]nd Congress too' (Philippines Free Press 1991), and open obstruction from the Bisayans. In Cebu province the governor refused to implement the decree and insisted instead that Cebuano, the major variety of Bisayan, be used as a language of education.

The future of Filipino is uncertain. As long as it remains non-existent it functions as a symbol of national unity. But as soon as it is given content it becomes divisive rather than uniting. Meanwhile Pilipino (whether or not considered to be Filipino) continues to be taught at schools all over the country. Knowledge of it is in fact undeniably increasing, which is also the result of increased mobility, ongoing urbanization and the influence of the film industry and mass media.

The polyglossic situation has not changed: the local vernaculars have kept their function within the family, as auxiliary languages (alongside English and Pilipino) in the lower grades of state schools, and as the daily language in rural areas. In the urbanized centres and in interethnic communication, Tagalog-based Pilipino has remained the major medium. In business, industry, higher education and in private schools English continues to be the main language.

7 MADAGASCAR

The linguistic situation of Madagascar is markedly different from that of other countries discussed in this chapter. Madagascar has the unique characteristic of being practically monolingual, i.e. the indigenous language varieties which collectively form the Malagasy language are closely related dialects. There was once an allegedly Arabic-speaking settlement in the southeast, and there is a small community of Bantu-speaking Comorans in the northwest. Furthermore, there are some Indian, Pakistani, Chinese and French immigrants and expatriates. By and large, however, the country may be said to be linguistically homogeneous. Yet ecologically and economically it is not, and this is ultimately the reason why the development of the national language shows similarities with the Philippine case.

Although Madagascar was frequented by European ships on their way to Asia – one of the oldest European sources on an Austronesian language is De Houtman's remarkable study on Malay and Malagasy (first published in 1603; see Lombard et al. 1970) – the island appeared not to be attractive enough for a lasting European settlement until the beginning of the nineteenth century. Before that time it was never a political unit because of its widely diverging ecologies and economies: wet rice cultivation in the central highlands, fishery, dry rice cultivation and export crops along the small eastern coast, rain forests in the north and along the eastern mountain slopes, and cattle breeding in the savannahs of the broad western coastal areas and in the very dry bush and cactus land in the south and southwest.

Usually the Malagasy are subdivided into 18 different ethnic groups, and this roughly corresponds to the division into dialects (see Wermter and Rubino, this volume). The most important groups in order of their numbers are the Merina (northern central mountains), the Betsimisaraka (along the east coast), the Betsileo (southern central mountains), the Tsimihety (northern mountains), the Sakalava (western savannahs), and the Antandroy (southern dry lands).

Before the age of colonialism groups of clans were united into kingdoms, among which those of the Sakalava and the Merina became the most prominent. Society in these kingdoms was stratified into a hierarchy of castes, with nobility (*andriana*), commoners (*hova*) and (descendants of) slaves (*andevo*). A king or queen stood at the head of the kingdom. This social stratification facilitated the slave trade, in which the coastal kingdoms of the Sakalava became most involved. These kingdoms consequently had regular contacts with Europeans well before the nineteenth century.

Towards the end of the eighteenth century the Merina kingdoms in the central mountains were united under King Andrianampoinimerina (1782–1810). He was succeeded by his son Radama I (1810–28), who defeated the Sakalava and extended Merina power over practically the whole of Madagascar. Only the extreme south remained independent until the beginning of French colonization.

Until the nineteenth century Malagasy was rarely written. If it was, it was in Arabic script, nowadays called *sorabe* 'big writing' (the traditional name is *volan'onjatsy*). The Antaimoro in the south had been the exclusive owners of this script, and what they wrote was chronicles, divinations, and treatises on astrology and medicines (the oldest records go back as far as the fifteenth century). Faced with the necessity to keep the European colonial powers at a distance, Radama I decided to modernize his country, among other things by introducing literacy. In 1823 he proclaimed the Latin script, as it had been introduced for Malagasy by the Reverend Jones of the London Missionary Society (LMS), to be the official alphabet of the kingdom. He also gave the LMS a free hand to establish schools and to develop teaching materials. The new education system was concentrated in the central highlands, and first among the literates were the children of the Merina nobility. The number of schools rose from one with three pupils in 1820 to 23 with an average of 100 pupils (one third of whom were girls) in 1828 (Heseltine 1971:105).

Under Radama's daughter, Queen Ranavalona I, however, a backlash caused the demise of the school system. First it was forbidden for slaves to become literate, then for everybody who did not belong to the government service, and finally all schools were closed (1835). French Catholics profited from the temporarily low profile of the British Protestants by establishing their first mission in 1837. In 1862 after the death of Ranavalona I the schools were reopened and the LMS reappeared on the scene. Again education was concentrated in the central highlands and insofar as Malagasy was used as language of instruction, it was the Merina dialect.

Until the end of the nineteenth century Madagascar remained an internationally recognized, independent state with ambassadors in London and Paris. Its sovereignty came to an end when Galliéni conquered the country for France by force of arms in 1896. As the first governor-general of the new colony, Galliéni vigorously stimulated French-style education. At the same time he encouraged all French officials to learn Malagasy. Until World War II many of them did. After the war the French policy of assimilation was continued, but in 1958 the Malagasy opted for independence, which was effectuated in 1960, on which occasion the French were proclaimed to be Madagascar's nineteenth tribe. Many French citizens continued working as teachers, especially in secondary and higher education, which remained completely French. It was not until 1965 that Malagasy became a compulsory subject in secondary schools.

In the 1970s Madagascar followed a leftist policy, which on the cultural plain aimed at the '*malgachisation*' of secondary and higher education. However, the policy was weakly planned and finally had to be aborted. Nonetheless, several bodies have continued working on standardization and terminology development for all fields of science. The avowed idea is to enrich a Merina-based Malagasy with lexicon from other dialects in order to achieve a truly national language. For the moment, however, both French and Malagasy are official languages. A major reason why French may be expected to suppress the rise of (Merina-based) Malagasy as the main or only official language in the future (apart from pressure from France itself) is the continued resentment of the peripheral tribes towards Merina dominance.

8 LANGUAGE POLICY IN OTHER SOUTHEAST ASIAN COUNTRIES

8.1 Guam

In 1521 Guam became a midway station in the Spanish galleon trade between Mexico and the Philippines. Vigorous efforts by the Spaniards to save the souls of the indigenous Chamorro population almost resulted in their termination: from an estimated 65,000 to 85,000 at the arrival of the Spaniards the population had dwindled to some 5000 in 1741. The Spaniards killed and deported the Chamorro male warriors in particular. If the Chamorro language continued to be spoken, albeit with heavy Spanish influences, this was largely due to the matrilineal culture of Chamorro society.

As a result of the Spanish–American War, Guam became American (1898). Henceforth all instruction was given in English and 'No Chamorro' became the rule. In schools the use of Chamorro was forbidden on penalty of a fine or even physical punishment.

After World War II Guam became a major military base, which further marginalized the original population, who were outnumbered by American army personnel. Yet thanks to the Naval Clearing Act, Guam was closed for tourists and non-military immigrants. This relatively quiet situation changed in 1962 when Kennedy lifted the Clearing Act, which caused an influx into Guam of Asians, Americans and Pacific islanders.

As a reaction, the government installed the Chamorro Language Commission, which had the task of writing a grammar and a dictionary. A few years later the Chamorro Language and Culture Program was set up with the purpose of reviving and preserving the Chamorro language through the school system. In the mid-1970s Chamorro was accepted by law as a subject (20 minutes daily in the first three grades of primary education, and 30 minutes in the higher grades). And as a language of instruction it was allowed for teaching Chamorro and foreign languages; all other courses, however, had to be conducted in English only. In 1993 the first courses in Chamorro were given at the University of Guam, as part of a teacher training program (see Clampitt-Dunlap 1995 for details).

8.2 Singapore

Established as a trading station by Sir Stamford Raffles in 1819, Singapore became a major port of call in the trade between Europe and China in the course of the nineteenth century, especially after the opening of the Suez Canal (1869). With the development of rubber planting in mainland Malaysia in the last decades of the nineteenth century, it also became the main centre of the rubber trade in the world. Its prosperity attracted immigrants on a large scale, turning it into the multi-ethnic city it is today. The majority (78%) of the 3 million Singaporeans are now of Chinese descent (consisting of Hokkien, Teochew, Cantonese, and others). Indians (mainly Tamil) constitute a minority of 7%, whereas the original population of the island state, the Malay, have dwindled to some 14%.

Already at an early stage Singapore acquired a special status within the British colonial system. In 1867 it came under direct control of the Colonial Office. After the Japanese occupation in World War II Singapore was made a separate Crown Colony. In 1959 it acquired internal self-governance and in 1963 it joined the Federation of Malaysia as an independent member. Two years later, however, it seceded from the Federation to become a fully independent state.

Because of the common history with Malaysia and the economic importance of the Malay peninsula as Singapore's immediate hinterland, Malay still is the national language of the state. This official Malay is the Malaysian standard variety. Alongside Malay and English, Tamil and Mandarin Chinese have also been proclaimed official languages. All four of them may be used in parliament. In practice, however, English remains the primary language of administration and commerce.

Education under direct British rule had been exclusively English. After independence it remained English-based with English as language of instruction. However, in line with the constitution Malay, Mandarin and Tamil are taught as 'mother tongues' in primary and secondary education, even though few Chinese have Mandarin as their home language, and not all Indians speak Tamil. The idea behind this educational policy is to wipe out linguistic dividing lines within the different ethnic communities: Indians speak Tamil, Chinese speak Mandarin, and Malays speak Standard Malay. Subsequent 'Speak Mandarin' campaigns have had the additional benefit of easing access to the emerging mainland Chinese market. Since the economic incentive to choose Tamil is less obvious, an increasing number of pupils of Indian descent appear to choose Malay as their 'mother tongue'.

8.3 Taiwan

In 1624 the Dutch established a post in western Taiwan, and in the 37 years they maintained themselves on the island they introduced the roman script for at least two of the aboriginal Formosan languages (Siraya and Favorlang). Long after they had been defeated by the Chinese admiral Zheng Chenggong (known in contemporary Dutch sources as Koxinga), this script was used by descendants of the first users at least until the early nineteenth century (cf. Adelaar 1999). The conquest of Zheng Chenggong meant the sinification of the island, first by large-scale immigration of speakers of Ho Lo (a Fukien dialect), later followed by Hakka speakers.

From 1895 until the end of World War II Taiwan was part of the Japanese empire. During that time Japanese was the national language, and the indigenous languages (both the Austronesian and the Chinese) had no status whatsoever. In 1945 Taiwan became part of China. But with the victory of the communists over the armies of the Kuomintang in mainland China in 1949 it was separated again. Taiwan was flooded by a third wave of immigrants from the mainland, many of whom spoke Mandarin. They were the remnants of the Kuomintang armies and their supporters, and considered themselves the rightful rulers of the whole of China. Under this fiction they established martial law and continued the one-language policy of the Japanese, substituting Mandarin Chinese for Japanese. During martial law broadcasting in the local varieties of Chinese (Taiwanese/Ho Lo and Hakka) was allowed on condition that they should in time be completely replaced by Mandarin. Towards the end of martial law broadcasts in these languages were reduced to one hour daily. In communist China spelling reforms were implemented for Mandarin Chinese, but for political reasons these were not accepted in Taiwan.

In 1988 martial law was finally lifted. The subsequent democratic process led to a new political perspective, according to which Taiwan was no longer an appendix of the great Chinese empire but a country in its own right. Local languages and cultures, including those of the Austronesian minorities, came to be reevaluated. For the past few years, Mandarin has no longer been the only language of instruction. In the lower grades the local languages are beginning to be used as such (insofar as teachers are available), and since 1996 one 'period' per week has been allotted to the teaching of these languages in the elementary education curriculum.

8.4   Thailand

In Thailand all state education is in Standard Thai, with centralized control and a curriculum determined in Bangkok. The major regional languages as well as the smaller minority languages are all part of a language hierarchy dominated by Standard Thai. The languages of the Austronesian sea-nomads scattered along the west coast of southern Thailand, Moken/Moklen (approximately 2500–3000 speakers per group; see LARISH, MOKEN AND MOKLEN) and Urak Lawoi' (with some 3000 speakers) are at the bottom of this hierarchy (Smalley 1994:366–367). No efforts are made to preserve these languages. A Thai-based writing system for Urak Lawoi', developed by missionaries, has not reversed the process of cultural deprivation and language decline.

Since its conversion to Islam in 1474, Pattani had been the Malay-speaking centre of an independent and at times powerful sultanate. Periodically it had to pay tribute to the Thai kings, but it was not until 1893 that it came under direct Thai rule. Today Pattani Malay is spoken by probably over a million speakers in the southeastern provinces of Yala, Pattani, Narathiwat and the southern part of Songkhla (Smalley 1994:155). In the southwestern province of Satun another variety of Malay is endemic, although its speakers are mostly bilingual (Satun Malay and Paktay (Southern Thai)) and the Thai system of education has generally been accepted. In the Pattani Malay area, however, Thai educational policy met with much resistance. Until the 1960s the impact of state schools was minimal. Most education was private, centered around a local Muslim teacher. The main activity in this private education was the reading of religious texts. These texts were Standard Malay written in Arabic script, and they were discussed in Pattani Malay. During the major waves of Thai chauvinism (under King Vajiravudh at the beginning of the twentieth century, and under Prime Minister Phibunsongkhram during World War II and again in the 1950s) attempts to force assimilation of the national minorities had had the opposite effect among the Malays. In the 1960s, however, the Thai government succeeded in bringing the private schools under its control. Since 1968 no new schools for Islamic education have been able to be established any more, and the existing Islamic schools have had to adopt a common Thai curriculum as well as Thai as the main language of instruction. Malay is only allowed for religion. Today the number of private schools in the Pattani-speaking provinces still exceeds the number of state schools (Zaphir Nikhab, p.c.), but their former function of teaching Islamic values and religion has been taken over by extracurricular courses and weekend schools.

8.5 Vietnam

Of the five Austronesian languages of Vietnam, only Cham used to be a literary language. It was the language of the Champa kingdom (seventh–fifteenth century) which once covered large parts of mainland Southeast Asia. This kingdom was regularly at war with the Vietnamese kingdom of Annam in the north and the Khmer in the west, and it was finally annexed by the Annamites in 1471. The subsequent influx of Vietnamese into the southern regions of Indochina drove most of the Austronesians to the mountains of central Vietnam. This created a state of relatively stable symbiosis, in which the Cham and the other Austronesian ethnic groups had become minorities vis-à-vis the Vietnamese. This situation continued to exist for centuries. Even under colonial French rule no dramatic changed occurred. The French hardly interfered with the minorities, who had an illiteracy rate of almost 100%. No minority language was used in any of the few schools that were accessible to children from the minorities.

The situation began to change with the anti-colonial struggle during and after World War II. Especially after the Americans had succeeded the French in their efforts to 'save' Vietnam for the West, the minorities came under pressure. The jungles of the central highlands provided the best hiding place for the anti-colonial/communist forces, and the Ho Chi Minh Trail ran through the regions populated by the Austronesian minorities. The logic of war required the destruction of their habitat by continuous bombardments and defoliation of the jungle. The Cham and other minorities were deported and/or concentrated into fortified settlements from where they no longer had access to their ancestors' territories.

After the defeat of the American forces and their South Vietnamese allies, the situation hardly improved for the Austronesian minorities. Vietnamese nationalism and communist ideology did not leave much room for independent cultural development. Streams of landless Vietnamese began to settle in the areas which were once exclusively inhabited by the minority groups. Mass education (in Vietnamese) was introduced and large infra-structural works (industry, mines, roads and dams) further transformed the traditional way of life of the minorities. As a consequence they were marginalized in their own traditional lands.

Officially the need for preservation and cultivation of the minority cultures is acknowledged, but in practice other priorities prevail. As regards the Austronesian languages, only for Cham is some provision made in education, and that only in the provinces of Binh Tuan and Ninh Thuan, some 200 km north of Ho Chin Minh City. In Ninh Thuan a large cultural centre for the Cham ethnic group has been set up. A Committee for Drafting School Textbooks in Cham (Ban Biên Soan Chu Cham) has been installed. The committee also supervises the 150 schools in the two provinces where the books are to be used. So far five schoolbooks have been produced. However, the committee does not have at its disposal typewriters adapted to the traditional Cham writing system, let alone computers. The books therefore have had to be written by hand (see Po Dharma 2001 for further details).

9 CONCLUDING REMARKS

Recurrent in the above discussions is the problem of legitimation. The multi-ethnic and multi-cultural states of Southeast Asia (including Madagascar) are ultimately the product of European and American wars, greed, and political agreements. A major *raison d'être* of the modern states (also outside Southeast Asia) is the existence – either imagined or not – of one particular language functioning as an emblem of the nation. Such a language may indeed be purely imaginary (such as Filipino), or of no practical consequence (such as Malay in Singapore). But in most cases the language chosen as the national language is meant also to be used as an official language, i.e. in official communication, education, and/or the media.

In the colonial period it was in most countries the language of the (European) colonizing power which fulfilled these official functions: English in Malaysia, Brunei Darussalam and Singapore; Dutch in Indonesia; Portuguese in East Timor; French in Madagascar and Vietnam; and Spanish and subsequently English in the Philippines and Guam. Malay became a secondary official language in the Dutch Indies and Brunei Darussalam, and to a lesser extent in Malaysia. With independence, indigenous languages were proclaimed to be national: Malay in Malaysia, Brunei Darussalam, Singapore, and – in another variety – in Indonesia, Pilipino/Tagalog in the Philippines, and Malagasy in Madagascar.

Taiwan and East Timor were exceptional in that they were (also) colonized by Asian powers. The consequence was that Japanese and subsequently Mandarin were imposed upon the Taiwanese as *their* national language, whereas Indonesian became the 'national' language of East Timor from its annexation by Indonesia in 1975 until the withdrawal of the Indonesian armed forces in 1999. East Timor continues to be an exception since it is the only country in the region which since its independence has two national languages, namely Tetum and Portuguese.

In most countries the choice of an indigenous language not only as a national language but also as an official language implied subsequent provisions for corpus planning (standardization of spelling and grammar, terminology development) and propagation (education, publication, language campaigns, etc.). The success of these efforts varies from country to country. For a country such as East Timor it is too early to point to any results. The degree of success in other countries depends on funds, expertise, and political will, but above all on the acceptability of the language choice to the majority of the population. Wherever this choice was felt as a takeover bid by an identifiable section of the population it was resented by others. This was obviously the case in the Philippines and in Madagascar with regard to Pilipino/Tagalog and Merina Malagasy. In Malaysia the position of Malay as the national and official language is not undisputed either, precisely because of its function as a compensation for the position of the '*bumiputra*' (indigenous) Malay vis-à-vis the (descendants of the) Chinese and Indian newcomers. Even in Indonesia, where the status of the national language had never been seen as unduly advantageous for any ethnic or social group, and which therefore had been most successful in its language policy, critique has recently been raised against the position of the standard language. Because of its centralized standardization it is now sometimes identified with a specific section of the population, to wit all those who had positions within the centralized Suharto regime.

Nevertheless there is neither an indigenous nor a foreign alternative for Indonesian in Indonesia. Dutch language policy failed to make Dutch indispensable in the Dutch Indies. But in the other countries the old colonial language was never completely abolished. Not without strong political support from Portugal, Portuguese was reintroduced as a national and official language in East Timor. Pressure from France contributed to the failure of the drive for *malgachisation* in Madagascar. In the former American and British colonies the role of English is still prominent. This is obviously the case in the Philippines and Singapore (as well as in Guam), but it is also very noticeable in Malaysia and to a lesser extent in Brunei Darussalam. The status of English as the global language can only result in a greater role at the national level, and not only in the former British and American colonies.

The decision to give one language a special status automatically entails a lesser status for other languages. The Southeast Asian linguistic scene is so complicated that even trained linguists will have a very limited understanding of the existing variety of languages. Policy-makers have even less to go on. They may deny the existence of other languages (as used to be the policy in Brunei), largely neglect them (such as in Malaysia and Thailand), or confine themselves to unspecified assurances that these languages should be preserved. Within Southeast Asia the Philippines, Indonesia and especially East Timor stand out for their attention to the local languages other than the national and official languages. Nonetheless, it may be expected that the mere existence of the national and official languages in these countries (with its various implications for education and mass communication) may cause many of the minor languages to become extinct within a few generations.

ACKNOWLEDGEMENTS

I am grateful to John Hajek for his information on East Timor, to Willem Wolters for his data on the Philippines, and to the editors for their fruitful suggestions and remarks, and stimulating reminders.

REFERENCES

Adelaar, K.A. (1999) 'Retrieving Siraya phonology: A new spelling for a dead language', in E. Zeitoun and P. Jenkuei Li (eds), *Selected papers from the Eighth International Conference on Austronesian Linguistics*, 313–354, Symposium Series of the Institute of Linguistics, Academia Sinica, Number 1, Taipei: Institute of Linguistics, Academia Sinica.
Bonifacio, A.F. (1969) 'Pilipino as Medium of Instruction at the University Level', *The Dilliman Review* 17–2:105–130.
Clampitt-Dunlap, S. (1995) *Maintenance and the spread of English: a comparative study of the cases of Guam, the Philippines and Puerto Rico*, PhD thesis, University of Puerto Rico, <http://ponce.inter.edu/vl/tesis/sharon/diss.html>.
Eccles, L. (2000) 'East Timorese Language Policy and the Language Policies of Other Small Pacific Nations', *Studies in Languages and Cultures of East Timor*, vol. 3:1–30.
Tsao, Feng-fu (1994) *Preserving Taiwan's indigenous languages and cultures: a discussion in sociolinguistic perspective*, <www.kokugakuin.ac.jp/ijcc/global/07/tsao.html>.
Gonzalez, A.B. (1980) *Language and Nationalism, The Philippine Experience thus Far*, Quezon City: Ateneo de Manila Univesity Press.
Hajek, J. (2000) 'Language Planning and the Sociolinguistic Environment in East Timor: Colonial Practice and Changing Language Ecologies', *Current Issues in Language Planning* 1:400–415.
Hassan Ahmad (1999) *The Language Policy of Malaysia*, Kuala Lumpur: Art Printing Works.
Heseltine, N. (1971) *Madagascar*, New York: Praeger.

Jones, G.M. (1996) 'The Bilingual Education Policy in Brunei Darussalam', in Martin *et al.*, 123–132.

Llamzon, T.A. (1968) 'On Tagalog as Dominant Language', *Philippine Studies. A Quarterly* vol. 16(4):729–749.

Lombard, D., W. Arifin, and M. Wibisono (1970) *Le 'Spraeck ende woord-boek': première méthode de malais parlé (fin du XVIe s.)/Frederick de Houtman*. Paris: Ecole française d'Extrême-Orient.

Martin, P.W., Ožóg, C. and Poedjosoedarmo, G. (eds) (1996) *Language Use and Language Change in Brunei Darussalam*, Ohio University Center for International Studies. Southeast Asia Series Number 100, Athens, Ohio.

Martin, P.W. and Poedjosoedarmo, G. (1996) 'An Overview of the Language Situation in Brunei Darussalam', in Martin *et al.*, 1–23.

Minde, Donald van (1997) *Malayu Ambong. Phonology, Morphology, Syntax*, Leiden: Research School CNWS School of Asian, African, and Amerindian Studies.

Ophuijsen, Ch.A. van (1901) *Kitab Logat Melajoe. Woordenlijst voor de spelling der Maleische taal*, Batavia: Landsdrukkerij.

Ophuijsen, Ch.A. van (1910) *Maleische Spraakkunst*, Leiden: Doesburgh.

Ožóg, A.C.K. (1996) 'The Unplanned Use of English: the Case of Brunei Darussalam', in Martin *et al.*, 156–172.

Philippine Free Press (1991) *Independent Weekly*, Manila.

Po Dharma (2001) 'The intangible cultural heritage of two provinces of central Viet Nam-Ninh Thuan and Binh Thuan', in O. Salemink (ed.), *Viet Nam's cultural diversity: approaches to preservation*, Paris: UNESCO.

Smalley, W.A. (1994) *Linguistic diversity and national unity. Language ecology in Thailand*, Chicago/London: The University of Chicago Press.

CHAPTER FOUR

RITUAL LANGUAGES, SPECIAL REGISTERS AND SPEECH DECORUM IN AUSTRONESIAN LANGUAGES

James J. Fox

1 INTRODUCTION

Ritual languages, special registers and speech decorum reflect the social and cultural features of the societies in which they occur. They thus constitute linguistic usages that are significantly shaped by extra-linguistic factors. Yet the patterning of these usages in Austronesian languages shows remarkable similarities across a wide range of diverse societies. Such similarities point to the operation of some of the basic features of language within a common cultural heritage.

The subject is both complex and diverse. This chapter will focus on several distinct phenomena: (1) the use of what are called 'ritual languages' or 'ritual speech'; (2) the use of 'avoidance vocabulary' and 'word tabooing'; (3) the use of special purpose hunting and fishing registers; and (4) the use of 'speech decorum' or 'honorific speech'. Although these phenomena – and much in the interstices between them – have generally been discussed separately, they share enough similarities to argue that they are related to one another. Each involves, primarily, an elaboration or a specific restriction of the lexicon.

Thus, in linguistic terms, it is the patterning of what Roman Jakobson referred to as the 'metaphoric or paradigmatic pole of language' that features most prominently in the expression of these phenomena. Selection and synonym are of prime consideration (Jakobson and Halle 1956). In cultural terms, this patterning reflects a tendency of speakers to attune speech acts to particular contexts and to discriminate among categories of addressees. Thus speech among the Austronesians becomes a multi-levelled event. In social terms, special lexicons involve a range of possibilities: their use may be widely distributed throughout the society or may be confined to specific subgroups or specialized practitioners.

This chapter is as much a survey as an analysis and will therefore endeavor to provide background understanding through an illustration of each of these phenomena and a discussion of the development of the literature on them.

2 RITUAL LANGUAGES AMONG THE AUSTRONESIANS

'Ritual language' or 'ritual speech', as it has come to be defined in the Austronesian context, involves the use of pervasive semantic parallelism which can be further embellished
with other forms of parallelism, grammatical and phonological. The critical feature of
such compositions is to establish a relationship between semantic elements in separate
lines or utterances. A simple illustrative example of this is the following set of lines from
a Rotinese mortuary chant in which each parallel element is marked (a1//a2), (b1//b2),
(c1//c2). In the literature on parallelism, '//' is conventionally used to distinguish two
elements of a dyadic set (see Gevirtz 1963, Fox 1971):

1 Soku-la (a1) Pinga (b1) Pasa (c1)	They carry Pinga Pasa
2 (Ma) ifa-la (a2) So'e (b2) Leli (c2)	(And) they lift So'e Leli
3 De ana sao (d1) Kolik (e1) Faenama (f1)	She marries Kolik Faenama
4 Ma tu (d2) Bunak (e2) Tunulama (f2)	(And) weds Buna Tunulama

In this example, the verbs *soku//ifa* 'to carry//lift' and *sao//tu* 'to marry//wed' form
dyadic sets (a1//a2) and (d1//d2). The chant from which these opening lines have been
taken consists of 234 parallel lines composed of 117 distinct dyadic sets plus a variety of
dyadic personal and place names. The structure of this chant is analyzed in detail in Fox
(1971:224–255). Whereas lexical positioning of elements is crucial to composition of
utterances, the underlying combinatorial possibilities of elements which form dyadic sets
is critical to the semantic understanding of these ritual or poetic languages. Hence much
of the recent literature on these languages is concerned with 'semantic' rather than simple 'lexical' parallelism.

Such use of parallelism is by no means confined to Austronesian languages. As a near
universal feature of the poetic discourse, the study of parallelism has been the subject of
considerable comparative study (see Jakobson 1966, Fox 1977, for two extended surveys). Since the history of the study of parallelism begins with Robert Lowth's research
on Hebrew (1753), it is not surprising that early missionaries in different Austronesian
societies were the first to signal its existence in special speech registers.

3 RITUAL LANGUAGES AS 'PRIEST, PRIESTESS AND
   SPIRIT' REGISTERS

The Bible translator A. Hardeland, in his *Versuch einer Grammatik der Dajackschen
Sprache* (1858), was the first to note the Hebraic parallels in Dayak 'spirit language'
(*basa sangiang*). Although Hardeland provided only a single textual illustration of this
'spirit language' with translation and commentary, the posthumous publication of the
Swiss missionary H. Schärer's two-volume compilation of texts in *basa sangiang*, *Der
Totenkult der Ngadju Dajak in Süd-Borneo* (1966), provides a substantial corpus for
study. M. Baier (1987) continued this work of more than a century by publishing a
dictionary of *basa sangiang* based on materials from both Hardeland and Schärer.
This corpus on the Ngaju has been further extended by the substantial work of Sri
Kuhnt-Saptodewo (1993, 1999).

Other large compilations of ritual language texts are those assembled by Dunselman
(1949, 1950a, 1950b, 1954, 1955, 1959a, 1959b, 1961) from the Kendayan and Mualang
Dayak of West Borneo; by Sandin (1977), Sather (2001) and Masing (1997) from the
Iban; by Lagemann (1893, 1906), Sundermann (1905) and Steinhart (1934, 1937a, 1938,
1950, 1954) from Nias; by Dunnebier (1938, 1953) from Bolaang Mongondow; by
van der Veen (1929, 1950, 1965, 1966) from the Sa'dan Toraja; by Middelkoop (1949)

from the Atoni Pah Meto of West Timor; and by Quack (1981, 1985) and Schröder and Quack (1979) for the Puyuma of Taiwan. These collections of texts, with accompanying translations, were produced by their various authors primarily for purposes of cultural exegesis.

Van der Veen's monograph *The Merok Feast of the Sa'dan Toradja* provides a good illustration. It begins with a brief outline of the phases of a complex ritual and then launches into an ordered presentation of texts with extensive explanatory footnotes to the text. These footnotes give further explanation of particular lexical items or information on context or reference. The principal chant, which takes the form of a journey, consists of 791 couplet lines filled with paired metaphoric images in an array of successive formulaic frames. As an example, it is useful to cite a few such parallel lines in several different formulaic frames (van der Veen 1965:38–39).

The first of these formulaic frames is: *Ammi pokinallo ilalan//ammi pokokong dilambanan*, which is translated as 'As sustenance for the journey//as provisions on the way'. This is followed by a specific set of objects. After a long recitation of these provisions, the chant sets forth the path that should be followed, using the same dyadic set (*lalan// lambanan*) as in the earlier sequence.

As sustenance for the journey, take the three-eared rice
(*Ammi pokinallo ilalan, pare tallu bulinnna*)
As provisions on the way, take the cut one, branched in three…
(*ammi pobokong dilambanan, ke'te tallu etengna*)…
As sustenance for the journey, take an auspicious dream
(*Ammi pokinallo ilalan, tindo maelo*)
As provisions on the way, take a pregnant nocturnal vision…
(*ammi pobokong dilambanan, mamma' makatongan-tongan*)

Open the door of thy sky
(*Bungka'mokomi ba'bana langi'*)
Throw open the window of the all-covering roof…
(*killangmokomi petiroanna to paonganan*)

Then shalt thou take the rainbow as thy path
(*Ammi ma'lalan tindak sarira*)
Thou shalt make thy way along the arch of the sky…
(*ammi ma'lambanan taraue*)

Most of these older textual collections provide relatively little linguistic analysis. The texts themselves are generally not recordings of particular performances or specific poetic recitations but rather texts compiled by language assistants with local knowledge working with groups or individuals.

Given the nature of these materials and the missionary linguists who were the first to record them, it is understandable that they were frequently referred to as 'spirit language', 'priestly litanies' or 'ceremonial chants'. The concern of these writers was primarily philological, with a focus on the origin of lexical items used in these registers. Hardeland was the first to attempt to classify different classes of vocabulary (1858:4–5). He distinguished (1) ordinary as well as slightly altered Dayak words, (2) Malay words, also slightly altered and (3) special words, whose meaning and form were confined exclusively to use in the 'spirit language'. His dictionary (1859) includes some 900 of these *basa sangiang* words. Following Hardeland, B.F. Matthes (1872) noted the use of similar sorts of lexical items in the parallel language of the transvestite priests of the Bugis, as did the missionary linguist N. Adriani who wrote a brief comparative paper in Dutch on 'Indonesian priest languages' (1920, reprinted 1932, 3:1–21) and another similar paper in German on 'Magic speech' (1926, 3:167–175, reprinted 1932). In fact, both of these papers draw on a more detailed study which Adriani wrote on 'The Toraja Woman as Priestess' (1917, reprinted 1932, 2:190–215). Reflecting this tradition, the Dutch anthropologist D.Th. Fischer prepared a short monograph, *Priestertalen: Een Ethnologiese Studie* (1934) on the subject.

The concern with the origins of the lexicon of these liturgical registers has continued to interest researchers to the present. In his study of Dusun 'sacred language', Evans (1953: 495–496) distinguished five classes of words that made up this register: (1) 'ordinary Dusun words'; (2) 'special but easily recognizable forms of ordinary words – poetic forms – derived from ordinary Dusun'; (3) 'words not usually current in the village…but found in other villages, near or far away'; (4) 'loan words from Malay' and (5) 'words used, as far as known, only in the "sacred language", for which derivations are not obtainable'.

Writing of the Timugon Murut priestesses (*babalian*), whose ritual curing performances require a strict pairing of all ritual utterances, D.J. Prentice gives particular attention to the origin of the lexicon of these utterances. In such performances, which can last for days, the principal priestess utters the first line to which her acolyte, who accompanies her, responds with the second. Prentice describes the first line of each couplet as 'couched in a style of language which has much in common with the poetic style normally used in non-ritual singing', whereas the 'response' (*taam*) is 'couched in a special ritual language' (1981:130–131). Prentice identifies various sources for such response words: (1) 'a small number of cases where the ritual substitute is a synonym that already exists in the normal language'; 'numerals may also be reckoned as belonging to this category since a numeral "X" is replaced in the *taam* by the numeral "X + 1"'; (2) 'more frequently, the *taam*-word exists in normal Timugon, but with a different (sometimes even contradictory) meaning'; (3) '*taam*-words which exist in normal language, but in a different form (i.e. a derivative rather than as a base, or vice versa)'; (4) 'a very large number of ritual terms…known only from cognates in some other Murut dialect or in another language'; and, finally, as in the case with Evans' analysis of Dusun, (5) 'a number of substitute words for which no connections are known, either in Timugon or in any other dialect or language' (1981:133–135).

Schärer (1966:8), using Hardeland's textual material, discovered that ordinary Dayak words of Hardeland's time had come to be regarded, within a hundred years and in areas where Schärer worked, as special *basa sangiang* terms. Although the vocabulary of *basa sangiang* as a whole had not changed radically, changes had occurred to the ordinary language of Ngadju, thus affecting its relationship to *basa sangiang*.

In a study of ritual language from Termanu on the island of Roti, based on chants of various sorts comprising approximately 5000 lines, Fox has compiled a dictionary of over 1000 dyadic sets (Fox 1972a,b, revised 1993). In total, this dictionary comprises more than 1400 items, not including a large corpus of personal names which constitute critical cultural knowledge. Since many lexical items can have more than one pair, the dictionary was specially constructed to map all relationships between pairs. Knowledge of approximately 1000 conventional pairs or dyadic sets is the minimum necessary for the fluent and acceptable use of this ritual language.

As noted by Hardeland, Evans and Prentice for other similar registers, the largest number of lexical terms in the ritual language of Termanu which are not found in the ordinary speech of this area derive from other dialects on the island. A systematic identification of items in the lexicon requires a thorough investigation of the dialect communities of the island (Fox 1974:70–73). Dyadic sets, made up of words from different dialects, appear to be conventionally stable across most of the island. Such sets selectively encode and effectively highlight particular local features among the different, diverse dialects of the island. The fact that 'dialect' pairs are stable across the island makes formal ritual speech more intelligible than ordinary speech at gatherings of individuals from different parts of the island. The relative stability of the lexicon of this register is evidenced by the fact that a long text gathered by J.C.G. Jonker in 1900 and published in 1911 was assumed to be a contemporary text when it was first recited, in 1965, to an audience of knowledgeable Rotinese (Fox 1988b:162–166).

4 RITUAL LANGUAGES AS PRAYER, ORATION, POETRY AND SONG

At the same time that in the 19th century some missionary linguists were focusing attention on priestly registers among the Austronesians, other missionaries had begun to recognize the more general nature of such registers based on parallel composition. Thus for example in 1880, writing of Malagasy, the British missionary James Sibree noted:

> It is most pleasant therefore to listen to a native orator, especially as in the more formal Malagasy speeches the parts of every sentence are regularly balanced in construction, form a kind of rhythm very closely resembling the parallelism of Hebrew poetry (1880:148).

As a special register for oratory, prayer, poetry or song, such formal socially elevated composition is not necessarily confined to a specific class of practitioners and is therefore more likely to be used in a variety of settings. Whereas in the case of 'priestly registers', identification is generally couched in relation to particular performers or religious performances, oratorical registers (based on similar modes of composition but often with a less obscure lexicon) are generally discussed in terms of different speech genres or literary productions. Often, however, oral poets in Austronesian societies are regarded as 'spirit-enlightened' figures whose role is similar to, and often overlaps with, that of priest, priestess or shaman. Based on his research among the Berawan of Sarawak, Peter Metcalf has published a collection of prayers in parallelism by which, for example, individuals instruct sacrificial animals to convey their words to specific deities (1989, 1994). In a different context, Margaret Florey has studied the preservation of a local genre of 'incantations' among the Alune of Seram in Central Maluku who are undergoing rapid social and linguistic change (Florey 1998, Florey and Wolff 1998).

The literature on these various poetic registers is diverse. Thus, for example, L. Sabatier has published the text of a major 'epic' in pervasive parallelism for the Rhade (1933); in his commentary on the *Salasilah of Kutai*, W. Kern has commented on the comparative significance of parallelism in Malay *penglipur-lara* tales, Middle Malay *anday-anday* and Minangkabau *kaba* (1956); and N. Phillips has produced an exemplary study of Sijobang, the sung narrative poetry of West Sumatra (1981). H.J. Wigglesworth has emphasized the role of parallelism as a rhetorical device in Manobo narrative discourse (1980); J.P.B. de Josselin de Jong has written a critical study of eastern Indonesian poetry (1941). Kaartinen has examined the parallelism of a song tradition among the displaced 'Bandanese' in the Kei islands (1998) and van Engelenhoven has provided a preliminary study of the parallelism of 'royal speech' and 'song speech' among the people of Leti in the southern Moluccas (1997). His article includes the translation of a parallel text first recorded in 1846. Similarly, Sankoff has done an analysis of parallelism in poetry of the Buang, an Austronesian-speaking population of Papua New Guinea (1977). The

Kumulipo, the long Hawaiian narrative chant translated by Beckwith (1951), provides an excellent example of similar forms of extended literary parallelism.

An ethnographically focused comparison of poetic uses of these registers can be found in Fox, *To Speak in Pairs: Essays on the Ritual Languages of Eastern Indonesia* (1988). This volume consists of ten studies of different ritual languages on Sumba, Flores, Roti and Sulawesi. The collection as a whole provides an indication of the diversity of social contexts in which these registers continue to be used in societies of eastern Indonesia: for divination and spirit communication, prayers and sacrificial invocations, bride wealth negotiations, ordeals, mortuary ceremonies, complex origin cycle rituals, and a variety of other critical oratorical contexts. Several authors focus on the ritual language traditions of different groups in west Sumba: Janet Hoskins examines the formal etiquette of communication with spirits in Kodi; David Mitchell explicates the metaphoric couplets in oratory among Wanukaka speakers; Brigitte Renard-Clamagirand focuses on the speech used in a ceremony for 'banishing transgression'; and Joel Kuipers discusses the pattern of prayer among the Weyewa. Gregory Forth contrasts the invocatory and oratorical speech in Rindi in eastern Sumba. For Flores, Eriko Aoki provides a detailed examination of a sequence of divination and ordeal to discover stolen objects among Lio speakers and Satoshi Nakagawa considers the formal idioms of marriage among Endeh speakers, while Douglas Lewis examines the performance of a narrative history in Tana Ai. Fox examines the formulaic structure of a long mortuary chant on Roti and Charles Zerner and Toby Volkman consider the language of one ritual in a complex cycle of Toraja ceremonies.

Contributors focus both on textual coherence and codes of communication required for different genres. Janet Hoskins in her analysis of spirit communication among the Kodi, for example, distinguishes between forms of speech addressed to the 'spirits of the outside' as opposed to deities and 'spirits of the inside'. For addressing deities and spirit deputies, she identifies six characteristics of spirit-speech etiquette: (1) exclusive use of paired couplets; (2) mediated communication in a public forum (no one can speak directly on his own behalf); (3) indirectness involving metaphoric expressions of deference and respect; (4) recognition of the strict hierarchy of the spirits and deities who may only be approached through an intermediary; (5) expression of an attitude of submission and pleading; and (6) the merging of individual responsibility with the destiny of the group. An example of this kind of deference speech from Hoskins (1988:54–55) is the following:

Only we are left, spiders with no livers
(*Ghica kanehengoka ha nggengge nja pa ate*)
Only we are left, snails with no thoughts...
(*Ghica kanehengoka ha buku nja pa koko*)...

There is no one here to tell us the many long myths
(*Njaingo na kedeko pa danga*)
There is no one here to teach us more of our customs
(*Njaingo na nughalo pa rehi*)

I am alone like a child holding the net for a discus toy
(*Di kaluka yayo enga pada pokatao kalaiyo*)
I am alone like a child grasping the rope on a spinning top...
(*Di kaluka yayo enga pada lereho kadiyo*)

We are only the lips told to pronounce
(*Ghica pimoka wiwi canggu tene*)
We are only the mouths told to speak.
(*Ghica pimoka ghoba tanggu naggulo*).

In ritual language usage among the Rindi, Gregory Forth contrasts 'speeches of invocation' addressed to ancestors and spirits with the 'oratorical speech' used in formal transactions between affines and other parties. Although both forms of speech require the use of carefully 'fashioned' couplets, oratorical speech, in particular, invariably involves complex communicative exchanges of messages among one or more pairs of orators, each with their deputies.

This 'weaving' of speech contrasts with the individual narrative performances of single chanters among the Rotinese, the recitations of specific individuals with privileged clan knowledge in Tana Ai, or the long ritual utterances of the priests of Toraja. The words of Mo'an Robertus Rapa of clan Ipir in Wai Brama (quoted in Lewis 1988:271) give an indication of this proud narrative style:

I am clan Ipir, the great ebony tree
(*A'u Ipir leten geté*)
I am exalted like the large birds of the mountains
(*A'u sodor wodon ilin*)
The domain of Wai Brama and Wolobola
(*Wai Brama Wolobola*)
Raja as far as Balénatar
(*Ratu wutun Balénatar*)
Speaking to the sky and earth
(*Ora nian tana kiring*)
Addressing the sun and moon...
(*Ora lero wulan harang*)...

Among the Rotinese the narrative structure of some mortuary chants relates to narratives of the origin of a variety of cultural artefacts; together these narratives appear to be fragments of a longer epic-like cosmological narrative of the lords of the sun and moon, ocean and sea depths (Fox 1997a). The use of ritual language to recount clan histories is one of the chief usages of such ritual language among the Atoni Pah Meto (McWilliam 1989, 1997) and among the Tetun of Timor (Therik 1995, 2004). Louis Berthe (1972) has published a substantial textual collection of 'ancestral journeys' in Bunak, a non-Austronesian language heavily influenced by the oral traditions of neighbouring Tetun. For the Mambai of East Timor, similar ritual narratives, in strict parallelism, recount both the origins of the earth and accounts of the 'walk of the flag' (Traube 1980, 1986). As a native speaker of Mambai, Benjamin Corte-Real has written with singular perception on the use of ritual language in different verbal genres of the Mambai of Suru-Ainaro (1998, 2000).

Joel Kuipers (1990, 1998) has written extensively on the specific linguistic features and social contexts of ritual speech in Weyewa. His work has been particularly useful in its discussion of a continuum of ritual speech styles associated with different social authority. Although the Weyewa tradition appears to lack an extended narrative genre like some found on neighboring islands, the use of ritual speech extends to a great variety of what Kuipers refers to as political, religious and personal genres of speech. Kuipers identifies no less than 19 such genres (Kuipers 1998:37). He has also addressed the question of ongoing changes in the use of ritual speech styles, noting the marginalization of an aggressive performance genre expressing the anger of politically powerful figures in favor of nostalgic laments and school-sanctioned children's performances (1998). In a different context, Fox has documented the adoption by Rotinese speakers of ritual language for new performance genres such as church services and sermons (Fox 1982) and for recasting biblical stories in traditional narrative modes (Fox 1983). The formal structure of such narratives takes on a resemblance to the structure of the Malay translations of the Old Testament that have been used by Christian Rotinese since the eighteenth century.

5 FORMS OF PARALLEL COMPOSITION

Ritual languages among Austronesian speakers are all based on some form of semantic parallelism, which may be further embellished by various other forms of parallelism, grammatical and phonological. The critical feature of such compositions is to establish a relationship between semantic elements in separate lines (or utterances). Each set of parallel lines constitutes a potential frame of variable complexity. Two parallel lines or utterances can be taken to represent the minimum form of composition, though the repeated utterance of identical lines could be considered as parallelism reduced to identity. The couplet is by far the most frequent format of parallelism but by no means the only format even in oral traditions that overwhelmingly favor this format. A succession of parallel lines is also a common device for particular purposes, especially the recitation of place names.

Parallel lines may vary in their complexity, from lines with a single lexical substitution in concurrent utterances to lines involving two, three, four or more substitutions per set of parallel lines. Further embellishments may also figure in composition: a tendency, if not a formal requirement, that paired terms in successive lines have a similar number of syllables or display vowels that are either similar or contrastive. Often levels of embellishment and complexity reflect the competence of individual performers within a particular tradition.

Roman Jakobson coined the term 'canonical' to refer to traditions of parallel composition in which there were culturally defined and generally accepted conventions concerning the pairing of particular semantic elements (see Jakobson 1966, Fox 1977). In Jakobson's terms, such traditions define a significant degree of congruence in their paradigmatic or metaphoric dimension, thus enhancing both the 'poetic' and 'ritual' aspects of language. Among Austronesian speakers, traditions vary considerably in the 'strictness' of their canonical requirements. In most traditions, the strictness of pairing of terms depends on the genre in which parallelism is used. Love songs or bride wealth negotiations may be far less strict in their pairings than those genres that recount origins, convey the words of the ancestors or guide the spirits of the dead. Thus among Rotinese performers, a poor chanter whose pairings go awry may be quickly tongue-clicked into embarrassed silence by his audience; more seriously still, ritual speakers at major ceremonies among the Ata Tana Ai of Flores are believed to risk death if their compositions fail; by contrast, among the Weyewa, the heated ritual speech of 'angry' big men is not necessarily judged on the strictness of its parallelism.

In traditions where strict conventions hold, as in Rotinese, it is possible to trace formal relations between pairs or fixed 'dyadic sets' within the language. Although some lexical elements may only occur in one dyadic set, others may occur in more than one set. Some elements may conjoin with five or more other lexical elements to form specific dyadic sets. As a result it is possible to trace formal interrelations among semantic elements and indeed to produce a dictionary of all lexical items used in ritual language arranged in terms of their formal pairings (see Fox 1972b/1993, 1974:73ff, 1975:121ff).

These formal interrelations can be represented as a complex network. In this network, a small number of lexical elements function semantically as critical nodes of a large configuration in which most lexical elements have only one or at most two specific pairings.

A small core of just 21 elements (from a lexicon of approximately 1400 such lexical items) appears to constitute the 'core' of the network as a whole (Fox 1975:111–129). Relying on this network, it is also possible to trace formal interrelations among categories of related lexical elements.

Formulaic conventions also figure prominently in most traditions of parallelism. Such formulae consist of a sequence of semantic elements, often of a poetic, highly metaphoric nature, that must conjoin with another equally elaborate sequence of elements. Thus, in Weyewa, 'horse with a standing tail, dog with a black tongue' is the conventional couplet formula for a good orator. 'Horse' and 'dog' form a dyadic set and occur in many other contexts. Similarly, in Rotinese, the lines 'they give gold-chains with snakes' heads, they give buffalo with crocodile-marked bodies' are formulaic lines that refer to a certain kind of bride wealth. This formula is itself composed of several dyadic sets: gold(-chain)// buffalo, crocodile//snake, and head//body, all of which regularly form pairs in other contexts. Such formulaic syntagmatic coherence adds a further dimension to the rules of proper composition.

In the literature on parallelism, the term 'couplet' is used in a variety of senses: for what is here called a 'dyadic set', for formulaic sequences composed of several dyadic sets, or for whole lines of paired elements. Where canonical traditions do not require the strict pairing of all semantic elements, formulaic sequences often figure more prominently because of their relative fixedness in performances.

6 TOPOGENY

Topogeny is a frequent special feature often associated with parallel utterances. It consists in an ordered sequence of place names. As such, the recitation of topogenies is as common among Austronesian speakers as is the recitation of genealogies; and, in many instances, genealogies merge with topogenies.

Topogenies are relied upon for many purposes: to mark a ritual pathway, to recount the journey of an ancestor, to determine the boundaries of a group, to identify the settlements of allies and confederates, or to invoke a succession of spirits by citing their place of power (see Fox 1997b:8–12). Thus the recitation of a topogeny is a means of organizing social knowledge by location. Parallelism lends itself well to the recitation of the ordered sequences of places invoked in topogenies.

One portion of the text of *The Merok Feast* (van der Veen 1965:49–61), which consists of an invocation of the gods of the different local regions, comprises 74 couplet lines of a litany of the names of these gods and their specific territories. A few lines (1965:53) from the translation of this litany provide an illustration of the use of parallelism as topogeny. The listing of places from Tondon, Sa'dan, Bori' and onwards defines the social geography of the Sa'dan Toraja:

The God of the territory of the Tondon region
(*Deata lembangna padang di Tondon*)
The lord of the district of Batulobo'
(*puangna padang di Batulobo'*)
The God of the territory of the Balusu region
(*Deata lembangna padang di Balusu*)
The lord of the district of Bontong
(*puangna padang di Bontong*)

The God of the territory of the Sa'dan
(*Deata lembangna padang di Sa'dan*)
The Lord of the district of Bori'...
(*puangna padang di Bori'*)...

Among the Rotinese, topogenies are complex compositions that are intended to recount the origin and distribution of culturally important objects throughout the island (see Fox 1997c). The topogeny of the origin of rice and millet, for example, consists of the ritual invocation of a sequence of paired ancestral women's names, each of which is associated with a particular location. These women take seeds (represented as a paired personage) from one named area and plant them in another named area in a circular path around the island.

Now the woman, Fi Bau
(*Besak-ka inak-ka Fi Bau*)
And the girl, Seda Kola
(*Ma fetok-ka Seda Kola*)
Cradles and carries him away
(*Ko'o do ifa nenin*)

She plants him with care
(*De sele nakaboboin*)
And sows him with attention
(*Ma tane nasamamaon*)
In the field of Bau Peda Dele
(*Nai Bau Peda Dele fuan*)
And in the plain at Kola Sifi Ndai...
(*Ma Kola Sifi Ndai mon*)...

The topogeny thus operates congruently at two levels: at the level of women's names which are themselves evocative of specific places, and at the level of particular fields and locations throughout the island.

Some of the longest and most elaborate parallel compositions among the Atoni Pah Meto are extended topogenies of the journey of particular name groups through the Timorese landscape (see McWilliam 1997). Similarly, in a long topogeny performed only at the end of a five-to-ten cycle, the Koa of the island of Palu'e recite the voyage of the first ancestors who travelled from the rim of the earth in the west bringing with them the 'black patola stone' that provides the primordial substance of their island. This chant in strict parallelism consists of 'a series of some two hundred paired place names'. Knowledge of the first paired names in the sequence is restricted to ceremonial officiants whereas knowledge of ritual place names within Koa is less restricted (see Vischer 1992:92–106).

7   WORD TABOOING

'Word tabooing' was first discussed by Sir James Frazer in *The Golden Bough* (1911, II:318–418). Already in Frazer's time, word tabooing, although not confined to speakers of Austronesian languages, was seen as a distinctive practice among such populations.

The most comprehensive survey since Frazer is that by G.F. Simons (1982:157–226). Simons' study provides a systematic examination of the distribution of various types of word tabooing practices among 75 Austronesian languages from Madagascar to the Cook

Islands. The only significant languages missing from Simons' survey are the Central-Malayo-Polynesian languages of Nusa Tenggara and Maluku.

Word tabooing covers a variety of usages. In particular it refers to the prohibition on the use of names (or of words resembling such names) for particular categories of relatives, especially affines, or for those who have died. Such tabooing is individually focused and in general the knowledge of the particularities of these taboos extends within a network of relatives and local co-residents. For some communities, word tabooing refers to the prohibition on the public utterance of the names of chiefs or leading men, either while they are alive or after their death. This usage extends more generally through a speech community. As a consequence of the tabooing of names, individuals or groups in these various speech communities are required to adopt acceptable lexical substitutes for prohibited names.

On the basis of his survey, Simons identifies various distributional patterns for these different prohibitions among Austronesian societies. Parent-in-law/children-in-law name tabooing is the most widespread of these practices, leading Simons to postulate these reciprocal prohibitions as a 'cultural practice of the Proto-Austronesian speech community' (1982:178). By contrast, sibling-in-law name prohibitions are confined almost exclusively to Melanesian communities of New Guinea, the Solomon Islands and Vanuatu, as are cross-sex (brother–sister) name prohibitions. A number of western Austronesian language communities in the Philippines, Borneo and Sumatra maintain a prohibition on the naming of senior consanguineal relatives or on the reciprocal use of names between generations.

The prohibition on the names of chiefs or persons of high rank is largely confined to Oceanic language communities from New Britain through Fiji and most of Polynesia, whereas the prohibition on naming the dead is concentrated in the islands at the southeast tip of New Guinea, New Britain, New Ireland, the Solomons, Vanuatu and Micronesia. In two-thirds of the societies where names are tabooed, prohibitions are extended to lexemes from which these names derive and often to other words that resemble the prohibited names.

In their analysis of Kwaio word tabooing, R.M. Keesing and J. Fifiʔi (1969) have provided the best single account of these linguistic practices in their cultural context. Thus among the Kwaio, the name of a person is associated with the 'essence' (toʔofuŋana) of that person; names of ancestors (both male and female) are revered in rough proportion to the number of their descendants who recognize them and continue to sacrifice pigs to them. Individual status derives from the number of sacrificial pigs one raises to offer the ancestors (adalo).

Descendants may declare the mention of the names of their most important ancestors as prohibited in their presence. Often a precipitating event (illness or misfortune) may trigger the declaration of the prohibition on the utterance of particular ancestors' names. Prohibitions can be extended to (1) the pseudonyms used for the pig(s) consecrated to these ancestors; (2) euphemisms used in divination addressed to the ancestors; and (3) the shrines that are the burial places of these ancestors and the sites of important sacrifice. Names of individuals who have died of either leprosy or tuberculosis are considered particularly dangerous and are the subject of immediate tabooing, as are the names of the recent dead among surviving relatives.

A variety of linguistic associations between ancestral names and other lexical forms that are either morphologically related or phonologically similar may lead to the prohibition of use of these lexical forms as well. Keesing and Fifiʔi found that more than one third (38%) of tabooed lexical forms referred to persons, body parts, sensations, sub-stances, and activities; another 22% referred to plants and plant parts, and natural objects and phenomena (see 1969:165, Table 2). Word tabooing requires linguistic resort to elab-orate lexical substitution in different social settings (that is, in the presence of individu-als with known linguistic prohibitions). This lexical substitution draws on the productive resources of Kwaio speakers. It includes the creation of numerous alternative lexemes (five different terms, for example, for 'bamboo fire-tongs', four terms for 'pudding bowl', etc.) for the same specific object, but can also include the adoption of loanwords from other Kwaio dialects or other Malaita languages as well as from Pidgin.

8   SPECIAL PURPOSE REGISTERS FOR HUNTING, FISHING, AND OTHER ACTIVITIES

In his survey of word tabooing, Simons also plots the distribution of special purpose reg-isters for hunting, fishing, mining, and even harvesting (1982:185). The majority of these registers are found in the Indonesian islands. They appear to be directed at 're-portraying' particular risk-prone or precarious activities through the systematic use of an alternate vocabulary comprised of synonyms and euphemisms intended, in some instances, to disguise (principally for a spirit audience) the ongoing conduct of these activities. C.E. Grimes and K.R. Maryott (1994) have described two such registers, *li garan*, a hunt-ing register used on Buru, and *sasahara*, a fishing register used by Sangir speakers. *Sasahara*, the better known of these registers, was first documented by N. Adriani (1893) and its vocabulary was included in Steller and Aebersold's Sangir–Nederlands dictionary (1959). C.L. van Klinken has described a similar fishing register, *lia tasi*, for the southern Tetun of Timor (1999:8–10; see also Therik 1995:40–43, 2004:39–44).

Maryott describes *sasahara* as a special register because it is unintelligible to uniniti-ated Sangir speakers, is used in well-defined social situations, is named as a special form of speech by the Sangir themselves, and clearly contrasts with ordinary speech. *Sasahara* is used primarily by men who fish, travel, and conduct business at sea; or, as was once the case, engaged in fighting at sea or conducted raiding from the sea. According to Grimes and Maryott (1994:298), although the use of some morphemes is markedly dif-ferent, 'affixes and compounding formatives in *sasahara* morphology are the same as those of common Sangir'. *Sasahara* differs from common Sangir primarily in its lexicon.

According to Steller and Aebersold (1959:405), *sasahara* consists of 'hidden words that the Sangir use at sea so that the spirits of the sea will not be able to overhear and interfere with their plans or intentions'. Interestingly, *sasahara* has affinities with other Sangir speech forms: 'a Sasahara term will often occur in parallel with its non-Sasahara equivalent in the same specimen of...versified chanting known as Sasambo, or in a quick-tempered variety of Sasambo known as Sasahola' (Grimes and Maryott 1994:289). It contrasts with *sasalili*, which is a form of honorific speech among the Sangir.

Maryott identifies a variety of mechanisms for the creation of *sasahara* terms. These include phrase characterization, substitution by association, formal resemblance or semantic disguise: rope: 'that which twists'; dog: 'barker'; anchor: 'that which sinks'; boat: 'forward-thrusting log'; look at: 'blind oneself to'. Although there are *sasahara* words for pairs such as 'big' and 'small', 'near' and 'far', 'many' and 'few', 75% of the statives that take antonyms have only one word for each antonymous pair: thus, 'long' but not 'short'; 'fast' but not 'slow'; 'old' but not 'young'. The missing paired element is produced by negation: 'not long'; 'not fast' or 'not old'.

The Tetun sea register is much less elaborate than that of Sangir. According to van Klinken (1999:8–10), *lia tasi*, whose use is believed to prevent accidents while fishing, is distinguished by a vocabulary of approximately 60 words used by men, women and children on fishing trips, mainly in local mangrove swamps. While engaged in such activities, the emphasis is placed on speaking as little as possible. The phonology, morphology and syntax of *lia tasi* are like that of ordinary language. Some adjectives and intransitive verbs in everyday speech serve as nouns in the sea register. Crocodiles, which are not uncommon, are referred to either as 'lords of the fish trap' (*kesak na'in*) or 'noble men' (*usi mane*). Some 'self-humbling' terms in this register also occur in the Tetun noble register (*lian na'in*).

Buru provides another case of a well-described hunting register. In his discussion of linguistic usage on Buru, Grimes notes the existence of persistent affinal taboos: prohibitions on uttering the names of parents-in-law, children-in-law and siblings-in-law but no prohibition on the utterance of ancestral names. Common word taboos on Buru, however, are not confined just to these person-based prohibitions but extend to both territorial- and seasonal-based prohibitions. Thus, in certain areas there exist restrictions on the use of the words for animals and fish, specifically those that are hunted or trapped, and on terms relating to water, thirst or drinking, with a corresponding set of lexical substitutes; similarly, during the heavy monsoon, hunters observe elaborate linguistic prohibitions and adopt lexical substitutions. It is also reported that women observe similar sorts of taboos during menstruation. Observation of these taboos is seen as a 'cooperative effort' with the ancestors and thus a form of respect.

Li Garan is a particular form of territorially based register that is used by approximately 3000 speakers of one subdialect of Rana when they travel in an uninhabited area of the island known as Garan. The syntax and phonology of *li Garan* is the same as ordinary Buru, as are pronouns, prepositions, conjunctions, and adverbials. The difference is entirely in its special vocabulary, for which Grimes has recorded some 400 lexical items. Some animals (pig and chicken but not dog), most but not all body parts (arm, leg and eye but not head, ear or breast), some kin terms (mother, father and child but not other relatives), the numerals one, ten and a hundred, many verbs, both active and stative, plus negatives have special *li Garan* terms. Earlier investigations by Schut (1919) and Jansen (1933) suggest that these lexical terms are relatively stable. Children are taught the register from an early age, allowing Rana speakers to use this register as a secret language in the presence of other Buru speakers (Grimes and Maryott 1994:280–286).

9 *PROKEM*: A SPECIAL REGISTER AMONG THE YOUTH OF JAKARTA

Prokem is a special register of Indonesian whose origins are obscure and whose popular use among the youth of Jakarta is difficult to define. Even the term, *prokem*, for this form of 'slang' speech is uncertain. Commentators suggest that a portion of this register was derived from the disguised speech used by criminal elements in urban centers on both Jawa and Sumatra (Chambert-Loir 1988:6–8; see Teguh Esha 1978 and also Dreyfuss 1983). It is clearly distinguishable from, but shares some features with, the disguise register used by transvestites in Jakarta (van der Meij 1983).

Prokem developed in the 1970s and 1980s as a distinct linguistic marker of a school-age generation whose vocabulary drew heavily on the local Jakarta dialect of Indonesian. A short dictionary of this register (Prokem/Indonesian and Indonesian/Prokem) consisting of just over 1000 words was published in 1988 at the height of its local social popularity (Prathama Rahardja and Chambert-Loir 1988).

Much of the vocabulary of *prokem* consists of simple transformations of recognizable words or phrases. One such transformation involves the infix *-ok-*: thus *bapak* 'father' is shortened to *bap* and the infix is added to form *bokap*; similarly, *bini* 'wife' becomes *bokin*; *rumah* 'house' becomes *rokum*. Variations on this transformation involve the retention of the second syllable: thus, *berat* 'heavy' becomes *berokat* (which can also take the form *rebat*); *mesin* 'machine' becomes *mesokin*. The infix *-in-* is also used, though less frequently than *-ok-*: thus, *cewe* 'girl' can be transformed to *cinewine*. Final consonants may also be changed: *becak* 'tricycle' becomes *boket* and *tujuh* 'seven' becomes *tokud*.

Prokem is also popularly referred to as *ngomong labik* 'backwards speech' because of its various forms of metathesis: thus, for example, *balik* 'return' becomes *labik*; *bikin* 'do, make' becomes *kibin*. Abbreviations abound in *prokem*: *botay* from *bau tahi* means 'shit smell'; *Fanta* [the drink] stands for *fanatik tapi agresip*: 'fanatic but aggressive'. Many ordinary words have different meanings: *kuda* 'horse' refers to a motorcycle; *hotel* to a jail. Abbreviations also combine with changed, often reversed, meanings: thus, *benci* 'to hate' is said to stand for *benar benar cinta* 'to really love someone'. Much of this special vocabulary focuses on drugs, drink, and sexual relations and it is claimed that *prokem* is more commonly used by young men than women (Chambert-Loir 1988:8–17).

Prokem was the street fashion of the 1980s, especially in Jakarta, and it has since given way to – or developed into – other slang registers, one of which is known as *bahasa gaul*. A distinguishing feature of this register is its greater use of the infix *-in-*, in some cases twice in the same word. Thus *bule*, the term for 'white person, westerner' becomes *binuline*; by the same process, *banci* 'transvestite' becomes *binancini* (see Sahertian 1999).

10 SPEECH LEVELS AND HONORIFIC REGISTERS

There is a great range of honorific registers among Austronesian-speaking populations. Raffles was one of the first of a long succession of commentators to describe honorific speech levels of Javanese (1817, I:356–372; reprint 1978). He viewed this register as a distinct 'dialect' used between 'higher and lower classes of society'. In his words, 'there is no feature in the language more deserving of notice, than the difference of dialect, or the distinction between common language and what may be termed the polite language or language of honour' (1978, I:366). Interestingly, in a somewhat similar vein, in 1882, three noted commentators published their initial observations on other, less elaborate, registers at different ends of the Austronesian world. Sibree remarked on the 'curious words' associated with the Malagasy royalty (1882); while Ray published a brief note on the 'chief's language' for Lifu and Ponape to accompany Newell's longer examination of chief's language on Samoa (1882).

Studies of Javanese speech levels include works by Damais (1950), Gonda (1947), Poedjosoedarmo (1968), Uhlenbeck (1978:278–335), and Suharno (1982). Errington (1985, 1988, 1998) provides an excellent, ethnographically grounded examination of the use of these speech levels in contemporary central Javanese speech communities. Clynes' MA thesis presents a comparative study of Javanese and Balinese 'speech styles' (1989). There also exists in Javanese a special 'palace language' (*basa kedaton*) which is used exclusively by members of the former Javanese courts and their staff in the presence of the ruler and in written communication. Poedjosoedarmo (1968:58) notes the existence of this register, but does not present an analysis of it. Errington (1982), on the other hand, examines this 'Javanese palace language' in some detail. There are also contemporary analyses of speech levels in Sundanese (Satjadibrata 1956, Hardjadibrata 1985) and

Madurese (Stevens 1965). Wolfowitz's (1991) study of 'stylistic choice' in Suriname Javanese extends these analyses to an overseas Javanese community.

Recent studies of honorific registers in the Pacific include Milner (1961) for Samoa; Lenormand (1990) for Lifou; and Tryon (1997) for the Loyalty Islands. Blixen (1969) has done a general survey of the distribution of these honorific 'languages' in Oceania. For eastern Indonesia, van Klinken has reported on the 'noble register' for the Tetun of Wehali (1999:8–9); van Engelenhoven has noted the existence of *lirmarna* 'royal language' or 'royal speech' on Leti (1997) while Bowden has noted 'speech levels' in Taba, whose refined lexicon consists of loans from Ternate (2001:21f).

Javanese, Sundanese, Madurese, Balinese and Sasak are the most prominent Austronesian languages that continue to maintain speech levels as a fundamental feature of proper speech decorum. Of these, Javanese registers have been the subject of the greatest linguistic attention, and are the only ones to be discussed here.

Although the formal structure of almost any simple sentence may seem unproblematic, in standard Javanese there can occur at least five or more acceptable, yet lexically different, ways of rendering such a sentence. By this same standard, using similar constituent elements, it is possible to generate other syntactically correct, but wholly unacceptable, expressions of the same sentence. A linguistic analysis of Javanese has, therefore, to link syntactic correctness with the specification of the system of constraints involved in the proper choice of lexical items for the production of acceptable sentences.

The traditional view has been to see Javanese as consisting of a layered number of speech levels reflecting distinct social gradations. These levels may vary from two to ten, depending on the analyst. Thus, for example, a contrast is drawn between a 'non-polite, informal' register known as *ngoko* and a 'polite, formal' register known as *krama* with an intermediate 'semi-polite, semi-formal' level, known as *madya* ('middle'). *Krama* is popularly differentiated into an unmarked form which is widely used for addressing people who are older or of a higher social status, and what is referred to a 'high *krama*', *krama inggil*, whose vocabulary is marked by respectful words referring to the person or actions of a noted dignitary and a 'humble *krama*', *krama andap*, whose vocabulary demeans one's own and others' actions in relation to a respected personage. Thus the marked forms of *krama* depend on the person referred to whereas ordinary *krama* depends on the person addressed. Certain affixes in Javanese are regarded as distinguishing features of the two basic contrasting levels: *ngoko: di-, -é, -(a)ken; krama: dipun-, -ipun, -aken*. A substantial portion of Javanese vocabulary can be grouped as either high or low; many *krama* words are marked by distinct formatives that identify them as *krama*; and the choice of first and second person personal pronouns according to speech level is a critical factor in appropriate speech.

Suharno (1982) has argued that this multiple-layer approach to Javanese is not based on precise semantic criteria and consequently gives a misleading impression of Javanese social strata as well as a blurred view of actual language usage. In its place he offers an alternative approach based on a speaker's choice of address reference for his interlocutor. This choice determines the speech relationship, for which there are only a limited number of possibilities. He describes this sociolinguistically as a system of 'speech decorum'. Instead of regarding the vocabulary of *ngoko* as the basis of Javanese, with an additional special vocabulary piled on in layers, he divides the Javanese lexicon into two subsets: one subset that is entirely neutral to any relationship between speaker and addressee and another subset of 'decorum-oriented words' that consists of variously ordered lexical pairs, triplets and quadruplets. The first subset comprises the overwhelming bulk of the Javanese vocabulary, whereas the second subset, which includes all pronouns and a host of important person-related nouns and verbs, constitutes a critical but limited portion of the lexicon amounting to about 14% of Javanese lexical elements.

'Speech levels' of a sort also emerge in Suharno's analysis, but instead of being designated in terms of supposed social gradations, these speech levels are based on 'basic types of relationships' reflected in the use of different sets of pronouns. He is thus able to concentrate on a limited number of recognizable 'you–I' pronominal relationships (1982:122–126). Three of these types he regards as fundamental. These pronominal types he labels as K: *kowe–aku*; M: *sampeyan–kula*; and P: *panjenengan–kula*. Although these types of relationships may resemble the distinctions between the speech levels of *ngoko*, *madya*, and *krama*, Suharno's analysis gives a different cast to an understanding of these forms. Other types of pronominal relationships he sees as either minor variants of his three main types or regional variants. Thus the *sampeyan–aku* type of pronominal relationship is an identifiably east Javanese relationship variant.

Suharno adopts, as have most analysts since the nineteenth century, the language patterns of the central courtly cities of Solo and Yogyakarta as 'standard Javanese'. With this as the lexical foundation of his model, he is able to delineate carefully a range of common 'mistakes' made in everyday spoken Javanese. Since 'decorum' remains a socially grounded notion and this has been built into his model, his analysis is able to distinguish between grammatical competence and communicative competence, implying that full communicative competence can only come from mastering the lexical manipulations associated with relationships of a particular speech community.

This model offers the possibility for an historical examination of the different regional speech communities on Java with different standards of decorum. The elaboration of the present Javanese lexicon of courtesy had its principal locus at the Mataram court, which was established in the sixteenth century. Sir Stamford Raffles, for example, provides a long list of Mataram's *basa krama* for the early nineteenth century (Raffles 1978, II: Appendix E). In spite of the historical influences of this court, not all of Java followed the same pattern. There were rival courts and alternative traditions: in particular, the north coast principalities, especially Banten and Cirebon that were in closer proximity to the Sundanese populations of West Java, the so-called 'Osing' at the far end of East Java, who were influenced by Balinese traditions, and the mountain peoples of Tengger, who actually resisted the development of speech levels. One indication of the variability of speech levels can be seen in Bernd Nothofer's dialect mapping of the lexical items considered appropriate for different speech levels in the Javanese dialect regions that interpenetrate Sundanese areas along the north coast of West Java and on the border between West and Central Java (1980). This important study of a selected portion of the lexicons of speakers from 154 villages throughout this mixed Javanese-, Sundanese- and Malay-speaking area points out a variety of instances where the relative positions of 'high' and 'low' terms (as judged from the standard of south central Java) are reversed. Although not as elaborate as the registers of Solo and Yogyakarta, levels of decorous speech are recognized everywhere, but the assignment of particular lexical items to specific levels is far from uniform, varying from one locality to another.

11 CONCLUSIONS

Raffles, in his discussion of Javanese speech registers, made a particularly perspicacious observation that has wider applicability. He noted that Javanese 'is remarkable for the profusion of words it contains...and the consequent extent of synonimes' (Raffles

1978, I:365). To underscore this observation, Raffles included, as an appendix to his *History of Java*, an extract from the *Dása Náma*, a Javanese 'collection of synonimes' which served as a linguistic teaching aid for children. He explained the function of the *Dása Náma* as follows:

> In order to facilitate the acquirement of the language, it is usual to collect all the words in the different dialects with their synonimes, and to connect them together by stringing them in classes following each other according to the natural chain of our ideas. Thus after commencing with the word *man*, and giving an explanation of every word in the vernacular, polite and Káwi languages, applicable from his birth to his death, as *infant, boy, youth*, and the like, it proceeds to *woman, child*; from thence to the deities, afterwards to the various avocations of mankind, &c. This collection of synonimes is called *Dása Náma*, literally the 'ten names', a term probably given to it on account of few important words in the language having less than ten synonimes…These collections are varied in their contents and order of arrangement, according to the acquirements and notions of the compiler (Raffles 1978, I:365).

Raffles' observation of the pervasiveness of synonymy in Javanese, particularly because of its speech levels, can in fact be applied to all of the various speech forms discussed in this essay. Word tabooing, for example, requires elaborate lexical substitution in a variety of social settings. Thus Keesing and Fifiʔi's comment on word tabooing in Kwaio echoes Raffles' observations on Javanese:

> the institutionalisation of word tabooing in Kwaio culture appears to produce and require the availability in the language of far more alternative monolexemic labels for the same cultural segregates, i.e. synonyms, than any other language with which I am familiar (1969:166).

The same may be said of the special purpose registers for hunting, fishing or other circumscribed social activities used among Austronesian-speaking populations. Each is a particular elaboration of a specialized lexicon, based upon culturally recognized resemblances, associations and substitutions, that are applied in specific social contexts. Such lexicons may vary in their elaboration from approximately 60 lexical items in the Tetun 'sea' register to some 400 lexical items in the Buru 'hunting' register to more than 1000 lexical items in the popular slang register used, for a time, among the school age population of Jakarta.

Where synonymy and lexical elaboration is most evident is in the 'ritual language' registers, based on parallelism, that are relied upon for a wide repertoire of oral performances among Austronesian speakers. Writing of a particular West Sumatran narrative tradition, Phillips, like Raffles and Keesing, was particularly struck by the 'rich vocabulary and capacity for variety of expression which parallelism demands'. When Phillips raised the subject with the oral poet Munin, whose performances he was studying, his response was to reel off synonyms for particular words, thus *kato, rundieng, tutue, koba, andai* and *kécék* for 'speech' (1981:116).

This elaboration of synonymy is precisely what defines the importance of these registers from a linguistic perspective. Such synonymy places the linguistic emphasis on what Jakobson has referred to as the 'metaphoric or paradigmatic pole' of language where the nuanced selection of lexical elements is particularly critical to culturally appropriate expressions of speech and where 'metaphor' consists of the culturally defined connections between lexical elements. This proliferation of synonyms provides new possibilities for lexical investigation. It is possible, for example, to trace a network of formal interrelations among the 1000 or more lexical elements in Rotinese ritual language based on what are culturally defined as dyadic sets. One such illustrative network traces the interrelations between twenty-five Rotinese verbs for speaking, asking, and answering, based on their connection in ritual language to the general Rotinese verb *fada* 'to speak' (Fox 1974:77–79). More significantly, it is possible to define the core set of semantic elements of the Rotinese ritual register (Fox 1975). The characteristic feature of this network is that of a 'small world' – a network containing many nodes with only a few links combined with a few nodes with many links (see Watts 1999). The nature of this system can therefore be understood, to some extent, from its formal properties.

It is also critically important to recognize that many of the features of Austronesian special registers are not confined to the Austronesian-speaking world. Systems of parallelism, for example, are found among all the language families of the world and are therefore a universal phenomenon of general theoretical interest (Jakobson 1966, Fox 1977, 1988a).

REFERENCES

Adriani, N. (1893) *Sangireesche Spraakkunst*, Leiden: A.H. Adriani.
——(1932) *Verzamelde Geschriften*, 3 vols, Haarlem: De Erven F. Bohn N.V.
Aoki, E. (1988) 'The case of the purloined statutes: the power of words among the Lionese', in Fox (ed.), 202–227.
Baier, Martin, Hardeland, A. and Schärer, H. (1987) *Wörterbuch der Priestersprache der Ngaju-Dayak*, Verhandelingen van het Koninklijk Instituut voor Taal-, Land- en Volkenkunde 128, Dordrecht: Foris.
Beckwith, M.W. (1951) *The Kumulipo*, Chicago: University of Chicago Press.
Berthe, L. (1972) *Bei Gua Itinéraire des Ancêtres*, Paris: Éditions du Centre National de la Recherche Scientifique.
Blixen, O. (1969) 'La dispersion del lenguaje honorifico en Oceania', *Moana: Estudios de Antropologia Oceanica* 1/3:1–17.
Bowden, J. (2001) *Taba: Description of a South Halmahera language*, Canberra: Pacific Linguistics.
Chambert-Loir, H. (1988) 'Prakokat', in Prathama Rahardja and Chambert-Loir, 1–17.
Clynes, A. (1989) *Speech Styles in Javanese and Balinese*, M.A. Thesis, Australian National University.
Corte-Real, B. de Araújo (1998) *Mambai and its Verbal Art Genre: A Cultural Reflection of Suru-Ainaro, East Timor*, unpublished PhD Thesis, Macquarie University.
——(2000) 'Social Order and Linguistic Symmetry: The Case of the Mambai, Suru-Ainaro', *Studies in Languages and Cultures of East Timor* 3:31–56.
Damais, L.C. (1950) 'Les formes de politesse en javanaise moderne', *Bulletin de la Société d'Études Indo-Chinoises* XXV:263–280.
Dreyfuss, J. (1983) 'The backwards language of Jakarta youth (JYBL), a bird of many language feathers', *NUSA* 16:52–56.
Dunnebier, W. (1938) 'De plecht 'waterscheppen' in Bolaang Mongondouw', *Tijdschrift voor Indische Taal-, Land- en Volkenkunde* 78:1–56.
——(1953) *Bolaang Mondondouw teksten*. Koninklijk Instituut voor Taal-, Land- en Volkenkunde 's Gravenhage: Nijhoff.
Dunselman, D. (1949) 'Bijdrage tot de kennis van de taal en adat der Kendajan Dajaks van West-Borneo', *Bijdragen tot de Taal-, Land- en Volkenkunde* 105:59–105,147–218.
——(1950a) 'Over de huwelijksadat der Moealang-Dajaks van West-Borneo', *Bijdragen tot de Taal-, Land- en Volkenkunde* 106:1–45.

——(1950b) 'Bijdrage tot de kennis van de taal en adat der Kendajan-Dajaks van West-Borneo II', *Bijdragen tot de Taal-, Land- en Volkenkunde* 106:321–73.
——(1954) 'Kana Sera of Zang der Zangerschap', *Bijdragen tot de Taal-, Land- en Volkenkunde* 110:52–63.
——(1955) *Kana Sera*, Verhandelingen van het Koninklijk Instituut voor Taal-. Land- en Volkenkunde 17, 's-Gravenhage: Nijhoff.
——(1959a) 'Gezangen behorend tot het huwelijksceremonieel der Mualang-Dajaks', *Anthropos* 54:460–74.
——(1959b) *Uit de literatuur der Mualang-Dajaks*, 's-Gravenhage: Nijhoff.
——(1961) 'Ngebau tadjau, een Kosmogonie der Mualang-Dajaks', *Anthropos* 56:409–37.
Engelenhoven, A. van (1997) 'Words and Expressions: Notes on Parallelism in Leti', *Cakalele* 8:1–25.
Errington, J.J. (1982) 'Speech in the royal presence: Javanese palace language', *Indonesia* 34:89–101.
——(1985) *Language and Social Change in Java: linguistic reflexes of modernization in a traditional royal polity*, Monographs in International Studies, Southeast Asia Series No. 65, Athens, Oh.: Ohio University Center for International Studies.
——(1988) *Structure and Style in Javanese: a semiotic view of linguistic etiquette*, Philadelphia: University of Pennsylvania Press.
——(1998) *Shifting Languages: interaction and identity in Javanese Indonesia*, Studies in the Social and Cultural Foundations of Language No. 19, Cambridge: Cambridge University Press.
Evans, I.H.N. (1953) *The Religion of the Tempasuk Dusun of North Borneo*, Cambridge: Cambridge University Press.
Fischer, D.Th. (1934), *Priestertalen: Een Ethnologiese Studie*, 's-Gravenhage: Nijhoff.
Florey, M.J. (1998) 'Alune incantations: continuity or discontinuity in verbal art?', *Journal of Sociolinguistics* 2:205–231.
Florey, M.J. and Wolff, X.Y. (1998) 'Incantations and herbal medicines: Alune ethnomedical knowledge in a context of change', *Journal of Ethnobiology* 18:39–67.
Forth, G. (1988) 'Fashioned speech, full communication: aspects of eastern Sumbanese ritual language', in Fox (ed.), 129–160.
Fox, J.J. (1971) 'Semantic parallelism in Rotinese ritual language', *Bijdragen tot de Taal-, Land- en Volkenkunde* 127:215–55.
——(1972a) *Rotinese Ritual Language: Texts and Translations* (Multilith, 303 pp).
——(1972b) *Dictionary of Rotinese Formal Dyadic Language* (Multilith, 270 pp).
——(1974) '"Our ancestors spoke in pairs": Rotinese views of language, dialect and code', in R. Bauman and J. Sherzer (eds), *Explorations in the Ethnography of Speaking*, 65–85, Cambridge: Cambridge University Press.
——(1975) 'On binary categories and primary symbols: some Rotinese perspectives', in R. Willis (ed.), *The Interpretation of Symbolism*, 99–132, London: Malaby Press.
——(1977) 'Roman Jakobson and the comparative study of parallelism', in C.H. van Schooneveld and D. Armstrong (eds), *Roman Jakobson: Echoes of his Scholarship*, 59–90, Lisse: Peter de Ridder Press.
——(1982) 'The Rotinese chotbah as a linguistic performance', in A. Halim, L. Carrington and S.A. Wurm (eds), *Accent on Variety*, 311–18, Canberra: Pacific Linguistics.
——(1983) 'Adam and Eve on the island of Roti: a conflation of oral and written traditions', *Indonesia* 36:15–23
——(ed.) (1988) *To Speak in Pairs: Essays on the Ritual Languages of Eastern Indonesia*, Cambridge: Cambridge University Press.
——(1988a) 'Introduction' in Fox (ed.), 1–28.
——(1988b) '"Manu Kama's road, Tepa Nilu's path": theme, narrative and formula in Rotinese ritual language', in Fox (ed.), 161–201.

Fox, J.J. (1992) '"Bound to the Core, Held locked in all our Hearts": Prayers and Invocations among the Rotinese', *Canberra Anthropology* 14(2):30–48.
——(1993) *Dictionary of Rotinese Formal Dyadic Language*, revised with English to Rotinese glosses, unpublished MS, Canberra: Anthropology, Research School of Pacific and Asian Studies.
——(1997a) 'Genealogies of the Sun and Moon: Interpreting the Canon of Rotinese Ritual Chants', in E.K.M. Masinambow (ed.), *Koentjaraningrat dan Antropologi di Indonesia*, 321–330, Jakarta: Asosiasi Antropologi Indonesia/Yayasan Obor Indonesia.
——(1997b) 'Place and Landscape in Comparative Austronesian Perspective' in J.J. Fox (ed.), *The Poetic Power of Place: Comparative Perspectives on Austronesian Ideas of Locality*, 1–21, Canberra: Anthropology, Research School of Pacific and Asian Studies.
——(1997c) 'Genealogy and Topogeny: Toward an Ethnography of Rotinese Ritual Place Names', in J.J. Fox (ed.), *The Poetic Power of Place: Comparative Perspectives on Austronesian Ideas of Locality*, 91–102, Canberra: Anthropology, Research School of Pacific and Asian Studies.
Frazer, J. (1911) *The Golden Bough, II: Taboo and the Perils of the Soul*, London: Macmillan.
Gevirtz, S. (1963) *Patterns in the Early Poetry of Israel*, Chicago: Chicago University Press.
Gonda, J. (1947) 'The Javanese Vocabulary of Courtesy', *Lingua* I: 333–373.
Grimes, C.E. and Maryott, K.R. (1994) 'Named Speech Registers in Austronesian Languages', in T. Dutton and D.T. Tryon (eds), *Language Contact and Change in the Austronesian World*, 275–319, New York: Mouton de Gruyter.
Hardeland, A. (1858) *Versuch einer Grammatik der Dajackschen Sprache*, Amsterdam.
——(1859) *Dajacksch–Deutsches Wörterbuch*, Amsterdam.
Hardjadibrata, R.R. (1985) *Sundanese: A Syntactical Analysis*, Canberra: Pacific Linguistics.
Harmonic, G. (1987) *Le Langage des Dieux: Culte et Pouvoir Pré-Islamiques en Pays Bugis Célèbes-Sud, Indonésie*, Paris: Éditions du CNRS.
Hoskins, J. (1988) 'Etiquette in Kodi spirit communication: the lips told to pronounce, the mouths told to speak' in Fox (ed.), 29–63.
Jakobson, R., (1960) 'Concluding Statement: Linguistics and Poetics', in T.A. Sebeok (ed.), *Style in Language*, Cambridge, Mass.: MIT Press.
——(1966), 'Grammatical Parallelism and its Russian Facet', *Language* 42:398–429.
Jakobson, R. and Halle, M. (1956), *Fundamentals of Language*, 's-Gravenhage: Mouton.
Jensen, H.J. (1933) 'Gegevens over Boeroe (1928)', *Adatrechtsbundels* 36:463–489.
Jonker, J.C.G. (1911) *Rottineesche Teksten*, Leiden: E.J. Brill.
Josselin de Jong, J.P.B. de (1941) 'Oost-Indonesische poëzie', *Bijdragen tot de Taal-, Land, en Volkenkunde* 100:235–254.
Kaartinen, T. (1998) 'Voices of the other: authenticity and consciousness of language in an eastern Indonesian song tradition', *Akademika* 53:87–112.
Keesing, R.M. and Fifiʔi, J. (1969) 'Kwaio word tabooing in its cultural context', *The Journal of the Polynesian Society* 78:154–177.
Kern, W. (1956) *Commentaar op de Salasilah van Koetai*, Verhandelingen van het Koninklijk Instituut voor Taal-, Land- en Volkenkunde Vol 19, 's-Gravenhage: Nijhoff.
Klinken, C.L. van (1999) *A Grammar of the Fehan Dialect of Tetun: An Austronesian Language of West Timor*, Canberra: Pacific Linguistics.
Kuipers, Joel C. (1988) 'The Pattern of Prayer in Weyéwa', in Fox (ed.), 104–128.
——(1990) *Power in Performance: The Creation of Textual Authority in Weyewa Ritual Speech*, Philadelphia: University of Pennsylvania Press.
——(1998) *Language, Identity and Marginality in Indonesia: The Changing Nature of Ritual Speech on the Island of Sumba*. Cambridge: Cambridge University Press.
Lagemann, H. (1893) 'Das niassische Mädchen von ihrer Geburt bis zu ihrer Verheiratung', *Tijdschrift voor Indische Taal-, Land- en Volkenkunde (Bataviaasch Genootschap)*, Van Kunsten en Wetenschappen 36, 296–324.

Lagemann, H. (1906) 'Ein Heldensang der Niasser', *Tijdschrift voor Indische Taal-, Land- en Volkenkunde* (Bataviaasch Genootschap Van Kunsten en Wetenschappen) 48:341–407.

Lenormand, M.H. (1990) *Le Miny: la langue des chefs de l'île de Lifou (Iles Loyauté, Nouvelle-Calédonie)*, Noumea: Edipop.

Lewis, E.D. (1988) 'A quest for the source: the ontogenesis of a creation myth of the Ata Tana Ai', in Fox (ed.), 246–281.

Lowth, R. (1753) *De Sacra Poesia Hebraeorum Praelectiones Academicae* [translated as *Lectures on the Sacred Poetry of the Hebrews*, Boston, 1829].

——(1778) *Isaiah X–X1* [translated as *Isaiah*, 1834], Boston.

Masing, J. (1997) *The Coming of the Gods: An Iban Invocatory Chant (Timang Gawai Amat) of the Baleh Region, Sarawak*, Canberra: Research School of Pacific and Asian Studies.

Matthes, B.F. (1872) *Over de Bissoe's of Heidensche Priesters en Priesteressen der Boeginezen*, Amsterdam.

McWilliam, A. (1989) *Narrating the Gate and Path: Place and Precedence in South West Timor*, unpublished PhD thesis, The Australian National University.

——(1991) '"Prayers of the Sacred Stone and Tree": Aspects of Invocation in West Timor', *Canberra Anthropology* 14:49–59.

——(1997) 'Mapping with Metaphor: Cultural Topographies in West Timor', in J.J. Fox (ed.), *The Poetic Power of Place: Comparative Perspectives on Austronesian Ideas of Locality*, 103–115, Canberra: Research School of Pacific and Asian Studies.

Meij, Th. C. van der (1983) *Enige aspecten van geheimtaal in Jakarta*, unpublished dissertation, Leiden University.

Metcalf, P. (1989) *Where are You, Spirits: Style and Theme in Berawan Prayer*, Washington: Smithsonian Press.

——(1994) '"Voilà ce que je dis": la projection de la parole dans la prière berawan', *L'Homme* XXXIV/4:59–76.

Middelkoop, P. (1949) *Een Studie van het Timoreesche Doodenritueel*, Verhandelingen van het Bataviaasch Genootschap van Kunsten en Wetenschappen, vol. 76, Bandoeng: A.C. Nix and Co.

Milner, G.B. (1961) 'The Samoan vocabulary of respect', *Journal of the Royal Anthropological Institute of Great Britain and Ireland* 91:296–317.

Mitchell, D. (1988) 'Method in the metaphor: the ritual language of Wanukaka', in Fox (ed.), 64–86.

Nakagawa, S. (1988) 'The journey of the bridegroom: idioms of marriage among the Endenese' in Fox (ed.), 228–245.

Newell, J.E. (1882) 'Chief's language in Samoa', *Transactions of the 9th Congress of Orientalists* 2:784–799.

Nothofer, B. (1980) *Dialektgeographische Untersuchungen in West-Java und im westlichen Zentral-Java*, 2 vols, Wiesbaden: Harrassowitz.

Ooy, F. van (1994) 'Ritual language of Sawu Dimu, eastern Indonesia', Paper presented at the 7th International Conference on Austronesian Linguistics, Leiden.

Phillips, N. (1981) *Sijobang: Sung narrative poetry of West Sumatra*, Cambridge: Cambridge University Press.

Poedjosoedarmo, S. (1968) 'Javanese Speech Levels', *Indonesia* 6:54–81.

Prathama Rahardja and Chambert-Loir, H. (1988) *Kamus Bahasa Prokem*, Jakarta: Pustaka Utama Grafiti.

Prentice, D.J. (1981) 'The Minstrel-Priestess: A Timugon Murut exorcism ceremony and its liturgy', in N. Phillips and Khaidir Anwar (eds), *Papers on Indonesian Languages and Literatures*, 121–144, University of London: Indonesian Etymology Project, SOAS.

Quack, A. (1981) *Das Wort der Alten: Erzählungen zur Geschichte der Pujuma von Katipol (Taiwan)*, Collectanea Instituti Anthropos 12, St Augustin: Anthropos-Institute.

——(1985) *Priesterinnen, Heilerinnen, Schamaninnen?: Die po'ringao der Puyuma von Katipol (Taiwan)*, Collectanea Instituti Anthropos 32. Berlin: Reimer.

Raffles, T. Stamford (1978[1817]) *The History of Java*, London, Kuala Lumpur: Oxford University Press.

Ray, S.H. (1882) 'Note on chief's language in Lifu and Ponape', *Transactions of the 9th Congress of Orientalists* 2:800–801.

Renard-Clamagirand, B. (1988) 'Li'i marapu: speech and ritual among the Wewewa of west Sumba', in Fox (ed.), 87–103.

Sabatier, L. (1933) 'La Chançon de Damsan', *Bulletin de l'École Française d'Extrême-Orient* 33:143–302.

Sahertian, D. (1999) *Kamus Gaul*, Jakarta: Pustaka Sinar Harapan.

Sandin, B. (1977) *Gawai Burong: The Chants and Celebrations of the Iban Bird Festival*, edited with an introduction by C.A. Sather, Pulau Pinang: Penerbit Universiti Sains Malaysia.

Sankoff, G. (1977) 'Le parallélisme dans la poésie Buang', *Anthropologica* (N.S.) XIX(1):27–48.

Sarumpaet, J.P. (1982) 'Linguistic varieties in Toba-Batak', in A. Halim, L. Carrington, and S.A. Wurm (eds), *Accent on Variety*, 27–78, Canberra: Pacific Linguistics.

Satjadibrata, R. (1956) *Unda-usuk basa Sunda*, Jakarta: Balai Pustaka.

Sather, C. (2001), *Seeds of Play, Words of Power: An Ethnographic Study of Iban Shamanic Chants*, Tun Jugah Foundation jointly with the Borneo Research Council. The Borneo Classic Series: vol. 5.

Schärer, H. (1966) *Der Totenkult der Ngadju Dajak in Süd-Borneo*, Verhandelingen van het Koninklijk Instituut voor Taal-, Land- en Volkenkunde, 51, 's-Gravenhage: Nijhoff.

Schröder, D. and Quack, A. (1979) *Kopfjagdriten der Puyuma von Katipol (Taiwan)*, Collectanea Instituti Anthropos 11. St Augustin: Anthropos-Institute.

Schut, J.A.F. (1919) 'Een Tijl Uilenspiegel verhaal in de Boeroetaal', *Bijdragen tot de Taal-, Land-, en Volkenkunde* 75:303–362.

Sibree, J. (1880) *Madagascar: The Great African Island*, London.

——(1882) 'Curious words and customs connected with chieftainship and royalty among the Malagasy', *The Journal of the Royal Anthropological Institute of Great Britain and Ireland* 21:215–229.

Simons, G.F. (1982) 'Word Taboo and Comparative Austronesian Linguistics', in A. Halim, L. Carrington, and S.A. Wurm (eds), *Accent on Variety*, 157–226, Canberra: Pacific Linguistics.

Sri Kuhnt-Saptodewo, J. (1993) *Zum Seelengeleit bei den Ngaju am Kahayan. Auswertung eines Sakraltextes zur Manarung-Zeremonie beim Totenfest*, München: Akademischer Verlag.

——(1999) 'A Bridge to the Upper World: Sacred Language of the Ngaju', *Borneo Research Bulletin* 30:13–27.

Steinhart, W.L. (1934) 'Niassche teksten met Ned. vertaling en aanteekeningen', *Tijdschrift voor Taal-, Land- en Volkenkunde* 74:326–75, 391–440.

——(1937a) *Niassche Teksten*, Verhandelingen van het Bataviaasch Genootschap 73, Bandoeng: A.C. Nix and Co.

——(1937b) 'De Evangelie-prediker en zijn houding ten opzichte van de Inheemsche cultuur', *Zendingstijdschrift De Opwekker* 82(4):147–160.

——(1938) *Niassche Priesterlitanieën*, Verhandelingen van het Bataviaasch Genootschap 74, Bandoeng: A.C. Nix and Co.

——(1950) 'Niasse teksten met Ned. vertaling en aantekeningen', *Tijdschrift voor Taal-, Land- en Volkenkunde* 84, 33–109.

——(1954) *Niassche Teksten*, Koninklijk Instituut voor Taal-, Land- en Volkenkunde, 's-Gravenhage: Nijhoff.

Steller, K.G.F. and Aebersold, W.E. (1959), *Sangirees-Nederlands Woordenboek met Nederlands-Sangirees register*, 's-Gravenhage: Nijhoff.

Stevens, A.M. (1965) 'Language Levels in Madurese', *Language* XLI:294–302.

Suharno, I. (1982) *A Descriptive Study of Javanese*, Canberra: Pacific Linguistics.

Sundermann, H. (1905) *Niassisch–Deutsches Wörterbuch*, Moers: J.W. Spaarmann.
Teguh Esha (1978) 'Kamus Preman' in *Ali Topan Detektip Partikelir*, Jakarta: Cypress.
Therik, G.T. (1995) *Wehali, The Four Cornered Land: The Cosmology and Traditions of a Timorese Ritual Centre*, PhD Thesis, The Australian National University.
Therik, T. (2004) *Wehali, The Female Land: Traditions of a Timorese ritual centre*, Canberra: Pandanus Books.
Traube, E. (1980) 'Mambai Rituals of Black and White', in J.J. Fox (ed.), *The Flow of Life: Essays on Eastern Indonesia*, 290–314, Cambridge, Mass.: Harvard University Press.
——(1986) *Cosmology and Social Life: Ritual Exchanges among the Mambai*, Chicago: University of Chicago Press.
Tryon, D. (1997) 'Honorific Languages in the Loyalty Islands (New Caledonia)', unpublished paper presented at the 8th International Conference of Austronesian Linguistics, Academia Sinica, Taipei (28–31 December 1997).
Uhlenbeck, E.M. (1978) *Studies in Javanese Morphology*, Koninklijk Instituut voor Taal-, Land-, en Volkenkunde, Translations Series 19, The Hague: Nijhoff.
Veen, H. van der (1929) 'Een wichel-litanie der Sa'dan-Tordja's', in *Feestbundel uitgegeven door het Koninklijk Bataviaasch Genootschap van Kunsten en Wetenschappen bij gelegenheid van zijn 150-jarig Bestaan 1778–1928*, vol. II, Weltevreden: G. Kolff and Co.
——(1940) *Tae'–Nederlandsch woordenboek met register Nederlandsch–Tae'*, Koninklijk Instituut voor Taal-, Land- en Volkenkunde, 's-Gravenhage: Nijhoff.
——(1950) 'De Samenspraak der beide priesters, de woordvoerders van bruid en bruidegom bij de huwelijksplechtigheid der Sa'dan-Toradja's', in *Bingkisan Budi* (Een Bundel Opstellen aangeboden aan Dr. Philippus Samuel van Ronkel), Leiden: Sijthoff.
——(1952) 'Gebruik van literaire of dichtertaal bij de vertaling van poëtische gedeelten van de Bijbel in de Indonesische taal', *De Heerbaan* 5, 211–40.
——(1965) *The Merok Feast of the Sa'dan-Toradja*, 's Gravenhage: Nijhoff.
——(1966) *The Sa'dan-Toradja Chant for the Deceased*, 's-Gravenhage: Nijhoff.
Vischer, M. (1992) *Children of the Black Patola Stone: Origin Structures in a Domain on Palu'e Island*, unpublished PhD Thesis, The Australian National University.
Watts, D. (1999) *Small worlds: the dynamics of networks between order and randomness*, Princeton: Princeton University Press.
Wigglesworth, H.J. (1977) 'Tualang Slays the Dragon: A complete song from Ilianen Manobo Epic of Tulalang', *Philippine Quarterly of Culture and Society* 5:123–165.
——(1980) 'Rhetorical devices distinguishing the genre of folktale (fiction) from that of oral history (fact) in Ilianen Manobo narrative discourse', *Philippine Journal of Linguistics* 1:45–80.
Wolfowitz, C. (1991) *Language Style and Social Space: Stylistic Choice in Suriname Javanese*, Illinois Studies in Anthropology 18, Urbana and Chicago: University of Illinois Press.
Zerner, C. and Volkman, T.A. (1988) 'The tree of desire: A Toraja ritual poem', in Fox (ed.), 282–305.

THE AUSTRONESIAN LANGUAGES OF ASIA AND MADAGASCAR: TYPOLOGICAL CHARACTERISTICS

Nikolaus P. Himmelmann

1 SOME PRELIMINARY DIVISIONS AND DEFINITIONS

When discussing typological characteristics of a genetically coherent group of languages, there are two points of view, an external and an internal one. Externally, the focus is on features which characterize the group as a whole vis-à-vis other language families or linguistic areas. Internally, the focus is on features which characterize one (typological) subgroup as opposed to another. The two points of view are obviously interrelated in that a complex internal typology – i.e. a group of languages differs with regard to a large number of features – usually makes it difficult, if not impossible, to reach significant external generalizations.

The Austronesian languages of Asia and Madagascar provide a paradigmatic example of this difficulty. They are typologically much more variegated than the Oceanic languages (and many other language groups and families). There are only very few features which are sufficiently general and widespread to be considered typological characteristics of the group as a whole, including reduplication (see section 2.2), the distinction between inclusive and exclusive pronouns (see section 3.7) and morphological causatives (see section 4.3).

The complex internal typology of the Austronesian languages of Asia and Madagascar entails a number of expository problems and inconveniences. Most importantly, for almost every generalization one has to give at least a rough indication of the set of languages to which it applies. To this end, occasional reference is made to the genetic groupings discussed in ADELAAR (A HISTORICAL PERSPECTIVE). But two other ways of specifying the relevant set are used much more frequently. First, the relevant set is often specified in geographic terms, referring either to national territories (e.g. *Philippine languages*) or major islands or island groups (e.g. *the languages of Borneo, the Moluccas*, etc.). See section 1.1 for further comments. Second, major use is made of a somewhat rough but still useful distinction between two basic types of languages, i.e. symmetrical voice languages and preposed possessor languages, as discussed further in section 1.2.

Finally, in order to keep the amount of hedging and repetition to an absolute minimum, it will be useful to identify right at the outset the most important exception to almost any typological generalization regarding the Austronesian languages of Asia and Madagascar. The Chamic and Moken-Moklen languages spoken in Vietnam, Cambodia, Myanmar (Burma) and Thailand have long been in intensive contact with non-Austronesian Southeast Asian mainland languages and have taken on their basic structural characteristics. These include regular tonal distinctions, fairly rigid SVO order, lack of affixation, etc, and are discussed further in the chapters on Cham and Moken-Moklen (see also Thurgood 1999 for the most thorough and up-to-date exposition of the contact history in this area). Unless explicitly mentioned, these languages are excluded from generalizations or divisions discussed in this chapter.

1.1 Geographical groupings

It has proved a rather difficult task to find a suitable label for the languages under investigation in this volume. There is a well-established term covering all but two Austronesian languages outside Asia and Madagascar, i.e. *Oceanic Languages*. These are the Austronesian languages of the Pacific with the exclusion of Palauan (Belau) and Chamorro, which geographically belong to Micronesia. However, no well-established term for non-Oceanic Austronesian languages exists, and since *Austronesian languages of Asia and Madagascar (plus Palauan and Chamorro)* is a rather clumsy way to refer to them, the rather loose geographical expression *western Austronesian* will be used here instead. A possible problem with this expression is that it has been used in the literature in various, and often imprecise, ways. In the present chapter, *western Austronesian languages* is strictly equivalent to *non-Oceanic Austronesian languages*. It is not to be confused with the term *Western Malayo-Polynesian* which is used in genetic classifications (cf. ADELAAR, A HISTORICAL PERSPECTIVE) and which covers only some of the languages dealt with here.

Apart from *western Austronesian*, there are a few other geographical references which have been used in different ways in the literature and thus require brief comment.

- *Philippine languages*: Philippine languages are the Austronesian languages spoken in the Republic of the Philippines. The Sama varieties spoken in the Sulu Archipelago in the southern Philippines (see Map 13.1), although spoken within the Republic of the Philippines, differ morphosyntactically from other Philippine languages and are generally not included in generalizations about Philippine languages. The same would appear to be true of the South Mindanao languages (Blaan, Tboli, Tiruray and possibly Bagobo (or Giangan)) but very little is known about them.
- *Philippine-type languages*: This term, though widely used, has never been precisely defined. It is used to refer to the Philippine languages (as just defined) and languages from neighboring islands which share typical Philippine characteristics. Roughly, they also include the Formosan languages and the languages of northern Borneo and northern Sulawesi. Sometimes Malagasy, Chamorro and Palauan are included too. Obviously an accurate delimitation of Philippine-type languages depends on what is considered a typical Philippine characteristic. As discussed in the next section, a somewhat narrower definition of Philippine-type languages is used here which excludes Malagasy, Chamorro, Palauan and a few Formosan and northern Bornean languages.
- *Languages of western Indonesia*: This refers to all languages spoken on Indonesian territory west of Lombok. This includes Bali, Java, Kalimantan, Sumatra and the minor islands in between them, but excludes the languages of Sulawesi. Most statements regarding the languages of western Indonesia will be sufficiently qualified so as to exclude Acehnese and the Barrier Island languages.

- *Barrier Island languages* are the languages spoken on the island chain west of Sumatra. They include Nias, Enggano, Mentawai, Sichule, and Simeuluë. Morphosyntactically, these languages differ significantly from the languages spoken on Sumatra.
- *Lesser Sunda languages* refers to the languages spoken on the island chain extending from Lombok to Alor, including Sumba and Savu but excluding Wetar and languages further east which belong to the Southwest Moluccan languages. Most languages spoken on Pantar and Alor, the two easternmost islands of the chain, are non-Austronesian and hence excluded here from any generalization referring to Lesser Sunda languages. Although often considered Lesser Sunda languages, the languages spoken on Timor and Roti are also excluded here since they have a somewhat different typological profile (see also section 6).

1.2 Symmetrical voice vs. preposed possessor languages

Even if the Chamic languages and Moken-Moklen are excluded, the structural variety attested by the remaining western Austronesian languages is still considerable. In order to be able to propose any generalizations at all, it will be useful to make a distinction between two basic types of languages found in the area, with a third group of languages not clearly aligning with either type. The first type of languages will be called *symmetrical voice languages*. The defining characteristic of these languages is the presence of at least two voice alternations marked on the verb, neither of which is clearly the basic form. Compare the following Malay examples:

(1) *Anak   saya   me-lihat   orang   itu.*
     child   1s   AV-see   person DIST
     'My child saw that person.'

(2) *Orang   itu   di-lihat   anak   saya.*
     person DIST   PV-see   child 1s
     'My child saw that person.'

The voice alternation illustrated by these two examples is symmetrical in that both the actor voice form *melihat* and the undergoer voice form *dilihat* are morphologically overtly marked by a prefix (*me-* and *di-* respectively). Thus, morphologically speaking, there is no unmarked or basic form from which the other form is derived. Furthermore, both examples appear to be syntactically equivalent in that both involve two nominal arguments (*anak saya* and *orang itu*), one preceding and the other following the verb without further overt marking by a preposition or case marker. The only obvious syntactic difference between the two voices pertains to the fact that in actor voice the experiencer precedes the verb and the stimulus follows it, while in undergoer voice the order is reversed. In contrast, in an English passive construction such as *That person was seen by my child* the experiencer does not only occur in postverbal position but is also marked as oblique, hence rendering the overall construction intransitive.

Both the above examples and the notion of a *symmetrical voice alternation* require further discussion and elaboration which will be found below in sections 3.3, 3.6 and 4.2. Here it will be sufficient to note that the question to what extent the alternation illustrated by the two examples is in fact symmetrical continues to be a matter of controversy. But this controversy is only of marginal relevance to present purposes. It is widely agreed that many western Austronesian languages show voice alternations which differ significantly in form and function from the passive alternation in, for example, European languages (the fact that example (2) is not given a passive translation is intended to reflect this difference). For much of the exposition of this chapter, it does not matter whether or not one agrees with a symmetrical voice analysis of these alternations. What does matter is the (uncontroversial) observation that these alternations are found in only some western Austronesian languages, thus providing a criterion for dividing these languages into two sets. Symmetrical voice languages in the sense intended here include the Austronesian languages of Taiwan, the Philippines, Malaysia, Madagascar, western Indonesia (with the exception of Acehnese and the Barrier Island languages) and the northern half of Sulawesi (Saluan (but not Banggai), Kaili-Pamona, Tomini-Tolitoli, Gorontalo-Mongondow, Minahasan and Sangiric).

The *Philippine-type languages* are a subset of the symmetrical voice languages. As mentioned above, the defining characteristics for this subset have never been explicitly defined (see also Himmelmann 2002a/b). Here the following preliminary definition is used. Philippine-type languages are symmetrical voice languages which have

(a) at least two formally and semantically different *undergoer* voices (see section 4.2.2);
(b) at least one non-local phrase marking clitic for nominal expressions (e.g. Tagalog genitive *ng*; see further section 3.5);
(c) pronominal second position clitics (see section 3.2).

This definition of Philippine-type languages excludes Malagasy, Chamorro, Palauan and the Austronesian languages of Brunei and Sarawak as well as Tomini-Tolitoli, Gorontalo-Mongondic, Sama-Bajau, and South Mindanao languages, all of which have occasionally been called Philippine-type languages. Among the Formosan languages, the Tsouic and Rukai languages are clearly not Philippine-type according to this definition, and the status of others (e.g. Bunun) needs further investigation. Similarly, the status of the Sangiric and Minahasan languages in northern Sulawesi needs further investigation since it is not clear to what extent the pronominal clitics in these languages are in fact second position clitics.

The advantage of this preliminary definition of Philippine-type languages is that the group of languages thus delimited would appear to be quite homogeneous and to share a number of further morphosyntactic features in addition to the three defining features (for example, infixes, aspect-mood marking, a strong preference for predicate-initial clause structure, etc.). The exact extent of their commonalities, however, needs further testing.

The second basic type of languages found in the western Austronesian area will be called *preposed possessor languages*. In these languages, possessors regularly precede the possessum as in the following Ambai examples: *Yani ne munu* (Yani POSS house) 'Yani's house', *ne-mu tarai* (POSS-2s.POSS body) 'your body'). Once again, this definition is in need of further elaboration and discussion which will be found in section 3.11. Here it is important to note that the criterion refers to the most common or unmarked order found in possessive constructions. That is, it is not required that all possessive constructions in a preposed possessor language show the order POSSESSOR-POSSESSUM, and conversely, non-preposed possessor languages may optionally allow a POSSESSOR-POSSESSUM order. Preposed possessor languages in this sense are the non-Oceanic Austronesian languages of Timor, the Moluccas and West Papua as well as the Pidgin-Derived Malay varieties (see ADELAAR, MALAYIC VARIETIES).

The two parameters *preposed possessor* and *symmetrical voice alternation* tend to correlate with other features (which makes them typologically useful). Most importantly, they tend to correlate negatively with each other in that languages with symmetrical voice alternations generally show postposed possessors, and languages with preposed possessors either do not show any grammaticized voice alternations at all or the voice alternations are clearly asymmetrical. Importantly, the reverse implications do not hold: languages with postposed possessors are not necessarily symmetrical voice languages, and languages with asymmetrical voice alternations are not necessarily preposed possessor languages, as the transitional languages discussed below show in particular. For further correlations, see section 6.

The distinction between symmetrical voice and preposed possessor languages is not new in the sense that the occurrence of preposed possessors was noted as a major feature of Moluccan languages as early as Van Hoëvell (1877:15f). This feature has continued to play a major role in discussions of the subgrouping of the Austronesian languages of eastern Indonesia (see Collins 1983:27–29 and Grimes 2000:3–6 for succinct discussion and references). In this regard, it is important to note that preposed possessor order is used here as a parameter in a *typological* classification, not a genetic one (its value for genetic subgrouping is rather doubtful, as already noted by Jonker (1914)).

In the present typological classification it is possible that a language is neither a preposed possessor language nor a symmetrical voice language. Such languages are found in the southern half of Sulawesi (e.g. Bugis, Makassar, Banggai, Mori Bawah, Muna, Tukang Besi), in the Lesser Sunda islands (e.g. Keo, Kambera) and in northwest Sumatra (Barrier Island languages and Acehnese). Most of these languages do not have verbal voice morphology. If they do (e.g. Makassar, Mori Bawah), it involves asymmetric voice alternations. Possessors are generally postposed (a major exception is Banggai in eastern central Sulawesi). With regard to other parameters, these languages differ quite substantially (many have elaborate person marking systems, but others do not; only a few have infixes; etc.). That is, they do not adhere to a common typological core profile. For expository purposes, it will be convenient occasionally to refer to these languages as *transitional languages*, reflecting the fact that most of them (except the northwest Sumatran languages) are geographically located in between the symmetrical voice and the preposed possessor languages. However, it should be emphasized that this is *not* a typological category. It is thus of a very different nature than *symmetrical voice languages* and *preposed possessor languages*.

In terms of numbers of languages, roughly 60% of the ca. 800 western Austronesian languages are symmetrical voice languages and 25% are preposed possessor languages, while the remaining 15% do not clearly align with either type and hence are called transitional here.

Note that there is also the converse of a transitional languages as just defined, i.e. languages that are both symmetrical voice languages and preposed possessor languages. Such languages appear to be extremely rare, but there is at least one example, i.e. the Formosan language Pazeh. Apart from having preposed possessor order in the basic possessive construction, this language is very similar to its neighboring symmetrical voice languages and should therefore actually be considered a symmetrical voice language (see also section 3.11).

1.3 Sources and conventions

This typological overview partly draws on the language sketches found in the remainder of this book. The names of these languages are given in bold in the remainder of the present chapter. The sketch chapters will usually contain further information, bibliographic references and examples for the issue under discussion. With very few exceptions, this information is not repeated here.

To broaden the typological variety documented in the language sketch chapters, data from languages with somewhat different typological profiles are also included. Unless indicated otherwise, data on these languages are from the following sources: Atayal (Taiwan, Rau 1997), Pazeh (Taiwan, Li and Tsuchida 2001, Blust 1999), Rukai (Taiwan, Li 1973), Paiwan (Taiwan, Egli 1990), Bontok (northern Philippines, Reid 1970, 1992), Cebuano (central Philippines, Wolff 1966, 1972), Ratahan (northern Sulawesi, Himmelmann and Wolff 1999), Lauje, Totoli and other Tomini-Tolitoli languages (central Sulawesi, Himmelmann 2001 and field notes), Urak Lawoi' (Malayic variety/southern Thailand, Hogan 1999), Standard Indonesian (Malayic variety, Sneddon 1996, Musgrave 2001), Acehnese (northern Sumatra, Durie 1985), Madurese (Madura/Java, Davies 1999a), Sundanese (Java, Müller-Gotama 2001), Balinese (Bali, Clynes 1995, Arka 1998, Pastika 1999), Muna (southeastern Sulawesi, Van den Berg 1989), Tukang Besi (southeastern Sulawesi, Donohue 1999), Keo (Flores/Lesser Sunda islands, Baird 2002), Kedang (Lembata/Lesser Sunda islands, Samely 1991), Waima'a (East Timor, Hull 2002, author's field notes), Tetun Dili (East Timor, Hull and Eccles 2001, Williams-van Klinken, Hajek, and Nordlinger 2002), Selaru (southeastern Moluccas, Coward and Coward 2000), Dobel (Aru/southeastern Moluccas, Hughes 2000), Buru (central Moluccas, Grimes 1991), Alune (Seram/central Moluccas, Florey 2001), Ambai (West Papua, Silzer 1983).

Despite this relatively broad range of languages that have been consulted, it will soon become obvious that the present survey is somewhat biased towards symmetrical voice languages. One reason for this bias is the fact that the author is most familiar with these languages. There are also far fewer publications about preposed possessor languages although, fortunately, descriptive work on these languages has increased noticeably in recent times (see references above, Grimes (ed.) 2000, and also Hull 2001 for the languages of Timor).

Examples in the phonology section are sometimes written with IPA symbols rather than in the established practical or standard orthography. Otherwise, the practical or standard orthography is used. Note that in these orthographies glottal stop is often represented as <'> or as <q>, or it remains unrepresented. Stress is only indicated if it does not fall on the penultimate syllable.

The orthographic representation of clitics as orthographically 'free' or 'bound' forms also follows the standard orthography. Note in particular that clitics in Meso-Philippine languages, including **Tagalog**, are generally represented as orthographically independent words.

Examples without source references are from the author's own corpora. In examples from other sources, the glosses have been adapted to the conventions followed throughout this book.

2 PHONOLOGY AND MORPHONOLOGY

Viewed crosslinguistically, Austronesian languages tend to be fairly inconspicuous with regard to basic phonological features. Segment inventories typically consist of three to five vowels and 16–20 consonants, with up to four nasals matching corresponding voiced and voiceless stop series and only few fricatives. The most common syllable structures are (C)V and (C)VC, frequently with restrictions on the consonants allowed in coda position. If consonant-clusters are allowed syllable-internally, they are typically restricted to onset position and usually consist of either nasal plus obstruent or obstruent plus glide or liquid. Consonant clusters across syllable boundaries are also fairly restricted. Often only clusters consisting of an obstruent preceded by a homorganic nasal (so-called NC-clusters) are allowed for. Stress is usually non-distinctive and occurs on the penultimate syllable. Lexical bases tend to be disyllabic and there is also a widespread tendency to reduce affixed words with more than two syllables to disyllabic words. In disyllabic lexical bases of the structure $C_1V(C)C_2V(C)$ there tend to be numerous co-occurrence restrictions on C_1 and C_2 and on the two vowels (this has been documented in detail for **Javanese**, Balinese, Malay and Muna, inter alia). It is very common to insert glides in between a high vowel and a following non-high vowel (hence /ia/ → [ija], /ua/ → [uwa], etc.), to palatalize dental or alveolar stops and fricatives before /i/, and to leave final stops unreleased.

Less commonly occurring consonants include implosives (in fact, these are fairly widespread in central and southeastern Sulawesi, northern Borneo and the Lesser Sunda islands, but also found in **Tsou**), interdental fricatives (e.g. some Formosan languages such as Thao and Rukai), retroflex stops (in, for example, **Javanese**, Madurese and Rukai) and uvular stops in addition to velar stops (in, for example, Formosan languages). The allophones of the alveolar lateral approximant which occurs in most segment inventories may include lateral fricatives, retroflex lateral flaps or palatal lateral approximants (e.g. in Formosan languages, **Buol**), a few languages actually having two lateral phonemes in addition to an alveolar trill or flap which is also part of the standard inventory (e.g. Rukai, Thao). **Nias** is unique among western Austronesian languages in having a bilabial trill but note that bilabial fricatives are widely attested as phonemes or allophones throughout the area. In the Lesser Sunda islands and the southern half of Sulawesi prenasalized consonant series frequently occur.

Some languages with larger consonant inventories have a three-way distinction between voiceless aspirated, voiceless unaspirated and voiced stops (e.g. Madurese, Urak Lawoi'). Waima'a, a language of East Timor, appears to have a significantly larger consonant inventory, with aspiration and glottalization providing for additional phonemic contrasts (Hull 2002, Hajek and Bowden 2002). Preglottalized consonants have also been reported for other languages, including Keo (spoken on Flores) and some Formosan languages (**Tsou**, Thao). **Biak** represents languages with somewhat smaller consonant inventories which appear to be more common in the southeastern Moluccas and West Papua (e.g. Selaru, Dobel, Ambai).

With regard to vowels, even closely related languages vary as to whether or not schwa is part of the basic inventory. In some languages, an unrounded back vowel [ɯ] or [ɤ] occurs, either in place of its rounded counterpart (e.g. Tukang Besi) or in addition to it (e.g., Sundanese, Madurese, Land Dayak varieties). Diphthongs are found in many descriptions but here one has to be careful to separate substantial phonetic or phonological differences from differences in descriptive practice. More often than not, what is described as a diphthong by one author is described as vowel plus glide sequence by another (e.g. /ay/ or /aw/). As Clynes (1997) convincingly argues (with regard to the root-final diphthongs of Proto-Austronesian, but the argument also applies to many synchronic descriptions), the vowel-plus-glide analysis is to be preferred on phonological grounds in most instances (possible exceptions include **Moken-Moklen** and Acehnese). Another widespread lack of agreement in descriptive practice (and occasionally also in actual fact) pertains to the phonological analysis of the glides themselves which sometimes are considered allophones of vowels and sometimes as consonant phonemes.

More complex vowel inventories are found in the Southeast Asian mainland languages (**Chamic, Moken-Moklen**), on Java, and in some parts of Sumatra and the Lesser Sunda islands. Acehnese, in fact, is said to have ten oral monophthongs plus seven nasal monophthongs and ten diphthongs (Durie 1985:16f, but see also Stokhof 1988:329–331). Kedang is described as distinguishing a neutral vowel series from one articulated with an advanced tongue root (Samely 1991:13–35).

Hardly any restrictions on the coda in CVC-syllables occur in Formosan and Philippine languages which also allow a wide range of consonant clusters across syllable boundaries. **Tsou**, in fact, is crosslinguistically remarkable for its broad range of consonant clusters. **Tsou** is also among the languages which allow a range of syllable-initial consonant clusters. Such languages are found in Taiwan (another example is Thao) and in Halmahera and the Moluccas (e.g. **Taba**, **Leti**). While Formosan and Philippine languages generally do not allow sequences of like consonants (or geminate consonants), such sequences are a prominent feature of South Sulawesi languages (**Makassar**, Bugis, etc.). More sporadically and mostly as a result of morphophonological processes, they are also found elsewhere in, for example, **Leti**, Dobel, **Taba**, Tukang Besi, Totoli, Bontok, Madurese, Toba Batak and various **Malayic varieties**; see also Blust 1995).

A fair number of languages, including Dobel and many Philippine languages (e.g. **Iloko**, **Tagalog**), have mandatory onsets, i.e. there are no vowel-initial syllables (and hence no vowel-initial lexical bases). This fact is often overlooked or misinterpreted because the practical orthographies in use for the Philippine languages do not include a regular representation for syllable-initial glottal stops. There are both phonological and phonetic reasons to assume that these syllable-initial glottal stops are phonemic and not just automatically added in the absence of an onset. For instance, base-initial glottal stops, just like any other consonant, are not omitted when a prefix is added. Thus when Tagalog *mag-* is combined with *ʔingáy* 'noise' the result is [mag.ʔi.ŋáj] and not *[ma.gi.ŋáj]. Consequently, there is no need to develop complicated accounts for infixation and reduplication of supposedly vowel-initial bases in these languages (cf. also Halle 2001:156).

The Philippine languages provide the most significant exception to the generalization that stress is non-distinctive. In most of these languages, stress placement is not predictable and may occur on either the penultimate or the ultimate syllable. Small classes of lexical bases with unpredictable final stress are also said to occur in a few other languages, including Atayal, Thao (Blust 2001:327), Toba Batak and Dobel. In a number of other languages (e.g. Pazeh, Acehnese, Balinese, Iban, Kendayan, Land Dayak), stress regularly occurs on the ultimate syllable rather than the penultimate syllable.

The tonal distinctions found in **Cham** and **Moken/Moklen** are part of their Southeast Asian mainland typological profile. Otherwise, western Austronesian languages generally do not have lexical tones, a possible exception being Ma'ya, a language spoken on the Raja Ampat Islands in eastern Indonesia (cf. Van der Leeden 1997 and Remijsen 2002).

Sundanese is well known for extensive nasal spreading (Robins 1957, Cohn 1990). To a somewhat lesser extent, this also occurs in Madurese, Balinese, and a number of **Malayic varieties**, particularly in Sumatra and Borneo (e.g. Iban, Kendayan). In Borneo languages, one additionally finds nasal preplosion and related phenomena (Blust 1997a) which are also found in neighboring non-Austronesian languages on the Southeast Asian mainland.

A widespread phenomenon superficially contravening the preference for disyllabic lexical bases is the addition of paragogic vowels to consonant-final bases, a phenomenon particularly widespread in Sulawesi (**Buol**, Sneddon 1993) but also found in many other languages throughout the area (e.g. Atayal, **Tsou**, **Kambera**, Buru). This additional vowel is extra-metrical in that it is not counted for stress assignment and usually disappears in compounding and when suffixes are added to the base. Thus, for example, the Lauje word *luba?e* 'hair', which consists of the base *luba?* and paragogic *e*, is regularly stressed on the antepenultimate syllable [lúba?e]. The paragogic *e* disappears when the third person possessive suffix *-(o)nye* is added to the base as in *luba?onye* 'his/her hair'. See also the 'weak final syllables' in **Malagasy**.

Turning to morpho(pho)nology (or morphophonemics), the basic generalization would appear to be that Austronesian languages are morphonologically simple in that the relation between basic and derived words is formally transparent, often involving a straightforward concatenation of formatives. There are significant exceptions to this generalization, as briefly shown in section 2.3 below. But inasmuch as it is true, it results from the fact that most languages show only a very limited set of morphonological alternations. It would be wrong, however, to conclude from this that the inventory of morphonological alternations across the whole group is equally limited. On the contrary, there is hardly a morphonological process that is not attested in at least one western Austronesian language. **Leti** and Meto (Dawanese) have complex and pervasive metathesis rules (limited to a few affixes, metathesis occurs throughout the area, e.g. **Biak**, **Taba**, Buru, Cebuano, **Tagalog**, Bontok, Atayal). In central Sulawesi and northern Borneo, some affixations involve vowel harmony (e.g. Lauje, Totoli, **Kimaragang**). Ablaut is found in a number of Borneo languages including **Belait** (Blust 1997b). Umlaut-like alternations are attested in **Kambera**. Consonant mutation has been described for **Nias** and **Kambera**. This is not to mention various other kinds of alternations such as assimilation, dissimilation, deletion and addition of segments which are well-attested throughout the area. The two most pervasive and characteristic alternations, however, are reduplication and nasal assimilation and substitution, which will be discussed in more detail below.

2.1 Nasal assimilation and substitution (*N* and *-um-*)

Many symmetric voice languages have a prefix or a set of prefixes which end in a nasal (*CVN-*) or simply consist of a nasal (*N-*) which assimilates to, and sometimes also modifies, the initial segment of the base in various ways. A notable exception is Formosan languages where only fossilized reflexes of prefixes with *N* are encountered (Zobel, to appear). Such fossilized reflexes are also found throughout the rest of the Austronesian family, and it is in this sense that nasal assimilation and substitution can be considered a highly characteristic feature of the family even though it is no longer productive in half of the languages.

The homorganic nasal, as it is conventionally called, is typically realized as a velar nasal (/ŋ/) before vowels. It remains unrealized before nasals (and often also before liquids and glides), and before other consonants it assimilates to the place of articulation of the following consonant. Voiceless consonants other than /h/ are usually deleted after the homorganic nasal. The Lauje examples in Table 5.1 illustrate these general regularities. See Newman (1984) and Pater (2001) for a broader range of examples and a review of the theoretical issues involved.

As the examples in Table 5.1 make clear, the assimilation to the place of articulation of the following consonant is only an approximate one in several instances. While in the case of the glottal stop and fricative (/?/ and /h/) the non-existence of an appropriate nasal 'explains' the lack of a precise match, this is less clearly so in the case of the alveolar fricative /s/ which is frequently replaced by palatal /ɲ/ rather than expected alveolar /n/. When /s/ is not replaced, but only preceded by *N*, the homorganic nasal is always /n/ as in Lauje *monsau* 'rub (strongly)' (< *sau*).

TABLE 5.1: NASAL ASSIMILATION AND SUBSTITUTION IN LAUJE

Assimilation	Substitution	Examples involving the actor voice prefix *moN-* (given in practical orthography)
N → (ŋ/ __V	–	*mongupi* 'dream' < *upi*
N → 0/__l/r/m/n/ŋ	–	*molandas* 'pull' < *landas, morapang* 'give a speech' < *rapang, mompoyongaʔ* 'shut (eyes)' < *mpoyong, montuul* 'lie' < *ntuul, mongkelung* 'lie down' < *ngkelung*
N → m/ __b	–	*mombanit* 'bite off' < *banit*
N → m/ __p	+	*momangang* 'chew betelnut' < *pangang*
N → n/ __d/ɟ	–	*mondangoy* 'bake sago' < *dangoy, monjaʔang* 'cook' < *jaʔang*
N → n/ __t	+	*monapa* 'roast' < *tapa*
N → ɲ/ __s	+	*monyunsut* 'suck' < *sunsut*
N → ŋ/ __g	–	*monggeges* 'rub' < *geges*
N → ŋ/ __k/ʔ	+	*mongikib* 'gnaw' < *kikib, mongoyab* 'fan' < *ʔoyab*

Not covered by the regularities stated so far are stems beginning with fricatives other than /s/ and /h/. Such stems with an initial bilabial (/ß/, /Φ/), labio-dental (/v/, /f/), or velar fricative (/ɣ/, /x/) are found in a number of languages throughout the area (they seem to be particularly common in Taiwan and Sulawesi). Unlike /s/ and /h/, these fricatives are often strengthened to a stop when co-occurring with *N* (but see **Malagasy** where initial /f/ and /v/ are replaced by /m/). The bilabial and labio-dental ones generally become /b/ as in the Tomini-Tolitoli languages Taje *mombaßa* 'carry' (< *ßaßa*) or Tajio *mombeen* 'give' (< *Φeen*), while the velar ones become /g/ as in Ratahan *munggoreng* 'fry' (< *xoreng*), regardless of voicing.

The preceding remarks already indicate that there is a lot of variation regarding the morphonology of *N*, both within and across languages. Substantial variation also occurs, for example, with regard to substitution where just about everything is possible, except that nasals, liquids and glides appear never to be replaced. Voiced obstruents may also be replaced, e.g. Lauje *momambal* 'report, inform' (< *bambal*). And conversely, voiceless obstruents may remain in stem-initial position after *N*, e.g. Lauje *montanong* 'bury' (< *tanong*). Sometimes, forms both with and without substitution occur, e.g. Lauje *mombentet* or *momentet* 'tear' (< *bentet*). This variation is particularly pervasive with regard to initial /b/ which is replaced sporadically in almost all languages with a productive *N*-prefix, and in quite a number of languages substitution is the rule rather than the exception. Other voiced stops (in particular /d/ and /g/) are much more rarely substituted by *N*. Note that in a few languages, such as **Buol**, Iban, Salako and Balinese, substitution of stem-initial obstruents has been generalized and thus pertains to voiceless and voiced obstruents in the same way (in Balinese for lexical bases of two or more syllables only). In a few other languages, mostly in the central parts of Sulawesi (e.g. **Mori Bawah**, Kaili, Mandar), voiceless consonants regularly become prenasalized rather than being replaced by *N*.

For other examples of variation in the morphonology of *N*, see in particular **Nias**, **Karo Batak**, **Kimaragang**, **Malagasy** and **Makassar**.

In passing, it may be noted that the variation with regard to substitution allows a distinction of different kinds of segmentally homonymous *N*-prefixes. Thus, for example, in Tagalog there is a stem-forming prefix *paN-* after which base-initial voiceless obstruents are regularly omitted. And there is a second prefix *paN-* used to derive words meaning 'for (use in) X'. With this second prefix, substitution of voiceless obstruents is either impossible or optional, hence *pangkapé* 'for (use in) coffee' (< *kapé*) and *pansukláy* or *panukláy* 'for use in combing' (< *sukláy*). See DeGuzman 1978 and also **Karo Batak**.

While nasal assimilation and substitution is most common and widespread with *N*-prefixes, somewhat similar processes also occur with regard to the infix *-um-*, although on a much more restricted scale. The widely attested infix *-um-* is generally inserted between the first consonant and vowel of the base (i.e. *-um-* + CVCCVC → C<*um*>VCCVC). Before vowel-initial stems, it often simply becomes a prefix, sometimes changing its shape from *um* to *m* (i.e. *-um-* + VCCVC → *um*-VCCVC or *m*-VCCVC). Exceptions to these general regularities pertain to bases with an initial labial or nasal consonant and to derived stems with certain derivational prefixes. Languages differ quite significantly with regard to the number of exceptions.

Muna provides one of the more complex examples (Van den Berg 1989:28–31). In addition to showing many standard examples for the infixation of *-um-* such as *s*<*um*>*olo* 'flow', the morphonology of Muna *-um-* includes the following subregularities. Before vowels, *-um-* is regularly *m-* (e.g. *m-ala* 'take'). Voiceless labials (/p/ and /f/) are regularly replaced by *m* (e.g. *mongko* 'kill' < *pongko* and *mutaa* 'laugh' < *futaa*). Bases with initial voiced labials, nasals or prenasalized consonants remain unchanged (*baru* 'happy' may represent either the unmarked base or *-um-* + *baru*). Bases with initial *w* may remain either unchanged (e.g. *wanu* 'get up' representing *-um-* + *wanu*) or *w* is replaced by *m* (e.g. *maa* 'give' < *waa*). Prefixes either abide by these regularities (e.g. causative *fo-* becomes *mo-* when affixed with *-um-*, verb stem deriving *ka-* becomes *kuma-*) or remain unchanged (e.g. detransitivizing *fo-* remains *fo-* in contexts where use of *-um-* is required).

With regard to derivational prefixes, three different scenarios have to be distinguished in all western Austronesian languages. First, *-um-* may be affixed to the prefix according to the same rules as for lexical bases. Second, *-um-* may be affixed to the prefix, but there are special regularities (e.g. the *um*-form of the Tagalog social action prefix *paki-* is *maki-* (not **pumaki-*) while with most *p*-initial lexical bases *-um-* is regularly infixed after the initial consonant as in *p*<*um*>*untá* 'go to'). Finally, the prefix may block affixation of *-um-*, i.e. the stem has to be expanded further before affixation of *-um-* is possible (e.g. the Tagalog causative prefix *pa-* disallows the affixation of *-um-*).

While the morphonological alternations of *N* and *-um-* share some similarities, they must have quite different (historical) origins. The widespread manifestation of *-um-* + *p*-initial prefix as *m* as in the above Tagalog example (*-um-* + *paki-* → *maki-*) is probably due to clipping the first syllable of a trisyllabic prefix (e.g. **pumaki-* → *maki-*) rather than to *-um-* somehow replacing the prefix-initial *p*. In this view, at least some of the very common prefixes of the shape *ma-* may be considered to be reduced forms of (historically as well as synchronically) underlying **kuma-*, given that *ka-* is a very common stem deriving prefix (and despite the fact that *kuma*→ *ma* does not make sense in terms of assimilation and substitution).

Finally, all alternations relating to *N* and *-um-* should be kept distinct from the alternation between non-realis marking *m* and realis marking *n* which is common with prefixes in many Philippine languages (e.g. stative non-realis *ma-* vs. stative realis *na-*). This *m/n*-alternation never involves assimilation or substitution, and it easily creates confusion if it is also represented by a capital N.

2.2 Reduplication

Reduplication is probably the most pervasive morphonological process in western Austronesian languages in that it is a productive process in all of them (a possible exception is Keo). However, Austronesian languages differ greatly in the formal make-up of reduplication patterns and their functions, as will become evident throughout this section and by comparing the language sketches. Here as well as in the language sketches the focus is on formal patterns.

To begin with, it will be useful to recall the distinction between reduplication as a morphonological process of word formation and the mere repetition of words as a means to convey intensity, multiplicity or duration. The latter is a syntactic pattern which is not constrained by morphonological parameters and involves the repetition of whole (phonological) words regardless of their morphological make-up. Such repetitions are possible in all languages (e.g. English *go go go!*). While this distinction is fairly clear on a conceptual level, its application in practice is sometimes not straightforward, as the following example from Standard Indonesian shows.

In Standard Indonesian it is possible to repeat any noun in order to indicate a plurality of referents as in *rumah-rumah* 'houses' or *anjing-anjing* 'dogs'. Such repetition is possible regardless of the morphological complexity of the noun, compare *perubahan-perubahan* 'changes' (< *ubah*). Grammars generally treat this as an instance of reduplication, but it is a borderline case where the analysis as reduplication depends very much on whether the duplication can be shown to convey a grammaticized meaning or function. Full base reduplication can indeed have specific semantic effects in Standard Indonesian in that it allows the derivation of new lexemes (e.g. *guna-guna* 'magic' < *guna* 'use', 'purpose', *mata-mata* 'spy' < *mata* 'eye'), which however only applies to underived lexical bases. Furthermore, there are many instances where full base reduplication only pertains to the lexical base, e.g. *sebesar-besarnya* 'as big as possible' < *besar* 'big'. This also holds for verbs which may be reduplicated to indicate a repeated or ongoing event as in *berjalan-jalan* 'walk about', 'go for a stroll'. Since in the case of morphologically complex bases only the lexical base is repeated, it is plausible to assume that in instances such as *duduk-duduk* 'sit about' we are also dealing with reduplication rather than with simple repetition.

With regard to reduplication, two types of functions or meanings may be distinguished in Austronesian languages. On the one hand, there is the somewhat diffuse and supposedly iconic range of meanings associated with reduplication throughout the world's languages, i.e. distribution, variety, plurality; habitual, repeated or ongoing activity; intensity and emphasis; increase or decrease of size or amount; pejoratives. This range of meanings is often conveyed by full base reduplication (or simple repetition) rather than by the partial reduplication patterns exemplified below.

On the other hand, reduplication patterns in western Austronesian are part of a large number of clearly circumscribed derivations, often in combination with further affixes. Thus, for example, reduplication occurs quite regularly in nominalizations such as the formation of instrument nouns (e.g. Thao *ca-capu* 'broom' < *capu* 'sweep' (Chang 1998:282); see also Blust 1998). But it also serves more purely morphosyntactic functions such as marking adnominal modifiers (including the verb in relative clauses) in Dobel (see also **Leti** and Carpenter 1996):

(3) *ʔamu   sertáy   **m**-maray*   (vs: *ʔamu sertáy maray* 'your clothes are dry')
     2s.POSS   clothes   RDP-dry
     'your dry clothes' (Hughes 2000:172)

Among the most frequent and widespread uses of reduplication is the derivation of numerals where it forms restrictives (e.g. **Iloko** *dù-duá* 'only two'), ordinals (e.g. Siraya *ka-ra-ruha* 'second' (with prefix *ka-* preceding *Ca*-reduplication), grouping (Malay *dua-dua* 'two at a time'), etc. Somewhat unusual is its use when counting humans as opposed to other entities. Thus Thao *tusha* 'two' occurs in serial counting or when counting animals or inanimate objects while *ta-tusha* necessarily refers to human referents (Blust 2001:332f). Perhaps even more remarkable in this is Siraya (Adelaar 2000:41,48) where two different kinds of reduplication apply when counting non-humans (CV-reduplication) and humans (Ca-reduplication).

It has occasionally been suggested that a possible third type of function for reduplication consists in the formation of lexical bases (sometimes called *inherent reduplication*). As is well known, many disyllabic lexical bases in western Austronesian languages have the shape of duplicated monosyllables as in Balinese *gigi* 'tooth', *agag* 'wide open' or *cakcak* 'chop up'. These are generally deemed to be fossilized forms, reflecting earlier productive reduplication patterns (see Blust 1988). But Clynes (1995:166–170) argues that, at least in the case of Balinese, there is evidence to suggest that such bases are the result of synchronic base formation via reduplication. Thus, for example, Balinese duplicated monosyllables are stressed on both syllables (hence *gígí*) just like productive full-base reduplications (e.g. *lúh-lúh* 'female (plural)' < *luh*) and unlike other disyllabic lexical bases, which are generally stressed on the final syllable.

Apart from the full base-reduplication illustrated above, the following partial reduplication patterns are attested among western Austronesian languages:

- *C-reduplication*: the first consonant of the stressed syllable is directly prefixed to it as in Dobel **m**-*mata* 'raw' or *ʔa*-**d**-*dém* 'she does' (<*ʔa-dém*) (Hughes 2000:168; syllable onsets are always filled in Dobel) or **Iloko** *lalláki* 'males' (< *laláki* 'male'). This form of reduplication is quite rare, often being restricted to a small set of items as in the case of Iloko where it occurs in animate and kin plurals only (see also Thurgood (1997:144) on Bontok). Dobel and its closest relatives are possibly the only languages where this is the main productive reduplication pattern.
- *Ca-reduplication*: The first consonant is copied and prefixed to the base with a default vowel intervening, e.g. Thao *fa*-*finshiq* 'seed for planting', **sha**-*shishi* 'shake repeatedly' (Chang 1998:282) or Balinese **də**-*daar-an* 'food' (< *daar* 'eat'; Clynes 1995:152). The default vowel is often *a* (e.g. Paiwan, Ratahan, **Tetun Fehan**), which is why this pattern is referred to as *Ca*-reduplication. Other vowels are also possible, as shown by Balinese and **Javanese** which have schwa, or Buru which has *e* (Grimes 1991:77). In **Taba** a default vowel *a* also occurs in more complex reduplication patterns (e.g. *CaC-*). Clynes (1995:154f) suggests that Ca-reduplication is actually a variant of C-reduplication in those languages which do not allow geminate consonant clusters. See Blust (1998) for a more comprehensive survey. Note that the difference between Ca-reduplication and CV-reduplication is automatically lost in languages with antepenultimate vowel neutralization (e.g. Atayal, **Seediq**, Malay, **Javanese**, **Malagasy**, Madurese).
- *CV-reduplication* or *monosyllabic reduplication* (also *syllable reduplication*): The reduplicant consists of a syllable prefixed to the base. This syllable can be either light (monomoraic) or heavy (bimoraic), and some authors would restrict the term *CV-reduplication* to instances of light syllable reduplication as in **Tagalog** *pag*-**bi**-*bilí* 'selling' and *pag*-**la**-*lakbáy* 'travelling', where the first syllable of the base is heavy *lak* but the reduplicant is light *la*. In heavy syllable reduplication, either the vowel in the reduplicant is stressed or lengthened (e.g. **Tagalog** **bí**-*bilí* 'will buy') or the syllable is obligatorily closed, compare Bontok *ʔik*-*ʔik.kan* 'is doing' where the base-initial syllable is already

heavy (*ʔik*) with **lap-la.pú** 'is going first' where it is not (Thurgood 1997:137). In particular in Philippine languages, it is common to have both heavy and light syllable reduplication in clearly different functions. While the segments in the reduplicant are usually a copy of the base-initial segments, there are also examples where the reduplicant regularly consists of a copy of the base-final syllable (e.g. Madurese *les-toles* 'write (more than once)', *ku-buku* 'books' (Davies 1999a:13) or Urak Lawoi' *jiʔ-bajiʔ* 'well' (Hogan 1999:24)).

- *CV(C)CV-reduplication* or *disyllabic reduplication* (also *foot reduplication*): The reduplicant consists of a combination of two syllables (i.e. a foot) prefixed to the base. The second syllable is usually open, regardless of the shape of the second syllable of the base, e.g. Lauje *e-ʔinde-ʔinde* 'nod indiscriminately', *me-ito-itong* 'rather black', *ma-ale-alenda* 'rather long'. In the case of disyllabic bases with an open final syllable such as *ʔinde*, this kind of reduplication is indistinguishable from full base reduplication, which may be the reason why it is occasionally also called *full reduplication*. But as the preceding examples show, it is not a literally full duplication of the base. Note that in many languages, foot reduplication occurs in addition to full base reduplication as in Lauje *mong-ontong-ontong* 'watch (for some time)' (where the base-final *ng* is part of the reduplicant as opposed to *me-ito-itong* where it is not).

Recently, it has been proposed that some western Austronesian languages also allow triplication, i.e. adding a given reduplicant twice to the same base. The best documented example to date is Thao, for which Blust (2001:330) adduces the following example among others: *qa-qa-qucquc* 'to tie or bind tightly or securely' with doubled Ca-reduplication from the base *qucquc* 'tie, bind' (see Müller-Gotama (2001:16) for possible examples from Sundanese).

Very many western Austronesian languages allow Ca-reduplication or one or more variants of CV-reduplication in addition to foot reduplication and full base reduplication. It is rare that a language allows both CV- and Ca-reduplication as productive processes applying to the same set of lexical bases. One example, already mentioned above, is Siraya, where numerals occur both with CV- and Ca-reduplication (see also Chang (1998:285) and Blust (2001:326f) on Thao and Li and Tsuchida (2001:21f) on Pazeh). It is thus not impossible that C-reduplication, Ca-reduplication and (light-syllable) CV-reduplication are actually variants of each other (in the case of Siraya, an extinct Formosan language, it is unclear whether the reduplicant in CV-reduplication was heavy).

While the majority of reduplicants are clearly prefixes (i.e. they are attached to the left edge of the base), there are a few examples which suggest attachment further to the right (sometimes called rightward reduplication). Thus, Chang (1998) lists the following examples from Thao in which material from the end of the base, excepting the final C if there is one, is copied and appears to be attached close to the right edge of the base (similar formations are found in Rukai and Pazeh (Chang 1998:296) and Siraya (Adelaar 2000:40f):

(4)   **Thao 'rightward' reduplication** (cf. Chang 1998:284)

		BASE	REDUPLICATED FORM (reduplicant in italics)	
	(a)	su.hu.i	p-i-suhui*hui*	'to be put there repeatedly'
	(b)	shna.ra	pa-shnara*nara*	'to burn sth. repeatedly'
	(c)	ag.qtu	agqtu*qtu*	'think about'
	(d)	sig.ki	sigki*gki*	'to kneel'
	(e)	ma-ku.tnir	mia-kutni*tnir*	'to harden'
	(f)	dut.khun	mia-dutkhu*khun*	'to hunch over'
	(g)	m-ar.faz	m-arfar*faz*	'to keep flying around'

The reduplicant is either monosyllabic with a heavy onset (as in c-g) or disyllabic with simple onset(s) (a and b). The choice of the reduplicant depends on the shape of the base. Roughly, if the rightmost syllable of the base has a heavy onset, then this syllable is copied (c, e, f). If its onset is light and the preceding syllable is closed, the reduplicant consists of the coda of the penultimate syllable plus the final syllable (d, g). Otherwise the last two syllables are copied (a, b), a possibly complex onset of the penultimate syllable being simplified (b). This reduplication pattern is in complementary distribution to 'regular' foot reduplication which applies to monosyllabic bases and disyllabic bases without complex onsets or a coda in the penultimate syllable (Chang 1998:279).

Since the reduplicant occurs to the left of the final consonant of the base (if there is one) this is not a clear-cut example of suffixing a reduplicant. In fact, as it stands, there is no clear-cut evidence to consider the second string of identical segments as the reduplicant. That is, rather than *agqtuqtu* and *marfarfaz* it is also possible to analyze these forms as *agqtuqtu* and *marfarfaz*, locating the reduplicant to the left of the main (i.e. stressed) part of the base. In this way, these forms look much more like standard examples of CV- or CVCV-reduplication, the major difference being that the reduplicant is not attached to the left edge of the base but placed directly before the stressed syllable of the base. This is how Van Klinken analyzes somewhat less complex, but still similar forms in **Tetun Fehan**.

In Balinese, there are a few examples in which the case for suffixation is clearer in that the reduplicant in fact includes the base-final consonant as in *pə-cəpolpol* 'collapse (plural)' (< *-cepol*) or *ngəbətbət* 'throb (plural)' (< *-kəbət*). But Clynes (1995:157) notes that the first syllable(s) in bases allowing final syllable reduplication is always from a severely restricted set (*kə, cə, kati/kali/katu, nərə/nylə*), which has prefix-like characteristics. Consequently, he argues for leftward attachment (i.e. *pə-cəpolpol*) in analogy to the standard cases such as *me-laib-laib* 'run (plural)' (< *laib*) where prefixes are also excluded from reduplication. See also Li and Tsuchida (2001:22) on Pazeh.

As the preceding examples from Thao and Balinese show, the structure of the base often determines the choice of reduplication pattern. Consequently, reduplication patterns are often in at least partial complementary distribution within a given language. In addition to the number of syllables, a major parameter here is whether the base is vowel- or consonant-initial. Thus, for example, in Lauje CV-reduplication is only possible for consonant-initial bases (e.g. *me-ní-nimpis* 'rather narrow' (< *nimpis*)). Vowel-initial roots only allow foot reduplication as in *me-ito-itong* 'rather black' (Himmelmann 2001:81f). Other languages allow the reduplicant to consist simply of a vowel which then is usually separated by a glottal stop from the base (e.g. in Ratahan *Ca*-reduplication for vowel-initial roots consists in prefixing the vowel /a/ to the root as in *a-ingkaʔ-en* [ʔaʔiŋkaʔen] 'messenger' < *ingkaʔ* (Himmelmann and Wolff 1999:15)).

A very complex area with much crosslinguistic variation is the interaction of reduplication and 'regular' affixation. The general tendency here is that many affixes, in particular monosyllabic ones, do not take part in reduplication but rather appear to be added to a derived stem consisting of reduplicant+lexical base. Thus, for example, infixes are almost always added to the reduplicant and not to the lexical base (e.g. Tagalog *biní-bili* 'bought', not *bí-binili*; see **Kimaragang** for a noteworthy exception to this generalization). When prefixes involve the homorganic nasal, however, it is generally the case that nasal assimilation and replacement modify the base before reduplication takes place (e.g. Tagalog *mamúmútol* 'will cut (a lot)' (< *maN-putol*) not *mamúpútol*).

Further morphophonological aspects of reduplication relevant to western Austronesian languages pertain to the simplification of base-initial onset clusters (e.g. Tagalog *mag-tá-trabaho* 'will work', not *mag-tra-trabaho), the insertion of nasals or glottal stops in between reduplicant and base, metathesis and various assimilation processes at the boundary of reduplicant and base. See the language sketches most of which contain data on reduplication.

2.3 Lack of morphonological transparency

Lack of morphonological transparency as understood here means that the relation between basic and derived words is formally not transparent in that the constituent formatives of a morphologically complex word are not easily identifiable. Once the changes brought about by the homorganic nasal are mastered, identifying constituent formatives in a western Austronesian language is generally not very difficult. However, there are two important and often ignored types of exceptions. On the one hand, there are a few languages such as **Leti** which lack morphonological transparency due to pervasive metathesis (and apocope). On the other hand, there are a few languages such as Atayal, Siraya, **Seediq**, **Tsou** or Gorontalo where in particular verbal derivations involve a whole set of largely reductive alternations, the combined application of which tends to obscure the relation between base and derived formation. This second type of exception is briefly illustrated here with data from Atayal.

The most pervasive morphonological alternation in this language is the reduction of all antepenultimate vowels to schwa. Thus, when a disyllabic root with penultimate stress is suffixed, the formerly stressed vowel is reduced to schwa as in *tápih* 'call' → *təpíhun* (*-un* is the patient voice suffix). (Since schwa is predictable, Atayal words are usually written without schwa, i.e. *təpíhun* is represented as *tpíhun* in standard orthography.) If a suffixed formation is stressed on the final syllable, all prefinal vowels are reduced to schwa: *tehúk* 'arrive' → *təhəkán*, *laqúx* 'win' → *ləqəxán* (<q> represents a uvular stop and *-an* is the locative voice suffix). In addition to this regular and pervasive reduction, whole syllables are dropped under various conditions. For example, when the two last syllables of a base are segmentally identical, one of them may be dropped in suffixation, e.g. *kəŋúŋuʔ* 'fear' → *kəŋún* (with suffix *-un*) and *kəŋúi* (with suffix *-i*).

In addition to these reductions, various consonant alternations occur. As the previous example *kəŋúŋuʔ* → *kəŋún* shows, root-final glottals may be dropped with subsequent contraction of sequences of identical vowels. But sometimes glottals are retained (e.g. *həŋəʔán* 'dip in water' < *həŋúʔ*), or they become a glide, which happens in roots ending in /iʔ/ or /uʔ/ (e.g. *siyun* < *siʔ* 'to place').

This does not yet complete the inventory of morphonological alternations in Atayal. But the following examples suffice to show what happens to morphonological transparency when several of these alternations apply together to a given derivation: *gálan* < *ágan* 'take' + *-an* (consonant alternation, stress shift, syllable loss), *kətón* < *kítaʔ* 'see' + *-un* (loss of glottal stop, vowel contraction, stress shift, vowel reduction), *həbəgán* < *həgúp* 'do magic' + *-an* (consonant alternation, metathesis, vowel reduction).

2.4 A note on morphological type

The large majority of western Austronesian languages shows a moderate inventory of affixes, mostly prefixes and a few suffixes (less than five, not counting pronominal suffixes). Productive infixation (involving usually two infixes) is largely confined to the northwest (Taiwan, Philippines and northern Borneo and Sulawesi). The typical number of prefixes is somewhat difficult to determine since it depends very much on whether complex prefixes are counted as prefixes in their own right (e.g. Tagalog *maka-* could be analyzed as an unanalyzable prefix of its own or as a combination of the two independently attested formatives *ma-* and *ka-*). The number of clearly monomorphemic prefixes rarely exceeds thirty, many of which have very special functions (e.g. the **Iloko** prefix *agat-* deriving words for smelling as in *agat-layá* 'smell like ginger'). Prefixes with a high functional load and text frequency typically do not exceed a dozen (counting person marking prefix sets as single prefixes). Such prefixes, as well as all suffixes, tend to be highly multifunctional.

Major exceptions to these generalizations are found on the Southeast Asian mainland, in western Borneo, where various Land Dayak languages exhibit very little morphology, and the Flores-Timor region, where a number of (nearly) isolating languages occur (e.g. Keo, Waima'a). Keo, in fact, is said to have no affixes whatsoever, only a single proclitic and no productive native reduplication patterns (Baird 2002:171). **Kambera**, spoken in neighboring Sumba, is also rather poor in affixes (one productive prefix, possibly two suffixes), but very rich in clitics.

In terms of morphological typology, most western Austronesian languages have been considered to be agglutinative. This assessment needs to be qualified, however. First, there is a considerable number of languages which are clearly not agglutinative because they exhibit pervasive metathesis, consonant mutation, ablaut or reductive alternations of one form or another, as was briefly exemplified in the preceding section. Second, the traditional categories *agglutinative* and *fusional* are not simple properties, but sets of logically independent properties, as explained in Plank (1999:282f). The formally more transparent Austronesian languages are agglutinative only with regard to some of these properties.

In terms of the formal concatenation of formatives, in particular transparent segmentability and phonological cohesion, many Austronesian languages indeed show few signs of fusion. Fusion with regard to these properties is very much limited to the ubiquitous homorganic nasal and a few other assimilatory processes. But even these languages, with their easily identifiable morpheme boundaries, are not agglutinative in the same way as Turkish, for example, because they deviate quite significantly from the ideal of 'one form – one meaning'. The major formatives not only tend to be multifunctional, but they also often convey a *bundle* of morphosyntactic features rather than representing a single category (for example, many so-called voice affixes are strictly speaking voice-aspect-mood affixes because they always convey a combination of these categories; see section 4.2.2). Conversely, the same category (e.g. locative voice) may be represented by two different formatives (as with locative voice which is represented by both *-an* and *-i*). Furthermore, most languages allow combinations of affixes (prefix plus suffix, two or more prefixes, etc.), and while some of these affix combinations are semantically transparent, others are quite idiosyncratic and demand an analysis as unit morphemes.

3 BASIC MORPHOSYNTAX

3.1 Lexical and syntactic categories (parts of speech)

In discussing lexical and syntactic categories in western Austronesian languages, it is necessary to make a fundamental distinction between morphological and syntactic (distributional) levels and between lexemes (lexical bases) and morphosyntactic words. It is a prominent feature of these languages that categorial distinctions on these different levels do not necessarily align in the same way as in other language families. For instance, two morphosyntactic words may differ clearly in that they participate in different paradigms and thus belong to two distinct morphological categories. At the same time, however, their syntactic distribution may be identical, thus belonging to the same syntactic category. Similarly, morphosyntactic words in a given language may clearly belong to different morphological or syntactic categories but at the same time there may not be a corresponding distinction on the level of lexical bases (roots) (see Sasse 1993, Evans 2000 and Himmelmann (to appear a) for a more detailed overview of different alignment possibilities). In the following discussion, morphosyntactic words are taken up first.

A basic distinction with regard to morphosyntactic words which is widely attested in the languages of the world is the one between content words (open word classes) and function words (closed word classes). This distinction is also found in all western Austronesian languages, with most morphosyntactic words clearly belonging to one or the other category. Exceptions pertain to weakly grammaticized items such as **Belait** *saw'* which functions both as a main predicate 'use' and as an instrumental preposition. Many function words are clitics, which are further discussed in section 3.2.

Western Austronesian languages differ somewhat with regard to the further subdivision of content words. In many languages there is a clear-cut syntactic distinction between verbs and nouns in that there are syntactic slots in which only nouns may occur (note that in most languages nouns can occur without further modification in predicate function so that typically there are no syntactic slots that are exclusively filled by verbs). This is the case in most preposed possessor and transitional languages including **Biak**, **Taba**, **Leti**, **Mori Bawah**, and **Nias**, where verbs are marked for person. In **Kambera** there is some distributional overlap between nouns and verbs, but the basic distinction is still clear.

In many symmetrical voice languages, on the other hand, the syntactic distinction between nouns and verbs is often somewhat less clearly delineated in that word-forms which semantically appear to be verbs easily and without further morphological modification occur in nominal functions and vice versa. Compare the following examples from Riau Indonesian (see also **Tagalog** and **Seediq**):

(5) *orang* ***bahasa*** ***Inggeris*** *sama* *David*
     person language English with David
     'Did people speak English with you (i.e. David)?' (Gil 1994:182)

(6) ***tunggu*** ***taksi*** *susa* *sekali*
     wait taksi difficult very
     'Waiting for a taxi is very difficult.' (Gil 1994:182)

In (5) the 'noun' *bahasa Inggeris* 'English' is used in predicate function and then conveys the clearly verbal meaning 'speak English'. Conversely, in (6) the 'verb' *tunggu* 'wait' with its complement *taxi* is used in subject function and has to be rendered by a nominalization in English.

Sometimes a distributional distinction between nouns and verbs pertains only to one or two fairly specific syntactic contexts. Thus in Standard Indonesian a major distributional difference between nouns and verbs pertains to the fact that nouns cannot be negated with *tidak* and that when verbs are negated with the nominal negator *bukan* the negation is emphatic or contrastive (see also **Sama**, **Kimaragang** and **Belait**).

The analytical consequences of a pervasive overlap in the syntactic distribution of putatively nominal and verbal word-forms remain controversial. Some authors (e.g. Gil 1994, 2000, Himmelmann 1991, to appear a) argue for a basic lack of a morphosyntactic noun/verb distinction. Most descriptive grammars and formal analyses of symmetrical voice languages assume underlying syntactic differences based on the semantics of the forms and analyze the examples above as involving zero conversion. Apparently nominal uses of 'verbs' are often also considered headless relative clause formations (see **Kimaragang**).

Analysts also differ widely as to whether it is useful and necessary to distinguish a separate morphosyntactic class of adjectives in addition to nouns and verbs. Here, however, one has to be particularly careful to determine the level at which such a distinction is claimed, and to distinguish differences in actual fact from differences in descriptive practice. It would appear that in most western Austronesian languages putative adjectives have the same kind of syntactic distribution as intransitive (particularly stative) verbs. Thus, for example, in languages where negators provide a diagnostic context for distinguishing nouns and verbs, putative adjectives always behave like verbs. Exceptions usually pertain to very small classes of words conveying property concepts which show some minor distributional differences distinguishing them from verbs (e.g. **Biak** *kasun* 'small' and *babo* 'new'; see also **Seediq**).

While there is thus little evidence to set up *adjective* as a distinct syntactic category, in various languages throughout the area there are good reasons to set up *adjective* as a distinct morphological category (e.g. **Iloko, Karo Batak, Malagasy, Leti, Tetun Fehan**). In these languages, adjectives are distinguished from other morphological categories by their distinctive morphological potential. Perhaps the most widespread distinguishing feature of adjectives is the fact that they have a specific way for expressing plural in agreement with some nominal constituent (this is generally optional and usually involves some form of reduplication). In some languages (e.g. **Iloko, Karo Batak**) adjectives additionally occur with specific comparative or superlative affixation unavailable for other classes.

As with adjectives, it is usually also possible to define a category of verbs in purely morphological terms, i.e. as the class of morphosyntactic words which are marked for either voice (and aspect/mood) or for person (and mood). An important difference exists between these two basic types of morphologically defined verbs in that for person-marked verbs the morphological category corresponds to a syntactic one (a person-marked verb usually has a clearly distinct syntactic distribution). Such a correspondence is generally much less clear in the case of voice-marked verbs. Their distribution, in particular in Philippine-type languages, often very closely resembles the distribution of (morphological) nouns (see **Seediq** and **Tagalog** for examples).

From a morphological point of view, nouns in western Austronesian languages are usually unmarked. That is, they are not overtly marked for case, number or gender but rather occur in their lexical base form in most uses (a major exception is **Nias**, where nouns occur in either mutated or unmutated form). Optional plural marking (usually via reduplication) is fairly widespread.

Turning now to the lexeme level, it is frequently noted in descriptions of western Austronesian languages that lexical bases (roots) are underdetermined in allowing both nominal and verbal derivations or uses. Alternatively, a basic distinction between nouns and verbs (and possibly adjectives) is made for lexical bases but then it is stated elsewhere in the grammar that nominal bases can be used as (morphosyntactic) verbs essentially in the same way as verbal bases (for example, by prefixing person markers). Once again one has to separate here differences in actual fact from differences in descriptive practice. The issue tends to be further confounded by the terms *root* and *precategorial*, which are used in widely differing ways in the literature. The following basic scenarios have to be distinguished:

- precategorial bound roots, i.e. lexical bases which do not occur without further affixation or outside a compound in any syntactic function and from which items belonging to different morphological or syntactic categories (nouns and verbs, for example) can be derived, without there being clear evidence that one of the possible derivations from a given root is more basic than the other one(s). This is the way Verhaar (1984:2) defined the term *precategorial root*. There is no western Austronesian language where this type of root is very common although sporadic examples are attested in a number of languages, including **Nias** and a number of **Malayic varieties** (Adelaar 1992:145f). In any event, it would be useful to restrict the use of the term *precategorial* to precisely this state of affairs (see also Clynes 1995:203–205).
- morphologically or syntactically subcategorized bound roots, i.e. lexical bases which do not occur without further affixation in any syntactic function but which clearly belong to one particular morphological or syntactic category because of the affixations they occur with. This type of root is attested in some preposed possessor and transitional languages, including **Nias** and **Biak**. It usually concerns verbal roots which obligatorily have to be marked with a person marking prefix before they can function as predicates. Note that such bound verbal roots typically may also co-occur with nominal derivational morphology (for example, to form instrumental nouns or action nominals). But this does not mean that the roots per se are precategorial because the same derivational morphology also occurs with free or derived verbal bases. It is obviously the function of this morphology to turn verbs into nouns regardless of whether the derivational base is a bound verbal root or some other kind of verbal base form.
- multifunctional lexical bases, i.e. lexical bases which occur without further affixation in a variety of syntactic functions. This type of lexical base is attested on the one hand in the isolating languages of Flores and East Timor (e.g. Keo, Waima'a). On the other hand, it occurs with some frequency in the languages of western Indonesia (e.g. Acehnese, many **Malayic varieties**, Ngaju Dayak and possibly Balinese) where 'verbs' are not necessarily marked for voice or person and the same base allows for verbal as well as nominal uses (e.g. Acehnese *jeu* which denotes both 'a type of net' and 'to catch with a net' (Durie 1985:44)).
- morphologically or syntactically subcategorized lexical bases.

In the large majority of western Austronesian languages, most lexical bases would appear to be of the morphologically or syntactically subcategorized type. Note that this assessment allows the possibility that lexical bases are only morphologically but not syntactically subcategorized (or vice versa) or that they are both morphologically and syntactically subcategorized but that morphological classes do not match syntactic classes.

In some languages (e.g. **Kambera**, **Tetun Fehan**), the evidence for a subcategorization of lexical bases is clear and uncontroversial because there are clear-cut distributional differences between nouns and verbs and most (underived) lexical bases fit either one or the other slot. In many of these languages (e.g. **Leti**), there are very productive conversion processes which, for example, allow all non-human nouns and many adjectives and numerals to be turned into verbs simply by adding a subject-marking prefix. But there appears to be sufficient evidence to assign each lexical base to one basic category which then serves as input to the conversion process.

It is exactly the lack of such evidence which causes the problem of assigning a given base to a single basic category in languages with a large number of multifunctional lexical bases. Three types of analyses for multifunctional bases are found in the literature: (a) The bases are assumed to be 'precategorial' in the sense of being unspecified for a morphological or syntactic category. (b) Lexical bases are assumed to occur in homonymous doublets, one subcategorized as a noun, the other as a verb. (c) Each base is subcategorized as a noun or as a verb (or an adjective), with productive conversion processes allowing for non-basic uses. This last option is primarily applied in those instances where lexical bases differ in morphological potential.

In another set of languages, notably the Philippine-type languages, evidence for the subcategorization of lexical bases also appears to be lacking, and in more recent literature these bases have repeatedly been classified as 'precategorial'. A major characteristic of these languages is that almost all lexical bases can be affixed with voice and aspect-mood affixes. For example, Tagalog *p<um>utol* 'to cut down' from *putol* 'cut' and *b<um>ató* 'to stone/throw stones at' from *bató* 'stone' both contain the actor voice marking infix *-um-*. Consequently, one cannot claim that *bató* and *putol* are different kinds of lexical bases because only one of them needs extra derivational morphology in order to become available for voice and aspect-mood morphology. On first sight, then, it may indeed appear that there is little evidence for a morphological subcategorization.

However, such an assessment is somewhat misleading because lexical bases in these languages typically differ with regard to their morphological potential. Thus, for example, Tagalog lexical bases differ as to whether they take either *-um-* or *mag-* or both of these affixes for actor voice marking (see also **Iloko**, **Tsou**, **Seediq**). Consequently, each Tagalog lexical base has to be subcategorized as belonging to the *-um-*, the *mag-* or the *-um-/mag-* class. Morphological classes of this kind are widely considered to be of purely morphological import, comparable perhaps to the inflection and declension classes well known from Indo-European languages. At least, they are usually ignored in the literature on lexical categories and it is a matter for further research whether there are morpholexical classes which are of interest and relevance beyond the realms of morphology (see Himmelmann (to appear a) for further discussion).

As for a possible syntactic subcategorization of lexical bases in Philippine-type languages, the assessment presented above for morphosyntactic words – i.e. that there is no distributional evidence for distinguishing major syntactic categories – of course also applies to lexical bases. The interesting and often overlooked observation here is that almost all lexical bases in these languages may occur without affixes. This is no surprise in the instance of a putatively nominal basis such as *bató* 'stone'. But putatively verbal bases such as *putol* 'cut' may also be used without affixes (in the same slots as putatively nominal bases), and perhaps even more surprisingly, they convey nominal meanings when used in this way. Thus, *putol* without verbal affixations means 'a cut, a piece' as in:

(7) *ang* **putol** *ng* *buhók* *ni* *Huán*
     SPEC   cut   GEN   hair   PN.POSS John
     'John's hair-cut' (Bloomfield 1917:220)

On first sight, these Philippine-type lexical bases may resemble the multifunctional lexical bases mentioned above. However, there are two important differences. In languages with multifunctional bases, there is a genuine morphosyntactic (distributional) difference between nouns and verbs, with verbs being excluded from at least some nominal slots and vice versa. Concomitant with this morphosyntactic difference, multifunctional bases also convey two clearly different meanings depending on which slot they occur in

(Acehnese *jeu* denotes 'a/the net' in a nominal slot and 'to catch with a net' in a verbal slot). In Philippine-type languages, there are no clearly nominal and verbal slots and consequently the meaning of lexical bases does not (in fact, cannot) change in correspondence with a different morphosyntactic function. Instead, it only changes via affixation. In this view, Philippine-type lexical bases are not precategorial, but belong to the last type of bases listed above (i.e. morphologically or syntactically subcategorized): they are syntactically subcategorized as content words and morphologically as belonging to different (derivational) paradigms.

3.2 Clitics

Clitics are probably attested in all western Austronesian languages although there are considerable differences in the number and type of clitics found in a given language (see **Kambera** for a particularly complex example). Formally, a distinction needs to be made between peripheral and second position clitics. Peripheral clitics appear at the beginning or end of the constituent to which they belong (immediately before the verb or at the end of a clause, for example). They are found in practically all western Austronesian languages.

Second position clitics are confined to Philippine-type languages and a few transitional languages (e.g. **Makassar** (only the absolutive pronoun in intransitive clauses), **Mori Bawah** (aspectual clitics only)). They are called second position clitics because they occur after the first constituent of the phrasal unit to which they belong (another term for these clitics is *Wackernagel clitics*). In the following Tagalog examples, the clause core is this unit and the two second position clitics *namán* and *namin* follow its first constituent. In example (a), the first constituent is the predicate *alam*. In example (b), it is the negator *hindí'* and the clitics now occur before the predicate *alam*. Non-clitic expressions such as the personal name phrase *ni=Pepito* do not change their position when a negator precedes the predicate (example (c)).

(8) (a) *alam=**namán**=**namin***
          knowledge=really=1pe.POSS
          'of course we knew'

     (b) *hindí=**namán**=**namin**   alam*
          NEG=really=1pe.POSS   knowledge
          'of course we didn't know'

     (c) *nguni't   hindí   alam   ni=Pepito*
          but   NEG   knowledge   GEN.PN=Pepito
          'but Pepito did not know'

Note that conjunctions such as *nguni't* in (c) do not belong to the clause core and hence do not attract second position clitics. Therefore, 'but of course we knew' is rendered by *nguni't alam=namán=namin* (**nguni't=namán=namin alam* is ungrammatical). See **Tagalog** (section 3.3) and **Kimaragang** (section 3.1.3) for further examples and discussion.

What counts as 'the first constituent of the phrasal unit to which they belong' is not quite as easily determined as the above examples might suggest. Schachter and Otanes (1972:187–193) list a number of complex constructions which appear to function as an uninterruptible unit with regard to clitic placement (see also Kroeger 1993:118–123). Thus, according to Schachter and Otanes, in *isáng taón at apat na buwan siyá* (one LK year and four LK month 3s) 'he is one year and four months old' the second position clitic *siyá* cannot be placed earlier in the clause (**isá siyá-ng taón at* …, **isáng taón siyá at* …, etc.). Unfortunately, such restrictions on clitic placement have been very little studied to date. The Tagalog regularities are not yet completely uncovered, and next to nothing is known about this topic in other Philippine-type languages (see Sneddon (1975: 238–246) for the basic rules in Tondano, which are quite different from those found in Tagalog).

Both peripheral and second position clitics are usually unstressed and form a prosodic unit with either the following word (proclitics) or the preceding word (enclitics). While the lack of stress and the concomitant need to attach to a phonological host are core features of clitics, second position clitics in western Austronesian languages present conflicting evidence in this regard. Most disyllabic clitics such as Tagalog *namán* and *námin* and some monosyllabic ones carry their own stress and thus could be considered independent words. But the fact that with regard to their position they clearly pattern with unstressed second position clitics strongly suggests an analysis as clitics. There is probably also evidence for a clitic analysis in the way the stress of the second position clitics interacts with the stress of the base, but this once again is a topic which has not yet been investigated.

Because of their positional variability, it is generally easy to distinguish second position clitics from affixes. This distinction, however, can be a problem in the case of peripheral clitics, especially proclitics. Thus, for example, the preposed pronouns *ku* and *kau* which are widely attested in **Malayic** constructions such as *buku ini sudah ku=baca* (book PRX already 1s=read) 'I already read this book' are sometimes analyzed as prefixes (*ku-*, *kau-*), and sometimes as proclitics (*ku=*, *kau=*). In many varieties, including Standard Indonesian, there appears to be no clear-cut evidence for preferring one or the other analysis (see also the discussion of cognate forms in **Javanese** and **Karo Batak**). In other instances, there are essentially three types of evidence for distinguishing clitics from affixes: (1) As opposed to affixes, clitics generally do not trigger morphonological alternations of the stem to which they are attached (this includes, for example, the fact that suffixes may cause stress shifts, while enclitics do not). (2) Clitics tend to be less selective than affixes with regard to the category of their hosts (for example, clitics may attach to nouns and verbs, while affixes usually are restricted to (a subclass of) either nouns or verbs). (3) Clitics are sometimes somewhat variable with regard to their position while affix order tends to be rigid.

The phonological attachment of a clitic does not have to match its morphosyntactic function. For example, in Central (or Guinaang) Bontok (northern Philippines) a number of phrase-marking clitics phonologically attach as enclitics to the preceding word while morphosyntactically they indicate the function of the following phrase (cf. Reid 1970, 1992). In example (9) this mismatch of phonological attachment and morphosyntactic function is illustrated by the general locative marker *as* which is usually reduced to just =*s* after vowel-final words (the square brackets indicate syntactic constituency).

(9)   *in-manok*   *nan*   *babái* = [$_{PP}$**s**   *nan*   *masdem]*
      AV-chicken   SPEC   woman=LOC   SPEC   night
      'the woman performs a chicken sacrifice' [$_{PP}$ in the evening] (Reid 1970:23 and p. c.)

The orthographic representation of clitics differs widely across the area. Thus, for example, in the northern Philippines enclitics are usually not separated from their host (and are thus orthographically indistinguishable from suffixes), while in the central Philippines all kinds of clitics are represented as independent orthographic words (compare the examples in the **Iloko** chapter with the ones in the **Tagalog** chapter; the indication of clitic boundaries in the Tagalog example (8) above does not conform to the standard orthography, which is otherwise adhered to throughout this chapter).

With regard to their function, the following major types of clitics are attested in western Austronesian languages:

• **Pronominal clitics**, which are widely attested throughout the area both as peripheral and as second position clitics (see section 3.7).
• **Aspectual/modal clitics**, which are also widely attested throughout the area. In Philippine-type languages they are usually second position clitics, while in the other languages they cluster around the verb as in the following example from Buru:

(10)   *kami*   ***la=ma=te=****iko.*
      1pe   IRR=1p=ABLE=go
      'we want to be able to go' (Grimes 1991:217)

• **Clitic particles**, which cover a wide range of interaction-related functions such as question and politeness markers, evidentials, etc. In Philippine-type languages these are often also second position clitics, while in the other languages they tend to be non-clitic particles, i.e. phonologically and morphosyntactically independent words which do not belong to a major word class.
• **Phrase-marking** and **determiner clitics** such as the Bontok locative preposition *as* (example (9)), the **Tagalog** phrase markers *ang, ng* and *sa* (see also section 3.6), definiteness marking *=nya* in **Colloquial Indonesian** and other **Malayic varieties** (see also section 3.7) or nominalizing proclitics such as Ratahan *to* in *tapi [to napók tee] nangule taa* (but NR AV.PST-CUT DIST AV.PST-return AND.DIR) 'but [those who split them] returned' (Himmelmann and Wolff 1999:34). Most western Austronesian languages have at least one clitic of this type but the distribution across the languages is very uneven and not easily amenable to generalizations.
• **Emphatic clitics** such as Standard Indonesian=*lah* or Buru=*an* which give various kinds of pragmatic prominence to the constituent to which they are attached. Compare the following Buru example:

(11)   *tawe,*   *yako=**an***   *naa*   *te=keha*   *moo.*
      friend   1s=FOC   PRX   ABLE=ascend   NEG
      'Friend, it is me here who can't climb (the tree).' (Grimes 1991:193)

3.3 Clause types I: multiple basic verbal clauses

In most western Austronesian languages, there are a number of verbal clause structures which appear to be equally basic in that they do not seem to be derived from each other or to be clearly rankable with regard to some markedness metric. The best known and most widely discussed example of such multiple basic clause structures is the different voices in symmetrical voice languages to be discussed further below. But there are also other types of variation in basic clause structure for both transitive and intransitive clauses.

Here and in the remainder of this chapter, the terms *transitive* and *intransitive* refer to semantic transitivity, which does not necessarily match morphosyntactic transitivity. A mismatch between the two types of transitivity is found, for example, in English passives such as *I was hit by the guy behind me* where a morphosyntactically intransitive predicate (*be hit*) denotes a transitive state of affairs (see also section 3.4, Clynes 1995:189f, 297–300 and Van Valin and LaPolla 1997:147). Similarly, 'verbal clause' is to be understood in purely semantic terms, i.e. a clause which denotes an event ('going', 'falling', 'digging', 'throwing', etc.). It is of no concern whether the predicate of such a clause is a verb in morphosyntactic terms.

Furthermore, it will be convenient to make use of the widely used abbreviations S for the single core argument of an intransitive clause, A for the more actor-like core argument of a transitive clause, and O for the more undergoer-like argument of a transitive clause. Note that S, A, and O here are convenient abbreviations for referring to the core arguments of verbal predicates and not syntactic-semantic relations of some kind (as in Dixon 1994:6 passim).

With regard to intransitive clauses, there is a phenomenon that has been called split intransitivity, i.e. the availability of two (or more) basic constructional patterns for intransitive verbal clauses in a given language. The most typical split pertains to (semantic) control and volitionality (cf. Mithun 1991). Thus, for example, in Acehnese the S argument is obligatorily cross-referenced by a proclitic if it is conceived of as being in full control of the action denoted by the predicate, as in (12) (the full pronoun *gopnyan* is optional).

(12) *(gopnyan)* ***geu=jak*** '(s)he goes' (Durie 1987:370)
      3s   3s=go

If the S argument is conceived of as undergoing rather than controlling the action (cf. Durie 1985:55–71), it is *optionally* cross-referenced by an *en*clitic, as in:

(13) *(gopnyan)* *rhët (= geuh)* '(s)he falls' (Durie 1987:369)
      3s   fall (= 3s)

These coding properties mirror the properties of the A and O arguments of transitive clauses, where the A argument (*lôn* in (14)) is also obligatorily cross-referenced by a proclitic while the O argument may optionally be cross-referenced by an enclitic.

(14) *(gopnyan)* *ka* ***lôn**=ngieng (=geuh)*
      3s   CPL 1s=see (=3s)
      'I saw him/her.' (Durie 1987:369)

Durie (1987) argues that these similarities between A and S_a arguments (i.e. those S arguments which share their cross-referencing properties with A arguments) on the one hand and O and S_o arguments on the other are not just superficial similarities but rather reflect the fact that Acehnese grammar is basically organized around the macro-roles of Actor and Undergoer. He claims that arguments with the same macro-role exhibit the same set of coding and behavioral properties, regardless of whether they occur in transitive or intransitve constructions (for a further illustration of relevant behavioral properties, see section 3.8.1). On this account, Acehnese is a Split-S language (cf. Dixon 1994:70 passim; Dixon's further distinction between Split- and Fluid-S languages is ignored here). Other possible examples for split-S languages in the area are Dobel (Hughes 2000:147f), Selaru, and **Mori Bawah**, where syntactic factors (rather than control and volitionality) play a major role in determining the choice of a given intransitive construction.

Not all split-intransitive languages are also split-S languages in the strict sense. That is, there may be no single basic intransitive verbal clause type in a given language, but the structural differences between the two (or more) basic intransitive clauses do not have to align with distinctions in transitive clauses in a straightforward way. **Kambera** has been described in this way. **Taba** is another possible candidate since here clear-cut alignments are complicated by the fact that O arguments also appear to be split into two basic types (see below and the detailed discussion in Bowden 2001:154–166).

Arka (1998:50–65) analyzes Balinese as a split-intransitive language based on the fact that intransitive predicates differ with regard to their morphological marking: some are prefixed with *N-* or *ma-*, and others remain unmarked. This difference in morphological marking resembles the kind of morphological marking found on transitive predicates. In undergoer voice, the predicate is morphologically unmarked; in actor voice it is usually prefixed with *N-* (compare example (15)b below). Note, however, that the fact that transitive predicates are never marked with *ma-*, and that therefore the proposed alignment between the intransitive and transitive system is only partial, remains unexplained. Furthermore, it is unclear whether the differences in morphological marking correlate with differences in clause structure.

In a similar spirit, Donohue (1999:482–484) proposes to analyze Tukang Besi as a split-intransitive language based on the fact that intransitive verbs fall into different classes with regard to their morphological potential: only some intransitive verbs may occur with the comitative applicative suffix *-ngkene*, while others may occur with factitive causative *hoko-*, etc. Grimes (1991:99 passim) makes a similar point for Buru. In both instances, however, there appears to be only a single basic intransitive clause structure in which S precedes V (in Tukang Besi, S is also cross-referenced by a pronominal prefix on V).

In most of the world's languages, dynamic and stative intransitives in all likelihood differ with regard to at least one morphological or syntactic property. It is therefore not quite clear whether it is useful to expand the notion of split-intransitivity in line with the proposals just sketched for Balinese, Tukang Besi and Buru, where differences between intransitive predicates primarily pertain to morphology (and semantics). There is, however, no doubt about the fact that the distinction between dynamic and stative predicates is of fundamental importance to the grammar of most western Austronesian languages, as further discussed in section 4.1. If the notion of split-intransitivity is applied to instances of differing morphological marking or potential, then all these languages are split-intransitive. Otherwise, split-intransitivity which is clearly manifest on the level of clause structure would appear to be found only in a number of transitional and preposed possessor languages, a (probably relatively small) subset of these being Split-S languages in the strict sense.

Turning now to transitive clauses, symmetrical voice systems provide one extremely common example of multiple basic transitive clauses in that for any transitive event there are at least two representations, one in actor voice and one in undergoer voice. This was already illustrated with the Standard Indonesian examples (1) and (2) above. Here is another example pair from Balinese:

(15) (a) *bawi-ne punika tumbas tiang.* UNDERGOER VOICE
           pig-DET   DIST   UV:buy 1
      (b) *tiang numbas bawi-ne punika.* ACTOR VOICE
           1   AV:buy   pig-DET DIST
           'I bought the pig.' (Arka 1998:10)

As already mentioned in section 1.2, it is a matter of controversy whether actor and undergoer voice clauses in such pairs are in fact equally basic. For Balinese and some other symmetrical voice languages, it has been argued that the undergoer voice clause is in fact the more basic one. Thus, for example, the undergoer voice verb form *tumbas* in example (a) is morphologically unmarked, while the actor voice form consists of the prefix *N-* plus the base *tumbas*. Note that such an argument does not hold in the case of the Standard Indonesian examples (1) and (2) because in Standard Indonesian both actor and undergoer voice forms are usually prefixed.

Other arguments that are usually invoked in order to show that undergoer voice clauses are more basic or less marked than actor voice clauses include claims that they are more frequent in discourse, that they occur in a wider range of discourse contexts, often being the required construction in a given context, or that they are acquired earlier in language acquisition. We will have the opportunity to look at some of these arguments in more detail in sections 3.8 and 5. Here it will suffice to note that none of these arguments appears to be without problems and that all contributions on symmetrical voice languages in this volume consider the relevant alternations to instantiate different, but equally basic transitive constructions.

Apart from symmetrical voice alternations, other types of multiple basic transitive clause constructions are attested in western Austronesian languages, usually involving some kind of pronominal marking. One type is found in Standard Indonesian and many other **Malayic varieties** (except **Old Malay**) as well as in most symmetrical voice languages of western Indonesia (prominent exceptions are Balinese and Sundanese). In Standard Indonesian, there is a third basic transitive construction type next to the two constructions exemplified in (1) and (2) above. In it, a pronominal actor occurs immediately before the (unaffixed) verb:

(16) *orang*   *itu*   **ku**=*lihat*.
      person   DIST   1s.ACT=see
      'I saw that person.'

It is widely agreed that in this construction the undergoer (*orang itu*) is the subject and the actor pronominal (*ku=*) is a non-subject core argument and that therefore the overall construction is equally transitive as the actor voice construction *anak saya melihat orang itu* in (1) (see Musgrave 2001 for references and discussion). Once again, however, it is a matter of debate whether the constructions are equally basic. Most important in this regard is the fact that the actor+unaffixed verb construction is restricted to pronominal actors and terms of address, including kin terms (*bapak* 'father, Mr.') and personal names (see also **Javanese** and **Karo Batak**).

A somewhat different type of multiple basic transitive clause construction appears to exist in Tukang Besi (cf. Donohue 1999:51–54, 2002). In one type of transitive construction, the A argument is marked with the so-called nominative marker *na* and cross-referenced by a verbal prefix. The O argument is preceded by the so-called core argument marker *te* and not cross-referenced on the verb (schematically: A-V *te* O *na* A):

(17) *no-kiki'i te*   *iko'o*   *na*   *beka*
      3.RLS-bite CORE   2s   NOM   cat
      'The cat bit you.' (Donohue 1999:53)

In a second type of transitive construction, the O argument is cross-referenced by an enclitic on the verb and is also marked with *na*. The A argument is still cross-referenced by a verbal prefix but now it is marked with the so-called core argument marker *te* (schematically: A-V=**o** **na** O *te* A).

(18) *no-kiki'i=ko*   *na*   *iko'o*   *te*   *beka*
      3.RLS-bite=2s.OBJ   NOM   2s   CORE   cat
      'The cat bit you.' (Donohue 1999:53)

Donohue (1999:53f) suggests that despite its greater morphological complexity, this second construction is the more basic one of the two constructions because it occurs more frequently in texts and also has a somewhat wider distribution. At the same time, he considers this alternation a symmetrical voice alternation, the construction with an O-enclitic (example (18)) corresponding to an undergoer voice construction, and the one without it (example (17)) to an actor voice construction (Donohue 1999:160–164). While there are some conspicuous similarities with Philippine-type voice alternations, the fact that there are no voice-marking affixes involved makes it doubtful whether this is really best analyzed as a *voice* alternation (rather than some other kind of symmetrical alternation between transitive construction types).

Note that the specific interaction of person markers and nominal phrase markers illustrated by examples (17) and (18) appears to be attested only in Tukang Besi. But in neighboring Muna a somewhat similar alternation in person marking occurs, which is called *definiteness shift* by Van den Berg (1989: 59–66). In this alternation, (mostly) transitive verbs change their subject class prefix when occurring with a definite object. In the following examples, the two subject prefix classes are simply glossed as I and II respectively:

(19)   (a)   ***ne-rabu   nuhua***   (b)   ***no-rabu-e***
            3sI.RLS-make   pitcher   3sII.RLS-make-3s.OBJ
            'She is making a pitcher.'   'She is making it.' (Van den Berg 1989: 59f)

As this example shows, the different subject marker is triggered inter alia by the presence of an object marking suffix.

Furthermore, other characteristic features of Tukang Besi, including the person markers and the occurrence of a clear passive construction (e.g. *'u-to-kiki'i na iko'o* (2s.RLS-PASS-bite NOM 2s) 'you were bitten' (Donohue 1999:53)), are frequently found in other transitional languages of Sulawesi such as **Mori Bawah** and **Makassar**. For this reason, Tukang Besi is considered a transitional language here rather than a symmetrical voice language. Nevertheless, the example of Tukang Besi shows that the occurrence of multiple transitive constructions is not restricted to symmetrical voice languages.

Finally, it should be mentioned that in a number of transitional and preposed possessor languages, a distinction is made between transitive and semi-transitive clause types which possibly also constitutes an example for multiple transitive constructions. Bowden (this volume) correlates the distinction between transitive and semi-transitive constructions in **Taba** with two types of O arguments, direct and remote undergoers, which differ in that remote undergoers may be optionally marked with an adposition. Inasmuch as this can be usefully analyzed as a split-O system (Bowden 2001:164–166), it would instantiate another type of multiple transitive constructions.

3.4 Clause types II: existential, possessive and equational clauses

It is a common feature of most western Austronesian languages that there are at least one or two non-verbal clause types which play a major role in grammar and discourse. These are, on the one hand, existential clause constructions which often also form the basis for possessive constructions, and on the other hand, equational (equative) clause constructions which play a role in cleft (emphatic focus) and question formation.

The most common existential construction in western Austronesian languages consists of an existential particle or verb which is immediately followed by its complement. Existential particles are unaffixed and thus differ clearly from verbs. Existential verbs usually differ from other verbs by combining only with a small subset of the verbal morphology available in the language (see **Nias**, **Mori Bawa**, **Leti** and **Kambera** for examples). The following Cebuano example illustrates an existential particle:

(20)   ***may***   *tulú*   *ka*   *tawu-ng*   *nangita?*   *nimu.*
       EXIST   three   LK   person-LK   AV.RLS:see   2s.DAT
       'There were three people looking for you.' (Wolff 1972:679)

This example also illustrates a very typical use of existential constructions, i.e. as presentative constructions introducing a new participant into the universe of discourse. In this use, the complement is often further expanded by a relative construction (as in (20)). The other major function of existentials is to indicate availability (or, in negated form, non-availability), as in Cebuano *may sigarilyu* 'there are cigarettes/we have cigarettes'.

The following three features of existential constructions appear to be restricted to symmetrical voice languages, in particular Philippine-type languages. First, in these languages it is possible to combine an existential particle directly with a voice and aspect-mood-marked form, as in Cebuano:

(21)   *may*   ***miinom***   *ug*   *tubig*   *sa*   *kusina.*
       EXIST   AV.PST:drink   OBL.NSPEC   water   OBL   kitchen
       'Someone drank water in the kitchen.'

This use of voice and aspect-mood-marked forms is just another indication of the lack of distributional differences between nouns and verbs characterizing these languages (see section 3.1 above).

Second, numerals and other quantifiers may be used in the function of an existential operator as in **Tagalog** *ma-rami-ng tao-ng na-matáy doón* (ST-amount-LK person-LK RLS.ST-dead DIST.LOC) 'there were many people who died there' (further examples in the **Seediq** chapter).

Third, it is very common that negative existentials are expressed by a negative existential particle which is not in any obvious way derived from the positive one. In Cebuano this is *walá?*:

(22)   ***walá?***   *na=y*   *tubig*
       NEG.EXIST   CPL=LK   water
       'There is no more water.' (Wolff 1972:1122)

The alternative is illustrated by **Malayic varieties** where existential *ada* is negated by the common verbal negator *tidak* (e.g. *tidak ada air* 'there is no water'). This is also the standard pattern attested in transitional and preposed possessor languages.

In a few languages, the element functioning as existential operator also functions as a locative preposition, as in Tetun Dili *iha foos iha ka'ut* (EXIST rice LOC sack) 'there is rice in the sack' (Hull and Eccles 2001:99; see also Muna *bhe*, Van den Berg 1989:160f). **Taba** is claimed to have no native existential expression. And in **Biak** there is an existential verb (based on a deictic root) which appears to be a full verb.

The existential construction also widely functions as the predicate in a clausal possessive construction, to which then another NP denoting the possessor is added. The NP denoting the possessor may occur in two grammatical functions. It may be the subject of the overall construction as in the following examples from Tetun Dili and Cebuano respectively (in (24) the subject pronoun *ka* is a second position clitic):

(23)   **ami**   *iha*   *telemovel*   *ida*
        1pi   EXIST   mobile phone   one
        'We have a mobile phone.' (Hull and Eccles 2001:100)

(24)   *may*   *sigarilyu*   **ka**   *dihá??*
        EXIST   cigarettes   2s   MED.LOC.PST
        'Do you have any cigarettes on you?' (Wolff 1972:679)

Alternatively the possessor NP may be expressed as a genitive attribute to the possessum (so that the literal meaning of the overall construction is something like *X's Y exists*). Compare the following Muna example:

(25)   *miina*   *bhe*   *doi-**ku***
        NEG   EXIST   money-1s.POSS
        'I do not have any money.' (Van den Berg 1989:161)

Possessive constructions built from a more basic existential construction are by far the most common strategy for possessive clauses throughout the area. The major alternative is an equational construction in which the possessum occurs in subject position and is ascribed to the possessor which functions as the predicate of the overall construction. In Tetun Dili, the possessor occurs in a special form, marked with the possessive suffix *-nian*:

(26)   *ne'e*   *sira-nian,*   *la'ós*   *ami-nian.*
        PRX   3p-POSS   NEG   1pi-POSS
        'This is theirs, not ours.' (Hull and Eccles 2001:34)

In most languages which allow such a construction, however, the possessor predicate is marked as a dative or locative phrase, as in Tagalog *sa nanay ang relos* (LOC mother SPEC watch) 'the watch belongs to mother' (Schachter and Otanes 1972:273).

Full verbs meaning 'have', 'own' or 'belong' are only sporadically attested. Where they exist, they tend to be used infrequently (major exceptions include Balinese where the most common possessive clause type involves the verb *ngelah* 'possess, own'). See **Taba** for a very unusual derived possessive verb based on possessive pronominals.

The Tetun Dili and Tagalog examples just mentioned also illustrate the basic pattern for equational clauses. These consist of a simple juxtaposition of a subject and a predicate phrase. There is no copula in most western Austronesian languages (major exceptions are West Papuan languages such as Ambai and **Biak**). In Philippine-type languages the basic order in equational clauses tends to be PREDICATE–SUBJECT while in most other languages, including many symmetrical voice languages in Indonesia, the order is SUBJECT–PREDICATE. Typical predicates are simple nouns (Madurese *Siti ghuru* 'Siti is a teacher') or prepositional phrases (Madurese *Buku-na nəng meja* (book-DET at table) 'the book is on the table' (Davies 1999a:26)).

The equational clause format is often used in clefts and content questions. In questions, the question word usually becomes the predicate while the remainder of the clause functions as the subject, often in the form of a headless relative construction or some other kind of nominalization. Compare the following example from Tukang Besi:

(27)   *te*   *emai*   *na*   *'umelo-'elo-aku*   *iso?*
        CORE   who   NOM   REL: RDP-call-1s.OBJ   DIST
        'Who is it that's calling me there?' (Donohue 1999:57)

In Tukang Besi and most other languages, this strategy is either optional or restricted to a subset of questions. In Tukang Besi, for example, it is obligatory only for subject questions (Donohue 1999:451f). In these languages, there is usually also a question-forming strategy where the question word remains in situ. **Biak** is somewhat exceptional in requiring the fronting of question words without imposing an equational structure.

In many Philippine-type languages, the equational clause-strategy is obligatory for clefts and content questions (at least for core roles; there are exceptions, in particular in Taiwan, e.g. Pazeh). In fact, starting with Bloomfield (1917) it has repeatedly been suggested that the basic clause structure in these languages is equational (see, for example, Scheerer 1924, Lopez 1937, Capell 1964, Lemaréchal 1991, Naylor 1995, Egerod 1988, DeWolf 1988, Himmelmann 1991). That is, the structure of verbal (or narrative) clauses is said to be essentially identical to that of equational clauses. Schachter and Otanes (1972:62) hint at this possibility with the following observation:

> It may, in fact, quite reasonably be argued that the distinction made above between equational and narrational sentences in Tagalog is a somewhat arbitrary one, and that all Tagalog basic sentences, including those here treated as narrational, are essentially equational in nature, involving a balancing of two elements – the predicate and the topic [i.e. subject, NPH] – against one another.

Compare the following Tagalog examples (based on Schachter and Otanes 1972:61f), where the (a) examples are generally considered equational, while the (b) examples are generally considered verbal:

(28) (a) *artista   ang   babae*   (a′) *babae   ang   artista*
           artist   SPEC   woman   woman   SPEC   artist
           'The woman is an artist.'   'The artist is a woman.'

      (b) *y<um>aman   ang   babae*   (b′) *babae   ang   y<um>aman.*
           <AV>riches   SPEC   woman   woman   SPEC   <AV>riches
           'The woman got rich.'   'The one who got rich is a woman.'

The only difference between these sentences is that in the (b) examples there is a voice and aspect/mood-marked word (*yumaman*). But it is questionable whether voice and aspect/mood marking has any clause-structural consequences. Thus, for example, voice and aspect/mood-marked words like other content words may appear in predicate as well as in subject position without any concomitant morphosyntactic changes. Furthermore, there are many ways of rearranging the content words in these examples (for example, one could topicalize *babae* as in *ang babae ay artista/yumaman*), but there is not a single alternative pattern which would clearly distinguish the (a) from the (b) examples. Note that essentially the same possibilities hold for semantically transitive expressions:

(29) (a) *asawa   ko   siyá*   (b)   *m<in>ura   ko   siyá*
           spouse   1s.POSS   3s   <RLS(UG)>scolding   1s.POSS   3s
      (a′) siyá   ang   asawa   ko   (b′) siyá   ang   minura   ko
      (a″) siyá   ang   aking   asawa   (b″) siyá   ang   aking   minura
      'She is my wife/he is my husband.'   I scolded him/her.

The equational clause hypothesis rests on the fact that essentially the same set of pronominal forms and phrase makers are used for arguments and adjuncts regardless of whether the predicate is (semantically) nominal or verbal. There are also no particles, negators or other kinds of grammatical markers which would clearly distinguish between a verbal and an equational clause type.

Nevertheless, there are two major empirical problems for this hypothesis. First, it is unclear how to account for control constructions and other kinds of multipredicate constructions under this hypothesis. In particular, the fact that in some languages (not standard Tagalog) verbal subjunctive forms occur in these constructions would appear to be not easily explainable within this framework (see sections 3.9 and 4.2.2). Second, there are in fact some minor differences in the marking of adnominal and verbal arguments, as is further discussed in section 3.6.

To date, these two problems have not yet been explicitly addressed by the proponents of the equational hypothesis. Hence it is unclear whether and in which form this hypothesis can be upheld. But in line with the quote from Schachter and Otanes (1972) given above, it should be obvious that verbal and equational clauses are very similar indeed in many Philippine-type languages and that the degree of their similarity constitutes an important parameter for both the internal and external typology of western Austronesian languages.

Very roughly, western Austronesian languages fall into three major types of languages with regard to this parameter: (1) languages where the two clause types are so similar that their distinction may be questioned (many symmetrical voice languages of the Philippine type); (2) languages where the distinction is not in doubt but where there are still quite a number of important similarities (the remaining symmetrical voice languages and some transitional languages); and (3) languages where the distinction between the two clause types is very clear and little overlap exists (some transitional languages and most preposed possessor languages).

3.5 Word order and constituency

Western Austronesian languages differ with regard to preferred basic word order and the strictness of ordering relations. Symmetrical voice and transitional languages are either predicate-initial, with a tendency to be also subject-final (i.e. 'VXS'), or favor a subject-predicate ('SVO') order. In most of these languages, however, there is some word order flexibility and more often than not it is unclear whether the so-called basic or unmarked order reflects a syntactic constraint or a pragmatic preference (see also Cumming 1991). Preposed possessor languages tend to follow an SVO pattern and to be somewhat more rigorous in adhering to this basic pattern.

The preceding generalizations are easily challengeable on methodological and empirical grounds. There is no need to repeat here the well-known methodological problems of statements on basic word order (see LaPolla and Poa (to appear), for a recent summary). Empirically, we may note that in symmetrical voice languages, for example, statistically manifest preferences vary according to voice type. For Balinese, Pastika (1999, chapter 6) finds that in more than 90% of the actor voice clauses in his corpus, the subject (=actor) NP precedes the predicate. In undergoer voice clauses, on the other hand, there is no such clear-cut preference, undergoer voice subjects being equally likely to precede or follow the predicate (see also Artawa et al. 2001).

Other word order generalizations are empirically much more robust. Adpositions are generally prepositions in western Austronesian languages (some of which may not have any adpositions at all, see section 3.6), although the odd postposition is also sporadically attested (e.g. **Karo Batak, Taba**). Auxiliaries generally precede main verbs. Negators also generally precede the negated constituent, with the exception of most preposed possessor languages, where negators usually occur in clause-final position (not in **Tetun Fehan** and only in part in **Leti**). Possessors generally follow the possessum, except of course in preposed possessor languages where non-pronominal possessors precede the possessum (see section 3.11). For (cardinal) numbers and other quantifiers the converse tendencies hold: they generally follow the head noun in preposed possessor languages, but precede it in most symmetrical voice and transitional languages. Otherwise, adnominal modifiers generally follow the head, with demonstratives being placed at the very end of an NP. In Philippine-type languages, however, the order of constituents in noun phrases is highly flexible and there are no clear-cut ordering rules, except that cardinal numbers tend to be placed at the beginning of an NP and genitive-marked possessors have to follow the possessum.

It has occasionally been claimed in the literature that some western Austronesian languages are free word order languages, sometimes even allowing every possible commutation of a verbal predicate and its core arguments (Uhlenbeck 1975 is an example). This is almost certainly an overstatement of the facts. To begin with, no western Austronesian language allows the constituents of noun phrases or prepositional phrases to be distributed discontinuously across the clause as is found in Latin or in Australian languages. Hence, if anything, western Austronesian languages could be free phrase order languages.

But even phrase order is probably not completely free in any of these languages. As shown by Davies (1999b) for Madurese and Javanese and Arka (1998:119–182) for Balinese, apparently free phrase ordering options are structurally constrained and usually intonationally marked in such a way that they clearly instantiate topic, cleft, or rightward expansion constructions. That is, for core constituents the phrase ordering options in a basic unmarked clause are usually restricted, allowing at most for one or two alternations. As in many other languages, the placement of adjuncts (including adverbs) tends to be somewhat less restricted. The alternation between absolute vs. oblique forms in Kerinci (**Malayic varieties**, section 5) provides strong historical evidence for the relevance of phrasal boundaries on various levels.

In many western Austronesian languages there is, in fact, good evidence for a VP constituent which contains the predicate and all non-subject core arguments. Non-subject core arguments generally have to occur in immediate post-predicate position. That is, neither the subject nor adjuncts may intervene in between the predicate and its non-subject arguments (exceptions include postverbal clitics and sometimes a restricted set of adverbs). Compare the following example from Totoli (see also Donohue (1999:151 passim) for Tukang Besi and Artawa *et al.* (2001:15) for Balinese):

(30)   *gaukan*   [$_{VP}$*no-gutu*   *ponguman*   *itu]*
      king   AV.RLS-make   story   DIST
      (Yesterday) the king made this announcement: ...
      (a)   *nogutu **gaukan** ponguman itu
      (b)   ***ponguman itu** nogutu gaukan

As the (a) example shows, it is not possible to place the subject (*gaukan*) in between the verb (*nogutu*) and the non-subject argument (*ponguman itu*). Furthermore, it is not possible to exchange the positions of subject and non-subject argument, as seen in (b). It is, in principle, possible to place the non-subject argument in clause-initial position (i.e. *ponguman itu, gaukan nogutu*). But this is clearly a topicalization construction in which the non-subject argument occurs outside the clause core and, among other things, forms a prosodic unit of its own (as indicated by the comma).

In symmetrical voice languages, the same kind of evidence points to the fact that in undergoer voice clauses the verb and the non-subject actor argument form a kind of VP constituent, as seen in the following example from Totoli:

(31) *kopi*   *ia*   [*vp ni-pogutu*   *i*   *Andris]*.
      coffee   PRX   RLS(UG)-make   PN   Andrew
      'Andrew made this coffee.'

Once again, subjects (*kopi ia*) or adjuncts cannot intervene in between verb (*nipogutu*) and non-subject actor argument (*i Andris*). The topicalization of the non-subject actor argument (i.e. placing *i Andris* in clause-initial position) is strongly dispreferred by speakers and not attested in spontaneous data.

It is a matter for further debate whether the 'VP' constituents in (30) and (31) are indeed sufficiently similar to warrant the same label. In fact, the nature of clausal constituents in western Austronesian languages has been very little studied to date and there are almost certainly many details still to be uncovered (useful but far from complete discussion can be found in Kroeger 1993:118–166, Arka 1998, Davies 1999b, and Musgrave 2001). Two problems, however, are already reasonably clear at this point.

First, while there is good evidence that the predicate and non-subject arguments form a constituent in most western Austronesian languages, it is also clear that the evidence varies with the nature of the non-subject argument. Thus, as just mentioned, non-subject undergoer arguments in actor voice constructions (such as *ponguman itu* in (30)) can usually be topicalized without any problems, but non-subject actor arguments in undergoer voice constructions (*i Andris* in (31)) cannot (see also **Karo Batak**). Furthermore, Arka (1998:124f) claims that in Balinese there is a significant difference between indefinite or non-referential and definite non-subject undergoer arguments. Only definite non-subject undergoer arguments (such as *ia* in *cang ng-runguang ia ditu* (1 AV-care.for 3 DIST.ADV) 'I cared for him/her there') can be topicalized and allow the insertion of certain adverbs after the verb.

Second, for some Philippine-type languages it is occasionally claimed that the order of arguments in post-predicate position is essentially free. In particular, the subject is said to be allowed to intervene in between predicate and non-subject arguments, resulting in a VSX order as in the following widely used Tagalog example:

(32) *b<um>ili*   **ang**   **babae**   *ng*   *tinapay*   *sa*   *tindahan*   *para*   *sa*   *bata'*
      <AV>buy   SPEC   woman   GEN   bread   LOC   store   for   LOC   child
      'The woman bought some bread at the store for the child.'

While sentences such as these are judged acceptable by some native speakers, they do not occur in natural discourse and are thus of questionable value. There are two problems with these examples. First, in Tagalog natural discourse, as probably in most languages, clauses containing more than one full NP are rare (see DuBois 1987). Second, and more importantly, full (non-pronominal) subject NPs never precede genitive-marked arguments and usually also follow locatives and benefactives (i.e. in natural discourse *ang babae* in (32) would always follow *ng tinapay* and in most instances in fact occur at the very end of the clause).

For Tagalog, there is one type of exception to this claim. Subject expressions consisting of a (short) personal name, which are marked by *si* rather than by *ang*, sometimes occur in immediate post-predicate position:

(33)   *nag-pa-sundó'*   **si Andrés**   *ng*   *isa-ng*   *pare'*
        RLS.AV-CAU-fetch   PN   GEN   one-LK   priest
        'Andrés sent for a priest' (Bloomfield 1917:92)

Bloomfield calls this ordering *enclitic positioning* (1917:153) since in this example the proper noun occupies the clitic position that is usually occupied by second position clitics (see section 3.2). This analysis implies that there are severe restrictions on the placement of non-pronominal subject expressions before other argument expressions. So far, however, the nature of these restrictions has not yet been investigated in any Philippine-type language.

3.6 Case marking, adpositional phrases and the core vs. peripheral distinction

Western Austronesian languages are generally not case-marking languages. No western Austronesian language has case affixes. However, in a very few instances alternations exist which are similar to affixal case alternations. These include the alternation between mutated and unmutated forms in **Nias** and the absolute vs. oblique alternation in Kerinci (cf. ADELAAR, MALAYIC VARIETIES). Furthermore, many symmetrical voice languages and a few transitional languages have paradigms of phrase-marking clitics which are often called case markers but which usually also convey specificity, definiteness or even deictic distinctions.

   Before looking more closely at these phrase-marking clitics, a few remarks on adpositions are in order. Since there are only very few postpositions in western Austronesian languages (see section 3.5 above), the discussion here will be limited to prepositions. Compared to Indo-European languages, the inventory of primary (or simple) prepositions tends to be fairly small. A typical inventory contains a smallish number of local prepositions (e.g. Standard Indonesian static locative *di* 'in, on, at', etc., allative *ke* 'to', ablative *dari* 'from') and a comitative-instrumental preposition (e.g. Standard Indonesian *dengan* 'with'). It is not uncommon that a single primary preposition can be used for stative locative as well as source and goal relations (e.g. **Kambera** *la*, Muna *we*). Local prepositions may usually also be used for temporal relations (**Kambera** *la mbaru* 'in the morning'). Further additions to the basic inventory tend to have fairly specific meanings and to be attested only in a few languages (Standard Indonesian, for example, also has *untuk* 'for', *oleh* (for agents in passives), and *tentang* 'about, concerning').

   More specific local relations are usually expressed with the help of relational expressions for body parts ('head', 'back', etc.) or relational object parts ('front', 'centre', etc.). These relational expressions are often combined with a locative primary preposition as in Standard Indonesian *di atas* 'above', *di bawah* 'beneath', or *di muka* 'in front'. Another strategy is the use of deictic or directional particles in prepositional functions. Thus, for example, Buru proximal *na(a)* may not only be used as a pronoun or adnominal modifier but also as a locative preposition. In the following example, it occurs in both functions (the short form *na* is conditioned by the non-final position).

(34)   *da*   *kaduk*   *na*   *huma*   *naa.*
        3s   come   PRX   house   PRX
        'He came here to this house.' (Grimes 1991:172)

In fact, much of what Lichtenberk (1991) observes for directional and prepositional elements in Oceanic languages also holds for western Austronesian languages, especially preposed possessor languages.

TABLE 5.2: CEBUANO AND TAGALOG NON-PERSONAL PHRASE MARKERS

	Cebuano	Tagalog	
SPECIFIC (ARTICLE)	ang	ang	SPECIFIC (ARTICLE)
OBLIQUE SPECIFIC	sa	ng [naŋ]	GENITIVE
		sa	LOCATIVE
OBLIQUE NON-SPECIFIC	ug	ng/LINKER	

TABLE 5.3: CEBUANO AND TAGALOG PERSONAL NAME MARKERS

	Cebuano	Tagalog
(NOMINATIVE)	si	si
POSSESSIVE	ni	ni
DATIVE	kang	kay

Apart from primary prepositions and complex prepositions consisting of a primary preposition and another relational expression, many western Austronesian languages also show weakly grammaticized prepositions, i.e. words which may be used as content words (usually verbs) and as prepositional function words. Standard Indonesian *sampai*, for example, functions both as a preposition 'until, as far as' (as in *sampai sekarang* 'until now') and as a verb 'arrive, reach' (as in *pukul enam pagi kami sampai* (strike six morning 1pe arrive) 'we arrived at six a.m.'). See also **Belait** and **Tetun Fehan**.

Philippine-type languages (and Tsou and Rukai) are languages with absolutely minimal inventories of primary prepositions. In fact, several of these languages have been analyzed as having no primary preposition at all (e.g. **Tsou**, see also **Kimaragang**). Such an assessment depends very much on the analysis of the phrase-marking clitics which occur in most of these languages. These clitics usually come in two paradigms, one for personal names and one for all other kinds of nominal expressions. Table 5.2 and Table 5.3 give the paradigms for two closely-related Meso-Philippine languages, Cebuano and **Tagalog**.

The personal name markers are always obligatory. Considerable variation exists with regard to the obligatoriness of the non-personal phrase marking clitics. In many languages, including Cebuano and Tagalog, the specific article *ang* may be omitted in a number of contexts, for example when the nominal expression occurs in topic position preceding the predicate. The other non-personal phrase markers generally cannot be omitted in Cebuano and Tagalog. In Pazeh, however, most non-personal phrase markers are said to be optional (Li and Tsuchida 2001:31).

Perhaps the most important fact to note about the paradigms given in Table 5.2 is that the distribution of the non-personal markers differs significantly despite the great formal similarities of the markers and the relative closeness of the two languages in geographical as well as typological terms (see **Seediq, Tsou, Iloko, Kimaragang,** and **Buol** for examples of further variation). Their distribution is roughly as follows: the unmarked specific form is used in both languages for subjects, topics and predicates of identificational clauses (e.g. Cebuano *si Ana ang guapa* 'the pretty one is Ana'). The specific oblique form *sa* in Cebuano is used in all other functions, including possessors (e.g. *nanay sa bata?* (mother OBL child) 'the child's mother'), adjuncts (*sa kusina* in (21)), actors in undergoer voice clauses and undergoers in actor voice clauses. The non-specific oblique form is used for obliques the referential identity of which is unknown or irrelevant (e.g. *anák ug hari?* (offspring OBL.NSPEC king) 'a king's offspring'). With regard to adjuncts, it mostly occurs with expressions corresponding to English manner adverbials, as in *milakáw siyá ug kusúg* (PST.AV:walk.away 3s OBL.NSPEC fast) 'she walked away fast' (Wolff 1972:1077).

In Tagalog, specificity plays a less prominent role in the distribution of the phrase markers. For possessors and actors in undergoer voice constructions only genitive *ng* is used and most kinds of adjuncts are marked by *sa*. The marking of undergoers in actor voice constructions is split among locative *sa* and genitive *ng*, animate and definite undergoers usually being marked by *sa*, and all others by *ng* (see below and **Tagalog** for further details and examples). Thus, there is no single marker corresponding to Cebuano *ug* which in Tagalog is sometimes rendered by *ng*, sometimes by the linker *na*.

The distribution of the personal name markers differs in some important details from those of the non-personal markers and is essentially identical across both languages (and most other Philippine-type languages). Possessive *ni* is used only for possessors and actors in undergoer voice clauses, never for undergoers in actor voice clauses or adjuncts. Dative *kang/kay* is used for recipients, addressees and other core undergoer roles in actor voice clauses. If personal names are used as adjuncts – not a frequent occurrence – the non-personal phrase marker *sa* precedes the *kang/kay*-marked personal name, as in Tagalog:

(35) *t<um>anggáp   sila   ng   isá-ng   gawáng   ka-bait-an*
      <AV>received   3P   GEN   one-LK   made:LK NR-kindness-NR
      sa   kay   Maria
      LOC   DAT.PN   Maria
      '(there were not any who could say that) they had received any kindness from Maria.' (Bloomfield 1917:76)

From a cross-linguistic point of view, the distribution of the non-personal markers in particular is somewhat unusual. To date, there is no standard analysis and terminology in use for these forms in the literature on western Austronesian languages. A recent survey by Reid (2002:286f) shows that more than two dozen labels have been used in reference to them, including *articles/determiners*, *prepositions*, *case markers* and *relation markers*. Note that this lack of terminological agreement also holds for individual markers in individual languages. Thus, for example, Tagalog *ang* has been glossed 'nominative', 'absolute', 'specific', 'subject', 'topic', 'trigger', etc. Consequently, the labels used in Table 5.2 and Table 5.3 are not standard in any sense.

The analysis of the phrase markers is very closely related to the analysis of other aspects of Philippine-type morphosyntax, in particular basic clause structure, grammatical relations and voice alternations, as will be evident from discussion in the relevant sections (3.3, 3.8, 4.2). Regardless of the choices determined by these aspects, however, it is quite clear that the phrase markers have characteristics of both determiners ('articles') and prepositions. The split between non-personal and personal markers is typical for determiners. Note also that *ang*, Tagalog *ng* and in some uses Cebuano *sa* can be replaced by demonstratives (e.g. Tagalog *sundalo ng sultan* 'the sultan's soldiers' can also be rendered by *sundalo nitóng sultan* (soldier GEN.PRX sultan)). In some languages (e.g. **Tsou**), in fact, all phrase markers also convey deictic distinctions.

On the other hand, Tagalog *sa* (and to a lesser degree Cebuano *sa*) is preposition-like not only because of its uses for adjuncts but also because it is a (usually obligatory) constituent of all complex prepositions such as Tagalog *tungkól sa* 'about, regarding', *hanggáng sa* 'until' or Cebuano/Tagalog *para sa* 'for', Cebuano *human sa* 'after', etc. Perhaps even more importantly, Tagalog *sa* and phrases headed by *sa* allow stative affixations which clearly bring out its essentially local meaning, for example, *na-sá-sa loób ng katawán* (RLS.ST-RDP-LOC heart GEN body) 'being within the body' (Bloomfield 1917:44).

Historically speaking it is highly likely that some phrase markers were in fact prepositions and others were deictics, and that the present paradigms thus consist of these two types of elements (cf. Himmelmann 1998). This mixed origin also contributes to the problems of their analysis. Note, for example, that the answer to the question of whether there are any primary prepositions in Philippine-type languages depends on whether one considers the oblique marking phrase markers such as Tagalog and Cebuano *sa* prepositions.

Perhaps the most far-reaching problem posed by the phrase marking paradigms is the problem that they rarely, if ever, provide clear-cut evidence for distinguishing core arguments from peripheral arguments (or adjuncts). That is, it is rarely the case that a given marker only applies to core arguments and another only to peripheral arguments. Tagalog *ng*, for example, is not only used for patients, themes and goals – i.e. roles one would expect to occur in core argument positions – but also for instruments:

(36)   *p<in>utol*   *niyá*   **ng**   **gulok**   *ang*   *kahoy*
        <RLS(UG)>cut   3s.POSS   GEN   bolo   SPEC   wood
        'S/he cut the wood with a bolo.' (Bloomfield 1917:175)

Arguably, *ng* is also used for manner and time (see Schachter and Otanes 1972:437f, 452f and Ross 2002:29) which, however, is somewhat obscured by the fact that in these functions it is orthographically represented as *nang*. Recall from above that Cebuano *ug* is also used for manner expressions.

Similarly, while Tagalog *sa* is used for a broad range of more peripheral roles, including location and time, it is also the regular marker for goals, recipients and addressees, and for definite patients and themes as in:

(37)   *itó*   *ang*   *pusa-ng*   *k<um>ain*   **sa**   **dagá'**
        PRX   SPEC   cat-LK   <AV>eat   LOC   rat
        'This is the cat that ate the rat.' (McFarland 1978:157)

Thus, the distribution of the phrase-marking clitics in Philippine-type languages does not reflect in any direct way the distinction between core and peripheral arguments. One may, in fact, doubt that such a distinction exists in these languages, an assumption which forms the core of the equational clause hypothesis mentioned above (section 3.4; cf. also Ross 2002:30).

However, two caveats have to be added to this conclusion. First, there may be other ways to diagnose a core vs. peripheral distinction. Kroeger (1993:40–47), for example, argues that in Tagalog all *ng*-marked arguments, including instruments, are core arguments and that all *sa*-marked arguments are peripheral. The argument invokes control phenomena and the fact that only *sa*-marked arguments allow fronting into a position immediately preceding the predicate. Arka (1998) and Arka and Manning (to appear) use evidence from reflexive binding to argue that only some actors in undergoer voice constructions in Balinese and Standard Indonesian are core arguments, while others are peripheral arguments. Musgrave (2001:67ff) supports the analysis of the Standard Indonesian data with evidence from quantifier floating. (Note that according to this argument, the Standard Indonesian example (2) above (*orang itu dilihat anak saya* 'my child saw that person') is a passive construction, with *anak saya* functioning as an oblique adjunct. However, if the actor is replaced by a pronominal clitic (as in *orang itu di-lihat=nya* (person DIST PV-see=3.POSS) 's/he saw that person'), then the actor is a core argument and the overall construction a true symmetrical voice construction.)

Second, the distribution of the phrase marking clitics is also not fully accounted for by the equational hypothesis. The problem here is the definiteness alternation associated with *ng* vs. *sa* marking in **Tagalog** actor voice constructions (similar definiteness or specifity-related alternations in most other Philippine-type languages, but the details vary significantly). As shown by (37), undergoers in these constructions may be marked with *sa* and then are clearly definite. If *sa* in this example is replaced by *ng*, the preferred interpretation is specific-indefinite ('a rat') or even non-specific ('the cat that eats rats'). Contrary to what is often claimed in the literature, *ng* marking does not preclude a definite interpretation, as amply illustrated in McFarland (1978). In fact, as McFarland (1978:157) makes clear, there are four options in phrasing this sentence:

(38) (a) itó ang pusang kumain **sa** dagá'   unambiguously
                                                          definite=(37)

      (b) itó ang pusang kumain **ng** dagá'   indefinite or non-
                                                          specific preferred, but
                                                          definite also possible

      (c) itó ang pusang kumain **ng** **isáng** dagá' unambiguously indefi-
                                                          nite (*isá*='one')

      (d) itó ang pusang kumain **ng** dagáng **iyón** unambiguously definite
                                                          (*iyón*=DIST)

This definiteness-related *ng/sa* alternation is problematic for the equational hypothesis for the following reason. It seems to occur only in construction with voice-marked forms ('verbs'). In semantically clearly possessive constructions such as *bahay ng lalaki* (house GEN man) 'the/a man's house' there is (a) no preference for an indefinite interpretation of *lalaki* (in fact, a definite interpretation is more likely); and (b) *ng* cannot be replaced with *sa* (such a replacement would result in a barely acceptable expression meaning something like 'house at/on/in the man').

Cross-linguistically, this definiteness alternation is known as *differential object marking* (Comrie 1979, Lazard 2001). As is common in languages with differential object marking, the alternation is most consistently observed for animate beings. Thus, the basic rule is that definite expressions for animate beings receive a more oblique-like marking (in Tagalog *sa*) when occurring in non-subject undergoer functions. Personal pronouns and personal names, which are inherently definite, in fact tend to be restricted to an oblique (dative) form in these functions, as just noted for the Cebuano and Tagalog personal name markers.

The definiteness alternation is also of major relevance to the ergative hypothesis to be discussed in section 3.8.2 below. According to this hypothesis, actor voice constructions are antipassives, i.e. intransitive constructions where undergoers may occur only in oblique positions. Strictly speaking, this hypothesis would predict that in Tagalog all undergoers in actor voice constructions are marked with *sa*, which is evidently not the case. Alternatively, one could argue that *ng*-marked undergoers in these constructions are in some way incorporated objects, which makes sense for non-specific undergoers and perhaps also for indefinite-specific ones (as in (38)c). But the fact that examples such as (38)b allow a definite interpretation, and that (38)d is at all possible, is difficult to account for on the assumption that these are antipassive constructions.

The preceding discussion was mostly concerned with Philippine-type languages. The core-peripheral distinction is usually much clearer in the other western Austronesian languages. Nevertheless, many of these languages allow alternations where a construction with preposition alternates with one without it as in the following Tetun Dili example:

(39) *ha'u   hanoin   (kona-ba)   ha'u-nia   main.*
     1s   think   about   1s-POSS   mother
     'I'm thinking about my mother.' (Hull and Eccles 2001:156)

As indicated by the parentheses, the preposition *kona-ba* can be omitted in this example, which in turn raises the question of whether *ha'u-nia main* is a core or a peripheral argument. See Bowden (this volume and 2001:157–166) for a more detailed discussion relating to similar examples in **Taba**.

Finally, it should be noted that in *all* western Austronesian languages all kinds of arguments can be omitted, i.e. there are no clear syntactic constraints on argument omission which could be used for distinguishing core and peripheral arguments (see section 5 for examples).

3.7 Pronouns and person marking

Almost all Austronesian languages make a distinction between first-person inclusive (speaker + addressee) and exclusive forms (speaker(s) only). This distinction is found in all paradigms of personal pronouns, regardless of their form (full, clitic, affixed) or function (subject marker, possessive suffix, etc.). A notable exception to this generalization among the western Austronesian languages is some Malayic varieties where this distinction has been lost (cf. Donohue and Smith 1998 and ADELAAR, MALAYIC VARIETIES).

Western Austronesian pronoun systems do not usually include dual or trial forms (exceptions include Iban and **Biak**). Third person forms are often restricted to human or animate referents, demonstratives being used in pronominal reference to inanimates. Full pronominal forms often include a personal article (or politeness clitic). Second person singular forms are usually used only in addressing friends or inferiors. Otherwise, politeness rules of various complexity are to be observed, which often forbid the use of pronouns in addressing people, for whom special terms of polite address or personal names are used instead (particularly complex systems of this type are found in western Indonesian languages, see FOX, RITUAL LANGUAGES and **Javanese**).

Most western Austronesian languages have a special paradigm of possessive pronouns, usually enclitics or suffixes. More often than not, these possessive pronouns (or forms more or less identical to them) occur also in other functions such as actor pronouns in undergoer voice constructions, etc.

Western Austronesian languages differ significantly with regard to person markers. The term *person marker* is used here as a cover term for both agreement markers (for example, the third singular formative *-s* in English *play-s*) and person markers proper, which are also called *pronominal arguments* (a term avoided here because of its controversial implications). Agreement markers and person markers proper have two characteristics in common: (a) they are affixed or cliticized to the predicate (or occur in a special clitic position); and (b) they may occur with a coreferential full nominal expression within the same nuclear clause. In the following Uma example, the third person singular prefix *na-* co-occurs with the coreferential noun phrase *tobinena* 'his wife'.

(40) ***na-**manyu   **tobine-na**   pae   toe.*
     3s-pound   woman-3s.POSS   rice   DIST
     'His wife pounded the rice.' (Martens 1988b:248)

The condition 'within the same nuclear clause' is intended to exclude instances of pronominal crossreference to nominal expressions which occur in a clearly clause-external position, for example as topics or rightward expansions ('afterthoughts'). Such constructions are possible in many, if not all, languages (cf. English *it doesn't bring out the best in people, **divorce***) and hence they are of no diagnostic value for person marking.

One way of distinguishing between agreement markers and person markers proper is that agreement markers generally require the co-occurrence of a coreferential nominal expression within the same clause (as in English or German), whereas person markers proper do not. According to this criterion, all person markers in western Austronesian languages are person markers proper.

Otherwise, western Austronesian languages differ widely with regard to the form and function of person markers. In fact, the southern half of Sulawesi and the Lesser Sunda islands are something of a laboratory attesting a bewildering variety of person marking systems. See **Mori Bawah**, **Makassar**, and **Kambera** for a glimpse of this variety, Haaksma (1933) for an early comparative study, and Mead (2002) for more recent discussion and references. Here we will only list some of the more remarkable features.

Person markers occur, on the one hand, in most transitional and preposed possessor languages (major exceptions are the isolating languages in the Flores – Timor region). On the other hand, they also occur in a few of the northernmost languages, i.e. the Philippine languages of northern Luzon (Kapampangan and languages further to the north) and a few Formosan languages, including **Tsou**, Rukai, and Pazeh (which only has one person marker, i.e. the first person inclusive prefix *ta-*; cf. Li and Tsuchida 2001:33,37). Furthermore, they occur in the two Micronesian outliers Chamorro and Palauan.

However, there are important differences between these two main person marking areas. Most importantly, all person marking systems in preposed possessor and transitional languages include at least one series of pronominal prefixes or proclitics while person markers in the northern languages usually only involve enclitics (which are also often second position clitics; Pazeh *ta-* is an obvious exception). Furthermore, in the northern systems third person forms are sometimes missing ('third person is zero'), which does not happen in preposed possessor and transitional languages. With regard to these two features, the two Micronesian outliers clearly pattern with the transitional and preposed possessor languages.

The pronominal prefixes and proclitics in most preposed possessor languages and some transitional languages crossreference S and A arguments and thus are usually called subject prefixes/proclitics. These languages differ as to whether use of the person markers is obligatory (as in **Nias**, Muna, Tukang Besi, Kedang, **Leti**, **Taba**, **Biak**) or optional (as in Buru and Alune). The subject marking prefixes often show very strong fusional tendencies in that they require the setting up of different inflectional (or conjugation) classes (this is particularly widespread in the Moluccas, but it is also attested in Muna and Kedang). In some preposed possessor languages, including **Taba**, Dobel and Selaru, the prefixes only crossreference A and S_a arguments (S arguments of dynamic verbs), which is a typical characteristic of split-intransitive languages (see section 3.3 above).

A conspicuous feature of a number of transitional languages (including **Nias**, Muna, and Tukang Besi) is the presence of two series of pronominal prefixes/proclitics, one for realis mood and one for non-realis (or irrealis) mood, a feature which is also very common in western Oceanic languages (see also the future series in **Mori Bawah**). In these series, it is usually impossible to separate person marking from mood marking formatives. In this regard they are similar to the voice-mood affixes in Philippine-type languages, which also cannot formally be separated into voice and mood marking segments (see section 4.2.2).

With very few exceptions, two person-mood marking prefix series are found neither in symmetrical voice languages nor in preposed possessor languages (Chamorro is a major exception among the symmetrical voice languages). But quite a few symmetrical voice languages in Sulawesi and western Indonesia show one (often incomplete) series of pronominal proclitics marking person and non-realis mood (see section 4.2.2).

Person markers for O arguments are not attested in preposed possessor languages but they do occur in a number of transitional languages (e.g. **Kambera**, Tukang Besi). Note also that there are often special enclitic or suffixal forms for pronominal O arguments in preposed possessor languages (e.g. Alune =*ma* 'first person plural transitive undergoer') but these do not co-occur with coreferential nominal expressions and hence are not person markers according to the definition above.

In a number of transitional languages (including **Makassar**) and northern symmetrical voice languages, in particular Kapampangan, person markers show ergative alignment, i.e. there is one marker for S and O arguments (=*i* in (41) and (42)) and another one for the A argument (*ku*=in (42)), as in the following two examples from Konjo:

(41) *a'-lampa=**i***
      INTR-go=3.ABS
      'S/he goes.' (Friberg 1996:140)

(42) ***ku**=kanre=**i***
      1.ERG=eat=3.ABS
      'I am eating it.' (Friberg 1996:153)

However, in most of these languages, there are a number of syntactic contexts where ergative alignment is suspended. In **Makassar** and Konjo, for example, S arguments are regularly crossreferenced by the 'ergative' prefix after negation and a number of adverbials (compare Konjo *anre' **ku**='-lampa* (NEG 1.ERG=INTR-go) 'I am not going' (Friberg 1996:152)). Perhaps even more remarkable from a crosslinguistic point of view is the fact that there are constructions where both core arguments are crossreferenced by 'ergative' prefixes. In Konjo this happens, for example, when the completive maker =*mo* is added to the predicate (see Friberg 1996:168):

(43) ***ku=na**=peppe'=mo   Ali.*
      1.ERG=3.ERG=hit=CPL   Ali
      'Ali hit me.' (Friberg 1996:168)

In a number of languages, including Uma and **Tsou**, only the A argument is regularly crossreferenced by a person marker, while the S and O arguments are expressed either by pronominal clitics or by full NPs but not both.

In addition to person markers, there are also definiteness or specificity marking clitics or suffixes which are identical to, or derived from, pronouns, in particular in the languages of Indonesia. Thus, for example, the third person possessive pronoun has clearly extended uses in many **Malayic varieties**, including **Colloquial Indonesian**, Balinese, Madurese, **Tetun Fehan**, etc. (cf. Himmelmann 1997:219f on possessive articles). See also the so-called indexer clitic in **Leti** and the pronominal articles in **Biak**.

3.8 Grammatical relations

In most preposed possessor languages the identification of a subject relation in verbal clauses is uncontroversial. The grammatical relation systems in these languages are usually characterized by nominative-accusative alignments (S and A arguments share the same coding and behavioral properties, while O arguments show a different set of properties; see **Tetun Fehan**, **Leti** and **Biak** for exemplification). However, there is also often some evidence for split-intransitivity (see section 3.3), and some languages (e.g. **Taba**) are explicitly analyzed as having a mixed nominative-accusative and split-S system.

The nature of grammatical relations in symmetrical voice languages and in many transitional languages continues to be a matter of controversy. The crux of this debate is the question of whether one can identify a subject relation in these languages. A related, though not identical question is whether they are best analyzed as ergative languages. Alternatively, they make up a type of their own or they are split-S languages ('active' languages in the sense of Klimov (1977)). Subjecthood will be discussed first.

3.8.1 Subjecthood

Following a paper by Keenan (1976), it has been widely accepted in the typological literature that the grammatical relation *subject* found in European languages applies to an argument expression which exhibits a specific set of coding (e.g. the subject is morphologically unmarked) and behavioral properties (e.g. the subject can be relativized), distinguishing it from other core arguments of the same predicate. While Keenan lists some thirty properties, the discussion of the distribution of such properties in western Austronesian languages has concentrated on the ones listed in Table 5.4. Following Schachter (1976) and Foley and Van Valin (1984), these properties are grouped in two subsets. Some properties are considered to be *reference-related* in that they reflect the fact that subjects tend to provide topical (or given) information. Other properties are called *role-related* because they appear to be linked to the fact that subjects tend to be actors (in basic underived transitive clauses).

The properties listed in Table 5.4 (and a few others) are discussed and illustrated in detail in Schachter (1976, 1995), Kroeger (1993:19–39), Cena (1995) and Donohue (1999:463–481), among others. Here it will be sufficient briefly to illustrate those properties mentioned in discussions of subjecthood in the grammar sketches assembled in this volume. For *relativization* see section 3.10.

Quantifier floating refers to the phenomenon widely attested in the languages of the world that quantifiers do not have to occur within the nominal expression they quantify. Thus, for example, the Tagalog quantifier *lahát* may occur either within the quantified NP (as in (44)) or immediately after the predicate, as in (45), where it is called a *floated quantifier*.

TABLE 5.4: SUBJECT DIAGNOSTICS COMMONLY USED FOR WESTERN AUSTRONESIAN LANGUAGES

Reference-related properties	Role-related properties
Coordinate conjunction reduction	Control of reflexives
Raising	Controllee in control constructions
Relativization	Addressee of imperatives
Agreement	
Quantifier floating	

(44) *sinúsúlat*   *ng   mga   bata'   ang   **lahát**   na   mga   liham*
RDP:RLS(UG):write   GEN   PL   child   SPEC   all   LK   PL   letter
'The children write all the letters.'

(45) *sinúsúlat*   **lahát**   *ng   mga   bata'   ang   mga   liham.*
RDP:RLS(UG): write   all   GEN   PL   child   SPEC   PL   letter
'The children write all the letters.' (Kroeger 1993:22)

Floated quantifiers in Tagalog and other western Austronesian languages are of relevance to the problem of subjecthood because they are often unambiguously related to only one of the two core arguments of a transitive predicate, i.e. the one marked with the specific article *ang* (or an equivalent pronominal form). Thus, example (45) cannot mean *All the children are writing letters*. In order to express this with a floated quantifier, one has to convert the clause from undergoer voice to actor voice so that *mga bata'* occurs in the *ang*-phrase:

(46) *sumúsúlat*   **lahát**   *ng   mga   liham   ang   mga   bata'.*
RDP:AV:write   all   GEN   PL   letter   SPEC   PL   child
'All the children are writing letters.' (Kroeger 1993:22)

If in a given language only one of the two core arguments of a transitive predicate is able to launch a floated quantifier, this is typically the subject argument. Therefore, so the argument goes, the ability of *ang*-phrases to launch quantifiers is one argument in favor of considering *ang*-phrases subjects.

A *raising* construction involves two clauses, a matrix clause and an embedded clause, the latter functioning as a complement of the matrix clause predicate (as in [*I expect [that Linda will sing the national anthem*]]). In many languages it is possible to *raise* to the matrix clause an argument which semantically belongs in the subordinate clause, and to make it structurally an argument of the matrix predicate. In (47), a 'normal' Tagalog complement clause construction without raising, *pambansáng awit* 'national anthem' is structurally part of the complement clause, functioning as subject of the complement clause predicate *awitin* 'sing'. In (48) it is raised, now functioning as the subject argument of the matrix clause predicate *inasahan* 'expect, hope'.

(47) *<in>asah-an*   *ko   [na   awit-in   ni   Linda*
<RLS(UG) >hope-LV   1s.POSS   COMP   song-PV   PN.POSS   Linda
ang   pambansáng   awit]
SPEC   GER:nation:LK   anthem
'I expected (for) Linda to sing the national anthem.' (Kroeger 1993:28)

(48) *<in>asah-an*   *ko   **ang   pambansáng   awit***
<RLS(UG)>hope-LV   1s.POSS   SPEC   GER:nation:LK   anthem
[na   awit-in   ni   Linda]
COMP   song-PV   PN.POSS   Linda
'I expected the national anthem to be sung by Linda.' (Kroeger 1993:28)

The diagnostic value of the raising construction resides in the fact that typically not all core arguments of the complement clause predicate can be raised in this way. For Tagalog, it is claimed that only phrases marked by *ang* (or an equivalent pronominal form) allow raising (but see Kroeger 1993:28f for some complications). Thus, in (47) it is not possible to raise the other core argument of the complement clause predicate *awitin*, i.e. *Linda*, which is marked by the possessive marker *ni* (**inasahan ko si **Linda** na awitin ang pambansáng awit* is ungrammatical).

Control (or *Equi-NP deletion*) constructions also consist of a matrix and an embedded clause. In these constructions, the matrix predicate and the embedded predicate share one core argument (thus in *I avoided looking at Linda* the pronoun *I* is an argument of both *avoid* and *looking at*). In many languages, this shared argument can be overtly expressed only once in the overall construction, leaving one of the argument slots of the embedded predicate empty (it is impossible to say in English **I avoided I/me looking at Linda*). But there is never a doubt as to the reference of the omitted argument, the empty argument slot of the embedded predicate (the controllee) being controlled by an argument of the matrix predicate (the controller). Often there are restrictions on the choice of the controllee in that not all argument slots of the embedded predicate can become controllees. In English, the controllee has to be the subject of the embedded predicate. Hence, both *I$_i$ want e$_i$ to look at Linda* and *I want Linda$_i$ e$_i$ to look at me* are fine, but it is impossible to omit the object *me* in the second clause (**I$_i$ want Linda to look at e$_i$*).

In Tagalog and many other western Austronesian languages no such clear-cut grammatical constraint on controllee choice seems to exist. In fact, the relevant facts appear to be quite complex and continue to be a matter of controversy (cf. Kroeger 1993:38f, 71–107 and Schachter 1995:21–27). Here it will suffice to note that at least in some control constructions the grammatical function of the controllee (whether it appears in an *ang*-phrase or in a genitive phrase) is irrelevant as long as the omitted argument is the actor of the embedded predicate:

(49) (a)   *<um>iwas*   *akó-ng*   *t<um>ingín* *kay*   *Linda.*
           <AV>avoidance 1.SG-COMP <AV>look   DAT.PN Linda

      (b)   *<um>iwas*   *akó-ng*   *tingn-án* *si*   *Linda.*
           <AV>avoidance 1.SG-COMP look-LV   PN   Linda
           'I avoided looking at Linda.' (Kroeger 1993:39)

In (49)a, the controllee, if overtly expressed, would have to occur in the *ang*-form (*tumingín akó kay Linda*) because it is the actor in an actor voice construction. In the (b) example, an undergoer voice construction, it would have to occur as a possessive pronoun (*tingnán ko si Linda*). Given such examples, it is clear that *ang*-phrases in Tagalog are not the only possible controllees in control constructions, a point where they differ quite clearly from subjects in European languages.

In *coordinate conjunction reduction* two conjoined main clauses share an argument which remains unexpressed in one of the conjuncts. Thus, in *Peter looked at me and left without another word* the subject of *left* remains unexpressed but, importantly, there is absolutely no ambiguity as to who actually left (i.e. *Peter*). As Kroeger (1993:33f) points out, Tagalog seems to allow basically any core argument to be omitted in such constructions, regardless of its semantic role or grammatical function. In the following example, the actor of the predicate *hinugasan* in the second clause remains unexpressed:

(50) *ni-luto'*   *ni*   *Josie* *ang* *pagkain*
     RLS(UG)-cooked PN.POSS Josie SPEC GER:eating

     at   *h<in>ugas-an*   *ang* *mga* *pinggán*
     and   <RLS(UG)>washing-LV SPEC PL   dish
     'The food was cooked by Josie, and the dishes washed (by her).' (Kroeger 1993:34)

Overtly expressed, the actor would have to be a possessive pronoun *niyá*, hence the 'complete' version of the second clause would read *hinugasan **niyá** ang mga pinggán*.

Kroeger (1993:36) argues that omissions such as the one illustrated in example (50) are actually instances of zero anaphora for which the same constraints hold within a sentence and across sentence boundaries (see section 5 below). Zero anaphora is to be distinguished from 'true' or logical conjunction reduction in which it is possible to omit an argument in the first conjunct, i.e. before its 'antecedent' has actually been mentioned:

(51) *hú-hugas-an*   *ko*   *at*   *pú-punas-an*   *mo*
      RDP-washing-LV   1s.POSS   and   RPD-wipe-LV   2s.POSS

     ang   *mga*   *pinggán*
     SPEC   PL   dish
     'I will wash and you dry the dishes.' (Kroeger 1993:34)

Here the undergoer of *húhugasan* (i.e. *ang mga pinggán*) remains unexpressed in the first clause. According to Kroeger, logical conjunction reduction is only possible for *ang*-phrases. For example, it would be unacceptable to omit the actor expression in the first conjunct of two undergoer voice clauses (as in ?**húhugasan ang mga pinggán at púpunasan ko* for 'I will wash and dry the dishes').

After this brief review of the subjecthood diagnostics most commonly used in the Austronesian literature, we will now turn to a discussion of their application to western Austronesian languages. It will be useful to begin with a brief review of the discussion of subjecthood in Tagalog (see also McKaughan 1973, Matsuda French 1988, Kroeger 1993:19–22). The Spanish grammarians in the seventeenth and eighteenth centuries as well as authors such as Bloomfield (1917), Blake (1925) and Lopez (1937) use the term *subject* in their descriptions of Tagalog without further comment and consistently apply it to the *ang*-phrase in post-predicate position. In the 1950s, a number of researchers affiliated with the Summer Institute of Linguistics saw the need to highlight the differences between Philippine and European languages with regard to grammatical relations and used *topic* for the *ang*-phrase in post-predicate position (and *focus* instead of *voice*). McKaughan, who seems to be the first to have used *topic* in this sense in print (McKaughan 1958), in a later paper (1973) considers this an unfortunate and possibly misleading move and reverts to calling the *ang*-phrase in post-predicate position a subject.

Schachter (1976) reopens the debate by arguing that in Tagalog subject properties such as the ones listed in Table 5.4 are distributed among the two core arguments of a transitive construction and that therefore neither of them can truly be considered a subject. Schachter's claim continues to be widely quoted and accepted in the typological as well as the formal syntax literature. Within the Austronesianist literature, however, support for this analysis has been on the wane, especially since Kroeger's (1993) detailed and largely convincing critique of Schachter's results (DeWolf's (1979:67–86, 1988:144–150) very similar argument has been largely ignored in the literature). Kroeger argues that there are quite a number of subject properties (including the reference-related ones in Table 5.4) which uniquely apply to the *ang*-phrase. Furthermore, he shows that the subject properties which do not uniquely apply to the *ang*-phrase (most importantly control of reflexives and target in control constructions) also do not uniquely apply to any other core argument of a transitive verb and hence are irrelevant to determining subjecthood in Tagalog. Consequently, the only sensible candidate for subjecthood in Tagalog is the *ang*-phrase in post-predicate position (see Cena 1995 and Schachter 1995 for a critique of this argument and conclusion).

From Kroeger's argument it does not necessarily follow, however, that the *ang*-phrase is indeed the subject of a Tagalog clause. Such a conclusion very much depends on the additional assumption that it is sufficient for a given argument expression to exhibit a number of subject properties to qualify for subjecthood. That is, it is still possible to argue that *ang*-phrases are not subjects because they do not show enough subject properties or the right subset of subject properties (which in turn presupposes a catalogue of properties that have to hold uniquely of an argument expression in order to qualify for subjecthood).

Although the property list-approach to subjecthood is the one most widely used in the more recent literature, it should be noted that this is not the only possible approach. The original intuition of the Greek and Latin grammarians who coined the terms *subject* and *predicate* pertained to equational (or nominal) clauses such as *She is an actress*. Such clauses are clearly bipartite, consisting of a referential expression denoting the entity about which an assertion is made – the subject – and an expression conveying the assertion – the predicate. It is a matter of cross-linguistic variation to what degree this simple bipartite structure can also be applied to narrative (or verbal) clauses such as *She collects doors*. Transitive narrative clauses consist of a verb (*collects*) and two arguments (*she, doors*). Applying the bipartite structure of equational clauses to narrative clauses presupposes an asymmetry in the relationship of the two arguments to the verb in such a way that one argument forms a closer unit with the verb and thus is interpreted as being part of the predicate (assertion) while the other argument provides the referential anchor or basis for the predication, denoting the entity about which the predication is made.

Languages differ with regard to the degree to which equational and narrative clauses are structurally similar. In Arabic, for example, the two clause types have very little in common (equational clauses have subject-predicate order, narrative clauses have verb-actor-undergoer order, etc.). In Indo-European languages, there are significant overlaps between equational and (many) narrative clauses in that, for example, one argument in a narrative clause usually receives the same case marking as the subject of an equational clause (i.e. nominative case) and the verb of the narrative clause agrees with this argument (and only with this argument) in the same way as the predicate agrees with the subject of an equational clause. This, essentially, is the reason why in grammatical analyses of Indo-European languages the term *subject* has been applied to the one argument in narrative clauses which is most similar to the subject of an equational clause.

The traditional approach to subjecthood outlined in the preceding paragraphs has been repeatedly criticized for being too vague to be of much practical value. The properties approach to subjecthood can be seen as a way to make one insight of the traditional approach more operational by providing tests for diagnosing asymmetries between the core arguments of narrative clauses. And this is in fact the major use that has been made of Keenan's putative subject properties in the Austronesian literature. They are used to test for morphosyntactic asymmetries between core arguments. Since in Austronesian languages these properties rarely cluster in the same way as in European languages, it is a widespread practice to use the term (syntactic) *pivot* instead of *subject* for arguments which are privileged vis-à-vis other arguments in that they uniquely show a number of morphosyntactic properties. (Note that there is a second, overlapping but more restricted use of *pivot* where it refers to the argument which is privileged in clause combining, for example, the omitted argument in coordinate constructions (cf. Dixon 1994:11). On its likely first appearance in Heath (1975:99), *pivot* refers only to the controllee in control constructions.)

However, the asymmetry between the core arguments of a narrative clause is only one aspect of the traditional subject intuition. The other major aspect demands that the privileged argument of a narrative clause displays morphosyntactic properties also displayed by the subject in an equational clause. These two aspects do not necessarily correlate with each other. To give just one, somewhat superficial example: in most preposed possessor languages, it is possible to mark the A argument in a transitive narrative clause by a prefix or proclitic on the verb (see also section 3.7). In the following Buru example, it is a proclitic:

(52)   *Ya=paha*   *ringe*   'I hit him.' (Grimes 1991:151)
      1s=hit   3s

There is no comparable paradigm of forms to mark the O argument on the verb, hence the existence of the proclitic series could be taken as evidence for an asymmetry between A and O arguments, privileging the A argument. However, the proclitics are restricted to verbal predicates (Grimes 1991:373). They cannot be used with the nominal predicates characteristic of equational clauses. Therefore, the existence of a series of pronominal proclitics does not render A arguments similar to the subjects of equational clauses, and their diagnostic value for determining subjecthood in the traditional sense is thus questionable.

If formal similarity to the subjects of equational clauses is taken to be the major criterion for diagnosing subjecthood in narrative clauses, one could argue that subjects of narrative clauses in Tagalog and many other symmetrical voice languages are in fact *more* subject-like than subjects of narrative clauses in European languages, simply because narrative and equational clause structures in Tagalog are very similar indeed. As discussed in section 3.4 above, proponents of the equational hypothesis in fact hold that there is no narrative clause type in Tagalog and that with the exception of a few minor clause types (e.g. existential clauses) all clauses follow an essentially equational pattern. But even if one does not subscribe to this hypothesis, many analysts would agree that the similarities between the two clause types are considerable in these languages (see, for example, the quote from Schachter and Otanes (1972:62) presented above in section 3.4).

From this point of view it would appear to be ironic that a group of languages where the subject relation is clearly manifest has been at the center of recent discussions concerning subjecthood. In this regard, it will be helpful to take note of the fact that all discussions of subject properties in symmetrical voice languages which are framed within Keenan's property list-approach fail to adhere to a very basic parameter set by Keenan. At the beginning of his 1976 paper, Keenan makes a considerable effort to define the notion of *semantically basic sentences*, and the ensuing subject property list only holds for *basic subjects* which occur in such *basic sentences*. In English, the basic sentence is identified with an active transitive clause. Consequently, the properties of subjects of passive sentences, for example, do not appear on the list.

In discussions of symmetrical voice languages, on the other hand, actor voice as well as undergoer voice clauses are used in the argument (without further discussion!), on the assumption that they are both equally basic. The fact that subject properties appear to be distributed across different arguments in these languages is a direct consequence of this use of multiple basic transitive constructions. It is not clear, however, whether Keenan's methodology is in fact applicable to languages with multiple basic transitive constructions.

3.8.2 Alignment systems: ergative, split-S or none of the above?

As mentioned in the introduction to this section, there is little controversy with regard to the assessment that preposed possessor languages show either nominative-accusative or mixed nominative-accusative and split-S alignments in their systems of grammatical relations. For symmetrical voice languages and many transitional languages, however, the issue of their basic alignment system continues to be heavily contested. Yet to begin with, we may note that it is widely agreed that most of these languages are *not* nominative-accusative. Furthermore, Acehnese has been forcefully argued to be a split-S language (Durie 1985, 1987). Split-S characteristics are also found in most other symmetrical voice and transitional languages but it is questionable whether these characteristics actually pertain to the clause level and thus are relevant for determining the alignment system (see section 3.3 above).

The major controversy, then, pertains to the question of whether symmetrical voice languages show ergative alignment or rather constitute a type of their own (for a brief illustration of ergative alignment, see examples (41) and (42) above). Ergative analyses of symmetrical voice and transitional languages have been proposed in quite a number of ways (for example, by Payne 1982, DeGuzman 1988, Martens 1988a, Blake 1988, Mithun 1994, Wechsler and Arka 1998). Practically all aspects of these proposals have been criticized in an equally varied number of ways (see, for example, Cumming and Wouk 1987, Shibatani 1988, DeWolf 1988, Kroeger 1993:47f, Schachter 1995:38–51, Foley to appear). Here no attempt is made to review the debate in detail but the following three general observations may be of use in assessing its relevance to typological concerns.

As mentioned in section 3.7, clear cases of ergative alignments in western Austronesian languages usually pertain to the distribution of person markers in languages such as Kapampangan, **Makassar**, Bugis, etc. The interesting point to observe here is that the distribution in western Austronesian languages is the converse of that found in many other ergative languages in, for example, Australia. That is, while in Australian ergative languages it is very common to find a split between a nominal case marking system showing ergative alignment and a pronominal or person marking system showing nominative-accusative alignment, in western Austronesian languages clear-cut cases of ergative alignment are restricted to person marking systems, with little or no evidence of an ergative distribution of noun phrase markers.

A second point that seems to be widely overlooked in the sometimes heated debate regarding ergativity in western Austronesian languages is the fact that very little follows from the assessment that a given language shows evidence of ergative alignment, as stated clearly in Dixon's recent survey of the phenomenon (where western Austronesian languages are excluded from further consideration):

> What then does it mean for a language to be ergative? Exactly what we said in the first paragraph of Chapter 1– that S is treated in the same way as O and differently from A in some part or parts of the grammar. *Nothing else necessarily accompanies this.* (Dixon 1994:219, emphasis added)

That is, showing that a given language is ergative is of comparatively little typological import in that nothing else correlates with it. And it is probably fair to say that most proponents of an ergative analysis would agree that putatively ergative western Austronesian languages have very little in common with ergative languages in other parts of the world, with the possible exception of Mayan languages (Martens 1988a:270f).

Third, it bears emphasizing that diagnosing ergativity or accusativity presupposes a reasonably clear distinction between syntactically transitive and intransitive constructions in a given language. Furthermore, it helps a lot when core arguments are clearly distinguishable from peripheral arguments. It would appear that these two preconditions are not, or at least not very clearly, fulfilled in many symmetrical voice languages, as argued in sections 3.3 and 3.6. In this view, much of the ergativity debate misses an essential point in that it focuses on providing evidence for ergative alignments rather than for the transitive/intransitive and core/oblique distinctions presupposed by such an alignment.

The last point indicates one possible venue for determining the place of symmetrical voice languages in a comprehensive typology of systems of grammatical relations. That is, in addition to the well-established distinction between nominative-accusative, ergative and split-S ('active') languages, one would need a superordinate parameter which distinguishes languages with clear-cut syntactic transitivity distinctions from those where transitivity is less clearly manifest in the morphosyntax (see also Egerod 1988). Nominative-accusative and ergative-absolutive systems presuppose grammaticized transitivity distinctions while syntactic transitivity distinctions are largely irrelevant for symmetrical voice and split-S systems.

3.9 Multi-predicate constructions: auxiliaries, complex predicates, serial verbs, and the like

Western Austronesian languages are rich in multi-predicate constructions, i.e. constructions which involve two or more phonologically independent predicate expressions within a single clause. However, there are many unresolved descriptive and theoretical issues with regard to these constructions, and it would be premature to attempt any typological generalizations at this point. The purpose of the present section is simply to point out some of the phenomena which eventually would have to be covered by typological generalizations.

Elements termed *auxiliaries* are widely attested in descriptions of western Austronesian languages. Such elements usually convey notions of tense, aspect, mood, negation, or manner. Some of them are clearly clitics and hence do not qualify as phonologically independent predicates in multi-predicate constructions. But others are phonologically independent and also often have some other characteristics of independent predicates. For example, **Tsou** auxiliaries – which are obligatory in all verbal clauses – do not only determine the tense and mood of the clause but are also marked for voice and are suffixed with person markers (in some contexts):

(53) ***mo-'u***   *bonɯ*   *to*   *tacɯmɯ*
     AV.RLS-1s   AV:eat   OBL   banana
     'I ate a banana.'

Some auxiliaries determine the form of the following predicate expression. Thus, the Cebuano past tense negator *walá?* (which also serves as negative existential, see (22) above) requires that the following 'main' predicate occurs in subjunctive form (see also section 3.7 in **Seediq**):

(54) *walá?*   *niya*   *lutu-a*
     NEG.PST   3s.POSS   cook-PV.SUBJ
     'He did not cook it.' (Wolff 1972:1121)

Kroeger (1993:139) proposes a complex predicate analysis for a similar construction involving the Tagalog negative imperative auxiliary *huwág*. He also notes (1993:181–201) that so-called 'pseudo-verbs' such as Tagalog *gusto* allow for two alternative constructions, one a biclausal control construction (55), the other a monoclausal complex predicate construction (56).

(55) **gusto**   ng   nanay   (na)   **p<um>untá**   sa   tindahan
     liking   GEN   mother   COMP   <AV>direction   LOC   store
     'Mother wants to go to the store.' (Kroeger 1993: 184)

(56) **gusto-ng   p<um>untá**   sa   tindahan   ang   nanay
     liking-LK   <AV>direction   LOC   store   SPEC   mother
     'Mother wants to go to the store.' (Kroeger 1993:184)

Note in particular the different phrase marking for 'mother' in the two examples. In (55) *nanay* is preceded by genitive *ng*, as required by the 'pseudo-verb' *gusto*. In (56) it is marked with *ang*, as required when functioning as the subject of actor voice *pumuntá*.

Tagalog 'pseudo-verbs' (Schachter and Otanes 1972:261–273) are auxiliary-like in that they convey modal meanings ('want, like', 'must', 'ought', 'able', etc.) and are not marked for aspect/mood and voice (or only allow a reduced set of such markers). They differ from typical auxiliaries in that they also allow for main predicate uses (e.g. *gusto ko itó* (liking 1s.POSS PRX) 'I want this').

Many other western Austronesian languages also have predicative expressions which occur both as independent predicates and in some kind of complex predicate construction with other predicates. These are not restricted to modal expressions. Another typical and widely attested class of such predicates are directionals. In the following two examples from Ratahan, the first illustrates the use of a directional as an independent predicate (with further directional proclitics). The second example shows the same directional in construction with another predicate:

(57) *ku=ta=sá*   *e*   Kinaepesan
     MOTION=AND=DIR   CPL   Kinaepesan
     '(We) **went on down** to Kinaepesan.' (Himmelmann and Wolff 1999:79)

(58) *te*   *tintúr*   **sá**   *ngkami*
     te   in -ntur   sa   ni=kami
     CON   PST-deliver   DIR   GEN=1pe
     'So we carried it **down there**.' (Himmelmann and Wolff 1999:79)

Compare also the discussion of **Buol** *maa* 'go' and *magi* 'come' and sections 3.3 in **Mori Bawah**, 3.4 in **Nias**, 3.8 in **Seediq**, and 3.7 in **Belait**.

In a number of western Austronesian languages a second predicate within a clause is used to introduce an additional argument, as in the following Tukang Besi example:

(59) *no-helo?a*   *te*   *roukau*   **ako**   *te*   *ana-no*
     3.RLS-cook   CORE   vegetable   do.for   CORE   child-3.POSS
     'He cooked the vegetables for his children.' (Donohue 1999:182)

Such constructions are considered prototypical examples of *serial verb constructions* in the literature. They have been sporadically reported for western Austronesian languages, including some **Malayic Varieties**, **Taba** and **Tetun Fehan** (and of course **Moken/Moklen** and **Cham**, where their occurrence is part of the typological profile of Southeast Asian mainland languages).

Finally, as noted by Kroeger (1993:196), in Tagalog and possibly other western Austronesian languages it appears that some controlled complement constructions show features of complex predications (i.e. they are mono- rather than biclausal) quite similar to the 'pseudo-verb' example (56) given above. In the following Tagalog example, the standard linker *na* is missing and only a few clitic elements would be allowed to appear in between the two predicates:

(60) *ang*   *tuláy*   *ay*   **ipinagbawal**   **gamitin**
      ang   tuláy   ay   i-in-pag-bawal   gamit-in
      SPEC   bridge   PM   CV-RLS(UG)-GER-forbidden   use-PV
      'The bridge was condemned (forbidden to be used).' (English 1986)

Appropriate ways to analyze the preceding constructions are still very much a matter of debate. Apart from considering them auxiliary or complex predicate constructions (with serial verb constructions being one type of complex predicates), some of these constructions are perhaps best analyzed as verbal compounds, as advocated by Klamer for **Kambera**.

3.10 Relative clauses

Western Austronesian languages are famous for their restrictions on the formation of relative clauses and have been of major import for the noun phrase accessibility hierarchy proposed by Keenan and Comrie (1977). The basic and central observation is that among the core arguments of a predicate, only subjects may be relativized. That is, the head to which the relative clause is attributed has to be the subject of the relative clause. Compare the following examples from Tagalog widely cited in the literature (in Tagalog, relative clauses are attached to their heads with a linker):

(61) (a) *isdá-ng*   *i-b<in>igáy*   *niyá*   *sa*   *bata'*
           fish-LK   CV-<RLS(UG)>gift   3s.POSS   LOC   child
           'the fish which she gave to the child'

      (b) *bata-ng*   *b<in>igy-án*   *niyá*   *ng*   *isdá'*
           child-LK   <RLS(UG)>gift-LV   3s.POSS   GEN   fish
           'the child to whom she gave the fish'

      (c) **isdá-ng*   *nag-bigáy*   *siyá*   *sa*   *bata'*
           fish-LK   RLS.AV-gift   3s   LOC   child

      (d) **isdá-ng*   *b<in>igy-án*   *niyá*   *ang*   *bata'*
           fish-LK   <RLS(UG)>gift-LV   3s.POSS   SPEC   child

In the (a) and (b) examples, the head of the relative clause (*isdá'* in (a) and *bata'* in (b)) is also the subject of the relative clause predicate which shows the appropriate voice affixation (conveyance voice in (a) and locative voice in (b)). There is also no nominal expression within the relative clause which formally could function as a subject (in which case it would have to appear in the *ang*-form). In the (c) and (d) examples, this is not the case, and these examples are therefore ungrammatical. In (c), the head of the relative clause (*isdá'*) is the theme argument of the predicate *bigáy*, but the predicate is marked for actor voice, not conveyance voice, which indicates that the actor (*siyá*) is its subject. Similarly, in (d) the relative clause predicate is marked for locative voice, indicating that the recipient (*ang bata'*) is the subject.

Note that the grammatical function of the head of the relative clause in the main clause is of no relevance to the grammaticality of the overall construction. Thus, the Tagalog equivalents of *The fish which she gave to the child smelled bad* (*fish* is subject), *I could smell the fish which she gave to the child* (*fish* is object), or *They returned with the fish which she gave to the child* (*fish* is oblique) are all grammatical.

There are two important qualifications with regard to the subjects-only constraint on relativization. First, this constraint is widely attested only in symmetrical voice languages. Transitional languages and preposed possessor languages usually allow all core arguments to head relative clauses. Occasionally, essentially the same relativizing strategy may be used for all core arguments (e.g. **Tetun Fehan**, **Taba**). More commonly, however, there are a number of different relative clause structures depending on the grammatical role of the head noun within the relative clause. This is briefly illustrated here with examples from Tukang Besi (see also **Kambera, Leti, Nias, Biak**). Donohue (1999:367) distinguishes four major types of relative clauses, only two of which are mentioned here. In subject relative clauses the head noun functions as A or S argument of the embedded predicate which lacks subject prefixes but instead is infixed with *-um-*. Otherwise, subject relative clauses are structurally identical to main clauses.

(62)   *no-lagu-mo*   *na*   *La*   *Judi*   *[b<um>alu*   *te*   *loka*
         3.RLS-song-PRF   NOM   PN   <REL>buy   CORE   banana

       ako   *te*   *ina-no]*
       for   CORE   mother-3.POSS
       'La Judi, who bought some bananas for his mother, is singing.' (Donohue 1999:372)

In object relative clauses the head noun is the O argument of the embedded predicate, which also lacks subject prefixes and is prefixed with *i-* (also *di-* or *ni-*). The other arguments of the embedded predicate do not receive their main clause marking (with nominative *na* or core *te*) but are coded as possessives or genitives, thus giving object relative clauses a distinctly nominalized appearance.

(63)   *te*   *po'o*   *[i-tompa-api-su*   *u*   *La Mar]*
         CORE   mango   REL-throw-APP-1s.POSS   GEN   Mark

       no-sangka-mo   *ki'iki'i*
       3.RLS-exceed-PRF   little
       'The mango that I threw over to Mark is a bit overripe.' (Donohue 1999:383)

Note that Tukang Besi relative clauses are marked by formatives (*-um-*, *i-*) which are widespread as voice-marking formatives in symmetrical voice languages (see also Donohue 2002:92f). Such specialized and sometimes also fossilized uses of originally voice-marking morphology are very common in transitional languages and are occasionally also found in preposed possessor languages.

   The second qualification with regard to the subjects-only constraint on relativization pertains to the fact that in many symmetrical voice languages it appears to be possible to relativize on some non-core arguments or adjuncts, in particular possessors. It is not unusual that in these instances the head noun is overtly represented in the relative clause by a resumptive pronoun such as the enclitic *=nya* in the following Standard Indonesian example:

(64)   *sopir*   *yang*   *nama=nya*   *Ali*
         driver   REL   name=3.POSS   Ali
       'the driver whose name is Ali' (Sneddon 1996:288)

Sneddon (1996:288f) suggests that this type of relative clause, which in Standard Indonesian and some other Malayic varieties can also be used for other non-subject core arguments and adjuncts, basically instantiates an embedded topic-comment structure (see Musgrave 2001, chapter 5 for extensive discussion). The independent (non-embedded) version of this topic-comment structure is *sopir itu nama=nya Ali* (driver DIST name=3.POSS Ali) 'that driver's name is Ali (lit. as for that driver, his name is Ali)'.

Related to these topic-comment structures are relative clause-like constructions where a word meaning 'place', 'time' or 'reason' is followed by a main clause structure, the overall construction serving as an adverbial clause ('(at the time) when', '(at the place) where', 'the reason why'). A Standard Indonesian example is given in (65) (for other examples, see **Belait**).

(65) *waktu   saya   masih   sekolah*
      time   1s   still   school
      'At the time when I was still going to school' (the following incident happened).

Such constructions are widely attested in symmetrical voice languages. While very general words meaning 'place' or 'time' are the most common 'heads', some more specific items are also possible as seen in the following Tagalog example:

(66) ***isá-ng   hapon***   *na   silá-ng   dalawá   'y   nag-lá-laró'*
      one-LK afternoon LK   3p-LK   two   PM RLS.AV-RDP-play

      sa   halamanan
      LOC garden
      'One afternoon when the two of them were playing in the garden' (...a butterfly came flying past the two children). (Bloomfield 1917:88)

Other noteworthy facts about relative clauses in western Austronesian languages are as follows. In most languages, relative clauses (like other modifiers) follow their head. In Philippine and Formosan languages, however, they may precede or follow the head (see **Seediq**, **Tsou**, and **Tagalog** for examples). In a few instances, the (semantic) head may also appear within the relative clause, as in the following Tagalog example:

(67) *Wala*   *pa*   *rín*   *yung*   *[pinangako*ng
      walá'   pa   rin   iyón-ng in-paN-ako'-ng
      NEG.EXIST still also DIST-LK RLS(UG)-GER-promise-LK

      lamsyed *sa*   *akin]*
      lamsyed sa   akin
      lamp   LOC 1s.DAT
      'The lamp that was promised to me still hasn't come.'

Gil (1994) and Donohue (1999:386f) report internally headed relative clauses for Riau Indonesian and Tukang Besi respectively.

Finally, it may be noted that the functional load of (usually headless) relative clauses in some western Austronesian languages is much higher than in many other languages because they form a regular part of information question and cleft (contrastive focus) constructions as in the following Standard Indonesian example (see also **Buol**, **Javanese**, **Kambera**, **Nias**).

(68) *siapa   yang   kau=undang?*
      who   REL   2s=invite
      'Who did you invite?' (Sneddon 1996:316)

3.11 Adnominal possession

As will be recalled from section 1.2, adnominal possessive constructions provide one major criterion for distinguishing symmetrical voice languages from preposed possessor languages. This section provides further details on the structure and distribution of the relevant constructions.

In symmetrical voice languages, adnominal possessive constructions are straightforward: the possessor generally follows the possessum, often without any intervening grammatical marker (e.g. Sundanese *imah₁ paman₂ kuring₃* 'my₃ uncle's₂ house₁' (Müller-Gotama 2001:36)). If there is a grammatical marker, it is usually a suffixed or enclitic third person possessor pronoun as in Sundanese *imah-**na** paman kuring* 'my uncle's house' (similar to many cognate forms in other Indonesian languages, Sundanese *-na* is no longer strictly a third person possessive pronoun but is also used in definiteness marking and nominalizations (Müller-Gotama 2001:25)). Alternatively, the possessor is preceded by a genitive or oblique proclitic as in Cebuano *maestro sa=bata?* (teacher OBL=child) 'the child's teacher'.

There is one type of exception to the otherwise strict ordering of possessum-possessor in symmetrical voice languages. Quite a number of these languages allow an alternative construction in which pronominal possessors precede the possessum. This is quite regular in Philippine languages where the construction of the form POSSESSUM + ENCLITIC POSSESSIVE PRONOUN (e.g. Tagalog *bahay mo* 'your (sg) house') regularly alternates with a construction of the form DATIVE/OBLIQUE PRONOUN + LINKER + POSSESSUM (e.g. Tagalog *iyong bahay* (2s.DAT-LK house) 'your (sg) house'). In other symmetrical voice languages, this alternative order is more restricted. In Sundanese, for example, it is restricted to the polite first and second person possessive pronouns *pun* and *tuang* (e.g. *pun bojo* 'my wife' (Müller-Gotama 2001:37)). In the Formosan language Paiwan, a special proclitic series exists only for first and second pronouns (e.g. *su=umaq* 'your house' (Egli 1990: 155)). In addition, Paiwan allows all kinds of pronominal possessors to be preposed with a linker intervening (e.g. both *umaq ni=maju* (house GEN=3s) and *ni=maju a umaq* (GEN=3s LK house) are possible for 'his/her house'). The variant with a preposed genitive pronoun appears to be the regular position in Pazeh (Li and Tsuchida 2001:35f) where nominal possessors also generally precede their possessum (e.g. *ni taruat a babizu* (GEN Taruat LK book) 'Taruat's book' (Li and Tsuchida 2001:32)). Li and Tsuchida (2001:35f) suggest that this rather remarkable and exceptional preposing of possessors in a symmetrical voice language could be due to contact with Southern Min.

In preposed possessor languages there are typically two types of possessive constructions, an alienable and an inalienable one. In the alienable construction, the possessor precedes a possessive marker or ligature inflected for person which in turn precedes the possessum as in Buru *ya nango todo* (1s POSS.1s machete) 'my machete' or *ka namo huma* (2s POSS.2s house) 'your house'. The possessor expression is optional, and the inflected possessive ligature, which essentially looks like a preposed possessive pronoun, may appear in reduced form (e.g. *nang todo* instead of *ya nango todo*). As Grimes (1991:279–282) shows for Buru, the possessive ligature sometimes has verb-like characteristics, as it can also occur with typical verbal affixes.

In the inalienable construction, the possessor also precedes the head but there is no ligature intervening in between possessor and possessum. Instead, the possessum is marked with a possessive enclitic (e.g. Buru *fafu olo=n* (pig head=3s.POSS) 'pig's head'). The possessor may be omitted and then the construction looks very much like the typical pronominal possessive construction in symmetrical voice languages (e.g. Buru *olo=m* (head=2s.POSS) 'your head'). This construction is used in Buru primarily for part-whole relationships, including body parts, but not for kinship terms (Grimes 1991:282).

In Buru the distinction between alienable and inalienable is on the constructional level, not on the lexical level (Grimes 1991:287–289). That is, nouns are not subcategorized as alienable or inalienable. In principle, all nouns can occur in both types of constructions. In fact, the two constructions can occasionally even be merged, as in *nak olo=n* (POSS.3s head=3s.POSS) '(she went away with) her (pig's) head' where the two possessive markers refer to different possessive relationships: the pronominal enclitic=*n* refers to the pig, the 'inalienable' possessor of its own head, and the inflected possessive ligature *nak* refers to the (alienable) owner who in some way acquired a pig's head (Grimes 1991:288).

There is considerable variation regarding the details of the alienable vs. inalienable distinction in preposed possessor languages. In **Leti**, there is actually only a single basic construction (POSSESSOR POSSESSUM + POSSESSIVE SUFFIX) but there is an alienable/inalienable distinction on the lexical level in that inalienable nouns obligatorily take a possessive suffix. In **Tetun Fehan**, the paradigm of the possessive enclitics has been merged into a single genitive marking enclitic =*n* (this has also happened in at least one Buru dialect (Grimes 1991:283)). Furthermore, the pronominal markers precede rather than follow the possessive ligature =*kan*. In Ambai both prefixes and suffixes occur with the ligature, hence *ne-ku* (POSS-1s) 'my' but *u-ne* (3d-POSS) 'their (dual)' (Silzer 1983:124). In **Biak**, which shows perhaps the most complex possessive marking attested in the area, the inflected possessive marker in the alienable construction typically follows rather than precedes the possessum.

Finally, it may be noted that in addition to the position of the possessor and the presence of an alienable vs. inalienable distinction, symmetrical voice languages and preposed possessor languages differ also with regard to another important detail of possessive constructions. Preposed possessor languages typically have pronominal forms (possessive suffixes and inflected possessive markers) which occur exclusively in possessive constructions. In symmetrical voice languages, possessive pronouns typically have at least one additional function: they are also used for actors in undergoer voice constructions (compare Tagalog *tingnán **mo*** (look:LV 2s.POSS) 'look!').

With regard to the position of the possessor, the transitional languages tend to align with the symmetrical voice languages (possessors are usually postposed; a major exception is Banggai in eastern central Sulawesi). With regard to the uses of the possessive pronouns, they often show a closer affinity to the preposed possessor languages in that possessive suffixes or enclitics generally occur only with nouns or nominalized constituents (e.g. Muna, **Nias**, Tukang Besi).

4 MAJOR VERBAL ALTERNATIONS

Western Austronesian languages usually have very little nominal morphology, if any, but they tend to provide for a fairly rich inventory of verbal affixations (in particular Philippine-type languages). The present survey briefly looks at the most widely attested verbal affixations: aktionsart (dynamic vs. non-dynamic), voice, causative and applicative. Zobel (to appear) provides a much more comprehensive survey on these alternations. See **Iloko** for a fuller presentation of a typical Philippine inventory, which usually also includes affixes for requestives, reciprocals, plural actors, etc.

4.1 Dynamic vs. non-dynamic (stative and potentive)

In most western Austronesian languages expressions for non-dynamic events are morphologically overtly marked while those for dynamic events remain unmarked. Expressions for dynamic events typically refer to actions which involve a volitional agent who is in control of the action (e.g. 'kiss', 'give', 'run', 'throw'). In addition, the dynamic class also includes expressions for meteorological events ('rain', etc.). The two major types of non-dynamic expressions are statives, i.e. states of affairs which in principle do not involve an agent (e.g. 'fall', 'be alive', 'be broken'), and potentives, i.e. events which involve an agent but one who is not in full control of the action. Expressions for processes ('grow', 'turn red', 'freeze', etc.) and spontaneous events ('explode', 'burst', etc.) are fairly variable in their class membership. In some languages they are generally coded as non-dynamic and in others as dynamic, while a third group will allow them to appear in either class. In the remainder of this section we will briefly review some of the forms and meanings typical of non-dynamic expressions.

One major reason to treat statives and potentives together is the fact that in many languages they are marked with the same prefix. One good example is the Acehnese prefix *teu-* which occurs in statives as in (69).

(69)   **teu-***hah*   *babah=kah*   *sabê*
       ST-open   mouth=2s   always
       'Your mouth is always open.' (Durie 1985:73)

The same affix occurs in potentives, which usually convey at least the following three kinds of meanings. First, potentives may refer to *accidental* actions, i.e. the action is done intentionally but the outcome is not the intended one:

(70)   *ka=***teu-***koh*   *bak=kayee=nyan*   *lê=kamoe*
       ??=POT-cut   tree=wood=DIST   by=1pe
       'We accidentally cut down that tree.' (Durie 1985:76)

Second, potentives are used for *involuntary* actions, i.e. someone happens to do something without having any specific intentions to do so:

(71)   *jih*   **teu-***batôk-batôk*
       3s   POT-RDP-cough
       'S/he is coughing a lot.' (Durie 1985:74)

Finally, and somewhat remarkably, potentives may convey an *abilitative* meaning, referring to actions someone is able to do or (just) manages to do:

(72)   *batee=nyan*   *h'an=***teu-***grak*
       stone=DIST   NEG=POT-move
       'That stone cannot be moved.' (Durie 1985:75)

Not all languages mark all of these event types as non-dynamic, and only some languages follow Acehnese in using a single prefix for these uses. Note also that the most common and widespread non-dynamic prefix is *ma-*.

Also part of the non-dynamic system are so-called adversative passives, which are usually marked by the affix combination *ka--an* (or its cognates) as in Pazeh *ka-udan-an* 'be rained on, be caught in the rain' (<*udan* 'rain') or *ka-lamik-an* 'to catch a cold' (<*lamik* 'cold') (Blust 1999:352). In many Philippine languages, *ka--an* is part of a productive voice alternation paradigm for statives, as seen in **Tagalog**.

4.2 Voice (and aspect/mood)

Two types of voice alternations are attested in western Austronesian languages: passives and symmetrical voice alternations. The latter are also known as *Philippine-type focus* alternations, but *focus* is widely agreed to be a misleading term in this context (cf. Himmelmann 2002b).

4.2.1 Passives and antipassives

A number of western Austronesian languages have voice alternations which are quite similar to the active/passive alternation familiar from European languages. Such passives are characterized by three features: (a) the verb is overtly marked with a passive formative; (b) the undergoer of a transitive verb is the subject of the construction; and (c) the actor may be left unexpressed or if expressed it is clearly marked as oblique, usually by a preposition. Compare the following Standard Indonesian example:

(73) *Orang   itu   di-lihat **oleh** anak   saya.*
      person DIST PV-see   by   child 1s
      'That person was seen by my child.'

This example is almost identical to example (2) above, with the exception of the agent-marking preposition *oleh*. Standard Indonesian is thus a language with both 'standard' passive (as in (73)) and symmetrical voice alternations (as in (2)). This probably also holds true for many symmetrical voice languages other than Philippine-type ones (see Arka (1998) for an analysis of Balinese along these lines).

Passive constructions are also fairly widely attested among transitional languages (e.g. **Makassar**). In **Mori Bawah** the agent argument is obligatorily deleted. In preposed possessor languages, passives are rare (but see **Biak**).

Antipassives are only rarely attested in the region. See **Mori Bawah** for one of the very few good examples. Of course, proponents of ergative analyses for western Austronesian languages (see 3.8.2 above) consider all actor voice constructions to be antipassives.

4.2.2 Symmetrical voice alternations

As mentioned in section 1.2, more than half of the western Austronesian languages are characterized by the occurrence of symmetrical voice alternations. There is a substantial body of literature concerning these alternations, beginning as early as Humboldt (1838: 347 passim). See Constantino (1971) and Matsuda French (1988) for surveys of the older literature, and Sells (1997) and the contributions in Klamer (1996) and Austin and Musgrave (to appear) for more recent discussion.

Basic morphosyntactic properties of symmetrical voice alternations are discussed in sections 3.3 and 3.8. In the current section we briefly review three major parameters of morphological variation: (a) the number of alternations; (b) the interaction with aspect/mood; and (c) the integration of person markers into the paradigm of voice alternations.

The typical Philippine and Formosan system, which is also attested in northern Sulawesi and Sabah (northern Borneo), has four alternations, as seen in the following Cebuano examples:

Actor voice

(74) *akú=y   **mu**-palít ug   isda?*
      1s=TOP AV-buy   OBL.NSPEC fish
      'I will buy some fish.' (Wolff 1972:xv)

Patient voice

(75) *palit-**ún**   ku   ang   isda?*
      buy-PV   1s.POSS   SPEC   fish
      'I will buy the fish.' (Wolff 1972: xv)

Locative voice

(76) *bantay-**án**   ninyú   ang   prisu*
      watch-LV   2P.POSS   SPEC   prisoner
      'You will watch the prisoner.' (Wolff 1972:38)

(77) *palit-**án**   ku   siyá=g   kík*
      buy-LV   1s.POSS   3s=OBL.NSPEC   cake
      'I will buy some cake for/from her.' (Wolff 1972:38)

Conveyance voice

(78) ***i*-butáng   niya   ang   kwarta*
      CV-put.down   3s.POSS   SPEC   money
      'S/he will put the money down.' (Wolff 1972:361)

(79) *wa?   ku=y   kwarta-ng   **i**-palít   ug   bugás*
      NEG.EXIST   1s=LK   money-LK   CV-buy   OBL.NSPEC   rice
      'I have no money to buy rice with.' (Wolff 1972:361)

The use of these voices is discussed in the chapters on **Seediq, Iloko, Tagalog, Kimaragang, Sama, Buol** and **Malagasy**. Note that there is a broad range of terms in use for the different voices. But the forms are usually easily recognizable since there is only very little cross-linguistic variation.

It is not uncommon to find references to more than four voice alternations in these languages in the literature. To give just one example, up to eleven voice alternations have been proposed for Tagalog (Schachter and Otanes 1972:344). However, in most instances the additional voice alternations are morphologically complex, consisting of a stem-forming affix plus a basic voice affix (e.g. the Tagalog 'instrumental voice' prefix *ipaN-* consists of the stem-forming prefix *paN-* and the conveyance voice prefix *i-*). More often than not, such formally complex voice affixes are also semantically compositional and there is little reason to consider them unit morphemes. In a few instances, however, there may be good morphological reasons for proposing a fifth basic voice (see **Iloko** (section 5.1), **Sama** (section 4.1) and **Kimaragang** (sections 3.1 and 4)).

The basic voices usually occur in a number of different aspects and moods. One type of system widely attested in the central Philippines consists of three moods: non-realis, realis, and subjunctive, as seen for Cebuano in Table 5.5. This table also shows that voice

TABLE 5.5: CEBUANO VOICE-MOOD PARADIGM FOR DYNAMIC VERBS (cf. Wolff 1972:xvi, 2001:123)

	Non-realis	Realis	Subjunctive
Actor voice	mu-	mi-/ni-	mu-
Patient voice	-un	gi-	-a
Locative voice	-an	gi--an	-i
Conveyance voice	i-	gi-	i-

TYPOLOGICAL CHARACTERISTICS   169

and mood marking are closely linked to each other, forming a paradigm. In most instances, it is impossible to formally separate a voice formative from a mood formative. Instead, most formatives represent a combination of these categories.

Voice-aspect-mood paradigms with four or five voice distinctions are formally heterogeneous in that they involve a mixture of prefixes, suffixes and very often also infixes. There are usually a number of different formatives for actor voice (e.g. Cebuano also has *mag-* and *maN-*) while the undergoer voices are represented by just one set of formatives. Patient voice is usually suffixless in realis mood but marked by a suffix in other moods. The voice affixes occur with both semantically transitive and intransitive lexical bases, with only a few lexical bases occurring unaffixed when referring to events or states.

The paradigmatic organization is also evident from the fact that in some instances one formative represents two voice-mood categories. Thus, Cebuano *gi-* represents both realis patient and realis conveyance voice. Only the alternations make it clear which voice-mood category it represents in a given instance (in patient voice, realis *gi-* alternates with non-realis *-un*, in conveyance voice, it alternates with non-realis *i-*). Such multifunctional formatives are found in practically all symmetrical voice-mood paradigms, as amply illustrated by the sketches for **Seediq, Iloko, Tagalog, Buol, Kimaragang,** and **Sama.** See also Himmelmann (to appear b) for further discussion.

The subjunctive forms are commonly used in imperatives, in some subordinate clause types, after certain adverbials, and (more sporadically) in narrative sequences (see section 5). The details vary from language to language. In Cebuano, only the undergoer voice forms are used in imperatives as in:

(80) *Bantay-i*   *uná?*   *siyá*   *ha?*
      watch.over-LV.SUBJ then   3s   okay?
      'Take good care of her/him, will you?' (Wolff 1966:440)

The adverbials which induce subjunctive mood in Cebuano mark all reference to time and include expressions such as *kagahapun* 'yesterday', *anus?a* 'when (with future time reference)', and *sa miaging Duminggu* 'last Sunday' as well as tense-marked negators and deictics:

(81) *wa?*   *niya*   *saky-i*   *ang*   *taksi*
      NEG.PST   3s.POSS   ride.on-LV.SUBJ   SPEC   taxi
      'He did not ride in the taxi.' (Zorc 1977:151)

In a number of languages, especially in Taiwan (e.g. **Seediq**) but also in **Buol**, there are two non-indicative moods rather than just one (the subjunctive). Ross (2002 and elsewhere), who reconstructs these two moods for Proto-Austronesian, calls them *atemporal* and *projective* respectively (see also ADELAAR, A HISTORICAL PERSPECTIVE).

In symmetrical voice languages which do not belong to the Philippine-type, the most common system of symmetrical voice alternations is a simple two-way alternation between actor voice and undergoer voice, as in the Standard Indonesian examples (1) and (2) above (see also **Belait, Karo Batak, Javanese**). There are also a few languages with three voice alternations (e.g. **Malagasy**). Zobel (to appear) provides a comprehensive survey of the attested systems.

A major characteristic of the symmetrical voice languages found in Indonesia (with the exception of northern Sulawesi) pertains to the fact that pronominal proclitics or prefixes have been integrated into the system of voice markers. In Da'a, a central Sulawesi language, for example, the non-realis undergoer voice prefix is *ra-* as seen in the following example:

(82)   *Loka*   *etu*   *ma-tasa*   *kana*   **ra-***koni*.
       banana   DIST   ST-ripe   must   UV-eat
       '(When) that banana is ripe it must be eaten.' (Barr 1988:21)

However, if the actor of an undergoer voice verb is first or second person singular, then *ra-* is replaced by the proclitic person markers *ku=* or *mu=*, as in:

(83)   *Da'a*   *ma-mala*   *aku*   **mu=***raga*.
       not   ST-able   1s   2s.ACT-chase
       'You can't chase me.' (Barr 1988:40)

As in the case of Da'a, these pronominal markers are often restricted to the first or second person. If a mood difference is marked on the predicate, the pronominal markers always occur in the non-realis forms. See also **Karo Batak, Colloquial Indonesian, Javanese**, and Zobel (to appear).

4.3 Causative and applicative

A causative formation involving the prefix *pa-* (or a cognate form) is probably the most widely attested productive morphological derivation in western Austronesian languages. Notable exceptions include Keo and **Biak** which lack productive morphological causatives altogether, and **Malayic varieties** and Modern **Javanese** which allow morphological causative derivations but primarily with suffixes rather than with a prefix (see below). Causatives are mentioned and illustrated in practically all language sketch chapters, but see in particular **Seediq, Kimaragang, Belait, Malagasy, Buol, Nias** and **Kambera** for examples and discussion.

Most western Austronesian languages, with the exception of Philippine-type languages, also have applicative morphology and constructions (**Tetun** and **Leti** are exceptions among the preposed possessor languages). There are typically two applicative suffixes, one (*-i* or a cognate form) for locative applicatives and one (often *-akan* or a cognate form) covering a broader range of semantic roles, usually including instruments and beneficiaries. Both suffixes also regularly occur in causative derivations (e.g. **Old Malay, Colloquial Indonesian, Javanese, Nias**). See **Mori Bawah** and **Kambera** for more extensive exemplification of applicatives and Sirk (1996) for historical discussion.

Although the morphosyntax is quite different, there is no doubt that the conveyance and locative voice alternations in Philippine-type languages have much in common semantically with applicative alternations in the other languages. There is furthermore a formal similarity in that the most widely attested applicative formative *-i* is also widely attested as (subjunctive) locative voice suffix (in the recent comparative literature (e.g. Wolff 1996, Ross 2002) it is sometimes assumed that the two suffixes are historically speaking identical but this is a conjecture rather than a proven fact). Another related, but not identical phenomenon appears to be the *affectedness alternation* described by Kroeger for **Kimaragang**.

One crosslinguistically remarkable feature of both causative and applicative derivations in western Austronesian languages is that these derivations are not always valency-increasing but convey a broader range of sometimes quite elusive meanings, including intensity and iterativity (cf. **Mori Bawah** and **Kambera**). Once again, Philippine-type languages would appear to be somewhat exceptional in that their causative *pa-* prefix generally only conveys causation. Since intensity and iterativity are often conveyed by the derivational prefixes *pag-* and *paN-* in Philippine-type languages, it may well be the case that what is described as polysemy of causative *pa-* for a number of transitional and preposed possessor languages is actually a case of homophony, due to a merger of **pa-*, **paR-* and **paN-*.

5 CLAUSE LINKAGE PATTERNS AND ANAPHORA

In all western Austronesian languages, there are few (if any) morphosyntactic constraints on the omission of coreferential arguments in clause sequences. That is, the possibility to omit a coreferential argument is not restricted to subject arguments, as in the following Balinese example where both *nuut* and *rauh* occur without overt subject expressions (see also example (50) above):

(84)   *lantas   ida   malayar   nuut   pasisi.*
     then   3.HON   INTR:sail   AV:follow   beach

     Rauh   di   pasisi   Pajarakan-ne
     arrive   LOC   beach   Pajarakan-DEF
     '...then she sails along the beach. When she arrives on the beach of Pajarakan, ...'
     (Pastika 1999, chapter 7)

Instead, it is also possible to omit all kinds of non-subject arguments. In the following Tetun Dili example, the subject and the non-subject patient of *hemu* 'drink' are omitted:

(85)   *nia   halo   kafé,   hemu.*
     3s   make   coffee   drink
     'He makes coffee and drinks it.' (Hull 1999:5)

In the following Tagalog example (originally from Martin 1981:313), the recipient of the predicate *ibíbigay* 'give to' in the second clause remains unexpressed:

(86)   *kung   ma-kí-kita   ko   siyá,   i-bí-bigáy   ko*
     if   POT-RDP-seen   1s.POSS   3s   CV-RDP-gif   1s.POSS

     ang   sulat   mo
     SPEC   letter   2s.POSS
     'If I see him, I will give [him] your letter.' (Kroeger 1993:34)

Overtly expressed, the recipient would have to be marked with the general locative preposition *sa*, hence the 'complete' version of the second clause would read *ibíbigáy ko **sa kaniyá** ang sulat mo*.

This (syntactically) free omissibility of argument expressions accounts for the fact that the coordinate conjunction reduction tests widely used in the typological literature on grammatical relations are generally inconclusive in western Austronesian languages (cf. Kroeger 1993:36, Cena 1995:15–18, and section 3.8.1 above).

Given that all kinds of argument expressions are freely omissible, it is somewhat remarkable that actor expressions in undergoer voice constructions are rarely omitted in symmetrical voice languages (cf. Shibatani 1988:93, Himmelmann 1999). Compare the following Balinese example:

(87) *raris   kenten   pepetan   padi-n-e   nika   kaat=a*
      then   like.that   husks   rice-LK-DEF   DIST   (UV:)cut.off=3.ACT

   jang=a   samping   jineng-e
   (UV:)put=3.ACT   beside   rice store-DEF

   nika   tunjel=a   pepet=ne   nika
   DIST   (UV:)burn=3.ACT   husks=3.POSS   DIST
   'Then she cut off those rice husks, put them beside the rice store, and burned
   them, those husks.' (Pastika 1999, chapter 7)

In this action sequence, all three verbs (*kaat, jang, tunjel*) are in undergoer voice and
have the same actor ('she') and undergoer ('rice husks'). But while the undergoer is not
mentioned in the second clause, the third person actor clitic=*a* occurs on all predicates.
In transitional and preposed possessor languages, transitive actors are also generally
overtly expressed in the sense that in many of these languages the use of subject marking proclitics or prefixes is obligatory.

   Related to the preceding phenomenon, there is a remarkable pattern of clause linkage
which is highly characteristic for symmetrical voice languages and somewhat unusual
from a cross-linguistic point of view. Compare the following example from Balinese (and
examples (40) and (41) in the **Tagalog** chapter):

(88) *lantas   ia   nyemak   punggalan-e   tur*
      then   3   AV:take   head-DEF   and

   entung-ang=a   ke   tukad-e
   (UV:)throw-APP=3.ACT   to   river-DEF
   'then he took the (severed) head and threw it into the river.' (Clynes 1995:296)

This example consists of two transitive clauses which share the same set of core arguments.
The first clause is in actor voice, the actor (*ia*) being the subject and the undergoer
(*punggalane*) the non-subject argument. In the second, undergoer voice clause, the linking
relations are switched around: the actor (=*a*) is the non-subject argument and the undergoer the subject argument (which is usually no longer overtly expressed, as noted above).

   This pattern is found in sequences of main clauses (which do not have to be overtly
coordinated) as well as in sequences consisting of a subordinate and a main clause (in
either order), as seen in the following Balinese example:

(89) *Mara   ia   ningeh   pamunyin   panak=ne   buka   keto,*
      when   3ᵢ   AV:hear   voice   childⱼ=3.POSS   as   like.that

   dadi   ampak-in=a   dogen   ia   jelanan.
   thus   (UV:)open-APP=3.ACTᵢ   just   3ⱼ   door
   'When she heard the voice of her child like that, she opened the door for him.'
   (Pastika 1999, chapter 7)

These examples are remarkable from a cross-linguistic point of view since a similar
switch in construction is not attested in other language types. A typical nominative-
accusative language, for example, would use two active voice clauses as in the English
translations of the two preceding examples.

   The examples are also noteworthy with regard to the definiteness constraint on actor voice
constructions already briefly discussed in section 3.6 above. It is often claimed that actor
voice constructions generally disallow definite undergoers. Examples (88) and (89)

show that this is not true. In both examples, the first clause is an actor voice construction but it still involves a definite undergoer (*punggalane* in (88) and *pamunyin panakne* in (89)). Unlike a number of other 'exceptions' to the definiteness constraint, there are no grammatical reasons for the choice of an actor voice construction (such as the occurrence of an actor voice construction in a relative clause, see **Tagalog** and **Karo Batak** for examples and further discussion). Consequently, the definiteness constraint in the strong form it is usually given is certainly wrong in relation to symmetrical voice languages.

Nevertheless, examples (88) and (89) are also good illustrations of the extent to which the definiteness constraint actually holds true. In both examples, it is practically impossible to use actor voice in the second clause. It is not yet clear whether this is a rather strong pragmatic or stylistic preference which allows the odd exception or whether it in fact constitutes a grammatical constraint on clause linkage. Note that the constraint holds between clauses regardless of their syntactic relationship (coordination, subordination, or simple juxtaposition).

A clearly more grammaticized pattern requiring a constructional switch in clause sequences pertains to certain uses of the subjunctive in a number of Philippine-type languages, mostly in Sabah (e.g. **Kimaragang**) and Taiwan (e.g. Paiwan, possibly also **Seediq**). In these languages, use of the subjunctive is required in 'narrative sequences', i.e. action sequences involving the same set of participants. In some languages, including Paiwan, use of the subjunctive is triggered by certain coordinators such as *sa* in the following example:

(90) *pacun-an   a   zu'   a   gang,   qucə-quc-ən*
      see-LV   SPEC   DIST   LK   crab   RDP-crush-PV

      sa   *kan-**i***   *aya*
      and.then   eat-PV.SUBJ   thus
      '... he saw the crabs, and crushed and ate them.' (Ross 2002:23, originally from Egli 1990:330)

In this example, the subjunctive only occurs in the last predicate, which is preceded by *sa*. In other languages, subjunctive forms occur throughout the narrative sequence (see example (52) in **Kimaragang**).

6 A FINAL LOOK AT TYPOLOGICAL DIVERSITY WITHIN WESTERN AUSTRONESIAN LANGUAGES

The preceding sections have surveyed some of the major typological characteristics of western Austronesian languages, both from an internal and an external point of view. The survey is obviously far from complete. Among the topics which have been omitted for lack of space are the following ones.

(i) Numeral classifiers

Many western Austronesian languages have small to medium-sized inventories of numeral classifiers, usually involving a special classifier construction. See **Sama, Belait, Cham, Moken/Moklen, Mori Bawah, Nias, Kambera, Tetun Fehan**, and **Taba** for examples and discussion. This list already indicates that numeral classifiers are found in both symmetrical voice and preposed possessor languages as well as transitional languages. They appear to be lacking in the Philippine-type languages and Taiwan.

(ii) Plural marking

There is a wide variety of usually optional plural markers for nominal expressions. Next to reduplication (see section 2.2), there are plural words (cf. Dryer 1989) such as **Javanese** *padha* or Tagalog *manga* (orthographically *mga*) and third person plural pronouns, which are used to indicate plural in **Tetun Fehan** (and Tetun Dili) and Buru (Grimes 1991:159), for example. Associative plurals, which refer to a group of people associated with a given person (e.g. Tagalog *sina Maria* 'Maria and company/the others'), are widely attested in Philippine-type languages (more sporadically also elsewhere, for example in Ambon Malay and **Nias**). There is also the possibility to indicate plurality in adjectives (usually by reduplication) and verbs (by prefixes). Apart from a number of languages in western Indonesia, where elaborate politeness rules have led to considerable changes in the pronoun systems (e.g. **Javanese**, Balinese), most western Austronesian languages also clearly distinguish plural from singular pronouns.

(iii) Deictics and reference to space

Western Austronesian languages differ significantly with regard to the basic structure of their (local) deictic systems. Parameters of variation include the number of degrees of distance which are distinguished in a given system (often two (proximal/distal) or three (proximal/medial/distal), but four and five are also attested; **Malagasy** is in fact famous for distinguishing seven different degrees). Visibility plays a role in, for example, **Tsou**, **Seediq**, **Iloko**, **Malagasy**, and **Leti**. In a number of languages, including **Malagasy** and **Iloko**, local deictics are obligatorily tense-marked. In **Leti** the deictics also convey speaker's attitude. Furthermore, in many languages, the basic deictics are closely linked to a system of directionals which specify locations and movements as being UP, DOWN, ACROSS or the like. See in particular **Buol**, **Mori Bawah**, **Taba** and **Biak** for examples. The wider systems of spatial orientation in Austronesian languages have only recently been explored (cf. the pioneering studies edited by Senft 1997 and Bennardo 2002).

(iv) Nominalization/subordination

Western Austronesian languages usually have a few derivational affixes to nominalize action expressions, regardless of whether or not nouns and verbs are clearly distinguished morphosyntactically. The most widespread derivations include instrumental nominalizations such as Pazeh *saa-kudung* 'hammer' (cf. *mu-kudung* 'hit with a hammer', Li and Tsuchida 2001:51), abstract qualities such as Muna *ka-ghosa* 'strength' from *ghosa* 'strong' (Van den Berg 1989:294) and gerunds/action nominalizations such as Ratahan *pangangaaq* 'action of taking/upon taking' from *a(l)aq* 'take' (Himmelmann and Wolff 1999:71). The voice affixes found in Philippine-type languages also have nominalizing functions, and in these functions they are found in many other languages as well. Nominalizing morphology is also widely found in subordinate constructions such as relative, complement and adverbial clauses. Almost every language sketch chapter in this volume provides further exemplification for these observations.

Finally, the proposed typological grouping for western Austronesian languages is also in need of further testing and refinement. Table 5.6 summarizes some of the characteristics of the two major types, symmetrical voice languages and preposed possessor languages.

TABLE 5.6: CHARACTERISTIC FEATURES OF SYMMETRICAL VOICE AND PREPOSED POSSESSOR LANGUAGES

Symmetrical voice languages	Preposed possessor languages	See section
Symmetrical voice alternations	No or asymmetrical voice alternations	3.3, 3.8, 4.2
Postposed possessor	Preposed possessor	3.11
No alienable/inalienable distinction	Alienable/inalienable distinction	3.11
Few or no differences between narrative and equational clauses	Clear-cut differences between narrative and equational clauses	3.4, 3.6
Person marking only sporadically attested	Person marking prefixes or proclitics for S/A arguments	3.7
Numerals/quantifiers precede head	Numerals/quantifiers follow head	3.5
Negators in pre-predicate position	Clause-final negators	3.5
V-initial or SVX	V-second or -final	3.5

With regard to refinements, it is certainly possible to distinguish further subgroups within these larger groupings. One well established and widely used typological subgroup within the symmetrical voice languages is the *Philippine-type languages*. In addition to the defining features already mentioned in section 1.2 (i.e. multiple undergoer voices, paradigms of phrase marking proclitics, pronominal second position clitics), these languages share a number of other features, including productive infixation, honorific articles, a realis/non-realis distinction, and the lack of (numeral) classifiers (these features are of course also found outside the Philippine-type languages). Nevertheless, despite the fact that these languages are very similar indeed in many respects one should be very careful when generalizing from one language over the whole group (practically every article on a Philippine-type language at some point starts to make claims for all Philippine-type languages). Standard Tagalog, for example, is in a number of regards not at all representative of Philippine-type languages (most importantly, perhaps, it lacks subjunctive affixation; see also section 3.6).

A second subtype of symmetrical voice language is the *Indonesian-type languages* (see Wolff 1996, Ross 2002, Zobel 2002 and to appear). Defining features for this subtype are the combination of a symmetrical voice system (with two or three symmetrical voice alternations), applicative morphology and the integration of proclitic actor markers into the paradigm of voice markers. This definition, which is narrower but also more precise than the ones employed in the literature to date, covers roughly the symmetrical voice languages of western Indonesia (including **Javanese**, **Colloquial Indonesian**, and **Karo Batak**), and central Sulawesi (Tomini-Tolitoli and Kaili-Pamona languages) as well as Chamorro and Palauan. It remains to be seen whether this is indeed a useful typological grouping in the sense that there are further features correlating with the defining features.

It is questionable whether the *Formosan languages* form a useful typological grouping, as it is sometimes implied in the literature. All Formosan languages are symmetrical voice languages but not all of them are also Philippine-type languages (see section 1.2 above). Furthermore, even for the Formosan languages which clearly are Philippine-type languages (e.g. Paiwan, Atayal, **Seediq**, Puyuma, Pazeh) it is not at all clear whether they share features which set them as a group clearly apart from other Philippine-type languages. In fact, it would appear that the Formosan languages are morphosyntactically much more heterogeneous than, for example, the northern or central Philippine languages.

Among the preposed possessor languages, the Austronesian languages of Timor form a special subtype due to the rather strong isolating tendencies found in many of them. These are shared with some languages of Flores (and the close-by islands Solor, Adonara, and Lembata), which are transitional languages according to the definitions employed here. However, once again more detailed investigations are required in order to see whether these languages share enough characteristics to warrant a (sub-)type of their own.

ACKNOWLEDGMENTS

I would like to express my gratitude to Sander Adelaar for his valuable comments on an earlier version of this chapter and to John Hajek for comments on the phonology section. Thanks also to Markus Greif, Emina Kurtić and Jan Strunk for feedback from a student's point of view.

REFERENCES

Adelaar, K.A. (1992) *Proto-Malayic: a reconstruction of its phonology and part of its morphology and lexicon*, Canberra: Pacific Linguistics.
——(2000) 'Siraya Reduplication', *Oceanic Linguistics* 39: 33–52.
Ameka, F., Dench, A. and Evans, N. (eds) (to appear) *Catching Language*, Berlin: Mouton de Gruyter.
Arka, I Wayan (1998) *From morphosyntax to pragmatics in Balinese*, PhD Thesis, University of Sydney.
Arka, I. Wayan and Manning, C.D. (to appear) 'Voice and grammatical relations in Indonesian: A new perspective', in P. Austin and S. Musgrave (eds).
Artawa, Ketut, Artini, Putu and Blake, B.J. (2001) 'Balinese Grammar and Discourse', in Austin et al (eds), 11–46.
Austin, P. and Musgrave, S. (eds) (to appear) *Voice and grammatical functions in Austronesian languages*, Stanford: CSLI.
Austin, P., Blake, B. and Florey, M. (eds) (2001) *Explorations in valency in Austronesian languages*, La Trobe Papers in Linguistics 11, Bundoora: La Trobe University.
Baird, L. (2002) *A Grammar of Keo: An Austronesian language of East Nusantara*, PhD Thesis, Australian National University.
Barr, D.F. (1988) 'Da'a Verbal Affixes and Clitics', in H. Steinhauer (ed.), 11–49.
Bennardo, G. (2002) *Representing Space in Oceania: Culture in Language and Mind*, Canberra: Pacific Linguistics.
Blake, B.J. (1988) 'Tagalog and the Manila-Mt Isa Axis', *La Trobe Working Papers in Linguistics* 1:77–90.
Blake, F.R. (1925) *A Grammar of the Tagalog Language*, New Haven: American Oriental Society.
Bloomfield, L. (1917) *Tagalog Texts with Grammatical Analysis*, 3 vols., Urbana, Ill.: The University of Illinois.
Blust, R.A. (1988) *Austronesian root theory. An essay on the limits of morphology*, Amsterdam: Benjamins.
——(1995) 'Notes on Berawan consonant gemination', *Oceanic Linguistics* 34:123–138.
——(1997a) 'Nasals and nasalization in Borneo', *Oceanic Linguistics* 36:149–179.
——(1997b) 'Ablaut in Western Borneo', *Diachronica* XIV:1–30.
——(1998) 'Ca-Reduplication and Proto-Austronesian Grammar', *Oceanic Linguistics* 37:29–64.
——(1999) 'Notes on Pazeh phonology and morphology', *Oceanic Linguistics* 38:321–364.
——(2001) 'Thao Triplication', *Oceanic Linguistics* 40:324–335.

Bowden, J. (2001) *Taba: Description of a South Halmahera language*, Canberra: Pacific Linguistics.

Capell, A. (1964) 'Verbal systems in Philippine languages', *Philippine Journal of Science* 93:231–249.

Carpenter, K.L. (1996) 'Subordination by reduplication in Wetan', *Studies in Language* 20:37–51.

Cena, R.M. (1995) 'Surviving without relations', *Philippine Journal of Linguistics* 26:1–32.

Chang, M.L. (1998) 'Thao reduplication', *Oceanic Linguistics* 37:277–297.

Clynes, A. (1995) *Topics in the Phonology and Morphosyntax of Balinese*, PhD Thesis, Australian National University.

——(1997) 'On the Proto-Austronesian 'Diphthongs', *Oceanic Linguistics* 36:347–361.

Cohn, A.C. (1990) *Phonetic and phonological rules of nasalization*, PhD Thesis, Univ. of California Los Angeles.

Collins, J.T. (1983) *The Historical Relationships of the Languages of Central Maluku, Indonesia*, Canberra: Pacific Linguistics.

Comrie, B. (1979) 'Definite and animate direct objects: a natural class', *Linguistica Silesiana* 3:13–21.

Constantino, E. (1971) 'Tagalog and other major languages of the Philippines', in T.A. Sebeok (ed.), *Current Trends in Linguistics*, vol. 8/1: 112–154) The Hague: Mouton.

Coward, D. and Coward, N. (2000) 'A phonological sketch of the Selaru language', in C.E. Grimes (ed.), 9–54.

Cumming, S. (1991) *Functional Change. The Case of Malay Constituent Order*, Berlin: de Gruyter.

Cumming, S. and Wouk, F. (1987) 'Is there "Discourse Ergativity" in Austronesian Languages?', *Lingua* 71:271–296.

Davies, W. (1999a) *Madurese*, München: Lincom (Languages of the World/Materials 184).

——(1999b) 'Madurese and Javanese as strict word order languages', *Oceanic Linguistics* 38:152–167.

DeGuzman, V.P. (1978) 'A case for nonphonological constraints on nasal substitution', *Oceanic Linguistics* 17:87–106.

——(1988), 'Ergative Analysis for Philippine Languages: An Analysis', in R. McGinn (ed.), *Studies in Austronesian linguistics*, 323–345, Athens, Ohio: Ohio University Monographs in International Studies.

DeWolf, C.M. (1979) *Sentential Predicates: A Cross-Linguistic Analysis*, PhD Thesis, University of Hawaii.

——(1988) 'Voice in Austronesian languages of Philippine type: passive, ergative, or neither?', in Shibatani (ed.), 143–193.

Dixon, R.M.W. (1994) *Ergativity*, Cambridge: Cambridge University Press.

Donohue, M. (1999) *A grammar of Tukang Besi*, Berlin/New York: Mouton De Gruyter.

——(2002) 'Voice in Tukang Besi and the Austronesian focus system', in Wouk and Ross (eds), 81–99.

Donohue, M. and Smith, J.C. (1998) 'What's happened to us? Some developments in the Malay pronoun system', *Oceanic Linguistics* 37:65–84.

Dryer, M.S. (1989) 'Plural words', *Linguistics* 27:865–895.

DuBois, J.W. (1987) 'The discourse basis of ergativity', *Language* 63:805–955.

Durie, M. (1985) *A grammar of Acehnese on the basis of a dialect of North Aceh*, Dordrecht: Foris.

——(1987) 'Grammatical Relations in Acehnese', *Studies in Language* 11:365–399.

Egerod, S. (1988) 'Thoughts on Transitivity', *Bulletin AS* 59:369–384.

Egli, H. (1990) *Paiwangrammatik*, Wiesbaden: Harrassowitz.

English, L.J. (1986) *Tagalog–English dictionary*, Manila: National Book Store.

Evans, N. (2000) 'Word classes in the world's languages', in G. Booij, C. Lehmann and J. Mugdan (eds), *Morphologie – Morphology. An international handbook on inflection and word-formation*, Berlin: de Gruyter, 708–732.

Florey, M. (2001) 'Verb and valence in Alune', in Austin *et al.* (eds), 73–120.

Foley, W.A. (to appear) 'The place of Philippine languages in a typology of voice systems, in P. Austin and S. Musgrave (eds).

Foley, W.A. and Van Valin, R. (1984) *Functional Syntax and Universal Grammar*, Cambridge: Cambridge University Press.

Friberg, B. (1996) 'Konjo's peripatetic person markers', in H. Steinhauer (ed.) 137–171.

Gil, D. (1994) 'The structure of Riau Indonesian', *Nordic Journal of Linguistics* 17: 179–200.

——(2000) 'Syntactic categories, cross-linguistic variation and universal grammar', in P. Vogel and B. Comrie (eds), *Approaches to the typology of word classes*, 173–216, Berlin: de Gruyter.

Grimes, C.E. (1991) *The Buru language of Eastern Indonesia*, PhD Thesis, Australian National University.

——(2000) 'Introduction: new information filling old gaps in eastern Indonesia', in Grimes (ed.), 1–8.

——(ed.) (2000) *Spices from the East. Papers in languages of eastern Indonesia*, Canberra: Pacific Linguistics.

Haaksma, R. (1933) *Inleiding tot de Studie der Vervoegde Vormen in de Indonesische Talen*, Leiden: Brill.

Hajek, J. and Bowden, J. (2002) 'A phonological oddity in the Austronesian area: ejectives in Waimoa', *Oceanic Linguistics* 41:222–224.

Halle, M. (2001) 'Infixation vs. onset metathesis in Tagalog, Chamorro, and Toba Batak', in M.J. Kenstowicz (ed.), *Ken Hale: a life in language*, 153–168, Cambridge, Mass.: MIT Press.

Heath, J. (1975) 'Some functional relationships in grammar', *Language* 51:89–104.

Himmelmann, N.P. (1991) *The Philippine Challenge to Universal Grammar*, Arbeitspapier 15, Köln: Institut für Sprachwissenschaft.

——(1997) *Deiktikon, Artikel, Nominalphrase: Zur Emergenz syntaktischer Struktur*, Tübingen: Niemeyer.

——(1998) 'Regularity in irregularity: Article use in adpositional phrases', *Linguistic Typology* 2:315–353.

——(1999) 'The lack of zero anaphora and incipient person marking in Tagalog', *Oceanic Linguistics* 38:231–269.

——(2001) *Sourcebook on Tomini-Tolitoli Languages. General Information and Word Lists*, Canberra: Pacific Linguistics.

——(2002a) 'Voice in two northern Sulawesi languages', in Wouk and Ross (eds), 123–142.

——(2002b) 'Voice in Western Austronesian: An update', in Wouk and Ross (eds), 7–16.

——(to appear a) 'Lexical categories and voice in Tagalog', in P. Austin and S. Musgrave (eds).

——(to appear b) 'How to miss a paradigm or two: Multifunctional *ma-* in Tagalog', in F. Ameka *et al.* (eds).

Himmelmann, N.P. and Wolff, J. (1999) *Toratán (Ratahan)*, München: Lincom.

Hogan, D. (1999) *Urak Lawoi'*, München: Lincom.

Hughes, J. (2000) 'The morphology of Dobel, Aru, with special reference to reduplication', in C.E. Grimes (ed.), 131–180.

Hull, G. (1999) *Mai Kolia Tetun: a course in Tetum-Praça, the lingua franca of East Timor*, 3rd edition, Sydney: Caritas Australia.

——(2001) 'A morphological overview of the Timoric Sprachbund', *Studies in Languages and Cultures of East Timor* 4:98–205.

——(2002) *Waimaha (East Timor Languages Profiles No. 2)*, Dili: Instituto Nacional de Linguística.

Hull, G. and Eccles, L. (2001) *Tetum Reference Grammar*, Winston Hills: Sebastião Aparício da Silva Project.

Humboldt, W. von (1838) *Über die Kawi Sprache*, Bd. II, Berlin: Dümmler.

Jonker, J.C.G. (1914) 'Kan men bij de talen van den Indischen archipel eene westelijke en eene oostelijke afdeeling onderscheiden?', *Verslagen en mededeelingen der Koninklijke Akademie van Wetenschappen, Afdeeling Letterkunde* (4) XII:314–417.

Keenan, E.L. (1976) 'Towards a Universal Definition of "Subject", in Li (ed.), 305–333.

Keenan, E.L. and Comrie, B. (1977) 'Noun phrase accessibility and universal grammar', *Linguistic Inquiry* 8:63–100.

Klamer, M. (ed.) (1996) *Voice in Austronesian*, NUSA 39, Jakarta: Universitas Atma Jaya.

Klimov, G.A. (1977) *Tipologija jazykov aktivnogo stroja*, Moskau: Nauka.

Kroeger, P.R. (1993) *Phrase Structure and Grammatical Relations in Tagalog*, Stanford: Stanford University Press.

LaPolla, R.J. and Poa, D. (to appear) 'On describing word order', in F. Ameka *et al.* (eds).

Lazard, G. (2001) 'Le marquage différentiel de l'objet', in M. Haspelmath, E. König, W. Oesterreicher and W. Raible (eds), *Language Typology and Language Universals*, 873–885, Berlin: de Gruyter.

Lemaréchal, A. (1991) 'Dérivation et orientation dans les langues des Philippines', *Bulletin de la Société de Linguistique de Paris* 86:317–358.

Li, C.N. (ed.) (1976) *Subject and Topic*, New York: Academic Press.

Li, P.J. (1973) *Rukai Structure*, Taipei: Academia Sinica.

Li, P.J. and Tsuchida, S. (2001) *Pazeh Dictionary*, Language and Linguistics Monograph Series No A2, Taipei: Academia Sinica.

Lichtenberk, F. (1991) 'Semantic change and heterosemy in grammaticalization', *Language* 67:475–509.

Lopez, C. (1937) 'Preliminary Study of the Affixes in Tagalog', in E. Constantino (ed.) (1977) *Selected writings of Cecilio Lopez in Philippine linguistics*, 28–104, Diliman: University of the Philippines Press.

Martens, M. (1988a) 'Focus or Ergativity? Pronoun sets in Uma', in H. Steinhauer (ed.), 263–277.

——(1988b) 'Focus and Discourse in Uma', in H. Steinhauer (ed.), 239–256.

Martin, J.R. (1981), 'Conjunction and continuity in Tagalog', in M.A.K. Halliday and J.R. Martin (eds), 1981, *Readings in Systemic Linguistics*, 310–336, London: Batsford.

Matsuda French, K. (1988) 'The focus system in Philippine languages: A historical overview', *Philippine Journal of Linguistics* 18/19:1–29.

McFarland, C.D. (1978) 'Definite objects and subject selection in Philippine languages', in C. Edrial-Luzares and A. Hale (eds), *Studies in Philippine Linguistics*, vol. 2, 139–182, Manila: Linguistic Society of the Philippines.

McKaughan, H.P. (1958) *The Inflection and Syntax of Maranao Verbs*, Manila: Bureau of Printing.

——(1973) 'Subject versus Topic', in A.B. Gonzales (ed.), *Parangal kay Cecilio Lopez*, 206–213, Quezon City: Linguistic Society of the Philippines.

Mead, D. (2002) 'Proto Celebic focus revisited', in Wouk and Ross (eds), 143–177.

Mithun, M. (1991) 'Active/agentive case marking and its motivations', *Language* 67:510–546.

——(1994) 'The Implications of Ergativity for a Philippine Voice System', in B.A. Fox and P.J. Hopper (eds), *Voice: Form and Function*, 247–277, Amsterdam: Benjamins.

Müller-Gotama, F. (2001) *Sundanese*, München: Lincom.

Musgrave, S. (2001) *Non-subject Arguments in Indonesian*, PhD Thesis, The University of Melbourne.

Naylor, P.B. (1995) 'Subject, Topic, and Tagalog syntax', in D. Benett, T. Bynon and G.B. Hewitt (eds), *Subject, Voice and Ergativity*, 161–201, London: SOAS.

Newman, J. (1984) 'Nasal replacement in western Austronesian: an overview', *Philippine Journal of Linguistics* 15:1–17.

Pastika, I Wayan (1999) *Voice selection in Balinese narrative discourse*, PhD Thesis, Australian National University, Canberra.

Pater, J. (2001) 'Austronesian nasal substitution revisited', in L. Lombardi (ed.) *Segmental phonology in Optimality Theory: Constraints and Representations*, 159–182, Cambridge University Press.

Payne, T.E. (1982) 'Role and reference related subject properties and ergativity in Yup'ik Eskimo and Tagalog', *Studies in Language* 6:75–106.

Plank, F. (1999) 'Split morphology: How agglutination and flexion mix', *Linguistic Typology* 3:279–340.

Rau, D.V. (1997) *A Grammar of Atayal*, Taipei: The Crane Publishing Company.

Reid, L.A. (1970) *Central Bontoc: Sentence, Paragraph and Discourse*, Norman/ University of Oklahoma: Summer Institute of Linguistics.

——(1992) *Guinaang Bontoc Texts*, Tokyo: Institute for the Study of Languages and Cultures of Asia and Africa.

——(2002) 'Determiners, nouns or what? Problems in the analysis of some commonly occurring forms in Philippine languages', *Oceanic Linguistics* 41:295–309.

Remijsen, B. (2002) 'Lexically contrastive stress accent and lexical tone in Ma'ya', in C. Gussenhoven and N. Warner (eds) *Laboratory Phonology VII*, 585–614, Berlin: Mouton de Gruyter.

Robins, R.H. (1957) 'Vowel Nasality in Sundanese', in *Studies in Linguistic Analysis* (Special volume of the Philological Society), 87–103, Oxford: Blackwell.

Ross, M.D. (2002) 'The history and transitivity of western Austronesian voice and voice-marking', in Wouk and Ross (eds), 17–62.

Samely, U. (1991) *Kedang (Eastern Indonesia). Some Aspects of its grammar*, Hamburg: Buske.

Sasse, H.-J. (1993) 'Das Nomen – eine universale Kategorie?', *Sprachtypologie und Universalienforschung* 46:187–221.

Schachter, P. (1976) 'The Subject in Philippine Languages, Topic, Actor, Actor-Topic or None of the Above', in Li (ed.), 491–518.

——(1995) *The Subject in Tagalog: Still none of the above*, UCLA Occasional Papers in Linguistics vol. 15, Los Angeles: UCLA, Department of Linguistics.

Schachter, P. and Otanes, F.T. (1972) *Tagalog reference grammar*, Berkeley: University of California Press.

Scheerer, O. (1924) 'On the Essential Difference Between the Verbs of the European and the Philippine Languages', *Philippine Journal of Education* 7:1–10.

Sells, P. (1997) 'The functions of voice markers in the Philippine Languages', in S.G. Lapointe, D.K. Brentari and P.M. Farell (eds), *Morphology and its relation to phonology and syntax*, 111–137, Stanford: CSLI.

Senft, G. (ed.) (1997) *Referring to space: studies in Austronesian and Papuan languages*, Oxford: Clarendon Press.

Shibatani, M. (1988) 'Voice in Philippine languages', in Shibatani (ed.), 85–142.

——(ed.) (1988) *Passive and Voice*, Amsterdam: Benjamins.

Silzer, P.J. (1983) *Ambai: an Austronesian language of Irian Jaya, Indonesia*, PhD Thesis, Australian National University.

Sirk, Ü. (1996) 'On the history of transitive verb suffixes in the languages of western Indonesia', in H. Steinhauer (ed.), 191–205.

Sneddon, J.N. (1975) *Tondano Phonology and Grammar*, Canberra: Pacific Linguistics.

——(1993) 'The drift towards final open syllables in Sulawesi languages', *Oceanic Linguistics* 32:1–44.

——(1996) *Indonesian. A comprehensive grammar*, London: Routledge.

Steinhauer, H. (ed.) (1988) *Papers in Western Austronesian Linguistics No. 4*, Canberra: Pacific Linguistics.

——(ed.) (1996) *Papers in Austronesian Linguistics No. 3*, Canberra: Pacific Linguistics.

Stokhof, W.A.L. (1988) 'A modern grammar of Acehnese: Some critical observations', *Bijdragen tot de Taal-, Land- en Volkenkunde* 144:323–350.

Thurgood, E. (1997) 'Bontok reduplication and prosodic templates', *Oceanic Linguistics* 36:135–148.

Thurgood, G. (1999) *From Ancient Cham to Modern Dialects: Two Thousand Years of Language Contact and Change*, Honolulu: University of Hawai'i Press.

Uhlenbeck, E.M. (1975) 'Sentence segment and word group. Basic concepts of Javanese syntax', *Nusa* 1:1–10.

Van den Berg, R. (1989) *A Grammar of the Muna Language*, Dordrecht-Holland: Foris.

Van der Leeden, A.C. (1997) 'A tonal morpheme in Ma'ya', in C. Odé and W. Stokhof (eds), *Proceedings of the Seventh International Conference on Austronesian Linguistics*, 327–350, Amsterdam: Rodopi.

Van Hoëvell, G.W.W.C. (1877) 'Iets over de vijf voornaamste dialecten der Ambonsche landtaal (bahasa tanah)', *Bijdragen tot de Taal-, Land- en Volkenkunde* 4:1–136.

Van Valin, R.D. and LaPolla, R.J. (1997) *Syntax. Structure, Meaning and Function*, Cambridge: Cambridge University Press.

Verhaar, J.W.M. (1984) 'Affixation in contemporary Indonesian', in B. Kaswanti Purwo (ed.), *Towards a description of contemporary Indonesian: Preliminary Studies*, Part I (=NUSA 18), 1–26, Jakarta: Universitas Atma Jaya.

Wechsler, S. and Arka, I Wayan (1998) 'Syntactic Ergativity in Balinese: an Argument Structure Based Theory', *Natural Language and Linguistic Theory* 16:387–442.

Williams-van Klinken, C., Hajek, J. and Nordlinger, R. (2002) *A short grammar of Tetun Dili*, München: Lincom.

Wolff, J.U. (1966) *Beginning Cebuano*, part I, New Haven: Yale University Press.

—— (1972) *A Dictionary of Cebuano Visayan*, 2 vols, Ithaca: Cornell University Southeast Asia Program.

—— (1996) 'The development of the passive verb with pronominal prefix in Western Austronesian languages', in B. Nothofer (ed.), *Reconstruction, classification, description — festschrift in honor of Isidore Dyen*, 15–40, Hamburg: Abera-Verlag.

—— (2001), 'Cebuano', in J. Garry and C. Rubino (eds), *Facts about the world's languages*, 121–126, New York: New England Publishing Associates.

Wouk, F. and Ross, M.D. (eds) (2002) *The history and typology of western Austronesian voice systems*, Canberra: Pacific Linguistics.

Zobel, E. (2002) 'The position of Chamorro and Palauan in the Austronesian family tree: evidence from verb morphosyntax', in Wouk and Ross (eds), 405–434.

—— (to appear) *A diachronic study of Austronesian verb morphosyntax*, PhD Thesis, Universität Frankfurt.

Zorc, R.D. (1977), *The Bisayan dialects of the Philippines: subgrouping and reconstruction*, Canberra: Pacific Linguistics.

CHAPTER SIX

OLD MALAY

Waruno Mahdi

1 INTRODUCTION

1.1 Sources

Old Malay (OM) is the conventional designation for the language of the earliest Malay epigraphy (seventh to tenth centuries AD). The language of Malay inscriptions of the subsequent period, though also preceding Classical Malay (CM), the language of Malay classical literature, is usually not considered OM (see e.g. Kridalaksana 1991:168). In this chapter, comparisons will be made with corresponding items in CM, in modern Indonesian Malay (IM), or in both of these (C/IM).

The known OM inscriptions are limited in number (see Table 6.1) and dialectally not uniform. Several (Kota Kapur, Karang Brahi, Palas Pasemah, and the Sabokingking Naga stone) have a non-OM introductory formula. Its language, called 'language B' by Damais (1968), bears similarities with Malagasy (Aichele 1954, Damais 1968, Adelaar 1989:36–37 who also compared Maanyan, Dahl 1991:49–55 who proposed to call it 'Old Maanyan').

Many inscriptions are damaged, or rather short. Three long ones, Karang Brahi, Palas Pasemah, and Kota Kapur are practically identical (wherefore only the latter will be quoted here). The fragmentary Sabokingking B and incomplete Kedukan Bukit inscriptions represent partly overlapping passages of the same text. OM texts abound with Sanskritisms retaining original Sanskrit spelling. In all, the available non-Sanskrit OM vocabulary covers barely 150 basic lexical units (Vikør 1988:81–83 lists 144). All this sets certain limits to a description of the language.

Major works on decipherment and on the language, with source texts and wordlists, are Cœdès (1930), Ferrand (1932), and Casparis (1950, 1956). Suhadi (1983) provides a collection of source texts. Various aspects of the language are dealt with by Kern (1931), Aichele (1942–1943), Teeuw (1959), Kähler (1983:22–31), Vikør (1988:67–84, 88), Kridalaksana (1991), Adelaar (1992 and in press), Ogloblin (1998), Tadmor (2000), and Wolff (2001).

1.2 Archaeological and historiographic data on chronology and distribution

Reviews on archaeological, palaeographic, and historiographic aspects of the epigraphy of the Malayan Archipelago, including OM inscriptions, have been made by Damais (1952, 1955), Wolters (1967), Casparis (1975), Boechari (1977), Edwards McKinnon (1985), Hall (1985:78–102), and Manguin (1987, 1993).

The bulk of OM inscriptions are from Sumatra and immediately neighboring Bangka island, being typically set up by rulers of Sriwijaya (*Śrī-Vijaya*). This thalassocracy was first identified by Cœdès (1918), and its location in Palembang has now been archaeologically confirmed (Manguin 1987, 1993). With exception of the Laguna copper plate found in the Philippines (Postma 1992), the remaining OM inscriptions were discovered in Java.

The development of OM before the seventh century AD is not documented, but archaeological studies (Solheim 1980:334) and other data (Mahdi 1994:188–191, 1995: 162–165) suggest that Malay-speaking seafarers became involved in sea trade with China, India, and the Near East between 200 BC and AD 200.

The apparently Malay polity of Yavadvipa emerged in the second century AD, being mentioned as *Yavadvīpa* (Sanskrit *dvīpa* 'island') in Valmiki's *Rāmāyaṇa*, as *Iabadíou* and *Sabadeîba* in Ptolemy's *Geography*, and as *Ye⁴diao⁴* with 132 AD dating in the Later Han Annals (*Hou⁴han⁴shu¹*), subsequently sometimes misspelled *Si¹diao⁴* (Mahdi 1994: 173, 204–205 nn. 25–26, 215 n. 93, 469–470 n. 111, 1995:165–166). Historiographic data imply a location on the east coast of Sumatra between the latitudes of Bangka and Singapore (Mahdi 1994:206 n. 27, 1995:167–170, cf. also Obdeyn 1941: map 3 at back of issue), i.e. in the region of later Malayu (whence C/IM *Məlayu* 'Malay').

Consequently, Malays and places they inhabited or ruled were referred to as *Jāvaka* in Pali, *Cavakam* in Tamil, (*az-*)*Zābağ* in Arabic, and as either *She²po²* ~ *She⁴po²* (< **jaba*) or *She⁴bo²* ~ *Zhu⁴bo²* (< **jabak[a]* ~ **jəbak[a]*) in Chinese (Mahdi 1994:205–206 n. 26, 214 n. 84, 474 n. 138, 1995:170–171). Middle Khmer had *Cvā* (Çœdès and Dupont 1943: 106 fn.1), from Old Khmer *Javā* ~ *Jvā*. The Modern Khmer reflex *Cvie* means 'Malay[an]' as well as 'Java[nese]' (Headley *et al.* 1977:264) but in fixed expressions it only refers to the former, e.g. *Srokcvie* 'Malaya' (*srok* 'land', 'country'). Malay itself has *Jawi* 'Malay[an]' borrowed from the Arabic (Wilkinson 1901–1903:218).

Since the third century AD, Chinese sources referred to Malay-speaking sailors as *Gu³lun²* ~ *Ku¹lun²* ~ *Jue²lun²* (the latter a misspelling). By the seventh century, one also finds the non-cognate *Kun¹lun²* as reference to Malay language and people (Mahdi 1999a:163–165). Yijing reports that three pilgrims visiting Sriwijaya (*Shi⁴li⁴fo²shi⁴*) learned the *Kun¹lun²* language (I-Tsing 1894:63, 159, 183), thus identifying this as OM (the language of Sriwijaya).

1.3 Dialectal variety

The precise relationship between OM and CM is still subject to discussion (Ronkel 1924: 16, 21, Aichele 1942–1943:45–46, Teeuw 1959:141–144, Adelaar 1985:191 and in press, Ross in press). The most conspicuous contrast involves the prefixes of the passive voice and of the stative verb forms, being respectively *di-* and *bər-* (*bar-* in early documents) in CM, but *ni-* and *mar-* (read *mər-*) in the original official OM dialect of Sriwijaya epigraphy. Later OM inscriptions from outside Sumatra typically feature *di-* and *bar-* or *var-* respectively, being in agreement with the CM.

Dialectal variety is thought to have existed at the time of OM epigraphy, and nonstandard dialects featuring *di-* and *bar-* must have existed parallel to the official OM dialect having *ni-* and *mar-* (Aichele 1942–1943, Teeuw 1959). Appearance of the former prefixes in later inscriptions is seen as influence of non-standard dialects. The latter also played an important role in the transition to CM (Adelaar in press).

There is indeed evidence that the two dialects coexisted at the time Sriwijaya arose in the second half of the seventh century. The dialect with *mar-* is attested by the name of the West-Sumatran volcano Merapi (< *mər-*prefix + *api* 'fire') – apparently having ritual significance for Yavadvipa – subsequently also conferred to a volcano in Central Java by a ruler originating from, or affiliated to, Yavadvipa. Meanwhile, the dialect with *bər-* is attested to by the original coining of C/IM *pohon bəringin* 'willow fig (*Ficus benjamina* L., often treated as sacred)' (*pohon* 'tree', *ingin* 'wish'; Aichele 1928:28 fn. 4). This tree name corresponds to Sanskrit *kalpavṛkṣa* 'wishing tree, a mythical banyan tree (*Ficus indica* L., resembling the willow fig in many features)', and was borrowed into Javanese as *waringin* 'willow fig'. The *b>w* shift in the latter suggests very early borrowing, apparently before the seventh century (cf. Mahdi 1999b: 196–197, 210–212).

Although OM *ni-* and *mar-* reflect relatively widespread Austronesian proto-affixes *<in>/ni-* and **maR-*, they are unique within the Malayic group. All other Malayic isolects have *di-* and *b[aə]r-/ba-* respectively. Three alternative treatments of this situation have been proposed:

(1) Proto-Malayic had **di-* and **baR-*, so that OM is not a descendant of Proto-Malayic (Ross in press); (2) Proto-Malayic had **ni-* and **maR-*, the former was replaced by *di-* and the latter shifted to *bər-* in colloquial dialects of OM, subsequently determining the prevalent dialect and influencing all other Malayic isolects (Adelaar in press); and (3) Proto-Malayic had **di-* and **baR-*, retained in OM colloquial dialects that subsequently became prevalent, while *mar-* (and *ni-*) were borrowed from Batak (Aichele 1942–1943:45–46, cf. also Ronkel 1924:16, 21). Aichele had simply too automatically taken the situation in CM as 'standard', thus requiring an external source as explanation for the deviant prefixes of OM (Teeuw 1959:141–144). In my opinion, it is nevertheless quite likely that the ruling elite in second-century Yavadvipa was at least partly of Batak extraction, which would explain Batakisms in the court language. Considering the numerous megalithic and early Hinduist monuments of Central Sumatra (see Schnitger 1939–1943, 1964), the adjacency to Barus, and other circumstances, Bataks must have played an important role in the late prehistoric period of the region.

What is undisputed, however, is that one must distinguish an original nuclear OM epigraphy featuring the verbal prefixes *ni-* and *mar-*, and a later dialectally contaminated OM with *di-* and *var-/bar-*. Another distinctive feature of later inscriptions is the appearance of retroflex *ḍ* in many indigenous words, whereas in the nuclear inscriptions of Sumatra it only occurred in a few honorific words (see 2.2).

For the sake of dialectal uniformity, the further discussion will be based on inscriptions featuring the prefixes *mar-* and *ni-*, and not having *ḍ* in non-honorific indigenous words. This nuclear OM corpus encompasses inscriptions BS, KB, KK, SKB, SKN, and TT as indicated in Table 6.1. One dialectally divergent inscription, SHW, will be quoted for comparative data. Cited passages will be identified by the abbreviated inscription name and the line number.

2 SPELLING AND PHONOLOGY

2.1 Basic characters for consonants

OM phonology can only be inferred from the spelling. An overview was provided by Vikør (1988:67–84). The Later Pallava script developed from an earlier South Indian version (see Casparis 1975:20–25) and was used in the nuclear corpus of OM epigraphy – in which usage it is often referred to as Old Sumatran script. It is illustrated in a table by Boechari in Kridalaksana (1982:xxi).

The script is syllabic, with basic characters (*akṣara*-s) denoting syllable-initial consonants with *a* as a default vowel, and with additional marks placed above, before, behind, or under a basic character, mainly in order to replace the default vowel by another syllabic element, or to suppress it. There are special basic characters for syllables without consonant initial. Various ligatures are used for consonant clusters.

TABLE 6.1: LIST OF OLD MALAY INSCRIPTIONS (INCL. DIALECTALLY DEVIANT ONES; INSCRIPTIONS USED HERE ARE HIGHLIGHTED)

Inscription name	Year	Prefix[a]	Region	Source references
Bukateja	c. 840	—	Central Java	Casparis (1956:207–211 #8), Suhadi (1983:76)
BS=Bukit Seguntang		ni-, mar-	Palembang	Casparis (1956:2–6 #1a)
Dang Puhawang Glis (Gandasuli)[b]	827	—	Central Java	Brandes (1913:3–4 #3), Damais (1955:133–136 #A.11), Suhadi (1983:74)
Dièng – Namaççiwaya Déwadrawya		—	Central Java	Brandes (1913:227–228 #96), Suhadi (1983:75)
Hujung Langit (Bawang)	997	—	Lampung	Damais (1955:130–133 #E.5), Damais (1960a)
Karang Brahi (similar to Kota Kapur)		ni-, mar-	Jambi	Krom (1920:426–431 #XVI), Çœdès (1930:45 #3), Boechari (1979), Suhadi (1983:78)
KB=Kedukan Bukit	683	mar-	Palembang	Ronkel (1924:19–21), Çœdès (1930:33–37 #1), Ferrand (1932:273), Poerbatjaraka (1952:33–34), Suhadi (1983:76)
Kebon Kopi[c] – Rakryan Juru Pangambat	942	bar-/ /mar-	West Java	Bosch (1941), Suhadi (1983: 70, 76)
KK=Kota Kapur	686	ni-, mar-	Bangka	Kern (1913), Çœdès (1930: 46–50 #4), Ferrand (1932:280–281), Poerbatjaraka (1952:39–41), Suhadi (1983:77)
Laguna copper plate	900	di-, bar-	Luzon	Postma (1992)
Manjuçrigrha	793	not seen	Central Java	Boechari unpublished (Suhadi 1983:68)
Palas Pasemah (similar to Kota Kapur)		ni-	Lampung	Boechari (1979), Suhadi (1983:78–79)
SKB=Sabokingking B (Telaga Batu)[d]		—[e]	Palembang	Casparis (1956:11–15 #1e)
SKN=Sabokingking Naga stone (Telaga Batu)[d]	c. 840	ni-, mar-	Palembang	Casparis (1956:15–47 #2), Suhadi (1983:79–81)
SHW=Sang Hyang Wintang (Gandasuli)[b]	832	di-, var-/ /mar-[f]	Central Java	Brandes (1913:236–238 #105), Casparis (1950: 50–73 #4), Suhadi (1983: 74–75)
Sojomerto		—	Central Java	Boechari (1966), Suhadi (1983:74)
TT=Talang Tuwo	684	ni-, mar-	Palembang	Ronkel (1924:12–19), Çœdès (1930:38–44 #2), Ferrand (1932:276–277), Poerbatjaraka (1952:35–38), Suhadi (1983:76–77)
Ulu Belu		—	Lampung	Damais (1960b)

a Critical prefix variants for dialect identification (ni- versus di-; mar- versus var-/bar-).

b References to a Gandasuli (also Kedu) inscription usually imply Sang Hyang Wintang rather than Dang Puhawang Glis.

c The Kebon Kopi – Rakryan Juru Pangambat (also Bogor, or Buitenzorg) inscription should not be confused with King Purnawarman's Sanskrit inscription also referred to as the Kebon Kopi-, Bogor-, or Buitenzorg inscription.

d Archaeologists have recently re-allocated sites near Telaga Batu to Sabokingking as new location referent. References to a Telaga Batu inscription typically imply the Sabokingking Naga stone rather than the lesser inscriptions of Sabokinging/Telaga Batu, of which only SKB is clearly OM.

e The only fragmentarily preserved SKB does not feature any of the diagnostic prefixes, but the text seems to coincide with that of the likewise incomplete KB which does feature the prefixes in complementary passages.

f SHW has var- repeatedly, and mar- only once (in a possibly fossilized form).

TABLE 6.2: CONSONANTS NOMINALLY IMPLIED BY OLD SUMATRAN-SCRIPT BASIC CHARACTERS

	Voiceless stop	Aspirated voiceless stop	Voiced stop	Aspirated voiced stop	Nasal
Velar	*k*	(*kh*)	*g*		*ṅ* [*ng*, *ŋ*]
Palatal	*c*		*j*		*ñ*
Retroflex			*ḍ*		*ṇ*
Dental	*t*	(*th*)	*d*	(*dh*)	*n*
Bilabial	*p*			(*bh*)	*m*
Continuants	*y*	*r*	*l*	*v* [*b* ~ *w*]	*h*
Sibilants		(*ś*[*ç*])	(*ṣ*)	*s*	

Basic characters occur for syllable-initial consonants listed in Table 6.2 (classified according to place and mode of articulation in Sanskrit). Entries in parentheses only occur in Sanskrit loanwords. Alternative transcriptions in the literature are in square brackets.

The OM inventory of consonants suggested by the spelling mainly differs from that of C/IM in featuring the retroflex consonants *ḍ* and *ṇ*, and the voiced fricative *v*. These are the problematic initial consonants in reading OM texts.

In the nuclear OM corpus, *ḍ* and *ṇ* in indigenous words are restricted to the honorific article *ḍa-* and enclitic *-ḍa* ~ *-ṇḍa*. Casparis (1956:208) suggested that this 'exotic' spelling merely served to stress the honorific character of special words without implying actual retroflex articulation (see also Vikør 1988:73).

The interpretation of written *v* either as *b* or *w* remained a problem (Kern 1931:509, Ferrand 1932:283–284, Aichele 1942–1943:40 fn. 1) until Damais (1968:527) indicated that the original Pallava script had a distinct character for *b*, hence written *v* could only represent *w*. With few exceptions (e.g. Kähler 1983:23), this remained the accepted treatment even after Vikør (1988:74) noted a decisive weakness of the argumentation: the Old Sumatran script evidently did not have a distinct character for *b*, because even a *b* in Sanskritisms was spelled *v* (e.g. TT-9 *vodhi-* for Skt. *bodhi-*, TT-13 *vrahma-* for Skt. *brahma-*). That written *v* could indeed be read as *b* rather than *w* in OM is suggested by renderings of *Śrī-Vijaya* in Chinese as *Shi[4]li[4]fo[2]shi[4]* (< *shə-li-but-jay < *səri bəjay[*a*]) and *Shi[4]li[4]pi[2]shi[4]* (< *shə-li-bit-jay < *səri bijay[*a*]), and in Arabic as *Sribuza* (< *sri bəja[*ya*]), see Ferrand (1929:294–297).

Therefore, one cannot generally determine whether a written *v* spelled *b* or *w*. The only reliable mode of transcription is retaining the *v*, leaving the concrete reading unspecified. For less exacting purposes, the C/IM cognate provides some guidance, but as the name of Sriwijaya demonstrates, this is not reliable. In India, the use of the same character to write both *b* and *v* was a widespread feature of Prakrit manuscripts (Cowell 1962:xii–xiii) to which belonged Buddhist scriptures (Sriwijaya was Buddhist, later OM epigraphy featuring distinct *b*/*w* spelling was perhaps Hinduist). As Malayic historical phonology excludes an inherited word-initial *w-* (see Adelaar 1985:67–69, 85–86), I will provisionally assume wordbase-initial *v-* to represent a voiced stop rather than a glide.

The script has no character for glottal stop. Proto-Malayic *k in final position is reflected in C/IM as final glottal stop (spelled with Jawi-script *qāf*) that alternates with *k* (Jawi *kāf*) before vowel-initial suffix. In OM cognates it is rendered *k* in both final and prevocalic position. This possibly reflected the actual pronunciation (Vikør 1988:77).

A C/IM word-final glottal stop that does not reflect an original *k is not reflected in the spelling of OM cognates, e.g. *tīda* 'no', 'not' (C/IM Jawi-script *tīdaq*, Latin-script *tidak*). One can only speculate whether final glottal stop indeed did not occur, or whether merely a means to write it was missing.

2.2 Consonant alternations

The situation in OM with regard to prefixes ending in a homorganic nasal, i.e. *maN-* and *paN-*, is for the greater part similar to that in C/IM, but the data is very limited. Table 6.3a lists the relevant forms (verb bases not explicitly attested by an OM form without nasal-final prefix are given with an asterisk). Note that no examples involving initial *d-*, *j-*, and *g-* are attested.

A major difference between OM and C/IM involves base-initial *l* and *r*, where the nasal is apparently retained as *ŋ* (spelled *ṃ* , see next section) in OM, rather than being dropped as in C/IM. See Table 6.3b.

With regard to the final *r* of the prefixes *mar-* and *par-*, OM apparently agrees with C/IM in dropping it before base-initial *r*, but there is only one diagnostic example: *rūpa-* → SKN-13 *marūpa-* 'apply forms'. In another single example, the prefixal *r* is dropped due to the presence of a final *r* in the following syllable: *kāryya* → SKN-27 *makāryya* 'perform transactions' (cf. Casparis 1956:348), which is in agreement with C/IM *kərja* → *bəkərja* 'work'.

A base-initial stop is often spelled geminated after prefixal *r*, in OM (SKN-10 *parddatuan* 'kingship'; KK-7 *marjjahati* 'do evil to'; KK-4, SKN-17 *marppādaḥ* 'report', 'relate'; TT-9 *marvvaṅun* 'rise, get up'), but this was not followed consistently (SKN-15 *parvvā = ṇda* ~ KB-2, TT-2 *parvā = ṇda* 'their auspices', 'the auspices of', and textually duplicate Karang Brahi-9 *marpādaḥ*~KK-4 *marppādaḥ*). Adelaar (1992:400) is probably right in reading SHW-13 *parttakan* as **parətakan* 'bean field', and written -*r*CC- seems

TABLE 6.3A: OM NASAL SANDHI SIMILAR TO THAT IN C/IM

Base-initial segment	Examples
V	**alap* → KB-3 *maṅalap*
	KK-3 [*ni*]*ūjar* → KK-3 *maṅujāri*
c	**caru* → SKN-11 *mañcaru*
h	**hidup* → TT-6 *maṃhidupi*
k	**kalit* → SKN-11 *maṅalit* (see Adelaar 1992:399)
m	TT-5,12 *mañcak* → BS-13 *mamañcak*
s	SKN-21 [*ni*]*suruḥ* → KK-6/7 *mañuruḥ*
t	KK-4 *tāpik* → KK-10 *manāpik*
v	**vali* (C/IM *balik* ~ [*kəm*]*bali*) → SKN-25 *pamvalya=ṅku*

TABLE 6.3B: OM NASAL SANDHI DIFFERENT FROM THAT IN C/IM

Base-initial segment	Examples
l	SKN-6 *larī* → SKN-9 *maṃlarī*
r	SKN-8 [*ni*]*rakṣa* → SKN-18 *maṃrakṣa*
	*ruru → SKN-10 *maṃruruā*
v	SKN-26 [*ni*]*vava* → SKN-9 *mamāva* (C/IM *bawa* → *məmbawa*)

indeed to have been a means of spelling *-rəC-*. Apparently, an anaptyctic schwa was optionally inserted between prefixal *r* and base-initial stop.

2.3 Vowels and other segments of the syllable rhyme

The basic characters (*akṣara*-s), discussed in 2.2, are complemented by additional marks that mainly serve to replace the default vowel *a* by another vowel, or to suppress it. Additionally, the *anusvāra* mark, conventionally transcribed as *ṃ*, indicates nasalization of the vowel in Sanskrit, and the *visarga*, transcribed *ḥ*, spelled a syllable-final spirant. Table 6.4 lists all these items; those only occurring in Sanskritisms are in parentheses; alternative transcriptions in the literature are in square brackets.

By comparing OM words with C/IM cognates, Vikør (1988:76) inferred that *anusvāra* is used for non-prevocalic *ŋ* and for part of the instances of non-prevocalic *m*, but not for *n*. A *visarga* is only used for word final *h*, alternating with the basic character for *h* in suffixed forms: SKN-5 *sumpaḥ* 'curse' → KK-2 *parsumpahan* 'invocation of the curse'. Examples of such alternation with *anusvāra* were not detected.

Assuming a similar vocalism as in C/IM, Casparis (1975:26–27) and Vikør (1988:71) noted three modes of handling schwa /ə/, which is not provided for in the script: (1) as short *a*; (2) as zero vowel – the flanking consonants appear as consonant cluster; and (3) as short *a* with doubling of the subsequent consonant. Adelaar (1992:400) established another one: (4) as zero vowel with doubling of the subsequent consonant (see 2.2 above).

Alternation of spelling modes (1) and (2) is attested, e.g. KK-5, SKN-8 *makalaṅit* ~ BS-20 *makalñit* 'cause to disappear' (see Adelaar 1992:394, 397–398). Mode (3) occurs only once, TT-3 *pattuṃ* 'k.o. bamboo' (C/IM *bətung*, Javanese *pətung*), but is widespead in later periods (Poerbatjaraka 1957, Vikør 1988:71–72). One additional contemporaneous example is the name of the last king of Yavadvipa, spelled *Səna* in the Sundanese chronicle *Carita Parahiyangan*, and *Sanna* in the 732 AD Canggal inscription (see Poerbatjaraka 1958:256–257).

The *ṛ* transcribes a syllabic rhotic in Sanskrit, not a retroflex consonant. The regular C/IM rendering is *ər*, and the same probably applied for Sanskritisms in OM. Thus, TT-6 *vṛddhi* 'growth' is spelled as in Sanskrit, but SKN-20 *nisamvarddhi=ku* 'be empowered by me' has *ar* for the *ṛ* in Sanskrit *samvṛddhi* 'power', 'might' (see Casparis 1956:351).

Symbols for the two diphthongs only occur in a single Non-Sanskrit word each: SKN-6, TT-5 *lai* 'other' (Casparis 1956:21–24, Ogloblin 1998), and KB-3 *sāmvau* 'ship'. The only other word with a diphthong was spelled differently: TT-2 *hanāu* 'toddy palm' (C/IM *ənau*). The vowels *e* and *o* only occur in Sanskritisms. The only exception, SHW-5,6 *sapopo* 'first degree relative in collateral line' (C/IM *səpupu*), is in a dialectally divergent inscription, probably reflecting local substrate influence (Teeuw 1959:146).

TABLE 6.4: SYLLABLE-NUCLEUS AND SYLLABLE-FINAL SEGMENTS INDICATED BY ADDITIONAL MARKS

Short V	Long V	*a*+V fused	*a*+V diphthong
a	*ā*		
i	*ī*	(*e*)	*ai*
u	*ū*	(*o*)	*au*
(*ṛ*)			
Syllable-final	segments	-*ṃ* [-*ṁ*, -*m*/-*ŋ*]	-*ḥ*

2.4 Vowel length, word stress, and word structure

The remaining three vowels, *a*, *i*, and *u*, are spelled either as short or long vowel. Vowel quantity is not a phonological feature in IM, nor is it reconstructed for Proto-Malayic. Means for noting vowel length however serve to indicate place of stress in Jawi-script spelling, and this is apparently also the case in Old Sumatran-script spelling (Kern 1913:399, Çœdès 1930:62, Casparis 1975:26, Vikør 1988:70–71, Tadmor 2000:157–158). A noteworthy feature, first noted by Blagden (1913:70), is that spelled vowel length (i.e. stress) shifts to the following syllable upon suffixation or before an enclitic: *dātu – ka-datū-an*; *dīri – dirī=ña*. Long (i.e. stressed) vowels typically stand in the penultimate syllable, otherwise in the ultimate syllable. In a large number of words, however, no vowel length (stress) was indicated at all.

The OM basic lexical unit was typically bisyllabic. Consonant (C) clusters had either a nasal (N) or an *r*, as first segment. With the sole exception of the reduplicated monosyllable *maṃmaṃ* (read *maŋmaŋ*), all NC-clusters were homorganic. Based on a corpus that also included texts with *bar-* and *di-*, Vikør (1988:81–83) made the following inventory of observed structures: 61 CVCVC, 42 CVCV, 12 VCVC, 6 VCV, 8 (C)VNCV(C), 2 CV*r*CV(C), altogether 131 bisyllabic basic words. Monosyllabic words numbered 6, all having the structure CVC (Vikør seems to have missed the two monosyllabic prepositions *di* and *ka* with structure CV). There are 7 trisyllabic basic words, encompassing 4 CVCVCV, and one each CVCVCVC, CVNCVCV, CVCVNCVC.

3 BASIC MORPHOSYNTAX

3.1 Word classes

The limited size of the OM corpus and interpretational uncertainties in the decipherment set limits to a morphosyntactic analysis. Analogy to C/IM remains an important aid for studying OM morphosyntax but this has its obvious problems.

Open word classes distinguished apriorically on a semantic basis can only be confirmed by distinctive morphosyntactic features in some individual examples. The open word classes of noun and verb are contrasted among others in combinations with prepositions, locatives, numeration, and in the active-passive voice alternation exclusive to verbs. One must bear in mind that apparent contrasts may be due to lack of data. Thus, OM data includes examples of quantification of nouns, but not of verbs, suggesting the rule: 'nouns can be quantified, verbs not'. In C/IM, verbs can be quantified too, but require the mediation of *kali* 'times'. Something similar probably existed in OM, but is simply not reflected in the available material.

It is difficult to distinguish adjectives from verbs in C/IM, and the same situation probably existed in OM. There are a few words that could be adjectives, but could also be intransitive verbs, e.g. *bhakti* 'submissive', 'be submissive' (KK, SKN), *māti* 'dead', 'be dead', 'die' (SKN), *sākit* 'hurt', 'sick', 'be sick' (SKN). A semantically likely example of an adjective is perhaps *jāhat* 'evil', 'wicked' in SKN-14 *yaṃ vuat jāhat* which could be glossed as 'that does/causes evil', but also as 'that is an evil deed'. The OM corpus does not include obvious examples of degrees of comparison.

A number of closed word classes can be tentatively identified. Personal pronouns, demonstratives and locatives will be dealt with in 3.3, prepositions in 3.4, while numerals and conjunctions follow here.

The following numerals are attested: *sa*= '1, all/whole' (KB, SKN), *dua* '2' (BS, KB, SKB), *tlu* '3' (KB), *sa=pulu ~ sa=puluḥ* '10' (KB, SKB), *sa=pulu dua ~ sa=puluḥ dua* '12' (KB, SKB), *dua–ratus* '200' (KB), *tlu–rātus* '300' (KB), *sa=rivu* '1000' (KB), *dua–lakṣa* '20,000' (KB, SKB). An example of a lengthy composed numeral is KB-6/7 *sa=rivu tlu–rātus sa=pulu dua* '1312'. Sanskrit *lakṣa* means '100,000', but the C/IM borrowed cognate (*sǝ=*)*laksa* means '10,000' and Çœdès (1930:76) plausibly assumed the same for OM *lakṣa*. Noteworthy is *tlu* '3' (C/IM *tiga*), and the formation of teens with a preposed *sa=pulu[ḥ]* (C/IM has postpositioned *–bǝlas*).

Unlike C/IM, OM does not feature quantifiers (classifiers), see Ferrand (1932:294). Numerals were placed immediately before a noun (BS-14 *dua tānḍa* 'two officers') or behind it (KB-5-6 *kośa dua–ratus* 'two hundred containers').

The interrogative numeral, BS-10 *pira* 'how much/many', appears only once. The indefinite numeral *vañak* 'much/many' only occurs in combination with the oblique-genitive form of a personal pronoun: SKN-5 *vañak=māmu* '[all] the lot of you'; KK-2 *kita sa-vañak=ta devata* 'ye all of ye gods'; KB-7 *tlu–rātus sa=pulu dua* **vañak=ña** *dātaṃ* (3 100 1 10 2 **many 3s**.GEN come) 'three hundred and twelve **in number** arrived'. Ordinal numbers are only attested in statements of the day of the Śaka-calendar month: TT-1 *dvitīya* '2nd', KB-8 *pañcamī* '5th', KB-3 *saptamī* '7th' (also partly illegible SKB-3 *..ptamī*), and KB-1 *ekadāśī* '11th', all being Sanskritisms.

The following words can be identified as conjunctions:

SKN-6,passim,27 *athavā* 'or' (C/IM *atau* 'or');
SKN-22,25 *graṃ* [*kadāci*] 'if [on the contrary]' (CM *gǝraṅ* 'might it be')
KK-3,4, SKN-5,passim,25 *kadāci* 'if', 'when', 'whenever';
KK-5,6, SKN-12, TT-3,7,10,12 *tathāpi* 'and', 'moreover' (C/IM *tǝtapi* 'but').

3.2 Basic clause structure

In spite of a surprising variety of clause structures, the corpus does not include specimens of the interrogative or imperative moods (though the proclamatory imprecations in TT and SKN have been interpreted to be in the imperative, see Kridalaksana 1991:171).

As in C/IM, transitive clauses occur in active and passive voice. Verb fronting seems to be frequent in OM, and particularly passive verbs often occur clause-initially. The following word orders are attested for passive transitive clauses.

*UG–**Vpass**–ACT*:

SKN-5   *vañak=māmu*   *uraṃ*   **ni-vunuḥ**   *sumpaḥ*
         many=2p.GEN   person   PASS-**kill**   curse
         'all of you people **will be killed** by the curse'

TT-1   *parlak*   *śrīkṣetra*   *ini*   **ni-par-vuat**
        garden   NAME   PRX   PASS-CAU-**make**
        parvā=nda   *punta*   *hiyaṃ*
        auspices=3s/hon.GEN   TITLE   NAME
        'this Sriksetra garden **was made** under auspices of the noble Punta Hiang'

Note that the actor argument in the passive clause in OM is not introduced by an instrumental or other preposition (in C/IM a preposition is optional).

Vpass–UG–ACT:

KK-7   *tuvi*   **ni-vunuḥ**   *ya*   *sumpaḥ*
        verily   PASS-**kill**   3s   curse
        'verily will he **be killed** by the curse'

SKN-5   **ni-vunuḥ**   *kāmu*   *sumpah*
          PASS-**kill**   2p   curse
          'you will **be killed** by the curse'

The latter clause is repeated at least 23 more times in the same SKN inscription, while *nivunuḥ ya sumpah* 'he will be killed by the curse' occurs altogether 4 times in KK.

There do not appear to be examples of this construction with a noun as UG, so that the latter position in this highly unusual construction is perhaps restricted to pronouns. Note that the corresponding structure in C/IM is Vpass–ACT–UG, for example in the CM *Malay Annals* (Situmorang and Teeuw 1958:245):

CM: *həndak*   **di-bunuh**   *baginda*   =*lah*   *anak*=*ku*   *ini*
      want   PASS-**kill**   majesty EMPH   child=1s.GEN PRX
      'shall then this child of mine **be killed** by his majesty' (i.e. his majesty must apparently be wanting to kill my child)

The following example suggests an even more unusual word order, namely the ACT argument preceding a verb in the passive voice and its UG argument:

SKN-25 *tīda*   *iya*   *akan* –   **ni-mākan**   *kāmu*
         NEG   3s   towards   PASS-**eat**   2p
         'you will not be **devoured** by it [?]'

But we probably have two clauses here, the first of which is a negated existential clause with a zero copula where *iya* '3s' functions as complement of the existential operator. It is thus not an argument of the passive verb and a more literal translation would be 'it will not [be] that you will **be devoured**'. This is also how it was apparently understood by Casparis (1956:45). The second clause at the same time illustrates instances of a passive verb immediately followed by the UG argument without there being an overt actor expression.

In active transitive clauses, the actor often precedes the verb and its undergoer argument, hence ACT–**Vact**–UG:

SKN-9   *jana*   **ma-māva**   *dravya*
        people   ACT-**carry**   property
        'people **transport** property'

SKN-20 *kāmu*   **mam-rakṣā**=*ña*
         2p   ACT-**protect**=3s.OBL
         'you **protect** them'

But verb fronting is attested here too. In this case, the actor argument precedes the undergoer in postverbal position.

Vact–ACT–UG

SKN-25 *tīda*   **mar-vuat**   *kāmu doṣa*   *ini*
         NEG   ST-**make**   2p crime   PRX
         'you do not commit these crimes'

For this construction too there are no certain examples with a noun as actor argument, and the corresponding construction in C/IM again has a different order of arguments, i.e. Vact–UG–ACT, as in the following line (from the CM *Hikayat Hang Tuah*, Balai Pustaka 1956:70):

CM: *Bər-mula*   ...   *akan*   **bər-buat**   *istana*   *raja*   *itu*
      ST-beginning...   FUT   ST-**make**   palace   king   DIST
      'At first...the king will **have** a palace **built**'

In intransitive clauses, the subject is in clause initial position. Clear examples with the verb in initial position, which is possible in C/IM, were not found. (In the following example and a few others further down, Ø indicates a formally unmarked verb form.)

KB-2/3   *ḍa   punta   hiyaṃ   **nāyik**   di   sāmvau*
       ART   TITLE   NAME   **ascend**.ø   at   ship
       'the noble Punta Hiang **boarded** ship'

SKN-11   *tida   kāmu   **mar-ppādaḥ**   dari huluntuhā=ṅku*
       NEG   2p   ST-**report**   from vassal-chief=1s.GEN
       'you do not **report** from my vassal chiefs'

SKN-5/6   *yaṃ   **mar-vuddhi**   lavan*
       REL   ST-**mind**   adversary
       'who **is** hostilely **disposed**'

The examples also show that the negation *tīda* can stand immediately before the verb as in SKN-25, or before the subject when this precedes the verb, as in SKN-11. The OM cognate of C/IM *jangan* 'don't' seems to be *jāñan*, cf.:

TT-6   *ya   **jāñan**   ya   ni-knā-i   sa=vañak=ña   yaṃ   upasargga*
    oh   **don't**   3s   PASS-hit-APP   one=many=3s.GEN   ART   calamity
    'and **may** they **not** be afflicted by all kinds of calamities'

Whereas C/IM *bukan* 'be not' is a negative existential-clause copula, the OM cognate *vukan* (SKN, TT) corresponds to C/IM *lain* 'other' (Kridalaksana 1991:170, Adelaar 1992:392–393). Its apparent synonym *lai* 'other' (SKN, TT) could however stand before as well as after the nucleus, and was perhaps cognate with C/IM *lain* (see Ronkel 1924: 16, Casparis 1956:21–22, but also Çœdès 1930:77, Adelaar 1988:71). The semantic shift from 'other' to 'be not' is reported for Sundanese and Javanese (Adelaar 1985:168, Ogloblin 1998).

3.3 NP-structure

SKN presents a number of paratactic listings without copulative conjunction (SKN-5 *mar-sī-haji hulun–haji* 'the king's countrymen, the king's vassal subjects'; SKN-20 *yuvarāja pratiyuvarāja rājakumāra* 'crown prince, second crown prince, [other] prince'), and one even lists at least 21 coordinate items, denotations of officials and professionals (SKN-3/4; some items are illegible, some have uncertain meaning). On the other hand, in TT the preposition *dñan* 'with' serves as copulative conjunction (in C/IM it has been compressed to *dan* 'and' in this function):

TT-9   *vodhicitta   **dñan**   maitri*   'Bodhi-thoughts **and** friendship'

In a longer listing it appears only between the last two items:

TT-2/3   *ñiyur   pinaṃ   hanāu   rumviya   **dñan**   samiśrā=ña   yam   kāyu*
      coconut   areca   toddy   sago [palms]   **and**   mixed=3s.GEN   ART   tree

      ni-mākan   vuaḥ=ña
      PASS-eat   fruit=3s.GEN
      'coconut palms, areca palms, toddy palms, sago palms and all varieties of trees whose fruit are eaten'

The combination of two nouns denoting different species of a common genus as collective term for the genus (e.g. IM *sendok garpu* 'cutlery', lit. spoon fork) is apparently productive:

TT-4   *parlak   vukan   dṅan   **tavad**   **talāga***
         garden   other   with   **embankment   pond**
         'other gardens complete with **hydraulic installations** [that belong in a garden]'

TT-5   *sa=vañak=ña   vuat=ña   **huma   parlak***
         one=many=3s.GEN   make.Ø=3s.OBL   **swidden   garden**
         'he set up a great deal of **horticultural sites**'

SKN-11   *ma-ṅalit   **mas   mani***
           ACT-steal   **gold   gems**
           'steal **treasures**'.

Combinations of two nominals, of which the first serves as generic determinator of the second, are relatively frequent, but the second component is often a proper name: KB-2 *vulan vaiśākha* 'the month of Vaisaka'; KK-4,8, SKN-15,20 *sanyāsa datūa* 'office of regent'; KK-10 *bhūmi jāva* 'the land of Java'; TT-10 *hyaṃ ratnatraya* 'the divinity Three-Jewels'. C/IM nouns denoting fish, snakes, birds, trees, days of the week, months, rivers, mountains, islands, and countries normally do not appear independently in nominal function, but only as descriptive attribute. In the former function, they require a preceding 'empty' target of attribution, a noun serving as generic determinator (cf. Mahdi 1993:191–192). The limited data suggests that this applied in OM for months (KB-2,4,8, KK-9, SKN-28, TT-1), but apparently not for trees (cf. TT-2/3 *ñiyur pinaṃ hanāu rumviya* 'coconut palms, areca palms, toddy palms, sago palms'). Country and place names usually occur as attribute, e.g. *Śrī-Vijaya* 'Sriwijaya' modifies: KK-2 *kadat-uan* 'palace/kingdom'; KK-4/5 *dātu* 'king'; KK-10 *vala* 'army'. However, there is also a counter-example in KK-10 *tīda bhakti ka śrī-vijaya* 'is not submissive to Sriwijaya'.

Personal pronouns are widely represented in OM texts, but the paradigm shown in Table 6.5 is perhaps a simplification.

While there is only one enclitic form respectively for 2p and 3s, one finds two variants for each of the three other pronouns: with and without nasal linker. The variants once possibly represented different morphological forms (e.g. genitive with nasal linker, oblique without it) but this is not strictly followed anymore in the inscriptions.

The enclitic form of *āku* '1s' without nasal linker typically appears in the oblique case: SKN-20,21,22 *ni-samvarddhi=ku* 'empowered by me', KK-4, SKN-18,19 *nigalar=ku* 'named [by] me'. In the genitive, the enclitic apparently does include an underlying nasal linker which only surfaces after a vowel, not after a consonant: SKN-6 *śatru=ṅku* 'my

TABLE 6.5: OM PERSONAL PRONOUNS

Person	Independent	Enclitic (oblique/genitive)
1s	*āku* (KK, SKN)	=*ku* (KK, SKN) ~=*ṅku* (SKN, TT)
2p	*kāmu* (SKN)	=*māmu* (SKN)
3s	*iya* (BS, KK, SKN) ~ ~ *ya* (KK, SKN, TT)	=*ña* (BS, KK, SKN, TT)
3p/honorific	*sida* (BS).	=*da* (BS) ~=*ṇḍa* (BS, KK, SKN, TT)
(2p)/divine	*kita* (KK),	=*ta* (KK) ~=*nta* (TT)

enemy', SKN-9 *huluntuhā=ṅku* 'my vassal chiefs' versus SKN-8 *kadātuan=ku* 'my royal residence', TT-4 *vuat=ku* 'my making'. But there is one exception with nasal in the oblique case: SKN-8 *ni-rakṣā=ṅku* 'be protected by me'. Thus, the distinction between oblique and genitive modes seems to be inconsistent, and free variation may have existed between uses with or without nasal after a vowel.

The independent form for 3p/honorific also occurs with retroflex *ḍ* in SHW-3 *siḍa*, but the inscription is dialectally divergent. It is possible that the alternatively spelled modes refer to plural (*sida/=da*) and honorific (*siḍa/=ṇḍa*) implementations respectively, but the material is too meagre for drawing reliable conclusions. Beside the enclitic, the honorific third person pronoun also seems to have a monosyllabic prosthetic article mode *ḍa*, as in KB-4 *ḍa pu=nta hiyaṃ* '**the noble** master of gods [?]' (see below).

For enclitic forms of *sida* '3p/honorific' and *kita* '2p/divine', only examples for the genitive are found. Appearance of the nasal linker seems to be governed by a similar morphophonological rule as described above for 1s, but there is too little data. For 3p/honorific the situation is complicated by alternative spellings with *d* or *ḍ*, and possible semantic shift between plural and (singular?) honorific (BS-3 *anak=da* 'their children' versus TT-2 *par-vā=ṇḍa* ~ KK-4 *par-vvā=ṇḍa* 'auspices of the noble...').

For the divine second person there is KK-2 *kita sa=vañak=ta devata* (2p/divine one many 2p/divine.GEN gods) 'ye all of ye gods' versus TT-2 *pu=nta hiyaṃ* 'master of gods[?]'. However, the latter interpretation is questionable, and Çœdès (1930:72–73) cites convincing comparative data from Khmer, Mon, and Thai suggesting that *pu=nta* was a title meaning 'our master', implying that *=nta* was 1p rather than 2p. It occurs twice in the cited line: TT-2 *par-vā=ṇḍa pu=nta hiyaṃ śrī jayanāśa* 'auspices of the noble Punta Hiang Sri Jayanasa', and TT-2 *praṇidhānā=ṇḍa pu=nta hiyaṃ* 'provision of the noble Punta Hiang'. Note also KK-4/5 *par-vvā=ṇḍa dātu śrī–vijaya* 'auspices of the noble king of Sriwijaya'.

Remarkable is the use of the genitive enclitic=[*n*]*ḍa*, perhaps also=[*n*]*ta*, as possessive copula analogously to 3s=*ña* (e.g. SKN-12 *sthānā=ña śatru=ṅku* 'position/residence of my enemy', TT-4 *puṇya=ña sarvva–satva* 'benefit of all beings') also occasionally used this way in C/IM. Mediation of such a possessive copula in possessive attribution is optional, and two nouns of which the second denotes the possessor can follow each other directly: KB-1/2, KK-9 *śuklapakṣa vulan* 'bright half of the month'; SKN-4 *vatak–vuruh* 'groups of workmen', SKN-5 *hulun–haji* 'vassal subjects of the king'. In such cases, however, it is difficult to differentiate between possessive attribution ('group of workmen') and a qualitative or descriptive one ('workmen group').

Only two demonstratives are attested in OM, *ini* 'this (PRX)' (BS, KK, SKB, SKN, TT), and *inan* 'that (DIST)' (KK), while a cognate of C/IM *itu* 'that' is not found. Their attributive use is well attested: SKB-8 *vihāra ini di vanua ini* 'this monastery in this country'; KK-10 *mamaṃ sumpaḥ ini* 'this curse imprecation'; KK-4 *uraṃ inan* 'those people'. Their pronominal use is less clearly documented, e.g. SKN-13 *ini maka-laṅit–prana uraṃ* (PRX CAU-disappear mind person) 'these [who] take away people's minds'.

Two definite article-like words have been identified: *iyaṃ* ~ *yaṃ* (neutral) and *daṃ* (honorific), thought to derive from combinations of *iya* ~ *ya* and *da* with a nasal linker *ŋ* (Kähler 1983:24). The use of the honorific one as article is relatively unproblematic: BS-20 *daṃ svāmi* 'the master'; TT-10 *daṃ hyaṃ ratnatraya* 'the divinity Three-Jewels'.

The use of *iyaṃ* ~ *yaṃ*, of which the C/IM cognate *yang* is a relative marker, is more diversified and one can distinguish three constructions (this is based on an earlier analysis by Kridalaksana 1991:172):

(a) as a relative pronoun followed by the verbal predicate of a relative clause:

TT-2   *sa=vañak=ña*   **yam** *ni-tānam* *di* *sini* *ñiyur*   *pinam...*
            one=many=3s.GEN **REL** PASS-plant at D.PRX coconut areca...
            'all of the coconut, areca, etc. palms **that** are planted here'

KK-4   *dṅan* *di* *iyam* *ni-galar=ku*   *sanyāsa* *datūa*
            with at REL PASS-name=1s.OBL office regent
            'with regard to [those] **who** have been named by me to the office of regent'

(b) as an article followed by a noun that is the head of a clause with predicate:

KK-10   *di vela=ña*   **yam** *vala* *śrī-vijaya* *ma-nāpik* **yam** *bhūmi jāva*
            at time=3s.GEN ART army NAME   ACT-attack ART land   NAME
            'at the time that **the** army of Sriwijaya attacked **the** land of Java'

(c) as an article followed by a noun that is the head of an NP group with attribute:

KB-5   *ma-māva* **yam** *vala*   *dualakṣa*
            ACT-lead ART army 20000
            'lead **an** army of 20000'

KK-2   *mam-raksa* **yam** *kadatuan* *śrī-vijaya*
            ACT-protect ART palace   NAME
            'protect **the** palace of Sriwijaya'

In the function under (c), *yam* cannot be literally translated into IM as *yang*, whereas in the function under (b), such a translation would sound awkward, as pointed out by Kridalaksana. The use of a relative marker was apparently optional, compare:

KK-10   *manāpik* *yam* *bhūmi* *jāva*   *tida* *bhakti*   *ka* *śrī-vijaya*
            ACT-attack ART land   NAME [ ] NEG submit.Ø to NAME
            'attacks the land of Java **that** is not submissive to Sriwijaya'

TT-3   *kāyu* *ni-mākan* *vuaḥ=ña*
            tree [ ] PASS-eat fruit=3s.GEN
            'trees **whose** fruit are eaten'

SKN-25   *ni-vunuḥ* *kāmu* *sumpaḥ* *ni-minu[m]=māmu* *ini*
            kill.PASS 2p curse [ ] PASS-drink=2p.OBL PRX
            'you will be killed by this curse **which** is drunk by you'

In C/IM, *yang* would have been expected in these environments.

3.4 Prepositional phrases

In OM, the prepositions *di* 'in', 'at', *ka* 'to', *dari* 'from', can apparently precede various subgroups of nominals:

(a) common nouns and proper names: SKB-8 *di vanua ini* 'in this country'; SKN-6 *dari śatru=ṅku* 'from my enemy'; KB-6 *di sāmvau* 'on ship'; KB-4 *dari mināṅa tāmvan* 'from Minanga Tamban'; TT-10 *di dam hyam ratnatraya* 'at the divinity Three Jewels'; KK-10 *ka śrī-vijaya* 'to Sriwijaya';

(b) personal pronouns: SKN-8 *dari kāmu* 'from you'; SKN-9 *ka kāmu* 'to you', SKN-12 *dy–āku* ~ KK-9 *diy–āku* 'at/to me'; KK-6 *ka iya* 'to him';

(c) locatives (a closed class of relational space nominals also occurring in languages of mainland Southeast Asia and South China) being in turn always followed by a possessive attribute: KK-7 *di dalaṃ=ña bhūmi* (at inside=3s.GEN earth) 'inside the earth'; TT-5 *di antara mārgga* 'in the midst of the way/journey'; SKN-9 *di luar huluntuhā=ṅku* (at outside vassal-chief=1s.GEN) 'outside [the territory] of my vassal chiefs';

(d) pro-locatives: TT-2 *di sini* 'here'; TT-9 *di sāna* 'there'; SKN-28 *ka-māna* 'where to';

(e) temporal nominals (e.g. TT-5 *di āsannakāla* 'in time-of-stopover'; KK-10 *di velā=ña* 'at the time of').

Another preposition, *dṅan* ~ *daṅan* 'with', mainly combines with a noun: SKN-12 *daṅan darah* 'with blood'; SKN-20 *dṅan śatru=ṅku* 'with my enemy'; KB-5/6 *daṅan kośa dua-ratus* 'with two hundred [supply] containers'; KB-6 *daṅan jālan* 'by road'. In one example that noun is preceded by *yaṃ* serving as article: SKB-21 *dṅan yaṃ uraṃ pradhāna* (with ART person high-ranking) 'with high-ranking persons'. (On *dṅan* as an NP-conjunction, see §3.3.)

The probable preposition *akan* 'to', 'into', 'as', is attested before a noun three times in the identical phrase SKN-20,21,22 *ni-samvarddhi=ku akan–datūa* 'empowered by me as regent'. However, it also occurs before verbs, seemingly as future tense modifier (as in C/IM). But it is conceivable that *akan* in these examples functions as a conjunction meaning 'in order to', 'with the aim of' instead: SKN-22 *akan–ni-mulaṅ śāsanā=ña* 'will/in-order-to be determined by his orders'; SKN-25 *akan–ni-mākan* 'will/in-order-to be devoured'. In one further example it is followed by a preposition, but here too it perhaps functions either as temporal modifier or as conjunction: SKN-22/23 *akan-dari kāmu ni-muah=ña* 'will/in-order-that from you be made available by him' (the translation is very uncertain).

C/IM has numerous temporal-aspectual modifiers (e.g. C/IM perfective *təlah*, durative *sədang*, etc.) and temporal adverbs (e.g. *d[ah]ulu* 'previously', *tadi* 'just now', *nanti* 'later', *kəlak* 'in future', *esok* 'tomorrow', etc.). No obvious equivalents of these are found in the OM corpus. Whenever temporal circumstance is expressed, this is either done with an elaborate statement of the date, or with a phrase like 'that was the time when…'.

4 MAJOR VERBAL ALTERNATIONS

The OM verb is the word class with the most comprehensive paradigm of forms. However, as in C/IM, OM verbs differ quite strongly as to which formations they allow. The exact grammatical meanings of the respective verb forms are difficult to determine purely from the inscription texts, and interpretation often relies on analogy with C/IM or related languages. The present treatment will therefore be mainly concerned with listing attested combinations of affixes and comparing OM with C/IM on this point.

PAn had an active voice marker which appeared as an infix *<um> in bases with initial consonant, and as a prefix *um- before bases with initial vowel. OM has only one possible reflex of this affix: BS-16 *um-aṃgap* 'devour', 'swallow'. (There is a C/IM cognate <əm> which is not productive.) But in fossilized items with a reflex of this historical *um-/*-um- affix, OM has *m-* (not um-), cf. SKN-24 *minuṃ* 'drink' < *<um> + *inum (C/IM *minum* 'id.', *maju* 'advance' ← <əm> + *aju* 'forward'). It seems likely, therefore, that BS-16 *um-aṃgap* is a contamination from 'language B'/'Old Maanyan' for which (in KK-2) a form *um-enteṃ* '?' is attested.

The two C/IM transitivizing verbal suffixes -*i* (locative applicative) and -*kan* (causative, benefactive applicative) are also attested in OM where, as a rule, they appear in combination with the prefix *maN-* or *ni-*. But they also transitivize stative *mar-* verbs (as they do with *bər-* verbs in CM, though not in IM): KK-7 *mar-jjahāt-i* 'do evil unto' (SKN-14 *jāhat* '[be] evil'). There is one example of such a suffixed form without prefix: TT-4 *prayojanā-kan* 'intending/aiming to/towards' (Sanskrit *prayojana* 'cause', 'intention', 'aim'). Two examples seem to provide evidence of -*akan* as variant mode of –*kan*. One is SKN-9/10 *larīy-ākan* 'run off with, take away' (cf. SKN-6 *larī* 'run'), but the double accentuation, and the split location (*larî-* at the end of line 9, *yākan* on line 10), strongly diminishes its significance as evidence for -*akan*. In the other example, SKN-20 *ni-par-sumpah-akan–kāmu* 'you shall be cursed[?]' (cf. SKN-5 *sumpah* 'curse'), the scribe seems to have simply written together three words (*ni-par-sumpah, akan*, and *kāmu*) in a row. Compare SKN-20,21 *ni-samvarddhi=ku akan–datūa* 'be empowered by me as regent'.

The comparison of OM and C/IM verbal prefixes in Table 6.6 reveals other discrepancies beside the much discussed *mar-/bər-* and *ni-/di-* contrasts. Thus, OM has *maka-* for which there is no C/IM cognate. Kähler (1983:28f) compared it with C/IM *məm-pər-*, but C/IM semantic correspondents of the OM forms have *məN-X-kan* (where *X* is the verb base). In a single example of the accidental perfective, normally formed in C/IM with *tər-*, OM has *ka-*, corresponding to C/IM *kə-* which in this function only appears in some fossilized forms as far as IM is concerned (e.g. *kə-təmu* 'meet'). For C/IM *bər-X-an* forms denoting joint action, OM has an equivalent *mar-sī-X* in one instance: SKN-5 *mar-sī-haji* '[those who] share the same king', 'the king's own countrymen' (see Adelaar 1992: 393–396). No OM correspondents have been found for C/IM reciprocal-voice *X-məN-X*.

The active-passive voice opposition is perhaps the best documented verbal alternation in OM. Attested *maN-/ni-* pairs are: SKN-18 *maṃraksa* 'protect' – SKN-8 *ni-rakṣā* [=*ṅku*] 'be protected [by me]'; KK-6/7 *mañuruh* 'order' – KK-4 *ni-suruh* 'be ordered'; SKN-26 *ma-nāpik* 'attack', 'invade' – SKN-26 *ni-tāpik* 'be attacked[?]'; SKN-7 *maṅ-ujār-i*

TABLE 6.6: OM PREFIXED VERB FORMS AND PROBABLE CORRESPONDING PREFIX IN C/IM

C/IM	OM	Formant of: /examples
bər-	*mar-*	Stative (also with -*i*, see above), possessional: TT-9 *mar-vvaṅun* 'rise', 'get up' SKN-5 *mar-vuddhi* 'have mind/character' (C/IM *bər-budi*).
di-	*ni-*	passive voice (also with -*kan*, -*i*): TT-2 *ni-tānaṃ* 'be planted' (C/IM *ditanam*); BS-19 *ni-kāryyā-kan* 'be processed/performed' (C/IM *di-kərja-kan*); TT-6 *ni-knā-i* 'be afflicted' (C/IM *di-kəna-i*).
di-pər-	*ni-par-*	passive causative: TT-1 *ni-par-vuat* 'be made' (C/IM *di-pər-buat*).
məN-	*maN-*	active voice (also with -*kan*, -*i*): KK-6/7 *mañuruh* 'order' (C/IM *mənyuruh*); TT-6 *maṃ-hidup-i* 'raise [cattle]' (C/IM *məng-hidup-i*).
tər-	*ka-*	coincidental perfective: KK-10 *ka-livat* 'was passed through' (C/IM *tər-liwat*).
	maka-	causative stative: KK-5, SKN-14,15 *maka-laṅit* ~ ~ BS-20 *maka-lṅit* 'cause to disappear' (C/IM *məng-hilang-kan*); SKN-14 *maka-gīla* 'make crazy' (C/IM *məng-gila-kan*).

'speak to'– SKN-23 *ni-ujār-i* 'be spoken to'; SKN-9 *mamāva* 'lead (army)', 'bring', 'carry' (things) – SKN-26 *ni-vava* 'be led', 'be sent' (army).

Some C/IM verbs are active transitive in their basic form, adding the passive prefix to this basic active voice form (C/IM *minum* 'drink' → *di-minum* 'be drunk'). OM apparently also has such verbs: SKN-24 *minuṃ* 'drink' → TT-5 *ni-minuṃ*[=*ña*] 'be drunk [by them]'; perhaps also SKN-8 *muaḥ* 'there be [?]', 'have [?]' → SKN-22/23 *ni-muaḥ*[=*ña*] 'be made available [?] [by him]', but the translation is uncertain.

There are OM verb forms with the suffix -*a*, identified by Kern (1913: 399) as formant of the subjunctive (SUBJ) by analogy to the same suffix in Javanese, Malagasy, and Bisaya (reflecting the PAn projective suffix *-a*).

TT-6/7   *varaṃ*   **vuat-ā**=*ña*
whatever   **make**-SUBJ=3S.GEN
'whatever they **should do**'

SKN-10   *athavā kāmu*   **larĭy-a**   **maṃ-larĭy-a**   *lai*   *kāmu*
or   2p   **run**-SUBJ   ACT-**run**-SUBJ   other   2p
'or **should** you **flee** or **let** others of you **flee**.'

5 NOMINALIZATIONS AND NOMINAL MORPHOLOGY

C/IM features a number of derivational means to form nouns denoting action, actor, or undergoer (i.e. *pəN-*, *pəN-...-an*, *pər-...-an*, *kə-...-an*, -*an*), but the same affixation occasionally leads to attributive or nominal forms within the paradigm of the verb (i.e. participles, infinitives, etc. which differ morphosyntactically from "true" nominalizations; cf. Mahdi 1993:202). Furthermore, the basic form of a verb can also be converted into a noun without explicit affixation. The situation in OM was probably similar. The following will take benefit of the doubt by provisionally assuming nominal derivation. When the base word itself is a noun, there is greater certainty that the derivation is nominal. Base words with an asterisk in Table 6.7 are not explicitly evidenced in the inscriptions.

In C/IM, deverbal nouns with -*an* typically name the act of the verbal denotatum, its target, or product, and the available data does not contradict a similar function of -*a* and -*an* in OM. When the basic word is a noun, the derivation with -*an* in C/IM typically

TABLE 6.7: LIKELY NOMINAL DERIVATIONS FROM NOUNS (N) AND VERBS (V) IN OM

Affix	Derivations
-*a*	*dātu* 'king (n)' → KK-4, SKN-15 *datū-a* 'regent'
	vuat 'make, do (v)' → SKN-15, TT-6/7 *vuat-ā* [=*ña*] '[their] action'
-*an*	**kasih* 'love (v)' → KK-6 *kasīh-an* 'love potion'
	vuat 'make, do (v)' → **vuat-an* (→ *ka-vuat-an-ā*=*ña*, see below)
ka-...-a	*vuat* 'make, do (v)' → KK-8 *ka-vuat-ā* [=*ña*] '[their] undertakings'
	*vuat-an 'deed (n)' → SKN-26 *ka-vuat-an-ā* [=*ña*] '[their] undertakings'
ka-...-an	*dātu* 'king (n)' → KK-2, SKN-8 *ka-datu-an* 'royal residence'
paN-...-a	**vali* 'return (v)' → SKN-25 *pam-valy-a*[=*ṅku*] '[my] recompense'
par-	**avis* 'be finished (v?)' → BS-7 *par-āvis* 'all', 'without exception'
	*va 'carry, lead (v)' →
	→ SKN-15 *par-vvā* [=*ṇḍa*] ~ KB-2 par-vā [=*ṇḍa*] 'auspices [of]'
par-...-a	*vuat* 'make, do (v)' → SKN-17 *par-vuat-ā* [=*ña*] '[their] machinations' [?]
par-...-an	*dātu* 'king (n)' → SKN-10 *par-ddatu-an* (BS-1 *par-dātv-a[n]?*) 'kingship'
	sumpah 'curse (n)'→ KK-2 *par-sumpah-an* 'invocation of the curse'

refers to an image, imitation, or analogue of the original signified, which agrees with the derivation *dātu* 'king' → *datū-a* 'regent (territorial governor)', further obscuring any differences between the two suffixes.

In SKN-21 *ni-minu=māmu* 'be drunk by you' there is fusion of the final nasal of *minuṃ* 'drink' and the initial nasal of *=māmu* 'your' (but TT-5 *ni-minuṃ=ña* 'be drunk by them'). It is possible that the assumed suffix *-a* in *vuat-ā=ña* 'their action', *ka-vuat-ā=ña* 'their undertakings', *ka-vuat-an-ā=ña* 'id.', and in *pam-valy-a=ṅku* 'my recompense', was actually *-an* with similar fusion of final *-n* with the nasal of the pronominal enclitic. That would still leave the suffix in *datū-a* 'regent' which is too widely represented to suspect an error in either writing or reading.

REFERENCES

Adelaar, K.A. (1985) *Proto-Malay, the reconstruction of its phonology and parts of its lexicon and morphology*, PhD thesis, Leiden University [rev. ed. 1992, Canberra: Pacific Linguistics].

——(1988) 'More on Proto-Malayic', in Mohd. Thani Ahmad and Zaini Mohamed Zain (eds), *Rekonstruksi dan cabang-cabang Melayu Induk*, 57–99. Kuala Lumpur: Dewan Bahasa dan Pustaka.

——(1989) 'Malay influence on Malagasy: Linguistic and culture-historical implications', *Oceanic Linguistics*, 28:1–46.

——(1992) 'The relevance of Salako for Proto-Malayic and for Old Malay epigraphy', *Bijdragen tot de Taal-, Land- en Volkenkunde*, 148:381–408.

——(in press) 'On the classifiability of Malayic', in D. Gil (ed.), *Malay/Indonesian linguistics*, London: Routledge-Curzon.

Aichele, W. (1928) 'Oudjavaansche bijdragen tot de geschiedenis van den wenschboom', *Djåwå* 8:28–40.

——(1942–1943) 'Die altmalaiische Literatursprache und ihr Einfluß auf das Altjavanische', *Zeitschrift für Eingeborenen-Sprachen*, 33:37–66.

——(1954) 'Sprachforschung und Geschichte im indonesischen Raum', *Oriens Extremus*, 1:107–122.

[Balai Pustaka] (1956) *Hikayat Hang Tuah*, tjet. ke-3, Djakarta: Balai Pustaka.

Blagden, C.O. (1913) 'The Kota Kapur inscription', *Journal of the Straits Branch of the Royal Asiatic Society*, 64:69–71, 65:37.

Boechari (1966) 'Preliminary Report on the Discovery of an Old-Malay Inscription at Sodjomerto', *Madjalah Ilmu-ilmu Sastra Indonesia*, 3:241–251.

——(1977) 'Epigrafi dan Sejarah Indonesia', *Majalah Arkeologi*, 1/2:1–40.

——(1979) 'An Old Malay inscription of Sriwijaya at Palas Pasemah (South Lampung)', in Satyawati Suleiman (ed.), *Pra Seminar Penelitian Sriwijaya (Jakarta, 7–8 Desember 1978)*, 18–42. Jakarta: Pusat Penelitian Purbakala dan Peninggalan Nasional.

Bosch, F.D.K. (1941) 'Een Maleische inscriptie in het Buitenzorgsche', *Bijdragen tot de Taal-, Land- en Volkenkunde van Nederlandsch-Indië*, 100:48–53.

Brandes, J.L.A. (1913) *Oud-Javaansche Oorkonden* (uitgegeven door N.J. Krom), Verhandelingen van het Bataviaasch Genootschap van Kunsten en Wetenschappen 60/1, Batavia: Albrecht/'s-Hage: M. Nijhoff.

Casparis, J.G. de (1950) *Prasasti Indonesia*, I, *Inscripties uit de Çailendra-tijd*, Bandung: A.C. Nix.

——(1956) *Prasasti Indonesia*, II, *Selected Inscriptions from the 7th to the 9th Century A.D.*, Bandung: Masa Baru.

——(1975) *Indonesian palaeography. A history of writing in Indonesia from the beginning to c. A.D. 1500*, Handbuch der Orientalistik, 3. Abt. Bd. 4, Lieferung 1, Leiden/Köln: E.J. Brill.

Çœdès, G. (1918) 'Le royaume de Çrīvijaya', *Bulletin de l'École Française d'Extrême-Orient*, 18/6:1–36.

——(1930) 'Les inscriptions malaises de Çrīvijaya', *Bulletin de l'École Française d'Extrême-Orient*, 30:29–80.

Çœdès, G., and P. Dupont (1943) 'Les stèles de Sdok Kak Thom, Phnom Sandak et Prah Vihar', *Bulletin de l'École Française d'Extrême-Orient*, 43:56–154.

Cowell, B.E. (1962) *The Prākṛta-Prakāśa, or the Prākṛt grammar of Vararuchi*, 3rd edn. Calcutta: Punthi Pustak [1st ed. 1854].

Dahl, O.C. (1991) *Migration from Kalimantan to Madagascar*, Instituttet for Sammenlignende Kulturforskning, Serie B: Skrifter 82. Oslo: Norwegian University Press.

Damais, L.-C. (1952) 'Études d'épigraphie indonésienne III. Liste des principales inscriptions datées de l'Indonésie', *Bulletin de l'École Française d'Extrême-Orient*, 46:1–105.

——(1955) 'Études d'épigraphie indonésienne IV. Discussion de la date des inscriptions,' *Bulletin de l'École Française d'Extrême-Orient*, 47:7–270.

——(1960a) 'Études soumatranaises I; La date de l'inscription de Hujung Langit ('Bawang')', *Bulletin de l'École Française d'Extrême-Orient*, 50:275–288.

——(1960b) 'Études soumatranaises II; L'inscription de Ulu Bəlu (Soumatra méridional)', *Bulletin de l'École Française d'Extrême-Orient*, 50:289–311.

——(1968) 'Études soumatranaises III; La langue B des inscriptions de Srī Wijaya', *Bulletin de l'École Française d'Extrême-Orient*, 54:523–566.

Edwards McKinnon, E. (1985) 'Early Polities in Southern Sumatra: Some Preliminary Observations Based on Archaeological Evidence', *Indonesia* (Ithaca), 40:1–36.

Ferrand, G. (1929) 'Le K'ouen-louen et les anciennes navigations interocéaniques dans les mers du sud', *Journal Asiatique* 11ᵉ série 13:239–333, 431–492, 14:5–68, 201–241.

——(1932) 'Quatre textes épigraphiques malayo-sanskrits de Sumatra et de Baṅka', *Journal Asiatique*, 221:271–326.

Hall, K.R. (1985) *Maritime trade and state development in early Southeast Asia*, Honolulu: University of Hawaii Press.

Headley, R.K. Jr., K. Chhor, Lam K.L., Lim H.K., and Chen C. (1977) *Cambodian–English Dictionary*, Washington (D.C.): Catholic University of America Press.

I-Tsing [=Yijing] (1894) *Les religieux éminents qui allèrent chercher la Loi dans les pays d'occident*, Mémoire composé a l'époque de la grande dynastie T'ang, traduit en français par Édouard Chavannes. Paris: Ernest Leroux.

Kähler, H. (1983) *Grammatik der Bahasa Indonésia*, Wiesbaden: Otto Harrassowitz.

Kern, H. (1913) 'Inscriptie van Kota Kapoer (eiland Bangka; 608 çāka)', *Bijdragen tot de Taal-, Land- en Volkenkunde*, 67:393–400.

Kern, R.A. (1931) 'Enkele aanteekeningen op G. Çoedès' uitgave van de Maleische inschriften van Çrīwijaya', *Bijdragen tot de Taal-, Land- en Volkenkunde*, 88:508–513.

Kridalaksana, H. (1982) *Kamus Linguistik*. Jakarta: Gramedia.

——(1991) 'Peri Hal Konstruksi Sintaksis Dalam Bahasa Melayu Kuna', in H. Kridalaksana (ed.), *Masa Lampau Bahasa Indonesia: sebuah bunga rampai*, seri ILDEP, 166–174. Yogyakarta: Penerbit Kanisius.

Krom, N.J. (1920) 'Epigraphische Aanteekeningen (XIV–XVI)', *Tijdschrift voor Indische Taal-, Land- en Volkenkunde*, Afdeeling Letterkunde, 59:420–431.

Mahdi, W. (1993) 'Distinguishing homonymic word forms in Indonesian', in G.P. Reesink (ed.), *Topics in Descriptive Austronesian Linguistics*, Semaian 11, 181–216. Leiden: Vakgroep Talen en Culturen van Zuidoost-Azië en Oceanië.

——(1994) 'Some Austronesian maverick protoforms with culture-historical implications', *Oceanic Linguistics*, 33:167–229, 431–490.

——(1995) 'Wie hießen die Malaien, bevor sie "Malaien" hießen?', in A. Bormann, A. Graf, M. Meyer, M. Voss (eds), pp. 162–176 *Südostasien und wir*, Austronesiana: Studien zum austronesischen Südostasien und Ozeanien 1. Hamburg: Lit.

——(1999a) 'The dispersal of Austronesian boat forms in the Indian Ocean', in Roger Blench and Matthew Spriggs (eds), *Archaeology and Language III: Artefacts, languages and texts*, 144–179. London: Routledge.

——(1999b) 'Linguistic and philological data towards a chronology of Austronesian activity in India and Sri Lanka', in Roger Blench and Matthew Spriggs (eds), *Archaeology and Language IV: Language change and cultural transformation*, 160–242. London: Routledge.

Manguin, P.-Y. (1987) 'Études Sumatranaises I. Palembang et Sriwijaya: Anciennes hypothèses, recherches nouvelles', *Bulletin de l'École Française d'Extrême-Orient*, 76:337–401.

——(1993) 'Palembang and Sriwijaya: an early Malay harbour-city rediscovered', *Journal of the Malaysian Branch of the Royal Asiatic Society*, 66/1:23–46.

Obdeyn, V. (1941) 'Zuid-Sumatra volgens de oudste berichten, I. De geomorfologische gesteldheid van Zuid-Sumatra in verband met de opvatting der ouden', *Tijdschrift van het Koninklijk Nederlandsch Aardrijkskundig Genootschap* 2e reeks 58:190–216.

Ogloblin, A.K. (1998) 'On the history of negation in Malayo-Javanic languages', Paper: North-Western International Academic Session on South-East Asia, St. Petersburg.

Poerbatjaraka (1952) *Riwajat Indonesia*, djil. I. Djakarta: Jajasan Pembangunan.

——(1957) 'Swara e (pepet)', *Bahasa dan Budaja*, 5(3):18–23.

——(1958) 'Çrīvijaya, de Çailendra- en de Sañjayavaṃ ça', *Bijdragen tot de Taal-, Land- en Volkenkunde*, 114:254–264.

Postma, A. (1992) 'The Laguna copper-plate inscription (LCI). A Javanese connection?', *Philippine Studies*, 40:183–203.

Ronkel, P.S. van (1924) 'A preliminary notice concerning two Old Malay inscriptions in Palembang (Sumatra)', *Acta orientalia*, 2:12–21.

Ross, M.D. (in press) 'Notes on the prehistory and internal subgrouping of Malayic', in J. Bowden and N.P. Himmelmann (eds), *Papers in Austronesian Linguistics*, Canberra: Pacific linguistics.

Schnitger, F.M. (1939–1943) 'Monuments mégalithiques de Sumatra-septentrional', *Revue des arts asiatiques*, 13:23–27 and plates VI–VIII.

——(1964) *Forgotten Kingdoms in Sumatra*, with contributions by C. von Führer-Haimendorf and G.L. Tichelman. Leiden: E.J. Brill.

Situmorang, T.D. and A. Teeuw (1958) *Sedjarah Melaju. Menurut terbitan Abdullah (ibn Abdulkadir Munsji)*, tjet. ke-2. Djakarta: Djambatan.

Solheim, W.G. II (1980) 'Neue Befunde zur späten Prähistorie Südostasiens und ihre Interpretation', *Saeculum,* 31:275–317, 319–344.

Suhadi, M. (1983) 'Seven Old-Malay inscriptions found in Java', in *SPAFA Final Report: Consultative Workshop on Archaeological and Environmental Studies on Srivijaya* (T–W3) Bangkok and South Thailand, 67–81. Bangkok: Southeast Asian Ministers of Education Organization.

Tadmor, U. (2000) 'Rekonstruksi Aksen Kata Bahasa Melayu', in Bambang Kaswanti Purwo and Yassir Nasanius (eds), *Pertemuan Linguistik (Pusat Kajian) Bahasa dan Budaya Atma Jaya Ketiga Belas*, 153–171. Jakarta: Pusat Kajian Bahasa dan Budaya Unika Atma Jaya.

Teeuw, A. (1959) 'The history of the Malay language. A preliminary survey', *Bijdragen tot de Taal-, Land- en Volkenkunde*, 115:138–156.

Vikør, L.S. (1988) *Perfecting Spelling. Spelling discussions in Indonesia and Malaysia 1900–1972*, Verhandelingen van het Koninklijk Instituut voor Taal-, Land- en Volkenkunde 133, Dordrecht: Foris Publications.

Wilkinson, R.J. (1901–1903) *A Malay–English Dictionary*. Singapore: Kelly & Walsh.

Wolff, J.U. (2001) 'A historical account of the origin of the Malay verbal affix *di-nya*', Paper: Fifth International Symposium on Malay/Indonesian Linguistics, Leipzig.

Wolters, O.W. (1967) *Indonesian Commerce. A Study of the origins of Śrīvijaya*. Ithaca: Cornell University Press.

CHAPTER SEVEN

STRUCTURAL DIVERSITY IN THE MALAYIC SUBGROUP

Alexander Adelaar

1 MALAYIC VARIETIES: AN INTRODUCTION

Malayic languages consist of Malay in all its regional and sociolinguistic variety and furthermore of various languages that are sufficiently close to it so as to form a genetic subgroup. A formal criterion for the Malayic subgroup consists of a set of phonological changes since Proto-Austronesian (PAn) which the Malayic varieties have commonly undergone (cf. Adelaar 1992:2).

Malayic varieties are spoken all over Indonesia, Malaysia, South Thailand, Brunei and Singapore (see Map 7.1; they are also spoken in diaspora, see FLOREY, LANGUAGE ENDANGERMENT). However, the traditional habitat of the Malayic varieties is roughly the land areas around the South China Sea, and more particularly, Sumatra, West Borneo, and West Malaysia or the Malay peninsula. Each of these areas have been proposed as the original homeland of Malay(ic). Linguists tend to favor West Borneo (Blust, Adelaar, Collins, Nothofer), with some of them (Adelaar, Blust) distinguishing between West Borneo as the homeland of the entire Malayic subgroup and South Sumatra as the cradle (later on) of the Malay language and civilization (Adelaar 2004 and ADELAAR, HISTORICAL PERSPECTIVE).

The internal classification of Malayic varieties is a controversial matter among scholars. Various subgrouping hypotheses have been proposed, and the data tend to favour a separate primary branch constituted by some of the inland varieties of West Borneo (including Kendayan and possibly Iban). Nevertheless, classification at the higher nodes remains inconclusive due to the lack of research in a historically complex area where many varieties of Malayic are spoken and a great deal of language contact has taken place (see ADELAAR, HISTORICAL PERSPECTIVE). The record is somewhat more positive regarding lower order subgrouping, where Kerinci seems to subgroup with Minangkabau (Prentice and A. Hakim Usman 1978). Furthermore, there seems to be a direct genetic link between Brunei Malay, Banjarese and Bacan Malay (Collins 1996a), and there is possibly also a direct link between the Malayic languages of Northwest Borneo and those of Bangka Island (Nothofer 1997) (see Adelaar to appear).

Adelaar and Prentice (1996) have proposed an alternative classification along sociolinguistic lines dividing Malayic into (1) literary Malay varieties, (2) trade Malay or Pidgin-Derived Malay (PDM) varieties, and (3) 'vernacular' Malay varieties.

(1) Literary Malay varieties include products of the literary Malay tradition that existed in Malacca and at various Malay courts elsewhere in Southeast Asia (usually referred to as 'Classical Malay'). These literary products were not always written in the same kind of Malay but they testify to an effort to adhere to principles of the same literary standard as those upheld at the court of Riau-Johore, which after Malacca fell to the

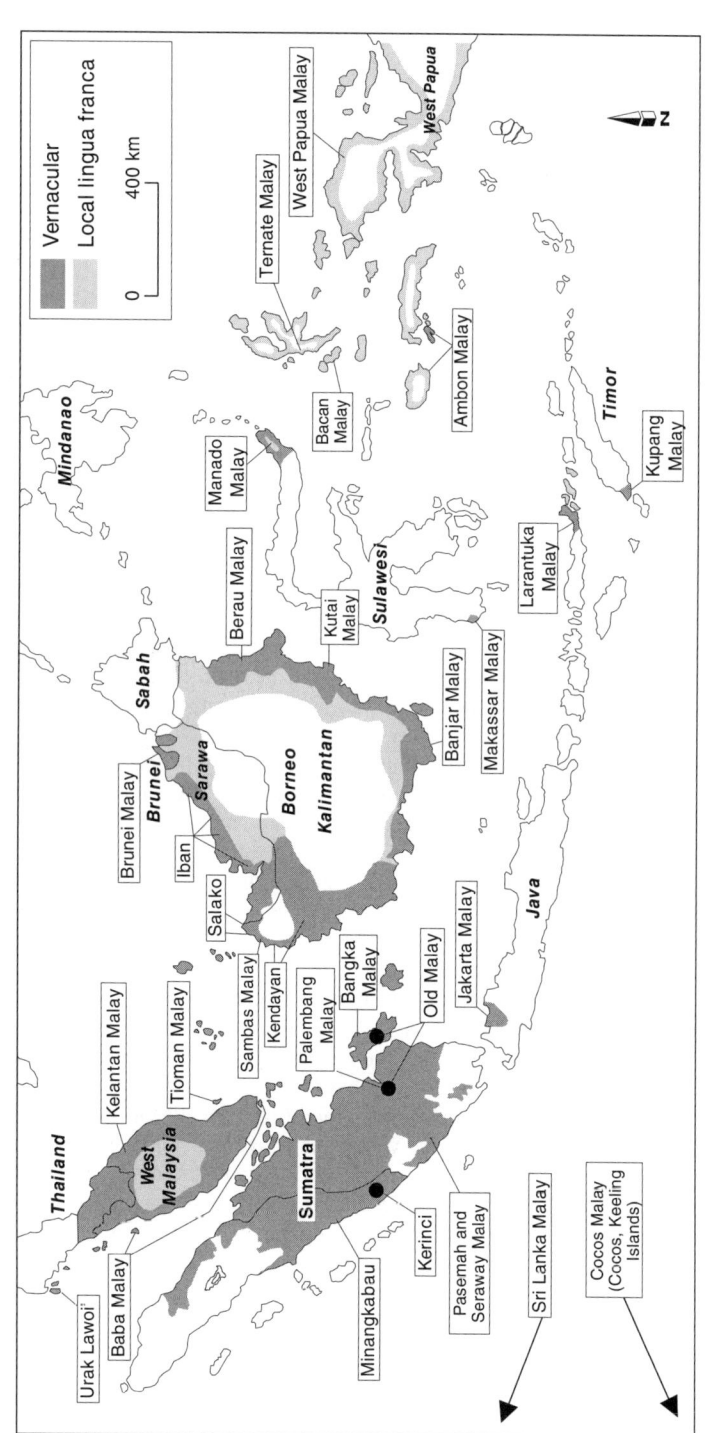

MAP 7.1 MALAYIC VARIETIES REFERRED TO IN CHAPTER 7

Portuguese in 1511 became the cultural heir of the kingdom of Malacca. Literary Malay varieties also include official Malaysian Malay and Indonesian (henceforth standard Malay or SM) which are ultimately also based on this literary standard.

(2) PDMs have a number of structural features in common which are neither inherited from PAn nor from Proto-Malayic (PM, the hypothetical common ancestor of Malayic varieties) suggesting that they have a pidginized form of Malay as a common source. They must have come into being as languages for trade and other forms of informal interethnic communication, but many of them developed into the mother tongues of sometimes sizeable speech communities. Examples of PDM are Bazaar Malay, Ambon Malay, Manado Malay, Sri Lanka Malay and Cocos Keeling Malay (the last four of which have become mother tongues).

(3) Malayic vernaculars are varieties of Malayic that are spoken in traditionally Malayic speech communities and appear to be regularly inherited from Proto-Malayic. They include Minangkabau (West Sumatra), Kelantan Malay (northeastern part of West Malaysia), Iban (Sarawak), Kendayan (West Borneo), and most other forms of native Malayic spoken in Sumatra, Borneo, the Malay peninsula and on islands in the South China Sea.

This division is clearly not based on genetic considerations. From a historical linguistic perspective the category of PDMs probably developed as an offshoot of literary Malay, and they most likely share their origins with various Malay dialects from South and East Sumatra and the Malay Peninsula's west coast. Other forms of Malayic (such as Kendayan) seem to be genetically further removed. But genetic distance is not always commensurate with criteria involving a dialect/language distinction. Given two Malayic varieties at (say) genetic equidistance to literary Malay, one may have undergone strong literary Malay influence whereas the other may have been heavily influenced by a non-Malayic language. In the end the former may look very 'Malay-like' and appear as a next-of-kin dialect of Malay, whereas the latter has become very different and may even have become a language in its own right, a development that can easily be misinterpreted as an indication of genetic distance.

Furthermore, the division between literary Malay, PDMs and Malayic vernaculars is not always a rigid one. Nowadays the categories have to some extent shaded into one another due to language contact and mutual influencing. Many PDMs have become mother tongues and behave sociolinguistically like vernacular Malay varieties. Probably all PDMs have borrowed (Malayic and non-Malayic) vernacular features into their structure, whereas forms of vernacular Malayic and literary Malay may on occasion have borrowed from PDMs. Varieties like Jakarta Malay are hard to classify because they show inherited features (e.g. the retention of last syllable *ə) as well as various PDM features (e.g. in its use of prepositions and determiners and (occasionally) in its possessive and causative constructions). Both PDMs and vernaculars have been under constant influence from literary Malay, which as a rule is considered the linguistic norm, especially in its standardized official language forms. Nevertheless, the division has some practical and historical merit and serves its purpose as a working hypothesis in this chapter.

Vernacular and PDM varieties of Malayic are sometimes very different from literary Malay in their phonological and morphosyntactic make-up. The present chapter tries to capture some of these differences. Section 2 gives an overview of the phonological diversity of vernacular and PDM varieties, paying special attention to the phonological structures of Minangkabau and Kelantan Malay. Section 3 surveys the morphosyntactic features that are particular to PDMs. The last two sections constitute to a closer look at two varieties, Salako (a dialect of Kendayan, West Borneo) and Kerinci (West Sumatra), which are unusually idiosyncratic in their morphosyntactic structure within the context of the Malayic subgroup.

Due to its emphasis on the typological diversity within the Malayic subgroup, the organization of this chapter is neither strictly by topic area nor does it give a systematic treatment of each of the Malayic varieties under discussion. It also does not include literary Malay varieties. For a succinct description of the structure of the phonology and morphology of one of these varieties (SM), the reader is referred to EWING, COLLOQUIAL INDONESIAN which discusses some of the discourse features of 'colloquial Indonesian' in contrast to textbook descriptions of standard Indonesian.

Some Malayic varieties are dialects of Malay, but other varieties are languages in their own right. In this chapter, the latter do not have the word 'Malay' in their name (e.g. Minangkabau, Salako, Urak Lawoi'). However, in many cases the dialect vs. language distinction remains unclear and somewhat random because of lack of linguistic data and also because of conflicting criteria that are applied to make the distinction. I admit that there is a certain randomness in labeling Banjar Malay and Kelantan Malay as Malay dialects while giving a separate language status to Minangkabau, given the measure of difference between each of these varieties and SM. In this chapter I simply follow common practice and do not claim any scholarly authority for the way the distinction is made in each individual case.

The linguistic data used in this chapter were taken from the following sources unless indicated otherwise: Ambon Malay: Van Minde (1997); Baba Malay: Pakir (1986); Banjar Malay: Abdul Djebir Hapip (1977); Berau Malay: Collins (1994); Brunei Malay: Clynes (in press); Cocos (Keeling) Malay: Adelaar (1996); Iban: Asmah Haji Omar (1981); Kelantan Malay: Abdul Hamid Mahmood (1994); Kerinci: Prentice and A. Hakim Usman (1978), Steinhauer and A. Hakim Usman (1978); Larantuka Malay: Steinhauer (1991); Manado Malay: Solea [Salea] Warouw (1985); Minangkabau: Adelaar (1992); North Moluccan Malay (Ternate Malay): Voorhoeve (1983); Salako: Adelaar (1991a, 2002); Sri Lanka Malay: Adelaar (1991b); Urak Lawoi': Hogan (1988).

2 PHONOLOGICAL CHARACTERISTICS

Malayic varieties usually differ in several phonological aspects from SM. Some of the more salient cases are treated below. The phonological changes that happened in Minangkabau and in Kelantan Malay have had a considerable effect on the overall phonological system of these varieties, and they require a more extensive discussion (cf. §§2.2–3). The phonological changes of Kerinci have affected its morphosyntactic structure to the extent that they need to be discussed together in a separate section (§5).

2.1 Some general trends

The following phonological features are observed in various parts of the Malayic-speaking area.

- PAn and PM had four vowels (*a, *ə, *i, *u) which occurred in penultimate and final syllables. Jakarta Malay maintained last syllable schwa but it was lost in almost all other varieties of Malayic, although traces of it have survived in a few varieties such as Tioman Malay (Collins 1985), Iban (Adelaar 1992:38) and Bangka Malay (Nothofer 1997), e.g. *hitəm 'black' > itəm (SM hitam); *ənəm 'six' > ənəm (SM ənam).

- The Jakarta Malay subdialect of Mester furthermore lost *h* (< PMP *q*) and raised and fronted final *-a(h)* to *-ɛ* (some other Jakarta Malay sub-dialects have *ə*, or maintained *a*, in this position), e.g. *ayɛ* 'father' (SM *ayah*); *siapɛ namɛ-ɲɛ?* 'what is his/her name?' (who name-3, SM *siapa nama-ɲa*). Heightening and backing or fronting of *-a* is also shown in various other Malayic varieties, e.g. Sambas Malay *-ɛ*, various Sumatran and Peninsular Malay varieties *-ə*, Minangkabau *-o*. These changes usually do not extend to final *a(h)* sequences, as they do in Jakarta Malay. They seem to be part of an areal trend that has affected many more West Indonesian languages including Javanese and Balinese (Clynes 1989). The trend may also include Lampung and possibly even the languages of South Borneo (including Malagasy) which all show the same tendency.
- In most forms of Malayic the original high vowels have split into sets of high and mid-vowels. Some varieties of Banjar Malay (Hulu variant; South Kalimantan), Brunei Malay and Berau Malay (East Kalimantan) never developed mid vowels (cf. *uraŋ* 'person' > Banjar Hulu, Brunei, Berau *uraŋ* vs. SM *oraŋ*) and reduced the original PMP four vowel system to *a*, *i* and *u*, by merging *a* and *ə* in *a*. In Berau Malay, the former presence of a schwa is still partly testified by gemination of the following consonant, although consonant gemination is not limited to this environment (Collins 1992), e.g. *bəsar* 'big' > Banjar Hulu, Brunei *basar*, Berau *bassar* vs. SM *bəsar*; *dəŋər* 'to hear' > Banjar Hulu, Brunei *daŋar*, Berau *daŋŋar* (SM *dəŋar*); but also: *nini* 'grandparent' > Banjar Hulu, Brunei *nini*, Berau (with unexplained loss of *n-*) *inni* (SM *nɛnɛ/k* 'grandmother').
- East Indonesian varieties (which are all PDMs) tend to show various phonological simplifications. They include the following ones (exemplified with Ambon Malay [Van Minde 1997] unless indicated otherwise): loss of *h* (*hati* 'liver' > *ati*; *lihat* 'to see' > *lia*; *rumah* 'house' > *ruma*); loss of final stops in part or all of the lexicon (*əmpat* 'four' > *ampa*; *anak* 'child' > *ana*); merger of final nasals into a velar nasal (*bəlum* 'not yet' > *baloŋ*; *ikan* 'fish' > *ikaŋ*; *təraŋ* 'clear' > *teraŋ*); merger of schwa and *a* in *a* (*əmpat* > *ampa*), or mutual assimilation of schwa and a last syllable high vowel to a mid vowel such that schwa and *i* both become *e*, and schwa and *u* both end up as *o* (*ləbih* > 'more' > *lebe*; (*bəlum* 'not yet' > Ambon Malay *baloŋ*, but North Moluccan Malay *boloŋ*).
- Realizations of *r* (historically a velar fricative, cf. Adelaar 1992) vary from a velar (sometimes uvular) fricative (e.g. in various parts of the Malay Peninsula and West Borneo) to an apical trill (e.g. in Java, Singapore, Brunei, East Indonesia) or both a velar fricative and apical trill (as in the case of the Pasemah and Seraway dialects of South Sumatra). Various Malayic varieties have a corresponding *h* (such as Kerinci, §5).
- Consonant gemination happens in various Malay dialects. It often happens after a historical schwa which has become *a*, as in Berau Malay *bassar* and *daŋŋar* (see above). It can also be the result of syllable reduction in avoidance of heterorganic consonant clusters, cf. Iban *llapan* 'eight' (< *dəlapan*, Scott 1956:VII) and §2.3 on Kelantan Malay.
- Vowel nasalization is basically regressive in e.g. Kelantan Malay (§2.3) and Larantuka Malay, where it is attested in syllables which historically end in a nasal except if the vowel is preceded by a nasal or by a nasal + voiced stop cluster, compare *ikã* 'fish' (SM *ikan*), *kucĩ* 'cat' (SM *kuciŋ*) with *guno* 'mountain' (SM *gunuŋ*), *aɲi* 'wind' (SM *aŋin*) and *aɲji* 'dog' (SM *aɲjiŋ*), which have no nasal vowel.

Vowel nasalization is progressive in Salako. Here a nasal may nasalize a following vowel, e.g. *saŋõ* [saŋɔ̃] 'nasal (voice)'. It may also nasalize a string of following vowels as long as there is no intermediate consonant other than a glottal consonant or a semivowel, e.g. *muhà* [mũhɔ̃] 'face'; *ɲuà* [ɲũɔ̃] 'to sell', and (with subjunctive suffix *-àʔ* (-[ɔʔ]) which is realized *-ʔàʔ* (-[ʔɔʔ]) when occurring after final *-a*), *ɲuà-ʔàʔ* [ɲũɔ̃ʔɔ̃ʔ] '(in order to) sell'.

In some cases, vowel nasalization appears to be phonemically distinctive in Salako, as shown in a few minimal pairs involving *o* including /maoʔ/ [maoʔ] 'drum' vs. *maõʔ* [mãõʔ] 'to want to', and *saɲo* [saɲo] 'rambutan' vs. *saɲõ* [saɲɔ̃] 'nasal (voice)'.

Note also the 2s possessive suffix *-ɲũ*, which has the allomorphs *-ɲũ*, *-nũ* and *-ũ*. The allomorph *ũ* occurs after *n*, *r*, velars and glottals, and therefore also in an environment where it is preceded by a consonant other than a nasal, as in *kamar-ũ* 'your room'; *bapaʔ-ũ* 'your father'.

- Nasal preplosion and cluster reduction involving nasals. Preploded nasals vary from one dialect to the other in their pronunciation. In Salako and in Kendayan dialects in general, they consist of an unreleased voiceless stop + homorganic nasal, but in other (Malayic and non-Malayic) speech forms in West Kalimantan, the first component can also be a voiced stop or a glottal stop.

In at least one Kendayan dialect, Belangin, original preploded nasals were further reduced to their corresponding final voiceless stops. Such a reduction of original preploded final nasals must also have happened in Urak Lawoi', which is spoken off Thailand's west coast from Phuket Island to the Adang Island group (Hogan 1988:1). Compare the following correspondence sets:

(1) | SM | | Salako | Urak Lawoi' |
|---|---|---|---|
| *kirim* | 'to send' | *kiripm* | *kirip* |
| *turun* | 'to descend' | *turutn* | *turot* |
| *oraŋ* | 'human, person' | *urakŋ* | *urak* |
| *bintaŋ* | 'star' | *bintakŋ* | *bitak* |

Nasal preplosion did not take place if the final nasal was immediately preceded by another nasal in the onset of the final syllable:

(2) | SM | | Salako | Urak Lawoi' |
|---|---|---|---|
| *dəmam* | 'fever' | *damam* | *demam* |
| *kanan* | 'right-hand' | *kanan* | *kanan* |
| *kəniŋ* | 'forehead' | *kaniŋ* | *keniŋ* |

Furthermore, preploded nasals alternate with simple nasals when their root is suffixed with *-an/-atn* (Salako dialect *-an/àtn* [ɔtn]), cf. *atàkŋ* 'come' and *ŋ-ataŋ-an* 'to evoke'. The examples in set (3) seem to contradict the previous observation. However, in these cases the immediately preceding nasal is not 'historical'. It is the result of another general change, the reduction of an older homorganic nasal + voiced stop cluster to its nasal component (cf. also SM *tuŋgu*, Salako *tuɲu*, Urak Lawoi' *tuɲu* 'to wait', 'to guard'; and SM *tambah*, Salako *tamàh*, Urak Lawoi' *tamah* 'to add').

(3) | SM | | Salako | Urak Lawoi' |
|---|---|---|---|
| *pijam* | 'to borrow' | *iɲàpm* | *iɲap* |
| *əmbun* | 'dew' | *amutn* | *mot* |

The reduction of a homorganic nasal + stop cluster took place in both Kendayan and Urak Lawoi' if the original stop was voiced. However, if the stop was voiceless, reduction only took place in Urak Lawoi', with the effect that the nasal was eliminated (not the stop) as the following set shows:

(4) SM   Salako   Urak Lawoi'
    təmpat 'place'   tampat   tepac
    bintaŋ 'star   bintakŋ   bitak
    aŋkat 'to lift'   aŋkat   akët

Nasal preplosion as a rule affects word-final nasals and occurs in languages that have no suffixes (e.g. Urak Lawoi'). In such languages, the phenomenon tends to lack phonemic relevance. However, in Kendayan dialects they also occur intervocalically in suffixed forms, cf. Salako ŋiɲɔpm 'to borrow' vs. ŋ-iɲapm-iʔ 'to lend to'. Moreover, affixation often conditions the occurrence of preploded nasals: the latter never occur when adjacent to another nasal. For instance, karikŋ 'dry' loses its preplosion when it obtains an applicative suffix -AN cf. ŋariŋ-an 'to dry [something]' (-AN appears as -an after nasals and as -àtn [-ɔtn] elsewhere). Likewise, the root buàkŋ [buɔkŋ] loses its preplosion when it obtains nasal prefixation: muaŋ [muaŋ] 'to throw away'. However, preplosion is not affected when the adjacent nasal is not historically derived from a nasal but from a cluster. For instance, in tumuhɔtn 'to graft' (← tumuh 'to grow'), preplosion in the suffix is not affected because the preceding nasal was historically a consonant cluster (cf. PM *tumbuh 'to grow'; cf. also Blust 1997 for a discussion of various nasalization phenomena in Borneo).

- In Malayic varieties, stress is not phonemic and generally falls on the penultimate syllable of the root. However, it regularly occurs on the last syllable of the root in Kerinci and in the Kendayan and Iban(ic) varieties of West Kalimantan. Indonesian speakers from Java tend to have predictable word stress, that is, stress is moved to the last syllable of the root if suffixation takes place.

For phonological data on various other Malayic varieties, see also the numerous publications by Collins and other authors listed in Collins (1990, 1995a, 1995b, 1996b).

2.2 Minangkabau

Minangkabau (West Sumatra) has many different dialects. The present phonological description concerns the standard dialect of Koto Gadang (near Bukittinggi).

This dialect developed mid-vowels e and o and merged penultimate *ə and *a in a (some other Minangkabau dialects merged *ə with either one of the newly developed mid-vowels; cf. Tamsin Medan 1980:78). Furthermore, in final syllables vowels underwent various diphthongizations, mergers and splits, whereas the original PM final stops merged in ʔ, *-s and *-h merged in -h, and the liquids are dropped word-finally but reappear in the process of suffixation.

These last syllable changes must have happened in stages (see Table 7.1). In last syllables which contained *a or ə, there was a first stage in which this *a and ə merged to a. In a second stage, the resulting a was raised to o word-finally and before *-p, and it was raised to e before *-t and *-s. Most likely, *a before *-p changed to o via an intermediate diphthong [aw], and *a changed to e via a diphthong [ay]. (As a matter of fact, other dialects and some written texts occasionally have ay instead of e.) Finally, in a third stage final stops merged in ʔ, final *s and *h merged in h, and final *l and *r were lost in word-final position (but kept before a suffix). Last syllables consisting of *a or ə followed by a nasal, semivowel or *h did not undergo any change.

In last syllables which contain a historical high vowel, there was a first stage in which *-m and *-n merged to -n, and *-p and *-t merged to –t. In a second stage, the high vowels were diphthongized: before final velars, final liquids and *-h, *u and *i became respectively uə and iə, and before final t (< *-p, *-t) and *s, *u became uy. In a third stage final stops merged in ʔ, final *s and *h merged in h, and final *l and *r were lost in word-final position (but were kept before a suffix). (No change happened to original high vowels in absolute word-final position.) These developments are shown in Table 7.2.

TABLE 7.1: CHANGES IN MINANGKABAU LAST SYLLABLES CONTAINING *a OR *ə

PM	Short gloss	I *ə > a in last syllables	II a > o or e in last syllables	III merger or loss of final consonants
*dua	two		⁺duo	duo
*hatəp	roofing	⁺(h)atap	⁺(h)atop	atoʔ
*sayap	wing		⁺sayop	sayoʔ
*səŋat	sting	⁺səŋat	⁺səŋet	saŋeʔ
*lumpat	jump		⁺lumpet	lumpeʔ
*anak	offspring			anaʔ
*baləs	reply	⁺balas	⁺bales	baleh
*bəras	rice		⁺bəres	bareh
*dəŋər	hear	⁺dəŋar		daŋa(r)
*akar	root			aka(r)
*jual	sell			jua(l)
*gatəl	itchy	⁺gatal		gata(l)

TABLE 7.2: CHANGES IN MINANGKABAU LAST SYLLABLES CONTAINING *i OR *u

PM	Short gloss	I *-p, *-t > -t *-m, *-n > -n	II diphthongization	III merger or loss of final consonants
*bəlum	not yet	⁺bəlun		balun
*puhun	stem			puun
*turut	follow		⁺turuyt	turuyʔ
*tutup	cover	⁺tutut	⁺tutuyt	tutuyʔ
*kirim	send	⁺kirin		kirin
*sisip	insert	⁺sisit		sisiʔ
*jahit	sew			jaiʔ
*duduk	sit		⁺duduək	duduəʔ
*jatuh	fall		⁺jatuəh	jatuəh
*pukul	beat		⁺pukuəl	pukuə(l)
*təlur	egg		⁺təluər	taluə(r)
*hituŋ	count		⁺(h)ituəŋ	ituəŋ
*tarik	pull		⁺tariək	tariəʔ
*putih	white		⁺putiəh	putiəh
*kəniŋ	forehead		⁺kəniəŋ	kaniəŋ
*lihər > ⁺lihir	neck		⁺li(h)iər	liiə(r)
*paŋgil	call		⁺paŋgiəl	paŋgiə(l)
*habis	finished			abih
*tərus	continue		⁺təruys	taruyh

Note that other varieties of Minangkabau may not have undergone some of the changes described above, or may show developments that do not apply to the Koto Gadang subdialect (see Tamsin Medan 1980 for an overview of Minangkabau dialect variety). Steinhauer (1987:86) points out that the Minangkabau dialect variety does not stop at the (cultural-historical) borders of the Minangkabau area. In fact, this area is part of a dialect continuum which also includes Malayic speaking areas in East Sumatra. On the other end of the continuum it probably also includes Kerinci (West Sumatra), although sound changes in the latter have brought about a rather unique realignment of its phonology and morphosyntax (see §5).

2.3 Kelantan Malay

Kelantan Malay also shows various vowel changes in last syllables. The sound changes reflected in Abdul Hamid Mahmood (1994) are sometimes ambiguous, and the following statement is somewhat generalized.

Final-syllable *a became ɔ before *-k, *-h and *-ø (cf. budɔk 'child' [SM budak]; gɔtɔh 'rubber' [SM gətah]; sayɔ '1s'; [SM saya]), and ẽ before a historical nasal (cf. bitẽ 'star', (see (5) below) and makẽ 'to eat' [SM makan]; itẽ 'black' [SM hitam]).

Final-syllable *i remained i word-finally (cf. kuci, below), ĩ before *ŋ (cf. kucĩ 'cat' [SM kuciŋ]), ẽ before *n or *m (cf. maẽ 'to play' [SM main]; yatẽ 'orphan' [SM yatim]), e and (sometimes) i before *s (cf. mənuleh 'to write' [SM mənulis]; bəlateh 'to exercize' [SM bərlatih], but also mənaŋih 'cry, weep' [SM mənaŋis]); *i became e elsewhere (cf. paŋe (see (5) below); ɣapeʔ 'close, tight' [SM (Malaysia) rapit]; mudeʔ 'upstream' [SM mudik]).

Final-syllable *u remained u before *s (cf. hapuh) and word-finally (cf. batu 'stone' [SM batu]); it became ũ before *m (cf. minũ), õ before *n or *ŋ (cf. ɣacõ (above); tgatõ 'depending' [SM tərgantuŋ]), u or o before a final stop (cf. sayo 'faint, blurred' [SM sayup]; patoʔ 'proper' [SM patut], masoʔ 'to go in' [SM masuk], but also lɔtuʔpẽ 'explosion' [SM lətupan]; ɣupuʔ 'grass' [SM rumput]; busũʔ 'rotten' [SM busuk]), and o or ɔ in all other cases (cf. tuboh 'body' [SM tubuh]; puko 'to beat' [SM pukul]; tido 'to sleep' [SM tidur]; bətəlɔ 'to lay eggs' [SM bərtəlur]).

The loss of a final nasal left traces in the preceding vowel which became nasalized and was raised to ẽ if it was an *a and lowered if it was a high vowel *u or *i (e.g. makẽ, ɣacõ, yatẽ, and see below). Nasalized vowels also occur in non-final syllables (e.g. minũmẽ 'a drink'; tmãka 'tobacco' (Ajid Che Kob 1985:289); note that the nasalization in tmãka is progressive, in contrast to the general (regressive) nasalization pattern in Kelantan Malay).

As a result of the loss of final nasals and the nasalization of their preceding vowels, nasal vowels became phonemic in final position, (cf. kuci [SM kuɲci] 'key' vs. kucĩ [SM kuciŋ] 'cat'; kəyi [SM kəri] 'k.o. small sickle' vs. kəyĩ [SM kəriŋ] 'dry').

Kelantan Malay shows the following consonant developments: in intervocalic position: homorganic nasal + voiced stop clusters were reduced to their nasal component and homorganic nasal + voiceless stop (or *s) clusters were reduced to their obstruent component. *r is realized as a velar fricative. Examples:

(5)   Standard Malay   Kelantan Malay
      gambar 'picture'   gama
      panday 'able'   pana
      paŋgil 'to call'   paŋe
      tər-lampaw 'exceedingly' tə-lapa

baŋsal 'shed, warehouse'	*basa*
kuɲci 'key'	*kuci*
bintaŋ 'star'	*bitẽ*
harimaw 'tiger'	*yimã*
racun 'poison'	*yacõ*

In word-final position, most consonants are not realized: *ʔ* appears instead if the underlying final consonant is a stop, and *h* appears if the underlying consonant is *s* or *h*; other final consonants (including semivowels) are not realized. Examples:

(6) Standard Malay   Kelantan Malay

harap 'to hope'	*haya?*
iŋat 'to remember'	*iŋa?*
busuk 'rotten'	*busũ?*
hapus 'to wipe'	*hapuh*
tulis 'to write'	*tuleh*
gətah 'rubber'	*gətɔh*
minum 'to drink'	*minũ*
bər-main 'to play'	*ba-maẽ*
urus 'to organize, take care of'	*uyuh*
bintaŋ 'star'	*bitẽ*
tidur 'to sleep'	*tido*
baisikal 'bicycle'	*basika*
panday 'able'	*pana*
harimaw 'tiger'	*yimã*

The underlying morpheme-final consonants do reappear on morpheme boundaries when *–ẽ* or *–i* are suffixed. However, the final glottals that emerged instead of stops or *s* in word-final position are also maintained, cf. *hara?pẽ* 'hope'; *iŋa?tẽ* 'memory'; *tulehsẽ* 'something written'; *minũmẽ* 'a drink'; *uyuhsẽ* 'business, concern'; *məlapawi* 'to exceed'; *kəpanayẽ* 'skill'. Furthermore, a non-historical glottal stop appears after a historical **a*, when *–ẽ* is suffixed, cf. *yajɔ* 'ruler' vs. *kəyajɔ?ẽ* 'kingdom'.

Finally, consonant gemination often takes place through the reduction of doubled root morphemes, trisyllables or quadrisyllables, whether these are polymorphemic or not. This gemination is the result of the reduction of original antepenultimate syllables, and the affected consonant is the initial consonant of the penultimate syllable. Examples:

(7) *ppuwẽ* 'woman' (cf. SM *pərəmpuan*)
     kkuyɔ 'turtle' (SM *kura-kura*)
     ttupa? or *kɔtupa?* 'rice cake'
     ppayẽ or *təpayẽ* 'k.o. water jar'
     bqŋɔ?-bqŋɔ? or *bbqŋɔ?* 'very many' (p. 59)
     pə- (+ transitive) + *puteh* 'white' → *pputeh* 'to whiten'
     məN- (+ active) + *basoh* '<cleaning>' → *bbasoh* 'to clean'

Sometimes, different derivational processes lead to the same reduced form:

(8) *pə-* + *tido* 'to sleep' →   *ttido* 'to put to sleep'
     tə- (+ non-volitional) + *tido* →   *ttido* 'fallen asleep'

Gemination of the initial consonant of a root optionally takes place if this root is the head of a locative prepositional phrase introduced with *di* 'in', 'at', *ko* 'towards' or *dari* 'from', e.g. [ssini] is the optional variant of *di sini* 'here', *ko sini* 'hither' or *dari sini* 'from here'; *di* + *kəda* 'shop' → [kkəda] 'at the shop'; *ko* + *luẽ* 'outside' → [lluẽ] 'to go outside' [SM *kəluar*].

Abdul Hamid Mahmood (1994:78) claims that gemination may affect any consonant except liquids. However, this is contradicted by the previous example [lluẽ].

Furthermore, from the various examples in Abdul Hamid Mahmood (1994) and Ajid Che Kob (1985), it rather seems that gemination does not happen to voiced stops or nasals if the preceding syllable begins with a voiceless stop, e.g. *t-glijaʔ* 'twisted'; *tamãka* (Ajid Che Kob 1985:289) 'tobacco'.

3 MORPHOSYNTACTIC FEATURES OF PIDGIN-DERIVED MALAY VARIETIES

The PDMs are characterized by a configuration of morphosyntactic features that as a rule do not occur in other forms of Malayic, and that do not seem to be inherited from PM. Although all PDMs have this configuration in common, some of them may have lost some individual features.

Adelaar and Prentice (1996:675) propose an inventory of morphosyntactic features specific to PDMs. All of these are discussed in this section (§3.1–7), except for one. This is the use of a multifunctional preposition (usually at the expense of other prepositions with a more specialized application). As it turns out, this feature does not apply to most PDMs as they appear today. Moreover, it is not only typical of some PDMs but also of many other Austronesian languages, as is demonstrated in various descriptive chapters in this volume. Instead of this feature another one is included here which is not mentioned in Adelaar and Prentice (1996), i.e. the lack of a typical Malayic voice system (§3.8).

The PDM features are demonstrated below with examples from Ambon Malay, Cocos Malay and occasionally data from other PDMs. Conforming to their notation in Van Minde 1997, Ambon Malay words are marked for stress if this is not on the penultimate syllable.

Various other noteworthy features are particular to individual PDMs, including the (for a western Austronesian language quite unusual) Subject–Object–Verb structure of Sri Lanka Malay (cf. Adelaar 1991b), and the complicated reduplication patterns found in Ambon, Manado and Ternate Malay, which also involve the reduplication of prefixes. However, the present section will not discuss these features as they are not part of a common PDM typology.

3.1 Plural pronouns based on *oraŋ*

Plural pronouns are mainly compounds consisting of singular pronouns + *oraŋ* 'human being', 'people'. The most complete paradigm is found in Baba Malay (traditionally spoken by communities of mixed Chinese-Malay descent in Penang, Malacca and Singapore). This dialect also has inclusive and exclusive first person plural forms, a distinction not made in other PDMs:

(9)   *gua* '1s' (< Hokkien)   *gua oraŋ* '1pe'/*kita oraŋ* '1pi'
       lu '2s' (< Hokkien)   *lu oraŋ* [loraŋ] '2p'
       dia '3s'   *dia oraŋ* [joraŋ] '3p'

Other PDMs lost some of these plural forms or have changed their original meaning. Ambon Malay generally has *kat'oŋ* '1p' (< *kita oraŋ*) and *doraŋ* and its short form *doŋ*

'2p; 3p' (< *dia oraŋ). Nevertheless, some other forms survive, such as bat'oŋ '1pe' which contrasts with kat'oŋ '1pi' in the Booi dialect of Saparua (Van Minde 1997: 68 fn.6), and osoraŋ, a plural of the second person pronoun ose (also os or se < Portuguese voce). Cocos Malay has doraŋ or doŋ '2p' (< *dia oraŋ) and oŋ '3p' (< *oraŋ). Both dialects have dia '3s' but only Cocos Malay retained an isolated form kita '1p'. Compare also Manado Malay toraŋ/toŋ '1p' (< *kita oraŋ) and doraŋ/doŋ '3p'; Sri Lanka Malay kitaŋ '1p', lu oraŋ or [loraŋ] '2p' vs. lu '2s' and deraŋ '3p' vs. de '3s'.

An additional feature common to most of the PDM pronoun systems is that they reflect a singular meaning for the Proto-Malayic first person plural inclusive pronoun *kita. Ternate and Manado Malay explicitly have kita '1s'. Sri Lanka and Ambon Malay have a reflex of *kita oraŋ for '1p', and, as seen above, Baba Malay has kita oraŋ for '1pi'. None of these latter varieties have a reflex of *kita without *oraŋ. All these cases point to an original singular meaning of *kita. Incidentally, this is also the case in Jakarta Malay which cannot unequivocally be classified as a PDM (§1). Jakarta Malay has the pronouns guè or kitè '1', lu '2' and diè '3' (which combine with the particle padè preceding the predicate in order to express an explicit plural). The only PDM contradicting the above analysis is Cocos Malay which has kita '1p' matching gua or (polite) saya '1s'.

3.2 Possessive constructions on the basis of a linker

Possessive constructions consist of possessor + linker + possessed. The linker is puɲa or an allegro form of puɲa (cf. Ambon Malay puɲ, poŋ, pu, ŋ or even ø, Baba Malay miya, Ternate-, Manado- and Sri Lanka Malay pe). Examples:

(10) beta puɲa/puɲ/ŋ/ø kals'aŋ 'my trousers' (Ambon Malay)
      1s   LK   trousers

(11) Se   poŋ mata 'your eyes' (Ambon Malay)
      2s   LK   eye

(12) Beta ŋ   tam'aŋ puŋ kaka
      1s   LK   friend LK   older sibling
      'my friend's older brother' (Ambon Malay)

Similar constructions are also used for several other functions in some PDMs, including genitive constructions and, sometimes, locative constructions. In Baba Malay, it seems to occur in a fairly broad range of attributive constructions, including simple attributive – Head phrases. Examples are Sri Lanka Malay ru:ma-pe da:laŋ (house-LK inside) 'inside the house', Sri Laŋka pe te daɔŋ (Sri Lanka LK tea leave) 'tea from Sri Lanka); and Baba Malay jahat miya oraŋ (wicked LK person) 'a wicked person', dulu miya baraŋ (past LK thing) 'things from the past'.

3.3 Progressive aspect with ada

The existential marker ada also functions as a verbal auxiliary indicating progressive aspect. Examples:

(13) kat'oŋ ada   dudu tad'o-tad'o, doŋ dataŋ ba-hoɲe   sa
      1p   PROG sit   RDP-quiet   3p   come   INTR-make noise just
      'We were sitting very quietly and they came to disturb us.' (Ambon Malay)

(14) *dia   ada   tuŋgu disini,   dia   maw   bicara   ma   Ne?*
      3s   PROG   wait   PRX   3s   want   talk   COM   term of address
      'She's waiting here because she wants to talk to you.' (Cocos Malay)

3.4 Directional *pigi*

A form corresponding to Standard Malay *pərgi* (usually *pigi* or its short form *pi*)
functions as a verb as well as a directional particle or a preposition 'to(wards)'. Ambon
Malay has partly idiomatic expressions where *pigi* is a preposition, e.g. *pigi pante* '(go)
to the beach', but also: 'go to the beach to relieve oneself' (Van Minde 1997:243). Cocos
Malay uses *pigi* in conjunction with a locative preposition *di*. It functions as a verb in (15)
but as a directional particle in (16):

(15) *Tu   pəɲu   pigi di   kolam   situ*
      DET   turtle go   LOC   pond   MED
      'The turtles go to the pond over there.' (Cocos Malay)

(16) *Ada   barat   dari   Pulu   Paɲjaŋ   sana   tu*
      EXIST   westerly (wind) from   island long   DIST   DET

      pukul   ombaʔ pigi di   ruma   sini
      beat   wave   DIR   LOC   house   PRX
      'There are westerly winds that blow over all the way from West Island (lit. long
      island) beating waves against the houses here.' (Cocos Malay)

Sri Lanka Malay uses *piggi/pi* as a verb 'to go' as well as in the meaning 'last', 'gone'
in temporal adverbial phrases (e.g. *piggi wik* 'last week').

3.5 Reduced demonstratives functioning as definite markers

In Baba Malay and Sri Lanka Malay (and apparently also in Manado Malay), demonstratives
as a rule precede the head, whereas in Ambon Malay there is a strong tendency to follow it.
   Ini 'PRX' and *itu* 'DIST' often developed short forms (*ni* and *tu*). These have somewhat
bleached deictic meanings and behave more like definite markers with anaphoric or contextual reference (but without totally losing their deictic meaning). Compare the following examples, where in (18) distal *tu* co-occurs with a first person pronoun, clearly
indicating that it is no longer strictly speaking a deictic element referring to something
at a distance from the speaker:

(17) *La   ose   mo   bikiŋ   apa?*
      Then   2s   want   make   what

      Ya   beta   mo   nae,   mar   beta   ni   bodo   nae
      yes   1s   want   climb   but   1s   DET   stupid climb
      'So what do you want to do? Well, I want to climb up, but I'm not good at it.'
      (Ambon Malay)

(18) *Ana   kikis   beta tu   abis-abis!*
      Child   scrape 1s   DET   RDP-finished

      Rasa-rasa   mo   manaɲis,   mar   so   talalu   bas'ar
      RDP-feel   want   cry   but   already too   big
      'The girl ripped me (as I was then) off completely! I felt like crying, but I'm too
      old for that.' (Ambon Malay)

In Cocos Malay, *ini* and *itu* precede their head, whereas the semantically bleached short forms *ni* and *tu* have a tendency to follow it (see (15) and (16) above for an example). Sometimes there occur concatenations of short forms and (at least in Ambon Malay) of short and long forms which precede the head in various combinations. The concatenation seems to combine deictic reference, definiteness and anaphoric reference (Van Engelenhoven unpublished). Compare the following Cocos Malay case, where *kita puɲa bəras tu tu* tentatively carries the literal meaning 'the [that] rice that we used to have at the time':

(19) *Dulu   kita   bəli   bəras   ari Saptu . . .   kita   puɲa*
      Before 1p   buy   rice   Saturday   1p   have

      bəras   tu   tu   satu   miŋgu,   man!
      rice   DET   DET   one   week   uncle; sir
      'In the past, we used to buy rice on Saturdays – the rice that we used to have at the time, you know – would last a week, Sir!' (Cocos Malay)

3.6 Periphrastic causatives

Kasi 'give' and *bikin* 'make' are used in periphrastic causative constructions. *Kasi* (Ambon Malay *kasi* or *kas*) can be combined with all verbal categories; *bikin* (Ambon Malay *bikiŋ*) only combines with stative verbs. These periphrastic constructions are very frequent in all PDMs under investigation, although in some PDMs there are also morphological causatives derived with *-kan* (Cocos Malay, Baba Malay) or *-kiŋ* (in Sri Lanka Malay). Compare examples (20) and (21), where *kasi* and *bikiŋ* are used as verbal heads, with examples (22), (23) and (24), where they are used as auxiliaries in causative constructions:

(20) *Kasi   kat'oŋ   tulaŋ   jua*
      Give   1p   bone   only, just
      'Please give us a bone.' (Ambon Malay)

(21) *Kat'oŋ   bisa   bikiŋ   nasi*
      1p   can   make   steamed rice
      'We can make rice.' (Ambon Malay)

(22) *Kase   makaŋ   ana-ana   tu   dolo,*
      CAU   eat   RDP-child ANAPH   first

      doŋ   su   lapar
      3p   already   hungry
      'Feed the children, they are hungry.' (Ambon Malay)

(23) *toloŋ   taŋaŋ   kas   kac'il   kompor   tu*
      help   hand   CAU   small   cooker   ANAPH
      'Help (me, and) turn the cooker lower.' (Ambon Malay)

(24) *Kal   os   pake   paku,   lama-lama   la   de   ba-tai*
      If   2s   use   nail   RDP-long.time   then   3s   INTR-excrement

      besi,   la   de   bikiŋ   rusak   kayo
      iron   then   3s   CAU   damaged   wood
      'If you use a nail, in the long run it will rust and it will damage the wood.'
      (Ambon Malay)

Note that there are other verbs that obtain a grammaticalized meaning in periphrastic constructions. For instance, *dapa* 'get', 'obtain', as an auxiliary adds an adversative notion to the following verb (cf. Ambon Malay *dapa brenti* 'get dismissed' [Van Minde 1997:325]; Cocos Malay *dapa mara* 'get angry'). However, it is unclear how general such other periphrastic constructions are in PDMs.

3.7 Loss of inherited morphology

PDMs as a category seem to have undergone a drastic reduction of the original Malayic morphology. Some PDMs exhibit a fair number of affixes that have their formal counterpart in other Malayic varieties. However, many of these seem not to be inherited. Adelaar and Prentice (1996:675) assert that the only affixes that have been maintained through most PDMs are cognates of the SM intransitive *bə(r)-* and non-controlled *tə(r)-* prefixes. However, even these are missing in some PDMs.

Baba Malay and Sri Lanka Malay have lost almost all Malayic morphology. Baba Malay only has a non-controlled prefix *tə(r)-* and a transitive suffix *-kan*. Sri Lanka Malay has a transitive suffix *-kiŋ* (which may or may not be related to *-kan*) and a suffix *-an* forming deverbal nouns.

In the case of Cocos Malay, the reduction of inherited Malayic morphology is not immediately obvious. However, at closer inspection much of the Cocos Malay morphology appears to be the result of borrowing and regrammaticalization due to SM influence. Cocos Malay has the following seven verbal affixes:

bə(r)-, an intransitive verb marker;
baku- a marker of reciprocality or repetitive and diffuse action;
tə(r)- forms intransitive verbs denoting lack of control;
kə- . . . -an forms intransitive verbs denoting lack of control and adversativity;
məN- (also *N-*) is unproductive and has no clear function;
di- marks an agentless passive.
-kan is basically a intransitive suffix. Moreover, with transitive verbs it indicates the contextual presence of a recipient (i.e. the recipient is not necessarily expressed in the sentence in which the *-kan* verb occurs). (This use of *-kan* is typical of Javanese and of Java Malay, another PDM. As in Java-Malay, *-kan* may co-occur with *di-* but not with *(mə)N-*.)

There are furthermore two nominalizing affixes, *-an* and *pəN-*, of which the latter is improductive.

Looking more closely at the verbal affixes, it become clear that several of them are not inherited. The prefix *baku-* is not Malayic: it occurs in various eastern Indonesian PDMs and is currently spreading into SM (colloquial Indonesian). *-kan* and *di-* are much more widespread in the Malayic subgroup but they are not inherited from PM either (cf. Adelaar 1992 and in press). Moreover, as seen above, the use of *-kan* betrays influence from Javanese. *(mə)N-* is unproductive and without clear function: it is either an archaism that has lost its original function or it is an unanalyzed part of some word forms borrowed from SM. This leaves Cocos Malay with only three verbal affixes (*bə(r)-*, *tə(r)-*, *kə- . . . -an*) and one nominal suffix (*-an*), which could possibly be inherited from an earlier PDM stage.

A similar picture arises from the evidence for Ambon Malay, which has a large inventory of affixes, but only very few of these seem to be inherited. As for Manado Malay, the only affixes that are listed as productive in Solea Warouw (1985:xvi–xvii) are *paN-*, *ba-*, *ta-* and *baku-*.

3.8 Loss of original voice system

In general outline, the voice system of SM (cf. Chapters 6 and 8) is common to many other varieties of Malayic and must be inherited from PM. However, PDMs do not share such a 'symmetrical voice system' (cf. HIMMELMANN, TYPOLOGICAL CHARACTERISTICS).

Ambon, Sri Lanka and Manado Malay do not make voice distinctions (cf. Van Minde 1997:189). Cocos Malay and Baba Malay do, but only in rudimentary and idiosyncratic ways.

Cocos Malay has a passive-marking prefix *di-*. In contrast to SM *di-*, it occurs only in agentless passive constructions and is not paradigmatically related to an active voice marker.

(25) *Di-stem   dia   puɲa   blakaŋ   tu*
     UV-stamp   3   LK   back   DET
     'Their backs were marked with a stamp.'

(26) *...dua   səkoci   dia   taŋkap.   Di-abiskan   sama səkali*
     ...two   boat   3s   catch   UV-finish-TR   completely
     '...He caught two boatloads [of turtles]. They were all eaten.'

Baba Malay has several passive constructions. One is formed with the non-controlled passive prefix *tə(r)-* which is generally used in Malayic varieties. The other is formed with *kəna* (lit. 'to hit the mark'), which is usually agentless and often adversative in nature. The *kəna* construction is also common in certain varieties of SM and vernacular Malay (especially in West Malaysia). It is demonstrated in (27) and (28):

(27) *Teŋok   itu   budak   yaŋ   kəna   buno   tu*
     look   DIST   youth   REL   UV   kill   ANAPH
     'Look at the case of the youth who was murdered.' (Baba Malay, Pakir 1986:182)

(28) *Bulat   kəna   maki*
     Bulat   UV   scold
     'Bulat was scolded.' (Baba Malay)

A third construction requires an agent which is introduced by *kasi* (lit. 'to give') and precedes the main verb. Pakir (1986: 136) considers this a calque construction derived from Hokkien. Compare sentence (29) which, in contrast to sentence (28), has an agent *mak dia* 'her mother'.

(29) *Bulat   kasi   mak   dia   maki*
     Bulat   Agent   mother   3s   scold
     'Bulat was scolded by her mother.' (Baba Malay)

4 MORPHOSYNTACTIC FEATURES OF SALAKO

As mentioned earlier on, Salako is a dialect of Kendayan, a Malayic vernacular in terms of the classification proposed in section 1. The Kendayan dialects are remarkable for their morphosyntax, which is richer than that of most other Malayic varieties, has retained various features lost in SM, and has undergone several developments not shared by other Malayic varieties. Among others, it developed a morphological opposition between completed and non-completed aspect. Salako differs from most other Kendayan dialects in the use of some lexical items, the partial loss of *l* and the rounding of *a* (which happens word-finally or before a final glottal, a final preploded nasal or another rounded *a*).

4.1 Proclitic *di=* in Undergoer Voice constructions

Salako Actor-oriented (AV) sentences are of an Actor–Verb–Undergoer word order, and UV sentences are of an Undergoer–Actor–Verb word order. The prefix *N-* is prefixed to AV verbs as well as to some UV verbs, see §4.2.

In SM, *di-* is a common prefix for undergoer-orientation (UV) occurring in verbs with a third person agent. However, in Salako *di=*is a proclitic which has not fully developed into a undergoer-oriented (UV) prefix and plays a rather supplementary role in marking undergoer-orientation. It has two functions. If the Actor is not expressed, it is cliticized to the verb and it indicates undergoer-orientation:

(30) *Uma-e   akà?   di=ŋa-rumput*
      field-3POSS   finished   UV=CPL-weed
      'Her field was already weeded.'

If the Actor is expressed, *di=* may precede it and function as an Actor preposition, as in sample sentences (31) an (32). However, the Actor often appears without *di=*, as is demonstrated in sentences (33) and (34). Apparently, the use of the Actor preposition *di=* puts more emphasis on the Actor (this needs further investigation). Whether *di=* is present or not, the Actor as a rule directly precedes the verb. Note also that the use of *di=* is not restricted to third person agents, as can be seen in (32).

(31) *Buuh bàà   aŋ-ɲian   gaʔe   di=ià   ŋosok-atn-i?   /N-gosok – AN-i?/*
      bamboo bàà   PRX   also   ACT=3   CPL-rub-APP-PL

      ka   tubuh-e
      LOC   body-3POSS
      'She also rubbed the "*bàà*" bamboo all over her body.'

(32) *Aŋ-koà-lah   tuàkŋ   kaleŋ*
      DIST-EMPH   bone   catfish

      di=kau   matàh-matàh   /N-RDP-patàh/   aŋ-koà.
      ACT=2s   CPL-break-RDP   DIST
      'That's the catfish-bone you've broken into many pieces.'

(33) *Dààpm   saʔ-ari   abis   uma-e   ià   ŋa-rumput*
      in   one-day   finished   field-3POSS   3s   CPL-weed
      'In a day he had finished weeding her field.'

(34) *Nanà   naŋe   kalo   dah   maɲak   padi   anà?*
      soon   EMPH   if   already   many   paddy   not

      kità?   piharà   anà?   kità?   hormat-i?
      2p   take care not   2p   respect-APP
      'Soon when there is a lot of paddy, you won't look after it, you won't treat it with respect.'

4.2 Completive marking in UV constructions

As is the case in SM and many other western Indonesian languages, Salako verbs are prenasalized (with *N-*) when they are actor-oriented. However, in contrast to other western Indonesian languages, in Salako prenasalization is also possible in UV verbs. The conditioning factor for the use with UV verbs is whether the event expressed by the verb is completed (in which case prenasalization applies) or not (in which case prenasalization does not apply). Events that are not completed either have not taken place at all or have not yet completely taken place, which includes repetitive, habitual, or recurrent acts and events. Non-completive aspect also applies to descriptions (for instance of a custom, a ritual or a technique), as they are instances of recurrent and habitual acts and events.

Sample sentences (35) and (36) exemplify completed acts (cf. also sentences (30–33):

(35)　*Eɲekŋ-e*　　*dah*　　　　*dimunuh*　*/di=N-bunuh/*
　　　 pig-3POSS　already　　　　　　　　 UV=CPL-kill
　　　 'His pigs were killed.'

(36)　*Tanàh*　*aŋ-koà*　*dah*　　　*di=ŋ-umà*
　　　 land　　DIST　　already　UV=CPL-work.a.field
　　　 'That land has already been worked.' (=The work is done)

Compare with the following instances of non-completed acts/events:

(37)　*Neʔ Kulup*　　　*aɲ-ɲian*　　*tai*　　　*anàʔ*　*jaji*　　*di=bunuh*
　　　 Grandpa Kulup　PRX　　　　ANAPH　　not　 really　UV=kill
　　　 'Kulup wasn't really killed.' (=The killing never took place)

(38)　*Si Kulup*　　*harus*　　　*di=bunuh*
　　　 Si Kulup　　have to　　UV=kill
　　　 'Si Kulup must be killed.' (=The killing has not yet happened)

(39)　*Tanàh*　*aŋ-koà*　*anàʔ*　*muih*　*/N-puih/*　*di=umà,*　　　　　*jahat.*
　　　 land　　DIST　　not　　　　　　　AV-allowed　UV=work.a.field　bad
　　　 'That land may not be worked, it's bad.' (=The work has not yet been done)

(40)　*Ame*　*ku*　*di=tiŋà-ʔàtn*　*di*　　*sià*　*aku*　*sorokŋ!*
　　　 don't　I　　UV=leave-APP　LOC　PRX　1s　　alone
　　　 'Don't leave me behind here all by myself!' (=I am not yet left behind)

(41)　*Jadi*　*tabat*　*bubu-e*　　　　　*di*　　*Pasir Panjaŋ*
　　　 so　　fence　 fishtrap-3POSS　LOC　PP

　　　masih　*dapat*　*di=tanaŋ*　*sampe*　*kanià*
　　　 still　　can　　　UV=see　　 until　　now
　　　 'So, the fence of his fishtrap can still be seen at *Pasir Panjang* (lit. 'long beach').' (=Seeing it remains a possibility)

Completive aspect is only marked in UV verbs: with AV verbs prenasalization applies irrespective of whether the event has been completed. The following two sentences (42) and (43) both denote non-completed acts/events in AV, in contrast to the above sentences

(37–41), which are non-completive in UV and hence without prenasalization:

(42) *Jadi   maoʔ-taʔ-maoʔ   diriʔ   aŋ-koà   harus*
So   like.it.or.not   1i   DIST   obliged

mayariʔ   /N-bayar-iʔ/   ià
AV-pay-APP   3s
'So, whether we like it or not, we have to pay him.'

(43) *Ame   sidi   kau   ŋataiʔ   /N-katàʔ-iʔ/   aku.   Aku   anàʔ   muih*
Don't   very   2s   AV-talk-APP   1s   1s   not

/N-puih/   ŋataiʔ   kau   pokoʔe   diam-diam   toʔokŋ   diriʔ
AV-allowed   basically   RDP-silent   really   1i
'Don't you talk to me at all. I'm not allowed to talk to you, so let's not say
a word to each other.'

The following AV sentence combines prenasalization with a subjunctive verb (marked with
-àʔ) which is non-completed *per se* because it expresses an intention (see further §4.4):

(44) *Ame   kitàʔ   dari,   ame   kitàʔ   gaiʔ,*
Don't   2p   run away   don't   2p   afraid

aku   anàʔ   munuhàʔ   /N-bunuh-àʔ/   kitàʔ?
1s   not   TR-kill-SUBJ   2p
'Don't you people run away, don't be afraid, I won't kill you.'

4.3 Applicative *-iʔ* vs. plural *-iʔ*

In Salako, it is expedient to distinguish two homonymous suffixes *-iʔ* (unlike in SM
where there is a suffix *-i* with similar functions but a different distribution). One is
a marker of plural action and is suffixed to a variety of intransitive verbs and to verbs
having the applicative suffix *-AN*. The other is an applicative suffix forming transitive
verbs that often have a location or direction as undergoer.

In combination with the intransitive prefix *ba-*, the plural marker *-iʔ* adds the notion
of reciprocality, plurality of Actor or repeated action to a base:

(45) *ba-juà (kayu)* 'sell wood',   *ba-jua-iʔ jukut* 'sell various products',
'be a seller of wood'   'sell (one's) products everywhere'
taʔap 'hold'   *ba-taʔap-taʔap-iʔ* 'hold each other'
-abuh   *baʔ-abuh-iʔ* 'be involved in an incestuous marriage'
                                    (lit. 'to fall (to lose one's social position), of a
                                    couple' < PM *labuh* 'to fall')
tumàkŋ 'fall down,   *ba-tumakŋ-iʔ* 'be trampled down (e.g. of grass)'
topple (long things)'

When co-occurring with the circumfix *ba- -AN* it adds a notion of 'many or all
people/things participating in an act or event' or also 'repetitiveness of act or event':

(46) *dari* 'run'   *ba-dari-atn-iʔ* '(everybody) run'
ukàʔ 'a wound'   *ba-ukaʔ-atn-iʔ* 'be covered by wounds'
turutn 'go down'   *ba-turun-an-iʔ* '(everybody) go down'
atàkŋ 'come'   *baʔ-ataŋ-an-iʔ* 'come (in huge numbers)'

It also adds this notion to transitive verbs with or without the applicative suffix -*AN*:

(47) *juà* 'sell'   *ɲua-iʔ* 'sell (many things)'
      taban-an 'take away'   *naban-an-iʔ* 'take (many) away, take (along many
                                              places), keep taking'
      apas-àtn 'set free'   *ŋ-apas-atn-iʔ* 'set (everything/everybody) free'

Text examples:

(48) *Ba-dari-atn-iʔ-lah*   *uràkŋ*   *Saboyoʔ*   *ba*   *uràkŋ*
      INTR-run-PL-PL-EMPH   people   Saboyoʔ   with   people

      Saribas   *aɲ-ɲian.*
      Saribas   this
      'All Saboyoʔ and Saribas fled' or 'The Saboyoʔ and Saribas people fled in all
      directions.'

(49) *Tubuh*   *neʔ*   *Diboʔ-pun*   *ba-ukaʔ-atn-iʔ,*   *ba-daràh.*
      body   Grandpa   Diboʔ-TOP   INTR-wound-PL-PL   INTR-bleed
      'Grandpa [ancestor] Diboʔ was covered with wounds, (and) he was bleeding.'

(50) *Ba-turun-an-iʔ-lah*   *samueɲe*   *uràkŋ*   *ka*   *dààpm*
      INTR-go down-PL-PL-EMPH   all   people   LOC   inside

      kapal   *aŋ-koà*   *tai.*
      boat   DIST   ANAPH
      'Out came all the people who were in that boat.'

(51) *Uràkŋ*   *kan*   *supàtn*   *kalaw*   *diriʔ*   *nabananiʔ*
      people   isn't it   embarrassed   if   1i

      /N-taban-AN-iʔ/   *bini-e*   *ka*   *sià*   *ka*   *naʔan*
      AV-take-APP-PL   wife-3POSS   LOC   PRX   LOC   DIST
      'People would get embarrassed if we took their spouses around, right?'

(52) *Di=ŋ-apas-atn-iʔ*   *burukŋ-e*   *dinatakiʔ*   */di=N-tatak-iʔ/*
      UV=TR-free-APP-PL   bird-3POSS   UV=N-cut-TR

      tali-e   *samueɲe.*
      rope-3POSS   all
      '(All) the birds were released, the ropes (holding them) were all cut.'

(53) *Kaniàʔ*   *dah*   *maɲak*   *tapayàtn*   *antik*   *aŋ-koà*
      nowadays   already   many   jars   antique   DIST

      dah   *uràkŋ*   *ɲuaiʔ*   */N-juà-iʔ/*
      already   people   CPL-sell-PL
      'Nowadays many of those antique jars have been sold.'

The applicative marker -*iʔ* forms transitive verbs on the basis of nouns and (stative and dynamic) intransitive verbs, compare *tatamà* 'medicine' and *natama-iʔ* 'cure', 'apply medicine to s.o.'; *salàh* 'bad' and *ɲalah-iʔ* 'do wrong to s.o.'; (*N + paniʔ* →) *maniʔ* 'bathe' and *maniʔ-iʔ* 'wash s.o.'. It can also be added to transitive verbs, turning locational or directional adjuncts into core arguments, e.g. *mayar* 'pay (something)' and *mayar-iʔ* 'pay (someone)'. (This is not unlike the standard Malay suffix -*i* when suffixed to transitive verbal roots, as in *məmbayar* 'pay (something)' and *məmbayar-i* 'pay (someone)'.)

Examples (cf. also (42)):

(54) *Dayaŋ-dayaŋ*   *mani?-i?*   /N + pani?-i?/   *ià*
     Lady.in.waiting-RDP   AV-bathe-TR   3s
     'Ladies-in-waiting gave him a bath.'

(55) *Ià*   *ɲuruh*   *pardana-mantari-e*   *aŋ-koà*   *ŋago*   /N-gago/
     3s   AV-send   prime-minister-3POSS   DIST   AV-look for

     uràkŋ   *am-pane-pane*   *natamai?*   /N-tatamà-i?/   *ià*
     person   REL-RDP-able   AV-medicine-APP   3s
     'He sent his prime minister to look for someone who had the expertise to cure him.'

4.4 Subjunctive *-à?*

Salako retains a subjunctive marker *-à?* (< Proto-Austronesian *-a*, also a subjunctive marker, and cognate to Old Malay *-a*). It indicates a purpose or intention ('in order to'). It has an allomorph *-?à?* which is suffixed to a base ending in *-à*, cf. *ka umà-?à?* in (58). Note that in sentence (58) *-à?* is suffixed to the prepositional phrase *ka umà* 'to the field' to derive a purposive clause. Examples:

(56) *Si Bunsu?*   *ampus*   *ka*   *rumàh*   *Si Pakapuràtn,*
     SB   go   LOC   house   SP

     ŋ-icakŋ-à?   *kaleŋ*   *sabap*   *anà?*   *di=puaŋ-an*   *tumare?*
     AV-look.for-SUBJ   catfish   because   not   UV=go.home-APP   yesterday
     'Si Bunsu? went to Si Pakapuràtn's house to look for the catfish, because it hadn't been returned the day before.'

(57) *tampat*   *burukŋ*   *aŋ-koà*   *ba-mani-atn-i-à?*
     place   bird   DIST   INTR-bathe-PL-PL-SUBJ
     'a bathing place for birds' (i.e. a place where all birds come together to bathe).

(58) *Ne?*   *Ibo*   *aŋ-ɲian*   *anà?*   *sampat*   *sidi*   *ka*
     Grandparent   Ibo   PRX   not   have opportunity   very   LOC

     Umà-?à?.
     field-SUBJ
     'Grandpa-of-Ibo had no opportunity at all to go to the field.'

4.5 Vocative *-à*

Salako also has a vocative suffix *-à* (without a final glottal stop!) which is not found in other Malayic varieties:

(59) *Am-bagà*   *mati*   *kau*   *aŋ-ɲian,*   *pa?*   *Aiai-à!*
     REL-stupid   dead(ly), very   2s   PRX   daddy   Aiai-VOC
     'Gee, how dumb you are, Pa? Aiai!' (literally 'Father-of-Aiai', a teknonym).

5 KERINCI: NEW MORPHOSYNTAX THROUGH SOUND CHANGE

Kerinci has part of its phonological history in common with Minangkabau. However, some of its phonological developments are different and more far-reaching to the extent that they have had a marked effect on Kerinci morphosyntax. In the Sungei Penuh subdialect of Kerinci two conditioned changes have resulted in the occurrence of up to four variant forms per root morpheme (see Steinhauer (2002) for a detailed study of the phonological changes that have led to these variant forms).

(1) The height of the vowel in the final syllable is conditioned by the presence or absence, anywhere in a word, of a voiced stop that is not part of a consonant cluster. Generally, the nuclear vowel in the final syllable of a word containing a voiced stop is raised vis-à-vis the corresponding vowel in words without voiced stop. This is demonstrated in Table 7.3, where the SM words to the left have a voiced stop and form minimal pairs with those to the right, which have not. (Note that in the final instance, *kalambaw* does have a voiced stop but it is part of a cluster.)

The height of the final syllable vowel can be changed through prefixation. For instance, the last vowel in *jaleŋ* 'way' is lowered when this root obtains prenasalization, because the resulting derivation has no voiced stop any more, cf. *ɲalaŋ* 'make go, do'. *Sapaw* 'broom' raises its last vowel when *ba-* is prefixed to it in *basapèw* 'with a broom', because this prefix contains a voiced stop. When *di-* is prefixed to the root of *ma-laraŋ* 'to prohibit', it becomes *dilareŋ*, and so on.

(2) An originally phonological distinction between words in phrase-final position and words in other positions gave rise to a morphosyntactic distinction that has been termed the 'absolute'/'oblique' opposition in a large part of the lexicon of the Sungey Penuh dialect. The distinction concerns last syllable vowels as well as final consonants (see Table 7.4).

The oblique form applies, for instance, to noun-heads followed by possessors, determiners, modifiers etc., AV verbs followed by an undergoer, or UV verbs followed by the agent (cf. Prentice and A. Hakim Usman 1978:147–148). Compare absolute *binateŋ* 'an animal' with oblique *binatòn itoh* 'the/that animal'. In absolute + absolute *umah gədeŋ* 'the house is big' both words are phrase final and contrast with oblique + absolute *umoh*

TABLE 7.3: KERINCI FINAL SYLLABLE VOWELS IN WORDS WITH AND WITHOUT A VOICED STOP

SM	Kerinci	Short gloss	SM	Kerinci	Short gloss
garam	gaheŋ	salt	karam	kahaŋ	sink
kəbal	kəbeŋ	invulnerable	kəpal	kəpaŋ	take in fist
jəriŋ	jəhoyn	tree species	kəriŋ	kəhayn	dry
jahit	jaoyʔ	sew	pahit	paayʔ	bitter
təbus	təbéwh	redeem	tərus	tərawh	straight
kəlabu	kalabèw	grey	kəlambu	kalambaw	mosquito-net

TABLE 7.4: KERINCI ABSOLUTE VS. OBLIQUE FORMS

SM	Short gloss	Kerinci: absolute	Kerinci: oblique
air	water	ayè	ayey
binataŋ	animal	binateŋ	binatòn
di-pəluk	embraced	dipəlòʔ	dipəlowʔ
—— (Minangkabau: gadaŋ)	big	gədeŋ	gədòn
mata	eye	matò	mato
putəri	princess	putay	putey
rumah	house	umah	umoh

gədeŋ 'big house', which is a noun phrase in which only *gədeŋ* is phrase-final. The following two examples are compounds: Their first components are therefore oblique forms per definition, whereas their last components can be absolute or oblique depending on whether they are phrase-final or not: absolute *mato ayè* vs. oblique *mato ayey* 'source', 'well'; absolute *ayey matò* vs. oblique *ayey mato* 'tear(s)'. Compare also absolute + absolute *dipəlò? putay* 'embraced was the princess' vs. oblique + absolute *dipəlow? putay* 'embraced by the princess': in the first case each word constitutes an independent phrase, whereas in the second case, *putay* is the Actor in an undergoer-oriented verb phrase.

However, the conditioning of whether a word occurs phrase-finally or not became blurred later on in the history of Kerinci (in contrast with the distinction between words with a voiced stop and those without, which is still productive). Nowadays, various words do not make the absolute vs. oblique distinction. They include loanwords that were adopted after the absolute/oblique split had ceased to be productive. They also include members of various word classes that only occur phrase-finally and therefore only obtained an absolute form, such as personal pronouns, deictic determiners, and members of word classes that never occur phrase-finally, such as prepositions and complementizers, which only developed an oblique form. They also include words that historically had a suffix. Original PM suffixes were lost in Kerinci: consequently, all original derivations with a suffix lost their final syllable, and with it the evidence for an absolute/oblique distinction. As a result, the derivations in question now exhibit the original penultimate syllable as their last syllable, which only has an oblique form. For instance, the original form **kə-lapar-an* 'starvation' became *kalapo*, which morphologically derives from an oblique form *lapo* 'hungry' (cf. absolute *lapa*). The original form **pəŋ-hidup-an* became *paŋidu?* 'livelihood', which morphologically derives from (oblique) *idu?* 'alive' (cf. absolute *idew?*).

There are several other categories of words that do not make the distinction, and, to complicate matters, some words allow the use of both absolute and oblique forms in certain positions (Steinhauer and A. Hakim Usman 1978).

Regarding its function, Prentice and A. Hakim Usman write that

> the absolute-oblique distinction has become associated with such wider syntactic distinctions as indefinite-definite (in nouns) and intransitive-transitive (in verbs), as the functional load is borne more by the phonological distinctiveness of the oblique form and less by the presence of, say, a following *itoh* (as determiner) or *ɲo* (as possessor or as object pronoun). (Prentice and A. Hakim Usman 1978:148)

Although this is an adequate summary of what the distinction is about in general, some of its applications are much more complicated, as is demonstrated in Steinhauer and A. Hakim Usman (1978).

The distinction gives rise to such contrasting sentences as *binateŋ minawŋ* 'an animal is drinking' and *binatòn minon* 'the animal is drinking it' (Prentice and A. Hakim Usman 1978:148). Another indication that the historical conditioning for absolute and oblique forms is becoming blurred is the fact that both *binatòn* and *binatòn itoh* (see above) nowadays mean 'the animal'. Here we see that the functional load of definite marking is shifting away from *itoh* and has become associated with oblique marking.

The absolute/oblique distinction is quite independent from the phonological distinction between words with a voiced stop and those without. It is consequently possible that a set of related words has four different endings, as is the case with *jaleŋ* (absolute), *jalòn* (oblique) 'way', which have a voiced stop, as opposed to (absolute) *ɲalaŋ*, (oblique) *ɲalan* 'make go, do', which have not. Compare also (absolute) *sapaw*, (oblique) *sapow* 'broom; to sweep', and (absolute) *basapèw*, (oblique) *basapu* 'with a broom'.

ACKNOWLEDGEMENTS

I am very grateful to Adrian Clynes (Universiti Brunei Darussalam), Don van Minde (Leiden University) and Nikolaus Himmelmann for their valuable comments on an earlier version of this chapter. They are not responsible for any errors in the present version.

REFERENCES

Abdul Djebar Hapip (1977) *Kamus Banjar – Indonesia*. Jakarta: Pusat Pembinaan dan Pengembangan Bahasa.
Abdul Hamid Mahmood (1994) *Sintaksis dialek Kelantan*, Kuala Lumpur: Dewan Bahasa dan Pustaka.
Adelaar, K.A. (1991a) 'A phonological sketch of Salako (West Kalimantan)', in Ray Harlow (ed.), *Papers of the 5th International Conference on Austronesian Linguistics Part II: West Austronesian*, 21–40, Auckland: Te Reo, the Linguistic Society of New Zealand.
——(1991b) 'Some notes on the origin of Sri Lanka Malay', in H. Steinhauer (ed.), *Papers in Austronesian linguistics No.1*, 1–22. Canberra: Pacific Linguistics.
——(1992) *Proto-Malayic: a reconstruction of its phonology and part of its morphology and lexicon*, Canberra: Pacific Linguistics.
——(1996) 'Malay in the Cocos (Keeling) Islands', in Bernd Nothofer (ed.), *Reconstruction, Classification, Description. Festschrift in honor of Isidore Dyen*, 167–198, Hamburg: Abera Verlag (Asia Pacific).
——(2002) 'Salako morphology and the interrelation between voice, mood and aspect', in K.A. Adelaar and R.A. Blust (eds), 1–27.
——(in press) 'On the internal classifiability of Malayic', in D. Gil (ed.), *Malay/Indonesian Linguistics*, London: Routledge/Curzon Press.
——(2004) 'Where does Malay come from? Twenty years of discussions about homeland, migrations and classifications', *Bijdragen tot de Taal-, Land- en Volkenkunde,* 160/1:1–30.
Adelaar, K.A. and Prentice, D.J. (1996) 'Malay: its history, role and spread', in S.A. Wurm, P. Mühlhäusler and D. Tryon (eds), *Atlas of languages of intercultural communication in the Pacific, Asia and the Americas*, 673–693. Berlin and New York: Mouton – de Gruyter.
Adelaar, K.A. and Blust, R.A. (eds) (2002) *Between worlds: linguistic papers in memory of David John (Jack) Prentice*, Canberra: Pacific Linguistics.
Ajid Che Kob (1985) *Dialek geografi Pasir Mas*, Monograf 3, Institut Bahasa, Kesusastraan dan Kebudayaan Melayu, Kuala Lumpur: Universiti Kebangsaan Malaysia.
Asmah Haji Omar (1981) *The Iban language of Sarawak: a grammatical description*, Kuala Lumpur: Dewan Bahasa dan Pustaka.
Blust, R.A. (1997) 'Nasals and nasalisation in Borneo', *Oceanic Linguistics,* 36:149–179.
Clynes, A. (in press) 'Brunei Malay: an overview', in D. Gil (ed.), *Malay/Indonesian Linguistics*, London: Routledge/Curzon Press.
——(1989) *Speech styles in Balinese and Javanese*, Unpublished MA thesis, Australian National University.
Collins, J.T. (1985) 'The phonology of Tioman and the reconstruction of Proto-Malay', in Suriya Ratanakul *et al.* (eds), *Southeast Asian linguistic studies presented to André G. Haudricourt*, 541–566, Bangkok: Mahidol University.
——(1990) *Bibliografi dialek Melayu di pulau Borneo*, Siri Monograf Bibliografi Sejarah Bahasa Melayu, Kuala Lumpur: Dewan Bahasa dan Pustaka.

Collins, J.T. (1994) 'Preliminary notes on Berau Malay', in P. Martin (ed.), *Shifting patterns of language use in Borneo*, 297–333, Williamsburg (Virginia): Borneo Research Council.

——(1995a) *Bibliografi dialek Melayu di pulau Sumatera*, Siri Monograf Bibliografi Sejarah Bahasa Melayu, Kuala Lumpur: Dewan Bahasa dan Pustaka.

——(1995b) *Bibliografi dialek Melayu di pulau Jawa, Bali dan Sri Lanka*, Siri Monograf Bibliografi Sejarah Bahasa Melayu, Kuala Lumpur: Dewan Bahasa dan Pustaka.

——(1996a) 'Borneo and Maluku: the evidence from the language of Bacan', in P.W. Martin, G. Poedjosoedarmo and C. Ozog (eds), *Language use and language change in Brunei Darussalam*, 73–88, Athens: Ohio University Centre for International Studies.

——(1996b) *Bibliografi dialek Melayu di Indonesia Timur*, Siri Monograf Bibliografi Sejarah Bahasa Melayu. Kuala Lumpur: Dewan Bahasa dan Pustaka.

Hogan, D.W. (in collaboration with S.W. Pattemore) (1988) *Urak Lawoi': basic structures and a dictionary*, Canberra: Pacific Linguistics.

Muhadjir (1981) *Morphology of Jakarta dialect: affixation and reduplication*, Nusa 11, Jakarta: Badan Penyelenggara Seri Nusa.

Nothofer, B. (1997) *Dialek Melayu Bangka*, Bangi: Penerbit Universiti Kebangsaan Malaysia.

Pakir, Anne Geok-In Sim (1986) *A linguistic investigation of Baba Malay*, Ph.D. thesis, University of Hawaii, Honolulu.

Prentice, D.J. and A. Hakim Usman (1978) Kerinci sound-changes and phonotactics, in S.A. Wurm and L. Carrington (eds), *Second International Conference of Austronesian Linguistics: proceedings, Fascicle I: Western Austronesian*, 121–163, Canberra: Pacific Linguistics.

Scott, N.C. (1956) *A dictionary of Sea Dayak*, London: School of Oriental and African Studies.

Solea [Salea] Warouw, M. (1985) *Kamus Manado – Indonesia*, Jakarta: Pusat Pembinaan dan Pengembangan Bahasa.

Steinhauer, H. (1987) 'Standaard Indonesisch: norm en ontwikkeling', in J. de Rooy (ed.), *Variatie en norm in de standaardtaal*, 85–114, Amsterdam: P.J. Meertens Instituut voor Dialectologie, Volkskunde en Naamkunde (Deel 7).

——(1991) 'Malay in East Indonesia: the case of Larantuka (Flores)', in H. Steinhauer (ed.), *Papers in Austronesian linguistics No.1*, Canberra: Pacific Linguistics.

——(2002) 'More (on) Kerinci sound-changes', in K.A. Adelaar and R. Blust (eds), 149–176.

Steinhauer, H. and A. Hakim Usman (1978) 'Notes on the morphemics of Kerinci (Sumatra)', in S.A. Wurm and L. Carrington (eds), *Second International Conference of Austronesian Linguistics: proceedings, Fascicle I: Western Austronesian*, 483–502, Canberra: Pacific Linguistics.

Tamsin Medan (1980) *Dialek-dialek Minangkabau di daerah Minangkabau/Sumatra Barat (Suatu Pemerian dialektologis)*, Jakarta: Pusat Pembinaan dan Pengembangan Bahasa.

Van Engelenhoven, A. (unpublished) *De rol van de definietmarkers in the Moluks Maleis*, Minor thesis, Leiden University.

Van Minde, D. (1997) *Melayu Ambong: phonology, morphology, syntax*, Leiden: Research School CNWS, School of Asian, African and Amerindian Studies.

Voorhoeve, C.L. (1983) 'Some observations on North Moluccan Malay', in J.T. Collins (ed.), *Studies in Malay dialects Part II*, Nusa Linguistic Studies of Indonesian and other languages of Indonesia Volume 17, 1–13, Jakarta: Badan Penyelenggara Seri Nusa.

CHAPTER EIGHT

COLLOQUIAL INDONESIAN

Michael C. Ewing

1 INTRODUCTION

Indonesian is a variety of Malay, a language spoken throughout much of insular and peninsular Southeast Asia. Malay occurs in many indigenous varieties, as a lingua franca, and in creolized forms. The variety known as Indonesian has developed from language planning work initiated by colonial scholars and administrators under Dutch rule. These scholars reinforced an indigenous distinction between 'high' and 'low' forms of the language in an effort to valorize one (artificially produced) variety of High Malay for their colonial purposes, in contrast to the numerous seemingly unwieldy varieties of Low Malay flourishing throughout the archipelago. This language-planning agenda has been continued in the post-colonial era by Indonesian linguists and educators with the goal of transforming Indonesian into a standardized 'high' language deemed suitable for a modern, culturally and intellectually forward-looking people, and shielded from the corrupting influences of 'low' forms of the language (see Steinhauer, Chapter 3, this volume, for more discussion).

The spread of this standardized form of an Indonesian language through the development of education and the media has indeed been one of the great successes of the Indonesian nationalist agenda (Errington 1998). Yet despite the efforts of the language planners, speakers of Indonesian still continue to use a wide range of fluid and constantly interacting codes, styles, and lects, which are neither easily nor appropriately separated into neatly distinct varieties. All speakers of Indonesian recognize a contrast between the government-sanctioned form of Indonesian and more spontaneous varieties. The former is known officially as *bahasa baku* 'standard language', characterized as *bahasa yang baik dan benar* 'language that is good and correct' and popularly referred to with such descriptors as *bahasa resmi* 'official language', *bahasa formal* 'formal language', or *bahasa EYD* 'the language of the definitive spelling system' (see section 2). Other forms of Indonesian or Malay used spontaneously throughout the country might be referred to by speakers as, for example, *bahasa lisan* 'spoken language', *bahasa pasar* 'market language', or *bahasa sehari-hari* 'everyday language'. Indeed in something of a continuation of this division, the present chapter on Colloquial Indonesian can be seen to complement Prentice's 1990 sketch of Standard Indonesian and fill out some of the observations made there about characteristics of colloquial language. The history of Indonesian has been chronicled in Alisjahbana 1962, Anwar 1980, Errington 1998, Hoffman 1979, and Maier 1993.

Although Colloquial Indonesian is often called *bahasa lisan* 'spoken language' by those who use it, these are not equivalent terms. While probably the best exemplar and most frequently occurring genre of Colloquial Indonesian is indeed casual conversation, salient features of the conversational exemplar include not only that it is spoken, but also that it is interactive, unplanned, and, crucially, emblematic of relaxed interpersonal relations. There are formal genres of spoken language that lack these characteristics, such as speeches and certain styles of drama. Indeed Badudu *et al.*'s (1984) research on spoken Indonesian morphology explicitly examines only *bahasa resmi* 'official language' with results that are very close to the prescribed standard. Conversely, the informal characteristics of conversational Indonesian occur in non-conversational genres and non-spoken channels, for example in personal letters, electronic forums, and popular magazines. Nonetheless, conversation remains the primary locus of Colloquial Indonesian and many writers of informal language strive to capture the feel of this genre.

This chapter presents Colloquial Indonesian not as a separate variety of Malay but as a social style, one register among the many ways that the national language of Indonesia is used by its speakers. This informal style is identifiable, to both speakers and researchers, by a convergence of lexical, morphological, syntactic, and discourse markers. In casual interactions, speakers and writers use these markers in conjunction with the wider resources of Standard Indonesian, and with resources from other varieties of Malay (e.g. Betawi Malay and Jakartan Indonesian), as well as other Indonesian and international languages (e.g. Javanese, Arabic, and English). Colloquial Indonesian is at once this set of markers and also the ways in which speakers use these markers together with other linguistic resources to simultaneously reflect and constitute an informal and casual quality of interaction. Because there is variation in how speakers constitute Colloquial Indonesian across educational, economic, regional, and ethnic groups, the description in this chapter is based on the type of language typically used by educated speakers of Indonesian using the language in ethnically (or first-language) mixed, informal interactions.

In this social style model of Colloquial Indonesian, speakers are seen to draw frequently on the grammatical resources of Standard Indonesian in their informal interaction. Because Standard Indonesian has been extensively described elsewhere, these features will not be covered in detail in the present chapter. Readers can turn to any of the reference grammars or linguistic descriptions of Standard Indonesian, including Kaswanti Purwo 1984, 1988, MacDonald and Dardjowidjojo 1967, Moeliono and Dardjowidjojo 1988, Musgrave 2001, Prentice 1990, Sneddon 1996, and Verhaar 1984. In this chapter, emphasis will be placed on issues noticeably divergent from the standard language: features that are pervasive in Colloquial Indonesian and features that are particularly characteristic of informal face-to-face interaction. Previous work on Colloquial Indonesian has been less extensive than that on the standard language, but there has been a recent strong upsurge of interest in the topic. See for example, Cumming 2002, Englebretson 2003, Ewing and Cumming 1998, Gil 2002a, 2002b, Sneddon 2002, Wouk 1989, Wouk 1999. Wolff *et al.* 1986 include extensive descriptions of both standard and informal usage, while Anderson 1966 and Hooker 1995 discuss the political implications of different styles of Indonesian. Other related work includes Grijns 1991, Ikranegara 1980, Muhadjir 1981, Tanner 1967.

The discussion in this chapter is based largely on a corpus of transcripts from naturally occurring conversational Indonesian recorded in Jakarta, various parts of Java, and among Indonesians residing in Australia. It therefore tends to represent Colloquial Indonesian as spoken in Java, although the conversations do generally include speakers with different first-language backgrounds, including speakers from outside Java. This study thus focuses on informal Indonesian in its role as a second language of national integration. Because prosody carries important grammatical information in spoken language on a par with morphology and syntax, the conversational data are transcribed into intonation units. Each intonation unit is 'a stretch of speech uttered under a single coherent intonation contour' (Du Bois *et al.* 1992:17) and is transcribed on a separate line, which is closed with punctuation to indicate whether the terminal pitch contour has final, continuing, or appeal intonation. See the list of transcription conventions at the end of the chapter for these and other conventions. The conversational data are augmented with examples of naturally occurring informal written language from the internet. The written data, of course, do not have prosody, and these examples are given as punctuated by the original writers.

2 PHONOLOGY AND ORTHOGRAPHY

In the context of the data used for this description, the phonological system of spoken Colloquial Indonesian is not strikingly different from the standard. The basic phoneme inventory of Indonesian includes the six vowels in Table 8.1 and the twenty-two consonants in Table 8.2.

The orthography used in this chapter follows Standard Indonesian, i.e. the Definitive Spelling System (*Ejaan yang Disempurnakan* or *EYD*, Moeliono *et al.* 1988). The orthographic symbols of the *EYD* correspond to the segmental symbols in Tables 8.1 and 8.2, with the following differences: $<e>$ = /ə/, $<é>$ = /e/, $<j>$ = /ɟ/, $<ny>$ = /ɲ/>, $<sy>$ = /ʃ/, $<y>$ = /j/, $<ng>$ = /ŋ/, $<kh>$ = /x/, and $<k>$ = /ʔ/ and /k/.

There will be variation in the phonetic realizations of some aspects of this system, differing both by individual speakers and from one region of the country to another. But because a description of regionally identifiable varieties of Colloquial Indonesian is not the goal of this chapter, such variation will not be addressed here. There are, however, a few frequent variations in Colloquial Indonesian phonology which stand out as salient to speakers themselves, especially those of the Jakarta/Java areas. These include, among others, the realization of the diphthong /ai/ as [e] and /au/ as [o]; unrealized /h/; the loss of initial syllable schwa before liquids as in /bəlum/ [blum] 'not yet'; and realization of /a/ as [ə] in the final syllables of some words, as in /sənaŋ/ [sənəŋ] 'happy'. In addition, other examples of reduced forms in Colloquial Indonesian are not part of the phonological system, but are limited to a small set of specific function words, e.g. Standard

TABLE 8.1: VOWELS IN INDONESIAN

i			u
	e	ə	o
		a	

TABLE 8.2: CONSONANTS IN INDONESIAN

		Labial	Interdental	Alveolar	Palatal	Velar	Labio-velar	Glottal
Stops	voiceless	p	t		c	k		ʔ
	voiced	b		d	ɟ	g		
Nasal		m		n	ɲ	ŋ		
Fricative		f		s	ʃ	x		h
Lateral				l				
Trill				r				
Glide					j		w	

sama – Colloquial *ama* 'same', Standard *saja* – Colloquial *aja* 'just', Standard *sudah* – Colloquial *udah* 'PFV', and Standard *mémang* – Colloquial *émang* 'indeed'.

The salience of such features for speakers is seen in colloquial spelling, a fluid set of informal orthographic conventions differentially applied by writers to give the 'sound' of familiarity to the written word. Some of the phonological variation discussed above appears in the colloquial spelling used in the following lines taken from internet interactions. These include the spellings <kalo> for *kalau* and <pake> for *pakai*, as well as <kasi> for *kasih* and <trus> for *terus*. In the interlinear glossing of examples taken from the internet, a line in standard spelling is placed before the gloss line.

(1) *kalo*   *udah*   *kepikir*   *gue*   *kasi*   *comment*   *lagi*
     kalau   udah   kepikir   gué   kasih   *comment*   lagi
     if   PFV   POT:think   1s   give   comment   again
     'If (I)'ve thought of (something), I'll give some more comments.'
     <http://www.geocities.com/SouthBeach/Pier/4375/geobook.html>

(2) *Trus*   *email*   *untuk*   *Slackware*   *itu*   *pake*   *yang*   *mana?*
     terus   *email*   untuk   *Slackware*   itu   pakai   yang   mana
     next   email   for   Slackware   DIST   use   REL   which
     'And what's the email to use for Slackware?'
     <http://www.vlsm.org/linux-archive/i7/msg00694.html>

Other aspects of colloquial spelling (not illustrated above) do not necessarily reflect phonological features of spoken Colloquial Indonesian, but are alternative forms for graphemes in the standard language, for example <nk> for standard <ng> or <ch> for standard <h>. Prior to 1972, use of the number <2> to mark reduplication was accepted in standard spelling, but is now restricted to informal contexts, as in example (68) below. Colloquial spelling is another indication of the salience for speakers of Colloquial Indonesian in all its various forms of expression. All examples of spoken language are presented with standard orthography while examples taken from the internet are presented with their original spelling.

3 BASIC MORPHOSYNTAX

3.1 Word classes

There are two open word classes in Colloquial Indonesian, nouns and verbs (both eventive verbs and stative verbs, including 'adjectives'). Words of both classes may either be monomorphemic or morphologically complex. Words with derivational or inflectional morphology can generally be more easily categorized as nouns or verbs based on form alone, because specific morphology tends to be associated primarily with either the argument or predicate functions within clauses. Most monomorphemic forms can be categorized as nouns or verbs based on whether they more frequently occur in argument or predicate functions in clauses and on patterns of interaction with negation markers (see section 3.5). However, monomorphemic forms tend to be rather flexible, and speakers of Colloquial Indonesian will unflinchingly use a word that might generally be taken as a verb in a nominal function or vice versa without the derivational morphology prescribed by Standard Indonesian to mark the shift in word class. Examples (3) through (5) illustrate the flexibility of word class membership. In (3) the speaker, in a more standard style, uses the monomorphemic form *cerita* 'story' as a noun in the first line, and then the derived verbal form, *menceritakan* 'to tell a story' in the second line. However, in (4) *cerita* is used as a verb without benefit of derivational morphology.

(3)   N: *kita   e: punya   cerita,*
         1p   HES   have   story
         terus   kita   men-cerita-kan   ke   teman-teman   kita,
         then   1p   AV-story-APP   to   friend-RDP   1p
         'We have a story, and then we tell (it) to our friends.'

(4)   C: ..   *Kalau   saya   cerita   begini,*
               if   1s   story   like.this
               'If I tell a story like this,'

Example (5) illustrates the use of *makan*, usually a verb meaning 'to eat' but in this context clearly a nominal meaning 'food'. The prescriptively appropriate derived form would be *makanan* 'food'.

(5)   C: *Makan   juga   nggak   boléh   di-taroh   di   situ.*
         food   also   NEG   allow   UV-put   LOC   MED.ADV
         'Food also isn't allowed to be put there.'

Derivational morphology is a major part of Indonesian grammar, in both standard and colloquial styles. Colloquial Indonesian includes a set of non-standard forms as well as the full range of forms found in Standard Indonesian; although standard forms may be put to colloquial usage as illustrated above. Colloquial derivational morphology mainly occurs with verbs and is discussed in Section 5. There is no nominal derivational morphology specific to Colloquial Indonesian: speakers draw morphologically complex nouns from the general stock of vocabulary common to Standard Indonesian and Colloquial Indonesian. Standard derivational morphology is discussed fully in the grammars of Standard Indonesian cited above. Prentice (1990) points out that Standard Indonesian has a larger inventory of derivational morphology than most non-standard forms of Malay. But because speakers of Colloquial Indonesian draw on standard, colloquial and regional linguistic resources, their language displays an even richer range of morphology than is displayed by Standard Indonesian.

3.2 Basic clause structure

A clause consists of a subject and a predicate or a predicate alone. The predicate is frequently a verb, either intransitive or transitive and either monomorphemic or with some sort of morphological marking. Common non-verbal predicate types include noun phrases, prepositional phrases, and some adverbs.

The subject and most other core arguments of an Indonesian clause are generally unmarked as opposed to oblique arguments, which are usually marked with a preposition. The subject is distinguished from other core arguments primarily by the fact that its position relative to the predicate is somewhat variable while that of non-subject core arguments is relatively fixed (examples are given below). In addition, the subject argument may have one or more of the following features. It is generally referential and identifiable; it is often highly accessible in the discourse context and so is often not expressed explicitly. In clause-combining contexts where a single argument is shared, that argument is usually the subject of the subordinate clause. In certain transitive clauses, the subject can trigger voice morphology on the verb, which marks the subject's role as actor or undergoer of the clause (see sections 3.2.1 and 5). The juncture between subject and predicate is an important position for adverbial expressions and for discourse particles, which may be placed here, clause-initially or clause-finally, but not within phrasal constituents in the clause. This is illustrated in section 3.2.3. Finally, plural subjects can be indicated with the plural marker *pada* preceding the predicate. Nonetheless, not all clauses will contain an argument that exhibits any of these features. This possibility, together with the prevalence of unexpressed arguments, frequent lack of verbal morphology, and flexibility in constituent order, can mean that not all naturally occurring clauses in Colloquial Indonesian will have a clear subject argument.

3.2.1 Verbal predicates

Transitive clauses have two core arguments, one more agent-like, here called the actor, and one more patient-like, the undergoer. Either the actor or the undergoer can serve as the subject of the clause, with any or all of the characteristics noted above. Most transitive clauses in which both core arguments are explicitly expressed have the constituent order SVX, where S is the subject, V the verb, and X the second, non-subject core argument, as in the actor voice (AV) example (6) and the undergoer voice (UV) example (7).

(6)   S: *Pak   Razi   mau   bawa   buah.*
           Mr   Razi   want   carry   fruit
           'Mr Razi is going to bring fruit.'

(7)   M: *Masa   dia   di:-ikut-in   sama   Intél,*
           D.PTCL 3s   UV-follow-APP   by   intellegence.office
           'No way she was followed by someone from *Intel*.'

There are in fact two different constructions which are both classified as UV. In the first, exemplified in (7), the verb is prefixed with *di-* and the actor argument is optionally marked by a preposition, either colloquial *sama/ama* or standard *oléh* 'by'. If the actor is not marked with a preposition, the word order is SVX and no intervening material can come between the verb and the actor. If the actor is marked with a preposition, that prepositional phrase is less restricted in its order relative to other elements in the clause. *Di-*form UV constructions have been prescriptively associated with third person actors in Standard Indonesian, but in modern Colloquial Indonesian they can also be used for first and second person actors, as in example (8).

(8)   *Katanya   cowo   itu   teh   pinter   pisan*
       kata-nya   cowok   itu   téh   pintar   pisan
       say-DEF   guy   DIST   D.PTCL smart   very

       tapi   kalo   diliat-liat   sama   saya
       tapi   kalau   di-lihat-lihat   sama   saya
       but   if   UV-see-RDP   by   1s

       cowo   ini   teh   tingkah laku-nya   agak   aneh,   jarang   ngobrol.
       cowok   ini   téh   tingkah laku-nya   agak   anéh   jarang   ngobrol
       guy   this   D.PTCL behavior-DEF   rather strange   rarely   AV:talk
       'They say that guy is very smart, but if I take a look at (him), that guy's actions are rather strange; (he) rarely talks.' <members.nbci.com/pd2online/cinta/yenni.html>

The words *téh* and *pisan* in this example are from Sundanese. As Sundanese uses a cognate *di-* construction for first person agent UV clauses, this is a likely source for this usage in Colloquial Indonesian, at least in the case of this particular writer.

In the second UV construction, the verb is unaffixed; the actor is expressed as a pronominal form (or name, kinship term, or title used pronominally) and precedes the verb so that the order is SXV, as in example (9).

(9) D: *Dia   juga   saya   undang,*
       3s   also   1s   invite
      'I invited him too.'

A specialized pronoun *tak* '1s', from Javanese, is used by some speakers to indicate the first person actor of a UV construction, as in example (10).

(10) W: *terus   yang   satu   untuk   saya.*
       next   REL   one   for   1s
       tak   pikir   gitu.
       1s   think   like.that
       'Then that one is for me, that's what I thought.'

Often in Colloquial Indonesian, as it is prescriptively in the standard language, the pronominal actor is cliticized to the verb such that nothing can intervene between them; aspect and negation particles all occur before the actor-verb complex, as in example (11).

(11) C: *ada   dua   hal   yang   mau   saya   kasih   tahu,*
       EXIST two matter REL   FUT   1s   give   know
       sama   anda-anda   ya?
       to   2s-RDP   yes
       'There are two things I want to tell you all.'

However, it is also common in Colloquial Indonesian for this cliticization to be loosened so that pre-predicate particles occur between the pronominal actor and the unaffixed verb, as in the relative clause in (12) (but note that the core constituent order is still SXV).

(12) D: *Yang   kaya   gitu   yang   saya   mau   cari.*
       REL   like   like.that REL   1s   FUT   look.for
       'That kind is what I want to look for.'

The UV construction with proclitic actor has been prescriptively associated with first and second person actors in Standard Indonesian, but it is also used with third person actors in modern Colloquial Indonesian.

(13) *dan   dia   bingung   apa   yang   harus   dia   lakukan   untuk*
     dan   dia   bingung   apa   yang   harus   dia   laku-kan   untuk
     and   3s   confused what REL   must   3s   do-APP   for
     ngelupain   mantannya   itu.
     nge-lupa-in   mantan-nya itu
     AV-forget-APP former-DEF   DIST
     'And he's confused about what he has to do to forget his ex.'
     <www.gudeg.net/isi/konsultasi/item/28-2443.html>

Pragmatically marked subject-final constituent order (VXS or XVS) can be used when the referent of the subject is highly accessible, yet still explicitly expressed, as in example (14).

(14)   *Sudah   saya   makan   tuh,*
      Sudah   saya   makan   tuh
      PFV   1s   eat   DIST
      'I've already eaten it.' <http://www.gammamagazine.com/Server-Docs/
      gammamagazine/th_1/6/LPU3-6.html>

Highly accessible and continuous referents in discourse are often not explicitly expressed. This might apply to either the actor, undergoer, or both of a transitive clause. Thus, a transitive clause in natural discourse may consist of the verb plus one explicit argument (15) or the verb alone (16).

(15)   W: *Malah   hampir   nyaing-i   Bapak,*
          in.fact   almost   AV:compete-APP   father.2s
          'In fact (I)'m almost in competition with you.'

(16)   N: *Nyari.*
          AV:search.for
          '(I)'m searching for (them).' or '(I)'m searching.'

In the context of (16) we understand that the speaker is talking about her search for newspaper clippings. However, this clause, like many produced in natural interaction, does not provide enough grammatical clues for us to determine whether it is transitive or intransitive. This indeterminacy is reflected in the alternative English translations.

Intransitive clauses usually have the order SV, as in (17). VS order is also possible and usually signals that the referent of the subject argument is highly accessible. In this constituent order, the subject is most commonly represented by a personal pronoun or a reduced demonstrative, as in (18).

(17)   M: *Si   Atin   juga   dulu   kan   belajar.*
          PN   Atin   also   before   D.PTCL   INTR:study
          'You studied before too, you know.'

(18)   C: *Hanya   satu   dua   bulan   ini   berantakan   kita.*
          only   one   two   month   PRX   messy   1p
          'We'll only be in a mess for one or two months.'

In Colloquial Indonesian, as in the standard language, the verb *ada* 'EXIST' can be used to introduce a referent into the discourse, in which case the unmarked constituent order is *ada* NP, that is VS. The referent is often contextualized with a locative or temporal expression.

(19)   D: ..   *Jadi   ada   karapan sap:i   dong,*
            so   EXIST   bull chariot race   D.PTCL
          di   sana.
          LOC   DIST.ADV
          'So there's *karapan sapi* there.'

Ada can also be used with a given or identifiable subject, in which case the unmarked order is SV. This construction can be used in a copula-like function to link the subject with a locative prepositional phrase as in example (20).

(20)   C: ...   *Map   hitam=nya,*
              folder   black=DEF
          dia   ada   di   lemari   sini.
          3s   EXIST   LOC   cupboard   PRX.ADV.
          'The black folders, they are in this cupboard here.'

Ada can also be used to indicate possession as in (21), in which the order is always possessor-ADA-possessed.

(21)   *Tuh   temen   kan   ada   sepéda   di   sini   tuh,*
       DIST   friend   D.PTCL   EXIST   bicycle   LOC   PRX.ADV   DIST
       lenyap.
       vanished
       'You know my friend had a bike here; (it) disappeared.'

3.2.2 Non-verbal predicates

Although predicates prototypically consist of verbs, essentially any phrase-forming element can be a predicate in Indonesian, including nominals, prepositional phrases, and other adverbials. Non-verbal predicates are juxtaposed with their subject, without a copula or any other linking morphology. While an optional copula, *adalah*, can be used with predicate nominals in Standard Indonesian, this is a formal marker and is not used in Colloquial Indonesian. As with intransitive verbal clauses, the unmarked constituent order in most non-verbal clauses is S PRED, while the marked PRED S order also occurs. Certain clause types, such as cleft constructions, have PRED S as the most frequent order. The subject argument need not be explicitly expressed.

Nominal predicates usually function to classify or identify the referent of the subject.

(22)   W: *Saya   tuh   orang   baru,*
            1s   DIST   person   new
            'I'm a new person,'

The predicate nominal may be used metaphorically, metonymically, or in some other way such that the relationship that holds between it and the subject must be inferred from the context. In example (23) the interactants have been discussing who will cook what dishes to bring to a social gathering and Nadar is the person to bring fried rice.

(23)   D: *Pak   Nadar   nasi   goréng.*
            Mr   Nadar   rice   fry
            'Mr. Nadar is the fried rice [person].'

An important type of predicate nominal clause is the cleft construction, in which a headless relative clause serves as the subject in the matrix clause, while a specific nominal referent acts as the predicate. The unmarked order in cleft constructions is PRED S.

(24)   C: *Saya   yang   ambil   Bu.*
            1s   REL   take   ma'am.
            'I'm the one who took (it), ma'am.'

Locative and temporal expressions (including prepositional phrases) are common predicates (25), as are demonstrative adverbs (26).

(25) D: *Dia   dari   Jawa.*
          3s   from   Java
          'He's from Java.'

(26) C: *Kalkulator   aja   kok   begitu.*
          calculator   just   D.PTCL   like.that
          'Why is it, even a calculator is treated in that way!'

3.2.3 Clausal adverbs

Clauses can be modified by adverbial expressions which can occur at any major juncture. This means clausal adverbials most frequently occur clause-initially, between the subject (if present) and the predicate, or clause-finally. They do not occur between the predicate and a non-subject argument. Examples (27) through (29) illustrate the use of *nanti* 'later' in three positions.

(27) D: *Nanti   saya   bikin   lah.*
          later   1s   make   EMPH
          'I will make (some).'

(28) D: *saya   nanti   coba   yang   di-goréng.*
          1s   later   try   REL   UV-fry
          'I'll try something fried.'

(29) D: *Kita   bisa   lihat   nanti.*
          1p   can   see   later.
          'We'll look at it later.'

Other temporal expressions, including adverbs and prepositional phrases, can occur in these positions, as can adverbials indicating evidentiality or speaker attitude toward the truth or relevance of what is being said. Many of these include derived adverbs, which are often marked with the enclitic *=nya*. These may be based on nouns as in (30), or verbs as in (31).

(30) W: *Dan   rupa=nya   Bapak   bisa   mendayung   eh?*
          and   appearance=DEF   father.2s   can   row   huh
          'And apparently you can row, huh?'

(31) D: *itu   biasa=nya   pakai   daun   pepaya,*
          DIST   usual=DEF   use   leaf   papaya
          'That usually uses papaya leaves,'

These adverbials are erstwhile nominals (see discussion of gerunds in section 3.3.2). Thus the structure of (30) might be represented by the alternative translation 'And the appearance is that you can row, huh?'. These forms are, however, best understood to be functioning as adverbials. This is evidenced by that fact that, like other adverbials, they can occur between the subject and predicate of the modified clause as in (31), in addition to occurring before or after the clause they modify.

3.3 Noun phrases

3.3.1 Noun phrase structure

Full noun phrases may consist of a single lexical noun or a lexical item with one or more modifiers. Nouns may be monomorphemic or may have derivational morphology. A few nouns are markers of informal style, for example Colloquial *duit* 'money' (Standard *uang*). Generally the order in the noun phrase is head-modifier. Modifiers which follow the head noun can include other nouns, stative verbs (and sometimes eventive verbs), possessors, relative clauses, and demonstrative determiners, usually in that order (32). Quantifiers usually precede the head (33).

(32)   B: *Garis-garis   mata   yang   sudah   tua   tuh   nampak   sekali.*
            line-RDP   eye   REL   PFV   old   DIST appear   very
            'The wrinkles of those old eyes are really visible.'

(33)   C: *dalam   satu   kantor   itu   ada   systém.*
            in   one   office   DIST   EXIST   system
            'In that one office there [should] be a system.'

3.3.2 =nya marking definiteness, possession and gerunds

Sometimes called a third person possessive, the enclitic = *nya* functions more generally as a definite marker and is so glossed in examples. = *nya* serves to indicate that the referent of the NP to which it is cliticized is identifiable through association with some other identifiable referent in the discourse. This association may be one of ownership as in (34) or other relationship often expressed by possessive constructions, such as family or part-whole relationships.

(34)   M: *Tapi   radio=nya   ke-temu   kan?*
            but   radio=DEF   POT-meet   NEG.Q
            'But (you) found your radio didn't you?'

In Standard Indonesian, lexical possessors are expressed as noun phrases following the head noun phrase, and this construction also occurs in Colloquial Indonesian. In Colloquial Indonesian, speakers also use a construction derived from Javanese, in which the enclitic =*nya* occurs together with the noun phrase possessor, as in (35).

(35)   D: .. *pecel   sih,*
               k.o.salad   D.PTCL
            gampang,
            easy
            bisa   bikin   di ..   tempat=nya   Bu   Sicil.
            can   make   LOC   place=DEF   Ms   Sicil
            '*Pecel* is easy, (we) can make (it) at Ms Sicil's place.'

Returning to the associative meaning of =*nya*, another kind of association – not always considered possession cross-linguistically, but regularly marked with =*nya* in Indonesian – is one of an evoked frame or scheme. This is illustrated in (36), where the speakers are talking about how to operate a tape player.

(36) D: *Waktu   kami   coba   gini,*
           time   1pe   try   like.this
           baru   ke-dengar-an   suara=nya.
           immediate.PFV   POT-hear- POT sound=DEF
           'When we tried this way, only then was the sound audible.'

The referent of *suaranya* 'sound=DEF' (the sound) has not been previously mentioned. It is marked as definite because it is understood to be associated with playing the tape recorder, already established as a discourse referent.

As a definite marker, =*nya* is also used to contrast one referent from another previously mentioned referent. These can occur with noun phrases that are inherently definite such as proper names (37) or pronouns (38).

(37) D: ..   *Bapak   aja   yang   di   sini.*
                father.2s just REL   LOC   PRX.ADV
           Ibu   ..   Sicil=nya   duduk   situ.
           Ms   Sicil=DEF   sit   MED.ADV
           'You just [sit] here. Ms Sicil [can] sit there.'

(38) S: ..   *Tapi   nanti,*
                but   later
           kalau   jadi   —
           if   become
           itu=nya   jadi   pecel,
           DIST=DEF become   k.o.salad
           ..   *sama   ya?*
                same   yes
           [Comparing the procedures for making two different kinds of salad:] 'But if it's going to be *pecel*, you do the same thing right?'

In addition to marking definiteness and possession, =*nya* is also used to form gerunds by simply adding it to verbs (which may be marked with voice and applicative morphology). Gerunds frequently function as the subject of a clause. In this way the information focus shifts from the erstwhile predication, which is presented as presupposed information, to some other element, such as an adverb or prepositional phrase, which now stands as the grammatical predicate and the information focus of the clause.

(39) W: *Ng-goréng=nya   nanti,*
           AV-fry=DEF   later
           'The frying [will happen] later.'

(40) U: *Diforwardnya   dulu,   Pak.*
           UV-fast.forward-DEF   first   sir
           'The fast-forwarding [should happen] first, sir.'

A number of gerundive forms with =*nya* have grammaticized as clausal adverbials, mentioned in section 3.2.3 above.

3.3.3 Headless relative clauses

Headless relative clauses, i.e. clauses introduced by the relative marker *yang* without a preceding head noun, are also a type of nominalization. Like=*nya* gerunds, they are based on a predicate, but unlike gerunds, which refer to the action of the predicate, headless relative clauses refer to the subject of the predicate. Headless relative clauses commonly function as part of a cleft construction (see section 3.2.2), in which the information focus shifts from the predicate to the erstwhile subject.

As in many other western Austronesian languages, relative clause formation in Colloquial Indonesian is constrained in that the head noun in general must also be the subject of the relative clause. However, as speakers produce relative clauses in real-time interaction, somewhat more complex structures can result, such as (41).

(41) S: *Nasi*   *yang* *nyiap-in*   *Pak* *Nadar.*
          cooked.rice   REL   AV:prepare-APP   Mr   Nadar
          '[As for] rice, the one who'll prepare [it] is Pak Nadar.'

Here *nasi* 'rice' is a topicalized nominal, juxtaposed to a comment which is a cleft construction consisting of the subject *yang nyiapin* and the predicate *Pak Nadar*. What makes this example unusual is that both arguments of the verb in the relative clause are shared with the matrix structure, one as a topic and the other as predicate of the cleft.

Yang constructions can also be used to create referents from non-verbal predicates. In (42), the speakers are sorting out various tasks they will undertake and these tasks are identified with *yang* plus NP constructions.

(42) D: *Kalau* *Bapak*   *yang* *ayam,*
          if   father.2s   REL   chicken
          saya   *yang sayur.*
          1s REL   vegetable
          'If you're [the one cooking] chicken, I'm the [one cooking] vegetables.'

3.4 Aspectual and modal markers

Aspect markers occur as auxiliaries directly before the predicate. High-frequency colloquial aspect markers include perfective *udah* (Standard *sudah*) and progressive *lagi* (Standard *sedang*). The continuous marker *masih* and recent perfective *baru* are standard forms regularly used in informal interaction. The negative perfective auxiliary *belum* 'not yet' is also Standard Indonesian; it is commonly used in Colloquial Indonesian but has the informal variant *belon*. Example (43) illustrates aspect being manipulated interactionally through the use of contrasting markers.

(43) M: *Lu* *udah* *mandi* *kan?*
          2s   PFV   bathe   NEG.Q
          'You've bathed, haven't you?'

      N: ... *Belum.*
               NEG.PFV
          'Not yet.'

M: .. *La:h,*
  INTJ
kata=nya *lagi* *mandi* *tadi.*
say=DEF PRG bathe earlier.
'Hey, earlier (you) said (you) were bathing.'

These auxiliaries also occur with non-verbal predicates, as in (44).

(44) D: *Sudah* *kota* *administratif* *ya?*
    PFV city administrative yes.
    '(Batu) is already an incorporated city, isn't it?'

Modality markers also occur as auxiliaries before the predicate and most are common to Standard and Colloquial styles. They include *bisa* 'ability', 'possibility', *boléh* 'permission', 'possibility', 'appropriateness', *harus/mesti* 'obligation', 'need', *akan* 'future', *mau* 'volition, future', *ingin* 'volition, desire'. *Pingin* and *péngén* are colloquial variants of *ingin*. The standard *tidak usah* 'lack of obligation, lack of need' can be formed with any of the colloquial negative particles (see Section 3.5), e.g. *nggak usah*. Examples illustrating modals with verbs include (5) and (6) above. Example (45) illustrates the use of modals with a prepositional predicate. Note also the doubling up of two markers of obligation.

(45) N: *mesti=nya* *harus* *ke* *biro* *pendidikan* *nih.*
    must=DEF must to bureau education PRX
    'I (lit. this one) should have [to go] to the Bureau of Education.'

Aspect and modal markers can co-occur. They can occur in any order, depending on the scope of each in the particular proposition being presented. The more common order in informal interaction is aspect followed by modal as in (46), but modal before aspect also occurs (47).

(46) S: *Aku* *émang* *lagi* *mau* *berdiri* *aja,*
    1s indeed PRG want stand just
    'In fact I want to just stand up.'

(47) *Cuma* *kayaknya* *sekarang* *harus* *sudah* *berhenti*
   cuma kaya=nya sekarang harus sudah berhenti
   only like:DEF now must PFV INTR:stop
   'Only it seems now (we) should have already stopped.'
   <http://student.unpar.ac.id/~4194117/album/koleksi.htm>

3.5 Negation

Negation is marked with a negative particle preceding the predicate. Various informal negative particles include *nggak*, *ndak*, *kagak*, and *gak*, all corresponding to the standard *tidak*. Negation generally precedes modal markers, e.g. (5); but order depends on the scope of negation, and a negative marker can occur between a modal and verb as in (48).

(48) *Dan* *lagian* *apa* *sih* *hubungan* *PDIP* *dg* *kasus* *BB*
   dan lagian apa sih hubungan PDIP dengan kasus BB
   and moreover what D.PTCL connection PDIP with case BB

sehingga	*saya*	*harus*	*nggak*	*suka*	*dg*	*PDIP?*
sehingga	saya	harus	nggak	suka	dengan	PDIP
until	1s	must	NEG	like	with	PDIP

'And moreover what's PDIP's connection with the BB case such that I have to not like PDIP?' <http://www.mail-rchive.com/itb@itb.ac.id/ msg07465.html>

Nominal predicates are frequently negated with the form *bukan*, as they are in Standard Indonesian:

(49) D: *Tapi*   *bukan*   *penduduk*   ..   *setempat?*
　　　　　but　　　NEG　　　resident　　　　　　local
　　　　itu　　*kan?*
　　　　DIST　　NEG.Q

'But (they) aren't local residents? Isn't that the point?'

But negative forms associated with non-nominal predicates (e.g. *nggak*, *ndak*, *kagak*) also occur with nominals in Colloquial Indonesian:

(50) D: *mungkin*   *kalau*   *ndak*   *kalimat,*
　　　　　maybe　　　if　　　NEG　　　sentence
　　　　..   *kata:*   *gitu.*
　　　　　　word　　like.that

'maybe if (it)'s not a sentence, (it)'s a word, like that.'

As in Standard Indonesian, *bukan* can negate a non-nominal predicate when a contrast is either stated or implied, as in (51).

(51) W: *Bu>*   *bukan*   *me-nikmat-i*   *sana*   *Pak.*
　　　　　　　　　NEG　　　AV-enjoy-APP　　DIST.ADV　sir

'[I went there but] (I) didn't enjoy going there, sir.'

3.6 *Kalau* constructions: conditionals and topics

The conditional particle *kalau* 'given, if, when' is important in both Standard and Colloquial Indonesian and is pervasive in informal, interactional language use. *Kalau* marks either hypothetical conditions as in (52) or real conditions as in (53). *Kalau* is also used in temporal adverbial clauses indicating a future time frame (54).

(52) D: ..   *Misal=nya*   *kalau*   *dari*   *Jawa,*
　　　　　　　example=DEF　if　　　from　　Java
　　　　kami   ..   *prioritus-kan,*
　　　　1pe　　　　priority-APP
　　　　e:,
　　　　uh
　　　　ini   *campur*   *gitu,*
　　　　PRX　　mix　　　DIST
　　　　seolah-olah,
　　　　as.if

eh,
uh

pakai .. kata-kata   tertentu.
use   word-RDP   certain

'For example if (we) were Javanese, we would prioritize, uh, mixing like that, like using certain words.'

(53) N: *Kalau   masih   sering-sering   korupsi,*
          if   still   often-RDP   corruption
          gimana   mau   makmur,
          how   want   prosperous
          .. negara   Indonésia.
              nation   Indonesia
          'When there's still often lots of corruption, how can Indonesia become prosperous?'

(54) C: *Jadi,*
          so
          .. kaya=nya,
              like=DEF
          kalau sudah di   gedung   baru itu,
          if   PFV   LOC   building   new   DIST
          kita sudah mesti   tega:s,
          1p   PFV   must   strict
          'So like when we're in the new building, we'll already have to be strict.'

The general meaning of *kalau* across these three examples is one of 'given' as in 'given situation X then Y holds', and is neutral as to the real or hypothetical nature of the given situation. Whether the clause is interpreted as realis or irrealis is a function of other elements in the utterance or context, not the particle *kalau*. Thus, the generic conditional in (53) has no explicit time frame. Example (52) is also conditional but has the added markers *misalnya* 'for example' and *seolah-olah* 'as if' (together with the knowledge shared by the speakers that speaker D is in fact not Javanese) to indicate a hypothetical condition. In contrast, (54) refers to a specific event, planned to take place in a few days.

Kalau can also mark a topicalized element. Rather than introducing a new referent, a *kalau* construction is usually contrasting an identifiable referent with some other entity. In (55) the speakers have been discussing the rising cost of university tuition according to the years that different acquaintances began studying; this example gives information about one of those years.

(55) N: *Kalau   Yoni,*
          if   Yoni
          nggak   nyampai   dua   juta.
          NEG   AV:reach   two   million
          'As for Yoni, [his year] didn't reach two million [rupiah].'

Prepositional phrases can also form the basis of a *kalau* constructions, and function to orient the proposition expressed by the main clause in space or time, usually in contrast to some other orientation. In the following example the speaker was discussing the employment situation first in Jakarta and now in Yogyakarta (referred to as Jogja).

(56)   M: *Mungkin kalau di   Jogja lebih   cocok   untuk   wirausaha,*
            maybe   if   LOC   Jogja more   appropriate   for   entrepreneurship
            'Maybe Jogja is more appropriate for entrepreneurship.'

These topicalization and orientation functions of *kalau* constructions are consistent with the general meaning of 'given' in which some situation, referent, or orientation is established as a foundation or background on which the information in the main clause holds (see Haiman 1978).

Kalau constructions regularly precede their main clauses, but can also follow them. Additionally, being a kind of adverbial construction, *kalau* constructions also often appear between the subject and predicate of the main clause. In these cases, the main clause and the *kalau* clause usually share the same subject as in (57) where *orang-orang atas* 'high level officials' is the subject of both *ngomong* 'talk' in the *kalau* conditional and *pakai* 'use' in the matrix clause.

(57)   M: *Eh   bukti=nya   orang-orang   atas   juga   kalau   ng-omong*
            uh   fact=DEF   person-RDP   above   also   if   AV-talk
            kan,   nggak   nggak   pakai   EYD   kan?
            NEG.Q   NEG   NEG   use   standard.Indonesian   NEG.Q
            'The fact is that even high level officials don't use Standard Indonesian when they talk.'

Note that in the second line of the above example *nggak* is not grammatically reduplicated, rather it is a repetition in the context of real-time production.

3.7 Other clause combining in discourse

Following verbs of speaking and cognition, the complement clause, which expresses that which was spoken or conceived, can be marked with *kalau*, as in (58); however, it is more common in Colloquial Indonesian that such clauses are not introduced with any linking particle, as in (59). Use of the Standard *bahwa* 'COMP' to link a complement clause with a verb of speaking or cognition is rare and indicates a more formal style.

(58)   D: ..   *Nggak   sadar,*
                 NEG   aware
            kalau   lagi   di-rekam.
            if   PRG   UV-record
            '(He) wasn't aware that (he) was being recorded.'

(59)   D: *tadi   bilang   daérah   turisme   untuk   perkebunan   ya?*
            earlier   say   area   tourism   for   plantation   yes
            'Earlier (you) said (it)'s an area for plantation tourism right?'

Temporal clause markers such as *sesudah* 'after', *sebelum* 'before', and *waktu* 'when (realis)' can be used in Colloquial Indonesian, but are not common in informal conversational interaction, where time relationships are more often developed iconically in sequence. If temporal sequence is marked explicitly, it will often be with a coordinating conjunction such as *terus* 'then, next'.

It is very common in informal interaction for clauses to be juxtaposed without any explicit conjunctions. The relationship between them must be inferred based on their relevance to each other within the context in which they were uttered. This is illustrated in example (60) where the speakers are discussing who will bring rice to a party they are planning. The rhetorical relationships implied in this economical Colloquial Indonesian utterance are presented explicitly in the rather liberal free translation.

(60)   S: *Takut=nya*   *nanti,*
            afraid=DEF   later
            nasi   lagi,
            rice   again
            kebanyakan.
            too.much
            gitu.
            like.that
            'What I'm afraid will happen is that another person will also bring rice and then we will have too much. That's what I'm afraid will happen.'

4 PRONOUNS AND DEMONSTRATIVES

4.1 Personal pronouns

The commonly used pronouns of Colloquial Indonesian include:

(61)   1s: *saya, aku, kita, gua ~ gué*   1p: *kita* (1pe: *kami*)
       2s: *kamu, lu ~ elu*   2p: *kalian*
       3s: *dia*   3p: *meréka*

These free forms are not marked for case and can occur in any position where a lexical noun can occur. In addition to the special UV actor proclitic *tak* '1s' mentioned in 3.2.1 above, two pronominal enclitics, =*ku* '1SPOSS' and =*mu* '2SPOSS', are also found in Colloquial Indonesian and are discussed in section 4.2 below. Besides the pronouns listed in (61), other forms may be used, especially for first and second person, according to a speaker's sociolinguistic background. In Colloquial Indonesian the class of pronouns is more porous and accepts new members more easily than a similar closed class might in other languages.

4.1.1 First person

In the corpus used here, *saya* is the most common first person pronoun used, although some speakers tend to prefer *aku*. Javanese also has the form *aku* and some Javanese speakers will use *aku* in their Colloquial Indonesian. Use of *aku* is not limited to Javanese speakers, however; nor do all Javanese use it when speaking Indonesian. *Kita* as a first person singular pronoun and *gua* (*gué*) are often associated in speakers' minds with

Jakartan usage, and the former is particularly familiar, even coarse to some people. Another strategy in more intimate relationships is to use name, kinship term, or combination of kinship term and name for first person reference. Assigning levels of informality and intimacy to different pronouns and choosing which to use in a given context is based on complex sociolinguistic factors and will vary from speaker to speaker. While ethnic background can suggest possible variation in the use of Colloquial Indonesian, it is not a reliable predictor, at least not in terms of simple transfer (see for example the discussion of avoidance of *aku* by Javanese speakers of Indonesian in Errington 1998).

In Colloquial Indonesian the meaning of *kita* is not restricted to first person plural inclusive as it prescriptively is in Standard Indonesian, but is generalized to include both first person inclusive and exclusive meanings and is also used for first person singular and generic. Various possible referents of *kita* are exemplified below.

(62)   Inclusive: the speaker is making plans which include his interlocutor.

D: *Nggak,*
       no
       kalau   jam   dua,
       if   hour   two
       .. *kita bisa   bareng   pak.*
          1p   can   together sir
       'No, at two o'clock we can go together, sir.'

(63)   Exclusive: the speaker refers to himself and his colleagues at another institution where none of his interlocutors work.

W: *Jadi kita share   denga:n   ..   PDP.*
       so   1p   share   with   PDP
       'So we share [facilities] with PDP.'

(64)   Singular: D is asking what he himself should bring to the party in contrast to others who are attending.

D: *Kita   mau   nyiap-in   apa?*
       1s   want   AV:prepare-APP   what
       .. *Daging   atau   sayur?*
          meat   or   vegetable
       'What should I make, meat or vegetables?'

(65)   Generic: speaking hypothetically about what might happen to anyone.

W: *Tapi kalau   kalau   ndak   bisa   ya,*
       but   if   if   NEG   can   yes
       (H) .. kita nambah   ..   nambah   ongkos.
             1p   increase   increase payment
       'But if (one) can't [row], well one has to pay more [to hire an oarsperson].'

The previous examples were chosen because the context makes interpretation relatively clear. But as with *we* in English, which may be vague between inclusive or exclusive meanings, the actual intent of a token of *kita* in Colloquial Indonesian may be ambiguous or even indeterminate.

(66)   C: .. *Nah,*
                  D.PTCL

    itu   yang,
    DIST   REL

    .. *eh,*
       HES

    saya   sudah ngomong-ngomong   panjang   lébar,
    1s   PFV   AV:talk-RDP   long   wide

    dengan   Yuda   semalam,
    with   Yuda   last.night

    tapi,
    but

    kita   belum   terlalu   stressing ke   sana.
    1p   NEG.PFV too   stress   to   DIST.ADV

    'OK, that's what I spoke to Yuda about for a long time last night but we haven't really stressed that much yet.'

The speaker and Yuda have been established as a pair of referents who have made plans together, and *kita* in the last line may refer to the two of them, exclusive of the present audience, who are fellow office workers at a meeting. However, the issue at hand has already been briefly mentioned in the present meeting as well, and *kita* may be inclusive of the audience. But in fact it is the speaker himself who has done almost all the talking up to now and he could well mean that he himself has not yet covered the issue in too much detail, and a first person singular reading is also possible. If we assume that the speaker had a specific referent in mind when this utterance was produced, than we can say that *kita* is ambiguous in this context. However, another possibility is that any or all of the interpretations listed above could have been intended by the speaker and heard by his audience, such that the 'real' identity of the referent of *kita* in this context is not only indeterminate, but irrelevant.

The first person exclusive pronoun *kami* can also occur in Colloquial Indonesian, where its meaning is always first person singular or first person plural exclusive, but never plural inclusive or generic. Choice between *kami* and *kita* with the singular or plural exclusive meanings will vary by speaker and intended level of informality. Exclusive *kami* evokes a more standard style than *kita*, while *kami* with singular reference is highly officious and its use in an otherwise informal context would produce a particularly jarring (and potentially very effective) juxtaposition of styles.

4.1.2 Second and third persons

Many speakers consider *kamu* '2s' appropriate for addressing any close friend, or even causal acquaintances in informal interaction, while other speakers consider *kamu* too coarse for use with equals and may use it only to small children or animals, if at all. Also very familiar is *lu* (*elu*), associated with Jakartan Indonesian and sociolinguistically complementary to first person *gua* mentioned above. Also important for second person reference is the use of names, classificatory kinship terms, or both, as seen in numerous examples throughout this chapter, where the literal meaning in the gloss line is appended with the abbreviation 2s to indicate the intended referent. Other second person pronominal forms are used from time to time according to the interactional needs of speakers, including those that are very familiar, e.g. *engkau*, more impersonal, e.g. *saudara* and *Anda*, or that would imply specialist knowledge, e.g. *you* (English) or *énté* (from Arabic via Betawi Malay).

Dia '3s' is typically reserved for human referents, as in (7). However, very topical non-human animate or even inanimate referents will be referred to with *dia* by some speakers, as in (20). *Meréka* '3p' is likewise usually reserved for human referents, as in (67).

(67) N: *Meréka   ceramah   pakai   mic*
   3p   lecture use microphone
   'They lectured using a mike.'

4.2 Possessive pronouns

The enclitics *=ku* '1sPOSS' and *=mu* '2sPOSS' can occur in Colloquial Indonesian among those speakers who use the corresponding full forms *aku* and *kamu* (68). More common in the data used for the present study is the use of full pronominal forms directly following the head noun for first or second person pronominal possessors (69).

(68) *He ...   ngapain   mukul-2   suamimu ????*
  Hé   ng-apa-in mukul-mukul suami=mu
  Hey   AV-what-APP AV:hit-RDP husband=2sPOSS
  'Hey, what are you doing hitting your husband?'
  <http://centrin.net.id/~erganov/humor3.html>

(69) S: *Karena   tante   kos   saya dulu   juga   orang   Menado.*
   because aunt boarding.house 1s before also person Menado
   'Because my previous landlady was also from Menado.'

These two enclitics formally and historically form a paradigm with the enclitic *=nya* which marks third person possessors. But as shown in section 3.3.2, current use of *=nya* far exceeds typical uses of possessive pronouns. It has become an important grammatical marker in Standard Indonesian and is even more frequently used in Colloquial Indonesian.

One other informal possessive construction should be mentioned in passing. It is often used by speakers from eastern Indonesia, among others, and comprises a possessor preceding the possessed, linked by *punya* (have, POSS), as in (70).

(70) A: *Dia   curi   saya   punya   uang,*
   3s steal 1s POSS money
   'She stole my money.'

4.3 Demonstratives

4.3.1 Demonstrative pronouns

The demonstrative system formally makes a simple two-way contrast between proximal and distal reference. Proximal *ini* ~ *nih* and distal *itu* ~ *tuh* are commonly used for pronominal reference. Demonstrative pronouns may point to things in the physical context as in the second line of (71).

(71)   A: *Foto   ini   cantik   lho.*
            photo   PRX   beautiful   PART
            'This photo is really nice.'
       T: ...   *Ini   Wiwi?*
                  PRX   Wiwi
            'Is this Wiwi?'

Demonstrative pronouns also commonly refer to referents already established in discourse, as in the last line of (72).

(72)   C: *Calculator aja   kok   begitu.*
            calculator   just   PART   like.that
            'How could just a calculator be thought that [important].'
            ..   *Tapi   lama-lama   gué   pikir-pikir,*
                 but   long-RDP   1s   think-RDP
            Iya   ya,
            yes   yeah
            itu   kan   sarana   kerja.
            DIST   NEG.Q facility   work
            'But after a while I was thinking, oh yeah, it is a part of our work equipment, you know.'

Demonstrative pronouns are especially common for non-human referents, which usually are not referred to with *dia* '3s', but can also refer to humans of any person, as with the use of *nih* for first person reference in (45). Demonstrative pronouns can also refer to propositional content, see the second line of (77) below, and can be used non-referentially as discourse markers to introduce a proposition as in (73).

(73)   C: *Ini   nanti   biar   Mbak   Yayu,*
            PRX   later   let.it.be sister   Yayu
            yang   nentu-kan   siapa.
            REL   AV:fix-APP   who
            'So here, Mbak Yayu's going to be the one to say who ['ll do what].'

A common marker of Colloquial Indonesian is the use of the reduced demonstrative pronouns *nih* 'this' and *tuh* 'that'. These can stand alone as in example (14) or in combination with the full-form equivalents, as *itu tuh* 'that that' in example (78). In general, reduced demonstratives do not occur clause initially, but otherwise can occur in any syntactic position where a full demonstrative can occur. A discussion of the functional differences between these forms awaits further research.

4.3.2 Demonstrative determiners

Demonstrative determiners have the same form as the demonstrative pronouns, including full and short forms, as well as the combination of full and short forms together. A major function of demonstrative determiners is to indicate that the referent of the noun phrase they modify is identifiable from the discourse context, as in the first line of (71) where *foto ini* 'this photo' is a photograph physically in front of the speakers, or that it is identifiable by having been previously established in the discourse as in (54) where *gedung baru itu* 'the new building' has already been mentioned in the conversation. In this function demonstrative determiners can be seen to complement =*nya*, discussed above, which indicates a referent which is identifiable by association with some other identifiable referent, but which itself need not have been previously mentioned or otherwise present in the discourse context.

Additionally, demonstrative determiners can also occur with noun phrases that are otherwise marked as identifiable, either inherently so, such as proper names or pronouns, as in (74), or in conjunction with =*nya*, as in (75).

(74) *Orang itu   benci sekali sama saya karena   saya itu   tidak serius.*
      Orang itu   benci sekali sama saya karena   saya itu   tidak serius
      person DIST   hate   very   with 1s   because 1s   DIST   NEG serious
      'That person really hates me because I'm not serious.'
      <http://www.perspektif.net/beta/teror/adil09.htm>

(75) D: *Kalau   saya,*
           if   1s
           teri=nya   itu,
           anchovy=DEF   DIST
           di-goreng,
           UV-fry
           'As for me, (I) fry the anchovies.'

4.3.3 Demonstrative adverbs

The demonstrative 'manner' adverbs *begini* 'like this' and *begitu* 'like that' and their short forms, *gini* and *gitu* respectively, are very important in Colloquial Indonesian discourse. Unlike true manner adverbs, these adverbs can be used anaphorically to refer to a previously mentioned proposition. In example (76) two interlocutors have agreed on a time and place to meet and D concludes the discussion using *begitu* to refer back to the circumstances just agreed on.

(76) D: *Udah,*
           PFV
           kalau   begitu.
           if   like.that
           'It's settled, if that's the case.'

The short form, *gitu*, is often used to refer back to the proposition which the speaker has just expressed; this usage usually occurs at the end of a short cluster of intonation units and is an important rhetorical device to marked unit boundaries in Colloquial Indonesian, as in (60).

As well as referring to whole propositions, a demonstrative adverb can refer to a previously established predicate, which then becomes the predicate of a different referent. In (77) the speaker first outlines a problematic situation involving office files. He then uses *begitu* to assert that the same problematic situation applies to stationery and other resources.

(77) C: *Di   laci   masing-masing   itu   masih   ada   file-file   kantor.*
          LOC   drawer   each   DIST   still   EXIST   file-RDP   office
          Nggak   bener   itu.
          NEG   correct   DIST
          ... *Sudah.*
                       PFV
          .. *Begitu   juga   dengan   kop surat,*
              like.that   also   with   letterhead
          dan   sebagainya.
          and   so.forth
          '(Each of you) still keeps office files in your own drawers. That's not right. That's the bottom line. That also goes for letterhead and other supplies.'

Begitu and *gitu* usually refer anaphorically to a predicate or proposition previously mentioned or implied within the discourse. *Begini* and *gini* are often used cataphorically to signal that a proposition is about to be expressed, as in (78).

(78) M: *pertama   kali   itu   tuh,*
          first   time   DIST   DIST
          .. *pikiran=nya   gini,*
              thought=DEF   like.this
          .. *pikiran=nya   jelék   melulu.*
              thought=DEF   bad   exclusively
          'The first time, they think this way, they think everything is completely bad.'

In contrast to demonstrative pronouns and demonstrative manner adverbs, locative deictics form a three-term system: proximal *sini,* medial *situ,* and distal *sana.* These are commonly used in conjunction with the general prepositions, locative *di,* allative *ke,* and ablative *dari,* as illustrated in (5), (21) and (19) among others. Example (37) illustrates locative deictics both with and without a preposition.

5 ON THE USE OF VERBAL MORPHOLOGY

5.1 Transitive and intransitive verbs

A clear distinction between transitive and intransitive clauses is central to discussions of Standard Indonesian morphosyntax, and grammatical transitivity is regularly marked morphologically on verbs. The situation is quite different in Colloquial Indonesian. Much of the verbal morphology of Standard Indonesian is not regularly employed during informal interaction. Additionally, understood referents are routinely not expressed explicitly. These features together contribute to cases in which it is not clear whether a given clause might be best categorized as transitive or intransitive.

The most frequently occurring Colloquial Indonesian intransitive verbs are monomorphemic. Several of these verbs, like *pergi* 'go', *duduk* 'sit', and *tidur* 'sleep' are also monomorphemic in Standard Indonesian. But many common intransitive verbs that might prescriptively take the intransitive prefixes *ber-* or *meN-* in Standard Indonesian, for example *bertanya* 'ask', and *menyanyi* 'sing', regularly occur as monomorphemic forms in conversational Indonesian, i.e. *tanya* (79), and *nyanyi* (80).

(79) U: *Kita   bisa   langsung   tanya   ya?*
          1p   can   direct   ask   yes
          'We can ask directly, can't we?'

(80) *Gara-garanya   waktu   itu   Fadly   sakit   cacar,   trus*
       gara-gara=nya   waktu   itu   Fadly   sakit   cacar,   terus
       result=DEF   time   DIST   Fadly   sick   smallpox   NEXT
       nggak   bisa   nyanyi.
       nggak   bisa   nyanyi
       NEG   can   sing
       Akhirnya   Nanang   yang   gantiin.
       Akhir=nya   Nanang   yang   ganti-in
       end=DEF   Nanang   REL   replace-APP
       'Since Fadly had smallpox at that time, and he couldn't sing, in the end Nanang replaced him.' *<http://sobatpadi.tripod.com/crew1.htm>*

The use of unaffixed intransitive verbs is a sign of informal style, but by no means are all intransitive verbs unaffixed in the type of Colloquial Indonesian described here. Nor is it the case that intransitive affixes are simply 'dropped' at random in Colloquial Indonesian. It is the most frequent verbs in discourse that regularly do not have affixes. Less commonly used and more specialized words tend to show fully affixed forms and can be analyzed as being drawn by speakers from the extensive stock of Standard Indonesian vocabulary, rather than the more limited (but pervasive) stock of informal vocabulary. Other factors that may motivate the use of prefixation include the following. In cases where a contrast in affixation bears an important semantic contrast, the affixes will tend to be retained, as in *belajar* 'study' and *ngajar* 'teach' from the base *ajar* 'having to do with the teaching/learning process'. Other prefixed verbs have developed specialized semantic functions in which the prefix no longer marks a transitive–intransitive distinction and tends to be retained in Colloquial Indonesian. The base *tinggal* 'depart, reside, remain' with the Standard Indonesian prefix *meN-*, *meninggal*, is a euphemism meaning 'to die' and in this function never occurs without the standard prefix, even in informal contexts.

5.2 Voice

As with Standard Indonesian, Colloquial Indonesian can mark a distinction between Actor Voice (AV) and Undergoer Voice (UV) transitive clause constructions (see section 3.2 above). As a marker of informal register, an AV verb may either be unprefixed, as in (6) or have the nasal prefix *N-* as in (15). Alternatively, AV verbs may have the Standard Indonesian prefix *meN-*. N represents either a velar nasal or a nasal homorganic with the initial consonant of the base as shown in Table 8.3. When *N-* is applied to base forms with initial voiced consonants, there are two alternative realizations – one consisting of a homorganic nasal alone, which is similar to the cognate construction in Javanese; and one consisting of *nge-*, which is similar to the cognate construction in Sundanese. Both

TABLE 8.3: NASAL PREFIX ALLOMORPHS

Initial phoneme	N-	meN-
p (*panggil* 'call')	m- (p elided) *manggil*	mem- (p elided) *memanggil*
b (*bantu* 'help')	m-, nge- *mbantu, ngebantu*	mem- *membantu*
t (*tentukan* 'set')	n- (t elided) *nentukan*	men- (t elided) *menentukan*
d (*dengar* 'hear')	n-, nge- *ndengar, ngedengar*	men- *mendengar*
s (*sebut* 'call')	ny- (s elided) *nyebut*	meny- (s elided) *menyebut*
c (*cari* 'look for')	ny- (c elided) *nyari*	men-* *mencari*
j (*jawab* 'answer')	n-*, nge- *njawab, ngejawab*	men-* *menjawab*
k (*kasih* 'give')	ng- (k elided) *ngasih*	meng- (k elided) *mengasih*
g (*ganggu* 'bother')	ng-, nge- *ngganggu, ngeganggu*	meng- *mengganggu*
h (*habisin* 'finish')	nge- *ngehabisin***	meng- *menghabisin*
w (*wawancara* 'interview')	nge- *ngewawancara*	me- *mewawancara*
liquids (*lédék* 'ridicule')	ng-, nge- *nglédék, ngelédék*	me- *melédék*
nasals (*nikmati* 'enjoy')	0- *nikmati*	me- *menikmati*
vowels (*ambil* 'take')	ng- *ngambil*	meng- *mengambil*

*   Orthographic <n> pronounced as palatal nasal [ɲ].
** This form is not common; a less marked alternative would be to use a more colloquial base without
    initial h-, plus ng-, *ngabisin*.

alternatives are commonly used in Colloquial Indonesian and individual speakers may alternate between them.

Use of AV clauses is generally associated with undergoers that are indefinite or non-referential. Actors in AV clauses tend to be definite and topical. There is also a tendency for speakers to prefer AV clauses in irrealis contexts and when expressing background information.

In both types of UV clauses, those with a *di*-prefixed verb as well as those with a proclitic actor (section 3.2 above), the undergoer subject tends to be referential and definite. In all UV clauses with a proclitic actor, the actor is also referential and definite. Many UV clauses with the *di*- construction also have referential and definite actors. There is a tendency for UV clauses to be used in realis contexts and when expressing foregrounded information. There is also a second type of *di*-verb construction, the agentless UV clause, in which the actor is non-referential or unimportant and is usually unmentioned or only expressed with a general term such as *orang* 'person, someone, anyone'. This is exemplified in (58) in which the actor of *direkam* 'be recorded' is unknown and inconsequential.

This brief functional description of AV and UV clauses only presents general tendencies. Speaker usage varies according to medium and genre, as well as first-language background and socio-economic status. The complexities of this system and its usage are topics which continue to occupy researchers.

5.3   Applicatives

In Colloquial Indonesian the standard applicative suffixes -*kan* and -*i* are used in addition to the exclusively colloquial -*in*. In Standard Indonesian, applicative suffixes generally form transitive verbs from transitive or intransitive verbal bases or from non-verbal bases. The suffix -*kan* can indicate causative (*memanaskan* 'to heat something up' < *panas* 'hot'), benefactive (*membelikan* 'to buy for someone' < *membeli* 'to buy') or controlled perception (*mendengarkan* 'listen to' vs *mendengar* 'hear'). The suffix *-i* can indicate directional (*mendatangi* 'come to' < *datang* 'come') or iterative (*memukuli* 'hit repeatedly' < *memukul* 'hit'). In Standard Indonesian, semantically related pairs of transitive and intransitive verbs are often found, in which the intransitive takes a prepositional complement, while the transitive has an applicative suffix and the erstwhile prepositional argument is the undergoer; for example *berbicara tentang* 'talk about' and *membicarakan* 'discuss', *duduk di* 'sit on' and *menduduki* 'occupy'.

The colloquial applicative suffix *-in* is a robust marker of informal style. It can often replace *-kan* or *-i*, retaining the same meaning as the form with the standard suffix, as in (81) where the standard forms would be *di-balik-kan* 'UV-return-APP' and *menyelidik-i* 'AV:investigate-APP'.

(81) N: .. *Terus   di-balik-in.*
           then   UV-return-APP
      ... *Dia   pingin   nyelidik-in   kita,*
           3s   want   AV:investigate-APP   1s
      'Then (he) returned (it) [my diary]. He had wanted to investigate me.'

The form with *-in* may cover both *-i* and *-kan* meanings for some verbs, or in other cases the *-in* form has no Standard Indonesian equivalents; for example Colloquial *ngerjain* 'beat up on' (physically or emotionally), but Standard *mengerjakan* 'employ' and *mengerjai* 'work on'. In Colloquial Indonesian, there may be no applicative used when one would be prescriptively required, e.g., the Colloquial unsuffixed *ngewawancara* 'to interview' is used instead of the standard applicative form *mewawancarai*. Conversely applicative forms may be used, when no such form is accepted in Standard Indonesian. This is illustrated in (82), where the standard form for 'help' would be *membantu* without a suffix.

(82) M: *Kenapa   Pak   RT=nya   nggak   nge-bantu-in,*
           why   Mr   neighborhood.head=DEF   NEG   AV-bantu-APP
          waktu   itu.
          time   DIST
      'Why didn't the neighbourhood head help at that time?'

While there is a preference by speakers to use the colloquial *N-* rather than *meN-* if a nasal prefix is used in conjunction with *-in*, forms which juxtapose the formal prefix and informal suffix do occur as in (83).

(83) C: *Kita   mem-bayang-in   ini,*
           1s   AV-image-APP   PRX
      'I'm imagining this,'

There is not as strong a preference for avoiding *N-* when standard applicative suffixes are used. Forms such as *ngadakan* and *ngadain* 'arrange' (< *ada* EXIST) are both common. Variation in the use of applicatives is seen throughout examples in this chapter.

5.4 Stative and potentive verbs

In Standard Indonesian the prefix *ter-*, used on verbal roots to indicate potential or adversative passive, is often replaced with informal *ke-* in Colloquial Indonesian: Standard *terbiasa*, Colloquial *kebiasa* 'accustomed to'; Standard *tertawa*, Colloquial *ketawa* 'laugh'; Standard *tertangkap*, Colloquial *ketangkap* 'to get caught'.

(84) M: ... *Ya   itu   ng-ada-in   pertemuan gelap   tuh,*
              yes DIST AV-conduct-APP meeting   dark   DIST
              yang di   Sibi.
              REL   LOC Sibi
              'Yeah, they had the secret meeting, the one in Sibi.'

           ... *Kan   ke-tangkep,*
                   NEG.Q POT-capture
           kamu nggak ngeli> nggak dengar,
           2s   NEG   NEG   hear
           .. *di-marah-marah-in.*
              UV-angry-RDP-APP
           'They were caught you know. You didn't hear it; they were reprimanded.'

Not all *ke*-V constructions in Colloquial Indonesian correspond to Standard Indonesian *ter*-V forms. For example, *ketemu* 'meet' corresponds to Standard Indonesian *bertemu*; it can also have the connotation of accidentally meeting someone and in that sense does not have a direct Standard equivalent.

6 DISCOURSE PARTICLES

Extensive use of discourse particles is a pervasive feature of Colloquial Indonesian, as will have been observed in many of the previous examples. As well as being general markers of informal style, each particle has an individual semantic, grammatical, or affective function. Their frequent occurrence at the end of intonation units also helps to signal breaks in the discourse which aid information processing. Only a few are discussed here.

Many colloquial discourse particles express speaker affect. *Dong*, associated with Jakartan Indonesian, indicates that the hearer is expected to have already known what the speaker is saying, as in example (19) above. *Lho*, from Javanese usage, in intonation unit-initial position indicates surprise, while intonation unit-finally indicates that what the speaker is saying is a reminder to the hearer. *Masa* or *masak* indicates disbelief that something is the case, as in (7). The Javanese *kok* also indicates surprise or disbelief, as in (26), and appeals for a response from the hearer. *Toh* 'nonetheless' is a concessive marker from Dutch.

Two common question particles are *ya* 'yes' and *kan* (from the negator *bukan*). *Ya* is a pervasive intonation unit-final particle used as a comprehension check, see example (44). Intonation unit-finally, *kan* is a negative question tag, see example (43). Intonation unit-initially or in pre-predicate position indicates that the speaker expects that the hearer should have known the information being presented, as in example (17). A third form is *ta* or *to*, which is exclusively an intonation unit-final question-forming particle.

(85) T: *Belum   di-tulis   di   papan   to?*
             NEG.pfv UV-write LOC   board   Q
             '(It') hasn't been written on the board yet, has it?'

The reduced deictic forms *tuh*, *nih*, *gini*, and *gitu* were discussed in 4.3 above in their deictic and information flow functions. Because these forms frequently occur at the end of intonation units, they can simultaneously function to mark the ends of discourse units while performing their other semantic or pragmatic functions. *Gitu* is especially common in informal interaction as a framing device marking the end of a larger discourse unit.

(86)   W: .. *Kalau   ingin   men-dapat-kan   sesuatu,*
             if   want   AV-receive-APP   something
             ikhtiar   dulu.
             endeavor   first
             gitu   Pak.
             like.that sir
             'If (you) want to get something, you have to work [for it] first, that's how it is, sir.'

This example also illustrates the juxtaposition of registers common in Indonesian interaction. Here the speaker's pronouncement is presented in a standard style, including the use of *meN-*, *-kan*, and the rather formal *sesuatu* 'something', yet is framed with the conversational *gitu* 'like that'.

Déh, *sih*, and *mah* mark the information status of elements within a clause. *Sih* and *mah* are topic markers, indicating given, often resumptive or contrastive, information in a statement; see for example *sih* in (35) above, or *mah* in (87). *Déh* highlights information focus in a statement, as in (87), and is also used as a softener in commands. *Déh* and *sih* are associated with Jakartan Indonesian, while *mah* is from Sundanese (see further discussion of regional particles below).

(87)   M: .. *lucu   déh,*
             funny   D.PTCL
             dia   mah.
             3s   D.PTCL
             'He's funny.'

Sih is also used as a softener after a question word, as in (88).

(88)   M: *Apa   sih   tuh   nama=nya.*
            what   D.PTCL   DIST   name=DEF
            'Now what was it called?'

Nah marks a transition between segments of discourse larger than a clause. For example, in (66) the speaker uses *nah* to indicate a summing up of what he has just been talking about. *Nah* can also be used to introduce a new topic of conversation, or to draw a hearer's attention to an item in the discourse or environment.

As seen with a few of the discourse markers discussed above, speakers frequently incorporate regional particles into Colloquial Indonesian. Some of these, such as *sih*, *déh* and *kok* have become very common in the Colloquial Indonesian of many speakers regardless of first-language or regional background. Other regional discourse markers, such as the Sundanese *mah*, or *jé*, a quotative or surprise marker common in some varieties of Javanese, especially on the North Coast of Java, will normally occur only in the Colloquial Indonesian of speakers from that specific area, and will not have gained wider currency throughout the archipelago. Other elements emblematic of Colloquial

Indonesian speech that may be associated with specific regional languages include, for example, the variation in allomorphs of *N-* mentioned in section 5.2.

When speakers use such regional features, they need not necessarily be regarded as speaking a separate variety of Colloquial Indonesian. Rather, one of the hallmarks of Colloquial Indonesian is that its speakers draw on a broad and varied set of linguistic resources in order to indicate an informal style of speech. One of the resources available to all speakers is the use of regionally identifiable linguistic elements and the option of using these to assert a sense of personal identity or social affiliation while speaking. That is, in the context of interpersonal interaction, speakers of Colloquial Indonesian regularly deploy morphological and syntactic resources from a variety of sources as they convey not only propositional and pragmatic information but a strong sense of identity embedded in the socially and emotionally salient context of informal interaction. This is exemplified by the juxtaposition of discourse markers from different regional sources in (87) and of different registers in (86), and is emblematic of the vitality of informal interaction. The result is the lively, personal, and constantly evolving language style that is modern Colloquial Indonesian.

ACKNOWLEDGMENTS

In addition to the two editors of this volume, I would also like to thank Susanna Cumming, Novi Djenar, and Robert Englebretson (who also provided examples 21 and 70) for their helpful comments. Umar Muslim greatly assisted me in the collection and transcription of much of the data. Research for this project was partially funded by an Australian Research Council Small Grant and I was supported as an Associate Fellow at the International Institute for Asian Studies, Leiden University during the initial writing phase.

TRANSCRIPTION CONVENTIONS

.	final pitch contour
,	continuing pitch contour
?	appeal pitch contour
–	truncated intonation unit
line break	separate line used for each complete or truncated intonation unit
..	short pause
...	long pause
:	lengthening of preceding segment
>	truncated word
A:	speaker attribution
[ ]	overlapping segment of speech
(H)	inhalation

REFERENCES

Alisjahbana, T.S. (1962) *Indonesian Language and Literature: Two Essays*, New Haven, Conn.: Yale University Southeast Asia Studies.
Anderson, R.O'G. (1966) 'The Languages of Indonesian politics', *Indonesia* 1: 89–116.
Anwar, K. (1980) *Indonesian: the Development and Use of a National Language*, Yogyakarta, Indonesia: Gadjah Mada University Press.

Badudu, J.S. *et al.* (1984) *Morfologi Bahasa Indonesia (Lisan)*, Jakarta: Departemen Pendidikan dan Kebudayaan.

Cumming, S. (2002) 'On *-in*', paper presented at the 9th International Conference on Austronesian Linguistics, Canberra.

Du Bois, J.W., Schuetze-Coburn, S., Paolino, D., and Cumming, S. (1992) *Discourse Transcription*, Santa Barbara: University of California, Santa Barbara Department of Linguistics.

Englebretson, R. (2003) *Searching for Structure: the Problem of Complementation in Colloquial Indonesian Conversation*, Amsterdam: John Benjamins.

Errington, J. (1998) *Shifting Languages: Interaction and Identity in Javanese Indonesia*, Cambridge: Cambridge University Press.

Ewing, M.C. and Cumming, S. (1998) 'Relative clauses in Indonesian discourse: Face to face and cyberspace interaction', in S.L. Chelliah and W.J. de Reuse (eds.) *Papers from the Fifth Annual Meeting of the Southeast Asian Linguistics Society*, 79–96, Tempe, Arizona: Arizona State University.

Gil, D. (2002a) 'The prefixes di- and N- in Malay/Indonesian dialects', in F. Wouk and M. Ross (eds.) *The History and Typology of Western Austronesian Voice Systems*, 241–283, Canberra: Pacific Linguistics.

—— (2002b) 'Riau Indonesian *-kan* in synchrony and diachrony', paper presented at the 9th International Conference on Austronesian Linguistics, Canberra.

Grijns, C.D. (1991) *Jakarta Malay: A Multidimensional Approach to Spatial Variation*, Leiden: KITLV Press.

Haiman, J. (1978) 'Conditionals are topics', *Language* 54: 564–589.

Hoffman, J. (1979) 'A foreign investment: Indies Malay to 1901', *Indonesia* 27: 65–92.

Hooker, V.M. (1995) 'New Order language in context', in V.M. Hooker (ed.) *Culture and Society in New Order Indonesia*, 272–293, Oxford: Oxford University Press.

Ikranegara, K. (1980) *Melayu Betawi Grammar*, Jakarta: Badan Penyelenggara Seri NUSA.

Kaswanti Purwo, B. (1984) *Towards a Description of Contemporary Indonesian: Preliminary Studies, Part II*, Jakarta: Badan Penyelenggara Seri NUSA.

—— (1988) *Towards a Description of Contemporary Indonesian: Preliminary Studies, Part III*, Jakarta: Badan Penyelenggara Seri NUSA.

MacDonald, R.R. and Dardjowidjojo, S. (1967) *A Student's Reference Grammar of Modern Formal Indonesian*, Georgetown: Georgetown University Press.

Maier, H.M.J. (1993) 'From heteroglossia to polyglossia. The creation of Malay and Dutch in the Indies', *Indonesia* 56:37–65.

Moeliono, A.M. and Dardjowidjojo, S. (eds.) (1988) *Tata Bahasa Baku Bahasa Indonesia*, Jakarta: Departemen Pendidikan dan Kebudayaan.

Moeliono, A.M. *et al.* (1988) *Kamus Besar Bahasa Indonesia*, Jakarta: Balai Pustaka.

Muhadjir (1981) *Morphology of Jakarta Dialect: Affixation and Reduplication*, Jakarta: Badan Penyelenggara Seri NUSA.

Musgrave, Simon (2001), *Non-subject Arguments in Indonesian*, PhD Dissertation, University of Melbourne.

Prentice, D.J. (1990) 'Malay (Indonesian and Malaysian)', in B. Comrie (ed.) *The World's Major Languages*, 913–935, London: Routledge.

Sneddon, J. (1996) *Indonesian: A Comprehensive Grammar*, London: Routledge.

—— (2002) 'Variation in informal Jakartan Indonesian: a quantitative study', paper presented at the 9th International Conference on Austronesian Linguistics, Canberra.

Tanner, N. (1967) 'Speech and society among the Indonesian elite: A case study of a multilingual community', *Anthropological Linguistics* 9:15–40.

Verhaar, J. (1984) *Towards a Description of Contemporary Indonesian: Preliminary Studies, Part I*, Jakarta: Badan Penyelenggara Seri NUSA.

Wolff, J.U., Oetomo, D., and Fietkiewicz, D. (1986) *Beginning Indonesian through Self-instruction*, Ithaca, NY: Cornell University Southeast Asia Program.

Wouk, F. (1989) *The Impact of Discourse on Grammar: Verb Morphology in Spoken Jakarta Indonesian*, PhD dissertation, University of California, Los Angeles.

—— (1999) 'Dialect contact and koineization in Jakarta, Indonesia', *Language Sciences* 21: 61–86.

CHAPTER NINE

TSOU

Elizabeth Zeitoun

1 INTRODUCTION

Tsou is spoken by around 4000 people living in Mt Ali, in the southwest of Taiwan. It is also known as 'Northern Tsou' in opposition to Saaroa and Kanakanavu or 'Southern Tsou'. Geographical maps on the location of the Tsou tribe are given in Wurm and Hattori (1983), Tsuchida (1995:294) and Wright (1996:45–46).

According to Tung *et al.* (1964), Tsou consists of four dialects, Tapangʉ /tapaŋʉ/, Tfuya /tfuya/, Luhtu /ɗuhtu/ and Iimucu /imucu/, the last of which is now extinct. The Tapangʉ and the Tfuya dialects are spoken in some scattered villages in Alishan township, Chia-yi county. The Luhtu dialect is spoken in only one village, located in Hsin-yi township (Nantou county) in Central Taiwan but is now on the verge of extinction, because the village where it is spoken has gradually become a Bunun habitat (Tsuchida 1976 and 1995). These three dialects exhibit only a few lexical and phonological variations, no significant grammatical divergences having ever been reported (see Tung *et al.* 1964, Li 1979 and Tsuchida 1995).

The position of Tsou among the Formosan languages remains rather unclear (see the section on subgrouping in the introduction to this volume). Ferrell (1969) classified the Formosan languages into three main groups: Atayalic (Atayal and Seediq), Tsouic (Tsou, Kanakanavu and Saaroa) and Paiwanic (all the remaining Formosan languages). Tsuchida (1976) argued that Tsou was more closely related to Rukai and that they formed an independent Rukai-Tsouic group. Ho (1983) and Li (1990) rejected such a subgroup and posited that Rukai was more closely related to Paiwan. Such divergent conclusions are partly due to the different comparative data used by these scholars: Tsuchida's (1976) analysis was based on a lexical comparison between Tsou and the geographically contiguous Rukai dialects belonging to the 'Lower Three Villages' (Maga, Mantauran and Tona), whereas Ho's (1983) conclusions were founded on a lexical comparison between Tsou and Budai, a Rukai dialect geographically closer to Paiwan. Other hypotheses have, since then, been advanced, where Tsou(ic) is treated as either a primary branch (Blust 1999) or a secondary offshoot (Starosta 1995) of Proto-Austronesian.

Tsou is one of the better documented Formosan languages. Tung *et al.* (1964) wrote a very comprehensive grammar, which not only deals with the phonology, morphology and syntax of the Tsou language, but also provides abundant texts and a glossary. More recently, another grammar has been compiled (Szakos 1994), which in terms of data collection surpasses the study carried out by Tung *et al.* (1964). Other works provide descriptions and analyses on various aspects of the language including its phonetics and phonology (cf. Tsuchida 1972 and 1976, Ho 1976, Li 1979, Ladefoged and Zeitoun 1993, Wright 1996 and 1999, Wright and Ladefoged 1997, Hsin 2000), morphology (cf. Stanley 1979 and Tsuchida 1990) and syntax (among others, Hen-li Lin 1955, Starosta 1974 and 1997, Zeitoun 1992, 1993, 1996 and 2000a, Chang 1998) as well as detailed ethnographic accounts (cf. Ogawa and Asai 1935 and Wei *et al.* 1952). However, many syntactic and semantic aspects of the language are still poorly understood, and though several vocabulary lists are available (cf. Nevskij 1935, Tung *et al.* 1964, Tsuchida 1995), no comprehensive dictionary has yet been published.

Unless mentioned otherwise, the data in the present analysis is based on the Tfuya dialect, which I have investigated on and off since 1991.

2 PHONOLOGY AND ORTHOGRAPHY

The Formosan languages generally exhibit fairly simple phonological systems consisting of no more than twenty consonants and four vowels. However, Tsou developed a more complex vocalic system as a result of, among others, vowel deletion.

2.1 Phonemic inventory

In the present analysis, the Tsou phonemic inventory includes 15 consonants, 1 glide and 6 vowels. In Tables 9.1 and 9.2, phonemes are represented by the orthographic symbols adopted in this presentation (see the discussion on orthography below). Wherever the phonetic value of the phoneme is not adequately represented through orthographic means, the relevant IPA symbol is added in square brackets (as it is elsewhere in this chapter).

The present Tsou phonemic description varies slightly from other major sources. The main differences might be partially due to dialectal variation. They are: (i) the description of the implosive [ɗ] (as a preglottalized lateral in Tung *et al.* 1964 and Szakos 1994), (ii) the place of articulation of [h] (a velar fricative [x] in Tsuchida (1976, 1995) but a glottal fricative in most other works), (iii) the vowel quality of [e] and [o] (described as 'midhigh' in Wright 1996 and Wright and Ladefoged 1997 but 'midlow' in Tsuchida 1995), (iv) the analysis of the high central vowel as [ɨ] or [ʉ].

Two more crucial divergences to be discussed here in more detail concern the phonemic status of the glide *w* and vowel length.

TABLE 9.1: TSOU CONSONANT PHONEMES

	Labial	Dental	Palatal	Velar	Glottal
Stop vl	p	t		k	'[ʔ]
Implosive	b [ɓ]	l [ɗ]			
Affricate		c [ts]			
Fricative vl	f	s			h
vd	v	z			
Nasal	m	n		ng [ŋ]	
Glide			y [j]		

TABLE 9.2: TSOU VOWEL PHONEMES

	Front	Central	Back
High	i	ʉ [ɨ]	u
Mid	e		o
Low		a	

Tsou was described by Tung *et al.* (1964:20) as having two 'non-syllabic' vowels, treated as the counterparts of /e/ and /o/. Ho (1976) showed that these 'non-syllabic' vowels are better analysed as glides (*y* and *w*, respectively), to account more uniformly for the stress and reduplication patterns as well as the syllable structure in this language. Ho's analysis has the advantage of avoiding long strings of vowels (up to six) in polysyllabic words (e.g. Tung's *pooeóeo* 'shirt' is Ho's *pooyóyo*) and is basically sound. Nevertheless, the phonemic status of [w] remains problematic because it hardly ever occurs in initial position (cf. Wright 1996:48, Zeitoun 1996). While maintaining /y/, I therefore decide not to treat [w] as a distinct phoneme.

Wright (1996 and 1999) proposes length contrast for all vowels. Compare, for example, *pitu* 'seven' with *pi:pia* 'spirit', *pepe* 'sky', 'heaven' with *pe:la* 'be able to', *pai* 'rice plant' with *pa:jai* 'place name' (Wright 1996:50). These long vowels are in opposition to disyllabic vowel clusters, which consist of two distinct vowels. This analysis is not adopted here for two main reasons. First, it is more economical to posit only one set of vowels, given that in word-medial position, long vowels are very scarce in number. Second, the assignment of stress (see section 2.4) is more regular when phonetically long vowels are simply considered sequences of two like vowels. Stress then generally falls on the penultimate syllable.

Two further allophonic variations need to be mentioned: (i) the preglottalized dental implosive is realized as a preglottalized lateral flap before /a/, e.g. [ɗiŋki] 'muddy' vs. [ʔlauja] 'maple' (see Wright 1996:53 and 1999:284); (ii) /c/ and /s/ are usually palatalized before /i/, e.g. *meosi* [meoʃi] 'big', *ci* [tʃi] 'REL(ativizer)'. These allophonic variations are not indicated in this presentation.

The orthographic system used here was developed by the 'Tsou literacy group' which consists of Tsou native speakers, church staff and linguists working together for the development of teaching materials. In 1993 the group adopted a roman alphabet, which includes the same number of phonemes as in the present analysis and differs only in a few details from a representation using only IPA symbols: the implosive [ɗ] is represented by <1>; the glottal stop [ʔ] is indicated by an apostrophe <'>; the velar nasal [ŋ] is represented by <ng>, the glide [j] by <y>, and the high central vowel [ɨ] is transcribed as <ʉ>.

2.2 Consonant clusters

Tsou allows a wide range of consonant clusters, some of which are rarely attested in languages of the world (Wright 1996 and 1999). Some examples of possible consonant clusters are given in (1):

(1)   Consonants clusters in Tsou (cf. Wright 1996:184–195)

	Word-initial	Gloss	Word-medial	Gloss
a.	*ptusu*	pimples	*smoetaptaptf*	flap wings to no avail
b.	*tposf*	write	*tatposa*	colorful
c.	*chumu*	water	*machachana*	all the rice paddies
d.	*vzovzo*	tall and thin	*avzovzo*	be penniless
e.	*f'ue*	sweet potato	*faaf'ohf*	broad, wide
f.	*msipngi*	wedge	*amsuhza*	get rid of

The possible combinations are constrained in the following way:

(i)   no more than two consonants are allowed either in word-initial or word-medial position.
(ii) geminate consonants such as **pp*, **kk*, **mm* (found, for instance in Maga Rukai) are not allowed.

(iii) only nasals and stops sharing the same place of articulation can occur together, e.g. *mputu* 'hold', *tnuyu* 'sudden downpour'.

(iv) with the exception of /h/ and /'/, e.g. *h'isi* 'grain husks', *h'oh'o* 'wound', no combinations of homorganic stops and fricatives are found.

Tung *et al.* (1964), Hsin (2000) and Wright (1999:289) claim that regardless of its position in a word, a Tsou consonant cluster always occurs in syllable onset position (i.e. word-medial clusters do not belong to different syllables). Their arguments are that consonant clusters obey the same phonotactic constraints in word-initial and word-medial positions and furthermore that in case of CV-reduplication the whole cluster is reduplicated (see also section 2.5). The following examples are extracted from Hsin (2000):

(2) Reduplicated consonant clusters
    a. *fsuju*   'bow'   *fsu-fsuju*   'hunting bows'
    b. *hcuju*   'hill'   *ma-hcu-hcuju*   'hills'
    c. *nanghia* 'friend, friendly' *na-na-nghi-nghia* 'friendly to all'
    d. *na'vama* 'father and son' *na-na-'va-'vama* 'father and sons'

2.3 Tsou syllable structure and stress

Most Formosan languages exhibit a CVC syllable structure. At an earlier stage of their history, echo vowels were added in Tsou, altering the PAn canonical CVC syllable structure to CVCV. This CVCV pattern was later reanalyzed, as Tsou developed consonant clusters as a result of vowel deletion. Thus the currently attested syllable structure can be represented by the formula (C)(C)V. The occurrence of the onset is optional and there is no coda. There are no (C)V roots except for grammatical words, which are usually monosyllabic. The following words exemplify some of the most common syllable patterns.

(3) V.CV   *a.mo*   'father'
    CV   *ho*   'and'
    CV.V   *ʔu.a*   'deer'
    CCV.V *fʔu.e* 'sweet potato'
    V.CV.V *e.mo.o* 'home'

The last vowel of a base is often an echo vowel, which either gets deleted or undergoes certain morphophonemic alternations after suffixation (see section 2.4). The phonetic value of the echo vowel is determined by the preceding vowel, e.g. it is *i* if the preceding vowel is /i/ or /e/, as in *hisi* 'tooth', *emi* 'wine', *u* if the preceding vowel is /u/, as in *puzu* 'fire', *u* if the preceding vowel is /u/, /a/ or /o/, as in *ngucu* 'nose', *pasu* 'a type of bamboo', *zomu* 'bird' (Tsuchida 1976:88).

Stress usually falls on the penultimate syllable of a word (4a–b), whether or not the last vowel is an echo vowel, and suffixation always causes stress to shift to the right of the stem (4c–d). In other words, stress falls on the (new) penultimate syllable.

(4) a. *ámo*   'father' ~ *amó-'u*   'my father'
    b. *tacúmf* 'banana' ~ *tacumú-su* 'your banana'
    c. *emóo*   'house' ~ *emoó-si*   'his house'
    d. *mcóo*   'eyes' ~ *mcoó-ta* 'our eyes'

2.4 Morphophonological alternations

Tsou exhibits a number of morphophonological alternations (see Szakos 1994:28–32) which include deletion of unstressed antepenultimate vowels (e.g. *emucu* > *mucu* 'hand', *emoo* > *moo* 'house'), assimilation (e.g. *onko* > *ongko* 'name'), and dissimilation, whereby:

(i) /s/ is realized as [h] when immediately followed by a suffix beginning with /s/, /c/ or /t/ (examples drawn from Tsuchida 1990:46 and 40):

(5)   a.   /*tas-*/ 'pull'   >   *t-m-ah-sa-sre'u* 'call out someone secretly (AV)'
                                        (*-m-* 'AV'; *sa-* 'RED'; *sre'u* 'avert')
                                but *t-m-as-pepe* 'pull up (AV)' (*pepe* 'high')
      b.   /*sa-*/ 'hit the mark'   >   *h-taicv-a'* 'hit the center (PV)'
                                        (*taico* 'center'; *-a* 'PV')
                                but *s-fungv-a* 'hit at the head (PV)'
                                        (*fnguu* 'head'; *-a* 'PV')

(ii) /h/ is realized as [k] when following /s/ (examples adapted from Szakos 1994:28):

(6)   a.   *s-m-uhnu*   'send s.o to do sthg (AV)'   ~ *skuna*   'send s.o to do sth (PV)'
      b.   *s-m-ohpici*   'pinch (AV)'   ~ *skopica*   'pinch (PV)'

Two other major morphophonological alternations are closely linked to suffixation of the undergoer voice affixes (PV *-a*, LV *-i* or BV/IV *-(n)eni*, see also sections 3.2 and 4). The first is *ɨ/u/o* with *v* and *e/i* with *z* when a verb is suffixed with an undergoer voice affix, as illustrated in (7) (see also Tsuchida 1976 and Li 1977).

(7)   a.   **ɨ/u/o ~ v**
           to'tohɨngɨ   >   *to'tohɨngv-a*   'think'
           bohsifou   >   *bohsifov-a*   'climb'
           yoyoso   >   *yoyosv-a*   'play'
      b.   **e/i ~ z**
           opcoi   >   *opcoz-a*   'kill'
           matyoɨe >   *patyoɨz-a* 'change clothes'

The second is the deletion of unstressed vowels, a recurrent process which usually also takes place when undergoer suffixation applies.

(8)   a.   *t-m-opsɨ* 'write (AV)' >   *tpos-i*   'write (LV)'
           (*-m-* and *-i* are AV and LV affixes respectively; *toposɨ* is the root)
      b.   *b-ochio* 'know (AV)' >   *cohiv-i*   'know (LV)' (root: *cohio*)
           (*b-* and *-i* are AV and IV affixes respectively; *toposɨ* is the root)

2.5 Reduplication

Tsou reduplication patterns have never been examined in detail. However, CV-reduplication and Ca-reduplication are well established:

CV-reduplication involves the reduplication of the first syllable of the base regardless of whether the onset is simple (C) or complex (CC), cf. *zomɨ* 'bird' > *zozomɨ* 'birds', *cmoi* 'bear' > *cmocmoi* 'bears'. If the root is vowel-initial, the initial vowel is reduplicated with a glottal stop preceding both the reduplication and the base-initial vowel (e.g. *oko* > *'o'oko,* but see Wright 1996 for a different analysis).

In Ca-reduplication, the first consonant of the base is copied and followed by the vowel /a/, e.g. *mefcueu* (*fcuei*) 'castrate' > *fafcuea* 'castrated man'. This process seems not to be productive anymore, because (i) in many instances, the base is not retrievable (cf. **hocngu* > *hahocngu* 'man', **mespingi* > *mamespingi* 'woman'), and (ii) it often involves the obligatory occurrence of further affixes (e.g. *fnguu* 'head' + *doe-* 'big' > *doe-fa-fnguu* 'big head' and *fnguu* 'head' + *-a* 'PV' > *fafngu-a* 'hit on the head (PV)' while **fafnguu* is disallowed).

Tung *et al.* (1964:170) mention two other very rare reduplicative processes: (i) the reduplication of two distinct syllables, e.g. *nat'ohaesa* 'brothers' > *nanat'ot'ohaesa* 'two brothers', and (ii) CVC reduplication *mahafo* 'take' > *mahmahafo* 'take many times'.

As in other Austronesian languages, reduplication is used as a morphological device that indicates different types of intensification (e.g. plurality in nouns, repetition in dynamic verbs and intensification in stative verbs).

3 BASIC MORPHOSYNTAX

3.1 Word classes

Though certain lexical items exhibit ambivalent grammatical functions (e.g. *oko* 'child/small', *bnuvu* 'flower/blossom'), nouns in Tsou can usually be distinguished from verbs because of their structural properties:

(i) they are always preceded by a case marker (9a); verbs never are, unless they modify a noun (9b).

(9) a. *mo*   *mongsi*   *'e*   *oko*
         AV   AV:cry   NOM   child
         'The child is crying.'

     b. *'e*   *mongsi*   *ci*   *oko*
         NOM   AV:cry   REL   child
         'The crying child.'

(ii) they can be suffixed with a genitive pronoun (10); verbs cannot.

(10) a. *mi-'o*   *tmalu*   *to*   *oko-su*
         AV.RLS-1S.NOM   AV:hear   OBL   child-2S.GEN
         'I hear your child.'

     b. *i-'o*   *talui*   *'o*   *oko-su*
         UV.RLS-1S.GEN   hear:LV   NOM   child-2S.GEN
         'I (just) heard your child.'

Verbs, on the other hand, are characterized by their overt voice marking (cf. *m-ofi* 'give (AV)', *fi-i* 'give (LV)', *fa-eni* 'give (BV)').

Some authors (e.g. Szakos 1994) propose to distinguish other major lexical categories, such as adjectives, adverbs or prepositions. However, only the status of temporal adjuncts referring to a point in time, e.g. *hohucma* 'tomorrow', *nehucma* 'yesterday' can, at this point, be ascertained. These temporal adjuncts form a small class. Unlike nouns, they are never preceded by a case marker, and unlike verbs they are unmarked for voice, and (usually) occur in sentence-final position as in the following example:

(11)   *moh-ta*   *bonʉ*   *to*   *tacʉmʉ*   **nehʉcma**
     AV.RLS-3S.NOM   AV:eat OBL banana   yesterday
     'He ate a banana yesterday.'

On the other hand, the equivalents of English adjectives (e.g. *beautiful, bad, cold*), past participles (e.g. *broken*), durative or frequentative time adverbs (e.g. *always, often, sometimes*), and degree adverbs (e.g. *very, little*) function as verbs in Tsou: they undergo voice inflection and they occur in the same sentential position, i.e. after the string of 'preverbs' (auxiliary verb, pronoun, aspectual suffixes and/or evidentials, see section 3.2 below).

(12) a. *la-ta*   **aacni**   **na'no**   **onaa'o**   *ho*
        AV.HAB-3S.NOM always:AV very:AV a long time:AV and
        la-ta   **bonʉ**
        AV.HAB-3S.NOM AV:eat
        'He always eats for a long time.' (actor voice)
   b. *la-ta*   **aacnia**   **na'na**   **onaava**   *ho*
        UV.HAB-3S.GEN always:PV very:PV a long time:PV and
        la-ta   *ana*
        UV.HAB-3S.GEN eat:PV
        'He always eats for a long time.' (undergoer voice)

There are no preposition-like elements (*in, at, from, to, on top of, behind*, etc.) in Tsou, these notions being rendered either by nouns (13a) or by verbs (13b).

(13) a. *ta skovskovna-si*   'on top of'
   b. *pan*   *to*   *mo*   *con*   *ci*   *evi*   *ci*   *mo*
        EXIST OBL   AV.RLS one REL tree REL AV.RLS
        bicibi   *to*   *emoo*
        adjacent to:AV OBL   house
        'There is a tree beside the house.'

Basic numerals include: *coni* 'one', *yuso* 'two', *tuyo* 'three', *sʉptʉ* 'four', *imo* 'five', *nomʉ* 'six', *pitu* 'seven', *voyu* 'eight', *sio* 'nine' and *m-as-kʉ* 'ten'. As is demonstrated by *m-as-kʉ*, tens are derived from the confix *m-* . . . *-hʉ*. The formation is subject to the following (regular) phonological constraints: (i) the last vowel of the confix becomes *u* is the preceding syllable has *u*, *ʉ* if it is *ʉ*, i.e. it echoes the preceding vowel (cf. section 2.3); (ii) *h* dissimilates to *k* before *s* (as in *m-pus-ku* 'twenty') and involves the occurrence of untressed antepenultimate vowels deleted in simple forms (as in *m-onmʉ-hʉ*). cf. *m-as-ku* 'ten', *m-pus-ku* 'twenty', *m-tuyu-hu* 'thirty', *m-sʉptʉ-hʉ* 'forty', *m-eimo-hʉ* 'fifty', *m-onmʉ-hʉ* 'sixty', *m-pʉtvʉ-hʉ* 'seventy', *m-voyvʉ-hʉ* 'eighty', *m-sio-hʉ* 'ninety'. Basic numerals used in counting can also function as adnominal modifiers, cf. *'o mo coni oko* (NOM AV.RLS one child) 'one child'.

3.2 Basic clause structure

Like most other Formosan languages, Tsou is basically a verb-initial language – or more specifically a 'predicate-initial' language, where 'predicate' refers to a verb phrase or a noun – with the subject usually occurring in clause-final position, unless followed by spatio-temporal adjuncts.

(14) a. [*mo*   *bonʉ*]_{Pred} [*to*   *tacʉmʉ*]_O [*'o*   *amo*]_S (*maitan'e*)
          AV.RLS AV:eat   OBL   banana   NOM father (today)
          'Father ate a banana (today).'

      b. [(*zou*) *oko-su*] _{Pred} [*na*   *a'o*]_S
          (be)   child-2s.GEN   NOM 1s.
          'I am your child.'

Grammatical relations are encoded through two morphosyntactic devices: (i) full NPs are obligatorily preceded by a (nominative or oblique) case marker; (ii) the subject (i.e. the NP marked as nominative) is morphologically marked on the verb by means of a voice affix.

(15) a. *mo*   ***m-osi***   *ta*   *pangka* *to*   *emi*   *'o*   ***amo***
          AV.RLS   AV-put   OBL   table   OBL   wine   NOM father
          'Father put some wine on the table.'

      b. *i-si*   *si-**a***   *ta*   *pangka* *to*   *amo*   *'o*
          UV.RLS-3S.GEN   put-PV   OBL   table   OBL   father NOM
          emi
          wine
          'Father put the wine on the table.'

      c. *i-si*   *si-**i***   *to*   *emi*   *to*   *amo*   *'e*
          UV.RLS-3S.GEN   put-LV   OBL   wine   OBL   father NOM
          pangka
          table
          'Father put the wine on the table.'

As shown by these examples, there are a number of different undergoer voice (UV) constructions in addition to an actor voice (AV) construction (see also section 4). Apart from the voice marking (on both the initial auxiliary verb and the main predicate) actor and undergoer voice constructions also differ in that a pronominal suffix representing the agent is obligatory in UV constructions, regardless of whether or not a co-referential full NP occurs in the same clause (as in 15b–c). In AV constructions, pronominal suffixes are usually used when no co-referential NP is present in the same clause.

3.2.1 Tsou auxiliary verbs and their interaction with preverbal constituents

A major feature of Tsou morphosyntax is the obligatory occurrence of auxiliary verbs. Auxiliary verbs exhibit the following syntactic properties:

(i) They usually occur in every verbal clause:

(16) a. ***moso*** *etamaku* *'o*   *ohaesa*
          AV.RLS smoke:AV   NOM younger sibling
          'My younger brother smoked.'

      b. * Ø   *etamaku* *'o*   *ohaesa*

(ii) They usually appear in clause-initial position unless preceded by a topicalized element (17a), an emphatic particle (17b), a negator (176c) or a conjunction (17d):

(17) a. *'o*   *ohaesa*   ***moh-**ta*   *la*   *etamaku*
          Top younger sibling   AV.RLS-3S.NOM   EXP   smoke:AV
          'As for my younger brother, he (once) smoked.'

b. *'a*   ***moso*** *la*   *etamaku*   *'o*
   it is the case that   AV.RLS   HAB   smoke:AV   NOM
   ohaesa
   younger sibling
   '(It is the case that) my younger brother (has had the experience of) smoking.'

c. *o'a* ***moso*** *s'a*   *la*   *etamaku*   *'o*
   NEG   AV.RLS   EVD   EXP   smoke:AV   NOM
   ohaesa
   younger sibling
   'My younger brother (has) never smoked.'

d. *moso-n'a*   *etamaku*   *'o*   *ohaesa*   *ne*
   AV.RLS-still   smoke:AV   NOM   younger sibling   when
   mo-'u   *esmi*
   AV.RLS-1s.NOM   enter:AV
   'When I entered, my younger brother was still smoking.'

(iii) They attract pronominal (17a) and aspectual (17d) suffixes and are immediately followed by aspectual, modal and evidential particles (17a–d):

Morphologically, the Tsou auxiliary verbs are either overtly or covertly marked for voice. Based on this criterion, they can be divided into three distinct classes: the first set (*mio, mo, mi-, moso,* and *mo(h)-*) only occurs in AV constructions; the second set (*i-* and *o(h)-*) only appears in UV constructions; the third set (*te, ta, tena, nte, ntoso, nto(h)-* and *la*) may be found in both AV and UV constructions.

Auxiliary verbs and main (lexical) verb(s) occurring in the same clause usually agree in voice. In other words, if the auxiliary verb is marked as AV, the following verb(s) will be marked as AV and the NP selected as subject is the Agent, as in (18a). If the auxiliary verb is marked as UV, the following verb(s) will be marked for one of the undergoer voices (PV, LV or BV/IV), depending on which of the nominal arguments is the subject of the clause, as in (18b) and (18c). If the auxiliary verb is unmarked for voice, morphological distinctions on the verb will usually help to determine which of the nominal NPs is regarded as the subject of the clause, as in (18d) and (18e).

(18) a. ***mo***   ***m-***ofi   *to*   *emi*   *ta*   *amo*   *'o*   *ino*
     AV.RLS   AV-give   OBL   wine   OBL   father   NOM   mother
     'Mother gave some wine to father.'

   b. *i-si*   *fi-**i***   *to*   *emi*   *to*   *ino*   *'o*
     UV.RLS-3s.GEN   give-LV   OBL   wine   OBL   mother   NOM
     amo
     father
     'Mother gave some wine to father.' (Lit. Father was given wine by mother)

   c. *i-si*   *fa-**eni***   *to*   *amo*   *to*   *ino*
     UV.RLS-3s.GEN   give-IV   OBL   father   OBL   mother
     'o   ***emi***
     NOM   wine
     'Mother gave the wine to father.' (Lit. The wine was given to father by mother)

   d. ***te***   ***m-***ofi   *to*   *emi*   *ta*   *amo*   ***'o***   ***ino***
     AV.IRR   AV-give   OBL   wine   OBL   father   NOM   mother
     'Mother will give some wine to father.'

e. **te**-*si*   *fi-i*   *to*   *emi*   *to*   *ino*   **'o**
   UV.IRR-3S.GEN   give-LV   OBL   wine   OBL   mother   NOM
amo
father
'Mother will give some wine to father.' (Lit: Father will be given the wine by mother)

Beside marking voice, auxiliary verbs also encode temporal/aspectual and modal information (see section 3.4 for details), the main dichotomy lying in the notion of 'realization' of an event (Realis vs. Irrealis).

The Tsou auxiliary verbs exhibit various distributional constraints, which are either phonologically or syntactically conditioned resulting in allomorphy, as Table 9.3 illustrates. Phonological variants occur in the same cell (separated by ~), while syntactic variants (bound vs. free forms) occur in the same row but in different columns.

Phonologically, an auxiliary verb with an /o/-ending (cf. *mo-*, *o-*, and *nto-*) is realized as /oh/- (yielding *moh-*, *oh-*, *ntoh-*) when followed by a (pronominal/aspectual) suffix/clitic with an initial -*t* (cf. -*ta* 'he', -*to* 'we') or -*c* (cf. -*cu* 'already').

(19) a. **mo-**'u   *bonи*   *to*   *тасити*   (**moh-*'u)
      AV.RLS-1S.NOM   AV:eat   OBL   banana
      'I ate a banana.'
   b. **moh**-ta   *bonи*   *to*   *тасити*   (*mo-ta)
      AV.RLS-3S.NOM   eat   OBL   banana
      'He ate a banana.'

Syntactically, as already mentioned above, any auxiliary verb occurring in UV constructions must be suffixed with a genitive pronoun. Hence, there are only bound forms for those auxiliaries which can only be used in UV constructions (i.e. *i-* and *o-/oh-*).

In AV constructions, *mo*, *moso* and *ntoso* are in complementary distribution with *mi-*, *mo(h)-* and *nto(h)-*, depending on their compatibility with pronominal and aspectual suffixes.

(i) *mo*, *moso* and *ntoso* cannot occur with pronominal suffixes (20a); *mi-*, *mo(h)-* and *nto(h)-*, on the other hand, cannot appear unaffixed (20b):

(20) a. **mo/moso** *mimo*   *ta*   *emi*   (***mo/*moso*-ta)
      AV.RLS   AV:drink   OBL   wine
      'He is drinking wine.'

TABLE 9.3: AUXILIARY VERBS IN TSOU

	Realis		Irrealis	
	Bound	Free	Bound	Free
AV	mi-	mo		
		mio		
	mo- ~ moh-	moso		
AV/UV				la
				te, tena, ta
				nte
			nto(h)- ~ ntoso-	ntoso
UV	i-			
	o- ~ oh-			

b. ***moh**-ta   mimo   ta   emi   (***mi-Ø**)*
   AV.RLS-3s.NOM   AV:drink   OBL   wine
   'He is drinking wine.'

(ii) *mo, moso* and *ntoso* can co-occur with -*n'a* 'still' (21a), *mi-, mo(h)-* and *nto(h)-*
cannot; conversely (21b), while the former cannot appear with -*cu* 'already' (21c),
the latter can (21d).

(21) a. ***mo**-n'a   mimo   ta   emi*
        AV.RLS-still   AV:drink   OBL   wine
        'He is still drinking wine.'

    b. ****mi**-n'a   mimo   ta   emi*
        AV.RLS-still   AV:drink   OBL   wine

    c. ****mo**-cu   mimo   ta   emi*
        AV.RLS-already   AV:drink   OBL   wine
        'He is still drinking wine.'

    d. ***mi**-cu   mimo   ta   emi*
        AV.RLS-still   AV:drink   OBL   wine
        'He is already drinking wine.'

Two minor variations must be pointed out regarding the occurrence of the aspectual
suffixes: the first is phonological in nature, the second is semantic. Among the four aspectual suffixes in Tsou (-*cu*/-*c'u* 'already', -*n'a* 'still, just, about to', and -*la* 'once'), the first
three interact closely with auxiliary verbs, distributionally and semantically (the semantic
contrast between *la*, as an auxiliary verb and -*la*, as an aspectual suffix will further be
discussed in section 3.4). The suffixes -*cu* and -*c'u* can be treated as allomorphs, because
the latter immediately follows auxiliary verbs ending with the vowel /a/, but never
co-occurs with pronominal suffixes (cf. *ta-c'u* but *tena-ta-cu* and not
*ta-cu or **tena-ta-c'u*; *la-c'u* and not *la-cu). The former appears elsewhere (cf. *mi-cu*
but not **mi-c'u*, *mi-ta-cu* but not **mi-ta-c'u* etc.).

The suffix -*n'a*, on the other hand, carries a different meaning, depending on the type
of auxiliary verb or main lexical verb it occurs with: in co-occurrence with activity or stative verbs, -*n'a* can be translated as 'still' (e.g. *mi-ta-**n'a** etamaku* 'He is smoking.'); in
co-occurrence with achievement verbs, -*n'a* can be glossed as 'just' (e.g. *mi-ta-**n'a**
uhtan'e* 'He has just arrived'); in co-occurrence with auxiliary verbs such as *te*, *ta* or
tena, which indicate an event has not happened yet, it means 'about to' (e.g. *te-ta-**n'a**
etamaku* 'He is about to smoke').

3.2.2 Clause types

Based on the occurrence of auxiliary verbs, three kinds of clause structures can be distinguished: the first is verbal, the second equational and the third existential. They are
examined and compared in turn below.

Verbal clauses include declarative (22a), imperative (22b) and (verbal) interrogative
sentences (22c).

(22) a. *la-ta   huhucmasi   eobako   to   oko-taini*
        AV.HAB-3s.NOM   everyday:AV   beat:AV   OBL   child-3s.GEN
        'He beats his child everyday.'

    b. *te   mimo   to   emi!*
        AV.IRR   AV:drink   OBL   wine
        'Drink wine!'

c. *mo*   *pio*   *na*   *i-si*   *eobaka*   *to*
    AV.RLS   how many:AV   NOM   UV-3S.GEN   beat:PV   OBL
    mo'o   *ci*   *'o'oko?*
    Mo'o   REL   children
    'How many children were beaten by Mo'o?'

They differ from equational and existential clauses in that they are headed by an auxiliary verb. If a verbal clause contains only two nominal arguments, the permutation of the two NPs may either lead to a different meaning as in (23d) or to its ungrammaticality as in (23c).

(23) a. *mo*   *bonʉ*   *to*   *tacʉmʉ*   *'o*   ***amo***
          AV.RLS   AV:eat   OBL   banana   NOM   father
          'Father ate a banana (today).'

      b. *i-si*   *ana*   *to*   *amo*   *'o*   ***tacʉmʉ***
          UV.RLS-3S.GEN   eat:PV   OBL   father   NOM   banana
          'The banana has been eaten by father (today).'

      c. **mo*   *bonʉ*   *'o*   ***amo***   *to*   *tacʉmʉ*
          AV.RLS   AV:eat   NOM   father   OBL   banana

      d. *i-si*   *ana*   *'o*   ***tacʉmʉ***   *to*   *amo*
          UV.RLS-3S   eat:PV   NOM   banana   OBL   father
          'Father's banana has been eaten.'

If a verbal clause includes more than two nominal arguments, word order is relatively free, and both VOS and VSO are found.

(24) a. *mo*   *meo'eoi*   *to*   *peisu*   *to*   *ino*   *'o*   *o'yu*
          AV.RLS   AV:steal   OBL   money   OBL   mother   NOM   thief
          i. 'The thief stole stole money from mother.'
          ii. 'The thief stole mother's money.'

      b. *mo*   *meo'eoi*   *to*   *ino*   *'o*   *o'yu*   *to*   *peisu*
          AV.RLS   AV:steal   OBL   mother   NOM   thief   OBL   money
          'The thief stole mother's money.'

      c. *mo*   *meo'eoi*   *'o*   *o'yu*   *to*   *peisu*   *to*   *ino*
          AV.RLS   AV:steal   NOM   thief   OBL   money   OBL   mother
          'The thief stole mother's money.'

NPs can function predicatively and introduce a nominative NP as its subject, yielding an equational sentence as in (25a). Equational sentences may be introduced by the particle *zou* 'be' as in (25b), which, in turn, can be preceded by *'a* 'it is the case that' or *o'a* '(it is) not (the case that)'.

(25) a. *cou*   *na*   *a'o*
          Tsou   NOM   1s
          'I am Tsou.'

      b. (***zou***)   *cou*   *na*   *a'o*
          (be)   Tsou   NOM   1s
          'I am Tsou.'

      c. *'a*   (***zou***)   *cou*   *na*   *a'o*
          it is the case that   (be)   Tsou   NOM   1s
          '(It is the case that) I am Tsou.'

      d. *o'a*   (***zou***)   *cou*   *na*   *a'o*
          NEG   (be)   Tsou   NOM   1s
          '(It is not the case that) I am Tsou.'

The order of the two NPs constituting the equational clause can be reversed:

(26) a. (zou) *mo'o* *'o* *mo* *eobako* *to* *oko-su*
    (be) Mo'o NOM AV.RLS beat:AV OBL child-2s.GEN
    'It is Mo'o who beat your child.'

  b. *'o* *mo* *eobako* *to* *oko-su* (zou) *mo'o*
    NOM AV.RLS beat:AV OBL child-2s.GEN (be) Mo'o
    'The one that beat your child is Mo'o.'

  c. (zou) *sia* *'o* *mo* *eobako* *to* *oko-su*
    (be) who NOM AV.RLS beat:AV OBL child-2s.GEN
    'Who beat your child?' (Lit: Who is the one who beat your child?)

  d. *'o* *mo* *eobako* *to* *oko-su* (zou) *sia*
    NOM AV.RLS beat:AV OBL child-2s.GEN (be) who
    'Who is the one that beat your child?' (Lit: The one that beat your child is who?)

The structure of existential sentences remains ill-understood because they do not fit the general clause pattern of the language: they differ from verbal clauses in that no auxiliary verb is allowed and from equational clauses in that there is no nominative marked NP. In the affirmative, existential clauses are headed by *pan* 'there is', which is followed by an oblique noun phrase; in the negative, they are introduced by *uk'a*, usually followed by the relativizer *ci*.

(27) a. (*mo/*moso) ***pan*** *to* *oko* *ne* *emoo*
    (*AV.RLS) EXIST OBL child OBL house
    'There are (a) child in the house.'

  b. ***uk'a*** *ci/*to* *oko* *ne* *emoo*
    NEG.EXIST REL/*OBL child OBL house
    'There is no child in the house.'

In existential sentences, the word order is rather fixed, the locative argument (if any) occurs) appearing in final position. Thus, it is not possible to reverse the order of the two NPs in (27a or b).

Existential sentences are also used to express possession:

(28) a. ***pan*** *to* *oko-'u*
    EXIST OBL child-1s.GEN
    'I have a child.' (Lit: My child exists.)

  b. ***uk'a*** *ci* *oko-'u*
    NEG.EXIST REL child-1s.GEN
    'I have no child.' (Lit: My child does not exist.)

If, however, the possessum is quantified, the existential pattern is not permitted (29a). In this case, the quantifier has to be made the predicate of a verbal clause (29b).

(29) a. **pan* *to* *mo* ***tuyo*** *ci* *'o'oko-'u*
    EXIST OBL AV.RLS three REL children-1s.GEN

  b. *mo* ***tuyo*** *'o* *'o'oko-'u*
    AV.RLS three NOM children-1s.GEN
    'I have three children.'

Locative sentences, which have the same structure as existential sentences in some Formosan languages (see Zeitoun *et al.* 1999), are instances of verbal clauses in Tsou.

(30) **mo** **eon** *ta* *emoo* *'e* *oko*
AV.RLS be.at:AV OBL house NOM child
'The child is at home.'

3.2.3 Negation

There are four major types of negators in Tsou (for details, see Li-May Sung 1999) which differ not only semantically but also syntactically. They can be categorized as follows:

(i) negation of an event/fact is rendered by *o'a*. The syntactic distribution of this negator is the broadest: it occurs before any auxiliary verb in verbal sentences, and before the predicate in an equational sentence:

(31) a. **o'a** *tena* *eon* *to* *pnguu* *'o* *mo'o*
          NEG AV.IRR be.at:AV OBL Pnguu NOM Mo'o
          'Mo'o will not be in Pnguu.'
      b. **o'a** *(zou)* *oko-'u* *na* *sico*
          NEG (be) child-1s.GEN NOM 3s
          'He is not my child.'

(ii) negation of the existence of a referent is indicated by *uk'a* as shown in (27b) and (28b) above.

(iii) prohibition is obtained through *'o* in AV constructions (32a) and *av'a* in UV constructions (32b). While *'o* precedes the auxiliary verb *te(na)*, *av'a* follows it.

(32) a. **'o-te** *mimo*
          NEG-AV.IRR AV:drink
          'Don't drink!'
      b. *te-**av'a*** *ima* *'e* *emi*
          UV.IRR-NEG drink:PV NOM wine
          'Don't drink (this) Wine!'

(iv) deontic negation is expressed through *o'*, Which appear before *te* 'will':

(33) **o'-te-'o** *mimo* *ta* *emi*
      NEG-AV.IRR-1s.NOM AV:drink OBL wine
      'I will not drink wine.'

3.3 Structure of the noun phrase

3.3.1 Nominal modifiers

In Tsou, every nominal argument must be preceded by a nominative or oblique case marker as amply illustrated by the examples throughout this chapter. As further discussed below, these case markers also convey deictic notions. In addition to the case markers full demonstratives may occur which are always placed after the noun:

(34) *'e* *oko* **eni**
      NOM child PRX
      'this child'

Two structures can be distinguished regarding the nominal vs. verbal modification of a noun. If a noun modifies another noun, the modifier occurs after the modified and is marked by an oblique case marker.

(35) a. *'o   mcoo   **to**   ino*
       NOM   eye   OBL   mother
       'Mother's eyes'

If, on the other hand, the noun is modified by a verb, then the modifier usually occurs before the modified, and is followed by the relativizer *ci*, which cannot be replaced by the oblique case markers *to/ta*.

(35) b. *'o   enghova   **ci**/*to/*ta   mcoo*
       NOM   blue   REL/*OBL   eye
       'blue eyes'

Of course, nominal and verbal modification can occur simultaneously:

(35) c. *'o   enghova   **ci**   mcoo   **to**   ino*
       NOM   blue   REL   eye   OBL   mother
       'Mother's blue eyes'

In verbal modification or relativization, the modified noun always has to be the subject of the predicate in the relative clause, as the following examples illustrate:

(36) a. *mo   uh   tan'e   'o   moso   eobako   to   mo'o*
       AV.RLS   go:AV   here   NOM   AV.RLS   beat:AV   OBL   Mo'o
       nehucma   ci   cou
       yesterday   REL   man
       'The man who beat Mo'o yesterday has come.'
    b. *os-'o   umnʉa   'o   moso   uh   ta*
       UV.RLS-1s.GEN   like:UV   NOM   AV.RLS   go:AV   OBL
       emoo-'u   nehucma   ci   oko
       home-1s.GEN   yesterday   REL   child
       'I like the child that came to my house yesterday.'
    c. *os-'o   eobaka   'o   i-si   pasunaenoveni*
       UV.RLS-1s.GEN   beat:UV   NOM   UV.RLS-3s.GEN   sing:BV
       to   paicʉ   ci   cou
       OBL   Paicʉ   REL   man
       'I beat the man for whom Paicʉ sang.'

Relative clauses do not have to precede the modified noun. Chang (1998:69ff) shows that in a restrictive relative clause, the subordinate clause precedes the head noun, as in (37a) whereas in a non-restrictive relative clause, the subordinate clause follows the head noun, as in (37b).

(37) Based on Chang (1998:69)
    a. *o-'u-cu   aiti   'o   [o-si   tposi*
       UV.RLS-1s.GEN-already   see:LV   NOM   UV.RLS-3s.GEN   write:PV
       *to   pasuya   ci   [**tposʉ**]]*
       OBL   Pasuya   REL   book
       'I have read the book that was written by Pasuya.'

b. *o-'u-cu*   *aiti*   *'o*   [*tposɨ*]   *ci*
    UV.RLS-1s.GEN-already   see:LV   NOM   book   REL
    [*o-si*   *tposi*   *to*   *pasuya*]
    UV.RLS-3s.GEN   write:PV   OBL   Pasuya
    'I have read the book, which was written by Pasuya.'

3.3.2 *Nominal case marking system*

Tsou exhibits a very complex nominal case marking system that differs quite drastically from other Formosan languages, and has given rise to different analyses which will not be discussed here in detail (cf. Tung *et al.* 1964, Zeitoun 1992, 1993 and 2000a, Szakos 1994, Chang 1998). As in other Formosan languages, Tsou case markers encode grammatical relations: they can be divided as nominative vs. oblique. They also carry meaningful information concerning the location of the referent with respect to the speech act participants, i.e. they locate the referent in the universe of discourse. They can be divided into two major classes, 'referential' vs. 'non-referential' and further be classified as 'identifiable' vs. 'non-identifiable'. The notion of referentiality

> involves, roughly, the speaker's intent to 'refer to' or 'mean' a nominal expression to have non-empty references – i.e. to 'exist' – within a particular universe of discourse …If a nominal is 'non-referential' or 'generic' the speaker does not have a commitment to its existence within the relevant universe of discouse. Rather, in the latter case, the speaker is engaged in discussing the genus of its properties, but does not commit him/herself to the existence of any specific individual member of that genus. (Givón 1978:293)

'Identifiability', on the other hand, involves the recognition of the referent by the speaker. This system is shown in Table 9.4. Two case markers *co* and *nca* are not indicated in this table because their interpretation is problematic and they will not be further discussed in this chapter.

TABLE 9.4: TSOU CASE MARKERS

The case-marked NP is:	Case markers	
	Nominative	Oblique
Referential		
Identifiable		
Visible and/or near (spatially, metaphorically) from:		
speaker	'e	
hearer	si	ta
Visible but away from		
speaker and hearer	ta	
(Non-)identifiable	'o	to
Invisible and far (spatially, metaphorically) from speaker and hearer or newly introduced in the discourse		
Non-referential		
Non-identifiable (usually implies a scanning of a class of elements)	na	no, ne

'e, si, ta (NOM/OBL) all indicate that the referent is identifiable to the addressee, but they differ in terms of their (joint/disjoint) reference to the speaker. If they locate the referent in space, they can usually substitute with one another as in (38a–c), because the speaker and the addressee are viewed as a 'joint' reference with respect to the referent.

(38) a. *mo   bonʉ   ta   tacʉmʉ   'e   oko*
          AV.RLS   AV:eat   OBL   banana   NOM   child
          'The child is eating a banana.' (implied: The child is located near the speaker)

      b. *mo   bonʉ   ta   tacʉmʉ   si   oko*
          AV.RLS   AV:eat   OBL   banana   NOM   child
          'The child is eating a banana.' (implied: The child is located near the hearer)

      c. *mo   bonʉ   ta   tacʉmʉ   ta   oko*
          AV.RLS   AV:eat   OBL   banana   NOM   child
          'The child is eating a banana.' (implied: The child is located away from the speech act participants; however, he is visible to them)

If they are used metaphorically, they cannot be substituted with one another, because the speaker and the addressee are then treated as a 'disjoint' reference. As an illustration, compare (39a–b):

(39) a. *i-su   talʉa   'e   ino-'u*
          UV.RLS-2s.GEN   think.about:PV   NOM   mother-1s.GEN
          'You have thought about my mother.' (Metaphorical usage)

      b. **i-su   talʉa   si/ta   ino-'u*
          UV.RLS-1s.GEN   think.about:PV   NOM   mother-1s.GEN

The occurrence of *'e* in (39a) is allowed because the speaker emphasizes the relation that exists between his mother and himself, i.e. the identification of the referent is not spatial but metaphorical; the speaker and the addressee are treated as a 'joint' reference. *si* and *ta* cannot take over this metaphorical interpretation because they indicate that a certain distance separates the referent from the speaker, i.e. the speaker and the addressee are viewed as a 'disjoint' reference.

The use of *o* and *to* indicates that the referent may or may not be identifiable to the addressee. If identifiable (i.e. absent or invisible but familiar), *'o* can usually substitute with *'e, si, ta* (NOM) and *to* with *ta* (OBL) as shown in (40a–b).

(40) a. *i-ta   eobaka   to   ino   'o   oko*
          UV.RLS-3s.GEN   beat:PV   OBL   banana   NOM   child
          'Mother has beaten the child.' (implied: The child and his mother are not being seen by the speech act participants at S(peech) T(ime), henceforth ST)

      b. *i-ta   eobaka   ta   ino   'e/si/ta   oko*
          UV.RLS-3s.GEN   beat:PV   OBL   banana   NOM   child
          'Mother has beaten the child.' (implied: The child and his mother are being seen by the speech act participants at ST)

If unidentifiable, because newly introduced in the discourse, for instance, the substitution of *'o* and *to* by *'e, si* or *ta* yields the ungrammaticality of the sentence in question.

(41) a. *pan   to   oko   ta   emoo*
          EXIST   OBL   child   OBL   house
          'There is a child in the house.'

      b. **pan   ta   oko   ta   emoo*
          EXIST   OBL   child   OBL   house

Both *no* and *na* refer to the scanning of a class of elements, e.g. in interrogative sentences, as in (42a–c), and carry a generic meaning, as in (42e). As a consequence, their substitution with other case markers is disallowed in many contexts.

(42) a. *cuma* ***na*** *i-si*   *ana* *ta* *oko?*
          what   NOM UV.RLS-3S.GEN   eat:PV OBL child
          'What has the child eaten?'
    b. **cuma* *'e/si/ta* *i-si*   *ana* *ta* *oko?*
          what   NOM   UV.RLS-3S.GEN eat:PV OBL child
    c. *mo*   *bonʉ* ***no*** *cuma* *ta* *oko?*
          AV.RLS AV:eat OBL what NOM child
          'What is the child eating?'
    d. **mo*   *bonʉ* ***ta/to*** *cuma* *ta* *oko?*
          AV.RLS AV:eat OBL   what NOM child
    e. *hoci* *moso* *o'te* *eaa* *uh* *ta*   *pepe* *ci*   *oko*
          if   AV.RLS NEG have go OBL heaven REL child
          uk'a   *ci*   *te*   *la*   *tamzi* ***no*** *nte*   *la* *hia*
          not.exist RLS UV.IRR HAB ask   OBL AV.IRR HAB
          yaezoi
          cultivate
          'If there was not the boy (who) went to the heaven, there would be no one to ask how to cultivate…' (Tung *et al.* 1964:362)

The foregoing discussion should not lead to the premature conclusion that nominative and oblique case markers always agree in referentiality and identifiability. In complex NPs (where the referent is treated as only one entity), it is true that there exists such an agreement between the two case-marked NPs.

(43) a. *mo* *enghova* *'e*   *psoevohngu* *ci*   *mcoo* ***ta***   *ino-'u*
        AV   blue   NOM beautiful   REL eyes OBL mother-1S.GEN
        'The beautiful eyes of my mother are blue.'
    b. **mo* *enghova* *'e*   *psoevohŋu* *ci*   *mcoo* ***to***   *ino-'u*
        AV   blue   NOM beautiful   REL eyes OBL mother-1S.GEN

NPs referring to two different entities/referents need not, however, be preceded by the same 'type' of case markers.

(44) a. *moso* *eobako* ***to*** *oko* *'o*   *ino*
         AV.RLS beat:AV OBL child NOM mother
         'Mother beat the child.' (Neither the child nor the mother are present at ST)
    b. *moso* *eobako* ***ta*** *oko* *'o*   *ino*
         AV.RLS beat:AV OBL child NOM mother
         'Mother beat the child.' (The child is present at ST; the mother is not)
    c. *moso* *eobako* ***to*** *oko* *'e*   *ino*
         AV.RLS beat:AV OBL child NOM mother
         'Mother beat the child.' (The mother is present at ST; not the child)
    d. *moso* *eobako* ***ta*** *oko* *'e*   *ino*
         AV.RLS beat:AV OBL child NOM mother
         'Mother beat the child.' (Both the mother and the child are present at ST)

3.3.3 Pronominal system

Personal pronouns divide into a set of free pronouns and a set of bound pronouns which appear in nominative and genitive functions (see Table 9.5).

Free pronouns are generally not marked for case distinctions. They are 'neutral', in that like full NPs, they may occur in topic (45a), subject (45b) or non-subject (45c) position. Free pronouns can optionally be preceded by *na* in topic or in subject position, but they cannot be marked with an oblique case marker when they occur in non-subject position. Third person singular pronominal forms are identical to the demonstratives.

(45) a. (*na*) ***a'o*** *zou* *lepemo'os'o*
          1s   be   doctor
      'I am a doctor.'

   b. *o-su*   *eobaka* (*na*) ***a'o***
       UV-2S.GEN   beat:PV   (NOM)   1s
       'You beat me.'

   c. *mo-su*   *eobako* ***a'o***
       AV-2S.NOM   beat:AV   1s
       'You beat me.'

The bound pronouns form phonological words with their hosts and cause stress to shift to the penultimate syllable of the complex word. It is a matter of ongoing research whether these forms should be analyzed as clitics or suffixes. In this chapter, they are tentatively treated as suffixes.

With the exception of the third person invisible forms, the same formatives may be used in two syntactically quite different functions, i.e. nominative and genitive, but always refer to the agent/actor of the sentence, cf. Starosta (1988). In nominative function, the bound pronouns appear immediately after actor voice auxiliary verbs, as in (46).

(46) *mo-'u*   *mavo*   *ta*   *pingi*
      AV.RLS-1S.NOM   AV:open   OBL   door
      'I opened the door.'

In genitive function, pronouns either attach to undergoer voice auxiliary verbs (47a) or to nouns to indicate a possessive relation (47b). This syntactic distinction is morphologically unmarked except for the third person, where *-ta* only occurs after auxiliaries while *-taini* exclusively marks adnominal possessors (48a–b).

TABLE 9.5: THE TSOU PRONOMINAL SYSTEM

Number	Person		Free	Bound	
			Neutral	Nominative	Genitive
Singular	1		a'o	-'o/-'u	
	2		suu	-su/-ko	
	3	+VIS	taini	-ta, -taini	
		−VIS	ic'o	—	-si
Plural	1	IN	a'ati	-to	
		EX	a'ami	-mza	
	2		muu	-mu	
	3	+VIS	hin'i	-hin'i	
		−VIS	hee	—	-he

(47)   a.   *oh-**ta**/*Ø*   *pavi*   *ta*   *pingi*   *'e*   *amo*
            UV.RLS-3S.GEN   open:LV   OBL   door   NOM   father
            'Father opened the door.'

       b.   *pan*   *to*   *oko-**'u***
            EXIST   OBL   child-1S.GEN
            'I have child(ren).'

(48)   a.   *oh-**ta**/*-**taini***   *pavi*   *ta*   *pingi*
            UV-3S.GEN   open:LV   NOM   door
            'He opened the door.'

       b.   *pan*   *to*   *oko-**taini**/*ta*
            EXIST   OBL   child-3S.GEN
            'He has child(ren).'

Note, finally, that the distribution of the first person suffixes *-'o* and *-'u* is phonologically conditioned: *'o* occurs after the vowel /i/ (as in *mi-'o*, cf. **mi-'u* AV.RLS-1S.NOM) and
'u after the remaining vowels (as in *mo-'u*, cf. **mo-'o* AV.RLS-1S.NOM). The distinction
between *-su* and *-ko* is mostly dialectal (*-su* is more commonly used by Tapangu speakers, and *-ko* by Tfuya speakers).

Possessive pronouns functioning as noun phrases (i.e. expressions corresponding to
English 'mine', 'yours' etc.) are derived from the genitive series by prefixing *nuu*, hence
nuu'u 'mine', *nuusu* 'yours'. They are unmarked for case and may occur, like (full)
nouns, in argument and adjunct positions (49a–b) as well as in predicative function (49c):

(49)   a.   ***nenu***   *na*   ***nuusu**,*   *nenu*   *na*   *nuu'u*
            which   NOM   yours   which   NOM   mine
            'Which is mine and which is yours?'

       b.   *mo*   *eon*   *ta*   *pangka*   *si*   ***nuusu***
            AV.RLS   be.at   OBL   table   NOM   yours
            'Yours is on the table.'

       c.   *mi-'o*   *mayo*   *to*   ***nuusu***
            AV.RLS-1S.NOM   AV:take   OBL   yours
            'I am taking yours.'

Tsou demonstratives are numerous. Szakos (1994:82–89) surveys the forms and
provides dozens of examples to illustrate their usage. I will therefore limit myself to the
following observations: first, demonstrative pronouns, like personal pronouns, are
unmarked for case. Second, there has to be agreement in referentiality/identifiability
between the case marker which precedes a noun and the demonstrative that follows it:

(50)   a.   ***'e**/*si/*ta/*/'o*   *oko*   *eni*
            NOM   child   PRX
            'this child'

       b.   ***si**/*'e/*ta/*'o*   *oko*   *sico*
            NOM   child   MED
            'that child' (visible, close by)

       c.   ***ta**/*'e/*si/*'o*   *oko*   *ta'e*
            NOM   child   DIST
            'that child there' (visible to speaker and addressee but, at a certain distance)

       d.   ***'o**/*'e/*si/* ta*   *oko*   *ic'o*
            NOM   child   DEM.INVIS
            'that child' (invisible to speaker and addressee)

3.4 The Tsou tense/aspect system

Auxiliary verbs play a major role in Tsou grammar because beside encoding voice variations, they also carry modal and temporal/aspectual information. Morphosyntactic constraints on the occurrence of one form or another were explained in section 3.2.1. In this section, we mainly look at how modal and temporal/aspectual distinctions are expressed.

The whole system (see Table 9.6 below) is based on a modal dichotomy, where the *realis* contrasts with the *irrealis*. In the realis, situations are viewed as having occurred or as actually taking place; in the irrealis, they are regarded as having not (yet) occurred, whether or not they may happen. Both in the realis and in the irrealis, events can be seen as 'immediate' as in (51a–b) or 'remote' (in time and/or space) as in (52a–b). These two notions must be understood as gradients and usually encode the speaker's perception of an event. However, they may also reflect contextual presuppositions, e.g. the event in question bears some/no relevance to what the speaker is talking about or what he may have experienced before; the situation may have just happened or it may have taken place some time ago, etc. They are moreover reflected on the morphological level: situations seen as immediate are expressed by an auxiliary verb ending with *-i* or *-e* (cf. *mi-*, *te-* etc.) while those viewed as remote are referred to by an auxiliary verb ending with *-o* (e.g. *moso*, *moh-*, *o(h)-*, *nto(h)-*).

(51)   a.   **mi**-*ta-cu*   *moyafo*
            AV.RLS-3s.GEN-already   AV:go out
            'He has already gone out.' (Not long ago)

       b.   **te**-*ta-cu*   *moyafo*
            AV.IRR-3s.GEN-already   AV:go out
            'He is going out/will go out.' (very soon)

(52)   a.   *upena*   *ne*   *moso*   *muchu*   *nehucma*,   **moh**-*ta*
            though   when   AV.RLS   AV:rain   yesterday   AV.RLS-3s.GEN
            c'o   *moyafo*
            only   AV:go out
            'Though it rained yesterday, he (still) went out.'

       b.   *upena*   *hoci*   *muchu*   *nehucma*,   **ntoh**-*ta*   *c'o*   *moyafo*
            though   if   AV:rain   yesterday   AV.IRR-3s.GEN   only   AV:go out
            'Even if it had rained yesterday, he would have (still) gone out.'

mi-, *mo*, *mio* and *i-* all refer to an event that bears some relevance to what the speaker is talking about but differ from one another in terms of the evidentiality.

TABLE 9.6: THE TEMPORAL/ASPECTUAL AND MODAL SYSTEM OF TSOU

	Immediate		Remote
Realis AV	mi-	mio, mo	mo(h)- moso
Realis UV	i-		o(h)-
Irrealis AV/UV			
Habitual			la
Predictive	te	tena, ta	
Hypothetical	nte		
Counterfactual			nto(h)- ntoso

The contrast between *mi-* and *mo* lies in the direct/indirect grasp of an event. By using the former (53a), the speaker asserts that he has/is witnessed/witnessing the situation he is talking about. With the latter (53b), he indicates that the situation in question is taking place away from him, i.e. that he is not a direct witness of its occurrence but knows of its happening.

(53) a. **mi**-*ta*   *mimo*   *ta*   *emi*
          AV.RLS-3S.NOM   AV.drink   OBL   wine
          'He is drinking wine.' (The speaker can see him drinking.)

      b. **mo**   *mongsi*   *co*   *oko*
          AV.RLS   AV.cry   NOM   child
          'A child is crying.' (The speaker can hear a child cry but cannot see him.)

As already mentioned above, *mo(h)*-, *moso* and *o(h)*- indicate a rupture, i.e. they refer to an event that has no direct discursive relevance.

(54) **moh**-*ta*   *mosi*   *ta*   *pangka*   *ta*   *emi*
      AV.RLS-3S.NOM   AV.put   OBL   table   OBL   wine
      'He put wine on the table.'

As a consequence, while *mi-* and *mo* (the same is true of *i-* and *mio*) are incompatible with temporal adjuncts (e.g. *nehucma* 'yesterday') or aspectual clitics (e.g. *la* 'used to') indicating a certain remotness in time, *mo(h)*- and *moso* (as well as *o(h)*-) can occur with such constituents.

(55) a. **mo-'u/moso**   *bonu*   *to*   *taсиmи*   *nehucma*
          AV-1S.NOM/AV.RLS   eat   OBL   banana   yesterday
          'I ate a banana yesterday.'

      c. **mo-'u/moso**   *la*   *bonu*   *to*   *taсиmи*
          AV-1S.NOM/AV.RLS   EXP   eat   OBL   banana
          'I (have the experience of having) eaten banana(s) (in the past).'

The voice alternation in the realis correlates with an aspectual distinction. In AV constructions, the speaker focuses on the activity carried out by the agent/actor; the situation must be interpreted as imperfective (or more specifically, as progressive) and the patient is regarded as only partially affected. In UV constructions, on the other hand, the speaker focuses on the result of that activity. Whether the situation is understood as completed or not, the patient is viewed as more (if not totally) affected.

(56) a. *mi-ta*   *etamaku*
          AV.RLS-3S.NOM   smoke:AV
          'He is smoking.'

      b. *i-ta*   *etamakua*
          UV.RLS-3S.GEN   smoke:PV
          'He has (just) smoked.'

This imperfective/perfective dichotomy is not found in the irrealis:

(57) a. *te-ta*   *etamaku*
          AV.IRR-3S.NOM   smoke:AV
          'He will smoke.'

      b. *te-ta*   *etamakua*
          UV.IRR-3S.GEN   smoke:PV
          'He will smoke.'

The irrealis auxiliary verbs *te, tena, ta, nte, nto(h)-, ntoso* convey a range of (epistemic and deontic) modal meanings. Among other things, they can occur in imperative (affirmative and negative) sentences.

(58) a. **te-to-n'a**   *mimo*
          AV.IRR-1p.NOM-again   AV:drink
          'Let's have (another) drink!'

      b. **te-av'a**   *ima*   *'e*   *emi*
          UV.IRR-NEG   drink:PV   NOM   wine
          'Don't drink the wine!'

The distinction between *te, ta* and *tena* is imperfectly understood.

(59) a. **te-'o-n'a**   *etamaku*
          AV.IRR-1s.NOM-again   smoke:AV
          'I am going to smoke again (at once).'

      b. **ta-'o-n'a**   *etamaku*
          AV.IRR-1s.NOM-again   smoke:AV
          'I will smoke again (in a moment).'

The contrast between *te* and *nte* lies in the degree of certainty with which the event will occur. With *te*, the situation is understood as likely to happen; with *nte*, on the other hand, the speaker is unable to determine whether the situation in question will effectively take place.

(60) a. **te-ta**   *mosi*   *ta*   *pangka*   *ta*   *emi*
          AV.IRR-3s.NOM   AV:put   OBL   table   OBL   wine
          'He is going to/will put the wine on the table.'

      b. **nte-ta**   *mosi*   *ta*   *pangka*   *ta*   *emi*
          AV.IRR-3s.NOM   AV:put   OBL   table   OBL   wine
          'He may put the wine on the table.'

nte and *nto* (or *ntoso*) refer, respectively, to an event which may occur (hypothetical reading) or was to happen in the past but did not take place (counterfactual reading). Compare (61a–b).

(61) a. *honci-'u*   *eaa*   *peisu,*   **nte-'o**   *mihia*   *emoo*
          if-1s.NOM   have   money   AV.IRR-1s.NOM   AV:buy   house
          'If I have money, I will buy a house.'

      b. *honci-'u*   *eaa*   *peisu,*   **nto-'u**   *mihia*   *emoo*
          if-1s.NOM   have   money   AV.IRR-1s.NOM   AV:buy   house
          'If I had had money, I would have bought a house.'

The habitual aspect is indicated by *la*.

(62) **la-ta**   *huhucmasi*   *etamaku*
      AV.HAB-3s.NOM   every day:AV   smoke:AV
      'He smokes every day.'

la occurs in initial position as in (63) only when it refers to an 'habitual present'. It can also co-occur with the other auxiliaries discussed in this section but must, in that case, be positioned after the auxiliary verb.

(63) a. *moh-ta*   **la**   *huhucmasi*   *etamaku*
          AV.RLS-3s.NOM   HAB   everyday:AV   smoke:AV
          'He used to smoke everyday.'

b. *tena*   ***la**-ta*   *huhucmasi*   *etamaku*
   AV.IRR   HAB-3S.NOM   everyday:AV   smoke:AV
   'He will (get in the habit of) smoking everyday.'

When occurring in second position, *la* 'HAB' might easily be confused with its homonym *la* 'EXP', which indicates that an event has been experienced/happened in the past. These two *la*s exhibit quite different distributional positions and thus different semantic functions (cf. Szakos 1994 for divergent views on their semantic functions), as the following examples illustrate:

(64) a. *o'a*   *moh-ta*   ***la***   *s'a*   *bonʉ*   *to*   *tacʉtʉ*
         NEG   AV.RLS-3S.NOM   HAB   EVD   AV:eat   OBL   banana
         '(In the past), he would not eat bananas.'
      b. *o'a*   *moh-ta*   *s'a*   ***la***   *bonʉ*   *to*
         NEG   AV.RLS-3S.NOM   EVD   EXP   AV:eat   OBL
         tacʉtʉ
         banana
         'He (has) never (eaten) bananas.'

(65) a. *moh-ta*   ***la***-n'a   *tmopsʉ,*   *mo-ʉ-cu*
         AV.RLS-3S.NOM   HAB-still   AV:read   AV.RLS-1S.NOM-already
         la   *eohioa*
         EXP   work
         '(At the time) when he was attending school, I was already working.'
      b. *moh-ta*-n'a   ***la***   *tmopsʉ,*   *mo-'ʉ-cu*
         AV.RLS-3S.NOM-still   EXP   AV:read   AV.RLS-1S.NOM-already
         la   *eʉteʉtʉ*
         EXP   enter: AV
         'I entered (the room) while he was still reading.'

3.5 Question words

There are three main types of questions in Tsou: yes–no questions, alternative questions and information (or so-called *wh-*) questions. While the first two have not received a lot of attention (see Chuo 1998 and Zeitoun 2000a), the latter have been well-examined during the past recent years (see Chang 1998, 2000, and Huang *et al.* 1999). Yes–no questions differ from their declarative counterparts only in that the intonation rises at the end of the sentence.

An alternative question can be asked about an event (e.g. 'Will you eat first or rather go to sleep right now?') or a person (e.g. 'Is it Mary or John who beat the child?'). Although the same expression (*honte no/na o'te* 'or OBL NEG') appears in both clause types, the first is verbal, and the second equational. If an alternative question is asked concerning the realization of an event, the sentence must be treated as verbal; the part of the sentence being interpreted as the alternative choice (its negated questioned form) functions as an oblique argument of the first (lexical) verb and is introduced by *no* 'OBL'.

(66) a. *te-ko*   *bonʉ*   ***honte***   ***no***   *o'te*   *oengʉtʉ?*
         AV.IRR-2S.NOM   AV:eat   or   OBL   NEG.AV.IRR   sleep:AV
         'Will you eat or sleep?'
      b. *la-ko*   *kaebʉ*   *bonʉ*   *to*   *yoskʉ*   ***honte***   ***no***
         AV.HAB-2S.NOM   like:AV   AV:eat   OBL   fish   or   OBL

    o'te   *(bonɨ to)*   *fou?*
    NEG.AV.IRR   (AV:eat OBL)   meat
    'Do you like eating fish or meat?'

If an alternative question is asked concerning a participant, the sentence must be treated as equational. Here, the part of the sentence expressing the choice functions as predicate and the remainder is put into a nominal clause introduced by *na* 'NOM', and becomes the subject of the sentence.

(67) a. *zou   yangui **honte** o'te*   *mo'o   **na**   te   uh*
        be   Yangui or   NEG.AV.IRR Mo'o NOM AV.IRR go
        ne   taihoku?
        OBL   Taipei
        'Is it Yangui or Mo who will go to Taipei?'
    b. *zou   yangui **honte** o'te*   *mo'o   **na**   mo   eobako*
        be   Yangui or   NEG.AV.IRR Mo'o NOM AV.RLS beat:AV
        ta   pasuya?
        OBL   Pasuya
        'Is it Yangui or Mo'o who beat Pasuya?'

Huang *et al.* (1999) show that so-called *wh*-words may function as nominals, verbals or adverbials. Two main criteria allow such a distinction: (i) their sentential position either in predicate or argument position and (ii) their co-occurring in an equational or verbal sentence (see Chang 1998 for a detailed study of *wh*- words in Tsou in a generative perspective).

Nominal question words (*sia* 'who', 'whom', *cuma* 'what', *nenu* 'which') may occur sentence-initially as predicates of an equational sentence, or remain *in situ*, preceded by the case markers *na* or *no*. *sia* is the only question word to be semantically affected by this distributional variation but it remains to be explained why it carries out a different meaning:

(68) a. *zou **sia** na   suu?*
        be   who NOM 2s
        'Who are you?'
    b. *zou oko   no   **sia** 'o   i-ko   ɨmnɨa*
        be   child OBL who NOM UV.RLS-2S.GEN like:PV
        'Whose child do you like?'

Verbal question words (*mainenu* 'how', *pio* 'how many', *mainci* 'why', 'how') are verbs and thus are usually positioned after the auxiliary verb (and other preverbal constituents).

(69) *te-mza   **mainci** cohivi   'e   conɨ eni*
     UV.1p.GEN UV:how know:LV NOM road this
     'How could we know the road.' (Adapted from Szakos 1994:186)

Adverbial question words (e.g. *nenu* 'where', *nehomna* 'when:RLS', *hohomna* 'when:IRR') occur in sentence-final position, like other temporal adjuncts (e.g. *maitan'e* 'today', *nehucma* 'yesterday') and are never preceded by a case marker.

(70) a. *moh-ta   la   uh ne   taipahu **nehomna?***
        AV.RLS-3S.NOM EXP go OBL Taipei when:RLS
        'When did you go to Taipei?'
    b. *te-ta   uh ne   taipahu **hohomna?***
        AV.IRR-3S.NOM go OBL Taipei IRR:when
        'When are you going to Taipei?'

4 MAJOR VERBAL ALTERNATIONS

Tsou verbs are typically marked for voice. The three undergoer voices are marked by suffixes, i.e. patient voice *-a*, locative voice *-i*, and instrumental/benefactive voice *-(n)eni*. These suffixes do not reflect the indicative neutral voice affixes found in other Formosan languages (PV *-un*, LV *-an* and IV/BV *si-*) but rather the non-indicative atemporal ones (Starosta *et al.* 1982 and Ross 1995).

The semantic relations between the subject and the UV marked verb are the ones found in a wide range of western Austronesian languages, i.e. patients in PV, locations, recipients, goals and sources in LV, and instruments (inanimate arguments) or beneficiaries (animate arguments) in IV/BV. These relations are illustrated in the following example sets in which the first example is in AV while the other examples illustrate two or more UV derivations from the same root.

(71) a. *mo* **t-m-eaphʉ** *to oko ta skayʉ si ino*
  AV.RLS put-AV OBL child OBL cradle NOM mother
  'Mother put the child into a cradle.'

  b. *i-si* **teaph-a** *ta skayʉ to ino*
  UV.RLS-3s.GEN put-PV OBL cradle OBL mother
  to oko
  NOM child
  'Mother put the child into a cradle.'

  c. *i-si* **teaph-i** *to oko ta ino*
  UV.RLS-3s.GEN put-LV OBL child OBL mother
  ta skayʉ
  NOM cradle
  'Mother put the child into the cradle.'

  d. *i-si* **teaph-neni** *to тасʉmʉ to ino*
  AV.RLS-3s.GEN put-BV OBL banana OBL mother
  'e oko
  NOM child
  'Mother put bananas (in a cradle) for the child.'

(72) a. *mo* **c-m-ofu** *to yoskʉ 'o mameoi*
  AV.RLS wrap-AV OBL fish NOM old.man
  'The old man wrapped a fish.'

  b. *i-si* **cfu-a** *ta mameoi 'o yoskʉ*
  UV.RLS-3s.GEN wrap-PV OBL old.man NOM fish
  'The old man wrapped the fish.'

  c. *i-si* **cfu-neni** *to yoskʉ 'o hungʉ to*
  UV.RLS-3s.GEN wrap-IV OBL fish NOM leaf OBL
  mameoi
  old man
  'The old man used leaves to wrap the fish.'

(73) a. *mo* **b-aito** *ta yangui 'e mo'o*
  AV.RLS AV-see OBL Yangui NOM Mo'o
  'Mo'o is looking at Yangui.'

  b. *i-si* **ait-i** *ta mo'o 'e yangui*
  UV.RLS-3s.GEN see-LV OBL Mo'o NOM Yangui
  'Mo'o has been looking at Yangui.'

c. *i-si*   ***ait-neni***   *no*   *yusʉ*   *ta*   *ino*   *'o*
   UVRLS-3S.GEN   see-BV   OBL   clothes   OBL   mother   NOM
   oko
   child
   'Mother helps the child look at the clothes.' (implied: to see whether they fit well)

Actor voice marking is formally somewhat more complex, mostly involving a prefix or an infix. Tsou verbs fall into five major classes (indicated by I, II etc.) with regard to actor voice marking, as illustrated in Table 9.7. The prefix or infix indicated in the second column refers to the main AV affixes, which may alternate with up to three allomorphs. Thus, the verb class I *-m-* is infixed to a stem beginning with *c*, *s* or *t*, as in *c-m-uhu* 'roast' but is realized as *b-* when infixed to a stem beginning with a glottal stop, as in *baito* 'see', and occurs as *m-* when infixed to a stem beginning with a vowel, as in *m-imo* 'drink'. Verb class *mo-* (e.g. *mo-si* 'put') has two allomorphs, *mʉ-* as in *mʉ'ʉho* 'hit the mark', *mu* as in *mu-fun* 'spurt water out of the mouth'. Both verbs marked as class I and II affixes occur as zero-marked in UV constructions. Compare for instance *mo-si* 'put (AV)' vs. *si-a* 'put (PV)'. Verb classes III-1 and III-2 have *m-* and *m-* . . . *m* as AV affixes, as in *masaho* 'take in the arms (AV)' and *mamteezoyʉ* 'stab fish (AV)'. These two affixes alternate respectively with *p-* and *p...p* in UV constructions, cf. the PV forms *pasha-a* 'take in the arms (PV)'and *papteezoy-a* 'stab fish (PV)'. Verbs belonging to class IV are unmarked in AV constructions, e.g. *etamaku* 'smoke (AV)' vs. *etamaku-a* 'smoke (PV)'. Verb classes V-1 and V-2 take the AV prefix *m-* which alternates with *t-* and *r-/e-* in UV constructions: *m-ongsi* 'cry (AV)' vs. *t-ngs-i* 'cry (LV)', *mainca* 'say (AV)' vs. *eainca-a* 'say (PV)'. Further details on these classes are given in Tsuchida (1976).

As mentioned above in section 3.2.1, auxiliary verbs determine the orientation of the voice in each clause (AV or UV). Except for the causative construction (see discussion below), main verbs must agree in basic voice orientation (AV or UV) with the auxiliary verb (74a–b). However, two verbs marked for different undergoer voices (e.g. PV and LV) can occur within the same clause (75a–b).

(74)   a.   *mo*   ***baito/*aiti***   *ta*   *yangui*   *'e*   *mo'o*
            AV.RLS   AV:see/*see:LV   OBL   Yangui   NOM   Mo'o
            'Mo'o is looking at Yangui.'
       b.   *i-si*   ***ait-i/*baito***   *ta*   *mo'o*   *'e*   *yangui*
            UV.RLS-3S.GEN   see-LV/*AV:see   OBL   Mo'o   NOM   Yangui
            'Mo'o has been looking at Yangui.'

TABLE 9.7: MORPHOLOGICAL ALTERNATIONS OF TSOU VERBS (AFTER TSUCHIDA 1976:101)

Verb class	Actor voice	*Stem*	Undergoer voice		
			Patient voice	Locative voice	Instrumental/ benefactive voice
I	-m-	Ø			
II	mo-				
III-1	m-	p-			
III-2	m...m	p...p	-a	-i	-(n)eni
IV	Ø	Ø			
V-1	m-	t-			
V-2		r-/e-			

(75) a. *i-si*   **mimh-a**   **fi-i**   *to*   *av'u*   *'o*   *oko*
          UV.RLS-3s.GEN   willing-PV   give-LV   OBL   dog   NOM   child
          to   *ak'i*
          OBL   grandfather
          'Grandfather is willing to give the child a dog.'

      b. *i-si*   **mimh-a**   **fa-eni**   *to*   *oko*   *'o*   *av'u*
          UV.RLS-3s.GEN   willing-PV   give-BV   OBL   child   NOM   dog
          to   *ak'i*
          OBL   grandfather
          'Grandfather is willing to give the dog to the child.'

Because of the major role played by auxiliary verbs, Tsou main verbs do not exhibit the large array of morphological distinctions found in many other Formosan languages:

(i)   They do not encode temporal/aspectual distinctions (see section 3.4).
(ii) They are not marked differently in the imperative (compare: *te eobako ta oko* (AV.IRR beat:AV OBL child) 'Beat the child!' vs. *te-ta eobako ta oko* (AV.IRR-3s.NOM beat:AV OBL child) 'He will beat the child').
(iii) They do not distinguish between dynamic and stative verbs. In other Formosan languages, this distinction manifests itself on the morphological level through the use of a different affix in their finite/non-finite forms (e.g. Paiwan *-em-*/zero for dynamic AV verbs vs. *ma-/ka-* for stative verbs) and the use of a different reciprocal form (e.g. Paiwan *ma-* for dynamic verbs vs. *mare-* for stative verbs), cf. Zeitoun (2000c), Zeitoun and Huang (2000) and Huang (2000). As shown in the following two pairs of examples, the verbs 'beat' and 'love' do not undergo any morphological alternations in the reciprocal construction, marked by *yupa*. Note also that in the reciprocal constructions in (77) the auxiliary and the main verb may occur in either actor or undergoer voice.

(76) a. *mi-ta*   **eobako**   *ta*   *pasuya*
          AV.RLS-3s.NOM   beat:AV   OBL   Pasuya
          'He beats Pasuya.'

      b. *mi-ta*   **kaebʉ**   *ta*   *pasuya*
          AV.RLS-3s.NOM   like:AV   OBL   Pasuya
          'He likes Pasuya.'

(77) a. *mi-hin'i*   **yupa**   *eobako*
          AV-3p.NOM   RCP   beat:AV
          'They beat each other.'

      b. *i-hin'i*   **yupa**   *kaebʉ*
          UV-3p.GEN   RCP   love:PV
          'They love/hate each other.'

Tsou has preserved, nonetheless, the causative prefix *poa-*, which has *p-* and *pa-* as allomorphs (see Starosta 1974). There seems to be no distinction whatsoever between *poabonʉ* and *pabonʉ*. The difference that lies between *poa-* and the formative *p'-*, on the other hand, is still ill-understood in terms both of syntactic structure and semantic interpretation. Compare, for instance, *i-ta poabonʉ si oko.* 'He fed the child' vs. *mi-ta p'onʉ to fou ta moahioya* 'He made/invited the workers (to) eat meat'. The causative formatives may be attached to verbs marked as AV or UV. In AV, the causer appears in the nominative (78a), in PV the causee (78b). If the theme is to appear in nominative function, then IV is chosen (78c).

(78) a. *te-ko-n'a*   ***poa-mofi***   *to*   *mameoi*   *to*   *paisu*
          UV.IRR-2S.GEN-still CAU-AV:give   OBL   old.man   OBL   money
          'o   *amo-su*
          NOM   father-your
          '(You) tell your father to give the money to the old man.'

      b. *i-si*   ***poa-mofi-a***   *to*   *mameoi*   *to*   *paisu*
          UV.RLS-3S.GEN   CAU-give-PV   OBL   old.man   OBL   money
          'o   *oko-su*
          NOM   child-your
          'The old man told your child to give (him) the money.'

      c. *te-ko-n'a*   ***poa-fae-neni***   *to*   *amo-su*   *to*
          UV.IRR-2S.GEN-still CAU-give-IV   OBL   father-your   OBL
          mameoi   *'o*   *paisu*
          old.man   NOM   money
          '(You) tell your father to give the money to the old man!'

In addition to the simple causative construction which only involves a single main verb
marked with the causative prefix, there is also a more complex construction involving the
formally non-causative verb *ahʉya* 'force' in PV and another verb morphologically
marked as causative. This second verb may occur in either AV or UV, which in the first
instance (illustrated in 79a) leads to a mismatch between the voice affixes that occur on
the auxiliary verb (UV) and the verb marked as causative (*pa-bonʉ* AV), a mismatch
otherwise not attested in Tsou:

(79) a. *i-si*   *'ahʉya*   ***pa-bonʉ***   *'o*   *oko*   *to*   *ino*
          UV-3S.GEN   force:PV   CAU-eat:AV   NOM   child   OBL   mother
          'The mother forced the child to eat.'

      b. *i-si*   *'ahʉya*   ***pa-ananeni***   *to*   *oko*   *to*   *ino*
          UV-3S.GEN   force:PV   CAU-eat:IV   OBL   child   OBL   mother
          'o   *tacʉmʉ*
          NOM   banana
          'The mother forced the child to eat the banana.'

ACKNOWLEDGEMENTS

Sections of this chapter were read at the monthly meeting of the Institute of Linguistics
(Preparatory Office), Academia Sinica, March 13, 2000. I would like to thank all the
participants for their comments, in particular Paul Li, Jackson Sun and Tien-hsin Hsin.
I would also like to express my deepest appreciation to my Tsou informants, Ming-hui
Wang, Zheng-zhong Zheng and Shan-shen Wu for their help with the Tsou data, and thier
friendship over the years. Last but not least, I wish to thank the editors of the present volume (and most especially Nikolaus Himmelmann) for their editing work – which they
might have felt tedious and discouraging, but which helped shape this chapter into a more
readable form through very constructive suggestions.

REFERENCES

Blust, R. (1999) 'Subgrouping, circularity and extinction: some issues in Austronesian
    comparative linguistics', in E. Zeitoun and P. Li (eds) *Selected Papers from the Eighth*

International Conference on Austronesian Linguistics, 31–94, Symposium Series of the Institute of Linguistics (Preparatory Office) No.1, Taipei: Academia Sinica.

Chang, M.Y. (1998) *Wh-constructions and the problem of wh-movement in Tsou*. MA Thesis, Hsinchu, Taiwan: National Tsing-hua University.

——(2000) 'On Tsou *Wh*-Questions: movement or in situ?', *Language and Linguistics* 1.2: 1–18.

Chuo, F.P. (1998) 'A comparative study of interrogatives in Tsou and Yami', *Fu Jen Studies* 31:1–18.

Ferrell, R. (1969) *Taiwan Aboriginal Groups: Problems in Cultural and Linguistic Classification*, Academia Sinica Monograph No. 17, Taipei: Institute of Ethnology.

Fuller, M. (1990) 'Pulmonic ingressive fricatives in Tsou', *Journal of the International Phonetic Association* 20.2:9–14.

Givón, Talmy (1978) 'Definiteness and referentiality', in C. Ferguson and E. Moravcsik (eds) *Universals of Human Language*, vol. 4: *Syntax*, 291–330. Stanford: Stanford University Press.

Ho, D. (1976) 'Tsou phonology', *Bulletin of the Institute of History and Philology* 47.2: 245–274 [in Chinese].

—— (1983) 'The position of Rukai in the Formosan languages', *Bulletin of the Institute of History and Philology*, 47.2:243–274 [in Chinese].

Hsin, T. (2000) 'Consonant clusters in Tsou and their theoretical implications', *Proceedings of the Eighteenth West Coast Conference on Formal Linguistics*, 206–217.

Huang, L. (1995) *A study of Mayrinax Syntax*, Taipei: Crane.

——(2000) 'Verb classification in Atayal', *Oceanic Linguistics*, 39.2:364–390.

Huang, L., E. Zeitoun, M. Yeh, J. Wu and H. Chang (1998) 'A typological overview of nominal case marking of the Formosan languages', *Proceedings of the Second International Symposium on Languages in Taiwan*, 21–48, Taipei: Crane.

Huang, L.M., E. Zeitoun, M.M. Yeh, A.H. Chang and J.J. Wu (1999) 'Interrogative constructions in some Formosan languages', in Yin Yuen-mei, Yang I-li, Chan Hui-chen (eds) *Chinese Languages and Linguistics*, V: *Interactions in Language*, 639–680, Symposium Series No. 2. Taipei: Institute of Linguistics (Preparatory Office), Academia Sinica.

Ladefoged, P. and E. Zeitoun (1993) 'Pulmonic ingressive phones do not occur in Tsou', *Journal of the International Phonetic Association* 23.1:13–15.

Li, Hen-li (1955) 'On the quasi indirect passive voice in the Tsou grammar in Ali mountain', *Journal of Chinese Ethnography* 1:207–216.

Li, P. (1977) 'Morphophonemic alternations in Formosan languages', *Bulletin of the Institute of History and Philology* 48.3:375–413.

—— (1979) 'Variations in the Tsou dialects', *Bulletin of the Institute of History and Philology* 50.2:273–297.

—— (1990) 'Classification of Formosan languages: Lexical evidence', *Bulletin of the Institute of History and Philology* 61.2:811–837.

Li-May Sung (1999) 'Negation in Tsou.' Paper presented at the Sixth Annual Meeting of the Austronesian Formal Linguistics Association (AFLA-6), April 16–18, Toronto, Canada.

Nevskij, N.A. (1935) *Materialy po Govoram Jazyka Cou*, Moscow: Trudy Instituta Vostokovedenija.

Ogawa, N. and E. Asai (1935) *The Myths and Traditions of the Formosan Native Tribes*, Taipei: Taipei Imperial University.

Ross, M. (1995) 'Reconstructing Proto-Austronesian verbal morphology: evidence from Taiwan', in P. Li, C. Tsang, Y. Huang, D. Ho and C. Tseng (eds) *Austronesian Studies Relating to Taiwan*, Symposium Series of the Institute of History and Philology No. 3: 727–791, Taipei: Academia Sinica.

Stanley, P. (1979) 'Morphophonemics of verb suffixes in Tsou', in Nguyen Dan Liem (ed.) *Southeast Asian Linguistic Studies* 3:187–198, Canberra: Pacific Linguistics.

Starosta, S. (1974) 'Causative verbs in Formosan languages', *Oceanic Linguistics* 12: 279–369.

—— (1985) 'Verbal inflection versus deverbal nominalization in PAn: the evidence from Tsou', in A. Pawley and L. Carrington (eds) *Austronesian Linguistics at the 15th Pacific Science Congress*, 282–312, Canberra: Pacific Linguistics.

—— (1988) 'A grammatical typology of Formosan languages', *Bulletin of the Institute of History and Philology* 59.2:541–576.

—— (1995) 'A grammatical subgrouping of Formosan languages', in P. Li, C. Tsang, Y. Huang, D. Ho and C. Tseng (eds) *Austronesian Studies Relating to Taiwan*, Symposium Series of the Institute of History and Philology No. 3: 683–726, Taipei: Academia Sinica.

—— (1997) 'Formosan clause structure: Transitivity, ergativity, and case marking', in Tseng Chiu-yu (ed.) *Chinese Languages and Linguistics: Typological Studies of Languages in China, Symposium Series of the Institute of History and Philology*, 4: 125–154, Taipei: Academia Sinica.

Starosta, S., A. Pawley and L. Reid (1982) 'The evolution of focus in Austronesian', in A. Halim, L. Carrington and S. Wurm (eds) *Papers from the Third International Conference on Austronesian Linguistics, vol. 2: Tracking the travellers*, 145–170, Canberra: Pacific Linguistics.

Szakos, J. (1994) *Die Sprache der Cou: Untersuchungen zur Synchronie einer austronesischen Sprache auf Taiwan*, PhD Dissertation, Bonn: Rheinische Friedrich-Wilhelms-Universität.

Tsuchida, S. (1972) 'The origins of the Tsou phonemes /b/ and /d/', *Gengo Kenkyu* 46: 42–52.

—— (1976) *Reconstruction of Proto-Tsouic Phonology*, Study of Languages and Cultures of Asia and Africa, Monograph Series No. 5, Tokyo: Institute for the Study of Languages and Cultures of Asia and Africa.

—— (1990) 'Classificatory study of Tsou verbs', *Tokyo University Linguistics Papers* 89: 17–52.

—— (1995) 'Tsou', in Darrell T. Tryon (ed.) *Comparative Austronesian Dictionary: An Introduction to Austronesian Studies*, 293–296. Berlin: Mouton de Gruyter.

Tung, T., S. Wang, T. Kuan, T. Cheng and M. Yan (1964) *A Descriptive Study of the Tsou Language, Formosa*, Institute of History and Philology, Academia Sinica, Special Publications No. 48, Taipei: Academia Sinica.

Wei, H., C. Yu and H. Li (1952) *Ethnography of the Ethnic Group Tsou*, Taipei: Commission of Historical Research of Taiwan.

Wright, R. (1996) *Consonant Clusters and Cue Preservation in Tsou*. PhD dissertation, Los Angeles: UCLA.

—— (1999) 'Tsou consonant clusters and cue preservation', in Elizabeth Zeitoun and Paul Jen-kuei Li (eds) *Selected Papers from the Eighth International Conference on Austronesian Linguistics*, 277–312, Symposium Series of the Institute of Linguistics (Preparatory Office), Academia Sinica No. 1, Taipei: Academia Sinica.

Wright, R. and P. Ladefoged (1997) 'A phonetic study of Tsou', *Bulletin of the Institute of History and Philology* 68.4:987–1028.

Wurm, S. and S. Hattori (eds) (1983) *Language Atlas of the Pacific Area*, part II: Japan area, Taiwan (Formosa), Philippines, mainland and insular south-east Asia, Canberra: Pacific Linguistics.

Yeh, M. (1991) *Saisiyat Structure*, MA Thesis, Hsinchu, Taiwan: National Tsing-hua University.

Zeitoun, E. (1992) *A Syntactic and Semantic Study of Tsou Focus System*, MA Thesis, Hsinchu, Taiwan: Tsing-hua University.

—— (1993) 'A semantic study of Tsou case markers', *Bulletin of the Institute of History and Philology* 64.4:969–989.

Zeitoun, E. (1996) 'The Tsou temporal, aspectual and modal system revisited', *Bulletin of the Institute of History and Philology* 68.1:503–532.

—— (2000a) *A Reference Grammar of Tsou*, Taipei: Yuan-liu [In Chinese].

—— (2000b) 'Notes on a possessive construction in the Formosan languages', in Videa DeGuzman and Byron Bender (eds) *Grammatical Analysis: Morphology, Syntax and Semantics*, 241–257, Honolulu: Oceanic Linguistics Special Publications 29.

—— (2000c) 'Dynamic vs. stative verbs in Mantauran (Rukai)', *Oceanic Linguistics* 39.2:415–427.

Zeitoun, E. and L. Huang (1997) 'Toward a typology of tense, aspect and modality in the Formosan languages: a preliminary study' in Chiu-yu Tseng (ed.) *Chinese Languages and Linguistics, 4: Typological studies of languages in China*, 595–618, Symposium Series of the Institute of History and Philology, Taipei: Academia Sinica.

—— (2000) 'Concerning *ka-*, an overlooked marker of verbal derivation in Formosan languages', *Oceanic Linguistics* 39.2:391–414.

Zeitoun, E., L. Huang, M. Yeh and A. Chang (1999) 'Existential, possessive and locative constructions in the Formosan languages', *Oceanic Linguistics* 38.1:1–42.

Zeitoun, E., L. Huang, M. Yeh, J. Wu and A. Chang (1996) 'The temporal/aspectual and modal systems of the Formosan languages: a typological perspective', *Oceanic Linguistics* 35.1:21–56.

CHAPTER TEN

SEEDIQ

Naomi Tsukida

1 INTRODUCTION

Seediq is a Formosan language spoken in the northeastern part of Taiwan (see Wurm and Hattori 1983: Map 30). Together with neighboring Atayal it forms the Atayalic group. Anthropologists usually regard Seediq as a subgroup of Atayal.

The Seediq population is about 25,000. Most of the speakers can speak Chinese, because Chinese has been the language of school education and mass media for nearly 50 years. Those who are younger than twenty usually cannot speak Seediq. Old people can speak Japanese because they were educated under the Japanese occupation (1895–1945).

Seediq consists of three dialects: Teruku (or Truku), Te'uda (or Tuuda), and Tekedaya (or Tkdaya, Paran). The Teruku community (living predominantly in Hualian prefecture) has about 20,000 members. The Te'uda and Tekedaya communities (living mainly in Nantou prefecture) have about 2500 members each. However, none of these dialect communities is entirely Seediq-speaking. The three dialects differ mainly in phonology and lexicon although there also seem to be slight differences in grammar. This description is based on the Teruku dialect.

There are no names for the language group as a whole. The Teruku speakers call themselves by dialect names. The neighboring Amis call them Taroko. Scholars have called the language Seediq, Sediq, Sedeq, Seedakka, or Sedik, a word originating from the word meaning human in the Tekedaya dialect: *seediq*. It is *se'diq* in the Teruku dialect.

The major sources for Seediq are as follows. Ogawa and Asai (1935) is a large collection of texts from 12 Formosan languages, including Seediq, and provides a brief sketch of each language. Asai (1953) is a descriptive grammar with texts based on the Tekedaya dialect. Unfortunately it does not distinguish between *k* and *q* or *x* and *h*, and the description of the syntax is rather weak. Yang (1976), Holmer (1996), and Zhang (1997, 2000) are also based on the Tekedaya (=Paran) dialect. Yang (1976) and Li (1991) deal with phonology. The vowel deletion process dealt with in Li (1991) does not take place in the Teruku dialect. Holmer (1996) is an attempt at analysing Seediq grammar within the Principles and Parameters framework. Zhang (1997) also employs the Principles and Parameters theory. He deals mainly with voice phenomena in two Formosan languages: Seediq and Kavalan. Zhang (2000) is a descriptive grammar of Tekedaya. Tsukida (1999, 2000) are based on Teruku and are a thorough examination of the locative, existential and possessive clauses and the use of goal voice forms, respectively. Pecoraro (1977) is the only Seediq dictionary so far, but it is mimeographed. It is based on the Teruku dialect. Unfortunately, it does not consistently mark major phonological distinctions such as the distinction between /h/ and /x/.

2 PHONOLOGY

2.1 Phoneme inventory, syllable structure and stress

Table 10.1 displays the 19 consonant phonemes that can be set up for Seediq, using the practical orthography employed throughout this chapter. $<l>$ stands for a voiced lateral fricative, $<ng>$ stands for a velar nasal, $<'>$ for a glottal stop, and $<g>$ for a velar fricative. The other symbols have their standard IPA values. The consonants /t/, /d/, and /s/ are palatalized when followed by /i/ or /y/. The affricate /c/ appears only in interjections (see 3.1), gerunds and loanwords.

The vowel phonemes are given in Table 10.2. The letter $<e>$ stands for a schwa. Three vowel-glide sequences are observed: *ay*, *aw* and *uy*.

Seediq syllable structure is C, CV, or CVC. *m* and *n* are syllabic in word-initial position before homorganic stops. As such they are found only in words of more than two syllables. Some interjections have an irregular syllable structure, i.e. CVCC, as in *saws* 'shout uttered when offering food to the soul of ancestors', and *sawp* 'sound of something blown by the wind'.

A disyllabic word is CVCV, CVCCV, CVCVC, or CVCCVC. The vowel in the final syllable is /i/, /u/, or /a/, and that in the penultimate syllable is /i/, /u/, /a/, or /e/ (schwa), i.e. the schwa phoneme does not appear in the final syllable of a word. This distribution of vowels is a very important indicator of word boundaries.

In longer words the vowels in the antepenultimate syllables are usually /e/. This is because of a phonological alternation discussed below in section 2.2. An antepenultimate vowel can be /i/ before or after /y/. So a trisyllabic or longer word has the following structure: (Ce)(Ce)(Ce)CeCV(C)CV(C). The longest word observed consists of six syllables. /e/ in antepenultimate syllables is deleted under several conditions some of which can be stated using natural classes. For example, it is deleted between a nasal and a homorganic stop (always), between voiceless fricatives (not in all combinations), and

TABLE 10.1: SEEDIQ CONSONANT PHONEMES (PRACTICAL ORTHOGRAPHY)

		Labial	Alveolar	Palatal	Velar	Labio-velar	Uvular	Glottal
Stops	voiceless	p	t		k		q	'
	voiced	b	d					
Fricative	voiceless		s		x			h
	voiced				g			
Affricate	voiceless		(c)					
Lateral fricative	voiced		l					
Nasal		m	n		ng			
Tap or approximant			r					
Glide				y	w			

TABLE 10.2: SEEDIQ VOWEL PHONEMES (PRACTICAL ORTHOGRAPHY)

	Front/unrounded	Back/rounded
High	i	u
	e	
Low	a	

between a voiceless stop and a fricative (not in all combinations). Other environments for deletion have to be stated with reference to individual segments (/e/ is also deleted between /m/ and /d/, and between /n/ and /k/, for example). Li (1991) and Holmer (1996) regard the /e/ in antepenultimate syllables as non-phonemic, but as the conditions for its deletion are not completely predictable it is regarded as phonemic here.

Seediq words carry stress on the penultimate syllable. The stressed syllable is pronounced with high pitch. Note that /e/ can also receive stress.

2.2 Phonological alternations

What is most characteristic about Seediq morphophonology is the weakening of vowels in antepenultimate syllables. Even when a syllable of a bare stem has an /a/, /i/ or /u/ vowel, or an /aw/ or /ay/ sequence, the vowel is weakened to /e/ if the syllable occurs in antepenultimate position through suffixation.

(1) /qita/ 'to see' + /-an/ 'GV2'   → /qeta-an/
     /qada/ 'to throw' + /-an/ 'GV2'   → /qeda-an/
     /baytaq/ 'to spear' + /-an/ 'GV2'   → /betaq-an/

Weakening of the vowel is also observed in reduplicated segments attached before the stem.

(2) /laqi/ 'PLURAL (reduplication)' + /laqi/ 'child'   →   /leqe-laqi/

In addition, there are some less regular instances of vowel weakening. One frequent condition for such a weakening is a V'V-sequence.

(3) ke–an 'GV2' + sa'ang 'to be angry'   →   *ke-se'eng-an
     → ke-se'ng-an 'angry-GV2'

The final form ke-se'ng-an also illustrates another process, i.e. the dropping of /e/ which was already briefly mentioned above. One environment in which such dropping occurs is when the sequence e'e fills the antepenultimate and penultimate positions (as a result of derivation or inflection). In this environment the penultimate /e/ drops.

(4) me- 'AV.FUT' + 'ekan 'to eat'   →*me-'ekan   →me-'kan 'AV.FUT-eat'

Another rule pertaining to schwa is: When the immediately neighboring consonant is /y/, the /e/ is assimilated to /i/.

(5) gayig 'to burn' + -an 'GV2'   → *geyig-an   → giyig-an
     bekuy 'to bind' + -anay 'CV.HORT'   → *bekey-anay → bekiy-anay
     kuyu 'Plural (reduplication)' + kuyuh 'woman'   → *keye-kuyuh → kiyi-kuyuh

All vowels in prefixes are /e/, but it is assimilated to the vowel in the next syllable if the following syllable begins with /'a/ or /'i/.

(6) me- 'AV' + 'isug 'to fear'   –› mi-'isug
     me- 'AV.FUT' + 'angal 'to take'   → ma-'angal

Seediq has several consonant alternation or neutralization rules. Several consonants are neutralized when they appear in word final position. Morpheme-final /p/ and /b/ become /k/ when they appear in word-final position. They are /p/ and /b/ when they are not word-final, that is, when suffixed.

(7)   /sebesip/ 'to sip'   → *sebesik*, cf. *sebesip-an*
      /karib/ 'to cut with scissors' → *karik*, cf. *kerib-an*
      /sekesik/ 'to sweep'   → *seksik*, cf. *seksik-an*

Morpheme-final /d/ and /t/ both become /t/ when they appear in word-final position.

(8)   /pelatad/ 'to make go out' → *pelatat*, cf. *peletad-un*
      /qiyut/ 'to bite'   → *qiyut*, cf. *qiyut-un*

Morpheme-final /m/ becomes /ng/ when it appears in word-final position.

(9)   /qequm/ 'to sip'   → *qequng*, cf. *qeqem-an*
      /perading/ 'to begin' → *perading*, cf. *pereding-an*

Morpheme-final /iy/ and /uy/ both become /uy/ when they appear in word final position.

(10) /sepiy/ 'to plug' → *sepuy*, cf. *sepiy-an*
      /hapuy/ 'to cook' → *hapuy*, cf. *hepuy-an*

Morpheme-final /ag/ sequences become /aw/ when they appear in word final position.

(11) /rengag/ 'to talk' → *rengaw*, cf. *rengag-an*

However, in this instance there also seems to be a reverse rule which turns all non-final /aw/ sequences into /ag/ sequences so that no /aw/ sequences are found word-medially. Consequently, one cannot really say which form is the base form. It is therefore an alternation rather than a neutralization.

2.3 Reduplication

Two kinds of reduplications are observed. One is partial (or Ce-) reduplication. It consists in the reduplication of the first syllable of the stem, as in (12) and (13). The vowels are weakened to *e* because of the weakening rule referred to in 2.2. Partial reduplication is observed in reciprocal verb formation (see 4.4), in plural form of nouns (see 3.3), and when emphasizing future (see 4.1).

(12) *sipaq* 'to hit'   → *me-se-sipaq* 'AV-RCP-hit'
(13) *qehuni* 'tree' → *qe-qehuni* 'PL-tree'

If the stem begins with a glottal stop, two subtypes of partial reduplication have to be distinguished. In subtype A partial reduplication involves the initial consonant of the second syllable of the stem, schematized as follows: 'VC$_1$V(C) → C$_1$e-'VC$_1$V(C). The *e* is assimilated to the following V if this is an /a/ or /i/, as already noted in 2.2. Examples are:

(14) *'usa* 'to go'   → *me-se-'usa* 'AV-RCP-go'
(15) *'ayug* 'valley' → *mi-ya-'ayug* 'AV-RCP-valley' (= 'for paper or cloth: to have wrinkles')

In subtype B the glottal stop is retained, as shown in the following schema: 'VC$_1$V(C) → 'e-'VC$_1$V(C). Assimilation operates here as well. Examples:

(16) *'iyah* 'CV-FUT.come' → *'i-'iyah* 'RDP-CV.FUT.come'
(17) *'uq-un* 'eat-GV1'   → *'e-'uq-un* 'RDP-eat-GV1'

The second type of reduplication is bisyllabic (or full) reduplication. In this type the first two syllables without syllable-final consonants are reduplicated, as in (18), (19), (20) and (21).

The vowels in the reduplicated part is weakened to *e*. Full reduplication is observed in the plural form of nouns (see 3.3 for details).

(18) *rudan* 'old man' → *rede-rudan* 'old men'
(19) *dawras* 'cliff' → *dere-dawras* 'cliffs'
(20) *se'diq* 'person' → *sede-se'diq* 'people'
(21) *'ayug* 'valley' → *'iya-'ayug* 'valleys'

3 BASIC MORPHOSYNTAX

3.1 Word classes

The words of Seediq are classified into one of the following word classes: nouns, verbs, adjectives, numerals, personal pronouns, deictics, adverbs, conjunctives, prepositions, interjections, and sentence final particles. The first three are open classes whereas the others are not. Before discussing some of these classes in more detail, note that two personal pronoun sets (see section 3.3) and some adverbs are clitics. Seediq clitics differ from affixes in that they do not cause phonological alternations when they are attached to a word: they do not cause weakening of vowels, for example. In addition, the clitics usually appear after the first word of the predicate phrase (i.e. they are second position clitics), regardless of the word class of the word. Yet they are dependent upon the preceding word in that the enclitic and preceding word form one stress unit: the penultimate syllable of the whole unit is stressed. A syllable of an enclitic receives stress if the clitic is longer than one syllable or if there is more than one clitic.

3.1.1 Open classes

As is reported for many north-western Austronesian languages such as Tagalog, Seediq nouns and verbs behave almost the same syntactically: they both can be predicate (example (22) and (23)), subject (example (24) and (25)), non-subject argument (example (26) and (27)), and noun-modifier (example (28) and (29)) in the same way. As will be explained later on in more detail, case markers are distributed as follows: subjects and time adjuncts are NOM (nominative); GEN (genitive) is used with non-subject agents or possessors; OBL (oblique) appears with other semantic roles and grammatical functions.

(22) **terema-an**=*nami*   *kedediyax*   *ka*   *hini.*
      bathe-GV2=1pe.GEN   everyday   NOM   PRX.LOC
      'We bathe here everyday.'

(23) **laqi**=*nami*   *ka*   *'uwa*   *gaga.*
      child=1pe.GEN   NOM   girl   DIST
      'That girl is our child.'

(24) *lelabang*   *ka*   **terema-an**   *hini.*
      be:wide   NOM   bath-GV2   PRX.LOC
      'This place where one bathes (=bathroom) is wide.'

(25) *'ini*=*su*   *kela-i*   *ka*   **laqi**=*nami.*
      NEG=2s.GEN   know-GV.NFIN   NOM   child=1pe.GEN
      'You do not know our child.'

(26) ga   tegehuy **terema-an** hiya   ka   laqi.
      DIST.PRG   AV.play   bathe-GV2   DIST.LOC NOM   child
      'The child is playing at that place where one bathes' (=bathroom).

(27) ga   sipaq **laqi**   ka   tama.
      DIST.PRG   <AV>hit   child   NOM   father.
      'The father is hitting a/the child.'

(28) sapah **terema-an** ka   hini.
      room   bathe-GV2   NOM   PRX.LOC
      'Here is the bathroom.' (=the room where one takes a bath)

(29) sapah **laqi** ka   hini.
      room   child   NOM   PRX.LOC
      'Here is the childrens' room.'

The differences between the two classes are mainly morphological. Nouns do not inflect for voice while verbs do, for example. Nouns have plural forms with prefix *de-* or (partial) reduplication, but verbs do not.

Adjectives can be regarded as a subcategory of verbs. Their morphology is quite similar to that of verbs, the morphology typical for adjectives being rather limited. Some of the adjectives have plural forms resembling that of nouns, that is (partial) reduplication. They differ from verbs mainly with regard to one syntactic feature: Verbs (and nouns, too) always appear after the head noun when in modifying function, but some adjectives can appear either before or after the modified noun.

(30) me-taqi=ku   sapah   paru.
      AV-sleep=1s.SBJ   room   big

(31) me-taqi=ku   paru   sapah.
      AV-sleep=1s.SBJ   big   room
      'I sleep in a big room.'

Derivation among these three major classes is quite commonly observed. Nouns can be derived from verbs and numerals, verbs from nouns, adjectives and numerals, adjectives from nouns and verbs through derivation. It is not unusual that the same base form can either be a verb stem or a noun. The base *karik*, for example, can be a noun, meaning 'scissors', or a verb stem meaning 'to cut'. Some of the more productive derivations are dealt with in section 4.4.

3.1.2 Closed classes

The present section gives a brief treatment of conjunctions, numerals and interjections. Other closed classes will be dealt with in some of the sections further below. Seediq has six conjunctions: *ni* 'and', *deni* 'and then' and furthermore *'u*, *du'u*, *ga* and *dega*, which all share the meaning 'in case that'. These conjunctions appear in between clauses. *'u* and *ga*, and *du'u* and *dega* are usually interchangeable. The clause before the conjunction may contain adverbs like *nasi* 'if' or *'ana* 'even'.

(32) **'ana** 'ini   'iyah   ka   hiya   **'u,**
      even   NEG   AV.NFIN.come   NOM   3s   CNJ
      mawsa=ku   ka   yaku.
      AV.FUT.go=1s.SBJ   NOM   1s
      'Though he won't come, I will go.'

The conjunction *ni* 'and' can appear between nouns (see 3.5), and the conjunction *'u* (and less frequently *ga*) also appears between topic NP and main clause (see 3.2).

The subordinating conjunction for embedded clauses is *ka*.

(33) *me-kela=ku*   [*ka   m-iyah   pa'ah   tehipaq   ka   kumu*].
      AV-know=1s.SBJ   CMP   AV-come   from   Taipei   NOM   Kumu.
      'I know that Kumu comes from Taipei.'

The basic numerals are *kingal* 'one', *deha* 'two', *teru* 'three', *sepat* 'four', *rima* 'five', *mataru* 'six', *mpitu* 'seven', *maspat* 'eight', and *mengari* 'nine'. *mataru* 'six' is an exception to the vowel distribution generalization in 2.1, since here an /a/ appears in antepenultimate position. There are two other expressions for 'one': *taxa* expresses that there is only one human, and *'uwin* is used when counting things. 10, 20, 30, 40, and 50 are formed with the circumfix *ma—(u)l*. The /u/ of the suffix disappears when the stem ends with an open syllable. The vowel of *ma-* is weakened to *e* when it appears in antepenultimate position. For 10 and 20, the stems are *xa* and *pusa*, respectively, whose origin is unclear. For 30, 40, and 50, the basic numerals are used as stems. Thus: *ma-xa-l* 'ten', *m-pusa-l* 'twenty', *me-teru-l* 'thirty', *me-sepat-ul* 'forty', and *me-rima-l* 'fifty'. 60, 70, 80, and 90, are expressed in such a way that the basic numerals modify the unit noun *ke-mexal-an* 'counter for higher multiples of ten'; e.g. *mataru kemexalan* '60'. Hundreds and thousands are likewise formed with unit nouns, i.e. *kebekuy* and *k<en>bekiy-an*, respectively. Thus: *sepat kebekuy* 'four hundred', *rima kenbekiyan* 'five thousand', and *mataru kenbekiyan mpitu kebekuy maspat kemexalan mengari* 'six thousand seven hundred eighty nine'. Ordinal numerals are formed by attaching the prefix *tege-* to the independent numerals; thus *tege-kingal* 'first', *tege-deha* 'second', etc.

The class of interjections includes onomatopoeic expressions. A few examples: *'ay* is the typical reply when called by someone, *hang* 'uh huh' (signalling agreement), *te'cu* 'Oh, no/How dirty!/What a mess!', *'akay* 'ouch', *puy* 'shout of setting dog(s) to something/somebody', *'ax* 'Oh, how noisy/bothersome!', *tix* 'shout uttered when one is tired', and *tip* 'a shout expressing one feels disappointed'. Onomatopoeic expressions include: *bih* 'sound of fire starting', *raq* 'sound of bamboo cracking', *ngar* 'growl of dogs', *saws* 'sound of a sword or bamboo stick striking against something', *paq* 'sound of someone jumping into water', *bas* 'sound of cutting grass', and *pus* 'sound of water dripping'. As mentioned in section 2.1, some interjections have an unusual syllable structure. Furthermore, *te'cu* 'What a mess!' contains the phoneme /c/, which is observed only in this word and in the gerund forming prefix *cese-*.

3.2 Basic clause structure

Seediq clauses are of three types: interjection clauses, basic clauses and existential/possessive clauses. The last one is dealt with in 3.10.

Interjection clauses function as expressions of emotion or are used to call the attention of a person (or animal); they are not related to other parts of the sentence (if there are any). They are typically made of interjections or names of persons and some kin terms. The latter may be in vocative form (see 3.3).

(34) *rubiq!*   Rubiq!
(35) *'iq.*   Yes.
(36) *tak.*   (Sound of cutting something with knife or ax.)
(37) *tar!*   Bang! (Sound of shooting guns and rifles.)

Basic Seediq clauses consist of a predicate, a subject, and optionally non-subject arguments and adjuncts. Predicates and non-subject arguments can form clauses by themselves if other information is recoverable from the context. The second clause of the example (38) consists only of non-subject arguments.

(38)   *niyi   'u,   teqi-an   rubiq   hug?*
      PRX   CNJ   sleep-GV2   Rubiq   Q
      'adi 'uri 'u,   rabay   hug?
      or   Rabay   Q
      'As for this, Rubiq sleeps [in it]? Or Rabay [sleeps in it]?'

The basic word order is: the predicate occurs in clause-initial position and the subject, which bears nominative case, comes at the end (example (39), see 3.2.1 for details), though some adverbs and clause final particles may appear after the subject.

(39)   *m-ahu   lukus   ka   masaw.*
      AV-wash   clothes   NOM   Masaw
      'Masaw washes clothes.'

The clause final particles express question/confirmation ((*de*)*hug*, (*de*)*heki*, *pini*, *binaw*), suspicion/surprise (*huwa*), suggestion (*binaw*), surprise/emphasis (*wah*, *'u*), and the like. Examples include (see also example (44) below):

(40)   *me-'iyah   hini   ka   hiya   deheki?*
      AV.FUT-come   PRX.LOC   NOM   3s   Q
      'Will he really come?'

(41)   *mah-i   binaw!*
      drink-GC.NFIN   TRY
      'Try and drink it!'

Predicates may be single verbs, adjectives or NPs. Example (42) illustrates an NP predicate and (43) an adjectival predicate.

(42)   *laqi   rubiq   ka   niyi.*
      child   Rubiq   NOM   PRX
      'This is Rubiq's child.'

(43)   *bilaq   niyana   ka   laqi   rubiq.*
      small   still   NOM   child   Rubiq.
      'Rubiq's child is still small.'

One can form complex predicate phrases from a simple predicate by adding preverbal adverbs, deictics, and some of the prepositions (example (44) and (45), see 3.7 for details). A topic NP may appear before the clause (example (46)), usually delimited by the conjunction *'u*. The coreferent NP in the main clause may be omitted in that case.

(44)   *gaga   m-ahu   lukus   ka   masaw   niyana   'u.*
      DIST.PRG   AV-wash   clothes   NOM   Masaw   still   EMPH
      'Masaw is still washing clothes.'

(45)   *hana   m-en-ahu   lukus   ka   masaw.*
      at:last   AV-PRF-wash   clothes   NOM   Masaw
      'Masaw washed clothes at last.'

(46) *patas*   *'u,*   *wada=na*   *se-begay*   *leqi-an.*
      book   CNJ   PST=3s.GEN   cv-give   child-OBL
      'As for the book, he gave it to a/the child.'

3.2.1 Subjects

Seediq subjects can be recognized on the basis of the following properties: voice affix, clitic pronoun, quantifier floating, relativization, and possessum demotion. First, the semantic role of the subject is shown in the verbal predicate through affix(es). In examples (39), (44) and (45), the semantic role of the subject is Agent. The verbs are in actor voice (AV) form, which signals that the semantic role of the subject is Agent. We may call such clauses AV clauses. In example (46) the semantic role of the subject is the thing conveyed, and the verb is in conveyance voice (CV) form. Voice marking of verbs and the phenomena of voice will be discussed in detail in section 4.3.

Second, only subjects are represented by agreeing clitic pronouns in the predicate phrase (for third persons, however, the clitic pronoun is *zero*, as seen in the above examples). This clitic pronoun is obligatory, while use of a full noun phrase expression for subjects is optional.

(47) *gisu=su*   *m-ahu*   *lukus*   *(ka*   *'isu).*
      PRG=2s.SBJ   AV-wash   clothes   (NOM   2s)
      'You are washing clothes.'

Quantifier floating and relativization are discussed elsewhere in this volume (see Himmelmann, Chapter 5, for more discussion). Possessum demotion refers to the following phenomenon. Those clauses that contain both a possessor and possessum in a subject NP, such as (48) and (50), have corresponding clauses that have the possessum demoted out of the subject NP (and the possessor becomes the head of the subject NP, but see section 3.10 below) such as in (49) and (51).

(48) *m-banah*   *ka*   *lukus*   *masaw.*
      AV-red   NOM   clothes   Masaw
      'Masaw's clothes are red.'

(49) *m-banah*   *lukus=na*   *ka*   *masaw.*
      AV-red   clothes=3s.GEN   NOM   Masaw
      'Masaw is wearing red clothes.'

(50) *q<en>iyut-an*   *huling*   *ka*   *baga*   *laqi.*
      <PRF>bite-GV   dog   NOM   hand   child
      'A dog bit the/a child's hand.'

(51) *q<en>iyut-an*   *baga*   *huling*   *ka*   *laqi.*
      <PRF>bite-GV   hand   dog   NOM   child
      'A dog bit the child on his/her hand.'

This alternative positioning is only possible if the possessor occurs in subject position; in all other syntactic functions possessum and possessor have to be part of the same NP.

Subjects bear nominative case, but not all nominative NPs are subjects. Expressions of time can bear nominative case, too.

(52) *masaw*   *'u,*   *m-bahu*   *lukus*   *(ka)*   *ke'man*   *sayang.*
      Masaw   CNJ   AV.FUT-wash   clothes   (NOM)   night   now
      'As for Masaw, he will wash clothes tonight.'

It is clear from the above example that *ka* is not a subject marker but only a nominative case marker. In (52) the syntactic subject, that is, *masaw*, is topicalized and not overtly expressed in the main clause. In a simple clause only one overt nominative NP can appear. So, if the subject appears as a nominative NP then expressions of time cannot appear as a nominative NP.

(53)   **m-bahu   lukus   ka   ke'man   sayang   ka   masaw.*
        AV.FUT-wash   clothes   NOM   night   now   NOM   Masaw
        'Masaw will wash clothes tonight.'

Word order is not relevant here (i.e. **m-bahu lukus ka masaw ka ke'man sayang* is equally ungrammatical).

3.2.2 Non-subject arguments

When the agent is not the subject, it bears genitive case if it is expressed by a pronoun.

(54)   *b<en>ahu=mu   ka   lukus   niyi.*
        <CV.PRF>wash=1s.GEN   NOM   clothes   PRX
        'I washed these clothes.'

NPs other than pronouns do not have a formally distinct genitive form. They just appear in direct case, that is, their citation form (see 3.3 below), as in example (58) below. The agent is usually expressed in most non-AV clauses when the agent is specific, either as a full NP or a pronoun.

When NPs with semantic roles other than actor, that is, patient, recipient, goal, beneficiary, etc., appear as non-subject arguments, they bear oblique case, though only pronouns, personal names and a limited number of the kin terms have formally distinct oblique forms.

(55)   *ga   taga   sunan   ka   masaw.*
        DIST.PRG   <AV>wait   2s.OBL   NOM   Masaw
        'Masaw is waiting for you there.'

Those nouns that do not have a distinct oblique form appear in direct form, as *lukus* in (52) does, for example.

3.2.3 Negation and imperative

There are two negative particles for basic clause predicates, i.e. *'ini* and *'adi*. *'ini* requires the non-finite form of the verb (the different aspectual and modal forms of verbs are further discussed in section 4).

(56)   *'ini   'usa   degiyaq   sayang   ka   tama.*
        NEG   AV.NFIN:go   mountain   now/today   NOM   father
        'Father did not go to mountain today.'

Such predicates express non-future meanings.

'adi is used to negate NP predicates and the future and perfect forms of verbs.

(57)   *'adi   m-bahu   lukus   ka   masaw.*
        NEG   AV.FUT-wash   clothes   NOM   Masaw
        'Masaw will not wash clothes.'

(58)   'adi   b<en>ahu   masaw   ka   lukus   niyi.
       NEG   <CV.PRF>wash Masaw NOM clothes PRX
       'Masaw did not wash this clothes.'

(59)   'adi   laqi   rubiq   ka   niyi.
       NEG   child Rubiq   NOM   PRX
       'This is not Rubiq's child.'

There are two ways to negate an adjectival predicate: *'adi* plus the non-future form and *'ini* plus the non-finite form. The former expresses simple negation.

(60)   'adi   bilaq   ka   laqi   rubiq.
       NEG   small NOM   child Rubiq.
       'Rubiq's child is not small.'

The latter expresses that something did not or does not or will not enter the state expressed by the adjective.

(61)   'ini   qe-bilaq   ka   lukus   niyi.
       NEG   AV.NFIN-small NOM clothes PRX
       'This clothes does/did/will not get small.' (e.g. after washing)

Verbal and adjectival predicates in their non-finite forms also occur in imperative clauses. In these clauses no subject and genitive clitics can be used. To negate an imperative the particle *'iya* is used.

(62)   'usa   degiyaq.
       AV.NFIN.go mountain
       'Go to the mountains.'

(63)   'iya   'usa.
       NEG.IMP AV.NFIN.go
       'Don't go.'

3.3 Morphology of nouns and pronouns

Most Seediq nouns have very simple case marking: direct case (=citation form) and nominative case (preceded by the case marker *ka*). Personal names, a limited number of kin terms and *se'diq*, the word for 'people', have a distinct oblique case: stem with suffix -*an*: e.g. *rubiq* (person name)+-*an* > *rebiq-an*, *tama* 'father'+-*an* > *tema-an*. Some animate nouns may be prefixed with *ne-* to refer to something possessed by the entity denoted by the noun, e.g. *ne-rubiq* 'Rubiq's possession, thing possessed by Rubiq'.

Personal names and some kin terms also have a vocative form which consists of the last syllable of the stem.

(64)   ga=su   huya   hug, saw?
       DIST.PRG=2s.SBJ <AV>do:what Q   Masaw:VOC
       'What are you doing, Masaw?'

(65)   'imah   qesiya, yi.
       AV.drink water   old:lady:VOC
       'Drink water, old lady.'

Seediq nouns have two ways to express plurality overtly. One is to use a prefix. Personal names and some nouns referring to human beings form a plural with the prefix *de-*.

(66) *kuyuh* 'woman'   → *de-kuyuh* 'women'
      rubiq (person name)   → *de-rubiq* 'Rubiq and other person(s)'

Nouns other than personal names have reduplicated forms. Bisyllabic roots show full reduplication, as in (18), (19), (20), (21) and (67). Roots with three or more syllables show partial reduplication, as in (13) and (68).

(67) *kuyuh* 'woman'   → *kiyi-kuyuh* 'women'
(68) *berigan* 'store' → *be-berigan* 'stores'

Some adjectives can also undergo this process to express plurality of the theme, e.g. *paru* 'big' → *pere-paru* as in:

(69) *pere-paru*   *ka*   *laqi*   *da.*
      PL-big   NOM   child(ren)   NEWSIT
      'The children are already big.'

It is possible to express past tense in nouns by prefixing *ne-*. Examples are:

(70) *kuyuh* 'woman, wife' → *ne-kuyuh* 'former wife'
      dangi 'fiance'   → *n-dangi* 'ex-fiance'. (/e/ is dropped between
                              homorganic nasal and stop, cf. 2.2.)

The personal pronoun system distinguishes first, second and third person as well as singular and plural. Inclusive and exclusive are distinguished for first person plural. Personal pronouns have a more complicated case system than nouns. There are five different forms: direct, oblique, independent possessive, subject and genitive, as shown in Table 10.3.

The direct case is the citation form which may be preceded by the nominative case marker *ka*, which also applies for nouns. The oblique forms all contain the suffix *-an*, which is also found with personal names. The independent possessive form, which refers to something possessed by the referent, e.g. *naku* 'my possession', 'thing possessed by me', may contain the additional prefix *ne-* (so *ne-naku*) which in fact is obligatory in the third person, as it is for nouns.

TABLE 10.3: PERSONAL PRONOUN SETS

	Direct	Oblique	Independent possessive	Subject	Genitive
1s	*yaku*	*kenan*	*(ne-)naku*	=*ku*	=*mu*
2s	*isu*	*sunan*	*(ne-)nisu*	=*su*	=*su*
3s	*hiya*	*hiyaan*	*ne-hiya*	/	=*na*
1pi	*'ita*	*tenan*	*(ne-)nita*	=*ta*	=*ta*
1pe	*yami*	*menani*	*(ne-)nami*	=*nami*	=*nami*
2p	*yamu*	*munan*	*(ne-)namu*	=*namu*	=*namu*
3p	*dehiya*	*dehiyaan*	*ne-dehiya*	/	=*deha*

The genitive and subject sets are enclitics. There are special merged forms of the clitic pronouns for the following three combinations: 1s.sbj+2s.gen=*saku*, 2s.sbj+1s.gen=*misu*, 2p.sbj+ 1s.gen=*maku*. Sentence (71) is an example of the use of *saku*.

(71) *gisu=**saku***   *biq-un*   *lala*   *patas*.
      PRG=1s.SBJ: 2s.GEN   give-GV1   many   book
      'You (sg.) are giving me many books.'

3.4 Deictics

Seediq has two demonstratives, distinguishing relative distance from the speaker. Deictic adverbials referring to places distinguish an additional category, namely visibility (or not) to the speaker. Table 10.4 summarizes the forms.

Demonstratives may modify a noun or be used as NPs by themselves. When they modify nouns, they follow the noun.

(72) *lukus*   *masaw*   *ka*   *niyi*.
      clothes   Masaw   NOM   PRX
      'These are Masaw's clothes.'

(73) *b<en>ahu*   *masaw*   *ka*   *lukus*   *gaga*.
      <CV.PRF>wash   Masaw   NOM   clothes   DIST
      'Masaw washed those clothes.'

Another use of the demonstratives is that of a locative predicate, expressing 'something (subject) is at...'. Thus, *gaga* also means 'be at a place far from the speaker' and *niyi* 'be at a place near to the speaker'. Examples are:

(74) *ga(ga)*   *selaq*   *hi*   *ka*   *katin*.
      DIST   paddle   DIST.LOC   NOM   cow
      'The cow is at the paddle there.'

(75) *niyi*   *berigan*   *yawyaw*   *ka*   *laqi=su*.
      PRX   store   Yawyaw   NOM   child=2s.GEN
      'Your child is here at Yawyaw's store.'

The verb *m-eniq* 'to exist, live, stay' is also used for predicating locations. However, the neutral form of this verb requires its subject to be animate, while *gaga* or *niyi* can appear with animate or inanimate subjects (*m-eniq* in non-neutral aspect/mood also allows inanimate subjects). Example (77) also shows that demonstratives may co-occur with deictic adverbials in the same sentence, provided that they are semantically compatible.

TABLE 10.4: SEEDIQ DEICTICS

	Demonstrative	Deictic Adverbial
Near speaker	niyi 'this', 'this one' (PRX)	hini 'here' (PRX.LOC)
Far and visible to speaker	ga/gaga 'that', 'that one'	hi/hiya 'there' (DIST.LOC)
Far and invisible to speaker	(DIST)	ga hiya, gaga hiya 'over there' (DIST.LOC)

(76) *m-eniq   hini   ka   laqi=su/*pastas=su.*
     AV-exist   PRX.LOC   NOM   child=2s.GEN/book=2s.GEN
     'Your child/*Your book is here.'

(77) *niyi   hini   ka   laqi=su/patas=su.*
     PRX   PRX.LOC   NOM   child=2s.GEN/book=2s.GEN
     'Your child/Your book is here.'

Probably related to their use as locative predicates is the use of the demonstratives with verbal predicates. They immediately precede the neutral form of verbs which are then interpreted as expressing a state or progressive action taking place near or far from the speaker. Note that the basic spatial meaning conveyed by the demonstratives is preserved in this usage, to which the gloss PRG is added here in order to facilitate the parsing of the examples.

(78) *ga(ga)   h\<em\>angut   rudux   ka   'ina.*
     DIST.PRG   \<AV\>cook   chicken   NOM   son's:wife
     'The son's wife is cooking there.'

(79) *niyi   'ul-an   qehuni   ka   katin.*
     PRX.PRG   hitch-GV2   tree   NOM   cow
     'The cow is hitched here to a tree.'

3.5 NP structure

The basic word order inside an NP is head-modifier. Modifiers include nouns that express a possessor (ex. (80)) or a quality (ex. (82)), adjectives (ex. (83)), relative clauses (ex. (84) and (85)), numerals and deictics. No linker appears between the elements. When possessor is a noun, it occurs in the direct case (ex. (80)). When it is a pronoun, it occurs in the genitive case (ex. (81)). Numerals are exceptional in that they come before the head (ex. (82)). Deictics come after all other modifiers (ex. (80) to (83)).

(80) *lukus   masaw   niyi*
     clothes   Masaw   PRX
     'These clothes of Masaw's'

(81) *lukus=su   gaga*
     clothes=2s.GEN   DIST
     'That dress of yours'

(82) *sepat   sapah   betunux   niyi.*
     four   house   stone   PRX
     'These four stone houses'

(83) *deha   'uwa   me-deremut   gaga.*
     two   girl   AV-diligent   DIST
     'Those two diligent girls'

Relative clauses can modify a noun in two possible ways. They either follow the head, without any special marker, as in (84); or they precede the head, with *ka* functioning as a linker, as in (85). The head noun has to be the subject of the relative clause predicate, as is also observed in other Formosan and Philippine languages.

(84) *wada   qeduriq   ka   se'diq   [p<en>ehuqil   rubiq].*
    PST   AV.escape NOM person AV.PRF-kill   Rubiq
    'The person who killed Rubiq escaped.'

(85) *wada   qeduriq   ka   [p<en>ehuqil   rubiq   ka]   se'diq.*
    PST   AV.escape NOM <AV.PRF>kill   Rubiq LK   person
    'The person who killed Rubiq escaped.'

As already mentioned in section 3.1, adjectives may follow or precede the head when they modify a noun.

(86) *m-en-da=nami   'elug   m-beqeru.*
    AV.PRF-pass=1pe.SBJ   road AV-bumpy
    'We passed a bumpy road.'

(87) *m-en-da=nami   m-beqeru   'elug.*
    'We passed a bumpy road.'

Plural personal pronouns and nation/tribe names can form appositive NPs.

(88) *yami teruku* 'we Teruku people'
(89) *yamu nihung* 'you Japanese'

Kin terms/names for professions, and personal names can also form appositive NPs. In some instances the order of the constituent is reversible, but in the following examples the word order is fixed in the way shown.

(90) *baki*   *masaw*
    uncle/grandfather Masaw
    'Uncle/Grandfather Masaw'

(91) *kumu*   *'ising*
    Kumu   doctor
    'Dr. Kumu.'

The order shown in (90) is ambiguous because one can also interpret such examples as head noun plus possessor noun (i.e. 'Masaw's uncle/grandfather').

The first person plural exclusive and second person plural pronouns can form inclusive NPs with personal names or nouns that refer to humans.

(92) *mawsa=nami   tehipaq   ka   yami   rubiq*
    AV.FUT:go=1pe.SBJ Taipei NOM 1pe   Rubiq
    'We, including Rubiq, will go to Taipei.'

For nominal coordination, *ni* 'and' is used.

(93) *lawking   ni   rubiq   'u,   me-nsewayi.*
    Lawking and Rubiq CNJ AV-sibling
    'Lawking and Rubiq, they are brother and sister.'

3.6 Prepositional phrases

Seediq has the following six prepositions: *quri* 'toward', 'about', 'in the direction of', *pa'ah* 'from', *bitaq* 'till', *saw* 'like', *'asaw* 'because of', *nawxay* 'for the sake of'. Note that there is no preposition for stative locatives ('on the mountain' etc.) which are simply put in postverbal position without further marking, as seen in the following examples:

(94)   *m-aduk   degiyaq   ka   senaw   rubiq.*
       AV-hunt   mountain   NOM   man   Rubiq
       'Rubiq's husband hunts in the mountain.'

(95)   *m-eniq   tehipaq   ka   laqi   rubiq.*
       AV-exist/live   Taipei   NOM   child   Rubiq
       'Rubiq's child lives in Taipei.'

Prepositional phrases can function as adverbials (as in (96)), predicates (as in (97)) or as noun modifiers (as in (98)).

(96)   *me-'iyah   pa'ah   tehipaq   ka   kingal   senaw.*
       AV.FUT-come   from   Taipei   NOM   one   man
       'One man will come from Taipei.'

(97)   *'asaw   sapuh   ka   me-huqil   ka   qesurux.*
       because   medicine   CMP   AV-die   NOM   fish
       'It is because of the (poisonous) medicine that the fish died.'

(98)   *m-arig=ku   kippu   bitaq   tehipaq.*
       AV-buy=1s.SBJ   ticket   up:to   Taipei.
       'I bought a ticket to Taipei.'

The prepositions appear to derive from different sources. As shown by the following example, *quri* and *saw* have noun-like features; they are marked as nominative. Unlike other nouns, however, they always have to be followed by an NP.

(99)   *'ini   biyaw   bu-an   hidaw   ka   quri   degiyaq   telewa'un.*
       NEG   long:time   hit-GV2   sun   NOM   direction   mountain   Telewaun
       '[The side of] Mountain Telewaun will soon be covered by sunshine.'

The preposition *pa'ah* 'from' is like a verb morphologically. It has a perfect form with infix *-en-*: *p<en>a'ah*. This form means 'came from...'. Its complement, that is, the source NP, cannot be omitted, at which point it differs from ordinary verbs. Ordinary verbs can usually have their complements omitted if recoverable from context. Both forms can be main predicates, as in (100) and (101), but for adverbial use *pa'ah* tends to be used, as in (96), whereas for adnominal uses *p<en>a'ah* NP tends to be used, as in (102).

(100)   *pa'ah   tehipaq   ka   laqi   niyi.*
       from   Taipei   NOM   child   PRX
       'This child is from Taipei.'

(101)   *p<en>a'ah   tehipaq   ka   laqi   niyi.*
       <PRF>from   Taipei   NOM   child   PRX
       'This child is from Taipei.'

(102)   *tege'inu   ka   se'diq   p<en>a'ah   tehipaq?*
       which   NOM   person   <PRF>from   Taipei
       'Which is the person who came from Taipei?'

Finally, *bitaq* 'till', 'up to' and *saw* 'like' can function as predicate extenders (see section 3.7 for details).

(103) *bitaq   me-sedara   me-sesepung   ka   dehiya.*
      till   AV-bleed   AV-wrestle   NOM   3p
      'They wrestle so much that they bleed.'

3.7 Predicate extenders (preverbal elements)

As mentioned in section 3.2, one can form extended predicate phrases from simple predicates by adding preverbal adverbs, demonstratives and prepositions *bitaq* 'up to…' (see example (103) above) and *saw* 'be like…'. I will call such elements predicate extenders. The use of demonstratives as predicate extenders is discussed in section 3.4. Some of the predicate extenders are semantically similar to 'auxiliaries', like *wada* 'past', *na'a* 'had better, could have done…' or *'ini* 'negative', some have 'adverbial' meanings, such as *dima* 'already' and *hana* 'just', and some are like conjunctions, such as *nasi* 'if'.

(104) *wada=na   se-begay   leqi-an   ka   patas.*
      PST=3s.GEN   CV-give   child.OBL   NOM   book
      'He gave the book to a/the child.'

(105) *dima=ku   m-en-ahu   lukus.*
      already=1s.SBJ   AV-PRF-wash   clothes
      'I have already washed clothes.'

(106) *nasi=su   m-en-iyah   hini   sehiga   ka   'isu   'u,*
      if=2s.SBJ   AV-PFR-come   PRX.LOC yesterday   NOM   2s   CNJ
      na'a=su   qeta-an   ka   patas   niyi.
      could=2s.GEN   see-GV2   NOM   book   PRX
      'If you had come yesterday, you could see this book (now).'

More than one predicate extender may appear at the same time.

(107) *pekelug   gaga   spug   patas   ka   laqi.*
      exactly   DIST.PRG <AV>read book   NOM   child
      'The child is reading a/the book right now.'

The predicate extenders are all alike in attracting clitic pronouns as shown by examples (104)–(106) above. In all of these examples the clitic pronouns representing subjects or non-subject agents appear immediately after the predicate extender rather than after the main predicate. That is, these clitics are all placed after the first word of the predicate phrase. Note that predicate initial-position is distinct from clause-initial position since there are some words which may appear in pre-predicate position but do not attract clitic pronouns:

(108) *ya'asa   hana=ku   m-en-ehedu   m-ahu   lukus.*
      because   just=1s.SBJ   AV-PFR-finish   AV-wash clothes
      'It is because I just finished washing clothes.'

Here *hana* 'just' is a part of the predicate but *ya'asa* 'because' is not because it does not attract the clitic pronoun.

Each predicate extender specifies in which form the following verb can appear. For example, *'asi* 'suddenly, at once' requires the following verb to be non-finite, but it does not matter whether it is AV, GV or CV.

(109)   *'asi*   *tuting*   *wah!*
        suddenly/at:once   AV.NFIN:fall   SURPRISE
        'It fell down suddenly!'

Predicate extenders usually determine aspect/mood but not voice.

The following is a partial list of the words that can function as predicate extenders. They are arranged according to which form they require the following verb to be in.

A. Extenders which require neutral verb forms: *wada* 'PAST', *ga(ga)* 'DISTAL PROGRESSIVE', *niyi* 'PROXIMAL PROGRESSIVE', *gisu* 'PROGRESSIVE, STATE', *meha* 'FUTURE, is going to do…', *(me-)teduwa* 'be able to do…', *nasi* 'if', *na'a* 'could have done something but did not'.

B. Extenders which require non-finite verb forms: *'asi* 'at once, suddenly', *kasi* 'at once, suddenly', *pasi* 'at once', *kani* 'one did not have to do something but did it', *'ini* 'negative', *'iya* 'negative imperative'.

C. Extenders that require future forms: *saw* 'is/was about to do…', *rubang* 'was about to do…'.

D. Extenders that require future or perfect forms of verbs or nouns: *'adi* 'negative'.

E. Extenders that are combined with adjectives or nouns: *ma'a* 'become'.

F. Extenders without specific requirements: *pekelug* 'just', *dima* 'already', *hana* 'at last', 'just', *'ida* 'surely', 'probably', *ya'a* 'uncertainty', *wana* 'only', *'ana* 'even', *ma* 'why', *'alung/'alaw/'arang* 'as is expected', *pida* 'exactly', *lengu* 'planned to do…', *binaw* 'confirmation', *'atih* 'at the last moment', 'nearly', *seperang* 'purposefully'.

There are no predicate extenders that select hortative verb forms.

Nouns can function as predicates, as is shown by examples (23) and (42) above. When one wants to express the meaning 'become X', the noun has to be preceded by the predicate extender *ma'a*.

(110)   *ma'a*   *'ising*   *ka*   *laqi=mu.*
        become   doctor   NOM   child=1s.GEN
        'My child will become a doctor.'

In contrast, adjectives usually express such a meaning by the future form.

(111)   *mpeke-paru*   *ka*   *laqi=mu.*
        AV.FUT-big   NOM   child=1s.GEN
        'My child will become big.'

However, when in construction with *gisu* 'state/progressive', some adjectives also need *ma'a*.

(112)   *gisu ma'a paru.*   It is becoming big.   (*ma'a* is necessary.)
(113)   *gisu (ma'a) me-keray.*   It is becoming hard/expensive.   (*ma'a* is optional.)

Some predicate extenders consist of two words phonetically, judging from the distribution of vowels, but their meaning is not compositional. The clitic appears after the first phonological word. An example is *asi ka* 'have to' in:

(114)   *'asi=ta*   *ka*   *m-usa* *karingku* *saman.*
        have:to=1pi.SBJ   have:to   AV-go   Hualian   tomorrow
        'We have to go to Hualian tomorrow.'

Other examples include *'asi lux* 'suddenly', *kani lux* 'one did not have to do something but did it', *haw ka* 'may', *'ana rabang* 'it was good that...'.

Some of the predicate extenders can be used as predicates by themselves. In example (115) *wada* is the main predicate and means 'is gone, already moved away from the speaker'.

(115) *wada   karingku   ka   masaw.*
       is:gone   Hualian   NOM   Masaw
       'Masaw already is gone to Hualian.'

Similarly, *meha* may be a main predicate meaning 'will be going', 'is going', *gisu* 'is coming, approaching toward the speaker', *teduwa* 'be possible, able', and *'adi* 'do not want'. The demonstratives *niyi* and *gaga* also allow for main predicate and predicate extender uses (cf. section 3.4 above).

3.8 Serial verbs

Seediq has two types of serial-verb constructions. In the first type, which bears some similarities with complex predicate constructions, the first verb immediately precedes the second (cf. (116) and (117)) and the second verb is always in neutral form, as seen more specifically in (117).

(116) *me-deremut   m-atas   ka   laqi   niyi.*
       AV-diligent   AV-study   NOM   child   PRX
       'This child studies diligently.'

(117) *m-en-sa   m-arig   bawa   daya   ka   hiya.*
       AV-PRF-go   AV-buy   bread   upper:place   NOM   3s
       'He went to buy steamed bread at the upper place.'

Pronominal clitics occur immediately after the first verb:

(118) *me-qaras=ku   m-ita   sunan.*
       AV-glad=1s.SBJ   AV-see   2s.OBL
       'I am glad to see you (sg.).'

The subject of the second verb has to be coreferential with the actor or theme of the first verb. In the above examples, both verbs are in AV, in which case this constraint is not particularly noticeable. In (119), however, which is a variant of (118), the first verb is in GV and hence the actor is marked as genitive. But the second verb is still in AV because the argument coreferential with the actor of the first verb is the actor argument.

(119) *qeras-un=misu   m-ita   ka   'isu.*
       glad-GV1=1s.GEN: 2s.SBJ   AV-see   NOM   2s
       'I am glad to see you (sg.).'

This example makes it clear that it is the first verb that determines the voice of the whole clause.

In the next example the goal argument of the second verb is coreferential with the actor/theme argument of the first verb. So the second verb is in GV form.

(120) *malu   qeta-an   ka   degiyaq   teruku.*
       good   see-GV2   NOM   mountain   Truku
       'The Truku mountains are beautiful.' (lit. The Truku mountains are good to be seen)

TABLE 10.5: SEMANTIC RELATIONSHIPS BETWEEN THE TWO VERBS
IN A SERIAL CONSTRUCTION

First verb	Second verb
manner	action
'to go/come'	purpose of going/coming
action/state	similar action/state
abstract action/state	specific action/state
adjective of emotion	event or action that caused the emotion
like, dislike, begin, finish, stop, be able	action/state

In (121), the actor/theme of the first verb *sekuxul* 'to like' is *laqi* 'child' and it is the conveyed object of the second verb *'apa* 'to carry'. So the second verb has to be in CV form.

(121) *sekuxul   sa-'apa   ka   laqi   niyi.*
       <AV>like   CV-carry:on:back NOM   child PRX
       'This child likes to be carried on the back.'

The semantic relationships between the two verbs which can be observed in this construction are summarized in Table 10.5.

In the second type of serial-verb construction, the two verbs also share at least one argument (the actor/theme argument of the first verb) but the relationship between the two verbs is less tight. Most importantly, the first verb has at least one argument not shared with the second verb. This argument then appears immediately after the first verb such as *qabang* does in (122).

(122) *hilaw   qabang   me-taqi   ka   laqi.*
       <AV>cover   blanket AV-sleep NOM   child
       'The child covers [her/his body] with a blanket to sleep.'

Moreover, the second verb may be followed by a subject clitic when it is in perfect form (cf. 123) or in future form (124), but not when it is in neutral form.

(123) *h<en>ilaw=ku   qabang   me-n-taqi (= ku)   (ka yaku).*
       <AV><PFR>cover=1s.SBJ blanket AV-PFR-sleep (= 1s.SBJ) (NOM 1s)
       'I covered (myself) with blanket and slept.'

(124) *me-hilaw=ku   qabang   mpe-taqi (= ku)   (ka yaku).*
       AV.FUT-cover=1s.SBJ   blanket AV.FUT-sleep (= 1s.SBJ) (NOM 1s)
       'I will cover (myself) with blanket and will sleep.'

Aspect and mood of the second verb are determined by the first verb according to the following rules. If the first verb is neutral, perfect or future then the second one agrees in aspect/mood (see the above examples). If the first verb is non-finite or hortative then the second verb is in neutral form.

(125) *halag-i   qabang   me-taqi.*
       cover-GV.NFIN blanket AV-sleep
       'Cover (yourself) with a blanket and sleep.'

3.9 Adverbs

Adverbs may appear (a) immediately after the predicate, (b) after all the non-nominative arguments, (c) in clause final position (but before clause final particles if they exist), (d) in clause initial position (outside the predicate phrase). Table 10.6 contains a fairly complete list of these adverbs.

Examples for the different positions:
(a) Immediately after the predicate

(126)   *quyux* **tih**   *ka*   *sehiga.*
        <AV>rain   a:little   NOM   yesterday
        'It rained a little yesterday.'

(b) After all the non-nominative arguments

(127)   *'ini   bahu*   *lukus*   ***niyana*** *ka*   *baki.*
        NEG   AV.NFIN.wash   clothes   still   NOM   old:man
        'The old man has not washed the clothes yet.'

(c) Clause final position

(128)   *m-en-ahu*   *lukus*   *ka*   *baki*   ***da.***
        AV-PRF-wash   clothes   NOM   old:man   NEWSIT
        'The old man already washed the clothes' (i.e. he does not have to do any more washing).'

(129)   *'ini   bahu*   *lukus*   *ka*   *baki*   ***niyana.***
        NEG   AV.NFIN.wash   clothes   NOM   old:man   still
        'The old man has not washed the clothes yet.'

An example of (d) is (108).

Some adverbs may appear as an argument. In (130) the adverb *kana* 'all' appears as a subject argument.

(130)   *me-gerung*   *ka*   ***kana*** *da.*
        AV-break   NOM   all   NEWSIT
        'Everything is broken.'

TABLE 10.6: LIST OF ADVERBS AND THEIR POSITION

Adverbs	Position
bi/ba/balay 'really'	(a)
ha 'beneficiary marker'	(a)
hari 'a little'	(a)
tih 'a little'	(a)
nanak 'by oneself, alone (intensifier)'	(a) or (b)
nehari 'soon'	(a) or (c)
'uri 'also'	(b) or after the NP focused by *'uri*
kana 'all'	(b) or in NP
duri 'again'	(b) or (c)
han 'for a while'	(b) or (c)
kiya 'a little later'	(b) or (c)
na/niyana 'still'	(b) or (c)
da 'new situation'	(c)
ya'asa 'because'	(d)

3.10 Expressions of existence/possession

Existential and possessive clauses contain the existential predicate *niqan* or its negative counterpart *'ungat*. These lack some important verbal properties, as they do not inflect for aspect/mood or voice (morphologically speaking, *niqan* is the GV form of the verb *m-eniq* 'to live (somewhere), to stay (somewhere), to be (somewhere)').

(131) *niqan   qesurux.*
       EXIST   fish
       'There are fish.'

(132) *'ungat   pila=mu.*
       NEG.EXIST   money=1s.GEN
       'I do not have money.'

Expressions for locations or possessors are optional. They occur in nominative case. The possessum is often followed by a genitive pronoun that agrees with the person and the number of the possessor.

(133) *niqan   qesurux   ka   yayung   gaga.*
       EXIST   fish   NOM   river   DIST
       'There are fish in that river.'

(134) *niqan   pila(=na)   ka   rubiq.*
       EXIST   money(=3s.GEN)   NOM   Rubiq
       'Rubiq has money.'

(135) *'ungat   pila(=na)   ka   masaw.*
       NEG.EXIST   money(=3s.GEN)   NOM   Masaw
       'Masaw does not have money.'

The nominative NP does not allow a clitic subject pronoun to appear (and hence lacks an important subject property).

(136) *'ungat   pila=mu   ka   yaku.*
       NEG.EXIST   money=1s.GEN NOM   1s
       'I do not have money.'

(137) * *'ungat=ku   pila=mu   ka   yaku.*
       NEG.EXIST=1s.SBJ money=1s.GEN NOM   1s

Numerals and quantifying adjectives can also function as existential predicates.

(138) *mataru   laqi=na   ka   rubiq.*
       six   child=3s.GEN   NOM   Rubiq
       'Rubiq has six children.'

(139) *hebaraw   se'diq   ka   hini.*
       many   person   NOM   PRX.LOC
       'There are many people here.'

A very similar alternative to (138) is (140):

(140) *mataru   ka   laqi   rubiq.*
       SIX   NOM   child   Rubiq.
       'Rubiq's children are six.'

In clauses with a demoted possessum introduced in 3.2 (cf. examples (49) and (51)), the possessor seems to be the subject. It is in nominative case and appears in clause final position. However, possessors in such clauses do not generally cause subject clitic pronouns to occur after the predicate. Likewise, possessors do not generate subject clitic pronouns in possessive clauses, as seen in (137) (above). We can see this clearly if the possessor is represented by a first or second person pronoun.

(141)   *m-banah   lukus=mu   ka   yaku.*
        AV-red   clothes=1s.GEN   NOM   1s
        'I am wearing red clothes.'

(142)   **m-banah=ku   lukus=mu   ka   yaku.*
        AV-red=1s.SBJ   clothes=1s.GEN NOM   1s

The matter is further complicated by the fact that this observation does not hold for all possessors. Some possessors appear to become 'true' subjects in that they are represented by clitic pronouns. Compare the following two examples:

(143)   *terema-un=ku   baga   baki.*
        wash-GV1=1s.SBJ   hand   old man   (*terima* 'to bathe, wash body parts')
        'The old man will wash my hands' (lit. 'I will be washed on the hands by the old man').

(144)   **behu-un=ku   lukus   'ina.*
        wash-GV1=1s.SBJ clothes   son's wife (*bahu* 'to wash clothes, dishes, etc.')
        'My daughter-in-law will wash my clothes.'

The relevant difference here may be alienability: possessors of inalienable items such as body parts can be 'raised' to become 'true' subjects, while possessors of alienable items cannot. However, this issue needs further research.

4 MAJOR VERBAL MORPHOLOGY

4.1 Voice and aspect/mood paradigms

Seediq verbs always occur in one of three voices (Agent voice or AV, Goal voice or GV or Conveyance voice or CV) which in turn are always inflected for aspect/mood. The four basic aspect/mood categories are neutral, perfect, non-finite, and hortative. For AV and GV forms there is in addition a distinct future form. No such special future form exists for GV. Instead, for GV two neutral forms are distinguished, one consisting of the stem plus suffix *-un* (GV1) and one of the stem with suffix *-an* (GV2). Although neutral forms are not markers of the future, clauses expressing future use the neutral form with *-un* (see 4.3 for further discussion). In such clauses it is sometimes accompanied by partial reduplication.

The infix *-em-* (or its allomorphs *me-* or ø) mark Agent voice in neutral and perfect aspect/mood. On the basis of their AV marking Seediq verbs and adjectives can be classified into five classes, as further discussed in section 4.2. Here it is sufficient to note that class IV and V verbs or adjectives generally are stative and will be referred to as such throughout this section.

The neutral form of a verb is basically non-future and imperfective. In this chapter, the 'neutral' form is not indicated in the glosses, i.e. all verb forms unmarked for aspect/mood are in neutral form.

Perfect is marked by the infix -en- in all three voices. When it is infixed, the GV voice marker is -an and the CV voice marker se- (see Table 10.7) do not appear. Perfect usually denotes past experience, but may express perfective in complex sentences expressing time relation.

The future AV form is marked with the prefixes me-, mpe-, or mpe-ke-. The CV future form is not marked overtly; its form is the bare stem, but this is sometimes accompanied by partial reduplication. Future usually expresses an event/situation that takes place after the point of utterance. It may, however, express an event or situation after a certain point in the past when they are used in combination with preverbal adverbs.

The non-finite AV form for typical transitive verbs is the bare stem; it is thus homophonous with the CV future form. For stative verbs the prefix ke- is added to the stem in nonfinite AV-forms. The GV and CV non-finite forms are marked with the suffixes -i and -ani, respectively. The non-finite form is used as imperative, but it can also appear in other types of clauses if it is combined with predicate extenders (see 3.7). In (109), for example, the non-finite form appears in combination with preverbal adverb 'asi and expresses a realis event. So it would be misleading to say that non-finite forms express irrealis situations.

The hortative forms are marked with suffixes for all voices: -a for AV, -ay for GV (or -aw or both for some verbs) and -anay for CV. For stative verbs the hortative is generally not used, probably because of semantic or pragmatic reasons.

Table 10.7 illustrates the aspect/mood paradigm of typical transitive dynamic verbs based on the root kerut 'cut'.

When the AV infix is infixed to a stem beginning with p, b or glottal stop, the first syllable is dropped, and the resulting forms begin with m.

(145)   patas 'to tattoo, write, study'   *patas   →   m-atas
        barig 'to buy'   *barig   →   m-arig
        'usa 'to go'   *'usa   →   m-usa

Table 10.8 illustrates the paradigm for stative verbs based on the root dakil '(for plants) to grow'. Note that all GV and CV verbs involve the prefix ke- which is not found in the

TABLE 10.7: VOICE AND ASPECT/MOOD PARADIGM FOR K<EM>ERUT 'CUT'

	AV	GV1	GV2	CV
NEUTRAL	kerut	kerut-un	kerut-an	se-kerut
PERFECT	k<en>erut	k<en>erut-an		k<en>erut
FUTURE	mpe-kerut	——		(ke-)kerut
NON-FINITE	kerut	keret-i*		keret-ani
HORTATIVE	keret-a*	keret-ay*		keret-anay

*The weakening of penultimate u to e in keret-i, keret-a and keret-ay is irregular, see further below.

TABLE 10.8: VOICE AND ASPECT/MOOD PARADIGM FOR ME-DAKIL 'FOR PLANTS TO GROW'

	AV	GV1	GV2	CV
NEUTRAL	me-dakil	ke-dekil-un	ke-dekil-an	(se-ke-dakil)
PERFECT	me-n-dakil	k<en>dekil-an		(k<en>dakil)
FUTURE	mpe-ke-dakil	——		((ke-)ke-dakil)
NON-FINITE	ke-dakil	ke-dekil-i		(ke-dekel-ani)
HORTATIVE	(ke-dakil-a)	(ke-dekil-ay)		(ke-dekel-anay)

paradigm for dynamic verbs given in Table 10.7. The forms in parentheses are rarely used (which holds true for most of the cv forms). The morphonological changes are explained in section 2.2.

Some roots alter their forms irregularly. The weakening of penultimate *u* to *e* in the root *kerut* 'to cut' before a suffix (cf. Table 10.7) is such an irregularity. Other examples include:

(146) *sipaq* 'to hit'   *paq-an* (GV neutral 2) (deletion of the antepenultimate syllables)

    pehapuy 'to cook'   *puy-an* (GV neutral 2) (deletion of the antepenultimate syllables)

    'eniq 'to exist'   *niq-an* (GV neutral 2) (regular+deletion of the antepenultimate syllable), *qeniq-i* (GV non-finite) (addition of initial *q*)

    tinun 'to weave'   *tun-an* (GV neutral 2) (syllable contraction)

    begay/buway 'to give'   *biq-an* (GV neutral 2) (syllable contraction)

    'ekan 'to eat'   *'uq-an* (GV neutral 2), *q<en>uq-an* (GV perfect), *q-ani* (CV non-finite) (alternation of vowel and consonant)

4.2 Classification of verbs according to their AV form

Verbs can be classified on the basis of their neutral and non-finite AV forms. The five classes are illustrated in Table 10.9.

Classes IV and V which contain stative verbs and adjectives are clearly set apart as they are prefixed with *ke-* in the AV future and non-finite (and also in all GV and CV forms, as already mentioned in 4.1). Furthermore in classes IV and V perfect is marked with the prefix *ne-*, a feature they share with class III verbs. The patterns II and V are not marked overtly for voice in neutral and perfect.

Examples of the members that take each pattern are shown below in their AV neutral form. Note that class III includes intransitive dynamic as well as stative verbs:

I *qita* 'to look, see', *(q-e)m-bahang* 'to listen, hear', *sipaq* 'to hit', *sekuxul* 'to like', *dengu* 'to dry something', *m-atas* 'to study', *m-arig* 'to buy', *m-ekuy* 'to bind', *m-adas* 'to carry', *m-usa* 'to go', *m-iyah* 'to come', *tapaq* 'to swim', *talang* 'to run', *sehungi* 'to forget', *lenglung* 'to think', *m-elukus* 'to get dressed', *quti* 'to excrete', *sehemu* 'to urinate', *quyux* 'to rain'.

II *dehuq* 'to arrive', *pehuqil* 'to kill', *pesakur* 'to cultivate', *qeduriq* 'to flee', *dengdang* 'to boil water', *terima* 'to bathe', *tegeli'ing* 'to hide oneself', *sekiya* 'to fly', *sete'tu* 'to go up (slope, mountain, stairs)', *pelukus* 'to make somebody get dressed'.

TABLE 10.9: THE FIVE ASPECT/MOOD INFLECTION PATTERNS FOR AV

	I	II	III	IV	V
Example	kerut	dehuq	me-karaw	me-udus	paru
	'to cut'	'to arrive'	'to climb'	'to be alive'	'to be big'
NEUTRAL	kerut	dehuq	me-karaw	me-udus	paru
PERFECT	k<en>erut	d<en>ehuq	me-ne-karaw	me-ne-udus	ne-paru
FUTURE	mpe-kerut	mpe-dehuq	mpe-karaw	mpe-ke-udus	mpe-ke-paru
NON-FINITE	kerut	dehuq	karaw	ke-udus	ke-paru
HORTATIVE	keret-a	deheq-a	(kerag-a)	——	——

III *me-takur* 'to stumble', *me-tuting* 'to fall, stumble', *me-kela* 'to know', *me-sangay* 'to rest', *me-temay* 'to enter', *me-karaw* 'to climb (tree)', *me-tuku* 'to be enough', *me-diras* 'to shout', *me-teqita* 'to appear', *me-huqil* 'to die, be dead', *me-hiyug* 'to stand up', *me-taqi* 'to sleep, be asleep'.

IV *me-'udus* 'to be alive', *me-dengu* 'to be dry', *me-nihur* 'to be astringent (taste)', *me-'uwit* 'to be tired', *me-keray* 'to be hard, expensive', *me-qalux* 'to be black', *m-banah* 'to be red', *me-rutiq* 'to be dirty', *me-sa'ang* 'to be angry', *me-siqa* 'to feel ashamed', *me-deremut* 'to be deligent'.

V *paru* 'to be big', *bilaq* 'to be small', *malu* 'to be good', *naqih* 'to be bad', *tehiyaq* 'to be far', *sesibus* 'to be sweet', *bebaraw* 'to be long', *behegay* 'to be white'.

This classification does not apply to roots, but to the voice marked forms. The same root can be used in different classes (sometimes involving some additional stem-forming prefixes) and then express different meanings. Examples are:

(147)   *dengu*: *dengu* (class I) 'to dry something' and *me-dengu* (class IV) 'to be dry'

   tutuy: *tutuy* (class I) 'to wake somebody up' and *me-tutuy* (class III) 'to be awake'

   rudu: *redu* (class I) 'to make nest' and *me-rudu* (class III) 'for the hair to be dishelved'

   gerung: *gerung* (class I) 'to destroy sth.' and *me-gerung* (class IV) 'to be broken'

   hurah: *hurah* (class I) 'to destroy sth.' and *me-hurah* (class IV) 'to be broken'

   qita: *qita* (class I) 'to see sth.' and *me-te-qita* (class III) 'to appear, be seen'

   lehelah: *lehelah* (class I) 'to make sth. loose' and *te-lehelah* (class V) 'to be loose'

   rawah: *rawah* 'to open' (class I) and *meke-rawah* (class IV) 'to be open'

Compare also the following two sentences:

(148)   qita=ku   degiyaq.
   <AV>see=1s.SBJ   mountain
   'I see a mountain.'

(149)   me-teqita   pa'ah   hiya   ka   degiyaq   kelebiyun.
   AV-appear   from   DIST.LOC   NOM   mountain   Kelebiyun
   'Mt. Kelebiyun is seen from there.'

As shown by these examples, the meaning difference roughly corresponds to the dynamic vs. stative distinction found in many western Austronesian languages. However, there are only a few of such pairs. There is consequently no systematic or productive way to derive stative verbs from dynamic ones (or vice versa). Furthermore, unlike many Philippine languages, Seediq also lacks productive derivations for potentives. Note in particular that the prefix *te-* which occurs in two of the above examples is not a productive prefix (it occurs in about 10 verb stems; cf. also section 4.4). The prefix *te-* is part of a set of stem-forming prefixes which can be applied to some verb roots and also to some nouns, numerals, and interjections to derive verbs. Other such prefixes are *ge-*, *ke-*, *pe-*, *se-*, and partial reduplication. The resulting stem always belongs to one of the five classes shown above. Which class applies depends on the prefix. Examples are given in Table 10.10.

The more productive and semantically transparent derivations for reciprocal, causatives, and reflexives are dealt with in 4.4.

4.3 Use of voices

Seediq is similar to Phillipine languages with regard to voice selection. Definite undergoers, if present, are generally chosen as the subject of the clause. The voices generally indicate the semantic role of the subject as stated in Table 10.11.

I will sometimes refer to the semantic roles using the cover terms shown as above.

The following examples illustrate the major roles on the basis of *kerut* 'cut'. The English counterpart of the Seediq subject is bold-faced in the translation.

(150) *ga*   *kerut*   *rudux*   *ka*   *'ina.*
      DIST.PRG   <AV>cut   chicken   NOM   son's:wife
      'The daughter-in-law (=Agent) is cutting chicken.'

(151) *kerut-un*   *'ina*   *ka*   *rudux.*
      cut-GV1   son's:wife   NOM   chicken
      'The daughter-in-law will cut **the chicken**.' (=Patient)

(152) *kerut-un*   *'ina*   *rudux*   *ka*   *qehuni*   *niyi.*
      'The daughter-in-law will cut the chicken on **this cutting board**.' (=Location)

(153) *se-kerut*   *'ina*   *rudux*   *ka*   *yayu*   *niyi.*
      CV-cut   son's:wife   chicken   NOM   knife   PRX
      'The daughter-in-law will cut chicken with **this knife**.' (=Instrument)

(154) *se-kerut*   *'ina*   *rudux*   *ka*   *baki.*
      CV-cut   son's:wife   chicken   NOM   old:man
      'The daughter-in-law will cut chicken for the **old man**.' (=Beneficiary)

With ditransitive verbs such as *begay* 'to give' or *rengaw* 'tell', the thing conveyed, including information or medium (=language), is the subject in CV.

TABLE 10.10: VERB STEM-FORMING FROM VARIOUS PARTS OF SPEECH

Roots	Resulting stem	Pattern (AV neutral)
huriq 'to be wet' (adjective)	ge-huriq 'to make something wet'	I (gehuriq)
rabi 'night' (noun)	peke-rabi 'to stay at night'	I (m-eke-rabi)
qequ 'cock-a-doodle-doo' (interjection)	qe-qequ '(for a rooster) to crow'	I (qeqequ)
hulis, me-hulis, 'to laugh' (verb)	te-hulis 'to mock somebody'	II (te-hulis)

TABLE 10.11: VERB FORMS AND THE SEMANTIC ROLE OF THE SUBJECT

Verb forms	Semantic roles	Cover terms	Examples
AV form	Agent, Experiencer, Theme	AGENT	(150)
GV form	Patient, Recipient, Goal, Location	GOAL	(151), (152)
CV form	Thing conveyed, Information, Instrument, Beneficiary	CONVEYED OBJECT	(153), (154)

(155) *se-rengaw=na sediq-an   ka   malu   kari.*
       cv-tell=3s.GEN people-OBL NOM   good   story
       'S/He tells **the good news** to people.'

With verbs such as *risuh* 'to paint' and *bubung* 'to cover', such objects as *pingki* 'paint'
or *qabang* 'blanket' are treated as the thing conveyed and become the cv subject.

(156) *beng-ani 317   mbuyas   ka   qabang   niyi.*
       cover-CV.NFIN   stomach NOM   blanket PRX
       'Cover the/your stomach with this blanket.'

With verbs such as *sebu* 'to throw', such objects as *betunux* 'stone' are treated as the
thing conveyed and become the CV subject.

(157) *se-sebu=deha   kumay ka   bedi.*
       RDP-CV.FUT.shoot=3p.GEN bear   NOM   arrow
       'They will shoot an arrow at a/the bear. They will shoot a/the bear with
       an arrow.'

Some of the class IV verbs have a **GOAL** argument and in such cases they can appear in
GV form, as is demonstrated in sentence (158).

(158) *k<en>se'ng-an   tama   ka   laqi.*
       <PRF>be:angry-GV father NOM   child
       'Father scolded the child.'

Class V verbs generally appear only in AV, reflecting the fact that they take only one
argument (= theme). Class IV/V verbs usually do not appear in cv except in those cases
dealt with in section 5.
   As indicated in Tables 10.7 and 10.8 above, two forms exist for the neutral GV, one
involving -*un* (GV neutral-1) and one involving -*an* (GV neutral-2). Nominal expression
with the same semantic role can appear as subjects with both forms, so one cannot consider these different voice forms on a par with AV and CV. Each suffix, however, conveys
somewhat different meanings which vary along a number of parameters. One factor concerning the distribution of -*un* vs. -*an* is the affectedness of the subject. Location, goal,
recipient are usually not affected and hence marked with -*an*.

(159) *hepuy-an damat   ka   hini.*   (non-affected location)
       cook-GV2 vegetable NOM   PRX.LOC
       'This [place] is where vegetables are cooked.'

Patients vary: some are more affected and others are less affected. In some instances this
amounts to the difference between a non-partitive and a partitive reading:

(160) *wada=mu   hepuy-un ka   seqemu.* (affected patient)
       PST=1s.GEN   cook-GV1 NOM   corn
       'I cooked (all) the corn.'

(161) *wada=mu   hepuy-an ka   seqemu.* (less affected patient)
       PST=1s.GEN   cook-GV2 NOM   corn
       'I cooked (some of) the corn.'

Another factor is aspect/mood. Future is expressed by the -*un* form, regardless of the
affectedness of the subject. Thus the predicate in (162) is marked with -*un* even though
the semantic role of the subject is location.

(162) *tepaq-**un** laqi ka yayung hini.*   (non-affected location)
      swim-GV1 child NOM river PRX.LOC
      'The/A child(-ren) will swim in this river.'

Extension of the predicate (e.g. by *wada* 'past' or *gaga*/*niyi* 'progressive', see 3.7) can also affect the distribution of the two forms. The verb *seqet* 'to cut', for example, is marked with *-an* when it appears as a simple predicate, as in (163), but it gets *-un* when extended by *wada*, as in (164). On the other hand, *peseqama* 'to burn' appears with *-un* regardless of whether or not it appears as simple predicate, as shown by (165) and (166).

(163) *seqet-**an** laqi kedediyax ka waray.* (less affected patient; simple)
      cut-GV2 child everyday NOM thread
      '(The/A) child cuts thread everyday.'

(164) *wada seqet-**un** laqi ka waray.* (less affected patient;
      PST cut-GV1 child NOM thread   complex (wada +))
      '(The/A) child cut the thread.'

(165) *peseqema-**un** tama kedediyax ka sudu.* (affected patient; simple)
      burn-GV1 father everyday NOM trash
      'Father burns trash everyday.'

(166) *wada peseqema-**un** tama ka sudu.* (affected patient;
      PST burn-GV1 father NOM trash   complex (wada +))
      'Father burnt trash.'

Finally, as already indicated in Tables 7 and 8, perfect forms marked with the infix *-en-* always occur with the suffix *-an*.

(167) *p<en>eseqema-**an** tama ka sudu.*
      <PRF>burn-GV father NOM trash
      'Father burnt trash.'

The distribution of the two forms is summarized in Table 10.12.

   Another interesting issue concerning Seediq voice selection concerns the use of CV perfect forms. Some perfect verbs can be marked as either CV or GV apparently without any difference in meaning when the Patient argument is the subject.

(168) *p<en>teluk-an tama ka laqi.*
      <PRF>hit:with:fist-GV father NOM child
      'Father hit the child with his fist.'

(169) *p<en>teluk tama ka laqi.*
      <CV.PRF>hit:with:fist father NOM child
      'Father hit the child with his fist.'

TABLE 10.12: USE OF GV NEUTRAL-1 AND -2

	Affected GOAL	Less affected GOAL	Not affected GOAL
Future	-un	-un	-un
Auxiliary +	wada -un	wada -un	wada -an
(wada: past	gaga -un	gaga -un	gaga -an
gaga: progressive)			
Present habitual	-un	-an	-an
-en- (perfect)	-en–an	-en–an	-en–an

Such verbs include: *pesetalux* 'to make hot', *gerung* 'to destroy', *pehuqil* 'to kill', *geheriq* 'to make wet', *getegut* 'to grind', *gedara* 'to make blood flow', *saruk* 'to burn body hair/feather,' *peseqama* 'to burn', *'uduh* 'to burn', *sipaq* 'to slap', *sikul* 'to push', *berbil* 'to pull', *basaw* 'to move from oven to table'.

Some meanings are expressed only through GV. The following expressions do not have an AV counterpart.

(170)   *da-an=ku   muda.*
        pass-GV2=1s.SBJ   flu
        'I am hit by the flu.'

(171)   *serelung-an   ka   degiyaq.*
        be:cloudy-GV2   NOM   mountain
        'The mountain is cloudy.'

4.4 Causatives, reciprocals, and reflexives

4.4.1 Causatives

Table 10.13 lists the types of morphological relationships that are observed between non-causative and causative verbs.

Among the types listed in Table 10.13, A, B, and B' are most often observed and productive. Type B and B' are the same in that the causative stem contains prefix *se-* and it is often observed that one non-causative base allows both formations. They differ, however, in the following three respects: (1) the causative stem of B does not contain the prefix *pe-* but that of B' does, (2) the causative stem of B inflects in pattern I but that of B' in pattern II, and (3) no GV perfect form can be derived from a B' stem. The same difference is observed in the pair C and C'. The types B through D all pertain to stative verbs while dynamic verbs follow the pattern in A. Examples of each pair are given in Table 10.14.

Some non-causative verbs have more than one corresponding causative verb. Among the above examples *me-rutiq* 'to be dirty', *me-dengu* 'to be dry', and *dalih* 'to be near' illustrate such a case.

Causative verbs take the Causer as AV subject, as in (172), and the Causee as GV subject, as in (173). If the non-causative verb is transitive, then its patient becomes CV subject with the corresponding causative verb, as in (174).

(172)   *m-pe-sepug   patas   kenan   ka   rubiq.*
        AV-FUT-CAU-read   book   1s.OBL NOM   Rubiq
        'Rubiq will make me read a book.'

TABLE 10.13: MORPHOLOGICAL TYPES OF CAUSATIVE FORMATIONS

Type	AV.NEUTRAL (non-causative)	Causative prefix	AV neutral (causative)
A	-em-, me- (class I or II)	pe-	pe- (class II)
B	(me-) (class IV or V)	se-	se- (class I)
B′	(me-) (class IV or V)	pe-se-	pe-se- (class II)
C	(me-) (class IV or V)	ge-	ge- (class I)
C′	(me-) (class IV or V)	pe-ge-	pe-ge- (class II)
D	me- (class IV)	Ø	-em- (class I)

(173)   *pe-sepug-un=ku*   *patas   rubiq.*
        CAU-read-GV1=1s.SBJ   book   Rubiq
        'Rubiq will make me read a book.'

(174)   *se-pe-sepug   leqi-an/laqi*   *bubu   ka   patas   niyi.*
        CV-CAU-read   child-OBL/child.DIR   mother   NOM   book   PRX
        'Mother makes child read this book.'

A non-subject causee appears in oblique case if it is a pronoun or a proper name, as in example (172), and either in oblique or in direct case if it is a noun referring to a human, as in example (174). For other nouns, there is no extra oblique case form, as mentioned in 3.3.

4.4.2 Reciprocals

More than one process exists to form reciprocals (see Table 10.15). Type A (and probably also B) involves partial reduplication. One can also derive reciprocal verbs from nouns (See Table 10.16). Reciprocal verbs are all in class III with regard to aspect/mood inflection.

TABLE 10.14: EXAMPLES OF CAUSATIVE VERBS

	Non-causative (AV neutral form)	Causative (stem/AV neutral form)
A	m-usa 'to go'	pawsa/pawsa 'to make something go, to send something'
	m-unuh 'to suck milk'	pe-'unuh/pe-'unuh 'to make (a baby) suck milk'
	me-huqil 'to die'	pe-huqil/pe-huqil 'to kill'
	sinaw 'to wash'	pe-sinaw/pe-sinaw 'to make wash'
	rawah 'to open sth.'	pe-rawah/pe-rawah 'to make s.o. open sth.'
	me-hiyug 'to stand'	pe-hiyug/pe-hiyug 'to make sth. stand'
B	dalih 'to be near'	se-dalih/sedalih 'to approach'
	me-rutiq 'to be dirty'	se-rutiq/serutiq 'to make dirty'
	me-hungul 'to be sharp'	se-hungul/sehungul 'to make sharp'
	me-dengu 'to be dry'	se-dengu/sedengu 'to make dry'
B'	dalih 'to be near'	pese-dalih/pese-dalih 'to approach'
	me-rutiq 'to be dirty'	pese-rutiq/pese-rutiq 'to make dirty'
	me-dengu 'to be dry'	pese-dengu/pese-dengu 'to cook rice dry (not into porridge)'
C	me-huriq 'to be wet'	gehuriq/ge-huriq 'to make something wet'
C'	me-kela 'to know'	pege-kela/pege-kela 'to notify'
D	me-dengu 'to be dry'	dengu/dengu 'to dry (something)'
	me-qurug 'to be round'	qurug/qurug 'to make (something) round'
	me-takur 'to stumble'	takur/takur 'to make (something) stumble'

TABLE 10.15: MORPHOLOGICAL TYPES OF RECIPROCAL FORMATIONS

Type	Non-reciprocal (AV.NEUTRAL)	Reciprocal (AV.NEUTRAL)
A	-em-	me-RDP- (pattern III)
B	-em-	m-pe-pe- (pattern III)
C	-em-	me- (pattern III)
D	-em-, me-	me-ne-(pattern III)
E	NOUN	me-se-NOUN/me-ke-NOUN (pattern III)

TABLE 10.16: EXAMPLES OF RECIPROCAL VERBS

Type	Non-reciprocal verbs	Reciprocal verbs
A	dayaw 'to help'	me-de-dayaw 'to help one another'
	galik 'to head-hunt'	me-ge-galik 'to head-hunt one another'
	m-asug 'to share'	me-sa-'asug 'to share with one another'
	m-ekan 'to eat'	me-ke-'kan 'to fight against one another'
	m-usa 'to go'	me-se-usa 'to visit one another'
B	rengaw 'to talk'	m-pe-pe-rengaw 'to discuss'
C	sterung 'to meet'	me-sterung 'to meet (with plural subject)'
	skuxul 'to like'	me-sekuxul 'to like each other.'
D	me-deka 'to be same'	me-n-deka 'to be alike'
	kiyux 'to push'	me-ne-kiyux 'to push one another'
E	lupung 'friend'	mese-lupung, meke-lupung 'to be friends with one another'
	dangi 'fiancé(e)'	mese-dangi, meke-dangi 'to be engaged to each other'
	dungus 'spouse'	mese-dungus, meke-dungus 'to be husband and wife'
	baki 'grandfather, uncle'	meke-baki '(of men:) to be related through the marriage between their children or grandchildren'

Examples of reciprocal verbs follow. Note the variation in the meaning of the reciprocal verbs which include 'to V one another', 'to V with one another', 'to V against one another', 'to V one another's N', etc.

Some reciprocal forms seem to express reflexive (or middle) meanings.

(175) Non-reciprocal   Reciprocal
       gimax 'to mix (tr.)'   *me-ge-gimax* 'to mix (intr.)'
       seli 'to gather, collect(tr.)'   *me-se-seli* 'to gather, come together (intr.)'

An important morphosyntactic feature common to reciprocal verbs is that they appear in AV only.

(176) *rubiq   ni   masaw   'u,   m-pe-pa'adas   patas.*
       Rubiq   and   Masaw   CNJ   AV-RCP-send   letter
       'Rubiq and Masaw are sending letters to each other.'

(177) **se-pe-pa'adas=deha   ka   patas.*
       CV-RCP-send=3p.GEN   NOM   letter
       'They send letters to each other.'

The Agent (=subject) of reciprocal verbs is always plural.

(178) *me-de-dayaw   ka   rubiq   ni   masaw.*
       AV-RCP-help   NOM   Rubiq   and   Masaw
       'Rubiq and Masaw help each other.'

If the Agent involves a first or second person, it may either be an 'incorporated' NP or a coordinate NP. The subject *pronoun* is always plural.

(179) *m-en-de-dayaw=nami   ka   yaku   ni   rubiq.*
       AV-PRF-RCP-help=1pe.SBJ   NOM   1s   and   Rubiq
       'Rubiq and I helped each other.'

(180) *m-en-de-dayaw=nami   ka   yami   rubiq.*
       AV-PRF-RCP-help=1pe.SBJ   NOM   1pe   Rubiq
       'We, including Rubiq, helped each other.'

4.4.3 Reflexives

Reflexive meanings are rarely expressed through verb morphology. *te(ge)-* seems to be the only prefix which may convey reflexivity, but it is not very productive.

(181)   *li'ing* 'to hide (tr.)'   *tege-li'ing* 'to hide (intr.)'
        besequr 'to hang someone'   *te-besequr* 'to hang oneself, to suffocate'
        m-aytaq 'to spear sth.'   *te-baytaq* 'to stick'

Seediq expresses reflexives using independent pronouns plus the intensifying adverb *nanak*. The pronoun may be either direct (ex. (182)), oblique (ex. (182)), or nominative (ex. (183)) case. In the latter case, the reflexive expression is the subject of the clause.

(182)   *tendahu=su*   *'isu/sunan*   *nanak*   *ka*   *'isu.*
        <AV>praise=2s.SBJ   2s.DIR/2s.OBL   INTSF   NOM   2s
        'You praise yourself.'

(183)   *masaw*   *'u,*   *se-pege-kela=na*   *rebiq-an*   *ka*
        Masaw   CNJ   CV-CAU-know=3s.GEN   Rubiq-OBL   NOM
        hiya   *nanak.*
        3s   INTSF
        'Masaw (male) let Rubiq (female) know about himself (=Masaw).'

As is shown in (183), reflexive sentences may occur in different voices.

Nanak basically has an intensifying meaning, i.e. 'by oneself', 'alone', and can also be used without an accompanying pronoun. It then always occurs in immediate postverbal position, or after all the non-nominative arguments and relates to the actor argument, regardless of voice.

(184)   *puy-un=na*   *nanak*   *ka*   *'idaw.*
        cook-GV1=3s.GEN   INTSF   NOM   rice
        'He himself will cook rice.'

(185)   *wada*   *me-huqil*   *nanak*   *ka*   *'isaw.*
        PST   AV-die   INTSF   NOM   Isaw
        'Isaw died alone.'

5 NOMINALIZATIONS AND NOMINAL MORPHOLOGY

As described in 3.1, inflected forms of verbs except the hortative form, the AV non-finite form, and the CV non-finite form can be used as noun phrases without further derivation, aid of any particle or any suprasegmental changes (see Table 10.17). The GV non-finite form in such uses refers to a patient/place to which or in which one should perform the action.

(186)   *hini*   *ka*   *seqeda-i*   *sudu.*
        PRX.LOC   NOM   throw-GV.NFIN   trash
        'The place for throwing trash is here.'

The verb form and their meaning when used as noun phrases are summarized below.

TABLE 10.17: NOMINAL DERIVATION FROM VERB FORMS

Forms	Meanings	Examples
AV future form and AV neutral form	agent	*mpe-tegesa* 'teacher'
GV neutral-1 form	patient	*'uq-un* 'food'
GV neutral-2 form	place	*teqi-an* 'bedroom'
CV neutral form	instrument, beneficiary, or thing conveyed	*se-baytaq* 'what is used to spear'
CV future form	what will be used, person for whose sake someone will do something, what will be conveyed	*(be-)baytaq* 'what will be used to spear'
AV perfect form	person who has done something'	*m-en-sa nihung* 'a person who has been to Japan
GV perfect form	person/thing that has undergone something or place where one did something	*t<en>epaq-an* 'place where one has swum'
CV perfect form	person/thing that has undergone something	*t<en>egesa* 'what has been taught'
GV non-finite form	patient/place to which or in which one should do the action	*qeda-i* 'the place for throwing trash'

The AV future form, the GV neutral-1 form, and the CV future form may involve reduplication of the first syllable, as in *be-baytaq* 'what will be used to spear'. However, this is not unique to nominal usage as it is also observed in predicate uses, as already mentioned in 4.1. The following sentences contain such nominals (indicated in italics).

(187)   *q<en>ita=su*   **mpe-tegesa**   *laqi=su*   *hug?*
      <AV><PRF>see=1s.SBJ   AV.FUT-teacher   child=2s.GEN   Q
      'Have you seen your child's teacher?'

(188)   *mawsa*   **berig-an**   *'ipay   ka*   *bubu.*
      AV.FUT.go   buy-GV2   Ipay   NOM   mother
      'Mother will go to Ipay's store.'

The GV or CV perfect forms of stative verbs/adjectives, when used as nominals, have the meaning of abstract nouns rather than expressing 'place where one had been ...'.

(189)   *me-huqil* 'AV-dead'   *q<en>heqil-an/q<en>huqil* 'death'
      paru 'AV:big'   *k<en>pera-an/k<en>paru* 'bigness, size'
      me-kela 'AV-to know'   *k<en>kela-an/k<en>kela* 'knowledge'

The CV neutral and future forms with reduplication of dynamic verbs and verbs of emotion (such as *sa'ang* 'to be angry') are used to mean purpose or reason. A typical construction for such usage is as follows: RDP-CV *future-verb +agent/patient+ka* CV *neutral-verb +agent/patient*. (190) is an example.

(190)   *ge-garang=na*   *malu   kari   ka   se-'uda=na*
      RDP-CV.FUT:convey=3s.GEN   good   story   NOM   CV-pass=3s.GEN
      peteraqil
      hardship.
      'The reason why she had a hard time is that she preached the Gospel.'
      (= good story)

It is unique to this construction which involves two CV forms that a CV-marked main predicate refers to reason. In all other constructions a clause whose predicate is a CV form does not take reason as subject but only beneficiary, instrument, or thing conveyed.

One can regard the above usage of the second (neutral) CV form as a kind of clausal nominalization where all the arguments of this second predicate occur in non-nominative case. Other than this Seediq has no morphological device to nominalize clauses. The marker *ka* is also used as a complementizer for embedding clauses.

(191)   *nawxay*   *pila*   *laqi*   *ka*   *pehiyug*   *sapah*   *ka*   *lawking.*
        creditable:to   money   child   CMP   AV.build   house   NOM   Lawking
        'It was thanks to his child's money that Lawking built his house.'

Example (33) in 3.1 and (97) in 3.6 are also examples of this usage.

ACKNOWLEDGEMENTS

I would like to express my gratitude to Nikolaus Himmelmann and Tasaku Tsunoda for helpful comments on an earlier draft of this essay, although of course I am solely responsible for any errors. And I wish to thank The Mitsubishi Trust Yamamuro Memorial Scholarship Foundation for their generous financial assistance.

REFERENCES

Asai, E. (1953) *The Sediq language of Formosa*, Kanazawa, Japan: Kanazawa University.
Holmer, A. (1996) *A parametric grammar of Seediq*, Lund: Lund University Press.
Li, P.J. (1991) 'Vowel Deletion and Vowel Assimilation in Sediq', in R.A. Blust (ed.) *Currents in Pacific Linguistics*, 163–169, Canberra: Pacific Linguistics.
Ogawa, N. and Asai, E. (1935) *Myths and Traditions of the Formosan Native Tribes*, Taipei: Linguistics Department, Taihoku Imperial University.
Pecoraro, F. (1977) *Essai de Dictionnaire Taroko-Français*, Cahier d'Archipel 7, Paris: S.E.C.M.I.
Tsukida, N. (1999) 'Locative, existential and possessive clauses in Seediq', in E. Zeitoun and P.J-K. Li (eds) *Selected Papers from the Eighth International Conference on Austronesian Linguistics*, 599–636, Taipei: Institute of Linguistics (Preparatory Office), Academia Sinica.
—— (2000) 'The CX-*un* and CX-*an* forms in Seediq', in R. Kikusawa and K. Sasaki (eds) *Modern Approaches to Transitivity*, 53–78, Tokyo: Institute for the Study of Languages and Cultures of Asia and Africa.
Wurm, S.A. and Hattori, S. (eds) (1983) *Language atlas of the Pacific area, Part II*. Canberra: Pacific Linguistics.
Yang, X. (1976) 'The phonological structure of the Paran dialect of Sediq', *The Bulletin of the Institute of History and Philology, Academia Sinica*, Vol 47 (4), 611–706.
Zhang, Y. (1997) *Voice, case and agreement in Seediq and Kavalan*, PhD Thesis, National Tsinhua University.
—— (2000) *Seediq reference grammar*, Taipei: Yuanliou Press.

CHAPTER ELEVEN

ILOKO

Carl Rubino

1 INTRODUCTION

Iloko (Ilocano, Ilokano, Iluko, Samtoy), the language of the Ilocano people, is spoken by nine million people in northwest Luzon Island. It is the third largest language in the Philippines after Tagalog (the basis of the Philippine national language Pilipino) and Cebuano (Sugbuhanon). It is a member of the Cordilleran language family of Northern Philippine languages. Within the family, it forms its own branch and has no close relatives, but does share certain syntactic and lexical affinities with the Itneg languages of Abra, shared by borrowing rather than direct genetic relationship. Other Cordilleran languages include: the Alta branch which includes Baler Dumagat, the South Cordilleran languages of Kallahan, Ibaloi, Pangasinan, and Ilongot; the Central Cordilleran languages of Isinai, Ifugao, Balangao, Bontok, Kankanay, Kalinga, and Itneg; Arta; and the Northern Cordilleran languages which can be subdivided into the Cagayan Valley languages of Gaddang, Itawis, Agta, Ibanag, Atta, Yogad, and Isneg, and the North East Luzon branch which comprises Paranan and Casiguran Dumagat (Reid 1989, 1991, R. Himes, p. c.).

The original Ilocano provinces include Ilocos Norte, Ilocos Sur, and La Union, but Ilocanos have migrated extensively and even predominate in many localities in the neighboring provinces of Abra, Pangasinan, Tarlac, Benguet, and Cagayan. In the provinces of Abra and Pangasinan, many of the Iloko speakers are ethnically Tinguian or Pangasinan, respectively, who have traded in their native tongues for the more prestigious lingua franca. There are also large communities of Iloko speakers in the major urban centers of the United States, most notably in California and Hawaii.

Two major dialects of Iloko exist, each with minor subdialects which minimally vary in lexicon and intonational patterns. The major dialects are usually categorized by the pronunciation of the *pepet* vowel /e/, which is pronounced as [ɛ] in the Northern dialects of Ilocos Norte and parts of Ilocos Sur, and as a high, central-back unrounded vowel [ɯ] in Abra, the southern parts of Ilocos Sur, La Union, Tarlac, and Pangasinan.

The history of Iloko grammar writing has been rather prolific, although much of the earlier pre-twentieth-century work of the Spanish friars has received very little attention. Early Iloko grammars include the Spanish works by Naves (1892), and Lopez (1895), and the English work by Williams (1929). Williams (1904) wrote the first Iloko grammar in German. The first widely publicized description is Bloomfield's (1942) article outlining Ilokano syntax followed ten years later by the impressive grammar by the missionary Vanoverbergh (1955). Widdoes (1950) is rarely cited in the literature, but he was perhaps the first linguist to recognize ergative patterning in Philippine languages, predating Gerdts (1988) and Rubino (1997). Generative grammars of the language include Buell (1960), Constantino (1959), and a relational grammar by Wimbish (1987). The most notable dictionaries are Carro (1888), which was augmented by Vanoverbergh (1956), Laconsay (1993), Geladé (1993), and Rubino (2000). Pedagogical materials include McKaughan (1952), Bernabe *et al.* (1971), Espiritu (1984), and Rubino (1998).

Iloko does not have official status in the Philippines, but does enjoy impressive literary activity. Associations of Iloko writers have sprung up all over the world and frequently put out literary anthologies. They are organized in an umbrella association called GUMIL which stands for *Gunglo dagiti Mannurat nga Ilokano* or Association of Ilokano writers. Iloko writers also use the weekly *Bannawag* 'Dawn' magazine, and a monthly web magazine *Burnay* 'Jar' as outlets for their creativity in their native tongue. The Iloko *Bukanegán* 'poetical joust', coined from the fabled father of Iloko literature, Pedro Bukanég, is still practiced today where contestants can practice their impromptu literary skills in public or on the air.

2 PHONOLOGY

2.1 Segments

Iloko has fifteen native consonantal phonemes, and a glottal fricative used in loanwords and one native word, *haán* 'no', the colloquial variant of *saán* (cf. Table 11.1). Fourteen of the consonants (all but the glottal stop) may appear geminate in roots, e.g. *lawwalawwá* 'spider', *tengngá* 'center', *ballá* 'crazy', *saibbék* 'sob', *saiddék* 'hiccup', *sayyét* 'immodest lady', and *bannáwag* 'dawn'. The glottal stop only occurs geminate across morpheme boundaries: *agaC-ʔárak* [agaʔʔá:rak] 'smelling of alcohol'.

Stops are unaspirated and, in final position, unreleased. The voiceless velar stop is pronounced quite far back and tends towards slight fricativization before vowels. Unlike in Tagalog, glottal stop does not phonemically appear word-finally. Orthographically, glottal stop is not represented word-initially. Word-medially, at a morpheme boundary, it is represented with a hyphen. Since in this sketch hyphens are used to indicate morpheme boundaries, word-medial glottal stop at morpheme boundaries will be transcribed here as <ʔ>.

Syllables have mandatory onsets, so the basic syllable structure of the language is CV(C): *aba* 'taro' [ʔá:.ba], *samʔít* 'sweet' [sam.ʔít]. Consonant clusters occur in both onset and coda positions in foreign loans and recently coined slang expressions which do not follow the native phonological structure: *kláts.bag* 'handbag' (f. English), *ták.werts* 'money' (slang, f. *kuartá* [Sp. *cuarta*]), and *brúha* 'witch', 'sorceress'; 'mythological monster' (f. Spanish *bruja*).

The phonemes /t/, /d/ and /s/ palatalize to [tʃ], [dʒ], and [ʃ] before the palatal glide /y/ or its equivalent (i + vowel), e.g. *siák* 'I' [ʃak], *tián* 'belly' [tʃan], *idiáy* 'there' [idʒay].

TABLE 11.1: ILOKO CONSONANTS (IN PRACTICAL ORTHOGRAPHY)

	±Voice	Labial	Dental	Alveolar	Palatal	Velar	Glottal
Stops	−	p	t			k	ʔ
	+	b	d			g	
Fricative	−			s			(h)
Affricates	−			ts			
Lateral	+			l			
Tap/trill	+			r			
Glide	+	w			y		
Nasal	+	m		n		ng	

TABLE 11.2: ILOKO VOWELS (IN PRACTICAL ORTHOGRAPHY)

	Front	Central	Centralized Back	Back
High	i		e	u
Mid	(ɛ)			(o)
Low		a		

Because of many borrowings from English, Spanish, and colloquial Tagalog where these palatal sounds are not complex phoneme sequences, the phonemic status of [tʃ], [dʒ], and [ʃ] is open to debate.

All consonants except the glottal stop can appear as onsets phonemically, and all non-glottal or non-palatalized consonants may occur phonemically as codas. The glottal stop [ʔ] occurs phonetically in words beginning in a vowel, and may surface as a coda phonetically when it replaces a coda *t* or *k* preceding another onset consonant: *pukráy* 'crumbly squash' > [*puʔ.ráy*].

Iloko has four native vowel phonemes /i, e, a, and u/ (cf. Table 11.2). The new phonemes /o/ and /ɛ/ are found only in loanwords. In the northern dialects, the phoneme /e/ is pronounced as /ɛ/, not differentiated from its pronunciation in Spanish loanwords.

The high vowel [u] is lowered considerably in word-final syllables, and is thus represented in the orthography, e.g. *búlo* 'kind of bamboo' /bú:.lu/, *agsaó* 'to speak' /agsaú/; *ások* 'my dog' /á:su=k/.

Sequences of two vowels other than the diphthongs /ia/, /io/, and /ua/ are pronounced as two syllables, with an intervening glottal stop in careful speech, *siít* 'thorn' [si.ʔít], *kées* 'crazy' [ké:.ʔes], *bigáo* 'winnow' [bi.gá:.ʔo], *saán* 'no' [sa.ʔán], and *dissúor* 'waterfall' [dis.sú:.ʔor], but: *alʔaliá* 'ghost' [ʔal.ʔal.ya], *bagió* 'storm' [bag.yó], and *luá* 'tear of eyes' [lwa].

2.2 Stress and vowel length

Stress is phonemic, e.g. *siká* 'you', 'familiar' vs. *síka* 'dysentery'. There, are, however, certain environments that attract stress. Stress falls on the last syllable if the penultimate syllable is closed, i.e. the last vowel is preceded by two consonants (including a sequence of glottal stop + consonant): *paltóg* 'gun', *takkí* 'excrement', *kulagtít* 'jerking movement', *tig-ʔáb* 'belch', *lisʔá* 'nit', 'lice egg', *pugtó* 'guess'. Exceptions to this rule include words of foreign origin or words with a velar nasal coda preceding a final syllable: *súngka* 'kind of native game', *bibíngka* 'rice cake', *karámba* 'jar' (Spanish loan), *kuárto* 'room' (Spanish loan).

Stress also falls on the last syllable if the last vowel is preceded by a consonant and glide: *sadiá* 'renowned', *bituén* 'star', *aniá* 'what'. Exceptions include borrowed words: *aránia* 'chandelier' (f. Spanish), *hópia* 'bean cake' (f. Chinese).

Orthographic vowel sequences, which comprise two syllables, usually take stress on the first vowel when following two consonants, e.g. *manabtúog* [ma.nab.tú:.ʔog] 'thump', *kulláaw* [kul.lá:.ʔaw] 'owl'. Words that include two identical CVC sequences separated by a vowel usually will carry the stress on the vowel separating them: *salísal* 'compete', *batíbat* 'nightmare', *arimasámas* 'red skies at moonrise', *bugábog* 'mixed varieties of rice'. There are, however, a few exceptions: *yakayák* 'sieve', and *pidipíd* 'closely set together'.

TABLE 11.3: ILOKO REDUPLICATION PATTERNS

Reduplicant shape	Use	Examples
-C-	Animate/kin plurals	laláki 'male' > la*l*láki 'males' babái 'female' > ba*bb*ái 'females' ubíng 'child' > u*bb*íng 'children'
CV-	Plural argument	ag-*pi*-p<inn>a-básol=da AV-PL-CAU<RCP>-blame =3p.ABS 'they are blaming each other'
	Animate plural	ka-ili-án 'townmate' > *ka*kailián 'townmates'
CVC-	General plurals	kaldíng 'goat' > *kal*kaldíng 'goats'
	Imperfective aspect	ag-bása 'read' > ag-*bas*bása 'reading (in the process of)'
	Comparison	dakkél 'big' > *dak*dakkél 'bigger' na-samʔít 'sweet' > na-*sam*samʔít 'sweeter'
CVC(C)V-	Lexical iterativity	ag-tilmón 'swallow' > ag-*tilmo*tilmón 'swallow repeatedly'
CVC(C)V+N-	Mutuality	rúpa 'face' > *rupan*rúpa 'face to face'
Full Reduplication	Lexicalized items	bánga 'pot' > *banga*bánga 'skull' tukák 'frog' > *tukak*túkak 'wart'

Vowels before geminate consonants and in stressed open (CV) syllables are automatically lengthened: *sála* 'dance' [sá:.la], *babbái* 'females' [bà:b.bá:.ʔi]. Open reduplicated syllables in roots that contain a vowel sequence also bear secondary stress/lengthening: *naka-bà-baín* (POT-RDP-shame) 'shameful'.

2.3 Reduplication

Reduplication in Iloko is used for both inflectional and derivational purposes. Formally speaking, there are six possible shapes of the reduplicant with the most common uses given in Table 11.3. Aside from the consonant gemination found in animate and kin plurals, all reduplicative morphemes in Iloko are prefixal, copying the first part of a given stem (root or prefix+root):

3 BASIC MORPHOSYNTAX

3.1 Word and morpheme classes

The open lexical classes are noun, verb, adjective, and adverb. All roots, however, may derive nominal and verbal forms because of the very productive morphological system of the language. Nouns, adjectives, and adverbs may occur as simple roots, but verbs, with very few exceptions, are decomposable into a root and a voice affix. Nouns are differentiated from verbs in that they do not take aspectual morphology and, unlike verbs, many show idiosyncrasies in their plural formation. Verbs consist of a root with a portmanteau affix denoting their voice class and aspect (see section 5.1 and 5.2). Adjectives are words that may follow the moderative adverb *medio* 'somewhat'. Most can take specific comparative, superlative, attenuative, and admirative affixation.

(1) Basic Adjective: *na-pigsá*   'strong'
     Comparative   *na-pig-pigsá*   'stronger'
     Superlative   *ka-pigsá-an*   'strongest'
     Attenuated   *pamigsáen* /paN-pigsa-en/   'rather strong'
     Admirative   *nag-pigsá=n*   'how strong!'

Adverbs are unlike nouns in that they cannot occur pluralized, and they are unlike verbs
in that they do not take voice affixation. Adverbs come in two forms, roots that may take
affixes and enclitics (such as *dandaní* in 2) vs. invariable particles. The latter include
kanó 'evidential hearsay particle', *met* 'extra information; also; emphasis', *pay* 'continued occurrence, still, yet', *ngatá* 'maybe', *gayam* 'surprise', *kadí* 'interrogative particle',
laeng 'limitation, only, just', *lattá* 'just, simply', *ngamín* 'particle of cause', *ngay* 'particle of elicitation', *ngarúd* 'particle of consequence or assertion, then'. These particles are
enclitic-like in their positional requirements (they usually occur in second position), but
not their segmental shape, as they do not phonologically fuse to their hosts (cf. 3).

(2) *Panunót-e=m   komá   a   dandaní=akó=n   ag-pa-sngáy*
     think-PV-2s.ERG   OPT   LK   almost=1s=now   AV-CAU-born
     'You should think that I am about to give birth.'

(3) *Ag-ka-probínsia-an=ta   gáyam.*
     AV-RCP-province-NR=1d.ABS   SURPRISE
     'So you and I are from the same province!'

Closed grammatical classes include the pronouns (enclitic and independent), articles/
prepositions which mark the case of the nouns following them, demonstratives, conjunctions, existentials, and ligature (linker).
    The ligature in Iloko is used to link heads and attributes. In formal written Iloko, it
manifests itself as *nga* before vowels, and *a* before consonants. In speaking, however, *nga*
is preferred regardless of environment. Environments requiring the ligature include
Number/Adjective + *nga* + Noun, Verb/Predicate + *nga* + Subordinate/Complement
Clause, Noun + *nga* + Relative Clause, and Negator *saán* + *nga* + Negated
Constituent. It is optional after demonstratives, e.g. *daytóy (nga) kayo* 'this (LK) tree'.
    Iloko speakers employ two number systems, a native one used in counting, and a bor-
rowed Spanish system used in telling time, dates, and calculation. The native numbers are:
maysá '1', *duá* '2', *talló* '3', *uppát* '4', *limà* '5', *inném* '6', *pitó* '7', *waló* '8', *siám* '9',
sangapúlo '10' (< *maysa-nga-púlo*), *sangapúlo ket maysá* '11', *duapúlo* '20', *tallopúlo*
'30', *uppát nga púlo* '40', *limapúlo* '50', *sangagasút* '100', *sangaríbo* '1000'; *sanga-
riwríw* '1,000,000'. Numbers may also be considered to be a class of their own due to the
number of morphological distinctions available to them. The possible derivations include
ordinals *maikaduá* 'second', indefinites *sumagdùduá* 'about two', restrictives *dùduá*
'only two', fractions *kaguduá* 'half', multiplicatives *maminduá* 'twice', multiplicative
ordinals *kapaminduá* 'second time', distributives *sagdùdua* 'two each', distributive multiplicatives *sagpaminduá* 'each twice', and grouping *dua-duá* 'two by two'. Numbers
may likewise take other morphology to derive nouns and verbs, e.g. *kapiduá* 'second
cousin', *piduá* 'second time', *paminduaén* 'to do twice', *pagduaén* 'to divide into two;
do two things at the same time', and *sinagduduá* 'fiber consisting of two strands twisted
together'.
    Words in Iloko can be monomorphemic or derived by one or more affixes which
include prefixes, suffixes, infixes, and combinations thereof. Productive prefixes may

function like proclitics (Rubino 1997), as they may attach to constituents that are longer than a word: *agat-[natáy a baó]=ka* (smell.of-[dead LIG mouse]=2s.ABS) 'You smell like a dead rat'. Furthermore, they are sometimes uttered independently with a pause before their root (... here represents a brief pause between the prefix and stem): *n-ag-... pandág* (PFV-AV-press) 'pressed'.

3.2 Basic clause structure

The central feature of the Iloko clause is the predicate which occurs in initial position. Three clause types can be distinguished (a) verbal, (b) equational, and (c) existential.

Verbal clauses are those that take a verb as the head of the predicate. The verb may be transitive (with two core arguments), e.g. *S<in>ipát ti lakáy ti ubíng* (spank<PFV.PV> CORE old.man CORE child) 'The old man spanked the child', intransitive (with one core argument), e.g. *Na-táy ti lakáy* (PFV-POT-die CORE old.man) 'The old man died', or ambient (containing a verb which cannot take an argument, e.g. a meteorological verb like *N-ag-túdo* (PFV-AV-rain) 'It rained'.

Core arguments are those that appear in either the ergative or absolutive case when pronominalized. That is, the ergative/absolutive distinction manifests itself only in the pronouns. The ergative case is marked on pronouns that are used for agents of transitive verbs (and for possessors), while the absolutive case is reserved for single arguments of intransitive verbs and nominal predicates, or the patientive arguments of transitive verbs. If the core arguments are pronominal, they will be enclitics as in (4) and (5). An exception is the third person singular absolutive which remains unmarked (see Table 11.5 below for an overview of the forms). If they are nominal, they will be preceded by a core noun marker (article or demonstrative), such as *Dallíng* and *kulibangbáng* in (6). Adjuncts (oblique arguments) will also be preceded by either an article or demonstrative in the oblique case. See Table 11.4 below for an overview of the forms of the article.

(4) *Ay-ayat-én=na=ka.*
     CONT-love-PV=3s.ERG=2s.ABS
     'He loves you.'

(5) *Gayyém=na=ka?*
     friend=3s.ERG=2s.ABS
     'You are his friend?'

(6) *Na-kíta   ni   Dallíng   ti   kulibangbáng   iti   ka-niog-án.*
     POT.PFV-see   PN.CORE   Dallíng   CORE   butterfly   OBL   LOC-coconut-NR
     'Dalling saw the butterfly in the coconut grove.'

Only vocative and predicative nouns may appear without an overt noun marker. The canonical constituent order of a verbal clause is verb (+ ERG) + ABS (+ adjunct).

Equational clauses are those that take a nominal predicate, i.e. a noun phrase or prepositional phrase. They have traditionally been called equational because of the absence of a copular verb, not because their primary function is that of equating. Equational clauses are often used in Iloko to contrast or identify a referent, e.g. *Ti kaldíng ti n-ag-saruá* (CORE goat CORE PFV-AV-vomit) 'The goat (is the one who) vomited', *Siák ti taga-Dagúpan.* (1s CORE from-Dagupan) 'I am (the one) from Dagupan'.

In existential clauses an existential particle occurs in the predicate position. Iloko has two existential particles, *addá* 'there is, there are', and its negative counterpart *awán* 'there is not, there are not'. The existentials are used to express both existence and possession, e.g. *Addá=ak ditóy.* (EXIST=1s.ABS PRX.ADV) 'I am here', *Adda áding=ko.* (EXIST younger.sibling=1s.ERG) 'I have a younger sibling'. In possessive constructions, the possessor appears in the ergative case, unlike in Tagalog, and the positive and negative existentials differ somewhat with regard to case marking. The article *ti* is used in conjunction with *awán* when the possessed noun is concrete and indefinite. It is left out, however, in the same circumstances with *addá*, e.g. *Awán ti baláy=ko.* (NEG.EXIST core house=1s.ERG) 'I do not have a house', *Addá kuartá=m?* (EXIST money=2s.ERG) 'Do you have any money?' Existentials in Iloko may also be used with partially reduplicated roots to express attenuation:

(7) *Médio   addá   dang-dang?ás   ti   saludsód-na.*
     somewhat   EXIST   RDP-haughtiness   CORE   answer=3s.ERG
     'His answer was a bit arrogant.'

(8) *Adda   ke-kées=na.*
     EXIST   RDP-crazy=3s.ERG
     'He is a bit crazy.'

Interrogative clauses come in two types, those mirroring an equational clause in which the interrogative occurs as the predicate and is followed by a verb (9, 10) or nominalization (11) which reflect the absolute status of the interrogative, or those in which the interrogative precedes a predicate, separated by a ligature (12). The choice between the two strategies is dependent upon the interrogative element involved.

(9) *Asíno   ti   <im-m>áy?*
     who   CORE   come<PFV-AV>   'Who came?'

(10) *Aniá   ti   g<in>átang=mo?*
     what   CORE   buy<PFV.PV>=2s.ERG   'What did you buy?'

(11) *Kaanó   ti   ya-?áy=na?*
     when   CORE   GER-come=3s.ERG   'When is he coming?'

(12) *Apay   nga   ag-sang-sángit=ka?*
     why   LK   AV-CONT-cry=2s.ABS   'Why are you crying?'

Non-existential clauses are negated with the negators *saán* (colloquially *haán*) or *di*. *Saán* may be used to negate nominal or verbal predicates, while *di* is preferred for verbal clauses only in spoken Iloko. The negator *saán* requires a ligature before the negated constituent while *di* does not: *Saán=da nga Insík* (NEG=3p.ABS LK Chinese). 'They are not Chinese', *Di=ka ay-ayat-en* (NEG=1s.ERG:2s.ABS CONT-love-PV) 'I do not love you'.

Imperatives are usually identical to verbal clauses, as the addressee is expressed by an enclitic pronoun, except in some cases in which the verb is contracted in very informal contexts: *guráy* 'wait!' (from *aguray* 'to wait'). Imperatives may be marked for continuous aspect: *Mangánkan!* /Mang-kaán=ka=n!/ (AV-eat=2s.ABS=already) 'Eat!', *Ag-sing-singpét=ka!* (AV-CONT-behave=2s.ABS) 'Behave!'. Disregarding intonational differences, prohibitives are formally identical to negative declaratives.

(13) *Haán=mo   nga   alá-en.*
     NEG=2s.ERG   LK   get/take-PV
     'Don't take it.'

Finally, a very common occurrence in verbal clauses are a number of aspectual or modal enclitics to the verb phrase aside from the core pronominals. They include *=(e)n* encoding a change of state, or a verbal action that is completed sooner than expected, =*(n)to* indicating future actions, and =*(n)sa* expressing doubt, e.g. *Na-táy=en* (PFV.POT-die=already) 'He already died', *Um-áy=kami=nto manén* (AV-come=1pe.ABS=FUT again) 'We'll come again', *Ag-tag-tagainép=ka=nsa* (AV-CONT-dream=2s.ABS=I.think) 'I think you're dreaming (hallucinating)'.

Iloko has also two lexical verbs that have grammaticized into auxiliaries, *um-áy* (AV-come) 'to come', and *ma-pán* (AV-go) 'to go'. As auxiliaries, they precede their main verbs in monoclausal constructions without the ligature *nga*, and take personal enclitics governed by the main verb. That is, although *mapán* and *umáy* are both intransitive verbs, they may take ergative pronouns if the main verb is transitive: *Um-áy=ka alá-en* (AV-come=1s.ERG:2s.ABS get-PV) 'I'll come get you', *Mapán=ko danón-en* (go=1s.ERG fetch-PV) 'I'll go fetch it'.

3.3 Noun phrase structure

Noun phrases are phrases that have a noun or pronoun as their head. Nouns may be classified into two categories depending on what articles they take, personal vs. non-personal. Personal nouns require a nominal marker at all times unless they are used vocatively. Non-personal nouns, however, may appear without an article or demonstrative when used predicatively (compare *Ubíng.* 'It is/was a child' (predicative NP) and *Ni Maria.* (PERS. CORE Maria) 'It is/was Maria.'). Articles distinguish two numbers (singular vs. plural), two cases (core vs. oblique), and personal vs. non-personal nouns (cf. Table 11.4), e.g. *N-ag-kantá ti ubíng iti paraángan* (PFV-AV-sing CORE child OBL yard) 'The child sang in the yard'. *Diáy*, an abbreviated form of the distal demonstrative *daydiáy* is also used in Iloko discourse as an article for identifiable referents.

Iloko has six sets of pronouns which encode eight personal distinctions (see Table 11.5). Independent pronouns are used predicatively. Ergative and absolutive pronouns are second position enclitics (see HIMMELMANN, TYPOLOGICAL CHARACTERISTICS, section 3.2, for

TABLE 11.4: ILOKO ARTICLES

	Non-personal		Personal	
	Singular	Plural	Singular	Plural
Core	ti (neutral), diay (definite)	dagití	ni	da
Oblique	ití	kadagití	kenní	kadá

TABLE 11.5: ILOKO PRONOUNS

Person	Number	Independent	Ergative	Absolutive	Oblique	Gloss
Speaker	sg.	siák	=k(o)	−ak	kaniák	1s
	pl.	dakamí	=mi	=kamí	kaniámi, kadakamí	1 pl excl
Addressee	sg.	siká	=m(o)	=ka	kaniám, kenká	2s familiar
	pl.	dakayó	=yo	=kayó	kaniáyo, kadakayó	2 pl, (2 formal)
Other	sg.	isú(na)	=na	2	kaniána, kenkuána	3s
	pl.	isúda	=da	=da	kaniáda, kadakuáda	3p
Speaker–Addressee	sg.	datá	=ta	=ta	kaniáta, kadatá	1 dual incl
	pl.	datayó	=tayó	=tayó	kaniatayó, kadatayó	1 pl incl

more discussion). In addition to their positional variability, these enclitics are unlike suffixes in that they do not cause stress shift. The oblique pronouns are formed with the absolutive enclitics attached to the stems *ken-* (for singular referents) and *kada-* (for plural referents). Alternatively, the ergative enclitics are attached to the stem *kania-* (most of these forms, however, are non-standard).

Monosyllabic enclitics are usually not immediately segmentable by native speakers and some show allomorphic variation dependent upon phonological environment. After the suffixes *-an* and *-en*, the first and second person ergative enclitics fuse with the final *n* to *k*, and *m*, respectively, e.g. *basáek* /basa-en=k(o)/ (read-PV = 1s.ERG) 'I'll read it'. The first and second person ergative enclitics also lose their final vowel after vowels, e.g. *adi=m* (younger.brother=2s.ERG) 'your younger brother', unless they are followed by the adverbial enclitic *=(e)n* 'now, already' or follow the monomorphemic functors *di* 'negation' or *sa* 'then', in which case they maintain their full forms (see 14). The following examples demonstrate both the fusional (14) and distributional (15) nature of the enclitic pronouns:

(14) *Surátemon!*
      súrat-en=mo=n
      write-PV=2s.ERG=now/already
      'Write it!'

(15) ...*sá=monto   surát-en kalpasánna?*
         then=2s.ERG=FUT   write-PV afterwards
      '...then you'll write it afterwards?'

When two enclitic pronouns appear on a transitive verb, sometimes a fair amount of agent neutralization occurs. The first person singular ergative enclitic, for example, cannot appear before the second person singular absolutive. Thus, *Kayát=ka* may mean either 'You are wanted' or 'I want you'. With first and second person patients, only the number of the agent is encoded, e.g. *Kayát=da=ka* may mean either 'We want you' or 'They want you' and *Kayat=n=ak?* means either 'Does he want me?' or 'Do you want me?'.

Some enclitics appear to be fossilized derivations of older forms that have nowadays become ungrammatical: *Indiák, diák, mandiák* are first person negators for transitive verbs using the absolutive clitic *=ak* instead of the ergative clitic *=k(o)*, e.g. *Diak maawátan* (NEG.1s POT:understand:DV) 'I do not understand it'. This may also be expressed as *Saán=ko a maawátan* (NEG = 1s.ERG LK POT:understand:DV) 'I do not understand it'.

Not included in Table 11.5 are the independent possessive pronouns formed with the stems *kukúa* 'thing' or *bági* 'share' followed by an ergative enclitic, e.g. *kukuák, kukuám, bágik, bágim*, etc. An example is *Kukuák daytá* (mine MED) 'That is mine'. Reflexive pronouns are formed by the stem *bagí* 'body' followed by an ergative enclitic, e.g. *bagík, bagím, bagína*, etc; cf. also *P<in>a-táy=na ti bagí = na* (CAU<PFV.PV>-die = 3s.ERG CORE body=3s.ERG) 'He killed himself'.

Both independent and enclitic pronouns must specify all the relevant participants of an event. 'Mary and I' in Iloko is rendered *Dakamí ken Maria* (1pe and Mary) 'We (exclusive) and Mary'. If the pronoun is an enclitic it may occur separated from the rest of the expression:

(16) *Saán=mi   a   kasapúlan ken Cedríng ti   túlong=mo.*
      NEG=1pe.ERG   LK   need:DV   and Cedring CORE help=2s.ERG
      'Cedring and I do not need your help.'

Like the articles, numerals, adjectives and quantifiers also precede their nominal head, but they are linked to the head with the ligature *nga*. Possessors are marked by the core article and follow their heads, as do contrastive adjectives, e.g. *ti baláy ni Gracia* 'Gracia's house', *ti ruángan ti baláy* 'the door of the house,' *ti baláy a nangína* 'the expensive house (as opposed to the other one)'. Demonstratives (section 4) precede their nominal head with or without a ligature: *daytóy (a) káyo* 'this (LK) tree'. Unlike other quantifiers, *tunggál* 'every', and *kadá* 'each' do not require the ligature *nga* before their head nouns.

Relative clauses are dependent on their head noun in the same formal way as most attributes in Iloko are dependent on them, with the ligature *nga*. Relative clauses follow their head noun which acts as the absolutive argument of the verb in the relative clause, i.e. NP = [article] [head noun] [ligature] [clause] (for examples, see section 5.1).

4 DEICTICS

Iloko deictics include spatial/temporal demonstratives (which have abbreviated short forms), and temporal adverbs that mark relative time. The temporal adverbs are *itá* 'now, today', *itattá* 'right now', *itattáy* 'just a while ago, immediate past', *itáy* 'a while ago, recent past', and *idí* 'a while ago, remote past'. The time frames covered by these adverbs vary considerably according to speakers' subjective assessment. They may all be used to indicate hodiernal events, and only *idí* can be used to express a time frame one day before the speech event. Temporals can mark both verb phrases and temporal nouns: *N-ag-paráng idí* (PFV-AV-appear REM.PST) 'It appeared a while back', *idí rabií* (REM.PST night) 'last night'. There is also a future marker *(in)ton(o)* which precedes temporal nouns, e.g. *intón bigát* (FUT morning) 'tomorrow'; it cannot be used as a temporal adverb.

The non-temporal Iloko demonstratives mark three degrees of spatial orientation, proximal (near the speaker), medial (near the addressee, or near both speaker and addressee), and distal (far from both interlocutors), and the out-of-sight demonstratives have two degrees of temporality (recent vs. remote). The full demonstratives inflect for two cases and two numbers, while their shortened forms do not. In most dialects of Iloko, the singular oblique forms are formed with the singular form preceded by the oblique article *iti*, but only the *ka-* prefixed variants are given in Table 11.6.

The recent and remote demonstratives are used for referents that are not visible in the speech event. They mark referents that may be dead, non-actual, or somehow distanced

TABLE 11.6: ILOKO DEMONSTRATIVES

Visibility	Range	Short forms	Full forms			
			Core		Oblique	
			Singular	Plural	Singular	Plural
Visible	Proximal	toy	daytóy	dagitóy	kadaytóy	kadagitóy
↓	Medial	ta	daytá	dagitá	kadaytá	kadagitá
Neutral	Distal	diay	daydiáy	dagidiáy	kadaydiáy	kadagidiáy
Out-of-sight	Recent	tay	daytáy	dagitáy	kadaytáy	kadagitáy
	Remote	di	daydí	dagidí	kadaydí	kadagidí

from the speech event. Referents that are recently activated into the consciousness of the speaker may also appear with a non-visible demonstrative. Compare *N-ag-paráng ni Sinting* (PFV-AV-appear PN Sinting) 'Sinting appeared/showed up' vs. *Nagparáng daydí Sinting* 'The late Sinting appeared (as a ghost)'; *Ania ti nágan=mo* (what CORE name=2s.ERG) 'What is your name' vs. *Ania tay náganmo [manén]* 'What was your name [again], (I used to know it)'.

5 MAJOR VERBAL ALTERNATIONS

Of all the morphological systems in the language, verbal morphology is the most complex. All verbs are marked for voice, by which the semantic relationship between the absolutive argument, which is highly thematic and syntactically privileged, and the verb is explicitly detailed by the morphology of the verb (section 5.1). Aspect can be either inflectional or derivational in Iloko, as regular paradigms and lexicalized reduplicative morphology both exist (section 5.2). All verbs belong to one or two moods: dynamic (unmarked), or potentive/stative (marked with the prefixes *maka-* or *ma-*) to denote an action or event which is abilitative, coincidental, unintentional, stative, or performed with less volition than its dynamic counterpart (section 5.3). Other morphological categories that pertain to the verbal template include causation/indirect action/direction with the prefix *pa-* (section 5.4), reciprocity with the infix *-inn-* (section 5.5), and joint action, indicated by the prefix *maki-* (section 5.6).

5.1 Voice

The Iloko voice system consists of five main voices, and two lesser voices (cf. Table 11.7). The different voices can be categorized into two dimensions, based on whether or not they may take a core argument in the ergative case. Actor voice verb forms take one core argument in the absolutive case, and non-actor voice verb forms take two core arguments, an agent in the ergative case, and another argument in the absolutive case. The actor voice (AV) is marked with one of three prefixes, *ag-* (durative), *-um-* (punctual/inchoative), and *mang-/maN-* (distributive; detransitive). Because actor voice verbs take maximally one core argument, they are grammatically intransitive. Meteorological verbs which do not take an argument also take AV morphology, e.g. *N-ag-túdo* (PFV-AV-rain) 'It rained'.

The AV prefix *ag-* is the most versatile of the Iloko prefixes and forms verbs with varying semantic case frames. Unlike in Tagalog, the actor arguments of *ag-* verbs are not

TABLE 11.7: VOICE MARKING MORPHOLOGY

Transitivity	Voice	Affix	Perfective	Example	Gloss
Intransitive	Actor	ag-	nag-	*ag*katáwa	to laugh
		-um-	-imm-	*du*makkél	to grow, become big
Detransitive		mang-	nang-	*mang*án	to eat
Transitive	Patient	-en	-in-	suráten	to write something
	Directional	-an	-in--an	surátan	to write to someone
	Conveyance	i-	in-; iny-	*i*súrat	to write down
	Benefactive	i- -an	in(y)- -an	idaítan	to sew for someone
	Comitative	ka-	kina-	*ka*tugáw	to sit with someone; seat mate
	Instrumental	pag-	pinag-	*pag*íwa	to slice with; knife

necessarily volitional: *agtúdo* 'to rain', *agsángit* 'to cry', *agláti* 'to rust', *agkatáwa* 'to laugh', *agsipílio* 'to brush the teeth', *agbúnga* 'to fruit (trees, plants)', *agukrad* 'to open (of flowers)'. The AV infix *-um-* may be used to designate events that are inchoative: *dumakkél* 'to grow, become big', *bumaknáng* 'to become rich', *lumaíng* 'to become intelligent', *tumáo* 'to be born (become a person)'. Like *ag-* verbs, the absolutive argument of *-um-* verbs may be volitional or non-volitional: *dumáwat* 'to ask for', *ngumáto* 'to rise', *bumabá* 'to lower', *pumúsay* 'to die', *umuttót* 'to fart'. With verbs that can take both the prefix *ag-* and the infix *-um-*, usually the *-um-* verb will express a telic action: *tumakdér* 'to stand up' vs. *agtakdér* 'to stand'.

The AV prefix *maN-/mang-* also only takes one core argument and is grammatically intransitive, but semantically *maN-* verbs pattern closely with their transitive counterparts and are therefore better considered detransitive: e.g. *tippúog* 'sound of crumbling' (from the root *tipóg*) > *agtippúog* 'to crumble down, collapse resoundingly (AV, intransitive)', *mangtippúog* 'to topple down, cause to crumble (AV, detransitive, one core argument)', *tippuógen* 'to topple down, cause to crumble (DV, transitive, two core arguments)'. The nominalized forms of the *maN-* verbs clearly show that the orientation of the verb is toward the agent of the action, and not the goal or patient: *ti mangtippúog* 'the person toppling down (a building, etc.)', *ti tippuógen* 'the thing being toppled'.

Of the non-agent voice verbs, six distinctions can be noted, based on the semantics of the corresponding absolutive argument which is usually identifiable from the context, and is the most highly thematic argument of a clause. The voice morphology differs when the absolutive argument is a patient, direction (partially affected referent or location), conveyed entity (theme), beneficiary, comitative referent, or instrument. Among the six non-agent voice formations, four are basic. The remaining two (the comitative and instrumental forms) should be classified midway between bona-fide verbs for taking aspectual morphology, and nominals for appearing in speech quite frequently in non-predicative position. It should be noted here that voice morphology is derivational and not fully productive with every root (Rubino 1997).

Verbs in the patient voice take an absolutive argument which is the target of the action of the verb: *Ania 't k<in>nan=mo* (what CORE eat<PFV.PV>=2s.ERG) 'What did you eat', *Siká ti kit-kitá-en=na* (2s CORE CONT-see-PV=3s.ERG) 'You're the one he's looking at', *Uráy-en=d=ak* (wait-PV=2/3p=1s.ABS) 'Wait for me'. The directional voice verbs take arguments that are either a source, a goal or a partially affected patient. Thus, aside from appearing on verbs that indicate addition or removal, e.g. *iwá-an* (slice-DV) 'to slice off a piece, carve, make a cut into' vs. *iwá-en* (slice-PV) 'to cut, slice fully', directional voice verbs may be used to take a human absolutive argument which is affected indirectly by the action of the verb, e.g. *takáw-en* (steal-PV) 'to steal something' vs. *takáw-an* (steal-DV) 'to rob someone'.

Conveyance verbs are those that take a theme absolutive argument, i.e. an entity that is physically or psychologically conveyed: *Iny-áwid=na ti pagiwarnák* (CV.PFV-to.home=3s.ERG CORE newspaper) 'He took home the newspaper', *In-salikád=na ti petáka* (CV.PFV-waistband=3s.ERG CORE wallet) 'He inserted the wallet in his waistband', *iy-ebkás* 'to express (in words)'. The prefix *i-* combined with the suffix *-an* forms benefactive verbs in which the absolutive argument is the beneficiary of the action of the verb, or the person in whose place the action was performed: *i-bagá=m ta i-dasar-án=ka=n* (CV-tell=2s.ERG CONJ BV-set.table-BV=1s.ERG:2s.ABS = now) 'tell me and I'll set the table for you'. *I-gatáng-an=n=ak man iti bagás* (BV-buy-BV=2/3s=1s.ABS please OBL rice) 'Please buy some rice for me'. The *i- -an* affix combination does not always encode benefactive verbs, however. Many lexicalized expressions take the same form: *ibuksílan* 'to express, expose, explain (absolutive argument=entity expressed)', *igasátan* 'to tell the fortune to', etc.

It should be noted here that the selection of voice morphology based on the semantics involved between the action of the verb and the role of the absolutive argument is valid only in main clauses. In relative clauses, and certain controlled clauses which take finite verbs (i.e. words marked for voice and aspect), the choice of voice morphology is constrained by a stringent requirement of Iloko syntax. Verbs in relative clauses take voice morphology which reflects the absolutive status of the head noun. Head nouns that are agentive with respect to the verb in the relative clause take an intransitive (agent voice) relative clause verb; non-agentive head nouns take a transitive verb in the relative clause. Thus, in (17) the verb *nangtemplá* appears in the agent voice, reflecting the agentive role of the head noun, *balásang*:

(17) *Ayán=na*   *[ti   balásanga   nang-templá   iti   kapé=k?]*
      where=2s.ERG CORE   maiden LK   AV-mix   OBL   coffee=1s.ERG
      'Where is the unmarried woman who prepared my coffee?'

And in (18), the verb *linútom* appears in the patient voice, reflecting the patientive role of the head noun *pinakbét*:

(18) *In-íbus=ko*   *[ti   pinakbét   a   l<in>úto=m]*
      PFV.CV-finish=1s.ERG CORE   dish   LK   cook<PV.PFV>=2s.ERG
      'I finished the *pinakbet* (vegetable dish) that you cooked.'

In complement clauses that function as the absolutive argument of transitive verbs (preceded by the core marker *ti*), the verb is controlled by the A (ergative) argument of the main predicate.

(19) *Kayát=mo*   *ti*   *ag-dígos?*
      want=2s.ERG CORE   AV-bath
      'Do you want to take a bath?'

Since the complement clause functions as the absolutive argument of a transitive main clause, the main predicate cannot take another absolutive argument, e.g. **Kayát=n=ak ti agdígos?* (want-2/3.ERG=1s.ABS core AV-bath) *'Do you want to bathe me (grammatically incorrect)?'

5.2 Aspect

Aspect in Iloko may be inflectional or derivational. Inflectional aspect is indicated by prefixes and infixes. Completed aspect is indicated with the infix *-in-* (or prefix *n-* with *ag-* AV verbs and *i-* CV verbs), and progressive aspect (for continuous or habitual actions) is encoded with initial CVC reduplication of the verbal root: *N-ag-sángit=da.* (PFV-AV-cry=3p.ABS) 'They cried', *Ag-sang-sángit=da.* (AV-CONT-cry=3p.ABS) 'They are crying'. A glottal onset does not participate in CVC progressive reduplication, but rather results in the addition of an open syllable with a long vowel: *ag-saó* (AV-talk) 'to talk' [ʔag.sa.ʔo] > *ag-sà-saó* 'is talking' [ʔag.sá:.sa.ʔó]. Table 11.8 provides an overview of the forms.

The completed aspect infix *-in-* cannot co-occur with the PV suffix *-en*: *saplít-en* 'thrash-PV', *s<in>aplít* 'thrashed'. With *-um-* AV verbs, the completive infix *-in-* appears as -*imm*-, historically derived from *-*in-um-* > *inm (attested in modern Pangasinan and in numerous other languages such as Bontok) > -*imm*: *g<um>átang* 'buy' vs. *g<imm>átang* 'bought'. This affix is also used to express similarity: *timmígre* 'like a tiger', *pimmúsa* 'like a cat'. The perfective form of conveyance verbs has two realizations, *in*- before consonants, and *iny*- before vowels, historically **ʔ<in>i-*.

Future actions are encoded either with an infinitive verb or with the enclitic =*(n)to* (-*nto* after vowels and -*to* after consonants). Verbs in the imperative mood may occur in the infinitive form or the progressive, and verbs expressing facts occur in the infinitive.

Derivational (lexical) aspect is indicated with bisyllabic reduplication to express the iterative, durative, continual, distributional, intermittent, or intensive nature of the action expressed by the reduplicated root: *agbannibanníkes* 'to repeatedly scold with the arms akimbo' (from *banníkes* 'akimbo'), *agtilmotilmón* 'to swallow repeatedly or forcefully' (from *tilmón* 'swallow'), *silawsiláwan* 'to light up various places' (*siláwan* 'to light up a place'), *naisiglosiglót* 'to be entangled, tied up in knots' (from *naisiglót* 'to be tied'). This is the only reduplicative process in which part of a suffix may be reduplicated with the rest of the stem (cf. 21):

(20) *N-ag-sarde-sardéng   nga   ag-eskuéla   tapnó   tulóng-an=na*
      PFV-AV-ITER-stop   LK   AV-school   so.that   help-DV=3s.ERG

      dagití   da-dakkél=na   nga   ag-múla   ití   lasoná.
      PL.CORE   PL-big=3s.ERG   LK   AV-cultivate   OBL   onions

'He went to school irregularly so he could help his parents farm onions.'

TABLE 11.8: ASPECTUAL MORPHOLOGY OF DYNAMIC VERBS

Voice	Affix	Perfective/ complete	Progressive	Future
Actor	ag-	nag-	ag-CVC-	ag- =(n)to
	agkatáwa 'laugh'	*nagkatáwa*	*agkatkatáwa*	*agkatáwanto*
	-um-	-imm-	C<um>VC-	-um- =(n)to
	tumakdér 'stand'	*timmakder*	*tumaktakdér*	*tumakderto*
	mang-, maN-	nang-, naN-	mang-CVC-; maN-CVC-	mang- =(n)to
	mangdáit 'sew'	*nangdáit*	*mangdàdáit*	*mangdáitto*
Patient	-en	-in-	CVC- -en	-en .. =(n)to
	suráten 'write'	*sinúrat*	*sursuráten*	*surátento*
Directional	-an	-in- -an	CVC- -an	-an .. =(n)to
	adaywán 'leave'	*inadaywán*	*adʔadaywán*	*adaywánto*
Conveyance	i-	in(y)-	i-CVC-	i- =(n)to
	iyáwid 'bring home'	*inyáwid*	*iyawʔáwid*	*iyáwidto*
Benefactive	i- -an	in(y)- -an	i-CVC- -an	i- -an .. =(n)to
	isurátan 'write for/ on behalf of'	*insurátan*	*isursurátan*	*isurátanto*
Comitative	ka-	kina-	ka-CVC	ka- =(n)to
	kasaó 'speak to'	*kinasaó*	*kasàsaó*	*kasaónto*
Instrumental	pag-	pinag-	pag-CVC-	pag- =(n)to
	pagtugáw 'chair'	*pinagtugáw*	*pagtugtugáw*	*pagtugáwto*

(21)   *Pinuluapuluánna*   *ti*   *búkot=ko*   *iti*   *lugít.*
    \<in\>RDP-pulu-an=na   ti   búkot=ko   iti   lugít
    \<PFV.PV\>RDP-smear -DV=3s.ERG   CORE   back=1s.ERG   OBL   guano
    'He smeared my back with guano.'

Continuous aspect can also be indicated with full reduplication of the verbal root: *N-ag-rikus-ríkos=da iti pantalán* (PFV-AV-RDP-circle/lap=3p OBL pier) 'They went around the pier several times'. Intensity is expressed by the infix *-an-*: *sumanaó* 'to chatter' (f. *saó* 'talk'), *agtanaúl* 'to bark loudly or repeatedly' (f. *taúl* 'bark'), *tumanaráy* 'to constantly be in a hurry' (f. *taráy* 'run').

Recently completed actions take the prefixes *ka+CV reduplication* (action verbs), or *ka+C reduplication* (resultatives). Actors in these constructions appear in the ergative case even if there is only one core argument: *Ka-sa-sangpét=ko* (REC.PFV-RDP-arrive=1s.ERG) 'I just arrived'; *ka-s-singtáw* (REC.PFV-RDP-slash) 'just slashed'. The prefix *apag-* 'as soon as' also takes ergative actors in the same way: *apag-sangpét=na* (as.soon.as-arrive=3s.ERG) 'as soon as he arrives'.

5.3 Potentive and stative mood

Potentive verbs are those which typically lack an element of volition, encompassing the following semantic areas: states of being, ability, need, involuntary activity, coincidental activity, or abilitative activity, e.g. *maka-dungpár* (POT-collide) 'to accidentally collide, happen to run into, be able to crash'. Dynamic verbs, which are unmarked for volition but usually carry a volitional reading, can be contrasted with potentive ones in: *Lipát-e-mo-n* (forget-PV-2s.ERG-already) 'Forget her already, get her out of your mind (dynamic reading)' vs. *Na-lipát-an=na manén* (PFV.POT-forget-DV=3s.ERG again) 'He forgot it again! (potentive reading)'.

Verbs in the potentive and stative mood are classified together because of their formal similarities (usually taking a form of the prefix *ma(ka)-*). Potentive verbs may occur in five voices, which more or less correspond to their dynamic counterparts (cf. Table 11.9).

Potentive verbs denoting uncontrolled perceptions can take either a non-volitional meaning or an abilitative one, e.g. *Diák na-kíta* (NEG.1s PFV.POT-see) 'I didn't see it' or 'I wasn't able to see it'. Verbs that correspond to events that may involve a slight element of volition can take a potentive prefix, to contrast them with non-potentive events in which the agent initiates a more controlled, volitional action, e.g. *kayáw-an* 'capture with intent', *ma-kayáw-an* 'to be able to capture (with intent); charm (without intent)'.

TABLE 11.9: POTENTIVE VERB FORMATION

Voice	Dynamic	Potentive	Example verb	Gloss
Actor	ag-, -um-, mang-	maka-	makalangóy	be able to swim
Patient	-en	ma-	madungpár	accidentally collide
Directional	-an	ma- -an	masagádan	happen to sweep; be swept
Conveyance	i-	mai-	maikábil	manage to put
Benefactive	i- -an	mai- -an	maisurátan	be able to write for

(22) *Na-laíng   a (..)   g\<um\>itára   ket   na-kayáw-an=na*
ADJ-good   LK   guitar\<AV\>   PM   POT.PFV-charm-DV=3s.ERG

ti   balásang
CORE   maiden

'He was good at guitar playing, so he charmed (was able to charm) the lady (by his playing, not through force).'

The prefix *maka-* may also encode non-volitional causation: *maka-disturbár* (POT-disturb) 'to disturb, annoy (frequently used with inanimate agents)', as well as non-causative states with some roots: *maka-ruród* (POT-anger) 'to be angry', *maka-úma* (POT-bore) 'to be bored', *maka-básol* (POT-guilt) 'to be guilty'.

Other combinations of affixes with potentive prefixes exist. The potentive prefix *makapag-*, e.g., encodes a sort of instrumental ability (as opposed to innate or absolute ability), specifying that the actor had the means to perform the action at the time of the utterance. Contrast *Saán = da a maka-dáit* (NEG = 3p.ABS LIG POT-sew) 'They can't (don't know how to) sew' to:

(23) *Saan=da   a   maka-pag-dáit.*
NEG=3p.ABS   LK   POT-INS.NR-sew
'They don't have the means to sew.'

The aspectual distinctions detailed for non-potentive verbs vary considerably for potentive verbs. Perfectivity (marked by *naka-* (intransitive) or *na-* transitive) usually denotes an attained state or abilitative/coincidental action which most likely continue to exist at the time of the utterance. The perfective stative form *na-* is commonly used for adjectives, unlike in Tagalog where the *ma-* (irrealis) prefix is preferred. A few adjectives that denote bodily states or human qualities generally take the nonperfective *ma-* prefix, for example, *mabisin* 'hungry', *manákem* 'wise', *mawáw* 'thirsty', *masirib* 'wise', *masdáaw* 'surprised'. A few other adjectives meaningfully contrast the perfective and non-perfective form: *maúyong* 'crazy' vs. *naúyong* 'cruel, mean', *masakít* 'sick' vs. *nasakít* 'sore, aching', *maíngel* 'brave' vs. *naíngel* 'strong (liquor, tobacco)'.

Potentive *maka-* verbs with CVC reduplication usually express desire or impending action, rather than progressive action, as their formal dynamic equivalents encode: *Maka-is-isbú=ak* (POT-RDP-urine=1s.ABS) 'I feel like urinating', *Maka-ba-baéng=ak iti ingel* (POT-RDP-sneeze=1s.ABS OBL alcohol.smell/strength) 'I feel like sneezing from the strength of the liquor'.

Stative verbs differ from potentive verbs primarily in their causative formation. The prefix *ika-* (perfective form *inka-*) is used with a few stative verbs to encode a type of causation, quite different from the *pa-* potentive causatives which are always non-volitional or non-controlled (see section 5.4). *Ika-* causatives can express enlargement, e.g. *ikaláwa* 'to widen', *ikadakkél* 'to enlarge', or the volitional causation of a state: *ikarigátan* 'to strive to do' from the root *rígat* 'hardship'.

(24) *Úray   kasáno-'t   rígat=da,   inka-rigát-an=da   a*
even   how-CORE   hardship=3p.ERG   PFV.ST.CAU-hard=3p.ERG   LK

p\<in\>ag-ádal   ni   Raul.
CAU\<PFV.PV\>-study   PN   Raul

'No matter how poor they were, they exerted all their efforts to put Raul through school.'

The situation exists where a *ma-* potentive verb can take an agent in the oblique case, the closest construction Iloko has to a passive voice. Like a prototypical passive construction, there is morphological evidence that the verb in this construction is de-transitivized. It does not have two core pronouns which cross-reference the agentive and patientive arguments. Only the patientive argument is cross-referenced by an absolutive enclitic. The agentive argument in the oblique case cannot be cross-referenced with an ergative pronoun unless it is promoted to core status and the verb is thereby transitivized:

(25) *Na-riíng=ak   ití   karibusó   iti   babá   ti   baláy.*
     POT-awake=1s.ABS OBL commotion OBL under CORE house
     'I was awakened by the commotion under the house.'

(26) *Na-riíng=da=k*
     POT-awake=3p.ERG=1s.ABS
     'They were able to wake me up.'

Stative stems can take the directional voice suffix *-an* to denote an exposure: *mapudó-tan* 'to be warmed up' (f. *púdot* 'warm'), *mainítan* 'to be exposed to the sun' (f. *init* 'sun'), *marabiián* 'to be overtaken by the night' (f. *rabií* 'night').

(27) *No   ag-sidá-t (iti)   síli,   isú't (ti)   ma-gasáng-an.*
     if   AV-eat-OBL   chili 3-CORE   POT-spice-DV
     'If one eats chili pepper, one gets burnt by the spice (proverb).'

5.4 Indirect action: the prefix *pa-*

A Pan-Philippine formative, the prefix *pa-* has a variety of functions in Iloko. It may mark indirect action, direction of an action, or causation. Table 11.10 contrasts direct action verbs with their indirect *pa-* counterparts.

The causative prefix *pa-* does not increase the valence of the verbs to which it attaches. The valence of the verb is indicated by its voice morphology. Thus, when a causative stem is marked for agent voice as in (28) it has one core argument. If it is marked for patient voice, it has two, as shown in (29):

(28) *Ag-pa-púkis=ak=to   no   bigát.*
     AV-CAU-haircut=1s.ABS.FUT FUT morning
     'I'll get a haircut tomorrow.'

(29) *Pa-kan-é=m /pa-kaan-en=mo/   dagití   piék!*
     CAU-eat-PV = 2s.ERG   PL.CORE chick
     'Feed the chicks!'

TABLE 11.10: THE PREFIX *pa-*

Direct action verb		Indirect action/Causative verb	
ma-túrog	to sleep	pa-turóg-an	put to sleep
mangpúkis	cut hair	ag-pa-púkis	get a haircut
ma-táy	die	pa-tay-én	kill
kan-én /kaán-en/	to eat something	pa-kan-én /pa-kaán-en/	feed
ag-kaán	devour	ag-pa-kaán	host a feast

The prefix is also more of a stem formative than an inflectional prefix, as can be seen by its behavior in reduplications. As other stem forming prefixes, *pa-* takes part in reduplications, compare *kanén* 'eat something (infinitive form)' with *kankanén* 'eating something (progressive form)', and *pa-kanén* (CAU-eat) 'feed' with *pak-pakanén* 'feed (progressive form)'. The prefix can be used with both dynamic and potentive morphology. With potentive morphology, the causation of the action or state expressed in the root is non-volitional. Contrast the dynamic causative verb *pa-dakkel-én* (CAU-big-PV) 'enlarge (by building)' to the potentive causative verb *maka-pa-dakkél* (POT-CAU-big) 'cause to grow (as of vitamins)'.

(30)   *Maka-pa-salunʔát   ti   salúyot.*
       POT-CAU-health   CORE   species of leaves
       '*Saluyot* leaves are healthy (cause health without volition).'

Another use of the prefix *pa-* is to indicate direction: *ag-pa-amiánan* 'to go to/towards the north (actor voice)', *i-pa-amiánan* 'to send to/towards the north (conveyance voice)', *pumalaém* 'to go inside', *agpaíli* 'to go to town'.

5.5 Reciprocity

There are a variety of ways to express reciprocal relationships in Iloko: with the prefix *ag-* whose use is restricted lexically, with derivational CVCV+N reduplication, and with the inflectional infix *–inn-*. The agent voice prefix *ag-* is most commonly used with roots that are inherently reciprocal, in which case the subject argument is plural: *N-ag-salliwásiw da.* (PFV-AV-fail.to.meet=3p) 'They missed each other (coming from different directions)'. The prefix *ag-* is similarly used with kinterms to denote a reciprocal relationship *ag-amá* 'father and child' (< *amá* 'father'), *ag-iná* 'mother and child' (< *iná* 'mother'), *ag-ulitég* 'uncle and nephew' (< *ulitég* 'uncle'), *ag-siúman* 'stepparent and stepchild' (< *siúman* 'stepchild'). The prefix is also employed with family names, e.g. *dagití ag-Galvez* 'the members of the Galvez family'.

The CVCV+N prefix is used with nouns to express a reciprocal notion: *ʔayanʔayát* (RCP-love) 'sweethearts, mutual loving', *balembáles* (RCP-revenge) 'avenging each other', *ngiwanngiwat* (RCP-mouth) 'mouth to mouth', *karinkarí* (RCP-promise) 'mutual promise', *guranggúra* (RCP-hate) 'mutual hatred', *talentalék* (RCP-trust) 'trusting each other, depending on one another', *rupanrúpa* (RCP-face) 'face to face'.

The reciprocal infix *-inn-* is much more general in its use. It is applied before the first vowel of its stem, which may be a simple root as in *N-ag-p<inn>ádas=da ití pigsá* (PFV-AV-compete<RCP>=3p OBL strength) 'They competed with each other in strength', or a polymorphemic stem as in *Ag-pi-p<inn>a-básol=da* ... (AV-PL-CAU<RCP>-blame=3p) 'They are blaming each other...'. It can be used with all verbs or gerunds to which a reciprocal meaning can be applied.

5.6 Joint actions (requestives)

Joint action verbs are intransitive verbs that take the prefix *maki-* (perfective *naki-*), with or without other affixes. They are similar to *ka-* transitive comitative verbs (cf. Table 11.7) in that they describe actions performed by a number of people, but they are different in a number of lexical ways. With roots that designate actions, *maki-* verbs describe actions that are performed in the company of others. The person participating in the joint action is the argument encoded in the absolute case, while the other participants, if specified, get oblique case marking: *Nakipag-púyat=ak kadakuáda* (JNT-up.all.night=1s.ABS 3p.OBL) 'I stayed awake all night with them', *In=kayó maki-ápit* (go=2p.ABS JNT-harvest) 'Go participate in the harvest'.

Maki- verbs are also commonly used in requests, in which the root can designate the activity or the thing requested: *Ma-balín ti maki-ka-tugáw?* (POT-able CORE JNT-PL-sit) 'May I sit with you?', *Maki-sindí=kami man* (JNT-light=1pe.ABS please) 'May we please have a light (borrow your fire)?' *In=kayó maki-naténg* (go=2p.ABS JNT-vegetable) 'Go ask for vegetables'. The prefix *maki-* has a peculiar use with terms referring to kin and other members of the household (including slaves): *makiamá* 'to treat/consider as a father', *makiadípen* 'to treat as a slave', *makiiná* 'to treat/consider as a mother'. The infix *-inn-* may be used with joint action verbs to indicate reciprocal actions: *Naki-t<inn>úlag=da idí kalmán* (JNT-contract<RCP>=3p.ABS REM.PST yesterday) 'They made a contract with each other yesterday'.

5.7 Frequentatives

Frequentatives are an interesting class of words in Iloko as they cannot be easily classified as nouns or verbs. Unlike referential nouns, they cannot be morphologically pluralized, and unlike verbs, they do not take voice or aspectual morphology. Like gerunds, they can only be formed off agent voice verbs; the formal similarities between the frequentatives and gerunds are shown in Table 11.11 Because the punctual/inchoative agent voice infix *-um-* is most likely not a voice affix historically, formal and semantic discrepancies in the paradigm exist.

(31)   *agsugál*   to gamble   *managsugál*   prone to gambling, always gambling
     makigubát   join a battle   *mannakigubát*   warrior, habitual fighter in wars

5.8 Other derivational affixes

Derivational prefixes not previously mentioned include: *agin*+CV-reduplication, a prefix indicating pretense as in *n-agin-la-langóy=da* (PFV-PRETEND-RDP-swim=3p) 'they pretended to swim', and *sangka-*, an habitual prefix which takes ergative actors, as in *sangka-dámag=na=ka* (HABIT-ask=3s.ERG=2s.ABS) 'he keeps on asking about you'. The prefix *mara-* is used to express similarity:

(32)   *Núpay*   *lakáy=en,*   *mara-kápas* *pay láeng* *ti*   *úbet=na.*
     though   old.man=now like-cotton still just CORE buttocks=3s.ERG
     'Although he is already an old man, his buttocks are still like cotton.'

TABLE 11.11: ILOKO FREQUENTATIVES

Mode	Class	Basic affix	Gerund	Frequentative
Dynamic	Durative	ag-	panag-	manag-
	Punctual/Inchoative	-um-	i-CV-*	C-um-V-*
	Distributive	mang-	panang-	manang-
Potentive		maka-	pannaka-	mannaka-
Joint action		maki-	pannaki-	mannaki-

* CV here represents CV reduplication.

The Spanish infinitive endings -*ar*, -*er*, and -*ir* can be applied to borrowed roots to form lexical stems that are clearly not Spanish, even though only the ending -*ar* was productive in the Spanish spoken at the time of contact, e.g. *i-submitir* 'to submit' (f. English), *maka-disturbár* 'to be disturbing' (f. English), *mang-atendár* 'to attend' (f. English).

6 NOMINALIZATIONS AND NOMINAL MORPHOLOGY

6.1 Nominal morphology

Iloko nominal morphology is derivational in nature. As already mentioned in section 3.1, referential nouns are distinguished from other lexical classes by their derivational plural formation. Iloko plural nouns are derivational because plurality is optionally expressed, and when it is, it usually denotes distributiveness, rather than general plurality: *dagití sábong* (PL.CORE flower) 'the flowers' vs. *dagiti sab-sábong* (PL.CORE PL-flower) 'the flowers here and there, the flowers of various kinds'. Most nouns form their plural by initial CVC reduplication, e.g. *kaldíng* 'goat' > *kalkaldíng* 'goats', *ruángan* 'door' *ru:ruángan* 'doors', *sílaw* 'light' > *silsílaw* 'lights'. Some animate nouns (mostly kinterms and proper nouns) form their plural by CV reduplication: *gayyém* 'friend' > *gagayyém* 'friends', *ulitég* 'uncle' > *ùulitég* 'uncles', *kabsát* 'sibling' > *kakabsát* 'siblings', *kailián* 'townmate' > *kakailián* 'townmates', *baknáng* 'rich person' > *babaknáng* 'rich people'. A few common terms denoting animate referents form their plural by geminating the first medial consonant of the root: *laláki* 'boy' > *lalláki* 'boys', *ubíng* 'child' > *ubbíng* 'children', *amá* 'father' > *ammá* 'fathers', *iná* 'mother' > *inná* 'mothers', *anák* 'child' > *annák* 'children'. Finally, a few non-personal nouns have irregular plural forms: *táo* 'person' > *tattáo* 'people', *baró* 'bachelor' > *babbaró* 'bachelors', *balásang* 'bachelorette' > *babbalásang* 'bachelorettes', *lakáy* 'old man' > *lallakáy* 'old men', *bakét* 'old woman' > *babbakét* 'old women'.

Common morphological devices used to form nouns aside from the nominalizations used with verbal stems (see Sec. 6.2), include the prefixes *ka-* for nouns of measurement: *ka-akába* (NR-wide) 'width', *ka-atiddóg* (NR-long) 'length', *ka-táyag* (NR-high) 'height', *ka-dakkél* (NR-big) 'size'; *kina-* for abstract nouns formed from stative roots: *kina-sadút* (NR-lazy) 'laziness', *kina-gagét* (NR-hard.working) 'industriousness', *kina-lagdá* (NR-durable) 'durability', and *ka-* (+ CV reduplication) (-*an*), which forms comitative nouns: *ka-ili-án* 'townmate' (*íli*=town), *ka-klase* 'classmate'.

Prefixes used only with nominal stems include: *sinan-* indicating resemblance: *sinam-pána* 'arrow-like thing', *sinan-táo* 'manlike thing', *sinan-bilóg* 'toy boat', *sinam-bituén* 'star-like entity'; *pagat/pagaC-* indicating physical extent: *pagab-barúkong* 'reaching the chest', *pagat-táo* 'size of a man'; and *agat/agaC-* indicating smell: *agab-barániw* 'smell of lemon grass (indicating a scandal)', *agal-layá* 'smell of ginger', and *agat-tsíko* 'smell of sapodilla fruit (indicating intoxication)'.

The agent voice infix -*um-* may be used with locative roots to designate residents: from *baláy* 'house' > *dagiti bumaláy* 'residents of the house', from *íli* 'town' > *dagití umíli* 'citizens; residents of a town or city', from *purók* 'village' > *dagití pumurók* 'villagers'. Degrees of kinship are indicated with the prefix *kapi(n)-*: *kapiduá* 'second cousin', *kapitló* 'third cousin', *kapimpát* 'fourth cousin', *kapinlimá* 'fifth cousin'. A related form *kapamin-* is used with numbers to express nominal ordinals: *kapamin-limá* 'the fifth time'.

Spanish nominal loan morphology is quite productive with many roots, sometimes borrowed with gender. The locative ending *-eria* can be seen in both loans and with native roots: *karinderia* 'Philippine-style cafeteria', *labandéria* 'laundromat', and *pansiteria* 'noodle house'. The agentive suffix *-ero* (feminine *-era*) is also used with both Spanish and native roots: *partera* 'midwife' (loan from Spanish), and *karaykayéra* 'female raker' (from *karaykáy* 'rake'). Gender is also morphologically expressed in a few Spanish loans, *mánong* 'older brother' vs. *mánang* 'older sister' (Sp. *hermano* 'brother', *hermana* 'sister'), *lólo, lélong* 'grandfather' vs. *lóla, lélang* 'grandmother' (Sp. *abuelo, abuela*), *bastonéro* 'conductor of an orchestra' vs. *bastonéra* 'majorette' (Sp. *bastón* 'cane, rod'), etc.

Not all borrowings can be traced directly to words or morphemes in a particular lending language. Words like *bentáhe* 'advantage' are hybrids with two language sources, Spanish *ventaja* + English *advantage*.

The velar nasal suffix *-ng* is widely used for nicknaming and with kinterms to express familiarity or vocative reference: *Maning* (nickname for Manuel), *Agong* (nickname for Santiago), *Polong* (nickname for Apollo), *táta* 'father' > *tátang* 'dad', *iná* 'mother' > *inang* 'mom', *ádi* 'younger sibling (reference)' > *áding* 'younger sibling (reference or vocative)'.

6.2 Nominalizations

Nominalizations in Iloko are formed on the basis of agent voice verbs as shown in Table 11.12. There are three basic nominalization types: (1) Instrumentals with *pag-/paN-/paka-/paki-*, etc. (2) Locative/Reason aspectual nominalizations (= instrumental gerund + *-an*); and (3) Manner gerunds (*panag-, panang-, pannaka-,* etc.).

TABLE 11.12: ILOKO NOMINALIZATIONS

Mode	Verbal affix	Gerund (Manner)	Instrument	Locative/Reason	
				Neutral	Perfective
Dynamic	ag-	panag-	pag-	pag- -an	nag- -an
	-um-	i-CV-*	–	-um- -an	-imm- -an
	mang-	panang-	pang-	pang- -an	nang- -an
	mangi-	panangi-	pangi-	pangi- -an	nangi- -an
	mangipa-	panangipa-	pangipa-	pangipa- -an	nangipa- -an
	mangpa-	panangpa-	pangpa-	pangpa- -an	nangpa- -an
	mangpai-	panangpai-	pangpai-	pangpai- -an	nangpai- -an
	mangpag-	panangpag-	pangpag-	pangpag- -an	nangpag- -an
Potentive	maka-	pannaka-	paka-	paka- -an	naka- -an
	makai-	pannakai-	pakai-	pakai- -an	nakai- -an
	makaipa-	pannakaipa-	pakaipa-	pakaipa- -an	nakaipa- -an
	makapa-	pannakapa-	–	pakapa- -an	nakapa- -an
	makapai-	pannakapai-	pakapai-	pakapai- -an	nakapai- -an
	makapag-	pannakapag-	pakapag-	pakapag- -an	nakapag- -an
	makapagi-	pannakapagi-	pakapagi-	pakapagi- -an	nakapagi- -an
Joint action	maki-	pannaki-	paki-	paki- -an	naki- -an
	makipag-	pannakipag-	pakipag-	pakipag- an	nakipag- -an
	makipagi-	pannakipagi-	pakipagi-	pakipagi- -an	nakipagi- -an

* CV here represents CV reduplication.

Gerunds are widely used in Iloko discourse as (1) core arguments of intransitive predicates (33); (2) adverbial clauses (34, 35); and (3) complement clauses (36). Following temporals and interrogatives, they are rather common:

(33) *Mayát ti   panag-dáit=na.*
      good   CORE   GER-sew=3s.ERG
      'Her sewing is good.'

(34) *Ma-súya=ako=n   ití   pan-agin-si-singpét=na!*
      POT-fed.up=1s.ABS=already   OBL   GER-PRETEND-RDP-behave=3s.ERG
      'I'm fed up with his pretending to be well behaved!'

(35) *In-arámid=ko   sakbáy ti   panag-áwid=da*
      PFV.PV-do=1s.ERG   before CORE   GER-go.home=3p.ERG
      'I did it before they went home (before their going home).'

(36) *Kaanó ti   panag-áwid=mo?*
      when   CORE   GER-go.home=2s.ERG
      'When are you going home?'

Locative nominalizations differ from instrumental or manner gerunds because they may inflect for perfective aspect. They may be used in interrogative main clauses to ask the reason, source or location of an event. After the interrogative *aniá* 'what', they specify reason:

Locative use:

(37) *Nag-adál-a=m?*
      NR.PFV.AV-study-NR=2s.ERG
      'Where did you go to school?' (from *Sadíno ti nagadálam?* (where CORE *nagadálam*))

Source/Reason use:

(38) *Aniá'-t   pag-apál-an=da*
      what-CORE   NR-envy- NR=3p.ERG
      'What are they envious about (what is the reason/source of their envy)?'

(39) *Naka-ammu-án=yo   a   kasangáy=ko   itá?*
      NR.PFV.POT-know-NR=2p.ERG LK   birthday=1s.ERG now/today
      'How did you find out it's my birthday today (what is the source of your knowledge)?'

Manner gerunds may take CVC progressive reduplication, but they do not inflect for perfective aspect like the locative/reason nominalizations.

(40) *... gapú ngatá   iti   panag-kur-kúrang=da   ití   taraón.*
          cause perhaps OBL   GER-RDP-lack=3p.ERG   OBL   nourishment
      '(they are quite thin...) probably because of their lack of nourishment.'

Instrumental gerunds are the least morphologically marked, formed with a variant of the affix *paC(V)-* (see Table 11.12). Instrumentals are *not* formed off intransitive *-um-* verbs. Instrumentals are widely used as nominals in spoken language, e.g. *pag-surat* (INS.NR-write) 'pen', *pag-sa-sao* (INS.NR-RDP-talk) 'language', *panait /paN-dait/* (INS.NR-sew) 'thread'. Example 42 shows the instrumental prefix used like a clitic, attaching to a tri-lexemic noun phrase:

(41) *Aniá   ti   nailián   a   pag-sa-saó   ditóy?*
      what   CORE   national   LK   INS.NR-RDP-talk   PRX.ADV
      'What is the national language here?'

(42) *Aniá   ti   pang-[anák=ko   iti   buniág]?*
      what   CORE   INS.NR-child=1s.ERG   OBL   baptism
      'What will I use to be a godfather (what will my sponsorship payment be)?'

Agent nominalizations are formed with *maNN-*, with or without CVC iterative reduplication, or with CV reduplication of an agent voice verb form: *mannurat* (maNN-surat) 'writer', *mannursúro* (maNN-RDP-suro) 'teacher', *mangngálap* (maNN-kalap) 'fisherman', *kumakánta* (RDP<um>-kanta) 'singer'.

ACKNOWLEDGMENTS

Special thanks to Lawrence Reid and the editors for their comments on a previous version of this chapter. They are not responsible for any mistakes herein.

REFERENCES

Bernabe, E., Fonacier, J. and Sibayan, B. (1971) *Ilokano Lessons*, Honolulu: University of Hawaii Press.
Bloomfield, L. (1942) 'Outline of Ilokano Syntax', *Language* 18:193–200.
Buell, W. (1960) *A generative grammar of the Ilocano language*, Ann Arbor: University Microfilms International.
Carro, A. (1888) *Vocabulario Ilocano-español trabajado por varios religiosos del orden de N. P. S. Agustín*, Manila: M. Pérez e Hijo.
Constantino, E. (1959) *A generative grammar of a dialect of Ilocano*, PhD Dissertation, Indiana University.
Espiritu, P. (1984) *Let's speak Ilokano*, Honolulu: University of Hawaii Press.
Geladé, G. (1993) *Ilokano–English dictionary*, Quezon City: Congregatio Immaculati Cordis Mariae.
Gerdts, D.B. (1988) 'Antipassives and Causatives in Ilokano: Evidence for an Ergative Analysis', in R. McGinn (ed.) *Studies in Austronesian linguistics* (Ohio University Monographs in International Studies. Southeast Asia Series 77), 295–321, Athens, Ohio: Ohio University Press.
Laconsay, G. (1993) *Iluko-English–Tagalog dictionary*, Quezon City: Phoenix Publishing House.
Lopez, F. (1895) *Gramática ilocana: compuesta por el Padre Predicador Fray Francisco López; corregida y aumentada por el Padre Carro, tercera edición*, Malabon: Asilo de huérfanos de Malabon.
McKaughan, H. (1952) *Ilocano: an intensive language course*, Glendale: Summer Institute of Linguistics.
Naves, J. (1892) *Gramática Hispana-Ilocana*, 2a. edición, Tambobong: Asilo de huérfanos.
Reid, L.A. (1989) 'Arta: another Philippine Negrito Language', *Oceanic Linguistics* 28(1):47–74.
——(1991) 'The Alta Languages', in R. Harlow (ed.) *Papers from the Fifth International Conference on Austronesian Linguistics*, Te Reo Special Publication, 265–297, Auckland: Linguistic Society of New Zealand.

Rubino, C. (1997) *A reference grammar of Ilocano*, PhD Dissertation, University of California, Santa Barbara.

——(1998) *Ilocano dictionary and phrasebook*, New York: Hippocrene Books.

——(2000) *Ilocano dictionary and grammar*, Honolulu: University of Hawaii Press.

——(2001) 'Ilocano', in J. Garry and C. Rubino (eds) *The encyclopedia of the world's languages: past and present*, 331–335, New York: H.W. Wilson.

Vanoverbergh, M. (1955) *Iloko grammar*, Baguio: Catholic School Press.

——(1956) *Iloko-English dictionary*, Baguio: Catholic School Press.

Widdoes, H.W. (1950) *A brief introduction to the grammar of the Ilocano language*, Philippines: United Brethren Church.

Williams, H.W. (1904) *Grammatische Skizze der Ilocano Sprache mit Berücksichtigung ihrer Beziehungen zu den anderen Sprachen der malayo-polynesischen Familie*, München: F. Strauss.

Williams, H.P. (1929) *English–Ilocano manual and dictionary*, revised and enlarged by Angel Guerrero, Manila: Christian Mission.

Wimbish, J. (1987) *A relational grammar of Ilocano*, MA Thesis, University of Texas at Arlington.

CHAPTER TWELVE

TAGALOG

Nikolaus P. Himmelmann

1 INTRODUCTION

Tagalog is perhaps the best-known Philippine language. Its 17 million native speakers make it one of the two largest Philippine languages (along with Cebuano). In 1937 it was chosen as the basis for the national language, Filipino (formerly Pilipino), which was officially declared the national language of the Philippines in 1946 (see STEINHAUER, COLONIAL HISTORY, for further details). The differences between Filipino and Tagalog are mainly lexical, the Filipino lexicon being systematically expanded by the Institute of National Language. Because of its prestige as the national language and the fact that it is a medium of education and public discourse throughout the Philippines, Tagalog is also widely known as a second language (estimates vary between 70 and 90 per cent of the population).

Since the beginning of Spanish colonization in 1565, the Tagalog area has been the center of political power in the Philippines, and Tagalog has been the primary medium of communication between the colonial powers and the native population. Not surprisingly, then, Tagalog has been strongly influenced by the colonial languages, Spanish and, from 1898 to 1946, American English (other important and older sources for loan words in Tagalog are Malay (Wolff 1976) and Chinese (Chan Yap 1980)). This influence is most visible in its lexicon and phonology. However, there has also been some normative influence on its morphosyntax (clear examples are comparative constructions and the use of adverbials/conjunctions). The Spaniards began using Tagalog very early as a missionary language, preparing catechisms in Tagalog and writing grammars. A *Doctrina Christiana*, dated 1593, is the oldest preserved Tagalog document and shows that the standard language has changed very little in the last 400 years.

Most Tagalog native speakers live in the southern parts of Luzon, including the capital Manila. They are also found in many other parts of the Philippines, in particular on Mindoro, Palawan and in some parts of Mindanao (cf. McFarland 1983:29, 80). In addition, there are major Tagalog communities outside the Philippines, for example, in the United States and in Canada.

No in-depth study of Tagalog dialects exists. McFarland (1983:80) claims that Tagalog exhibits surprisingly little dialectal diversity. The following eight major regional dialects are mentioned in the Ethnologue (Grimes 1999): Bataan, Batangas, Bulacan, Lubang, Manila, Marinduque, Tanay-Paete, and Tayabas. For Tayabas, Arsenio (1971) provides an impressive dictionary. Furthermore, Lopez (1970) and Soberano (1980) have drawn attention to some lexical and morphological idiosyncrasies in the Tagalog dialect spoken on the small island of Marinduque.

Of all Philippine languages, Tagalog is the one that has been studied most intensively and that has had the greatest influence in linguistics. There are a number of grammars in Spanish, the most influential one being the one written by Totanes (1865, first published in 1745). It served as the basis for many analyses of Tagalog until the turn of the century (e.g., Humboldt 1838, Müller 1882:87–163, Marre 1901). In the Spanish tradition, Tagalog grammars were cast in the framework and terminology of Latin grammars, the last and most comprehensive one being Blake (1925). Tagalog played an important role in the emergence of American structuralism because it was the first non-Indo-European language Leonard Bloomfield worked on. Bloomfield (1917) is among the earliest and finest pieces of structuralist grammatical analysis, attempting to present Tagalog in its own terms. Tagalog also plays a major role in Bloomfield's classic book *Language* (1933).

Beginning with Humboldt (1838), Tagalog has served as *the* prototypical example of a Philippine-type language in modern comparative grammar and typology. As pointed out in HIMMELMANN, TYPOLOGICAL CHARACTERISTICS, section 6, this choice is somewhat unfortunate in that Tagalog differs in some important regards from its nearest relatives, the Central Philippine languages (not to mention the distinctly different Northern Philippine languages). The ongoing debate surrounding grammatical relations in Tagalog has been sparked by Schachter's (1976) paper on the distribution of subject properties.

A review of linguistic work on Tagalog is given in Constantino (1971:118–145) and Reid (1981). Major grammatical reference sources for Tagalog include Bloomfield (1917) and Schachter and Otanes (1972). Wolff *et al.* (1991) is the most comprehensive textbook to date, which also contains a wealth of grammatical observations and data. Major dictionaries include Panganiban (1972), English (1977, 1986), Santos (1983), Rubino (1998) and Constantino (1999). Bearing further witness to its prominent position as a national language and as a linguist's favorite, Tagalog is also the object of a substantial number of survey articles and encyclopedia entries (e.g. Schachter 1987, 1995, Zorc 1994, DeGuzman 2001).

Many issues in Tagalog grammar engender considerable controversy. Among the prominent topics are stress, reduplication, voice marking and grammatical relations, and lexical categories (the distinction between nouns and verbs). For reasons of space, no attempt has been made here to provide for a detailed account of these controversies. However, ample references are given for all of these issues, which should make it easy to follow them up if required.

Most examples in this chapter come from the author's own corpus of spontaneous spoken narratives which includes stories from Wolff *et al.*'s (1991) textbook (see Himmelmann 1999:245f for details). Other sources are Bloomfield's (1917) text collection and the example clauses found in Father English's (1986) dictionary and Schachter and Otanes's (1972) reference grammar. The examples from the narrative corpus retain features of the spoken language (in particular common reductions).

2 PHONOLOGY AND ORTHOGRAPHY

2.1 Segment inventory, syllable structure and stress

The segment inventory of Tagalog does not include any unusual sounds. The vowels are /a,e,i,o,u/ and the consonants are listed in Table 12.1. Consonants in parentheses occur only in loans (and in a few colloquial forms such as [can] for *tiyán* 'stomach').

The most common syllable types are CV and CVC. That is, there are no vowel-initial syllables. In native words, syllable-internal consonant clusters only arise if unstressed vowels are deleted before glides as when the pronoun *siyá* is realized as [ʃja] or *tuwíd* 'straight' as [twid]. A small number of syllable-internal consonant clusters are allowed in loans, e.g. *trabaho* 'work' and *lipstik*.

TABLE 12.1: TAGALOG CONSONANT PHONEMES

		Labial	Dental	Alveolar	Palatal	Velar	Labio-velar	Glottal
Stops	voiceless	p	t		(c)	k		ʔ
	voiced	b	d		(ɟ)	g		
Nasal		m	n			ŋ		
Fricative		(f)		s				h
Lateral				l				
Tap or trill				r				
Glide					j		w	

Lexical bases are typically disyllabic and any combination of the two basic syllable types is allowed (i.e. CV.CV, CV.CVC, CVC.CV, and CVC.CVC). Clitics and affixes are often monosyllabic (either CV or CVC). Since many Tagalog words consist of a lexical base and at least one affix, words with three or four syllables frequently occur. Moreover, since most affixes can be combined with each other, words with even higher numbers of syllables are also common (e.g. *makipagtáwánan* 'join in laughter' <*tawa* 'laugh').

Stress in Tagalog appears to be closely interrelated with vowel length. For some authors (e.g. Bloomfield 1917, Matsuda French 1988) stress is the primary phenomenon while vowel length is an epiphenomenon. Others (e.g. Schachter and Otanes 1972, Wolff *et al.* 1991) consider vowel length to be primary. Only one instrumental study exists (Gonzales 1970) and many of the relevant facts are still unclear. Here some of the important (and mostly uncontroversial) facts are presented as primarily stress-related, for reasons of expository convenience.

Most importantly, stress is distinctive in Tagalog. That is, segmentally identical word forms are distinguished by the fact that stress falls on a different syllable, either the final syllable (e.g. *bukás* 'open') or the penultimate syllable (e.g. *búkas* 'tomorrow'). However, stress cannot fall on just any syllable. CVC-syllables in non-final position are generally not stressed (exceptions are *mínsan* 'once' and *pínsan* 'cousin').

Stressed syllables are made prominent by pitch changes (in isolation it is usually a strong rise), increased duration and/or loudness (intensity). Various factors contribute to the choice among these stress marking devices, including the syntactic context and socio-linguistic variables. When stress falls on a non-final syllable, the vowel in this syllable is distinctly lengthened while a stressed final syllable may be short.

Affixes and reduplicated syllables may bear their own stress, resulting in multiply stressed words, e.g. *má-kíta* 'be seen', *púpuntá* 'will go', *máka-limút-an* 'to forget'. Consequently, not only lexical bases but affixed forms as well can be distinguished solely by a difference in stress. Compare *magkákásáma* 'do things together' with *magkakasáma* 'people who accompany each other'.

Affixation may involve stress shifts. For example, it is common that the addition of a suffix to a lexical base causes the stress to shift one syllable to the right. Hence, *táwag* 'call' + *-an* is *tawágan* 'to call someone', and *laró?* 'game' + *-an* is *laruán* 'toy'. Not infrequently, different affixes (more precisely: different derivations) are distinguished by their interaction with stress. Thus, there is another derivation from the lexical base *laró?* involving the suffix *-an* which results in the form *lárúan* 'playground'.

Within intonational phrases, lexical stress (i.e. the stress pattern that occurs on words in isolation) is modified in a number of ways as a result of its interaction with pitch changes related to intonation contours. For example, the phrase *kaharíang itó* 'this kingdom' may be realized as *kahariang ito* or *kahariang itó*, in which one of the two inherently stressed syllables loses its stress (see also Bloomfield 1917:143f and Schachter and Otanes 1972: 30–56).

2.2 Orthography

Tagalog orthography, which makes use of the Roman alphabet, matches pronunciation fairly well in most words. That is, most letters in Tagalog represent the same value they have in the phonetic alphabet (for many English loans, however, the conventional English spelling is retained, e.g. *cylinder* instead of *silinder*). Only one native sound, the velar nasal [ŋ], is represented by a combination of two letters, i.e. <ng>. The alveo-palatal stops in loans (/c/ and /ɟ/) are frequently rendered by <ts> and <dy>, respectively. And as in most western Austronesian orthographies, the palatal glide /j/ is represented by <y>.

A major deviation from the close match between spelling and pronunciation results from the fact that glottal stops and stress are not indicated in the standard orthography. Consequently, words such as *abó* 'ashes' that appear to be vowel-initial in writing actually have an initial glottal stop, i.e. <abó> represents /ʔabó/. Similarly, two vowels which occur adjacent to each other in writing are separated by a glottal, thus *tao* 'person, people' is /táʔo/. And many orthographically vowel-final words such as *sira* 'break, damage' actually include a final glottal stop, hence /síraʔ/.

The lack of an indication for final glottal stops in writing may create confusion since two words may differ only with regard to this feature. Compare /báta/ 'robe' with /bátaʔ/ 'child', both conventionally spelled as *bata*. Similarly, stress distinguishes otherwise identical word forms, as illustrated above. In order to make this important information available, the better dictionaries and textbooks (as well as Bloomfield 1917) indicate both stress and final glottal stops. The convention for stress is to indicate it with an acute accent whenever it does not fall on the penultimate syllable, or when two adjacent syllables are stressed. Thus, conventional *abo* is written *abó* in the dictionaries and conventional *laruan* either *laruán* (for 'toy') or *lárúan* (for 'playground'). But *bata* 'robe', which has penultimate stress, is just written *bata* in the dictionaries.

The convention for final glottal stops is to indicate them by a grave accent on the final vowel (conventional *bata* 'child' is *batà* in the dictionaries). Words having both final stress and a final glottal stop are marked by a circumflex on the final vowel, e.g. *hindî* 'no'. In this chapter, all examples are presented according to the dictionary conventions, except that final glottals are indicated by <ʔ> (thus *hindî* is spelled *hindíʔ*).

Two further orthographic conventions are of practical importance: First, in the Tagalog alphabet the letter <k> takes the place conventionally occupied by <c>. Thus, the beginning of the alphabet reads *a, b, **k**, d, e*, etc. Furthermore, the digraph <ng> representing the velar nasal is placed in between <n> and <o>, hence *l, m, n, **ng**, o, p*, etc. Second, it is conventional to abbreviate the following two frequent grammatical function words: the genitive marker /naŋ/ is written as *ng* and the plural marker /maŋá/ as *mga*. This convention is also adhered to in the present chapter.

2.3 Phonological alternations

There are very few phonologically conditioned alternations in Tagalog. That is, when affixes are added to lexical bases (or clitics to their hosts) neither affix nor base undergo many formal changes. Note in particular that initial glottal stops are not deleted when preceded by a consonant-final formative. For example, *mag+aral* 'to study' is [mag.ʔá.ral] and not *[ma.gá.ral]. However changes in the stress pattern occur fairly regularly, in particular when suffixes are involved (see 2.1 above).

With a few exceptions, prefixes which involve a homorganic nasal follow the general rule given in HIMMELMANN, TYPOLOGICAL CHARACTERISTICS, section 2.1. Initial /s/ is regularly replaced by /n/ (e.g. *maN+sakít → manakít* 'to hurt'). Before glides, *N* regularly becomes /ng/ (e.g. *maN+wikaʔ → mangwikaʔ* 'say sth. insulting'). The deletion of the voiced stops /b/ and /d/ is not uncommon (cf. *maN+bilí → mamilí* 'to go shopping' and *maN+daʔig → manaʔig* 'to prevail'). Somewhat exceptional is the fact that initial glottal stops are often retained (*maN+apí → mang-apí* [maŋʔapí] 'to oppress'). Furthermore, the replacement of voiceless obstruents is optional in some formations (e.g. *paN+takíp* is either *pantakíp* or *panakíp* 'sth. used for covering'; cf. DeGuzman 1978b).

Another fairly general process is the deletion of the vowel in a stressed base-final CVC-syllable when a suffix is added. Thus, *bigáy+an* is *bigyán* 'give sth to someone' and *sunód+in* is *sundín* 'to obey'. Occasionally this deletion is accompanied by metathesis: *taním+an → tamnan* 'to plant on'. Final glottal stops are generally deleted in this context: *gawáʔ+in → gawín* 'to make sth'.

When suffixes are added to vowel-final bases, an /h/ is inserted between base and suffix as in *basa+in → basahin* 'to read sth' or *sabi+in → sabihin* 'say sth'. H-insertion together with base-final vowel deletion account for derivations such as the following: *bilí+in → bilhín* 'to buy sth', *sará+an → sarhán* 'to shut sth'. Sporadically, there is also the insertion of an /n/ when bases end in a vowel or a glottal stop (e.g. *tawa+an → tawanan* 'to laugh at someone'). Completely irregular is the form *kunin* 'to get sth' from *kuha+in* (which occurs along with *kuhanin* (same meaning)).

A final glottal stop is regularly deleted, and the preceding vowel lengthened, when an enclitic follows. Thus, *hindíʔ=na* 'no longer' is pronounced [hindí:na], *gawáʔ=nya* 'his/her deed' [gawá:ɲa]. Note that no such change occurs with suffixes.

A few other automatic changes occur on the level of phonological words and phrases. In native words, a final /o/ is regularly raised to /u/ when not occurring in phrase-final position. Thus, the proximal demonstrative *itó* is [ʔitó] when phrase-final (as in *bundók na itó* 'this mountain') but it is [ʔitú] in other positions (*itúng bundók*). The base for 'game' is *laróʔ*, but the suffixed form for 'toy' is *laruán*. Similarly, an /i/ occurring in a phrase-final syllable may be lowered to /e/ as in the common pronunciation [gabé] for *gabí* 'night' ([gabí] is also possible). Furthermore, /d/ often becomes /r/ in intervocalic position, although this is by no means always the case. Compare *doón* 'there' with *maroón* 'be there', *tawad* 'discount' with *tawaran* 'ask for a discount on sth', etc. Note that /r/ does not occur in initial position or after a consonant in Tagalog native words.

2.4 Reduplication

From a purely formal point of view, there are three kinds of reduplication processes in Tagalog. In two of these processes the first consonant and vowel of the base are copied (CV-reduplication). The two processes differ with regard to the fact that in one the reduplicated syllable is assigned stress (RDP1), and in the other it is not (RDP): *mang-gá-gamót* 'will practice medicine' vs. *mang-ga-gamot* (or *manggagamót*) 'physician'. If a base starts with a consonant cluster, only the first consonant is copied, cf. *trabaho* 'work' → *mag-tá-trabaho* 'will work'. Recall from sections 2.1 and 2.2 that all Tagalog syllables are consonant-initial even though initial glottal stops are not indicated in the orthography (hence a form such as *mag-íígi* /mag?í?ígi/ 'to adjust' (base *igi* /?ígi/) is not an example for the reduplication of a vowel-initial base).

The third process consists in copying the first two syllables of the base (RDP2). In the case of disyllabic bases, the complete base is copied including its stress pattern, e.g., *mura* 'cheap' → *mura-mura* 'rather cheap', *lakad* 'walk' → *mag-lakád-lakád* 'to stroll, to walkabout'. If bases contain more than two syllables, the second syllable is copied only up to its nucleus, which is then also assigned stress, cf. *tahimik* 'peaceful' → *tahí-tahimik* 'rather peaceful', *baluktót* 'crooked' → *balú-baluktót* 'variously bent'. RDP and RDP2 generally apply to lexical bases only, while RDP1 freely applies to prefixes as well (*mag+RDP1+pa+putol* → *magpápapaputol* 'will cause to be cut').

A certain kind of reduplication may occur only once in a derivation, but different kinds of reduplication may co-occur within the same derivation. When RDP1 and RDP2 co-occur, RDP2 derivationally precedes RDP1: *magsásakít-sakitan* 'will pretend to be sick'. RDP1 and RDP may also co-occur, in which case RDP derivationally precedes RDP1. Thus from *takbó* 'run' *mág-ta-takbó* 'run wild' is derived by prefixing *mag-* and RDP. From the latter the imperfective aspect *mag-tá-ta-takbó* is derived by RDP1.

In addition to reduplication, there is also the possibility to repeat complete (grammatical) words in order to express various forms of intensification. In this case, the word forms remain unchanged and there is usually a linker (see below 3.2) inserted in between the two repeated forms. Examples: *pagód na pagód* 'very tired', *magandá-ng-magandá* 'very beautiful', etc.

3 BASIC MORPHOSYNTAX

3.1 Basic clause structure and phrase marking

Tagalog clauses are basically of two types. In simple main clauses, the predicate occurs in clause-initial position and the subject comes at the end. If the subject is a common noun (such as *aswáng* in (1)) it is usually preceded by the specific article *ang*:

(1) *dumatíng   na   ang   aswáng*
    AV:arrive   now   SPEC   vampire
    'The vampire came.'

Typically, there is also at least one clitic particle in clauses of this type (in (1), *na* is such a particle). These clitics are second position clitics, i.e. roughly speaking, they occur after the first word of the predicate. If the predicate consists of only one word (such as *dumatíng* in (1)), this is equivalent to saying that second position clitics come immediately after the predicate (see also section 3.3).

The second clause type is the existential clause which consists of the existential operator *may* (or *mayroon*) or its negative equivalent *walá?* and a complement (*bigás* in (2)). Other, optional constituents in this clause type are clitics (*na* and *raw* in (2)) and local adjuncts (*sa tindahan* in (2)):

(2) *may   bigás   na   raw   sa   tindahan*
    EXIST   rice   now   RPRT   LOC   store
    'There's rice in the store now, they say.'

Existential clauses may be expanded by a subject phrase (typically in final position) and then convey a possessive meaning (cf. McFarland 1978a):

(3) *may*   *kápitbahay*   *naman*   **silá**
    EXIST neighbor   also   3p
    'They had (or have) a neighbor,...'

In colloquial Tagalog, clauses often end in an emphatic particle (*e*, *a*, *ha*, or *o*) which may express regret, sympathy, surprise, urgency, sarcasm, reason or the like:

(4) *napakagandáng*   *dalaga*   *iyón*   **e**
    ELATIVE:beauty:LK young.woman DIST EMPH
    'She (that one) is a very beautiful girl, you see.'

The preceding example also illustrates the fact that all kinds of expressions may serve as the predicate in simple main clauses. In (4) the predicate consists of the complex expression *napakagandang dalaga* 'very beautiful girl'. The typical predicative expression in simple main clauses, however, is a voice-marked word which is roughly equivalent to an English verb (see 3.3 below for some pertinent differences between English verbs and Tagalog voice-marked words). Voice-marking will be discussed in detail in section 4.1. Here it is sufficient to note that there are essentially two basic types of voice constructions. In actor-oriented voice, the predicate is marked for actor voice (by the infix *-um-* in (5)) and the subject expression refers to the actor of the event denoted by the predicate:

(5) *hum**anap*   *na*   *ng*   *bahay*   **ang**   **mga**   **bata?**
    um-hanap na ng bahay ang mga bata?
    AV-search now GEN house SPEC PL   child
    'The children looked for houses/a house.'

In undergoer-oriented voices, the predicate is marked for an undergoer voice (by the infix *-in-* in (6)) and the subject expression refers to the undergoer of the event denoted by the predicate:

(6) *hin**anap*   *na*   *ng*   *bata?*   **ang**   **bahay**
    in-hanap   na ng bata? ang bahay
    RLS(UG)-search now GEN child SPEC house
    'The children looked for the house(s).'

That is, a special relation exists between the subject and the predicate in that the voice affix on the predicate marks the semantic role played by the subject in the event expressed by the predicate. Thus, for example, the infix *-um-* in (5) makes it clear that the subject (*ang mga bata?*) is the agent of the search and not its undergoer. This special relation between voice-marked predicates and subjects is one of the reasons for assigning the grammatical relation *subject* to the *ang*-phrase in clauses such as (5) and (6) (see HIMMELMANN, TYPOLOGICAL CHARACTERISTICS, section 3.8.1, for references and discussion regarding the controversy surrounding subjecthood in Tagalog).

Note that the specific article *ang* is not a subject marker since *ang*-phrases may also occur in other syntactic functions. In the following example, the first *ang*-phrase (*ang langgám*) functions as the predicate while the second *ang*-phrase (*ang tumulong sa mga bata?*) is the subject (for a different analysis of this construction, see Constantino 1965,

DeGuzman 1986, and Kroeger 1993:148–152):

(7) **ang langgám** rin ang tumulong sa mga bata?
SPEC ant also SPEC AV:help LOC PL child
'The ants also helped the children (lit. The ones who helped the children were also the ants).'

Furthermore, subjects (and some, but not all, non-predicative constituents) may occur in pre-predicate position. In the most common type of construction in which the predicate is not initial, the predicate marker *ay* ('y after vowels) signals the beginning of the predicate. Thus, instead of *dumatíng ang aswang*, the following is also possible (same meaning as in (1)):

(8) **ang aswáng ay** *dumatíng*

Although a subject is always implied in a Tagalog simple main clause (except in meteorological expressions and the like), this subject does not have to be overtly expressed. Compare the following sequence of two clauses where the subject of the second predicate (*inilagáy*), which is coreferential with the subject of the first predicate (*kinuha*), is not overtly expressed:

(9) *at* *kinuha* *niyá* *ang langgám*
at in-kuha niyá ang langgám
and RLS(UG)-getting 3s.POSS SPEC ant

at **inilagáy** *niyá* *sa* *pampáng*
at in-i-lagáy niyá sa pampáng
and RLS(UG)-CV-position 3s.POSS LOC river.bank
'And he got the ant and put (it) on the riverbank.'

The preceding examples also show that non-subject arguments and adjuncts are marked with either the genitive preposition *ng* (i.e. [naŋ]) or the general locative preposition *sa*. The choice among these two markers for a given argument or adjunct depends on its semantic role and, in one instance, on its animacy (human vs. non-human). Non-subject actors (including experiencers) are generally marked as genitives (cf. *ng mga bata?* in (6)). Non-subject patients and themes are also marked as genitives, if non-human (cf. *ng bahay* in (5)). If they are human and specific, they are usually marked by *sa* (cf. *sa mga bata?* in (7)). All other semantic roles – except non-subject instruments, which may also be marked as genitives – are expressed by *sa*-phrases or complex prepositional expressions, which in Tagalog always include the general locative marker *sa* (e.g., *tungkól sa* 'about, regarding', *para sa* 'for'). This includes a large variety of temporal and local adjuncts as in (10) as well as recipients/goals (*sa pampang* in (9) above):

(10) *at* *dun* *na* *silá* *tátabunan* **sa** **lugar** **na** **iyón**
at doón na silá RDP1-tabon-an sa lugár na iyón
and DIST.LOC now 3p RDP1-complete.cover-LV LOC place LK DIST
'And there they were covered (with earth) at that place.'

Tagalog argument and adjunct expressions, then, are generally preceded by a grammatical function marker (i.e. *ang*, *ng*, and *sa* in the case of common noun phrases). Their order is not totally fixed but there is a strong tendency for them to occur in the following order: genitives almost always occur immediately after the predicate, subjects tend to be placed in clause-final position, and locative-marked phrases typically precede the subject when expressing an argument. They may either precede or follow the subject when expressing an adjunct.

Not all nominal expressions in Tagalog are marked by one of the three markers *ang*, *ng*, and *sa*. These markers only occur in common noun phrases. For personal names there is a different series of markers, and demonstratives and personal pronouns have their own *ang*, *ng*, and *sa* forms which are not preceded by a marker. Table 12.2 lists some of the forms.

Overall, the syntactic distribution of the forms in each column is very similar. In fact, the distribution of the *ang*, *ng*, and *sa* forms of the demonstratives is completely identical to the distribution of the *ang*, *ng*, and *sa* forms of common noun phrases. In particular in the spoken language, *ang, ng,* and *sa* are often replaced by the corresponding forms of the demonstratives. Compare the following example in which *yung*, a variant of the distal demonstrative *iyón* plus linker, has taken the place of *ang*:

(11)   *sumigáw*   **yung**   *anák*
      AV:shout   DIST.LK   child
      'That child shouted:...'

With regard to the *ng* and *sa* forms of personal pronouns and personal names, however, there are some minor, but still important distributional differences which warrant slightly different glosses. The *ng*-form of personal pronouns and personal names is used only to express possessors (as in *ang bahay niyá* 'his/her house') and actors in undergoer-oriented constructions (as in (9) above). It cannot be used to mark the undergoer in actor-oriented constructions (i.e. *ng bahay* in (5) cannot be replaced by the *ng*-form of a personal pronoun or a personal name). To indicate this difference, the *ng*-form of personal pronouns and personal names is glossed here as *possessive* (rather than as *genitive*). Similarly, the *sa*-form of personal pronouns and personal names is glossed as *dative* (rather than as *locative*) because of a number of distributional differences (cf. Schachter and Otanes 1972:91, 136).

TABLE 12.2: NOUN PHRASE MARKERS AND PRONOUNS

	ANG-FORM (SPEC)	*NG*-FORM (POSS/GEN)	*SA*-FORM (LOC/DAT)
Noun phrase markers			
COMMON NOUNS	ang	ng	sa
PERSONAL NAMES	si	ni	kay
Pronouns			
1.SG	akó	ko	akin
2.SG	ikáw/ka	mo	iyo/iyó
3.SG	siyá	niyá	kaniyá
1.DU.IN	kitá/katá	nitá	kanitá
1.PL.IN	tayo	natin	atin
1.PL.EX	kamí	namin	amin
2.PL	kayó	ninyó	inyó
3.PL	silá	nilá	kanilá
Demonstratives			
PRX	itó	nitó	dito, rito
MED	iyán	niyán	diyán, riyán
DIST	iyón	niyón, noón	doón, roón

3.2 Noun phrase structure and linkers

The structure of noun phrases is very straightforward. As just noted, all noun phrases are introduced by a proclitic phrase marker. Possessors follow their head and are genitive-marked:

(12) *ang   hari   **ng   lamók***
    SPEC   king   GEN   mosquito
    'the king of the mosquitos'

An exception are pronominal possessors which can also precede their head and then occur in dative rather than in possessive form (i.e. a semantically fully equivalent alternative to *ang bahay niyá* 'his/her house' is *ang kaniyá-ng bahay* (SPEC 3s.DAT-LK house)).

All non-possessive modifying constructions involve the linker *na* (*-ng* after vowels, /n/ or glottal stop) between each major constituent:

(13) *ang   ma-liít   **na**   hayop*
    SPEC   ST-smallness   LK   animal
    'the small animal'

The order of the constituents in the linker construction is not fixed ('the small animal' could also be rendered by *ang hayop na maliít*). Only numerals generally precede all other constituents, except demonstratives, as in:

(14) *ang   **apat   na**   ma-lalim   **na**   balón*
    SPEC   four   LK   ST-depth   LK   well
    'four deep wells'

Attributively used demonstratives occur at the very periphery of noun phrases and may in fact be used twice, both at the beginning and the end:

(15) ***itó-ng*   *isá-ng*   *tasa*   *-ng*   *itó***
    PRX-LK   one-LK   cup   -LK   PRX
    'this one cup'

Relative clauses are also constructed with a linker and may precede or follow their head. In the following example, there are two relative clauses, one preceding, the other following the head (*isáng ibon*):

(16) ***kanyáng   nákítang***   *isáng   ibon   **na   mayroóng   pugad***
    kanyá-ng   na-kita-ng   isá-ng   ibon   na   mayroón:LK   pugad
    3s.DAT-LK   RLS.POT-seen-LK   one-LK   bird   LK   EXIST:LK   nest
    '(There was) a bird he happened to see that had a nest.'

The head remains formally unexpressed in the relative clause. With a few exceptions, it has to correspond to the missing subject argument of the relative clause predicate (cf. HIMMELMANN, TYPOLOGICAL CHARACTERISTICS, section 3.10).

The linker does not only occur in noun phrases but generally links the major constituents of modifying constructions. Thus, it also links adverbial expressions, as in:

(17) ***lalo-ng***   *malakí   ang   takot*
    surpassing-LK   big   SPEC   fear
    'The fear was very great...'

(18) ***biglá-ng***   *dumatíng   yung   utusan*
    sudden-LK   AV-arrival   DIST:LK   servant
    'Suddenly that servant came...'

3.3 Lexical categories (word classes)

With regard to the grammatical categorization of lexical items, a first and very basic distinction can be made between content words and function words (or full words and particles). Content words have a meaning of their own and fall into large classes of items with similar grammatical properties. Function words signal often elusive grammatical or interactional meanings and form small, closed classes with regard to their grammatical properties.

Most Tagalog function words are clitics (i.e. phonologically they are not independent words). The noun phrase markers (*ang, ng, sa*, etc.) are proclitics, i.e. they form a phonological constituent with the following content word. Apart from the proclitics, there is also a relatively large number of second position clitics. Second position clitics occur after the first content word of the constituent to which they belong (exceptions are discussed in Schachter and Otanes 1972:187–193, 433–435 and Kroeger 1993:118–123, 152–154). That is, clause-level clitics come right after the predicate if the predicate is in clause-initial position (as in examples (5) and (6) above). If another constituent, for example, an adverbial or a negation, precedes the predicate proper, the clitic will occur right after that constituent. In the following example, the politeness clitic *hó?* follows the (non-clitic) negation marker *hindí?* (note that clitics in Tagalog are represented as independent words in standard orthography):

(19) *nakú   hindí   **hó?**   pwede*
      my!   NEG   FRM   possible
      'Hey! That's impossible, Sir.'

However, there are some clause initial constituents which are ignored for purposes of clitic placement. These include interjections such as *nakú* in the preceding example and *ay*-inverted constituents (cf. (8) above).

If the prepredicate constituent is linked to the predicate proper by a linker, the clitic (*siyá* in the following example) occurs before the linker:

(20) *biglá   **siyá**-ng   nagbangon*
      sudden   3s-LK   RLS.AV:rising
      '...she got quickly up (from her bed),...'

The domain for the placement of a clitic can also be smaller than a clause. In the following examples, it is a noun phrase. Note that the clitic (here *ko*) always comes after the first content word, regardless of whether or not this is also the semantic head of the construction:

(21) *ang   anak   **ko**-ng   dalaga*   'my daughter'
      SPEC   child   1s.POSS-LK   young.woman

(22) *sa   dalawá   **ko**-ng   kasama*   'to my two companions'
      LOC   two   1s.POSS-LK   companion

There are two basic types of second position clitics: pronouns and a fairly heterogeneous set of particles, including the aspectual particles *na* 'already, now' and *pa* 'still', the question marker *ba*, the politeness markers *hó?* and *pó?*, *yata?* expressing uncertainty, *palá* expressing surprise, etc. With regard to pronouns, it should be noted that not all forms of the pronouns are second position clitics. The *ng*-forms of the pronouns (such as *ko* in the preceding examples, see also Table 12.2 above) are always second position clitics. The *ang*-forms of the pronouns can be used as second position clitics (cf. *siyá* in (20)) but they can also be used as phonologically independent words. They may, for example, occur in clause-initial position preceding *ay*. Thus, an alternative order for (20) is *siyá 'y bigláng nagbangon*. No alternative orders exist for 'true' second position clitics such as *ho* in (19) or *ko* in (21) or (22).

When two or more clitics co-occur, the general rule is that monosyllabic pronominal clitics come first, followed by the clitic particles (among which monosyllabic ones precede disyllabic ones), and disyllabic pronominal clitics come last, as in *bigyán **mo namán akó*** (gift-LV 2s.POSS truly 1s) 'give me (some) please' (cf. also Schachter 1973).

Content words fall into a number of subcategories. These subcategories do not correspond very closely to the categories noun, verb and adjective familiar from English and other Indo-European languages. One major distinction between the Tagalog categories and the English ones pertains to the fact that in the English scheme morpho-lexical and syntactic categories closely correspond to each other. That is, an English verb such as *betray* is a verb both on morphological grounds (for example, it forms a past tense with *-ed*) and with regard to its syntactic distribution (it may be used as a predicate but not, without further derivation, as the head of a noun phrase (*the betray)).

In Tagalog, there is no such close correspondence between morpho-lexical and syntactic categories. In fact, content words do not have to be subclassified with regard to syntactic categories. They all have the same syntactic distribution, i.e. they all may occur as predicates, as (semantic) heads of noun phrases and as modifiers (cf. Lemaréchal 1982, 1989, Himmelmann 1991, to appear, Gil 1993, Shkarban 1995, or Naylor 1995). For example, voice-marked words, which generally have a verb-like meaning, are not restricted to the predicate function. They may occur in other syntactic functions as well. In the following example, the undergoer voice form *sásabihin* 'will be said' functions as the patient argument of the actor voice predicate *naghintáy* 'waited for' and is marked accordingly by the genitive marker *ng*:

(23) *at*   *ang* *pare* *at*   *siyá* *ay* *nag-hintáy*
     and SPEC priest and 3s   PM RLS.AV-wait
     ng **sá-sabih-in**   ng sundalo
     GEN RDP1-statement-PV GEN soldier
     'And the priest and he waited for what the soldier would say.'

Furthermore, voice-marked words may be in construction with quantifiers, including the existential quantifier *may*:

(24) ***may*** ***i-pá-pa-kita***   *akó* *sa* *iyo*
     EXIST CV-RDP1-CAU-seen 1s LOC 2s.DAT
     'I have something to show you.'

The fact that content words have essentially the same syntactic distribution means that phrases marked by *ang, ng*, and *sa* are not noun phrases in the strict sense (i.e. phrases headed by a noun). Instead, they are *determiner phrases* which are headed by a function word. The function word determines the syntactic distribution as well as the basic meaning type of the phrase (they are all referential expressions). Thus, the term *noun phrase* in this chapter is to be understood in its wide sense as a cover term for both determiner phrases and noun phrases in the strict sense.

As opposed to the syntactic level, Tagalog content words clearly fall into different classes on the morpho-lexical level. That is, they do not all have the same morphological possibilities and they differ with regard to the meaning alternations associated with various formal derivations. Here it is useful to make a distinction between affixed forms and non-affixed forms. Some affixed forms belong to more or less extensive paradigms of formations so that given one form it is possible to predict the availability of a number of other formations involving the same lexical item. This holds true in particular for voice-marked forms, all of which allow for aspect/mood inflection and a number of other regular derivations (see section 4 below). Because of these morphological characteristics, voice-marked words may be considered a morpho-lexical class of their own which, on the basis of their meaning, could also be called 'verbs', keeping in mind that Tagalog 'verbs' are very different from English verbs.

Non-affixed forms, here called *lexical bases*, belong to different classes according to the kinds of affixes with which they occur. The actual number and kind of classes is a matter of ongoing research and controversy (for different ways of classifying lexical bases with regard to voice marking, see Blake (1925:38f), Schachter and Otanes (1972:295–310), Cruz (1975), McFarland (1976), Ramos (1974), DeGuzman (1978a), Ramos and Bautista (1986)). Once again, however, it appears to be the case that one cannot distinguish formally between nominal and verbal bases, as is shown by the following lexicographic practice, among other things.

In standard dictionaries, the basic meaning of most lexical bases is rendered by an English noun, adjective or past participle. This may appear to be odd in the case of bases which denote actions or states, such as *lagáy* 'condition, state, location, position', *kuha* 'a helping, act of getting', *hanap* 'quest, object of search', *alís* 'departure', *kita* 'seen, obvious' or *hirám* 'borrowed'. When these bases are affixed with a voice affix, the meaning is clearly verbal (thus, for example, *umalís* is glossed 'to go/go away (actor-oriented)' and *hiramán* as 'to borrow from someone (undergoer-oriented)'). Most of these bases are used with such affixes most of the time. However, if the unaffixed base is used (which is possible for a great many of them), the meaning is clearly nominal (or adjectival). For example:

(25) *subali't* *tuluy-tulóy* *pa*   *rin*   *ang* **kain**   *ni*   *matsíng*
      but   RDP2-continue   still   also   SPEC   eating   PN.POSS   small.monkey
      'But the monkey's eating continued nevertheless.'

(26) *biglaan*   *ang*   *kanyáng*   **alís**
      bigláʔ-an   ang   kanyá-ng   alís
      sudden-??   SPEC   3s.DAT-LK   departure
      'His departure was sudden.'

Because of examples such as these, the lexicographic practice of glossing lexical bases as either nouns or adjectives/participles has some validity. Note that all the glosses for bases in this chapter are taken from a single source (English 1986), for reasons of consistency.

4 MAJOR VERBAL ALTERNATIONS

Like many other western Austronesian languages, Tagalog verbs exhibit an elaborate set of morphological distinctions. Recall from the preceding section that overt voice-marking is the defining feature of verbs. So Tagalog verbs are, by definition, voice-marked. Two further categorial distinctions are – explicitly or implicitly – expressed by all verbs. One of these is aspect/mood (cf. section 4.1). The other one is the distinction between dynamic and stative verbs. Dynamic verbs generally refer to the volitional and controlled doing of an action. Stative verbs refer to states of affairs which do not involve any kind of agent. For dynamic verbs there is a special morphology, called *potentive* here, which signals that the volitional and controlling agent typically involved in the state of affairs expressed by a dynamic verb is not in full control of the event. Stative and potentive morphology are similar both semantically and formally, and therefore are dealt with together in section 4.2.

In addition to the three major verbal categories of voice, aspect/mood and dynamic/stative, a number of other concepts exists which are morphologically marked on the verb. Most of these concepts are in one way or another related to the way in which the actor is involved in a given state of affairs. They include causation, joint and reciprocal action, making a request and various forms of multiple actions. See Lopez (1937) for an extensive illustration of these affixes and RUBINO (ILOKO) for a similar range of derivations from Iloko, often involving cognate affixes.

4.1 Voice and aspect/mood

The Tagalog voice system consists of at least four voices. Actor voice is marked by the infix *-um-* or the prefixes *mag-* or *maN-*, patient voice by the suffix *-in*, locative voice by the suffix *-an*, and conveyance voice by the prefix *i-*. The latter three voices share several semantic and formal characteristics, which makes it convenient to use *undergoer voices* as a cover term for them.

Most lexical bases may be combined directly with one or more of the voice affixes. Some bases, however, require the use of the stem forming-prefixes *pag-* or *paN-* before voice marking can be applied.

For each voice form it is possible to distinguish two aspects and two moods. Imperfective aspect is marked by accented CV-reduplication (RDP1), perfective aspect is unmarked. Realis mood is marked by the infix *-in-* in the undergoer voices, non-realis mood remaining formally unmarked. In actor voice, the expression of mood is somewhat less straightforward. When actor voice is expressed by *mag-* or *maN-*, there is a special *n*-initial form of the prefix, i.e. *nag-* and *naN-*, which signals realis mood while the *m*-initial form signals non-realis mood (the initial nasals in these forms, *n* and *m*, are historically related to the infixes *-in-* and *-um-*, respectively; cf. Reid 1992). When actor voice is marked by *-um-*, a mood distinction is formally expressed only in the imperfective aspect, where *-um-* is lacking. Table 12.3 illustrates these formations based on the base *bilí* 'purchase, sale'.

TABLE 12.3: ASPECT/MOOD PARADIGM FOR *bilí* 'purchase, sale'

	AV ('buy')	AV ('sell')	PV	LV	CV
NON-REALIS/ PERFECTIVE	b\<um\>ilí	mag-bilí	bilh-ín	bilh-án	i-bilí
NON-REALIS/ IMPERFECTIVE	bíbilí	mag-bíbilí	bíbilh-ín	bíbilh-án	i-bíbilí
REALIS/ PERFECTIVE	b\<um\>ilí	nag-bilí	b\<in\>ilí	b\<in\>ilh-án	i-b\<in\>ilí
REALIS/ IMPERFECTIVE	b\<um\>íbilí	nag-bíbilí	b\<in\>íbilí	b\<in\>íbilh-án	i-b\<in\>íbilí

In addition to the lack of *-um-* in the non-realis/imperfective form of the actor voice, there is one further idiosyncrasy in this paradigm: the realis forms of the patient voice lack the suffix *-in* (for further comments on the asymmetries cf. Himmelmann 1987:171–178).

The *m/n*-alternation signaling mood in the actor voice is also found with a number of *p*-initial bases (e.g., the non-realis form of *panoód* 'watch' is *manoód*, realis *nanoód*). For this and other reasons, the actor voice prefixes *mag-* and *maN-* can be analyzed as consisting of the stem-deriving prefixes *pag-* and *paN-*, respectively, plus *m/n*-alternation signaling voice and mood (see DeGuzman 1978a:149ff). The stem-deriving prefixes *pag-* and *paN-* also occur in the undergoer voices, i.e. there are formations involving *pag- -in*, *pag- -an*, *i-pag-*, etc.

Table 12.3 is somewhat misleading in that it fails to bring out a very important difference between aspect/mood and voice. Aspect/mood-marking is completely general and regular. That is, given a voice-marked word it is clear that it will occur in all four aspect/mood-forms shown in Table 12.3. In this sense, it is legitimate to speak of aspect/mood-inflection of verbs in Tagalog.

Voice marking is different. It is common to illustrate the workings of Tagalog voice morphology with multiple derivations from the same base, as it is done here in Table 12.3. This procedure easily leads to the misconception that it is possible to derive a large number of different voices from every base. This is not the case. Instead, even in those instances where several derivations are possible from the same base, there are typically only one or two derivations in common use while the other ones are marginal and marked in that they convey special semantic and/or pragmatic meanings and implications (cf. McFarland 1976). That is, the voice affixes are essentially derivational when viewed from a crosslinguistic perspective (cf. DeGuzman (1997) and Rubino (1998a) for recent contributions to the inflection vs. derivation controversy).

Before looking more closely at the different voice formations, a few comments on the four aspect/moods are in order. There are a number of alternative terminologies in use for these forms (cf. Werlen in Bader *et al.* (1994:95–100) and Kroeger (1993:15–18) for an overview). The terminology used here reflects the formal make-up of the paradigm but it is not quite felicitous in all instances with regard to the function of the forms.

The form labeled non-realis/perfective here is formally the most unmarked form (and therefore also called the *basic form* or *infinitive*). It has essentially the distribution of a subjunctive. That is, it is used in imperatives (27) and in various dependent constructions (reduced complement and adverbial clauses, in construction with modal auxiliaries (28), etc.):

(27)　*hindí?!*　**tingnán**　*mo*　*ika?*　*si*　*Maria!*
　　　hindí?　tingín-an　mo　ika?　si　Maria
　　　NEG　look-LV　2s.POSS　said　PN　Maria
　　　'Don't (panic)! Just look at Maria (she said)!'

(28)　*gusto*　*ni*　*Pepito*　*na*　**sagip-in**　*ang*　*dahon*
　　　liking　PN.POSS　Pepito　COMP　salvage-PV　SPEC　leaf
　　　'Pepito wanted to catch the leaf.'

The non-realis/imperfective form (also called *contemplated aspect* or *future*) generally refers to states of affairs which have not yet taken place at reference time:

(29)　**gágawá**　*kamí*　*ng*　*kubó*
　　　RDP1-made　1pe　GEN　hut
　　　'We will make a hut.'

The realis/imperfective forms (*imperfective aspect* or *present tense* in alternative terminologies) are used for states of affairs which are ongoing at reference time:

(30) | di | yong | lalaki | ... ***nag-íígi*** | | ng | pantalon |
|---|---|---|---|---|---|---|
| di | iyón:LK | lalaki | nag-RDP1-igi | | ng | pantalón |
| so | DIST:LK | man | RLS.AV-RDP1-all.right | | GEN | trousers |

'So the man was adjusting his trousers...'

These forms are also used for habitual or iterative states of affairs (cf. (40) below).

The realis/perfective forms (*perfective aspect* or *past tense*) are used for states of
affairs which have been completed at reference time (see examples (7) and (9) above,
among others).

Turning now to the voice formations, note first that the ensuing discussion primarily
concerns dynamic verbs. The meanings of the voices in stative and potentive formations
are slightly different, as discussed in 4.2. In dynamic formations, the actor voice forms
usually imply that the subject is a volitional and controlling instigator of the event. The
major exception to this rule are self-regulated processes (also known as "achievements")
and natural phenomena, which are generally marked by the actor voice infix *-um-* as well.
The subject of process verbs is a theme rather than an actor:

(31) | ***g<um>anda*** | na | ang | buhay | nilá |
|---|---|---|---|---|
| <AV>beauty | now | SPEC | life | 3p.POSS |

'(...and) their life became beautiful.'

Expressions for natural phenomena are usually subjectless (*umúulán na* 'it's raining'). The
choice of one or the other of the three actor voice affixes *-um-*, *mag-* and *maN-* sometimes
conveys semantic differences pertaining to reflexivity, the intensity of the action and the
like (cf. Pittman 1966, Lopez 1937:46–49, Drossard 1984:87–92; Himmelmann 1987:101f,
185–188). It is rare, however, that one base occurs with all three actor voice affixes, as in:
pumutol 'cut', *magputol* 'cut several things', *mámutol* 'cut selectively or in quantity'.

Of the three affixes, *maN-* is the least common. It generally indicates intensive, distributive or repeated action, e.g., *bumilí* 'buy' vs. *mamilí* 'shop', *humampás* 'hit with a
whip' vs. *manghampás* 'go whipping'.

The major contrast is the one between *-um-* and *mag-*. Often *mag-* indicates a greater
frequency or intensity of an action, cf. *bumasa* 'read' vs. *magbasa* 'to read a lot/study'.
mag- and *-um-* may even co-occur to indicate a very high degree of intensity, cf.
mag<um>aral 'study diligently' or *mag-s<um>igáw* 'shout (long and very loud)'.
With regard to bases denoting position or motion, there is a regular contrast in transitivity: *t<um>ayó? kami* (<AV>stand.upright 1pe) 'we stood up' vs. *nag-tayó? kami ng*
bahay (RLS.AV-stand.upright 1pe GEN house) 'we erected a house'. That is, the *-um-*-form
denotes actors who move themselves while the *mag-*-form denotes actors who move
something else. A similar contrast exists with respect to bases denoting qualities, e.g.,
um-init 'become/get hot' vs. *mag-init* 'make hot, heat'. Much quoted, but unique is the
contrast between *bumilí* 'buy' and *magbilí* 'sell'.

In other instances, however, it is difficult to determine what exactly the choice of the actor
voice affix contributes to the meaning of the overall formation. That is, it appears to be simply a lexical feature of some bases to occur with *mag-* and others to occur with *-um-*.

Unlike the three actor voice affixes, the three undergoer voice affixes consistently
differ with regard to the semantics of the undergoer. Hence it is customary to distinguish
at least three undergoer voices in Tagalog. Ignoring several details and complications,
it generally holds true that if the predicate is marked with the conveyance voice prefix

i-, the subject expresses an argument bearing the semantic role of a displaced theme. Compare:

(32) *ibinalík*   *nilá*   **ang**   **bata?**
      i-in-balík   nilá   ang   bata?
      CV-RLS(UG)-return 3p.POSS   SPEC   child
      'They returned the child.'

Here the subject (*ang bata?*) is the displaced theme (i.e. the entity viewed as moving) of the event expressed by the predicate (*ibinalík*). Instruments are also viewed as moving entities and hence marked with the conveyance voice prefix:

(33) *ipangpúpútol*   *ko*   *na*   *lang*   **itóng**   **kutsilyo**
      i-paN-RDP1-putol   ko   na   lamang   itó-ng   kutsilyo
      CV-INS-RDP1-cut   1s.POSS   now   only   PRX-LK   knife
      'I will just cut it with this knife.'

In instrumental uses, it is common that the conveyance voice prefix is added to a derived stem (as in the preceding example) rather than directly to the base. For this reason, a distinction is sometimes made between the conveyance voice proper and an instrumental voice.

A third use of *i-* which is often mentioned is its use for beneficiaries, as in *I-hanap mo akó ng trabaho* (CV-look for 2s.POSS 1s GEN work) 'Look for some work for me'. It is quite difficult to establish a semantic link between this use and the two preceding ones. Note that benefactive use of *i-* is less frequent than the other two uses both in terms of tokens (text frequency) and types (bases for which a benefactive derivation is in common use; see also Himmelmann 1987:141–143).

In locative voice (marked with *-an*), the subject expresses a locative argument, understood in a very broad sense. This may be the location at which something happened:

(34) *tinirhán*   *ko*   **ang**   **bahay** **na**   **itó**
      in-tirá-an   ko   ang   bahay   na   itó
      RLS(UG)-dwelling-LV 1s.POSS   SPEC   house   LK   PRX
      'I stayed at this house.'

Or the location to which (or from which) motion occurred:

(35) *pinuntahán*   *na*   *namán*   *nilá*   **ang**   **bata?**
      in-puntá-an   na   namán   nilá   ang   bata?
      RLS(UG)-direction-LV now   also   3p.POSS   SPEC   child
      'They went to the child.'

Locative voice is also used for recipients, addressees, and beneficiaries inasmuch as these are also (more or less direct) recipients or goals of the action as in (36):

(36) *títirán*   *ninyó*   **akó**
      RDP1-tirá-an   ninyó   akó
      RDP1-leftover-LV   2p.POSS   1s
      'Will you (please) set some aside for me.'

Even more generally, locative voice may be used for all kinds of undergoers which are not directly affected by the action denoted by the verb, as in (27) above and (37):

(37) *tulung-an* *ninyó*   **akó**
      help-LV   2p.POSS   1s
      '(If) you help me,...'

The different uses of locative voice as illustrated here are sometimes considered to be different voices. So a distinction is made between directional (or goal) voice, benefactive voice, and locative voice proper (which often involves stem-formation via *pag-* or *paN-*).

The suffix *-in*, marking patient voice, is the unmarked member of the undergoer-voice-marking affixes and is used for a broad variety of undergoers, including prototypical patients, i.e. entities directly affected or effected by the event denoted by the predicate:

(38) *patay-ín*   *natin*   **itó-ng dalawá-ng Hapón**
      dead -PV   1pi.POSS   PRX-LK   two-LK   Japan
      'Let's kill these two Japanese!'

As already mentioned above, in realis mood patient voice is simply marked by the realis undergoer voice infix *-in-*:

(38') *p<in>atáy*   *natin*   *itó-ng dalawá-ng Hapón*
       <RLS(UG)>dead   1pi.POSS   PRX-LK   two-LK   Japan
       'We killed these two Japanese.'

The choice among the different voices is determined by considerations of semantic role, referentiality/definiteness and some other discourse pragmatic factors which are still poorly understood (cf. Naylor 1975, McFarland 1978b, Adams and Manaster-Ramer 1988, and the discussion in HIMMELMANN, TYPOLOGICAL CHARACTERISTICS, section 3.1. One fairly robust rule is the following: If there is a definite patient or theme participant in the state of affairs to be expressed by a simple main clause, then patient or conveyance voice are chosen (cf., for example, (32) and (38) above). That is, definite patients or themes are extremely rare in actor voice constructions. But it is not completely impossible for a formally definite patient or theme to occur in an actor voice construction in a simple main clause. It can happen if the patient or theme participant is either in possession of the subject of the construction (39) or it receives a partitive interpretation (40):

(39) *nag-dá-dalá*   *silá* **ng**   **sarili** **nilá-ng**
      RLS.AV-RDP1-bring   3p   GEN   own   3S.POSS-LK

      banda **ng**   **músika**
      band   GEN   music
      'They bring their own band.'

(40) *namúmúlot*   *silá* **noón**
      naN -RDP1-pulot   silá   noón
      RLS.AV-RDP1-pick.up   3p   DIST.GEN

      at   *ipinagbíbili*   *nilá*
      at   i-in-pag-RDP1-bilí   nilá
      and   CV-RLS(UG)-SF-RDP1-sale   3p.POSS
      '(Okay, their means of living was to pick fruit, those fruits which are used in
      chewing betel nuts...) They would pick (some of) those and then sell
      them,...'

Note that if one continues to speak about such a formally definite patient or theme it has to be made the subject of the following predicate (thus *ipinagbíbili* is chosen here rather than *nagbíbilí*). Similarly if an indefinite patient or theme is referred to again in a subsequent predication, it has to be made the subject. Thus, *ibenta* rather than *magbenta* has to be chosen in the following context:

(41) *nangúngúha*   *ngá*   *ng*   *baging*   **para**   **ibenta**
      naN -RDP1-kuha   ngá?   ng   bagin   para   i-benta
      RLS.AV-RDP1-getting indeed   GEN   vine   for   CV-sales
      '(My husband hasn't arrived yet) he is collecting vine for selling it.'

It is also common to make indefinite patients and themes the subject if they are going to be major participants in the ongoing discourse, in particular if they are animate.

(42) *doón*   *ay*   *ná-kita*   *nilá*   **ang**   **isá-ng**   **ma-lakí-ng**   **higante**
      DIST.LOC   PM   RLS.POT-seen   3p.POSS   SPEC   one-LK   ST-size-LK   giant
      'There they saw a great giant...[the giant is going to be the main protagonist of the ensuing episode]'

For other undergoer roles such as goals, beneficiaries, locations and instruments, similar tendencies exist. That is, whenever a participant bearing such a role is identifiable for speaker and hearer it tends to be made the subject, unless there is also a definite patient or theme participant involved. Actor voice, then, is a marked choice in all states of affairs which involve undergoers, in particular if the undergoers are definite. However, this does not mean that actor voice constructions are very infrequent in natural discourse. Since many semantically intransitive constructions involve actor voice marking, its overall text frequency is at least as high as the overall frequency of all undergoer voices combined.

The whole issue of choosing a voice is complicated by the fact that the preceding observations only hold for simple main clause constructions in which the verb functions as predicate. Different rules obtain in cleft constructions, relative clauses, and existential constructions, in which the verb does not occur in predicate position. Most importantly, in these constructions there is no restriction on definite patients or themes for actor voice verbs. Compare the following example where the actor voice verb *mangibig* occurs in a relative clause and takes a definite undergoer argument:

(43) *sa*   *mga*   *lalaki*   *na*   **mangibig**   **nung**   **kanyáng**   **anák**
      sa   mga   lalaki   na   maN-ibig   noón:LK   kanyá-ng   anák
      LOC   PL   man   LK   AV-love   DIST.GEN:LK   3s.DAT-LK   child
      '(So he held a contest) between the men who courted his child...'

That is, in these constructions there is no inherent preference for the undergoer voices. Instead, the syntax of the overall construction determines which voice has to be chosen.

Thus, a complete account of voice choice also has to include a discussion of the factors which determine the choice of a construction in which the verb is not a main clause predicate. There are in particular two such constructions, the existential construction and the cleft construction.

Existential constructions can be used whenever a state of affairs involves an indefinite participant, especially participants for which no basic lexical designation exists. In this instance, it is common to use the verb itself as a description for the participant. Thus, in the following example, *nagáalaga* is used as a descriptive label for the person looking after the birds:

(44) *ay*   *mayroón*   *paláng*   **nagáalaga**   *doón*   *sa*   *ibun*
      ay   mayroón   palá-ng   nag-RDP1-alaga?   doón   sa   ibon
      PM   EXIST   so! -LK   RLS.AV-RDP1-cared.for DIST.LOC   LOC   bird
      '(But he didn't know) there was already someone looking after those birds.'

In cleft constructions, focal participants (and in particular, contrastive ones) are put in predicate position while the remainder of the clause, including the verb, occurs in a noun phrase. This construction is regularly chosen for most question words (cf. also example (7) above):

(45) ***ano***   *ang*   *gágawín*   *ng*   *langgám*   *sa*   *dahon*
      anó   ang   RDP1-gawá?-in   ng   langgám   sa   dahon
      what   SPEC RDP1-act-PV   GEN   ant   LOC   leaf
      '(He thought:) What will the ant do on the leaf?'

To summarize: In choosing a voice form, a Tagalog speaker has to decide first which construction will be appropriate. If a construction is chosen in which the verb does not occur in predicate position, voice choice is determined by the syntax of the construction. If a simple main clause construction is chosen for expressing a transitive state of affairs, there is a strong preference for undergoer voices, in particular if definite patient or theme participants are involved.

Despite the large number of options existing in principle for the expression of a particular state of affairs, the freedom of choice remains limited. For most everyday situations there are conventional ways in which these situations can be referred to. In terms of voice affixation this means that for each base there are typically only one or two voice affixes it frequently combines with.

4.2 Stative and potentive

With a few exceptions, the verbs discussed in the preceding section are only used for states of affairs which involve a volitional and controlling actor (regardless of whether or not this actor is overtly expressed). States of affairs which do not involve a controlling actor are expressed by a related but different set of formations. Two different scenarios have to be distinguished here. On the one hand, the state of affairs may be such that it excludes the involvement of an actor for principled conceptual reasons. This is the case for *stative* expressions such as 'be hungry', 'be angry', 'be adrift', and the like. On the other hand, the state of affairs may be such that in principle it allows for controlling actors but in the specific instance at hand the actor is not in full control of the event. This is the case when someone happens to do something without having the intention to do it. Formations expressing this second possibility are called *potentive*.

A completely regular correspondence exists between dynamic and potentive formations. That is, for each dynamic verb form there is a corresponding potentive form. The major potentive formatives are *maka-* for actor voice and *ma-* for the undergoer voices. For details compare Table 12.3 with Table 12.4.

TABLE 12.4: POTENTIVE ASPECT/MOOD PARADIGM FOR *bilí* 'purchase, sale'

	AV ('buy')	AV ('sell')	PV	LV	CV
NON-REALIS/ PERFECTIVE	maka-bilí	maka-pagbilí	ma-bilí	ma-bilh-án	ma-i-bilí
NON-REALIS/ INPERFECTIVE	maka-bíbilí	maka-pagbíbilí	ma-bíbilí	ma-bíbilh-án	ma-i-bíbilí
REALIS/ PERFECTIVE	naka-bilí	naka-pagbilí	na-bilí	na-bilh-án	na-i-bilí
REALIS/ IMPERFECTIVE	naka-bíbilí	naka-pagbíbilí	na-bíbilí	na-bíbilh-án	na-i-bíbilí

The typical use of potentive forms is for involuntary actions:

(46) *biglá*   *niyá-ng*   **ná**-*bigkás*   *iyón*
      sudden   3s.POSS-LK   RLS.POT-enunciation   DIST
      '(Terrified) she suddenly exclaimed:...'

This includes actions done accidentally, i.e. the actor may be in control of the action but did not really intend its outcome:

(47) **na-i**-*luto*   *ko*   *na*
      RLS.POT-CV-cooked   1s.POSS now
      'I happen to have cooked it already (by mistake).'

It also includes perceptions over which the actor (=experiencer) has no control (cf. (42) above).

In a second, somewhat different use potentive forms express the ability of an actor to perform the action in question:

(48) *kung*   *inyóng*   **ma**pagtiis**án**   *iyán*
      kung   inyó-ng   ma-pag-tiís-an   iyán
      if   2p.DAT-LK POT-SF-suffer-LV   MED
      'If you are able to endure this...'

(49) *at*   *hindí*   **maka**baríl   *sa*   *kanyá*
      at   hindí?   maka-baríl   sa   kanyá
      and   NEG   POT.AV-gun   LOC   3s.DAT
      '(The man got bitten by the ants) and wasn't able to shoot at him.'

Turning now to stative verbs, these also come in four different voices, two of which are formally identical to the potentive voice forms. But despite these formal similarities and the fact that essentially the same glosses are used for dynamic and stative voices, the syntax and semantics of the stative voices differs quite clearly from the potentive formations so that the category labels are not really indicative of their functions.

In the basic voice form for statives, which is simply called *stative* here, the subject is a theme, i.e. an entity which is in, or currently is undergoing, a given state. The forms are identical to the patient voice forms of the potentive paradigm, i.e. base plus prefix *ma-*. The forms of the stative actor voice are morphologically identical to the potentive actor voice forms, i.e. base plus *maka-*. The stative locative and conveyance voices are marked by the prefix *ka-* to which the basic voice affixes *-an* and *i-*, respectively, are added. See Table 12.5 for an overview of the forms.

TABLE 12.5: VOICE AND ASPECT/MOOD PARADIGM FOR STATIVE VERBS (base *galit* 'anger')

	ST	ST.LV	ST.CV	ST.AV
NON-REALIS/ PERFECTIVE	ma-galit	ka-galit-an	i-ka-galit	maka-galit
NON-REALIS/ IMPERFECTIVE	ma-gágálit	ka-gágalit-an	i-ka-gágalit	maka-gágálit
REALIS/ PERFECTIVE	na-galit	kina-galit-an	i-kina-galit	naka-galit
REALIS/ IMPERFECTIVE	na-gágálit	kina-gágalit-an	i-kina-gágalit	naka-gágálit

Once again it is essential to note that the forms listed in Table 12.5 differ substantially with regard to their productivity. The only really productive formation is the basic stative formation. Almost every Tagalog content word base (and many derived stems) can be prefixed with *ma-* and express a state:

(50) **na-*galit*   *siyá*
      RLS.ST-anger   3s
      'She was/got angry.'

With bases such as *basag* 'crack, break', which allow both a state and an action reading, the form *nabasag* is ambiguous: it can mean 'be in a broken state' (stative) or 'happen to break/able to break' (potentive patient voice). In context, these readings are generally distinguished by the presence of an overt actor expression in the potentive use (*nabasag niyá* 's/he happened to break it/was able to break it').

The stative locative voice is common with bases expressing emotions. The subject expresses the person or thing at which the emotion is directed:

(51) **kina*galitan*   *siyá* *ng*   *Nanay*
      in-ka-galit-an   siyá   ng   nanay
      RLS(UG) -ST-anger-LV 3s   GEN   mother
      'Mother was angry with him/her.'

Frequently, stative locative voice derivations take on some more specialized meanings. Thus, *kagalitan* also means 'to reprove, to scold, to rebuke'. In addition, stative locative voice derivations are possible with a (relatively small) number of stative expressions which do not pertain to emotions. They then denote the place at which a given state occurs (e.g., *ka-hulug-an* 'place where someone falls' (<*hulog* 'fall')).

The stative conveyance voice is also most common with bases expressing emotions. Stative conveyance voice formations always have the connotation of causation, that is, the subject specifies the reason for the emotion:

(52) *ikinagalít*   *niyá*   *akó*
      i-in-ka-galit   niyá   akó
      CV-RLS(UG)-ST-anger   3s.POSS   1s
      'She got angry at me (I was the reason for her being angry).'

The stative conveyance voice is found with a somewhat broader range of bases than the stative locative voice. These include *ikabasá?* 'get wet on account of', *ikabagsák* 'fall on account of', *ikatawa* 'laugh on account of', *ikaiyák* 'cry on account of', etc.

The stative actor voice is very similar in meaning to the stative conveyance voice since it also specifies the cause for a given state. But the two formations differ in their grammar and productivity. In the stative conveyance voice construction (as in the stative locative voice construction), the theme argument (i.e. the one who experiences an emotion in the case of emotion verbs) is grammatically coded as a genitive argument. In the stative actor voice construction it is a locative argument:

(53) *lahát* *ng* *kanyáng*   *sabihin*   *ay*   *nakagágalit*   *sa*
      lahát   ng   kanyá -ng   sabi-in   ay   naka-RDP1-galit   sa
      all   GEN   3s.DAT-LK   statement-PV   PM   RLS.ST.AV-RDP1-anger   LOC
      akin
      akin
      1s.DAT
      'Everything he says irritates me.'

The subject expression in the stative actor voice construction usually refers to an inanimate cause (some state of affairs or a thing). With regard to productivity, the stative actor voice forms are the least common of all stative formations and whenever they occur they often take on somewhat specialized meanings (thus *makagalit* is 'irritate, antagonize, give offense' rather than a plain 'make angry'). Furthermore, the stative actor voice derivations are often conventionalized in one of the four aspect/mood forms, for example, *naka-áawaʔ* 'arousing pity, pitiable' (<*awaʔ* 'mercy, compassion'), *nakáka-litó* (or *naka-lílitó*) 'confusing' (<*litó* 'confused, at a loss'), or *nakáka-gandá* (or *naka-gágandá*) 'beautifying' (<*gandá* 'beauty').

5   NOMINALIZATIONS AND NOMINAL MORPHOLOGY

As pointed out in section 3.3, it is somewhat misleading to speak of nouns and verbs in Tagalog if these terms are understood to have a similar meaning as in English. Strictly speaking, we are dealing in this section with formations which are not voice-marked. Inasmuch as voice-marking is taken to be the defining characteristic of Tagalog 'verbs', these formations are clearly non-verbal. Whether it is useful to call them nominals or nominalizations is a moot question which will be ignored here. Considerations of space prevent the review of all relevant formations. The major focus is on gerunds.

5.1   Gerunds

Gerunds provide a way to refer to actions or states without orienting them towards one of the participants involved in the action or state via voice-marking. They may denote a type of activity as in:

(54)   **pag-lu-lutoʔ**   ng   pagkain   ang   trabaho   niyá
     GER-RDP-cook   GEN   food   SPEC   work   3s.POSS
     'His/her job is cooking food.'

Gerunds are regularly derived from actor voice forms, usually by replacing the voice affix with *pag-* or *paN-* (in some instances, unstressed CV-reduplication is also part of the process). Stative gerunds are derived from the basic stative voice by replacing *ma-* with *pagka-*.

Since gerunds are not voice-marked, all participants involved in the state of affairs denoted by the gerund have to be expressed as non-subject arguments (i.e. either as genitive or locative arguments). This, however, does not mean that gerunds cannot be used as predicates, as shown by example (54) above. As with all Tagalog content words, gerunds can be used in any syntactic function, provided their meaning fits. In the following example, a (stative) gerund functions as the subject of the potentive patient voice predicate *maáalis*:

(55)   *maáalís*   *lámang*   *ang*   *pagkaahas*   *mo*
     ma-RDP1-alís   lamang   ang   pag-ka-ahas   mo
     POT-RDP1-departure   only   SPEC   GER-ST-snake   2s.POSS
     '(You will become a snake and) you will only be able to leave your snakehood (your state of being a snake)...'

The most common use of gerunds, however, is their use in the function of reduced temporal clauses. In this use, they designate specific instances of the action or state denoted by the base:

(56) **pag-datíng** *namin* *doón*
    GER-ARRIVAL 1pe.POSS DIST.LOC

    in-iwan *namin* *don* *ang bangka?*
    RLS(UG)-abandon 1pe.POSS DIST.LOC SPEC boat
    'When we arrived there we abandoned the boat,…'

(57) *at* **pag-ká-sabi** *niyá* *nitó*
    and GER-ST-say 3s.POSS PRX.GEN
    '… and when he had said this…'

A gerund preceded by *sa* may also be used for reduced complement clauses:

(58) *pagbawalan* *mo* *ang* *batang* *iyón* *sa*
    pag-bawal-an mo ang bata?-ng iyó sa
    SF -forbidden-LV 2s.POSS SPEC CHILD-LK DIST LOC

    paglalaró? *sa* **lansangan**
    pag-RDP-laró? sa lansangan
    GER-RDP-play LOC street
    'Forbid that child to play in the street.'

5.2 Abstracts, instruments, locations, etc.

Among the other very productive 'nominalizing' processes are the formations for abstracts, instruments and locations. Most of these are segmentally identical, or at least very similar, to the verbal formations discussed in the preceding section. Note, however, that inasmuch as both verbal and 'nominal' derivations are possible from the same base they are usually distinguished by different stress patterns.

- *ka–an* derives abstracts and collectives: *kamurahan* 'cheapness' (<*mura* 'cheap'), *katámáran* 'laziness' (<*tamád* 'lazy'), *kasabihán* 'proverb' (<*sabi* 'statement'), *káratnán* 'possible result, outcome' (<*dating* 'arrival'), *kapuluán* 'archipelago' (<*puló?* 'island'), *kabundukán* 'mountains' (<*bundók* 'mountain').
- *-an* derives designations for places associated with the base: *bilíhan* 'market, trading place', *aklatan* 'library' (<*aklat* 'book'), *hiráman* 'place for borrowing' (<*hirám* 'borrowed', cf. locative voice *hiramán* 'to borrow from someone'), *pintuan* 'doorway' (<*pintó?* 'door'), *itlugan* 'place where eggs are laid' (<*itlóg* 'egg').
- *maN-* plus unaccented CV-reduplication derives a designation for someone professionally occupied with what the base designates: *mámimili* 'shopper, buyer, customer', *mambabasa* 'reader' (<*basa* 'read'), *manlalaro?* 'player' (<*laró?* 'play'), *manggagamot* 'physician' (<*gamót* 'medicine, cure').
- *paN-* (with, in some instances, optional replacement of the base-initial consonant) derives designations for instruments/means: *pambili* 'means for buying', *panghampás* 'sth. for hitting' (<*hampás* 'blow, strike'), *pansará/panará* 'fastener, lock' (<*sará* 'closed'), *pampatabá?* 'sth. which makes fat, fertilizer' (<*tabá?* 'fat, grease').

ACKNOWLEDGEMENTS

Many thanks to Dante O. Alatiit (Laguna) and Ning Vitto (Marinduque) for teaching me Tagalog and helping me with the Tagalog data. And to Sander Adelaar for very useful feedback on an earlier version of this chapter.

REFERENCES

Adams, K.L. and Manaster-Ramer, A. (1988) 'Some questions of topic/focus choice in Tagalog', *Oceanic Linguistics* 27:79–101.
Arsenio, M.E. (1971) *A lexicographic study of Tayabas Tagalog of Quezon Province*, Quezon City: University of the Philippines Press.
Bader, T., Werlen, I. and Wymann, A. (1994) *Towards a typology of modality*, Arbeitspapier 32, Bern: Institut für Sprachwissenschaft.
Blake, F.R. (1906) 'Expression of case by the verb in Tagalog', *Journal of the American Oriental Society* 27:183–189.
—— (1925) *A grammar of the Tagalog language*, New Haven: American Oriental Society.
Bloomfield, L. (1917) *Tagalog texts with grammatical analysis*, Urbana: The University of Illinois.
—— (1933) *Language*, London: Allen and Unwin.
Chan Yap, G. (1980) *Hokkien Chinese borrowings in Tagalog*, Canberra: Pacific Linguistics.
Constantino, E. (1965) 'The sentence patterns of twenty-six Philippine languages', *Lingua* 15:71–124.
—— (1971) 'Tagalog and other major languages of the Philippines', in T.A. Sebeok (ed.) *Current Trends in Linguistics*, 8/1: 112–154, The Hague: Mouton.
—— (1999) *The Contemporary English–Filipino Dictionary*, Quezon City: Center for Philippine Languages.
Cruz, E.L. (1975) *A subcategorization of Tagalog verbs*, The Archive Special Monograph No.2, Quezon City: University of the Philippines.
DeGuzman, V.P. (1978a) *Syntactic derivation of Tagalog verbs*, Oceanic Linguistics Special Publication 16, Honululu: University Press of Hawaii.
—— (1978b) 'A case for nonphonological constraints on nasal substitution', *Oceanic Linguistics* 17:87–106.
—— (1986) 'The subject of identificational sentences', in B.F. Elson (ed.) *Language in global perspective*, 347–362, Dallas: Summer Institute of Linguistics.
—— (1997) 'Verbal affixes in Tagalog: Inflection or derivation?', in C. Odé and W. Stokhof (eds) *Proceedings of the Seventh International Conference on Austronesian Linguistics*, 303–325, Amsterdam: Rodopi.
—— (2001) 'Tagalog', in J. Garry and C. Rubino (eds) *Facts about the world's languages*, 703–707, New York: New England Publishing Associates.
Drossard, W. (1984) *Das Tagalog als Repräsentant des aktivischen Sprachbaus*, Tübingen: Narr.
English, L.J. (1977) *English–Tagalog dictionary*, Manila: National Book Store.
—— (1986) *Tagalog-English dictionary*, Manila: National Book Store.
Gil, D. (1993) 'Tagalog semantics', *Berkeley Linguistic Society* 19:390–403.
Gonzales, A.B. (1970) 'Acoustic correlates of accent, rhythm, and intonation in Tagalog', *Phonetica* 22:11–44.
Grimes, B.F. (1999), *Ethnologue – Languages of the world*, 13th edition, Dallas: Summer Institute of Linguistics.
Himmelmann, N.P. (1987) *Morphosyntax und Morphologie – Die Ausrichtungsaffixe im Tagalog*, München: Fink.
—— (1991) *The Philippine challenge to universal grammar*, Arbeitspapier Nr. 15, Köln: Institut für Sprachwissenschaft.
—— (1998) 'Regularity in irregularity: Article use in adpositional phrases', *Linguistic Typology* 2:315–353.
—— (1999) 'The lack of zero anaphora and incipient person marking in Tagalog', *Oceanic Linguistics* 38: 231–269.
—— (to appear) 'Lexical categories and voice in Tagalog', in P. Austin and S. Musgrave (eds) *Voice and grammatical functions in Austronesian languages*, Stanford: Center for the Study of Language and Information.

Humboldt, W. von (1838) *Über die Kawi Sprache*, Bd. II, Berlin: Dümmler.

Kroeger, P.R. (1993) *Phrase structure and grammatical relations in Tagalog*, Stanford: Stanford University Press.

Lemaréchal, A. (1982) 'Sémantisme des parties du discours et sémantisme des relations', *Bulletin de la Société de Linguistique de Paris* 77:1–39.

—— (1989) *Les parties du discours. Sémantique et syntaxe*, Paris: P.U.F.

Lopez, C. (1937) 'Preliminary Study of the Affixes in Tagalog', in E. Constantino (ed.) (1977) *Selected writings of Cecilio Lopez in Philippine linguistics*, 28–104, Diliman: University of the Philippines Press.

—— (1970) 'On the Boak Tagalog of the island of Marinduque', *The Archive* (University of the Philippines) I/2:1–53.

Marre, A. (1901) 'Grammaire tagalog, composé sur un nouveau plan', *Bijdragen tot de Taal-, Land- en Volkenkunde* 53:547–92.

Matsuda French, K. (1988) *Insights into Tagalog. Reduplication, infixation, and stress from nonlinear phonology*, Dallas: Summer Institute of Linguistics.

McFarland, C.D. (1976) *A provisional classification of Tagalog verbs*, Tokio: Institute for the Study of Languages and Cultures of Asia and Africa.

—— (1978a) 'Tagalog existentials', *Philippine Journal of Linguistics* 9:1–13.

—— (1978b) 'Definite objects and subject selection in Philippine languages', in C. Edrial-Luzares and A. Hale (eds) *Studies in Philippine Linguistics*, 2/1:139–182, Manila: Linguistic Society of the Philippines.

—— (1983) *A linguistic atlas of the Philippines*, 2nd edn, Manila: Linguistic Society of the Philippines.

Müller, F. (1882) *Grundriss der Sprachwissenschaft*, II. Band II. Abt., *Die Sprachen der schlichthaarigen Rassen*, Wien: Alfred Hölder.

Naylor, P.B. (1975) 'Topic, focus, and emphasis in the Tagalog verbal clause', *Oceanic Linguistics* 14:12–79.

—— (1980) 'Linking, relation-marking, and Tagalog syntax', in P.B. Naylor (ed.) *Austronesian syntax. Papers from the Second Eastern Conference on Austronesian Languages*, 33–49, Ann Arbor: Center for South and Southeast Asian Studies.

—— (1995) 'Subject, topic, and Tagalog syntax', in D. Benett, T. Bynon and G.B. Hewitt (eds) *Subject, voice and ergativity*, 161–201, London: School of Oriental and African Studies.

Panganiban, J.V. (1972) *Diksyunario-tesauro Pilipino–Ingles*, Quezon City: Manlapaz.

Pittman, R. (1966) 'Tagalog -um- and -mag-. An interim report', in *Papers in Philippine Linguistics* 1, 9–20, Canberra: Pacific Linguistics.

Ramos, T.V. (1974) *The case system of Tagalog verbs*, Canberra: Pacific Linguistics.

Ramos, T.V. and Bautista, M.L.S. (1986) *Handbook of Tagalog verbs. Inflections, modes, aspects*, Honolulu: University of Hawaii Press.

Reid, L.A. (1981) 'Philippine linguistics: the state of the art: 1970–1980', in D.W. Hart (ed.) *Philippine Studies: political science, economics, and linguistics*, 223–230, Northern Illinois University: Center for Southeast Asian Studies.

—— (1992) 'On the Development of the Aspect System in Some Philippine Languages', *Oceanic Linguistics* 31:65–91.

Rubino, C.R.G. (1998) *Tagalog standard dictionary*, New York: Hippocrene Books.

—— (1998a) 'The morphological realization and production of a nonprototypical morpheme: the Tagalog derivational clitic, *Linguistics* 36:1147–1166.

Santos, V.C. (1983) *Pilipino–English dictionary*, Metro Manila: National.

Schachter, P. (1973) 'Constraints on clitic order in Tagalog', in A.B. Gonzales (ed.) *Parangal kay Cecilio Lopez*, 214–231, Quezon City: Linguistic Society of the Philippines.

—— (1976) 'The subject in Philippine languages: topic, actor, actor-topic or none of the above', in C.N. Li (ed.) *Subject and topic*, 491–518, New York: Academic Press.

—— (1987) 'Tagalog', in B. Comrie (ed.) *The world's major languages*, 936–958, London: Croom Helm.

—— (1995) 'Tagalog', in J. Jacobs *et al.* (eds) *Syntax*, II:1418–1430, Berlin: Mouton de Gruyter.

Schachter, P. and Otanes, F.T. (1972) *Tagalog reference grammar*, Berkeley: University of California Press.

Shkarban, L.I. (1995) *Grammatičeskij stroj tagal'skovo jazyka*, Moskva: Nauka.

Soberano, R. (1980) *The dialects of Marinduque Tagalog*, Canberra: Pacific Linguistics.

Totanes, S. de (1865) *Arte de la lengua tagala y manual tagalog*, 4th edition, Binondo: Miguel Sanchez y Ca.

Wolff, J.U. (1976) 'Malay borrowings in Tagalog', in C.D. Cowan and O.W. Wolters (eds) *Southeast-Asian history and historiography: essays presented to D.G.H. Hall*, 345–367, Ithaca: Cornell University Press.

Wolff, J.U. with Centeno, M.T.C. and Rau, D.V. (1991) *Pilipino through self-instruction*, 4 vols, Ithaca: Cornell Southeast Asia Program.

Zorc, R.D. (1994) 'Tagalog', in D.T. Tryon (ed.) *Comparative Austronesian dictionary*, 1:335–341, Berlin: Mouton de Gruyter.

CHAPTER THIRTEEN

SAMA (BAJAU)

Akamine Jun

1 INTRODUCTION

Sama languages, also known as 'Bajau' or 'Sama-Bajau' in the linguistic literature, are spoken mainly in the Sulu Archipelago (southern Philippines), Sabah (eastern part of Malaysian Borneo), and eastern Indonesia (see Map 13.1). The original homeland of the Sama is thought to be in the Zamboanga-Basilan area in the southern part of the Philippines (Pallesen 1985).

Bajau is probably a Malay ethnonym (Evans 1952) and it has gained wide acceptance in Sabah as a cover term for all speakers of Sama languages (Walton and Moody 1984:114; Sather 1997:5). In Indonesia, Sama-speakers are simply called *Bajo* by the Buginese and are known as *Bayo* or *Turijene* in Makassar (Grimes 1999). In the Philippines, the term *Bajau* or *Badjaw* refers to (formerly) nomadic Sama-Bajau populations whereas *Samal* or *Siyamal* refers to settled Sama populations.

Sama is an autonym, a term Sama speakers use to refer to themselves throughout the entire area where varieties of Sama are spoken. They call their various dialects *bahasa sama* in Malaysia (Walton and Moody 1984:114), *sinama* or *ʔəlliŋ sama* in the Philippines, and *baʔoŋ sama*, *baʔon sama*, or *bahasa Bajau* in Indonesia.

The Sama-Bajau are widely believed to be seafaring nomads, and they are generally known as *Bajau Laut* or *Sama Dilaut* in Malaysia and the Philippines. However, not all speakers of Sama are nomadic. In addition to the sea-nomadic and formerly nomadic communities, the Sama-Bajau also include shore-based people and land-based people. Naturally, these different communities have developed different cultures to fit their ecological, political and economical environments. See Sopher (1965) for general information on Sama-Bajau societies, Lapian and Nagatsu (1996) for reviews on Sama-Bajau studies in various disciplines, and particularly Warren (1978, 1981) for a dynamic Sama history showing the important role played by the Sama-Bajau people in the British-Sino-Insular Malay triangle trade two centuries ago.

Pallesen (1985) classified the Sama languages into 11 major varieties, but Grimes (1999) reduces these to the following nine: *Abaknon Sama, Balangingi Sama, Central Sama, Pangutaran Sama, Southern Sama, Yakan, Mapun, West Coast Bajau*, and *Indonesian Bajau*. Figure 13.1 displays the genetic relationship between these varieties as hypothesized by Grimes (1999). The following discussion of the different subgroups closely follows Grimes (1999).

Abaknon (or Inabaknon) is spoken mainly in Capul Island near San Bernardino Strait, Northwest Samar (Central Philippines), where it is sometimes referred to as Capuleño. It has an estimated 16,000 speakers, including 11,000 speakers on Capul Island and another 5000 speakers elsewhere in the Philippines. Abaknon shows little influence from Arabic (via Islam), but borrowed heavily from Spanish (Jacobson and Jacobson 1980:32). Its phonology is discussed by Jacobson and Jacobson (1980) and its grammar by Constantino (1965) and Merin (1992).

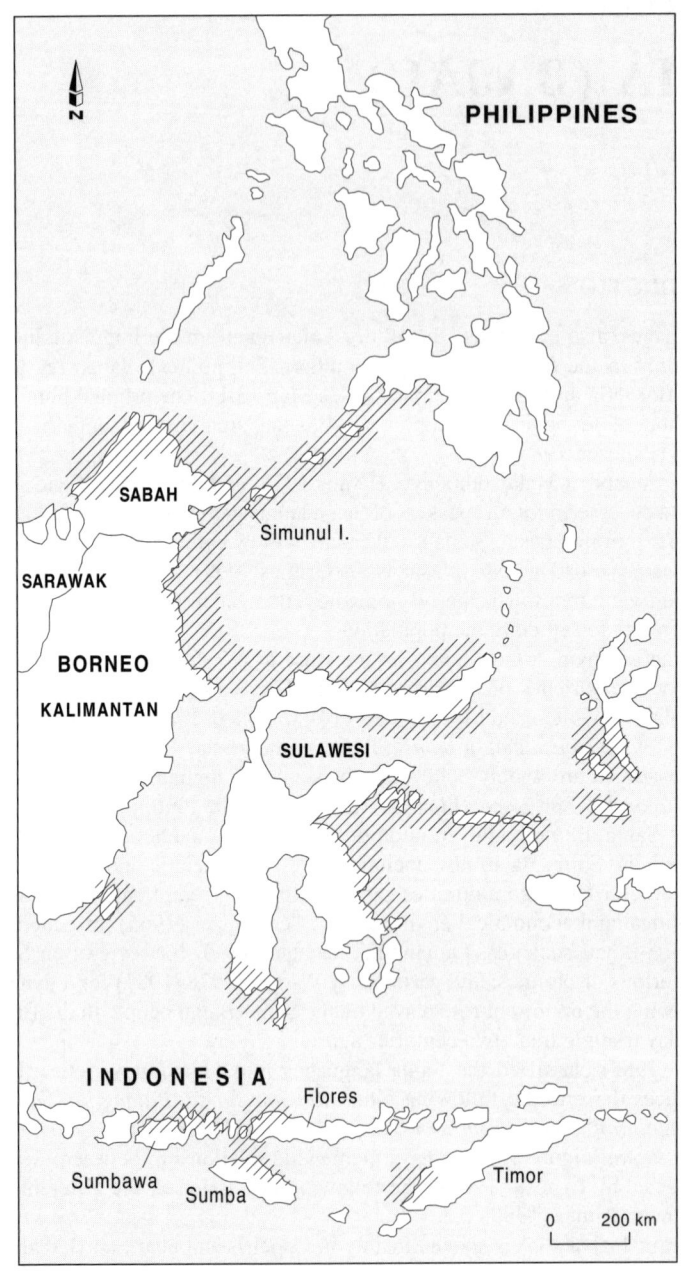

MAP 13.1 GEOGRAPHIC SPREAD OF THE SAMA-BAJAU LANGUAGES

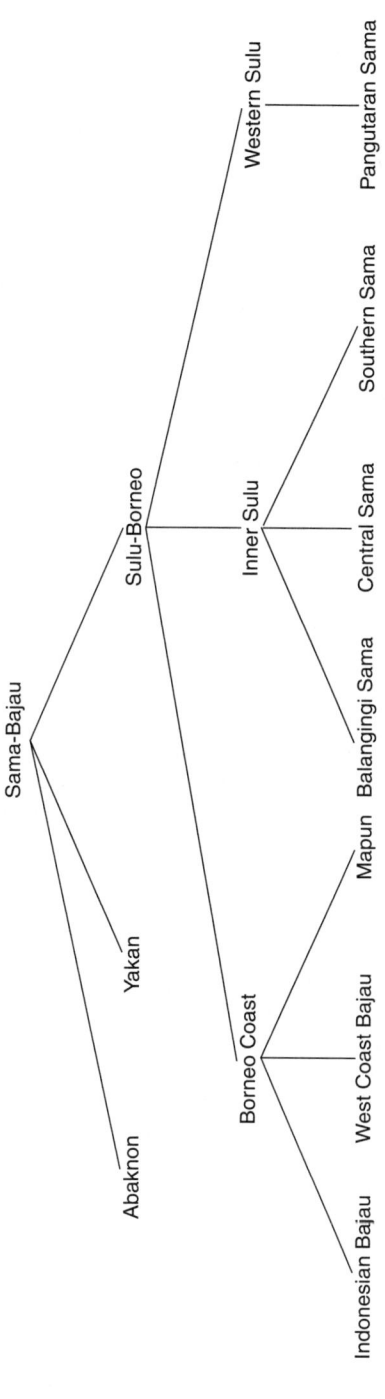

FIGURE 13.1 TREE DIAGRAM OF SAMA-BAJAU LANGUAGES (AFTER GRIMES 1999)

Yakan (ca. 70,000 speakers) is mainly spoken in the Sulu Archipelago, on Basilan Island and in western Mindanao. Some 5000 to 10,000 speakers are also found in Sabah, Malaysia. A few Yakan phrases and words can be found in Summer Institute of Linguistics (1979).

The Cagayan de Tawitawi Island in the mid-western Sulu Sea is densely populated by Mapun speakers. Mapun is also spoken on the southern coast of Palawan Island and in Sabah state (King and King 1984). In the early 1980s, there were around 15,000 Mapun speakers in the Philippines.

West Coast Bajau speakers (40,000 to 50,000 speakers) inhabit the area between Kuala Penyu and Kudat on Sabah's west coast. The language has borrowed heavily from Malayic languages in Borneo (Smith 1984:12). Abdul (1950) offers a few descriptive notes.

Indonesian Bajau is widely distributed throughout Sulawesi, northern Maluku (Bacan, Obi, Kayoa, and Sula Islands), eastern Kalimantan, and the lesser Sunda Islands. In the early 1980s, the population was an estimated 25,000 in Central Sulawesi; 8000 to 10,000 in South Sulawesi; 5000 or more in northern Maluku and several thousand in Nusa Tenggara. Aspects of the grammar are described by Abdul (1979), Donohue (1996), and Verheijen (1986), while Anceaux (1978) and Verheijen (1986) provide word lists.

Balangingi Sama, *Central Sama*, *Pangutaran Sama*, and *Southern Sama* are spoken in the Sulu archipelago and on Sabah's east coast. According to the national population census of 1995, the total number of speakers of these four languages in the Philippines is estimated to be around 330,000. These four ethnolinguistic groups share a similar sea-oriented culture. *Pangutaran Sama* is classified as Western Sulu Sama, whereas the other three are known as the *Inner Sulu Sama* languages.

A phonological analysis of *Pangutaran Sama* is given by Walton (1979) and a syntactic analysis by Walton (1986). An English–Pangutaran Sama dictionary was compiled by Walton and Walton (1992).

Of the three *Inner Sulu Sama* languages, Southern Sama has been studied most intensively, including a phonological study by Allison (1979) and word lists by Allison (1980), Summer Institute of Linguistics (1990), and Akamine (1997). Kunting (1989), a native speaker of the language, compiled a Sama–English dictionary. Grammatical and discourse analysis are found in Constantino (1965), Allison (1977), Akamine (1996, 2002), and Trick (1997). Gault (1979) discusses the phonemics of Balangingi Sama. For the grammar of Balangingi Sama, see Constantino (1965) and Gault (1986, 1999). Schneeberger (1937) recorded 790 Central Sama words and Summer Institute of Linguistics (1979) compiled a set of phrases and words for Central Sama. Concise notes on Central Sama morphology are given by Sather (1965, 1968).

Opinion varies on whether or not the Inner Sulu Sama languages make up a dialect chain extending through the Sulu Archipelago. Pallesen (1985) claims that the Central Sama speakers used to be nomads whereas the other Sama-Bajau speakers in this group were shore dwellers. This implies that the Central Sama speakers are culturally different from the other two groups. Current population movements in the Sulu Archipelago and population flow into Sabah, however, are complicating the linguistic as well as cultural situation. In the 1970s, for example, as a result of the conflict between the Moro National Liberation Front and the armed forces of the Philippines in the Sulu Archipelago, close to 100,000 refugees migrated out of the area.

The data for the present article are mostly from Simunul Island, which is located in the southernmost province of the Philippines, Tawitawi, where the author carried out intensive fieldwork from 1992 up to the present. Following local usage, this variety will be called *Sinama*.

2 PHONOLOGY AND ORTHOGRAPHY

2.1 Segments and syllable structure

Sinama has 17 consonant phonemes, which are summarized in Table 13.1. The major allophonic alternation to note here is that /d/ is realized as [r] in intervocalic position.

Simunul Sinama has, phonetically speaking, six vowels: [i, e, ə, a, o, u]. The mid-central vowel [ə], however, is not phonemic in Simunul Sinama (although it may be so in some other Sinama languages). In Simunul Sinama it always occurs in the first syllable of a word when it is followed by a cluster consisting of a nasal and a homorganic stop consonant, e.g. *ʔəmpat* 'four', *ʔənda* 'wife', and *ʔəŋgoʔ* 'ancestor'.

Stress is also not phonemic in Simunul Sinama. It always falls on the penultimate syllable, and the stressed vowel is phonetically lengthened. Again, the situation may be different in other Sinama languages.

The most common syllable types are CV and CVC. There are no vowel-initial syllables. Clitics and affixes are often monosyllabic (either CV or CVC). Lexical roots are typically disyllabic and any combination of the two basic syllable types is allowed.

Geminate consonant clusters are frequent except for geminate clusters consisting of ʔ, h and ŋ, which are not attested. Examples of a minimal contrast between a simple consonant and a geminate cluster are *kapal* 'thick' vs *kappal* 'ship' and *tanaʔ* 'land' vs *tannaʔ* 'put'.

2.2 Orthography

The vowels are orthographically represented as <i, e, a, o, u>. Note that <e> stands for /e/ as well as for schwa. Some native speakers prefer to employ an apostrophe <'> to indicate schwa but the sound is simply represented by <e> in the present orthography owing to its predictability. For the following consonants the orthographic representation deviates from the IPA standard: /ʔ/ is <q>, /ɟ/ is <j>, /ɲ/ is <ny>, /ŋ/ is <ng>, and /j/ is <y>. The word-final glottal stop is locally written as an <h> or an apostrophe <'>, and the one in intervocalic position is marked by a dash <->. For the sake of clarity, the present essay consistently employs the letter <q> to represent a glottal stop in all positions except proper nouns. Although [r] is an allophone of /d/ in intervocalic position, the letter <r> is employed in the orthography, following local standards. In reduplication, reduplicated segments are connected by a dash <-> as in *qanak-qanak*.

2.3 Morphonological alternations

There are a few phonologically conditioned alternations in Sinama. Note in particular that a base-initial consisting of a glottal stop followed by a mid-central vowel is deleted

TABLE 13.1: SINAMA CONSONANTS

		Labial	Dental	Palatal	Velar	Glottal
Stop	vl.	p	t		k	ʔ
	vd.	b	d	ɟ	g	
Nasal	vd.	m	n	ɲ	ŋ	
Fricative	vl.		s			h
Lateral	vd.		l			
Semi-vowel	vd.	w		j		

when it is preceded by a vowel-final formative. For example, *ka-* + *qempat* 'four' is realized as [kam.pat] 'fourth', not as *[ka.ʔəm.pat].

When a vowel initial suffix such as /-an/ or /-un/ attaches to a root or stem which ends with a vowel, an /h/ is added to the suffix, as seen in *billihan* 'to buy (LV)' < *billi* 'buy' and *bowahun* 'to bring (PV.IMP)' < *bowa* 'bring'. In some Sinama varieties, such as the Sitangkay dialect, a glide is observed instead: /y/ is employed after front vowels, and /w/ after back vowels, as in Sitangkay *billiyan* 'to buy (LV)' < *billi* 'buy' and *kinataquwan* to be known (LV.POT)' < *taqu* 'know'.

The symbol *N-* represents a prefixed nasal that interacts in various ways with the initial consonant of the stem. Preceding most stops, i.e. /p, b, t, k/, and preceding /s/, *N-* assimilates to the point of articulation of the stem-initial consonant, which is deleted. In other environments, it has the following realizations: /q/ is replaced by /ng/, and *N-* occurs as *nga-* preceding /h, l, m, n/, as *ngan-* preceding /d, j/ and as *ngang-* preceding /g/. Examples are *ngaq* 'to get/take (AV)' < *qaq* 'take', *ngahinang* 'to work/make (AV)' < *hinang* 'work', *ngandoleq* 'to make angry (AV)' < *doleq* 'anger', and *nganggamot* 'to grow (AV)' < *gamot* 'root' (for the slightly different rules in Indonesian Sinama see Verheijen 1986:9-10).

2.4 Reduplication

The only attested form of reduplication is full reduplication of the base (indicated by RDP). Reduplication often conveys a diminutive sense as in *lumaq-lumaq* 'small house' < *lumaq* 'house', and *lepa-lepa* 'small canoe' < *lepa* 'canoe'. An imitation of what the base designates is represented by the formation RDP- + base + -*an* as in *lumaq-lumaq-an* 'doll house'. A somewhat special case is *qanak* 'offspring' vs *qanak-qanak* 'children (in a general sense)'.

3 BASIC MORPHOSYNTAX

3.1 Lexical categories (word classes)

The open word classes are verbs and nouns. A major distributional difference between them pertains to negative markers (see section 3.7 below). Both verbs and nouns in Sinama may be either *primary* or *derived* forms. Primary forms simply consist of a root while derived forms consist of a base (either a root or a stem) plus a verbal or nominal-izing affix. Adjectives may be considered a subclass of stative verbs, most of which are unaffixed. The closed classes are pronouns, prepositions, determiner, various series of deictic elements and adverbial clitics.

Examples of primary nouns are *boheq* 'water', *sokaq* 'coconut', and *pay* 'rice paddy'. Some of the most productive nominalizing affixes are -*an*, *ka-*, *ka- -an*, *pa-*, *pa- -an*, *paN-*, and *paN- -an* which are briefly reviewed here in order to illustrate the kinds of nominal derivations common in Sinama. Verbal morphology is further discussed in section 4.

The suffix -*an* occurs in the following four formations: (i) with some verbal bases it derives action nominals: *sohoqan* 'command, order' < *sohoq* 'command to do'; (ii) from quality-denoting stative bases it derives words for the abstract quality, e.g. *lingkatan* 'beauty' < *lingkat* 'beautiful'; (iii) with another set of verbal bases it designates the place where the verbal activity commonly occurs, e.g. *liqisan* 'grater' < *liqis* 'grate'; and

(iv) with some nominal bases it derives collectives, e.g. *tabbahan* 'sea shells (in general)' < *tabba* 'coral reefs visible at low tide'.

In general, the prefix *ka-* is also used to nominalize a stative ('adjectival') base, as in *kallum* 'life' < *qellum* 'alive', *kaqaseq* 'mercy' < *qaseq* 'pity', and *kabansi* 'aversion' < *bansi* 'dislike'. Formations with *ka- -an* have three main meanings: (i) the product or result of the action denoted by the base *kaqampunan* 'forgiveness' < *qampun* 'forgive'; (ii) abstract qualities, e.g. *kabontolan* 'truthfulness' < *bontol* 'true'; and (iii) collectives *kabatuhan* 'stony area' < *batu* 'stone'.

The prefixes *pa-* and *pa- -an* are used for deriving nouns denoting instruments, e.g. *patuli* 'blanket' < *tuli* 'sleep' and *paboheqan* 'water container' < *boheq* 'water'. The prefix *paN-* also derives nouns denoting instruments as in *pamonoq* 'instrument used in killing' < *bonoq* 'kill'. In addition, it occurs in terms for seasons such as *pangallaw* 'dry season' < *qellaw* 'sun'. Combined with the suffix *-an* it may denote instruments or places, e.g. *pangisiyan* 'piggy bank' < *qisi* 'content', and *pameyaqan* 'means of transportation' < *beyaq* 'go'.

3.2 Basic clause structure and phrase making

Sinama clauses are basically of two types. In simple main clauses, the predicate occurs in clause-initial position and the subject comes at the end.

(1) *bey*   *nangis*   *qanak-qanak*
     CPL   N-tangis   child
     CPL   AV-cry   child
     'The child cried.'

The second clause type is the existential clause, which consists of the existential verb *niyaq* plus its complement and often an optional adjunct.

(2) *niyaq*   *manusiyaq*   *ma*   *lumaq*
     EXIST   person   LOC   house
     'There is somebody in the house.'

Existential predicates (i.e. *niyaq* plus complement) may also occur with a subject expression in final position, conveying a possessive meaning.

(3) *niyaq*   *awto*   *si*   *Soting*
     EXIST   car   PN   Soting
     'Soting has a car.'

The typical predicate in a simple main clause is a voice-marked verb. The voice marking determines the semantic relationship between the verb and its grammatical subject, which is one of the main features identifying the subject. Voice-marking will be discussed in detail in section 4.1. For the time being, it is sufficient to note that there are essentially two basic types of voice constructions, i.e. *actor voice* and *undergoer voice*. In the actor-oriented voice, the predicate is marked for actor voice (often by the prefix *N-*, see section 2.3) and the subject refers to the actor of the event denoted by the predicate. Non-subject complements such as *kendi* occur in immediate postverbal position.

(4) *bey*   *milli*   *kendi*   *qanak-qanak*
     bey   N-billi   kendi   qanak-qanak
     CPL   AV-buy   candy   child
     'The child bought some candies.'

There are a number of different undergoer voices that are marked by the affixes *-in-,*
paN-, -an, or a combination of these. In undergoer voice constructions, the subject refers
to the undergoer of the event denoted by the predicate. The agent of the event, if expressed,
may be marked with the agentive preposition *leq*. If it is marked with *leq*, its position is
variable; if it is not, it has to occur in immediate postverbal position. The rules for the use
of *leq* in marking actors are as follows: Non-pronominal actors are always marked by *leq*.

(5) *bey   binilli   leq   qanak-qanak   kendi*
     bey   in-billi   leq   qanak-qanak   kendi
     CPL   PV-buy   AGT   child   candy
     'The child bought the candies.'

(6) *heka   bey   takakan   leq   qanak-qanak*
     heka   bey   ta-kakan   leq   qanak-qanak
     many   CPL   PV.POT-eat   AGT   child
     'The child ate a lot.'

If the verb is in patient voice marked with the infix *-in-,* pronominal agents always
co-occur with *leq*.

(7) *bey   binalla   leq   na   buwas*
     bey   in-balla   leq   na   buwas
     CPL   PV-cook   AGT   3.MIN.GEN   rice
     'He cooked the rice.' (**bey binalla na buwas*)

On the other hand, when the verb is marked with other undergoer voice affixes, *leq* does
not occur with pronominal actors:

(8) *heka   bey   ta-kakan   ku*
     many   CPL   PV.POT-eat   1.MIN.GEN
     'I ate a lot.' (**heka bey takakan leq ku*)

Sentence (8) above should be compared with sentence (6) *heka bey takakan leq qanak-
qanak*, which has the full NP child as an actor. Examples for other voices with pronominal
actors are the following ones:

(9) *billi-han   ku   qinaq   ku   sayul*
     billi-BV   1.MIN.GEN   mother   1.MIN.GEN   vegetable
     'I will buy vegetables for my mother.'

(10) *dangey   sin   bey   pamilli   nu   manuk*
     how.much   money   CPL   IV:billi   2.MIN.GEN   chicken
     'How much did you pay for the chicken?'

(11) *say   bey   pamillihan   nu*
     who   CPL   LV:billi:LV   2.MIN.GEN
     'From whom did you buy (it)?'

Subjects can easily be topicalized, while non-subject complements generally cannot.
A topicalized subject may be followed by a short pause, which is represented in the
writing system by a comma.

(12) *qanak-qanak,   bey   nangis*
     child   CPL   N-tangis
     child   CPL   AV-cry
     'The child cried.'

In cleft sentences, the new or contrastive information occurs in clause-initial position, while the presupposed information (the remainder of the clause) is nominalized by the specific article (which is formally identical to the third person singular pronoun *qiya*).

(13) *qanak-qanak qiya bey nangis*
    child   SPEC CPL N-tangis
    child   SPEC CPL AV-cry
    'The child is the one who cried.'

3.3 Prepositions

Sinama has five prepositions, namely *leq*, *ma*, *ni*, *min*, and *maka*. Their meanings are shown in Table 13.2. Phrases formed with these prepositions often appear as predicates of a non-verbal clause as in *ma qaku duyan* (LOC 1.MIN durian). 'The durian is mine'.

Agentive *leq* differs from all other prepositions in that it takes genitive pronouns. Other prepositions take 'predicative' pronouns (see section 3.4). *Leq* marks the agent when it co-occurs with *in*- infixed verbs. With other verbs it marks reason.

(14) *bey matey qanak-qanak leq tibi*
    CPL AV:die child   RSN tuberculosis
    'The child died of tuberculosis.'

(15) *bey petak sigala leq qulan*
    CPL wet   3.NMIN RSN rain
    'They got wet because of the rain.'

The preposition *ma* has a number of uses. First, it marks static locations.

(16) *bey qaku ngiskul ma UP*
    CPL 1.MIN AV:study LOC UP
    'I studied at the University of the Philippines.'

In addition, *ma* introduces non-subject goals in non-motion sentences and ditransitive constructions. It introduces non-subject causees in causative constructions.

(17) *bilahi qaku ma kaqaw*
    like   1.MIN LOC 2.MIN.PRD
    'I love you.'

(18) *si Soting, bey manduq Tagalog ma si Akko*
    PN Soting CPL AV:teach Tagalog LOC PN Akko
    'Soting taught Tagalog to Akko.'

(19) *magpagumpit qaku ma qinaq ku*
    AV.CAU:scissors 1.MIN LOC mother 1.MIN.GEN
    'I have my hair cut by my mother.'

TABLE 13.2: SINAMA PREPOSITIONS

leq	*ma*	*ni*	*min*	*maka*
agent reason	location	goal	source	instrument comitative

The preposition *ni* marks directions (goals of motion) and *min* marks starting point or source:

(20) *bey   qaku   piqiq   ni   Sabah*
       CPL   1.MIN go.there   to   Sabah
       'I have been to Sabah.'

(21) *qembal   giq   qaku   maka-laqan   min   qopis*
       NEG   yet   1.MIN AV.POT-leave from   office
       'I am not yet able to leave the office.'

The preposition *maka* is used for (non-subject) instruments and comitatives.

(22) *ngulap   na   si   Soting   maka   boheq   panas*
       AV:wash.face   EMPH   PN   Soting   with   water   hot
       'Soting washes his face with warm water.'

(23) *mag-kaki   kami   maka   si   Soting*
       AV.GER-cousin   1.NMIN with   PN   Soting
       'Soting and I are cousins.'

3.4 Personal pronouns

Sinama has three basic sets of pronouns as shown in Table 13.3: nominative, predicative and genitive. Sinama pronouns have inclusive forms that include the person spoken to. The inclusive is a basic category in this system. Because it always contains more than one person, the terms *singular* and *plural* are avoided in the present chapter, the terms *minimal* and *non-minimal* being used instead.

The minimal set (MIN) refers to the minimal number of members in the set, while non-minimal (NMIN) refers to anything above what is required of the minimal set. For instance, the minimal set for the inclusive person (IN.MIN) is the speaker and the hearer (expressed by *kita*); the inclusion of anyone else (whether speaker or hearer) requires the use of the non-minimal inclusive person (IN.NMIN, expressed by *kitabi/tabi*). The pronoun in the first person non-minimal set is usually termed *first person plural exclusive* and the inclusive person non-minimal form *first person plural inclusive*. If inclusive person is considered a basic category in the system, there is no need for an explicit inclusive versus exclusive opposition. Apart from avoiding the problem of speaking about a singular and a plural inclusive form, the advantage of the present analysis will

TABLE 13.3: SINAMA PERSONAL PRONOUNS

	Person	Nominative	Predicative	Genitive
Minimal	1	*qaku*	*qaku*	*ku*
	2	*kaw*	*kaqaw*	*nu*
	IN	*kita*	*kita*	*ta*
	3	*qiya*	*qiya*	*na*
Non-minimal	1	*kami*	*kami*	*kami*
	2	*kam*	*kaqam*	*bi*
	IN	*kitabi*	*kitabi*	*tabi*
	3	*sigala*	*sigala*	*sigala*

become clear when one looks at the demonstrative pronouns and situationally bound adverbs which are organized in a parallel way to the personal pronominal paradigm (section 3.6).

Nominative pronouns occur as the grammatical subject of a sentence. They are second position clitics, i.e. they occur immediately after the verb if there is no auxiliary preceding it, but after the particle (e.g. *bey*) if there is one. Compare *milli qaku kendi* (AV:buy 1.MIN candy) 'I will buy candy' with *bey qaku milli kendi* (CPL 1.MIN AV:buy candy) 'I bought candy'. They never occur after full NPs (hence **bey milli kendi qaku*).

All of the predicative pronouns (PRD) except the second person have the same form as those in the nominative set. They occur as the predicate of cleft sentences, e.g. *kaqaw qiya bey mayad* (2.MIN.PRD SPEC CPL AV-pay) 'You are the one who paid'. As mentioned above, the 'predicative' forms also occur after all prepositions other than *leq*, which is always followed by a genitive pronoun.

The genitive pronouns are used as actors in undergoer voice constructions and as possessors in possessive constructions, e.g. *sin na* (money 3.MIN.GEN) 'his money' and *danakan ku lalla* (sibling 1.MIN.GEN male) 'my brother' (see also the next section).

3.5 NP structure

Any simple noun can be expanded into an endocentric construction with the noun as its head by the addition of other nominals and of adjectives. Modifiers generally follow the noun: *lansa mayor* (boat mayor) 'the mayor's boat', *lansa ku* (boat 1.MIN.GEN) 'my boat', *lansa heya* (boat large) 'large boat'. Genitive pronouns precede modifying nouns or adjectives: *qanak ku lalla* (offspring 1.MIN.GEN male) 'my son', *lansa ku heya* (boat my large) 'my large boat'.

The determiner *si* occurs before every proper name regardless of its grammatical function, e.g. *si Amil* 'Amil', *leq si Amil* 'by Amil', *maka si Amil* (with PN Amil) 'with Amil'. Classifiers and quantifiers also occur before the head of a NP: *tallu saging* 'three bananas', *qempat qanak* 'four children'.

There are various classifiers in Sinama. For instance, *mundaq* 'bow' is used with boats, ships and vessels, e.g. *dakayuq mundaq lansa* 'one motor launch', *duwa mundaq boggo* 'two boats', *dahatus mundaq* 'one hundred vessels'. *Batang* 'log' is used for oblong, cylindrical objects such as stems and cigarettes, e.g. *qennom batang pingi kayu* 'six cassava stems' and *pituq batang siga* 'seven cigarettes'. Numbers of persons below four are referred to by a numeral suffixed with *-ngan*, e.g. *da-ngan* 'one person', *duwa-ngan* 'two persons', and *tallu-ngan* 'three persons'. More than three persones, on the other hand, are referred to by a numeral followed by a classifier *puhuq*, e.g. *qempat puhuq* 'four persons'.

3.6 Deictics

Sinama has a four-way person-oriented system of spatial deixis, as shown in Table 13.4. The paradigm is parallel to that of the personal pronouns discussed in section 3.4.

The locational adverbs probably consist of the locative preposition *ma* plus the demonstratives. This is more transparent in Sitangkay Sinama, which has the corresponding forms *maqitu*, *maqilu*, *minaqan*, and *mahele*. Similarly, the manner adverbs, which can be rendered by 'like this' and 'like that' in English, consist of *bete* plus the demonstratives.

TABLE 13.4: SINAMA DEMONSTRATIVES AND DEICTIC ADVERBS

Person	Demonstratives	Locational Adverbs	Manner Adverbs
1 (= location near speaker)	*qitu*	*mitu*	*beteqitu*
2 (= location near addressee)	*qilu*	*milu*	*beteqilu*
IN (= location away but not far) from both speaker and addressee)	*qinaqan*	*minaqan*	
3 (= location far from both speaker and addressee)	*qili*	*mili*	*beteqili*

3.7 Auxiliaries

Auxiliaries occur in preverbal position, and, with the exception of the clitic nominative pronouns, no other elements may come in between auxiliary and verb. There are three auxiliaries which indicate aspect: completive *bey*, incompletive *lay* and contemplated *song*.

(24) *bey   ni-liqis   leq   na   pinggiq   kayu*
      CPL   PV-grate   AGT   3.MIN.GEN   tuber   tree
      'He grated the cassava.'

(25) *lay   na   ma   lansa*
      INCPL   EMPH   LOC   boat
      '(He) is already on board.'

(26) *song   tahak   na*
      CNTP   ripe   EMPH
      '(It) will soon be ripe.'

There are four kinds of negative auxiliaries, which appear first in line whenever there is a series of auxiliaries preceding the predicate: *maha*, *qembal*, *sikeyya*, and *daqa*. *Maha* negates stative and potentive (i.e. non-dynamic) predicates, including the existential *niyaq*.

(27) *maha   kagkag   si   Soting*
      NEG   thin   PN   Soting
      'Soting is not thin.'

(28) *maha   niyaq   sumping-sumping   ma   lumaq*
      NEG   EXIST   flower   LOC   house
      'There are no flowers in the house.'

Qembal negates verbal predicates.

(29) *qembal   giq   mayad   si   Abdul*
      NEG   yet   pay   PN   Abdul
      'Abdul has not yet paid.'

(30) *qembal   bilahi   paragan   si   Amil   ma   mayor*
      NEG   like   run   PN   Amil   LOC   mayor
      'Amil does not want to run for mayor.'

Nominals are negated by *sikeyya*.

(31) *sikeyya   mastal   si   Soting*
      NEG   teacher PN   Soting
      'Soting is not a teacher.'

(32) *sikeyya   buwas,   sikeyya   gandom,   sogaq   pinggiq   kayu*
      NEG   rice,   NEG   corn,   but   tuber   tree
      '(It is) not rice or corn but cassava.'

The fourth negative auxiliary *daqa* usually appears in imperatives.

(33) *daqa   kaw   sittowa   ma   qaku*
      NEG.IMP   2.MIN   laugh   LOC   1.MIN.PRD
      'Do not laugh at me.'

It also occurs with stative predicates:

(34) *daqa   na   kaw   hijul*
      NEG.IMP   EMPH   2.MIN   noisy
      'Don't be noisy.'

4 MAJOR VERBAL ALTERNATIONS

4.1 Voice and mode

The major verbal affixes combine the expression of voice and mode as shown in Table 13.5. Note in particular that there are four types of undergoer voice: the patient, locative, beneficiary, and instrument voices. The morphophonology of *N*- is dealt with in section 2.3.

In addition to *N*-, actor voice is also marked by the prefix *pa*-, which occurs in motion verbs such as *palaksu* 'to jump', *palabey* 'to pass by', *palege* 'to lie down'. Compare also *bey paragan qanak-qanak* (CPL AV-run child) 'The child ran'. The prefix *pa*- has the allomorph *pi*- in the fossilized deictic (ad)verbs *piqitu* and *pihiq*. These may be used as main predicates as in *piqitu giq kaw* (AV.PRX yet 2.MIN) 'come here' and *pihiq na kita* (AV.DIST EMPH IN.MIN) 'shall we (inclusive) go?' Adverbial use is illustrated below.

The infix *-in-* has an allomorph *ni*- prefixed to roots with initial *l* and *q*. It marks patient voice and, as already noted in 3.2 above, an actor NP occurring in a patient voice construction is always introduced by *leq*.

(35) *bey   ni-qadjal   deying   kurapuq   leq   qingkalla*
      CPL   PV-cook   fish   grouper   AGT   bachelor
      'The bachelor cooked the grouper fish.'

TABLE 13.5: SINAMA VERBAL AFFIXES

	Indicative	Imperative	Potentive
Actor	*pa-, N-*	*N-*	*maka-*
Patient	*-in-*, 0	*-un*	*ta-*
Locative	*paN- -an*	*paN- -in**	*kapaN-*
Beneficiary	*-in- -an*	*-in*	*ka-*
Instrument	*paN-*	*paN- -un*	*tapaN-*

*This form is quoted from Pallesen (1985: 99); it does not occur in the author's corpus.

In addition to signalling patient voice, the *-in-* infix often carries an incompletive sense as in *qay kinakan leq nu?* (what PV:eat AGT 2.MIN.GEN) 'what are you eating?' and *qay nindaq leq na?* (what PV:look.at AGT 3.MIN.GEN) 'what is he looking at?' This makes a striking contrast to unmarked verb roots, which may also be used in patient voice function but always carry a perfective or volitional sense.

(36) *qay   bey   billi   nu*
      what   CPL   BUY   2.MIN.GEN
      'What did you buy?'

(37) *qay   billi   nu*
      what   buy   2.MIN.GEN
      'What are you going to buy?'

An important feature of bare stem patient voice forms is that they only allow pronominal actors not marked with *leq*.

The infix *-in-* may also be used with some stative roots and then carries an *adversative* sense. Compare *tinenne qaku* (PV-cold 1.MIN 'I feel cold' with *tenne tangan na* (cold hand 3.MIN.GEN) 'her hand is cold'. Similarly, *nilantu na qaku* (PV-hungry EMPH 1.MIN) 'I feel hungry' is fine, but **nilosso na qaku* (PV-full EMPH 1.MIN) for 'I feel full (i.e. having eaten too much)' is not (the latter meaning is expressed by *losso na qaku*). Commonly used adversative statives include *kinaluq* 'feel sleepy', *niqulapay* 'have a cold', *nilango* 'have seasickness', *nirab* 'have morning sickness', *binaleq* 'get physically tired', and *sinumuq* 'get satisfied'.

Examples for patient voice imperative mode, which is marked by *-un-*, are *billi-hun qitu* (buy-PV.IMP PRX) 'buy this' and *bowa-hun piqitu* (bring-PV.IMP come:PRX) 'bring (it) here'.

Locative voice is marked by *paN- -an* in the indicative mode and with *paN- -in* in the imperative mode:

(38) *qanak-qanak   qiya   bey   pamillihan   na   duyan*
      qanak-qanak   qiya   bey   paN-billi-an   na   duyan
      child   SPEC   CPL   LV-buy-LV   3.MIN.GEN   durian
      'The child is the one from whom he bought durian.'

The beneficiary voice indicative mode is marked by *-in- -an* in the indicative mode and with *-in* in the imperative mode. Despite the fact that the infix *-in-* is part of the indicative formation, pronominal agents are not necessarily preceded by the agentive preposition *leq*.

(39) *qanak-qanak   qiya   bey   binillihan   na   duyan*
      qanak-qanak   qiya   bey   in-billi-an na   duyan
      child   SPEC   CPL   BV-buy-bv   3.MIN.GEN   durian
      'The child is the one for whom he bought durian.'

(40) *billihin   qaku   duyan*
      billi-in   qaku   duyan
      buy-BV.IMP   1.MIN   durian
      'Buy *me* durian.'

An example of the instrumental voice indicative mode prefix *paN-* is:

(41) *gasul   qiya   bey   pamalla*
      gasul   qiya   bey   paN-balla
      gasul   SPEC   CPL   IV-cook
      'Gas is what (he) cooked with.'

Potentive formations indicate that the agent is not in full control of the action. They are used for conveying ability or involuntary actions.

(42) *bang maha niyaq qinyawa, saga mata, bowaq, maka taynga,*
      if   NEG EXIST soul   PL   eye mouth and ear

      sogaq maha maka-kandaq, maha maka-bissala, maka maha
      but   NEG AV.POT-look NEG AV.POT-speak and NEG

      maka-kale
      AV.POT-hear
      'If there is no soul, eyes, mouth, and ears, (we) are not able to see, speak or hear.'

(43) *bey tandaq   ku   na*
      CPL ta-qendaq   1.MIN.GEN EMPH
      CPL PV.POT-look me
      'I happened to look at (it).'

Finally, we may note that there is a set of motion verbs that generally do not occur with verbal affixes. These are *takka* 'to arrive', *tulak* 'to leave', *kawut* 'to go towards the sea', and *kaleya* 'to move inland from the sea'. *Kawut* and *kaleya* are probably fossilized forms derived from +*kalawut* 'ka-sea' and +*kadeya* 'ka-inland' respectively (where *ka-* is a verbal motion prefix). Examples: *bey takka mastal* (CPL arrive teacher) 'The teacher arrived'; *kawut giq qaku* (go.sea yet 1.MIN) 'I am going to sea (for fishing)'.

4.2 The *leq*+*AV* construction

In addition to the constructions reviewed in the preceding section, there is a so-called 'derived-transitive' construction, in which the form *leq* occurs with an *N*- marked actor-voice verb. In this construction, *leq* functions as a verbal prefix that gives the clause a perfective sense. This construction is remarkable in a number of ways. To begin with, compare the actor-voice clause *ngadjal qaku manuk* (AV:cook 1.MIN chicken) 'I cooked chicken' with the following sentence:

(44) *leqngadjal   leq ku   manuk*
      leq.N:cook   AGT 1.MIN.GEN manuk
      'I have cooked the chicken.'

Although the verb *ngadjal* (< *N-qadjal*) here appears to be in actor voice, the grammatical subject is not the actor. Instead, the actor is marked by the preposition *leq*, a typical characteristic of undergoer voice clauses. Furthermore, the undergoer, *manuk* 'the chicken', is unmarked and in final position, which is typical for subjects. Its subject status is further supported by the fact that it can be topicalized without problems (i.e. *manuk leqngadjal leq ku* is also possible).

The *leq*+AV construction is also remarkable in that the agentive complement can also be topicalized, compare *leq ku ngadjal manuk* (by 1.MIN.GEN N-cook chicken) 'I have cooked the chicken'. In this case, the verbal *leq*-prefix has to be omitted (i.e. **leq ku leqngadjal manuk*). Note that in the usual patient – voice clause, an agentive complement cannot be topicalized, that is, **leq ku bey niadjal manuk* is impossible (as compared to *bey niadjal leq ku manuk* 'I cooked the chicken', which is correct).

TABLE 13.6: SEMANTIC TRANSITIVITY IN
LEQ+AV AND PV CONSTRUCTIONS

	Aspect	Mode	Affectedness
leq+ AV	+telic	+realis	total
-in-	±telic	±realis	partial

In cleft constructions with *leq+*AV, both the subject and the agentive complement precede the predicate resulting in *manuk qiya (bey) leq ku ngadjal*, where again the verbal prefix *leq-* must be dropped (**manuk qiya (bey) leq ku leqngadjal*). See also:

(45) *say   leq   nu   monoq   qinsiniq   siq*
       who   AGT   2.MIN.GEN   AV:fight   while.ago   EMPH
       'Who did you fight with just a while ago?'

The semantic and/or pragmatic differences between *leq ku ngadjal manuk* and *leqngadjal leq ku manuk* are unclear. The former, however, appears to be more frequent in texts.

Nevertheless, three semantic characteristics of the *leq+*AV-construction are clear. First, the construction carries a perfective sense. Second, the construction seems to be restricted to realis mode: only adverbs with a past sense can occur in a *leq+*AV construction. And finally, the grammatical subject of *leq+*AV constructions is interpreted as being totally affected, whereas the grammatical subject of patient voice sentences is only partially affected. Table 13.6 compares the two constructions with respect to semantic transitivity (see Akamine in print for further details).

(46) *leqmangan   leq   kuting*
       leq.AV:eat   AGT   cat
       'The cat has eaten (it) all.'

(47) *kinakan   leq   kuting*
       PV:eat   AGT   cat
       'The cat ate (some of) it.'

(48) *kakan-un   qintollo,   leqmalla   na*
       eat-PV.IMP   egg   leq.AV:cook   EMPH
       'Eat the eggs. (They are) already fully boiled.'

The *leq+*AV construction is not infrequent in Simunul texts. It is at least as common as the other major verb forms, i.e. actor and patient voice. However, not all Sinama dialects and languages have this construction. To my knowledge, the construction is observed only in the southwestern part of the Sulu archipelago and in the northwestern parts of Sulawesi, in particular the Dondo Bay area in the Tolitoli district.

5 TEXT EXAMPLE

Paghinang Landang (How to make Landang)

       Qisi   pinggiq   kayu   qiya   ni-hinang   landang.
       flesh   tuber   tree   SPEC   PV-make   landang
       'Cassava meat is made into a cake.'

Dahulu, ni-qupas-an kuwit pinggiq kayu.
first BV-peel-BV skin tuber tree
'First, the skin of the cassava root is peeled.'

Katis peqen bey ni-qupas-an qisi pinggiq kayu,
finish PTCL CPL BV-peel-BV flesh tuber tree,
'After the cassava root is peeled,

kinoseq-an lammis na maka boheq,
BV:clean-BV dirt 3.MIN.GEN with water,
the dirt is washed off with water,

qembohoq pinuhiq-an ma qellaw qasupaya tigang tagok na.
then BV:dry-BV LOC sun so.that dry.well resin 3.MIN.GEN
then (the cassava) is put in the sun to let its resin dry.'

Pamallaw qatawa pamuhi qisi pinggiq kayu ma qellaw,
IV:dry or IV:dry flesh tuber tree LOC sun,
'To let the cassava dry in the sun,

ta-qabut da pituq togol na.
PV.POT-reach one seven long 3.MIN.GEN
(it) takes a week.'

Bang tigang na qisi pinggiq kayu bey pinuhiq-an,
if dry.well EMPH flesh tuber tree CPL BV:dry-BV
'When the cassava flesh is dry,

qembohoq ni-liqis ma liqis-an.
then PV-grate LOC grate-NR
then (it) will be grated in a grater.'

Katis peqen bey ni-liqis, ginulung na maka tangan
finish PTCL CPL PV-grate, PV:roll EMPH with hand

ma ligu,
LOC basket
'After being grated, (it) will be rolled by hand (into a cake) in a winnowing basket,

qembohoq pinuhiq-an ma qellaw paballik.
then BV:dry-BV LOC sun again
and then (it) will be left to dry again in the sun.'

Da-nga-llaw qatawa duwa-nga-llaw pamuhiq ta ma qiya
one-LK-day or two-LK-day IV:dry IN.MIN.GEN LOC 3.MIN
'After it has been left to dry there for one or two days by us

qembohoq tigang toqongan.
then dry.well very.much
it will dry very well (get very hard).'

Qembohoq pinutu leq ta ma putuhan.
then PV:steam AGT IN.MIN.GEN LOC putuhan
'Then we will steam it on a *putuhan* (steaming instrument).'

Tahak peqen qembohoq na sab pa-tigang ta
cook PTCL then EMPH also PV.CAU-dry.well IN.MIN.GEN

ma   qellaw   paballik.
LOC   sun   again
'After cooking (it), we will dry (it) again in the sun.'

Tigang   peqen,   qembohoq   binalla   leq   ta   maka
dry.well   PTCL   then   PV:cook   AGT   IN.MIN.GEN   with

gataq   lahing.
milk   coconut
'After drying (it), we will cook (it) with coconut milk.'

Tahak   peqen,   qembohoq   pa-tannahan   ta   na   gula.
cook   PTCL   then   PV.CAU-place   IN.MIN.GEN   EMPH sugar
'After cooking (it), we will mix (it) with sugar.'

Mitu   makajari   na   kinakan   leq   ta.
PRX.ADV   possible   EMPH   PV:eat   AGT   IN.MIN.GEN
'At this point, we can eat (it).'

Nipakkal   leq   ta   ni   pa-lunuk-an,
PV-scatter   AGT   IN.MIN.GEN   DIR   NR-soft-NR
'We will break it into small pieces,

puwas   ngaq   kita   boheq   pamaseq   qiya.
after   AV:get   IN.MIN   water   IV:wet   3.MIN
and get some water to soften it.'

Qembohoq   ni   ni-gulum   ni-hinang   bete   lowa   bigi.
then   to   PV-roll   PV-make   like   shape   seed
'Then (it) will be rolled into a seed-like object.'

Lay   na   peqen   puwas   leqngahinang   ni-puhiq-an   na
INCPL EMPH   PTCL   after   leq.AV:make   BV-dry-BV   EMPH

ma   qellaw.
LOC   sun
'After this has been made, it will be dried in the sun.'

Pag-kassang   na   ni-qalaq   leq   ta
GER-dry   EMPH   PV-take   AGT   IN.MIN.GEN
'When dried, we will take it

Ni-qadjal   leq   ta   qasupaya   tahak.
PV-cook   AGT   IN.MIN.GEN   so.that   ripe
and cook it so that it is ready to eat.'

Pag-tahak   kinakan   na.
GER-cook   PV:eat   EMPH
'When ready, (it) will be eaten.'

ACKNOWLEDGEMENTS

I am grateful to Hadji Amilhamja S. Juaini in Manuk Mangkaw, Tawitawi Province, and Hadji Musa Malabong in Sitangkay, Tawitawi Province, who accommodated me and taught me Sinama. This research was mainly supported by the Asian Studies Scholarship Program from the Ministry of Education, Science and Culture in Japan. It was also funded by two grants from the same ministry as part of a project 'Culturo-Ecological

Structure of Network Society in Wallacea' (#07041057), headed by Tanaka Koji of Kyoto University and 'Fieldwork and Descriptive Grammatical Studies on Endangered Languages in the Philippines and Eastern Indonesia' (#12039221), organized by Kitano Hiroaki of Aichi University of Education. I am indebted to Ernesto Constantino, Lawrence Reid, Ricardo Nolasco and Nagatsu Kazufumi for their many helpful suggestions and comments on my field study.

REFERENCES

Abdul Djebar Hapip (1979) *Bahasa Bajau*, Jakarta: Pusat Pembinaan dan Pengembangan Bahasa.

Abdul Ghani Bin Bagul (1950) 'Notes on the Bajau language', *Sarawak Museum Journal* 5/2: 196–200.

Akamine, J. (1996) 'A grammatical analysis of Manuk Mangkaw Sinama', Ph.D. dissertation, University of the Philippines, Diliman.

—— (1997) 'Notes on Sinama languages: Phonology, orthography and wordlist', *The Journal of Sophia Asian Studies* 15: 3–39.

—— (2002) 'A Sinama derived transitive construction', in F. Wouk and M.D. Ross (eds) *The History and Typology of Western Austronesian Voice Systems*, 355–366, Canberra: Pacific Linguistics.

Allison, J. (1977) 'Discourse analysis of a southern Samal text: Abunawas and the beautiful widow', *Studies in Philippine Linguistics* 1: 143–169.

—— (1979) 'The phonology of Sibutu Sama: A language of the southern Philippines', *Studies in Philippine Linguistics* 3(2): 63–104.

—— (1980) *Sama Vocabulary*, MS.

Anceaux, J.C. (1978) 'A Samalan wordlist from southeast Sulawesi', in S.A. Wurm and L. Carrington (eds) *Second international conference on Austronesian linguistics: Proceedings, fascicle 1*, Canberra: Pacific Linguistics.

Banker, J.E. (1984) 'The West Coast Bajau language', in J.K. King and J.W. King (eds), *Languages of Sabah: A survey report*, 101–112, Canberra: Pacific Linguistics.

Constantino, E. (1965) 'The sentence patterns of twenty-six Philippine languages', *Lingua* 15: 71–124.

Donohue, M. (1996) 'Bajau: A symmetrical Austronesian languages', *Language* 72: 782–793.

Evans, I.H.N. (1952) 'Notes on the Bajau and other coastal tribes of North Borneo', *Journal of the Malayan Branch of the Royal Asiatic Society* 25(1): 48–55.

Gault, J.A. (1979) 'Phonemics and morphophonemics of Sama Balangingi', *Papers in Philippine Linguistics* 9: 49–67, Canberra: Pacific Linguistics.

—— (1986) 'Focal content in Sama Bangingi narrative discourse', *Studies in Philippine Linguistics* 6(1): 200–215.

—— (1999) 'An ergative description of Sama Bangingi', LSP Monograph 46, Manila: Linguistic Society of the Philippines.

Grimes, B.F. (1999), *Ethnologue – Languages of the world*, 13th edn, Dallas: Summer Institute of Linguistics.

Jacobson, M.R. and Jacobson, S.M. (1980) 'Sama Abaknon phonology', *Philippine Journal of Linguistics* 11(1): 32–44.

King, J.K. and King, J.W. (eds) (1984) *Languages of Sabah: A survey report*, Canberra: Pacific Linguistics.

Kunting, Y.C. (1989) *Sinama English dictionary*, 2nd edn., Zamboanga: Alliance Press.

Lapian, A.B. and Nagatsu, K. (1996) 'Research on Bajau communities: A maritime people of Southeast Asia', *Asian Research Trends: Humanities and Social Sciences Review* 6: 45–70.

Merin, E.M. (1992) 'A grammatical description of Inabaknon', MA thesis, University of the Philippines, Diliman.

Pallesen, A.K. (1979) 'The pepet in Sama-Bajaw', *South-east Asian Linguistic Studies* 3: 114–42. Canberra: Pacific Linguistics.

—— (1985) *Culture contact and language convergence*, Manila: Linguistic Society of the Philippines.

Sather, C. (1965) 'Bajau numbers of adjectives of quantity', *Sabah Society Journal* 2(4): 194–197.

—— (1968) 'Some notes concerning Bajau Laut phonology and grammar', *Sabah Society Journal* 3(4): 205–224.

—— (1997) *The Bajau laut: Adaptation, history, and fate in a maritime fishing society of south-eastern Sabah*, South-East Asian Social Science Monographs, Oxford: Oxford University Press.

Schneeberger, W.F. (1937) 'A short vocabulary of the Banggi and Bajau', *Journal of the Malayan Branch of the Royal Asiatic Society* 15(3): 145–164.

Smith, K.D. (1984) 'The languages of Sabah: A tentative lexicostatistical classification', in J.K. King and J.W. King (eds), *Languages of Sabah: A survey report*, 1–49, Canberra: Pacific Linguistics.

Sopher, D. (1965) *The Sea Nomads: A study of the maritime boat people of Southeast Asia*, Singapore: National Museum Singapore, reprinted in 1977 with postscript.

Summer Institute of Linguistics, Philippines (1979) *Languages of the Southern Gateway: Chavacano, Sinama, Tausug and Yakan*, Quezon City: Summer Institute of Linguistics, Philippines.

—— (1990) *Sinama-Pilipino-English: Bissara pondok-pondok*, Quezon City: Summer Institute of Linguistics, Philippines.

Trick, D. (1997) 'Equi-NP deletion in Sama Southern', *Philippine Journal of Linguistics* 28: 125–144.

Verheijen, J.A.J. (1986) *The Sama/Bajau language in the Lesser Sunda islands*, Canberra: Pacific Linguistics.

Walton, C. (1979) 'Pangutaran (Sama) phonology', *Studies in Philippine Linguistics* 3(2): 189–217.

—— (1986) *Sama verbal semantics: Classification, derivative and inflection*. Manila: Linguistic Society of the Philippines.

Walton, J. and D.C. Moody (1984) 'The east coast Bajau Languages', in J.K. King and J.W. King (eds), *Languages of Sabah: A survey report*, 113–123, Canberra: Pacific Linguistics.

Walton, J. and Walton, C. (eds) (1992) *English-Pangutaran Sama dictionary*, Quezon City: Summer Institute of Linguistics, Philippines.

Warren, J.F. (1978) 'Who were the Balangingi Samal? slave raiding and ethnogenesis in nineteenth century Sulu', *The Journal of Asian Studies* 37(3): 477–490.

—— (1981) *The Sulu Zone: The dynamics of external trade, slavery, and ethnicity in the transformation of a Southeast Asian maritime state*, Singapore: Singapore University Press.

CHAPTER FOURTEEN

KIMARAGANG

Paul Kroeger

1 INTRODUCTION

Kimaragang is a Dusunic language spoken by approximately 10,000 people living in the state of Sabah, East Malaysia. The Dusunic family, together with Murut-Tidong, Paitanic, and Bisayan, comprise the Northeast Borneo subgroup (Wurm 1983; Smith 1984). The wider genetic classification of this stock is a debated issue which will not be discussed here (see Blust 1998 and ADELAAR, A HISTORICAL PERSPECTIVE). The Dusunic languages share many lexical and phonological features with various Philippine languages; but the most striking parallels are found in morphology and syntax, where Dusunic shows a very high degree of similarity to languages of the central Philippines such as Tagalog and Cebuano.

Kimaragang is spoken in the Kota Marudu and Pitas districts of Sabah, near the northeastern tip of Borneo. The Kimaragang dialects spoken in these two districts are distinguished by a significant number of lexical differences, as well as a smaller number of morphological and phonological differences, but remain fully intelligible to each other. The Sonsogon dialects, spoken in the highland areas to the south and east, are closely related to Kimaragang but exhibit major phonological differences. The Kimaragang view Sonsogon as an extremely low-prestige speech variety.

The Kimaragang are a small minority in the Pitas district; but in the Tandek subdistrict of Kota Marudu they constitute the largest single ethnic group. Kimaragang functions as a local *lingua franca* in contexts such as the Tandek weekly market. A local variety of Sabah market Malay has long been used for interactions with local officials and people from other districts. Standard Malay is now the language of education, mass media, and government.

The Kimaragang were originally swidden rice farmers. After the British administration put an end to head-hunting and tribal warfare, some Kimaragang began to move down out of the hills onto the eastern edge of the large flood plain which lies immediately to the south of Marudu Bay. These people now farm wet rice on the plain, although most families continue to plant some dry rice and other crops in hillside gardens, and traditional religious beliefs are still centered on the dry rice farming cycle.

This chapter is based on the dialect spoken on the plain around Tandek.

2 PHONOLOGY AND ORTHOGRAPHY

2.1 Segment inventory, syllable structure and stress

2.1.1 Segmental phonemes

Kimaragang makes use of 18 phonemic consonants and 5 vowels. The five vowels are /i,e,a,o,u/. The back mid vowel /o/ in other Dusunic languages is usually a back unrounded or only slightly rounded vowel, roughly [ɤ], with considerable tensing of the tongue back.

TABLE 14.1: KIMARAGANG CONSONANT PHONEMES

	Labial	Dental	Palatal	Velar	Glottal
Vls. stops	p	t		k	ʔ
Vd. stops	b	d	j(ʤ)	g	
Implosives	ɓ	ɗ			
Nasals	m	n		ŋ	
Sibilant		s			
Flap		r			
Lateral		l			
Glides	w		y		

But in Kimaragang, this vowel is normally more rounded, roughly [ɔ]. In pre-penultimate syllables, /o/ is pronounced as schwa.

The 18 consonant phonemes of Kimaragang are shown in Table 14.1.

All stops are unreleased in word- or phrase-final position. /s/ is (by many speakers) palatalized to [ʃ] before a high vowel. The flap /r/ is usually trilled in word-final position. An epenthetic voiced stop is inserted between the flap and a preceding nasal, as in the form /san-rawoʔ/ [sandrawoʔ] 'one ear (of rice)'.

Some Kimaragang speakers pronounce the /r/ as a velar fricative, [ɣ], in all environments. This feature is characteristic of the deep Sonsogon dialect; but among the Tandek Kimaragang, the trait is considered a speech defect referred to as *ɓiraʔ*.

The semivowels /w/ and /y/ are contrastive even following homorganic high vowels, as seen in the following examples:

(1) *momuwaw* 'smoke out bees' *momuaw* 'scare away birds'
                                            (e.g. from rice field)

      siyam   'nine'   *sian*   'pity'

The implosive voiced stops /ɓ/ and /ɗ/ are exclusive features of the Tandek dialect; in the Pitas dialect, cognate forms show plain voiced stops /b/ and /d/. Implosives occur only in word-initial or intervocalic position, and the regular voiced stops /b/ and /d/ are very rare in these positions. However, the difference is contrastive as shown in the following examples:

(2) /monuduŋ/ 'look down'   vs.   /monuɗuŋ/, 'chop wood'
     /tadaw/ 'day, sun'   vs.   /kaɗaw/ 'banana species'
     /todoŋ/ 'enter'   vs.   /toɗuŋ/ 'nose'
     /obuli/ 'can'   vs.   /oɓutak/ 'muddy'
     /bas/ 'bus'   vs.   /ɓaju/ 'shirt'

The glottal stop is generally optional in non-final position, e.g. [raʔat] ~ [ra:t] 'sea'. The word-final glottal stop, which is highly contrastive in the Pitas dialect, is only marginally contrastive in the Tandek dialect. Most words which end with a vowel in the Pitas dialect are pronounced with a final glottal in Tandek, so that final (open) vowels are quite rare. All examples of open final vowels which have been identified so far are in functors, pronouns, question words, etc. (though many other words in these categories do have the final glottal). However, even in Tandek a few minimal pairs can be found:

(3) /ko/ 'you (sg.)'   vs.   /koʔ/ 'or'
     /kito/ 'we (dual)' vs.   /o-kitoʔ/ 'see'

2.1.2 Syllable structure

The basic shape of a syllable in Kimaragang is (C)V(C). Consonant clusters occur only word-medially, and the first element in the cluster is always a nasal or voiced stop. The second element is generally a homorganic obstruent, though across morpheme boundaries certain other combinations are possible. The allowable morpheme-internal clusters are illustrated below:

(4) -mp-   *pampaŋ*   'stone'
     -nt-   *puntiʔ*   'banana'
     -ns-   *nansak*   'ripe'
     -ŋk-   *kaŋkab*   'chest'
     -mb-   *simbar*   'answer'
     -nd-   *tandus*   'spear'
     -ŋg-   *taŋgaʔ*   'bamboo water container'
     -bp-   *tobpineeʔ*   'sibling'
     -dt-   *lodtuŋ*   'swell up'
     -ds-   *podsuʔ*   'bathe'
     -gk-   *lagkaw*   'hut'

Kimaragang follows the general Austronesian pattern in that root forms are usually two syllables long. Roots of three or more syllables are generally derived historically from disyllabic roots through infixation, reduplication, or some other morphological process.

Each syllable normally contains a single vowel. Thus vowel sequences are normally disyllabic, with each of the two segments functioning as nuclei in adjacent syllables. A glottal stop is optionally inserted within such sequences. However, when geminate vowel sequences are followed by one or more other syllables, the two vowels are shortened so that both together are only slightly longer than one normal vowel. No glottal stop can be inserted within these non-final geminates, and (at least in terms of the surface phonology) one must say that the two vowels have merged to form the complex nucleus of a single syllable with the non-standard shape CVV(C). This process leads to contrastive length in non-final syllables, as illustrated in the following examples:

(5) *taŋ.kap*   'sheath for parang'   *taaŋ.kap*   'sling for baby'
     to.luʔ   'three'   *too.luʔ*   'pestle'
     tu.kad   'ladder, stairs'   *tuu.kad*   'spade, trowel'
     ko.yu.wan   'body'   *ko.yuu.wan*   'able to part with'

2.1.3 Stress

Stress is not contrastive on the word level, but it is difficult to determine what rules govern the distribution of phonetic stress. Native speakers seem to have no intuitions about stress, being unaware of stress placement in their own pronunciation and often accepting variable stress patterns for the same word as being equally correct. Marked intonational (or focal) stress can be placed on different syllables within the same word, e.g. when a story teller repeats a particular phrase or clause for emphasis. Moreover, it is not uncommon for trained linguists listening to the same data to disagree about the position of stress in a particular word.

No detailed acoustic study has yet been attempted, but my impressionistic observations support the following basic generalizations. Normal stress may occur on the final or penultimate syllable of the word, or the last two syllables may receive equal stress. Final open syllables are generally unstressed, while words ending with the suffixes -an or -on tend to have final stress.

There are a few forms in which a marked focal stress seems to have become lexicalized, leading to some apparent 'minimal pairs'. The marked stress in the following examples differs from normal stress, in that it is signaled by a definite rise in pitch and a slight lengthening of the vowel. These same features (sometimes greatly exaggerated) are used to mark intonational (sentence level) focal stress.

(6) /to?on/   'year'   vs. /tóo?on/   'next year'
     /mantad/   'from'   vs. /máantad/   'previous'
     /banar/   'true, very'   vs. /báanar/   'for no reason, in vain'

The pattern illustrated in these examples can also be used to modify words borrowed from Malay. For example, /skáaraŋ/ is used in Kimaragang to mean 'later; some time today' and is derived from *sekarang* /skaraŋ/, which means 'now' in standard Malay.

2.2 Orthography

At the present time there is no officially recognized standard orthography for Kimaragang. The practical orthography described here and used in later sections of this chapter is specific to the Tandek dialect. The general design strategy has been to conform with the official orthography of the national language, Bahasa Malaysia, as far as possible. Only deviations from that norm will be discussed in this section.

A medial glottal stop is written with an apostrophe, as in the older Malay orthography. Since there are very few words in the Tandek dialect which end in a vowel, compared to the very large number that end in glottal stop, it is more economical to mark final open vowels rather than to write the final glottal stop. Following an orthographic convention formerly used in Penampang Kadazan, the letter -h is used to indicate the absence of a glottal stop (i.e. a final open syllable).

The official Malay orthography forbids the use of the letters w and y at the end of a word. The vowel sequences /-ai-/, /-oi-/, /-au-/ and /-ou-/ do not occur in Kimaragang, having merged diachronically to /-ee-/ and /-oo-/ (see also section 2.3.2). For this reason, the word final sequences /-ay/, /-oy/, /-aw/ and /-ow/ can be written as -ai, -oi, -au and -ou (as in Malay) without confusion. Where there is a contrast between a final glide and the corresponding high vowel, however, -y and -w are written as in *tikuw* 'tail'.

The letters b and d represent implosives /ɓ/ and /ɗ/ in word-initial or intervocalic position, and regular voiced stops /b/ and /d/ word-finally or following a nasal (environments where the contrast is neutralized). In the rare words where /b/ and /d/ occur in intervocalic position, they are written as -bb- and -dd- respectively, as in *taddau* 'day, sun'.

2.3 Morphophonemic alternations

2.3.1 Nasal merger and nasal assimilation

Like most Western Austronesian languages, Kimaragang has a verbal prefix (*poN-*) ending in a nasal which merges with, or replaces, a following voiceless obstruent. In Kimaragang the process of nasal merger also affects the voiced labials /b,bb,w/. This alternation is illustrated in the following examples (the merger of the prefix /m-/ with the

/p-/ of *poN-* will be discussed below; see §2.3.3 for the assimilation of /o/ to /a/):

(7) (a) -N + k → /ng/
          as in: m-poN- koruang   →   /mongoruang/ 'to accompany'

     (b) -N + {s,t} → /n/
          as in: m-poN- siddang   →   /moniddang/ 'to dry in the sun'
                  m-poN- tibas   →   /monibas/ 'to slash'

     (c) -N + {p,w,b,bb} → /m/
          as in: m-poN- panau   →   /mamanau/ 'to walk'
                  m-poN- waal   →   /mamaal/ 'to make'
                  m-poN- boli   →   /momoli/ 'to buy'

Before vowels, -N is realized as a velar nasal /ng/, as in the following examples:

     (d) m-poN- irak   →   /mongirak/ 'to laugh'
          m-poN- akan   →   /mangakan/ 'to eat'.

Before {d,dd,g,j,r,l}, an epenthetic vowel /o/ is inserted, and -N is again realized as a velar nasal /ng/:

     (e) m-poN- duat   →   /mongoduat/ 'to ask'
          m-poN- guring   →   /mongoguring/ 'to harrow'
          m-poN- jaga   →   /mangajaga/ 'to guard'
          m-poN- ragus   →   /mangaragus/ 'to plow'
          m-poN- lumbid   →   /mongolumbid/ 'to roll a cigarette'

Another sort of nasal merger is triggered by the actor voice marker (see section 3.1.1). It is this process which gives rise to the initial /m-/ in the preceding examples. Actor voice is marked by the prefix /m-/ before vowel-initial stems (8a). Before non-labial consonants it is marked by the infix /-um-/, which is inserted immediately following the initial consonant of the stem (8b). Before labial consonants, however, the /m-/ replaces the initial consonant of the stem, as in (8c).

(8) a. m-ogom   →   *mogom*   'sit'
         m-uli   →   *muli*   'return'

     b. m-toyog   →   *tumoyog*   'swim'
         m-sobu   →   *sumobu*   'urinate'

     c. m-podsu   →   *modsu*   'bathe'
         m-waliw   →   *maliw*   'move'
         m-bubus   →   *mubus*   'spill' (intrans.)

Other prefixes which end in nasals do not trigger nasal merger, but the prefix nasal does (in most cases) assimilate to a following obstruent. The behavior of these nasal elements before vowels and sonorants varies considerably from one prefix to another, and is beyond the scope of the present study.

2.3.2 *Vowel merger*

As mentioned in section 2.2, the vowel sequences *-ai- and *-oi-, *-au- and *-ou- have merged diachronically (following the loss of Proto-Dusunic **h*) to /-ee-/ and /-oo-/

respectively. The same merger operates synchronically where the sequences /o+i/ or /o+u/ occur across a morpheme boundary. Some examples are given in (9):

(9) po- + uli + -on   → /poolion/   'allow to return'
     noko- + ulok   → /nokoolok/   'accidentally stepped on'
     ko- + uma   → /kooma/   'enough; able to fit'
     no- + igit + -an   → /neegitan/   'accepted proposal of marriage'
     noko- + idu   → /nokeedu/   'has escaped'
     po- + inum + -on   → /peenumon/   'give someone a drink'

2.3.3 Vowel harmony

Vowel harmony in Kimaragang spreads from right to left, changing /o/ to /a/ when the vowel in the following syllable is an /a/. The following examples illustrate the effect of vowel harmony:

(10) noko-dagang   → *nakadagang*   'sold'
     poN-omot-an   → *pangamatan*   'harvest time'
     po-ogom-an   → *paagaman*   'place where you set something'
     poN-tanom-an   → *pananaman*   'time/place of planting'
     ondom-an   → *andaman*   'remember'
     -in-poN-olos-an   → *pinangalasan* 'the person you borrowed from'
       (< olos 'borrow')
     -in-poN-asok-an   → *pinangasakan* 'the place you planted'
       (< asok 'plant rice')

The reverse process does not apply; that is, /a/ does not spread from left to right, nor does /o/ spread to the left when preceded by /a/, as shown by examples like the following:

(11) dagang + -on → *dagangon* 'buy'
     surat + -on   → *suraton*   'write'
     lapak + -on   → *lapakon*   'split'

High vowels neither trigger nor undergo vowel harmony. In fact, the process is blocked when a high vowel intervenes between the /a/ and a preceding /o/. The /o/'s in the following examples do not undergo vowel harmony, even though a suffix containing an /a/ is added, because they are 'shielded' by an intervening high vowel:

(12) sogit + -an → *sogitan*   'cold'
     sobu + -an   → *sobuan*   'urinate'
     oling + -an → *olingan*   'forget'

Another interesting fact about vowel harmony in Kimaragang is that the process does not apply to mono-morphemic geminate vowels. This 'geminate inalterability' effect is illustrated in (13). Note that a sequence of identical vowels across a morpheme boundary does undergo vowel harmony in the normal way, as seen in *paagaman* (example 10).

(13)	woog-an	→	*woogan*	'wash'
	poN-woog-an	→	*pomoogan*	'washing place'
	no-loot-an	→	*nolootan*	'covered with sand/dirt'
	o-toor-an	→	*otooran*	'clutch'
	toboong-an	→	*toboongan*	'tie the mouth (of a dog)'
	poN-in-loow-an	→	*ponginloowan*	'term of address' (< loou 'call')

2.3.4 Vowel neutralization

The examples in (11) above demonstrate that 'reverse vowel harmony' does not occur; that is, /a/ does not change to /o/ when the following vowel is /o/. However, there is another context in which the change from /a/ to /o/ can be triggered. This process is illustrated in the following examples:

(14)	a.	talib + -an	→	*toliban*	'pass by'
	b.	lasu + -an	→	*losuan*	'to feel hot'
	c.	anu + -on	→	*onuwon*	'take'
	d.	sawo + -on	→	*sowoon*	'marry'

In these examples, /a/ is the first vowel in a disyllabic root whose second vowel is not /a/. When a suffix is added, the /a/ changes to /o/. If the suffix is /-an/, which would trigger vowel harmony, this change is only observed when the second root vowel is high, as in (14a–b). If the suffix is /-on/, which cannot trigger vowel harmony, the change is observed even when the second root vowel is not high, as in (14d). In general, any /a/ which would otherwise occur in pre-penultimate position (i.e. more than two syllables from the end of the word) is neutralized to /o/, unless it is preserved by vowel harmony.

2.3.5 Particle infixation

The unstressed aspectual particles *noh* 'completive' and *poh* 'incompletive' sometimes merge with pronouns which end in a semivowel (/w/ or /y/). More precisely, when the aspectual particle is immediately preceded by such a pronoun, the particle is inserted (or 'infixed') into the last syllable of the pronoun, just before the final semivowel. This infixation occurs only in the Tandek dialect, and not in the Pitas dialect. Some examples are given below:

(15)	/muli okoi no/	→	/muli okonoi/	'we (excl.) are going home now'
	/muli tokou no/	→	/muli tokonou/	'we (incl.) are going home'
	/muli tokou po/	→	/muli tokopou/	'let's (incl.) go home'

2.4 Reduplication

Reduplication in Kimaragang exhibits a number of phonological complications which have not yet been investigated in any systematic way. But in simplest terms, we can identify three basic patterns of reduplication: CV-reduplication, full root reduplication, and vowel lengthening (which can be viewed as reduplication of a single vowel).

CV-reduplication is used to mark a number of different morphological categories, including reciprocal actions, intensification or diminution of stative predicates, and repetitive, habitual or progressive aspect. When the root begins with a consonant and the word contains no infix, the first consonant and vowel of the root are copied, as in (16a). When an infix is present, the first CV of the infixed stem is copied, as in (16b).

(16) a.

Root		Underlying representation	Output	Gloss
gayo	big	o-RDP-gayo	*agagayo*	a little bigger
bisa	potent	o-RDP-bisa	*obibisa*	very powerful
patai	die/kill	m-pi-RDP-patai	*mipapatai*	kill each other; wage war
boros	speak	ko-RDP-boros	*koboboros*	reason for speaking

b.

Root		Underlying representation	Output	Gloss
laga	come	RDP -um- laga	*lulumaga*	always coming around
talib	pass	RDP -um- talib	*tutumalib*	keep passing by
goroi	tear	RDP -in- goroi	*giginoroi*	torn into little pieces
tanom	plant	RDP -in- tanom	*titinanom*	being planted

When the root begins with a vowel and the form includes a suffix, CV copying begins with the second syllable of the root, as in (17a). When there is no suffix, the full root is normally copied, as in (17b).

(17) a.

Root		Underlying representation	Output	Gloss
igit	betroth	RDP-igit-an	*igigitan*	getting engaged
ansak	cook	pi-RDP-ansak-an	*piansasakan*	cook quickly
ilug	snare	RDP-ilug-on	*ilulugon*	trying to snare
ampas	imply	RDP-ampas-on	*ampapason*	speaking indirectly

b.

Root		Underlying representation	Output	Gloss
uli	return	pi-RDP-uli	*piuli-uli*	return it quickly
ondom	remember	pi-RDP-ondom	*piondom-ondom*	keep remembering
owit	carry	n-RDP-owit-Ø	*nowit-owit*	always carried
imbas	show ability	m-RDP-imbas	*mimbas-imbas*	compete

Full root reduplication with consonant-initial roots is quite rare; Jim Johannson (p.c.) suggests that the attested forms may in fact be borrowings or calques. Forms exhibiting this pattern frequently involve an irregular alternation, with even non-labial initial consonants being replaced by the *m-* which marks actor voice. Some examples are given in (18).

(18)

Root		Reduplicated form	Gloss
panau	walk	*manau-panau*	take a walk
kombit	touch	*mombit-kombit*	touch repeatedly
sayau	dance	*mayau-sayau*	go on dancing

The lengthening of the first vowel in the word is used to mark habitual actions. It is most common with actor voice forms, but can also be used in other voices:

(19)	Root		Base form	Habitual	Gloss
	inum	drink	m-poN-inum	*moonginum*	drunkard
	patai	die/kill	m-poN-patai	*maamatai*	habitual killer
	wudut	tell lies	m-poN-wudut	*moomudut*	habitual liar
	iit	bite	m-poN-iit	*moongiit*	habitually bites (of dog)
	anu	take	m-poki-anu	*mookianu*	always asking for something
	intong	watch	m-pog-intong	*moogintong*	seer, diviner
	siddang	sun dry	po-siddang-an	*poosiddangan*	place for sun-drying things
	uli	return	uli-an	*uulian*	normal time for coming home

3 BASIC MORPHOSYNTAX

3.1 Verbal clauses

3.1.1 Voice and case marking

A basic verbal clause consists of a verb plus one or more arguments. One of these arguments has unique morphological and syntactic properties which identify it as the subject of the clause. These properties include: (a) nominative case marking when overtly expressed, whether by a pronoun or a full NP; (b) the argument's semantic role is indicated by the voice marking affix on the verb; (c) it is the obligatorily plural argument of a reciprocal verb (see section 4.5.2); (d) eligibility to be relativized or clefted; (e) eligibility to launch floating quantifiers; (f) eligible target (or controllee) in the Equi construction (unlike Tagalog). See HIMMELMANN, TYPOLOGICAL CHARACTERISTICS, section 3.8, for further discussion and references.

The patterns of case and voice-marking in Kimaragang are illustrated in the following examples. In each sentence, the subject is in bold:

(20) a. *Mangalapak*   **okuh**   *do*   *niyuw.*
   m-poN-lapak   okuh   do   niyuw
   AV-TR-split   1s.NOM   GEN   coconut
   'I will split a coconut/some coconuts.'

   b. *Lapak-on   kuh   **it**   **niyuw.***
   split-OV   1s.GEN   NOM   coconut
   'I will split the coconut(s).'

   c. *Lapak-an   kuh   do   niyuw   **it**   **wogok.***
   split-DV   1s.GEN   GEN   coconut   NOM   pig
   'I will split some coconuts for the pigs (to eat).'

   d. *Nokuroh.tu   n-i-lapak   nuh   do   niyuw*
   why   PST-IV-split   2s.GEN   GEN   coconut
   inoh   dangol   kuh?
   MED.NOM   bush.knife   1s.GEN
   'Why did you use my bush knife to split coconuts?'

In example (20a), the actor voice marker (*m-*) signals that the agent is the subject, and so the agent pronoun ('I') appears in NOM case. In example (20b), the objective voice marker (*-on*) indicates that the patient is the subject. In example (20c), the dative voice marker (*-an*) indicates that the subject is a beneficiary. In example (20d), the instrumental voice marker (*i-*) indicates that the subject is an instrument.

Subjects are normally definite (note the glosses of *niyuw* in (20a–b) above). Any argument of the verb can in principle be selected as subject; but the preferred subject in a simple declarative sentence is the patient or Undergoer. A definite Undergoer will normally be selected as subject unless some other argument of the clause is fronted or extracted.

Actor voice is used when the Actor (i.e. the most prominent semantic role) of a clause is selected as subject. Objective voice is used primarily when the subject of the sentence is the patient. Note that in the past tense, or in potentive aspect (see sec. 4.2), the OV suffix *-on* is replaced by a zero allomorph. Instrumental voice is used not only for instrumental subjects, as in (20d), but also when the subject corresponds to the displaced theme of verbs such as 'give', 'throw', 'hang up', 'plant', 'put away', etc.

Dative voice has a very wide range of uses in Kimaragang. Its primary use is to mark the subject as the goal or recipient of a ditransitive verb, or as the beneficiary of a transitive verb. Dative voice is also used when the subject is the goal or stimulus of a verb of cognition, such as 'know', 'remember', 'feel', etc. It is used when the subject is the Undergoer of actions whose effect is distributed over a wide area, e.g. sweeping, washing, burning, flooding, etc.; and it is also used for the adversative, as in *n-a-patay-an do tanak* (PST-POT-die-DV GEN child) 'suffered the death of a child'.

A fifth voice category, not illustrated in (20), is locative voice. The locative voice marker is homophonous with the objective voice suffix *-on*. The two forms are distinct only in the past tense, where the objective voice marker becomes *-Ø* while locative voice retains the *-on*. Locative voice is used primarily when the subject of the sentence is the location or destination of an intransitive verb of motion, posture or position. It is also used with verbs denoting infestation or affliction, e.g. *g-in-iyuk-on* 'attacked by maggots' from the root *giyuk* 'maggot'; *gorigit-on* 'suffering from *gorigit*' (i.e. ringworm).

Kimaragang, like most Philippine-type languages, distinguishes three morphological cases: nominative, genitive and dative. As the examples in (20) illustrate, overt subjects always appear in nominative case while non-subject arguments carry semantically determined case marking. Dative case is used for goals, recipients, and locations, while genitive case is used for possessors, Actors, and instruments.

In some Philippine languages, non-subject Undergoers may be marked with either genitive or dative case depending on factors like definiteness and animacy. In Kimaragang, non-subject pronominal Undergoers take dative case while other non-subject Undergoer NPs (including personal names) are marked with genitive case.

The case-marking particles used for non-pronominal NPs are listed in (21). See Kroeger (1996b) for a discussion of the origins and distribution of the 'moveable *-t*' in these forms. As the table shows, the case markers have distinctive definite vs. indefinite forms (which are usually not distinguished in the glosses). Apart from existential clauses (section 3.2), the subject is rarely if ever indefinite. Thus the 'indefinite' nominative marker *o(t)* is most commonly used for generic subjects, as illustrated in (22), or in cleft sentences (see section 3.1.4).

(21)

	NOM	GEN	DAT
PERSONAL NAME MARKERS	*i*	*di*	*sid+i*
COMMON NOUNS (DEFINITE)	*i(t)*	*di(t)*	*sid*
COMMON NOUNS (INDEFINITE)	*o(t)*	*do(t)*	*sid*
COMMON NOUNS (UNIQUE REF.)	*a(t)*	*da(t)*	*ad*

(22) *Mangakan do tinanom ot giyuk.*
      AV.TR:eat GEN crops NOM maggot
      'Worms eat up our crops.'

The paradigm of pronominal forms is listed in (23). The 'emphatic' forms are used primarily in preverbal or other contrastive positions. They function as a special kind of NOM case. (The first person dual inclusive forms *toh* and *ditoh* are rarely used in the Tandek dialect.)

(23) **Pronominal forms**

	EMPHATIC	NOM	GEN	DAT
1 SG.	*yokuh*	*okuh*	*kuh*	*dogon*
2 SG.	*ikau*	*ikau/koh*	*nuh*	*dikau*
3 SG.	*yalo*	*yalo*	*yoh*	*dialo*
1 DUAL INCL.	*ikitoh*	*kitoh*	*(toh)*	*(ditoh)*
1 PL. INCL.	*itokou*	*tokou*	*daton*	*daton*
1 PL. EXCL.	*yokoi*	*okoi*	*yah*	*dagai*
2 PL.	*ikoo*	*ikoo/kou*	*duyuh*	*dikoo*
3 PL.	*yaalo*	*yaalo*	*daalo*	*daalo*

3.1.2 Word order

The examples in (20) and (22) illustrate several facts about normal word order in basic verbal clauses: the verb always comes first, pronouns almost always precede full NPs, and NP subjects tend to occur in clause-final position. The position of pronominal elements is fairly strictly determined by various constraints which will be discussed below. The relative order of full NPs, on the other hand, is relatively free. Some general preferences are noted here, but these can often be overridden by discourse effects.

There is a general tendency for NPs to precede PPs, and for genitive NPs to precede dative NPs. When the verb is marked for actor voice, the nominative Actor NP may either occur in final position, as in (22), or immediately after the verb, as in (24a). In other voices, the Actor NP normally precedes all other non-pronominal elements of the clause (24b). But non-human Actors, as well as inanimate effectors, may also occur after the subject (24c).

(24) a. *Minangagamit i mama do karabau.*
          PST.AV:catch NOM daddy GEN buffalo
          'Dad went to catch a buffalo.'

      b. *S-in-unsub-Ø di tama i Dondomon.*
          PST-drive.out-OV GEN father NOM Dondomon
          'Dondomon was driven away (from home) by his father.'

      c. *N-o-soruwang-Ø i botung yah do karabau.*
          PST-POT-invade-OV NOM rice.field 1pe.GEN GEN buffalo
          'A/some buffalo got into our paddy field.'

3.1.3 Second position clitics

First and second person nominative and genitive pronouns are second-position (or '2P') elements; that is, they must always follow the first constituent in their clause. In a normal verb-initial clause, this means following the verb, as illustrated in (20a–d): all four of those examples contain a pronominal Actor immediately following the verb.

When a negative or other adverbial element is fronted to preverbal position, 2P clitics will also precede the verb; this is exemplified in (25). In addition to pronouns, a variety of other particles also occur in this position, as seen in (25c):

(25) a. *Suwab-suwab* **okuh**   *manalu*   *do*   *pulut.*
          every.day   1s.NOM   AV.TR:tap GEN   rubber
          'Every day I tap rubber.'

      b. *Sid* *tana*   **yah**   *n-odop-on.*
          DAT   earth   1pe.GEN   PST-sleep-LV
          'We slept on the ground (after the house burned down).'

      c. *Amu*   **okuh**   **poh**   **dati**   *ko-guli*   *dot*   *suwab*
          NEG   1s.NOM   yet   probably   POT.AV-return   ADV   tomorrow
          sitih   *kumaraja.*
          PRX.LOC   AV:work
          'Tomorrow I probably cannot return to work here.'

Sentence-level conjunctions do not function as a part of the minimal clause, and so do not affect clitic placement. In the following example, the clause begins after the conjunction *bang*, and the 2P clitic pronoun occurs after the fronted location phrase *id tana*.

(26) *Bang* *[id* *tana*   **koh**   *monumpa...]*
       if   DAT   earth   2s.NOM   AV.TR:swear
       'If it is on the ground that you swear (an oath)...'

In Kimaragang, as in Tagalog, genitive pronouns always precede nominative pronouns. But unlike Tagalog, in Kimaragang a first person pronoun always precedes a second person pronoun. When these two principles are in conflict, e.g. when the subject is first person and the genitive Actor is second person, the ordering of first person before second person takes precedence, and the Actor is expressed in the dative rather than the genitive as in the following examples:

(27) a. *Ong* *taak-an* **okuh**   **dikau**   *do*   *siin,*
          if   give-DV   1s.NOM   2s.DAT   gen   MONEY
          potolibon   *tekaw(<kuh-ikau).*
          CAU:pass.by:OV   1s.GEN-2s.NOM
          'If you give me money I will let you go past.'

      b. *Tulung-ai*   **okuh**   **poh**   **dikoo**...
          help-DV.IMP   1s.NOM   yet   2p.DAT
          'Help me, all of you,...'

3.1.4 Topicalization and clefting

The examples in (25) and (26) involve clause-internal fronting, which can be identified by the preverbal position of the 2P clitics. There are also several different constructions which involve fronting an element to a position outside the clause. One of the most common is the TOPICALIZATION of the subject NP. The topic phrase is often followed by the particle *nga* 'but', as illustrated in (28), but this is not obligatory.

(28)   a.   *It*   *bowang*   *nga*   *l-um-aga*   *sid*   *dogon.*
　　　　　NOM   bear　　　but   AV-come   DAT   1S.DAT
　　　　　'As for the bear, he came after me.'

　　　b.   *It*   *tulun*   *kikiawi*   *dirih*   *nga*   *noko-ongoi*   *sirih*   *manabang.*
　　　　　NOM   people   all　　　ANAPH   but   AV.POT-come   there   AV.TR:help
　　　　　'All the people went there (to the burning house) to help out.'

　　　c.   *It*   *tiwanon*   *kuh*   *dirih*   *nga*   *sampai*   *m-in-ulau.*
　　　　　NOM   father.in.law   1S.GEN   ANAPH   but   until　　　AV-PST-crazy
　　　　　'As for my father-in-law, he went crazy (from grief).'

Another common subject-initial construction is the CLEFT SENTENCE, illustrated in (29). This construction is a special type of equative clause (see sec. 3.2), i.e. a clause in which both subject and predicate are NPs. The subject NP appears in initial position, followed by a headless relative clause which functions as the predicate.

(29)   a.   *Korikot*   *it*   *koturu*   *taddau,*
　　　　　arrive   NOM   seventh   day
　　　　　i   ***Sompuun***   *dirih*   *ot*   *mongoi*   *mongomot.*
　　　　　NOM   Sompuun   ANAPH   NOM   AV:go   AV.TR:harvest
　　　　　'When the seventh day came, it was Sompuun who went out to harvest.'

　　　b.   ***Doyokuh***   *nogi*   *o*   *sowo-on.*
　　　　　1S.EMPH   then   NOM   marry-OV
　　　　　'I was the one who was to be married (i.e. the bride).'

A third sentence pattern which involves a pre-clausal NP is the EXTERNAL TOPIC construction. This sentence type features a topic NP which is not the subject and need not be an argument of the main clause at all. In (30a), which contains an external topic followed by a cleft sentence, the topic phrase corresponds to the theme of the following verb. In (30b) the external topic is not an argument of the following clause but a possessor. This pattern is quite similar to the so-called 'double subject' construction found in many languages of east and southeast Asia.

(30)   a.   ***Kikiawi***   ***dit***   ***tarata***   ***di***   ***moleeng***   ***yoh,***
　　　　　all　　　GEN   property   GEN   parents   3S.GEN
　　　　　yalo   *ot*   *p-in-a-taak-an.*
　　　　　3S.NOM   NOM   PST-CAU-give-DV
　　　　　'As for all of his parents' property, he was the one it was caused to be given to.'

　　　b.   ***Kikiawi***   ***do***   ***tulun***   *nga*   *duwo*   *noh*   *ot*   *mato.*
　　　　　all　　　GEN   person   but   two   FOC   NOM   eye
　　　　　'All people have two eyes.'

3.2 Other clause types

In addition to the verbal clauses discussed in section 3.1, there are three other principal clause types in Kimaragang: (a) STATIVE clauses, in which the predicate is an adjective, common noun or locative phrase; (b) EQUATIVE clauses, in which the predicate is another NP; and (c) EXISTENTIAL clauses, which involve a special existential predicate.

Examples of the three kinds of stative predicates are given in (31a–c). In example (31d) the subject of a stative clause has been topicalized, while in (31e) the subject has been clefted.

(31)   a.   *A-wagat   itih   kadut.*
           ST-heavy   PRX.NOM   sack
           'This sack is heavy.'

       b.   *Kusai   ot   tanak.*
            man   NOM   child
            'The baby was a boy.'

       c.   *Sid   sarayo   it   walay   yah.*
            DAT   up.stream   NOM   house   1pe.GEN
            'Our house is up the river.'

       d.   *It   tongondu   nopoh   dirih   nga   bambarayon.*
            NOM   woman   only   ANAPH   but   rice.spirit
            'As for those women, they were really rice spirits.'

       e.   *It   tagad   daalo   noh   ot   a-gayo.*
            NOM   field   3p.GEN   FOC   NOM   ST-big
            'It was really their rice field that was the big one.'

As mentioned above, the EQUATIVE clause is one in which both subject and predicate are NPs. There is no copular verb in Kimaragang; the two NPs are simply juxtaposed, as in the following examples:

(32)   a.   *I   Pawai   noh   ot   orang.tua   sitih.*
            NOM   Pawai   FOC   NOM   head.man   PRX.LOC
            'Pawai is the head man here (i.e., of this village).'

       b.   *Ikau   gaam   ot   tanak   gulu?*
            2s.NOM   Q   NOM   child   eldest
            'Are you the eldest child?'

Kimaragang has three existential predicates. Two of these are positive (*waro* and *ki-*, both meaning 'exist' or 'have') and one negative (*aso*, or more rarely *amuso*, meaning 'not exist' or 'not have'). *Waro* and *ki-* appear to be semantically interchangeable, but *waro* is a free form while *ki-* is a prefix which must attach directly to the noun which heads the subject NP. These existential predicates may express either existence or possession.

(33)   a.   *Waro   noh   iso   kusai,   tanak   do   raja...*
            exist   FOC   one   man   child   GEN   king
            'There was once a man, the son of a king,...'

       b.   *Aso   tulun   sitih.*
            NEG.exist   person   PRX.LOC
            'There is no one here.'

       c.   *It   tongo   torigi   dirih   nga   aso   noh.*
            NOM   PL   house.post   ANAPH   but   NEG.exist   already
            'Even the house posts were gone (burned up).'

d. Waro   tanak   nuh   oy?
   exist   child   2s.GEN   Q
   'Do you have any children?'

e. *Ki-anak   nuh   oy?*
   exist-child   2s.GEN   Q
   'Do you have any children?'

f. *Aso   si-siin   kuh   ditih.*
   NEG.exist   RDP-money   1s.GEN   PRX
   'I don't have any money.'

3.3 Noun phrase structure

The basic order of elements in a Noun Phrase is given by the following rule:

(34) NP → Determiner (Number) N (Possessor) (Modifier)

where 'Determiner' may be either a case-marker or a demonstrative (which also marks case; see below); and 'Modifier' may be an adjective, PP, or relative clause. Plural number is optionally indicated by the particle *tongo*.

Post-nominal possessor phrases, whether pronouns or full NPs, appear in the genitive as in (35a–b). Possessors may also be expressed by a pre-nominal dative pronoun followed by the linking particle *do*, as in (35c–d):

(35) a. *it   tanak   di   Ampalan*   'Ampalan's child'
          NOM   child   GEN   Ampalan

      b. *it   paray   yah*   'our (excl.) rice'
          NOM   rice   1pe.GEN

      c. *dogon do tanak* (1s.DAT LK child)   'my child'

      d. *dagai do paray* (1pe.DAT LK child)   'our (excl.) rice'

As illustrated in (31a, e), most adjectives require the stative prefix *o-/a-* (see section 2.3.3 for a discussion of vowel harmony). When these adjectives occur as post-nominal modifiers, an additional prefix *t-* is added before the stative prefix (Kroeger 1996b). Note the contrast between the predicative and modifying forms of the adjectives in the following examples:

(36) a. *O-kodok   itih   walai   kuh.*   b. *walai   t-o-kodok*
          ST-small   PRX.NOM   house   1s.GEN   house   LK-ST-small
          'My house is small.'   'small house'

(37) a. *A-gayo   ilo   tanak   nuh.*   b. *tanak   t-a-gayo*
          ST-big   DIST.NOM   child   2s.GEN   child   LK-ST-big
          'Your child is big.'   'big child'

The Kimaragang demonstratives are listed in (38). In addition to the familiar three-way distinction in terms of distance from the speaker (proximal, medial and distal), Kimaragang also employs a fourth demonstrative *irih* to mark an NP which is a current topic of discussion. Demonstratives may either replace the case marker in NP-initial position, as indicated in (34) and illustrated in (36a) and (37a), or may appear at the end of the NP, as in (39).

When the demonstrative introduces the subject NP, the nominative form is used. In all other contexts, the 'general' form is used. Each demonstrative also has a corresponding locative form meaning 'here' or 'there'.

(38)

	NOM	GENERAL	LOC
PRX: this	*itih*	*ditih*	*sitih*
MED: that (near)	*inoh*	*dinoh*	*sinoh*
DIST: that (far)	*ilo*	*dilo*	*silo*
the aforementioned	*irih*	*dirih*	*sirih*

(39) *it*   *tanak*   *nuh*   *dilo*
      NOM   child   2s.GEN   DIST
      'that child of yours'

In fact the pattern in (39) is relatively rare. It is much more common for a single NP to contain two copies of the same demonstrative, one at the beginning and one at the end:

(40) a. *itih*   *sada*   *ditih*   'this fish'
          PRX.NOM   fish   PRX

      b. *ilo*   *tanak*   *nuh*   *dilo*   'that child of yours'
          DIST.NOM   child   2s.GEN   DIST

3.4 Relative clauses

A relative clause construction is a noun phrase which contains a clausal modifier. The modifying clause in Kimaragang always follows the head noun, as indicated in (34), and is introduced by the linker *dot*, glossed as REL for 'relativizer' in the examples below.

The most important restriction on relative clauses in Kimaragang, as in most languages of the Philippines and northern Borneo, is that only subjects can be relativized; that is, the head noun of the matrix NP must be interpreted as the subject of the modifying clause. This is indicated by the use of the appropriate voice marker on the verb, as well as the lack of any overt subject NP within the modifying clause. Thus example (41a), in which the relativized argument is the subject, is fully grammatical, while the corresponding example (41b) is ungrammatical because the relativized argument is not the subject. Similarly, in example (42a) the head noun 'son' must be understood as the agent of the modifying clause, because the subordinate verb 'slash' is marked for actor voice; but in (42b), the head noun can only be understood as the patient because the subordinate verb is marked for objective voice.

(41) a. *Lingkosu-on*   *duyuh=i*   *oi*
          boil-OV   2p.GEN=EMPH   Q
          [it   we'eg   dot   [inum-on   duyuh?]]
          NOM   water   REL   drink-OV   2p.GEN
          'Do you boil the water that you drink?'

      b. **it   we'eg   dot   [monginum   ikoo]*
          NOM   water   REL   AV.TR:drink   2p.NOM
          '(for: the water that you drink)'

(42) a. *Ontok   nopoh   dit   tanak   dot   [minonibas   dit   tidi   yoh]…*
      about   only   GEN   child   REL   PST.AV.TR:slash   GEN   mother   3s.GEN
      'As for the son who slashed (i.e. murdered) his mother,…'

   b. *Ontok   nopoh   dit   tanak   dot   [t-in-ibas-Ø   dit   tidi   yoh]…*
      about   only   GEN   child   REL   PST-slash-OV   GEN   mother   3s.GEN
      'As for the son who was murdered by his mother,…'

The modifying clauses in the preceding examples are verbal, but stative clauses are also common in this context. This stative type of relative construction is frequently used instead of a modifying adjective; compare the relative construction in (43a) with the equivalent modifying adjective in (43b):

(43) a. *kayu   dot   a-sawat*   'tree that is tall'
      tree   REL   ST-high

   b. *kayu   t-a-sawat*   'tall tree'
      tree   LK-ST-high

Relative clauses are frequent in natural discourse, and carry a large amount of the information content in some texts. Nested relatives, in which the modifying clause itself contains another relative clause construction, and serial relatives like that in (44), in which a single head noun is modified by a sequence of two or more modifying clauses, are not uncommon. The example in (44) also illustrates the normal method of introducing a new participant into a narrative discourse, through the use of an existential predicate plus relative clause construction.

(44) *Waro   noh   tulun   sirih   [dot   sinumambat   di   Majabou]*
    exist   FOC   person   ANAPH.LOC   REL   PST.AV:meet   GEN   Majabou
    [dot   amu   mongoo   mindakod   i   Majabou   sirih].
    REL   NEG   AV.TR:agree   AV:climb   NOM   Majabou   ANAPH.LOC
    'There were people there who met Majabou and wouldn't allow him to climb up there.'

3.5 Lexical categories (word classes)

'Major class' categories are often defined as those whose members function as heads of phrasal constituents. By this definition, the only major class categories in Kimaragang would be Noun and Verb. Nouns can head Noun Phrases, as discussed in section 3.3, and verbs can function as clausal heads.

It is not easy to distinguish between these two categories on the basis of distribution, for two main reasons. First, since Kimaragang has no copula, nouns can function as clausal predicates (section. 3.2). Second, the headless relative construction allows verbal clauses to appear in NP positions with the verb occupying the position of the head noun (at least in terms of surface word order). However, nouns and verbs can be distinguished from each other on morphological grounds in that verbs always carry some kind of voice marking (except for intransitive imperatives, where actor voice is marked by Ø-; see section 4.1.3). Further, only verbs can be inflected for tense, aspect, and mood. Another basis for distinction is that nouns are negated by *okon* 'not', while verbs and adjectives are negated by *amu* 'not'.

We have been speaking thus far of actual words. It is somewhat more difficult to distinguish noun roots from verb roots, because a number of noun roots can also be used as verbs. However, this is by no means true for all nouns; and in the cases where it is allowed, the meanings of these derived verbal forms are semantically unpredictable. The surest way of classifying roots seems to be that only noun roots can appear without affixation, especially in an NP position where Ø-marked imperatives would be impossible.

It is not yet clear whether there is a distinct category of adjectives, or whether adjectives are simply a special kind of intransitive verb. Virtually all adjective roots seem to allow productive verbal affixation to produce verbs meaning 'to become X' or 'cause to become X'. The same stative prefix which occurs with adjectives in their most basic usage is also used with unaccusative verbs (i.e. intransitive verbs with Undergoer subjects; see also section 4.2). The only way to distinguish these two classes seems to be that unaccusative verbs are frequently marked for past tense, whereas 'true' adjectives are not. It remains to be investigated to what extent this difference is predictable from the inherent semantic content of the root, and whether it is possible for native speakers to assign any interpretation to adjectives which do bear the past tense marker.

In any case, there is no constituent corresponding to an Adjective Phrase (like the English phrase *very big*) which can appear within an NP. Adverbs of intensity, such as *banar* 'really, very much' or *sabat* 'a little', only modify clausal predicates, whether verbal or adjectival. Many adjectives can also be used as adverbs of manner, subject only to semantic plausibility. Other adverbial elements include time words, the negative elements mentioned above, etc.

Some words which correspond to English prepositions have verbal morphology, e.g. *mantad* 'from' and *kuma'a* 'to', and might plausibly be analyzed as serial verbs. Others are clearly nominal and are normally preceded by the dative case marker, e.g. *pialatan* '(space) between', *toning* '(space) beside', *saralom* '(space) inside', *siba* '(space) below', etc. Only a few Malay loan words (e.g. *sampai* 'until', *masam* 'like') would justify the existence of a distinct Preposition category.

Kimaragang has a very large inventory of 'particles' expressing various concepts relating to aspect, mood, modality, evidentiality, discourse prominence, speaker's attitude, etc. Some of these are second position elements, as mentioned in section 3.1.3, others occur in sentence-final position, and others have a variable distribution. The two most common members of this class are the aspectual particles *noh* 'completive' and *poh* 'incompletive'. The completive particle *noh* is also used as a focus marker, e.g. to mark foregrounded events in narrative (Kroeger 1991) and fronted NPs in a cleft sentence.

Conjunctions, including words such as *nga* 'but', *jadi* 'so', *tu* 'because', *om* 'and', *ko* 'or', *kadung* 'if, when', *pagka* 'since, because', *insan ko* 'even, although', appear to form a distinct category. Words in this class have unique distributional properties, in that they occur at the beginning of the sentence or clause which they introduce but do not 'count' as part of the clause for purposes of 2P clitic placement.

Kimaragang possesses a fairly typical range of basic question words, including *isay* 'who', *nunuh* 'what', *sera* 'when', *piroh* 'how many', etc. But in addition there is an interrogative verb root *kuroh* which is used productively to derive more question words. Some of the most commonly occurring forms include: *nokuroh* 'why', *kukuroh* 'how', *kumuroh* 'what time, what age', *songkuroh* 'how much', *monguroh* 'doing what', *mikukuroh* 'how related' (e.g. kinship), *kumukuroh* 'how in the world', *okukuroh* 'what conditions' (in place), *pengkukuroh* 'in what manner, like what'.

4 VERBAL AFFIXATION

Voice is in many ways the pivotal category of Kimaragang verb morphology, and inter-acts with every other category. The table in (45) summarizes the forms of the voice mark-ers in the main tenses and moods. The declarative past and non-past forms were already discussed in section 3.1.1. The imperative and subjunctive moods are discussed in 4.1.3, the potentive in 4.2. Tense marking affixation is discussed in 4.1.1.

(45)	Voice Category	Non-past	Past	Imperative/ subjunctive	Potentive
	Actor (AV)	m-/-um-	m-in-/-in-um-	-Ø-	(no)ko-
	Objective (OV)	-on	-in-__-Ø	-oʔ	(n)o-
	Dative (DV)	-an	-in-__-an	-ai	(n)o- -an
	Instrument (IV)	i-	n-i-	–	(no)ko-
	Locative (LV)	-on	-in-__-on	–	–

Section 4.3 discusses the 'transitivity' prefixes, which index the affected argument of the clause, and sections 4.4 and 4.5 discuss some of the very rich inventory of derivational affixes.

4.1 Tense/aspect and mood

4.1.1 Tense

Kimaragang exhibits a simple two-tense system, past vs. non-past. The past tense marker is the infix -in-, inserted after the initial consonant of the base form (i.e., the stem plus all other affixes). Before vowel-initial forms, this infix reduces to a prefixed n-. Verb forms which lack this tense marker are interpreted as non-past, i.e. either present, future, or unmarked for time reference. The following examples illustrate this contrast.

(46) a. *M-in-ongoi   oku   sid   talob.*
          AV–PST-go   1s.NOM   DAT   market
          'I went to the market (some time in past).'

      b. *M-ongoi   oku   sid   talob   (ditih).*
          AV–go   1s.NOM   DAT   market   PRX
          'I am going to the market (right now).'

      c. *M-ongoi   oku   sid   talob   suwab.*
          AV–go   1s.NOM   DAT   market   tomorrow
          'I will go to the market tomorrow.'

In addition to these two basic tenses, there is a prefix *koo-* which marks immediate past tense, i.e. events which have only just taken place. Some examples:

(47) *koo-susu*   'just newly born'
      koo-rikot   'only just arrived'
      kaa-tanom   'only just planted'

These immediate past forms are usually unmarked for voice and often seem to function as gerunds, appearing in clauses which lack any nominative NP. However, immediate past forms are occasionally marked for objective or dative voice, taking the subjunctive form of the voice suffix (see section 4.1.3) as in the following example.

(48)   *Koo-boli-yai*   *kuh*   *yalo*   *dot*   *sigup,*
       IMM.PST-buy-DV.SUBJ   1s.GEN   3s.NOM   GEN   tobacco
       moki-boli   *kembagu.*
       AV.RQV-buy   again
       'I only just bought him some tobacco and he asks me to buy for him again.'

4.1.2 Repetitive/Iterative/Habitual aspect

As mentioned in section 2.4, vowel lengthening (or copying) is used to mark habitual aspect (see examples in (19)), while CV-reduplication is used for a variety of aspectual senses which I will subsume under the cover term ITERATIVE. This category is used for actions which are distributed in time or space. Most frequently it signals that the action is repeated many times or performed by many Actors, but it has several other uses as well. In the following example, the reduplication indicates not a series of repeated events but a single on-going activity, i.e. continuous aspect:

(49)   *Subai.ko*   *ipapat-an*   *inoh*   *parai*   *tu*
       necessary   RDP:guard-DV   MED.NOM   rice   because
       a-awi-Ø   *dati*   *do*   *manuk*   *moninduk.*
       POT-finish-OV   likely   GEN   bird   AV.TR:peck
       'You must continually guard the rice, otherwise the birds may eat it all up.'

   The iterative form can also be used to signal progressive aspect. In the following examples, reduplication is used in the second clause to mark an event that was taking place at some prior time specified in the first clause. These examples also illustrate contexts in which Kimaragang employs relative tense marking, since the reduplicated verb is not marked for past tense but takes its time reference from the preceding clause.

(50)   a.   *Neemot-Ø*   *kuh*   *i*   *baju*   *kuh,*
            PST:see-OV   1s.GEN   NOM   shirt   1s.GEN
            boboju-on   *di*   *Medol.*
            RDP:shirt-OV   GEN   Medol
            'I saw my shirt being worn by Medol.'

       b.   *I*   *noko-rikot*   *okuh,*
            NOM   PST.AV.POT-arrive   1s.NOM
            boboyuk-on   *dialo*   *i*   *tanak*   *yoh.*
            RDP:swing-OV   3s.DAT   NOM   child   3s.GEN
            'When I arrived, she was swinging her child (in a sarong sling).'

   (Note: third person agent pronouns sometimes appear in the dative form, as in (50b), rather than the expected genitive.)

4.1.3 Imperative and subjunctive moods

Imperative mood is indicated by reduced or modified forms of the voice markers, as shown in (45). When used in a command, the imperative verb is usually followed by an aspectual particle: either *poh* 'yet', which marks polite commands or requests, or *noh* 'already', which marks more abrupt or urgent commands. The addressee of an imperative sentence (the participant to whom the command is addressed) is normally a second person pronoun, which need not be overtly expressed if it is singular. The addressee is always the Actor of the sentence, but it need not be the subject. The choice of subject (normally the Undergoer if definite) is indicated by the voice marking of the imperative verb. Some examples are given below.

(51) a. *Ø-Uli*   *noh!*
          AV.IMP-return   already
          'Go home now!'

    b. *Pomo'og*   *poh!*
          Ø-poN-wo'og   poh
          AV.IMP-TR-wash   yet
          'Wash (your hands)!'

    c. *Lapak-o*   *poh*   *itih*   *niyuw!*
          split-OV.IMP yet   PRX.NOM coconut
          'Split this coconut!'

    d. *Boli-ai*   *okuh*   *poh* *do*   *tasin!*
          buy-DV.IMP 1s.NOM yet   GEN   salt
          'Buy me some salt!'

In addition to imperative sentences, the reduced voice markers listed in table (45) have two other principal uses. We will refer to these forms as SUBJUNCTIVES when they are used in non-imperative contexts. The first important use of the subjunctive form is as a 'narrative tense', i.e. to mark verbs expressing the main events in a narrative discourse. This usage is illustrated in the following sentence, taken from a folk-tale:

(52) **Ongoy-o** *noh* *di*   *tasi-asi* *om* **patay-o**   *noh*
      go-OV.SUBJ FOC GEN orphan   and kill-OV.SUBJ FOC
      om   **tunuw-ai**   *noh.*
      and   roast-DV.SUBJ FOC
      'The orphan boy fetched (the lizard) and killed it and roasted it.'

The other main use of the subjunctive is following the auxiliary verb *mangan*. This verb, often shortened to *maan*, with past tense forms *minangan*, *minaan*, or *naan*, is sometimes used alone as a kind of pro-verb meaning 'do something'. Its most frequent use, however, is as an auxiliary introducing a transitive action verb marked for objective or dative voice. In this construction the main verb must appear in the subjunctive form, as illustrated in the following examples.

(53) a. *Minaan*   **akan-o**   *do*   *tusing* *ilot*   *sada.*
          PST.AUX   eat-OV.SUBJ GEN cat   DIST.NOM fish
          'That fish was eaten by a cat.'

    b. *Naan*   *okuh*   **iit-ai**   *do*   *tompolulu'u.*
          PST.AUX 1s.NOM bite-DV.SUBJ GEN scorpion
          'I was stung by a scorpion.'

4.2 Potentive mode

The POTENTIVE mode is used primarily to encode a possible action, an unintended result, or unspecified time. It is indicated by the use of two markers, both of which have past vs.

non-past tense forms: *(n)o-* (a specialized use of the stative prefix) for objective and dative voice, and *(no)ko-* for actor and instrumental voice. (As mentioned in section 3.1, objective voice is realized by a zero-allomorph in the presence of the potentive prefix.) No examples of potentive verbs bearing locative voice have been found.

When focusing on the contrast between potentive forms and verbs which are unmarked for modality, I will refer to the unmarked verb forms as INTENTIVE. Sample verbs showing the contrast between intentive vs. potentive mode for each voice category are given in (54).

(54)	Voice	Intentive form		Potentive form		Gloss
		Non-past	Past	Non-past	Past	
	Actor	*mang-akan*	*m-in-ang-akan*	*ka-akan*	*naka-akan*	'eat'
	Objective	*lapak-on*	*l-in-apak-Ø*	*a-lapak-Ø*	*n-a-lapak-Ø*	'split'
	Dative	*t-aak-an*	*t-in-aak-an*	*a-taak-an*	*n-a-taak-an*	'give'
	Instrumental	*i-taak*	*n-i-taak*	*ka-taak*	*naka-taak*	'give'

All of the verb roots in (54) are transitive. Intransitive verbs have only a single core argument, so in the unmarked intentive mode all intransitives take actor voice affixation. When they are marked for potentive mode, however, a split emerges. One group, the UNERGATIVE type, take the actor voice form *(no)ko-*; this group includes verbs meaning 'run', 'fly', 'bathe', 'swim', 'sit', 'sleep', etc. The other group, the UNACCUSATIVE type, take the stative or objective voice marker *(n)o-*; this group includes verbs meaning 'fall', 'drift', 'die', 'be born', 'break', 'split', 'collapse', 'dissolve', etc. Various other morphosyntactic differences correlate with this split; see Kroeger (1990) for details.

There are two crucial semantic contrasts between potentive and intentive verbs. First, the unmarked intentive form of the verb entails that the Actor intended to perform the described action, while potentive verbs are neutral with respect to intention or volitionality. Thus in the following example, the potentive form in (55a) allows the accidental interpretation shown in the gloss, which in most contexts would be strongly preferred as the most plausible reading. The corresponding intentive form in (55b) does not allow this accidental reading, and can only be interpreted to mean that the poison was eaten intentionally. This contrast in volitionality is further illustrated in (56).

(55) a. *Naka-akan   do   rasun   i   tanak kuh.*
       PST.AV.POT-eat   GEN   poison   NOM   child 1s.GEN
       'My child accidentally swallowed some poison.'

    b. *Minangakan   do   rasun   i   tanak kuh.*
       -in-m-poN-akan   do   rasun   i   tanak kuh
       PST-AV-TR-eat   GEN   poison   NOM   child 1s.GEN
       'My child intentionally swallowed some poison.'

(56) a. *N-o-lo'o   yalo   mantad   sid   sawat   do   kayu.*
       PST-OV.POT-fall   3s.NOM   from   DAT   high   LK   tree
       'He fell out of a high tree.'

    b. *L-in-um-o'o   yalo   mantad   sid   sawat   do   kayu.*
       PST-AV-fall   3s.NOM   from   DAT   high   LK   tree
       'He jumped down out of a high tree.'

Second, the potentive form of a verb entails that the described event has actually taken place, that the result-state has actually been achieved. The intentive form, in contrast, is neutral with respect to the outcome of the action. In most contexts the intentive form creates a pragmatic implicature that the event actually took place, but this implicature can be denied as in (57a). However, with the corresponding potentive form this negation would lead to self-contradiction, as in (57b).

(57) a. *Minamatay*   *okuh*   *do*   *wulanut*   *nga*   *amu*   *minatay.*
          -in-m-poN-patay   okuh   do   wulanut   nga   amu   -in-m-patay
          PST-AV-TR-die   1s.NOM   GEN   snake   but   NEG   PST-AV-die
          'I (tried to) kill a snake, but it didn't die.'

      b. **Naka-patay*   *okuh*   *do*   *wulanut*   *nga*   *amu*   *minatay.*
          AV.POT-die   1s.NOM   GEN   snake   but   NEG   PST.AV:die
          '*I killed a snake but it didn't die.'

In addition to marking non-volitional actions, potentive mode is also commonly used to encode possibility or potentiality, as in the following examples:

(58) a. *Amu*   *ka-akan*   *yalo*   *tu*   *o-ruol*   *it*   *nipon*   *yoh.*
          NEG   AV.POT-eat   3s.NOM   because   ST-hurt   NOM   tooth   3s.GEN
          'He cannot eat because his tooth hurts.'

      b. *Amu*   *a-akan*   *itih*   *sada*   *ditih,*   *n-a-pasa*   *noh.*
          NEG   OV.POT-eat   PRX.NOM   fish   PRX   PST-OV.POT-rot   already
          'This fish cannot be eaten, it is rotten.'

Another important use is to indicate non-specific time reference. The following pair of examples provide a minimal contrast. When the question is asked using the potentive form (59a), the time reference is not specified; the addressee would be expected to answer 'yes' if he had ever in his life climbed the mountain. When the question is asked using the intentive form (59b), a specific time reference is implied which would be identified in the discourse context, e.g. a recent visit to Sabah. The addressee would be expected to answer 'no' if he had not climbed the mountain at the time under discussion, even if he had climbed it any number of times on other occasions.

(59) a. *Naka-takad*   *koh*   *noh*   *ad*   *limpapak*   *dat*   *Nabalu*   *oy?*
          PST.AV.POT-climb   2s.NOM   already   DAT   peak   GEN   Kinabalu   Q
          'Have you ever climbed to the top of Mt. Kinabalu?'

      b. *T-in-um-akad*   *koh*   *ad*   *limpapak*   *dat*   *Nabalu*   *oy?*
          PST-AV-climb   2s.NOM   DAT   peak   GEN   Kinabalu   Q
          'Did you climb to the top of Mt. Kinabalu?'

In a usage which seems related to indefinite time reference, the potentive mode is often used in adverbial time clauses in narrative or procedural discourse, referring back to the main verb of the preceding sentence: 'Having done X, . . .'

4.3 Affectedness

As mentioned in section 3.1.1, the Undergoer (i.e. the affected argument, or the argument which the speaker views as being acted upon) is the preferred choice of subject when it is definite. When the Undergoer is not selected as subject, the verb must carry an additional prefix which I will refer to as a TRANSITIVITY PREFIX.

The transitivity prefix indicates something about the semantic features of the Undergoer. The most common prefix, *poN-*, is used when the Undergoer corresponds to the patient, recipient or goal of the action. The prefix *po-* is used when the Undergoer is a displaced theme or instrument. (This prefix is homophonous with the causative prefix discussed in section 4.4 below, but I analyze them as being two distinct morphemes. In some closely related languages, it appears that both of these prefixes can co-occur in the same word.)

The prefix *poG-* is used only with a limited set of verb roots, and generally marks the Undergoer as being plural, non-individuated, or indefinite. For example, words for hunting and fishing usually take the prefix *poG-*, as illustrated in (60), because the hunted object cannot be specified (which wild pig? which fish?) while the action is taking place.

(60)   *m-pag-asu*   go hunting (with dog)
       m-pag-urab   go hunting (with blowgun)
       m-pag-apon   go fishing (with hook)

For some roots there is a minimal contrast between *poN-* and *poG-*, with *poN-* being used when the action is directed at a specific object, e.g. *mong-inum* 'to drink (something)', while *poG-* is used when the object is indefinite or non-individuated, e.g. *mog-inum* 'drink to get drunk (e.g. at a drinking party)'. But overall the semantics of *poG-* is complex and somewhat irregular, and will not be discussed further here. Rather, we will focus on the contrast between *poN-* and *po-*.

Where there are more than two participants involved in a given situation, the speaker may choose to adopt different 'perspectives' on the same action. In a certain context, the speaker may view one participant as being primarily affected or acted upon (e.g. *John loaded the hay on the cart*), while in a different context the speaker may view another participant as being primarily affected or acted upon (e.g. *John loaded the cart with hay*). The choice of transitivity prefix in Kimaragang reflects this same kind of alternation in the speaker's perspective, that is, an alternation in the identity of the Undergoer. Consider the following examples, based on the root *ta'ak* 'give' (note that actor voice is always expressed by a Ø-allomorph before *po-*):

(61)   a.   *Ø-pa-ta'ak   okuh   do   siin   sid   tanak   kuh.*
            AV-TR-give   1s.NOM GEN   money   DAT   child   1s.GEN
            'I give money to my child.'

       b.   *Mana'ak   okuh   di   tanak   kuh   do   siin.*
            m-poN-ta'ak   okuh   di   tanak   kuh   do   siin
            AV-TR-give   1s.NOM GEN   child   1s.GEN GEN   money
            'I give my child money.'

The act of giving involves three participants: an actor (the giver), a theme (the gift), and a recipient. In (61b), with the prefix *poN-*, the Undergoer is the recipient; the action is viewed as primarily affecting, or being directed towards, the recipient. This event must involve a change of ownership: the actor (giver) must be the original owner, and the recipient (i.e. the child) must become the new owner. In (61a) on the other hand, with the prefix *po-*, the Undergoer is the theme, i.e. the money. In this case there need not be any change of ownership, but there must be a physical transfer of possession. This change in perspective is also reflected in the case marking of the recipient: dative in (61a), but genitive in (61b).

The semantic contrast is illustrated more clearly in (62). The noun *tana* is ambiguous between the meanings 'land' and 'dirt'. Thus example (62a) could mean either 'I will give you some land' or 'I will give you some dirt'; but the former meaning is more likely, since the *poN-* form implies change of ownership and dirt is seldom given as a gift. However, the *po-* form in (62b) implies a physical transfer of possession. Since a piece of land cannot be physically moved (at least, not by human agency), example (62b) can only mean 'I will give you some dirt'.

(62) a. *Mana'ak   okuh   dikau   do   tana.*
        m-poN-ta'ak   okuh   dikau   do   tana
        AV-TR-give   1s.NOM   2s.DAT   GEN   earth
        'I will give you some land.'

    b. *Ø-pa-ta'ak   okuh   dikau   do   tana.*
       AV-TR-give   1s.NOM   2s.DAT   GEN   earth
       'I will hand you some dirt (*land).'

A similar alternation is observed in the following pair of examples. Sentence (63a) implies that there is one fish, or at least some definite number of fish; and the basket need not be completely filled. Sentence (63b) implies that the basket is completely filled, but there is an indefinite number of fish.

(63) a. *Ø-po-suwang   okuh   ditih   sada   sid   pata'an.*
        AV-TR-enter   1s.NOM   PRX   fish   DAT   basket
        'I will put this fish in a/the basket.'

    b. *Monuwang   okuh   do   pata'an   do   sada.*
       m-poN-suwang   okuh   do   pata'an   do   sada
       AV-TR-enter   1s.NOM   GEN   basket   GEN   fish
       'I will fill a basket with fish.'

The more common type of transitive verb (e.g. 'hit', 'break', 'cut', 'build', 'pound', etc.) involves minimally an actor and a patient, but may also involve an instrument. Normally the Undergoer will correspond to the patient. In this case the prefix *poN-* must be used whenever the subject is some argument other than the Undergoer, e.g. in actor voice (64a–b) or instrumental voice (64c). (Compare example (20b) above, which has the Undergoer as subject.)

(64) a. *Mangalapak   okuh   do   niyuw.*
        m-poN-lapak   okuh   do   niyuw
        AV-TR-split   1s.NOM   GEN   coconut
        'I will split a coconut/some coconuts.'

    b. *Monibas   yalo   do   kayu.*
       m-poN-tibas   yalo   do   kayu
       AV-TR-slash   3s.NOM   GEN   wood
       'He is chopping wood.'

    c. *Tongoh   ot   pangalapak   nuh   dilo   niyuw?*
       tongoh   ot   Ø-poN-lapak   nuh   dilo   niyuw
       what   NOM   IV-TR-split   2s.GEN   DIST   coconuts
       'What will you split those coconuts with?'

But under certain special circumstances the action may be viewed as affecting, or being directed at, the instrument rather than the patient. In such cases the instrument can be encoded as the Undergoer, as illustrated in (65). Sentence (65a) carries the implication that the speaker wants to test the sharpness or strength of the instrument (the axe), while sentence

(65b) implies that the speaker is threatening to damage the instrument. Example (20d) above shows an instrument Undergoer as subject, i.e. with the verb marked for instrumental voice.

(65)   a.   *Ø-pa-lapak   okuh   poh   ditih   kapak   nuh   do   niyuw.*
            AV-TR-split   1s.NOM   yet   PRX   axe   2s.GEN   GEN   coconut
            'I will (or 'Let me') split some coconuts with your axe.'

       b.   *Ø-po-tibas   okuh   poh   ditih   dangol   nuh   do   pampang.*
            AV-TR-slash   1s.NOM   yet   PRX   bush.knife   2s.GEN   GEN   stone
            'I will slash a stone with your bushknife.'

In this section we have considered primarily examples in the actor voice. However, the transitivity prefixes *poN-* and *po-* function in much the same way in other voices, whenever the Undergoer is not selected as subject. Moreover, these prefixes also play a role in certain transitivity alternations, e.g. the contrast between *m-ongoy* 'go' vs. *m-poN-ongoy* 'fetch'. See Kroeger (1996a) for a more detailed discussion of these issues.

4.4 Causative constructions

Causative verbs in Kimaragang are formed by adding the causative prefix *po-*. As is true in virtually all languages which have morphological causatives, the CAUSER becomes the Actor of the causative verb. Note the use of actor voice when the causer is selected as subject, as in (66). (Recall from section 4.3 that actor voice is always expressed by a Ø-allomorph before *po-*.) The CAUSEE in Kimaragang, i.e. the original Actor of the root verb, assumes the status of a patient. This is reflected in the use of objective voice when the causee is subject, as in (67).

(66)   a.   *Ogom   poh   sinoh,   Ø-po-odop   okuh   poh   ditih   tanak.*
            sit   yet   MED.LOC   AV-CAU-sleep   1s.NOM   yet   PRX   child
            'Have a seat while I put the baby to sleep.'

       b.   *Kadung   aa   kou   pendakod   dogon,   tibas-on   tekoo.*
            Kadung   aa   kou   Ø-po-indakod   dogon,   tibas-on   kuh-ikoo
            if   NEG   2p.NOM   AV-CAU-climb   1s.DAT   slash-OV   1s.GEN-2p.NOM
            'If you don't let me climb up there, I'll slash you all to pieces!'

(67)   a.   *Po-odop-on   kuh   poh   inoh   tanak   om   mituturan   nogi.*
            CAU-sleep-OV   1s.GEN   yet   MED.NOM   child   and   AV.RCP:story   then
            'I will put the baby to sleep first, then we'll talk.'

       b.   *Ilo   sawo   nuh   poolion   yah   noh.*
            Ilo   sawo   nuh   po-uli-on   yah   noh
            DIST.NOM   spouse   2s.GEN   CAU-return-OV   1pe.GEN   already
            'As for your wife, we are already allowing her to go home.'

All of the above examples involve intransitive verb roots. When a causative verb is derived from a transitive root, there is a potential conflict between the causee, as derived patient of the causative, and the original patient of the root predicate. This conflict is resolved by 'demoting' the original patient to instrumental status.

The following examples illustrate the voice marking possibilities with transitive causatives. When the causee is selected as subject (68), the verb takes objective voice. When the original patient is selected as subject (69), the verb takes instrumental voice. As noted above, the causer functions as Actor of these causative structures. But Kimaragang systematically prohibits the use of actor voice with causative verbs derived from transitive roots; thus the causer cannot be selected as subject in these examples.

(68) a. *Pa-akan-on   kuh   poh   i   Jaiwan   tu   witilon.*
          CAU-eat-OV   1s.GEN   yet   NOM   Jaiwan   because   hungry
          'I'll have Jaiwan eat something (i.e. give him something to eat) first, because he's hungry.'

      b. *Peenumo   i   tanak   nuh   ditih   tubat.*
          po-inum-o   i   tanak   nuh   ditih   tubat
          CAU-drink-OV.IMP   NOM   child   2s.GEN   PRX   medicine
          'Get your child to drink this medicine.'

(69) a. *Nunuh   ot   i-pa-akan   nuh   do   tanak   dot   s-um-usu   poh?*
          what   NOM   IV-CAU-eat 2s.GEN   GEN   child   REL   AV-nurse   yet
          'What will you feed a child that is still nursing?'

      b. *Nipeenum   di   Majabou   dit   tanak   yoh   it   gatas,*
          n-i-po-inum   di   Majabou   dit   tanak   yoh   it   gatas
          PST-IV-CAU-DRINK   GEN   Majabou   GEN   child   3s.GEN   NOM   milk
          it   nan   urud-o   dit   sawo   yoh   sid   mangkuk.
          NOM   AUX   express-OV.SUBJ   GEN   spouse   3s.GEN   DAT   bowl
          'Majabou let the child drink the milk which his wife had squeezed into the bowl.'

These examples accurately illustrate the voice marking patterns for transitive causative verbs. However, they are misleading in one respect: the pattern *po-V-on* illustrated in (67) and (68) is characteristic of causatives derived from (a) intransitive roots or (b) transitive roots belonging to the INGESTIVE class. Ingestive verbs are a special class of transitive roots whose Actor is in some way affected by the action. The class includes verbs of eating, drinking, smoking, etc. as well as certain verbs of perception and cognition. Some further examples are given in (70):

(70) a. *Po-sigup-o   okuh   poh!*
          CAU-smoke-OV.IMP   1s.NOM   yet
          'Give me a cigarette!'

      b. *Pentongo   poh   i   Janama   do   gambar   nuh!*
          po-intong-o   poh   i   Janama   do   gambar   nuh
          CAU-look.at-OV.IMP   yet   NOM   Janama   GEN   picture 2s.GEN
          'Show Janama your pictures!'

      c. *Pelo'on   okuh   poh...*
          po-ilo-on   okuh   poh...
          CAU-know-OV 1s.NOM   YET
          'Please inform me...'

With all other transitive roots, however, the causative prefix *po-* gets replaced by *poN-* when the causative verb is marked for objective voice (i.e. when the causee is subject). This pattern is illustrated in (71). But in instrumental voice the causative prefix is retained; thus the examples in (72), with root verb's patient selected as subject, involve the same affixation as those in (69).

(71) a. *Pangalapako   yalo   dinoh   niyuw.*
          poN-lapak-o   yalo   dinoh   niyuw
          TR-split-OV.IMP   3s.NOM   MED.GEN   coconut
          'Get him to split those coconuts.'

b. *Isai   ot   pong-owit-on   nuh   ditih   surat?*
   who   NOM   TR-carry-OV   2s.GEN   PRX   letter
   'Who will you get to carry this letter?'

(72) a. *N-i-pa-lapak   kuh   di   ama   it   niyuw   tu*
       PST-IV-CAU-split 1s.GEN GEN   father NOM   coconut because
       amu   l-in-apak-Ø   di   iyai.
       NEG   PST-split-OV   GEN   mother
       'I got Dad to split the coconut, because Mom wouldn't split it.'

   b. *N-i-po-owit   kuh   di   Janama   inoh   surat.*
       PST-IV-CAU-bring 1s.GEN GEN   Janama   MED.NOM   letter
       'I had Janama deliver the letter.'

Semantically, causative verbs are potentially ambiguous between a coercive reading, as suggested for (71a) above, and permission, as in (66b) and (67b). The following example highlights this fact, since it allows only a permissive reading:

(73) *Pa-ansak-on   poh   ilo   punti   om   akan-on   nogi.*
       CAU-ripe-OV   yet   DIST.NOM banana   and   eat-OV   then
       'Let those bananas ripen first and then eat them.'

4.5 Other derivational morphology

4.5.1 Requestives (poki-)

The prefix *poki-* forms REQUESTIVE verb stems. It has the basic meaning 'ask for', but can also be used with related meanings such as 'look for', 'want', etc. Within this range of meanings, the specific meaning assigned to the combination of *poki-* with a particular root is often somewhat idiosyncratic. Some roots unpredictably fail to combine with *poki-*; but on the whole the prefix is quite productive.

The Actor of the derived verb (the participant who does the asking or seeking) corresponds to the recipient, beneficiary or goal of the basic predicate. For example, the predicate *tuduk* 'show, teach' takes an agent, a theme and a recipient. The derived form *mokituduk* can be translated 'ask someone to teach you something'. As the translation suggests, the Actor of the derived form is the recipient of the base verb, i.e. the one to whom something is taught.

(74) a. *Mokituduk   okuh   do   boros   do   momogun   siddi   Pangadap*
         m-poki-tuduk okuh   do   boros   do   momogun   siddi   Pangadap
         AV-RQV-teach 1s.NOM GEN   word   GEN   Dusun   DAT   Pangadap
         'I am asking Pangadap to teach me the Dusun language.'

   b. *Isai   ot   poki-tuduk-an   nuh   do   boros   do   momogun?*
       who   NOM   RQV-teach-DV   2s.GEN   GEN   word   GEN   Dusun
       'Who are you asking to teach you the Dusun language?'

   c. *Nunuh   ot   poki-tuduk-on   nuh   siddi   Pangadap?*
       what   NOM   RQV-teach-OV   2s.GEN   DAT   Pangadap
       'What are you asking Pangadap to teach you?'

As the examples in (74) indicate, requestive verbs can occur in at least three voices. Actor voice is used to select the asker as subject, dative voice for the source or addressee (the person asked), and objective voice for the thing asked for.

With intransitive roots, the requestive form often carries the meaning 'ask permission to X'. With some noun roots, the requestive prefix can be added to mean 'search for X' or 'gather X'. Other noun roots which can take this prefix have less predictable meanings. Some commonly used examples of various types are listed in the following table, all in actor voice:

(75)

Root	Gloss	Requestive form	Gloss
anu	take	*mokianu*	ask for
patay	die	*mokipatay*	risk or seek death
waya	follow	*mokiwaya*	ask to accompany someone
atod	send, take	*mokiatod*	ask for a ride
suwang	enter	*mokisuwang*	seek to enter
gangot	firewood	*mokigangot*	gather firewood
lo'o	to fall	*mokilo'o*	search for windfalls (fruit)
gambar	picture	*mokigambar*	have one's picture taken
gunting	scissors	*mokigunting*	get a haircut
(t)ubat	medicine	*mokiubat*	seek medical treatment
sawo	spouse	*mokisawo*	ask to marry
rayow	praise	*mokirayow*	seek praise; show-off
ambaya	friend	*mokiambaya*	try to make friends with

4.5.2 Reciprocals and reflexives

There are no reflexive or reciprocal pronouns in Kimaragang. Reflexive and reciprocal actions are indicated by derivational prefixes on the verb, *pising-* and *pi-* respectively. The reciprocal prefix *pi-* requires that the subject of the verb be plural (or a dual pronoun), since the subject NP names a group whose members stand in some relation to each other. Partial reduplication of the stem often accompanies this prefix, but is not obligatory. Reciprocal verbs most often occur in the actor voice. The sentence in (76), taken from a traditional flood narrative, contains three such examples.

(76) *Leed.sule'ed*   *om*   *ko-pi-sa-sambat,*
after.long.time   and   AV.POT-RCP-RDP-meet

miboboros   *nopoh*   *nga*   *amu*   *ko-pi-arati.*
m-pi-bo-boros   nopoh   nga   amu   ko-pi-arati
AV-RCP-RDP-speak   only   but   NEG   AV.POT-RCP-understand
'A long time passed (after people were scattered in the world), and when they met each other, they would speak to each other but could not understand each other.'

When the verb is marked for some other voice, there must be an Actor which is distinct from the subject. This construction generally has causative semantics, with the Actor functioning as causer. The Actor need not be plural, but the subject must be expressed by a plural NP, since it is the subject which names the group involved in a reciprocal action or relation. Note that the subject must be given a plural interpretation even when it is not explicitly marked as being plural, as seen in (77a).

(77)   a.   *Nokuroh.tu*   *pi-ansap-on*   *nuh*   *inoh*   *dangol?*
       why   RCP-scrape-OV   2S.GEN   MED.NOM   bush.knife
       'Why are you scraping those bush knives against each other?'

b. *P-in-i-toning-Ø   kuh   it   sapi   om   karabau   Ø-po-ogot.*
PST-RCP-near-OV   1S.GEN   NOM   cow   and   buffalo   AV-TR-tie
'I tied up the cow and the buffalo near each other.'

The reflexive prefix *pising-* has a variety of uses, similar to the range of meanings associated with the middle voice in many languages; but in Kimaragang this affix must co-occur with one of the regular voice markers. The primary use of the reflexive prefix is with transitive verb roots. In this context, the effect of the prefix is to signal that the Actor and Undergoer of the action are the same individual. A few examples of this usage are given in (78). Notice that the final nasal in this prefix does not assimilate to a following obstruent.

(78)

Root	Gloss	Reflexive form	Gloss
garas	slaughter	*misinggaras*	slit one's own throat
patay	die, kill	*misingpatay*	kill oneself
timbak	shoot	*misingtimbak*	shoot oneself
tobok	stab	*misingtobok*	stab oneself
wanit	poison	*misingwanit*	poison oneself
lapis	slap	*misinglapis*	slap oneself
(t)ubat	medicine	*misingubat*	treat/medicate oneself
(o)wiyaw	full (of food)	*misingwiyaw*	to eat one's fill
rayow	praise	*misingrayow*	to praise oneself
gambar	picture	*misinggagambar*	take one's own picture

As these examples indicate, reflexive verbs almost always appear in the actor voice (*m-pising-* becoming *mising-*). However, this is not the only possible pattern. Note the use of dative voice in the following example, derived from the root *liyuw* 'to learn, study':

(79)   *Ombot   awasi,   irih   noh   pising-liyuw-an.*
where   good   ANAPH.NOM   FOC   RFL-learn-DV
'Whatever is good, that is what you should study.'

With intransitive verbs and adjectival roots, the reflexive prefix can have several possible uses: 'make oneself X', 'pretend to be X', 'intentionally X', 'be excessively X', etc. Some representative examples are given below:

(80)   a.   *Amu   mangakan   yalo,   mising-gagas.*
NEG   AV.TR:eat   3S.NOM   AV.RFL-skinny
'She won't eat, she is trying to slim down.'

b.   *Mising-ba-basag   yalo   mana'an   dilo   gangot*
AV.RFL-RDP-strong   3S.NOM   AV.TR:hold   DIST   firewood

dot   amimi-i   o-owit-Ø.
REL   NEG:RDP-EMPH   POT-carry-OV
'He is pretending to be strong by lifting that firewood when in fact he can't carry it.'

c.   *Mising-sa-sama   yalo   do   manan-tapi...*
AV.RFL-RDP-Bajau   3S.NOM   COMP   AV:put.on-sarong
'He is acting like a Bajau by wearing a sarong (spoken of a Kimaragang man).'

Transitive and unaccusative verb roots can occasionally be used in an intransitive actor voice form with a middle or reflexive meaning, e.g. *sumiddang* 'to sunbathe', derived from the transitive root *siddang* 'to dry (something) in the sun'; and *gumaras* 'slit one's own throat', from the root *garas* 'slaughter'.

4.5.3 Other verbal affixes

Kimaragang has a considerable number of other derivational affixes, but only a few of them can be mentioned here. The prefix *ponoN-* changes noun roots into verbs which usually have the meaning 'to use, wear, put on X'. Some examples in actor voice are listed in (81); see also (80c).

(81)	Root	Gloss	Derived form	Gloss
	tapi	sarong	*manantapi*	wear a sarong
	kasut	shoe	*manangkasut*	wear shoes
	tiyan	stomach	*monontiyan*	be pregnant
	sawo	spouse	*manansawo*	(of man) to marry a woman
	ama	father	*manangama*	address or regard as father

The desiderative prefix *ti-* attaches to verb stems to form new verbs meaning 'want to X'. Some examples are given in (82). With most transitive roots, the *ti-* form includes one of the transitivity prefixes, but at least some ingestives appear to be exceptions to this pattern. A single example (*ti-odop-on* 'sleepy') has been found which includes a suffix.

(82)	Root	Gloss	Desiderative	Gloss
	sobu	urine	*tisobu*	feel need to urinate
	sayau	dance style	*tisayau*	want to dance
	odop	sleep	*tiodop*	want to sleep
	binit	pinch	*tipominit*	feel the urge to pinch
	apuy	fire	*tipagapuy*	want to light a fire
	akan	eat	*tiakan*	want to eat

The prefix *obing-* attaches to verb roots to produce adjectives meaning 'prone to X'. Some examples are given in (83). As with the reflexive prefix, the final nasal in this prefix does not assimilate. With some roots the dative voice suffix can co-occur, as shown in (84).

(83)	Root	Gloss	Derived form	Gloss
	babak	shatter	*obingbabak*	fragile, easily broken
	rasak	dried up	*obingrasak*	prone to dry up (river)
	rasang	angry	*obingrasang*	quick to anger, hot-tempered
	tigog	startled	*obingtigog*	easily startled
	labus	escape	*obinglabus*	prone to escape
	tarabang	help	*obingtarabang*	quick to help

(84)	*peet*	bitter	*obingpeet*	quickly becomes bitter (e.g. rice wine)
			obingpeetan	(person) very sensitive to bitter taste
	lonit	swell up	*obinglonit*	prone to swell (e.g. feet)
			obinglonitan	prone to suffer swelling (e.g. allergic person)

Another prefix, *otug-*, is used with similar meaning in a few forms, e.g. *otug-oling* 'forgetful'; *otug-irak* 'quick to laugh'.

ACKNOWLEDGMENTS

I would like to thank my colleague Jim Johansson, who provided much of the data for this study and collaborated on the analysis at a number of points. Thanks also to the editors of this volume, Nikolaus Himmelmann and Sander Adelaar, for their very helpful suggestions. Of the many Kimaragang friends who have helped in many different ways, special thanks are due to Janama Lantubon and Welin Ibal.

REFERENCES

Banker, J.E. and Banker, E. (1984) 'The Kadazan/Dusun language', in J.K. King and J.W. King. (eds) *Languages of Sabah: a survey report*, 297–324, Canberra: Pacific Linguistics.
Blust, R.A. (1998) 'The position of the languages of Sabah', in L. Bautista (ed.) *Pagtanaw: Essays on language in honor of Teodoro A. Llamzon*, 29–52, Manila: Linguistic Society of the Philippines.
Clayre, B.M. (1966) 'A comparison of some dialects of Dusun', *Sabah Society Journal* 3:3–12.
Hurlbut, H. (1988) *Verb morphology in Eastern Kadazan*, Canberra: Pacific Linguistics.
Kroeger, P.R. (1985) 'Linguistic relations among the Dusunic groups in the Kota Marudu district', *Borneo Research Bulletin* 17.1:31–46.
——(1988a) 'Verbal focus in Kimaragang', in H. Steinhauer (ed.) *Papers in Western Austronesian linguistics No. 3*, 217–240, Canberra: Pacific Linguistics.
——(1988b) 'Case marking in Kimaragang causative constructions', in H. Steinhauer (ed.) *Papers in Western Austronesian linguistics No. 3*, 241–276, Canberra: Pacific Linguistics.
——(1990) 'Stative aspect and unaccusativity in Kimaragang Dusun', *Oceanic Linguistics* 29.2:110–131.
——(1991) 'The event line in Kimaragang narrative', in S. Levinsohn (ed.) *Thematic continuity and development in languages of Sabah*, 93–104, Canberra: Pacific Linguistics.
——(1993) 'Kimaragang phonemics', in M.E. Boutin and Inka Pekkanen (eds) *Phonological descriptions of Sabah languages*, 31–45, Sabah Museum Monograph no. 4, Kota Kinabalu: Sabah State Museum.
——(1994) 'Vowel harmony systems in three Sabahan languages', in P. Martin (ed.) *Shifting patterns of language use in Borneo*, 279–296, Borneo Research Council Proceedings Series vol. 3.
——(1996a) 'The morphology of affectedness in Kimaragang Dusun', in H. Steinhauer (ed.) *Papers in Austronesian Linguistics No. 3*, 33–50, Canberra: Pacific Linguistics.
——(1996b) '*Asu* vs. *Tasu*: On the origins of Dusunic moveable *t-*', in J.T. Collins (ed.) *Language and Oral Traditions in Borneo*, 93–114, Borneo Research Council Proceedings Series vol. 2.
Prentice, D.J. (1971) *The Murut languages of Sabah*, Canberra: Pacific Linguistics.
Smith, K.D. (1984) 'The languages of Sabah: a tentative lexicostatistical classification', in J.K. King and J.W. King (eds) *Languages of Sabah: a survey report*, 1–49, Canberra: Pacific Linguistics.
Wurm, S.A. (1983) 'Map 41', in S.A. Wurm and S. Hattori (eds) *Language Atlas of the Pacific Area*, Canberra: Pacific Linguistics.

CHAPTER FIFTEEN

BELAIT

Adrian Clynes

1 INTRODUCTION

Belait is a little-described language spoken in Brunei Darussalam in a small number of villages in the Belait and Tutong districts, in the western and central areas of the country respectively. The Belait were formerly longhouse dwellers: the last longhouses are said to have been abandoned in the 1950s. Until recently the culture revolved around the cultivation of sago palm and rice. Speaker numbers were estimated at 700 by Martin (1995). Belait is now only very rarely learnt as a first language.

Belait is most closely related to languages and dialects spoken along tributaries of the lower Baram river in nearby Sarawak, such as Kiput, Narum and Miri – grouped by Blust (1974, 1997) in the Lower Baram subgroup of his North Sarawak group. The Tutong language, spoken in central Brunei, is also a member of the Lower Baram subgroup, although it is less closely related to Belait. Within Brunei, there are at least four mutually comprehensible dialects, differing mainly in details of phonology and lexis. Speakers are found in two discontinuous areas. The first area, with by far the largest number of speakers, is that centered until recently in the inland Belait district around Kuala Balai and Labi villages; these have distinct but closely related dialects. In the past fifty years many speakers have moved from these villages to the coastal oil towns of Seria and Kuala Belait. The second area is in the inland Tutong region, in the Kiudang subdistrict. Two distinct dialects of Belait, Metting and Bong, are found in the single village of Mungkom in Kiudang, spoken by perhaps 100 and 10 speakers respectively. The common term for the language across dialects is *tau(') kitah*, literally 'our speech'. 'Belait', the officially used name in Brunei, is originally an exonym and is not used by speakers from outside the Belait district.

The ancestors of the Belait people originally lived on a tributary of the Baram in present-day Sarawak. Hughes-Hallet (1980) estimated that they came to Brunei in the nineteenth century, probably some time between 1830 and 1890. One oral tradition has it that this was to escape the expanding and warlike Kayan ethnic group. Many Belait still have family ties in the Baram area (Noor Alifah Abdullah 1992, 1995, Peter Sercombe p. c.). Another not incompatible oral tradition also from the Belait district is that the Belait are descended from the former inhabitants of the Belait region, speakers of another language, 'Dusun', which was displaced by that of the arrivals, 'Metting'. Over time the newly acquired language came to be called Belait, but it is 'really' Metting (Noor Alifah Abdullah 1995). The Tutoh River, a tributary of the Baram close to the Brunei border, is referred to in Kenyah as the Metting (Martin 1990a), and in Berawan as the Lamating (Nelson Kalang, p. c.). According to Noor Alifah Abdullah (1995), some Belait speakers identify another Baram tributary, the Tinjar, with the original Metting river. The name *Metting* ([mətteŋ ~ məttɪŋ]) is still used as an autonym in Kiudang (*tau' Metting* 'Metting language', *idih Metting* 'Metting people'). All dialects of Belait are now threatened with extinction, with the language, like other minority languages in Brunei, being displaced by Brunei Malay (see §5 below).

Very little has been published on Belait. Wordlists are found in Ray (1913), where it is called *Lemeting* (as pointed out in Martin 1990a), in Martin (1990a) and in Nothofer (1991). Noor Alifah Abdullah (1992), an unpublished BA thesis at Universiti Brunei Darussalam, contains extensive texts in the Labi dialect. A monolingual dictionary of the Kuala Balai dialect is currently being prepared by Dato Kifli bin Bujang. Muhamad Islam Abdullah (1997) has some limited data on the Bong dialect. Kumanireng (1995) is a first sketch of verbal morphology. Martin has published on the history and ethnolinguistic situation of Belait speakers, and particularly on reasons for language shift (1995, 1996). Ethnographic writings on the Belait include Hughes-Hallet (1980), Harrisson (1958), Noor Ehsan Hj Noor Kaseh (1983), Ak Johani Pg Pungut (1983), Pudarno (1993). Relevant works on related languages include Blust (1974, 1997), Nothofer (1991) and Clayre (1996).

The present description, still preliminary in many respects, is of the Metting dialect, spoken in Kiudang, Tutong district, using data collected by the author from two fluent first-language speakers, Awang Kumpoh Labu and Dayang Dayang Agal, born in 1930 and 1938 respectively. As well, some data from the Labi and Kuala Balai dialects is given. Labi data derives exclusively from Noor Alifah Abdullah (1992) and (1993), Kuala Balai data from the author's fieldnotes.

2 PHONOLOGY

As with other Lower Baram languages (Blust 1974), Belait phonology offers a variety of descriptive challenges, due amongst other things to widespread free variation and partially overlapping realizations of phonemes. (These make the devising of an orthography acceptable to native speakers an equally challenging task.) Previous sketch descriptions of the phonology are Martin (1990b, Metting dialect) and Noor Alifah Abdullah (1992, Labi dialect).

2.1 Segments

Metting Belait is analysed here as having five monophthong vowels /i, u, e, o, a/, represented straightforwardly in the orthography as <*i, u, e, o, a*>, and one diphthong, /iə/ <*ie*>. In the absence of clear evidence, vowel length is not assumed to be distinctive in Metting Belait, though for the Labi dialect Noor Alifah Abdullah (1992) claims a length distinction for the vowels /i, i:/, /a, a:/ and /u, u:/, plus several diphthongs and triphthongs (see also Blust 1974 for similar analyses of related Baram varieties). The Metting dialect is similarly rich in diphthongs at the phonetic level, but (with the exception of /iə/) these are treated here as either non-distinctive realizations of monophthongs, or vowel-glide sequences. Note that the examples from Labi dialect, while taken from Noor Alifah (1992), are given in the present author's orthography, rather than in the original variable phonetic transcriptions, except as noted.

Phoneme /e/ is realized as [ə] in most non-final syllables, and as [ɛ] or [e] in (i) final syllables and (ii) in non-final syllables where /e/ also occurs in the final syllable. In the phonetic realization of the vowel phonemes, there is considerable optional diphthongization. The front vowels generally have a schwa offglide before dorsal or glottal consonants: *appe'* [ɐppeˀʔ] 'father (term of address)', *belalik* [bəlaliˀq] 'moon, month', *buik* [buiˀq ~ buyəq] 'flower'. Labi and Kuala Balai often (but variably) have [ya] in final syllables where Metting has [a], including in recent loanwords: [kyat] (Labi), [kad] (Metting) 'card'; [malyar] (L), [malaʁ]'always' (from Malay *malar* 'constant, always').

The vowels also show a variety of partially overlapping realizations or free variation, in the speech of a single speaker:

1 In final syllables the realizations of the high vowels /i/ and /u/ partially overlap with those of the mid, non-central vowels /e, o/. Both /i/ and /u/ vary freely in the range high to mid-low, thus /i/ [i ~ e ~ ɛ]: *durri* 'run' [duʁʁi(:) ~ duʁʁe(:) ~ duʁʁɛ(:)], *tuliw* 'body' [tulɪw ~ tulew ~ tulɛw]; and /u/ [u ~ o ~ ɔ]: *semmut* 'AV:meet' [səmmut ~ səmmot ~ səmmɔt], *mukkut* 'AV:suck' [mukkut ~ mukkot ~ mukkɔt]. The mid non-central vowels /e/ and /o/ are also realized with mid-low, [ɛ(:), ɔ(:)] to mid-close realizations [e(:), o(:)]. They are however distinguished from the high vowels, since they do not have high realisations: *ture* 'female' [tuʁɛ ~ tuʁe], but never *[tuʁi]; *mukot* 'hit with fist' [mukɔt ~ mukot], never *[mukut], *kratod* 'k.o. frog' [kratɔd ~ kratod], never *[kratud].

2 The high front vowel /i/ moreover often 'breaks' or diphthongizes in final syllables. This, together with the variation described in the previous paragraph, leads to a multiplicity of variant realizations by the same speaker: *kulit* 'skin' [kulɪt ~ kulyɪt ~ kulet ~ kuleyt ~ kulyet...], *tuliw* 'body' [tuliw ~ tulyiw ~ tulyew ~ tulyɛw ~ tuleow...], *blabiw* 'rat' [b(ɐ)labiw ~ b(ɐ)labyew...].

3 In non-final syllables underlying /a/ varies freely between [a ~ ɐ ~ ə]: *mattang* 'AV: say, pronounce' [mattaŋ ~ mɐttaŋ ~ məttaŋ]; however /e/ in the same context is realized as [ə], never as [ɐ ~ a], thus *seggim* 'morning' [səggɪm], not *[saggim].

4 In non-final syllables /e/ may vary with /i/, thus *seggim* or *siggim* 'morning' [səggɪm ~ sɪggɪm ~ siggɪm], *tejjih* or *tijjih* '3s.NSBJ' [təjjɪh ~ tɪjjɪh ~ tijjɪh], *nesaw'* or *nisaw'* 'UV:use'.

Still, despite the high degree of variation described in the preceding paragraphs, an underlying phonological representation can be posited for each morpheme. The reader should be aware though that the orthography used in this description abstracts away from these variable phonetic realizations, which are common to all dialects of Belait, and to other Lower Baram languages, see Blust (1974). Beatrice Clayre (p. c.) suggests that such phonetic variability is a wider areal feature in Sarawak.

The consonant phonemes of Metting Belait are given in Table 15.1:

TABLE 15.1: BELAIT CONSONANT PHONEMES (METTING DIALECT)

	Labial	Apical	Laminal	Dorsal	Glottal
Oral stops, voiceless	p	t	c	k	ʔ<'>
Oral stops, voiced	b	d	ɟ<j>	g	
Nasal stops	m	n	ɲ<ny>	ŋ<ng>	
Fricatives			s	ʁ<r>	h
Laterals		l			
Glides	w		j<y>		

All dialects share this inventory, though phoneme /r/, a dorsal fricative in Metting, is an alveolar trill or tap in other dialects. The orthographic symbols used to represent ɲ, ŋ, ɟ j, ʁ and ʔ are given in angled brackets in Table 15.1. The apicals are generally alveolar, the laminals alveolar to post-alveolar. /s/ patterns with the other laminals, not as an apical. /t/ can be realized as a dental affricate word-finally; /s/ is usually dental or alveolar, but is often post-alveolar before /i/ and /e/. The dorsals /k/, /g/ and /ŋ/ have generally uvular realizations word-finally; otherwise they have velar realizations.

Phonetically long consonants realise geminate sequences (clusters of two identical consonants) in Belait, see discussion below.

/c/ is relatively uncommon, particularly word-initially and is often replaced by /s/ in loanword adaptation and diachonic change: *sesseng* 'ring' (cf. Malay *cincin* 'id.'), *using* 'cat' (cf. Brunei Malay *ucing* 'id.') *seremin* 'glass'(cf. Malay *cərmin* 'id.'). On the other hand, /ŋs/ sequences in cognates or loans from other languages typically correspond to /cc/ clusters in Belait: *acca'* 'goose' (cf. Malay *angsa* 'id.'), *geccak* 'bronze food stand' (cf. Malay *gangsa* 'bronze'), *meccin* 'faint' (cf. Malay *pingsan* 'faint').

As with the vowels, some distinctive contrasts between consonants are partly neutralized in certain contexts. For example:

1 /k/ and /ʔ/: /k/ is realized as either uvular [q] or glottal [ʔ] word-finally, e.g. /anak/ 'child' [ana:ʔ ~ ana:q] However /ʔ/ is never realized as [k] or [q], thus /anaʔ/ 'may' [ana:ʔ], never *[ana:q].
2 /h/ and /ʔ/ both contrast morpheme-finally with their absence (*lay* 'male', *lay'* 'to'; *mara* 'dry', *marah* 'AV:burn'. Nonetheless, they both often elide in that environment, when not phrase-final.
3 Geminate consonant sequences may reduce to a single segment in rapid speech.
4 Nasal-obstruent sequences may elide to a geminate sequence, either of two nasals, *n-embit* 'UV-take'[nəmbeyt ~ nəmmeyt], or of two obstruents, *p-embit* 'CAU-take' [pəmbeyt ~ pəbbeyt].

2.2 Morpheme and syllable structure

Lexical roots are typically disyllabic, though monosyllabic and trisyllabic roots also exist: *tak* 'snap (intr), be cut off (of phone)', *namumbot* 'wasp', *kababik* 'butterfly'. No examples of quadrisyllabic roots have been noted. Since Belait words often consist of a root and at least one monosyllabic affix, derived lexemes of three syllables frequently occur. See also §2.3 on the preferred size of derived lexemes. Stress is predictably on the final syllable.

At the syllable level, there are different possibilities of segment occurrence according to whether a syllable is final or non-final. Final syllables in Metting Belait have the shape $(C)V_F((C)C))$. V_F can be any vowel. The sequence [iə] which occurs in final open syllables is here analysed as a diphthong /iə/: *padie* 'fishing rod'(cf. *padi* 'paddy'), *pidie* 'difference', *lussie* 'AV:take off (e.g. clothing)'. The onset consonant may be any consonant except /h/ (one exception noted, *ohon* 'classifier for fruit and flowers'). Labi and Kuala Balai allow onset clusters in final syllables, in one case only: they have [n.dr] where Metting has medial [n.d]: *mandaw'* (M), *mandraw'* (L) 'bathe'; *andaw* (M), *andraw* (L) 'day'; *sundab* (M), *sundrab* (L) 'clear land by burning'. A final-syllable coda can be filled by any single consonant except the laminals /c/, /j/, /ɲ/, /s/ occurs only rarely in this position. Coda clusters are restricted to the sequences /yʔ/ and /wʔ/: *ulay'* 'carry', *ukaw'* 'head', *siw'* 'below'.

Non-final syllables have the structure $((C)(C))V_{NF}(C)$. Only the vowels /a, e, i, u/ are distinctive in non-final syllables. While /a/ and /e/ contrast (*messa'* 'AV:bite', *massa'* 'cooked (intr)'), they have partly overlapping realizations in non-final syllables, with /a/ being realized in the mid-central area at times (see discussion of vowels above). [i] varies freely with [e], and [u] with [o]. Onset clusters occur only word-initially in Metting Belait. Simple onsets may be filled by any consonant except /h/; the glides /w/ and /y/ hardly occur in this position. The second element in an onset cluster is either /l/ or /r/ (*brungun* 'classifier for animals', *blabiw* 'rat'). Phonetically other clusters also often occur initially, though these are here taken to be underlyingly medial: *endong* [(ə)ndɔŋ] 'nose', *embay* [(ə)mbay] 'what', *ejjiw'* [(ə)jjiwʔ] 'tail', *ellit* [(ə)llit] 'cooked sago'. C$_{coda}$ is either a nasal homorganic with a following obstruent, or the first of two identical ('geminate') consonants. The main nasal-obstruent sequences are /mb/ and /nd/: *embah* 'which?', *timbak* 'stab'; *andaw* 'day', *nundek* 'AV:clear.land'; some morphemes with /mp/ also occur: *empay'* (or *meppay'*) 'nine'. Otherwise nasal-obstruent sequences generally do not occur, compare Belait *kappung* 'village' with Malay *kampung*; Belait *lappung* 'lamp' with Brunei Malay *lampung*; Belait *mukkom* 'place name' with Brunei Malay *mungkom*; or Belait *acca'* 'goose' with Malay *angsa*.

Geminate sequences may be of any consonant except *w*, *y* or *h*. Geminates are clusters and not unit phonemes in Belait. Evidence for this comes from syllabification tests (e.g. [kʊd.dʊq]'sit', not *[ku.d:ʊq]). It is also indicated by optional syllable-final devoicing in Labi dialect. In Labi dialect voiced obstruents in word-final position are often optionally realized as voiceless *patad* or *patat* 'accompany, bring', *kised* or *kiset* 'shift'. The same devoicing, also optional, is found with the first element of certain medial geminate sequences: *addiw* or *atdiw* '(be) many', *nepbit* or *nebbit* 'learn', *sikgim* or *siggim* 'morning'. The simplest explanation, one consistent with syllabification tests in the Metting dialect, is that geminate sequences must lie across a syllable boundary.

Morpheme-internally gemination of consonants is predictable after schwa (see examples above); after other vowels occurrence of geminate clusters is not predictable: *marat* 'AV:strike with side of fist', *marrat* 'AV:pull, tug', *puttay* 'banana', *putay'* 'white'. Gemination does not occur after schwa in prefixes and infixes in the Metting dialect: *ngesseng (N-kesseng)* 'AV:laugh', but *k[en]esseng* 'UV:laugh'; *s[en]uka'* 'UV:like', *t[en]ite* 'UV:leave'; *me-rato* [məratɔ] 'one-hundred', *se-durung* 'one-moment'.

2.3 Phonological alternations

In contrast to the considerable variation in phonetic outputs noted above, there are few phonological alternations in Belait. One manifestation of Actor voice (§4) is the replacement of an initial, usually voiceless, obstruent by a homorganic nasal *mulah (N-pulah)* 'AV:plant', *nugil (N-tugil)* 'AV:dibble', *ngesseng (N-kesseng)* 'AV:laugh', *nyusor (N-susor)* 'AV:playgong (in mourning)'. A similar alternation optionally occurs with the final nasal segment in the irrealis/imperative proclitic *an* 'IRR:make/do' (cf. §3.7), though this time without loss of the root-initial consonant: *am=pulah* 'plant [it]!', *ang=kadem* 'turn [it] off!'.

Of three reduplication patterns noted, only the first has been found in all three dialects:

(i) The entire base is copied. The base may be a single morpheme: *matay-matay* (RDP-be.dead) 'dead (pl)'; *semmi'-semmi'* (RDP-be.near) 'come nearer', *mengngod-mengngod* (RDP-be.young) 'young (pl)'; *kajew-kajew rajjih-rajjih* (RDP-tree RDP-be.big) 'big trees'. Or else it may be morphologically complex, with a prefix or infix: *k[in]an-k[in]an* (RDP-UV:eat) 'eat (pl)'; *pa'ut-pa'ut* (RDP-[CAU:fear]) 'frighten', from underlying (nonoccurring) /pe-ba'ut/.

(ii) In Labi and Kuala Balai dialects, just the first CV sequence of a monomorphemic base may be copied *tu-tubbiw* (RDP-origin) 'at first'. In a variant of this pattern, /e/ replaces the vowel of the base: *se-said* (RDP-sick) 'very sick, sick (durative)'.

(iii) All but the final consonant of the base is copied: *milay-milay'* (RDP-AV:choose) 'be.choosey'; *seggi-seggim* (RDP-morning) 'very early in the morning'; *rinu-rinut* (RDP-be.slow) 'do.slowly'. The base may be complex, as in *milay-milay'*. So far this pattern has been noted in Metting dialect only. The examples here are all with disyllabic bases.

Forms like *ti-tik* 'small (pl.)' are ambiguous between reduplication types (ii) and (iii). No trisyllabic or longer bases with type (iii) reduplication have been noted so far.

Where the causitive affix *pe-* (§4.3) attaches to a root with an initial labial consonant, it 'replaces' that consonant: *ba'ut* 'afraid', *pa'ut* (CAU:afraid) 'frighten'; *melley* 'AV:buy', *pelley* (CAU:buy) 'sell'; *messap* 'AV:drink', *pessap* 'cause to drink'.

Just as simple morphemes are generally disyllabic, morphonological processes suggest that the preferred derived lexeme size is two, and at most three, syllables. This can be seen in (i) ablaut effects in voice alternations, which retain the disyllabic syllable count of the base (see §4): *gekker* 'UV:slaughter', *gukker* 'AV:slaughter'; *tekke* (or *tikke*) 'UV:give', *tukke* 'AV:give'; *teppah* 'rice pestle', *tippah* 'UV:pound', *tuppah* 'AV:pound'; (ii) segmental prefixes on vowel-initial roots, which often maintain disyllabic root size: *-embit* 'carry', *p-embit* (CAU-carry) 'AV:carry', *nimbit* 'UV:carry'; (iii) prefixes on some consonant-initial roots 'replace' the first segment of the root. This occurs with Actor voice *N-* discussed above and also with the nominalizing prefix *ka-* (§3.3) as in *k-ajjih* 'size' from *rajjih* 'big'. Furthermore, the reciprocal action verbal prefix (§4.2) is *sare-* before a monosyllabic base, *sar-* before a disyllabic vowel-initial base, and *sa-* before a disyllabic consonant-initial base, giving in all cases a trisyllabic output: *sare-pok* (RCP-hit) 'hit each other' (cf. *mu-pok* 'AV:hit', *ni-pok* 'UV:hit'), *sar-atat* (RCP-pull) 'pull each other', *sa-timbak* (RCP-stab) 'stab each other'. (iv) in sporadic cases when prefixes are attached there is truncation of a disyllabic verb root, ensuring a di- or trisyllabic output. This also happens with *sare-* as seen in *sare-sseng* 'smile at each other' (from *-kesseng* 'laugh') and *sarettip* (or *sagettip*) 'bite each other', from *guttep* 'bite'.

Elision of segments and whole syllables is common. Most grammatical words have at least two forms: *nga'* or *nga* or *ng-* 'already, perfective aspect'; *nyeh* or *nye* '3s'; *yeh* or *=e(h)* 'DIST, that'; *kaw* or *ko* '1s'. Disyllabic lexical morphemes with initial /e/ ([ə]) are most often realized as phonetic monosyllabes: *ejjew* 'river' [əjjew ~ (j)jew], *errit* 'sand' [əʁʁɪt ~ (ʁ)ʁɪt]. Many other commonly used lexical morphemes are also often reduced to monosyllables: *itti'* [(it)tiʔ] 'small', *ammi'* [(am)miʔ] 'a little bit', *tukki* [(tuk)kɛ(:) ~ (tuk)ki(:)] 'AV:give', *mattang* [(mɐt)taŋ] 'AV:say, state', *ubin* [(u)bin] 'every'.

3 BASIC MORPHOSYNTAX

3.1 Morpheme and word classes

Morphemes occur either as free lexical bases, bound lexical bases (perhaps all of which are verbal roots, see §4), or as affixes. There is comparatively little derivational morphology in Belait: just a single noun-deriving affix, discussed in §3.3, and a limited set of verbal affixes described in §4. The very few segmental affixes are either prefixes (*ka-bit* (NOM-long) 'length', *pe-lakaw* (CAU-go) 'drive (e.g. car)'; *ng-injik* 'AV-inject', *n-injik* 'UV-inject') or infixes in the leftmost syllable (*k[en]eseng* 'UV:laugh at', *t[en]utok* 'UV:gnaw'). With ablaut or stem-internal vowel alternation the alternating vowel is again in the leftmost syllable: *timbang* 'UV:fell', *tumbang* 'AV:fell'. When they occur as postmodifiers of verbs or nouns, monosyllabic pronominals such as *kaw* (or *ko(h)*) '1s', *naw* (or *no(h)*) '2s', *nyeh* (or *nye*) '3s'(see Table 15.2 below), as well as the distal demonstrative *(y)eh*, are considered to be enclitics, and not suffixes, since they do not influence stress placement, which remains on the final syllable of the stem to which they attach. There is one proclitic, *an=*'UV.IRR:make, do', see §3.7.

Major word classes include verbs and nouns (both open classes, with potentially no limit on new members). Stative verbs provide the functional equivalent of both adjectives and adverbs in Belait. The minor, closed classes of grammatical words include pronouns (§3.4), prepositions (§3.5), classifiers (§3.3.2), numerals (see below), modals/aspectuals (§3.6), and deictics including demonstratives (§3.3.3).

There is some preliminary evidence that word category distinctions apply at the level of the root. Simple morphemes which function unaffixed as nouns must undergo affixation to function as verbs: *titay'* 'breast (n)', *mitay'* 'AV:breastfeed', *nitay'* 'UV:breastfeed'; *alod* 'boat', *ng-alod* 'travel by boat'. Similarly, no evidence has been found of monomorphemic verbs functioning unmodified as nouns. The fact that all bound morphemes noted so far surface with verbal morphology is not inconsistent with the possibility that they are inherently verbal, given that affixes signal information about the semantic status of verbal arguments.

On the level of the morphological word, verbs can be distinguished distributionally from nouns since verbs when functioning as predicate can be negated by *(e)ndeh* (1), whereas nouns functioning as predicates are negated by *kay'*, not by *ndeh* (examples 2, 3):

(1) *pra'=yeh*   *nga'*   *salit,*   *ndeh*   *ana'*   *umaw'*   *padi*
     rain=DIST   already   be.hard   NEG   able   AV:make   paddy
     'The rain has become hard, [we] are not able to grow rice.'

(2) *kad*   *macim*   *blabiw,*   *kay'*   *blabiw*
     tarsier   like   rat   NEG   rat
     'A tarsier is like a rat, but it is not a rat.'

(3) *kay' (*ndeh)*   *idih*   *lengngan*
     NEG   person   different
     '[He is] one of us (*lit.* not another people/ethnic group).'

Verbs moreover can be freely modified by aspectuals such as *nga'* in (1) above, whereas this is not always the case with nouns:

(4) a. *nga'*   *jadi'*   *guru*
         already   become   teacher
         '[She has] already become a teacher.'
     b. *??nga'*   *guru*
         [Same intended meaning]

An exception to this observation is the lexicalized discourse linker *nga' ieh* 'after that', where the distal demonstrative *ieh* refers to an entire proposition, rather than to an NP (see examples 8 and 76).

The basic numerals in Metting are *ceh* (also *se-*) '1'; *debbih* '2', *tellaw* '3', *pat* '4', *limah* '5', *nam* '6', *tujjiw'* '7', *maray* '8', *(e)mpay'* or *meppay'* '9', *pulo* '10'. Examples of more complex numbers: *pulo debbih* '12', *debbih pulo tellaw* '23'; *me-rato* '100', *me-ribiw* '1000' (both exceptionally with *me-* 'one'), but *limah ribiw tujjiw' rato* '5700'. *ceh* is used in counting in series, or as the 'unit' element in more complex numbers (*pulo ceh* 'eleven'); *se-* replaces it before classifiers and other 'countables' (*se-llang* 'one-CLF', *se-ray* 'once, one time'). *Sellang* itself also functions as a numeral, preceding another classifier: *puttay sellang ohon* (banana one CLF) 'one banana fruit'. Ordinals are produced by prefixing *ka-*: *kadebbih* '(the) second', *katellaw* 'the third', *kanam* 'sixth'. *Partama* 'first' is from Malay (ultimately from Sanskrit).

3.2 Basic clause structure

Belait is a head-initial language: head nouns generally precede modifying elements such as other nouns and pronouns (e.g. *adin tamah=kaw* 'my father's name'), stative verbs ('adjectives') as in *berejin ma'ang* (durian be.red) 'red durian (species)', and relative clauses (§3.3.1). Actor voice verbs precede 'objects' (Undergoers), e.g. *kuman ellit* 'eat sago paste'; while Undergoer voice verbs precede Actors, e.g. *kinan=ko* (uv:eat=1s) 'eaten by me'.

A clause consists of a predicate and usually (but not necessarily) at least one NP which is assumed here to take the subject grammatical relation. The subject NP may either precede or follow the predicate. Word order thus varies between subject-predicate (example 5, first clause) and predicate-subject (5, second clause; the subject being *pading=yeh* in both clauses):

(5) *pading=yeh   lassaw'*, [...]
     sword=DIST   hot
     'The sword was hot,

     nengngay'=nyeh   pading=yeh   lay'   mi'   dile'
     UV:throw=3s   sword=DIST   to   at   sea
     He threw the sword into the sea.'

This variable position of the subject NP distinguishes it from non-subject arguments which usually occur immediately after the predicate, unless (in the case of Undergoers only) they are topicalized (see examples 14 and 15 below). Other properties of the subject NP include: (i) where a noun is modified by a relative clause, that noun may only be coreferential with the (missing) subject NP within the relative clause, (ii) in transitive clauses, the subject NP is that 'indexed' by transitive verb morphology (Actor or Undergoer voice marking). The subject NP is typically definite. Negatively, one of the two pronoun sets, the non-subject pronouns (§3.4), can never occur in subject NP position.

The predicate may be a VP (§3.2.1) or an NP or PP (§3.5). In addition to a subject NP, the clause may also contain optional elements such as negators (§3.2.3), markers of mood and aspect (§3.6), and non-subject NPs which will be further discussed in §3.2.1.

A topicalized NP, external to the clause proper, may precede it. The resumptive pronoun *tijjih* in (6) is optional.

(6) *takke, bulun=yeh   ndeh bulih   kuman   tijjih*
     deer   person=DIST   NEG may   AV:eat 3SNSBJ
     'Deer, those people are not allowed to eat it.'

(7) *ubo   idih   metting,   adeh   tellaw   na'an*
     cemetery people   M.   EXIST   three   places
     'The Metting people's cemeteries are in three places.'

Verbal arguments, regardless of their grammatical function, are very frequently omitted where easily recoverable from context:

(8) *mana   anak   nangah=yeh,   nga'   ieh,*
     AV:take   child sago.palm=DIST already   DIST
     an=kitah   mulah
     UV.IRR:make=1pi   AV:plant
     '[We] take the young sago palm, then we plant [it].' (At the very beginning of a text on how to grow sago palm)

(9)   [*kalaw   padi paya'*]...   *bin-bin ta'on   umaw'   tiyeh*
      [if   paddy swamp]   RDP-every year   AV:make   MED.ADV
      '[As for wet rice (*in Malay*)], every year [they/people] grow [it] there.'

(10)   A: *takke?*   B: *adeh   sih   bulun kuman*
            deer   EXIST   PTCL   person AV:eat
       A: 'What about deer?' B: 'There are people who eat [them].'

3.2.1   Verbal predicates

A verbal clause has a VP predicate. The head of the VP may be a simple, semantically intransitive verb, one with only one NP argument and no voice marking:

(11)   *katew'   ungon=eh*
       fall   fruit=DIST
       'The fruit fell.'

It may alternatively be a transitive verb, that is (in the present understanding) a verb potentially occurring with two unmarked NPs, one the Actor of the event predicated by the verb, the other the Undergoer of that event:

(12)   *idih   unnah   kuman   salang*
       peopl   before   AV:eat   charcoal
       'The people before [first ancestors of the Belait] ate charcoal.'

Transitive verbs occur in two related voice forms, an Actor voice (AV) form (cf. *kuman* in 12), and an Undergoer voice (UV) form (*kinan* in 13), each with its distinctive morphology and syntax (see §4 for more details on voice morphology):

(13)   *brejin   kinan=lew   abey'*
       durian   UV:eat=3p   complete
       'The durian was all eaten up by them.'

UV is regularly associated with aspectually perfective events, AV with other contexts. The subject NP associated with the Actor voice verb is a semantic Actor; that with the Undergoer voice verb form, an Undergoer. Whether the Undergoer of an AV verb, or the Actor of a UV verb can be considered to bear the object grammatical relation is unclear. The Undergoer NP of an Actor voice verb, where present, almost always immediately follows it, as in *salang* in (12). Fronted (=topicalized) Undergoers of AV verbs occasionally occur:

(14)   *seluar   bit   ndeh   nyeh   melley*
       trousers   long   NEG   3s   AV:buy
       'Trousers he didn't buy.'

(15)   *adi'   nyeh   mana   lay'   mi'   langit*
       light   3s   AV:place   to   at   sky
       'The light, he put [it] in the sky.'

Similarly, in UV, the Actor NP, where present, generally immediately follows the verb:

(16)   *pading=yeh lassaw',   nengngay'   Baginda Ali   mi'   dile'*
       sword=DIST hot,   UV:throw   Baginda Ali   at   sea
       'The sword was hot, [it] was thrown by Baginda Ali into the sea.'

(17) *ne-saw' ujid   lah   sermin   matah   bulun   teh*
      UV-use monkey   PTCL   glass   eye   person   PRX
      'The person's glasses were put on by the monkey.'

(18) *motuka=beh   tenite=beh   teh?*
      car=3d   UV:leave=3d PRX
      'Did they two leave their car here?'

Aspect markers must occur after the Actor NP:

(19) *narah   unyiw   nga'   oras=yeh?*   (not **narah nga' unyiw…*)
      UV:burn   2p   already   rubbish=DIST
      'Has the rubbish been burnt by you?'

(20) *kiw'   kidin   sadey'   nda*
      EVIT   UV:hear   crocodile   later
      'Let it not be that [we are] heard by a crocodile later'

In Actor voice clauses, non-subject Undergoers similarly also precede aspect markers:

(21) *pujew   tellaw   tijjih   nda*   (not **tellaw nda tijjih*)
      AV:order   AV:inform   3SNSBJ   later
      'Tell [someone] to inform her later.'

In UV clauses, the Actor NP may also occur in a separate phrase headed by *(n)inaw'* 'UV:make, do':

(22) *long ubak   kennah   inaw'   ugang=nyeh*
      hole door   UV:contact   UV:do   antler=3s
      'The doors were touched by his antler.'

Such Actor phrases also occur in association with an intransitive main clause:

(23) *butin=yeh   tungaib   inaw'   baroy*
      coconut=DIST   fall   UV:do   wind
      'The coconut fell because of the wind.'

(24) *idih semmi'   mikat   inaw'=nyeh*
      person close   wake   UV:do=3s
      'The people close by woke up because of him.'

Although the Actor phrase in examples such as (22)–(24) has the structure of a clause, it is not clear whether such examples should be analysed as biclausal constructions. Alternatively, *inaw'* could be analysed as a (weakly grammaticized) preposition. In the somewhat similar case of instrumental adjuncts coded by *saw'* 'use' there is good evidence for grammaticization, including the fact that such adjuncts may precede the subject as in:

(25) *timbak=nyeh   saw'   upit   tuliw=nyeh*
      UV:stab=3s   UV:use knife   body=3s
      'He stabbed himself using a knife.'

In this usage *saw'* cannot take a clitic Actor pronominal, it must be immediately followed by an instrument, and may not occur in its longer 'matrix verb' form of *nesaw'* 'UV:use' (see example 17), suggesting that it is on the way to being grammaticised as a preposition. No similar evidence was found for *(n)inaw'* in examples like (22)–(24) above.

3.2.2 Existential clauses and non-verbal predicates

The existential particles *adeh* 'EXIST' and *n(d)adeh* 'NEG:EXIST' often function to introduce a new indefinite subject NP to the discourse:

(26) *adeh   anak   tellaw   tuliw*
      EXIST   child   three   CLF
      'There were three children.'

(27) *waris   kamay   ndadeh   kuman   kammal,   aram,   kad,*
      lineage   1pe   NEG.EXIST   eat   colugo,   pangolin,   tarsier
      ngan   kikay
      with   slow.loris
      '[In] our lineage, there is no one who eats colugo, pangolin, tarsier or loris.'

In a different construction, a topic-like NP is juxtaposed with a unit consisting of *adeh* plus NP. The latter NP is understood to be possessed by the initial NP:

(28) *nyeh   kay'   adeh   nipan*
      3s   NEG   EXIST   teeth
      'It [the pangolin] doesn't have teeth.'

In addition, *adeh* has emphatic uses in which it precedes a clause and means something like 'it (really) is the case that':

(29) *idih   abi   teh   pun   adeh   umaw'   padi sili'   temburung*
      people   Brunei.Malay   PRX   too   EXIST   make   rice side   T.
      'The Brunei Malay people too grow rice, over Temburong way.'

Non-verbal predicates may be formed with an NP or a PP. They are often semantically equational (30); but also include weather expressions (31) and time expressions (32):

(30) *baneh=nyeh Pangiran Mohamud,   nanang   idih   abi*
      husband=3s P. M   genuine   people   Brunei.Malay
      'Her husband is Pangiran Mohamud, [he is] a true Brunei Malay.'

(31) *andaw   pra'*
      day   rain
      'It is raining.'

(32) *tebbih sab,   din=yeh   bin-bin   ta'on*
      smoke fire   3nhum=DIST   RDP-every   year
      'The smoke haze, it [happens] every year.'

A classifier phrase (§3.3.2) can fill the predicate slot:

(33) *A: kudeh   ellang   anak=naw?   B: anak=kaw   pat tuliw*
            how.many   CLF   children=2s   child=1s   four CLF
      A: 'How many [are] your children' B: 'I have four children (*lit*. My children are four)'

Examples of prepositional phrases occurring as predicate include:

(34) *panay   ngan   tijin   padi=yeh*
      newly   with   stomach   rice=DIST
      'The rice has just begun to form grains (*lit*. 'is newly with stomach').'

(35)   *nyeh   mi'   spital   dalim   tellaw   lim*
      3s   at   hospital in   three   nights
      'He [was] at the hospital for about three nights.'

Unmarked noun phrases referring to locations also often occur in predicate position in Belait. They are here assumed to involve ellipsis of a preposition (see also §3.5):

(36)   *nyeh   Serie'*
      3s   Seria
      'He [lives/is] in Seria.' (*mi' Serie'* also possible)

3.2.3 Negation

As already mentioned in §3.1, predicate NP's are negated by *kay'*. Either *ndeh* or *kay'* negates a predicate VP or PP, with the difference that *kay'* adds a 'counter-to-expectations' semantic element. Both *kay'* and *ndeh* usually occur immediately before the verb/predicate noun (see (2), (3), (6), (41) and *passim*), but both may also occur clause-initially:

(37)   *kay'   nyeh   lay'   dajjih*
      NEG   3s   to   dry.land
      'It [a species of monkey] does not go onto dry land (away from the riverside).'

(38)   *ndeh   ko   ingat   batin=nyeh*
      NEG   1s   remember   appearance=3s
      'I don't remember what he looked like.'

(39)   *kaw   semmat   selliw,   ndeh   kaw   semmut*
      1s   AV:look.for 3pNSBJ NEG 1s   AV:meet
      'I looked for them, but didn't find [them].'

Paralleling the function of *adeh* mentioned in §3.2.2, *ndadeh* marks emphatic negation:

(40)   *nadeh,   ndadeh   nyeh   pulay'   kacalu'*
      NEG.EXIST, NEG.EXIST 3s   AV:carry shrimp.sauce
      'No, she *didn't* take any shrimp sauce.'

The following example illustrates all three ways of negating a clause:

(41)   *idih kudang   ndeh kuman,   ndadeh   bu'uy...   kay'*
      people Kiudang NEG AV:eat NEG.EXIST accustomed NEG
      kamay   kuman
      1pe   AV:eat
      'Kiudang people don't eat [pangolin], are not used [to it], we *don't* eat [it].'

3.2.4 Imperatives

The simplest imperative clauses have the word order of declarative clauses, with the Actor optionally marked:

(42)   *titeh   no   kudduk*
      PRX.ADV 2s AV:sit
      'Sit here!'

Imperative mood is expressed in Actor voice: *katay!* 'AV:kill [it]'. Imperatives in UV could not be elicited. With some verbs, a distinct irrealis AV form of the verb is used in imperatives. The verb *kan* 'eat' has such a form, used transitively: compare *kan!* (AV.IRR:eat): 'eat it! (tr)' with *kuman!* (av:eat) 'eat! (intr)'. Compare also *apan* 'take!' (av *mana*, UV *nana*) and *abin* 'wait!'(av *pabin*, UV *nabin*):

(43) *apan*   *nda*   *beg=kaw*   *a*
      AV.IRR:take   later   bag=1s   PTCL
      'Get my bag later!'

(44) *(naw)*   *abin*   *sedurung*
      (2s)   AV.IRR:wait   one.moment
      'Wait a moment!'

Another way of forming imperatives is with the defective complement taking verb *(u')an* (UV.IRR:make, do) discussed in §3.7.

Negative imperatives are formed using the evitative *kiw'* 'let it not be that [S]':

(45) *kiw' semmi'-semmi'*   *idih*   *melara'*   *ujid=eh*
      EVIT RDP-close   people   look.after   monkey=DIST
      'Don't go close to people who keep monkeys.'

(46) *kiw'*   *an=pa'ut-pa'ut*   *nyeh*
      EVIT   UV.IRR:make=RDP-CAU:fright   3s
      'Don't frighten him.'

kiw' is also used in non-imperative contexts, again with the meaning 'Let it not be that' (see also example 20):

(47) *tudong*   *geccak=yeh*   *saw'*   *tubbil*   *nukan [...]*   *kiw'*
      lid   tray=DIST   UV:use   AV:cover   rice,   EVIT
      nuak   *lalad*
      UV:enter   fly
      'The lid of the *geccak* is used to cover rice, lest it be entered by flies.'

3.3 Noun phrase structure

On criteria for distinguishing the category 'noun' in Belait, see §3.1. Only one affix derives nouns in Belait, the prefix *ka-,* which attaches to a limited set of stative verbs referring to measurable qualities to derive nominals. Examples include *ka-bi* 'length (of time)', from *bi* 'be a long time', *k-addew* 'amount (*addew* '(be) many')', *kajjih* 'size' (*rajjih* 'big'), *ka-bit* 'length (physical) (*bit* 'long'). The only other nominalization strategy is the use of headless relative clauses as NPs, described below.

The form *nukan* 'rice' in (47) reflects a 'fossilized' nominalizing affix no longer part of the synchronic grammar and not so far recorded elsewhere in the language, except in the related *nekan* 'food in general'; also irregular are related *kuman* 'AV:eat' and *kinan* 'UV:eat', directly reflecting PAn *-um-* and *-in-*, otherwise only recorded in the similarly exceptional *umaw'*, *(n)inaw'* (see section 3.7).

A noun phrase is normally headed by a noun, a pronoun (§3.4) or a demonstrative pronoun (§3.3.3). Most modifying elements follow the head of the NP. These include other nouns, relative clauses, and demonstratives. Quantifying expressions generally may either precede or follow the head noun (see §3.3.2 for examples of this), though some quantifiers occur only as pre-head modifiers: *(ubin-)ubin ta'on* '(RDP-)every year'. Demonstratives occasionally appear to occur in pre-head position (§3.3.3).

Exclusively post-head modifiers include other NP's functioning as possessors, as in *adin tamah=kaw* (name [father=1s]) 'my father's name'), or in other semantic relations with the head: *si'kupi'* 'coffee' (lit. 'water [of] coffee'), *na'an kabun* 'place [of] garden', *pena beri* 'storage.place [for] rice'.

3.3.1 Relative clauses

Relative clauses follow the head noun or are headless. Across dialects, three ways of marking relative clauses have been noted. (i) The head noun is directly followed by a VP, with no overt marker:

(48) *bulun lakaw   debbih   tuliw,   bulun   patad   sampay   nam   pulo*
person go   two   CLF   person AV:lead until   six   ten
'The people who were going were two, but the people who were accompanying [them] were sixty in number.'

(49) *puttay nulah=ko   matay-matay   sa'*
banana UV:plant=1s   RDP-dead   only
'The banana trees which I planted just all died.'

Unmarked stative verbs modifying head nouns, as in *berejin ma'ang* (durian red) 'red durian', are here assumed to occur in a relative clause, since relative clauses often have no overt marker.

(ii) The relative clause is preceded by *(a)naw* or *(a)no* (Labi) or (rarely) *no* (Metting):

(50) *embay   sa'=lah* [...]   *no*   *sau=nyeh   m-ulon,*
what   only=PTCL   REL   UV:use=3s   AV-life
'Anything at all which was used by him when alive,

nimbet   le'   tak   ubur,   natat   tikki   ticjih
UV-carry to   at   grave   UV:bring UV:give 3sNSBJ.
is brought to the grave, brought and given to him.'(Labi dialect, Noor Alifah 1992:609)

(iii) the relative clause is preceded by the third person singular pronoun *nyeh*. This last structure, synchronically still analysable as using a pronoun retention strategy (the head noun must be third person), is found only in Metting dialect, where it is far more common than the second method above:

(51) *nyeh   se-llang teh   ramat iseng*
3s   one-CLF PRX   finger
'This one is the *iseng* finger (little finger).'

The head noun may be missing in all three strategies:

(52) *nyeh   menynyit,   peretap   unyi,   adeh kidin=nyeh*
3s   AV:wake.up AV:listen.to sound EXIST UV:hear=3s
'He woke up, listened, there was something which he heard.'

The three structures illustrated in (48) to (51) appear to require the head noun to be coreferential with the (missing) subject NP of the relative clause. While non-subject arguments are excluded as heads of these relative clauses, the head noun may be a non-core NP in other relative-clause-like structures. In these structures a noun meaning 'place', 'time' or 'reason' may be simply juxtaposed with a following clause, which paratactically modifies it, thus *na'an* [S] 'the place where [S]' in (53, 54), *ator* [S] 'the reason why [S]' in (55):

(53) *na'an   nyeh   uppak   mukkom*
      place   3s   AV:live   M.
      'The place where she lives is Mungkom.'

(54) *nyeh surit   tad   amen   na'an   nyeh   mekkil*
      3s AV:go.down   from   house   place   3s   AV:sleep
      'he went down from the house, the place where he had been sleeping'

(55) *ator   no ndeh   messap   kupi'*
      reason   2s NEG   AV:drink   coffee
      '(the) reason you don't drink coffee' (Labi dialect, Noor Alifah 1992)

The general noun may in fact be missing when the construction functions as a complement of a preposition:

(56) *komputer=nyeh [...]   nebbit   tadey=nyeh [...]   mi' nyeh belajir*
      computer=3s   UV:carry younger.sibling=3s LOC 3s study
      'Her computer was taken by her younger sister [...] to [*the place where*] she is studying.'

3.3.2 Classifiers

When modifying nouns, numbers often occur before a classifier or measure word. Classifiers are used when counting small numbers of people or objects. A classifier must be preceded by a numeral: *karabaw debbih brungun* (buffalo two CLF) 'two buffalo'. The number-classifier sequence either follows the head noun as in the preceding example and in *pensil debbih lang* 'two pencils', *puttay sellang ohon* 'one banana fruit', or precedes it: *pat tuliw anak* (four CLF child) 'four children', *se-llang asaw* (one-CLF dog) 'a dog'. Classifying expressions may fill the head of NP position, though presumably with ellipsis:

(57) *se-llang=yeh   ramat   akang*
      one-CLF=DIST   finger   *akang*
      'That one is the middle finger.'

Classifiers and the semantic types they index include *tuliw* for people (also a noun 'body') and *(el)lang* for most inanimate objects. *(El)lang* is also the default classifier that can be used in place of other classifiers such as *brungun* for animals, fish and some birds, *ohon* for fruit and flowers, *po'on* for trees and woody plants, *rappun* for plants which grow in clumps (like bananas, lemon grass), *uar* for other non-woody plants and *belid* for mats.

Some 'typically counted' nouns, such as *igit* 'bundle', *ray* 'time, occasion' and other nouns referring to time (*andaw* 'day', *bulin* 'month') occur without a classifier:

(58) *nangah=yeh   pulo   limah   ta'on   baru   no dapit   tumbang*
      sago.palm=DIST   ten   five   year   new   2s may   AV:fell
      'Sago palms, only after 15 years can 'you' cut [them] down.'

(59) *tellaw   lim   tellaw andaw   ndeh   surit   sew'*
      three   night   three day   NEG   descend   down.'
      '[They] don't come down for three nights and three days.'

3.3.3 Deictics

The demonstratives *(i)teh* PRX and *(i)yeh* DIST occur both as modifiers of an NP head and as heads of NP. As postmodifiers, they occupy the 'rightmost' position in the NP, including after relative clauses (60). Demonstratives also occasionally appear in pre-head position (61). The intonation pattern in examples like (61) is consistent with them being a single phrase, rather than two juxtaposed NPs:

(60)   *anak   lay=koh   no   s-ellang   ieh*
        child   be.male=1s   REL   one-CLF   DIST
        'That one of my boys.'

(61)   *teh   melli'   t[en]utok   mammal*
        PRX   fruit   UV-gnaw   squirrel
        'This *melli'* fruit (a type of durian) was gnawed by a squirrel.'

As a postmodifier, the distal demonstrative *yeh* often occurs in a reduced form=*eh*. Both forms often mark the referential status of an entity as previously mentioned or presumed to be known to the hearer. As head of NP, the demonstratives may have disyllabic realizations *iteh, ieh*.

There is also a separate series of deictics for which three degrees of distance from the deictic center are distinguished (and not just two as in the case of the demonstratives): *inay* 'here/this place', *jey* 'there/that place', *ju* 'yonder/yonder place'. These (like the demonstratives) often co-occur with prepositions: *lay' inay* 'to here', *lay' jey* '(to) there'. A locative preposition, cognate with Labi and Kuala Balai *ta'* 'at', but no longer found in Metting is reflected in *tinay* or *titeh* 'at.here', *tejjey* or *tiyeh'* at.there', and *tejju* 'at.yonder':

(62)   *komputer=nyeh* [...]   *nebbit*   *tadey=nyeh*   *lay' ju*
        computer=3s   UV:carry   younger.sibling=3s   to DIST.ADV
        'Her computer was taken by her from home, taken by her younger sister to there.'

3.4 Pronouns

The personal pronouns of Metting Belait are given in Table 15.2. There is a distinction between singular, dual and plural number, and in the third singular pronouns, between human and non-human referents. In Metting dialect the distinction between human and non-human third singular pronouns is not strictly maintained: the former are at times used in reference to non-human, including inanimate, referents. The exact behaviour of the dual pronouns needs further study: for example, the 2/3 dual series can be used either for exclusive second person or exclusive third person reference, but whether they can be used, say, for combinations of second and third persons as in 'you and (s)he' needs investigation.

Formally, there are two sets of pronouns, a general set and a 'non-subject' (NSBJ) set. Phonologically the monosyllabic general series pronouns are enclitics when they occur as (i) Actors of Undergoer voice verbs, occurring in immediately postverbal position and (ii) Possessors of nouns. All other general series pronouns take stress in those two positions. While the general set is essentially the same in all dialects, the forms and perhaps the syntactic behavior of the NSBJ pronouns differ across dialects. The description here is of Metting usage.

TABLE 15.2: PERSONAL PRONOUNS OF METTING BELAIT

	General	Non-subject (NSBJ)
1s	*kaw (ko(h))*	*sakay'*
2s	*naw (no(h))*	*ciw'*
3s human	*nyeh*	*tijjih*
3s non-human	*din, dih*	*tijjih*
1dual	*beh-debbeh*	*beh-debbeh*
2/3dual	*beh(-debbeh)*	*sebbeh*
1pi	*kitah*	*nyakitah*
1pe	*kamay*	*sakamay*
2p	*unyiw*	*sunyiw*
3p human	*liaw (lew)*	*saliaw*

The two sets (general and non-subject) have largely complementary distributions; both occur in positions otherwise filled by NPs. In the Metting Belait of my informants, pronouns in the general series occur in a variety of contexts, including subject NP, external topic, Actor of an Undergoer voice verb (63), and Possessor of a noun head (64).

(63) *byaw   puta'   narah=ko   uni'*
      smell   fish   UV:burn=1s   earlier
      'the smell of the fish that I grilled earlier'

(64) *embah   tinah=no*
      where   mother=2s
      'Where is your mother?'

The non-subject pronouns never occur in the first three of those contexts, and only rarely in the last. The grammatical argument status of phrases filled by non-subject pronouns is as yet unclear. These appear to derive historically from a sequence of a preposition followed by a general series pronoun. They typically occur as Undergoer of an Actor voice verb (65). Speakers of both Metting and Kuala Balai dialects strongly reject the occurrence of general series pronouns in this position. (On the usage of younger speakers, see §5.)

(65) *imbulan   p-ulay'   tijjih   lay'   ospital*
      ambulance   AV.CAU-carry   3sNSBJ   to   hospital
      'An ambulance took him to the hospital' (*pulay' nyeh*)

(66) *asaw teh   guttep   ngan=nyeh...   asaw   ture   teh   guttep   tijjih*
      dog PRX   AV:bite   hand=3s   dog   female   PRX   AV:bite   3sNSBJ
      'The dog bit his hand...the woman's dog bit him.'

Example (66) clearly illustrates how the non-subject pronouns occur in positions otherwise filled by noun phrases.

Semantically, the NSBJ pronouns encode a variety of roles including transferred theme (65), true patient (66), recipient (67), or location/possessor (68):

(67) *tekki=nyeh   sakay'   se-llang ukaw*
      UV:give=3s   1sNSBJ   one-CLFwooden.stirring.paddle
      'He gave me an *ukaw*.'

(68) *teh   sakay',   ieh   tijjih*
     PRX   1SNSBJ   DIST   3SNSBJ
     'This is mine, that is his/hers.'

An equivalent clause to (68), but where *sakay'* and *tijjih* are replaced by prepositional phrases, could not be elicited. In elicitation sessions the NSBJ pronouns were rejected as Possessor of noun head. In texts, however, they do occur occasionally with this function, as in (69):

(69) *macam   Péhin Arip...   kemaman   sakay'*
     like   P. A.   uncle   1SNSBJ
     'Like Pehin Arip, my uncle.'

There is no reflexive pronoun; reflexive action is expressed analytically with the word for 'body' plus a general series pronoun (see also example (25)):

(70) *timbak=nyeh   tuliw=nyeh*
     UV:stab=3s   body=3s
     'He stabbed himself.'

The indefinite/interrogative pronoun *(e)mbay* 'anything, what' also fills a variety of NP positions, including Undergoer of an AV verb, which is usually negated (71), and, in questions, predicate position (72):

(71) *idih   spital   ndeh   m-ana'   umaw'   embay*
     people hospital NEG   AV-able   AV:do   what
     'The hospital staff weren't able to do anything.'

(72) *embay   adin   cen   teh*
     what   name   animal   PRX
     'What is the name of this animal.'

3.5 Prepositional expressions

Prepositions in Belait include *mi'* 'at' (*ta'* in Labi/Kuala Balai dialects), *lay'* or *li'* 'to', *tad* 'from', *ngan* 'with'. Prepositions do not undergo affixation processes and do not take pronominal clitics. Complexes of two independently occurring prepositions also occur: *lay' mi', tad mi', tad li'*. The functional difference between *lay'* and *lay' mi'* is not clear; both are common.

(73) *pingit=nyeh   putay'   tad mi'ukaw'   lay'   mi'   jud   teh*
     cheek=3   white   from at head   to   at   back   PRX
     'Its cheeks are white from on the head to the back here.'

More specific locative relations are expressed with relational nouns: *jud amen* '(at the) back (of the) house'. Others include *alim* 'in(side)' and *jung* 'upper area, area above':

(74) *idih matay   ndeh   nittil   alim   tana*
     people dead   NEG   UV:bury   inside ground
     'The dead were not buried in the ground' (Kuala Balai dialect).

(75) *bilun=eh   lakaw   jung   amen*
     plane=DIST   go   area.above   house
     'The plane went above the house.'

This is part of a more general pattern by which unmarked noun phrases often occur in positions and functions where a prepositional phrase can also occur (see also discussion of 36):

(76) *andaw   pat   nyeh   paneng   nga'   ieh   taros   spital*
    day   four   3s   headache   after   DIST   directly   hospital
    'On Thursday she had a headache, after that [she went] straight [to] hospital.'

As also shown by example (76), time adjuncts such as 'on Thursday' usually do not involve a preposition.

3.6 Aspect-mood markers and adverbs

There are a variety of aspect and mood markers, including *nga'* 'already', *(ndeh) sadeh* 'not yet', *akal* 'still', *acin* 'again', *kan* 'future action', *tuggeh* 'want to', *liaw* 'intend to', *nda* 'later, lest'. These markers most often immediately precede (77) or follow (78, 79) the predicate (and any accompanying non-subject argument); they may also occur clause finally (80):

(77) *sabah=nyeh   nga'   ng-alod*
    wife=3s   already   AV-boat
    'His wife had already gone off by boat.'

(78) *rajjih-rajjih   nga'   anak=nyeh*
    RDP-big   already   child=3s
    'Her children are already big.'

(79) *narah unyiw   nga'   oras=yeh?*
    UV:burn 2p   already   rubbish=DIST
    'Have you burnt the rubbish?'

(80) *narah unyiw   oras=yeh   nga'?*
    UV:burn 2p   rubbish=DIST   already
    'Have you burnt the rubbish?'

In addition to these particles, stative verbs like *abey'* 'be complete, finished; all', *apar* 'be.equal', *panay* 'do just recently', *apo* 'be finished' occur, always preceding the 'main' verb. They convey semantic information such as degree of affectedness or quantification. Structurally a kind of complex predicate formation may be involved, though this has not been investigated.

(81) *abey'   nga'   gettem   padi=yeh*
    complete   already   UV:harvest   paddy=DIST
    'The paddy has all been harvested.'

(82) *nga'   apar   lusit   ieh   padi*
    already   even   go.out   DIST   paddy
    'That paddy has all come out (produced seeds).'

(83) *nga'   apo   kaw messap*
    already   finished   1s AV:drink
    'I've finished drinking.'

Time expressions (e.g. *mem* 'yesterday, previous day', *jain* 'tomorrow, next day', *ubin lim* 'every night') often occur clause-initially (84) or -finally (85):

(84)   *mem*   *nyeh* *lay'* *long* *mana* *pencin* *idih* *rebban*
       previous.day   3s   to   town   AV:take pension   person old
       'The previous day he went to town to get the old age pension.'

(85)   *endeh ji'* *anyim=kaw*   *andaw* *teh*
       NEG good   feeling=1s   day   PRX
       'I don't feel good today.'

3.7 Complex predicates with *u'an*

This section discusses predicates formed with *u'an* 'UV.IRR:make, do', an irrealis variant of *(n)inaw'* 'UV:make, do' (AV *umaw'*). *U'an* occurs as the sole predicate in simple clauses:

(86)   *bambin=yeh*   *u'an=ko*   *kab*
       k.o.plant=DIST   UV.IRR:make=1s   container
       'I will make this *bambin* (rattan-like plant) into a container.'

However it also very commonly occurs in a complex predicate construction of this general structure: *u'an* (NP$_{ACTOR}$) VERB:

(87)   *u'an=naw*   *ngallah* *ukaw'* *anak=eh*
       UV.IRR:make=2s   AV:feel   head   child=DIST
       'Feel the child's head.'

That is, *u'an*, syntactically the main verb, occurs with an optional Actor NP, followed by a dependent verb, obligatorily in Actor voice if transitive, as in (87). The predicate is normally followed by a Undergoer NP, as in (87). With an intransitive dependent verb (88) the semantically causative nature of this construction is clear:

(88)   *tolong* *u'an*   *(it)ti'* *swara* *redio*
       please   UV.IRR:make   small   voice   radio
       'Please turn the radio down.'

Where there is no Actor participant, *u'an* commonly reduces to proclitic *(')an* which attaches to the following dependent verb (see §2.3): *am=purey' ngan=eh* 'wash [your] hands!', *ang=ngallah* 'feel!'. Although the dependent verb where transitive must be in Actor voice, complex predicates with *u'an* are consistently translated as though both verbs were in Undergoer voice. Consistent with this, the Undergoer NP appears to function as subject of the main verb *u'an*: its position is variable, it is referentially definite, and most importantly, its place cannot be filled by a non-subject pronoun:

(89)   *an=naw*   *tungaw* *nyeh/(*tijjih)*
       UV.IRR:make=2s   AV:call   3s
       'You call him.'

Clayre in a survey of cognate constructions in related Sarawak languages, refers to them as 'an alternative way of forming an undergoer focus construction' (1996:77). In Belait, complex predicates with *u'an* are functionally distinct from other UV predicates: whereas elsewhere UV verbs in simple clauses refer almost exclusively to modally realis, completed events (§4), complex *u'an* clauses are generally modally irrealis, functioning as imperatives or referring to non-realized events. Note that no other verb in Belait has a special irrealis UV form. As imperatives, such clauses are said to be more polite than the simple imperatives above.

(90) *an=guttep   ungon=yeh*
      UV.IRR:make=AV:bite   fruit=DIST
      'Bite the fruit!' [more literally 'make/have [someone] bite the fruit']

(91) *ana'   an=guttem   padi=kaw=yeh,   u'an=unyiw guttem*
      able   UV.IRR:make=AV:cut   paddy=1s=DIST,   UV.IRR:make=2p AV:cut
      '[It] can be "made cut", my paddy, [let it be] "made cut" by you!'

Some uses of *(u')an* refer to habitual, rather than irrealis, events in series (see also example (8) above):

(92) *segenip   buliw=nyeh   nuak   lalay,   nga'   ieh,   an=nyeh*
      all   hair=3s   UV:enter   termite   already   DIST   UV.IRR:make=3s

      embukuk,   an=nyeh   ngatup   tuliw=nyeh,   katay   lalay=yeh,
      curl.up   UV.IRR:make=3s   AV:close   body=3s   AV:kill   termite=DIST

      an=nyeh   menyug tuliw=nyeh.
      UV.IRR:make=3s   AV:shake body=3s

      kalaw nga'   lalay=yeh   matay...   an=nyeh   kan
      when already   termite=DIST   be.dead   UV.IRR:make=3s   AV:eat
      lalay=yeh
      termite=DIST
      'All of its [the pangolin's] hair is entered by termites. After that it will curl up, close its body up tight, kill the termites, [then] shake its body. When the termites are dead...it will eat them.'

4 VERBAL MORPHOLOGY

This section discusses the morphology of transitive verbs (§4.1) and intransitive verbs (§4.2). The reciprocal affix *sare-*, which typically derives verbs with reduced valency, is also discussed in §4.2. Formation of causatives, including periphrastic causative constructions, is discussed in §4.3. Formally, verbs occur either as simple morphemes, or with no more than one segmental affix; the derived form may be reduplicated (§2.3). There are just four segmental affixes in Belait. Unlike most of the languages in this volume, Belait appears to have no native morphology marking lack of control (though Brunei Malay *tar-* is sometimes appropriated for this function).

4.1 Voice

Many verbs occur in two 'alternate' forms, an Actor voice form and an Undergoer voice form, each with a distinct syntactic behaviour (see §3.2.1) and morphology. A small set of syntactically transitive verbs of cognition take only Actor voice morphology; they have no corresponding UV form (Kumanireng 1995). In Metting Belait these include *meci'* 'know, understand', *ketan* 'AV:see', *kelitah* 'AV:forget', *nu'aw* 'believe'. Other, syntactically intransitive verbs also occur with Actor voice morphology only, see §4.2.

There are several ways of marking both UV and AV, with variation from base to base in which of these are used. Blust (1997) reconstructs a relatively simple system behind the present complexity of voice marking in North Sarawak languages. As in other Baram languages, ablaut or root-internal alternation in the vowel in the first syllable of the lexeme is one means of marking voice: UV marked by *-i-* or *-e-* ([ə]), or both; and AV by *-u-*:

(93)   UV   AV
 gekker, gikker   *gukker*   'slaughter (by stabbing)'
 gettem   *guttem*   'harvest'
 kedduk   *kudduk*   'sit'
 lessie   *lussie*   'take off (clothing)'
 tekki, tikki   *tukki*   'give'
 tebbil   *tubbil*   'cover'
 tippah   *tuppah*   'pound' (cf. *teppah* 'pestle' (n))

An historically related alternation is the marking of UV by prefix *n-* and of AV by *m-*. Bases in this case are (or were, cf. Blust 1997) often vowel-initial:

(94)   UV   AV
 nulit   *mulit*   'skin (tr)'
 n-ana'   *m-ana'*   'take'
 n-ella'   *m-ella'*   'see'
 nuak   *muak*   'enter'
 n-engngay'   *m-engngay'*   'throw away'

A variation is the apparent affixation on a monosyllabic base of *mu-/me-*(AV) and *ni-* (UV): *messap/nissap* 'AV/UV:drink'; *mupok/nipok* 'AV/UV:hit', *mucceh/nicceh* 'AV/UV:strike (with sth.)'.

Otherwise, Actor voice is commonly marked by *N-*. This prefix is also used before some vowel-initial stems (then realized as *ng-*), in particular in loanwords:

(95)   UV   AV
 pukot   *mukot*   'hit'
 bitil   *mitil*   'bury'
 k[en]ambang   *ngambang* 'swell up'
 k[en]eseng, niseng   *ngeseng*   'laugh, laugh at'
 t[en]ukod   *nukod*   'prop'
 n-iñjin   *ng-injin* 'use an engine'(< Mly < English)
 n-iñjik   *ng-iñjik* 'inject' (< Mly < English)

As examples like *k[en]eseng* in (95) show, another common marker of UV is the infix *-en-* ([ən]) in the initial syllable, typically occurring after a voiceless obstruent:

(96)   UV   AV
 senuka'   *suka'*   'like (tr)'
 kenulun   *kulun*   'turn on, give life to' (cf. *ulon* 'life')
 penasang   *pasang*   'turn on (e.g. fan)'
 kenatay   *katay*   'kill'   (cf. *matay* 'die, be.dead')
 penelley   *pelley*   'sell'   (cf. *nelley/melley* 'buy')
 penakan   *pakan*   'feed'   (cf. *kan* 'eat')

The examples in (95) and (96) also show that different lexical bases occur with different combinations of the possible AV and UV markings listed above. In some cases, AV may be relatively less marked, as in (96) above, while in others, the UV form may be less marked:

(97)   UV   AV
     tapan   *napan*   'winnow (e.g. rice)'
     kallah   *ngallah*   'feel (tr)'

Occasionally either the AV form (for example *suka'* (96)) or the UV (*tapan* (97)) is a completely unmarked monomorphemic base. More typically however both UV and AV appear to involve affixation on an inherently bound root morpheme.

With a very few verbs, a distinct portmanteau Irrealis-Actor voice form also occurs, for example in imperatives (§3.2.4) and in noun compounds:

(98)   UV   AV   AV.IRR
     nabin   *pabin*   *abin*   'wait for, guard'
     nulay'   *pulay'*   *ulay'*   'carry'
     kinan   *kuman*   *kan*   'eat (tr)'

The Undergoer voice form is inherently aspectually perfective: it refers to a completed action. It is the preferred form in narrating a sequence of past (completed) events. Attempts to elicit UV forms in future contexts are rejected, for example **jain kan nana'=kaw* (tomorrow FUT UV:fetch=1s) 'tomorrow [it] will be fetched by me' was corrected to *jain kaw mana' deh* 'tomorrow I will (AV:)fetch it'. The UV form is nonetheless compatible with the 'future' marker *kan* (from Malay *akan*, also a future marker) which then is interpreted as irrealis (99) and also allows for other irrealis uses:

(99)   *kan*   *nulay'=kaw,*   *ndeh*   *kaw*   *semmot*
     FUT   UV:bring=1s   NEG   1s   AV:meet
     'I was going to bring [it, but] I didn't find [it].'

The Actor voice form is often used in irrealis contexts (e.g. contemplated actions, actions not performed, imperatives). In texts it co-occurs relatively rarely with the perfective marker *nga'*, though it does occur in past narratives, where for example the discourse focusses on the Actor participant, or aspect is non-perfective (for example, ongoing actions).

4.2 Intransitive verbs

While most transitive verbs can be considered to be inherently bound, many intransitive verbs occur without affixation. Others take Actor voice marking. These are discussed below, along with a prefix-like *me-* element here considered to be no longer part of the synchronic grammar. Intransitive verbs which occur without affixes generally have stative or adjectival senses: *ji'* '(be) good', *ma'ang* '(be) red', *bi* '(be) a long time', *sikiw* '(be) tall', *ngalih* '(be) tired'. These do not appear to have transitive counterparts. Some intransitive verbs of motion also occur unaffixed: *lakaw* 'go', *parabing* 'run'.

Some semantically 'dynamic' intransitive verbs take Actor voice marking (see below), otherwise found only on transitives: *ng-alod* 'AV-travel by boat' (*alod* 'boat'), *lusit* 'AV:come out (intr)', *kudduk* 'AV:sit', *tulod* 'AV:fly'. Evidence that forms like *lusit* are not monomorphemic (and that instead infix *-u-* marks Actor voice) comes from Undergoer voice counterparts or other alternants: thus *pe-lessit* 'CAU-come.out:make come out'; similarly for *kudduk* 'AV:sit' there is *kedduk* 'UV:sit on'. These AV verbs are nonetheless intransitive since they occur with an oblique locative Undergoer, rather than a bare NP as non-subject argument:

(100)   *nyeh   lusit   tad   long kellan*
       3s   come.out   from   window
       'He came out via the window.'

Other verbs occur in both intransitive and transitive contexts, for example *kuman* 'eat' (intr., tr.), *ngesseng* 'laugh; mock' and *dusseh* 'be angry; scold': *liaw ngesseng (tijjih)* 'they laughed (at him)'.

A few stative intransitive verbs take a fossilized prefix *me-*; its limited and variable occurrence within and across dialects suggests that it is no longer synchronically part of the grammar: *lusek* or *me-lusek* 'peeling (of skin)', *lipang* or *me-lipang* 'empty, of rice grain' (Labi), *me-rebbian* 'old' (Labi, Metting has *rebban*), Labi *m-abiy* 'all gone' (Metting has *abiy'*).

The verbal prefix *sare-* conveys either 'reciprocal action' (the more common usage), or 'joint action' as in *sare-kan* 'eat together' and *saresseng* 'laugh together' (compare *ngesseng* 'laugh'). It attaches to a base which may be distinct from both the UV and AV forms (see §2.3 for the morphophonological alternations and examples); most often it is identical to the UV form (*sa-tekki* 'RCP-give', *sa-gettip* 'RCP-bite'). In a few (elicited) cases, the base is identical to the AV form. Where it marks reciprocal action the resultant verb has one fewer argument: intransitives are formed from transitive bases (101, 102). Similarly, transitives appear to be formed from ditransitive bases (though the syntactic status of the semantic theme in examples like (103) requires investigation):

(101)   *nyeh   durep   sakay',   kaw   dure   tijjih,   kamay   kuba sa-direp*
       3s   AV:help   1sNSBJ   1s   AV:help   3sNSBJ   1pe   same RCP-help
       'He helps me, I help him, we help each other.'

(102)   *beh   sabah baneh   masa teh   beh   nga'   sar-engngay'*
       3d   wife husband   time PRX   3d   already   RCP-throw.away
       'They, the married couple, they have already divorced.'

(103)   *kuba-kuba   sa-tekki   baring*
       RDP-same   RCP-give   thing
       '[They] give each other things.'

4.3 Causatives

The causative prefix *pe-* or *pa-* (*p-* before a vowel, or 'replacing' a root-initial labial consonant, cf. §2.3) derives AV transitive verbs from bases which elsewhere function variously as intransitives (*pe-lakaw* (CAU.AV-go) 'drive (e.g. car)', nominals (*p-igit* (CAU.AV-bundle) 'tie into a bundle' < *igit* 'bundle (n)'), or transitive verbs (*pe-kan* 'feed' < *kan* 'eat').

(104) | Related form | Causative (AV) |
| --- | --- |
| *ba'ut* 'afraid' | *pa'ut* 'frighten' |
| *tau'* 'speech (n)' | *pe-tau'* 'speak (a language)' |
| *ubit* 'medicine (n)' | *p-ubit* 'have (a patient) take medicine' |
| *lusit* 'go out (intr)' | *pe-lessit tau'* 'emit speech: speak' |
| *mekkil* 'sleep' | *pakkil* 'put to sleep' |
| *messap* 'drink' | *pessap* 'cause to drink' |
| *kan* 'AV:eat' | *pa-kan* 'feed' |

The resulting verb has Actor voice syntax: the Actor/Causer is in subject function, the Undergoer/Causee, where present, follows the verb:

(105)   *merray   nyeh   pe-lakaw   motuka*
        fast   3s   CAU.AV-go   car
        'He drives his car fast.'

The corresponding UV form generally has *n(a/e)-*: *n-isi'* 'be filled' (cf. *p-isi'*(CAU.AV-contents (n)) 'fill'); *rabay* 'dry, of padi etc. (intr)', *pe-rabay* 'CAU.AV-dry' *nerabay* 'CAU.UV:dry'. Alternatively some forms mark UV with infix *-en-*: *na-kan* or *p-en-akan* 'be eaten', *penelley* 'be sold' (cf. *pelley* (CAU.AV:buy, sell).

(106)   *[kaw]   na-kan   idih   ubit*
        [1s]   CAU.UV:eat   people   medicine
        'I was made to eat medicine by people.'

pe- does not co-occur with inherently stative intransitive verbs. These instead occur in periphrastic constructions with various forms of *u'an* 'make, do', e.g. *umaw' (it)tiq/rajjih* 'make small/big'.

5 LANGUAGE LOSS

In 1991 more than 90% of ethnically Belait parents interviewed reported that they used Brunei Malay rather than Belait as the language of primary communication with their offspring, who generally do not speak the language (Martin 1995). As Martin argues, the impending disappearance of Belait and of all or most of the minority languages in Brunei has its origins in the development of the oil industry, and the associated economic and cultural dominance of the Brunei Malay ethnic group. In recent decades, oil has brought widespread affluence, near-universal education, and new aspirations and expectations. Traditional rural occupations, places of residence, and belief systems have been lost to an urbanized way life, and a new Bruneian ethnic and national identity. Frequent marriage across traditional ethnolinguistic boundaries has further hastened language loss (Martin 1995, 1996).

For speakers of Belait as for those of all minority languages in Brunei, code switching with Brunei Malay is common, even in the home (Martin and Poedjosoedarmo 1996). Even the Belait of speakers aged in their sixties often shows the influence of a lifetime of intimate contact with Brunei Malay. Among younger speakers lexis, syntax, morphology and phonology all converge with that of Malay. In the phonology, for example, geminate sequences, and other distinctions not found in Malay such as the final /ʔ/- /k/ contrast are often lost (Noor Alifah 1995, Kiudang data). Along with the many everyday lexical items borrowed from Malay, bound morphology is borrowed, including the verbal affix *ter-* 'non-controlled action', and the Malay applicative suffix *-kan* (realized with palatalization of the initial consonant in Labi Dialect):

(107)   *mana-kian   kaw   seluar   alim*   (cf. Malay *ambil-kan saya seluar dalam*)
        take-*kan*   1s   trousers inside
        'Get me some underpants.'   (Noor Alifah 1993:48)

An example of syntactic borrowing is the use of the '*kena*' passive construction, clearly a borrowing from Brunei Malay where it is used with high frequency:

(108)   *seremin   matah=nyeh   kennah rapas   ujid*
        glass   *eye*=3s   *kennah* UV:grab   monkey
        'His glasses were snatched by a monkey.'

Simplification of the grammar is also exemplified by changes in the usage of the NSBJ pronoun series, which are being displaced by the general series (§3.4). Younger speakers allow use of the general series pronouns in all positions, and seem to be losing the NSBJ pronouns.

Older Belait speakers are simplifying in the same direction, and acknowledge that they often deliberately simplify when speaking with younger speakers. This of course complicates the task of any learner of the language, including linguists doing fieldwork.

ACKNOWLEDGMENTS

This chapter was written in close cooperation with Awang Kumpoh Labu and Dayang Dayang Agal of Mukkom, Kiudang, who have tirelessly and generously devoted many long hours to teaching me their language. Thanks are also due to speakers from Kuala Balai, in particular Haji Busu Ahmad and Dato Kifli Bujang, as well as to Peter Martin and Beatrice Clayre for helpful comments. I owe special thanks to the editors of this volume for their considerable, invaluable help in the writing of this chapter, and for their infinite patience.

REFERENCES

Ak Johani Pg Pungut (1983) 'Adat beranak puak asli Belait', *Berita Muzium Brunei* 2:12–16.

Blust, R.A. (1974) *The proto-North Sarawak vowel deletion hypothesis*, unpublished dissertation, University of Hawai'i.

——(1997) 'Ablaut in Western Borneo', *Diachronica* XIV:1–30.

Clayre, B. (1996) 'The changing face of focus in the languages of Borneo', in H. Steinhauer (ed.) *Papers in Austronesian linguistics No. 3*, 51–88, Canberra: Pacific Linguistics.

Dzulkefli Hj Yusuf (1984) 'Adat kematian puak asli Belait', *Berita Muzium Brunei* 6:30–34.

Harrisson, T. (1958) 'Origins and attitudes of Brunei Tutong-Belait-Bukit-Dusun, North Borneo "Dusun" and Sarawak "Bisayan", Metting and other peoples', *Sarawak Museum Journal* 8/11:293–321.

Hughes-Hallet, H. (1980) 'An account of a berhantu ceremony called 'perakong' by the Orang Belait of Brunei', *Brunei Museum Journal* 5:41–48 (reprinted from *Journal of the Malaysian Branch of the Royal Asiatic Society* 16,1:102–108, 1938).

Kumanireng, A.D. (1995) 'Konstruksi pasif dalam bahasa Belait', in Cawangan Perkamusan DBP (ed.) *Dialek memperkaya bahasa*, 167–177, Bandar Seri Begawan: Dewan Bahasa dan Pustaka.

Martin, P.W. (1990a) 'Who are the Belait?', *Paper presented at the first extraordinary meeting of the Borneo Research Council*, Kuching, 4–10 August 1990.

—— (1990b) *Notes on the phonology of Belait*, (unpublished MS).

—— (1995) 'Whither the indigenous languages of Brunei Darussalam?', *Oceanic Linguistics* 34:44–60.

—— (1996) 'Sociohistorical determinants of language shift among the Belait community in the sultanate of Brunei', *Anthropos* 91:199–207.

Martin, P.W. and Poedjosoedarmo, G. (1996) 'Introduction: an overview of the language situation in Brunei Darussalam', in P. Martin, G. Poedjosoedarmo and C. Ozog (eds) *Language use and language change in Brunei Darussalam*, 1–26, Athens: Ohio University Centre for International Studies.

Muhamad Islam Abdullah (1997) *Refleks bunyi proto-Austronesia pada bahasa Belait*, unpublished BA thesis, Dept. of Malay Language and Linguistics, Universiti Brunei Darussalam.

Noor Alifah Abdullah (1992) *Struktur bahasa Belait*, unpublished BA thesis, Dept. of Malay Language and Linguistics, Universiti Brunei Darussalam.

——(1993) 'Ungkapan tabu dalam masyarakat Belait dari sudut sosiolinguistik', *Beriga* 13:45–60.

——(1995) *Latar Belakang: asal-usul puak Belait, bahasa Beliat dan dialek-dialek Beliat*, MS, Dept. of Malay Language and Linguistics, Universiti Brunei Darussalam.

Noor Ehsan Hj Noor Kaseh (1983) 'Adat perkahwinan puak asli Belait', *Berita Muzium Brunei* 7:34–43.

Nothofer, B. (1991) 'The languages of Brunei Darussalam', in H. Steinhauer (ed.) *Papers in Austronesian Linguistics, No. 1*, 151–176, Canberra: Pacific Linguistics.

Pudarno Binchin (1993) 'Upacara perakong sebagi sebuah upacara kepercayaan berpadi masyarakat puak Metting (Lemetting)', *Brunei Museum Journal* 8:29–46.

Ray, S. (1913) 'The languages of Borneo', *The Sarawak Museum Journal* 1/4:1–196.

CHAPTER SIXTEEN

MALAGASY

Janie Rasoloson and Carl Rubino

1 INTRODUCTION

1.1 Language area and speakers

Malagasy is an Austronesian language belonging to the Southeast Barito linguistic subgroup of the Western Malayo-Polynesian subfamily (cf. Dahl 1977). It is spoken by about 14 million people throughout Madagascar as well as by an ethnic group on the island of Mayotte (Comoros Islands; see Map 16.1).

The relationship between Malagasy and the Austronesian languages has been discussed by various scholars since Houtman (1603). An overview of their work is given in Dahl (1951, 1991) who also outlines that Maanyan, an Indonesian language spoken in South Borneo, shows striking phonetic, grammatical as well as lexical similarities with Malagasy and is the language most closely related to Malagasy. Adelaar (1989, 1994a, 1994b) demonstrates the existence of Malay and Javanese loanwords in Malagasy. He proposes the seventh century AD as the most likely migration date and argues for continued contacts between Madagascar and Southeast Asia until after the introduction of Islam in the latter. Adelaar (1995) shows the existence of South Sulawesi loanwords in Malagasy. The contacts of Malagasy with non-Austronesian languages are witnessed by elements from Swahili and other Bantu languages (cf. Dahl 1951, 1988), Sanskrit (Dahl 1951), Arabic (cf. Dahl 1983), French and English.

Malagasy is spoken in several dialects, which are often so closely related to one another that a clear group classification is uncertain and quite a number of different classifications have been put forward (cf. Vérin et al. 1969; Dez 1963, 1980; Simon 1988; Mahdi 1988). Andriamanantsilavo and Ratrema (1981:41–63) propose a detailed typological classification of Malagasy dialects based on comparisons of specific phonemes or phonemic groups within the regional dialects. They divide them into three main groups: the eastern dialects, the western dialects, and the intermediate dialects. The following phonemic oppositions distinguish eastern dialects from western ones (see also Beaujard 1998): /di/ vs. /li/ (e.g. *miàdy* vs. *miàly* 'to fight'), /tsi/ vs. /ti/ (e.g. *antsìka* vs. *antìka* 'ours'), /tr/ vs. /ts/ (e.g. *fahèfatra* vs. *fahèfatse* 'fourth'), /-z-/ vs. /ø/ (e.g. *àiza* vs. *àia* 'where'), /-i/ vs. /-e/ (e.g. *mihètsika* vs. *mihètseke* 'to move').

The eastern dialects include *Antakarana, Tsimihety, Sakalava avaratra, Bezanozano, Sihanaka* in the northeast, *Merina, Betsimisaraka atsimo, Betsileo avaratra* in the central east, and *Antaimoro, Antambahoaka, Antesaka, Antaifasy, Tanala, Zafisoro* in the southeast. *Antaimoro* has the oldest written literature, which is a consequence of the early encounter of its speakers with Islam. Already in the fifteenth century the *Antaimoro* made use of the Arabic script to write Malagasy. *Merina*, spoken in the central highlands, was also first written in Arabic script. In 1820 the Malagasy king Radama I adopted the Roman script using an orthography developed by British missionaries.

456

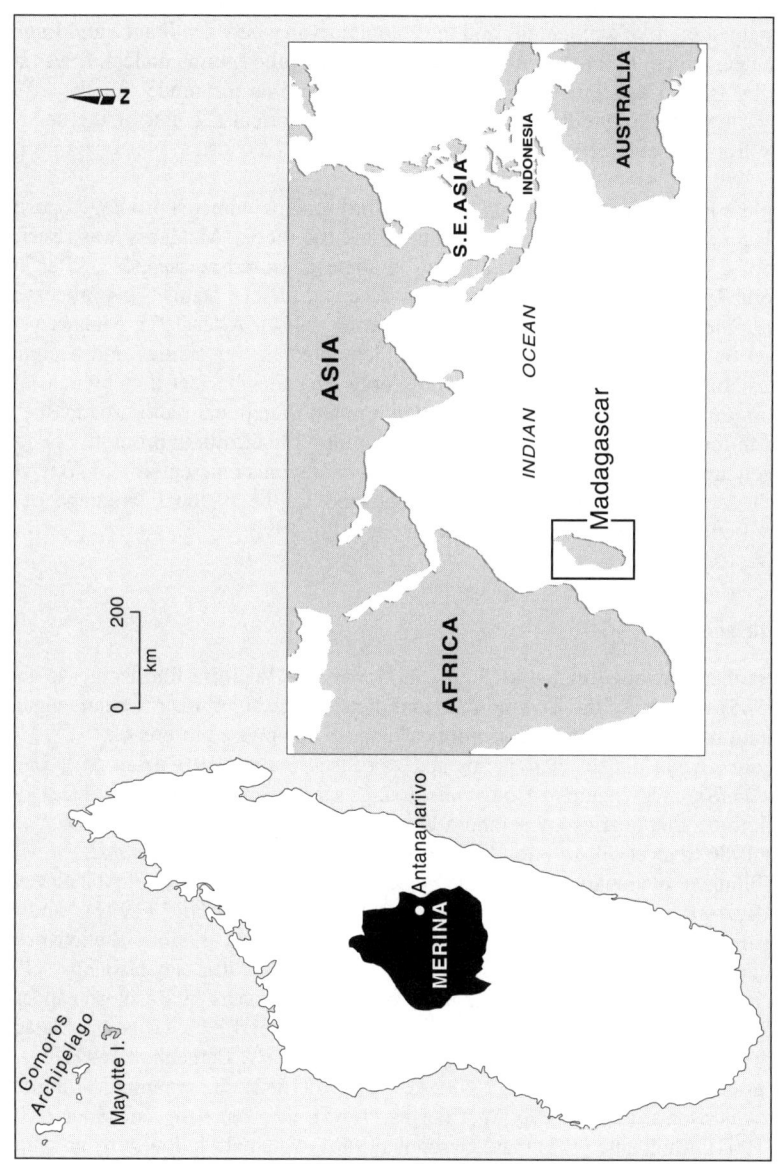

MAP 16.1 THE INDIAN OCEAN AND MADAGASCAR

The western dialects include *Sakalava of Menabe*, *Masikoro* and *Vezo avaratra* in the central west and *Antandroy*, *Mahafaly*, *Tañala* and *Vezo atsimo* in the south-west. The intermediate dialects, which share elements from both the western and eastern dialects, include *Bara*, *Antanosy* and *Betsileo*. The *Antalaotsy* dialect and two dialects spoken on Mayotte, *Kibosy Kimaore* and *Kiantalaotsy*, are not included in this dialect classification.

The establishment of a monarchy and the colonial rivalry between France and England in the nineteenth century contributed to the supremacy of the Merina dialect. It was standardized by British and French missionaries and served as the model for the official Malagasy language. Schmidt (1991:14–20) gives a historical account of the status of Malagasy from the eighteenth century to the early 1990s (see also STEINHAUER, LANGUAGE POLICY).

During the French colonial period (1895–1960), French obtained a privileged position over Malagasy in official functions, education, and the media. Malagasy was restricted to family use only, although it was allowed in some censored newspapers. After independence in 1960, both French and Malagasy received official status. This process was known as *fanagasiana* or *malgachisation* (Schmidt 1984). After 1975 Malagasy was introduced in education, but it was never implemented in universities and eventually became established in state primary schools only. Despite the fact that French is the medium in higher education, Malagasy is predominant in national radio broadcasts, and it is used in local newspapers and television. Although the efforts to promote Malagasy were largely unsuccessful (Schmidt 1983, 1984) – an obvious repercussion of sixty years of French occupation – Malagasy was established as the national language of the Malagasy Republic in an official referendum passed in 1992.

1.2 Major sources

The comprehensive monolingual Malagasy dictionary by Rajemisa-Raolison (1963, new edition 1985) was one of the first monolingual dictionaries of an Austronesian language. Its publication was an initiative to promote Malagasy as opposed to French.

There are several dialect dictionaries and wordlists: Dubois 1917 (*Betsileo*); Decary 1928 (*Antandroy*); Deschamps 1936 (*Antaisaka*); Descheemaeker (unpubl.) and Dez 1960, 1992 (all three dictionaries of southern *Betsimisaraka*); Mampitovy 1978 (*Zafisoro*); Gueunier 1986 (dialect of Mayotte); Elli 1988 (*Bara*); Beaujard 1998 (*Tanala*).

Major bilingual dictionaries include the French–Malagasy dictionaries of Abinal/Malzac (1888), Rajaonarimanana (1995b), Rajaonarimanana and Vérin (1997), and the Malagasy–French dictionary of Webber (1853), the Malagasy–English dictionaries of Freeman and Johns (1835), Richardson (1885), Paginton (1970), and Hallanger (1969, 1973). A compact Malagasy–English/English–Malagasy dictionary by Rasoloson appeared in 2001. There is also a Malagasy–Russian dictionary (Korneev 1966), a Russian–Malagasy dictionary (Korneev 1970) and a Malagasy–German dictionary (Bergenholtz 1991).

Older grammars include Ailloud (1873), G. Cousins (1882), the grammatical introduction in Richardson's dictionary by W. Cousins (1885), the works of Caussèque (1886), Malzac (1908), Montagné (1931) and Gerbinis (1946), which are followed by an outpour of Malagasy grammars written by native speakers as exemplified by Rahajarizafy (1960), Rajemisa-Raolison (1969), Rajaona (1972), Domenichini-Ramiaramanana (1976), Rabenilaina (1983), and Rajaonarimanana (1995a). Further grammars include Dez (1980) and Builles (1998). An array of works on different aspects of Malagasy morphology and syntax has recently appeared, e.g. Keenan (1976, 1994), Randriamasimanana (1986),

Dahl (1986), Mahdi (1988), Manaster-Ramer (1992), Pearson and Paul (1996), Keenan and Polinsky (1998), Keenan and Ralalaoherivony (1998), Paul (1998), Rackowski (1998), Fugier (1999), Randriamasimanana (1999), Paul (1999, 2000), Pearson (1996, 2001), Keenan and Rabenilaina (2001).

Major Malagasy textbooks in French include Berthier (1922), Rajaobelina (1966), Rabearivelo (1976), Razafindrabe (1984), Razafindrakoto (1990) and Rajaonarimanana (1995c). Stark (1969) published a Malagasy course for English-speaking students. Razafindrabe, Ralahatra and Ravaomalala (1980) provide an outstanding bilingual textbook in French and English. The first Malagasy textbook for German speakers is Rasoloson (1997).

Corpus-based studies of spoken Malagasy are rare (Rasoloson 1994, 1995). Most of the examples in this chapter originate from our own corpus of spontaneous spoken language.

2 PHONOLOGY

2.1 Segments

The Malagasy consonantal inventory is detailed in Table 16.1, using the standard Malagasy orthography. Phonemes attested only in some dialects are given in parentheses.

Voiceless stops are unaspirated. There is an asymmetry in the velar stops; the voiceless velar stop has a palatalized allophone preceding the vowel i, and all velar stops palatalize following the vowel i, e.g. *alìka* 'dog' [alík^{j}a], *hàingana* 'fast' [(h)áj^{n}g^{j}ana]. All stops may appear prenasalized. They are then pronounced either with a short homorganic nasal onset or, less frequently, as stops following a heavily nasalized vowel. The voiceless prenasalized consonants *mp, nt, ntr, nts*, and *nk* only appear word-medially. (The nominal prefix *mp-* in words like *mpiàsa* 'worker' is pronounced [p].) The five fricatives in Malagasy include two labio-dentals, f and v, two alveolar, grooved fricatives articulated with spread lip position, s and z, and the weak glottal fricative h. Fricatives may be syllabic when they precede devoiced vowels. The four affricates in Malagasy are the apical dento-alveolars *ts* and j (*dz*), and the blade alveolars *tr* and *dr*. Like the stops, they may appear prenasalized. The resonants are l, a voiced, dento-alveolar lateral, and r, a trill

TABLE 16.1: MALAGASY CONSONANTS

	Bilabial	Labio-Dental	Dental	Alveolar/Retroflex	Velar	Glottal
Stops	p b		t d		k g	(ʔ)**
Prenasalized stops*	mp [^{m}p]		nt [^{n}t]		nk [^{ŋ}k]	
	mb [^{m}b]		nd [^{n}d]		ng [^{ŋ}g]	
Fricatives		f v	s z			h
Affricates			ts j [dz]	tr dr		
Prenasalized affricates*			nts [^{n}ts]	ntr [^{n}tr]		
			nj [^{n}dz]	ndr [^{n}dr]		
Nasals	m		n		(ñ [ŋ])	
Laterals			l			
Trills			r			

* Prenasalized stops and affricates are represented in the official orthography with a hyphen following the nasal in cases of a morpheme break.

** The glottal stop has phonemic status only in a few dialects, e.g. Antaimoro.

which may also appear as a single flap. All consonants except *h* are slightly palatalized before *i*, and may be slightly labialized before the vowel *u*. The velar nasal ñ is present in most varieties of Malagasy; however, it is not phonemic in Merina.

All consonants except the voiceless prenasalized consonants may occur in initial position. The one exception to this rule is *ntàolo* 'ancestors' which lost a historical initial /u/ (Keenan and Polinsky 1998). The glottal fricative is often dropped in medial position, especially between two distinct vowels. It alternates with k in certain morphologically complex forms, reflecting an older stage of the language (*k > h): *òlon-kèndry* (/òlona-hèndry/'person-wise') 'wise person', *haingankàingana* 'somewhat fast' (/RDP-hàingana/'fast').

Although geminate consonants do not exist in underlying form, they may result from the devoicing and dropping of an unstressed *i* or *o* vowel, e.g. *inona* 'what' [ínna]. When an unstressed vowel is dropped before the nasal *n*, the nasal may assimilate to the preceding consonant, causing gemination: *làmina* 'set, arrange' [lámma], *tèlina* 'swallow' [télla], *òlona* 'person' [úlla].

Malagasy has a four vowel system, *i* (spelled <y> in word-final position), *u* (orthographic <o>), *e*, and *a*, with four diphthongs, *ai*, *ia*, *oa*, and *au*. The vowel [o] may result from shortening of the vowel sequences *ao* or *oa* (except word finally where it is pronounced as *u*), e.g. *misàotra* 'to thank' [misótra], *lòatra* 'too much' [lótra], but *tokòa* 'indeed' [tukú]. The vowel [o] also frequently occurs in loan words, where it may be represented orthographically as *ô*, e.g. *kamiônèty* 'pick up truck', *môtôsikilèty* 'motorcycle', *biôlôjìa* 'biology'. Although the vowel [o] does occur as a phoneme in nonstandard dialects, the only native Merina word with the vowel is the vocative interjection *ô*. The vowel sequence *ia* and the diphthong *ai* may be pronounced as [e], e.g. *dia* 'focus particle' [de], *ianào* 'you' [enáu], *hàino* 'listen' [héno]. The vowel /a/ may reduce to [ə] in unstressed environments, or just to a simple release of the preceding consonant, especially word-finally, e.g. *mahita* [mahítə] 'see'.

Vowels have weak nasalization preceding a nasal consonant, and heavy nasalization preceding prenasalized consonants. They do not occur long.

All vowels may occur root-initially, but the vowel *e* is rare as the second vowel of native roots. In final position with some verbs, the vowel *i* (orthographic *y*) alternates with *e* in suffixed forms, e.g. *mambòly* (<maN-voly) 'plant (active)' vs. *volèna* 'plant (passive)'. No sequences of identical vowels occur, and only the sequence /ai/ functions as a stable diphthong, retaining the stress pattern v'v instead of becoming v.v' with stress attracting suffixes (Garvey 1964:19).

The unstressed vowels *i* and *o* are often devoiced in Malagasy, especially in final position or between two consonants.

2.2 Syllable structure and stress

Malagasy syllable structure is CV; no codas are allowed word-finally and the maximal onset is one segment, except in a few loanwords, e.g. *frantsày* 'French'. Only vowels may function as syllable peaks, all other segments must be treated as onsets phonologically.

Most Malagasy words are stressed on the penultimate syllable, e.g. *mahita* 'see', *màmba* 'crocodile', *sikìdy* 'divination', *vàry* 'rice', *paràky* 'tobacco' (in standard Malagasy orthography, stress is indicated by a grave accent, as in the preceding examples). However, there are cases where stress is not predictable, e.g. *àty* 'liver' vs. *atỳ* 'here (not in sight)' and in the imperative formation of some active verbs and adjectives, as a result of a suffix -*a* that has merged (contracted) with a final root vowel, e.g. *manàsa* 'wash (indicative)' vs. *manasà* 'wash (imperative)'; *tsàra* 'good' vs. *tsarà* 'be good'. If a word ends in a diphthong, it bears final stress, e.g. *papày* 'papaya', *manào* 'do'. Moreover, words ending in the 'weak final syllables' -*na*, -*ka*, or -*tra* take stress on the antepenultimate syllable, e.g. *filàmatra* 'principle', *kàmbana* 'twin', *fàntatra* 'know', *manòmboka* 'begin'. A regular exception to this rule is that words, which end in weak syllables have penultimate stress when the preceding vowel is /e/, /e/ being a regular stress-attractor in Malagasy, e.g., *pôkètra* 'purse, hand bag'.

Weak final syllables in Malagasy behave peculiarly in that they function as extrametrical stem formatives, which delete in compounding, reduplication, and before clitics and suffixes: *antànana* 'fall into the hands of' + *màmba* 'crocodile' =*antàna-màmba* 'fall into the hands of a cruel person'; *fihina* 'to clutch, clasp' + *màmba* > *fihi-màmba* 'refusal to let go of something', *zànaka* 'child' + =*ko* '1s.GEN' > *zànako* 'my child'. The deviant behavior of -*ka*, *tra*, and -*na* reflects the fact that they are a product of a default vowel /a/ added after historically consonant-final words as part of the development towards the modern CV structure in Malagasy, e.g. *vòlana* 'moon' (< **bùlan*), *sòratra* 'writing' (< **surat*). The resulting forms should be treated as 'extended roots' which are involved in a variety of synchronic alternations.

Roots of four or more syllables assign secondary stress to every second syllable working back from the main stress. Compound words receive primary stress on the second word of the compound, e.g. *tòro-hèvitra* (point-idea) 'advice'; *manòso-pòtaka* (/maN-hòsotra-fòtaka/=ACT-smear-mud) 'smear with mud, slander'.

In suffixation, root stress shifts one syllable to the right (e.g. *bàbo* > *babòina* 'be captured') unless the root is stressed on the final syllable, is monosyllabic, or has a weak ending in which case an additional consonant may be inserted, e.g. *to* > *toàvina* 'be obeyed', *fàoka* > *fàohana* 'be carried off'. With bi-syllabic enclitics, the enclitic often attracts heavy stress, but does not alter the stress of the root.

2.3 Morphophonemics

A homorganic nasal is inserted between reduplicant and base in reduplication and between the two components of a genitive construction or compound if the first component does not end with a weak final syllable -*tra*, -*ka*, or -*na*, e.g. *rèsin-tòry* (/resy-tory/=overcome-sleep) 'overcome by sleep'; *sòlom-bodiakòho* (/sòlo-vody-akòho/=substitute-rump-chicken) 'a gift given to one's elder (different from the traditional chicken rump)', *akànjon-jàza* (/akànjo-zàza/=clothing-child) 'children's clothing', *fetim-pianakavìana* (fèty-fianakavìana/=feast-family) 'family feast' (for further details of genitive formation, see section 3.2.1).

If the first component of a compound or reduplication ends on -*tra* or -*ka*, the weak final syllable is dropped before a consonant. If this consonant is a fricative or liquid it becomes a stop or affricate based on the rules given in Table 16.2 (see Erwin 1996 for a more detailed phonological account). Examples: *hèna-màso* (/henatra-maso/= shame-eye) 'behaving in the presence of others', *hàta-pìso* (/hataka-piso/=request-cat) 'persistent request', *pòa-bàsy* (/poaka-basy/=explosion-gun) 'gunshot'; *vòso-dràtsy* (/vosotra-ratsy/=joke-bad) 'buffoonery'; *mandàtsa-bàratra* (/mandàtsaka-vàratra/=lay/ cast.down-thunder) 'to cause misfortune from a wrongdoing'. Before a vowel the final *a* of the weak syllable is dropped, the dropped vowel in this environment being indicated in the orthography by an apostrophe e.g. *sàsak'àlina* (/sasaka-alina/=half-night) 'midnight'.

TABLE 16.2: MORPHOPHONEMIC ALTERNATIONS IN COMPOUNDING

v > b	tòsi-bòhon-tànana	rejection showing disdain
	(/tosika-vòho-tànana/=push-back-hand)	
f > p	fitandrèmam-pahasalamàna	health care
	(/fitandrèmana-fahasalamàna/=caring for-health)	
h > k	fanavakavàham-bòlon-kòditra	racial discrimination
	(/fanavakavàhana-volo-hoditra/)=discrimination-color-skin	
s > ts	fàdin-tserànana (/fàdy-serànana/=taboo-port.of.entry)	customs duties
z > j	mihètsi-jàza (/mi-hètsika-zàza/=ACT-move-child)	to be in labour
r > dr	mangìran-dràtsy (/mangìrana-ràtsy/=light.beam-bad)	first dim light of the morning
l > d	an-dàlana (/an-làlana/=on-road)	on the way

Words ending with the weak final syllable *-na* drop final *a* before consonants, and the nasal is realized as homorganic to the following consonant. The latter may be occlusivized following the rules discussed in Table 16.2, e.g. *èntana vàrotra* (baggage-commerce) > *èntam-bàrotra* 'merchandise' (see also the examples in Table 16.2).

In words with prefixes ending with a homorganic nasal such as present tense active *maN-*, the homorganic nasal of the prefix assimilates to a following obstruent, after which the obstruent deletes if it is voiceless, e.g. *mamìhina* (from *fihina*) 'to clutch, clasp', *manàfy* (from *tàfy*) 'to dress', *manàfotra* (from *sàfotra*) 'to submerge', but *mambòntsina* (from *bòntsina*) 'to mislead'. Before vowel-initial bases, the prefix ends in /n/: *manàfaka* (from *àfaka*) 'to set free'. If the base begins with an /h/, the /h/ is replaced either by a prenasalized glottal stop as in *mangàtaka* (from *hàtaka* < *kataka*) 'to ask for' or by /n/ as in *manàntona* 'hang' (from *hàntona*). See Keenan and Polinsky (1998:595f) for further details.

2.4 Reduplication

Malagasy verbs and adjectives may undergo full root reduplication to encode attenuation, iterativity or unsystematic (non-motivated) event processing, e.g. *màinty* 'black', *maintimàinty* 'slightly dark skinned', *mandèha* 'to go, walk' > *mandehandèha* 'to walk about'. The weak endings *-ka*, *-tra*, *-na* do not participate in the reduplication, e.g. *pìtsoka* 'foolish' > *mi-pitso-pìtsoka* 'a little bit stupid, foolish', *mi-pètraka* 'to sit' > *mi-petrapètraka* 'to sit about'.

As detailed in Table 16.2 for compound constructions, reduplications undergo similar phonological alternations involving consonantal substitution, e.g. *maN-fàntsika* 'to nail' reduplicated becomes *mamantsipàntsika* 'to nail repeatedly', *maN-hàntona* 'to hang' becomes *manantonkàntona* 'to hang about', and *mi-vàntana* 'to be direct' becomes *mivantambàntana* 'to be somewhat direct'.

3 BASIC MORPHOSYNTAX

3.1 Basic clause structure

In unmarked phrases, Malagasy clauses are predicate-initial. The predicate can be verbal or non-verbal (e.g. noun/proper name, adjective, numeral, prepositional phrase, possessive (genitive) phrase, temporal adverb, deictic). The following examples for non-verbal predicates show that these are not introduced by a copula. Note also that the Malagasy predicates do not always correspond to the English ones:

Possessive:

(1) **Anày**   *ilày   fìàra   sìmba.*
    1pe.DAT   DET   car   broken
    'The broken car is ours.'

Adjective:

(2) **Lehibè**   *tokòa   ny   aerodròme.*
    big   indeed   DEF   airport
    'The airport is big indeed.'

Numeral:

(3) **Fòlo**   *ihàny   ny   òmbi=này.*
    ten   only   DEF   ox=3pe.GEN
    'We only have got ten oxes.' (lit. Our oxes are only ten)

Deictic in presentative function:

(4) **'ty**   *ny   famèrim-bòlanào,   tòmpoko.*
    intỳ   ny   famèrim-bòla=nào   tòmpo=ko
    PRX.VIS.PRD   DEF   change=2s.GEN   lord=1s.GEN
    'Here is your change, Sir.'

In verbal clauses, both transitive and intransitive verbs are marked for voice and tense. Active verbs take an active prefix, the most common ones being *mi-* and *maN-*, where the prefix *m-* changes to *h-* or *n-* depending on tense (see section 5).

(5) *N-i-salasàla*   *i*   *Nàivo.*
    PST-ACT-hesitate   PN   Nàivo.
    'Nàivo hesitated.'

(6) *N-a-hìta*   *òmby   àho.*
    PST-ACT-see   ox   1s
    'I saw an ox.'

Malagasy simple main clause subjects are generally placed in final-position in non-verbal clauses as well as in verbal clauses, as seen in the preceding examples. In the majority of cases where undergoer arguments appear with active verbs, they occur immediately after the verb and are indefinite as in (6) unless specified by a demonstrative or the definite article *ny*, as in (7):

(7) *Làsa*   *n-i-làhatra*   *nanòhana*   **ny**   **grévistes**   *an!*
    Gone   n-i-làhatra   n-aN-t òhana   ny   grévistes   an!
    Gone   PST-ACT-stand.in.line   PST.ACT:support   DEF   strikers   INTJ
    'Gone [on strike] to support the strikers!' (emphatic)

Passive verbs are marked with the affixes *-ina*, *-ana* or *a-*. The undergoer argument appears in subject position and is generally definite (Manaster-Ramer 1992:276). The actor argument immediately follows the verb, often in the form of a clitic pronoun. Contrast (6) with (8):

(8) *An, napètrako*   *t-èo*   ***ny tômôbila*...
     An, n-a-pètraka=o   t-èo   ny tômôbila...
     INTJ PST-PASS-put=1s.GEN PST-MED.VIS DEF car
     'Uh, I left the car there...'

Other arguments and adjuncts typically occur in between the two core arguments of transitive verbs:

(9) *Nanàovan'ny*   Croix Rouge ***kermèsy*** *ny*
     n-aN-tào-v-ana=n'ny   *Croix Rouge* kermèsy ny
     PST-CIRC-do-SF-CIRC=GEN.DEF Cross Red   fair   DEF
     vòla   voaàngona.
     vòla   voa-àngona.
     money   RES-raise
     'The money raised was used by the Croix Rouge to organize a fair.'

(10) *Natàon'ny*   Croix Rouge ***tàmin'ny***   *vòla*
     n-a-tào=n'ny   *Croix Rouge* t-àmin'ny   vòla
     PST-PASS-do=GEN.DEF   Cross Red   PST-with:GEN.DEF money
     voaàngona *ny*   *kermèsy.*
     voa-àngona   ny   kermèsy.
     RES-raise   DEF   fair
     'The Red Cross organized the fair with the money raised.'

(11) *Nanàovan'ny*   Croix Rouge ***kermèsy***
     PST:CIRC.do.SF:CIRC=GEN.DEF Cross Red   fair
     t-àmin'ny   **zomà**   **t-ào**   **Mahavòky**
     PST-on:GEN.DEF   Friday   PST-MED.INVIS   Mahavòky
     ny   *vòla*   *voa-àngona.*
     DEF   money   RES-raise
     'The money raised was used by the Red Cross to organize a fair in Mahavòky on Friday.'

Adjuncts occurring after the subject can be interpreted as modifying the subject rather than the overall predication, as in (12).

(12) *Nanàovan'ny*   Croix Rouge *kermèsy* *ny*   *vòla*
     PST.CIRC:do:SF.CIRC.GEN.DEF Cross Red   fair   DEF   money
     voa-àngona *t-àmin'ny*   *zomà*   *t-ào*   *Mahavòky.*
     RES-raise   PST- on:GEN.DEF   Friday   PST-MED.INVIS   Mahavòky.
     'The money raised on Friday in Mahavòky was used by the Red Cross to organize a fair.'

As shown in examples (10), (11), and (12), prepositional phrases always show tense agreement with the verb. Here they are inflected for past tense with the prefix *t-* (i.e. *t-ào* and *t-àmin'ny*).

The unmarked VXS word order may be altered by the fronting of a normally post-predicate subject followed by the focus marker *no*: **S + no + P**. The element preceding the particle *no*, which is the subject appearing here in clause-initial position, carries the greatest prominence in the clause, e.g.:

(13) *Ny   mpampiànatra   **no**   n-i-tèhaka.*
      DEF   teacher   FOC   PST-ACT-clap the hand
      'The teacher (and no one else) applauded.'

(13) encodes a restrictive meaning singling out this teacher from any other person who might be under consideration (e.g. the musician, the children, the spectators, etc.).

This type of focus construction is not restricted to subjects. Other non-predicate elements (e.g. an adverb) can also appear in initial position and be followed by the particle *no* indicating focus on this element. Thus, in the sentence: *Omàly **no** niàinga izy* (yesterday FOC PST:leave 3) the focus is on the temporal adverb *omàly* 'yesterday': 'He/she left yésterday (and not on another day)'. Compare also:

(14) **T-ào**   **Mahavòky**   **t-àmin'ny**   **zomà**   **no**
      t-ào   Mahavòky   t-àmin'ny   zomà   no
      PST-MED.INVIS   Mahavòky   PST-on:GEN.DEF   Friday   FOC
      nanàovan'ny
      n-an-tào-v-ana=n'ny
      PST-CIRC-do-SF-CIRC=GEN.DEF
      Croix   Rouge   *kermèsy*   *t-àmin'ny*   *vòla*   *voa-àngona.*
      Cross   Red   fair   PST-with:GEN.DEF   money   RES-raise
      'It was in Mahavòky on Friday that a fair was organized by the Red Cross with the money raised.'

Another inversion construction may be obtained simply by fronting the post-predicate subject, which yields an 'emphatic' SVO word order. The preposed subject is set off from the remainder of a sentence by a pause or by lengthening the last vowel (*fàrany:::*) of the preposed subject argument (cf. Rasoloson 1994:109–122):

(15) *Ìzy   mirahavàvy   fàrany:::   tsy   mbòla   n-a-hìta   ranomàsina.*
      3   sister   last   NEG   yet   PST-ACT-see   sea
      'The youngest two (sisters) of them, they have not seen the sea yet.'

This 'emphatic' SVO construction could be given as an answer to the question: 'Who has not seen the sea yet?'

In predicate focus constructions, the subject also occurs in clause-initial position, and the predicate is preceded by the particle *dia*: S + **dia** + P. The implication of this type of construction is that, of the set of potential events under consideration (put in brackets as shown below), there is only one which is carried out (16).

(16) *Ny   bibikèly   **dìa**   n-i-hìnana   ny   fàka=ny.*
      DEF   insect(s)   FOC   PST-ACT-eat   DEF   root=3.GEN
      'The insect(s) ate its roots (they did not damage them or play with them, etc.).'

Compare this example with the related subject-focus clause construction:

(17) *Bibikèly   **no**   n-i-hìnana   ny   fàka=ny.*
      insect(s)   FOC   PST-ACT-eat   DEF   roots=3.GEN
      'Insect(s) (not butterflies, not bees, not dragonflies, etc.) ate its roots.'

In a subtype of the predicate-focus construction, the clause-initial subject consists of a nominalized expression and the predicate of a nominal expression:

(18) *Ny   n-i-hìnana   ny   fàka=ny   **dia**   bibikèly.*
      DEF   PST-ACT-eat   DEF   roots=3.GEN   FOC   insect(s).
      'Insect(s) ate its roots (the ones who ate its roots were insects).'

3.2 Noun phrases

Basic order in full noun phrases is DETERMINER HEAD MODIFIER. Alternative orders of head and modifier are possible but usually also convey a different meaning. Thus, adjectives usually follow their head as in *ny kiràro malòto* (DEF shoes dirty) 'the dirty shoes'. If the adjective precedes its head, a nominalization results (cf. also section 6.1): *ny malòto kiràro* (DEF dirty shoes) 'the one with the dirty shoes'.

Common noun phrases are marked for definiteness by an article or a demonstrative, with a special set of markers occurring in the case of personal names (cf. Table 16.3).

In addition to the definite article *ny*, there is the determiner *ilày* which is used for referents known to speaker and hearer via specific shared knowledge without necessarily having been mentioned in the preceding discourse.

(19) *Àry   ilày   rangàhy   m-i-pìtsoka   hìta=nào?*
      and   DET   man   PRS-ACT-crazy   PASS:see=2s.GEN
      'What about that crazy man you saw?'

The personal article *i* is not used when the name begins with a proper name proclitic, *I-, Ra-, Ilai-* or *Ikàla-*. In addition to the personal article *i*, there is a further personal article *ry* which designates a group of persons in a family relationship or in a friendship relationship with the person denoted by the noun it precedes (20). *Ry* is also used before nouns to address someone directly (21).

(20) *Nandèfa   taratàsy   **ry**   Bakòly.*
      n-aN-lèfa   taratàsy   ry   Bakòly
      PST.ACT:send   letter   PN   Bakòly
      'Bakòly and her family sent a letter.'

(21) *N-ìsy   vòla   ve   t-ào   **ry**   Màma?*
      PST-EXIST   money   PTCL   PST-MED.INVIS   PN   Mum
      'Was there any money in there, Mum?'

The full genitive clitics of the group (A) in Table 16.3 are used as proclitics, forming possessive predicates (group B is discussed in the next section). *An'ny* [anní] and *an'ilày* are employed with definite common nouns whereas *an'i* [aní] is used with proper nouns:

(22) ***An'ny***   *mpampiànatr'i   Sèndra   'ty   pôkètra   'ty.*
      GEN.DEF   teacher:GEN.PN   Sèndra   PRX.VIS   bag   PRX.VIS
      'This bag belongs to Sendra's teacher.'

TABLE 16.3: NOUN PHRASE MARKERS

	DEF	GEN.DEF	
		(A)	(B)
Definite common nouns	ny/ilày	an'ny/an'ilày	=n'ny
Personal names	i	an'i	=n'i/=n

(23) *An'i   Rìna   'zào   e!*
GEN.PN   Rìna   now   INTJ
'It is Rìna's [turn] now!'

These possessive predicates can be nominalized by preposing the definite article *ny* and then function as subjects (preposed subjects in the following example):

(24) *Ny   an'   isè   dìso   fa   ny   an'   ialàhy   no   mèty.*
DEF   GEN   FAM   wrong   but   DEF   GEN   FAM.M   FOC   okay
' "Yours" (i.e. one trainee's performance) is wrong but "yours" (another trainee's performance) is okay.' (Teacher to his trainees.)

Pronouns come in three major sets rather than the two attested for common nouns (see Table 16.4 for a summary). The nominative case is used for pronominal subject arguments, e.g. *Lèo izy* (fed up 3) 'he/she is fed up'; the dative for non-subject arguments and for predicates conveying possession, e.g. *Lèo àzy àho* (fed up 3.DAT 1s) 'I am fed up with him/her, *Anarèo ìo.* (2p.DAT that) 'That is yours'. The genitive forms are used to indicate the actor of a non-active verb, e.g. *Vìta=ko ilày bòky.* (PASS-finish=1s.GEN DET book) 'I finished that book', or the possessor of a nominal, e.g. *ny solomàso=nào* (DEF glasses 2s.GEN) 'your glasses'. They are also used for most prepositional objects. The choice between the two genitive forms is morphonologically conditioned, as discussed in the next section.

Both forms of the first pronoun singular *àho* and *izàho* can function as a nominative subject. The difference between them is conditioned by word order: *Izàho* is the clause-initial counterpart of *àho*. E.g.: *Miàsa àho* (work 1s) 'I am working' vs. *Izàho dia miàsa* (1s FOC work) 'I am working (not sleeping)'.

The second singular pronoun *ianào* is not necessarily a familiar form. In most uses, it in fact excludes any kind of familiarity and is used as a distant form. In family relationship, however, *ianào* may express familiarity when used between a married couple or by an adult addressing a child. In other informal friendly relationships, a different set of *nominal* address forms is preferred which encode additional information about the speech act participants (sex, age, social status, personal relationship, etc.), e.g. *ialàhy* (high degree of familiarity, addressing a male), *indrỳ* (high degree of familiarity, addressing a female), *isè* (high degree of familiarity) (cf. example (24) above and Rasoloson 2000).

TABLE 16.4: FULL AND CLITIC FORMS OF MALAGASY PERSONAL PRONOUNS

	NOM	DAT	GEN	
			(I)	(II)
1.SG	izàho/àho	àhy	=ko	=o
2.SG	ianào	anào	=nào	=ào
1.PL.INCL.	isìka	antsìka	=ntsìka	=tsìka
1.PL.EXCL.	izahày	anày	=này	=ày
2.PL	ianarèo	anarèo	=narèo	=arèo
3 (SG or PL)	ìzy	àzy	=ny	=ny
3.PL	ìzy irèo	àzy irèo	=n'ìzy irèo	=ny

3.2.1 Genitive constructions

Genitive constructions are morphophonologically complex and differ for pronominal and nominal genitive modifiers. The head of a genitive construction can be a noun, a verb in passive or circumstantial voice, or a preposition.

The use of the genitive pronouns (Table 16.4) varies according to whether or not the final syllable of the head is a weak syllable. Heads not ending in a weak syllable take the genitive pronouns of group (I), e.g. *ny kiràro > ny kiràro=ko* (DEF shoe=1s.GEN) 'my shoes', *ny boky > ny bòki=narèo* (DEF book=2p.GEN) 'your book'. With heads ending in weak *-na*, the weak syllable drops and genitive pronouns of group (I) are used as well: *kàvina* 'earring' *> kàvi=này* (earring=1PE.GEN). If the head ends in weak *-ka* or *tra*, the final *-a* of the weak syllable is dropped and the genitive pronominal clitics of group (II) are used: e.g.: *pèratra* 'ring'*> pèratr=ào* (ring=2s.GEN) 'your ring'. If these clitics begin with a consonant (i.e. the third person and the first person plural inclusive clitics), then they replace the weak syllable, hence *pèrany* 'her/his/their ring' and *pèratsìka* 'our (incl.) ring'.

If the genitive argument consists of a noun or noun phrase, a number of different scenarios have to be distinguished. In the case of definite noun phrases and personal names functioning as genitive arguments, the genitive markers of group (B) in Table 16.3 above are used:=*n'ny* (phonologically /ni/) is employed with common nouns while=*n'i* (phonologically also /ni/) is employed with personal names: *ny bòky* 'the book(s)' *> ny bòki=n'ny mpampiànatra* 'the teacher's book', *ny kiràro* 'the shoes' *> ny kiràro=n'i Fàly* 'Fàly's shoes'. Major variants of this basic rule are as follows:

- If the personal name begins with /r/ (including names beginning with the personal name proclitic *Ra=*) the genitive marker is simply=*n*: *sàry* 'photograph' + *Rasòlo > sàrin-dRasòlo* 'Rasòlo's photograph' (r > dr is a phonologically regular alternation in reduplication, compounds and genitive constructions (cf. section 2.3)). The use of a dash in between head and genitive argument in this environment is a convention of standard Malagasy orthography. Another example with a verbal head is *Mbòla totòn-dRalày ny kafè* (still PASS-pound=GEN Ralày DEF coffee) 'Ralày is still pounding the coffee'.
- If the genitive argument is a personal name and the head ends in a weak syllable (*ka, tra,* or *na*) the vowel *a* of the weak syllable is dropped (in orthographic representations it is replaced with an apostrophe) and no special genitive marker is used: *kàvina* 'earring' *> kàvin' i Rìna* 'Rina's earring(s)'. As the preceding example shows, this rule also applies to personal names beginning with /r/, which then are preceded by the personal article *i*.
- If the genitive argument is a definite common noun and the head ends in weak *ka* or *tra,* the final *a* of the weak syllable is replaced with /i/ followed by the article *ny,* e.g.: *pèratra* 'ring' *> pèratry ny rahavàvi=ko* (ring:GEN DEF sister=3.GEN) 'my sister's ring', *zànaka* 'child' *> zànaky ny àlina* 'child(ren) of the night=children who are wandering about in the night'.
- If the genitive argument is a definite common noun and the head ends in weak *na,* the weak syllable is replaced by=*n'ny*, e.g. *hàvana* 'relative' + *ny sèfo* 'the boss' *> hàva=n'ny sèfo* 'relative(s) of the boss'.

Finally, if the genitive argument is an indefinite (common) noun phrase, then the genitive marker is =*n* as in *vinànto* 'son or daughter in law' + *andrìana* 'nobleman' *> vinànton'andrìana* 'a nobleman's son or daughter in law', *tràno* 'house' + *andrìana* 'nobleman' *> trànon'andrìana* 'a nobleman's house' (conventionally written as a single word in standard Malagasy orthography). If the genitive argument begins with a fricative or a liquid, this initial consonant is turned into a stop according to the rules stated in Table 16.2. Examples: *adàla* 'crazy' + *lalào* 'games' > *adàlan-dalào* 'game-mad (person)', *vinànto* + *sakàiza* 'friend' > *vinànton-tsakàiza* 'a friend's son in law or a friend's daughter in law'. Once again, somewhat different regularities hold for heads ending in weak syllables (see Keenan and Polinsky 1998:575f. for details and examples).

Adjectives may follow either the genitive argument or the head. In the latter case, the genitive case marker, if any, is directly appended to the adjective: *ny bòky malòto=n'ny mpampiànatra* (DEF book dirty=GEN.DEF teacher) 'the teacher's dirty book(s)'. If the adjective follows the genitive argument, this may result in two different constructions distinguished by context and intonational contour. One possibility is an unmarked restrictive relative clause (cf. section 3.2.2) as in *ny bòkin'ny mpampiànatra malòto* (DEF book:GEN.DEF teacher dirty) 'the teacher's book(s) which is/are dirty', the other an 'emphatic' subject construction (cf. section 3.1): *ny bòkin'ny mpampiànatra* (pause) *malòto* 'the teacher's book(s), they are dirty'.

3.2.2 Relative clauses

Malagasy relative clauses follow the noun they modify. They are optionally introduced by the relative clause marker *izày* and optionally followed by a demonstrative: DEF + N + (*izày*) + Predicate Phrase + (DEM) (Keenan 1994). Malagasy can only relativize on subjects and on possessors of subjects. Consequently, the verb in the relative clause has to appear in the appropriate voice, as illustrated in the following examples (in all of which *izày* is omissible):

(25) *i Bèma* [izày *nanòratra taratàsy ho an'ny nàma=ny*]
      PN Bèma REL PST.ACT:write letter to GEN.DEF friend=3.GEN
      'Bèma [who wrote a letter to his friend]'

(26) *ny taratàsy* [izày *nosoràtan'i Bèma ho an'ny nàma=ny*]
      DEF letter [REL PST:write:PASS.GEN.PN B. to GEN.DEF friend=3.GEN
      'the letter [that Bèma wrote to his friend]'

(27) *ny nàma=ny* [izày *nanoràtan'i Bèma taratàsy*]
      DEF friend=3.GEN REL PST.CIRC:write:GEN.PN Bèma letter
      'His friend [whom Bèma wrote a letter]'

(28) *ny tràno* [izày *hanàovana ny hasoàvan-jàza]*
      ny tràno izày h-an-tào-v-ana ny ha-sòa-v-ana=zàza
      DEF House REL FUT-CIRC-do-SF-CIRC DEF CIRC-good-SF-CIRC-child
      'The house [where the child's circumcision will be carried out]'

By using a non-active voice, it is also possible to relativize on the possessor in a possessive construction. Thus, from (29) one may form (30):

(29) *Nokapòhako tàmin'ny kifàfa ny*
      no-kapòka-ana=ko t-àmin'ny kifàfa ny
      PST-knock-PASS=1s.GEN PST-with:GEN.DEF broom DEF
      alìkan'ilày rangàhy.
      alìka=n'ilày rangàhy.
      dog=GEN.DET man
      'I hit the man's dog with a broom.'

(30) **Ilày   rangàhy** [izày   nokapòhako   t-àmin'ny
      DET   man   [REL   PST:knock:PASS=1s.GEN   PST-with:GEN.DEF
      kifàfa   ny   alìka=**ny**.]
      broom   DEF   dog=3.GEN
      'That man [whose dog I hit with a broom]'

Definite objects freely appear with active verbs in relative clause constructions, following the rigid constraint that only subject arguments (and their possessors) can be relativized:

(31) Ny   tròpy   Antananarìvo   teàtra   indrày   izày   h-i-sèhatra
      DEF   troupe   A   theatre   as.for   REL   FUT-ACT-stage
      izàny   tantàra   izàny
      DIST.INVIS   story   DIST.INVIS
      'As for the Antananarivo theatre troupe which will perform those (aforementioned) stories...'

If the relative clause is not formally marked by izày, it is only distinguished by intonation from an 'emphatic' subject construction (cf. Dez 1980:111ff.). Compare the following two examples:

(32) Ny   òlon-dehibè   m-i-rèsaka
      DEF   adults   PRS-ACT-talk
      'The adults who are talking.'

(33) Ny   òlon-dehibè   (..)   m-i-rèsaka.
      DEF   adults   (pause)   PRS-ACT-talk
      'The adults, they are talking.'

It is also possible to form headless relative clauses. Here, the relative pronoun izày cannot be omitted:

(34) Asehò=y   àhy   **izày**   n-a-tào=narèo   omàly.
      Show=PASS.IMP   1s.DAT   REL   PST-PASS-do=2p.GEN   yesterday
      'Show me what you did yesterday.'

(35) Tsy   hài=ko   ry   Fàra   **izày**   n-a-lèha=ny   a!
      NEG   know=1s.GEN   ART   F.   REL   PST-PASS-go=3.GEN INTJ
      'I do not know where he has gone, Fàra.'

4 DEIXIS

Malagasy has a rather elaborate deictic system. It involves the remarkably high number of seven degrees of distance from the speaker in addition to a visible/non-visible distinction. Apart from these semantic distinctions, there is also a grammatical distinction between adverbs and demonstratives. The deictic adverbs are listed in Table 16.5.

TABLE 16.5: DEICTIC ADVERBIALS

	Proximal	Medial	Distal
Visible	etỳ, èto	èo, etsỳ	èny, eròa, erỳ
Invisible	atỳ, àto	ào, atsỳ	àny, aròa, arỳ

(36)   *Làvitra   àvy   èto   ve   izàny?*
      far   coming.from   PRX.VIS   Q   DIST.INVIS
      'Is that (the road, not visible) far from here (close by, visible)?'

(37)   *àry   tsy   m-ìsy   ràhona   èny   àmin'ny   lànitra*
      and   NEG   PRS-EXIST   cloud   DIST.VIS   in:GEN.DEF   sky
      '…and there are no clouds there in the sky (distal, visible).'

(38)   *Mbòla àny   ìzy   àny.*
      still DIST.INVIS   3   DIST.INVIS
      'He's still (hanging about) there (distal, invisible).'

Like prepositions, deictic adverbs are marked for past tense with the prefix *t-* when occurring in a past tense context:

(39)   *ràha   tònga   **t-ào**   Ambòsitra   ìzy.*
      as   arrive   PST-MED.INVIS   Ambòsitra   3
      '…as he arrived there in Ambositra.'

Deictic adverbs can also be verbalized with the active voice prefix *mank-*, e.g. *Nank-àny àho* (PST.ACT-there 1) 'I went there'. This also holds for the corresponding locative question word *àiza* 'where' as in *Mank-àiza ianào?* (PRS.ACT-where 2s) 'Where are you going?'.

The demonstratives, which are obviously derived from the adverbs, are listed in Table 16.6. Note that there is a special, though not fully complete, series of plural forms for the visible demonstratives. The demonstratives can be used both as pronouns and as determiners. Examples for pronominal use are *Ìny no tìa=ko* (that DIST.VIS want=1s.GEN) 'That is what I want' and:

(40)   *Ka   omàly   ìo   sa   tsy   omàly   e?*
      so   yesterday   MED.VIS   or   NEG   yesterday   INTJ
      'So is that (fruit salad) from yesterday or not?'

When functioning as determiners, the demonstratives regularly occur at the beginning of a noun phrase, taking the place of the definite article. For emphasis, they may in fact flank the noun phrases they specify, e.g. *ho anào ìo labièra ìo* (for 2s.DAT MED.VIS beer MED.VIS) 'That beer is for you', *itỳ tràno lehibè itỳ* (PRX.VIS house big PRX.VIS) 'this big house'.

(41)   *Ìzy   no   nanào   an'ìny   retrarètra   **ìny**.*
      ìzy   no   n-aN-tào   an'ìny   rehetra-rehetra   ìny.
      3   FOC   PST-ACT-do   GEN.DIST.VIS   RDP-all   DIST.VIS
      'He did all of that!'

(42)   …   *na   **ìo**   fìtambàra=n'i*   *Allemagne   **ìo**   àrany*
      …   na   ìo   f-i-tàmbatra-ana=n'i   Allemagne   ìo   àry
      or   MED.VIS   NR-CIRC-unify-CIRC=GEN.PN   Germany   MED.VIS   even
      'even this German reunification…'

TABLE 16.6: MALAGASY DEMONSTRATIVES

	Proximal	Medial	Distal
Invisible	izatỳ, izàto	izào, izatsỳ	izàny, izaròa, izarỳ
Visible	itỳ, ìto	ìo, itsỳ	ìny, iròa, irỳ
Visible.Plural	irèto	irèo, irètsy	irèny, ireròa, irerỳ

The visible/nonvisible distinction permeates the system. This distinction does not only refer to visibility in a literal sense. Instead, the invisible forms are used for referring to places or entities which are only vaguely identified or have unclear boundaries. Conversely, highly topical referents may be encoded with a visible deictic, even if they are not actually present during the speech event.

(43)   *nefa   manào   ahoàna   sy   manào   ahoàna   izy   io?*
      nefa   m-aN-tào   ahoàna   sy   m-aN-tào   ahoàna   izy   io?
      but   PRS-ACT-do   how   and   PRS-ACT-do   how   3   MED.VIS
      '...but just how is he (emphatic)? (referring to someone not present in the speech event but just mentioned for the first time).'

This example also shows that in emphatic reference the demonstratives may occur with personal pronouns.

Furthermore, visible deictics are employed in narratives to refer to entities whose location is known or accessible to the addressee, even though the referents are clearly not visible in the actual speech event.

(44)   *ka   nanontanintàny   àzy   t-èny   an-dàlana.*
      and   PST.ACT:RDP.interrogate   3.DAT   PST-DIST.VIS   on-road
      '[His father approached him] and asked him there en route.'

In addition to deictic adverbs and demonstratives, there are also predicative deictics based on the same roots. Most of these are obsolete in modern Malagasy speech (but see (4) above for an example). The singular predicative deictics are from proximate to distal: *intỳ, ìndro, ìny, indrỳ, intsỳ, indròna, indrỳ* (visible); *injàto, inào, injào, inày, injày, inàny, injàny* (invisible).

5 VERBAL MORPHOLOGY

Malagasy verbs form the class of words that are marked for mood (section 5.4), mode (section 5.5) and voice (section 5.1). They can be classified into two primary classes, active and non-active, depending on whether they take an agentive argument in the genitive case. Non-active verbs (traditionally called 'passive' verbs) are those that take a genitive argument encliticized to the verb, which serves as an actor, and a subject argument in a non-actor case role. The non-active verbs may be subclassified into four groups based on their morphology: monomorphemic root passives, suffixal passives in *-ina* (with a stem-conditioned variant *-ena*), or *-ana*, prefixed thematic passives in *a-*, and circumstantial verbs which consist of the active prefix minus the *m-* and the suffix *-ana*. Malagasy verbs, like certain prepositions, are inflectionally marked for tense (cf. section 5.3), and can be derived to reflect causation (cf. section 5.6), and reciprocity (cf. section 5.7). This section also details the specifics of the Malagasy resultatives formed from the prefixes *tafa-*, and *voa-* (cf. section 5.2).

5.1 Voice

5.1.1 Active verbs

Active verbs in Malagasy are those verbs that take one of the following active prefixes: *m-, mi-, ma-, maN-, miaN-, miha-, mana-, maha-, mank-,* or *manka-,* and form their imperatives with *-a* (Sec 5.4). Among the very few exceptions to the bimorphemic nature of active verbs are the verbs *tìa* 'to like', and the following verbs of motion: *tàmy* 'about to arrive', *làsa* 'to be gone', *tònga* 'to arrive', and *àvy* 'to come'. The last three verbs can be used as auxiliaries:

(45)   *Tèna*   ***làsa***   ***nanòkatra***   *varavàrana*   *mihìtsy*   *anìe*   *i*   *Nìvo*   *e!*
        Tèna   làsa   n-aN-sòkatra   varavàrana   mihìtsy   anìe   i   Nìvo   e!
        even   gone   PST-ACT-open   gate   indeed   PTCL   PN   nivo   INTJ
        'Nivo has even gone to open the gate!'

The verb *tìa* 'to like' may also appear as *te=*before a verb in the future tense, where it functions as an auxiliary proclitic meaning 'to want': *te=hi-ànatra aminào àho.* (want=FUT.ACT-learn from.you 1s) 'I want to learn from you'.

Furthermore, the verbs *tìa, làsa* and *tònga* may also occur as root passive verbs, taking genitive agents, e.g. *Tìa=nào ve ny àsa=nào* (like(PASS)=2p.GEN Q DEF work=2p.GEN) 'Do you like your job?'.

Of the four basic active prefixes *mi-* and *maN-* are highly productive, whereas the prefixes *m-*, and *ma-* apply only to a closed class of roots. We will discuss the four prefixes by their order of productivity.

The *mi-* prefix is commonly used to form intransitive verbs such as *milàsy* 'to camp', *mièmpo* 'to dissolve, melt', *mitsinkàfona* 'to float', *mihàvana* 'to be friends'.

(46)   *Mbòla*   *mba*   *m-i-tèny*   *ve*   *izàny?*
        still   RQV   PRS-ACT-speak   Q   DIST.INVIS
        'Does that still make sense?'

Mi- verbs may also take objects, which are usually non-specific, unless qualified by the definite article or demonstrative: *Hi-sòtro (ny) labièra izy.* (FUT.ACT-drink (DEF) beer 3) 'He will drink (the) beer'. Very low on the transitivity continuum, *mi-* cannot be used to form ditransitive verbs, unlike the passive affixes and the active prefix *maN-*. *Mi-* is also used with verbs that are inherently reciprocal, e.g. *mi-anadàhy* 'to be siblings' and *misaobàdy /mi-saotra-vady/* (ACT-thank-spouse) 'to divorce each other'.

Many *maN-* verbs, with the less frequent variant *mana-*, can also be shown to be primarily intransitive, e.g. *mandèvy* 'boil, bubble', *mangasihàsy* 'to be timid', *manètroka* 'to give off smoke'. But *maN-* verbs are usually distinguished from their *mi-* counterparts in that they have one more argument in their semantic frame, putting them relatively higher on the transitivity continuum. Their semantics is therefore comparable to their passive counterparts. Compare the following triplets: *mi-sàraka* 'to be separated, divorced' vs. *manàraka* (active), *saràhina* (passive) 'to separate something, detach'; *mi-fòra* 'to be circumcised' vs. *mamòra* (active), *foràina* (passive) 'to circumcise somebody'; *mi-àmpy* 'to be added', *manàmpy* (active), *ampìana* (passive) 'to add, to augment'.

M- verbs are those in which a tense prefix (*n-* past, *m-* present, *h-* future) directly appends to the root. There are a few dozen such verbs, including *mànana* 'to have', *mìno* 'to believe', *mòdy* 'to go home', *mèty* 'to agree', *mèndrika* 'to deserve', *mèrika* 'to drizzle', *mìsy* 'to exist', and *màka* 'to take'.

Ma- verbs comprise a closed class of verbs, which are primarily stative, like their Philippine counterparts. They include *mahìta* 'to see', *matòry* 'to sleep', *maràry* 'to be sick', *madìo* 'to be clean', *mahìtsy* 'to be straight', *malàny* 'to be foul smelling', *masàka* 'to be ripe; well cooked', *maròroka* 'to grow rapidly'.

The remaining active voice affixes convey more specific meanings in addition to active voice: *miaN-* indicates direction (motion towards) or tendency, e.g. *mian-àla*

(ACT-forest) 'to go to the forest', *mian-tsèna* 'to go to the market'; *miha-* expresses the inchoative, e.g. *miha-mangatsiaka* 'to become cold'. For *mank-* see section 4, and for *manka-* section 5.6.

5.1.2 Passives

Formally speaking, passive verbs are the most heterogeneous kind of verbs in Malagasy, as they may be formed with prefixes, suffixes, or no morphology at all. Their common feature is that they take a genitive argument as actor, usually in a transitive verb frame, and do not take the imperative suffix *-a* associated with active verbs, but *-y* or *-o*. The nominative argument of passive verbs is non-agentive, which can be a variety of things with respect to the semantics of the passive verb: a patient, theme, location, or instrument. Although in the majority of tokens of passive verbs, a genitive argument is overtly expressed, there are cases in which no arguments are overtly expressed, and the subject is understood to be a non-agentive argument which must be inferred from the context.

(47) *Mbòla   voàsana.   Mbòla   kikìsana.*
      mbòla   voàsana.   mbòla   kìky-s-ana
      still   peel:PASS still   grate-SF-PASS
      'It's still being peeled off. Still being grated.' [talking about ginger fruit]

We will now discuss passives by their morphological form and function, differentiating the roles of the root passives, suffixing passives in *-ina* and *-ana* and the *a-* thematic passives.

Root passives are those verbs that are monomorphemic and take either an actor in the genitive case, or a patient in the nominative case or both.

(48) *Tsy   n-ìsy   zàvatra   **re**   àfatsy   ny   fi-patrapàtraky   ny   ràno.*
      NEG   PST-EXIST thing   PASS:hear except   DEF   NR-drip drop:GEN   DEF   water
      'Nothing was heard except the drip drop of the water.'

They are rather frequent in Malagasy discourse, cited in Keenan (1994) to comprise thirty percent of the occurrences of passive verbs, second in frequency to the *-ina* passives. Root passives in Malagasy include experiencer verbs such as *àzo* 'understood', *hìta* 'seen', *re* 'heard', *fàntatra* 'known', *hèno* 'listened to', *tsàpa* 'felt', *tsìnjo* 'perceived from above', *tadìdy* 'remembered', and a number of other verbs such as *hày* 'able to', *rèsy* 'defeated', *vàky* 'broken', *bàbo* 'captured', *vòa* 'afflicted', etc.

The most frequently occurring passive verbs in discourse are those taking the suffixes *-ina* (*-ena*), or *-ana*, with concomitant stress shift one syllable to the right for minimally bisyllabic roots. Unlike in Philippine languages, where the choice between the suffixes is dependent upon the semantics involved, the suffix choice in Malagasy is largely a feature of the root, except in the very few (dozen or so) cases where roots can accept both *-ana* and *-ina* with different meanings (Rahajarizafy 1960:190). While *-ina* is much more frequent than *-ana* for passive verbs, only *-ana* is used for circumstantial verbs, so the suffixes most likely carried different meanings in a paradigm that was productive earlier on in the history of the language.

The passive suffix is appended to the root formative, which is not necessarily identical to the root used with an active verb. The stem endings *-ka*, *-tra*, and *-na* are reduced before the suffixes, and many roots take a thematic consonant before the suffix. Some roots change their final vowel before the addition of the suffix, and non-final diphthongs

TABLE 16.7: FORMATION OF SUFFIXING PASSIVES

Root	Suffixing stem	Suffixed passive
(a) Reduction of stem endings		
tàpaka 'break'	tapàh-	tapàhina
sòratra 'write'	soràt-	soràtana
sàina 'think; mind'	sàin-	sàinina
(b) Addition of a thematic consonant with or without stem ending reduction		
hàfatra 'message, order'	hafàr-	hafàrana
tsìnjo 'see from afar'	tsinjòv-	tsinjòvina
dòka 'flatter'	dokàf-	dokàfana
tàratra 'see through'	taràf-	taràfina
(c) Change of final root vowel with or without a thematic consonant added		
jèry 'look at'	jerè-	jerèna
vòly 'plant'	volè-	volèna
rèfy 'fathom, measure'	refès-	refèsina
tèty 'pass through'	tetèz-	tetèzina
àndry 'wait'	andràs-	andràsana
tàndrina 'pay attention'	tandrèm-	tandrèmana
(d) Addition of stem formant -as-, -az- or –av-		
dìmby 'replacement'	dimbiàs-	dimbiàsina
be 'big'	beàz-	beàzina
tàdy 'look for'	tadiàv-	tadiàvina

within roots often become monophthongal in stems before the suffixes, e.g. *tàiza* 'a nursing child' > *tezàina* 'bring up children (passive)'. The major types of passive formations are summarized in Table 16.7.

In addition to these regular alternations, suffixing passives sometimes also involves suppletion. Verbs with suppletive active-passive pairs include: *m-aka* 'take (ACT)', *alà-ina* 'take (PASS)'; *mi-tòndra* 'carry (ACT)', *ènt-ina* 'carry (PASS)'; *mi-vàrotra* 'sell (ACT)', *amìdy* 'sell (PASS)'; and *mamàofy (vàofy)* 'peel (ACT)', *voàsana* 'be peeled (PASS)'. It should be noted that the infix *-in-*, the perfective or realis counterpart of the cognates of *-ina/-ana* undergoer voice suffixes in a number of western Austronesian languages, is not a productive morpheme in Malagasy, although it surfaces as an infix in a few passive verbs, e.g. *vàky* 'broken', *vinàky* 'be broken'.

A number of stative verbs share the ability to derive passive forms, e.g. *vòlo* 'hair' + *-ina* > *volò-ina* 'hairy' (adj.) but *vòlo + -àna* > *volò-s-ana* 'to be plucked (of fowl)'; *ma-dìo* 'clean', *dìo + -ìna* > *diòvina* 'to be cleaned' (pass.).

The prefix *a-* forms passive verbs that, like the suffixal passives, are most often encountered with an overt genitive actor. However, they differ from the suffixal passives in that the nominative argument is most likely to be either an instrument, a theme or an argument which is physically or psychologically conveyed, *a-sòritra* 'to mark with (instrument)' vs. *sorìt-ina* (< *soritra-ina*) 'to mark something, that which is marked (patient)'; *a-dìka* 'to translate, copy (theme)' vs. *dikàina* 'to cross (location)'. Common verbs which specify conveyance include *a-hàtaka* 'move away, separate', *a-òlaka* 'turn something aside', *a-ròso* 'push, put forward', *a-rònjina* 'push out of the way', *a-tèlina* 'swallow', *a-tòlotra* 'present to, give as a gift', *a-tòtotra* 'fill up with earth', etc. *A-* passive verbs may also denote themes which are transformed, e.g. *a-òlana* 'to twist'.

The prefix *a-* carries secondary stress and maintains its syllabic integrity before vowel-initial roots; *aòlaka* 'turn something aside' syllabifies as *a.ò.la.ka*. Although the *a-* passives are formally quite different from the suffixal passives, they take the same tense marking, reduplication and imperative marking as their suffixal counterparts, maintaining the appropriate consonant mutations, and stem alternations (cf. §5.3).

It should be noted here that all thematic passives with the prefix *a-* have suffixing passive or circumstantial counterparts.

5.1.3 Circumstantial verbs

Circumstantial or 'relative' verbs in Malagasy are readily identifiable as those verbs, which have both an active prefix (*i-, aN-, a-, Ø-*) and the passive suffix *-ana*. Table 16.8 presents a few typical examples.

The name 'circumstantial' was coined to reflect the nature of the subject as being a semantically peripheral argument of the verb. They are usually cited in paradigms with active and passive examples as in (49–51), giving the somewhat false impression that they are fully productive as main predicate verbs.

(49)   *Mandràkotra   làmba   ny   tòngony   àho.*
       m-aN-ràkotra   làmba   ny   tòngotra=ny   àho
       PRS-ACT-cover   blanket   DEF   leg=3.GEN   1s
       'I cover his legs with a blanket.' (Active)

(50)   *Rakòfako   làmba   ny   tòngony.*
       ràkotra-ana=ko   làmba   ny   tòngotra=ny.
       cover-PASS=1.SG.GEN   blanket   DEF   leg=3.GEN
       'I cover his legs with a blanket.' (Patient passive)

(51)   *Aràkotro   ny   tòngony   ny   làmba.*
       a-ràkotra =o   ny   tòngotra =ny   ny   làmba.
       PASS-COVER=1s.GEN   DEF   leg=3.GEN   DEF   cloth
       'I cover his legs with a blanket.' (Thematic passive)

(52)   *Andrakòfako   ny   tòngony   ny   làmba.*
       aN-rakotra-ana=ko   ny   tòngotra=ny   ny   làmba.
       CIRC-cover-CIRC=1s.GEN   DEF   leg=3.GEN   DEF   blanket
       'I cover his legs with a blanket.' (Circumstantial)

Examples (50) and (51) are different in that in (50) the subject argument is the patient *ny tongon'* while in (51) it is the instrument *ny làmba*. Structurally, the prefix passive clause (51) and the circumstantial clause (52) are identical. One major difference between them is that circumstantials ordinarily are not used as main predicates in natural discourse. They typically appear as modifiers to nouns in relative clause constructions (with or without the relativizer *izày*), or after the focal particle *no*.

TABLE 16.8: MALAGASY VERBS IN THREE VOICES

Root	Active	Passive	Circumstantial
sàsa 'wash'	manàsa	sasàna	anasàna
vòno 'kill'	mamòno	vonòina	amonòana
rèsaka 'converse'	mirèsaka	resàhina	iresàhana
hàino 'hear'	mihàino	henòina	ihainòana
àraka 'follow'	manàraka	aràhina	anaràhana

(53) *ilày   zazavàvy   nampiàkariny   ho   vàdy*
      ilày   zazavàvy   n-amp-i-àkatra-ina=ny   ho   vàdy
      DET   young woman   PST-CAU-CIRC-lift up-CIRC=3.GEN   for wife
      'that young woman he married'

(54) *Aiza   intsòny   no   **hahatadidiàvako**   an'izàny?*
      àiza   intsòny   no   h-aha-tadidi-àv-ana=ko   an'izàny?
      where   ever   FOC FUT-POT-remember-SF-CIRC=1.GEN   GEN.DIST.INVIS
      'How am I ever supposed to remember that?'

In nominal frames after an article or existential, the circumstantial verb specifies the purpose, reason, or circumstance of an act, not the actor (as expressed by an active verb counterpart), or the patient (as expressed by a passive verb counterpart).

(55) *Tsy   m-ìsy   niomànan'ny   òlona   mihìtsy.*
      Tsy   m-ìsy   n-i-òmana-ana=n'ny   òlona   mihìtsy.
      NEG PRS-EXIST   PST-prepare-CIRC=GEN.DEF   person   a little
      'There was no time at all for the people to prepare.' (lit. there was no way/means at all in which the people could get ready)

Circumstantial verbs may also be employed to modify nouns in lexicalized compound constructions: *vàlan-drèsaka niaràha=ny* (interview accompany:CIRC=3.GEN) 'his joint interview'.

Circumstantial verbs may also be formed with the secondary prefixes *-anka-*, *-amp-*, with the reciprocal prefix *-if-*, and with reduplicated stems. Their imperatives are formed in the same way as passive imperatives, taking either *-y*, or *-o*, as determined by the vocalic nature of the root (Sec 5.4).

5.2 Voa- and Tafa- resultatives

The resultative prefixes *voa-* and *tafa-* are considered together here because they share a few morphosyntactic similarities. They do not inflect for imperative mode or past tense, e.g. *voa-tòntan'ny latàbatra ny lòha=ny* (RES-fall:GEN.DEF table DEF head=3.GEN) 'The table fell on his head'.

Contrary to many grammatical analyses of Malagasy, we do not categorize these resultatives with passives. The behavior of *voa-* and *tafa-* resultatives is strikingly different from *a-*, *-ina* and *-ana* passives, as the agent, typically coded in the genitive case, is usually absent.

The differences between *voa-* and *tafa-* resultatives are as follows: *voa-*, historically apparently related to the root *voa* 'fruit, seed', encodes completive states with experiencers (non-agents) in subject function. Examples of *voa-* resultatives include: *voa-ràkitra* 'preserved', *voa-fìdy* 'elected', *voa-tèry* 'forced', *voa-hàja* 'respected', and *voa-fàritra* 'demarcated'. They may participate in compounding to form new lexical items: *òlom-boafìdy* /òlona-voa-fìdy/ (person-RES-elect) 'elected official'.

Although the agent of *voa-* predicates is usually unexpressed, it may be expressed immediately after the *voa-* resultative, provided it is not in initial predicate position.

(56) *Fokontàny   èfatra   no   voa-kàsiky   ny   ràno.*
      fokontàny   four   FOC RES-affect:GEN   DEF water
      'Four *fokontany* (communities) were affected by the water' (in a flood).

Tafa- resultatives often encode a coincidental or unexpected state of affairs. The subject of *tafa-* resultatives exercises more control to bring about the resultant state than the subject of a *voa-* formative.

(57) *Tafa-vèrina   t-èto*   *Antananarìvo   ny   Fi-lòha   Zàfy.*
     RES-return   PST-PRX.VIS   Antananarìvo   DEF   NR-head   Zafy
     'President Zafy happened to return to Antananarivo.'

Keenan and Polinsky (1998:590) notes that *voa-* may be used with reduplicated roots, while *tafa-* may not, e.g. *voalazalàza* 'said a bit'; *tafavèrina* 'returned', but not **tafaverimbèrina*.

5.3 Tense and aspect

Most Malagasy verbs take inflectional tense marking in accordance with the following patterns. Active verbs with the prefix *m-* change the initial prefix *m-* to *n-* to indicate past tense, and *h-* for the future tense, e.g. *manòmpo* 'serve', *nanòmpo* 'served', *hanòmpo* 'will serve'; *H-i-àraka amin'i nèny izy* (FUT-ACT-accompany with:GEN.PN mother 3) 'He'll go with Mother'. Like active verbs, stative verbs and the majority of adjectives beginning with the present active prefix *m-* take *n-* for the past tense and *h-* for the future tense, e.g. *ma-hòmby* 'successful' > *na-hòmby* 'was successful' > *ha-hòmby* 'will be successful'.

All circumstantial verbs, and passive verbs that begin with a vowel or take the prefix *a-*, also take the prefix *n-* for their past form, and *h-* for their future form, e.g. *oròhana* 'be kissed', *noròhana* 'was kissed', *horòhana* 'will be kissed'. Suffixal passives that begin with a consonant take the prefix *no-* for the past tense and *ho-* for the future tense (formerly written as separate words), e.g. *velòmina* 'is brought to life/started (engine/fire)' *novelòmina* 'was brought to life', *hovelòmina* 'will be brought to life'.

The particle *ho* is used to form the future of certain verb types that do not inflect for past tense: monomorphemic root verbs, or resultatives which take the prefixes *tafa-* or *voa-*: *Ho tonga=ko ny òvy* (FUT bring(PASS)=1s.GEN DEF sweet.potatoes) 'I'll bring the sweet potatoes', *Efa ho lasa izy* (done FUT depart 3) 'He is about to leave'. It may also be employed to express the future of nominal and deictic predicates *Ho mpitsàbo Rasoa* (FUT doctor R.) 'Rasoa will be a doctor', *Ho àny amin'ny tanàna i Koto* (FUT DIST.INVIS in:GEN.DEF village PN Koto) 'Koto will be in the village'.

Most verbs in Malagasy carry only one inflectional tense marker, but there are a few derived verbal compounds that can carry two, such as *miàra-mandèha* (PRS:with-PRS:go) 'go with' vs. *hiàra-handèha* 'will go with' (Ranaivoson unpublished).

Inflectional past tense is not only reserved for verbs and adjectives beginning with *m-*. As already noted above, demonstratives, prepositions and the locative interrogative *aiza* 'where' may also inflect for past tense, however, with a different prefix (*t-*). In auxiliary and complement constructions, both the auxiliary/matrix verb and the complement verb are marked for tense (59).

(58) *N-i-pètraka   n-an-gina   t-èo   izy   ròa   làhy…*
     PST-ACT-sit   PST-ACT-silence   PST-there   3   two   boy,
     fa   tsy   nìsy   òlona   nihelingèlina.
     fa   tsy   n-ìsy   òlona   n-i-RDP-hèlina.
     but   NEG   PST-EXIST   person   PST-ACT-RDP-pass_by
     'The two boys sat there silently, but nobody passed by.'

(59) *Tàiza   ianào   no   niànatra   namàky   tèny?*
     T-àiza   ianào   no   n-i-ànatra   n-aN-vàky   tèny?
     PST-where   2s   FOC   PST-ACT-learn   PST-ACT-read   word
     'Where did you learn to read?'

Malagasy verbs and adjectives may also encode aspectual distinctions through reduplication, e.g. *mi-tsàngana* 'to rise, stand' > *mi-tsangantsàngana* 'to promenade, stroll', *mihèrika* 'to look back' > *miherikèrika*, 'to keep looking around; to look behind one repeatedly'.

(60) *'Za   alòa   de   mipaozipàozy   isan'àndro   fa*
       izàho   alòa   dia   m-i-paozi-pàozy   isan'àndro   fa
       1s   first PART   PRS-ACT-RDP-appearance everyday   but
       'zany   hoe   tsìsy   mikitikitika
       <u>'izany   hoe</u> tsy   ìsy   m-i-kiti-kitika
       I.mean   NEG   EXIST PRS-ACT-RDP-touch
       'I always smarten up myself every day but – I mean – nobody touches me here and there.'

Some verbs with an inherent durative or iterative nature always appear in reduplicated form, e.g. *mi-vezi-vèzy* 'to wander, roam', *mi-kiti-kitika* 'tickle, touch in passing', *mi-dradra-dràdra* 'cry aloud', *mi-dridro-drìdro* 'squeal', *mi-safo-sàfo* 'caress', *mi-dodo-dodo* 'move with quick and noisy steps'.

Finally it may be noted that Malagasy uses repetition to express intensification. In such instances, the adjective or verb is repeated and the focus particle *dia*, functioning here as a linker, is usually inserted in between two elements, e.g. *gàga dia gàga àho* (surprised LK surprised 1s) 'I was very surprised indeed', *miànatra dia miànatra ianarèo* (PRS.ACT:learn LK PRS.ACT:learn 2p) 'You are learning a lot indeed'.

5.4 Imperative formation

Imperatives of adjectives and active verbs are usually formed by suffixing *-a* after the stem (sometimes with insertion of a final consonant to the root if the latter ends in a vowel). However, if the stem terminates in stressed *e*, no suffix is added. After stems that end in *-a*, the suffix *-a* and the final vowel merge while attracting stress: *milàza + -a=milazà* 'Tell!'. The addressee is not overtly expressed in the imperative, e.g. *Ma-zotò-a* (ACT-diligent-IMP) 'Be diligent!'. Imperatives of prefixing or suffixing passives are formed by adding the suffix *-y* to the full stem of the verb if the last syllable of the stem contains the vowel *o*, otherwise *-o* is suffixed. The suffix *-y* may also be applied if the penultimate syllable of the stem contains the vowel *o*, and the last syllable does not contain a high vowel *i* or *e* as illustrated with *loàh-y* in Table 16.9, which exemplifies the regularities just stated.

Prohibitives are formed with *aza* 'don't' and the verb in its present indicative form, and the particle *mba* is used for polite, less forceful suggestions.

(61) *Mba   atoròy   làlana   àho   azafàdy.*
       mba   a-tòro-y   làlana   àho   azafàdy
       RQV   PASS-point out-PASS.IMP way 1.SG please
       'Please show me the way!'

Less forceful suggestions may also be uttered using the indicative form of the verb instead of the imperative: *M-i-ànatra m-i-tsìtsy* (PRS-ACT-learn PRS-ACT-save) 'Learn to save money'. Future tense is yet another option for suggestives:

(62) *Mi-fòha-z-a   amin'izày,   'ndào   h-i-sakàfo   e!*
       PRS.ACT-WAKE-SF-IMP   then   PRPV   FUT-ACT-meal   INTJ
       'Get up then! Let's have breakfast!'

TABLE 16.9: IMPERATIVE FORMATION

Active imperatives

Root	Active	Stem	Imperative
tònga 'arrive'	tònga	tongav-	tongàva
hevitra 'think'	mihèvitra	hever-	mihevèra
fy 'delicious'	mankafŷ	fiz-	Mankafiza
omè 'give'	manomè	manomez-	manomèza
sòkatra 'open'	manòkatra	sokaf-	manokàfa

Passive imperatives

Root	Passive	Stem	Imperative
omè 'give'	omèna	omè-	omèo
tàpaka 'break'	tapàhina	tapàh-	tapàho
la 'refuse, deny'	làvina	lav-	làvo
foy 'give up'	afòy	afoiz-	afòizo
kàroka 'investigate'	karòhina	karòh-	karòhy
lòaka 'bore a hole'	loàhana	loàh-	loàhy
sòratra 'write'	soràtana	soràt-	soràty, soràto

Root verbs do not take special imperative marking: *Las'=nareo tèlo* (go=2p three) 'The three of you go!' Because the undergoer of an imperative is usually identifiable, passive imperatives are preferred to actives in the case of transitive verbs: *Amèo (omeo) vàry kèly a' hoe?* (give:IMP rice little 1s QUOT) 'Please will you give me some rice?'

5.5 Potentive mode

Potentive verbs are those that are morphologically marked to express states, or actions that are abilitative, non-volitional or accidental. They are formed with the prefix *ma(ha)-*.

(63)   *'Zày   m-ànana   posipòsy   'zào   no   tèna   maha-vòa.*
       Who   PRS.ACT-have   rickshaw   now   FOC   really   POT-hit.the.mark
       'Those who own rickshaws are really making profits now.'

(64)   *Tsìsy   mahàzo   miàsa?*
       tsy ìsy   maha-àzo   m-i-àsa
       NEG exist   POT-get   PRS-ACT-work
       'Nobody is allowed to work?'

Like the prefix *maka-* in Philippine languages (see RUBINO, ILOKO), *maha-* also forms verbs that express non-volitional causation. Non-volitional and especially inanimate causers frequently take *maha-* verbs in this capacity: *mahatsiràvina* 'to shock', *mahafinàritra* 'to please (by being beautiful)', *mahagàga* 'to surprise, astonish', *mahavèlona* 'to support, keep alive (nourishment)', *mahamènatra* 'to shame', *mahasàrika* 'to attract (as a magnet)', *mahasalàma* 'to make healthy'.

(65)   *Mahafinàritra   ilày   migrèvy   e?*
       m-aha-finàritra   ilày   m-i-grèvy   e
       PRES-POT-happy   DET   PRS-ACT-strike   INTJ
       'It's fun to go on strike, isn't it?' [Subject is *migrèvy* 'going on strike']

(66)   *Maha-lìana   àhy   ny   zavamanìry.*
       POT-interest   1s.DAT   DEF   plants
       'The plants interest me' (I am interested in the plants).

Verbs of cognition such as *mahafàntatra* 'know' and *mahalàla* 'know, learn' also take the *maha-* affix. Peculiar to the *maha-* affix is its ability to form verbs from locative deictics: *naha-t-èto* (PST.POT-PST-here) 'brought here'.

5.6 Causatives

There are three causative prefixes: *(m)amp-*, *(m)anka-*, and *(m)aha-*. The prefix *mamp-* is the most prototypical one, as it may encode a volitional agent and is the most productive of the causative affixes. It is used in both active and passive voices. Example clauses are *Ìnona no zàvatra m-amp-a-tàhotra anào* (what FOC thing PRS-CAU-ACT-afraid 2s.DAT) 'What things scare you?', and:

(67) *Èfa   nampanantèna   àho   fa   handòa.*
      èfa   n-amp-an-antèna   àho   fa   h-aN-lòa
      already   PST-CAU-ACT-promise 1s   that FUT-ACT-pay
      'I already promised (made a promise) to pay.'

(68) *Ampisambòry   vòla   àho   azafàdy.*
      amp-i-sàmbotra-y   vòla   àho   azafàdy
      CAU-SF-borrow-PASS.IMP money   1s   please
      'Please loan me some money.'

The prefixes *maha-* and *manka-* greatly differ from *mamp-* in their function. As noted in section 5.5, the prefix *maha-* may form causative verbs that denote actions in which the causation is non-volitional, e.g. *zàva-maha-domèlina* (thing-CAU-stupefy) 'narcotic, something that causes a stupefied state'. The prefix *manka-*, on the other hand, combines primarily with stative roots to form verbs which may express either causation or appreciation of a state: *mankarary* 'to cause illness', *mankasìtraka* 'consider pleasing, appreciate, enjoy'.

(69) *Tsìsy   mankaràry   vavòny   'zàny*
      tsy ìsy   m-ank-aràry   vavòny   izàny
      neg exist   PRS-CAU-sick   stomach   DIST.INVIS
      'That doesn't spoil the stomach...'

5.7 Reciprocals

The reciprocal prefix *if-* is a secondary prefix; it succeeds the tense marking prefixes, and may either precede or follow the causative prefixes as shown in Table 16.10. The reciprocal prefix is not fully productive as it does not co-occur with all active marking prefixes.

(70) *Mifanitsa-kìtro   ny   vahòaka.*
      m-if-aN-hìtsaka-kìtro   ny   vahòaka
      PRS-RCP-ACT-trample-ankle   DEF   people
      'People trample on each other's ankles' (at a fair).

(71) *Ampifandimbiàso   ny   vòly   àmin'ny   tàny   anankiràly.*
      amp-if-aN-dimbi-as-o   ny   vòly   àmin'ny   tàny   anankiràly
      CAU-RECIP-ACT-replace-SF-IMP   DEF   plants on:GEN.DEF land   one
      'Alternate the (planting of the) plants on a single plot of land' (for a better harvest).
      [Causative of a reciprocal action: *ampifandimbiàsina ny vòly* 'to successively exchange the plants.]

TABLE 16.10: CAUSATIVE AND RECIPROCAL MORPHOLOGY

Simple	Reciprocal	Causative	Causative-Reciprocal	Reciprocal-Causative
mi-		m-amp-i-		m-ifamp-i-
miha		m-amp-iha-		m-ifamp-iha-
maha-		m-amp-aha-		m-ifamp-aha-
ma-	m-if-a-	m-amp-a-		m-ifamp-a-
maN-	m-if-aN-	m-amp-aN-	m-amp-if-aN-	m-ifamp-aN-
mana-	m-if-ana-	m-amp-ana-	m-amp-if-ana-	m-ifamp-ana-
manka-	m-if-anka-	m-amp-anka-	m-amp-if-anka-	m-ifamp-anka-

(72)   *Tsy   n-if-amp-a-tòky*   *ìzy   roa-làhy.*
       NEG   PST-RCP-CAU-ACT-trust   3   two-male
       'The two of them (they) did not trust each other.' [Reciprocal of a causative action]

6 NOMINALIZATIONS

Malagasy has quite a few productive derivational nominalization patterns. Typical cases of derivational morphology involve affixes which form nominals from adjectives, verbs, as well as nouns. In every case, nominalizing affixation involves regular alternations in consonants, vowel fusion, and stress-shift (cf. section 2).

6.1 Agent nominals with prefix *mp-*

Malagasy agentive nominalizations are formed predominantly with the prefix *mp-* (pronounced [p]) based on active verbs. The derived form designates an individual whose regular activity is denoted by the root: *mpisòtro* /mp-i-sòtro/ (NR-ACT-drink) 'drinker, drunkard', *mp-aN-dìhy* (NR-ACT-dance) 'dancer, a person whose habit is to dance', *mpandròra* /mp-aN-ròra/ (NR-AC-spittle) 'a person who has the habit of spitting'. It also forms a large number of occupational nouns: *mpandràfìtra* /mp-aN-ràfitra/ (NR-ACT-carpentry) 'carpenter', *mpanjàka* /mp-aN-zàka/ (NR-AC-governing) 'king', *mpiànatra* /mp-i-ànatra/ (NR-ACT-advice) 'student, pupil', *mpanèty* /mp-aN-hèty/ (NR-AC-scissors) 'barber', etc.

An agent nominal can be formed from a predicate phrase, e.g. from the action verb *mitèndry* 'to perform on a musical instrument' and its object *valìha* 'a Malagasy lute made of bamboo' is formed the agent nominal *mpitèndry valìha* 'one who plays the valìha', from *mitsòka mozìka* 'to blow a musical instrument' is formed *mpitsòka mozìka* 'one who blows a musical instrument'. In this type of agentive formation active verbs like *manào* 'to do, to make' can be compounded with a specific field to designate profession. Thus, *manào + nìfy* 'teeth' yields *mpanào nìfy* 'dentist'; *manào + kiràro* 'shoes' yields *mpanào kiràro* 'shoemaker'.

Causative verbs (cf. section 5.6) and reciprocal verbs, including the complex reciprocals (causative reciprocal forms and reciprocal causative forms, cf. section 5.7), also form agent nominals in the same way: *mpampihomèhy* /mp-amp-i-homèhy/ (NR-CAU-ACT-laugh) 'someone who makes people laugh', *mpifampatòky* /mp-if-amp-a-tòky/ (RCP-CAU-ACT-trust) 'people who trust each other'.

Besides derivational patterns, agent nominals may be obtained from syntactic nominalizations (cf. section 6.3).

6.2 Prefix *f-*: action/result, object, instrument, manner and/or location

A productive morphological process for creating action or result nominals is based on active verbs where the nominaliser prefix *f-* replaces the present tense marker *m-*: *m-i-òva* 'to change' > *f-i-òva* 'change(s), the way of changing', *m-an-ontàny* 'to ask' > *f-an-ontàny* 'question'. In many instances, the derivative can have an instrumental interpretation, a fact/occurrence interpretation and a manner interpretation, e.g. *m-a-tòry* 'to sleep' > *f-a-tòry* 'the way of sleeping, the fact of sleeping', *m-i-hògo* 'to comb (intransitive)' > *f-i-hògo* 'instrument for combing/a comb, the way of combing one's hair, the fact of combing one's hair', *m-i-ràkotra* 'to cover' > *f-i-ràkotra* 'a covering, the way of covering, the fact of covering'. The transitive verb *mandràkotra* /m-aN-ràkotra/ (PRS-ACT-cover) 'cover' has the nominal derivative *fandràkotra* 'which is usually used to cover'.

A few passive verbs formed with the prefix *a-* may take the nominalizer *f-* to form a nominal designating something, which usually undergoes the action denoted by the passive verb: *f-a-lèfa* (NR-PASS-send) 'something which is usually sent or shipped', *f-a-lèha* (NR-PASS-go) 'something which is usually gone along (a road or a path)', *f-a-sèho* (NR-PASS-display) 'things which are usually displayed'.

The prefix *f-* may also be applied to circumstantial verbs (cf. section 5.1.3). For instance, *m-i-vòry* (PRS-ACT-meet) 'to meet' has a circumstantial form *i-vòri-àna* (CIRC-meet-CIRC), from which is derived the nominal *f-i-vori-àna* (NR-CIRC-meet-CIRC) 'a meeting'. The derivatives thus formed may have an action nominal interpretation, an instrument interpretation (*f-a-handrò-ana* 'something used for the purpose of cooking'), a location interpretation (*f-i-petràh-ana*, 'place of sitting') and a manner interpretation (*f-i-lomanò-s-ana* 'way of swimming'). In the following sentences, *fikapàna hàzo* ('the cutting of trees') allows all four of these interpretations depending on context:

(73) Fikapàko   hàzo   itỳ.
     f-i-kàpa-ana=ko   hàzo   itỳ
     NR.CIRC:cut:CIRC=1s.GEN   trees PRX.VIS
     'This is the implement with which I cut trees.' (instrument)

(74) Izào   no   fikapàna   hàzo.
     MED.INVIS FOC   NR.CIRC:cut:CIRC   trees
     'This is the way of cutting trees.' (manner)

(75) Fikapàna   hàzo   èo.
     NR.CIRC:cut:CIRC   trees MED.VIS
     'Trees are cut there.' (location)

(76) Fikapàna   hàzo   no   àntom-pivelòma=ny.
     f-i-kàpa-ana   hàzo   no   àntony-f-i-vèlona-ana=ny
     NR.CIRC:cut:CIRC   trees FOC   reason-NR-CIRC-living-CIRC=3.GEN
     'Cutting trees is his means of subsistence.' (action nominal)

The nominals derived from circumstantial verbs may be used like adjectives in attributive functions or as an unmarked relative clause construction as in (77):

(77) Ikètaka **fanirakirakày**   àto   an-tràno
     Iketaka f-an-iraka-iraka=ay   àto   an-tràno
     Iketaka NR-ACT-RDP-send=1pe.GEN   PRX.INVIS in-house
     'Ikètaka who used to be our messenger girl here in the house.'

Derivatives with *f-* may appear with reduplicated stems: *famerimberènana* /f-aN-vèrina-vèrina-ana/ (NR-CIRC-RDP-repeat-CIRC) 'the act of repeating many times', *fanavakavàhana* /f-aN-àvaka-àvaka-ana/ (NR-CIRC-RDP-discriminate-CIRC) 'discrimination'. And as with the agent nominals discussed in section 6.1., *f-* nominals can also be formed from a predicate phrase, e.g.: *mitèndry valìha* 'to play the *valìha*' yields the action nominal *fitendrèna valìha* 'the act of playing the *valìha*.

A related formation on the basis of adjectives consists in circumfixing *faha-…-ana* to the base, the derived form then denoting abstract qualities: *fahavokìsana* /faha-vòky-s-ana/ (NR-satiated-SF-NR) 'satiation, the fact of being satiated', *faharatsìana* /faha-ràtsy-ana/ (NR-wicked-NR) 'wickedness, the fact of being wicked', *fahadisòana* /faha-dìso-ana/ (NR-mistake-NR) 'mistake, guilt'. Note that the affixes *ha-* and *ha-…-ana* also form abstract nominals from adjectival roots: *ha-* expresses an intrinsic quality (Dez 1980), whereas *ha-…-ana* describes a quality which is not inherent to an object or a person but which results from a process of action practised on or by the subject. Compare *tsàra* 'nice, beautiful, kind' > *ha-tsàra* 'intrinsic kindness, natural beauty' vs. *hatsaràna* /ha-tsàra-ana/ 'kindness or beauty acquired through a transformation'.

6.3 Syntactic nominalization

Besides derivational formations, nominalization can also be realized by introducing a verbal phrase with the articles *ny* (78) or *ilày* (79), or by flanking the predicate phrase with demonstratives as in (80):

(78) *Ny*   *mitsangatsàngana*   *èny*   *àmin'ny*
      Ny   m-i-tsàngana-tsàngana   èny   àmin'ny
      DEF   PRS-ACT-RDP-stand   DIST.VIS to:GEN.DEF

      gàra   *no*   *tèna*   *maha-varìana*   *tokòa.*
      station   FOC   really   POT-absorb one's attention indeed
      '*Going for a walk at the (railway) station* is very absorbing indeed.'

(79) *Sàrotra*   *erỳ*   *ilày*   *nanòlotra*   *ny*   *sakàfo*   *fanajàna*
      sàrotra   erỳ   ilày   n-aN-tòlotra   ny   sakàfo   f-aN-hàja-ana
      difficult   really   DET   PST-ACT-offer   DEF   meal   NR-CIRC-honor-CIRC

      sy   *fandràisam-bahìny*
      sy   f-aN-rày-s-ana-vahìny
      and   NR-CIRC-receive-SF-CIRC-guests
      '*Offering a meal in order to honor and welcome the guests* was really difficult.'

(80) *Irèo*   *voa-làza*   *ambòny*   *irèo*   *àry*   *no*   *santiòna=n'ny*
      MED.VIS.PL   PASS-mention   above   MED.VIS.PL   and   FOC   sample=GEN.DEF

      kabàry   *fanào*   *àmin'ny*   *fandevènana.*
      kabàry   f-aN-tào   àmin'ny   f-aN-lèvina-ana/
      speech   NR-ACT-do   at:GEN.DEF   NR-CIRC-bury-CIRC
      '*And these aforementioned (oratories)* are samples of the oratories usually made at burial ceremonies.'

Agent nominals may also be obtained from a predicate phrase premodified by a definite article (81) or a demonstrative (82):

(81) *Ilày*   *nihèvitra*   *ho*   *nanào*   *ny*   *sòa*   *indrày*   *no*   *tàitra.*
      Ilày   n-i-hèvitra   ho   n-aN-tào   ny   sòa   indrày   no   tàitra
      DET   PST-ACT-think   PTCL   PST-ACT-do   DEF   good   again   FOC   shocked
      'That one who thought to have done good to someone was afterwards (the one to be) shocked.'

(82)   *Nòdy*   *irèo*   *n-i-àsa*   *àlina.*
       PST.ACT:go.home   MED.VIS.PL   PST-ACT-work   night
       'Those who worked at night went home.'

ACKNOWLEDGEMENTS

The authors would like to thank Matthew Pearson, Ed Keenan, Andoveloniaina Rasolofo, Ileana Paul, Waruno Mahdi and the editors of this volume for their helpful comments on previous versions of this chapter.

REFERENCES

Abinal, R.P. and Malzac, S.J. (1993) *Dictionnaire malgache–français*, Fianarantsoa [reprint of the original 1888 edition: Paris: Editions Martimes et d'Outre-Mer].

Adelaar, K.A. (1989) 'Malay Influence on Malagasy: Linguistic and culture-historical implications', *Oceanic Linguistics*, vol. XXVIII no. 11, 1989:1–46.

——(1994a) 'Malay and Javanese Loanwords in Malagasy, Tagalog and Siraya (Formosa)', *Bijdragen tot de Taal-, Land- en Volkenkunde* 1995:50–66.

——(1994b) Malagasy, in D. Tryon (ed.) *Comparative Austronesian Dictionary*, 393–406, Berlin: Mouton de Gruyter.

——(1995) 'Asian roots of the Malagasy: a linguistic perspective', *Bijdragen tot de Taal-, Land- en Volkenkunde* 151/3:325–356.

Ailloud, P. (1873) *Grammaire malgache-hova*, Tananarive.

Andriamanantsilavo, S. and Ratrema, W. (1981) *Ny fitsipi-pitenenantsika. Boky voalohany*, Antananarivo: Imprimerie d'Ouvrages Educatifs Ankatso.

Beaujard, P. (1998) *Dictionnaire malgache–français. Dialecte tanala, sud-est de Madagascar. Avec recherches étymologiques*, Paris, Montréal: L'Harmattan.

Bergenholtz, H. (ed.) (1991) *Rakibolana Malagasy–Alema. Madagassisch–Deutsches Wörterbuch*, Moers: Edition Aragon.

Berthier, H. (1922) *Manuel de la langue malgache*, Tananarive.

Builles, J.M. (1998) *Manuel de linguistique descriptive, le point de vue fonctionnaliste*, Paris: Nathan Caussèque.

Caussèque, P.R.P. (1886) *Grammaire malgache*, Antananarivo: Imprimerie Catholique.

Cousins, G. (1882) *Gramara Malagasy*, Antananarivo: London Missionary Society Press.

Cousins, W.E. (1885) 'A Concise Introduction to the study of the Malagasy Language as spoken in Imerina', In Richardson (1885). Republished in Jedele and Randrianarivelo (1998) with additions by T.P. Jedele.

Dahl, O.C. (1951) *Malgache et Maanjan*, Oslo: Egede Instituttet.

——(1977) 'La subdivision de la famille barito et la place du malgache', *Acta Orientalia* (Copenhagen) 38:77–134.

——(1983) *Sorabe révélant l'évolution du dialecte antemoro*, Antananarivo: Trano Printy Loterana.

——(1986) 'Focus in Malagasy and Proto-Austronesian', in P. Geraghty, L. Carrington, and S.A. Wurm (eds) *FOCAL I: Papers from the Fourth International Conference on Austronesian Linguistics*, 21–42, Canberra: Pacific Linguistics.

——(1988) 'Bantu substratum in Malagasy', in *Linguistique de Madagascar et des Comores*, Études Océan Indien, no. 9, Paris: Institut des Langues et Civilisations Orientales, 91–132.

——(1991) *Migration from Kalimantan to Madagascar*, Institute for Comparative Research in Human Culture series B, 82, Oslo: Norwegian University Press.

Decary, R. (1928) *Lexique français–antandroy*, Tananarive: Pitot (Mémoire de l'Académie Malgache).

Deschamps, H. (1936) *Le dialecte antaisaka (langue malgache)*, Antananarivo: Imprimerie Moderne de l'Emyrne, Pitot de la Beaujardière.

Descheemaeker, R.P.A. (unpubl.) *Vocabulaire des Betsimisaraka atsimo Zafindriamanaña*, unpubl. ms.

Dez, J. (1960) *Le dialecte betsimisaraka du sud*, unpubl. ms.

——(1963) 'Aperçus pour une dialectologie de la langue malgache', *Bulletin de Madagascar* 204, 205, 206, 210.

——(1980) *Structures de la langue malgache: Eléments de grammaire à l'usage des francophones*, Paris: Publications Orientalistes de France.

——(1992) *Lexique sommaire du parler vorimo, d'après l'étude grammaticale du dialecte betsimisaraka du sud de Pasteur J. Ruud* (unpubl.).

Domenichini-Ramiaramanana, B. (1976) *Le malgache. Essai de description sommairre*, Paris: SELAF (Société d'Études Linguistiques et Anthropologiques de France).

Dubois, R.P.H.M. (1917) *Essai de dictionnaire betsileo*, Tananarive: Imprimerie Officielle.

Elli, R.P.L. (1988) *Dizionario bara–italiano*, Fianarantsoa: Ambozontany.

Erwin, S. (1996) 'Quantity and moras: an amicable separation', in M. Pearson and I. Paul (eds) 2–30.

Freeman, J.J. and Johns, D. (1835) *A Dictionary of the Malagasy Language. In two parts. I. English and Malagasy. II: Malagasy and English*, Tananarive.

Fugier, H. (1999) *Syntaxe malgache*, Louvain: Peeters.

Garvey, C. (1964) *A Sketch of Malagasy Grammar*, Washington D.C.: Center for Applied Linguistics.

Gerbinis, M.L. (1946) *La langue malgache enseignée suivant la méthode directe*, Tananarive, Madagascar: Imprimerie Nationale.

Gueunier, N.J. (1986) *Lexique du dialecte malgache de Mayotte*, Paris: Institut national des Langues et Civilisations Orientales [= Etudes Océan Indien numéro spécial 7].

Hallanger, F.S. (1969) *An elementary English–Malagasy Dictionary*, Tananarive: Trano Printy Loterana.

——(1973) *Diksionera Malagasy–Englisy*, Antananarivo: Trano Printy Loterana.

Houtman, Frederick de (1603) *Spraeck ende woord-boeck, in de Maleysche ende Madagaskarsche Talen*, Amsterdam.

Jedele, T.P., and Randrianarivelo, L.E. (1998) *Malagasy Newspaper Reader*, Kensington, Maryland: Dunwoody Press.

Keenan, E.L. (1976) 'Remarkable Subjects in Malagasy', in C. Li (ed.) *Subject and Topic*, 303–334, New York: Academic Press.

——(1994) 'Predicate-Argument Structure in Malagasy', in C.S. Burgess, K. Dziwirek, and D. Gerdts (eds) *Grammatical Relations. Theoretical Approaches to Empirical Questions*, 171–216, Stanford: CSLI Publications.

Keenan, E.L. and Polinsky, M. (1998) 'Malagasy', in A. Spencer and A.M. Zwicky (eds) *Handbook of Morphology*, 563–623, Oxford: Blackwell.

Keenan, E.L. and Rabenilaina, R.-B. (2001) 'Malagasy', in J. Garry and C. Rubino (eds) *Facts About the World's Languages: An Encyclopedia of the World's Major Languages: Past and Present*, 448–451, New York: H.W. Wilson.

Keenan, E. and Ralalaoherivony, B. (1998) 'Raising from NP in Malagasy', in I. Paul (ed.) 50–64.

Korneev, L.A. (1966) *Maljgašško–russkij slovar*, Moscow: Sovetskaia entsiklopediia.

——(1970) *Russkij–Maljgašško slovar*, Moscow: Sovetskaia entsiklopediia.

Mahdi, W. (1988) *Morphophonologische Besonderheiten und historische Phonologie des Malagasy*, Berlin: Dietrich Reimer.

Malzac, S.J. (1908 [1960 Fourth edition]) *Grammaire malgache*, Paris: Société d'éditions géographiques, maritimes et coloniales.

Mampitovy, A. (1978) *Voambolana sy ohabolana zafisoro*, Antananarivo: Ministère de l'art et de la Culture Révolutionnaires.

Manaster-Ramer, A. (1992) 'Malagasy and the Topic Subject issue', *Oceanic Linguistics* 31:267–279.

Montagné, L. (1931) *Essai de grammaire malgache*, Paris: Société d'Éditions Géographiques, Maritimes et Coloniales.

Paginton, P. (1970) *English–Malagasy vocabulary*, Antananarivo: Trano Printy Loterana.

Paul, Ileana (2000) *Malagasy Clause Structure*. Unpublished PhD dissertation, Department of Linguistics, McGill University, Montreal, Quebec, Canada.

Paul, I. (ed.) (1998) *The structure of Malagasy, vol. II*, University of California in Los Angeles Occasional Papers in Linguistics 20, Los Angeles: University of California, Department of Linguistics.

——(1999) *Malagasy clause structure*, Doctoral dissertation, McGill University.

Pearson, M. (1996) *Raising and restructuring in Malagasy existentials*, MA thesis, University of California, Los Angeles.

——(2001) *The Clause Structure of Malagasy: A minimalist approach*, Ph.D. Dissertation, University of California, Los Angeles.

Pearson, M. and Paul, I. (eds) (1996) *The Structure of Malagasy vol. 1*, University of California, Los Angeles Occasional Papers in Linguistics 17, Los Angeles: University of California, Department of Linguistics.

Rabearivelo, A. (1976) *Le malgache facile: pour apprendre le malgache chez soi en 70 leçons*, Tananarive: Librairie de Madagascar.

Rabenilaina, R.-B. (1983) *Morpho-syntaxe du malgache. Description structurale du dialecte bara*, Paris: Société d'Études Linguistiques et Anthropologiques de France.

Rackowski, A. (1998) 'Malagasy adverbs', in I. Paul (ed.) 11–33.

Rahajarizafy, R.P.A. (1960) *Essai sur la grammaire malgache*, Antananarivo: Imprimerie Catholique.

Rajaobelina, P. (1966) *Parler malgache. Méthode pour apprendre le malgache usuel en quarante leçons*, Tananarive: Imprimerie Luthérienne.

Rajaona, S. (1972) *Structure du malgache – Etude des formes prédicatives*, Fianarantsoa: Ambozontany.

Rajaonarimanana, N. (1995a) *Grammaire moderne de la langue malgache*, Paris: L'Asiathèque, Collection 'Langues-INALCO'.

——(1995b) *Dictionnaire du malgache contemporain*, Paris: Éditions Karthala.

——(1995c) *Méthode de malgache*, Paris: L'Asiathèque.

Rajaonarimanana, N. and Vérin, P. (1997) *Dictionnaire français–malgache*, Dictionnaire des langues O, Paris: L'Asiathèque.

Rajemisa-Raolison, R. (1963 [1985]) *Rakibolana*, Librairie Ambozontany: Fianarantsoa.

——(1969) *Grammaire malgache*, Fianarantsoa: Librairie d'Ambozontany.

Ranaivoson, J.F. (unpublished) *Les constructions verbales à infinitive en malgache*, Université d'Antananarivo.

Randriamasimanana, C. (1986) *The Causatives of Malagasy*, Honolulu: University of Hawaii Press.

——(1999) 'Clausal architecture and movement verbs in Malagasy', in E. Zeitoun and P.J.-K. Li (eds) *Selected Papers from the Eighth International Conference on Austronesian Linguistics*, 509–527, Taipei: Academia Sinica.

Rasoloson, J. (1994) *Interjektionen im Kontrast – Am Beispiel der deutschen, madagassischen, französischen und englischen Sprache*, Arbeiten zur Sprachanalyse 22, Bern: Peter Lang.

——(1995) 'Das deutsche 'HM' und das madagassische 'M': funktionale Differenzen bei formaler Gleichheit', in G. Henrici and E. Zöfgen (eds) *Fremdsprachen Lehren und Lernen (FLuL): Kontrastivität und kontrastives Lernen*, 241–254, Bern: Peter Lang.

——(1997) *Lehrbuch der madagassischen Sprache*, Hamburg: Helmut Buske.

——(2000) *Terms of address in Malagasy*, Working paper 3 on *Language of Politeness in Intercultural Communication*, Hamburg: Germanisches Seminar, University of Hamburg.

——(2001) *Malagasy–English/English–Malagasy Dictionary and Phrasebook*, New York: Hippocrene Books, Inc.

Razafindrabe, M. (1984) *Cours de malgache pour les étrangers. Résultats de sept ans d'expériences et de recherches*, 2ème édition. Luxembourg: Imprimerie Saint-Paul.

Razafindrabe, M., Ralahatra, X. and Ravaomalala, E. (1980) *Je parle couramment le malgache – I speak Malagasy fluently*, Troisième Edition. Fianarantsoa: Ambozontany.

Razafindrakoto (1990) *Malaky miteny Malagasy aho: étude graduée du malgache à l'intention des étrangers francophones*, Antananarivo: FOFIPA.

Richardson, J. (1885) *A new Malagasy–English dictionary*, Westmead, Farnborough, Hants: Gregg International Publishers.

Schmidt, B. (1983) *Französisch auf Madagaskar. Eine soziolinguistisch-historische Untersuchung*, Dissertation A, Leipzig: Karl-Marx-Universität.

——(1984) 'Die Malgassisierung und das 'malagasy iombonana' – Bilanz der Verwendung und Schaffung einer Nationalsprache', *Zeitschrift für Phonetik, Sprachwissenschaft und Kommunikationsforschung* 57:618–629.

——(1991) 'Aus der Geschichte der madagassischen Sprache', in H. Bergenholtz (ed.) 21–27.

Simon, P. (1988) *Ny fiteny fahizay: reconstitution et périodisation du malgache ancien jusqu'au XIVe siècle*, Paris: Institut des Langues et Civilisations Orientales.

Stark, E.L. (1969) *Malagasy without moans; a first course in the Malagasy language for English-speaking students*, Tananarive: Trano Printy Loterana.

Vérin, P., Kottack, C.P. and Gorlin, P. (1969) 'The glottochronology of Malagasy speech communities', *Oceanic Linguistics* 8:26–83.

Webber, R.P. (1853) *Dictionnaire malgache-français*, Ile Bourbon: Etablissement Malgache de Notre-Dame de la ressource.

CHAPTER SEVENTEEN

PHAN RANG CHAM

Graham Thurgood

1 INTRODUCTION

The extraordinary French scholar Çoedès noted that Cham is the earliest attested Austronesian language. Çoedès dated the Cham inscription found at Trakiêu near the old Cham capital of Indrapura as being from the middle of the fourth century, describing the inscription as 'the oldest text, presently known, written in a Malayo-Polynesian dialect' (Çoedès 1939). The language of the text is associated with the once flourishing kingdom of Champa, a kingdom first mentioned by the Chinese *ca.* 190–193. Champa reached its zenith about the sixth century, continuing to flourish until the Vietnamese 'push to the South' in the tenth century began its slow demise. At the time of the first inscriptions, the Chamic languages were still a largely undifferentiated dialect continuum, but in the subsequent 1500 or so years of change, realignments in patterns of affiliation and language contact restructured stretches of the original dialect chain into distinct languages and distributed the speakers over a much wider area. No longer functioning as the lingua franca of the kingdom of Champa, Chamic lives on in its modern descendants: the Tsat spoken on Hainan, the Rade, Jarai, Haroi, Chru, and Roglai spoken in the southern Vietnam highlands, the Phan Rang Cham spoken in Vietnam, the various Western Cham communities of Cambodia, and the Acehnese of north Sumatra.

Quite correctly, the literature simply assumes that the mainland Chamic languages form a subgroup, but there have been minor questions about the relationship of Acehnese with the mainland Chamic languages. Niemann reached the correct solution as early as 1891, first subgrouping Acehnese and Cham together on the basis of similarities in the verbal morphology, the treatment of inherited vowels, and in various instances of apparent lexical agreement, and then positing a migration of Chams to Aceh (cf. Thurgood 1999 for extended discussion).

Phan Rang Cham (or, Eastern Cham) is a Chamic language spoken in southern Vietnam by 35,000 to 50,000 people in the area around the towns of Phan Rang and Phan Ri. It is closely enough related to Western Cham for the two to be considered dialects of one another. Baumgartner (1998:1) notes that the differences between the two are primarily matters of pronunciation and vocabulary with the grammars being almost identical. As for the number of speakers, he notes that Western Cham is the numerically larger of the two, with 300,000 to 350,000 speakers in Cambodia, and another 35,000 or so speakers in the Mekong delta region of Vietnam, particularly around Chau Doc, Tay Ninh, and Saigon.

1.1 Classification and history

Although as early as 1822, John Crawfurd, a British civil servant and a medical doctor, had recognized the Austronesian affiliation of Cham, which he termed the 'Malay of Champa', it was not until the second half of the twentieth century that scholarship would return to Crawfurd's position. Toward the end of the nineteenth century and for the first half of the twentieth, the classification of the Chamic languages was controversial due to the belief of scholars like Étienne Aymonier, who thought, along with many of his contemporaries, that the Austronesians had migrated to the islands from this part of the Southeast Asian mainland. Failure to distinguish between borrowed Mon-Khmer elements and inherited Austronesian elements led Aymonier to write (1889) that Cham formed a kind of transitional language genetically intermediate between Khmer and Malay. Schmidt (1906), influenced by Cham's Mon-Khmer-influenced typological characteristics and its numerous Mon-Khmer borrowings, described Cham as an Austroasiatic mixed language (Austroasiatic is Mon-Khmer plus Munda). In fact, as late as 1942 Thomas Sebeok was to misclassify Chamic languages as Austroasiatic.

From a modern perspective, it is evident the Chams reached the mainland from a site probably somewhere in West Borneo some 2000 years ago. The Chamic languages are far too closely related and far too easily reconstructed to date back much over 2000 years, let alone the six thousand or so that would be required to account for Austronesian. The borrowed Mon-Khmer elements can readily be distinguished from the inherited Austronesian elements, leaving a clearly Western Malayo-Polynesian language behind, and in the process providing a magnificent venue for studying the effects of language contact on language change.

As an aside, although Moken is sometimes classified as Chamic, careful comparative examination makes it clear that, despite certain areally expected typological similarities and their common membership in Austronesian, there is no special subgrouping relationship between Moken and Chamic (however, see LARISH (MOKEN AND MOKLEN) for an opposite view).

The breakup of ancient Cham into various modern languages followed an almost predictable pattern. For roughly the first millennium, the Chamic languages were a largely undifferentiated dialect chain that certainly extended along the coast of Vietnam and may even have stretched as far south as the east coast of the Malaysian peninsula (although Chamic-like features now found along the east coast of Malaysia certainly date from a much later Acehnese influence). The dialect chain along the coast of Vietnam broke into clearly distinct languages when the Vietnamese moved south down the coastline, a movement that pushed many Chamic speakers up into the highlands and destroyed much of the rich interactional network between the coastal communities. New sets of language networks developed for almost all Chamic speakers, with some like the Haroi eventually coming to be part of a Mon-Khmer social network, while others like the Phan Rang Cham eventually came to be part of the lowlands society dominated by the Vietnamese.

As for Cham itself, it mostly began its split into Western and Phan Rang Cham around the end of the fifteenth century with the fall of the southern capital to the Vietnamese.

Cham has its own literary tradition, one that dates back to the first inscriptions written in an Indic script in the middle of the fourth century. Various texts and inscriptions have been gathered, primarily through the work of various French scholars. However, much of the epigraphic work remains to be done and until then much of the early history of Champa and of Cham will remain beyond our reach.

1.2 Sources

The published sources on Cham are limited. The only phonological sketch that I know is a well-done sketch by David Blood (1967), which this work draws on heavily. Several other works have dealt with aspects of the historical phonology (Doris Blood 1962, Thurgood 1996, 1999) but more remains to be done.

No detailed grammars exist, although there is a good grammatical sketch of Western Cham by Baumgartner (1998). For Phan Rang Cham, there are a handful of articles, including David Blood (1977) on Cham sentences and Doris Blood (1977) on Cham clause and sentence-final particles. The discussion of discourse data in this chapter comes largely from Doris Blood (1978), which gives three Cham texts along with a sophisticated and insightful analysis. The numbers following the cited sentences below refer to these Blood sources; the citations are obvious, except for Blood 1978, which contains three separate texts; for this source the three texts are coded as 6.1, 6.2, and 6.3, plus a line number. Two other sources of Cham texts exist: an extensive French collection of Cham manuscripts catalogued in Pierre-Bernard Lafont, Po Dharma, and Nara Vija (1977) and six reels of microfilms of Cham documents in the Echols Collection of the Kroch Library at Cornell University.

Several good dictionaries exist: Aymonier and Cabaton (1906), written in French, has its idiosyncracies and naturally is somewhat dated, but it is still quite usable. Moussay (1971) is also useful; in addition to citation in the Cham, it has two additional representations, one a transliteration of the Chamic script, and the other a modified transliteration intended to approximate the contemporary pronunciation. Still another is a Cham-Vietnamese dictionary by Bui Khanh The (1995), which seems to take most of its entries from Aymonier and Cabaton (1906); this dictionary uses the same script as Aymonier and Cabaton, but replaces their transliteration with one that is more transparent.

Overall, more historical work than synchronic description seems to have been published on Chamic and Cham. Thurgood (1999) presents an overview that incorporates most of the available historical work.

This grammatical sketch is text-based, a necessary but not ideal constraint. Despite this limitation the attempt has been made to give a precise and succinct statement regarding the polysemy of various, often historically related formatives, although at times there was not enough data to do this.

2 PHONOLOGY

The phonotactics of the word are the key to the phonology of Cham (David Blood 1967). Like the surrounding Mon-Khmer languages, most words are disyllabic and iambic. The rare trisyllabic word is often morphologically complex and, as Blood notes, frequently collapses into a disyllable, following interesting but still unclear paths of reduction.

Contemporary Phan Rang Cham is rapidly going from disyllabic to monosyllabic. A small number of words of course were always monosyllabic, but under the internal influence of final stress and the external influence of Vietnamese now even the typically disyllabic words are increasingly becoming monosyllabic and motivating much of the phonological variation within Cham. Within the last several generations initial syllables were first omitted in informal, colloquial speech and now seem to have been dropped entirely by some speakers. Doris Blood (1962:11) gives a vivid instance, citing the following variants of the word 'new': *perèw ~ prèw ~ phirèw ~ phrèw ~ firèw ~ frèw*. She notes that the scholars tend to maintain the full forms in speech, but, typically, non-scholars modify the first syllable, reducing its vocalism, subjecting it to assimilation, or losing it entirely.

The segment inventories correlate directly with the syllable structure and its iambic stress pattern. The preliminary syllables (using terminology introduced by Blood 1967) are unstressed, shorter in duration, and typically CV, although occasionally a final -ŋ occurs that may assimilate to the following consonant. Blood (1967) notes that as the vowel disappears, the preliminary syllable is restructured, with the consonantal onset sometimes becoming syllabic and sometimes, where the phonetics are compatible, becoming the onset for a main syllable cluster (see the examples in the preceding paragraph).

2.1 Segment inventories

Consonantal contrasts are maximized in the onset position of the fully stressed main syllables (Table 17.1), as Blood makes clear. Consonant clusters are limited to a restricted set of CC- clusters in the main syllable with the second position occupied by either a semi-vowel or a liquid. The occasional appearance of a word like ɓlwaʔ 'more than' with a CCC-onset is only marginal as a counter-example, as the ɓ- in its onset labels it a loanword.

Certain individual segments are worth a brief mention. The /c/ is prepalatal to palatal. The imploded stops vary with corresponding voiced stops. Except for /tʰ-/, the aspirated stops all have fricative variants: /pʰ-/ varies with [f-], apparently under the influence of Vietnamese; /kʰ-/ varies with [x]; and /cʰ-/ varies with [çˢ-] and [s-].

Among the voiceless stops, the cluster written <tr-> is sometimes replaced by a retroflexed stop, e.g. ʈy for trày 'self'. In the speech of women, Blood reports a tendency to replace /tr-/ with /ty-/ which reflects the general tendency among women to substitute /y/ for /r/.

Two distinct phonation types occur after voiceless, unaspirated onsets: one with residual breathy voice and a lower pitch (indicated in the examples by the grave accent); the other with modal (or clear) voice is unmarked in the examples.

The preliminary syllable onsets (Table 17.2) are a subset of those found in main syllables. The imploded series is missing as are the palatal and the velar nasals and the semi-vowels. Among the aspirated stops, only the bilabial and the velar occur heading preliminary syllables.

TABLE 17.1: MAIN SYLLABLE ONSET CONSONANTS

	Labial	Alveolar	Palatal	Velar	Glottal
Vl. stops	p-	t-	c-	k-	ʔ-
Aspirated stops	pʰ-	tʰ-	cʰ-	kʰ-	
Implosives	ɓ-	ɗ-			
Fricatives			s-		h-
Nasals	m-	n-	ñ-		
Semivowels/liquids	w-	l-, r-	y-		

TABLE 17.2: PRELIMINARY SYLLABLE ONSET CONSONANTS

	Labial	Alveolar	Palatal	Velar	Glottal
Vl. stops	p-	t-	c-	k-	ʔ-
Aspirated stops	pʰ-	tʰ-			
Fricatives			s-		h-
Nasals	m-	n-			
Liquids		l-, r-			

TABLE 17.3: MAIN SYLLABLE CONSONANTAL CODAS

	Labial	Alveolar	Palatal	Velar	Glottal
Vl. stops	-p	-t		-k	-ʔ
Fricative					-h
Nasals	-m	-n		-ŋ	
Liquids		-l, -r			

TABLE 17.4: CHAM VOWELS

	Front	Central	Back	Front	Central	Back
High	i	ɨ	u	i	ɨ	u
Mid		ə		e	ə	o
Low		a		ε	a	ɔ
	Preliminary syllables			Main syllables		

The main syllable codas (Table 17.3) are not only even more limited than preliminary syllable onsets, but they also have special characteristics (Blood 1967).

The voiceless unaspirated stops are frequently unreleased utterance-finally. Word-finally /-t/ and /-k/ may be replaced by a glottal stop. As is evident from spectrographic evidence, the glottal stop in final position varies with laryngealization, according to Blood, a characteristic of the languages of the area. The final velar nasal has a labialized allophone occurring variably after the vowels /u/ and /o/, which is characteristic of women's speech. Final /l/, /r/, and /n/ vary among one another and with a retroflex nasal. Much of this reflects movement toward reducing all three to /n/, again an areal characteristic.

Blood writes several more finals but, although historically accurate (except for the <b> which historically would have been a /-p/), these are now orthographically rather than phonetically motivated: <-c> is /-i̢ʔ/, <-b> is /-i̯uʔ/, and <-s> is /-i̢h/.

The vowel system (Table 17.4) is typical of Southeast Asian mainland languages, with the number of vowels in the main syllable reflecting both borrowings and changes from the earlier, more limited inventory under the influence of the neighboring Mon-Khmer languages.

In the preliminary syllable, the vowel contrasts are significantly reduced; only schwa occurs with all the possible consonant onsets. In addition, all four other vowels frequently vary with schwa.

2.2 Tones

The Cham tones are an instructive example of true tonogenesis, namely, the development of tones in a formerly atonal language, not the far more common tone splitting in an already tonal language. The tones are well-described by the Bloods, by Fr. Gérard Moussay (1971:xiii–xiv), and by Han, Edmondson, and Gregerson (1992), who did valuable instrumental work on them. Despite minor disagreement about whether the rising and falling tones are phonemically or only phonetically distinct, the historical correlations of pitch distinctions with various consonant classes is quite straightforward. As Table 17.5 shows (for monosyllables), syllables that historically began with a voiced

TABLE 17.5: CHAM TONES

	Non glottal stop finals	Glottal stop finals
Formerly non-voiced obstruent initials	modal voice (+higher pitch) →mid tone	modal voice (+higher pitch) →falling tone
Formerly voiced obstruent initials	breathy voice (+lower pitch) →low tone	breathy voice (+lower pitch) →rising tone

obstruent developed breathy voiced vowels, while the syllables beginning with the other initials did not. Because breathiness is prototypically accompanied by lower pitch, the resulting breathiness versus modal voice contrast split Cham monosyllables into a low pitched set (low level tone) and a relatively higher pitched set (mid level tone).

The two tone classes are further split on the basis of finals: items ending in a final glottal stop (or a final stop accompanied by final glottal closure) became contour tones. The breathiness associated with the former voiced obstruents interacting with a final glottal gesture resulted in a rising tone, while the modal voiced items interacting with a final glottal gesture resulted in a falling tone. Much of the original voicing distinction in initial obstruents has since been lost, although it is retained orthographically.

Note that it was the breathy voiced quality induced by the voiced obstruents, not the voicing *per se*, that resulted in the low tones. The historical developments are complicated slightly by the spreading of voice quality differences from the preliminary to the main syllable but the conditions are still transparent. In fact, the overall transparency of the process makes Phan Rang Cham invaluable for its insights into the mechanisms of tonogenesis.

2.3 Reduplication

Blood (1967) makes a three-way phonological distinction depending on whether the base is fully reduplicated, partially modified, or segmentally reduced. He notes that instances of full reduplication are rare (e.g. *myet myet* 'forever', which does not have a non-reduplicated counterpart).

In partially modified reduplication (Table 17.6), the base (in italics) precedes the reduplication which still has the same number of segments, but generally involves some vowel and consonant changes.

In segmentally reduced reduplication (Table 17.7), the reduplicative sequence usually precedes the base, contains fewer segments than the base, and some of the occurring segments are phonologically less marked than those in the base form.

Note that the last example (Table 17.7) fits neither pattern particularly well. In any case, the function of reduplication seems to be to provide some sort of distributive meaning. That is, it functions much as do various matched pairs of words, both with the same meaning: *hya cɔʔ* 'cry', with both morphemes meaning 'cry' and *huaʔ baŋ* 'eat', with both morphemes individually also meaning 'eat'.

TABLE 17.6: PARTIAL REDUPLICATION PATTERNS

sənɯŋ-senəŋ	'to meditate'	from *sənɯŋ* 'to think'
likàh-likòy	'tired'	from *likàh* 'tired'
pəsrɛh-pəsrɔh	'compassion'	from *pəsrɛh* 'compassion'
kəruŋ-kəreŋ	'be in anguish'	from *kəruŋ* 'be worried'
rəbah-rəbup	'difficult'	from *rəbah* 'difficult'

TABLE 17.7: REDUCED REDUPLICATION

məʔ-*mɯk*	'to hiccough'	(always reduplicated)
ci-*cih*	'be clean'	from *(hə)cih* 'clean'
təri-*təreŋ*	'be industrious'	from *təreŋ* 'diligent'
təpi-*təpaʔ*	'morally good'	from *təpaʔ* 'straight'

3 BASIC MORPHOSYNTAX

Cham morphemes never consist of less than a syllable, and they always consist of whole syllables. Overwhelmingly, the morphemes are phonologically separate words, with the possible exception of the causative prefix *pa-* in Modern Cham, which may still be marginally productive.

Word classes are defined distributionally. Verbs can be negated, nouns can be pluralized and can occur with classifiers, classifiers can occur with numerals, and so on. The problematic cases are locative nouns and co-verbs, for which see sections 3.4 and 4.5.

3.1 Basic clause structure

Until recently Cham served for a long time as a lingua franca first along the coast and then in the highlands of southern Vietnam. This fact, combined with its relative lack of morphology, probably accounts for the fact that it is a configurational language with a fairly rigid word order. The staple of Cham clausal syntax is the verb-centered, basic declarative sentence. Most of the other clause types are essentially extensions of the declarative clause modified by sentential particles or by deletions required by inter-clausal cohesion. Within the basic clause, the number of arguments is determined by the semantics of the verb. The two core arguments, the subject and the object, are only marked by word order, with the subject preceding the verb and the object following it. Cham thus is a SVO language. Indirect objects never seem to appear as a third unmarked core argument, rather they are always marked as such by a preposition.

Stative intransitive clauses consist of a subject plus stative verb.

(1) *MəHləʔ (ø)   cəmɯn   lo.* (6.1.55)
     Hlok   desolate very
     'Hlok was desolate.'

(2) *pətaaw (ø)   on-təpon   paʔ   hətaay* (6.1.96)
     King   happy   at   liver
     'The king was overjoyed.'

This pattern is used for descriptive adjectives; equational sentences follow the topic-comment pattern discussed below. As is obvious from example (2) and others elsewhere, the stomach, the liver, or some major organ are seen as the seat of the emotions, and the metaphor of an emotion going into the stomach or liver is common in the languages in the area.

In some instances, Cham uses a topicalization construction in which the topic is marked with the distal demonstrative *nan*. This construction is the typical way for marking equative sentences – the apparent origin of the construction – and is also used widely for marking other kinds of topics. In her brief discussion of topic-comment sentences, Doris Blood (1977:63–64) presents the example in (3) with its double occurrence of *nan*, the first functioning as adnominal modifier, the second as a topic marker.

(3) oŋ   *nan nan uraaŋ toy.* (Blood 1977:63)
     mister DIST DIST CLF   guest
     'That gentleman is a guest.'

In example (3), the topic then is *oŋ nan nan*. The comment consists of the classifier *uraaŋ* 'person' followed by the head noun *toy* 'guest'.

The topic constituent is not limited to nouns but can involve more complex phrases and even clauses, as shown by the following two examples in which the topical constituent is non-Italic:

(4) pətaaw Taluy? ŋa? nan *oh   ?jɔw? pətaaw pya? o.* (Blood 1977:64)
     king   Taluch do   DIST NEG correct king   real NEG.
     'King Taluch's behavior was not that of a true king.'

(5) ŋa? kəñi nan *pyəh   ?wa? ŋa? yaaŋ,* (6.2.34–5)
     make kanhi DIST in.order rub   make spirits
     '(They) make the *kanhi* (a kind of instrument) to appease the spirits.'

As shown by (5), there need be no grammatical nexus between topic and comment, only semantic coherence.

Presentative clauses (sometimes termed existential clauses) introduce new entities onto the main stage. The verb *hu* 'have; get' functions as the existential predicate which is immediately followed by the expression for the newly introduced participant.

(6) *tha hray nan hu   tha muu?   təha...*(6.1.126)
     one day   DIST have one grandmother old...
     'One day there was an old woman...'

(7) *hu   tha uraaŋ cam   [__ŋa?   kəñi   khḱh   lo]* (6.2.21)
     have one CLF   Cham [__make kanhi skillful very]
     'There is a Cham man who makes the *kanhi* very skillfully.'

The verb *hu* 'have; get' can also be used as a main verb. It then is preceded by the subject, as in

(8) *tòm   uraaŋ   hu   ənu? tòra   hu   pĭnaay rup* (6.1.65)
     some people have child young have lovely appearance
     'Some people have young daughters who have a lovely appearance.'

When used as a presentative, as in (6), various adverbials may occur in the preverbal adjunct position, but the subject itself is always found post-verbally.

Aside from the presentative, the only construction in Cham with a non-canonical word order is left-dislocation. In this construction, a constituent which usually has to occur in postverbal position occurs in clause-initial [or pre-clausal?] position, preceding the subject.

(9) cərɔʔ   əmɛɛʔ MəKaam ŋaʔ ___   rilɔ   baŋ   plɔ̀h. (6.1.37)
     charok   mom   Kam   make ___ meat   eat   finish
     'Your *charok*, Kam's mother has already made (*it*) into food.'

(10) kəɲɪ   uraaŋ   oh   ʔwaʔ ___   məʔin (6.2.33)
     kanhi person NEG   rub ___   play
     'The *kanhi* (is an instrument) that people do not play ___ for fun.'

This construction is also found with embedded clauses:

(11) əmɛɛʔ   MəKaam   hmit   ənɪɪʔ   rimɔɔŋ   baŋ ___,   cɔʔ   hya (6.1.188)
     mother Kam   hear   child   tiger   eat ___   cry   cry
     'Kam's mother, hearing her daughter had been eaten by a tiger, wept.'

As for non-declarative moods, Cham has a rich array of imperatives, many with still transparent origins. In their simplest form, imperatives may consist of nothing more than an optional vocative followed by a VP.

(12) cərɔʔ   ləy,   (ø)   doŋ   təkò?   baŋ   lithay (6.1.22)
     charok hey,   (ø)   rise up,   eat   rice
     'Charok! Come on up and eat your rice.'

Imperatives may also use a sentence-final marker. In formal contexts, including written material, the marker is usually *pè?*, descended from a proto-Chamic negative imperative but of obvious Mon-Khmer rather than Proto-Austronesian origin. In less formal contexts, the most common marker is *mɛʔ*, which varies with *ɛʔ* in even more colloquial speech. Doris Blood (1977:45) notes that this is a more forceful command, described in Cham as *dom baʔ* 'speaking salty'. She gives these examples.

(13) *aay*   *huaʔ* mɛʔ   (14) tɔ̀ɔʔ   ɛʔ   (Doris Blood 1977:45)
     elder.sibling   eat   IMP   stay   IMP
     'Eat, brother!'   'Stay!' (to person staying)

Here, however, as elsewhere in Cham, an abundance of sentence final particles exist functioning to register a wide range of moods and functions (Doris Blood 1977:45–47). Thus, other sentential markers can follow *mɛʔ*, in which case they alter the mood (examples from Blood).

(15) ənɪɪʔ *huaʔ* mɛʔ   yə!   (16) *huaʔ* mɛʔ   kaay!
     child eat   IMP   (hurry)   eat   IMP   (coaxing)
     'Hurry and eat, child!'   'Oh come on and eat!

(17) naaw thaŋ   mɛʔ   ɲɪ!   (18) *huaʔ* mɛʔ   ah!
     go   house IMP   (softened)   eat   IMP   (coaxing)
     'Go home, okay!'   'Come and eat!'

Notice that the final particle *yi* has increased the directness of the command, but *kaay*, *ɲɪɪ*, and *ah* have taken away some of the bluntness.

Like many Southeast Asian languages, Cham has a non-compositional negative imperative *còy* 'don't'.

(19) còy   diʔ   còy   ah! (Blood 1977:47)
     don't climb don't PTCL
     'Better not climb (it)!'

In this example, the force of the imperative has been moderated by the use of the final particle *ah*. Note that the negative imperative may occur before the verb, clause-finally, or in both positions. However, in final position, it is 'preceded by a pause and is spoken on a higher level of intonation with a rather sharp fall' (Doris Blood 1977:47), a description suggesting a right-dislocated element more than a fully incorporated final particle.

Questions follow the same word order as the corresponding declarative sentences. Questions answerable with a yes or no typically are signaled with nothing more than a rise in intonation on the last element in the sentence (Doris Blood 1977:42). Less commonly a yes/no question may be signaled by the sentence-final particle *laay* 'Q'.

(20) *aay*   *takrı* *laay* (Doris Blood 1978:42)
      elder.brother want   Q
      'Do you want to?'

Additional sentence-final particles provide other nuances. For example, in (21), the tag *ʔjɔwʔ* laay 'right?' gives the flavor of a tag question to which a positive answer is expected. With this tag, the clause is followed by a slight pause before the tag is added.

(21) *aay*   *naaw* *thaaŋ* *o*   *ʔjɔwʔ* *laay* (Blood 1978:43)
      elder.brother go   home   NEG   correct Q
      'You're not going home, right?'

Some particles are more tightly incorporated than the one just discussed. Blood (1978:43) mentions *hu laay*, which has the nuance of possibility from the *hu* 'possible; able; get; have'.

(22) *tɘhlaʔ* *naaw* *thaŋ* *aay*   *hu*   *laay?* (Blood 1978:43)
      I   go   house   elder.brother able   Q
      'Can I go to your house?'

Content questions, like yes/no questions, use the same word order as the corresponding declarative sentences, but with the question word inserted in place of the questioned item. Examples for question words are *pa* 'where' < *paʔ hlaay* 'at which?', *taaw* 'where?', *kèʔ* 'what?', *thipàal* 'why?', etc.

(23) *tɘhlaʔ* *waʔ* *yaaw* hlaay *kayʔʔ* (Blood 1978:45)
      I   write like   what   (specifically)
      'How do I write (it)?'

The final particle *kayʔ* here, Blood notes, seems to demand a specific answer.

3.2 Noun phrase structures

The basic structure of the NP is quite stable in Cham. Schematically, it can be represented as: NUM CLF *Head* Modifier(s) Demonstrative. (24) illustrates these positions.

(24) *twà* *tàŋ* *tɘlay* *kapwàʔ* *nan* (6.2.20)
      two   CLF   string   silk   DIST
      'those two *strings* of silk'

More complex modifiers can, of course, be included replacing the genitive modifier *kapwàʔ* in the example given. As for genitive constructions, they are marked by simple juxtaposition with the head noun coming first and the genitive following. Other examples are *ɘmɛɛʔ MɘHlɘʔ* 'mother + Hlok' = 'Hlok's mother', *hɘtiwʔ tɘluyʔ* 'wife' + 'younger son' = 'wife of the younger son', and:

(25) *MəKaam tɔɔʔ tì la tuh əpìh* ikaan *MəHləʔ təmɪ tənɛh* (6.1.11)
    Kam   stay LOC down pour all fish Hlok   into basket
    'Kam stayed below and poured all of Hlok's *fish* into her basket...'

In Modern Cham, juxtaposition appears to be the only way to form genitives, whether the genitive marks possession, part of a whole, or whatever.

3.2.1 Pronouns and indexicals

Two types of indexing are used to track participants in a text: pronouns, which index speech act participants, and indexicals, which index personal and social identity.

The Cham pronouns themselves come from a variety of sources, some inherited from proto-Chamic (PC) or even as far back as Proto-Austronesian, others borrowed from Mon-Khmer sources. Table 17.8 provides an overview of the forms. The first person singular pronoun PC **kɔw* dates back to the earliest Austronesian sources, while the first person polite form PC **hulun*, which also means 'slave', is an innovation in its pronominal use that is no older than PC and possibly much younger. Similarly, **kaməy* 'we (EX)' and **ta* 'we (IN)' relate to Austronesian pronouns, while **drəy* 'we (IN); intensifier' derives from the still extant word for 'body'. In addition, Phan Rang Cham has yet another polite first person form **dahlaʔ*, also of recent origin.

The table includes one of the two plural markers: the plural form meaning *kàwʔ *gəp* 'group; other', which shows up in various plural pronouns, for instance the second person plural, which simply adds *kàwʔ* to the singular. The other, found in the combination *khɔl ñu*, is a pluralizer for the third singular pronoun *ñu*; the combination is identical to the combination *chúng nó* meaning 'they' in Vietnamese.

Nouns characterizing social roles such as grandmother, elder sister, stepmother, king, and such are frequently used in the place of pronouns. In the texts examined, the third person pronoun is only used for humans.

3.2.2 Demonstratives

Demonstratives can function pronominally or modify a noun in which case they follow the constituent they modify: only the minimal two-way distinction between a distal and a proximal demonstrative is made. Finer semantic distinctions are found in the directional coverbs (see section 4.3). The distal demonstrative *nan* is the one that has taken up the duties involved in marking NPs as anaphoric; the proximal *ni* is only used when a proximal meaning is emphasized.

(26) *trù   kìnrəh nan* (Blood 1978:2.3.3.3)
    medicine magic DIST
    'that magic medicine'

TABLE 17.8: THE PHAN RANG PRONOUNS

PC	PR Cham		PC	PR Cham	
*kɔw	kaw	'I (familiar)'	**kaməy*	kami	'we (EX)'
*hulun	halun	'I (polite); slave'	**ta*	ita	'we (IN)'
*dahlaʔ	tə̀hlaʔ	'I (polite)'	**drəy*	-tray	'we (IN); reflexive'
*hã	hĩ	'you; thou'			
*ñu	ñu	'he, she'	**gəp*	kàwʔ	'other; group'

In the corpus, demonstrative pronouns are most frequently found as objects of prepositions as in (27). Much more rarely are they found elsewhere, as in most cases coreferential NPs are omitted.

(27)   *...hmit   yaw   nan* (Blood 1978:2.3.3.1)
       ...hear   like   DIST
       '...heard about that'

In the texts, the demonstratives also do not seem to occur referring to humans or animates; whether this is an absolute restriction or just a strong tendency is not clear. In addition, and as mentioned in section 3.1, the demonstrative *nan* occurs as part of the topicalization construction.

3.2.3 Classifiers

Cham classifier constructions are as follows: (NUM) CLF (Head (Mod) (Demonstrative)), with the only necessary component being a CLF but with significant potential for elaboration.

(28)   *kràwʔ   trày   cim   niʔ   thɔŋ   kətraw* (6.1.81)
       PL   CLF   bird   sparrow   and   pigeon
       'some sparrows and pigeons'

(29)   *tha   plàh   pəpaan   lipth* (6.2.5)
       one   CLF   board   thin
       'a thin piece of wood'

(30)   *pɔ̀h   məkya   nan* (6.1.131)
       CLF   ebony   DIST
       'that *kya* (persimmon-like fruit)'

The analysis of examples like (30) is problematic as *pɔ̀h* 'fruit; CLF for fruit' can be analysed both as a head noun and as a classifier. Similarly, *phun* functions both as the word for 'tree' and as the CLF for trees.

(31)   *hu   təmuh   tha   phun   məkya* (6.1.124)
       have   grow   one   CLF   ebony
       'there grew an ebony (or *kya*) tree'

In discourse, the first appearance of the CLF introduces a new entity into the flow of discourse. Typically, this first mention of the CLF co-occurs with the number *tha* 'one', in which case it is marking the entity as indefinite as well as singular. Subsequent mentions of the CLF (with reference to the same entity), however, serve a different function and are often not accompanied by any quantifier. In such subsequent mentions the CLF serves as a sort of pronoun, parallel to the way that nouns characterizing social roles such as grandmother, elder sister, stepmother, king, and such are used in the place of pronouns. In fact, in the texts examined, pronouns are never used to track nonhumans; instead, the tracking is done with a combination of zeros (safely ignored in the discussion to follow), CLFs, and various (other) noun substitutes. Compare the following segments drawn from the same text.

(32)   *hu   tha   pɔ̀h   prɔŋ   yɔm   də   cəluʔ*...(6.1.125)
       have   one   CLF   large   compare   equal   bowl
       'having one fruit as large as a bowl'

(33) *tɔlaaʔ*   *mɔŋ*   *boh*   tha   pɔh   məkya   prɔŋ   kəcàan. ... (6.1.128)
      look.up   look   see   one   CLF   ebony   big   near.ripe
      'and looked up to see a large persimmon-like fruit almost ripe.'

(34) *min*   *cɔŋ*   *ka*   pɔh   məkya   nan   *lɛʔ*   *trun*   *tɔlam*
      but   wish   for   CLF   ebony   that   fall   down   inside
      liʔi   *muuʔ*. (6.1.131)
      basket   grandmother
      'She wished that the fruit would fall down into her basket.'

(35) pɔh   məkya   *truh*   *trun*   *təpaʔ*   *liʔi*. ... (6.1.133)
      CLF   ebony   fall   down   straight   basket
      'the ebony fruit fell down into her basket.'

(36) *pacɛ*   *both*   pɔh   mʌ̃əkya   plàh   twà   tɔ̀ɔʔ   kədɔh   thɔh. ... (6.1.153)
      peek   see   CLF   ebony   cut   two   stay   peel   only
      'peeked in and saw the ebony fruit cut in two with just the peel left.'

[Note that in this example it could also be argued that *pɔh* functions as a noun rather than a CLF, in particular in 32 and 33.]

Here, the CLF with *tha* 'one' is used to first introduce the fruit to the listener *tha pɔh prɔŋ yɔm də côluʔ* (6.1.125); that this is an initial introduction is made particularly obvious by the use of the presentational *hu* 'have'. Several lines later (6.1.128) the fruit is again introduced but this time to an old woman with *tha pɔh məkya prɔŋ kəcàan*, again marked with *tha* 'one' indicating that it is indefinite from the old woman's viewpoint. The next overt reference (6.1.131) *pɔh məkyanan* 'that ebony fruit' occurs without a numeral; here, the CLF is being used solely for reference tracking, with the deictic *nan* 'that' making the definite reference obvious. Two lines later (6.1.133) the form *pɔh məkya* occurs, again without *tha* 'one' and again being used pronominally. Twenty lines later (6.1.153) the form *pɔh məkya* occurs once more, again without *tha* 'one' and again being used pronominally.

As for the function of classifier constructions in counting, it is a decidedly minor one: Classifiers can and do co-occur with numbers, of course, but more often than not they occur without numbers and, with a great frequency, numbers occur without classifiers.

3.2.4 Relative clauses

With regard to relative clauses, one ultimately has to sympathize with the analysis implicit in David Blood's 1977 overview of Cham sentences in which he makes no mention of relative clauses. Certainly, the data examined showed no special relative clause construction. However, there are entities closely resembling the relative clauses found in other western Austronesian languages in which the head noun exceptionally is not the subject of the relative clause. They also involve words for 'time' and 'place', as illustrated by the following two examples.

(37) *əmɛɛʔ*   *MəHləʔ*   *mətaay*   tuʔ   *MəHləʔ*   tɔ̀ɔ   siit (6.1.2)
      mother   Hlok   die   hour   Hlok   stay   small
      'Hlok's mother died when she was small.'

(38) *lipiʔ*   *tàl*   *pyà*   *Hləʔ* (6.1.123)
      place   bury   queen   Hlok
      '...the place Queen Hlok was buried'

Nonetheless, this type of clause is marginal in Phan Rang Cham, both statistically and structurally. The closely related Western Cham certainly has a relative clause construction with its own relative clause marker *kung*. And the older Cham documents show a relative clause marker, which may be related to the Malay marker *yang*; however, the presence of *yang* in these documents mostly reflects contact with Malay speakers rather than a common inheritance.

3.2.5 Noun compounds

Although not pervasive throughout Cham, noun compounds certainly exist. The mechanism is juxtaposition and the construction is semantically driven: Two words describing characteristic features are combined.

(39) *baŋ mǝñum* (6.1.185)   (40) *mǝñin   cǝluʔ* (6.1.20)
    eat   drink   bowl   plate
    'a feast'   'dishes'

These are simple juxtapositions, typically composed of the two most salient members or characteristics of a class, an activity, or whatever, used as a general noun. These are exceedingly common in Southeast Asia.

3.3 Verb phrase structures

Several archaic verbal affixes occur in Proto-Chamic and in the older Cham records but now have been lost. Thus, older Cham records contain attestation of the causative verbal prefix **pǝ-*, which is apparently native to both Mon-Khmer and Proto-Austronesian, the nominalizing infix **-ǝn-*, which is definitely of Mon-Khmer origin, and the 'inadvertent' prefix, a prefix that appears to descend from Proto-Chamic **tǝ(r)*. Except for **pa-*, these affixes seem to be lost in modern Cham.

3.3.1 Aspect and tense

Cham does not mark tense, but it does mark basic aspectual distinctions. The two items most frequently used to mark aspectual distinctions are the forms *plɔh* 'finish' and *tɔɔʔ* which as a main verb means 'live; stay' but also may mean 'still'.. In their aspectual uses these two forms distinguish ongoing states and activities (PROGRESSIVE) from completed states and activities (COMPLETIVE).

The differences in the meaning of *tɔɔʔ* correlate with its placement in an overall construction: in (41a) *tɔɔʔ* 'live; stay' is used as a main verb; in (41b) where it precedes an attributive predicate *tɔɔʔ* indicates the continuance of a state and is best rendered by 'still'; and in (9) where it precedes an activity predicate *tɔɔʔ* indicates the continuance of an activity.

(41a) *MǝKaam   tɔɔʔ   tii   la   tuh   ǝpìh   ikkan   MǝHlǝʔ*
      Kam   stay   LOC   down   pour   all   fish   Hlok
      tǝmɪ   tǝnɛh (6.1.11)
      into   basket
      'Kam stayed below and poured all of Hlok's fish into her basket and....'

(41b) *ǝmɛɛʔ   MǝHlǝʔ   Mǝtaay   tuʔ   MǝHlǝʔ   tɔɔʔ   siit* (6.1.2)
      mother   Hlok   die   hour   Hlok   stay   small
      'Hlok's mother died when she was still small.'

(41c) *MəHlə?*   tɔɔ?   *məʔin*   oh   *mɪ?*   hu   *ikaan.* (6.1.14)
Hlok   stay   play   NEG   get   have   fish
'Hlok is still playing and she didn't get any fish.'

Example (42) shows still another use of *tɔɔ?*. Here it occurs at the beginning of a clause, marking an overlap of the activities in the ensuing paragraph and the activities in the previous paragraph.

(42) tɔɔ?   *MəKaam*   *təpià?*   *truh*   *məthìl*...(6.1.186)
stay   Kam   go.out   away   palace...
'Meanwhile Kam had left the palace...'

Similarly, the different functions of *plɔh* 'finish' also correlate with its distribution: as a main verb *plɔh* means 'finish; finished'; sentence-initially as in (43), *plɔh* marks the next significant event (a meaning roughly translated here as 'then'), and clause-finally, as (44), it marks one activity as completed with respect to the next one.

(43) plɔh   *mɪ?*   *kədɔh*   *məkya*   nan   *patàw?.* (6.1.155)
finish   get   peel   ebony   that   hide
'then took the skin of the fruit and hid it.'

(44) *rəmi?*   *məñin*   *cə̀lu?*   plɔh (6.1.20)
clean   bowl   plate   finish
'After she did the dishes,
ñu   pà   lithay   naaw   pa?   piŋun   ?ya   likuu?   thaaŋ...(6.1.21)
she   take   rice   go   at   well   water   back   house
'she took the rice to the well...,'

These forms are transparently related to the basic meaning 'finish; finished' with differences in scope related to differences in placement.

3.3.2 Negation

Negation may occur sentence-finally, before the verb, or in both positions, but it does carry different nuances in each position. Sentence-final negation, signaled by *o*, is described by Doris Blood as the normal way to express negation and it frequently appears in their notes.

(45) *mɪ̄kaw*   *poy?*   o. (Blood 1977:40)
father   I scold   NEG
'My father won't scold.'

None of the three texts examined contained any examples of this pattern, however. Instead, all instances of negation involved the negative particle placed just before the initial element of the verb string.

(46) *tə̀lam*   *tyaan*   *mɪ?*   *ŋa?*   *kəray*   min   oh   *dom*   *təpià?.* (6.1.120)
inside   stomach   get   make   different   but   NEG   speak   out
'Inwardly he wondered, but didn't say anything.'

(47) min   *əmɛɛ?*   *MəKaam*   oh   *prày*   naaw (6.1.70)
but   Mom   Kam   NEG   give   go
'but Kam's mother would not let her go,'

(48) *min   muuʔ*   oh   *mətà   dih   wal.* (6.1.149)
      but   grandmother   NEG   ever   sleep   sound
      'but grandmother never completely fell asleep.'

In (46) the negation is before the main verb, in (47) it precedes a permissive verb meaning 'let' (literally 'give'), and in (48) it precedes an adverb. Doris Blood notes that pre-verbal negation is typical of more formal styles, termed by the Cham *dom klɔ̀ŋ* 'speaking high'. The more formal pre-verbal negative, she notes, is often intensified by repeating the negative particle sentence-finally.

(49) ...*(ø)*   oh   *boh   ʔya   kìnrəh*   o, (Blood 1978:2.3.3.6)
      ...(ø)   NEG   see   water   magic   NEG
      '...(they) didn't see the magic water,'

(50) *plɔ̀h   ñu*   oh   *khin   pà   təkhɔ   tuy   tra*   o. (6.1.56)
      after   she   NEG   dare   take   shoe   follow   again   NEG
      'After that she didn't dare take the (other) shoe with her anymore.'

(51) *tàlam   raay   muuʔ*   oh   *mətà   hu   tòm   kəya   baŋ*
      inside   generation   grmother   NEG   ever   have   some   thing   eat
      yaw   nan   o. (6.1.144)
      like   DIST   NEG
      'In all her days the woman had never had food like that.'

3.3.3 Reflexives, joint action, and reciprocals

Cham reflexives are marked with *trày* /trèy/ 'self', a word that derives from the still extant word for 'body'. Note the idiomatic usage in (52).

(52) ...*plɔ̀h(ø)*   *likaw   trày   naaw   ʔyəʔ   məthìl   pətaaw.* (6.1.87)
      ...then(she)   beg   self   go   look   palace   king
      '...then (she) begged leave to go watch at the king's palace.'

(53) *saniŋ   yaaw   nan,   tapay   klaw   tha   trày.* (Blood 1977:54, 62)
      think   like   DIST,   rabbit   laugh   one   self
      'Thinking like that, the rabbit laughed to himself.'

Joint action can be marked explicitly with *càaʔ kàwʔ*, which in these texts is a construction always marked by a pronoun followed by *càaʔ* 'mutual' which, in turn, is followed by *kàwʔ* 'other'.

(54) *ñu   càaʔ   kàwʔ   maay   paʔ   thaaŋ   təluyʔ* (2.3.3.2)
      they   mutual   other   come   at   house   y.son
      'and they came together to the house of the youngest son,'

(55) *plɔ̀h   ñu   càaʔ   kàwʔ   naaw.* (2.3.3.14)
      finish   they   mutual   other   go
      'Then they left together.'

Reciprocal action is marked by using *kàwʔ* 'other' after the verb, which in certain contexts is extended to mean 'together' or 'each other'.

(56) twà   *ətày   aay   bɔɔʔ   məta   trɔ̀h   kàwʔ.* (6.1.118)
      two   y.sibling   e.sibling   cheek   eye   like   other
      'The two sisters looked just alike.'

(57) plɔ̀h   twà   *hətyuʔ*   *pəthaaŋ*   kol   kàwʔ   *hya*   *cɔʔ.* (6.1.180)
     finish two   wife   husband hug other cry   cry
     'Then the husband and wife hugged each other and cried.'

(58) twà   cəʔ   təcɔ   rɔɔŋ pà   kàwʔ. (6.1.163)
     two   grandmother grandchild keep take other
     'the two of them taking care of each other.'

Note that all three of the examples include *twà* 'two' used to indicate that the pair of entities that follow form a group.

3.4 Prepositions and locative nouns

Three morphological systems, largely complementary but occasionally overlapping, serve to mark the oblique cases: prepositions, locative nouns, and co-verbs (see section 4.5). Locative noun phrases mark stationary locations. Co-verbs, derived from motion verbs, tend to mark directional motion, among other things. Prepositions are the most diffuse in meaning but seem to mark the more core-like oblique cases. Here we first discuss the prepositions and then the locative nouns.

The marker *ka* 'for; BENEFACTIVE' has two related functions: within clauses it marks the benefactive and in embedded clauses it is often used to mark the subject NP (see section 4.2). Examples of benefactive *ka*:

(59) ñu   buyʔ   pìmaaw   ka   əmɛɛʔ   ñu. (Blood 1977:53)
     he   pluck mushroom for mother he
     'He gathered mushrooms for his mother.'

(60) mɛɛʔ   mətɔ̀h,   təkòʔ   naaw   mìʔ   lithay ka   ənìʔ
     mother woke   get.up, go   get   rice   for child
     hwaʔ (Blood 1977:54)
     eat.rice
     'The mother got up (and) went to get rice for (her) child to eat.'

Cham marks sources with *mɨ̃ŋ* 'from' and goals with *tal* 'arrive'. The word *tal* marks, as the gloss indicates, arrival at the goal. Movement toward a goal is marked either by the co-verb *naaw* 'go' or the preposition *tì* 'to; at', which will be discussed shortly. As for *tal*, unlike the other prepositions discussed here, it has a clearly verbal origin; it is neither an inherited preposition, nor does it originate in an earlier noun.

mɨ̃ŋ and *tal* occur before a full range of noun phrases, including gerunds and sentential complements, marking literal and metaphoric spatial and temporal movement.

(61) mɨŋ   tɔ́lam   khaan   pràh (6.1.150)
     from   inside   pot   rice
     'from inside the rice storage pot'

(62) oŋ   ŋaʔ   tha   tràv   rəŋ   mɨŋ   kəyaw (6.2.23)
     sir   make one   CLF   crab from wood
     'He makes a bridge (= a crab-shaped part) of wood'

(63) *tal*   MɔHlə maay mɨŋ   klàŋ   pəpè (6.1.30)
     arrive Hlok   come *from* watch goat
     'When Hlok came home from watching the goats,...'

(64) ñu   pəlih   mɨŋ   pəkè   tal   *sup*   yɔm   hu   tha   cɔ̀luʔ (6.1.77)
     she separate from morning arrive dark do   have one bowl
     'working (i.e. separating (seeds)) from morning till dark but had (filled) only one bowl'

The most general and thus least marked preposition is *tì* 'to; at' which seems to have a generalized locative function. It also occurs with locative nouns converting them into phrasal prepositions as in (67). It often codes a goal, including addressees and recipients.

(65)   *plɔ̀h   pa-doyʔ   hraʔ   tì   krɑ̀wʔ   nəkàl* (6.1.62)
       after   CAU-run   letter   LOC   PL   countries
       'he sent a letter to all countries.'

(66)   *ñu   càaŋ   likaw   tì   əmɛɛʔ   hmɔm   naaw   ʔyəʔ   thɔŋ*
       she   also   beg   LOC   mom-   step   go   look   with
       MəKaam (6.1.69)
       Kam
       'and she also asked her stepmother if she could go look with Kam...'

(67)   *MəKaam   tɔɔʔ   tì   la   tuh   əpìh   ikaan   MəHləʔ*
       Kam   stay   LOC   beneath   pour   all   fish   Hlok
       təmɩ   tanɛh, (6.1.11)
       into   basket
       'Kam stayed below and poured all of Hlok's fish into her basket.'

Other prepositions include *thɔŋ* 'with; and', *paʔ* 'at', *yaw* 'like'.

As is true for a number of the languages of the area, locative nouns supplement the work that is done by prepositions in English. Locative noun phrases are genitive constructions consisting of two juxtaposed nouns. The head noun (the locative noun) designates a place and the following noun designates whatever is located with reference to that place. Usually, but not always, the locative noun is preceded by a 'true' preposition, often the very general *tì*. In (38) and (39), the distinct words for 'put' notwithstanding, no preposition precedes the locative noun.

(68)   *pùh   rɔɔŋ   tàlam   piŋun   ʔya   likuuʔ   thaaŋ.* (6.1.18)
       put   feed   inside   well   water   back   house
       'and put it in the well at the back of the house to feed it.'

(69)   *ñu   cɛʔ   pɔɔʔ   təkhɔʔ   ŋɔʔ   təboʔ.* (6.1.53)
       she   put   package   shoes   top   bank
       she put the package of shoes on the bank.

In (70ff) the situation is more typical.

(70)   *tàlaaŋ   cərɔʔ   tàl   mɩŋ   likuuʔ   kìŋ.* (6.1.38)
       bone   charok   bury   from   back   kitchen
       'Its bones are buried at the back of the kitchen.'

(71)   *ñu   tɔɔʔ   mɩŋ   la   pan   phun   pənɩŋ   yuh.* (6.1.113)
       she   stay   from   underneath   hold   tree   betel   shake
       'She stayed down below, took hold of the betel tree, and shook it.'

(72)   *min   mɩŋ   liŋiw   ŋaʔ   on-təpon* (6.1.104)
       but   from   outside   make   happy
       'but on the surface appearing pleased.'

(73)   *klaaʔ   tha   wɛt   mɩŋ   kɔʔ   tal   krɩh   kəʔɩŋ.* (6.2.4)
       dispose   one   piece   from   head   arrive   mid   upper.back
       'taking off a piece from the head to the middle of the back.'

3.5 Older morphology

As already mentioned at the beginning of section 3.3, older documents record now lost morphology. The widely attested -*kan* suffix is also found in Cham (see ADELAAR on MALAYIC VARIETIES), although other Malay suffixes such as -*an* and -*i* had disappeared along with all the other suffixes (Aymonier and Cabaton 1906:xxiv). Remnants of PC **si-*, the honorific-marking prefix, are also found (Marrison 1975), but only as a fossilized prefix on certain kinship terms. The existence of other connectives such as *maka* 'well, then, because, and, thus', *pun* 'then, if; really; also', and *ampun* 'forgiveness, ask forgiveness' exist but may simply reflect later Malay influence, as does -*kan*, which is not inherited from Proto-Malayic and is missing in various Malayic varieties.

Although it has been lost in modern Cham, there is a verb marker, the so-called 'inadvertent' prefix, Proto-Chamic **tə(r)*, which is described by Aymonier and Cabaton (1906:xxiii–xxiv) as having a range of meanings for Cham including causativity, reciprocity, and stativity. This prefix is reconstructed not just back to the proto-Malayo-Chamic stage but to Proto-Austronesian. Remnants of it are still found in various Chamic languages (Thurgood 1999) and it has, in some cases, been borrowed into the neighboring Mon-Khmer languages.

Different devices are used to mark causation in Cham but the only affixal causative is *pa-* inherited from Proto-Austronesian. This morpheme, apparently fossilized, converts intransitives into transitives, adding an additional argument.

Compare the following sentences.

(74) *cərɔʔ   ləy,   doŋ   təkòʔ   baŋ   lithay* (6.1.22)
      charok   hey,   rise up,   eat   rice
      'Charok! Come on up and eat your rice'.

(75) *ñu   boh   ənuʔ   cərɔʔ   pa-doŋ   trày   təkòʔ   tì   ʔya.* (6.1.23)
      she   see   child   charok   CAU-rise self   up   LOC   water
      'She saw the baby fish rise to the top of the water.' (i.e. raise itself)

4 COMPLEX PREDICATES AND SENTENCES

Cham clause concatenation often involves little more than the juxtaposition of clauses with the coherence supplied by the context augmented by the iconicity of the sequencing. It is difficult to find textual examples of action sequences in which chronological order is not followed, for example. When the juxtaposed clauses share the same subject, this subject is deleted in subsequent clauses, thus providing additional cohesion to the coherence already established by the context and the sequencing of the clauses. Further cohesion is sometimes added through the addition of explicit markers of the relationship at the clausal peripheries, although it appears more typical not to mark relationships explicitly unless it is clearly necessary to do so.

4.1 Periphrastic causatives

The most common of the periphrastic causatives are formed with *ŋaʔ* which means 'make' and is used in its literal sense as a main predicate in (76). (77) illustrates a causative usage.

(76) *muuʔ   təkrɪ   kraʔ   ʔyəʔ   thay   uraaŋ   ŋaʔ   lithay   ka*
      grandmother   want   spy   see   who   person make rice   for
      muuʔ. (6.1.47)
      grandmother
      'The woman wanted to discover who had made rice for her.'

(77) *MəHlə   mɪʔ   ŋaʔ   raw   rilo.* (6.1.34)
      Hlok   get   make   sad   much
      'It made Hlok very sad.'

Permissive causatives are formed with *pràỳ* 'give'. In (78) *pràỳ* is a main verb meaning 'give'; in (79) and (80) it functions as a permissive auxiliary.

(78) *əmɛɛʔ   MəKaam   càaŋ   pràỳ   aaw   khan   kɔɔŋ   kərah* (6.1.66)
      mom   Kam   also   give   clothes   bracelet   ring
      'Kam's mother also gave clothes, bracelets and rings…'

(79) *min   əmɛɛʔ   MəKaam   oh   pràỳ   naaw* (6.1.70)
      but   Mom   Kam   NEG   give   go
      'but Kam's mother would not let her go,'

(80) *pràỳ   ka   təhlaʔ   likaw   ʔyəʔ   bɔɔʔ.* (6.1.76)
      give   for   me   beg   look   cheek
      'Please let me see (her) cheek (i.e. see her face).'

4.2 Complement clauses

The most straightforward clausal complements in Phan Rang Cham are found with verbs of perception and ordering.

(81) pədal   *MəHləʔ   koyʔ   mɪʔ   təlaaŋ   ikaan   pà   tàl   tì*
      order   [Hlok   dig   get   bone   fish   take   bury   LOC
      əla   tənɪŋ   dih (6.1.39–40)
      underneath   bed   sleep]
      '…ordered Hlok to dig up the bones and bury them beneath the bed.'

(82) *ñu   sənɪŋ   Po   Tèpita   trun   tɔ̀ŋ n-u,* (6.1.85)
      she   think   [God   down   help   her]
      'She felt that God had come down to help her.'

(83) *ənɪɪʔ   əmɛɛʔ   MəKaam   boh   pyà   Hləʔ   maay   thaaŋ* (6.1.102)
      child   mom   Kam   see   [queen   Hlok   come   house]
      'Kam and her mother saw Queen Hlok come to the house,'

Notice that in these three examples, beyond being embedded in the matrix sentence, nothing special marks these as complements.

Wish- and want-clauses are more distinctly marked: the embedded complement immediately follows the matrix verb, but here the subject of the complement clause is marked by *ka*, labeled 'for' as it occurs elsewhere as a benefactive preposition.

(84) *min   cɔŋ   [ka   pɔ̀h   məkya   nan   lɛʔ   trun   tàlam*
      but   wish   [for   CLF   ebony   DIST   fall   down   into
      liʔi   muuʔ]. (6.1.131)
      basket   grandmother]
      'She wished that the fruit would fall down inside her basket.'

(85) *məyah   uraaŋ   təkrɪ   [ka   kəñi   məñi   syaam   sap]* (6.2.30)
      if   person   want   [for   *kanhi*   call   good   sound]
      'If they want the instrument to sound good,…'

Quotative clauses are usually preceded by the quotative *lay?*, a morpheme obviously related to the verb *lay?* 'say'.

(86)   *muu?*   *doy? kol kəmay tə̀ra   nan   dom*
       grandmother   run   hug   woman   young   DIST   speak
       lay?   'təcɔ   lə̀y,..' (6.1.158–59)
       say   g.child   hey
       'The woman ran, hugged the young girl and said, "Hey grandchild…".'

In (87) the quotative *lay?* 'say' occurs immediately after *dom* 'speak', another verb of saying. This marker occurs with both direct and indirect quotations:

(87)   *ñu pathaw* lay? *prù?   nan   ñu   ŋa?   plɔ̀h   pajə.*   (Blood 1977:55)
       he inform   QUOT   work   DIST   he   do   finish   already
       'He stated that he had completed that work already.'

(88)   *dom   pəlɛ?   MəHlə?   ti   əmɛɛ?*   lay? (6.1.13)
       speak   lie   Hlok   to   mom   QUOT
       '…(she) lied about Hlok to her mother, saying,
       MəHlə?   tɔ̀ɔ?   mə?in   oh   mɪ?   hu   ikaan. (6.1.14)
       Hlok   stay   play   NEG   get   have   fish
       "Hlok is still playing and she didn't get any fish."'

4.3 Adverbial clauses

Multiclausal relationships are usually marked in Cham with iconic juxtaposition. Beyond that, one also finds markers such as 'before', 'arrive', and 'finish' helping to mark the relationship of one clause to another typically combined with the deletion of the coreferential subject, if appropriate. In addition to the highly iconic nature of the clause ordering, another striking aspect is the etymological transparency of many of the clause markers: *tal* 'when; arriving' < 'arrive', *plɔ̀h* 'then; PERFECTIVE' < 'finish', and *tɔ̀ɔ?* 'progressive' < 'live; stay' (cf. sections 3.3.1 and 3.4 above).

(89)   tal   *maay thaaŋ MəKaam pədal MəHlə?*   lay?,…(6.1.7)
       arrive   come   house   Kam   order   Hlok   saying,
       'Coming home, Kam ordered Hlok,…'

(90)   tal   *MəHlə?   maay mɪŋ klà   pəpè* (6.1.30)
       arrive   Hlok   come   from   watch   goat
       'When Hlok came home from watching the goats,…'

Other typical clausal conjunctions include *min* 'but', *mɪjah* (*jah*) 'if, since', *kaal* 'when', *kayua* (*yua*) 'because', and *ŋan* 'or' (cf. David Blood 1977).

Clausal expression of a purpose is also often done simply by juxtaposing two clauses with the purpose reading inferable from the context (91). If a more explicit purpose clause is needed, it is indicated with *pyəh* 'in order to', which appears to be used when the speaker thinks the purpose reading might otherwise not be obvious to the listener as in (92).

(91)   *min   ətày   oh   dii?   cɪŋ   pɛ?   ka   əmɛɛ?   baŋ.* (6.1.108)
       but   y.sibling   NEG   climb   able   pick   for   mom   eat
       'but I can't climb up to pick it for her to chew.'

(92)   *əpìh   pənoy?   ni   pyəh   prày   thaw   lay?* (6.1.190)
       all   word   PRX   in.order.to   give   know   QUOT
       'All these words are to let (you) know that…'

Purpose clauses usually share a subject with the prior clause and thus occur without an explicit subject, but if an overt subject occurs it is marked with the preposition *ka* 'for; BENEFACTIVE', as in (91).

4.4 Serial verb constructions

As already pointed out above related sequential actions are usually rendered by a sequence of clauses with the shared subject deleted in all but the first:

(93) *pɔtaaw tàŋ, dii? yun, naaw thaaŋ.* (Doris Blood 1977:61)
       king   stand climb.into hammock go   home.
       'The king stood up, climbed into his palanquin, and went home.'

Such sequences of clauses (or verb phrases) are completely transparent and do not involve any specific constructional properties other than the omission of the subject expression. However, in some juxtapositions of verb phrases certain conventionalized syntactic patterns have developed with semantics not fully predictable from the sum of the parts. These are often termed serial verb constructions, which differ primarily from other clausal coordination patterns through their conventionalization of a specific through reference to a series of events conceptualized in some way as constituting a single conceptual unit. Essentially one of the verbal elements takes on what is an adpositional character, and, as this characterization suggests, the deverbal adposition can no longer be independently negated or marked for aspect.

As in many other languages in the area, there are in particular two domains in Cham where one finds serial verb constructions: directionals and co-verbs, i.e. markers for peripheral (non-core) arguments.

The directionals are commonly used motion verbs that have occurred so frequently in a semantically secondary role in clausal concatenations that they have come to have the semantic properties more characteristic of prepositions or verbal particles. The two most common co-verbs are the two from the least marked motion verbs *naaw* 'go' > 'motion away from the center of action' and *maay* 'come' > 'motion towards the center of action'.

(94) *MəHlə? pà cərɔ? naaw thaaŋ* (6.1.17)
       Hlok   take charok go   house
       'Hlok took the fish home.'

These directionals can occur with a complement specifying a location:

(95) *aa? pal maay cəkɔɔŋ tha kàh.* (6.1.54)
       crow fly come pick.up one side
       'A crow flew by and snatched one shoe.'

Other directionals include 'get up; rise up' > 'up' and 'go down; descend' > 'down'.

(96) *əmɛɛ? MəKaam chɔ? pà təkò càn kɔ? ŋa? baŋ.* (6.1.29)
       Mom   Kam   scoop take up chop head make eat
       'Kam's mother scooped it up, cut off its head, and made it into food.'

(97) *pɔ̀h məkya truh trun təpa? li?i.* (6.1.133)
       CLF ebony fall down straight basket
       '…the ebony fruit fell down into her basket.'

As with 'go' and 'come' these directionals coexist with homophonous fully verbal forms.

Another frequent serial construction involves the verb *mıʔ* 'get; receive' which may mark a change of state. The literal meaning of *mıʔ* 'get; receive' is seen in (98).

(98) *plɔh   oŋ   mıʔ   tha   plàh   pəpaan   lipih* (6.2.5)
      finish sir get one   CLF   board   thin
      'Then he gets a thin piece of wood,...'

Example (99) involves both the literal meaning and the change of state meaning in that this example literally means something like 'Hlok came to have a lot of fish'.

(99) *MəHləʔ   mıʔ   hu   rilo.* (6.1.5)
      Hlok   get   have many
      'Hlok caught a lot of fish.'

Note that *mıʔ* is only used with stative expressions when a change of state occurs. Thus, in (100), which indicates not a change of state but simply the existence of a state, *mıʔ* does not occur. However, in (101), which records a change of state, *mıʔ* does occur. And, in (102), which indicates a caused change of state using *ŋaʔ* 'make' as the causative marker, *mıʔ* also occurs.

(100) *ñu   (ø)   on   lo   tòlam   tyaan* (6.1.84)
       she (ø)   happy deep inside stomach
       'she was very happy'

(101) *ñu   mıʔ   məpàay-cənıʔ.* (Blood 1978:2.3.3.9)
       they get   hateful
       'they became hateful.'

(102) *muuʔ   mıʔ   ŋaʔ   on   tòlam   tyaan* (6.1.146)
       Grandmother *get* make   happy inside stomach
       'She became happy.'

The verb *tuy* 'follow' may also mean 'according to' and 'with', thus functioning as a co-verb.

(103) *plɔh   ripùh   rawʔ   mətaay   tuy   ənıʔ.* (6.1.189)
       finish fall   sickness die   follow child
       'then (she) fell ill and followed her child in death.'

(104) *plɔh   ñu   oh   khin   pà   təkhɔʔ   tuy   tra   o.* (6.1.56)
       after she   NEG   dare   take shoe   follow again   NEG
       'After that she didn't dare take the other shoe with her anymore.'

Other co-verbs most likely exist, but the line between a verb and a co-verb is often difficult to pinpoint, especially where the metaphor involved is (cross-culturally) transparent and the iconic sequence of events is still retained. Thus, 'take' in (105), for example, could be analysed as expressing 'accompaniment'.

(105) *hray   nan   pətaaw pà   hlaw-pìlaaŋ   naaw   maal* (6.1.57)
       day   DIST   king   take soldier   go   hunt
       'That day the king took his men hunting...'

ACKNOWLEDGMENTS

The examples and a significant part of the analyses come from the work of David and Doris Blood done roughly a quarter of a century ago.

REFERENCES

Adelaar, K.A. (1992) *Proto-Malayic, the reconstruction of its phonology and parts of its lexicon and morphology*, Canberra: Pacific Linguistics.

Aymonier, É.F. (1889) *Grammaire de la langue chame*. Saigon: Imprimerie Coloniale.

——and A. Cabaton (1906) *Dictionnaire cham-français*. PEFEO 7. Paris, Leroux.

Baumgartner, N. (1998) 'A grammar sketch of Western (Cambodian) Cham', Papers in Southeast Asian Linguistics No. 15: Further Chamic Studies. Edited by D. Thomas. Pacific Linguistics, 1–20.

Blood, David L. (1967) 'Phonological units in Cham', *Anthropological Linguistics* 9.8, 15–32.

——(1977) 'A three-dimensional analysis of Cham sentences', Papers in South East Asian Linguistics No 4: Chamic Studies. Edited by D. Thomas, E.W. Lee, and Nguyen Dang Liem. Pacific Linguistics, 53–76.

Blood, Doris W. (1962) 'Reflexes of Proto-Malayo-Polynesian in Cham', *Anthropological Linguistics* 4.9, 11–20.

——(1977) 'Clause and sentence final particles in Cham,' Papers in South East Asian Linguistics No. 4: Chamic Studies. Edited by David Thomas, Ernest W. Lee and Nguyen Dang Liem. Pacific Linguistics Series A, No. 48:39–51.

——(1978) 'Some aspects of Cham discourse structure', *Anthropological Linguistics* 20.3, 110–132.

Bui Khanh The (1995) *Tu Dien Cham-Viet*. Nha Xuat Ban Khoa Hoc Xa hoi.

Çoedès, Georges (1939) 'La plus ancienne inscription en langue cham', *New Indian Antiquary* (Bombay) 48 (New Series 1):39–52.

Crawfurd, J. (1822 [1967]) *Journal of an embassy to the courts of Siam and Cochin China* [reprinted]; with an introduction by D.K. Wyatt. Kuala Lumpur, London, New York: Oxford University Press.

Han, Phu Van, Edmondson, J. and Gregerson K. (1992) 'Eastern Cham as a tone language'. *Mon-Khmer Studies* 20, 31–43.

Lafont, P.-B., Po Dharma and Nara Vija (1977) *Catalogue des manuscrits čam des bibliothèques françaises*. (Publications de l'Ecôle Française d'Extrême-Orient 114). Ecôle Française d'Extrême-Orient. Hanoi/Paris.

Marrison, G.E. (1975) 'The early Cham language and its relationship to Malay'. *Journal of the Malaysian branch of the Royal Asiatic Society* 48.2, 52–59.

Moussay, Fr. G. (1971) *Dictionnaire Cam-Vietnamien-Français*. Phan Rang: Centre Culturel Cam.

Niemann, G.K. (1891) 'Bijdrage tot de Kennis der Verhouding van het Tjam tot de Talen van Indonesië.' *Bijdragen tot de Taal-, Land- en Volkenkunde van Nederlandsch-Indië* 40, 27–44.

Ross, M. (1995) 'Reconstructing Proto-Austronesian verbal morphology: the evidence from Taiwan', in P. Li, C. Tsang, Y. Huang, D. Ho and C. Tseng (eds) *Austronesian Studies Relating to Taiwan*, Symposium Series of the Institute of History and Philology No. 3: 727–791, Taipei: Academia Sinica.

Schmidt, Pater W. (1906) 'Die Mon-Khmer-Völker, ein Bindeglied zwischen Völkern Zentralasiens und Austronesiens', *Archiv Anthropologie* n.s. 5:59–109.

Sebeok, T.A. (1942) 'An examination of the Austroasiatic language family', *Language* 18:206–17.

Thurgood, G. (1996) 'Language contact and the directionality of internal 'drift': the development of tones and registers in Chamic', *Language* 71.1:1–31.

——(1999) *From Ancient Cham to Modern Dialects: Two Thousand Years of Language Contact and Change*. Oceanic Linguistics Special Publication No. 28. Honolulu: University of Hawai'i Press.

CHAPTER EIGHTEEN

MOKEN AND MOKLEN

Michael D. Larish

1 INTRODUCTION

1.1 Language area and speakers

The Moken and Moklen are two closely related – yet culturally and linguistically distinct – groups of Austronesian people, who live along the rivers, beaches, and islands on the West Coast of the Thai-Malay Peninsula. The Moklen (Mkl) people live exclusively in peninsular Thailand, while their close relatives, the Moken (Mkn) live predominantly throughout the Mergui Archipelago in Burma, renamed Myanmar in 1989. Although both the Moken and Moklen are traditionally hunter-gatherers, the Moken, who are sea nomads, depend more on foraging than the Moklen. Most Moklen men have jobs (in road clearing, tin mining, and the rubber industry). Consequently, the Moklen only gather sea and forest products to supplement their diets. In addition, some Moklen have become agriculturalists.

The Moken-Moklen (Mkn-Mkl) speaking area extends 650 kilometers from Tavoy Island, Burma to Phi Phi Island, Thailand. In Thailand, the Mkn-Mkl speakers live in a northern, exclusively Moken-speaking region off Ranɔːŋ, a central exclusively Moklen-speaking region in Pʰaŋ-ŋaː Province (where the majority of the land-based Moklen speakers live), and a southern mixed Moken and Urak Lawoi'-speaking area at the southern end of Pʰuket Island. (Urak Lawoi' is a Malayic language.)

Burmese varieties of Moken include Jait, Lebi, and Niawi and Dung Moken, of which only the latter has been adequately described (Naw Say Bay 1995). While several of these Burmese varieties of Moken may also be encountered on the islands off Ranɔːŋ in Thai waters, the two major variants of Moken spoken in Thailand are Kɔ̂ʔ Surin Moken and Rawai Moken. These two varieties are often also referred to as Northern and Southern Jadiak, respectively.

There are eight Moklen villages in the northern part of the Moklen area; they range from Kɔ̂ʔ Pʰráʔ Tʰɔːŋ, where a high degree of Mkn-Mkl interaction is found (Court 1971), to Baːŋ Sak (77 km from the northernmost tip of Phuket Island). The northern Moklen area is approximately 40 km from the main concentration of Jadiak Moken speakers in Thailand. The central Moklen area, with nine villages, ranges from Paːk Wiːp (km 71) to Hɪn Laːt (km 31–32). The three Moklen villages in the southern Moklen area cluster around the northernmost tip of Phuket Island.

The Moken-Moklen varieties described in this sketch are spoken in Thailand. The Moklen examples were obtained in the central Moklen area mainly from Baːn Dɔːn Can, a village in Pʰaŋ-ŋaː Province. Most Moken examples come from Surin Island (Kɔʔ Surin), which is located just below the southernmost tip of Burma in Thai waters. In some cases, contrastive details are provided from Burmese Dung Moken and other Moken or Moklen varieties. Most of the data in this chapter come from Larish (1999).

Moken and Moklen are *endangered* Austronesian languages. Although the Moken people are maintaining their ethnolinguistic health better than the Moklen, it is questionable whether either group has sufficient speakers (approximately 2500–3000 per group) to sustain ethnolinguistic vitality. If the Moken can maintain their sea nomad lifestyle, they may be able to retain their language and culture. As for the land-based Moklen, it is quite likely that they will be unable to maintain their language and culture due to Thai influence. Convergence towards Thai has already occurred in Moklen at the phonological, morphological, and syntactic levels. In addition, there is some indication that young Moklen speakers are undergoing an interethnic shift and are becoming Thai (see Larish 1993).

The numerous linguistic differences between the Moken and Moklen varieties make it necessary to regard them as separate languages (Larish 1993:1307). They have in fact differentiated to the point where it becomes easier for their respective speakers to employ a third language, such as Thai, in face-to-face interactions rather than attempting the use of the sister language.

1.2 Major sources

Four unpublished master's theses, all written in English at Mahidol University, contain useful sources of Moken and Moklen data and description. Chantanakomes (1980) describes Rawai Moken, spoken on Phuket Island, whereas Swastham (1982) presents a sketch of Lampi: Moklen. Makboon (1981) includes Swadesh 200-word lists collected in three Moken and three Moklen villages. Leerabhandh (1984) is a comparative study of Moklenic – a broad term that includes all Moken and Moklen isolects. These studies were extensively used in Larish's PhD thesis (Larish 1999), which includes reconstructions of Proto-Moken-Moklen phonology and lexicon in addition to synchronic descriptions. It also presents a subgrouping hypothesis in which Proto-Moken-Moklen is closely related to Malayo-Chamic. Proto-Moken-Moklen–Aceh-Chamic-Malayic consists of two branches, Moklenic and Aceh-Chamic-Malayic. For further discussion, see ADELAAR, A HISTORICAL PERSPECTIVE.

Anthropological descriptions of the Moken are Ivanoff (1988; in French) and Hinshiranan (1996). Both studies concentrate on the Moken at Surin Island. Only a small number of articles in English have appeared that compare *both* Moken and Moklen. Court (1971) was the first to document the Moken-Moklen interaction on Pʰráʔ Tʰɔːŋ Island. Larish (1991) examines lexical affinities between Moklenic and Mon-Khmer languages. Hogan (1972) and Larish (1993) are ethnolinguistic introductions to the Moken, Moklen, and the Urak Lawoi'. Bishop and Peterson (1987) undertake mutual intelligibility testing and attitudinal research, and they also consider how much Thai is used among the Moklen. Larish (1997) typologically classifies Moken-Moklen, Acehnese (spoken on North Sumatra), and Chamic (Vietnam) as mainland-type Austronesian languages on account of their word-final stress. For further discussion, see THURGOOD, PHAN RANG CHAM.

Lewis (1960) compiled a 53-page Moken–English wordlist with 1430 entries from early Burmese Moken texts collected mainly by American or British missionaries and travelers during the British colonial period in Burma. The oldest text, *A Primer of the Selong Language* (first published in 1846), was transliterated by Lewis from the Pwo Karen script developed by American missionaries working in the Mergui Archipelago. Other texts were taken from Anderson (1890), Carrapiett (1909), White (1913, 1922), and Bernatzik (1938/58). The wordlist and accompanying texts found in Lewis (1960) are significant in that they represent the only published Burmese Moken texts. In addition, Lewis (1960) provides brief sketches of Burmese Moken phonology and morphosyntax.

2 MOKEN AND MOKLEN PHONOLOGY

Moken and Moklen have most phonological features in common: word structure, syllable structure, heavy ultimate stress, nasalization, contrastive vowel quantity, and nearly all consonant phonemes. Despite these similarities, Moken and Moklen sound considerably different – to the point that they have become mutually unintelligible.

2.1 Syllable structure and stress

Disyllabic word shape is common in Mkn-Mkl vocabulary, especially in isolated citation forms; however, disyllabic words are frequently reduced to monosyllabic ones through the optional deletion of unaccented initial syllables in actual connected speech. Many monosyllabic words also occur as the result of diachronic phonological reduction similar to that described by Lee (1974) for Chamic. Disyllabic structure is (CV).(C)CV(C); monosyllabic structure is (C)CV(C). Mkn-Mkl reduce loans with CVC.CVC structure to CV.CV(C) shape. For example, Thai *naŋsuː* 'book' has become Mkl *lacʰuː* and Surin Mkn *lasiː*. This example shows that initial syllables in Moklenic languages always have to be open.

Southeast Asian linguists customarily describe word and syllable structure by using the following terminology and conventions. To facilitate reference, each position within the phonological word is given a unique designation, namely $(C_pV_p).C_mV_m(C_f)$. Subscript p and m are used to distinguish the consonants (C) and vowels (V) of initial and final syllables, respectively. Subscript p stands for *p*resyllable or *p*retonic; subscript m marks *m*ajor or *m*ain syllable positions, and subscript f stands for *f*inal consonant (see Naw Say Bay 1995:201).

In Moken and Moklen words, primary stress *invariably* occurs on the last syllable. The stress that speakers of Moken and Moklen place on last two-mora syllables is generally heavier than English stress. Therefore, to give a native English speaker an impression of what mainland-Austronesian stress sounds like, let us examine the following atypical English utterance. When the English word *machine* [məʔ²¹.ˈʃiːn⁴⁵³] is emphasized as in 'I said *machine* – not *marine*', it closely approximates a typical Moklen sound pattern, for example [muɯ·²¹.ˈcʰiːn⁴⁵³] 'to comb'. (Superscript numbers represent pitch levels from low (¹) to high (⁵)). When disyllabic foreign names with penultimate stress such as *Michael* and *Eddie* are introduced into Moklen, the stress is invariably placed on the last syllable, as in [may²¹.ˈkɯːn⁴⁵³] 'Michael' and [ʔɛ·³³ˈdiː³⁴³] 'Eddie'.

The vowel of the initial syllable may be reduced to schwa or receive secondary stress. This difference is sometimes terminologically marked by using *presyllable* for the former and *minor syllable* for the latter type of initial syllable. The distinction between presyllable and minor syllables is probably dependent on speaking rate. Initial syllables normally have secondary stress in slower citation forms but are reduced to presyllables in faster speech.

2.2 Consonant phonemes

Tables 18.1 and 18.2 demonstrate that there are two major phonemic differences between Moklen and Surin Moken. Surin Moken retains two phonemes that Moklen lacks: /s/ and

TABLE 18.1: THE SYLLABLE-INITIAL (C_P AND C_M) PHONEME INVENTORY OF MOKLEN

	Phonemes				
Stops:					
Vl. Unasp.	p	t	c	k	?
Vl. Asp.	p^h	t^h	c^h	k^h	
Vd. Unasp.	b	d		g	
Spirants					h
Sonorants:					
Nasals	m	n	ɲ	ŋ	
Liquids		l			
Glides	w		y		

TABLE 18.2: THE SYLLABLE-INITIAL (C_P AND C_M) PHONEME INVENTORY OF Kɔʔ SURIN MOKEN

Stops:					
Vl. Unasp.	p	t	c	k	?
Vl. Asp.	p^h	t^h	c^h	k^h	
Vd. Unasp.	b	d [~r]	j	g	
Spirants		s			h
Sonorants:					
Nasals	m	n	ɲ	ŋ	
Liquids		l			
Glides	w		y		

/j/. Moklen lacks /s/ at the phonemic level but [c^h] and [s] are in free variation in Moklen. Since the Moklen people generally use [c^h] in slower, more careful speech and in citation forms, and [s] in colloquial speech, /c^h/ is chosen to represent this allophonic pair on the phonemic level.

Another salient difference between Moklen and all Moken varieties is that Moklen lacks the voiced palatal affricate /j/. Moken /j/ regularly corresponds to Moklen /y/ (palatal glide). Beyond these two main differences, both onset positions (C_p and C_m) in Moken and Moklen have essentially the same inventory of contrasts which are greater than the ones found in offsets (on which see below).

Table 18.1 (Moklen) and Table 18.2 (Kɔʔ Surin Moken) provide an overview of consonant inventories typical for Moklen and Moken.

In C_p position, free variation occurs between segments which are clearly distinctive in other positions. Compare, for example, Moken *gaci:* 'sea cucumber' with Moklen *gaci:, daci:,* and *laci:* 'sea cucumber'; Mkn *gutəy* 'lice' with Mkl *gutəy, dutəy,* and *lutəy* 'lice'; Mkn *midu:n* 'to sleep' with Mkl *nidu:n, didu:n, lidu:n,* and *ʔidu:n* 'to sleep'; and Mkn *gatɔ:n* 'spider' with Mkl *gatɔ:n, datɔ:n* 'spider'. These alternations occur only in C_p position, never in C_m or C_f position, and they appear to be more widespread in Moklen than in Moken.

Some of this variation appears to be sociolinguistically conditioned by the age of the speaker. Age correlates with education. While few Moklen speakers over the age of forty have received any formal education, those under thirty-five usually have three to six years of primary education. Since younger Moklen people use Thai more and Moklen less than their elders, we might predict that a high degree of Thai competency may

TABLE 18.3: MOKLEN CONSONANT CLUSTERS

Moken	*pəla:ŋ*	'sunlight'	Moken	*kəlaŋ*	'hard, strong'
Moklen	*pla:ŋ*	'sunlight'	Moklen	*klaŋ*	'hard, firm'
Moken	*kəla:n*	'bone'	Moken	*kəlu:n*	'egg'
Moklen	*kla:n*	'bone'	Moklen	*klu:n*	'egg'

influence the Moklen utterances of the younger generation. The Thai sound system does not have the phoneme /g/, but the Moklen sound system does. Therefore, we might expect younger Moklen speakers – those who use Thai more, and consequently have adapted more to Thai phonological norms – to use /g/ less in comparison of members of the elder generation. This hypothesis is supported by fieldwork data. When the data elicited from a 95-year-old Mkl man is compared to that of a 29-year-old Mkl man, we see a fairly regular variation between *g-* from the elder consultant and *d-* from the younger one (in 'bracelet', 'sea cucumber', 'lice', and 'spider').

Moken speakers in Thailand share some features with Moklen speakers that they do not share with Burmese Moken speakers. All Moken-Moklen varieties spoken in Thailand, including Surin Moken and Rawai Moken, lack /r/, while this phoneme is retained in Dung Moken (spoken in Burma). Moken dialects have at least several *r*-type allophones that alternate with [d] between vowels in C_m position. Like Surin Moken and Rawai Moken, Moklen has only /l/. The lack of /r/ and /j/ in Moklen, and the lack of /r/ in Moken varieties in Thailand, may be attributed to phonological convergence towards Thai, which also lacks /r/ and /j/ (Haas 1964:xi).

Consonant clusters result from the reduction of unstressed presyllables, giving rise to the merger of two syllables into one, particularly in Moklen. Concisely, $C_əCV(C)$ becomes CCV(C). The examples in Table 18.3 illustrate this process:

Additional examples of Moklen consonant clusters include: *(tʰə)kʰlup* 'all', *tuklɛt* 'to close (eyes)', *kapʰlɔk* 'coconut shell', *pla:k* 'clump (of bamboo)', *ticum-tuklu:* 'dove', *ʔipʰlɪk* 'dragonfly', *tʰupʰlat* 'to fall', *klak* 'husband', and *klɔ:n* 'to be hungry'.

All known Moken and Moklen isolects have an identical syllable-final consonant inventory: /p t k ʔ h m n ŋ w y/. That is, Mkn-Mkl share the following coda constraint: palatals (excluding the semivowel), aspirated stops, voiced stops, and the lateral approximant /l/ do not occur as syllable-final consonants. In this regard Moklenic languages have clearly converged toward Thai rather than Mon-Khmer languages. The Mkn-Mkl set of ten contrastive C_f consonants is indistinguishable from the Thai system with the exception of *-h*, which Thai lacks.

2.3 Vowel phonemes

A comparison between Moklen major syllable vowels in Table 18.4 and Dung Moken major syllable vowels in Table 18.5 reveals markedly diverse systems. The most salient difference between Tables 18.4 and 18.5 is that Moklen does not have the tense/lax distinction that is found in Moken. Although Moklen also has a fair number of diphthongs, these cannot be described as phonetic realizations of long tense vowels as in the case of Moken.

As in Tables 18.4 and 18.5, all reported isolects of Moken and Moklen have a vowel-quantity contrast. However, this vowel-length contrast occurs only in closed major syllables (Hogan 1983:15, Naw Say Bay 1995:196, Larish 1997:128). Open major syllables are always two-mora syllables, containing either long vowels or diphthongs.

TABLE 18.4: THE VOWEL PHONEME INVENTORY OF MOKLEN, MAJOR SYLLABLES (slightly revised from Swastham 1982:29)

	Front	Central	Back
HIGH	i iː	ɯ ɯː	u uː
MID	e eː	ə əː	o oː
LOW	ɛ ɛː	a aː	ɔ ɔː
	DIPHTHONGS		
	ia	ɯə	uy
	ɛo	əy	uə
	ay		aw

TABLE 18.5: THE VOWEL PHONEME INVENTORY OF DUNG MOKEN, MAJOR SYLLABLES (adapted from Hogan 1983:14, Naw Say Bay 1995:201). The ν-shaped diacritic above a vowel indicates tenseness

	Front	Central	Back	
HIGH	ĭ ĭː [əi]		ŭ ŭː [əu]	Tense
	i iː		u uː	Lax
MID	ĕː [əe]		ŏ ŏː [əo]	Tense
	e eː	ə	o oː	Lax
LOW	ĕː [ae]	ă: [ɛa]	ɔ̆: [ɔa]	Tense
	ɛ ɛː	a aː	ɔ ɔː	Lax
		DIPHTHONGS		
	ea		oa	

With the exception of a small number of cases, nasalization is predictable in Moken and Moklen (Chantanakomes 1980:27–33, Swastham 1982:53). Vowels are regularly nasalized when they follow the nasal consonants *m, n, ɲ*, and *ŋ*. Therefore, nasalization is only marked on vowels in exceptional cases, where no conditioning nasal consonant is evident (e.g. Mkl *hãh* 'not' and Mkl *hɛ̃ʔ* 'at', where presumably *h-* < * *ŋ*).

In minor syllables, with secondary stress, Moklen has eight contrasting vowel qualities: /i e ɛ ɯ a u o ɔ/. Moken, on the other hand, has only six vowel phonemes in minor syllables: /i ɛ a u o ɔ/ (Naw Say Bay 1995:201). Vowel quantity is not phonemically contrastive in minor syllables. There are two degrees of vowel length in the V_p position, i.e. short [V] and half-long [V·]. These phonetic differences are predictable in that they depend on the vowel length of the major-syllable vowel. A compensatory influence operates between minor and main syllables within a word. The vowel in the initial syllable is half-long when the major-syllable vowel is short (that is, CV·CVC); it is short when the major-syllable vowel is long (that is, CVCV:(C)).

Bradley (1977:1) impressionistically describes tonal contrasts with 'a low-to-high numbering system where [1] represents the lowest pitch and [5] the highest.' Using Bradley's system, the following phonetic pitch levels or contours can be distinguished:

(1) High-level	[44]		(6) Mid-falling	[343]		
(2) High-falling	[453]		(7) Low-level	[22]		
(3) High-sharp-rising	[45]		(8) Low-falling	[232]	(major syllables)	
(4) Mid-rising	[35]		(9) Low-falling	[21]	(minor syllables)	
(5) Mid-level	[33]		(10) Low-rising	[24]		

TABLE 18.6: MOKLEN REDUPLICATION

Non-reduplicated form		Reduplicated form	
amɔn	'good'	ʔamɔn-ʔamɔːn	'very good'
calɔːŋ	'beautiful'	calɔːŋ-calɔːŋ	'very beautiful'
ʔiət	'small'	ʔiət-ʔiːət	'very small'
suwaŋ	'morning'	suwaŋ-suwaːŋ	'early morning'

Eighty to 90 percent of Moklen tones can be predicted by looking at syllable type and consonant voicing (for details see Larish 1997:139). Since the majority of Moklen tones are predictable, they are not marked in this sketch. The remaining 10 to 20 percent of Moklen tones that are not predictable deserve further investigation. Larish (1997: 140–141) provides eighteen tonal minimal pairs which support the hypothesis that Moklen is in the process of developing a Southern Thai-type tonal system.

2.4 Reduplication

There is only one type of reduplication attested in present-day Moklen, i.e. full-stem reduplication. This is generally used for intensification, as shown by the examples in Table 18.6.

Although reduplication most commonly occurs with stative verbs, other word classes can undergo this process as well, as illustrated by *suwaŋ-suwaːŋ* 'early morning'.

3 BASIC MORPHOSYNTAX

As in phonology, Moken and Moklen converge morphosyntactically toward mainland Southeast Asian typological norms. They show fairly rigid SVO word order, with corre-lating head-modifier order and prepositions. Their basic morphosyntactic make-up may be linked phonologically to rising (final) phrase accent which, in turn, may be associated with word-final stress, as suggested by Donegan and Stampe (1983:338). Nevertheless, Moken-Moklen syntax differs in various ways from Thai syntax. Differences are most salient in the ordering of clitic pronouns (cf. section 3.1) and negators (section 3.2).

Moklen syntax is normally congruent with Moken syntax. That is, Moklen construc-tions can typically be translated word-for-word into Moken ones, as illustrated in (1–3):

(1a) *mɔklɛːn   kaməy   nahɔːŋ   kafɛː*   (Moklen)
(1b) *mɔkaɛn   kamɔy   nahɔːŋ   kupiː*   (Moken)
      Mok(l)en 1pe   call   coffee
      'We call (it) coffee.'

(2a) *ticaw   klaːw   laːy*   (Moklen)
(2b) *cicaw   makaːw   ʔaloh*   (Moken)
      tomorrow   speak   anew
      'Tomorrow (we will) speak again.'

(3a) *ʔekaːn   ʔɛːm   taʔaw*   (Moklen)
(3b) *ʔekaːn   məʔɛːm   taʔaw*   (Moken)
      fish   dwell   sea
      'Fish dwell (in the) sea.'

3.1 Basic clause structure

With regard to basic clause structure in Moklen, we may distinguish between verbal and verbless constructions. Sentence (4) illustrates a Moklen sentence with a nominal predicate. The compound *kaba:ŋ-laya:n* 'sail boat' is the main predicate, which is preceded by a noun phrase (*kaba:ŋ pʰalaŋ* 'boat (of) foreigner') in subject position.

(4) *kaba:ŋ   pʰalaŋ   kaba:ŋ-laya:n   ka:*
     boat   foreigner   boat-sail   Q
     '(Are the) boats (of) foreigners sailboats?'

Nominal predicates are common in Moken and Moklen in several types of constructions, especially in equational sentences (Chantanakomes 1980:99, Swasthan 1982: 77–78) and classifier constructions (see 3.4.2). In equational sentences, the Thai loan *pm* 'to be' (from Thai *pɛn* 'to be') frequently functions as a copula, as in (5):

(5) *cəy   pm   mɔklɛ:n*
     1s   COP   Moklen
     'I (am) Moklen.'

However, this copula is not necessarily present:

(6) *cəy   mɔklɛ:n*
     1s   Moklen
     'I (am) Moklen.'

In verbal clauses, the subject NP (if overtly expressed) also immediately precedes the predicate phrase. Non-subject complements and adjuncts usually follow the predicate:

(7) *bulaw   maykɯ:n   lubut   tʰuk   ʔaləy*
     wife   Michael   run   every day
     'Michael's wife runs every day.'

(8) *cəy   muɲa:m   ta:ŋ   ʔɔla:ŋ*
     1s   borrow   money   3p
     'I borrow their money.'

(9) *cəy   munɛ:m   ʔana:t   ʔuʔu:y*
     1s   raise   child   sibling
     'I (am) rais(ing) my younger sister's child.'

(10) *ʔɛnɔŋ   bɔh   sɔba:y   ʔɛka:n*
      mother   make   curry   fish
      'Mother (is) making fish curry.'

(11) *cəy   nɛpɔŋ   kuʔe:ow   kʰu:ₗ   pɛ:t-tu: ʔɔn   patak*
      1s   chop   tree   with   machete   make   fall
      'I chop (the) tree with (a) machete (to) make (it) fall (down).'

Verbal clauses include those formed with stative verbs which have essentially the same distribution as dynamic verbs. Stative verbs convey notions which are often rendered by adjectives in other languages.

(12) *dayo:ŋ   (du)wa:ʔ   hat   latah   pa:t   hat*
      high   two   cubit   (be) long four   cubit
      '[A motorcycle] is two cubits high, (and) four cubits long.'

(13) *cʰiŋɔʔ*   *lahan*   *kɯutəy*
      rubber tree   many   very
      '(The) rubber trees (are) very many.'

In addition to their position, subjects are also identified by the fact that clitic pronouns
co-referential with the subject NP optionally occur to the right of the verb.

(14) *manɔk-kanay*   *nɛɲəy*   *ɲaː*   *suwaːŋ-suwaːŋ*
      chicken-male   crow   3   early.morning
      'Roosters, they crow (in the) early morning (around 5 A.M.).'

(15) *ʔəy*   *nɛlɛːt*   *ɲaː*   *tʰuŋ*   *batik*
      dog   lick   3   bag   plastic
      'The dog is licking the plastic bag.'

Clitic pronouns also occur when no overt subject NP is present:

(16) *kaw*   *laːŋ*   *mɛt*   *kaʔ*
      go   3p   all   already
      'They all went already.'

(17) *bɔh*   *laːŋ*   *namaʔ*   *tʰaːw-tʰuat*
      make   3p   flag   grandparents.great-grandparents
      'They [Moklen people] make the ancestor flag.'

(18) *klaːw*   *cəy*   *ʔadaʔ*
      speak   1s   big
      'I complain loudly.'

(19) *dɪn*   *bəy*   *tʰaŋ*   *tam*   *may*
      come   2s   from   where   Q
      'Where did you come from?'

Clitic pronouns are commonly found in Thai as well, but the order of Moken-Moklen
and Thai clitic pronouns differs. While such pronouns follow the verb in Moklen, they
precede the verb in Thai, as shown in sentences (20) and (21):

(20) *manuy*   *dɪn*   *ɲaː*   *mutɔk*   *canaːt*   *maɲay*   *sɯutap*
      bee   come   3   sting   child   cry   loudly
      '(A) bee came (and) stung (the) child (who was) cry(ing) loudly.' (Moklen)

(21) *pʰuŋ*   *man*   *maː*   *cʰːy*   *dɛk*   *lɔːŋ*   *katʰuan*
      bee   3s   come   sting   child   cry   loudly
      '(A) bee came (and) stung (the) child (who was) cry(ing) loudly.' (Thai)

Moklen *hɛ̃ʔ* 'at', *tʰaŋ* 'from', *buːk* 'under', and *(da)lam* 'in' are the most frequently
used locative prepositions. Sentences (22–24) illustrate their use:

(22) *kaw*   *bɯuləy*   *ʔɛkaːn*   *hɛ̃ʔ*   *tulaːt*
      go   buy   fish   at   market
      '(I am) go(ing to) buy fish at (the) market.'

(23) *pɔlɔːk*   *ʔɛːm*   *(da)lam*   *tɯumɔk*
      termite   live   in   hill
      'Termite(s) live in (a) termite hill.'

(24) buːk   (ʔɔ)maːk   cut   kɯupʰut   nuɯŋɛːn   nalaːŋ
      under   house   light husk   chase   mosquito
      'Under the house, light (a) coconut husk to drive off the mosquitoes.'

Moken and Moklen sentences can be augmented by sentence-final particles (PTCL), which alter the function of a sentence. Thus, for example, imperatives are frequently marked by a sentence-final particle. Note that the addressee in example (25) is not overtly expressed.

(25) yɪp   paːkkaː   baːʔ   ʔɔn   cǝy   dǝy
      pass   pen   carry   give   1s   PTCL
      'Pass the pen to me.'

Wh-words normally co-occur with the interrogative sentence particle *lay* or one of its allomorphs (*may*, *ŋay*, *way*); the initial consonant of *lay* assimilates to preceding *Wh*-words, as is illustrated in (26) and (27):

(26) bǝy   kaw   tam   may
      2s   go   where   Q
      'Where (are) you go(ing)?'

(27) ŋɔːʔ   ʔanɔŋ   ŋay
      look   what   Q
      'What (are you) look(ing at)?'

As in Thai and Japanese, emphatic sentence particles in Moken and Moklen communicate a speaker's perspective, attitude, or emotion in a sentence. Emphatic sentence particles such as *dey* and *ʔiː* are difficult to translate because English does not have this syntactic class. Italics are used in the translations that follow to convey the nuance of the meaning of these particles.

(28) dan   hãh   dǝy
      know   NEG   PTCL
      '(I) *really* (do) not know, *you see*.'

(29) ʔɔlaːn   ɲuː   nɔkɔt   manut   matay   kaʔ   ʔiː
      snake   MED   bite   people   die   already   PTCL
      '(If) that snake bites people, (they will) *certainly* die!'

In addition to the sentence-final particles, there are a number of postverbal particles. Some of these mark aspect, as for example the completive aspect marker *kaʔ* illustrated in the preceding example and in (30). The question in (30) is the most common greeting among the Moklen.

(30) ɲam-cɔːn   kaʔ   kaː
      eat-rice   already   Q
      '(Have you) eat(en) already?'

Another postverbal particle is the reciprocal (RCP) marker *(ʔa)bɔːʔ* which is used in a variety of joint actions, as illustrated in the following two examples. Example (32) also shows that the postverbal particles follow the clitic subject pronouns if there are any.

(31) tɔlɔŋ   (ʔa)bɔːʔ   kaw   pɔk   kabaːŋ
      help   RCP   go   build   boat
      'Help each other build a boat.'

(32) bɔh   tʰaːw-tʰuat   tulǝy   buŋay   duyaː?   ?ɔlaːŋ   ?abɔː?
      do   grandparents great-grand-parents   three   night   dance   3p   RCP
      '(When) the ancestor worship ceremony is performed, people dance together
      (for) three nights.'

3.2 Negation

In Moklen (33 and 35) the negative marker always occurs in postverbal position, unless
it appears independently as an answer to a question. However, in Thai (34 and 36), it
precedes the verb. Compare the Moklen and Thai sentences below:

(33) bɔh   hãh   kaːn   lǝy   nǝy   cʰubaːy   hãh   (Moklen)
      do   NEG   work   day   PRX   well   NEG
      'I am not working today, (for) I do not feel well.'

(34) mây   tʰam   ŋaːn   wan   nîː   mây   sabaːy   (Thai)
      NEG   do   work   day   PRX   NEG   well
      'I am not working today, (for) I do not feel well.'

(35) klaːw   dan   luaŋ   hãh   (Moklen)
      speak   know   story NEG
      'I do not know what is being said.' (lit. (they) speak, (but I do) not know (the)
      story)

(36) pʰûːt   mây   rúː   ruâŋ   (Thai)
      speak   NEG   know   story
      'I do not know what is being said.'

An example illustrating the occurrence of hãh with a sentence-final particle is
presented in (37).

(37) ?a=liː?   naː?   balɛh   hãh   kaː
      PN=liː?   still   return   NEG   Q
      'Aliː? still (has) not return(ed) home?'

The main negator hãh may be accompanied by the emphatic negator la? which always
occurs in preverbal position:

(38) cǝy   la?   kuutɛːn   hãh
      1s   EMPH.NEG   lie   NEG
      'I (am) not lying.'

In prohibitive utterances, lay is used in place of hãh.

(39) pɪt   mataː?   bǝy   pǝːt   lay$_1$
      close   eyes   2s   open   NEG.IMP
      'Close your eyes and do not open them.'

(40) ?anaːt   bǝy   ?ɛn   lay$_1$
      child   2s   play   NEG.IMP
      'Your children shouldn't play (here).'

This prohibitive lay$_1$ is homophonous with the sentence-final particle lay$_2$ which is the
underlying form of the interrogative sentence-final particle in (26) and (27). As (41)

illustrates, however, *lay*$_2$ does not assimilate with non-*Wh* words:

(41) *(ʔa)caw   kaw   buləy   kʰunum   lay*$_2$
     who   go   buy   sweets   Q
     'Who went to buy sweets?'

3.3 Pronouns and deictics

Table 18.7 lists the pronoun forms for various Moken and Moklen varieties.

   Moklen has a four-way distinction in deictics, as do many Southeast Asian languages (cf. Harmon 1977:119), whereas Moken only has a three-way distinction (Chantanakomes 1980:194). Table 18.8 lists the forms.

   These deictics are most widely used as adnominal modifiers (42), but they may also function as adverbs (43; see also (55)):

(42) *ləy   nəy   kaw   tʰiaw   balɛh   ʔɔma:k*
     day   PRX   go   wander   return   house
     'Today (= this day) I am going (to have) fun (then) return home.'

(43) *cana:t   nulɔ:n   ɲa: ɲu:*
     child   (be) naked   3   MED
     'The child (is) naked there (near you) [consultant pointing].'

3.4 Noun-phrase structure

Noun phrases in Moklen in general consist of a head noun followed by one or more dependent attributes. We will briefly discuss the three most common

TABLE 18.7: MOKEN-MOKLEN PERSONAL PRONOUNS

Person/ number	Dung Moken	Surin Moken	Rawai Moken	Northern Moklen	Central Moklen
1s	*cwe*	*cɔy*		*ci:*	*cəy*
2s	*bĕ:ŋ*	*(bi)ʔĕ:ŋ*	*kaɲĕ:*	*bi:*	*bəy*
2s (girl)	*mĕ:*	*mĕ:*	*mĕ:*	—	—
2s (boy)	*bɔ*	*bɔ*	*bo*	—	—
1pi	*ʔɛta:ʔ*	*ʔɛta:ʔ*	*ʔɛtaʔ*	*ʔɛta:ʔ*	*ʔɛta:ʔ*
1pe	*kamɔy*	*kamɔy*	*kamoy*	*kaməy*	*kaməy*
2p	*kaɲĕ:*	*kaɲĕ:*	*kaɲĕ:*	*ɲaw*	*ɲaw*
3s/3p	*ɲa:*	*ɲa:*	*ɲa:*	*ɲa:* *pɔ:ʔ*	*ɲa:* *pɔ:ʔ*
3p	—	*(ʔɔ)la:ŋ*	—	*(ʔɔ)la:ŋ*	*(ʔɔ)la:ŋ*

TABLE 18.8: MOKEN AND MOKLEN LOCATIVE DETERMINERS

Mkn-Rw	Moklen	Gloss
ni:	*nəy*	PRX (near the speaker)
ɲu:	*ɲu:*	MED (near the addressee)
to:/tup	*dĕ:ʔ*	DIST (far from speaker/addressee)
	top	DIST (out of sight)

constructions: possessive constructions (3.4.1), nominal classifier constructions (3.4.2), and relative clauses (3.4.3).

Before turning to these constructions, we may note that there are also two kinds of proclictics which occur with nouns. First, personal names are often accompanied by a proclitic name marker, as in $A = k^hwak$ 'PN = k^{h}wak' and $I = li:a$ 'PN = li:a'. The male name marker [ʔa·] and the female name marker [ʔi·] are obligatory before Moken and Moklen names unless a kinship or respect term is used (as in $T^ha:w$ Nam 'Grandfather Nam', $wa?$ $sɔ:y$ 'Aunt Sɔːy', $?eba:p$ $Samp^han$ 'Respected Ancestor Samp^{h}an').

Second, a reduced form of the numeral 'one', the full form being Mkl $c^ha:?$, also occurs as a proclitic. Similar to the English indefinite article, whenever Mkl $c^ha:?$ 'one' is criticized to a following noun, it appears in the phonologically reduced form $?a$, as in $?a=pɔ:?$ 'one person', $?a=lam$ 'one boat', and $?a=(bu)lat$ 'one thing'.

3.4.1 Possessive constructions

Possession in Moklen is normally marked solely by word order. The possessor follows the possessum, as illustrated in (44) and (45):

(44) $?əy$ $cəy$ $?e:m$ top
      dog   1s   EXIST   DIST
      'My dog is way over there'

(45) $?ɔma:k$ $?enɔŋ$ $cəy$
      house   mother   1s
      'My mother's house'

Although possessive constructions are normally unmarked lexically, Moklen has borrowed the possessive noun $k^hɔ:ŋ$ 'thing' from Thai.

(46a) $?əy$ $k^hɔ:ŋ$ $?acaw$ way (Moklen)
(46b) mǎ: $k^hɔ̌:ŋ$ k^hray —   (Thai)
       dog   POSS   who   Q
       'Whose dog is this?'

3.4.2 Classifier constructions and quantifiers

The typical order of elements in Moklen classifier constructions is a head noun followed by a numeral and nominal classifier, as in the following examples:

(47) $kaya:?$ $pa:t$ $p^hɔh$ $nɔkɔ:t$ $manut$
      crocodile   four   CLF   bite   person
      'Four crocodiles bit a person.'

(48) $manɔk$ $nulu:n$ $ɲa:$ $klu:n$ $duwa:?$ $(bu)lat$
      chicken   lay   3   egg   two   CLF
      '(The) chicken laid two eggs.'

Moklen has a unique system which consists of two general classifiers – $(bu)lat$ and $p^hɔh$ – in complementary distribution. These pattern as follows: $(bu)lat$ is used for the numerals 1–2, 10–12, 20–22, 30–32 and so on, while $p^hɔh$ appears with 3–9, 13–19, 23–29, 33–39, and so on. The general classifier in Moken is $bulat$ which – like the two general classifiers in Moklen – can be used for counting animals and inanimates.

In addition to the general classifiers, more specific classifiers are common: Mkn-Mkl *lam* for counting boats, Mkn-Mkl (*di*)*luy* for people, Mkn-Mkl *caw* for families or houses, Mkn-Mkl *pɔkɔn* for tree(s), Mkl *nuŋɔːn* for factory-rolled cigarettes, Mkl *bakɔn* for meat, Mkl *bɔŋ* 'a piece', Mkl *cʰupiəŋ/suupiəŋ* 'half (for symmetrical or round objects)', Mkl *pucuʔ* for guns, Mkl *kanaː* for rattan, Mkn *kutum* for flowers, Mkn *mat* for bundles of grass or rice, Mkn *bup* for books, and Mkn *wiː* for bananas. These classifiers can also be used as independent nouns and can then be counted without the addition of another classifier:

(49) *waːʔ luy ɲuː dɔːk klaːw ʔabɔːʔ*
  two people MED sit speak RCP
  'Those two people sit talking together.'

(50) *cəy muutɛt kuway ʔɔn duwaːʔ kanaː*
  1s cut rattan make two piece
  'I cut (the) rattan into two pieces.'

A number of Moken and Moklen classifiers have been borrowed from Thai – especially ones used in counting manufactured products. Compared to Thai, Moken and Moklen have a less extensive repertoire of classifiers.

Note that quantifiers, most of which are borrowed from Thai, usually immediately precede the head noun and no classifier is used:

(51) *buulaw maykuuːn luubut tʰuk ʔaləy*
  wife Michael run **every** day
  'Michael's wife runs every day.'

(52) *yaŋ bɔːʔ nahɔːŋ kuway tɔcɔh*
  some people call thatch cross
  'Some people call it "cross thatch".'

Alternatively, quantifiers may 'float' and then occur in immediate postverbal position (after the subject pronoun if there is one):

(53) *kaw laːŋ mɛt kaʔ*
  go 3p all already
  'They all went already.'

3.4.3 Relative clauses

Relative clauses are generally unmarked in Moklen. They occur immediately after the head noun. Stative verbs are common in this position:

(54) *namɔk **kɛtam** ʔɛːm ɲaː panaːt nɔkɔt makɛt*
  fly (be) black dwell 3 beach bite hurt
  'Black flies live (at the) beach, (their) bite hurts.'

Moklen sometimes uses the Thai relative-clause marker (*tʰiː*), which Savetamalya (1989: 120) describes as a relative noun:

(55) *ʔəy tʰiː ʔɛːm nəy matay*
  dog REL live(d) PRX die(d)
  'The dog that lived here died.'

3.5 Serial verbs

As is common in Southeast Asian mainland languages, Moklen makes heavy use of serial constructions, as illustrated in (56) and (57):

(56) *Ɂanaːt baːɁ   cɔːn kaw   Ɂɔn   Ɂapɔŋ*
      child   carry rice go   give father
      '(The) child(ren) take rice to (the) father.'

(57) *klaːw   cəy   Ɂɛn   yaː*
      speak   1s   play only
      'I (am) only jok(ing).'

Serial-verb constructions frequently involve directional verbs such as Mkl *kaw* 'go' and *dɪn* 'come'. Mkl *baːɁ dɪn*, for example, literally means 'carry come', but can be synthetically translated as 'bring', and *baːɁ kaw* literally means 'carry go' hence 'take'. Cf. also Mkl *mɛn baːɁ dɪn* 'get carry come' for 'get (it) and bring (it)'. Some of the most common verbs appearing in serial chains also have more grammaticalized uses. Thus, for example, *mɛn* 'get' is used as a future marker:

(58) *bulaːn   naː   mɛn   kaw   tʰɔŋkʰaː*
      month   next   FUT   go   Pʰuket
      'Next month (I) will go to Pʰuket.'

As noted in section 3.2 above, the negative marker always occurs after the predicate. In serial constructions, its placement is somewhat variable in that it may occur after each verb in the chain while still retaining scope over the whole construction. (59) is considered to be the unmarked order for this serial-verb construction, but (60–61) are also possible:

(59) *Ɂa=kʰwak   naːɁ   dɪn   **hãh**   mɛn   bayəy*
      PN=kʰwak   still come NEG   take   shirt
      'Akʰwak still has not come to pick up the shirt.'

(60) *Akʰwak   naːɁ   dɪn   mɛn   **hãh**   bayəy*

(61) *Akʰwak   naːɁ   dɪn   mɛn   bayəy   **hãh***

4 MORPHOLOGY

4.1 Remnant affixation

There is no productive affixation in Moken-Moklen. All that remains of the fairly rich morphological apparatus reconstructed for Proto-Malayo-Polynesian are a few semi-productive patterns and statistical tendencies. To begin with, we may note that Moken and Moklen verbs generally have an initial nasal while nouns generally have not. In a few instances, some of which are listed in Table 18.9, we find in fact contrasting pairs of nouns with a non-nasal initial and semantically related verbs with a nasal initial.

In some instances, different varieties show different initial nasals in verbals, some reflecting the earlier *m*-initial non-perfective form, others the earlier *n*-initial perfective form (Lawrence A. Reid, pers. comm.). Compare Dung Moken *məbɔɁ* 'do' with Surin Moken *(lə)bɔɁ* 'do, make' (presyllable *l* is in free variation with *n* here and in the following examples), Dung Moken *mupʰuy* 'to sell' with Surin Moken *lupʰuy* 'to sell' and Moklen *lupʰluy*

TABLE 18.9: CONTRASTING PAIRS OF NOUNS AND NASAL-INITIAL VERBS (REFLECTING *N)

Moken examples

Gloss	Noun	Verb	Gloss
rudder	cəku:t	ɲəku:t	to steer (Rawai Moken)
earring(s)	cʰɔbaŋ	ŋɔbaŋ	put on earring (Dung Moken)
pointing finger	cʰuju:k	luju:k nuju:k	to point (Surin Moken)
medicine	ʔɔbat	ŋɔbat	to medicate (Dung Moken)
scale (fish)	cəcik	məcik	scale a fish (Rawai Moken)
comb	sola:y	ɲola:y	to comb (Rawai Moken)
claw (crab)	kapi:t	ŋapi:t	to clip, pinch (Rawai Moken)
fishing net	pəja:n	məja:n	throw a net (Rawai Moken)

Moklen examples

Gloss	Noun	Verb	Gloss
pointing finger	daluy duyu:k	duyu:k nuyu:k	to point
ear	tɛŋa:ʔ	neŋa:ʔ	to hear
egg	klu:n	nulu:n	to lay (an egg)
fishhook	cʰuwi:ək suwi:ək	nuwi:ək	to fish with a rattan reel from a boat
fishhook	tuman	numan	fish with a bamboo pole
gums (in mouth)	kuɲi:t	nuɲi:t	to put tobacco between upper gums and teeth
oar	pɯcay	mɯcay	to row
U-shaped rattan basket	sɛleŋ	nɛleŋ	scoop bait using a sɛleŋ

or *nupʰluy* 'to sell', Dung Moken *məba:ʔ* 'carry' with Rawai Moken *ləbaʔ* 'carry'. This variation makes it likely that the aspectual alternation marked by the initial nasals was still productive at the time Moken-Moklen split from the rest of the family.

There are also a few examples where a nasal-initial dynamic form of the verb contrasts with a *p*-initial stative causative form (the formal contrast is well known from other western Austronesian languages but the associated semantic contrast is remarkable). Dynamic forms typically involve a human actor who intentionally undertakes the action of a verb. For instance, Mkl *natak* 'to actively break' is used when a person breaks a stick of wood, and Mkn-Mkl *nayam* 'to actively extinguish' is employed if a human actor blows out a candle. Stative causative forms, on the other hand, typically involve a non-human effector, so the verb expresses an unintentional or natural occurrence. When the wind breaks a branch from a tree, Mkl *patak* 'to cause to break' is used. If the wind blows out a candle, both Moken and Moklen employ *payam* 'cause to become extinguished'. A similar, but somewhat more complex example is Mkl *muniŋ* 'to turn' versus Mkl *puniŋ* 'to feel dizzy (caused by drinking whiskey)'.

Some of the clearest examples of Moken and Moklen fossilized affixes can be observed in Thai loan-words such as those presented in Table 18.10. Monosyllabic Thai words – which become the major syllables of Moken and Moklen lexemes – are often

TABLE 18.10: THAI LOANS MORPHOLOGICALLY INCORPORATED INTO MOKEN AND MOKLEN

Moken examples

	Moken	*Thai*	*English gloss*
1.	kʰamuək	muək	hat
2.	matʰaːm	tʰaːm	to ask for
3.	macot	cut	to light fire (Dung Moken)
4.	manap	nap	to count (Dung Moken)
5.	metʰiaw	tʰiaw	walk about, wander, pass by (Mkn-1844)
6.	maan	aːn	to read (Mkn-1844)
7.	meŋap	ŋap	to catch (Mkn-1844)
8.	medut	duːt	to smoke (Mkn-1844)
9.	meshon	sɔːn	to teach (Mkn-1844)

Moklen examples

	Moklen	*Thai*	*English gloss*
10.	kɯpʰlɔk	pʰlɔk	coconut shell
11.	kapʰaːŋ	faːŋ	millet
12.	kapuːn	puːn	lime chewed with betel nut
13.	nuhaːk	haːk	to clear throat
14.	nuŋɔː	hɔː	to wrap
15.	napat	pʰat	to blow (wind)

made into Moken and Moklen disyllables by prefixation. The prefix *ka-* or *kɯ-* is often found with nouns; *na-, nu-, na-* or *ma-, mu-, ma-* with verbs.

Examples six through ten in Table 18.10 are found in the earliest known Moken text, '*A Primer of the Selong Language*' (§1.2), which makes it likely that this was a more productive process in the mid-1800s. Not all Thai loans in Moken and Moklen have prefixes; those without prefixes are probably recent loans.

Another indication that prefixation has become non-productive not too long ago is shown by the fact that a number of Moken words with verbal prefixes attested in older sources varied between monosyllabic and disyllabic form but can only be heard in monosyllabic form (without prefixation) in Moklen today. These include: Mkn-Lws *(me)bo/(ne)bo* 'make, do', Mkn-1844 *(ne)bo*, Moklen *bɔh* 'to do'; Mkn-Lws *nemoé*, Mkn *mɔy*, Mkl *bay* 'can, able to'; Mkn-Lws *(me)èm/maèm/neèm* 'remain, dwell, marry (of the man)', Moklen *ʔɛːm* 'to live, to exist'; Mkn-Lws *nyadin* 'come, assemble', Mkn-1844 *ngadén*, Surin Moken *ŋadin*, Moklen *din* 'to come'.

There is some evidence that infixation was also once productive in Moken and Moklen. Again, the best evidence comes from Thai loans. Moklen *sulɔt* 'vegetables' appears to be derived from the Thai stative verb *sòt* 'be fresh'. With the addition of an *-ul-* infix, Moklen *s-ul-ɔt* 'vegetables' probably meant literally 'something that is fresh'. Another example (with different semantics) is Mkl *culum* 'to dip (fingers) in water' (cf. Thai *cùm* 'to dip').

4.2 Compounding

As opposed to affixation, compounding is a highly productive process in Moklen. Most productive are noun + noun compounds of which there are various types exemplified by *laːŋ-pɔlaːw* (people-island) 'island people' (or 'Moken') in sentence (62), *tʰaːw-tʰuat* 'grandparents.great-grandparents (= ancestor)' in sentence (63), and *kuway-ʔuʔeːn* (rattan-water) 'water rattan' (a variety of rattan) in (64).

(62) *laːŋ-pɔlaːw*   *ʔaduːm*   *ʔɛːm*   *pʰaːmaː*   *ʔaduːm*   *ʔɛːm*   *tʰay*
      people-island   some   live   Burma   some   live   Thai
      'As for the Moken 'island people', some (of them) live (in) Burma and some live
      (in) Thailand.'

(63) *bɔh*   *laːŋ*   *namaʔ*   *tʰaːw-tʰuat*
      make   3p   flag   grandparents.great-grandparents
      'They [Moklen people] make the ancestor flag.'

(64) *kuway-ʔuʔěːn*   *mɔlaːt*   *lataːy*
      rattan-water   (be) twist   split bamboo
      'Water rattan (is) twist(ed) (over and around) split-bamboo flooring.'

General-specific N + N compounds such as *kuway-ʔuʔěːn* 'water rattan' are widely used for naming places, plants, and animals. For example, many fish names involve the generic noun *(ʔɛ)kaːn* 'fish' preceding a more specific designation as in Moklen *ʔɛkaːn-kuyəy pakɛːt* 'White-spotted shovelnose ray (*Rhynchobatus djiddensis*)', literally 'bitter fish-shark'.

Compounding is not restricted to N + N compounds. Other combinations – for example V + N – are also productively used (e.g. *ɲam-cɔːn* 'eat-rice', a single lexical verb meaning 'to eat'). Another common phenomenon is bilingual compounding involving a Moklen and a Thai word, e.g., *bɔh-kaːn* 'do-work' (= 'to work'), where *kaːn* is probably a Thai loan (cf. Thai *tʰam-ŋaːn* 'do-work').

5 TEXT

The teller of the following story is Aliːʔ Samutwariː, a Moklen man about forty years old who was born at Kɔʔ Pʰraʔ Tʰɔːŋ. He has spent over thirty years living in the Central Moklen speaking area and currently lives at the Moklen village of Baːn Dɔːn Can. In the story, Aliːʔ's fifteen-year-old son, Akəy, and a friend, Awat, are involved in a motorcycle accident. The motorcycle belonged to Imɛlaːk and Somchay, Aliːʔ's Thai neighbors. Thai words are boldfaced in the text:

(65) *ʔa=kəy*   *muɲaːm*   **lot**   **kluaŋ**   *tʰaŋ*   *ʔi=mɛlaːk*
      PN=kəy   borrow   vehicle   engine   from   PN=mɛlaːk
      'Akəy borrowed a motorcycle from Imɛlaːk.'

(66) *yaːy*   *ɲaː*   *kaw*   *muləy*   **kua**   *ʔɔn*   *maʔ*
      say   3   go   buy   shoes   give   mother
      '(He) said (that) he (was going to) buy shoes for [story teller's] mother
      [= Akəy's grandmother].'

(67) *ʔa=wat*   *cʰuən*   *ɲaː*   *ʔa=kəy*   *kaw*   *luɯsak*
      PN=wat   want   3   PN=kəy   go
      'Awat wanted to go (with) Akay to (the village of) Luɯsak.'

(68) *ʔa=kəy*   *ʔa=wat*   *balɛh*   *hãh*
      PN=akəy   PN=awat   return   NEG
      'Akəy and Awat did not return (home).'

(69) *ʔi=mɛlaːk*   *dɯn*   *ɲaː*   **tʰaːm**   *cəy*   *puɯnaːʔ*   *ʔa=kəy*   *naːʔ*   *dɯn*   *hãh*
      PN=mɛlaːk   come   3   ask   1s   see   PN=akəy   still   come   NEG
      'Imɛlaːk came to ask me why Akəy still had not returned.'

(70)   *dɯn*   *ɲaː*   *tulǝy*   *hɔn*   *ʔɔn*   *cǝy*   *kaw*   **taːm**   *ʔa=kǝy*
        come   3   three   time   have   1s   go   follow   PN=kǝy
        'She came three times to have me go look for Akǝy.'

(71)   *cǝy*   *kʰuː*   *somcʰay*   *kaw*   **taːm**   *ʔa=kǝy*
        1s   with   Somchay   go   follow   PN=kǝy
        'I and Somchay went to look for Akǝy.'

(72)   *ʔa=kǝy*   *ʔɔt*   *hɛ̃ʔ*   *pɔːm*   *kʰawlak;*   *puutʰaːʔ*   *hɛ̃ʔ*   *dugak*
        PN=kǝy   NEG.EXIST   at   check point   meet   at
        'Akǝy was not at the Khaw Lak (police) checkpoint; (we) met at Khuk Khak (the
        Thai name for the Moklen village of Dugak).'

(73)   *ʔa=kǝy*   *paliek*   *hɛ̃ʔ*   *na;*   *ʔa=wat*   *paliek*   *hɛ̃ʔ*   *ʔɔtak*
        PN=kǝy   tear   at   face   PN=wat   tear   at   head
        'Akǝy was cut on his face; Awat was cut on his head.'

(74)   *ʔa=kǝy*   *muɲiǝŋ*   *nɛmaːʔ*   *dalum;*   *ʔa=wat*   *nam*   *dalum*
        PN=kǝy   sew   five   stitch   PN=wat   six   stitch
        'Akǝy received five stitches; Awat (got) six stitches.'

(75)   *numɔh*   *cʰaŋ*   *ban*   *lay?*
        fall   how   Q
        Hearer: 'How did (they) fall?'

(76)   *ɲaw*   *numɔh*   *dalum*   *kʰuː*   *nalaŋ*
        2p   fall   in   ditch   grass
        'They fell in (a) grassy ditch.'

(77)   *ʔa=kǝy*   *lubut*   *tʰuːm*   *plɔh*   *lay?*
        PN=kǝy   run   how many   ten   Q
        Hearer: 'How many (kilometers per hour was) Akǝy driving?'

(78)   *canaːt*   *lubut*   *waley*   *plɔh;*   *tulaw*   **kɯːn**   *ʔamɔːn*   *hãh*
        child   run   eight   ten   fast   too   good   NEG
        '(The) child (was going) 80 (kilometers per hour); (that is) too fast – not good.'

(79)   **welaː**   **lot**   **kluɯaŋ**   *numɔh*   *kɔyaːn*   *nɔlɛŋ*   *lahan*   *hãh*   *kaː?*
        time   vehicle   engine   fall   rain   fall   much   NEG   Q
        Hearer: 'When (the) motorcycle fell, wasn't it raining heavily?'

(80)   **laː**   *numɔh*   *ɲuʔ*   *kɔyaːn*   *plɛʔ plɛʔ*   *yaː*   *laʔ*   *lahan*   *hãh*
        time   fall   that   rain   little   only   EMPH   much   NEG
        'When (it) fell, (there was) only little rain, not much at all.'

REFERENCES

A primer of the Selong language (1844/1846) Maulmain: American Mission Press [Transliteration of the original in M.B. Lewis (1960)].

Anderson, J. (1890) *The Selungs of the Mergui Archipelago*, London: Trübner & Co.

Bernatzik, H.A. (1938/58) *The spirit of the yellow leaves*, translated by E.W. Dickes, London: Robert Hale Limited. [First published in German as *Die Geister der Gelben Blätter, Forschungsreisen in Hinterindien*, Leipzig: Kohler & Voigtländer, 1938.]

Bishop, N. and Peterson, M.M. (1987) 'A preliminary language research survey report: the Moklen and Sakai language groups'. Bangkok: Summer Institute of Linguistics.

Bradley, D. (ed.) (1977) *Papers in Southeast Asian linguistics 5*, Canberra: Pacific Linguistics.

Carrapiett, W.J.S. (1909) *The Salons*, Ethnographical Survey of India. Burma No. 2. Rangoon.

Chantanakomes, V. (1980) *A description of Moken: A Malayo-Polynesian language*, M.A Thesis at Mahidol University, Nakhorn Pathom: Institute of Language and Culture for Rural Development.

Court, C. (1971) 'A fleeting encounter with the Moken (The Sea Gypsies) in Southern Thailand: Some linguistic and general notes', *Journal of the Siam Society* 59: 83–96.

Donegan, P. and Stampe, D. (1983) 'Rhythm and the holistic organization of language structure', in J. Richardson, M. Marks, and A. Chukerman (eds) *Papers from the parasession on the interplay of phonology, morphology, and syntax*, 337–53, Chicago: Chicago Linguistic Society.

Haas, M.R. (1964) *Thai–English student's dictionary*, Stanford: Stanford University Press.

Harmon, C. (1977) *Kagayanen and the Manobo subgroup of Philippine languages*, Ph.D. dissertation, University of Hawai'i.

Hinshiranan, N. (1996) *The analysis of Moken opportunistic foragers' intragroup and intergroup relations*, Ph.D. dissertation, University of Hawai'i.

Hogan, D.W. (1972) 'Men of the sea: Coastal tribes of South Thailand's West Coast', *Journal of the Siam Society* 60:205–235.

——(1983) 'A Thai Orthography for the Moken Language', unpublished manuscript, Melbourne: Pacific College of Graduate Studies.

Ivanoff, J. (1988) *Moken: Les naufragés de l'histoire*, Ph.D. dissertation, École des Hautes Études en Sciences Sociales, Paris.

Larish, M.D. (1991) 'The special relationship between Moken, Acehnese, Chamic and Mon-Khmer: Areal influence or genetic affinity?' Unpublished paper presented at the *Sixth International Conference on Austronesian Linguistics*, Honolulu: University of Hawai'i.

——(1993) 'Who are the Moken and Moklen on the Islands and Coasts of the Andaman Sea?' in: *Pan-Asiatic Linguistics: Proceedings of the Third International Symposium on Language and Linguistics*, Chulalongkorn University, January 8–10, 1992, volume III:1305–19, Bangkok: Chulalongkorn University Printing House.

——(1997) 'Moklen-Moken phonology: Mainland or insular Southeast Asian typology?', in C. Odé and W. Stokhof (eds) *Proceedings of the Seventh International Conference on Austronesian Linguistics*, 125–50, Amsterdam: Rodopi.

——(1999) *The Position of Moken and Moklen in the Austronesian Language Family*, Ph.D. dissertation, University of Hawai'i.

Lee, E.W. (1974) 'Southeast Asian areal features in Austronesian strata of the Chamic languages', *Oceanic Linguistics* 13:643–82.

Leerabhandh, S. (1984) *Phonological reconstruction of Proto Orang-Laut*, MA Thesis at Mahidol University, Nakhorn Pathom: Institute of Language and Culture for Rural Development, Salaya Campus.

Lewis, M.B. (1960) *Moken texts and word-list: A provisional interpretation*, Kuala Lumpur: Museums Department, Federation of Malaya.

Makboon, S. (1981) *Survey of Sea People's dialects along the West Coast of Thailand*, MA Thesis at Mahidol University, Nakhorn Pathom: Institute of Language and Culture for Rural Development.

Naw Say Bay (1995) 'The phonology of the Dung dialect of Moken', in D. Bradley (ed.) *Studies in Burmese languages* (= Papers in Southeast Asian Linguistics No. 13), 193–205, Canberra: Pacific Linguistics.

Savetamalya, S. (1989) *Thai nouns and noun phrases: A lexicase analysis*, Ph.D. dissertation, University of Hawai'i.

Swastham, P. (1982) *A description of Moklen: A Malayo-Polynesian language*, MA Thesis at Mahidol University, Nakhorn Pathom: Institute of Language and Culture for Rural Development.

White, W.G. (1913) 'St. Mark in Mawken', Rangoon: British and Foreign Bible Society.

——(1922) *The Sea Gypsies of Malaya. An account of the nomadic Mawken people of the Mergui Archipelago with a description of their ways of living, customs, habits, boats, occupations, &c., &c., &c.* London: Seeley, Service & Co.

CHAPTER NINETEEN

KARO BATAK

Geoff Woollams

1 INTRODUCTION

Karo Batak is the language spoken by the Karo people of North Sumatra. Karo people refer to themselves as *kalak Karo* in their own language (or *orang Karo* in Indonesian) and call their language *cakap Karo*. The term 'Batak' refers to a congeries of culturally related groups or tribes (Viner 1979:90) who inhabit the greater part of the hinterland of the province of North Sumatra (*Sumatera Utara*), in the centre of which is located Lake Toba. Each of these groups has its own distinctive language, social organization and history. The Toba Batak, who occupy the island of Samosir in Lake Toba, and the territory to the east, south and south-west of the lake, have been the subject of much anthropological and linguistic study for more than a century, with their language recorded by H.N. van der Tuuk in his classic 1864–67 grammar *Tobasche Spraakkunst* (since translated into English in 1971). Post-war migration of the Toba Batak led to their establishing sizeable communities along the east coast of North Sumatra, in Aceh and in Java, as well as in other Batak areas, so that the term 'Batak' has, for outsiders, become virtually synonymous with 'Toba Batak'. Other Batak peoples reject the label, preferring for instance to be known as *orang Mandailing* or *orang Angkola* (found further to the south of Lake Toba, and extending to the provincial border with West Sumatra), *orang Simalungun* (to the north-east of the lake), or *orang Pakpak* and *orang Dairi* (to the west and south-west of Lake Toba).

The Karo people live to the north-west of Lake Toba, occupying an area of some 5000 square kilometers, roughly between 3° and 3° 30′ north latitude, and 98° and 98° 30′ east longitude. Karoland comprises two main areas:

(a) The Karo highlands (Karo Gugung), which includes all of the Karo regency (Kabupaten Karo) whose administrative centre is the town of Kabanjahe, and extends southwards partially into Kabupaten Dairi and eastwards partially into Kabupaten Simalungun.

(b) The Karo lowlands (Karo Jahe), which includes the geographically southernmost subdistricts of Kabupatens Langkat and Deli-Serdang.

The highlands are regarded as the original homeland and cultural centre of the Karo people. There, the language is less subject to external influences, and kinship ties and traditional life are still strongly maintained. Most highland Karo practice small-scale agriculture (mostly fresh fruit and vegetables, with a variety of cash crops) for their own consumption as well as for regional and nearby international markets. The lowland settlements are more oriented towards plantation agriculture such as palm oil and rubber, and the people here are more subject to Malay cultural and linguistic influence, often embracing Islam, and sometimes abandoning their patrilineal clan names. From statistics obtained in 1984 it was estimated that the total Karo population of North Sumatra was around 570,000 with around 44% of Karo people living in the highlands, 46% in the lowlands, and the remaining 10% residing in the provincial capital of Medan. Besides proficiency in their own language, the most important mark of one's identity as a Karo Batak is the clan name, with all Karo people belonging to one of the five patriclans or *merga*, namely: Karo-karo, Ginting, Tarigan, Sembiring and Perangin-angin. Singarimbun's (1975) ethnography provides an excellent account of the workings of Karo society.

Following Voorhoeve (1955:9) the Batak languages may be divided into two mutually unintelligible groups: the Northern, which comprises Karo, Pakpak and Alas, and the Southern, which includes Toba, Angkola and Mandailing. Voorhoeve places the geographically intermediate Simalungun as linguistically midway, though in a more recent study, Adelaar (1981) concludes that Simalungun is more closely related to the Southern group. A comparison of 207 basic vocabulary items from Karo and its adjacent linguistic neighbours reveals cognate percentages of 76% for Alas, 81% for Pakpak, and 80% for Simalungun. With Indonesian/Malay, which it borders on the north, the percentage of shared vocabulary is only 30%. Karo and Toba Batak are not mutually intelligible.

Dialect differences are found within Karo itself, though not to the point of hindering mutual comprehension. At worst, such differences may give rise to amusement and teasing. A survey of key variants suggests the existence of a major boundary between eastern and western dialects, reflecting a relatively limited number of phonological and lexical differences. In broad phonological terms the western dialect is characterized by either a lowering or fronting of vowels found in the eastern dialect, and a tendency towards monophthongization of diphthongs, for example:

(1)   eastern dialect   western dialect
      /waluh/   /waloh/   'eight'
      /sitik/   /sitek/   'a little'
      /melëhé/   /melihé/   'hungry'
      /jauŋ/   /joŋ/   'corn'

Within this highly simplified major scheme, many subdialects may be identified, sometimes down to village level. Within this largely uncharted network of variation, however, the highlands' eastern dialect seems to be regarded as the 'standard' variety of Karo by many speakers, undoubtedly in no small part due to the fact that the town of Kabanjahe, the administrative and commercial hub of Kabupaten Karo, is located there.

The activities of Dutch missionaries and educators at the turn of the twentieth century saw the production of the first Dutch–Karo dictionary in 1907 by M. Joustra, who published a great deal on various facets of everyday Karo life. He was followed by another missionary, J.H. Neumann, who likewise contributed much to the documentation of Karo anthropological matters, as well as translating the Bible, producing a grammar of the language, and compiling a new Dutch–Karo dictionary. Neumann's grammar, like so many other studies of Indonesian languages at the time, was more devoted to morphological than syntactic aspects of the language. Nevertheless, together with his posthumously published dictionary (1951), it remains a thorough and reliable work. More recent contributions to the study of the Karo language have borne the name of Henry Guntur Tarigan, himself a Karo who also wrote voluminously on neighbouring Simalungun. A review of his works up to 1972 is provided by Chambert-Loir in *Archipel* (1974). A more recent comprehensive study of the language was made by Woollams (1996).

Despite the existence of an indigenous script – a legacy of earlier Indian influence (see Parkin 1978) – the Karo had no established written literary tradition in precolonial times.

Voorhoeve (1961) describes how the early Batak texts were essentially confined to works written by medicine men on matters of magic, astrology and divination, inscribed on concertina-like bark books and bamboo cylinders. On the basis of his studies of Karo lamentations, Kozok (1996:245) concludes that literacy in the Batak script was actually more widespread throughout the population until the advance of Islamic and Christian missions in the mid-nineteenth century. Nowadays, knowledge of their early alphabet has all but disappeared among Karo speakers.

Some traditional folktales were published by the early Dutch missionaries and educators (see Voorhoeve 1955:14; Joustra 1904), but little subsequent material appeared in print until the 1960s. Recent decades have seen an increase in the number of publications in the Karo language (using Latin orthography) inspired by the initiatives of Karo scholars such as Masri Singarimbun (1960) and Henry Guntur Tarigan (1965). These later publications embrace traditional folktales, modern short stories and novels, clan histories, descriptive and prescriptive texts on *adat* (= traditional law and customs), school texts and readers, poems, proverbs, songs, and translations of the Bible.

2 PHONOLOGY

2.1 Segment inventory

Karo has 24 segmental phonemes, 17 consonants and 7 vowels, as shown in Table 19.1. Voiceless stops are unaspirated, and unreleased before consonants and utterance finally; /k/ is realized as a glottal stop before consonants and utterance finally. The voiceless glottal fricative /h/ is sometimes realized as a voiceless velar fricative in syllable-final position. The vibrant /r/ is normally a voiced alveolar trill, but in syllable-initial position may occur as a flap.

Front and back vowels are relatively higher (= tense) in open syllables and relatively lower (= lax) in closed syllables. Additionally, /i/, /o/ and /u/ exhibit a kind of vowel harmony, whereby they are lowered in a stressed open syllable immediately preceding an occurrence of the same (lax allophone of the) vowel in a closed syllable. *ë* represents the unrounded high back vowel [ɯ]. It poses some descriptive challenges, as in unstressed syllables it is generally replaced by schwa, from which it is elsewhere

TABLE 19.1: KARO PHONEMES (in practical orthography)

Consonants		Labial	Alveo-dental	Palatal	Velar	Glottal
Stops	voiceless	p	t	c	k	
	voiced	b	d	j	g	
Nasals		m	n		ng	
Fricatives			s			h
Lateral			l			
Vibrant			r			
Semi-vowel		w			y	
Vowels		Front	Central	Back		
High		i		ë, u		
Mid		é	e	o		
Low			a			

phonemically distinguishable on the basis of minimal pairs such as /perëh/ 'manner of coming' and /pereh/ 'to wring out' (see Woollams 1996:20–22 for a more comprehensive discussion).

For everyday purposes, Karo is written in the Latin alphabet following the standards set by the 1972 *Ejaan Yang Disempurnakan* promulgated by the Indonesian Ministry of Education and Culture. The consonant phonemes are written as they appear in the inventory above. The letter *e* bears a triple functional load, representing /é/, /ë/ and /e/. This poses no problems for literate Karo, however, who readily recognize the limited number of words containing /é/ and /ë/.

2.2 Stress and prosody

Stress in Karo is predictable and therefore non-phonemic. Three kinds of stress can be distinguished: word stress, phrase stress, and vocative stress. Word stress, indicated here by ['] preceding the stressed syllable, normally falls on the penultimate syllable, e.g.:

(2)   /'nandé/ 'mother'

(3)   /ida'rami/
      i-daram-i
      UV-seek-ITER.APP
      'be sought'

(4)   /idara'mina/
      i-daram-i = na
      UV-seek-ITER.APP = 3.ACT
      'be sought by him'

If the penultimate syllable is open, and contains /e/, stress usually shifts to the last syllable: /me'dem/ 'sleep'. However, this stress shift does not occur if the final syllable begins with a velar nasal or glottal fricative, or if it contains the suffixes -*i* or -*en*: /'leŋa/ 'not yet', /ŋe'nehen/ 'see', /nim'pet-i/ 'extinguish', /ba'ges-en/ 'deeper'. Word stress is replaced by stronger stress on the last word of a phrase. This is called phrase stress and is indicated by ["]. Phrase stress may also be accompanied by a slight lengthening of the vowel, unless it is /e/. Compare the presence of phrase stress on *rumah* in /i "rumah/ 'in the house', and its absence in /i 'rumah pe"ŋulu/ 'in the house of the chief'.

Vocative stress is a particular kind of phrase stress, whereby a word or phrase used vocatively is strongly stressed on the last syllable. The vowel may also be lengthened: /nan'dé/ ~ /nan'dé:/ 'O mother!'

Vowel length is predictable and thus not phonemic. A vowel is lengthened when either: (a) it occurs root finally and is suffixed with -*en*, e.g. /uli/ + /-en/ → /ulien/ [ulɪ:n] 'better'; (b) it occurs in a monosyllabic word bearing phrase stress; compare /i das/ [i "da:s] 'on top' with /i das lemari/ [i 'das lə"mari] 'on top of the cupboard'; or (c) as the stressed vowel in a word bearing phrase stress it is lengthened for emphasis, e.g. /"aku/ ["a:ku] 'It was me!'

Intonation may be the sole distinguishing feature between two utterances of identical segmental material. Spoken with a declarative intonation contour (22221: low-mid pitch falling to low utterance finally), *ku juma ia* (to field 3) means 'He has gone to the fields', whereas with an interrogative contour (34223: initially higher pitch, rising to its highest level on the syllable which receives phrase stress, then falling and rising again) the utterance means 'Has he gone to the fields?'.

2.3 Syllable types

Six syllable types are possible: V, VC, CV, CVC, CCV, CCVC. Examples: /i.a/ 'he, she', /im.pal/ 'cousin', /ma.té/ 'die', /suŋ.kun/ 'ask', /nde.ha.ra/ 'wife', /nder.bih/ 'yesterday'.

Root morphemes are most typically disyllabic, though monosyllabic, trisyllabic and quadrisyllabic forms also occur: /kam/ 'you', /én.da/ 'this', /ru.bi.a/ 'animal', /ka.lin.ca.yo/ 'kind of flower'. All syllable types can occur anywhere within morphemes except for CCV and CCVC which are found only morpheme initially. The structure for words is the same as that for morphemes, except that in addition, the expansion of roots through affixation, reduplication and cliticization can yield words of up to eight syllables in length:

(5)   /i.ba.han.na/
      i-bahan=na
      UV-make=3.ACT
      'he made'

(6)   /i.pe.ga.jah.ga.jah.ken.ndu/
      i-pe-gajah-gajah-ken=ndu
      UV-CAU-RDP-elephant-CAU.APP=2s.ACT
      'you exaggerate'

In morphologically complex words CCV syllable types occur word finally, in the case of the second person enclitic pronoun =*ndu* '(by) you, your'.

All consonants may occur initially and medially in words (although word-initial instances of /h/, /w/, and /y/ are rare), and all consonants except voiced stops, affricates and semi-vowels can close syllables. Word initial consonant clusters comprise a nasal which is homorganic with the following obstruent, with all obstruents except /p/ able to occur as second member of the cluster. All vowels are found in all syllable types, except for /ĕ/ which occurs only in CV and CVC. Vowel clusters occur only across syllable boundaries.

2.4 Phonological alternations

A sequence of two vowels with a front vowel preceding may be punctuated with a phonemically non-distinctive /y/: /kiniulien/ [kiniulɪːn] ~ [kiniyulɪːn] 'beauty', whilst a sequence of two vowels with a back vowel preceding may be separated by a phonemically non-distinctive /w/: /ué/ [ue] ~ [uwe] 'yes'. A glottal stop is inserted between two identical vowels at a word boundary: /bidé é/ [bideʔe] 'that fence'. Schwa is optionally added to the beginning of a word starting with a consonant cluster whose second member is a voiceless stop: /nterem/ [ntərəm] ~ [əntərəm] 'many'. Phonetic consonant geminates may occur in disyllabic words with an open first syllable containing /e/: /besur/ [bəssur] 'satiated, full'; this phenomenon is mostly confined to situations where the speaker is articulating the word very carefully (such as to a learner), or emphatically ('I can't eat another thing – I'm full!').

Vowels are sometimes elided in fast speech; this commonly occurs with /e/ immediately following a vowel, across a morpheme or word boundary: /la ku = eteh/ [la kutəh] (NEG 1s.ACT = know) 'I don't know'. Sequences of two vowels with a low vowel occuring first (/ai/ and /au/) are frequently monophthongized, particularly medially: /ndauhsa/ [ndauhsa] ~ [ndohsa] 'too far'. Diphthongs are also often produced in words containing the sequence /-aw-/: /lawes/ [lawəs] ~ [laus] 'go'.

Word final /i/ and /é/ are lowered to [ɪ] and [ɛ] when followed by a word beginning with a consonant cluster; in such cases the nasal of the consonant cluster is interpreted as closing the previously open syllable of the preceding word: /si mbaru/ [sɪm.baru] 'which is new'.

When a root ending in a vowel is suffixed with -en, the schwa of the suffix assimilates to that preceding vowel, yielding a phonetically long vowel: /rana + -en/ → /ranaen/ [rana:n] 'discussion'. A front or back vowel in this situation is also lowered to its lax allophone: /duri + -en/ [durɪ:n] 'breadfruit'.

Free (non-conditioned) phonological variation also occurs on a word-by-word basis, usually involving loss of an initial syllable (/eŋko/ ~ /ko/ 'you'), consonantal variation (/banci/ ~ /danci/ 'can') or vowel alternation (/ué/ ~ /oé/ 'yes', /ula/ ~ /ola/ 'don't').

Finally, some variation is attested in the form of certain affixes. Principal among these is the prefix *N-*, of which there are five different morphemes posited. In general terms this is a homorganic nasal which assimilates to the place of articulation of the stem-initial consonant to which it is attached: {m-} before bilabial stops, {n-} before dental, alveolar and palatal stops and fricatives, and {ŋ-} before velar stops. The differences between the five N- prefixes are complex, varying in terms of their replacive effect on the stem-initial consonant (which is sometimes elided and sometimes retained) and their form preceding a vowel. They are described in detail in Woollams (1996:41).

Prefix *er-* has two allomorphs, {r-} when attached to a stem beginning with a vowel, and {er-} elsewhere: /er- + impal/ → /rimpal/ 'have a cousin', /er- + dalan/ → /erdalan/ 'walk'. Prefixes *ter-* and *per-* are reduced to *te-* and *pe-* when attached to a stem beginning with /r/; otherwise they remain intact: /per- + ridi/ → /peridi/ 'way of bathing'. The postposed formative *sa* manifests a number of different morphemes including the enclitic form of the third person pronoun; following a dental stop or nasal, = *sa* is often realized as {=ca}: /meteh =sa/ 'know it', /ŋenehen + -sa/ → /ŋenehenca/ 'see it'.

2.5 Reduplication

In formal terms, there are two types of reduplication processes in Karo: full reduplication and CV-reduplication. The latter involves reduplication of only the initial CV syllable of a stem, with a tendency for the vowel in the reduplicated syllable to alternate freely with schwa: *pagi* 'tomorrow' → *papagi* ~ *pepagi* 'tomorrow'. Although a distinguishing feature of the western dialects, this process is of much lower frequency than full reduplication, however, and applies only to a limited number of words in standard Karo.

Full reduplication occurs mainly with open word classes, and is characterized by a good deal of simultaneous intertwining and idiosyncrasy. Words from different classes are often reduplicated with the same semantic effect; conversely, words of the same class may have entirely different functions and meanings when doubled. For many words, doubling is an inherent structural feature of their lexical identity: *pekpek* 'hit', *sura-sura* 'ambitions'; such words have no undoubled counterparts. Some words mean the same whether reduplicated or not: *uruk* ~ *uruk-uruk* 'hill'.

Many reduplicated forms are onomatopoeic: *giring-giring* 'small bell', *circir* 'splash'. Reduplicated nominals often signify plurality or variety (*tulan* 'bone' → *tulan-tulan* 'bones', *suan* 'to plant' → *suan-suanen* 'plants'), imitation or similitude (*nahe* 'leg' → *nahe-nahe* 'stilts', *berku* 'coconut shell' → *berku-berku* 'skull'). Reduplicated verbs often convey repetition (*nungkun* 'ask' → *nungkun-nungkun* 'keep asking'), duration (*ngukuri* 'think' → *ngukur-ngukuri* 'ponder', *bulan* 'moon' → *erbulan-bulan* 'lasting for months'), or imitation (*medem* 'sleep' → *medem-medem* 'lie down, rest'). Other meanings include emphasis and intensity (*mbages* 'deep' → *mbages-mbages* 'deeply, intently'), indefiniteness (*piga* 'how many' → *piga-piga* 'several', *kundul* 'sit' → *kundul-kundul* 'sit around'). Preceded by a negative, a reduplicated form may indicate indefiniteness (*ku ja* 'to where' → *la ku ja ku ja* 'to nowhere'), or a failure of something which was expected (*nggeluh* 'live' → *la nggeluh-nggeluh* 'wouldn't start' (of a motor)).

3 BASIC MORPHOSYNTAX

3.1 Word and morpheme classes

In Karo a distinction needs to be made between 'phonological word' and 'grammatical word'. For instance, the utterance /rumahta/ is a single phonological word, with characteristic stress on the penultimate syllable, but grammatically it is a sequence of two units, *rumah* 'house' and =*ta* 'our'. The term *word* in this section refers to a grammatical word.

Clitics are a special subset of words; they are monomorphemic, unstressable forms which never occur freely but are phonologically bound to an adjacent word. Karo has two sets of clitics: (a) the pronominal agentive and possessive forms, *ku*=, =*ku*, =*ndu*, =*mu*, =*na*/ =*sa*, *si*= and =*ta* (see Table 19.2 in 3.3 below); and (b) the particles *nge* and *me*, which under certain conditions lose their vowel and merge with an adjacent word, e.g. *i jénda* = *nge* (at D.ADV EMPH) → *i jéndang* 'here!'.

Affixes are similar to clitics, in that they are also phonologically bound forms. However, whereas clitics combine with words to form grammatical phrases (e.g. *rumahta* 'our house' above), affixes are limited to the domain of word formation. In the simplest cases, affixes combine with roots to form words, e.g. *baba* 'carry' + -*en* → *baban* 'burden, load'. Many such affixed roots can have further affixes added to them to produce new words, e.g. *er-* + *baban* → *erbaban* 'to carry a load'. Words which can be further affixed in this way are called stems. Recursion or layering of stems within stems is quite common in Karo.

In terms of syntactic distribution, eight word classes may be distinguished in Karo: nouns, transitive verbs, intransitive verbs, adjectives, prepositions, conjunctions, operators and finally, a residual category comprising exclamations, interjections and responses. The first four classes are typically 'open', in the sense that there is an unlimited number of items which belong to them. By contrast, the latter four classes have finite membership. Nouns, transitive verbs, intransitive verbs and adjectives may all occur as predicates, but only nouns can occur as subjects. In order to occupy the same syntactic positions as nouns, verbs and adjectives must be nominalized (see Section 5).

This classification is reinforced by regularities in morphological processes. For example, the suffix -*en* has four different but predictable function-meaning combinations depending upon the class of word to which it is attached: (a) with nouns, -*en* generally means 'affected by...', e.g. *perkis* 'ant', *perkisen* 'ant-ridden'; (b) with transitive verbs, -*en* derives undergoer nouns, e.g. *inem* 'to drink', *inemen* 'a drink'; (c) with intransitive verbs it signifies plurality or multiplicity, e.g. *kiam* 'run', *kiamen* 'run everywhere'; (d) with adjectives it marks comparative degree, e.g. *gedang* 'long', *gedangen* 'longer'. Since most roots can freely occur as exponents of syntactic constructions, the classification of words according to the above scheme also applies to roots. However, mention must be made of a special subset of roots which are bound forms which need to be affixed before they can be occur in constructions at the word level. Classification of these roots is normally not problematical, as they can be generally assigned to one class or other on the basis of their affixational potential.

Although most roots belong to only one word class, dual categorial membership is possible. It is not uncommon for verbs (both roots and derived stems) to also function as prepositions or conjunctions, e.g. *seh* 1. (v.) 'reach, arrive', 2. (prep.) 'as far as, until'.

3.2 Basic clause structure

A major distinction can be made between transitive and non-transitive clauses. The latter embrace the following types: ambient, identificational, stative, intransitive and existential clauses. The central identifying characteristic of a clause is its predicate, which can be realized by a variety of constituents (most frequently adjectives and verbs) and which in Karo generally, but not necessarily, precedes the subject. The subject is mostly realized by a NP or some other nominalized form, sometimes even by a clause. Although most clause types in Karo have a subject as one of their nuclear constituents, some do not (notably ambient clauses, and certain kinds of undergoer-voice clauses, see 3.2.3).

3.2.1 Non-transitive clauses

Ambient clauses minimally contain a predicate referring to the meterological, temporal or environmental setting. They have no formal subject.

(7)　*Udan　me.*
　　　rain　　EMPH
　　　'It was raining.'

Identificational clauses have a subject and predicate both realized by nominals.

(8)　*Pangan=na　labang　　　entah　kirik.*
　　　food=3.POSS　grasshopper　or　　　cricket
　　　'His food was grasshoppers or crickets.'

(9)　*Si　Amin　nge　si　nulisi /N-tulis-i/　　　dinding　é.*
　　　PN　Amin　EMPH　REL　　AV-write-LOC.APP　wall　　ANAPH
　　　'It was Amin who wrote on the wall.'

The normal word order in identificational clauses is Subject-Predicate, but inversion may occur if the predicate is modified by a limiter or emphatic particle, as in the example above, or if it is realized by an interrogative pronoun:

(10)　*Kai　pindonndu /pindo-en=ndu/*
　　　 what　　　　　　　request-NR.UG = 2.POSS
　　　 'What is your request?'

Distinguishing subject from predicate can be readily accomplished by negating the
sentence, the negative phrase *la bo* occuring before the predicate, thus:

(11) *Pangan=na   la bo   labang   entah   kirik.*
      food=3.POSS   NEG   grasshopper   or   cricket
      'His food was not grasshoppers or crickets.'

(12) *La bo si   Amin si   nulisi /N-tulis-i/   dinding   é.*
      NEG PN   Amin REL   AV-write-LOC.APP   wall   ANAPH
      'It wasn't Amin who wrote on the wall.'

Subject and predicate may be linked by a copulative particle *émkap*, especially if either
constituent is relatively long, or if the predicate contains information which serves to
define the subject:

(13) *Puang   kalimbubu   émkap   kalimbubu   ibas   kalimbubu=nta,*
      puang   kalimbubu   LK   kalimbubu   at   kalimbubu=1pi.POSS

      mama   nandé=ta   tah   mama   ibas   mama=nta   nari.
      uncle   mother=1pi.POSS   or   uncle   at   uncle=1pi.POSS   from
      'The "*puang kalimbubu*" are the *kalimbubu* of the *kalimbubu*, our mother's
      maternal uncles, or the maternal uncles of our maternal uncles.'

Stative clauses have a predicate manifested by a prepositional phrase or an adjective;
word order is variable:

(14) *Ia   pecerén   nari.*
      3   Peceren   from
      'He's from Peceren.'

(15) *Gegeh-en   ia   asangken   aku.*
      strong-CMPR   3   than   1s
      'He is stronger than me.'

Stative clauses frequently contain a complement realized by a NP, dative PP, or a clause:

(16) *Agi=ngku   m-biar   biang.*
      younger.sibling=1s.POSS   ADJ-afraid   dog
      'My little brother is afraid of dogs.'

(17) *Aku   la   tëk   man   ba=na.*
      1s   NEG   believe   DAT   INTSF=3.POSS
      'I don't believe him.'

(18) *Me-hangké   aku   er-kuan   ras   ia.*
      ADJ-reluctant   1s   DTR-speak   with   3
      'I am reluctant to speak with him.'

As the sentence above illustrates, when coreferential with the subject of the main clause,
the subject of the complement clause is omitted, and the 'shared subject' is interposed
between the main (higher) and subordinate (lower) predicates. This is a particularly
common clause combining strategy in Karo.

Intransitive clauses contain predicates manifested by intransitive verbs of various
classes: root verbs, derived intransitive verbs bearing various affixes (*er-*, *N-*, *-en*, *ke-…-en*),
or transitive verbs in actor-voice used intransitively.

(19)   *Opé   bapa   berkat,   man /N-pan/   kami   lebé.*
     before   father   depart   AV-eat   1pe   first
     'Before father left, we ate.'

(20)   *Rubia-rubia   pé   kerina   kiam-en   ku   jah   ku   jé.*
     animal-animal   EMPH   all   run-PL   to   D.ADV   to   D.ADV
     'The animals were running about in all directions.'

(21)   *Udan   ras   kilap   sialo-alon /si-alo-alo-en/.*
     rain   and   lightning   RCP-RDP-welcome-RCP
     'Rain and lightning followed each other.'

It is possible for an intransitive verb to be followed by a NP, yielding a structure which appears to parallel the pattern of an actor-voice transitive clause:

(22)   (a) *Ia   er-daya   sepeda.*
         he   DTR-sell   bicycle
         'He sells bicycles.'

      (b) *Ia   n-daya-ken   sepeda.*
         he   AV-sell-APP   bicycle
         'He sells/sold his bicycle.'

Despite superficial similarities, however, these are quite different constructions, with only the latter capable of being transformed into undergoer-voice (see section 3.2.2). In contrast to (b), the postverbal NP in (a) above is non-referential, in the sense that it does not refer to any particular bicycle, but to bicycles in general. This NP cannot be modified by descriptives, possessors or determiners in the usual way that other NPs can. Furthermore, the restriction that no intervening material may be placed between the verb and postverbal NP in (a) leads us to analyse such structures as intransitive phrasal verbs, which have in effect been created by incorporating an undergoer NP into the intransitive verb phrase. Thus (a) could also be glossed as 'He is a bicycle seller'.

Existential clauses express the existence or non-existence of some entity, and are frequently associated with a presentative function, introducing upon the scene a new participant of some significance (Cumming 1988:137). They often contain a locative or temporal element:

(23)   *Pagi   lit   kerja-kerja   i   rumah   silih=ta.*
     tomorrow   EXIST   feast   at   house   cousin=1pi.POSS
     'There is a feast at our cousin's place tomorrow.'

(24)   *Tupung   si   é   enggo   lit   agama   islam   i   barus.*
     time   REL   ANAPH   already   EXIST   religion   Islam   at   Barus
     'At that time Islam was already in Barus.'

The existential predicate *lit* normally precedes the subject, but inversion may occur for the purpose of contrastive emphasis:

(25)   *Sén   pé   la   lit,   nakan   pé   la   lit.*
     money   EMPH   NEG   EXIST   rice   EMPH   NEG   EXIST
     'There was no money, there was no food.'

Although mostly the subject of an existential clause is non-identifiable/indefinite, when a possessed NP occurs in subject position, the major notion communicated by the clause is that of possession, rather than existence:

(26) *La   lit   sén=ku.*
      NEG EXIST money=1s.POSS
      'I have no money.'

Finally, *lit* frequently occurs with a sentential subject which it either precedes, or is found interposed between the fronted NP subject and predicate of this lower clause. The effect of *lit* in such structures is to convey a nuance of 'actuality' or greater emphasis on the complement clause.

(27) *Lit   baba=ndu   tambar?*
      EXIST (UV:)bring=2s.ACT medicine
      'Did you bring any medicine?'

(28) *É   la   lit   ku=begi*
      ANAPH NEG EXIST 1s.ACT=hear
      'I didn't hear that (=I wasn't aware of that).'

3.2.2 Transitive clauses

The canonical transitive clause in Karo contains a verb relating two nominal participants, identifiable in semantic terms as Actor and Undergoer, following Foley and Van Valin (1984:29). Transitive clauses may be realized as actor-voice or as undergoer-voice.

When the actor occurs as subject, it normally occupies clause-initial position, the verb is marked for actor-voice with the inflectional prefix N^1- (glossed here as AV), and the undergoer is placed postverbally:

(29) *Embun me-kapal nutupi /N-tutup-i/   matawari.*
      cloud   ADJ-thick   AV-cover-LOC.APP   sun
      'Thick cloud obscured the sun.'

Other constituents such as adverbs of frequency or auxiliaries may intervene between these three core constituents of the actor-voice clause:

(30) *Si limbeng   lalap   maba /N-baba/ ranan /rana-en/.*
      PN Limbeng always   AV-carry   conversation-NR.UG
      'Limbeng kept the conversation going.'

(31) *Raja acéh   nimai /N-tima-i/   denga putri hijau.*
      king Aceh   AV-wait-LOC.APP   still   Putri Hijau
      'The King of Aceh was still waiting for Putri Hijau.'

Although the normal word order is Actor-Predicate-Undergoer, Predicate-Undergoer-Actor order is commonly found when the undergoer is expounded by an interrogative pronoun such as *ise* 'who' or *kai* 'what':

(32) *Nukur /N-tukur/ kai   kam ku   tiga?*
                AV-buy   what you   to   market
      'What did you buy at the market?'

Transitive clauses also allow undergoers to become subjects, in which case the undergoer may occur clause initially and the verb is prefixed with undergoer-voice marker *i* (glossed here as uv). Compare (29) above with (33) below:

(33) *Matawari i-tutup-i embun me-kapal.*
    sun   uv-cover-LOC.APP   cloud   ADJ-thick
    'The sun was obscured by thick cloud.'

More frequently however, the undergoer occurs after the verb + actor. Compare (31) above with (34) below:

(34) *I-tima-i raja acéh denga putri hijau.*
    uv-wait-LOC.APP   Raja Aceh   still   Putri Hijau
    'Raja Aceh still waited for Putri Hijau.'

When undergoers occur as subjects, the clause is analysed as consisting of two core constituents, Subject and Predicate, with the actor being part of the predicate. That the actor becomes part of the predicate is supported by a number of considerations, such as the placement of phrase stress upon the postverbal actor rather than upon the verb itself, and the occurrence of various post-modifying auxiliaries and operators after the postverbal actor, rather than between the undergoer-voice verb and actor.

When the actor in an undergoer-voice clause is expounded by a first person singular or inclusive pronoun (1s, 1pi), it is realized as a *pro*clitic and no prefix *i-* occurs, e.g. *ku = pekpek biang* 'I hit the dog'. If the actor is a second person singular or a third person pronoun, special *en*clitic forms are used and the verb is prefixed with *i-*, e.g. *i-pekpek = na biang* 'He/she/they hit the dog'. When expounded by other pronouns (*kam, kena, kami*), the actor remains formally unchanged and is placed postverbally, just like common nouns: *i-pekpek kami biang* 'we (excl) hit the dog'. See also Table 19.2 below.

The undergoer-voice prefix *i-* has a free variant *ni-* which occurs in some older texts. The prefix *i-* is frequently dropped by speakers in informal contexts, or in situations where other syntactic or pragmatic clues exist to define the clause as undergoer-voice. In examples in this chapter, the potential but unrealized presence of the undergoer-voice prefix is indicated by the gloss in parentheses (uv). The actor-voice prefix N^I-, however, can never be dropped, a fact which suggests that it is the more marked construction of the two. This correlates with the observation that indeed the undergoer-voice construction occurs much more frequently in Karo, and this too seems to correlate with the greater tendency towards predicate-first structures in the language.

As described above, the actor in an undergoer-voice transitive clause is always immediately adjacent to and structurally linked with the verb. It may also be omitted from the predicate phrase, when the identity of the actor is unknown or irrelevant, or indeed known but not stated so as to avoid directness, such as in imperatives:

(35) *I-palu me gendang suari berngi.*
    uv-beat EMPH drum   day   night
    'The drums were beaten day and night.'

(36) *Ola ni-ambek-ken!*
    PRH uv-throw-APP
    'Don't throw it out!'

As subjects are also omissible under certain conditions (such as their identity being able to be established from the immediate context), undergoer-voice clauses containing only one nominal constituent are potentially ambiguous with respect to the role of that NP. In such cases, pragmatic factors and/or intonation will normally help to resolve whether the

NP is actor or undergoer. Alternatively, the post-predicative discourse particle *me* may serve to disambiguate the role of the solitary NP. Compare the following:

(37) (a) *I-daram-i*   *guru*   **me**   *ku*   *kerangen.*
             UV-seek-LOC.APP   medicine.man   PTCL   to   forest
             'The medicine man looked (for it) in the forest.'

      (b) *I-daram-i*   **me**   *guru*   *ku*   *kerangen.*
             UV-seek-LOC.APP   PTCL   medicine.man   to   forest
             '(They) looked for the medicine man in the forest.'

In (a) *guru* is part of the predicate phrase (modified by *me*), therefore actor. In (b) *guru* lies outside the predicate phrase, and is therefore subject of the clause, and thus undergoer. In the absence of a context, the sentence *I-daram-i guru ku kerangen*, without *me*, is ambiguous between these two interpretations.

3.2.3 Subjectless constructions

As illustrated in the preceding sections, subjects in Karo are identifiable by their variable position before or after the predicate while non-subject arguments generally occur in post-predicate position. Furthermore, subjects may be deleted from the clause when understood (see examples above), they may launch a floating quantifier (as in (38); see also section 3.3) and they can be relativised (as in 39):

(38) *M-bué*   *usur*   *dat*   *raja*   *é*   *kapur barus.*
          ADJ-much   always   (UV:)get   chief   ANAPH   camphor
          'The chief always got plenty of camphor.'

(39) *Galuh*   *si*   *i-tukur=na*   *i*   *tiga*   *ndai*   *enggo*   *macik.*
          banana   REL   UV-buy=3.ACT   at   market   RCT   already   rotten
          'The bananas she bought at the market are already rotten.'

Of particular interest in Karo is the fact that a number of undergoer-voice constructions are found to contain no subject whatsoever. Such subjectless constructions embrace three types: undergoer-voice reflexives, undergoer-voice clauses of direction and reference (by 'reference' here is meant the notion conveyed by prepositions meaning 'about, concerning'), and undergoer-voice constructions which take complement clauses.

Actor-voice reflexives parallel regular actor-voice transitive clauses, consisting of three core constituents as described above, with the predicate expounded by an active-voice verb and the undergoer expounded by the invariant reflexive marker *bana* 'self':

(40) *Kam*   *muji /N-puji/*   *bana usur.*
          2s   AV-praise   RFL always
          'You're always praising yourself.'

By contrast, an undergoer-voice reflexive consists of a predicate and a dative prepositional phrase. The predicate comprises the verb inflected for undergoer-voice, plus an obligatory actor pronoun. The dative PP comprises an optional preposition *man* 'to, for' plus an obligatory head consisting of the reflexive bound morpheme *ba-* plus an enclitic personal pronoun which agrees in person and number with the actor.

(41) *Engkai*   *maka*   *pekpek=ndu*   *man*   *ba=ndu?*
          why   that   (UV:)hit=2s.ACT   DAT   INTSF=2s.POSS
          'Why did you hit yourself?'

(42)   *I-bunuh=na   ba=na.*
       UV-kill=3.ACT   INTSF=3.POSS
       'He killed himself.'

Although such clauses contain both an actor and (coreferential) undergoer, they are technically subjectless, with the undergoer accorded only peripheral syntactic status by virtue of its being encoded as a prepositional phrase. It is interesting that agreement is maintained between actor and undergoer in the undergoer-voice construction, but not the actor-voice construction, where all reflexive undergoers are subsumed by the invariant *bana*.

Undergoer-voice clauses of direction and reference are constructions characterized by a predicate manifested by a verb denoting motion, volitional perception, cognition or communication, an optional (usually pronominal) actor, and a prepositional phrase expressing direction or reference.

(43)   *I-tatap=na   i   datas   nari   ku   kelewet=na.*
       UV-look=3.ACT   at   top   from   to   surroundings=3.POSS
       'He gazed down from above, towards the surrounding area.'

(44)   *Lanai   i-ukur-i   tingtang   uis   m-baru.*
       no.longer   UV-think-ITER.APP   about   clothes   ADJ-new
       'There was no further thought given to new clothes.'

(45)   *I-gawang-i   unduk-unduk   é   ku   kayu   tertentu.*
       UV-creep-LOC.APP   caterpillar-caterpillar   ANAPH   to   tree   certain
       'The caterpillars crawled to a particular tree.'

Undergoer-voice constructions also often occur with a predicate containing a verb plus actor, followed by a reduced complement clause whose actor is coreferential with that of the main clause, and thus omitted. The reduced complement clause lacks essential subject properties (for example, it is positionally restricted, while most subjects are not). Therefore, this construction is also considered to be a subjectless construction.

(46)   *Ku=pala-pala-i   nge-lupa-ken   ia.*
       1s.ACT=endeavour-ITER.APP   AV-forget-APP   3
       'I tried hard to forget her.'

(47)   *La   si=eteh   naksir=sa /N-taksir=sa/*
       NEG   1pi.ACT=know   AV-estimate=3.UG
       'We don't know how to estimate it.'

These kinds of subjectless constructions are by no means unique to Karo; analagous patterns are found in Toba and Dairi Batak (van der Tuuk 1971:159–161, 175).

3.2.4 Word order and dislocations

Word order, or more specifically, subject-predicate ordering, is a complex phenomenon in Karo, and is dealt with only incidentally in this overview. As stated above, the general preference exhibited is for predicates to precede subjects (around two thirds of the time), but systematic exceptions occur, determined by such structural factors as clause type, interrogative mood, the dependent or independent status of the clause, the presence of prohibitive markers and fronted negatives, or the presence of a quantifier in the subject.

These are described in detail in Woollams (1996:275–282). In general terms, fronting of a constituent confers upon it some special prominence, and in transitive verbs particularly, this has particular morphological implications. Sometimes a nominal constituent may be 'extracted' or 'dislocated' from its normal position in the clause, and rendered into a clause external topic (optionally marked with one of a number of topic markers). The dislocated NP may be moved to the left or right of the clause, from which it is marked off by a separate intonation peak and a potential pause. It remains linked to the clause by an anaphoric pronoun, frequently a possessive:

(48) *Deleng   sinabun,   m-bué   kertah=na.*
      mountain   Sinabun   ADJ-much   sulphur=3.POSS
      'Mt. Sinabun, it is abundant in sulphur.'

(49) *Kam,   kai   tukur=ndu?*
      2s   what   (UG):buy=2s.ACT
      'You, what did you buy?'

(50) *Pagit   nanam=na,   tambar   é   ndai.*
      bitter   taste=3.POSS   medicine   ANAPH   RCT
      'It tastes bitter, that medicine.'

3.3 Noun phrase structure

Noun phrases in Karo consist of a head and various modifiers, most of which follow the noun, in the following order: possessive, descriptive, determiner, and apposition. Quantifiers, however, normally precede. The noun head itself may be manifested by various types of pronoun (personal, interrogative or indefinite), nouns, demonstratives, numerals or other nominalized forms including headless relative clauses. Personal pronouns are listed in Table 19.2 and discussed first.

   Some of the first and second possessive pronouns vary in form according to whether the word they are attached to ends in a vowel or consonant: *agi* 'younger brother', *agingku* 'my younger brother', *aginta* 'our younger brother', *agim* 'your younger brother'; compare *rumah* 'house', *rumahku* 'my house', *rumahta* 'our house', *rumahmu* 'your house'. Special second person pronouns exist to indicate politeness (*kena*) or familiarity (*engko, ko*). The use of the latter instead of the neutral *kam* is sometimes a matter of dialect difference, but mostly one of attitude, potentially denoting an assertion of superiority by the speaker to the addressee (in terms of age or authority), or intimacy and friendliness, or anger, admonition or insult. Agentive pronoun forms are used in undergoer-voice constructions, whilst objective forms are found in actor-voice constructions and after prepositions.

TABLE 19.2: PERSONAL PRONOUN MATRIX

	Independent	Possessive	Agentive	Objective
1s	aku	=(ng)ku	ku=	aku
1pi	kita	=(n)ta	si=	kita
1pe	kami	kami	kami	kami
2s/p	kam	=ndu	=ndu	kam
2s (familiar)	engko, ko	=m(u)	=m(u)	engko
2p (polite)	kena	kena	kena	kena
3s/p	ia	=na	=na, =sa	=sa/=ca

Quantifiers pre-modify noun heads. They comprise quantifiers proper such as *kerina* 'all', *piga-piga* 'several', *tiep-tiep~tep-tep* 'every', various quantifying adjectives (which are further modifiable or inflectable for degree) such as *nterem* 'many' (for people), *melala* 'many' (with count nouns), *mbué* 'many, much', or simple numerals: *sada* '1', *dua* '2', *telu* '3', *empat* '4', *lima* '5', *nem* '6', *pitu* '7', *waluh* '8', *siwah* '9'. Examples: *kerina kalak ah* (all person DIST1) 'all those people', *nterem kalak* 'many people', *telu wari* 'three days'. Higher numerals are formed by combining the simple numerals with group numbers *pulu* 'tens', *ratus* 'hundreds', *ribu* 'thousands'; in such combinations *sada* is manifested as *se-*: *seribu* '1000'. Similar to group numbers are various subclasses of measure nouns, which express standard volumes (*sada tumba beras* 'one tumba of rice, approx 2.5 litres'), informal measures (*sejemput sira* 'a pinch of salt'), clusters of objects (*sentandan galuh* 'a bunch of bananas'), whole objects (*selambar belo* 'a leaf of betel'), and units of time, length and currency (*sejengkal* 'a handspan').

Of interest in Karo is the phenomenon of quantifier 'floating', whereby a quantifier may split off from the head which it modifies, and move to the left or right. This is confined to cases of noun phrases which are grammatical subjects. In the following example, the quantifier in the phrase *kami kerina* 'all of us', occurs separate from its head in post-predicate position:

(51) *Minter*   kami *man /N-pan/* kerina
      straightaway 1pe   AV-eat   all
      'We all ate straightaway.'

Postmodifiers of the noun head include possessives; sometimes multiple embeddings occur:

(52) *i* *tengah kesain*   *kuta*   *kami*
      i   tengah [kesain   [kuta   [kami]]]
      at middle square   village   1pe.POSS
      'in the middle of our village square'

Descriptive modifiers of the noun head include adjectives (*kalak$_1$ bayak$_2$* 'rich$_2$ people$_1$'), nouns (*kite$_1$ buluh$_2$* 'bamboo$_2$ bridge$_1$'), prepositional phrases (*perlawes = ku ku Medan* (going = 1s.POSS to Medan) 'my going to Medan'), ordinal numbers (*jumpa$_1$ pemena$_2$* 'first$_2$ encounter$_1$') and relative clauses (*kade-kade = na si deher* (RDP-relative = 3.POSS REL near) 'his close relatives'). Not infrequently, a noun head modified by a relative clause may be omitted, when the identity of the noun itself is well established and therefore recoverable from the context. The resultant 'headless' relative clause then takes over as exponent of the noun head:

(53) *Isé* *(kalak)* *si*   *rëh*   *ndai*
      who   person   REL   come   RCT
      'Who was that who came before?'

If present in the NP, determiners always follow possessive and descriptive modifiers. They include the demonstrative pronouns *énda* 'close to the speaker' (PRX), *éna* 'close to the addressee' (MID), *ah* 'relatively distant from both parties' (DIST1), *oh* 'quite distant or out of sight' (DIST2) and *é* 'previously mentioned' (ANAPH). All of these may also occur as the noun head.

Another common determiner is the temporal adverb *ndai* 'recently', used to identify a participant recently referred to or somehow relevant to the context of shared experience between speaker and addressee. It may occur alone or in conjunction with other determiners:

(54) *Meser-sa gulen /gulé-en/   ah   ndai.*
      hot-too   cook-NR.UG   DIST1 RCT
      'Those vegetables were too hot.'

The apposition slot always occurs finally in a string of nominals, and more than one may occur:

(55) *Ola   inget   aku ini = ndu   datuk   rubia gandé.*
      PRH   (UV:)remember 1s   grandfather = 2s.POSS Datuk   Rubia Gandé
      'Don't think back to me, your grandfather, Datuk Rubia Gandé.'

3.4 Adjuncts

Adjuncts amplify information about the event or situation, typically expressing such notions as time, location, manner, instrument, reason, and so on. Formally their exponents vary greatly: NPs, PPs, verbs, adjectives and subordinate clauses. Although positionally they are quite mobile, they tend to occur clause initially or finally:

(56) *Pagi   er-pagi-pagi   jam   lima kita   berkat.*
      tomorrow   DTR-RDP-morning hour   five 1pi   depart
      'Tomorrow we leave at 5 a.m.'

(57) *Anjar-anjar kam   ku   teruh.*
      slow-slow   2s   to   below
      'Go down slowly.'

(58) *Ku = angka   sitik-sitik.*
      1s.ACT = understand little-little
      'I understand a little.'

Adpositional phrases are quite varied in Karo. In addition to a large number of pre-positions there is one postposition, *nari* 'from'. Locational PPs frequently contain a loca-tional noun or pronoun which refers to a specific locative orientation: *i das méja* (at top table) 'on top of the table', *ku képar lau é* (to opposite-side river ANAPH) 'to the other side of the river', *i ja nari kam?*(at where from 2) 'where do you come from?' Etymologically prepositions in Karo are a mixed bag. Some are 'pure' prepositions (*i* 'at', *ku* 'to', *ras* 'with'), others also serve as nouns (*arah* 1. 'in the vicinity of, 2. direction') and adjec-tives (*deher* 'near'), and many are derived from verbs (*erkitéken* 'because of'; lit. 'having a bridge to'). The prepositions *i* 'at' and *man* 'to, for' (dative in sense) are sometimes dropped in speech:

(59) *(Man) ba=ngku   énda?*
      DAT   INTSF=1s.POSS   PRX
      'Is this for me?'

3.5 Negation and other clause-level particles

The class of operators is a heterogenous set of mostly morphologically simple forms which modify predicates, subjects and adjuncts, but which cannot themselves occur as exponents of those constituents. They include negatives, particles, adjective modifiers, quantifying markers and aspect markers. Only the first two of these are described here.

The main negative markers are *la* 'not', *lenga* 'not yet' and *lanai* 'no longer'. Although most commonly found preceding the predicate, they may also occur clause initially and finally for emphasis. They may also stand alone as responses.

(60) *Aku   lenga   er-jabu.*
      1s   not.yet DTR-household
      'I'm not (yet) married.'

(61) *...perban   la   engko   er-nande,   la   engko   er-bapa.*
      because   NEG   2s.FAM   DTR-mother,   NEG   2s.FAM   DTR-father
      '...because you don't have a mother, you don't have a father.'

(62) *Pagi   pé   lanai,   kedun   pé   lanai.*
      tomorrow   EMPH   no.longer,   day.after.tomorrow   EMPH   no.longer
      'Not tomorrow, not the day after.'

A small number of verbs in Karo permit 'negative raising', whereby a negative marker is moved from the complement clause with which it is logically associated, and attached to the predicate of the main clause:

(63) *La   ku=kap   ia   rëh*   *[← Ku=akap   (ia la   rëh)]*
      NEG   1s.ACT=think 3   come   [1s.ACT=think (3   NEG   come)]
      'I don't think he is coming.'   [I think that he is not coming.]

Particles are mostly monosyllabic forms which post-modify other constituents. They cannot stand alone, but enter into phrase level constructions with the constituents they follow. Semantically, however, they tend to modify the whole clause in which they occur, adding important 'attitudinal flavour' such as encouragement, assurance, nonchalance, reservation, uncertainty, conviction, annoyance, and so on to the utterance. The meaning of a particle often varies according to whether the clause is in declarative, interrogative or imperative mood. About 17 in number, they comprise softening particles, emphatic particles, and discourse particles. Some examples are:

(64) *Ras   gia   kita.*
      together   SOF   1pi
      'I suppose you may as well come along with us.'

(65) *Kai   keh   isi   kujam=na?*
      what   EMPH   contents   purse=3.POSS
      'Goodness! What *has* she got in her purse?'

(66) *Adi   enggo   m-belin,   r-ukur /er-ukur/   kin!*
      if   already   ADJ-big   DTR-think   EMPH
      'If you are a grown-up, then *think* like one!'

(67) *Aku   kin   min   ndehara=na,   sikap   mis   ku=bahan.*
      1s   EMPH   SOF   wife=3.POSS   in.order   directly   1s.ACT=make
      'Now if I were his wife, I'd have everything set straight at once.'

3.6 Interrogatives and imperatives

Yes–no interrogatives in Karo are mostly structurally identical to declaratives, differing only in respect of the intonation contour (see section 2.3). Confirmation questions use the particle *ari* utterance finally:

(68) *Ia   enggo   er-jabu,   ari?*
     3   already   DTR-household   Q
     'He's already married, isn't he?'

Interrogative particles may be used to convey subtle information concerning the speaker's expectations:

(69) *Banci   kang   ku=pinjam   sekin=ndu?*
     may   PTCL   1s.ACT=borrow   knife=2s.POSS
     'May I borrow your knife?'

This question contains no special expectation on the speaker's part. Replacing the particle *kang* with *kin*, however, would mean the speaker assumes the listener will readily comply with the request ('Lend me your knife, will you?'). Use of another particle, *nge*, on the other hand, would indicate disbelief or surprise on the part of the speaker ('May I *really* borrow your knife?'). Using the rhetorical marker *ma* clause initially implies that the listener indeed knows that the statement is true:

(70) *Ma   enggo   er-jabu   ia?*
     PTCL   already   DTR-household   3
     'But he's already married, isn't he?'

Content questions contain interrogative words which expound a variety of syntactic roles but typically occur clause initially:

(71) *Isé   gelar=ndu?*
     who   name=2s.POSS
     'What is your name?'

(72) *Apai   kin   merga=ndu?*
     which   PTCL   clan=2s.POSS
     'What is your clan? (Which of the five clans do you belong to?)'

(73) *Kai   dahin=ndu /dahi-en=ndu/?*
     what   work-NR.UG=2s.POSS
     'What's your job?'

(74) *Ndiganai   kam   rëh?*
     when   2s   come
     'When did you come?'

(75) *Piga   kam   sembuyak?*
     how.many   2s   sibling
     'How many brothers and sisters do you have?'

The interrogative pronoun *kai* can be used as a verb, then taking verbal morphology:

(76) *Er-kai   kam   é?*
     DTR-what   2s   ANAPH
     'What are you doing?'

(77) *Eng-kai   kam   ku   jénda?*
     AV-what   2s   to   here
     'Why have you come here?'

Imperatives embrace a broad range of constructions whose illocutionary force is directive. The simplest imperatives involve omission of the second person subject/actor from the clause: *kundul!* 'Sit!', *Burihi pinggan enda* (rinse dish PRX) 'Rinse these dishes'. The imperativizing suffix *-ken* may be attached to intransitive verbs, unaffixed transitive verbs, and even PPs: *kundulken!* (sit-IMP) 'Sit down!' *bukaken!* (open-IMP) 'Open up!', *mari, ku basken lebe!* (HORT to inside-IMP first) 'Please come in!'. Other imperative and hortatory markers convey varying degrees of politeness, encouragement or urgency. The presence of an identifiable undergoer in the clause triggers undergoer-voice in transitive verbs; the actor (= addressee) and verb prefix *i-* are normally omitted (but may be retained), and actor-voice is not possible in such situations:

(78) *Buat*   *sitik*   *ba=ngku*   *téh*
      (UV:)make   PTCL   INTSF=1s.POSS   tea
      'Please make me some tea.'

(79) *Takal=ndu*   *é*   *i*   *babo*   *lau*   *i-ban!*
      head=2s.POSS   ANAPH   at   top   water   UV-make
      'Keep your head above the water!'

Prohibitions are signalled by *ula/ola*, and the addressee is as often retained as omitted:

(80) *Ula*   *kam*   *rëh*   *pagi.*
      PRH   2s   come   tomorrow
      'Don't come tomorrow.'

(81) *Ula*   *tawa-i=ndu*   *ia.*
      PRH   (UV:)laugh-LOC.APP=2s.ACT   3
      'Don't make fun of him.'

3.7 On the meaning and discourse function of the voice alternation

In attempting to better understand and define the functions of actor- and undergoer-voice in Karo, it is instructive to compare their distributions and relative frequency of occurrence. With respect to frequency, it is striking that across all genres of Karo discourse, undergoer-voice is statistically dominant. Around 7 out of every 10 transitive clauses in Karo are in undergoer-voice, and 9 out of every 10 of those undergoer-voice constructions occur independently. For active-voice the tendency is reversed, with more than two thirds of them occurring in dependent clauses.

Similar observations of the preponderance of undergoer-voice constructions (variously termed object-focus, or patient-focus, or goal-topic) over actor-voice constructions have been made for a variety of western Austronesian languages, including Toba Batak (Percival 1981:72; Wouk 1984:195), Tagalog (Hopper 1979; Hopper and Thompson 1980; Naylor 1986), Chamorro (Cooreman 1982), and certain varieties of Indonesian and Malay (Rafferty 1982:48; Cumming 1988:105).

In Karo, undergoer-voice correlates closely with perfective aspect or accomplishment-type semantics. An action which is viewed as a complete whole is typically encoded in undergoer-voice. Thus the following clause refers to the weaving of a mat as an accomplished, whole event:

(82) *I-bayu*   *nandé*   *amak.*
      UV-weave   mother   mat.
      'Mother wove a mat.'

By contrast, actions which are progressive, continuous or habitual (termed 'imperfective')
are expressed via actor-voice:

(83)   *Nandé   m-bayu   amak.*
       mother   AV-weave   mat
       'Mother is weaving a mat.'

This important distinction was alluded to by Neumann (1922:41–42) who neatly illustrated
the semantic contrast with a pair of imperative clauses:

(84)   *Ula   bunuh   kaba-kaba   é.*
       PRH   (UV:)kill   butterfly   ANAPH
       'Don't kill that butterfly!'

(85)   *Ula   munuh /N-bunuh/   kaba-kaba.*
       PRH   AV-kill   butterfly
       'Don't kill butterflies!'

In attempting to account for the determinants of voice selection in Karo, it is more useful
to regard undergoer-voice as the general unmarked transitive construction, and to identify
the relatively restricted grammatical environments in which actor-voice clauses occur.
   In dependent clauses, actor-voice is found in the following circumstances:

(i)   in relative clauses, when the relativised nominal is an actor:

(86)   *kalak   si   nukur /N-tukur/   galuh   ah*
       person   REL   AV-buy   banana   DIST1
       'the person who bought those bananas'

(ii)   in various reduced complement clauses where the (omitted) actor is coreferential
       with a participant in the main clause:

(87)   *Aku   la   beluh   nukur /N-tukur/   galuh.*
       1s   NEG   clever   AV-buy   banana
       'I'm not good at buying bananas.'

(iii)   in various reduced adverbial clauses where the (omitted) actor is coreferential with
        a participant in the main clause:

(88)   *Aku   ku   tiga   lako   nukur /N-tukur/   galuh.*
       1s   to   market   to   AV-buy   banana
       'I went to the market to buy bananas.'

(iv)   in secondary predicate constructions sharing a common actor:

(89)   *Lawes   ia   nading-ken /N-tading-ken/   kami.*
       go   3   AV-stay-CAU   1pe
       'He went, leaving us.'

In independent clauses, actor voice is found when:

(i)   the actor is realized by a demonstrative or interrogative pronoun:

(90)   *Isé   nukur-sa /N-tukur-sa/   galuh   énda?*
       who   AV-buy-PFV   banana   PRX
       'Who bought these bananas?'

(ii) when the actor is emphasized or particularized, usually through extra phonological stress and/or post-modifying particles:

(91) *Kam   nge   rusur   muat /N-buat/   galuh   ah.*
      2s   EMPH   always   AV-take   banana   DIST1
      'You're the one always taking those bananas!'

(iii) when the actor in a reflexive clause is not a pronoun:

(92) *Bukti=na   n-cidah-ken   bana.*
      proof=3.POSS   AV-see-CAU   RFL
      'The evidence revealed itself.'

The perfective-imperfective aspectual distinction inherent in the actor-undergoer voice dichotomy is effectively confined to those independent clauses where voice is not grammatically determined. Thus when an actor-voice clause is employed in response to the circumstances of the superordinate construction or by virtue of the lexical identity or need for emphasis of the actor, it is no longer automatically to be interpreted as imperfective in meaning. Thus sentence (93) has a clearly perfective meaning, but is in actor-voice in accordance with the rules of relative clause formation:

(93) *Isé   si   man /N-pan/   galuh=ku   ndai?*
      who   REL   AV-eat   banana=1s.POSS   RCT
      'Who ate my banana?'

Where necessary, perfective aspect may be more explicitly signalled on a compulsorily active verb, by means of the suffix *-sa*. In the following examples, habitual or progressive readings are vitiated by the perfective suffix:

(94) *Isé   ndai   maké-sa   payung=ku?*
      who   RCT   AV-use-PFV   umbrella=1s.POSS
      'Who used my umbrella?'

(95) *Kalak   gutul   ah   nangko-sa /N-tangko-sa/   sen=ku.*
      person   bad   DIST1   AV-steal-PFV   money=1s.POSS
      'That bad fellow stole my money.'

4 MAJOR VERBAL ALTERNATIONS

Voice alternations in Karo are dealt with in sections 3.2.2 and 3.7. The morphology commonly found on intransitive verbs is mentioned in section 3.2.1. This section is concerned with other verbal morphology, in particular the marking of potentive verbs (4.1) and applicatives (4.2).

4.1 Decontrolled undergoer-voice constructions

The preceding account of undergoer-voice transitive clauses in section 3.2.2 describes such constructions as they occur in dynamic mode, marked by the prefix *i-*. Such constructions may also occur in decontrolled mode, which is marked by the prefix *ter-*. More precisely, there are two *ter-* prefixes, one expressing an abilitative or potential meaning glossed here as POT, the other conveying a sense of accidental, unintentional or spontaneous action glossed as ACL.

(96) *La   kal   ter-jabap   aku   penungkunen /peN-sungkun-en/ é.*
      NEG   EMPH   POT-answer   1s.ACT   NR-ask-NR   ANAPH
      'I wasn't able to answer that question at all.'

(97) *Ter-képar-i=ndu   nge   titi   é?*
      POT-other.side-LOC.APP=2s.ACT   EMPH   bridge ANAPH
      'Are you able to cross that bridge?'

(98) *Legi   sitik piso   é,   ter-ambek-ken   aku   ndai.*
      (UV:)fetch SOF   knife ANAPH ACL-throw-APP   1s.ACT before
      'Go and find that knife for me please, I threw it out by mistake.'

(99) *Ula kam kari   ter-sayat   dilah.*
      PRH   2s   later ACL-slice   tongue
      'Don't say something you'll regret later! (= Don't be cut by your own tongue!)'

Structurally these two constructions are virtually identical, with the actor always in immediate postverbal position. First person pronominal actors occur in full form, second and third person usually occur as enclitics, with the third person agentive pronoun realized as =sa. The constructions differ in that with abilitatives, the actor is freely omissible, but with accidentals, it is unusual for the actor not to be expressed. Furthermore, the actor in accidentals may sometimes be found encoded in a prepositional phrase:

(100) *Ter-begi   man   ba=na   sora   kalak   rendé /er-endé/.*
      ACL-hear   DAT   INTSF=3.POSS   voice   person   DTR-sing
      'Suddenly she heard somebody singing.'

In such cases the actor is really more an experiencer than an agent, and its relegation to a peripheral position is consistent with the diminution of responsibility for, or control over, the action. It is either performed without the actor's intention to do so, or it lies beyond the actor's capacity to perform it. This marking of non-volitional behaviour on the part of the actor is common in Indonesian languages (see Cartier 1978; Wouk 1980; Durie 1985). Although it is more transparently compatible with *ter-* accidentals, the notion of decontrol fits well with abilitatives too, in that these constructions typically occur in interrogative or negated clauses, in which cases there is explicit uncertainty or denial about the actor's degree of control over the action.

   Subjectless undergoer-voice clauses (see section 3.2.3) may also be marked for decontrol; these are mostly abilitatives:

(101) *La   ter-dahi=sa   ku   jah.*
      NEG   POT-visit=3.ACT   to   D.ADV
      'He was unable to go there.'

4.2 Verbal and adjectival derivations, including causatives and applicatives

Karo possesses a number of important derivational affixes whose function is to create new transitive verb stems from other word classes, as well as a set of affixes which derive intransitive verbs and adjectives.

   The major transitivising verb affixes are *-i*, *-ken*, *pe-* and *per-*, and their combinations *pe-...-i*, *per-...-i*, *pe-...-ken* and *per-...-ken*. The stems thus formed are subject to further affixation with the voice affixes, depending upon the circumstances of the clause in which they occur.

Suffix *-i* operates primarily on adjectives, intransitive verbs and nouns, to form transitive verbs with a locative applicative meaning: *dauh* 'far' → *dauhi* 'to avoid', *cirem* 'smile' → *ciremi* 'to smile at', *sira* 'salt' → *sirai* 'to put salt on', *laklak* 'bark' → *laklaki* 'debark'.

Suffix *-ken* operates on all open word classes, producing verbs with a variety of meanings. With some adjectives, intransitive verbs and nouns, the meaning is causative: *keri* 'depleted' → *keriken* 'to deplete', *pekara* 'lawsuit' → *pekaraken* 'turn into a legal matter'. With verb stems referring to cognition or communication, the *-ken* derivative acquires a prepositional meaning: *ertoto* 'pray' → *totoken* 'pray for', *ngerana* 'talk' → *ranaken* 'talk about, discuss'. Derivatives with *-ken* often take an undergoer which denotes the instrument employed in the action: *ambekken batu* 'throw a stone', *tukurken sén* 'spend money' (from *tukur* 'buy').

The prefix *pe-* is similar to *-ken* in mainly deriving causative verb stems from adjectives, intransitive verbs and nouns, but it is of much higher frequency: *malem* 'cured' → *pemalem* 'to cure', *pulung* 'to gather' → *pepulung* 'to collect', *darat* 'outside' → *pedarat* 'to send outside'. Not all roots which take *pe-* can also be suffixed with *-ken*, but when this does occur, the *pe-* derivative is mostly associated either with a human or personified actor, or a concrete rather than abstract undergoer, suggesting a greater degree of intentional causation. *Pe-* derivatives do not normally bear the active-voice prefix N^1-, though some have acquired the regular inflection: *uli* 'beautiful, good' → *pehuli* 'to repair' → *mehuli* 'to repair (AV)'.

Least frequent of the transitivizing prefixes is *per-*, which also has a causative meaning: *dua* 'two' → *perdua* 'to divide in half', *nandé* 'mother' → *pernandé* 'consider as one's mother'.

Combinations with *pe-*...*-ken* and *pe-*...*-i* have a more intensive causative meaning, 'to make more...': *ganjang* 'high', *peganjang* 'to put up high', *peganjangken* 'to put up even higher'; *bentar* 'white', *pebentari* 'to make whiter'. Derivations with the circumfixes *per-*...*-ken* and *per-*...*-i* are relatively few; they express prepositional and causative-cum-locative meanings, respectively: *ernipi* 'dream' → *pernipiken* 'to dream about', *sabah* 'wet rice field' → *persabahi* 'to utilize as a wet rice field'.

Various affixes serve to derive new intransitive verbs; of these, *er-* is the most productive, forming intransitive verbs with characteristically stative (rather than eventive) meanings, and often conveying a sense of possession or utilization: *jabu* 'household' → *erjabu* 'to be married', *uis* 'clothing' → *ruis* 'to wear clothes'. The related circumfix *er-*...*-ken* means 'to utilize...as': *uis* 'clothing' *guni* 'sack' → *ruisken guni* 'to wear a sack for clothing'.

Prefixes N^2- and N^5- (differing in allomorphic variation) create new intransitive verbs and adjectives respectively, often from bound roots; their meanings are not as predictable or systematic: *darat* 'outside' → *ndarat* 'to go outside', *kawil* 'hook' → *ngkawil* 'to fish', *erdang* 'sow' → *merdang* 'to sow rice'. Prefix *me-* makes adjectives from some nouns: *teruh* 'underneath' → *meteruh* 'low', anak 'child' → *meanak* 'doting'. The circumfix *si-*...*-en* has two distinct meanings; based on transitive verb stems, it denotes reciprocity (*tatap* 'look' → *sitatapen* 'gaze at each other', *pedauhi* 'avoid' → *sipedauhen* 'avoid each other', from *dauh* 'far'). With adjective stems, however, it means 'differing in respect of...': *gedang* 'long' → *sigedangen* 'of different lengths'. The circumfix *si-*.....*-na* makes intransitive verbs with a distributive sense: *sindarami panganna* (si-n-daram-i pangan = na) 'each look for their own food'.

Two forms create stative derivatives bearing the meaning 'adversely affected by the referent of the stem': *-en* and *ke-*...*-en*. These derive mainly from nouns, adjectives, intransitive verbs and bound roots: *panas* 'perspiration' → *panasen* 'sweating', *bergeh* 'cold' → *bergehen* 'feeling cold', *tading* 'remain' → *ketadingen* 'left behind', *biar* '(fear)' → *kebiaren* 'gripped by fear'.

Affixes on adjectives are a complex and often irregular set, which include the predicative prefixes *me-* and N^3- (*gegeh* → *megegeh* 'strong', *erga* → *meherga* 'expensive', *bergeh* → *mbergeh* 'cold', *dauh* → *ndauh* 'far', *anjar-anjar* → *manjar-anjar* 'slow'), the comparative suffix *-en* (*gegehen* 'stronger', *ergan* 'more expensive'), the circumfix *ter-...-en* which marks intensive comparative degree (*terbergehen* 'even colder', *terdauhen* 'further still'), and the excessive degree marker *-sa* (*mehergasa* 'too expensive', *ndauhsa* 'too far'). The latter sometimes occurs with intransitive verbs:

(102)   *Ola   ngandung-sa,   ola   tawa-sa.*
      PRH   cry-too   PRH   laugh-too
      'Don't cry too much, don't laugh too much.'

It should be noted that many of the affixes mentioned in this section also occur in non-derivational functions. Most importantly, *-ken* is also an imperative marker, attached to intransitive verb stems, unsuffixed transitive verb stems, and some adjectives (*sikap* 'ready' → *sikapken!* 'Get ready!'; *nangkih* 'climb' → *nangkihken!* 'All aboard!'). The suffix *-i* attached to transitive verb stems adds an iterative meaning: *pekpek* 'hit → *pekpeki* 'hit repeatedly'. The suffix *-en* attached to intransitive verb stems signals multiplicity of action or that the action occurs en masse: *mate* 'die' → *maten* 'all die', *cires* 'leak' → *ciresen* 'leak everywhere'.

5 NOMINAL MORPHOLOGY

Karo possesses an array of nominalizing affixes which frequently correlate with verbal affixes. Only productive formations are described here.

The prefix *peN-* forms nouns from (mostly transitive) verbs with prefix *N-*: *maké* 'to wear' → *pemaké* 'way of wearing '(from *paké* 'wear'), *ngisap* 'to smoke' → *pengisap* 'smoker' (from *isap* 'cigarette'). When based on verbs with *-i* or *-ken*, the resultant noun sometimes drops the suffix; this loss is not predictable: *ngerakuti* 'to bind' → *pengerakuti* 'way of binding' (<*rakut*), *nampati* 'help' → *penampat* 'assistance' (<*sampat*). Nouns with *peN-* have four possible meanings: (a) the agent of the action: *mindo-mindo* 'to beg' → *pemindo-mindo* 'beggar', (b) the way the action is performed: *ndabuh* 'to fall' → *pendabuh* 'way of falling', (c) action nominal: *meteh* 'to know' → *pemeteh* 'knowing, knowledge', or (d) the product or result of the action: *meréken* 'to give' → *pemeré* 'gift'.

Nouns with *per-* are derived mainly from adjectives and intransitive verbs (many with prefix *er-*, which *per-* parallels morphologically). Their meanings are similar to those for *peN-* above: (a) actor or doer, and bearing in mind that the meaning of the original verb/adjective is often more stative than dynamic, the resultant forms often refer to occupations or personality characteristics: *erjuma* 'to work the field' → *perjuma* 'farmer', *sinik* 'quiet' → *persinik* 'a taciturn person'; (b) way or manner: *turah* 'grow' → *perturah* 'way of growing'; (c) action nominal: *lawes* 'go' → *perlawes* 'going, departure'.

The circumfix *peN-...-en* also produces derivatives from verbs, similar to *peN-*, meaning either (a) action nominal: *mindo* 'ask for' → *pemindon* 'request', or (b) the place where the action is carried out: *nutu* 'pound (rice)' → *penutun* 'place to pound'. In similar fashion, *per-...-en* makes nouns from mostly intransitive stems, meaning (a) the fact of the action or situation: *pulung* 'assemble' → *perpulungen* 'gathering', or (b) place: *ridi* 'bathe' → *peridin* 'bathing place'. Additionally *per-*...*-en* makes collective nouns from count nouns: *bapa* 'father' → *perbapan* 'the fathers', *juma* 'field' → *perjuman* 'fields'.

Whereas *peN-* derives nouns which correspond to active verbs, the suffix *-en* derives nouns with undergoer type meanings. Examples of such correspondences are given with the verbs cited in undergoer voice: *ibaba* 'carried' → *baban* 'load, burden', *iranaken* 'to be discussed' → *ranan* 'discussion, talk', *itawai* 'to be laughed at' → *tawan* 'laughing-stock'. Such forms often occur in apposition with other nouns: *barang* 'goods' + *itangko* 'to be stolen' → *barang tangkon* 'stolen goods', *amak* 'mat' + *ikunduli* 'to be sat on' → *amak kundulen* 'a mat for sitting on'. Many *-en* nouns also appear in purpose prepositional phrases, expressing an obligative sense: *ibaba* 'to be carried' → *man baban* 'for carrying, to be carried', *ikunduli* 'to be sat on' → *man kundulen* 'for sitting on'. Interestingly, such purpose nouns on *-en* which are derived from verbs bearing a *pe-* or *-ken* affix retain that verb affix (note the position of *-en*!): *i-pe-sikap* 'made ready' → *man pesikapen* 'for preparing, should be prepared', *i-begi-ken* 'listened to' → *man beginken* (/begi-en-ken/) 'for listening to', *i-rana-ken* 'discussed' → *man rananken* (/rana-en-ken/) 'to be discussed'. That these forms are essentially nominals is attested by their potential for modification by possessives:

(103) *Kai   denga   si   man   rananken=ta /rana-en-ken=ta/?*
      what   still   REL   DAT   talk:NR.UG.APP=1pi.POSS
      'What else is there for us to discuss?'

The circumfix *ke-*...*-en* derives nouns from adjectives and intransitive verb roots, with a resultant abstract meaning: *bayak* 'rich' → *kebayaken* 'wealth', *nggeluh* 'to live' (from the bound root *geluh*) → *kegeluhen* 'life', *dung* 'finished' → *kedungen* 'conclusion'. The circumfix *kini-*...*-en* has a similar function and meaning, but it can also operate on negated adjectives: *uli* 'good' → *kiniulin* 'goodness', *latih* 'tired' → *kinilatihen* 'weariness', *la bujur* 'dishonest' → *kinilabujuren* 'dishonesty', *la beluh* 'not clever' → *kinilabeluhen* 'stupidity'.

Finally, the suffix *-na* creates nouns from adjective roots, compound adjectives and intransitive verb roots: *sui* 'ill, painful' → *suina* 'the pain of', *beluh* 'clever' → *beluhna* 'the cleverness of', *dabuh* 'to fall' → *dabuhna* 'the falling, descent of', *la lit* 'there is not' → *la litna* 'the absence of'. The English glosses of the forms above reflect some significant aspects of both the syntax and semantics of the nominalizer *-na*. Such nouns are always modified by a possessor, and linked to this is the observation that the derived nouns refer to a specific instance of the quality exhibited by, or event affecting, that possessor. Whereas *ke-*...*-en* and *kini-*...*-en* nouns are more abstract in meaning (as in 104), *-na* nouns refer to some 'concrete' or 'actual' situation (as in 105).

(104) *Kiniulinna /kini-uli-en=na/*   *enggo   ter-berita   ku   kerina   kuta.*
      NR-good-NR=3.POSS   already   POT-news   to   all   village
      'His reputation as a good man was well known in all the villages.'

(105) *...ng-inget   uli-**na**   ukur   appung   barus   man   ba=na*
      AV-remember   good-NR   heart   Appung   Barus   DAT   INTSF=3.POSS
      '... recalling the kindness of Appung Barus towards him.'

The use of *ulina* in the preceding example refers to some particular instance(s) of good behaviour on the part of Appung Barus, whereas *kiniulinna* in the sentence before that refers to the more abstract notion of the general personality trait possessed by him.

REFERENCES

Adelaar, K.A. (1981) 'Reconstruction of Proto-Batak Phonology', in R.A. Blust (ed.) *Historical linguistics in Indonesia*, Part 1, *NUSA* 10: 1–20.

Cartier, A. (1978) 'On *Ke-* Verb Sentences in Indonesian', in S.A. Wurm and L. Carrington (eds) *Second International Conference on Austronesian Linguistics*. Pacific Linguistics, C-61: 463–482.

Chambert-Loir, H. (1974) 'La sauvegarde des littératures régionales indonésiennes', *Archipel* 7: 175–198.

Cooreman, A. (1982) 'Topicality, ergativity and transitivity in narrative discourse: evidence from Chamorro', *Studies in Language* 6: 343–374.

Cumming, S.A. (1988) *Syntactic function and constituent order change in Malay*. PhD dissertation, University of California, Los Angeles.

Durie, M. (1985) 'Control and decontrol in Acehnese', *Australian Journal of Linguistics* 5: 43–53.

Foley, W.A. and Van Valin, Jr., R.D. (1984) *Functional syntax and universal grammar*, Cambridge: Cambridge University Press.

Hopper, P.J. (1979) 'Aspect and foregrounding in discourse', in T. Givon (ed.) *Syntax and semantics*, vol. 12: *Discourse and syntax*, 213–241, New York: Academic Press.

Hopper, P.J. and Thompson, S.A. (1980) 'Transitivity in grammar and discourse', *Language* 56: 251–299.

Joustra, M. (1904) *Karo-Bataksche Vertellingen*, Verhandelingen van het Bataviaasch Genootschap van Kunsten en Wetenschappen 56.

——(1907) *Karo-Bataksch woordenboek*, Leiden: E.J. Brill.

Kozok, U. (1996) 'Bark, bones and bamboo: Batak traditions of Sumatra', in A. Kumar and J. McGlynn (eds) *Illuminations. The writing traditions of Indonesia*, 231–246, Jakarta: The Lontar Foundation.

Naylor, P.B. (1986) 'On the pragmatics of focus', in P. Geraghty, L. Carrington and S.A. Wurm (eds) *FOCAL I: Papers from the Fourth International Conference on Austronesian Linguistics*, 43–57, Canberra: Pacific Linguistics.

Neumann, J.H. (1922) *Schets der Karo-Bataksche spraakkunst*, Verhandelingen van het Bataviaasch Genootschap van Kunsten en Wetenschappen 58.

——(1951) *Karo-Bataks-Nederlands woordenboek*, Djakarta: Lembaga Kebudajaan Indonesia.

Parkin, H. (1978) *Batak fruit of Hindu thought*, Madras: The Christian Literature Society.

Percival, W.K. (1981) *A grammar of the urbanised Toba-Batak of Medan*, Canberra: Pacific Linguistics.

Rafferty, E. (1982) 'Discourse Structures of the Chinese Indonesian of Malang', *NUSA* 12.

Singarimbun, Masri (1960) *1000 Perumpaman Karo*, Medan: Ulih Saber.

——(1975) *Kinship, descent and alliance among the Karo Batak*, Berkeley: University of California Press.

Tarigan, H. G. (1965) *Nuré-Nuré di Karo*, Bandung: Perhimpunan 'Sada Perarih'.

Tuuk, H.N. van der (1971) *A grammar of Toba Batak* (Koninklijk Instituut Voor Taal-, Land- en Volkenkunde Translation Series 13), The Hague: Nijhoff [first edition, 1864–1867, *Tobasche spraakkunst*, 2 vols, Amsterdam: Muller].

Viner, A.C. (1979) 'The changing Batak', *Journal of the Malaysian Branch of the Royal Asiatic Society* 52: 84–112.

Voorhoeve, P. (1955) *Critical survey of studies on the languages of Sumatra*, The Hague: Nijhoff.

——(1961) *The Chester Beatty Library: A catalogue of the Batak manuscripts, including two Javanese manuscripts and a Balinese painting*, Dublin: Hodges.

Woollams, G. (1996) *A grammar of Karo Batak, Sumatra*, Canberra: Pacific Linguistics.

Wouk, F. (1980) 'The *ter-* prefix in Indonesian: a semantic analysis', in P.B. Naylor (ed.) *Austronesian studies: papers from the second eastern conference on Austronesian languages*, 81–87 (Michigan Papers on South and Southeast Asia 15). Ann Arbor: Center for South and Southeast Asian Studies, University of Michigan.
——(1984) 'Scalar transitivity and trigger choice in Toba Batak', in P. Schachter (ed.) *Studies in the structure of Toba Batak*, UCLA Occasional Papers in Linguistics 5: 195–219.

CHAPTER TWENTY

NIAS

Lea Brown

1 INTRODUCTION

1.1 Language area and speakers

Nias is spoken on the island of Nias, one of a group of islands known as the Barrier Islands, which stretch along the west coast of Sumatra. It is also spoken on the Batu Islands to the south of the main island of Nias. The other large islands in the Barrier chain are Simeuluë to the north of Nias, and Siberut, Sipora, the Pagai Islands and Enggano to the south. The languages Sichule and Simeuluë are spoken on the island of Simeuluë. Sichule is clearly very closely related to Nias, as shown by Kähler (1955, 1963). Simeuluë is regarded by Kähler (1963) as Western Malayo-Polynesian but not closely related to Nias. Based on evidence from phonetic, semantic and lexical innovations, Nothofer (1986) claims that Simeuluë and Sichule, along with the Mentawai language, spoken on Siberut, Sipora and the Pagai Islands, and Enggano, the language spoken on Enggano Island, about 400 km to the south of the other islands, form a genetic subgroup with the Batak languages of Northern Sumatra (see also Nothofer 1994).

The population of Nias and the Batu Islands was estimated at 639,675 in 1998 (Kabupaten Nias 2000). There are three major speech varieties in Nias, one spoken in the north, which is the prestige variety and has the largest number of speakers, one spoken in the central region, and one spoken in the south, including the Batu Islands. This chapter describes the features of the southern dialect, Nias Selatan, with comments on variation when relevant.

Nias village chiefs have traded with Chinese and Acehnese merchants for a long time. The main exports of Nias used to be slaves and coconuts, and the main import was gold. Contact with Europeans has been known since the early seventeenth century, when both the Dutch and the English had trading interests in Nias. In 1756, the English set up a trading post in Gunungsitoli in the north-east of the island. This post was relinquished to the Dutch by treaty in 1825, who maintained it until the Japanese invasion in World War II.

1.2 Major sources

There have been two major grammatical studies of Nias published: one in German by Sundermann (1913), and one in Indonesian by Halawa *et al.* (1983). There is also a useful learner's grammar (Fries 1915) based on Sundermann (1913), which presents Sundermann's data in a systematic form and includes additional examples. Brown (2001) is a grammar of the southern dialect. Kähler (1936–7) is a series of three papers which analyse aspects of Sundermann's grammar, using then newly available historical material from Otto Dempwolff and insights from comparisons with other Austronesian languages.

Other articles concerned with Nias grammar are Pätsch (1964a,b), which examine pronominal and verbal morphology, and Catford (1988), on the phonetics and phonology of Nias. Pätsch (1978) analyses Nias words and morphosyntax in search of retentions from Proto-Austronesian. There are four dictionaries available: Nias–Malay–Dutch (Thomas and Taylor Weber 1887), German–Nias (Sundermann 1892a), Nias–German (Sundermann 1905a), and Nias–Indonesian (Laiya 1985). Although there is an immense corpus of anthropological studies of Nias, which include many song texts with translations into Dutch or German, the only non-poetic collection of texts in Nias which have translations (in German) are those in Sundermann (1905b), and a small number in Sundermann (1892b). Steinhart and Maier (1990) is a translation into Dutch and English of a song text from the Batu Islands.

All of the grammatical studies of Nias to date, except for Brown (2001) and brief comments in Sundermann's (1913) grammar, are concerned with the northern dialect. While there are significant numbers of lexical differences between dialects, as well as different grammatical morphemes, much of the basic morphosyntax of the dialects is the same. Where differences are known to exist between the northern and southern dialects, they will be noted in this chapter.

The data used in this article are taken from the author's own corpus of oral texts collected in 1993–4 and 1996 from speakers from the village of Botohilitanö.

2 PHONOLOGY AND ORTHOGRAPHY

2.1 Segment inventory, syllable structure and stress

The segment inventory of Nias Selatan consists of twenty-two consonants and six vowels. One consonant in Nias is quite rare in the world's languages (although it is found in a number of Austronesian languages): a bilabial trill, [ʙ]. According to Ladefoged and Maddieson (1996:130), the bilabial trill in Nias is unique because it can be followed by any vowel – in all other languages examined by them in which a bilabial trill occurs it is followed by [u], and has developed from increased labiality involved in anticipatory articulation of the rounded vowel. In slow speech it is sometimes possible to detect prenasalization of [ʙ] in intervocalic contexts in Nias Selatan, but not in utterance-initial position (although according to Catford (1988:154), it occurs in some instances in initial position in the northern dialect). Frequently in Nias Selatan the bilabial trill is pronounced as a bilabial fricative.

The consonant phonemes of Nias Selatan are listed in Table 20.1. Their phonetic realizations are given in square brackets.

The phoneme inventory for northern Nias includes an additional phoneme, a velar nasal, /ŋ/, but lacks the affricate /c/ ([t͡ʃ]). In addition the affricate /z/ ([d͡ʒ]) is pronounced as an alveolar fricative, [z], in northern Nias. Note that vowel-initial words are usually pronounced with an initial glottal when occurring in isolation (the phonemic status of this glottal remains to be determined).

The vowels in all dialects of Nias are the same, as listed in Table 20.2.

The syllable in Nias may have the form V or CV. There are no syllable-final consonants, and no consonant clusters. Affricates and the stop with trilled release are unit phonemes. There are no phonemic long vowels.

The majority of simple nouns and verbs are disyllabic. A number of simple nouns are trisyllabic, but very few verbs are. There is a small set of monosyllabic lexical forms, perhaps fifteen at most, of which all but two or three are nouns. Some examples of these are *bu* 'hair', *ö* 'food', *a* 'eat'.

TABLE 20.1: CONSONANT PHONEMES OF NIAS SELATAN

	Labial	Labio-dental	(Dento-)alveolar	(Alveo-)palatal	Velar	Labio-velar	Glottal
Stops							
voiceless			t		k		' [ʔ]
voiced	b		d		g		
trilled release			ndr [dʳ]				
Nasals	m		n				
Fricatives							
voiceless		f	s		kh [x]		h
voiced		v					
Affricates							
voiceless				c [tʃ]			
voiced				z [dʒ]			
Trills	mb [ʙ]		r				
Lateral			l				
Approximants		ß [ʋ]		y [j]		w	

TABLE 20.2:   VOWEL PHONEMES IN NIAS

	Front	Central	Back
High	i		u
Mid	e	ö [ɤ]	o
Low		a	

Apart from a small number of words which are inherently stressed on the final syllable (e.g. *ato* [ʔató] 'many (people)', *ara* [ʔará] 'be/take a long time') most full words are stressed on the penultimate syllable when spoken in isolation, e.g. *fanikhakha* [fanixáxa] 'advice'. All suffixes are counted as syllables for the assignment of stress, such that stress always falls on the syllable preceding monosyllabic suffixes and on the first syllable of the suffix if it is disyllabic. Compare, for example, *ína* 'mother' with *iná-gu* 'my mother' and *ina-nía* 'his/her mother'. No prefixes are counted as part of the word for the assignment of stress.

2.2 Morphophonological alternations: nasal assimilation

Transitive verb stems which are made imperfective with the prefix *aN-* and its derivations undergo changes to their initial segments (see 3.4.5 for discussion of the prefix *maN-*, section 5 for examples of *aN-* and *faN-*, section 3.5.2 and examples (8) and (79) for *saN-*). Since Nias allows neither syllable-final consonants nor consonant clusters, the nasal coda in these prefixes cannot be realized consonantally in front of a stem-initial consonant. The most common changes that occur to resolve this problem are listed below (with examples using the prefix *maN-*). For the sake of morphological clarity in glossing forms containing a prefix of the shape *(C)aN-*, prefixes are separated from the base before the fused consonant or before a stem-initial vowel:

/b/, /f/, /t/, /c/ and /s/ are generally replaced with homorganic nasals, e.g. *ma-me* 'giving' from *be* 'give', *ma-make* 'using' from *fake* 'use', *ma-nibo* 'throwing away' from *cibo* 'throw away'. Note that in about eight verbs, /b/ is replaced with a bilabial trill and the prefix vowel changes to /o/, e.g. *mo-mbaso* 'reading' from *baso* 'read', *mo-mböβöi* 'creating' from *böβöi* 'create'.

/z/ is replaced by /n/ in some verbs, e.g. *ma-nuzu* 'climbing' from *zuzu* 'climb'. In other verbs it remains, and the prefix vowel changes to /o/: *mo-zuzu-ni* 'splitting with wedge' from *zuzu-ni* 'split with wedge'.

In vowel-initial verbs, with the exception of verbs beginning with /o/, the default form of the prefix is attached, i.e. *man-*, e.g. *man-alui* 'looking for' from *alui* 'look for', *man-ötö* 'crossing' from *ötö* 'cross'. Verbs beginning with /o/ are anomalous in appearing to gain a prothetic /l/, and in taking the /o/ variant of the prefix, e.g. *mo-lohe* 'carrying' from *ohe* 'carry'.

In all of the remaining instances the prefix vowel is /o/ rather than /a/.

/β/ remains the same in most verbs, e.g. *mo-βuβusi* 'breathing' from *βuβusi* 'breathe'. In at least one verb /β/ is replaced with the bilabial trill, e.g. *mo-mbaβalö* 'borrowing' from *βaβalö* 'borrow'.

/d/ and /r/ are generally replaced by the alveolar stop with trilled release, /ndr/, e.g. *mo-ndröli* 'pulling' from *döli* 'pull', *mo-ndrino* 'boiling' from *rino* 'boil'.

/k/ and /kh/ are replaced by /g/, e.g. *mo-gaoni* 'calling out' from *kaoni* 'call out', *mo-gau* 'fining, sentencing' from *khau* 'fine, sentence'.

/ndr/, /n/, /l/ and /h/ remain the same, e.g. *mo-ndrandra* 'plaiting' from *ndrandra* 'plait', *mo-nönö* 'adding' from *nönö* 'add', *mo-lau* 'doing' from *lau* 'do', *mo-halö* 'holding, taking' from *halö* 'hold, take'.

The consonants /m/, /mb/, /v/, /g/ and /y/ do not occur in initial position of transitive verb stems and the consonant /w/ occurs only on one verb, *waö* 'say', which takes the form *maö* in those contexts in which other transitive verbs occur in their *maN-* forms.

2.3 Reduplication

Reduplication occurs with some measure of productivity only in verb stems in Nias, although historically it has played an important role in the derivation of nouns (see section 5). There are two kinds of reduplication processes, one which copies the initial syllable of a stem and one which copies the first two syllables. The two reduplication processes appear not to co-occur.

Initial syllable reduplication (RDP1) copies the initial consonant and vowel of consonant-initial verb roots and the initial vowel of vowel-initial verbs, respectively. In verbs which refer to physical actions, which are almost all consonant-initial, the process can indicate iterative action (usually of a quick and small nature), exhaustiveness of an action or plurality of the referent affected by the action. Examples of initial syllable reduplication in consonant-initial verb stems are given in (1) and (2):

(1)   *Ma=la-ci-cika*   *zagö*   *mao.*
      CPL=3p.RLS-RDP1-make.hole.in   roof:MUT   cat
      'The cats have made holes in the/some roofs.'

(2)   *I-tu-tunö*   *mböröta*   *niha.*
      3s.RLS-RDP1-tell   beginning:MUT   person:MUT
      'He recited in detail (the story about) the origins of people.'

Initial syllable reduplication in verbs referring to physical states or qualities, which are mostly vowel-initial verbs, indicates plurality of the argument. Reduplication of the initial vowel in these verbs requires a /g/ to be inserted between the copied vowel and the initial vowel of the verb, as shown in (3) and (4):

(3) *Ag-a-nau   za'a-nia.*
     RDP1-ST-long   finger.nail:MUT-3s.POSS
     'His nails were long.'

(4) *Oya   mbatu   s=eg-e-bua.*
     many   stone:MUT   REL=RDP1-ST-big
     'There were a lot of big stones.' (lit. 'The stones which were big were many.')

Disyllabic reduplication (RDP2) can indicate that an action is continued for long time or is continually repeated. It can also indicate that a quality or state is intensified or, in a few special cases such as colour terms, weakened. The process copies the first two syllables of the stem, ignoring prefixes, e.g. *e-bua-bua*, 'very big' from *e-bua* 'ST-big'; *base-base-'ö* 'keep on waiting for (s/o)' from *base-'ö* (rest-TR) 'wait for (s/o)', *o-ßuge-ßuge'e* 'greenish' from *o-ßu-ge'e* (HAVE-hair-parrot:MUT) 'green'. Because of the interaction of morphophonological alternations and syllable structure mentioned in 2.2, reduplicated syllables may include the coda of a prefix of the shape *(C)aN-*. For example in (5) below, the initial /n/ of the reduplicated stem is the fusion of the initial consonant of the verb *taba* 'cut up', and the coda of the imperfective prefix *maN-*:

(5) *Ma-naba-naba   ira.*
     IPF-RDP2-cut   3p.MUT
     'They kept on cutting (it) up.'

Disyllabic reduplication often involves voicing of one or both consonants in a stem, e.g. *i-zofu-zofu* 'he kept asking questions' from *sofu* 'ask a question', *a-vuzi-vuzi* 'whitish, sort of white' from *afusi* (ST:white) 'white'.

In the case of monosyllabic roots, it is impossible to tell formally which reduplication process applies. However, reduplicated monosyllables always have meanings that are similar to those expressed by disyllabic reduplication, e.g. *so-so* 'always be present' from *so* 'exist, be present', *be-be* 'always give, keep on giving' from *be* 'give'.

3 BASIC MORPHOSYNTAX

3.1 Word classes

The Nias lexicon contains two large open word classes: noun and verb. These two classes are clearly distinguished with regard to a number of features, including the fact that only nouns can have mutated and unmutated forms (see 3.2) and that only verbs may occur with pronominal prefixes (see 3.3.2). Many verbs and nouns are formed from bound roots that do not occur on their own in any syntactic function. Nias has no class of adjectives – it uses verbs to express meanings which are typical of adjectives in languages which have them, and makes use of relative clause constructions with verbal predicates to express attributive modification of nouns (see 3.5.2). Closed word classes include pronouns, demonstratives, question words, numerals, classifiers, adverbs, prepositions, conjunctions, subordinators, and verbal and sentential particles.

3.2 Case marking: nominal mutation

The most distinguishing feature of Nias morphosyntax is a system of segmental alternations, or 'mutations', which plays a role similar to case and ligatures in other languages. Mutation is a morphophonemic process which affects the initial segment of a nominal, i.e. a noun or other constituent which can take the same argument roles as nouns, such as personal pronouns, demonstrative pronouns and headless relatives.

The effect of mutation is most clearly observable in nouns. The unmutated form of a noun is usually its citation form. The mutated form differs from the citation form in its initial segment, in accordance with a set of regular morphophonemic alternations. Examples of citation forms of nouns (i.e. unmutated forms), their mutated forms, and a list of the alternations which occur are given in Table 20.3 (the initial consonant segments not illustrated in this table do not change when mutated).

The nouns exemplified in Table 20.3 are all consonant-initial. Vowel-initial nouns are preceded by one of two consonants in their mutation forms, /n/ or /g/. The choice between these two consonants does not appear to be phonologically conditioned, /g/ being clearly the more frequent choice. In some cases, in fact, minimal pairs exist in mutation forms of nouns. For example, the unmutated form *öri* can mean either 'village federation' or 'bracelet, amulet', but the mutated form *nöri* can only mean 'village federation', while the mutated form *göri*, only 'bracelet, amulet'; *ußu* can mean 'plank' or 'part of coconut with eyes', but *nußu* can only mean 'plank', and *gußu*, 'part of coconut with eyes'.

The main syntactic contexts in which nominals occur in mutated form are listed below, with an example of each context. In discussing these contexts the abbreviations S, P and A are used as terms for the functions of the obligatory arguments in prototypical clause types (following Comrie 1978): S represents the single argument of an intransitive verb, P represents the more patientive argument in a transitive clause and A represents the more agentive argument in a transitive clause.

Syntactic contexts in which mutated nominals occur:

(i) As the S argument of an intransitive verb, e.g. *nidanö* is the mutated form of *idanö* 'water' in *aukhu nidanö* 'the water is hot'.

(ii) As the P argument of a transitive verb in main clauses, e.g. *mbaßi* is the mutated form of *baßi* 'pig' in *la-bunu mbaßi* (3p.RLS-kill pig:MUT) 'they killed a/the pig(s)'.

(iii) As the possessor in a possessive phrase, e.g. *nomo* is the mutated form of *omo* 'house(s)' in *tova nomo* 'wall(s) of a/the house(s)'.

(iv) As the object of most prepositions, e.g. *mbanua* is the mutated form of *banua* 'village' in *ba mbanua* 'in, at, to a/the village'.

TABLE 20.3: MUTATION IN NOUNS: ALTERNATIONS IN INITIAL CONSONANT PHONEMES

Base form and meaning	Mutated form	Alternation
Voiceless consonants		
fakhe 'rice'	*vakhe*	f > v
tanö 'land'	*danö*	t > d
si'o 'stick'	*zi'o*	s > z [ʤ]
ci'aci'a 'gecko'	*zi'aci'a*	c [ʧ] > z [ʤ]
kefe 'money'	*gefe*	k > g
Voiced consonants		
baßi 'pig'	*mbaßi*	b > mb [ᵐb]
doi 'thorn; fishbone'	*ndroi*	d > ndr [dʳ]

(v) As both experiencer and stimulus with certain experiencer verbs, for example in (6) below, the experiencer *mba'e* is the mutated form of *ba'e*, 'monkey', and the stimulus *nono matua* is the mutated form of *ono matua* 'boy':

(6) *A-ta'u   mba'e   nono   matua.*
     ST-fear   monkey:MUT   child:MUT   male
     'The monkey is afraid of the boy.'

The main syntactic contexts in which unmutated nominals occur are the following:

(i) As the A argument in transitive clauses (e.g. (14) below).
(ii) As the predicate in nominal clauses (see 3.3.1).
(iii) As the P argument of transitive verbs in dependent clauses (e.g. (44), (80)), including relative clauses in which the A argument has been relativized (see (57)).
(iv) As the argument of the negative existential verb *löna* (see (22) and (23)).
(v) After certain prepositions, such as instrumental *faoma* 'with' (e.g. *faoma sinali* (with rope) 'with a rope/ropes').
(vi) As any topicalized argument (see (33), (49)).
(vii) As bare instrumental or locative nouns (see (73)).
(viii) As the non-initial noun in conjoined NPs or in lists. For example, in the prepositional phrase *khö nama-gu ba ina-gu* (DAT father:MUT-1s.POSS CNJ mother-1s.POSS) 'to/from my father and mother', note that the second noun, *ina*, is not mutated while the first noun, *nama*, is. As this example shows, mutation applies to the NP as a whole and not just to nominals individually.

As mentioned above, in simple main clauses mutated nominals occur as S and P arguments while unmutated nominals occur as A arguments. The case alignment which treats the S and P arguments in the same way and the A argument differently is typically described as an ergative pattern. In such a pattern, S and P arguments are regarded as occurring in absolutive case and the A argument as occurring in ergative case. Although the terms 'absolutive' and 'ergative' are appropriate for arguments in some contexts in Nias, there are numerous syntactic contexts in which these terms are potentially misleading. In particular, many of the uses listed above of unmutated forms are ones that are not ergative in the sense of the A argument of a transitive verb, such as the predicate in nominal clauses or the P argument in a dependent clause. Despite a possibly clumsy feel to the words, the terms given to nominal arguments in this chapter are simply 'mutated' and 'unmutated'. For simplicity, only mutated nominals, including those nominals which are phonetically unaffected by mutation but occur in contexts which require mutated NPs, are glossed in this chapter with 'MUT'; no extra gloss is used for unmutated nominals.

As mentioned above, personal pronouns also have 'mutated' and 'unmutated' forms (see Table 20.4). The forms of pronouns in Nias Selatan, however, are irregular in that the normal mutation processes do not apply. 'Mutated' and 'unmutated' pronouns correspond in use to almost all of the contexts in which mutated and unmutated forms of nouns occur. The exceptions are contexts (iii) and (iv) of those listed for mutated nouns (i.e. as possessors and as objects of prepositions). In these contexts, the possessive form of pronouns, as listed in Table 20.4, is used.

In the northern variety, the pronouns which are equivalent to the mutated forms for first and second singular and first plural exclusive differ from those of Nias Selatan in

**TABLE 20.4: PRONOUNS AND POSSESSIVE SUFFIX
IN NIAS SELATAN**

	Unmutated	Mutated	Possessive
1s	ya'o	ndrao	-gu
1s.EMPHATIC	ya'oto	ndraoto	
2s	ya'ugö	ndraugö	-u
3s	ya'ia	ya	-nia
1pi	ya'ita	ita	-da
1pe	ya'aga	ndraga	-ga
2p	ya'ami	mi	-mi
3p	ya'ira	ira	-ra

having a glottal stop after the initial syllable *ndra*, e.g. *ndra'o* '1s.MUT'. In addition, the northern variety has short form variants for these three pronouns which function as suffixes on the verb: *-do* '1s.MUT', *-'ö* '2s.MUT' and *-ga* '1pe.MUT'. For details see Sundermann (1913) or Fries (1915).

3.3 Basic clause structure

Nias has both nominal and verbal predicate clauses. The basic structure of all clauses, whether nominal or verbal, entails a predicate in initial position followed by an argument, usually in mutated form. If the predicate is verbal it may be preceded by auxiliaries or particles signalling negation, modality, aspect and/or manner (see 3.4). Schematically the basic constituent order in a simple verbal clause is the following: (preverbal auxiliaries/particles) – verb – (argument(s)). This order is illustrated in (7) below. The sentence contains a transitive verb *tandra* 'mark', preceded by a fused element consisting of the completive marker *m(a)=* and the quantifier *oi*, and followed by the P argument:

(7) *M=oi*   *la-tandra*   *geu.*
     CPL=most, all   3p.RLS-mark   tree:MUT
     'They had marked all of the trees.'

3.3.1 Nominal clauses

In nominal clauses the predicate nominal occurs in initial position and is unmutated, and the argument (or 'subject') follows the predicate and is mutated, e.g. *tome ndrao* (guest 1s.MUT) 'I am a/the guest'. There is no copular element. Nominal clauses are negated with the constituent negator *te'ana* before the predicate NP, which is unmutated, as illustrated in (8):

(8) *Te'ana*   *ya'ia*   *z=a-nura.*
     NEG   3s   [REL=IPF-write]:MUT
     'The writer (of it) is not him.'

Note that the subject of the negative predicate in (8) is a headless relative (see also 3.5.2). The relative clause marker *s=* is mutated, indicating that the relative clause is case-marked and is, therefore, functioning as an argument, not an NP adjunct.

A very common use of nominal clauses in Nias is in questions, which are cleft constructions in which the question word occurs in predicate position and, typically, a headless relative occurs as subject, as illustrated in (9).

(9)   *Hanata   zi=möi?*
      who   [REL=go]:MUT
      'Who is going?' (lit. 'The one who is going is who?')

3.3.2 *Verbal clauses*

What distinguishes verbal from nominal predicates at a morphosyntactic level in Nias is the capacity of verbs, but not nominals, to occur with person/number marking prefixes. In Nias Selatan, verbs can occur in one of two modes, realis or irrealis, which is coded primarily by the form of the person/number marking prefixes. Realis mode encodes notions of past and present (and sometimes immediate future), i.e. events that either have happened or are happening at the time of speaking. Irrealis mode encodes notions of future, possibility, intention or desire, i.e. events which have not yet happened. This distinction is not marked by pronominal prefixes in the northern dialect, which expresses the relevant notions with adverbs or other verbs. It is in this area of verbal predicate syntax and morphology that the northern and southern dialects differ most. Only the southern dialect will be described here. For details of the northern dialect see Sundermann (1913) or Fries (1915).

In realis clauses in Nias Selatan, only transitive verbs have pronominal prefixes, coding the person and number of the A argument. In irrealis mode, *all* verbs are marked with a pronominal prefix, encoding the person and number of the A or the S. The prefixes used in realis and irrealis modes in Nias Selatan are given in Table 20.5.

In realis mode an intransitive verb does not carry a pronominal prefix. The S argument follows the verb in mutated form, e.g. *anakhö ndao* (ST:tired 1s.MUT) 'I'm tired'. In irrealis mode, the S argument of an intransitive verb is obligatorily marked on the verb with an irrealis pronominal prefix indicating person and number. If the S argument is expressed also by a lexical NP, it is mutated, as in (10):

(10)   *Ya-ma-nana   nono-nia   ba   va-a-lio.*
       3s.IRR-DYN-hand   child:MUT-3s.POSS   LOC   [NR-ST-quick]:MUT
       'Her child will be crawling soon.'

With stative verbs (see 4.1) and with dynamic intransitive verbs beginning with /m-/ (see 4.2), the pronominal prefix is the only indication of the mode of the clause. An example of a stative verb in irrealis mode is given in (11).

TABLE 20.5: PRONOMINAL PREFIXES IN NIAS SELATAN

	Realis	Irrealis
1s	*u-*	*gu-*
2s	*ö-*	*gö-*
3s	*i-*	*ya-*
1pi	*ta-*	*da-*
1pe	*ma-*	*ga-*
2p	*mi-*	*gi-*
3p	*la-*	*ndra-*

(11) *Na*   *ma=e-bua*   *ya*   *dania* *ba*   *ya-a-lawa*
      when   CPL=ST-big   3s.MUT   later   CNJ   3s.IRR-ST-high

mboto-nia   *moroi* *khö* *nama-nia.*
body:MUT-3s.POSS   come   DAT   father:MUT-3s.POSS
'He'll be taller than his father when he's bigger' (i.e. older). (lit. 'When he has become big later, his body will be tall from his father.')

Without the pronominal prefix, the form *alawa* 'high' is the form which would occur in a simple realis clause: cf. *a-lawa niha* [ST-high person:MUT] 'the man is tall'.

Existential clauses are a subtype of intransitive verb clause – the existential verb *so* is followed by a mutated argument, in both realis and irrealis mode:

(12) *So*   *nösi*   *ma*   *ide'ide.*
      EXIST   contents:MUT   CNJ   ST:small
      'There is something inside but it's only little.'

(13) *Ya-so*   *daßila.*
      3s.IRR-EXIST   taßila(feast):MUT
      'There's going to be a taßila feast.'

In transitive clauses, the A argument is obligatorily marked on the verb by a pronominal prefix in both realis and irrealis clauses. If the A argument is also expressed lexically it occurs in unmutated form. There is no pronominal marking on the verb for the P argument, which if present occurs in mutated form. An example of a transitive sentence in realis mode containing an A and a P argument is given in (14):

(14) *I-rino*   *vakhe*   *ina-gu.*
      3s.RLS-cook   rice:MUT   mother-1s.POSS
      'My mother cooked rice.'

The normal constituent order in transitive clauses containing two lexical arguments is V-P-A, as in (14). The same order occurs in irrealis clauses, as illustrated in (15):

(15) *Ya-d<um>oro*   *nono*   *manu*   *andre*
      3p.IRR-<IRR>carry   child:MUT   chicken:MUT   DIST

ba   *Mbaßömataluo*   *Ama-da*   *Faoso.*
LOC   Baßömataluo:MUT   father-1pi.POSS   Faoso
'Ama Faoso wanted to take that baby chicken to Baßömataluo.'
(*Ama-da* (lit. 'father of ours') is a way of referring to any man of one's father's age or older, as well as ancestors.)

Ditransitive verbs are marked for A and P arguments in the same way as simple transitive verbs, but include also a third argument encoded in a prepositional phrase, as exemplified in (16) in realis mode and in (17) in irrealis mode:

(16) *I-be*   *zi=to-röi*   *gö-da*
      3s.RLS-give   [REL=RES-leave.behind]:MUT   food:MUT-1pi.POSS

ba   *nasu*   *ina-gu.*
LOC   dog:MUT   mother-1s.POSS
'My mother gave our leftovers to the dog.'

(17) *Gu-m-oturagö   ndraugö   khö-ra.*
1s.IRR-IRR-tell   2s.MUT   DAT-3p.POSS
'I'm going to tell them about you.'

In irrealis mode, all dynamic verbs except for verbs which begin with /m-/ (see 4.2) are marked with the infix /um/. This infix has four allomorphs: (1) it occurs as the infix *-um-* after the initial consonant of verbs which begin with consonants other than labials, e.g. *dumoro* 'carry:IRR' from *doro* 'carry' as in (15) above; (2) it is realized as *m-* in front of vowel-initial verbs, e.g. *m-oturagö* 'tell:IRR', as in (17); (3) it replaces initial /b/ with a bilabial trill, e.g. *mbe* 'give:IRR' (realis *be*; see example (21) below); (4) it replaces initial /f/ with /v/, e.g. *vake* 'use:IRR' (cf. realis *fake*).

As further discussed in section 3.4.5, P arguments do not always occur in mutated form. When a transitive verb occurs in imperfective form with an irrealis prefix (indicating definite future action), the P argument is unmutated, in contrast with P arguments of simple irrealis constructions.

In all clauses, continued reference to humans typically involves an overt expression, i.e. a pronoun or a lexical NP. In contrast, continued reference to inanimate objects is usually realized by zero anaphora, i.e. no further mention at all. In the case of non-human animates, there is usually a choice of repeating the lexical NP or using zero anaphora. To illustrate, if the referent of the S in the second conjunct in the following sentence is 'the boy', the clause must contain a pronoun, e.g.:

(18) *Ma=i-bözi   nasu   ono   matua   ba   ma=moloi   ya (*ø).*
CPL=3s.RLS-hit   dog:MUT   child   male   CNJ   CPL=run   3s.MUT
'The boy hit the dog and ran away.'

If, however, it is the dog who runs away, the NP can either be repeated or omitted, e.g.:

(19) *Ma=i-bözi   nasu   ono   matua*
CPL=3s.RLS-hit   dog:MUT   child   male

ba   ma=moloi   nasu/ø (*ya).
CNJ   CPL=run   dog:MUT/ø (*3s.MUT)
'The boy hit the dog and it ran away.'

3.3.3 Negation

Negation of verbal predicates in both realis and irrealis clauses in Nias Selatan is realized with the auxiliary verb *löna* 'not', as exemplified in (20) (realis) and (21) (irrealis). (See 3.3.1 for negation in nominal clauses.) Case marking and verb form in main clauses are not affected by *löna*.

(20) *Löna   la-faigi   nösi.*
NEG   3p.RLS-see   contents:MUT
'They didn't notice the contents.'

(21) *Löna   ndra-mbe   khö-ra   ndra-ono.*
NEG   3p.IRR-give:IRR   DAT-3p.POSS   [ASSPL-child]:MUT
'They do not intend to give them the children.'

The verb *löna* by itself can function as the negative existential verb. The NP which follows *löna*, in contrast with the NP following the affirmative existential *so* (see example (12)), is unmutated, as in (22) and (23):

(22) *Löna   fakhe   ba   mba'a.*
    NEG.EXIST rice   LOC   box:MUT
    'There's no rice in the box.'

(23) *Löna   ono-nia.*
    NEG.EXIST child-3s.POSS
    'S/he doesn't have any children.'

3.4 Preverbal auxiliaries and particles

Verbal predicates also differ from nominal predicates in the complexity of the predicate. Apart from the negator *löna*, a number of auxiliaries and particles may precede the verb to express notions of modality, temporal and manner aspects of the situation described by the verb, and quantification of one of the participants. Most of the auxiliaries can also function independently as verbs, but are used infrequently in this function. In their role as preverbal auxiliaries these forms cannot have any arguments, and essentially form a single complex predicate with the following verb. It is always the second verb which carries argument marking.

3.4.1 Completive ma=

In general, verbs in realis mode in Nias Selatan refer to the present or the past (and sometimes also to the immediate future) depending on the context of the utterance. The particle *ma=*, which cannot co-occur with a verb in irrealis mode, the negator *löna* or any modal auxiliary, adds some sort of 'completive' sense to realis verb forms. For example, a not unexpected comment after eating is the following:

(24) *Ma=a-buso   ndrao.*
    CPL=ST-replete   1s.MUT
    'I'm full.'

Note that *ma=* is not restricted to expressions with clearly past temporal reference. It may also be used to signal completion of an event in the immediate future:

(25) *Ma'efu   tö   ma=a-soso.*
    a.bit   more   CPL=ST-ready to eat
    'It will be ready to eat (cooked or ripe) in a little while.'

In addition to completion, *ma=* also appears to indicate that the situation is currently relevant. For example, if one asks 'What's new?' on return to an area one has left for some time, the answer should include *ma=* if the reply refers to a situation which is still current, such as the one described in the second conjunct of (26):

(26) *Ma=a-labu   ya   ba   ma=a-fatö   gahe.*
    CPL=ST-fall   3s.MUT   CNJ   CPL=ST-break   leg:MUT
    'He fell and has broken his leg.' (lit. 'He fell and his leg has been broken.')

Ma= precedes all other preverbal auxiliaries, and fuses with the preverbal quantifier *oi* 'most, all' (see 3.4.4 below).

3.4.2 Modal expressions

Nias has nine modal expressions which occur in preverbal position. The most frequently used are *tola* 'can, be able, be permitted', *tobai/tebai* 'can't, not be able, not be permitted' and *tebai lö'ö/tebai löna/lö tola lö'ö* 'have to', which consist of the verb *tebai* and either the emphatic negator *lö'ö* 'not' or the common negator *löna* 'not', or a reduced negator *lö* plus *tola* 'can' followed by *lö'ö*. The verb which follows a modal form can be in realis or irrealis mode. Examples containing modal forms are given in (27)–(29). In (27) and (28), the modal form precedes the irrealis form of the verb:

(27)   *Tola   da-t<um>elefo   ba   da-s<um>ofu   mböli-nia.*
      can   1pi.IRR-<IRR>phone   CNJ   1pi.IRR-<IRR>ask   cost:MUT-3s.POSS
      'We could phone them and ask the price.'

(28)   *Tobai   gu-r<um>öi   nama-gu.*
      can't   1s.IRR-<IRR>leave.behind   father:MUT-1s.POSS
      'I can't leave my father.'

In (29) the verb is in realis form:

(29)   *Lö.tola.lö'ö   la-doro   ba   Hilizondrege'asi.*
      NEG.can.NEG   3p.RLS-carry   LOC   Hilizondrege'asi
      'They had to carry (it) to Hilizondrege'asi.'

Other modal expressions are *moguna* 'need to', *sinanea* 'it is appropriate, should', *dörö* 'perhaps' and *nama* 'perhaps'. Two other forms that are occasionally used are presumably borrowed from Indonesian: *tepaksa* 'must, have to' (cf. Indonesian *terpaksa* 'must, have to'), and *tatu* 'of course, certainly' (cf. Indonesian *tentu* 'of course, certainly').

3.4.3 Time and manner

A number of auxiliaries can precede the main verb to indicate temporal or manner aspects of the action or process. Among these are *asese* 'often', *itaria* 'sometimes', *ero* 'every time', *ara* 'long time', *alio* 'quick', *asala* 'indifferently, in a perfunctory manner', *ahori* 'finished' and *faoma* 'same'. Some examples are given in (30)–(35).

(30)   *Asese   la-fake   gorokoro   ira-ina   meföna.*
      often   3p.RLS-use   scoop:MUT ASSPL-mother   in.the.early.days
      'In the early days women often used scoops.'

(31)   *Ero   mo-möi   mondri,...*
      every.time   JOINT-go   bathe
      'Every time they go to bathe,...'

(32)   *Ara   mörö   ndrao.*
      long.time   sleep   1s.MUT
      'I slept for a long time.'

(33)   *Ira-ina   ba   mbanua   mana,   asala   la-rino   manö.*
      ASSPL-mother   LOC   village:MUT   now   indifferently   3p.RLS-cook   just
      'Women in the villages these days, they just cook very perfunctorily.'

(34)   *Ahori   i-a.*
      finished   3s.RLS-eat
      'He ate (it) all up.'

(35)   *Faoma   la-ohe   doho.*
      same   3p.RLS-hold.in.hand   spear:MUT
      'They were all carrying spears.'

3.4.4 Quantifier

The particle *oi* 'most, all' also precedes the verb, as illustrated earlier in example (7). Usually when *oi* is preceded by the completive marker *ma=*, the vowel of *ma=* is elided and the particles fuse to become one word, *moi*, as occurs in (7). This fusion does not occur when *ma=* precedes any other vowel-initial word, nor does it apparently always have to occur with *oi*, as is evident from (36):

(36)   *Ma=oi   a-khozi   sa-mbua   banua.*
      CPL=most, all   ST-burn   one-CLF.MUT   village
      'Almost an entire village had been razed.'

The particle *oi* may refer to any argument, including datives and locatives. In (7) it refers to a P argument; in (36) it refers to an S argument; in (37) below it refers to the locative noun *mbanua* 'village(s)':

(37)   *Oi   ndra-va-sindro   sikola   ba   mbanua.*
      most,all   3p.IRR-[CAU-stand]:IRR   school   LOC   village:MUT
      'They will build schools in all the villages.'

3.4.5 Imperfective constructions

Certain aspectual notions are represented by changes to the verb. Reduplication is one form of aspectual marking (see 2.3). Nias makes a distinction in the form of the verb between actions that are punctual and those that are not (i.e. those which are imperfective – habitual, characteristic of the actor, ongoing or in progress). The simple realis form of a dynamic verb (i.e. one involving action) implies a punctual action. To signal that the action is not punctual, Nias uses affixation. In intransitive verbs referring to actions, the infix *-um-* indicates that the activity is carried on for some time, as exemplified in (38):

(38)   *A-hono   ma=t<um>ataro   ya   maefu   ba   gabera   nomo…*
      ST-calm   CPL=<IPF>sit   3s.RLS   towards   LOC   left:MUT   house:MUT
      'He was calmly sitting to the left of the house…'

The S argument of intransitive verbs with imperfective marking is often generic, as in (39) below, where the infix provides a habitual meaning:

(39)   *H<um>ago   niha.*
      <IPF>snore   person:MUT
      'People snore.'

Imperfective intransitives with *-um-* in Nias Selatan differ from irrealis intransitives with *-um-* in that the latter also have a pronominal irrealis prefix (see 3.3.2).

    Transitive verbs also have an imperfective form, marked with *maN-*. When prefixed with *maN-*, verbs are reduced in transitivity – the A argument is no longer marked on the verb but is realized as a mutated NP. An example of a main clause containing a transitive verb in its imperfective form is given in (40):

(40)   *Man-uri*   *zawi*   *ya.*
       IPF-keep.alive   cattle:MUT   3s.MUT
       'He keeps cattle.'

This sentence answers a question such as 'What's he doing now (in life)?' to which a response containing a simple transitive verb would be inappropriate because of its implied punctual nature. Note that both arguments of the verb are mutated (although it should also be noted that some speakers prefer that the P argument, *zawi*, be unmutated, and in the northern dialect the P argument in sentences such as these *cannot* be mutated). The order of arguments in main clauses containing imperfective forms of transitive verbs is fixed – it corresponds to the unmarked order of arguments in a simple transitive clause, i.e. V-P-A. However, imperfective forms of transitive verbs are infrequent in main clauses and usually lack one or both arguments when their referents are already known. In addition, P arguments are usually non-referential. A typical example of an imperfective form of a transitive verb without any overt arguments is given in (41):

(41)   *A-efa*   *hö'ö,*   *man-a.*
       ST-passed   DIST   IPF-eat
       'After that, (they) ate.' (Or, perhaps, 'After that, (there was) eating.')

Verbs to which *maN-* is attached are reduced in transitivity in four ways: (1) by the absence of pronominal prefixing on the verb for the A argument, (2) by mutation of the A argument, (3) by the fact that in most cases the P argument is non-referential and (4) by the fact that neither argument is obligatory. These features, and the aspectual notions of imperfectivity which are expressed by *maN-*, are characteristic of antipassive verb forms in other languages. Despite these observations, I will not refer to the *maN-* form of transitive verbs as 'antipassive' in this chapter. This prefix shows semantic and syntactic similarities to imperfective affixes which occur with intransitive verbs (such as *-um-* and *m-*) and has other functions which are related but cannot be described in terms of 'antipassive', and it would obscure the relationships amongst these prefixes to mark imperfective *maN-* as distinct from them.

   The kind of imperfective verb form just described for transitive and intransitive verbs is obligatorily used when a speaker wishes to indicate that a group of people do something together (i.e. 'joint action'), which is expressed by the prefix *mo-*. This construction can only be used when the participants involved, who may be many or just two, have already been mentioned. For most speakers, no pronominal argument may co-occur with a verb marked with *mo-*. However, a nominal argument referring to a group (i.e. with the associative plural prefix *ira-*) may optionally occur, and if so, is mutated. Examples of intransitive and transitive constructions with *mo-* 'joint action' are given in (42) and (43):

(42)   *Mo-s<um>indro*   *(?ira).*
       JOINT-<IPF>stand   (?3p.MUT)
       'They all stood.'

(43)   *Mo-ma-nunö-nunö*   *(ndra-Inti/?ira).*
       JOINT-IPF-RDP2-sing   ([ASSPL-Inti]:MUT/?3p.MUT)
       'They (or: Inti and her companion) are always singing together.'

   Imperfective forms of the verb are also used with the transitive verb *lau*, 'do', to express progressive aspect. In this case the imperfective form is a dependent form. An example of a transitive verb in progressive aspect is given in (44):

(44) *I-lau*   *ma-makha*   *balale*   *ina-gu.*
     3s.RLS-do   IPF-weave   basket   mother-1s.POSS
     'My mother is weaving a basket.'

Note that both the P argument and the A argument of the verb *fakha* 'weave' in (44) are unmutated. In all such dependent transitive clauses in Nias the P argument is unmutated. Note that semantically the A argument of *fakha* 'weave' is simultaneously the A argument of the verb *lau* 'do' but is expressed syntactically only as an A argument of *lau*, as illustrated both by its realization on the verb as the third person prefix, *i-*, and by its unmutated form. An example of an intransitive verb in progressive aspect is given in (45):

(45) *I-lau*   *t<um>ataro*   *ba*   *nora*   *nomo*   *ama-gu.*
     3s.RLS-do   <IPF>sit   LOC   step:MUT   house:MUT   father-1s.POSS
     'My father is sitting on the steps of the house.'

Note that in (45) *ama-gu* 'my father' is semantically the S argument of *tataro*, but is syntactically the A argument of *lau* 'do', as reflected by the pronominal prefix and its unmutated form.

     MaN- has another important function for transitive verbs in Nias Selatan: when an irrealis prefix attaches directly to an imperfective form of a transitive verb (prefixed with *maN-*) rather than its irrealis form (affixed with *-um-*), the construction expresses a definite, and often immediate, future – the conviction that an event will occur. This meaning contrasts with the meaning of vague possibility usually implied by the simple irrealis form. Compare the definite future in (46) with the simple irrealis (47):

(46) *Ya-ma-mu'a*   *ömö-nia.*
     3s.IRR-IPF-repay   debt-3s.POSS
     'He is about to pay off his debt' (i.e. he has the money ready to hand over).

(47) *Ya-mbu'a*   *gömö-nia.*
     3s.IRR-repay:IRR   debt:MUT-3s.POSS
     'He would like to/might repay his debt' (but he doesn't know where he would
     get the money).

Note that the P argument in the definite future construction (46) is unmutated, in contrast to realis clause instances of imperfective transitive verbs in which the P argument is mutated (see (40)).

3.5 NP structure

A noun phrase containing more than just a noun can be followed by any of the following modifiers: a possessive NP, one or two deictic adjuncts, and one or more relative clauses. If an NP is indefinite, a numeral phrase may precede it. If an NP is definite, a numeral phrase takes the form of a relative clause and follows the noun. Schematically, the order of constituents in a definite NP with noun as head is given in (48) (where the raised 'n' implies the theoretical possibility of any number):

(48)   N   (POSS)   (DEICTIC)   (RECOG)   (REL CL)^n (REL CL)
                                   (attrib)   (num)

There is also a small set of words which may follow a noun directly in certain common collocations. Words which belong to this set are: *matua* 'male', *alaße* 'female', *raya* 'south', *löu* 'north' and *kafu* 'cold' (this last only in collocation with 'water'). Some examples of phrases containing these words are: *ono alaße* (child female) 'young girl', *tanö raya* (land south) 'south land', *idanö kafu* (water cold) 'cold water'.

Possessors immediately follow their head and occur as a mutated nominal or possessive suffix. Possessors may be nested. For example in (49), the possessive modifier *nakhi dua-gu* itself contains the possessive modifier *dua-gu* which in turn contains the possessive suffix *-gu* (in this example *ina Moli* is the topicalized subject of the nominal predicate *ono nakhi dua-gu*):

(49)   *Ina*   *Moli,*   *ono*   *nakhi*   *dua-gu.*
       mother   Moli   child   younger.sibling:MUT   grandparent:MUT-1sg.POSS
       'The mother of Moli is the daughter of the younger brother of my grandfather.'

3.5.1 Deictics

The forms for deictic reference differ between dialects in Nias. This section describes the forms for the southern dialect. See Sundermann (1913) or Fries (1915) for details of demonstratives in the northern dialect.

There are two broad semantic types of demonstratives in Nias Selatan: a purely deictic type and a 'recognitional' type (see Himmelmann 1996), both of which have several forms. The first type is used to identify the physical or cognitive distance of the referent of the NP within the situational or speech context. The forms in this category are: *ha'a* 'PRX', *hö'ö* 'DIST', *andra* 'PRX' and *andre* 'DIST'. Except for *andre*, these demonstratives are used for deictic reference in situational use as well as for identifying referents in discourse (i.e. in discourse-tracking uses). There does not seem to be a difference in meaning between *ha'a* and *andra* in situational use, although *ha'a* has greater frequency in this context. In texts *andra* is very often used in reported speech where *ha'a* might be used in non-reported situational contexts (see (52) below, for example), suggesting that *andra* may have more formal connotations than *ha'a*. *Andre* is used adnominally only as a discourse-tracking device. Examples of these demonstratives are given in (50)–(53):

(50)   situational
       Haiya   *mo-guna*   *geu*   *ha'a.*
       what   HAVE-use   wood:MUT   PRX
       'What is this wood used for?'

(51)   discourse-tracking
       So   *mbambatö-ra*   *ba*   *mbanua*   *hö'ö.*
       EXIST   relative:MUT-3p.POSS LOC   village:MUT   DIST
       'They had relatives in that village.' (lit. 'Their relatives existed in that village.')

(52)   reported situational use in discourse
       ...la-waö   *"ta-hare-'ö*   *ba*   *mbanua*   *andra".*
       ...3p.RLS-say   2pi.RLS-seat-TR   LOC   village:MUT   PRX
       '...they said, "Let's settle in this village".'

(53)   discourse-tracking
       I-waö   *khö*   *zi'ila-nia*   *andre,...*
       3s.RLS-say   DAT   adviser:MUT-3s.POSS   DIST
       'He said to that adviser of his,...'

In texts *ha'a* 'PRX' and *andra* 'PRX' often imply that a referent has been mentioned recently, and *hö'ö* 'DIST', that it has been mentioned earlier, but the correlation between proximal vs. distal forms and recent vs. earlier mention is not consistent and can be influenced by a speaker's emotional proximity to a person, place or topic being discussed. The three forms, *ha'a* 'PRX', *hö'ö* 'DIST' and *andre* 'DIST' can be used pronominally as well as adnominally. The proximal form *andra* is not used pronominally. There are also two common enclitic forms, *=ndra* and *=ndre*, which can only be used adnominally and otherwise roughly have the same meanings and functions as *andra* and *andre*.

There are three recognitional adjuncts which have the function of drawing the hearer's attention to someone or something which has either been previously mentioned or is within the sphere of knowledge shared by speaker and hearer (frequently reference to family members or cultural detail, and not to the larger context of general knowledge, such as *the sun*). These recognitional forms function only as adjuncts, never as heads of NPs. They are: *no*, *noma'e* (or *nomae*) and *nomema'e* (or *nomemae*). Their meaning is something like 'the one I've been talking about' or 'you know?'. The first form, *no*, occurs infrequently and may well be a reduced form of the others. An example in which both *nomema'e* and *no* have the same referent is given in (54):

(54)   *Maoso*   *z=a-hatö*   *khö-ra=ndra*   *nomema'e,*
      get.up   [REL=ST-close]:MUT   DAT-3p.POSS=PRX   RECOG

      z=a-hatö   *khö*   *ni-khozi*   *no*   *la-waö…*
      [REL=ST-close]:MUT   DAT   PASS-burn   RECOG   3p.RLS-say

      'The relatives of those people I've been talking about, the relatives of those people who had been burnt, got up and said…'

The form *noma'e*, occurs primarily in proper names, e.g. *Amada noma'e Taögönaso* 'our ancestor Taögönaso, whom I know you know'. The longer form, *nomema'e*, may also occur in place of *noma'e* in this construction.

The form *nomema'e* may co-occur in a noun phrase with the deictic demonstrative *andre* 'DIST', as illustrated in (55). Note that the recognitional demonstrative follows the deictic demonstrative in this example:

(55)   *Ba*   *si'ulu=wa=e*   *nama-da*   *andre*   *nomema'e!?*
      CNJ   noble=D.PTCL=D.PTCL   father:MUT-1pi.POSS   DIST   RECOG
      'And you mean that ancestor you've been talking about was a noble!?'

3.5.2 Relative clauses

Relative clauses in Nias are formed by gapping the argument being relativized and marking the clause with the proclitic *s(i)=*. Example (56) below contains two relative clauses in which the S argument has been relativized (when *s(i)=* is attached to vowel-initial stative verbs its vowel is elided).

(56)   *ama-da*   *si=bihasa*   *s=a-tua-tua*
      father-1pi.POSS   REL=old   REL=ST-RDP2-mature
      'a wise old man'

As illustrated in (56), more permanent attributes occur closer to the head than temporary attributes. Example (57) contains a relative clause in which the A argument has been relativized. Note that the pronominal prefix is not present on the verb (i.e. the A argument has been gapped), and the P argument is unmutated:

(57) *Andrehe'e   nasu   si=usu   ya'o.*
      that.one   dog:MUT   REL=bite   1s
      'That is the dog that bit me.'

An alternative form is available when relativizing A arguments, which involves the use of the prefix *aN-* (see 2.2), e.g. *asu s=an-usu ya'o* (dog REL=IPF-bite 1s) 'the dog that bit me'. These two types of clauses are apparently interchangeable in most contexts – both can refer to punctual events or to ongoing activities. However, text examples reveal that the second type occurs much more frequently in reference to habitual qualities of the referent of the relativized noun or to events which are not related to a specific time.

Any argument can be relativized, including possessive arguments and obliques. S arguments in relative clauses in which possessives or obliques are relativized are unmutated. An example of a relative clause in which a possessive is relativized is given in (58), and one in which a locative is relativized is given in (59):

(58) *niha   si=ma=mate   fo'omo   meneßi*
      person   REL=CPL=die   wife   yesterday
      'the man whose wife died yesterday'

(59) *Andaha'a   nahia   si=tumbu   ya'o.*
      PRX   place   REL=born   1s
      'This is the place where I was born.'

Relative clauses are sensitive to negation. If a relative clause contains the negator *löna*, the verb must occur in imperfective form, e.g.:

(60) *Andehe'e   nono   matua   si=löna   mo-lau (*i-lau)   ohi.*
      that.one   child:MUT   male   REL=NEG   IPF-climb (*3s.RLS-climb)   tree
      'That is the boy who did not climb the coconut tree.'

If a P argument is relativized, the relative clause typically has a different form from those in which S's, A's, possessives or obliques are relativized. First, there is no relative marker unless auxiliaries precede the verb (e.g. (62) below). Second, the verb is marked with the prefix *ni-*, and has no pronominal prefix. Third, the A argument is realized as a possessive suffix or as a mutated noun following the verb. Relativization of a P argument, *sekhula* 'coconut', is illustrated in (61):

(61) *sekhula   ni-rökhi-nia*
      coconut   PASS-grate-3s.POSS
      'the coconut which she grated' (cf. *I-rökhi zekhula.* (3s.RLS-grate coconut:MUT)
      'She grated the coconut.')

Ni- forms of the verb resemble typical passives in other languages: the verb is explicitly marked, the patient is pivot in the sense of being the gapped argument and the agent is marked obliquely. Most uses of the *ni-* form of the verb, however, differ from a typical passive in that it is more common for the A argument to be present than for it to be omitted. It is also the case that *ni-* forms are restricted to use in relative clause formation, and do not occur as main clause verbs. Despite this restriction, the forms will be glossed as passive ('PASS') in this chapter. Note that *ni-* is not a substitute for *si=* in these clauses – *ni-* must be prefixed directly to the verb. There can be no preverbal elements intervening between *ni-* and the verb, as is possible between *si=* and the verb; if these occur they precede *ni-*, and the relative marker *si=* must be used, as exemplified in (62):

(62) *Andrehe'e   nohi   si=löna   ni-lau   nono   matua.*
      that   coconut.tree:MUT REL=NEG PASS-climb   child:MUT   male
      'That is the coconut tree that was not climbed by the boy.'

Relative clauses may function by themselves as arguments, and frequently occur in this function in nominal clauses (see 3.3.1). As heads of NPs, they are subject to the same mutation rules as occur with nouns – the initial segment is mutated in those contexts requiring mutation (hence *s(i)=* becomes *z(i)=*). Examples of relative clauses used as NPs occur in examples (8), (9), (54) and (79).

3.5.3 Classifiers and numerals

Classifiers are a small set of common nouns which are used with numerals when counting things below about ten in number. Above ten a numeral usually occurs without a classifier. The most common classifiers and the sorts of things they are used to count are given in Table 20.6 (their meanings as common nouns are given in square brackets).

The classifier for people, *da*, always precedes the numeral, e.g. *da tölu zi'ila* (CLF three adviser:MUT) 'three advisers'. (This classifier refers to people in general, but while it is used consistently for men and groups including men, it is not used consistently with women, children or slaves, who are sometimes classified with *bua*.) All other classifiers follow the numeral.

As mentioned earlier, when an NP has definite reference, numerals (and numeral + classifier constructions) occur in relative clauses and follow the head. As numerical reference is typically less permanent than other attribution, relative clauses containing a numeral follow any other relative clause, e.g.:

(63) *baßi-ra   s=a-fusi   si=öfa   geu*
      pig-3p.POSS   REL=ST-white   REL=four   CLF.MUT
      'their four white pigs'

When NPs have indefinite reference, numerals and numeral + classifier constructions occur *before* the head noun, e.g.:

(64) *öfa   geu   mbaßi   s=a-fusi*
      four   CLF.MUT   pig:MUT   REL=ST-white
      'four white pigs'

TABLE 20.6: CLASSIFIERS IN NIAS SELATAN

Classifier	Thing counted
da	people [no similar noun known]
eu	animals, coconut trees, some concrete things (bodies) [*eu* 'tree, wood']
bua	concrete things in general (eggs, chairs, houses, villages) [*bua* 'fruit']
balö	abstract things (thoughts, kinds of things) [*balö* 'end, heap, pile']
rozi	long things (wood, gold), baby animals [*rozi* 'pole for pounding rice']
roto	sections (e.g. of bamboo, sugarcane) [*roto* 'section of bamboo']
bulu	flat things (blankets, mats) [*bulu* 'leaf']

Classifiers are linked to the numeral in one of two ways: by mutation or with the linking particle *na*. Examples of a mutated classifier, *geu*, occur in (63) and (64) above. In contrast, the same classifier occurs in unmutated form in example (65) but is preceded by the linker *na*.

(65)   *tölu*   *na*   *eu*   *mbaßi*
      three   LK   CLF   pig:MUT
      'three pigs'

The alternation between mutated classifier and [linker + unmutated classifier] is predictable morphophonologically: classifiers following numerals ending in /a/ are mutated, while classifiers following numerals ending in vowels other than /a/ take unmutated form but are preceded by the linker *na*. Since a mutated classifier and the combination of *na* plus an unmutated classifier are in complementary distribution, this may be taken as circumstantial evidence that mutation has its origins in an earlier nasal linking particle, as such particles are widely attested throughout the Austronesian family.

3.6 Prepositional phrases

Nias has quite a few prepositions, most of which also function as verbs, adverbs or nouns, but there are two basic prepositions which do not have other functions in the language: *ba* and *khö*. *Ba* is used for location and direction, and can be used with animals and with reference to people in a generic sense. *Khö* is used also for location and direction but only with reference to people. *Ba* can have ablative meaning (motion from) and allative (motion towards), as well as locative. *Khö* can have ablative meaning as well as dative and benefactive. Both *ba* and *khö* are followed by mutated nominals, as shown by numerous examples throughout this chapter. *Ba* is also found in a set of lexicalized phrases referring to unique and common locations, in which it is affixed to unmutated vowel-initial nouns, e.g. *ba-omo* '(at/to) home' (from *omo* 'house'; see (67) below), *ba-ene* 'at/to the sea-shore' (from *ene* 'beach'), *ba-ero* 'outside' (from *ero* 'outside'). Some of these expressions have come to have meanings which are associated with the activity typically carried out in these places, e.g. to say that someone is *ba-ene* 'at the sea-shore' can imply that he has gone fishing, to say that someone is *ba-ero* 'outside' can imply that someone has gone outside to relieve themselves.

    Nias also has a number of complex prepositions in which the basic prepositions are in construction with words which function elsewhere in the language as verbs, adverbs or nouns. The most frequently occurring complex prepositions are *moroi ba* and *moroi khö*, both meaning 'from'. An example of *moroi khö* occurs in (11). The word *moroi* occurs elsewhere in the language as an intransitive verb meaning 'come from, start from'. In collocation with *ba* and *khö*, however, *moroi* has no verbal features, e.g. no adverbs or aspectual particles may precede or follow it; nothing can be inserted between the verb and the preposition and it cannot take an argument. Another verb which occurs frequently in collocation with *ba* is *möi* 'go'. The collocation has an allative meaning, i.e. 'towards'.

4 DERIVATIONAL VERBAL MORPHOLOGY

Verbs in Nias can be divided into two classes, stative and dynamic, according to morphological, semantic and derivational properties (for details see Brown 2001, sections 4.4, 4.5 and 5.2). Stative verbs in general are intransitive verbs which refer to physical or emotional states or qualities. Dynamic verbs refer to actions and may be intransitive or transitive.

4.1 Stative verbs

A large class of stative verbs begin with the stative prefix *a-*. Many of the verbs in this class never occur without this prefix, i.e. stative verb roots are often bound roots. Such verbs generally refer to states which persist for a relatively long time or describe some (often inherent) characteristic of the referent, e.g. *aoha* 'easy, light' from *-oha* (not otherwise used), *afusi* 'white' from *-fusi* (also not otherwise used). Other verbs in this class may have nouns or transitive verbs as stems. Such verbs have the meaning 'S is affected by N/V', e.g. *a-fau* 'hoarse' from *fau* 'sore throat', *a-huẞa* 'grey-haired' from *huẞa* 'grey-hair', *a-lulu* 'loosened' from *lulu* 'loosen', *a-rörö* 'distracted' from *rörö* 'distract'. Stative verbs derived from the transitive verbs *fatö* 'break' and *khozi* 'burn' are illustrated in (26) and (36) above. Some of the verbs derived with *a-* may have inchoative meanings (e.g. *a-fosu* 'starting to have breasts' from *fosu* 'breast of young girl'). No agents can be overtly expressed in these constructions. A small class of underived stative intransitive verbs are consonant-initial. These include *sökhi* 'good', *bohou* 'new', *bihasa* 'old' (referring to people), *bidöyö* 'blind', *biha* 'sated from eating too much pork', *bötö* 'wounded', and *taiha* 'lost'.

Another class of stative verbs is formed from transitive verbs or bound roots with the prefixes *te-* and *to-*, e.g. *te-rono* 'heard' from *rono* 'hear', *te-boka* 'open' (from *-boka*, cf. *boka-i* 'open sth.'), *to-bini* 'hidden' (from *-bini*, cf. *bini-'ö* 'hide sth'). Verbs beginning with *te-* or *to-* refer to states resulting from the action denoted by the root. The primary function of these prefixes appears to be to signal that the coming about of these states is not attributable to an agent. The states can be characterized generally as less permanent than those to which verbs derived with *a-* refer, or as having less effect on the referent of the argument. A few of the verbs derived with *te-* or *to-* have meanings which involve accidental action, e.g. *te-tutu* 'accidentally bumped' from *tutu* 'bump, hit', but this meaning is not primary to these prefixes. It is unclear whether there is a difference in meaning between *te-* and *to-* synchronically. Many verbs only ever occur with one prefix or the other, e.g. *te-söndra* 'found' (**to-söndra*), *to-ila* 'known' (**te-ila*). (See Brown 2001, section 5.1.1.4, for discussion.)

4.2 Dynamic verbs

The category of dynamic verbs in Nias is morphologically diverse. It includes vowel-initial intransitive verbs such as *a'ege* 'laugh' and *aekhu* 'fall', *atoru* 'drop', consonant-initial verbs such as *sindro* 'stand' and *tataro* 'sit', as well as most transitive verbs. There is a small set of dynamic intransitive verbs in Nias which all begin with *m-*. These verbs include *m-aoso* 'get up; stand up; wake up', *m-ofanö* 'leave', *m-örö* 'sleep', *m-e'e* 'cry', *m-oloi* 'run away', *m-oroi* 'come from', *m-uta* 'vomit', *m-ondri* 'bathe', *m-alu* 'go hunting', *m-iẞo* 'crow', *m-eẞo* 'chase birds' and possibly *möi* 'go'. These verbs take the same form in main and dependent clauses, realis or irrealis modes. The rest of the category of dynamic intransitive verbs consists almost entirely of verbs derived from nouns through the prefixes *maN-*, *mo-* and *fa-*, as described in the rest of this section.

The prefix *maN-* derives intransitive verbs with meanings such as 'S does sth. with N', e.g. *manoho* 'carry a spear' from *toho* 'spear' (noun), *manimbo* 'be smoking' from *simbo* 'smoke' (noun), *manana* 'crawl (use hands)' from *tana* 'hand' (illustrated in sentence (10) above). This prefix is glossed as 'DYN', although it should be noted that it has the same morphological form as the prefix which marks imperfective forms of transitive verbs (see 3.4.5 above).

The prefix *mo-* can attach to almost any noun to form an intransitive verb meaning 'have N', e.g. *mo-toho* 'have/hold a spear', *mo-ono* 'have a child/children', *mo-ndrewa* 'have pimples'. Although semantically many of these verbs suggest states rather than actions, the verbs are treated by causativization and nominalization processes as dynamic rather than stative (see 4.3.1 and 5.1). Without the initial segment *m-*, some of these verbs can function as stative verbs, e.g. *o-lofo* (HAVE-hunger) 'hungry'. *Mo-* can also attach to nouns referring to weather, e.g. *mo-teu* 'be raining', *mo-ani* 'be windy'. Weather verbs derived with *mo-* differ syntactically from HAVE-derivations in that they do not allow for an overt argument expression in realis mode, e.g. *mo-teu* (*ya*) 'it's raining'. In irrealis mode, however, a pronominal prefix must occur, e.g. *ya-mo-teu* (3s.IRR-HAVE-rain) 'it might rain, it's going to rain'.

The prefix *fa-* can derive transitive and intransitive verbs. It has two functions depending on the kind of noun to which it is prefixed. When affixed to nouns referring to movement, sound, instruments, activities or kinds of people, *fa-* derives verbs with meanings related to an activity associated with the referent of the noun, such as 'do N', '(actively) be N', 'do something with N', 'make N happen' or 'make P be N'. Some intransitive verbs derived with *fa-* are: *fa-liwaliwa* 'move' from *liwaliwa* 'movement', *fa-ßikhoßikho* 'whistle' (verb) from *ßikhoßikho* 'whistle' (noun), *fa-gai* 'fish with line and hook' from *gai* '(line and) hook'. Some transitive verbs are: *fa-guru* 'teach, learn' from *guru* 'teacher', *fa-tuturu* 'point the way to' from *tuturu* 'finger', *fa-bu'u* 'make a promise' from *bu'u* 'knot'. This prefix is glossed as 'DO' to indicate the most basic meaning of the morpheme.

The second function of *fa-* occurs when it is attached specifically to kin term nouns, and derives verbs meaning 'call s/o [kin term]', e.g. *fa-sibaya* 'call someone uncle', from *sibaya* 'uncle'. The derived verb requires two obligatory arguments – a mutated S argument, and a dative argument referring to the person who is called by the kin term. An example is given in (66):

(66) *Fa-ama   ndraga   khö-nia.*
      DO-father   1pe.MUT   DAT-3s.POSS
      'We call him "father" (because he is the same age and social rank as our father).'

A formative of the same shape occurs also with transitive verbs and bound roots to derive intransitive verbs which can have reciprocal meaning, e.g. *fa-bözi ira* (DO-fight 3p.MUT) 'they fought', *fa-lakhi ira* (DO-meet 3p.MUT) 'they met'. This reciprocal meaning, however, is not automatic, e.g. *fa-bözi ira* can also mean 'they fought (someone else)'. Participants can also be mentioned separately, in which case the verb obligatorily takes two arguments, one mutated and one oblique, as exemplified in (67):

(67) *Fa-lakhi   ndao   khö-nia   ba   v-anavuli-gu   ba-omo.*
      DO-meet   1s.MUT DAT-3s.POSS   LOC   [NR-return]:MUT-1s.POSS LOC-house
      'I met him on my way home.'

The prefix *fa-* which occurs on nouns and the prefix *fa-* which occurs on transitive verbs and bound roots, derive verbs which appear to behave in the same way with respect to nominalization – both types of derived verbs are nominalized with the suffix *-sa* (see 5.2). These prefixes are classed together under the term 'dynamic' *fa-*, to distinguish them from 'causative' *fa-*, which is discussed in the next section. Dynamic *fa-* also occurs as a part of a circumfix which derives causative verbs from transitive and ditransitive verbs; see 4.3.2 below.

4.3 Causative and applicative derivations

Causative and applicative verbs are derived with both prefixes and suffixes. Only one affix may attach to both transitive and intransitive verb stems in causative derivations – the prefix *f(V)*-, which is described in 4.3.1. Suffixes tend to have causative or applicative meanings when applied to intransitive stems, but their function with transitive verbs in general involves only subtle changes in meanings and rarely a rearrangement of argument structure. Suffixes are discussed in 4.3.2.

4.3.1 Causative prefix f(V)-

The causative prefix *f(V)*- occurs only on dynamic verbs. It has three forms, *fa-*, *f-* and *fe-*. *Fa-* occurs with consonant-initial verbs, e.g. *fa-sindro* 'make stand (with ropes and pulleys); build (e.g. a village)' from *sindro* 'stand', *fa-törö* 'make go, work' from *törö* 'go (by means of/via)'. The allomorph *f-* occurs in two contexts: (1) prefixed to vowel-initial intransitive verbs, e.g. *f-alua* 'make happen' from *alua* 'happen', *f-a'ege* 'make laugh' from *a'ege* 'laugh'; and (2) as a replacement for /m/ in verbs which begin with /m/, including those which are derived with the prefix *mo-* 'HAVE' e.g. *f-ofanö* 'send away' (cf. *m-ofanö* 'leave'), *f-e'e* 'make cry' (cf. *m-e'e* 'cry'), *fo-ömö* 'cause to have debt' (cf. *mo-ömö* (HAVE-debt) 'have debt'). In these causative derivations the A argument expresses the causer and the P argument the causee. The P argument corresponds to the (agentive) S argument of intransitive verb bases. Examples of causative forms with *fa-* and *f-* are given in (68) and (69):

(68)   *La-fa-sindro   gehomo.*
       3p.RLS-CAU-stand   pillar:MUT
       'They erected the pillar' (by using, e.g. ropes and pulleys).

(69)   *I-f-a'ege   ndaga   ba'e.*
       3s.RLS-CAU-laugh   1pe.MUT   monkey
       'The monkey made us laugh.'

In a number of causative derivations in which the causer is directly responsible for the action (i.e. by doing something with their own hands, not through the medium of tools or instruments), the causative prefix is *fe-*. *Fe-* occurs with bound roots, nouns, intransitive verbs and transitive verbs, e.g. *fe-ta'u* 'frighten' (from *-ta'u*, cf. *ata'u* 'afraid'), *fe-haga* 'signal with eyes' from *haga* 'ray (of sun, moon)', *fe-sindro* 'make stand' (e.g. a baby, by holding up with hands), *fe-a* 'feed' (from *a* 'eat'). An example of a causative construction with *fe-* is given in (70):

(70)   *Ma   i-fe-tataro   fefu   niha.*
       PST   3s.RLS-CAU-sit   all   person:MUT
       'He got everyone to sit down' (by asking, or by taking person to seat).

4.3.2 -Cö and -(C)i: Transitive derivations with causative and applicative meanings

Suffixes of the shape *-Cö* and *-(C)i* are used to derive transitive verbs from nouns, intransitive verbs and bound roots. The factors relevant for the choice between these two suffixes as well as the choice of the consonant (if any) are complex and will not be discussed in detail here (see Brown 2001, section 5.2 for more extensive treatment). In general, however, if a stem is stative, a derived verb is causative in meaning (i.e. the additional participant is coded as an A argument), while if the stem is dynamic the derived verb is applicative (i.e. the additional participant is coded as a P argument).

Suffixes of the shape *-'ö*, *-gö*, *-i* and *-ni* apply to nouns to derive transitive verbs with a meaning something like 'A makes/lets P have/be N', e.g. *lagö-'ö* 'cover' (verb) from *lagö* 'cover for large things', *balu-gö* 'cover' from *balu* 'cover for small things', *sagö-i* 'roof' (verb) from *sagö* 'roof' (noun), *ete-ni* 'bridge' (verb) from *ete* 'bridge' (noun).

Suffixes of the shape *-'ö*, *-gö*, *-i* and *-si* are used with stative intransitive verbs or bound roots to derive verbs with causative meanings. The causee in these constructions corresponds to the S argument of the stative verb, and is thus patientive in its semantic role. These suffixes are exemplified in (71)–(74):

(71) *Ö-ide'ide-'ö*   *ndrao   mana*, ...
      2s.RLS-ST:small-TR   1s.MUT   now
      'You look down on me now, ...' (cf. *Ide'ide ndrao.* 'I am small.')

(72) *Ma=u-hori-gö*   *gö-gu*   *kofi*
      CPL=1s.RLS-finish-TR food.MUT-1s.POSS   coffee
      'I have finished my coffee.' (cf. *A-hori gö-gu kofi.* 'My coffee is finished.')

(73) *La-fönu-i*   *zumo*   *batu.*
      3p.RLS-full-TR well:MUT   rock
      'They filled the well with rocks.' (cf. *A-fönu zumo batu.* 'The well is full of rocks.')

(74) *Ö-aila-si*   *ndrao*
      2s.RLS-embarrassed-TR   1s.MUT
      'You embarrassed me.' (cf. *Aila ndrao.* 'I am embarrassed.')

The suffix *-'ö* and suffixes of the shape *-(C)i* are used in applicative function with dynamic intransitive verbs. In verbs derived with these suffixes, the referent of the A argument corresponds to the S argument of the stem and a P argument is added, as exemplified in sentences (75)–(77):

(75) *Löna   u-a'ege-'ö*   *ndaugö.*
      NEG   1s.RLS-laugh-TR   2s.MUT
      'I did not laugh at you.' (cf. *Löna a'ege ndao.* (NEG laugh 1s.MUT) 'I did not laugh.')

(76) *Ma=i-cici-ni*   *mbatö*   *asu*
      CPL=3s.RLS-defecate-TR   floor:MUT   dog
      'The dog has defecated on the floor.' (cf. *Tebai cici ya* (can't defecate 3s.MUT) 'He is constipated.')

(77) *I-a-ta'u-fi*   *nama-nia.*
      3s.RLS-ST-fear-TR   father:MUT-3s.POSS
      'He is in awe/afraid of his father.' (cf. *Ata'u ya* 'He is afraid.')

Suffixes of the shape *-(C)i* are also used in applicative function with bound dynamic roots, e.g. *alu-i* 'look for' from *-alu* 'go hunting', *e'e-si* 'cry over' from *-e'e* 'cry', *eßo-khi* 'guard field from birds' from *-eßo* 'chase birds'.

Transitive verbs and ditransitive verbs are made causative by prefixation of dynamic *fa-* and suffixation of either *-'ö* (for transitive verbs) or *-gö* (for ditransitive verbs).

(See Brown 2001, sections 5.2.1 and 5.2.2 for details of this analysis.) These derivations are illustrated in (78) and (79) below. If the causee is present in these constructions it is realized by an oblique argument, such as *khö-gu* 'me' in (78):

(78) *I-fa-sura-'ö*   *zura*   *khö-gu*   *fandrita.*
      3s.RLS-DO-write-TR   letter:MUT   DAT-1sg.POSS   priest
      'The priest got me to write a letter/had me write a letter.'
      (cf. *u-sura zura* (1s.RLS-write letter:MUT) 'I wrote a letter.')

(79) *I-fa-be'e-gö*   *gefe*   *khö*   *z=o-ndröröu.*
      3s.RLS-DO-give-TR   money:MUT   DAT   [REL=IPF-make.medicine]:MUT
      'He sent money to the village healer.' (i.e. 'He got someone to give money to the village healer.')

5 NOMINALIZATIONS AND NOMINAL MORPHOLOGY

There are three main strategies used synchronically to derive nominals from verbs: relative clause formation (see 3.5.2), prefixation of formatives beginning with *f-*, and suffixation of *-(C)a*. Reduplication of verbs, bound roots and nouns has been used in the past to derive nouns, but this process does not appear to be productive synchronically. Some examples of nouns formed by reduplication are *sou-sou* 'scoop' from *sou* 'scoop' (V), *balo-balo* 'patch' from *balo* 'mend', *balu-balu* 'cover' from *-balu*, cf. *balu-gö* 'cover' (V), *ndro-ndro* 'food cooked in pig's blood', from *ndro* 'blood', *löfö-löfö* 'fireflies' (root does not occur elsewhere).

5.1 Prefixes

Prefixation is used to derive abstract nouns referring to actions, states, processes, manner of action and instruments. Prefixes do not derive nouns referring to places or things resulting from actions, which is the domain of suffixation (see 5.2). There are five forms of the nominalizing prefix: *fa-*, *fa'a-*, *f-*, *fe-* and *fe'a-*.

The forms *fa-* and *fa'a-* derive nominals with abstract meanings from stative intransitive verbs. The form *fa-* occurs on vowel-initial stems, e.g. *fa-auri* 'life' from *auri* 'alive', *fa-ide'ide* 'smallness' from *ide'ide* 'small', *fa-olofo* 'hunger' from *olofo* 'hungry'. The form *fa'a-* occurs on consonant-initial stems, e.g. *fa'a-sökhi* 'goodness' from *sökhi* 'good', *fa'a-mate* 'death' from *mate* 'dead', *fa'a-tumbu* 'birth' from *tumbu* 'born', *fa'a-te-kiko* 'ruination' from *te-kiko* (RES-destroy) 'ruined'.

F-, *fe-* and *fe'a-* derive nominals referring to the act or state described by the verb, or to instruments. *F-* replaces *m-* in most verbs which begin with *m-*, including those derived with *mo-* 'HAVE' and imperfective forms of transitive verbs, e.g. *f-eßo* 'the act of chasing birds from field' (cf. *m-eßo* 'chase birds from field'), *f-aluaya* 'dance' (noun) (cf. *m-aluaya* 'dance' (verb)), *f-o-ömö* 'state of having a debt' (cf. *mo-ömö* 'have debt'), *famunu* (*f-aN-bunu* (NR-IPF-kill)) 'the act of killing', *fanagö* (*f-aN-tagö* (NR-IPF-steal)) 'the act of stealing', *fondra'a* (*f-aN-ra'a* (NR-IPF-cut.small.things')) 'knife used for cutting small things'. In a number of cases, nominals derived with *f-* have the same form as the causative verb, e.g. *fo-ömö* 'state of having debt' can also mean 'cause to have debt'; *f-ofanö* 'act of leaving' also means 'send away' (cf. *m-ofanö* 'leave'). The form *fe-* occurs on consonant-initial dynamic verbs, including some of those verbs which begin with *m-* and some transitive verbs, e.g. *fe-bahö* 'the act of coughing' from *bahö* 'cough', *fe-miẞo* 'the act of crowing' from *miẞo* 'crow', *fe-halö* 'the act of holding/taking' from *halö* 'hold; take', *fe-bötö-si* 'anything used to hurt someone' from *bötö-si* (wounded-TR) 'wound'. The form *fe'a-* occurs on two intransitive verbs, *möi* 'go' and *so* 'arrive': *fe'a-möi* 'trip, journey', *fe'a-so* 'arrival, advent'.

Nominals derived from dynamic verbs with the forms *f-*, *fe-* and *fe'a-* correspond in meaning and some of their functions to present participles or gerunds in other languages. For example they are the preferred form of complement for a number of verbs which can take clausal complements. An example of a nominal derived from the verb *döli* 'pull' occurs as the complement of the verb *tandraigö* 'try' in (80):

(80) *I-tandraigö   vo-ndröli   sao.*
      3s.RLS-try   [NR-pull]:MUT   anchor
      'He tried to pull in the anchor.'

Note that the derived nominal is mutated, as expected of nominals in P function. The A argument of the complement is controlled by the matrix verb and is marked on that verb by a pronominal prefix; its P argument, *sao*, is unmutated. If a nominal derived from a transitive verb occurs with its A argument, that argument occurs as a possessive suffix, as exemplified by *-nia* in (81):

(81) *Ma=fa-lele   ya   khö-gu   v-a-nua-nia.*
      CPL=DO-tongue   3s.MUT   DAT-1s.POSS   [NR-IPF-say]:MUT-3s.POSS
      'She swore at me when she was speaking.' (lit. 'She swore at me (in) her saying (it).')

Note that the nominal in (81) is used adverbially, another function of these derivations. If possessive suffixes occur with nominals derived from intransitive verbs, the referent of the suffix corresponds to the S argument of the verb, e.g. *götö va-a-uri-gu* (during [NR-ST-keep.alive]:MUT-1s.POSS) 'during my lifetime', cf. *a-uri ndrao* (ST-keep.alive 1s.MUT) 'I am alive'; *aradö ma'efu ve'a-so-ra* (late a.bit [NR-arrive]:MUT-3p.POSS) 'They arrived a bit late' (lit. 'Their arrival was a bit late.'), cf. *so ira* (arrive 3p.MUT) 'They arrived.'

5.2 Suffixes

Suffixes of the shape *-(C)a* derive nominals referring to acts, places, and results of actions. These suffixes typically attach to verbs which are formally intransitive – that is, transitive verbs in imperfective form, prefixed with *aN-*. A suffix of the shape *-Cö*, which is found attached directly to unmodified transitive verb stems, is now fossilized and occurs in just a handful of nouns, e.g. *fohu-tö* 'girl ready for marriage' from *fohu* 'select', *tanö-mö* 'seed(ling)' from *tanö* 'plant', *uri-fö* 'domestic animal' from *uri* 'look after', *halö-wö* 'work' from *halö* 'hold, take'. There is some evidence that the consonants which occur in these suffixes, i.e. /s/, /t/, /l/, /w/, /m/, /n/, /kh/ and /f/, are reflexes of original word-final consonants (for discussion see Brown 2001, sections 3.8 and 6.6).

The suffix *-sa* occurs almost exclusively on verbs derived with dynamic *fa-*, e.g. *fa-lele-sa* 'swear words' (from *fa-lele* (DO-tongue) 'swear'), *fa-bö'ö-sa* 'difference' (from *fa-bö'ö* (DO-other) 'be different'), *fa-lakhi-sa* 'meeting' (from *fa-lakhi* (DO-meet)). Examples of nominals derived with other suffixes of the shape *-(C)a* are: *sao-ta* 'harbour' from *sao* 'anchor', *o-ndröi-ta* 'inheritance' from *röi* 'leave behind', *a-mua-ta* 'behavior' from *bua* 'act, behave', *ate-la* 'grave' from *m-ate* 'die, dead', *a-matö-la* 'bit broken off' from *fatö* 'break', *ofanö-wa* 'departure' from *m-ofanö* 'leave', *taro-ma* 'position, status' from *taro* 'put', *ötö-na* 'ford' (in river) from *ötö* 'cross', *ambu-kha* 'forge' from *ambu* 'forge metal', *auri-fa* 'life' from *auri* 'alive', *a-nunu-a* 'cremation' or 'place for burning' from *tunu* 'burn'. (For extensive treatment of nominalization strategies see Brown 2001: ch. 6.)

REFERENCES

BPS Kabupaten Nias (2000) *Nias dalam Angka* 1998 ('Nias in figures'), Gunungsitoli: Badan Perencanaan Pembangunan Daerah Tingkat II Nias dan Badan Pusat Statistik Kabupaten Nias ('Regional Development Planning Board and Statistical Office of Nias Regency.

Brown, L. (2001) *A Grammar of Nias Selatan*, PhD Dissertation, University of Sydney.

Catford, J.C. (1988) 'Notes on the phonetics of Nias', in R. McGinn (ed.) *Studies in Austronesian Linguistics*, 151–172, Athens, Ohio: Center for Southeast Asian Studies.

Comrie, B. (1978) 'Ergativity', in W.P. Lehmann (ed.) *Syntactic Typology: Studies in the Phenomenology of Language*, 329–394, Austin: University of Austin Press.

Fries, E. (1915) *Leitfaden zur Erlernung der Niassischen Sprache*, Ombölata: Missionsdruckerei.

Halawa, T., Harefa, A. and Silitonga, M. (1983) *Struktur Bahasa Nias*, Jakarta: Pusat Pembinaan dan Pengembangan Bahasa.

Himmelmann, N.P. (1996) 'Demonstratives in Narrative Discourse: A taxonomy of universal use', in B. Fox (ed.) *Studies in Anaphora*, 203–252, Amsterdam: Benjamins.

Kähler, H. (1936–1937) 'Untersuchungen über die Laut-, Wort- und Satzlehre des Nias', *Zeitschrift für Eingeborenen-Sprachen* 27:91–128; 212–222; 261–288.

——(1955) *Die Sichule-Sprache auf der Insel Simalur an der Westküste von Sumatra*, Berlin: Dietrich Reimer.

——(1963) *Texte von der Insel Simalur*, Berlin: Dietrich Reimer.

Ladefoged, P. and Maddieson, I. (1996) *The Sounds of the World's Languages*, Oxford: Blackwell.

Laiya, S.Z. (1985) *Kamus Nias – Indonesia*, Jakarta: Pusat Pembinaan dan Pengambangan Bahasa.

Nothofer, B. (1986) 'The Barrier Island languages in the Austronesian language family', in P. Geraghty, L. Carrington and S.A. Wurm (eds) *FOCAL II: Proceedings from the Fourth International Conference on Austronesian Linguistics*, 87–109, Canberra: Pacific Linguistics.

——(1994) 'The relationship between the languages of the Barrier Islands and the Sulawesi-Philippine languages', in T. Dutton and D.T. Tryon (eds) *Language Contact and Change in the Austronesian World*, 389–409, Berlin: Mouton de Gruyter.

Pätsch, G. (1964a) 'Reste einer personal-gegliederten Konjugation im Indonesischen', *Mitteilungen des Instituts für Orientforschung* X:171–181.

——(1964b) 'Verbale und nominale Fügungen im Nias', *Zeitschrift für Phonetik Sprachwissenschaft und Kommunikationsforschung* 17:597–608.

——(1978) 'Das Nias im historischen Vergleich', *Zeitschrift für Phonetik Sprachwissenschaft und Kommunikationsforschung* 31:58–72.

Steinhart, W.L. and Maier, Henk (1990) Song XXVII. In Volkenkundig Museum Nusantara, *Nias: Tribal treasures. Cosmic reflections in stone, wood and gold*, 137–182, Delft: Volkenkundig Museum Nusantara.

Sundermann, H. (1892a) *Deutsch–Niassisches Wörterbuch*, Moers: J.W. Spaarman.

——(1892b) 'Kleine Niassische Chrestomathie mit Wörterverzeichniss', *Bijdragen tot de Taal-, Land- en Volkenkunde van Nederlandsch Indië* 41:335–446.

——(1905a) *Niassisch–Deutsches Wörterbuch*, Moers: J.W. Spaarman.

——(1905b) 'Niassische Texte mit deutscher Uebersetzung', *Bijdragen tot de Taal-, Land- en Volkenkunde van Nederlandsch Indië* 58:1–72.

——(1913) *Niassische Sprachlehre*, 's-Gravenhage: Martinus Nijhoff.

Thomas, J.W. and Taylor Weber, E.A. (1887) *Niasch–Maleisch–Nederlandsch Woordenboek*, Batavia.

CHAPTER TWENTY-ONE

JAVANESE

Alexander K. Ogloblin

1 INTRODUCTION

The Javanese form the largest language community in the Austronesian language family. With about 80 million people at the end of the twentieth century, they make up about 40% of the Indonesian population. Their original habitat is Central and Eastern Java, but many Javanese live in Sumatra and elsewhere in Indonesia. There are also descendants of Javanese immigrants in Malaysia and Singapore (who tend to assimilate with Malays), Surinam, the Netherlands and New Caledonia. Outside Southeast Asia, their language is maintained best in Surinam, which had a Javanese community of about 50,000 members in 1980. With the Javanese outnumbering other ethnic groups in Indonesia and with the central position (in several respects) of Java in Indonesia, Javanese has had a considerable influence on Indonesian (the national language). On the other hand, more than half of the Javanese use Indonesian (particularly in formal situations). As a result, much Indonesian vocabulary is being borrowed into Javanese spoken and written language as well as Javanese mass media.

Nothofer classifies Javanese as a separate primary branch within the Malayo-Javanic subgroup facing another primary branch including Malay, Madurese, Sundanese and Lampung (Nothofer 1975, 1985). However, Adelaar excludes Javanese from his Malayo-Sumbawan subgroup. The latter consists of Balinese, Sasak, Sumbawa, the Malayic and Chamic languages, Madurese and Sundanese (ADELAAR, A HISTORICAL PERSPECTIVE).

Two partly overlapping periods are distinguished in the development of Javanese: an Old Javanese and a New Javanese period. Old Javanese (henceforth OJ) is the language of epigraphy and manuscripts. It is mostly written in verse, and it stems predominantly from the ninth to the tenth century in Central Java, from the tenth to the fifteenth century in East Java, and from the fifteenth century until present in Bali. The OJ script is of Old Indian origin, and about 50% of the vocabulary is Sanskrit, while there are also some loanwords from Old Malay and other neighboring languages (Aichele 1943, Kullanda 1992). The poetic tradition is elaborate and has remained stable throughout the centuries (Zoetmulder 1974:25). The OJ of certain texts written in the fourteenth century and later (mostly in Bali) is called *Middle Javanese*.

After 1500 AD, OJ works and poetic tradition were preserved and continued in Hindu-Buddhist Bali. In Java itself Islamization caused the erosion of the OJ literary system, and New Javanese (henceforth NJ) became the main literary language. Apart from influencing Balinese and Sasak, OJ also exercised lexical influence on Sundanese, Madurese and Malay (partly through the intermediary of NJ). Modern Indonesian uses OJ as a source for political and other terminologies. OJ is also called *kawi* 'of poets, poetical'; this term furthermore refers to archaic elements in NJ poetry. This chapter is mainly concerned with the description of NJ. Some notes on OJ structure are presented in §6.

The NJ standard seems to have experienced two shifts since the sixteenth century. A first shift was from the Hindu-Buddhist center in East Java to Java's north coast, where new Muslim states had emerged and much Islamic literature was produced. This literature includes translations from Malay and is often written in *pégon* (an adaptation of the Arabic script). A second shift took place from the northern coast area to the Central Javanese hinterland with the rise of the agrarian state of Mataram in the sixteenth century (cf. Pigeaud 1967). The Mataram literary tradition was continued by authors in the Surakarta and Yogyakarta principalities, where in the eighteenth and nineteenth centuries a literary standard was created based on the dialect of Central Java. Its stylistic repertoire was enriched with OJ words and affixes. NJ book printing started in the 1830s making use of the carakan script which is of OJ origin (cf. §6); later on Roman script was used which eventually became the standard writing system. It underwent some spelling reforms (cf. §2.3).

The mid-nineteenth century NJ saw the appearance of newspapers and travelogues, and in the twentieth century novels, short stories and lyrics in *vers-libre* emerged, although the traditional versification is practiced still today. There are books, journals and TV programs in NJ, and the language has its teaching hours in the school syllabus. According to Uhlenbeck (1949:26), the language of literature and media which emerged in the twentieth century probably deserves the name Modern Javanese.

Two main dialect groups can be distinguished. A western group has been in contact with Sundanese and is more archaic in phonology. It has retained voiced consonants and the pronunciation of the final [a]. On the other hand, a central-eastern dialect group changed [a] for [ɔ] (cf. Poerwadarminta 1953:2). Its voiced consonants have become voiceless aspirated ones. The eastern part of the central-eastern area has been in contact with Madurese for many centuries. A separate status should perhaps be given to the Osing (Using) dialect in the extreme east of Java (Banyuwangi district).

NJ is renowned for its etiquette synonymy with its oppositions 'informal' (*ngoko*) vs. 'formal' (*krama*, henceforth indicated with F; this opposition was absent or nearly absent in OJ) and plain vs. honorific (*krama inggil*, indicated with H). The synonyms are partly or entirely different in form. The number of formal synonyms is about 850 words and there are several formal affixes; the amount of honorific words (including those humbling oneself or anybody else in respect to another person) is about 280. There are also about 35 semi-formal words (*madya*, indicated with SF) and several words of court usage (Poedjosoedarmo 1968). Combinations of different style units result in several speech styles. This overgrowth of synonymy (much increased in the nineteenth century) and the rules for using it in various situations create an almost insurmountable hardship for most non-Javanese speakers. This contributed to the fact that NJ, the most widely spoken language in Indonesia with an ancient literary tradition, failed to become the official language of the state.

There also exists a traditional literary style (*basa rinengga* 'embellished language') with many archaic words and formatives. A discussion of these formal and literary styles is beyond the present outline (see Fox, Chapter 4, this volume, for additional notes).

The study of OJ as well as NJ was started in the nineteenth century by predominantly Dutch scholars. The main contributions to the study of OJ were made by H. Kern and H.N. van der Tuuk. The German linguist W. von Humboldt used OJ as a case study in his general theory of language. At present the main tools for the study of OJ are Zoetmulder's grammar (Zoetmulder 1950) and dictionary (Zoetmulder 1982) and articles by several scholars. There are textbooks and grammars in Indonesian including translations of Zoetmulder (1950) and (1982). There is also a short grammar in Russian (Teselkin 1972). Many data are found in publications of OJ inscriptions and literature which usually contain a few observations on language structure and use (e.g. Sarkar 1971–72 vol. I:xiii–xx).

NJ studies include several grammars and a major NJ–Dutch dictionary (2 volumes, in carakan script; Gericke and Roorda 1901); other dictionaries are NJ–Dutch (Jansz 1932; Pigeaud 1938), NJ–French (Favre 1870), NJ–German, (Herrfurth 1972), and NJ–English (Horne 1974 (with many examples on the usage) and Robson and Wibisono 2001). A NJ–Russian dictionary is in press. In the twentieth century a systematic structural description of NJ was produced by E.M. Uhlenbeck, including a grammar, a fundamental monograph on morpheme structure and a series of important papers (Uhlenbeck 1941, 1949, 1978 and its Indonesian translation of 1982).

There are descriptions of dialects (most recently, Adipitoyo *et al.* 1999 on the Surabaya dialect, Ewing 1999 on Cirebon Javanese, Setrowidjojo and Setrowidjojo 1994 and Vruggink 2001 on the Javanese of Surinam, Mohamed Subakir 1996 on language shift in Malaysia), of dialect geography (cf. Nothofer 1980–1981, Sudaryono *et al.* 1990), of etiquette styles etc., textbooks, short grammars, theses, papers on various subjects in French, Russian, German, Czech, Japanese, but most of all in English. Apart from the reference list to this section, the reader is also referred to critical bibliographies by Uhlenbeck (1964, 1971), a list of more recent studies by Clynes and Rudiyanto (1994), and a periodical newsletter (*Caraka*). A new textbook of modern spoken NJ (Arps *et al.* 2000) was issued by the University of Leiden, which has the only chair of Javanese studies outside Indonesia. Indonesian papers and monographs on NJ grammar, lexicology, dialects and other subjects are among others Soebroto (1998), Soebroto *et al.* (1991) and Sudaryanto (1992). Dictionaries compiled in Indonesia are NJ-Indonesian (Prawiroatmodjo 1957), monolingual NJ (Poerwadarminta *et al.* 1939, Prawiroatmodjo 1998) and Indonesian–NJ (Poerwadarminta 1945).

The NJ examples quoted below are mostly from prose texts of the 1950s onwards. The OJ examples are from tenth–eleventh century prose. Some NJ examples were kindly supplied and explained by Ms Henny S. Drajati.

2 PHONOLOGY, ORTHOGRAPHY AND MORPHOPHONEMICS

2.1 Phonemes

There are 25 consonants and 8 vowels. Four of the consonants occur in loanwords only and occur between brackets in Table 21.1.

TABLE 21.1: CONSONANTS

	Labial	Dental	Retroflex	Palatal	Velar	Glottal
Occlusive, non-sonorant	p b	t d	ṭ ḍ	c j	k g	ʔ
Occlusive, sonorant	m	n		ɲ	ŋ	
Fricative (non-sonorant)	(f)	s (z)		(š)	(x)	h
Liquid		l, r				
Semivowel	w			y		

TABLE 21.2: VOWELS

	Front	Central	Back
High	i		u
Mid-high	e		o
Mid-low	ε	ə	ɔ
Low		a	

/b/, /d/, /ḍ/, /j/, /g/ have two allophones. They are voiced postnasally in homorganic clusters (/mb/ [mb], /nd/ [nd], etc.). In other positions they are almost or totally voiceless and aspirated, whereas the following vowel is breathy with a harsh timbre ([pʰ], [tʰ], [ʈʰ], [cʰ], [kʰ], cf. the instrumental phonetic accounts in Fagan 1988, Hayward 1993). There is a tendency for monophonemization of /mb/ type clusters. /b/, /d/ and /g/, do not occur word-finally although the graphemes b, d and g, are still used in standard orthography (cf. §2.3 below).

The palatal occlusives are affricates whereby the front upper part of the tongue first touches the alveolum and the front part of the palate, and then moves down. The /n/ has a retroflex [ɳ] variant before /ʈ/, /ḍ/.

The phoneme inventory in Table 21.2 reflects analyses made by Horne (1961) and Samsuri (1961). An alternative phonological analysis recognizes only 6 vowel phonemes (Uhlenbeck 1949; Yallop 1982; Ras 1985). However, according to this system (which conforms to the traditional spelling), allophones of different vowels may appear in the same phonological environment. Furthermore, the rules of allophonic distribution and of vowel alternations are fairly complex and heterogeneous, which makes the system not quite realistic (Ogloblin 1993).

Post-nasal vowels, and also certain combinations of subsequent vowels, are nasalized: [mã], [nĩ], etc., [sãẽ] F 'good'. The vowel /ɔ/ is very open, approaching [ɑ]. The vowel /ə/ is relatively short and alternates phonetically with zero.

2.2 Syllable and morpheme structure

The main syllable types are V, CV, VC, CVC. There are also syllables beginning with a consonant cluster. These are initial homorganic clusters consisting of a nasal + voiced occlusive (NCV, NCVC): *mboten* [mbɔ.tən] F 'no', of an occlusive + sonorant non-occlusive: *krungu* [kru.ŋu] 'hear', *mlarat* [mla.rat] 'very poor', *ngwungu* [ŋwu.ŋu] 'awaken', *gebyar* [kʰə.pʰyar] 'shine', or of a homorganic cluster with a following non-occlusive sonorant (NCCV, NCCVC): *ngglambyar* [ŋgla.mbyar] 'insipid'. Word-initial three consonant clusters point to prefixation. Onset /h/ is exceptional. Aspirate and retroflex consonants, palatal occlusives, /w/ and /y/ are not allowed as coda. Coda occlusives are normally unreleased.

About 85% of morphemes have two syllables (Uhlenbeck 1949:31), other morphemes have one, three or four syllables; asyllabic morphemes are rare. There is a strong phonetic tendency to restore disyllables from monosyllables as well as to reanalyze quadrisyllables as two disyllables. The double CVC structure is a kind of reduplication: *wangwang* 'hesitant'.

Intervocalic clusters predominantly consist of a homorganic nasal + occlusive or are [ŋs]. They can also consist of any of these clusters with a following /r/, /l/, /y/, e.g. [mpr, mbl, mpy, ɲcr, ɲjr, ŋkr, ŋsr]: *wonten* 'be; (there) is (F)', *santri* 'pious Muslim' (Uhlenbeck 1949:181 sqq). A syllable before a homorganic cluster (also before /ŋs/, /ŋsr/ etc.) is open by convention, as is shown by the rounding of penultimate /a/ in *tampa* [tɔm.pɔ] 'receive', *bangsa* [pʰɔŋ.sɔ] 'nation'. Compare *tanpa* [tan.pɔ] 'without' (which has no homorganic cluster).

The vowels /i/ and /u/ are generally not permitted in closed last syllables, nor are final /ə/ and /ɛ/. Final /-a/ is permitted in right-bound morphemes: *ana-né* [ana-ne] '(its) being', but not word-finally; consequently, a loanword like *Amérikah* ends in [h] in order to avoid rounding of final [a]. Regressive vowel harmony applies in that the height of the penultimate vowel cannot be just one level lower than the height of the final syllable vowel. The vowel heights are as follows: /i/, /u/, /ə/ at the first level, /e/, /o/, /a/ at the second level, and /ɛ/, /ɔ/ at the third level. So sequences like /e...i/, /o...u/, /ɛ...e/, /ɛ...o/, /e...ə/ and /ɔ...a/ are not permitted. Other disallowed sequences are /e...ɛ/, /o...ɛ/ and /ɛ...ɔ/, but no such restrictions apply to sequences with central vowels /a...i/, /a...u/, and /a...ə/ (Ogloblin 1993, 1999). This harmony affects neither antepenultimate syllables nor affixes. Further exceptions from the restrictions are some loans and dialectal or expressive-affective words.

Word accent is not phonologically distinctive.

2.3 Orthography

The orthography is partly based on the morphological principle that different allomorphs are identical in writing.

The letters *b, c, d, f, g, l, m, p, r, s, t, w, y* are identical to their phonemic transcription and have only one phonemic value; *n* stands for /ɲ/ before *c, j; v* is usually realised as /f/, *z* may be fricative or affricative. The following digraphs denote one phoneme: *dh* /ɖ/, *th* /ʈ/, *ng* /ŋ/, *ny* /ɲ/, *sy* /š/, *kh* /x/. Word-finally, *b, d, g* denote voiceless /p/, /t/, /k/; if only morpheme-final, but not word-final before a vowel, alternation with original aspirates is possible in somewhat archaic usage: *oyod* [ɔyɔt] 'root' → [ɔyɔtʰe] instead of [ɔyɔte] 'its root'. Syllable-final *k* denotes /ʔ/, but in some loans, onomatopoeic words, and after /ə/ it is /k/: *butek* [pʰutək] 'turbid'. However, colloquial forms have [ʔ] in the same cases: *wektu* [wəktu], colloquial [wəʔtu] 'time'. The *h*, with some exceptions, is zero between different vowels, and nearly zero between the same vowels, cf. *olèhé* [olɛe] (nominalizer, see §5), *kahanan* [kaʰanan] 'situation', *-silihi* [siliʰi] 'lend'.

The letters for vowels have more than one reading. The correct reading of a vowel in the last syllable is obtained according to the rule that 'a higher vowel occurs in the open syllable and a lower one in the closed syllable'. A correct reading of the penultimate vowel is mainly governed by the rules of vowel harmony.

1 *a* stands for /ɔ/ if final, and in an open or conventionally open penult before the final /ɔ/; it is realized as /a/ in other positions: *dina* [tʰinɔ] 'day', *Jawa* [cʰɔwɔ] 'Java', *tampa* [tɔmpɔ] 'receive', but *tampi* [tampi] 'id.' F, *bapak* [pʰapaʔ] 'father', *alon* [alɔn] 'slow'; exceptions are *ora* [ora] 'no, not' and some loans, e.g. *Jakarta*. In the old Dutch transliteration 'å' was used for the /ɔ/ reading.

2 *e* stands for /e/, /ɛ/, and /ə/. Diacritics were used before 1973 for the distinction: *é* for /e/ and *è* for /ɛ/: *kéné* [kene] 'here', *yèn* [yɛn] 'if'. These diacritics are also used in this chapter. Another, not standard, orthography prefers only one diacritic: *ě* for /ə/. It is used following transliteration of OJ or sometimes in language learning (Arps *et al.* 2000).

3 *o* stands for /o/ if it is word-final or occurs in an open (or conventionally open) syllable preceding word-final /o/, as well as /e/, /ɛ/, /a/, and final /-ɔ/: *loro* 'two', *ombé*

'drink', *olèh* 'get', *bolah* [pʰolah] 'thread', *rosa* [rɔsɔ] 'strong'. In other positions, it stands for /ɔ/, as in *kori* 'door', *wolu* 'eight', *kothong* 'empty', *mboten* 'no, not' F.

4 in closed syllables *i, u* indicate /e/ resp. /o/; or, according to Ras (1985), they indicate the vowels intermediate between [i] and [e] resp. between [u] and [o]; in other positions, they stand for /i/ resp. /u/: *éling* [eleŋ] 'remember', *ésuk* [esoʔ] 'morning', *iki* 'this', *kuwi* 'that', *pulo* [pulo] 'island'.

The reading rules hold for all root morphemes, but only partly so for affixal words. Sometimes the spelling hides the morphemic structure of a word and yields ambiguous orthographic words such as *keboné* which stands for [kəpʰone] 'his buffalo' (← *kebo* [kəpʰo] 'buffalo' + *-né* 3POSS) as well as for [kəpʰɔne] 'his garden' (← *kebon* [kəpʰɔn] 'garden' + *-é* 3POSS); *kabecikan* 'goodness' (← *becik* 'good') is pronounced [kapʰəciʔan], but *kamardikan* 'freedom' (← *mardika* 'free') is pronounced [kamartʰikan], although both are derived with the confix *ka- -an*; compare also *ngana* [ŋɔnɔ] 'like that', but *mangana* [maŋanɔ] 'eat!' ← *mangan* + *-a* [-ɔ]. So there clearly remain some ambiguities in the orthography, especially if no diacritics are used.

2.4 Words, morpheme types and their variability

A morphological word is a unit equal to a root morpheme, to its combination with (one or more) affixes or to a reduplicated root morpheme or affixed word. Combinations of roots, affixed words and reduplicated words, may in most cases be considered as phrases, although some combinations are close to compound words. Composed roots consist of two roots one or both of which are truncated, e.g. *lunglit* 'very thin' < *balung* 'bone' + *kulit* 'skin'. Finally, Sanskrit-based compounds have an 'Attribute-Head' order of constituents while in native compound-like formations 'Head-Attribute' order is the rule.

Affixes are grammatically bound morphemes that are never separated from the adjacent morpheme. Most of them modify the phonemic composition of roots. There are about 40 affixes, monosyllabic, disyllabic as well as asyllabic (consonantal) ones. They include prefixes (about 20), infixes (1), infix-prefixes (2), suffixes (10), and confixes (with pre- and suffixal parts identical to separate prefixes and suffixes, 7). Ten of these affixes are stylistic variants of other affixes. Some prefixes are unproductive and of doubtful status.

Infixation of *-um-* happens after the first consonant: *tindak* 'pace' → *t-um-indak* 'proceed'. This infix has a prefixed variant which occurs with vowel-initial roots : *ili* 'current' → *m-ili* 'flow'; alternatively also with roots that have initial [r] or [l]: *laku* 'course' → *m-laku, l-um-aku* 'walk'.

A word may contain one or two prefixes and one or two suffixes (including prefix or suffix parts of a confix), but no more than four affixed elements in total. A small number of roots, mostly function words, never take affixes, e.g. *lan* 'and', *dhèk* 'then (in the past)'.

Besides roots and affixes there are proclitics and enclitics denoting the first and the second person; see §3.1 below.

There are several types of stylistic variation of root and affixal words:

(1) colloquial [ə] for [a] in antepenultimate syllables: *nagara* [nəkʰɔrɔ] 'city; state', *sakedhap* [sə-kətʰap] '(in) a moment'.

(2) colloquial elimination of [ə] in non-final syllables: *gamelan* [kʰaməlan] → [kʰamlan] 'indigenous classic orchestra'.

(3) colloquial elimination (truncation) of some or all non-final syllables: *bocah* → *cah* 'child', *rembulan* → *mbulan* 'moon' (in fact, some monosyllabic variants are more usual than disyllables).

(4) colloquial vowel contraction: *dhéwé* → *dhé* 'self', *ana ing* → *nèng* 'in, at', *di-ombé* → *d-ombé* 'be drunk, is being drunk' (Robson 1985:166; Horne 1974: xiv, xvi–xvii).

(5) expressive change of vowels: /e/, /a/ → /i/; /o/, /ɔ/ → /u/, in the last syllable, sometimes with special final vowel length: *gedhé* [kʰətʰe] 'big' → [kʰətʰi::] 'awfully big', *panas* [panas] 'hot' → [panis] 'very/ awfully hot'.

(6) expressive addition of [w] or [uʷ] as a prefix before the first vowel: *énak* [enaʔ] 'tasty' → [wenaʔ] 'very tasty', or an infix in the first or second syllable: *bodho* [pʰotʰo] 'silly' → [pʰuʷotʰo] 'what a fool', *abot* [apʰɔt] 'heavy' → [apʰwɔt] 'very heavy' (examples for (5) and (6) from Ras 1985:15; Horne 1961:416–17, Sudaryanto 1992:54–55, transcription adjusted).

(7) change of vowels or consonants to make a variant of the formal register: [kuraŋ] → [kiraŋ] F 'few', [luŋgoh] → [ləŋgah] F 'sit', [wəktu] → [wəktʰal] F 'time', [tʰinɔ] → [tʰintən] F 'day'. Semi-formal style variants are mostly obtained by deleting some initial syllable or consonant of the formal synonym: [mənɔpɔ] F → [nɔpɔ] SF 'what?', [wɔntən] F → [ɔntən] SF 'be'. The prefix *di-* has the formal variant *dipun-*.

Prefixation of *N-*, *paN-/ peN-*, *maN-/meN-* involves the replacement of the voiceless occlusives with their corresponding homorganic nasals; the consonants /c/, /s/ are replaced by /ɲ/: *-cakot* → *nyakot* 'bite'; alternatively they are replaced with /n/ if the following syllable also begins with /s/ or /c/: *-susul* → *nusul* 'follow'. The aspirate allophones are replaced by non-aspirate voiced ones when preceded by a homorganic nasal: *-gawa* [kʰɔwɔ] → *nggawa* [ŋ-gɔwɔ] 'carry'. Vowel-initial roots as well as roots with /r/-, /l/- and /y/-, take /ŋ/: [paŋ-rɔsɔ] 'feeling', [ŋ-laɲi] 'swim'. In roots with initial /w/ this /w/ is most often replaced by /m/: [wɔcɔ] → [mɔcɔ] 'read', and sometimes by /ŋ/: [wetan] 'east' → [ŋetan, maŋetan] 'go to the east'.

Some vowel-initial suffixes take an initial /n/ if the preceding word ends in a vowel: *-é* ~ *-né*, *-ipun* ~ *-nipun* , *-ing* ~ *-ning*, *-en* ~ *-nen*: *kebo* 'buffalo' → *keboné* 'his buffalo', *dangu* 'long' F → *sadangunipun* 'during, as long as' F, *warni* 'color' F → *warnining* 'color of (something)' F, *tuku* 'buy' → *tukunen* 'let it be bought! = buy it!'. In some derivatives with the confix *ke- -en* the suffixal part is *-n* after vowels: *amba* 'broad' + *ke- -en* → *k-amba-n* 'too broad' (besides *k-amba-nen*). The prefix [kə-] becomes [k-] before vowels, as in the previous example. Roots with final /-i/, /-e/ supply /y/ and roots with final /-u/, /-o/ supply /w/ to certain suffixes: *mréné* '(towards) here' + *-a* → *mrénéa* [mreneyɔ] 'come up!', *jago* 'cock' → *jagoan* [-owan] 'stalwart, hero'. For the phonemic status of /y/ and /w/ here, see Ogloblin (1996).

Vowel-final roots have '/n/-final'; and '/ʔ/-final' allomorphs before certain vowel-initial suffixes. In both cases the vowels of the root are lowered:

/ɔ/ → /a/, e.g.	[tipʰɔ] 'fall' → [tipʰan-i] 'fall on *(st.,so.)*', [tipʰaʔ-ake] 'let fall, drop'
/ɔ...-ɔ/→/a...a/, e.g.	[kɔndɔ] 'tell' → [kandan-i] 'tell to *(so.)*', [kandaʔ-ake] 'tell' *(sth.) n*
/o/ and /u/→/ɔ/, e.g.	[təmu] 'meet' → [təmɔn-i] 'visit' [kruŋu] 'hear' → [kruŋɔʔ-ake] 'listen'
/e/ and /i/→/ɛ/, e.g.	[isi] 'content' → [isɛn-i] 'fill'; [kʰawe] 'make' → [kʰawɛʔ-ake] 'make for (so.)'

Roots may therefore have up to two additional allomorphs, as with [kaṇḍan], [kaṇḍaʔ] for [kɔṇḍɔ] above, whereas other roots have only one additional allomorph, or none at all, if their combination with suffixes is restricted.

In derivations, a base with an epenthetic final /n/ may have the same shape as a suffixal derivative that obeys the same sandhi rule, compare *isèn* (<*isi* 'contents') 'contents', *temon* (<*temu* 'meet') 'sth.found' and *isèn -i, temon-i* above. In some words *-an* is used twice, as an accretion and as a suffix: *nesu* 'angry' → *neson, neson-an* 'short-tempered'. Some irregular analogical forms and alternative variants from the same root are possible (Uhlenbeck 1949:208–211).

The /-ɔ/ and /ɔ...-ɔ/ roots, in addition, have '/a/-allomorphs': *kira* [kirɔ] 'idea' → *kirané* [kira-ne] 'perhaps', *kandha* [kɔṇḍɔ] 'tell' → *kandha-né* [kaṇḍane] '(his) story'. Thus, there may be four allomorphs of the same root morpheme: [kɔṇḍɔ], [kaṇḍa], [kaṇḍan], [kaṇḍaʔ].

Vowel alternation also occurs in consonant-final roots. Roots having /e/, /o/ in the final closed syllable replace them with /i/ resp. /u/ if the root-final consonant is resyllabified with the following syllable: *wis* [wes] 'already' → *sawisé* [saʔ-wi.s-e] 'after (that)', *-rangkul* [raŋkol] 'embrace' →[raŋku.l-an] 'embrace each other'. Final /ʔ/ always remains as the syllable coda: *manuk-é* [manuʔ.e] 'the bird'. The suffixes *-ipun*, *-aké*, *-aken* do not cause the syllable boundary shift, nor does the prefix *dipun-* before vowels (it was written separately in earlier orthographies).

Roots with final /h/ lose this consonant before vowel-initial suffixes: *salah* 'mistaken' → *salah-é* [salae] 'his/her mistake', *adoh* 'far' → *kadohan* [katʰowan] 'far distance'.

2.5 Reduplication

In full reduplication, roots and complex stems can be copied entirely with or without vowel change: *wong* 'person' → *wong-wong* 'people', *se-dhéla* 'one moment' → *se-dhéla-se-dhéla* 'from time to time', *telu-las* 'thirteen' → *telu-las-telu-las* 'in groups of thirteen', *bali* 'again' → *bola-bali* 'again and again', *gruthal-grathul* 'with a coarse voice' (many patterns of vowel change exist). For a further variant of this pattern, see §4.3.

In Ce-reduplication the first consonant followed by /ə/ is prefixed to a root: *lara* 'ill' > *le-lara* 'illness', *griya* F 'house' → *ge-griya* 'have one's own household'. Ce-reduplication does not happen to roots with initial vowel.

Reduplication of suffixed forms may be preceded by morphophonemic changes: *omah* [omah] 'house' → *omah-é* [oma-e] 'his house' → *omah-omahé* [oma-oma-e] 'his houses'. The /ɔ..ɔ/ type seems to be exceptional: *kanca* [kɔɲcɔ] 'mate, friend' > *kanca-kanca-n é* [kɔɲcɔ-kaɲcane] 'mates'.

Nasal substitution of initial consonants is reproduced in the reduplicated segment, as if nasal substitution preceded reduplication: *-colong* 'steal' → *nyolong* 'steal' → *nyeny-olong* 'commit thefts (permanently)', *nyolong-nyolong* 'steal now and then', *krungu* 'hear' → *ngrungok-aké* 'listen' → *ngrungok-ngrungok-aké* 'listen continually'. The same applies when consonants are pre-nasalized: *dhepis* 'flat' → *n-dhepis* 'hide (flat)' → *ndhepis-ndhepis* 'hide (several times)', *-bungah* 'glad' → *m-bungah-aké* 'gladden' → *mbungah-mbungah-aké* 'gladden by various ways'. The reverse order (reduplication before pre-nasalization) occurs with initial vowels: *anèh* 'strange' → *ng-anèh-anèh-i* 'behave strangely'. It also occasionally occurs with initial consonants but seems more archaic: *m-bungah-bungah-aké* (Ras 1985:128–129), *donga* 'prayer' → *n-donga* 'pray' → *n-de-donga* 'offer prayers'. Monosyllables are reduplicated when suffixed with *-an* in order to adapt to a disyllabic root structure (Uhlenbeck 1982:104): -*peng* 'strive, try hard' → *pengpengan* 'best of all'.

3 BASIC MORPHOSYNTAX

3.1 Word classes

Word classes are mostly determined by their syntactic distribution, which for root words (including reduplicated roots which are attested in all classes) is the only criterium. Many affixes are either verbal or nominal. Other affixes allow us to identify certain forms or subclasses of verbals (verbs, adjectives) and nouns, but they are not diagnostic for any traditional part of speech in itself. For instance, the prefix *paN-* and the confix *paN- -an* are nominal: *pan-jaluk* 'request', *pang-gon-an* 'place'. On the other hand, the suffix -*an* and the confix *ka-/ke- -an* derive both nouns and verbs, and the prefix *sa-* derives adverbs, numerals, or nouns, and so on.

Transitive verbs possess an inflectional paradigm of voice and person, numerals possess a special derivational paradigm, and some demonstratives and directionals express relative distance (in space or time) vis-à-vis the speaker which is indicated by different vowels, e.g. *kéné* 'here', *kono* 'there', *kana* 'there (far)'.

Function words have constraints on autonomy and linear order (some have to be non-final, others non-initial), also on affixation and reduplication. Function words can be relativizers, articles, prepositions, subordinative and coordinative conjunctions, or particles.

Substitutes make up a subsystem parallel in distribution to autosemantic words. Verbal substitutes include *dikapakaké* 'what is done to (someone or something)?' and *dimengkonokaké* 'to be done in that way'. The major personal pronouns, substitutes of nouns, are listed in Table 21.3. Some other forms exist in different etiquette styles.

Plural in pronouns is unmarked or is expressed lexically in phrases such as *aku sakloron* 'we (lit. I) both', *aku kabèh* (lit. I + all) 'we', *awak-é dhéwé* 'we' (incl., lit. body-the own), *dhèwèké kabèh* 'they' etc. Basically, NJ has no plural personal pronouns except *kita* which is probably borrowed from Indonesian. Third person is also referred to with demonstratives (see example (52b) below).

TABLE 21.3: PERSONAL PRONOUNS

	Free forms	Proclitics (actor)	Enclitics (genitive)	Suffixes (genitive)
1s, 1p excl.	*aku, kula* (F), *kowé, pen- jeneng-an* (F, formerly H)	*tak=,* *(n)dak=*	=*ku*	
1p incl.	*kita*			
2s, 2p	*sampé-yan* (SF)	*ko(k)=* [kɔʔ], colloq. *tok=*	=*mu*	
3s, 3p	*dhèwèk-é,* *piyambak- ipun* (F)			-*(n)é,* -*(n)ipun* (F)

Clitics alternate with full pronouns. Proclitics and affixes are similar in that they are inseparable from the adjacent morpheme. Enclitics can be separated from their hosts by an attribute: *kanca-ku* 'my friend' → *kanca kenthel-ku* 'my bosom friend' (*kenthel* lit. 'thick'). The same holds for the suffix -*é*, as it has the same possessive pronominal function: *wajan-é* 'her frying pan' → *wajan emas-é* 'her golden frying pan'. This ability to become separated may be due to Indonesian influence on the noun phrase structure. The third person suffix -*é/-ipun* also has a wider range of functions and uses than the genitive enclitics (cf. in particular §3.5).

Verbals are typically negated with *ora* 'not' (*mboten* F). They may be further subdivided into transitive and intransitive verbals. The latter include adjectives with some derivational possibilities unusual in verbs, as, for instance, *pedhes* 'hot (of taste)' → *sa-pedhes-pedhes-é* 'as hot as possible' (Uhlenbeck 1982:67; Ras 1985:210–211). In general, however, adjectives and intransitive verbs are very close in syntactic behavior.

Verbal affixes delineate, more or less precisely, the semantic roles of the subject and complements. Root verbals are unmarked.

Nouns are typically negated with *dudu, dédé* F. They take numeral attributes and quantifiers.

Auxiliaries are intermediate between function words and full words, having some features of autonomy and allowing derivational affixation, reduplication or enclitization. They include negations, modal words, aspectual, taxis and tense markers, and nominalizers.

3.2 Basic clause structure

The main syntactic functions, or sentence parts, are predicate and its direct dependents: actants (arguments) and circumstants (adjuncts). Actants are for the most part obligatory sentence parts whereas circumstants are mostly optional sentence parts with predicative meaning. Actant types are subject and complements. Complements are in contact position to verbs or they are introduced by prepositions; either feature distinguishes them from the subject.

The most common order in a clause is Subject-Predicate-(Complement$_1$-Complement$_2$), or $SV(O_1O_2)$ in more popular notation.

There are no overt markers of the subject function. For most clause patterns we can identify the subject by the way it corresponds to the head of a relative phrase. For example, the head in (1a) corresponds to the subject in (1b); *sing* is a relativizing function word.

(1) a. *Angin-é   sing   adhem   isih   tumiyup*
         wind-the   REL   cold   still blow
         'The cold wind was still blowing.'

(1) b. *Angin-é   adhem*
         wind-the   cold
         'The wind was cold.'

Complements disallow this correspondence, e.g. from *Wong$_1$ kuwi$_2$ nulis$_3$ layang$_4$* 'That$_2$ man$_1$ is$_3$ writing$_3$ a$_4$ letter$_4$' we cannot obtain **layang sing wong kuwi nulis* 'a letter that the man is writing'. However, not all clause types have their counterparts in relative phrases.

The predicate can be a noun phrase, a numeral or a prepositional phrase: *Kula Oplet* 'I am Oplet'; *dhipan$_1$-é$_2$ loro$_3$* 'Her$_2$ sofas$_1$ were two$_3$' = She had two sofas; *Aku$_1$ menyang$_2$ kutha$_3$* 'I$_1$ to(wards)$_2$ town$_3$' = 'I am going to town'.

As for verbal predicates, the difference between transitive verbs and intransitive verbals and their associated constructions is essential. Transitives occur in active and passive constructions (and are marked accordingly), while intransitives occur only in one basic construction type, some in a more active-like construction, others in a more passive-like one. There are regular syntactic-semantic correspondences between transitive verb forms and the actants of active and passive transitive constructions, whereas such correspondences are irregular in intransitive constructions.

First, complements to active transitive verbs correspond to the subject of the passive clause (there are, however, passive clauses without active counterparts). Complements of an intransitive verbal have no such correspondence. Moreover, these complements often have a generic meaning and indefinite reference (cf. towards the end of this subsection). Note that according to these definitions, intransitives are not necessarily one-place predicates.

Transitive and intransitive verbals have different mood forms. The basic form of both may be labeled mood-irrelevant, or indicative. Other moods are the irrealis, the imperative, and the propositive, which is a first person imperative denoting urging oneself or expressing an intention to do something. Intransitive verbs have no imperative mood, hortative meanings being expressed by indicative and irrealis forms. As shown in Table 21.4, transitive verbs consist of a base and a voice or voice + person prefix: *N-*, *di-* or *ø*. The irrealis has forms for all persons in both voices; the propositive is by definition restricted to the first person in both voices. The imperative has only second person passive forms. It is not opposed to another voice or person form, and hence is without the zero prefix. The morpheme *tak* in the active propositive coincides with the first person proclitic, but here it is a part of the analytical verb form, cf. §3.3.

The base (here preceded by a hyphen) may coincide with a root morpheme: *-jupuk* 'take' or with a nominal derivative: *peng-anggé* F 'garments' → *-pengangé* 'dress up', or it may be derived from both with the suffixes *-i* or *-aké/-aken* F. Verbs with these suffixes have an increased valency and are sometimes called the first and the second transitive (henceforth TR1 and TR2; see further §4.1).

After vowel-final roots the suffix variant *-nen* is used instead of *-en* in imperatives: *waca* 'read' → *waca-nen* 'read (it)!'. The suffixes *-aké* and *-n* are synonymous, as well as *-i* and *-an* (which becomes [ɔn] before *-a* [ɔ]: [cʰupoʔɔnɔ].

The combinations *-an-a*, *-an-é* and *-n-a*, *-n-é* are often treated as single suffixes. However, in both of them the components retain their meanings: derivational in the first component (*-an*, *-n*) and modal (*-a*, *-é*) in the second one (cf. Soebroto *et al.* 1991:111).

TABLE 21.4: MOOD FORMS OF TRANSITIVE VERBS (NON-FORMAL STYLE)

-jupuk 'take', *-jupuk-i* 'pick up, take many *(sth.)*', *-jupuk-aké* 'fetch for *(so.)*'

	Indicative	Irrealis	Imperative	Propositive
Active	*n-jupuk*	*n-jupuk-a*	——	*tak n-jupuk*
	n-jupuk-i	*n-jupuk-an-a*	——	*tak n-jupuk-i*
	n-jupuk-aké	*n-jupuk-n-a*	——	*tak n-jupuk-aké*
Passive:	*ø-jupuk*	*ø-jupuk-a*	*jupuk-en*	*ø-jupuk-é*
1/2	*ø-jupuk-i*	*ø-jupuk-an-a*	*jupuk-an-a*	*ø-jupuk-an-é*
	ø-jupuk-aké	*ø-jupuk-n-a*	*jupuk-n-a*	*ø-jupuk-n-é*
Passive:	*di-jupuk*	*di-jupuk-a*	——	——
3	*di-jupuk-i*	*di-jupuk-an-a*	——	——
	di-jupuk-aké	*di-jupuk-n-a*	——	——

Some verbs lack the marker *N-* (e.g. *gawé* 'make; cause') and some have alternating roots in active and passive.

Active clauses with two actants contain a subject expressing the ACTOR (ACT) and a complement expressing the UNDERGOER (UG), usually in ACT-V-UG order. In (2) the subject (denoting the second person) is omitted anaphorically.

(2) *Ngancan-i   aku   ya?*
    AV:friend-TR1   1   OK
    '(Will you) accompany me, OK?'

The order VOS implies some emphasis on the action.

(3) *Wis   nemu   akal   aku*
    PFV   AV:find   sense   1
    'I've *got* a solution.'

The NJ passive is unusual in that the person category is irrelevant in the active, but is marked in the passive where it refers to the complement (denoting the ACT), not to the subject (denoting the UG). Passive clauses with third person actors differ from passive clauses with first or second person actors (henceforth 3-passive and 1/2-passive, respectively). Verbs with a third person ACT have the prefix *di-* (*dipun-* F); the ACT, if overtly expressed, immediately follows the verb and/or is introduced by *déning, ing, karo* or another preposition.

(4) *Kandha=ku   di- gugu   wong₁ akèh₂*
    say=1.GEN   PASS:3-believe   people₁,₂
    'People believed what I said.'

(5) *Dhokter   Santosa   tansah   di-seneng-i   déning   wong₁ akèh₂*
    doctor   PN   always   PASS:3-pleased-TR1   by   people₁,₂
    'People always liked Dr Santosa.'

Omission of the ACT is usually anaphoric.

(6) *Embok-é   Sarjana nandur   empon-empon.*
    mother-GEN PN   AV:plant   medicinal.root

    Slédri,   bawang   lan   tomat   uga   di-tandur.
    celery   onions   and   tomato   also   PASS:3-plant
    'Sarjana's mother plants medicinal roots. She also plants celery, onions and tomatoes.' (lit. 'Celery, onions and tomatoes are also planted [by her].')

In other semantic or contextual conditions the absence of the ACT denotes its unspecificity.

(7) *Ing   pakunjaran   panjenengané   di-siksa*
    LOC   prison   3 (H)   PASS:3-torture
    'He was tortured in prison.'

In the 1/2-passive the verb has a zero prefix. It is immediately preceded by a full pronoun or human noun representing the ACT. The ACT expression cannot be omitted in this construction which is another peculiar feature for a passive.

(8) *Upama   sampéyan   kula   ø-jak   mrika…*
    if   2 (SF)   1 (F)   PASS:1/2-invite   DIST.LOC (F)
    'If I invite you there,…'

In non-formal style proclitic pronouns are used.

(9) *Suk   liya   dina   mesthi   dak=ø-jak   mréné*
     FUT   other day   certainly 1=PASS:1/2-invite PRX.LOC
     'I will certainly invite [him] to come here some day.'

The alternation of proclitic bound morphemes with autonomous words implies that they are not prefixes, as usually stated in grammars. Both types of ACT exponents serve as complement. This is the only instance in NJ syntax where a complement without a preposition precedes the verb.

In casual speech the prefix *di-* may be dropped (Robson 1985:165), in which case the opposition between the two passive forms only appears from the syntactic context.

In three-place active and passive clauses, one of the two non-subject complements is semantically a location, 'dative' or other 'stable' non-actor participant, and the other complement is something which is passed on, handed over, or another 'moving' non-actor participant (cf. Alieva *et al.* 1991:159 on Indonesian). No prepositions are used if the 'stable' participant is the first complement. This construction may be labeled applicative. Most often the verb is marked with the suffix *-i* (TR1).

(10) *Ibu   mènèhi (/N-wènèh-i/) bocah lima dhuwit papat*
      mother AV-give-TR1   child five duwit   four
      'Mother gives five children four *duwits* (a small coin).'

In the corresponding passive clauses the 'stable' participant becomes the subject. Such constructions are preferable to those with active verbs which sometimes sound artificial, although they are well represented in grammars.

(11) *Aku   di-silih-i   pit*
      I   PASS:3-lend-TR1 bicycle
      'I was lent a bicycle.'

A locational subject alternates with a prepositional complement of the same meaning. The passive clause is consequently left with no subject.

(12) *Ing panggonan kono di-deg-i   kutha*
      LOC place   DIST.LOC PASS:3.build-TR1 town
      'A town was built in that place.'

In the other constructions the 'moving' participant is the first complement, and the 'stable' participant is represented by the second complement, prepositional or not. This construction may be labeled causative. Most often the verb is marked with the suffix *-aké* (TR2).

(13) *Pelayan nimbang   mau   mènèh-aké (/N-wènèh-aké/)*
      shopman AV:weigh ANAPH   AV-give-TR2

      barang-barang mau   marang juragan=é
      thing-PL   ANAPH   DIR   master=3.GEN
      'The shop assistant whose job was to weigh gave these things to his master.'

In the corresponding passive clauses the 'moving' participant is the subject:

(14) *Iwak-é   di- wènèh-ké   aku*
      fish-the PASS:3-give-TR2 I
      'The fish was given to me [by him].'

The second complement occurs with or without a preposition, cf. the verb -*pasrahaké* in the following two sentences:

(15) *Pati-urip*   *dak=ø-pasrah-aké*   *marang* *Sing* *Kuwasa*
     death-life   1=PASS:1/2-surrender-TR2 DIR   REL   Powerful
     'I give up my life and death to The Powerful.'

(16) *Tukon=é*   *di-pasrah-aké*   *embok=né*
     purchase=3.GEN PASS:3-surrender-TR2 mother=3.GEN
     'She handed her purchases over to her mother.'

Note that some kinship terms take -*né* instead of -*é*, as in *embok = né* in (16).

Imperative clauses are passive, because the linear order UG-Verb is quite common. Thus the UG is the subject of the imperative sentence. It always has definite reference. (Imperatives with indefinite UGs may be formed with hortative irrealis forms, cf. examples 30–31 below.) Contrary to the indicative with the zero prefix, imperative forms are never preceded by an ACT-complement. If the ACT (i.e. the addressee) is mentioned, it is in the form of a vocative (as in (18)).

(17) *Mripat = mu*   *tutup-an-a*
     eye = 2.GEN   close-TR1-IMP
     'Close your eyes.'

(18) *Waos-en,*   *bu*
     read(F)-IMP Ma
     '(Please) read (it), Mom.'

Basic intransitive predicates are root words, derivatives from other verbs or derivations from words of non-verbal classes. The most productive affix is the prefix *N*-, less productive are the prefix *meN-/maN-* and the infix-prefix -*um-/-em-/m*-. The prefixes are used on verbs denoting actions, movements, and visual or acoustic effects: *endhog* 'egg' → *ngendhog* 'lay eggs', *kadhaton* 'palace' → *ngadhaton* 'go to the palace', *kidul* 'south' → *mangidul* 'go to the south'. The infix-prefix denotes an action, a state or a transition to a state: -*lebu* (bound root) → *m-lebu* 'enter'.

The common order in one-place intransitive clauses is SV.

(19) *Oplet*   *m-èsem*
     PN   INTR-smile
     'Oplet smiled.'

The reverse order predicate-subject is common in presentative (existential) clauses.

(20) *Ana*   *wong*   *nini-nini, /...*/
     EXIST person old.woman
     'There is an old woman...'

With other types of predicates, reverse order puts some emphasis on the predicate.

(21) *Klèru* *banget* *pangira=mu*
     false   very   assumption=2.GEN
     'Your assumption is totally false.'

The prefix *a*- denotes 'being in a state of possessing [root]'. Such verbs are derived from nouns or verbals. They are somewhat archaic and bookish: *bebed* 'sarong' → *abebed* 'wear a sarong', *woh* 'fruit' → *awoh* 'have/ bear fruit', *urip* 'live' → *aurip* (embellished style) 'live'. This prefix does not co-occur with roots beginning with [a] or [ə]. Some originally monosyllabic stative verbs (adjectives) have a fossilized *a*-: *abot* 'heavy', *akèh* 'much, many'. This prefix can also derive verbs from an NP consisting of a head + attribute.

(22)   *A-mata   papat,   a-sikil   telu*
      POSS-eye four   POSS-leg three
      'With four eyes, with three legs.' (A riddle; the answer: 'An old man with spectacles and a stick')

One-place intransitives may have no subject at all. A locational prepositional complement is used instead, to describe a situation at a certain location. Cf. (12) for a parallel transitive passive construction.

(23)   *Ing   pasar   ramé*
      LOC   market crowded
      'The market is crowded.'

Two-place intransitive clauses are actional, stative or experiential/adversative. Their structure resembles either an active or a passive transitive construction, as exemplified by (24) and (25), respectively.

(24)   *Kupu   iku   duwé   tlalé*
      butterfly DIST have   feeler
      'Butterflies have a feeler.'

(25)   *Kulawarga = ku   kena   musibah*
      family = 1.GEN   affected misfortune
      'My family was struck by misfortune.'

The complement may be prepositional or not. In passive-like clauses the ACT is expressed mostly without prepositions as in 3-passive clauses, but there are no restrictions with regard to person. Prepositions can sometimes alternate with other prepositions or with their absence: *wedi karo asu = ku* 'is afraid *of* (lit. with) my dog', *wedi marang sang ratu* 'is afraid *of* the king', *wedi dhokter* 'is afraid of the doctor'. Cf. *karo* and *nyang* in (26):

(26)   *Dhèwèké   saiki   malih   seneng   karo   Tatiek   lan   wis   ora*
      3   now   change   like   with   PN   and   PFV   NEG

      seneng   nyang   aku
      like   to(wards) 1
      'He has now changed his liking from me to Tatiek.' (lit. 'liking (to) Tatiek and no longer liking (to) me')

Prepositions are usually absent in colloquial speech and when the complement is immediately adjacent to the verb.

    Some nouns have locative prenasalized forms: *omah* 'house' → *ngomah* 'in(to) the house', *Bandung* → *mBandung* 'to Bandung'.

    In active-like intransitives, the UG without preposition is often non-referential and/or the verb has a generic meaning: *mèlu kursus* 'attend courses', *réwang simbok* 'help one's mother' (usually, habitually), *golèk dhuwit* 'earn (lit. look for) money', *dodol pathi pohung* 'trade in tapioka flour'.

3.3 Non-indicative moods and uses (irrealis, propositive, hortative)

The irrealis suffix -*a* can join not only verbals, but also words of other classes: pronouns, adverbs, auxiliaries, conjunctions etc. For example, *aku* 'I' → *aku-a* 'if it was me' (Arps *et al.* 2000:508). Irrealis has several meanings.

(i) Potential (in broad sense, including possible or intended action/event):

(27) *Daya-daya   tekan-a   ing   omah*
      do.one's.best   arrive-IRR   LOC   house
      '[She] did her best to arrive at home.'

(ii) Conditional (irrealis here is marked on an auxiliary):

(28) *Aja-a   ana   lawa,   lemud   kuwi   rak   ndadi*
      NEG.IMP-IRR   EXIST   bat   mosquito   that   PTCL   multiply
      'If there were no bats, moskitoes would be breeding in mass.'

(iii) Optative:

(29) *Lelakon   iku   di-gawé-a   kaca*
      event   DIST   PASS:3-make-IRR   mirror
      'Let this event serve as an example.'

(iv) Hortative, which occurs with active transitive (30) and with intransitive (31) verbs. The UG is usually indefinite.

(30) *Ng-ombé-a   banyu   godhogan*
      AV-drink-IRR   water   boiled
      'Drink boiled water.'

(31) *Wis   meneng-a   ta,   Tar*
      enough   silent-IRR   PTCL   PN
      'Now be silent, Tar!'

Some hortative sentences use the irrealis form with nouns: *kemul* 'blanket' → *kemul-a* 'use (as) a blanket!' (lit. let it be blanket) (Herawati 1993:81). Deictics may also be the predicate of such sentences: *mréné* '[moving] here' → *Mréné-a!* 'Come here!; come this way!'

In sentences urging that an action be performed in a certain manner, the relative marker *sing* introduces the adjectival attribute of the verb, which is not usual with neutral modality.

(32) *Lungguh-a   sing   anteng*
      sit-IRR   REL   quiet
      'Sit quietly.'

The morpheme *tak/(n)dak*, which is segmentally identical with the first person passive proclitic, is used with intransitive and active transitive verbs in preverbal position to express a readiness or intention: *dak lunga* 'let me go', *dak ng-ombé* 'let me drink'. In contrast to the first person passive proclitic, its occurrence does not exclude the separate denotation of the first person as a subject. In the propositive it acts like a function word and can be separated from the following verb by another word (Uhlenbeck 1965:61, note; 1982:178, note).

(33) a. *Aku   tak   nusul   Bapak   dhéwéan*
         1   1.PRPV   AV:follow   father   alone
         'Let me follow father by myself.'

(33) b. *Aku   tak   dhéwéan   waé   nusul   Bapak*
         1   1.PRPV   alone   PTCL   AV:follow   father
         'Let me alone follow father.'

The passive forms are preceded by the same *tak* = /*(n)dak* = or *kula* F, however, here they represent the ACT-complement (the same as in the indicative and irrealis 1/2-passive). The propositive meaning is marked by the suffix *-é/-ipun* F. The UG in this construction cannot be a second person. This may be due to the fact that the suffixes marking the propositive are identical to the third person suffixes.

(34) *Tak=ø-plathok-an-é*   *kayu=mu*
       1 = PASS:1/2-chop-TR1-PRPV   wood = 2.GEN
       'Let me chop your wood.'

(35) *Mangké   kula   ø-pados-an-ipun*
       just.now   1(F)   PASS:1/2-look.for(F)-TR1-PRPV (F)
       nomer   tilpun=ipun
       number   telephone = 3.GEN (F)
       'Let me now look for her telephone number.'

Indicative forms, particularly the two passive forms of transitive verbs, are also common in commands and appeals, and also in mild urging.

(36) *Linggih   kéné*
       sit.down   PRX.LOC
       'Sit down here.'

(37) *Cobi   panjenengan   ø-pireng-aké*   *pethèk   kula*
       please(F)   2(F)   PASS:1/2-hear (F)- TR2   solution   1(F)
       'Please listen to my solution [of the puzzle].'

The *di-* form of the 3-passive is often used for indirect urging of the second person, also for joint first and second person action.

(38) *Mangga   dipun-unjuk   malih*
       please   PASS:3-drink(H)   more (F)
       'Please have some more.'

(39) *Ayo   padha   di-tulung-i*
       let   PL   PASS:3-help-TR1
       'Let us help [him].'

Before adjectives, *di-* expresses the urge for a certain quality: *di-becik baé* '(be) well'. Only the indicative is used in vetative sentences with the auxiliary *aja*.

(40) *Aja   ng-ombé   banyu   wantah*
       NEG.IMP   AV-drink   water   unboiled
       'Don't drink unboiled water.'

See Ramelan (1983), Herawati (1993) and Ogloblin (2001) for further reading on the hortative.

3.4 Circumstants, adverbial auxiliaries

Circumstants are represented by adverbs (time), noun phrases (time), prepositional phrases (place, time, manner), and simple and reduplicated adjectives (manner) including: *biyèn* 'formerly', *jam pitu* (hour seven) 'at seven o'clock', *ora suwé* (not long) 'soon', *alon-alon* 'slowly', *saka bungah=é* (from joyful=3.GEN) 'for joy', and *kanthi permana* 'sharply' as in: *nyawang Oplet kanthi permana* (look PN with sharp) 'looked at Oplet sharply'. Quantifiers may be considered a specific kind of circumstant: *wis asat kabèh* (PFV dry all) 'are all (already) dry', *methik-i lombok siji-siji* (AV:pluck-TR1 red. pepper one-by-one) 'to pluck red pepper pods one by one'.

Some circumstants are attributes of the preceding verb making up a stable phrase with it: *mèsem₁ kecut₂* 'smile₁ acidly₂', *ngguyung glègès* 'laugh softly'.

Meanings of modality, evidentiality, inference, textual coherence are conveyed by modal verbs and adverbs such as *mesthi*, *mesthi-né* 'should; certainly', *apik-é* 'it would be nice', *wangun-é* 'apparently', *jaré-né* 'they say', *cekak-é* 'in short', *kocap-a* 'let us tell; now' (beginning another topic), *dadi* 'thus', *adat-ipun* 'usually' F.

Auxiliaries (mostly preverbs) of taxis, aspect, tense, and modality specify the meaning of the verb. Some of them are oriented towards a certain moment that coincides with the moment of speech or is determined by the context: cf. *lenggah* F 'sit' or 'sit down', but *lagi lenggah* 'is/are/was/were sitting' (continuous); *wis asat* 'is/was/will be (already) dry', *wis lunga* 'is/was/will be gone' (perfective), *durung ana* 'is/was not yet available/ will not yet be available', *durung klakon* 'has/had not yet taken place/ will not yet have taken place' (negation of the perfective). The future and intentional marker is *arep*: *arep nuku* 'will buy/would buy/ is or was going to buy'. *Banjur* and *nuli* are markers of subsequent actions: *m-lebu₁, banjur₂ tepung-an₃ karo₄ réwang₅-é₆* 'came₁ in₁, then₂ met₃ with₄ the₆ maid₅'. Other preverbs are *sok* (habitual), *tansah* 'still, always', *saya* 'more and more'. Modal verbs, as *bisa* 'can', *kudu* 'must' are very much like these preverbs. Postverbally *manèh* '(any) more' is used. Some phrases composed of auxiliaries can be stable phrases by themselves: *ora tau* (not ever) 'never'. The past marker *dhèk* is initial in adverbials of time; the marker *suk* denotes future.

The plural marker *padha* means plurality of subject or, sometimes in passive clauses, of the complement (=ACT) (Hayward 1998).

(41) *Kabèh   padha   g<um>uyu*
      all   PL   -INTR-laugh
      'All of them laughed.'

(42) *Aku   padha   di-   tinggal*
      1   PL   PASS:3-leave
      (Context: the parents were gone,) 'I was left [by them].'

With nouns that are not countable it means locational distribution ('in several places').

(43) *Aspal   padha   gempal*
      asphalt   PL   chipped
      'The asphalt was cracked everywhere.'

3.5 Noun phrase structure

Definite reference of noun phrases is conveyed by the suffixes *-(n)é/-(n)ipun* F, demonstratives and personal articles. The suffixes are also markers of (i) the third person possessive or (ii) the genitive or, (iii) in combination with (i) or (ii), they can be nominalizers:

(i) omah=é, griya-nipun F (1) 'his/her/their house', (2) 'the house'
(ii) omah-é Sudin 'Sudin's house', *rega-né sing nomer limalas* 'the price of the fifteenth'
(iii + i) mulih-é 'her coming home' (*m-ulih* 'come home')
(iii + ii) mulih-é Sudin 'Sudin's coming home'

For *-(n)é/-(n)ipun* as markers of the propositive passive, see Table 21.4 and §3.3.

Demonstratives are *iki* PRX, *kuwi* DIST (colloquial), *iku* DIST (literary), *kaé* DIST (far away), and *punika* F which is neutral with regard to distance. They can be used as pronouns as well as adnominal modifiers in which case they follow their head. (The latter is also true for the anaphoric marker *mau* 'the one just mentioned'.) Pre-head determiners are *saben* 'every', the personal articles *si* (familiar), *sang* (honorific), *para* (PL:HUMAN), social determinatives which occur before human nouns (e.g. *dhi Èdi* '(younger) brother Edi', *Pak Lurah* 'Mr Village-head'), and the indefinite marker *sawijining* 'one, certain' (indefinite reference in most contexts is not overtly marked). Some quantifiers may also occur before the head. The demonstratives *iku* and *kuwi* are also used for generic subjects, cf. (24) and (69). However, if only one entity is presupposed by the context, no reference marker is required, cf. (23) and (43).

Nominal attributes follow the head. They may do so without special markers: *wit₁ kinah₂* 'cinchona₂ tree₁', *tanah Jawa* 'the country of Java', *bala₁ kethèk₂* 'army₁ of monkeys₂', *swarga₁ donya₂* 'paradise₁ on earth₂'. They may also take the GEN marker *-é/-ipun* F after the head in the possessive, which yields a restrictive relation: *omah-é Marsam* 'Marsam's house', *kuburané ratu* 'the king's grave' (cf. *pasaréyan* (F) *ratu-ratu* or *pasaréyan* (F) *kraton* 'royal grave(yard) F'). The head marker *-ing* (of bookish style and not used as a possessive pronoun) conveys various semantic relations between head and attribute: *ratu-ning buta* 'the king of giants', *rerenggan-ing griya* 'embellishment [for the] house (F)', *dèwi-ning kaéndahan* 'goddess of beauty'.

Attributes with the prefix *sa-* (variants are *se-* (colloquial), *sak-* stressing the quantity 'one' or a totality) + noun denote the full measure of what is denoted by the head, or joint ownership, or joint belonging to what is denoted by the head: *wong sa-pendhapa* 'all the people in the hall', *buku sak-lemari* 'a case full of books', *aku sa-kanca* 'I with my mates', *kanca sak-klas* 'a classmate' (Gina *et al.* 1987:43).

Adjectival attributes that supply a logical restriction to the notion of the head noun follow the head without special markers: *jaman₁ kuna₂* 'ancient₂ times₁', *sumur₁ jero₂* 'deep₂ well₁'; the same applies to non-passive verbs denoting potentiality or destination: *tandha₁ budhal₂* 'sign₁ (to) depart₂', *piranti₁ nenun₂* (N-*tenun*) 'equipment₁ (for) weaving₂'. Reduplication of adjectives means plurality and different degrees of the quality of [adjective]: *para priyayi gedhé-gedhé* 'big (and high) dignitaries'. The pattern 'noun + transitive verb root' seems to be a borrowing from Indonesian, as in *méja tulis* 'writing table'. In certain subordinated constructions the difference with the predicate is neutralized: *kaya₁ gajah₂ m-laku₃* 'as₁ a walking₃ elephant₂' or 'as an elephant walks'.

An attribute introduced by the relative markers *sing, kang, ingkang* F is usually contrastive, especially if it consists only of an adjective: *enggon₁ sing reged-reged₂* 'dirty₂ places₁' (as opposed to clean ones).

Numerals precede measure or count unit nouns: *se-puluh jam* 'ten hours', *ro-las rupiyah* 'twelve rupiahs'. The accretion *-ng* is used with some variation for most digits from 2 to 9 before such nouns and before the numeral base for tens, hundreds and thousands, while 'one' is rendered by *se-/s-* in these contexts: *lima* 'five' → *limang taun* 'five years', *atus* 'hundred' → *s-atus rupiyah* 'one hundred rupiahs'; *-ng* is also used with indefinite quantifiers: *pira* 'how much?' → *pirang-pirang dina* 'many days'. Other nouns mostly take numerals in post-position: *sumur loro* 'two wells', *candhi sèwu* '(one) thousand temples'. Numerals function as ordinal numbers when they follow the measure/count unit noun : *jam lima* 'five o'clock', *kelas nem* 'sixth class'; ordinal numbers may also be expressed by the prefix *kaping* or *ping* (which is written separately and usually expresses multiplicity, 'so many times'): *cap-capan₁ kaping₂ telu₃* 'third₂,₃ (time₂) edition₁'.

Coordinate nouns are joined with conjunctions (*lan, tur* 'and', *utawa* 'or', etc.) or just without markers: *bapa₁ biyung₂* 'father₁ and mother₂, parents', *pati₁-urip₂* 'life₂ and death₁', *se₁-taun₂ rong₃ taun₂* 'one₁ or two₃ years₂'.

An attribute may also be a prepositional phrase: *panggonan₁ ing₂ sa-kiwa-tengen₃=é₄* 'surrounding (*lit.* in₂ its₄ left-right₃) place₁', *pitulung₁=é₂ marang₃ menungsa₄* 'its₂ help₁ to₃ people₄'.

In phrases with several attributes, restrictive attributes generally precede possessive ones, and a GEN marker may be attached to the head or to the restrictive attribute: *anak₁-é₂ pembarep₃ Pak₄ Lurah₅* 'the eldest₃ son₁ of₂ Mr₄ Village-Head₅', *sipat-sipat₁ ala₂-né₃ wong₄* 'bad₂ qualities₁ of₃ people₄'.

Relativized or prepositional attributes follow other attributes: *kalung₁ mutiara₂ sing₃ ditinggalaké₄ Perisadhé₅* 'pearl₂ necklace₁ that₃ was left₄ for₄ Perisade₅', further to the right go demonstrative pronouns or the anaphoric *mau*: *putra₁ =né₂ kakung₃ loro₄ mau₅* 'his₂ (aforesaid₅) two₄ sons₁ ₊ ₃ (*lit.* child₁H male₃H)'.

The attribute of an attribute follows its own head: *ril₁ dalan₂ sepur₃* 'rails₁ of the rail (*lit.* train₃) way₂', *leluhur₁-ing ratu-ratu₂ Jawa₃* 'ancestor₁ of Javanese₃ kings₂'. Relativizers may be absent even in extended NPs: *rak₁ isi₂ buku₃ akèh₄ banget₅* 'shelf₁ containing₂ very₅ numerous₄ books₃'. (On noun phrases, see also Hayward 1995).

3.6 Topic and cleft constructions

The topic construction consists of a topic and a comment. The comment is a clause with its own subject and predicate and it contains the anaphoric suffix *-é/-ipun* F. This suffix refers to the topic of the whole sentence and is often attached to the subject of the comment clause, as *cagak* 'pile' in (67):

(44) *Omah-omah   iku   cagak=é   dhuwur*
      house-PL   DIST   pile=3.GEN   high
      'Those houses have high piles.'

But this suffix may also join other parts of the comment clause, e.g. the complement.

(45) *Mung   unta   kuwi   aku   lali   wujud=é*
      only   camel   DIST   1   forget   appearance=3.GEN
      'The only thing about the camel is, I have forgotten what it looks like.'

Two comment clauses with anaphoric *=é* may be inserted into one another. Cf. the following example from Uhlenbeck (1941:91):

(46) *Sekolahan   iku   guru=né   wis   misuwur   kapinteran=é*
      school   DIST   teacher=3.GEN   already   well-known   skill=3.GEN
      'The skill of the teacher at this school is well-known.' (*lit.* 'this school (the main topic), its teacher (2nd topic) is well-known his skill' (subject of the comment clause))

In cleft constructions, the subject is complex. It is a word or a phrase introduced by the relative marker. It is usually topical and may occur in sentence-initial position.

(47) *Sing gawé ora   ng-anggo, sing ng-anggo ora   weruh,*
      REL make NEG   AV-use   REL AV-use   NEG   see

      sing weruh ora   gelem
      REL see   NEG   want
      'He who makes [it] doesn't use [it], he who uses [it] doesn't see [it], he who sees [it] doesn't want [it].' (A riddle: 'Coffin'.)

The predicate is often a noun or personal pronoun.

(48) *Kang   rusak   mung omah   ng-arep*
      REL   collapse only   house LOC-front
      'Only the front house collapsed.'

Predicate-subject order indicates emphasis on the nominal predicate, as with *aku* in (49).

(49) *Ing   ng-omah   iki   aku sing   duwé   kuasa*
      LOC   LOC-house PRX 1   REL   have   power
      'It is me who is in control in this house.'

The cleft construction is commonly used in questions about the subject. The wh-word here functions as predicate:

(50) *Sapa sing   tunggu omah?*
      who   REL   guard   house
      'Who guards the house?'

(51) *Apa   sing   di-pethik-i?*
      what REL   PASS:3-pick-TR1
      'What are [they] picking?'

4 MAJOR VERBAL DERIVATIONS

The basic morphology marking the active-passive alternation as well as the markers for basic intransitives is dealt with in §3.2. This section provides more details on the applicative and causative suffixes (TR1, TR2) and introduces an archaic passive formation (§4.1). Derived intransitives (§4.2) mostly convey uncontrolled states of affairs (involuntary actions, adversative passive, etc.).

4.1 Transitive derivations

Derivation of transitive clauses from basic transitive or intransitive ones implies the change of the correspondence between participants and actants, while the basic verbal takes on the suffixes *-i* or *-aké* which often increases its valency.

   Derivatives with the suffix *-i* may be applicative, denoting an action towards a locational, dative or reciprocal UG: *-tandur* 'plant' → *-tandur-i* 'plant with *(sth.)*', *keplok* 'clap' → *-keplok-i* 'applaud *(so.)*', *padha* 'equal' > *-padhan-i* 'be equal to, compete with *(so./sth.)*'. Derivatives from transitive verbs may also denote extensive action and/or action with multiple UGS without valency increase: *-plathok* 'chop, split' → *-plathoki* 'chop/split many things, chop/split consistently, for a long time'. Compare also sentences (52)a and (52)b:

(52) a. *Sarjana kerep mangan tomat*
          PN   often AV:eat tomato
          'Sarjana often eats tomatoes.'

(52) b. *Kuwi   mangan-i   godhong   tèh*
        DIST   AV:eat-TR1   leaf   tea
        'They [= insects] devour tea leaves.'

These derivatives furthermore also denote intensive, purposeful action: *-tampa* 'receive' →
-tampan-i 'accept'. Some verbs are causative: *-ombé* 'drink' → *-ombèn-i* 'have/give *(so.)*
to drink', *becik* 'good' → *-becik-i* 'improve' (also with 'dative' meaning; 'to treat kindly').

The suffix *-aké* and its formal counterpart *-aken* forms causatives, mostly from intransitives: *m-lebu* 'enter' → *-lebok-aké* 'put into, insert'. From transitive verbs it derives
three-place benefactive- and instrument- or means-oriented verbs: *-jupuk* 'take' →
-jupuk-aké 'fetch, get' (lit. 'take for *so.*'), *-tuku* 'buy' → *-tukok-aké* (1) 'buy for *(so.)*',
(2) 'spend (money) for *(sth.)*'.

The suffixes *-i* and *-aké* are quite productive, and may form pairs from the same root
contrasting applicative with causative, cf. *mara* [N-*para*] 'approach' (usually with a prepositional complement) → *-paran-i* 'id.' (with a non-prepositional complement in the active
sentence) vs. *-parak-aké* 'move, direct (so./sth.)', or just change the syntactic-semantic
correspondences, as in *-pakan* 'food' → *-pakan-i* 'feed' (dative-causative) vs. *-pakak-aké*
'give (sth.) for food' (direct causative), without changing the verb meaning.

Both suffixes also derive verbs from nouns and words of other classes: *tamba* 'medicine'
→ *-tamban-i* 'treat with medicine', *temen* 'friend' → *-temen-i* 'keep (so.) company'; *pi-
takon* 'question' → *-pitakon-i* 'address a question to (so.)'.

In causative derivation the complement of the active clause corresponds to the subject
of the basic intransitive clause, while the newly introduced participant, the causer, is in
subject function.

(53) a. *Wong   Pejajaran   wis   Islam   kabèh*
        people (toponym) PFV Muslim all
        'All people in Pejajaran were already Muslims.'

(53) b. *Para   utusan   mau   uga   ng-islam-aké   wong-wong   ing   Pejajaran*
        PL envoy ANAPH also AV-Islam-TR2 people-PL LOC Pejajaran
        'These envoys have also islamized people in Pejajaran.'

The second complement corresponds to the subject of the basic active transitive clause.
It may be introduced by a preposition, as in (54b), or it may not, as in (54c).

(54) a. *Mangga   dhik   ng-unjuk   kopi*
        please younger.sibling AV-drink(H) coffee
        'Please have some coffee.' (Cf. also (38) for a passive use of this verb.)

(54) b. *Dhokter   kadhaton   énggal-énggal   ng-unjuk-aké   jamu-né*
        doctor palace quick-ADV AV-drink(H)-TR2 medicine-the
        marang   sang   prabu
        DIR ART king
        'The court doctor quickly gave the medicine to drink to the king.'

(54) c. *Kabèh   jamu   turu   gawé-an=é   wis   di-unjuk-aké   sang prabu*
        all medicine sleep make:NR=3.GEN PFV PASS:3-drink-TR2 ART king
        '[He] had the king drink all his sleeping draughts.'

The passive construction, already illustrated in the preceding example, is often preferred:

(55) a. *Laku=né   rikat*
        walk=3.GEN fast
        'He walked fast.'

(55) b. *Laku=né*   *di-rikat-aké*
          walk=3.GEN   PASS:3-fast-TR2
          'He accelerated his pace.'

As mentioned above, the new actant may also be a beneficiary.

(56) a. *Dak=ø-tuku*   *permèn*
          1=PASS:1/2-buy   candy
          'I bought candies.'

(56) b. *Anak-anak=ku*   *dak=ø-tukok-aké*   *permèn*   *endhog*   *cecak*
          children=1.GEN   1=PASS:1/2-buy-TR2   candy   egg   lizard
          'For my children I bought 'lizard's egg' candies.'

In addition to the standard passive forms reviewed in §3.2 above, there are archaic passive forms built with the prefix *ka-* or the infix-prefix *-in-/ing-*: *ka-irid* 'be lead/brought forth' instead of *di-irid*, *l-in-ebok-aké* 'be inserted' instead of the common *di-lebok-aké*. The category person is irrelevant in this formation. The ACT is expressed as in 3-passive clauses, with or without preposition.

(57) *Prau*   *ka-tempuh*   *ing*   *ombak*
      boat   PASS-strike   by   wave
      'The boat was struck by the waves.'

(58) *Sajak*   *punika*   *t<in>utur/*   *t<in>utur-aken/*   *ka-tutur-aken*
      poem   PRX/DIST(F)   -PASS-recite/   -PASS-recite-TR2(F)/   PASS-recite-TR2(F)
      déning   *panjenengan*
      by   2(F)
      'This poem was recited by you.'

The suffix *-i* is changed to *-an* in these passive forms: *-tangis-i* 'weep for'→ *ka-tangis-an* 'be wept for'.

(59) *Tindak-ipun*   *ibu*   *ka-tangis-an*   *déning*   *kula*
      go (H)-GEN(F)   mother   PASS-weep-TR1   by   1(F)
      ['Mother's passing away was wept for by me' →] 'I wept over mother's death.'

(60) *Samangké*   *nangkoda*   *mugi*   *ka-timbal-an-a*
      now (F)   captain   let (F)   PASS-invite(H)TR1-IRR
      'Now let the captain be invited.'

4.2 Intransitive derivations

In derived intransitives the valency of the verbal base is often decreased. Several affixes are connected with modal, aspectual and other meanings.

The prefix *ke-* denotes involuntary transition into a state, or the resultative state itself, or being affected by an action: *-tarik* 'attract' → *ke-tarik* 'attracted, interested', *-peksa* 'compel' → *ke-peksa* 'compelled', *-sindhir* 'make hints' → *ke-sindhir* 'stung'.

(61) *Basa Inggris*   *ke-pireng*   *ing*   *pundi-pundi*
      language English   INVOL-hear (F)   LOC   everywhere (F)
      'The English language is heard all around.'

The ACT is denoted by the complement mostly without preposition.

(62) ...*suk=é*   *kabar-é*   *s<um>ebar.* *Nganti* *ke-pireng* *sang* *prabu*
      tomorrow=3.GEN news-the -INTR-spread so.that INVOL-hear ART king
      'The next day the news spread. So that [it] was heard by the king.'

(63) *Amir* *ke-tabrak* *sedhan*
      PN   INVOL-hit   car
      'Amir got hit by a car.'

The confixes *ke- -an* and *ke- -en* denote that one is adversely affected by a state or experience beyond one's control (the so-called adversative passive): *lara* 'ache' → *kelaran* 'feel pain', *wengi* 'night' → *kewengèn* 'be overtaken by night', *remen* 'like, inclined to (sth.)' → *ke-remen-en* 'carried away, absorbed'. If such a derivative has a complement, then the subject and the complement relate as possessor and possessed (cf. (64)) or as place/space/vessel and something located therein (cf. (65) and Soebroto 1998).

(64) *Aku* *kélangan*   *sakabèhé*
      Aku   ka-ilang-an   sakabèhé
      1   ADVS-disappear-ADVS   all
      'I have lost all.'

(65) *Alun-alun* *ke-banjir-an*   *wong*
      square   ADVS-flood-ADVS   people
      'The square was flooded with people.'

Excessivity is a special sub-meaning of the adversative: *cilik* 'small' → *ke-cilik-en* 'too small'.

(66) *Kowé* *iku*   *kegedhèn*   (/ke-gedhé-en/) *pamrih*
      2   DIST   ADVS-big-ADVS   self-interest
      'You are too driven by self-interest.'

The suffix *-an* denotes an action or state extended in time or space: *n-jaluk* 'ask' → *njaluk-an* 'cadge, be of begging nature'.

(67) *Lawang-é* *tutup-an*
      door-the   close-ST
      'The door was closed.'

Other, less productive affixes are the prefix *sa-* denoting similarity with what is denoted by the root: *sa-endhog* 'like an egg', and the suffix *-en* meaning being affected physically by some negative influence: *jamur* 'mould' → *jamur-en* 'mouldy'.

The prefix *mak-* denotes a sudden punctual action: *mak-byur* 'fly suddenly'; *pating-* (generally with infixation of *-r-* or *-l-* into the following root) denotes variegated actions/states of a multiple subject: *pating-t-l-ècèk* 'lie in disarray', *pating-g-r-andhul* 'hang in various positions' (Uhlenbeck 1982:159–160).

Partly in combination with affixes, reduplication adds the notion of iterative, extensive, distributive or reciprocal action. It also expresses notions such as aimless or not serious action, mollified urging and concession: *mlaku* 'walk' → *mlaku-mlaku* 'take a walk, stroll about', *omong* 'speak' → *omong-omongan* 'talk, chat'. It can also decrease the verbal valency: *nonton* 'look at' → *ne-nonton* 'go to the movies', *tuku* 'buy' → *tetuku* 'go shopping'.

A special subclass of stative intransitives takes the shape of a transitive verb in AV form, but it is used without a complement: *maédahi* 'useful' (*N-paédah-i*) < *paédah* 'use, profit'; *ng-gumun-aké* 'astonishing' < *gumun* 'astonished'.

4.3 Reciprocals

Reciprocal verbs are derived with the suffix -*an* (often with root reduplication), or according to a special reduplication pattern 'Root-R-*in*-oot(-*an*)': -*tulung* 'help' → *tulung-t-in-ulung* 'help each other', -*ajèn-i* 'respect' → *ajèn-ing-ajèn-an* 'respect each other'.

In one reciprocal construction the complement which denotes the second participant ('co-actor') is introduced by the preposition *karo* 'with'.

(68) *Ana   ing   sepur,   omong-omong-an   karo   kanca-kanca=né*
      EXIST   LOC   train   talk-RCP   with   friend-PL=3.GEN
      'In the train [he] talked with his friends.'

In another reciprocal construction the subject denotes a plural participant. It may consist of two nouns joined by the same preposition *karo*.

(69) *Lawa   karo   wong   kuwi   tulung-t-in-ulung*
      bat   with   man   DIST   RCP-help
      'Bat and man help each other.'

(70) *Wiwit   samana si   kucing   karo   asu   terus   se-satron*
      Wiwit   samana si   kucing   karo   asu   terus   RDP-satru-an
      begin   so.long ART cat   with   dog   go.on   RCP-enemy-RCP

      tekan   saiki
      tekan   saiki
      till   now
      'The cat and the dog have had a feud ever since.'

Both constructions may also contain lexical (underived) reciprocal verbs.

5 NOMINALIZATION

As already mentioned in §3.5 above, the possessive clitics and suffixes are used also for nominalizing verbals. If no attribute follows, the nominalizing function of =*ku*, =*mu*, -*é*/-*ipun* combines with the possessive meaning: *teka* 'come' → *teka=né* 'his/ her/their arrival'. If followed by an attribute, the suffixes -*é*/-*ipun* as well as -*ing* unite the functions of a nominalizer and a genitive marker: *bungah* 'glad' → *bungah-é wong kuwi* 'joy of this man', *aran* 'be called' → *aran-ing negara* 'the name of the state'. This method is used only for intransitive verbs. Transitive verbs may be nominalized with the aid of the prefix *peN-/paN-*: -*jaluk* 'ask' → *pan-jaluk-é* 'his/her/their request'. Verbs nominalized in this way can function as subject or complement.

(71) *Tekan=é   layang=mu   gawé   kagèt=é   wong   sa-omah*
      come=NR   letter=2.GEN make   embarrassed=NR   people   all-house
      'The arrival of your letter caused embarrassment to the whole household.'

Another nominalization strategy is to use *olèh-/ angsal*- F (< 'get, obtain') or *enggon-/ anggon-/anggèn*- F (< 'place') plus a possessive pronoun followed by the verb. This

strategy is used for both transitive and intransitive verbs. Again, the nominalizations fulfil various syntactic functions including
(i) subject:

(72) *Anggon=é   bisu   ora   bisa   mari*
      NR=3.GEN   dumb   NEG   can   cease
      'His dumbness cannot be cured.'

(73) *Dak=ø-terus-n-é   olèh=ku   omong*
      1=PASS:1/2-go.on-TR2-PRPV   NR=1.GEN   speak
      'Let me continue what I was saying.'

(ii) predicate:

(74) *Jaran   iku   olèh=ku   tuku,   ora   olèh=ku   n-jaluk*
      horse   DIST   NR=1.GEN   buy   NEG   NR=1.GEN   AV-ask
      'I paid for the horse, I didn't [just] ask for it.' (lit. 'that horse [was] my purchase, not my request')

(iii) attribute:

(75) *Iwak=é   anggon=é   mancing* [N-pancing]   *dhéwé   iku*
      fish=3.GEN   NR=3.GEN   AV:fish.with.line   self   DIST
      bobot=é   sak-kilo
      weight=3.GEN   one-kilogram
      'That fish which he has got himself weighs (*lit.* its weight) 1 kilogram.'

Actants of the nominalized verb may be expressed by noun phrases immediately following the verb (see Uhlenbeck 1983b and Herrfurth 1984 for more data and discussion).

(76) *Olèh=é   nonton   bocah   loro iku   nganti   byar*
      NR=3.GEN   AV:watch   kid   two DIST   till   day.break
      'Both kids watched till day-break.' (lit. 'The watching of the two kids (lasted) till day-break')

6 NOTES ON OLD JAVANESE AND STRUCTURAL CHANGES IN THE HISTORY OF JAVANESE

6.1 Phonology

In OJ, the aspirates *ph, bh, th*, etc. were added to the consonant inventory due to Sanskrit influence (note the different value of these digraphs with NJ *th, dh*): *buddha* 'Buddha'. These aspirates often interchanged with OJ non-aspirates in inherited lexicon, and they eventually merged with the latter and were lost in NJ. The voiced consonants were probably much like those in modern Malay or Sundanese. In NJ, they generally became voiceless and aspirated (§2.1), e.g. OJ *jaba* → NJ [cʰɔpʰɔ] 'outside'.

Sanskrit sibilants *ṣ* and *ś* were later replaced by *s*. The interchange of *t* with *ṭ*, *d* with *ḍ*, *n* with *ṇ* in early texts makes it doubtful whether OJ had separate retroflex phonemes (Damais 1970:12). They were nevertheless reconstructed for protolanguages ancestral to Javanese (Nothofer 1975). NJ glottal stop had OJ /k/ as its predecessor in syllable codas.

The OJ vowels are *i, e, u, o, ě* [ə], and *a*. (It lacks the mid-high vowels /e/ and /o/).The long vowels *i:, u:, ě:*, and *a:* were phonologically relevant only for poetry and they often interchange with short ones. In native vocabulary, however, long vowels often compensate the loss of an earlier Proto-Austronesian *R: *tu:t* 'follow', *rĕŋĕ:* 'hear', cf. protolanguage forms **tuRut*, **deŋeR*. They disappeared in NJ. The Sanskrit vowel-like *r̥* was probably realised as [rə] or [ər], and *l̥* as [lə] or [əl].

The sequence *ay* alternates with *e* as in *way, we* 'sun', and the Sanskrit sequence *au* becomes *o*: *komara* < Skr. *kaumara* 'young'.

Although the majority of morphemes is disyllabic, there are still many monosyllabic morphemes. Many OJ mono- and trisyllabic morphemes turned into standard NJ disyllables (Casparis 1947). Often used non-syllabic function morphemes of high frequency (such as the article *ŋ* and the pronominal morphemes *k, t, r/n*) disappeared in NJ.

The clusters 'occlusive + semivowel' are common: *pya* 'dried fish', *lwir* 'appearance'. Word-initially, homorganic consonant clusters seem to be a later innovation. Intervocalic clusters include also [-ŋh-]: *saŋhub* 'mist', *tiŋhal* 'look, sight'. Roots consisting of two identical CVC syllables are frequent: *baŋbaŋ* 'red', *jamjam* 'quiet', *jugjug* 'straight, direct'. Their number and diversity has decreased in NJ.

Retroflex occlusives, palatal occlusives and *w* are not found as the syllable coda, nor is there a morpheme-final [ɲ]. Voiced auslaut *-b,-d,-g* are allowed. In NJ they became devoiced. Final OJ *-y* disappeared in NJ.

The typical NJ lowering of high vowels in closed final syllables and the raising and rounding of *a* in certain open syllables, did not take place in OJ, cf. OJ *kirim* > NJ [kirem] 'send', OJ *apa* > NJ [ɔpɔ] 'what?'. Restrictions on vowel distribution are also NJ innovations.

Doubling of consonants occasionally occurs, especially at morpheme boundaries before vowels: *wḍihh-an* 'cloth', *manusukk-a* 'to mark out' (cf. Sarkar 1971 vol. 1:xiii). It became a regular orthographic device for morpheme segmentation and probably yielded a higher readability of texts written without word breaks.

OJ applies sandhi rules for vowels '*a + a → a:*', '*i + i → i:*', '*u + u → u:*', '*a + i,e → e*', '*a + u → o*', '*vowel + ĕ → vowel*', '*i + a → ya*', '*u, ĕ + a → wa*', not only word-internally but also, imitating Sanskrit, at word boundaries, e.g. *ma- + anak* 'child' → *ma:nak* 'have a child', *pa- + ulah* 'action' → *polah* 'activity', *sira* 3p + *i* 'in' → *sire* 'he LOC'. Some exceptions exist, approaching the NJ sandhi rules: *(h)ulu* 'head (waters) + *ka- -an* → *kulwan, kulon* 'west' (*ka-* becoming *k-*, and later, *wa* becoming *o*) cf. §2.4).

In prenasalization *N-* becomes *ŋ* before *d, ḍ, j, w*-initial roots; *b-* is replaced (not preceded) by *m-*, and *s-* is replaced by *n-*.

Compared to NJ, OJ has more prefixes and infixes but less suffixes. Infixation applies not only to roots, but also to prefixes: *paka-* → *p-in-aka-*. New suffixal alternations appeared in NJ, partly through the introduction of etiquette oppositions.

OJ reduplication is less variegated than in NJ. Apart from full reduplication and Ce-reduplication, there is also reduplication with loss of the final consonant. Examples: *lipur* 'soothed, calm' → *aŋ-lipur-lipur-akĕn* 'to sooth, comfort', *l-in-ipur-lipur* 'be soothed', *rĕŋga* 'adornment' → *a-rĕ-rĕŋga* 'have (sth.) as adornment', *tuŋgal* 'one' → *tuŋga-tuŋgal* 'sole, single'.

6.2 Morphosyntax

The noun/verb distinction is less developed in OJ: the difference between verbals and nouns mainly seems to be that the former have imperative forms. It also seems that verbals cannot be introduced by the genitive marker *ni* without article (but this needs further research). Unlike NJ, verbals and nouns co-occur with the same negation *tan* 'not'.

Many root morphemes with predicative meanings are, syntactically, nouns, and the corresponding verbals are derived from them through affixation. This is reminiscent of the Philippine system and does not apply to NJ, cf. OJ *(m)a-liŋgih* 'sit' ← OJ *liŋgih* 'sitting', NJ 'sit', NJ *abot*, OJ *a-bwat* 'heavy' ← *bwat* 'weight'. The last OJ example is an affixal verb of quality, as distinct from the NJ root adjective.

Another Philippine-like feature is the status of transitive verbs. Some OJ passive forms are based on intransitives or nouns and have an additional causative or applicative semantic element: *putus* 'end' → *amutus* (*aN-* + *putus*, intransitive) 'to be the last', *p-in-utus* 'completed, perfect', *taŋis* 'weep' → *t-in-aŋis* 'be wept for, mourned over', *gajah* 'elephant' → *g-in-ajah* 'formed in the shape of an elephant', cf. Ogloblin (1991). However, like NJ and unlike Philippine languages, OJ has special transitive suffixes (*-i* and =*akĕn*).

Transitive verb bases are derived with the prefixes *pa-*, *paha-*, *pi-* 'causative', *paka-* 'have/ use as', the suffixes *-i* (applicative, extensive, causative) and *-akĕn* (causative, applicative), the confixes or prefix-suffix combinations *pa(N)- -akĕn* (benefactive among others): *a-hayu* 'good' → *-pa-hayu* 'put in order', *lĕba:* 'broad; tranquil in mind' → *-paha-lĕba:* 'to calm, dispel cares', *tasik* 'sea' → *-paka-tasik* 'have as its sea', *wijil* 'go out' → *-wijil-akĕn* 'produce', *-gi:ta* 'sing' → *-paŋgi:takĕn* (*-paŋ-gi:ta-akĕn*) 'sing for (so.)'. The suffix *-i* joins the vowel-final root with an optional sandhi accretion *-an*: *pati* 'death' → *-pati:, -patyani* 'kill', *anugraha* 'favor, gift' → *-anugrahe, -anugrahani* 'favor, bestow a gift'. Only the suffixes survived in NJ.

The active voice form prefixes are *aN-/maN-* (these allomorphs alternate without evident functional difference, but see the comment on the imperative below) and the affix *-um-* alternating with *m-*. Many verbs have forms with both *(m)aN-* and *-(u)m-*: *rĕŋĕ:* 'hear' (verb base) → *maŋ-rĕŋĕ:, r-um-ĕŋĕ:*; *kuliliŋ* 'around' → *kuliliŋ-i* 'surround' (verb base) → *k-um-uliliŋ-i*; *anak* 'child' → *paka:nak* 'have/obtain so. as a child' (verb base) → *maka:nak*; *hiḍĕp* 'mind, knowledge' → *pa-hiḍĕp* 'pay attention' (verb base) → *ama-hiḍĕp*.

Intransitive verbs are root verbs and verbs with the affixes *(m)a-* (denoting, among others, possession; the distribution of *ma-* and *a-* is uncertain), *(m)a- -an* (extensive, joint action, reciprocal), and *-ĕn* 'affected by sth.': *huntu* 'tooth' → *ma-huntu* 'have teeth', *gawe* 'work' → *(m)a-gawe* 'do', *a-toh* 'put up for stake' → *a-totoh-an* 'play for stakes', *gigir* 'fright' → *gigir-ĕn* 'in a fright'. Furthermore, intransitive verbs formed with *(m)aN-* and *-(u)m-* denote actions, transitions, movements, states: *pati* 'death' + *m-* → *mati* 'die', *ginḍal* 'going away' → *aŋ-ginḍal, g-um-inḍal* 'go away'. The prefix *ka-* denotes involuntary or accidental actions, or resultative aspect. Verbs with *ka-* are sometimes lexicalized: *an-gyat* 'doing sth., moving suddenly' → *ka-gyat* 'taken by surprise'.

The prefix *paka-* is used in formations meaning 'to have as/in the quality of sth. denoted by the verb-base'. Exceptionally, it may also mean 'to be, to serve as (sth.)' in both active (*maka-*) and passive (*pinaka-*) forms: *guru* 'teacher' → *maka-guru* 'be a teacher' (along with the regular 'have so. as a teacher'), *pawwat* 'present, offering' → *pinaka-pawwat-nya* 'serving as their presents'.

The most common linear order is VS(Complement₁)(Complement₂).

(77) *Liṇḍu ta ŋ pṛthiwi:*
    shake PTCL ART earth
    'The earth shook.'

(78) *Anon ta sira patapan.*
    aN-ton ta sira patapan
    AV-see PTCL 3 hermitage
    'He saw a hermitage.'

Complements may be prepositional or not. Subject V Complement order is also possible.

(79) *Irika: ta   saŋ   A:sti:ka   maŋ-astuti   ri   śri: maha:ra:ja*
      then   PTCL ART   PN   AV- praise   LOC   his.majesty   king
      'Then Astika sang praise to his majesty the king.'

The particle *ta* adds salience to the whole sentence or to a part of it (Uhlenbeck 1970, Hoff 1998).

Applicative and causative three-place clauses may be distinguished in OJ like in NJ. The former associate mostly with the suffix *-i* (TR1, Object₁='stable' UG) and the latter with the prefix *-akĕn* (TR2, Object₁='moving' UG).

(80) *Maha:ra:ja   [...]k<um>aluŋ-kaluŋ-i   ri   sira*
      king   -AV-necklace-RDP-TR1   LOC   3.HON

      yayah=ta   ula:
      father=2.GEN   snake
      'The king has put a snake around the neck of your (reverend) father.' (lit. 'neck-laced at your rev. father a snake').

(81) *Hana   ta   sira   maŋke   k<um>aluŋ- akĕn   ula: ri   gulu:=nira*
      EXIST PTCL   3   now   -AV-necklace-TR2   snake   LOC   neck=3.GEN
      'Indeed, he just has put a snake around his neck.' (lit. 'he necklaced a snake on his neck')

Passives are formed with *in-/-in-*: if the verb base contains the suffix *-i*, this is replaced by *-an*. The ACT is expressed by complements that may be enclitic: *=(ŋ)ku*, *=mami* 'by me/us', *=(n)ta*, *=mu*, *=(n)yu* 'by you', *=(n)ya*, *=(n)ira* 'by him/her/them'; these enclitics also function as possessive pronouns (cf. *yayah=ta*, *gulu:=nira* above).

(82) *S<in> rĕŋ=nira   ta   mantra=nira*
      -PASS-intensify=3.GEN   PTCL   mantra=3.GEN
      'He intensified his mantra.'

(83) *T<in>on=yu   ma-hulu   warana:ku [warana=aku]*
      -PASS-see=2.GEN   POSS-head   monkey-1
      'You see I have a monkey's head.' (lit. 'being seen by you am monkey-headed I').

Note that distinct from NJ, the same passive form is used with first, second and third person ACTS. Non-pronominal ACT complements are often marked with the preposition *de*.

(84) *S<in>rĕŋ   ta   ŋ   mantra   de   saŋ   yajama:na*
      -PASS-intensify   PTCL   ART   mantra   by   ART   priest
      'The priest intensified the mantra.'

As pointed out in Zoetmulder (1950:54) there are examples which are superficially similar to the NJ 1/2-passive. They are used mostly with a propositive meaning; the ACT is expressed with the proclitic *ndak*, cf. NJ *dak= /tak=*.

(85) *Ilu   ta,   ndak   wĕ:r-akĕn   kita*
      follow:IMP   PTCL   1.PRPV   flight-TR2   2
      'Come along, I will take you flying.'

They differ from NJ propositives in that the latter has a special form with the suffixes *-é/-ipun* (F) and does not allow a second person UG (cf. §3.3 above). Details of this historical change need further research.

Accidental/involuntative passive clauses have the same structure as those with -*in*- forms. Note the GEN ligature *ni* which often occurs between the preposition *de* and a following noun.

(86)   *Ka-pu:h-an   aku   de-ni   ŋ   paŋ -hrik=mu*
     INVOL-crush-INVOL   1   by-GEN   ART   NR-shrill=2.GEN
     'Your shrill perplexed me.'

The moods are the indicative, the irrealis and the imperative. As shown in Table 21.5 irrealis is marked by the suffix -*a*, except root verbs in the passive which are marked with -*ĕn*. The passive marker -*in*- is usually dropped.

The irrealis form conveys several meanings of potentiality in a broad sense.

(i) Intention, wish, purpose, future.

(87)   *Aku   tumamba:na   ri   ŋ   mantroṣadha*
     aku   -um-tamba-an-a   ri   ŋ   mantroṣadha
     1   AV-medicine-TR1-IRR   LOC   ART   curative.formula
     'I shall treat [him] with a curative formula.'

(88)   *A-hyun   aŋ -inum-a   wwai   sira*
     INTR-wish   AV-drink-IRR   water   3
     'He wished to drink water.'

(89)   *Lumampah   ta   sira: meta   stri: sanama=nira*
     l-um-ampah   ta   sira   aN-pet-a   stri: sa-nama=nira
     INTR-go   PTCL   3   AV-look.for-IRR   wife   one-name=3.GEN
     'He went to look for a wife of the same name as himself.' (Zoetmulder 1950:159)

(90)   *Sira   ta   tamba:nana*
     sira   ta   tamba$_1$-an$_2$-an-a
     3   PTCL   medicine$_{1,2}$-TR1-IRR
     'He will be cured.'

The future meaning is lost in NJ.

(ii) Mild hortative, optative.

(91)   *Sira:tah   (/sira   atah/)   sĕmbah-ĕn   maha:dewi:*
              3   PTCL   worship-IRR   queen
     'Please pay reverence to him, your highness.'

TABLE 21.5: OLD JAVANESE INDICATIVE AND IRREALIS FORMS OF TRANSITIVE VERBS

	Indicative	Irrealis
(a) root verbs, e.g. *pangan* 'eat'		
Active	*amangan, umangan*	*amangan-a, umangan-a*
Passive	*p-in-angan*	*pangan-ĕn*
(b) suffixal verbs, e.g. -*weh-i* 'give' (TR1)		
Active	*ameh-i*	*ameh-an-a*
Passive	*w-in-eh-i*	*weh-an-a*

(iii) Possible, allowed or urged action/event.

(92) *Tan   hana   sira   ratu   waneh   ma-gaway-a   yajña   sarpa*
      NEG   EXIST   3.HON   king   other   INTR-do-IRR   sacrifice   serpent
      'There are no other kings who can/may arrange the serpent sacrifice.'

(93) *Ya   ta   k-in-on=ira   ma-hwan-a   ŋ   lĕmbu*
      3   PTCL   -PASS-order=3   INTR-graze-IRR   ART   cow
      'He ordered him to graze cows.'

(iv) Appraisal, evaluation, conditional, concessive-conditional.

(94) *Yogya   haji   ma-gaway-a   ŋ   yajña   sarpa*
      proper   king   INTR-do-IRR   ART   sacrifice   serpent
      'It is proper for [you], king, to arrange/if you arrange the serpent sacrifice.'

(95) *Yadyan   uhut-akn-a,   apan   hana   kukus=nira*
      even.if   prevent-TR2-IRR   because   EXIST   smoke=3GEN
      '(Everyone will see the fire), even if being prevented [from it], because there is
      still the (lit. its) smoke.' (Zoetmulder 1950:161)

The irrealis applies also to nouns.

(96) *Marya   huluna   demami*
      m-ari-a   hulun-a   de=mami
      INTR-cease-IRR   slave-IRR   by=1.GEN
      '([...]so that she) will cease to be my slave.'

The irrealis passive form became the NJ imperative passive, perhaps due to the deval-
uation of mild tone in hortative usage.
    The imperative is expressed by three forms. The first, corresponds to the indicative
-um- and *(m)aN-* forms (intransitive and active transitive) and is formally equal to the verb
base: *lampah* 'go!', *paŋan* 'eat!', *rĕŋw-akĕn* 'listen!', *pi-siŋih* 'obey!'. The clause is
constructed in the passive (i.e. the UG is subject). The meaning is that of simple request,
ordering, command. The suffix *-i* does not become *-an*.

(97) *Weh-i   ta   kami   sa-kahyun=mami*
      give:IMP-TR1   PTCL   1   so.much.as-wish=1.GEN
      'Give me as much [food] as I want.'

Sometimes the second person marker *t-* is preposed to the root base; if the root base is
a noun, this *t-* has a disambiguating function.

(98) *T-iŋĕt-iŋĕt   ta   den=ta*
      2-remember:IMP-RDP   PTCL   by=2
      'Remember!'

    The two other imperative forms correspond with (intransitive)*(m)a-* verbs and (intran-
sitive and active transitive) *(m)aN-* verbs in the indicative. One of them uses the prefixes
pa- resp. *paN-* instead, cf. *tuŋgu* 'wait' → *(m)atuŋgu* (id.) → *patuŋgu* 'wait!', *aN-* +
-palaku 'demand' (verb base) → *amalaku* (id. AV) → *pamalaku* 'demand, request!',
huwus 'finished' → *ma-huwus-an* 'finish, cease'→ *pahuwusan* 'finish! stop!'. The other
has prefix *a-* resp. *aN-* preceded by the second person marker *t-*: *t-a-warah* 'say!',
t-aminta (← *aN-* + *-pinta*) 'request, demand!'.

(99) *T-a-wuɲu*   *ta*   *bapa*
2 -INTR-get.up (noun)   PTCL   father
'Get up, my dear.' (*bapa* here is a term of address for certain males)

Hybrid hortative forms are found, combining the *pa(N)-* imperative with the irrealis marker *-a*. All these imperative forms are lost in NJ, where the form equal to the transitive base became the indicative second person passive.

Thus the affixes *ma-*, *maN-*, and *-(u)m-* appear as a kind of 'non-imperative' mood markers. The infix-prefix *-in-*, being also dropped in irrealis, can be analyzed as a marker of the indicative, cf. Table 21.5.

The noun, as illustrated in the preceding examples, is often accompanied by the definite article *ŋ* or *aŋ*. The former variant is very frequent, supplying a remarkable contrast to NJ. The article *ŋ* can be combined with preceding demonstrative pronouns: *ika ŋ daitya* 'this demon'. There are also other articles (honorific *saŋ* etc.). They can nominalize the verb in actant functions: *mati* 'die', *saŋ mati* 'the dead'. Attributes follow the head noun without special markers, or (especially possessive ones) are joined by the genitive particle *ni*, as in *ratu ni ŋ pas* 'king of tortoises'. In NJ the combination *ni ŋ* became the monomorphemic genitive marker *-(n)iŋ* (§3.5). A verb with the article can also serve as an attribute: *maŋgala ni ŋ l-um-ampah-a* 'blessing of the forthcoming journey' (*l-um-ampah* 'go, walk').

REFERENCES

Adelaar, K. Alexander, (in press) 'The genetic affiliations of Balinese, Sasak and Sumbawa with Malayic and Chamic', *Working papers in Sasak* vol. 3, Melbourne: The University of Melbourne, Department of Linguistics and Applied Linguistics.

Adipitoyo, S., Yulianto, B., Tirtawijaya, T. and Hudiyono, E.Y. (1999) *Morfofonemik bahasa Jawa dialek Surabaya*, Jakarta: Pusat Pembinaan dan Pengembangan Bahasa.

Aichele, W. (1943) 'Die Altmalaiische Literatursprache und ihr Einfluss auf das Altjavanische', *Zeitschrift für Eingeborenen-Sprachen* XXXIII/1:37–66.

Alieva, N.F., Arakin, V.D., Ogloblin, A.K. and Sirk, Ju. H. (1991), *Bahasa Indonesia. Deskripsi dan teori*, Yogyakarta: Kanisius.

Arps, B., Bogaerts, E., Molen, W. van der, Supriyanto, I., and Veerdonk, J. van der (in collaboration with B. Litamahuputty) (2000) *Hedendaags Javaans*, Semaian series 20, Leiden: Leiden University, Opleiding Talen en Culturen van Zuid-Oost Azië en Oceanië.

Becker, A.L. and I Gusti Ngurah Oka (1974) 'Person in Kawi: an exploration of an elementary semantic dimension', *Oceanic Linguistics* 13:229–255.

Caraka. "The Messenger" (1982–2001) A Newsletter for Javanists, 1–36, Leiden: Leiden University.

Casparis, J.G. de (1947) 'L'importance de la disyllabie en javanais', in J. Ph. Vogel (ed.) *India Antiqua. A volume of oriental studies*, 63–76, Leiden: Brill.

Clynes, A. and Rudiyanto, C. (1994) 'Javanese', in D. Tryon (ed.) *Comparative Austronesian Dictionary. An Introduction to Austronesian Studies. Part 1*, 467–481, Berlin: Mouton De Gruyter.

Damais, L.Ch. (1970) *Répertoire onomastique de l'épigraphie javanaise* (Publication de l'École Française d'Extrême Orient, LXVI), Paris: École Française d'Extrême Orient.

Ewing, M.C. (1999) *The clause in Cirebon Javanese conversation*, PhD diss. University of California at Santa Barbara.

Fagan, J.L. (1988) 'Javanese intervocalic stop phonemes: the light/ heavy distinction', in R. McGinn (ed.) *Studies in Austronesian linguistics*, 137–197, Athens, Ohio: Monographs in International Studies, Southeast Asia Series 76.

Favre, P. (1870) *Dictionnaire javanais-français*, Vienne-Paris.

Gericke, J.F.C. and Roorda, T. (1901) *Javaansch–Nederlandsch handwoordenboek*, 2 vols, edited by A.C. Vreede, Amsterdam – Leiden (4th ed.).

Gina, Wedhawati, Arifin, S., Sukiyasri and Nardiati, S. (1987) *Frase nomina dalam bahasa Jawa*, Jakarta: Pusat Pembinaan dan Pengembangan Bahasa.

Gonda, J. (1949a) 'Over Indonesische werkwoordsvormen', *Bijdragen tot de Taal-, Land- en Volkenkunde* 105:333–380.

——(1949b) 'Prolegomena tot een theorie der woordsoorten in Indonesische talen', *Bijdragen tot de Taal-, Land- en Volkenkunde* 105:275–331.

——(1973) *Sanskrit in Indonesia*, New Delhi: International Academy of Indian Culture (2nd ed.).

——(1959) 'On Old-Javanese sentence structure', *Oriens Extremus* 6, 57–68.

Hayward, K. (1993) '/p/ vs. /b/ in Javanese: some preliminary data', *School of Oriental and African Studies Working Papers in Linguistics and Phonetics* 3. L.:1–33.

——(1995) 'Some notes on the noun phrase in Javanese', *Indonesia Circle* 65:42–56.

——(1998) 'The verbal auxiliary *padha* in contemporary Javanese', in Janse (ed.) 317–336.

Herawati (1993) 'Kalimat perintah dalam bahasa Jawa', *Widyaparwa. Majalah ilmiah bahasa dan sastra* (Yogyakarta, Balai Bahasa) 40:63–108.

Herrfurth, H. (1972) *Djawanisch–deutsches Wörterbuch*, Leipzig: VEB Enzyklopädie.

——(1984) '*Oleh/angsal* und *enggon/enggen* im Javanischen: Unterscheidung der vollsemantischen lexikalischen Einheit von deverbal-nominalisierenden und satzsteuernden Element', *Acta Orientalia* (Copenhagen) 45:97–106.

Hoff, B. J.(1998) 'Communicative salience in Old Javanese', in Janse (ed.) 337–347.

Horne, E. (1961) *Beginning Javanese*, New Haven: Yale University.

——(1963) *Intermediate Javanese*, New Haven: Yale University.

——(1974) *Javanese–English dictionary*, New Haven: Yale University.

Janse, M. (with the assistance of An Verlinden) (ed.) (1998) *Productivity and creativity. Studies in general and descriptive linguistics in honor of E. M. Uhlenbeck*, Berlin: Mouton de Gruyter.

Jansz, P. (1932) *Practisch Javaansch – Nederlandsch woordenboek met Latijnsche karakters*, Semarang: van Dorp (1st ed. 1876).

Keeler, W. (1984) *Javanese: a cultural approach*, Athens, Ohio: Ohio University, Center for International Studies.

Kullanda, S.V. (1992) *Istorija Drevnej Javy* [Early Javanese history], Moscow: Nauka.

Mardiwarsito L. and Kridalaksana H. (1984) *Struktur Bahasa Jawa Kuna*, Ende, Flores: Nusa Indah.

Mohamed Subakir Mohd. Yasin (1996) *Shift in language allegiance: the Javanese in Malaysia*, PhD thesis, University of Hawaii.

Nothofer, B. (1975) *The reconstruction of Proto-Malayo-Javanic*, 's Gravenhage: Nijhoff.

——(1980) *Dialektgeographische Untersuchungen in West-Java und im westlichen Zentral-Java*, Wiesbaden: Harrassowitz.

——(1981) *Dialektatlas von Zentral-Java*, Wiesbaden: Harrassowitz.

——(1985) 'The subgrouping of the languages of the Javo-Sumatran hesion: a recon-sideration', *Bijdragen tot de Taal-, Land- en Volkenkunde* 141:228–302.

Ogloblin, A. K. (1986) 'Some problems of diachronic typology of the Malayo-Javanic languages', in P. Geraghty, L. Carrington and S.A. Wurm (eds) *FOCAL II: Papers from the 4th International conference on Austronesian linguistics*, 111–122, Canberra: Pacific Linguistics.

——(1991) 'Old Javanese verb structure', in Lokesh Chandra (ed.) *The art and culture of South-East Asia*, Sata-pitaka series vol. 364, 245–259, New Delhi: International Academy of Indian Culture/Aditya Prakashan.

——(1993) 'Sistema javanskih glasnyh: garmonija po podjemu' [Vowel height harmony in Javanese], *Voprosy jazykoznanija* 6:57–63.

——(1996) *Ocherk diahronicheskoj tipologii malajsko-javanskih jazykov* [Aspects of diachronic typology of Malayo-Javanic languages], Moscow: Novoe tysjacheletie.

——(1998) 'A note on relative markers in Javanese', in Janse (ed.) 349–356.

——(1999) 'Keselarasan vokal dalam bahasa Jawa', in *Buku Panduan Kongres Linguistik Nasional IX*, Masyarakat Linguistik Indonesia, 66–69, Jakarta: Pusat Pembinaan dan Pengembangan Bahasa/Universitas Katolik Atma Jaya.

——(2000) 'The Old Javanese word *de*', in Lokesh Chandra (ed.) *Society and culture of South-East Asia. Continuities and changes*, Sata-pitaka series vol. 395, 179–190, New Delhi: International Academy of Indian Culture/Aditya Prakashan.

——(2001) 'Imperative constructions in Javanese', in V. S. Xrakovskij (ed.) *Typology of imperative constructions*, 221–242, München: Lincom Europa.

Pedoman ejaan bahasa Jawa yang disempurnakan (1977), Jakarta: Pusat Pembinaan dan Pengembangan Bahasa.

Pigeaud, Th.G.Th. (1938) *Javaans-Nederlands handwoordenboek*, Groningen: Wolters Noordhoff (2nd edn 1982: Leiden: Royal Institute of Linguistics and Anthropology).

——(1967) *Literature of Java. I. A synopsis of Javanese literature 900–1900 A.D.*, Leiden: Bibliotheca Universitatis.

Poedjosoedarmo, S. (1968) 'Javanese speech levels', *Indonesia* (Ithaca) 6: 54–87.

Poerwadarminta, W.J.S. *et al.* (1939) *Baoesastra Djawa* vol. I, A-L., Groningen/Batavia: Pakempalan Tiwikrama.

——(1945) *Baoesastra Indonesia-Djawi* (3rd edn), Jakarta: Balai Poestaka.

——(1953) *Sarining paramasastra Djawa*, Djakarta: Noordhoff-Kolff.

Prawiroatmodjo, S.P. (1957) *Bausastra Djawa-Indonesia*, Surabaja: Marfiah (3rd edn 1985).

——(1998) *Bausastra Jawa*, Surabaya: 'Djojo Bojo' (1st edn 1987).

Ramelan (1983) 'Javanese indicative and imperative passives', in A. Halim, L. Carrington and S.A. Wurm (eds) *Third International Conference on Austronesian linguistics* vol. 4, 199–214, Canberra: Pacific Linguistics.

Ras, J.J. (1985) *Inleiding tot het modern Javaans*, Dordrecht (Neth.)/Cinnaminson (CT): Foris (2nd edn).

Robson, S.O. (1985) 'Spoken Javanese in the countryside', *Review of Indonesian and Malaysian affairs* 19/1:106–176.

Robson, S.O. and Wibisono, S. (2001), *Javanese–English dictionary*, Singapore: Periplus.

Sarkar, H.B. (1971–72), *Corpus of the inscriptions of Java (corpus inscriptionum javani-carum) (up to 928 A.D.)*, vol. I (1971) vol. II (1972), Calcutta: Firma K.L. Mudhopadhyay.

Samsuri (1961) 'Javanese phonemes and their distinctive features', *Medan Ilmu Pengetahuan* 2/4:309–321.

Schoterman, J.A. (1981) 'An introduction to Old Javanese–Sanskrit dictionaries and grammars', *Bijdragen tot de Taal-, Land- en Volkenkunde* 137:419–442.

Setrowidjojo, B.S. and Setrowidjojo, R.T. (1994) *Het Surinaams-Javaans*, Den Haag: Suara Jawa.

Soebroto, D.E. (1998) 'Adversative-passive verbs in standard Javanese', in Janse (ed.) 357–368.

Soebroto, D.E., Soenardji and Sugiri (1991) *Tata Bahasa Deskriptif Bahasa Jawa*, Jakarta: Departemen Pendidikan dan Kebudayaan.

Sudaryanto (ed.) (1992) *Tata bahasa baku bahasa Jawa*, Yogyakarta: Duta Wacana University Press.

Sudaryono, Dewi, K., Anggrahini, M. and Subariyah, S. (1990) *Geografi dialek bahasa Jawa Kabupaten Demak*, Jakarta: Departemen Pendidikan dan Kebudayaan.

Suharno, I. (1982) *A descriptive study of Javanese*, Canberra: Pacific Linguistics.

Teselkin, A.S. (1961) *Javanskij jazyk* [The Javanese language], Moscow: Nauka.

——(1969) *Uchebnyj slovar' javanskogo jazyka* [A student's Javanese dictionary], Moscow: Voennyj institut.

——(1972) *Old Javanese*, Ithaca: Cornell University.

Uhlenbeck, E.M. (1941) *Beknopte Javaanse grammatica*, Batavia: Volkslectuur.

——(1949) *De structuur van het Javaanse morpheem*, (Verhandelingen van het Bataviaasch Genootschap 78), Bandoeng.

——(1964) *A critical survey of studies on the languages of Java and Madura*, 's-Gravenhage: Nijhoff.

——(1965) 'Some preliminary remarks on Javanese syntax', *Lingua* 15:53–70.

——(1968) 'Personal pronouns and pronominal suffixes in Old Javanese', *Lingua* 21: 466–482.

——(1970) 'Position and syntactic function of the particle *ta* in Old Javanese', in R. Jakobson and S. Kawamoto (eds) *Studies in General and Oriental Linguistics presented to Shiro Hattori*, 648–658, Tokyo: TEK Corporation for Language and Educational Research.

——(1971) 'Indonesia and Malaysia', in T.A. Sebeok (ed.) *Current trends in linguistics. Vol.8. Linguistics in Oceania*, 55–111, The Hague: Mouton.

——(1975) 'Sentence segment and word group. Basic concepts of Javanese syntax', *NUSA* 1:1–10.

——(1978) *Studies in Javanese morphology*, The Hague: Nijhoff.

——(1982) *Kajian morfologi bahasa Jawa*, Jakarta: Djambatan.

——(1983a) *Javanese linguistics. A retrospect and some prospects*, Dordrecht: Foris.

——(1983b) 'Two mechanisms of Javanese syntax: the constructions with *sing (kang, ingkang)* and with *olehe (enggone, anggenipun)*', in A. Halim, L. Carrington and S.A. Wurm (eds) *Third International Conference on Austronesian linguistics*, vol. 4, 9–20, Canberra: Pacific Linguistics.

——(1986) 'Clitic, suffix, and particle: some indispensable Distinctions in Old Javanese grammar', in C.M.S. Hellwig and S.O. Robson (eds) *A man of Indonesian letters. Essays in honour of Professor A. Teeuw*, 334–341, Dordrecht: Foris.

——(1991) 'Nouns, nominal groups and substitutional processes in Old Javanese', in R. Harlow (ed.) *Papers from the Fifth International Conference on Austronesian Linguistics. Vol. 2. Western Austronesian and Contact Languages*, 349–366, Auckland: Te Reo, The Linguistic Society of New Zealand.

Vruggink, H. (in samenwerking met J. Sarmo) (2001) *Surinaams–Javaans–Nederlands woordenboek*, Leiden: KITLV uitgeverij.

Wojowasito, S. (1980) *A Kawi lexicon*, edited by R.F. Mills, Ann Arbor, Michigan: University of Michigan, Center for South and Southeast Asian Studies.

Yallop, Colin, (1982) 'The phonology of Javanese vowels', in A. Halim, L. Carrington and S.A. Wurm (eds) *Third International Conference on Austronesian linguistics*, vol. 4., 299–319, Canberra: Pacific Linguistics.

Zoetmulder, P.J. (1950) *De taal van het Adiparwa. Een grammaticale studie van het Oudjavaans* (Verhandelingen Lembaga Kebudayaan Indonesia/Koninklijk Bataviaasch genootschap van kunsten en wetenschappen LXXIX), Bandung: Nix & Co.

——(1974) *Kalangwan. A survey of Old Javanese literature*, The Hague: Nijhoff.

——with the collab.of S.O. Robson (1982) *Old Javanese-English dictionary*, 2 vols, 's-Gravenhage: Nijhoff.

CHAPTER TWENTY-TWO

BUOL

Erik Zobel

1 INTRODUCTION

The Buol language (*apadu Vuolo*) is spoken by about 75,000 people (Grimes 1996) in the *kabupaten* (regency) Buol in Central Sulawesi (see Wurm and Hattori 1983, Map 43). Buol is the westernmost member of the Gorontalo-Mongondic subgroup and belongs to its Gorontalic branch. Within the Gorontalic branch, Buol is most closely related to Gorontalo, spoken to the east of the Buol area. The western neighbor of Buol is Totoli, which does not belong to the Gorontalo-Mongondic subgroup, but which has shared with Buol a long period of mutual influence, especially lexically. Language use is still vigorous, although in certain areas where many outsiders are present (e.g. at the harbor area of Leok or in parts of Paleleh that are rich in natural resources), some young people only have a limited command of Buol. Until now, dialect variation has hardly been investigated.

So far, the Buol language has gained only moderate scholarly attention. Minor sources from Dutch colonial times are Jansen (1855, wordlist), Riedel (1872, sixteen somewhat corrupted lines of a song), and van Andel (1929, customary law terminology). Adriani and Kruyt (1914) devoted a short section of their linguistic overview of the Sulawesi area to Buol, giving some lexical and grammatical data. A 'Holle-list' was collected in the late 1910s by van Andel (in Stokhof 1983), with almost a thousand lexical items and 25 sample sentences, plus additional notes on lexicon and function words. An article by van Wouden (1941) contains a text of seven pages on early Buol history from creation to the first kingdoms, together with a good Dutch translation. In recent times, two Indonesian research reports on the structure of Buol have been published (Garantjang *et al.* 1984, 1986). The phonological history of Buol and its place within the Gorontalo-Mongondic subgroup are discussed in Usup (1986) and Sneddon and Usup (1986).

2 PHONOLOGY

2.1 Segment inventory

The Buol phoneme inventory comprises five vowels and eighteen consonants. The vowel phonemes are: /a, e, i, o, u/, the consonants are listed in Table 22.1.

The most common root template is (C)V(C)V(C). The only allowed consonant clusters (apart from those in recent loanwords or arising through syncope, see 2.3) are combinations of nasals with a homorganic voiced stop, i.e. /mb, nd, ŋg/, which only occur medially, e.g. *umbat* 'mat', but exceptionally also in initial position in proper names (e.g. *Ndubu*). The consonants /h/, /ʔ/, /j/, /s/ and /β/ do not occur in final position. All vowel combinations are allowed, including the sequence of two like vowels, which phonologically is counted as two syllables, but phonetically is realized as a long vowel, e.g. /maata/

TABLE 22.1: BUOL CONSONANTS

	Labial	Apical	Palatal	Velar	Glottal
Voiceless stop	p	t		k	ʔ
Voiced stop	b	d	j	g	
Nasal	m	n		ŋ	
Fricative	β	s			h
Liquid		l, r			
Glide	w		y		

'unripe', pronounced [máːta] (here and further below, stress is indicated by an acute accent).

/h/, /s/, /j/ and /ʔ/ have marginal status and mostly occur in loanwords, e.g. *habar* 'news' (< Arabic *xabar*, probably via Malay), *sirita* 'story' (< Malay *cerita*), *sabe* 'silk' (< Makassarese *saʔbe*), *pajeko* 'plough' (< Makassarese *paʔjeko*), *duʔa* 'prayer' (Arabic *duʕaː*, via Malay *doʔa*). /h/, /s/ and /ʔ/ are also found in a small number of native words, e.g. *buahanga* 'k.o. cricket', *sio* 'nine' and *naʔal* 'bark slippers'.

The bilabial fricative /β/ (spelled *v* here, cf. 2.2) only occurs before /u/. Its phonemic status is apparent in (near) minimal pairs with /b/, e.g. *vungo* 'fruit' vs. *bungol* 'deaf'.

/t/ has a dental articulation, while /d/ is pronounced as an alveolar stop, except in the nasal cluster /nd/, in which case it is dental.

The lateral /l/ has three allophones: an alveolar lateral [l], a palatal lateral approximant [λ], and a retroflex lateral flap [ɽ]. The distribution of these allophones is conditioned by the front vowels /e/ and /i/. /l/ is realized as:

[l]   if preceded by a front vowel, e.g. *dila* [dila] 'tongue', *tunggil* [tuŋgil] 'mouth';

[ɽ]   if followed, but not preceded by a front vowel, e.g. *linug* [ɽinug] 'earthquake', *ale* [aɽe] 'chin';

[λ]   if not contiguous to a front vowel, e.g. *longit* [λoŋit] 'mosquito', *olo* [oλo] 'what', *tangul* [taŋuλ] 'name'.

An exception to the above rule is that the first /l/ in the sequences /lala/, /lola/ and /lolo/ is realized as [l], e.g. *lolo* [loλo] 'face', *lolaung* [loλaung] 'afternoon'.

The semivowel /y/ is acoustically similar to the [λ]-realization of /l/, and occurs in the same environment, i.e. it is never contiguous to /e/ and /i/. It is however clearly a distinct phoneme, as can be seen from near-minimal pairs such as: *mopoyok* 'short' vs. *polok* [poλok] 'smoke', *boya* 'face' vs. *mogola* [mogoλa] 'take'.

Stress regularly falls on the penultimate syllable, paragogic vowels not counted (see 2.3). Words with a sequence of like vowels in the antepenultimate and penultimate syllables receive stress on the antepenultimate mora (see the example of *maata* above). Enclitics and suffixes lead to stress shift to the right, as e.g. in *bolé-ku* 'my house' (house-1s.GEN) or *noitamó=lon* 'already arrived' (PV.ST:PST:arrive=CPL).

2.2 Orthography

There is no generally accepted orthography for Buol. Speakers mostly use Indonesian in formal and informal writing and correspondence, but when the native language is written down, as in song texts, *ad hoc* spellings based on the Indonesian orthography are used. With most phonemes, this does not cause problems, but some inconsistencies appear with sounds not present in Indonesian: /β/ is spelled <bw>, <b> or <v>, and the [ʎ] and [ɾ] realizations of /l/ are often spelled <y> and <r>, respectively, thus being confused with /y/ and /r/, which are distinct phonemes. Phonetically long vowels are often spelled with a single vowel letter.

The spelling used here follows Indonesian practice in writing <ng> for /ŋ/. /β/ is spelled <v>.

2.3 Paragogic vowels and syncope

A characteristic that Buol shares with all Gorontalic languages are paragogic vowels following final consonants: /u/ after voiced stops (in the present-day language often /o/), /o/ following all other consonants. For instance, the roots /βuok/ 'hair' and /iag/ 'moon' are realized as [βúoko] and [íagu]/[íago]. The addition of a paragogic vowel does not influence stress placement, and the vowel is dropped if a suffix or enclitic is added, e.g. /βuok-io/ (hair-3s.GEN) 'his hair'. In this sketch, words in isolation will be written without paragogic vowel, but whenever paragogic vowels appear in examples from actual speech, they will be marked by underlining, e.g. *vuoko* or *iagu*.

In older descriptions from Jansen (1855) to van Wouden (1941), this paragogic vowel is used consistently, as in the Gorontalic sister languages. In present-day speech however, the paragogic vowel is often dropped, especially in connected speech before consonants or if a word is cited in isolation, e.g. *unggag moinito* (< *unggago moinito*) 'hot water'. The paragogic vowel is usually heard before vowels or pause (e.g. *monginumo unggago* 'drink water'), although younger speakers also tend to drop it in these positions (*monginum unggag*).

Related to the optional occurrence of the paragogic vowel, unstressed /o/ before a consonant in the first syllable of a word can be subject to syncope in connected speech whenever it occurs in the same prosodic position as the paragogic vowel, i.e. two syllables after a stressed vowel. Examples of this syncope (indicated by an apostrophe) are: *día n'kopólongo* < *día* + *nokopólong* (NEG PV.ST.PST:sleep) 'was not able to sleep' or *táa m'toligútato* < *táa motoligútat* (NR cousin) 'cousin'. This syncope can also affect non-paragogic final /o/ in the words *maino* 'where, which' and *koda=ako* 'towards (away from speaker)' due to floating stress placement, e.g. *máin' ti Anto?* < *maíno/máino ti Anto?* (where PN *Anto*) 'where is Anto?' and *kodáak' dógoto* < *koda=áko dogot* (like=DIR sea) 'towards the sea'. Furthermore, syncope of unstressed /o/ is also found in a few other prosodic positions, notably in the second syllable of the complex affix *k<in>o- -an*, e.g. *kin'dovúan bongo* < *kinodovúano bongo* (DV.ST.PST:fall coconut) 'be fallen on by a coconut'.

Finally, syncope of any vowel may occur in the second syllable of CVCV-reduplications, see 2.6 below.

2.4 Instable final /n/

In many words, word-final /n/ can be optionally dropped. This /n/ always reappears if there is a following suffix or enclitic. Formatives with final /n/ can be grouped into three classes according to their behavior in this respect:

(a) Final /n/ is never dropped. This class includes the aspect marking enclitic =*lon*, and probably also some nouns and verbs.
(b) Final /n/ is optionally dropped. This class includes roots and affixes that can be followed by genitive pronouns and case markers, including many nouns and verbs.

Examples are *kaa(n)* 'eat' (cf. *mong-[k]aa(n)* 'eat (actor voice)', but *k<in>aan-um* 'eaten by you'), *uti(n)* 'penis', and the verbal suffix *-a(n)*. For these items, the dropping of final /n/ is more frequently encountered with older speakers who consistenly use the paragogic vowel, although often there is free variation, e.g. between *vulaa* and *vulaano* 'gold'. With younger speakers, dropping of final /n/ is rarely encountered.

(c) Final /n/ is always dropped. This class is represented by the deictics *tia(n)*, *tii(n)*, and *too(n)*. With these elements, final /n/ only comes to surface before clitics, e.g. *tian=on* 'already here'.

In the following sections, roots and affixes of classes a) and b) cited in isolation will be spelled with final /n/.

2.5 Morphophonology

The most common morphophonological processes in Buol are nasal replacement, vowel assimilation and raising, and strategies to avoid disallowed consonant clusters.

Nasal replacement is found with the verbal prefixes *noN-*, *moN-* and *poN-*. The realizations of *N-* are given in (1).

(1) $N + v\text{-}, b\text{-}, p\text{-}$ >   *m-*
   $N + d\text{-}, t\text{-}$ >   *n-*
   $N + g\text{-}, k\text{-}$ >   *ng-*
   $N + V\text{-}$ >   *ngV-*

Before the remaining consonants, *N-* is realized as zero.

Root initial /a/ becomes /o/ following the prefixes *mog-*, *nog-* or *pog-*, e.g. *mog-ola* 'take (actor voice, neutral tense)' from the root *ala*, cf. *ni-ala* (patient voice, past tense). /a/ also becomes /o/ in CV-reduplication, e.g. *to-taig* 'comb (noun)', cf. *monaig* 'to comb'. Raising of /o/ to /u/ is encountered after the voiced stops /b, d, g/ in CV-reduplication and optionally with the completion marker *=lon*, e.g. *du-dolo* 'character', *bu-bandi* 'hoe' (instead of **bo-bandi*); *nolaud=un* or *nolaud=on* (PV.ST.PST:finish=CPL) 'already finished'.

In certain combinations of clitics and function words, final /o/ assimilates to following /a/, as in *tila=a Tolitoli* (<*tilo* '3p.NOM' + *a* 'in, at') 'the people in Tolitoli', or *atade=pa=agi* (<*=po* + *=agi*) (DV.IMP:call=INCPL=DIR) 'call (him/her) first!'. Assimilation of /o/ to the preceding vowel is found with the dynamic patient voice suffix *-on* (see 5.2.1), which becomes *-an* and *-en* following verb roots with final /a/ and /e/, respectively, e.g. *pate-en* 'kill' (<√*pate*) or *ala-an* 'take' (<√*ala*).

There are several strategies to avoid disallowed consonant clusters that would arise from the combination of consonant-final prefixes and consonant-initial suffixes and enclitics with other formatives. The most common strategy is to delete the consonant of the affix/clitic and leave the host intact. This is found with the verbal prefixes *mog-*, *nog-*, and *pog-*, the genitive pronouns *-ku*, *=nio*, *=nami*, *=niu*, *=nilo*, the personal genitive case marker *ni*, and the completive enclitic *=lon*. E.g.:

(2) *mo-tali*   < *mog-* + *tali* 'buy (AV, neutral tense)
   utat-u   < *utat* 'sibling' + *-ku* '1s genitive'
   mongambuling=on < *mongambuling* 'return home' + *=lon* 'CPL'

A second strategy is the insertion of an epenthetic vowel /o/, which occurs before the suffixed genitive pronoun -*to* '1pi/2.HON.GEN', and the enclitics =*po* 'still, first' and =*laut* 'very':

(3) *utatoto* 'our brother'   <   *utat* 'sibling' + =*to*
     mobutogopo 'still full'   <   *mobutog* 'full, satisfied' + =*po*
     moinitolaut 'very hot'   <   *moinit* 'hot' + =*laut*

Allowed nasal clusters are formed by sandhi of formatives ending in /n/ with the enclitics -*ku* '1s.GEN', -*to* '1pi.GEN' and -*po* 'still, first', resulting in, respectively, /ŋg/ (often reduced to /ŋ/), /nd/ and /mb/:

(4) *podutiando*   <   *po-duti-an* 'seek (extended dative voice, neutral)' + -*to*
     kotaang(g)u   <   *ko-taan* 'know (stative dative voice, neutral)' + -*ku*
     alaambaagi   <   *ala-an* 'take, get (patient voice, imperative)' + =*po* + =*agi*

2.6 Reduplication

There are two types of reduplication in Buol: CV(N)CV- and CV-reduplication. Reduplication of the first two syllables (without the coda in case the second syllable is closed) is primarily found in the formation of progressive aspect of many verbs (cf. 5.2.3), and in some nominal derivations. Examples are: *undu-undu* 'carrying/being carried on the head', *kio-kiom* 'smiling', *manu-manuk* 'bird' (<*manuk* 'chicken').

The vowel of the second reduplicated syllable in CVCV-reduplications may be omitted under two conditions: First, syncope occurs to avoid the sequence of four syllables beginning with the same consonant as in *bib'-bibito̲* (rare in modern speech: *bibi-bibito̲*) 'carrying/being carried with a string hanging from hand'. Second, syncope regularly applies in the case of trisyllabic bases, e.g. *pot'-potaano̲* (also *pota-potaano̲*) 'carrying/being carried on shoulder'.

CV-reduplication is employed in noun formation (cf. 6), and also to express reciprocal action together with the suffix -*an*, e.g. *ko-kait* 'broom' (cf. *mongait* 'sweep'), *to-taup-an* 'winnow' (cf. *monaup* 'to winnow'), *mo-ko-kotau-an* 'know each other'. A variant of CV-reduplication is lengthening of the first vowel of the stem, which is always used to avoid the occurrence of three like syllables, e.g. *piipid* 'fan' (instead of *pi-pipid, cf. *momipid* 'to fan'). This variant is also preferred in the formation of reciprocal verb forms, e.g. *mo-paate-an* 'kill each other' (<√*pate* 'kill').

3 BASIC MORPHOSYNTAX

3.1 Word classes

With regards to morphosyntactic words, two major open word classes can be distinguished, nouns and verbs. They are distinguished by their syntactic and inflectional properties. Both nouns and verbs can appear as predicates, but only nouns (and some minor classes of function words) can be subject in a clause (see 3.2 below for the definition of subject). All verbs are marked for aspect, and in dynamic and stative aspect, verbs are always marked for voice and tense. In order to occur in the same syntactic functions as nouns, e.g. as subjects, verbs have to be nominalized (see 3.3 below).

On the root level however, the distinction between nouns and verbs is blurred, since many roots can be used as nouns and at the same time serve as verb roots without further derivation. An example is the noun *ini* 'urine', which can take the verbal inflectional prefix *moN-* (marking actor voice, neutral tense and dynamic aspect), yielding *mongini* 'to urinate'. Other nouns cannot immediately serve as bases for verbal formations, but have to take derivational affixes, e.g. *puluka* 'trousers', from which the verb *mogipuluka* 'wear trousers' is derived, containing the inflectional prefix *mog-* (actor voice, neutral tense and dynamic aspect), and the derived stem √*ipuluka* with the derivational prefix *i-*. Finally, some roots are bound roots in that they cannot appear as such, but always have to be modified by either affixation or reduplication (or both) in order to serve as verb or noun, e.g. the root √*kait* which combines with the verbal affix *moN-* to give the verb *mongait* 'to sweep', or with CV-reduplication to form the noun *kokait* 'broom'.

The remaining word classes are closed sets of function words. Pronouns and deictics can appear in the same syntactic positions as nouns. Temporal expressions (e.g. *kolaung* 'yesterday', *tongoma* 'day after tomorrow') usually appear either at the beginning or the end of a clause. Other function words include clitics such as case markers (3.3), directionals (4.2), and discourse particles (e.g. *ai* 'reported speech').

3.2 Clause types

Three clause types can be distinguished in Buol: basic, equational and existential clauses.

Basic clauses minimally consist of a predicate, which can be a verb or a non-specific noun or nominalization. Except for a small subclass of clauses with meteorological verbs, the basic clause further contains a *subject* NP. The function of a basic clause is to give new information about the subject. This subject NP is characterized by four features: (a) it has to be a pronoun or a definite noun, i.e. a known entity in the discourse; (b) it appears in nominative case, which has a distinct form for pronouns and personal nouns (see 3.3); (c) if the predicate is a verb, the semantic role of the subject NP is indicated by the voice marking on the verb (see 5.1); (d) the subject is the only positionally variable core NP in that it can either precede (5) or follow the predicate (6).

(5) *Inda   kodo-too [tilo]*_{SBJ} *[nomongat=ono]*_{Pred} *koda-agi Vuolo.*
    when   like-DIST 3p.NOM   AV.PST:depart=CPL   like-DIR   Buol
    'Then they departed for Buol.'

(6) *Noroe=lon   dondia   [n'kokotamoon]*_{Pred} *[kito   duia.]*_{SBJ}
    PV.ST.PST:long=CPL   just.now RCP.PST:meet   1pi.NOM   two
    'It's been a long time and only now we two meet.'

The subject-initial order often involves emphasis or contrast, or serves to bring an already known participant back into the discourse or narrative (7).

(7) *[Aku   kolo]*_{SBJ} *[mogulat doi.]*_{Pred}
    1s.NOM   also   AV:wait   money
    'I am also waiting for money.'

Often, the subject is left unexpressed if it is recoverable from context, as in (8), where the subject of both clauses is 'Anggatibone', mentioned in the preceding clauses.

(8) *Inda   noitamo   a   Goa, ni-nika   ni   madika no   Goa.*
    when   PV.ST.PST:arrive LOC   Goa   PV.PST-marry PN.GEN   king   GEN Goa
    'After [Anggatibone] had arrived in Goa, [she] was taken as wife by the king of Goa.'

Extensions of the predicate can be found before and after the verb. The most important extensions following the verb are non-subject core NPs: agent or instrument NPs in genitive case (9) or common noun undergoers in unmarked neutral case (10) (see 3.3 for nominal case marking). In the case of more than one nominal predicate extension, genitive nouns precede nouns in neutral case, and if there are two nouns in genitive case, the agent precedes the instrument. The subject NP cannot intercede between the verb and these extensions.

(9) *Inda   kodo-too   [noala   no   bali]*_{Pred} *[ti   Dai Bole.]*_{SBJ}
     when   like-DIST   PV.ST.PST:take   GEN   enemy   PN.NOM   Dai Bole
     'Then the enemies captured Dai Bole.'

(10) *[No-dolo   boyo]*_{Pred} *[tio.]*_{SBJ}
      AV.PST-bring   fish   3s.NOM
      'He brought (some) fish.'

Another important class of predicate extensions are the predicate-modifying clitics which include the proclitic progressive marker *du=* (5.2.3), the enclitic completion markers *=lon* and *=po* (3.5), and the enclitic directionals *=agi* and *=ako* (4.2).

Existential clauses are formed with *oulo* (archaic variant: *oluo*) as predicate, expanded by a complement NP. If this complement is an indefinite NP, *oulo* asserts its existence, as in (11) and (12).

(11) *Oluo   teetu   wakutu...*
      EXIST   one   time
      'Once upon a time...' (lit. 'There was a certain time...')

(12) *Oulo   taa   moduti   kunimu.*
      EXIST   NR   AV:seek   2s.OBL
      'Someone is looking for you.'

The complement of *oulo* can also be a definite noun. In this case, the existential clause does not express the existence of the complement (which is presupposed), but its actual presence, as in example (13), where the speaker refers to a specific amount of money already being sent to him.

(13) *Naali,   agu   oulo=lon   doi-ku...*
      PST:become   if   exist=CPL   money-1s.GEN
      'So, if I already have my money...' (lit. 'So, if there already is my money...')

In *equational* clauses, the identity of two definite noun phrases is asserted. Such clauses are often used for contrastive focus involving nominalizations as in (14) (see also 3.3), including WH-questions as in (15).

(14) *Aku   taa   nogola.*
      1s.NOM   NR   AV.PST:take
      'I was the one who took it.'

(15) *Olo   ku   du=nikaan-um?*
      what   NR   PRG=PV.PST:eat-2s.GEN
      'What are you eating?'

Negation is expressed by *dia* and *diila*. *Diila* is a free formative. It is used in isolation and to negate predicates in equational and basic clauses (16). *Dia* occurs only in basic clauses. It is a proclitic that immediately precedes verbal predicates (17).

(16)   *Diila   pinate-ku   bunia-mu.*
       NEG   PV.PST:kill-1s.GEN   hawk-2s.GEN
       'I didn't kill your hawk.'

(17)   *Dia   kotoloman-umo̲   lipu   no   Vuolo̲?*
       NEG   DV.ST:remember-2s.GEN   land   GEN   Buol
       'Aren't you homesick for Buol?'

Dia also combines with the enclitic completion markers to give *dia=po* 'not yet' and
diadun 'not any more' (in place of expected **dia=lon*). The negative form of the existential predicator *oulo* is *diauon* 'not existing, not present'. Negative commands are
marked by *nai* followed by the prohibitive form of the verb (18).

(18)   *Nai   kaan-e   kundii!*
       NEG.IMP   eat-PRH   NR.MED
       'Don't eat that!'

Like *dia*, *nai* also can combine with *=po* (*Nai=po!* 'Don't do it yet!', 'Wait first!')
and *=lon* (*Nai=lon!* 'It's not necessary any more!').

3.3 Noun phrases and case marking

A noun phrase consists of a pronoun or a noun with a case marker. Both pronouns and
nouns can optionally be further modified.

In principle, four cases can be distinguished: nominative, genitive, oblique and locative, but this distinction cannot be made for all classes of nominals, as further explained
shortly. The four cases are distributed as follows:

(19)   nominative: subject NP, topicalized NP;
       genitive: possessor, non-subject agent/cause, instrument;
       oblique: non-subject undergoer;
       locative: location.

For nouns (including nominalizations), there are two sets of nominal case markers,
common and *personal*, given in Table 22.2. The personal case markers are used with personal names. Definite human nouns also take personal markers, always so in genitive and
oblique case, but less consistently in nominative case. The case markers for common
nouns are employed with all non-human nouns and with indefinite human nouns. The case
marking paradigm for common nouns is much reduced. In particular, nominative and
oblique case are not distinguished. Instead, common nouns are in unmarked neutral case
when they appear in subject or topic position, or function as non-subject undergoers.

The case markers are proclitics to the following noun, except for the post-consonantal
personal genitive marker *i*, which is cliticized to the preceding noun or verb. Before

TABLE 22.2: NOMINAL CASE MARKERS

Personal		Common	
Nominative:	*ti*	Neutral:	Ø
Genitive:	*ni* following final vowel	Genitive:	*no* following final vowel
	i following final consonant		Ø following final consonant
Oblique:	*kuni*		
Local:	*a/ato kuni*	Local:	*a/ato*

a noun beginning with a consonant, the vowel of the common genitive marker *no* is usually subject to syncope, as e.g. in *bole n' tamaang* (house GEN friend) 'house of a friend' (*bole no tamaang* is also possible). The frequent zero marking of common nouns in genitive case, together with the fact that neutral case is regularly zero marked, shows the importance of constituent order for identifying the core roles in a verbal clause.

Locative case is indicated as follows: nouns taking common noun marking are immediately preceded by the preposition *a* (variant *ato*), whereas personal names and nouns that take personal case marking are preceded by *a/ato* and the oblique marker *kuni*.

The case marking paradigm for personal pronouns is similar to that for personal nouns, as shown in Table 22.3.

Nominative and oblique pronouns are independent words, while genitive pronouns are either suffixes (1s, 2s and 1pi forms except for=*noto*) or enclitics (remaining forms). Pronouns appear in essentially the same positions in a clause as nouns with the same syntactic function. That is, they are not second position clitics subject to fronting as in Tagalog and other Philippine languages (see HIMMELMANN, TYPOLOGICAL CHARACTERISTICS). Following the locative marker *a*, pronouns occur in oblique form.

In polite address to elders, one uses the 1pi form while referring to oneself by *kami ato-niu* (1pe.NOM slave-2p.GEN). The second and third person plural forms are used when speaking or referring to royals, e.g. *anak-iu* (child-2p.GEN) 'your child'.

The noun phrase can be expanded to the right by possessors and relative clauses. Possessor noun phrases are in genitive case and immediately follow the head noun, e.g. *bunia ni Anggatibone* 'Anggatibone's hawk'.

In relative clauses, verbs with their extensions can follow the nominal head without further marking, e.g. *botu moitomo* (stone PV.ST:black) 'a black stone' or *rusa [idokopo diuko]* (deer PV.PST:catch dog) 'the deer caught by the dog'. The head of the relative clause has to be the subject or the possessor of the subject of the relative clause. The two examples just given exemplify subject relatives. When the head functions as the possessor of the subject in the relative clause, it is represented by a pronoun in the relative clause as in *bodu [mopoyok limo=**nio**]* (shirt short hand=3s.GEN) 'a shirt whose sleeves are short'. Optionally, the verb in relative clauses can be preceded by a nominalizer (see below), which here serves as a kind of relativizing element, e.g. *gokito **ku** pongambulingan=io* (raft NR DV:return=3s.GEN) 'a raft on which he will return home'.

The nominalizing proclitics *ku* and *taa* are employed to form noun phrases from verbs or locative phrases. Formally, they are reduced forms of the nouns *kuon*

TABLE 22.3: PERSONAL PRONOUN SETS

	Nominative	Genitive		Oblique
		after V	after C	
1s	*aku*	*-ku*	*-u**	*kunaku*
2s	*iko*	*-mu*	*-um*	*kunimu*
3s	*tio*	=*nio*	=*io*	*kunio*
1pi	*kito*	*-to*/=*noto*	*-oto**	*kunoto*
1pe	*kami*	=*nami*	=*ami*	*kunami*
2p	*kamu*	=*niu*	=*iu*	*kuniu*
3p	*tilo*	=*nilo*	=*ilo*	*kunilo*

* After stem-final *n*, sandhi occurs, see 2.4.3.

'what-you-call-it' (also employed in absolute possessives, e.g. *kuon-um* 'yours') and *tau* 'person'. The nominalizer *ku* forms non-human noun phrases:

(20) ...*kotaang-gu=lono̲*   ***ku***   *a*   *ginaa-mu.*
      DV.ST:know-1s.GEN=CPL   NR   LOC   wish-2s.GEN
      '...I already know what is on your mind.'

(21) *Nai*   *ponokope*   ***ku***   *molongo,*   *ponokope=agi*   ***ku***   *mogite!*
      NEG.IMP   DV.PRH:catch   NR   PV.ST:fat   DV.IMP:catch=DIR   NR   PV.ST:thin
      'Don't catch fat ones [=deer] for him, catch him thin ones!'

Singular and occasionally also plural human noun phrases are formed with the nominalizer *taa*:

(22) ***Taa***   *no-bute*   *too*   *duia*   *no*   *pulu*   *agu*   *limo*   *no*   *tau.*
      NR   AV.PST-oar   DIST   two   GEN   ten   and   five   GEN   person
      'The ones who went to sea were twenty-five people.'

Note also *taa itol* 'old man', *taa diti* 'young person', or the ethnonyms *taa Vuol* 'Buol person', *taa Bolano* 'Dutchman', *taa Manol* 'Mandarese'. The third person plural pronoun *tilo* serves as the regular plural for *taa*, e.g. *tilo itol* 'the old folks', *tilo diti* 'young people', *tila a Tolitoli* 'the people in Tolitoli'. The genitive and oblique forms are also used in this function:

(23) ...*kinohabaran=on=**ila***   *a*   *Tolitoli...*
      DV.ST.PST:news=CPL=3p.GEN   LOC   Tolitoli
      '...the people of Tolitoli got news...'

Nominalizations have the same syntactic properties as regular nouns. They can appear as subject (20), non-subject undergoer (21) or non-subject agent (23), and also as predicates in basic clauses, e.g. in example (24), where *rusa idokopo̲ diuko̲* is the subject.

(24) ***Ku***   *molongo*   *rusa*   *idokopo̲*   *diuko̲,*   *io*   ***ku***   *mogite?*
      NR   PV.ST:fat   deer   PV.PST:catch   dog   CNJ   NR   PV.ST:thin
      'Are the deer caught by the dog fat ones, or thin ones?'

3.4 Numerals

The basic independent numerals are: 1 *teetu*, 2 *duia*, 3 *totolu*, 4 *opat*, 5 *limo*, 6 *onom*, 7 *pitu*, 8 *walu*, 9 *sio*. Most nouns are counted using independent numerals which can either precede or follow the noun without further linking, e.g. *manuko̲ teetu* 'one chicken' or *pitu gui* (seven night) 'seven days'. Independent numerals can also appear as predicates, e.g. *lavung-io kama opato̲ gotuto̲* (many-3s.GEN maybe four hundred) 'there were about 400 of them'. There is a small class of *unit nouns*, which are linked to the independent numerals in a genitive construction, e.g. *duia no tau* 'two people', with the exception of single units, which take the prefix *tongo-*, e.g. *tongo iagu* 'one month', and units of three using the shortened form *tolu*, e.g. *tolu no tau* 'three people'. Tens, hundreds and thousands are counted like unit nouns with the bases √*pulu*, √*gotut* and √*rivu*, respectively, with the exception of *mopulu* '10' and *mogotut* '100'. Higher decimals precede lower decimals, and are connected with *agu* 'and', e.g. *tolu no gotut agu duia no pulu agu onomo̲* '326'.

Ordinal numerals are formed by attaching the prefix *inggo-* to the independent numerals, multiplicative forms take the prefix *poko-*. Exceptional formations are: *pamula* 'first' (also 'beginning'), *miindan* 'once', *inggoulo* (variant: *inggoluo*) 'second', *inggotolu* 'third', *pokoulo* (variant: *pokoluo*) 'twice', *pokotolu* 'thrice'.

3.5 The completion markers =*lon* and =*po* and the order of verbal clitics

The clitics =*lon* and =*po* have completive and incompletive meaning, respectively. They immediately follow the (morphological) word they modify. When attached to the predicate of a declarative sentence, =*lon* indicates that the action or state described by the predicate has become fact, or is about to become fact and can often be translated with 'already', as in (25).

(25)   *Niunom=on*   *a*   *ruma sakit.*
       PV.PST:medicine=CPL LOC hospital
       '[He] has already been treated in hospital.'

In foregrounded clauses of a narrative, the predicate is often marked with=*lon*, while clauses providing background information are unmarked. In imperative clauses,=*lon* adds emphasis, and is used in direct commands, e.g. *Popolong=on!* (AV.IMP:sleep=CPL) 'Go to sleep!', or in offering something, e.g. *Alaan=on!* (PV.IMP:get=CPL) 'Just take it!'. In combination with noun phrases,=*lon* has a restrictive meaning, e.g. *iko=lon* 'just you (and no one else)'.

The incompletive marker=*po* indicates that what is expressed by the preceding word is still being extended or added to. In combination with a predicate,=*po* carries the meanings 'still, first' e.g.

(26)   *Aku*   *mongaan=opo,* *dondoo* *molako*
       1s.NOM AV:eat=INCPL   then   AV:walk
       'I eat first before I go.'

Following nominals,=*po* has an additive meaning, e.g. *olo=po?* 'what else?'. In imperative clauses,=*po* is usually employed when asking a favor and serves to soften the command, e.g. *Alaambaagi!* (<*alaan=po=agi* PV.IMP:get=INCPL=DIR) 'Please get it (for me)!'.

If the completion markers co-occur with other clitics such as the clitic genitive pronouns and the directionals (see section 4), they appear in the order given in (27).

(27)   (head)=completion marker=directional=enclitic pronoun

Examples (28), (29) and (30) illustrate some of the ordering possibilities.

(28)   ...*naa*   *iduti=**lon**=**ilo***   *taa* *madika.*
       PST:go   PV.PST:seek=CPL=3p.GEN NR   royal
       '...they went to look for the king.'

(29)   ...*naali*   *naa*   *pinoki-bulot=**agi**=**nio***   *diuko̲.*
       PST:become PST:go IV.PST.RQV-borrow=DIR=3s.GEN dog
       '...so she ordered to borrow the dog.'

Recall that the 1s, 2s and 1pi genitive pronouns are suffixes (cf. 3.3) and thus always precede enclitics (30).

(30)   *Alaang-u=**pa**=**agi***   *doi-ku.*
       PV:get-1s.GEN=INCPL=DIR money
       'I get my money first.'

3.6 Complement clauses and complex predicates

There are two constructions in Buol in which a verb is syntactically dependent on a matrix verb. The first type involves control constructions with a matrix clause having as predicate a verb of intention and motion, or a verb expressing commands or prohibition, followed by a complement clause with equi-NP deletion. In the complement clause, the controlled noun phrase has to be subject and the verb is always in actor voice, overriding pragmatic criteria for voice selection (as outlined in 5.1), as in (31) and (32). Often, the complement clause contains a complex predicate with *maa*/*magi* (see below), as in (32)

(31)   *Tondanangu*   ***mogotad***   *kunio.*
     DV:try:1s.GEN   AV:call   3s.OBL
     'I will try to call him.'

(32)   *Nosituru*   *taanda=nio*   *agu*   *tau*   *no*   *lipu*   ***maa***   ***mogola***=*agi*
     AV.PST:agree   all=3s.GEN   and   person   GEN   land   go   AV:get=DIR
     kuni   *anak*   *i*   *Dai Bole.*
     PN.OBL   *child*   PN.GEN   Dai Bole
     'They all [=the elders] together with the people [of Buol] agreed to go and get the son of Dai Bole.'

The second type of construction makes use of the verbs *maa* and *magi* (past forms are *naa* and *nagi*, respectively) which together with a locative expression can form independent predicates meaning 'go to X' and 'come to X (near speaker)', as in examples (33) and (34).

(33)   *Maa*   *maino*   *iko?*
     go.to   where   2s.NOM
     'Where are you going?'

(34)   *Naali*   *nagi*   *ato*   *tudu=lono*   *tilo.*
     PST:become   PST:come   LOC   top=CPL   3p.NOM
     'Thus, they came to the mainland.'

In combination with another verb, *maa*/*magi* form single complex predicates with tense/mood agreement. The meaning of *maa* in such constructions is 'go in order to VERB' or sometimes also 'set about to VERB', without implying change of place, while *magi* always expresses 'come here in order to VERB'. The logical subject of *maa*/*magi* is coreferential with the actor of the second verb, and the case marking of the arguments of the complex predicate is determined by the voice marking on the second verb. This is apparent in example (35) where the speaker is the logical subject of *naa* but expressed by a genitive pronoun, since the second verb is in instrument voice with the content of the question as subject. Example (36) illustrates the use of *magi* with a verb in actor voice.

(35)   *Naa*   *pinongindu-ku*   *a*   *kuni*   *Buyung*   *main'*   *ti*   *Anto.*
     PST:go   IV.PST:ask-1s.GEN   LOC   OBL   Buyung   where   NOM   Anto
     'I went to ask Buyung where Anto is.'

(36)   *Inda*   *kodo-too*   *buloli*   *nagi*   *nonginumo*   *a*   *tualungo*   *bole.*
     when   like.DIST   pig   PST:come   AV.PST:drink   LOC   space below   house
     'Then a pig came to drink underneath the house.'

3.7 Interrogatives

Buol has the following interrogative bases: *(ti) tai* (genitive *(n)i tai*, oblique *kuni tai*) 'who?', *olo* 'what?', *maino* 'which?', *monu* 'how many?', *katoo* 'why?'. Combinations with other formatives are:

(37) *olo*:   *tong-olo* 'how much?', *kodo-olo* 'how?', and the verb *mong-olo* 'do what?' (the past form *nongolo* can also mean 'why?'), which also has an instrument voice form *pong-olo* 'do what with SBJ?'

    maino: *ku maino* 'which one?', *a maino* 'where?', *maa maino* 'where to?'

    monu: *poko-monu* 'how many times?', *komonu* 'when (past)?', *komonuan* 'when (future)?'

The interrogative pronouns *(ti) tai* and *olo* appear usually in initial position in an equational clause, followed by a noun or nominalization, as in (38), but they can also appear *in situ* in basic clauses, if they are not subject, as in (39) where *olo* is non-subject agent.

(38) *Olo   ku   du=dution-um?*
    what   NR   PRG=PV:seek-2s.GEN
    'What are you looking for?'

(39) *Nikekelano   olo   iko?*
    DV.PST:bite   what   2s.NOM
    'What has bitten you?'

4 DEICTICS AND DIRECTIONALS

The deictic and directional system of Buol is relatively simple since its elements only express location and direction relative to the position of the discourse participants, without reference to topography or cardinal directions, as e.g. in the related Gorontalo or Bolaang Mongondow. Topographical terms such as *dualom* 'interior, away from the sea' (lit. 'inside'), *duli* 'mountainside' (lit. 'above') or *panau* 'relating to the sea' (lit. 'below'), are only used if one actually speaks about events that are directly related to these areas.

4.1 Deictics

Buol has three deictic bases: *tia(n)* 'near speaker', *tii(n)* 'near addressee', *too(n)* 'far from both speaker and addressee'. These bases can occur as predicate, with the meaning 'to be near speaker', etc. (40), and as modifier, e.g. *diuko too* 'that dog'. Deictic bases can also be used as independent noun phrases, but only in subject function (41).

(40) *Tian=on   ti   ina.*
    PRX=CPL   PN   mother
    'Mother is already here.'

(41) *O?o,   too   kotolomang-u.*
    yes   DIST   DV.ST:remember-1s.GEN
    'Yes, that one I am longing for.'

Explicitly nominalized forms are *kundia(n)*, *kundii(n)* and *kundoo(n)* (<nominalizer *ku(n)-* + *tia(n)* etc.), which can occur as free noun phrases (42) or as modifier following a noun (43). With human reference, *taa kundia(n)* 'this person' etc. are used.

(42)   *Kundia   sirita   no   Madika   Moputi.*
     NR.PRX   story   GEN   king   white
     'This is the story of the White King.'

(43)   *Kundi-kundi   kundi   kundii.*
     PRG-lock   door   NR.MED
     'That door is locked.'

The deictics also serve as bases for expressions relating to place, manner and time: *a tia(n)* etc. 'here', *kodo tia(n)* etc. 'like this', *don-dia(n)/don-dii(n)* 'just now', *don-doo(n)* 'just then'.

4.2 Directionals

Buol has two directional enclitics,=*agi* 'towards speaker' and=*ako* 'away from speaker'. They are very frequently used and can combine with verbal predicates, temporal expressions and other constituents. Examples (44) and (45) illustrate the use of the directionals.

(44)   *Maa   alaangu=agi.*
     go   PV:get:1s.GEN=DIR
     'I'll go and get it (and bring it here).'

(45)   *Ondonge=lon=ako   tio!*
     DV.IMP:see=CPL=DIR   3s.NOM
     'Just look at him!'

The directionals, usually =*ako*, can also express comparative degree with stative verbs (46).

(46)   *Kundia   modoka=ako.*
     NR.PRX   PV.ST:big=DIR
     'This one is bigger.'

The directionals can function as prepositions when combined with *kodo* 'like', giving *koda=agi* 'towards' (coming to speaker, often shortened to *daagi*) and *koda=ako* 'towards' (away from speaker, often *daako*, *daak*), followed by place nouns (47).

(47)   *Diaduno̱   nokokambulingo̱   koda=ako   Vuolo̱.*
     not.anymore   AV.ST.PST:return   like-DIR   Buol
     '[He] could not return anymore to Buol.'

Directionals can also be cliticized to deictics that function as predicates, e.g. *toon=on=ako* 'already gone there' and *tiin=on=agi* 'already come here'.

5 MAJOR VERBAL ALTERNATIONS

5.1 Voice and tense/mood

Buol verbs can be marked for one of four voices: *actor voice*, *patient voice*, *dative voice* and *instrument voice*. When a verb is the predicate of a main clause, voice indicates the semantic role of the subject in the event denoted by the verb:

- In actor voice, the subject is the performer of an action or the experiencer in the case of verbs of perception and mental activity.

- In patient voice the subject is an undergoer that is directly affected, or transferred in space, e.g.: *kaan-on* 'eat sth.', *pate-en* 'kill someone', *po-gutu-on* 'make sth.', *undud-on* 'escort someone', *igi-on* 'give sth. (to someone)'.
- In dative voice the subject is an undergoer that is externally affected, as in *digum-an* 'hold sth.', *pipi-an* 'wash sth. (clothes)', *init-an* 'heat up sth.'. It can also be a location, direction, recipient (also beneficiary) or source: *po-digu-an* 'take a bath at some place', *kiki-an* 'laugh at someone', *igi-an* 'give someone (sth.)', *po-tali-an* 'buy for someone'.
- In instrument voice the subject is either an instrument or, with communication verbs, the message conveyed: *pom-[p]aki* 'throw with sth.', *pom-[b]ubog* 'hit with sth.', *pong-indu* 'ask about sth.', *po-guman* 'say sth.'.

Voice selection depends on syntactic and pragmatic factors. In independent clauses, the voice of the predicate is determined by the definiteness of its arguments: if there is a definite patient or theme, it will usually be chosen for subject (48). If the patient is indefinite, actor voice is used (49), unless there are other highly topical arguments, such as an instrument, beneficiary or goal, which can also be selected for subject, as in (50), where the beneficiary is subject.

(48) *Pinate-mu=lono̱*   *bunia-ku!*
      PV.PST:kill-2s.GEN=CPL   hawk-1s.GEN
      'You have killed my hawk!'

(49) *Aku,*   *kakai,*   *mogile*   *manuko̱*   *teetu.*
      1s.NOM   grandfather   AV:ask.for   chicken   one
      'Grandfather, I would like to ask for one of the roosters'

(50) *Potalie=ako*   *gau*   *tio!*
      DV.IMP:buy=DIR   cigarette   3s.NOM
      'Buy him cigarettes!'

In many cases, the voice of the verb is determined by its syntactic environment, such as in relative clauses or many WH-questions, where the relativized or questioned noun has to be subject. This is illustrated in example (51), where the recipient is questioned, which requires the verb *igi* 'give' to occur in dative voice.

(51) *Ti*   *tai*   *taa*   *niigian-um*   *bodu-ku?*
      PN.NOM   who   NR   DV.PST:give-2s.GEN   shirt-1s.GEN
      'To whom did you give my shirt?'

The patient and instrument voices are only minimally distinguished. Formally, they are only kept apart in neutral tense in dynamic aspect (cf. 5.2.1 Table 22.4). With many bases, they are in (near-)complementary distribution: plain roots and stems formed with the causative prefix *poko-* (cf. 5.3) only combine with patient voice; stems formed with *pog-*, *poN-* or the causative prefix *po-* rarely appear in patient voice, but instrument voice forms are common; stems formed with requestive *poki-* (cf. 5.4) never take patient voice marking. In stative aspect (cf. 5.2.2) there is only a single voice category corresponding to patient and instrument voices in dynamic aspect.

Voice marking in Buol verbs is closely linked to tense/mood marking, as shown by Table 22.4. Four tense/mood categories are distinguished: past, neutral, imperative and prohibitive. *Past* tense is used to express past events. *Neutral* tense covers present tense, but also describes future events or events that occur regularly. With many verbs, neutral tense also expresses progressive aspect, both in the past and at present. The *imperative* and *prohibitive* moods are used in positive commands and negative commands, respectively.

For certain verb forms, a plural variant is available that indicates the plurality of the performer. So far, distinct plural forms have been recorded for verbs in dynamic aspect in actor voice (cf. 5.2.1 below) and in progressive aspect (cf. 5.2.3); in both cases, the use of these plural forms is optional, i.e. they can always be replaced by the corresponding forms without number agreement.

5.2 Aspect

Buol has three morphologically marked aspects, dynamic, stative and progressive. *Dynamic* aspect profiles the beginning of an action or event, but does not indicate whether its endpoint is reached. In *stative* aspect, the result of an action or event is highlighted, disregarding the nature of its beginning. *Progressive* aspect focuses on the action or event as an ongoing process.

Only dynamic and stative aspect receive distinct marking for tense and voice. In progressive aspect, tense is not distinguished while voice is only marked with verb roots that have a progressive form based on one of the other two aspects plus the progressive marker *du-* (cf. 5.2.3).

Verb roots can be classified according to the aspect they can take. With dynamic roots, the actor initiates the action and usually has control of it. Such roots can naturally occur in dynamic aspect, but they can also take stative aspect in which case the intention is deemphasized in favor of the result. Typical dynamic roots are those where the actor has full control over the action, such as *kaan* 'eat', *pate* 'kill', *lako* 'walk'. Dynamic aspect is also found in expressions for uncontrolled processes such as *mon-[t]iuk* 'blossom' and for events or activities that are not or only partially controlled, but which are initiated by the actor, e.g *mong-ini* 'urinate', *mog-undud* 'fart'. Stative roots are intransitive roots that only appear in stative aspect, because they describe events or states which are not brought about by an actor, e.g. *maate* 'die', *mo-ono* 'cold', *moi-tamo* 'arrive'. Some roots are ambivalent in that they can either have a dynamic or stative meaning, e.g. *tutung* 'set something to fire (dynamic)' vs. 'burn (stative)', or *dovu* 'drop something (dynamic)' vs. 'fall down (stative)'.

5.2.1 Dynamic aspect

In dynamic aspect, all four voices are distinguished, occurring in all four tense/mood categories (Table 22.4; infixes are indicated by pointed brackets). Almost all dynamic verb roots can appear in actor voice, with the performer of the action as subject. If the verb is in one of the other three voice forms (called *undergoer* voices in the following discussion), the subject is a participant other than the actor, while the actor noun phrase itself takes genitive case marking.

The first set of AV affixes is not productive and is found with a small number of verbs expressing motion or process, e.g. *mo-t<um>ulod* 'enter', *mo-t<um>umul* 'grow, live', *mo-l<um>andik* 'jump'. The imperative forms seem to be in free variation, for example: *Tulod!*, *Tumulod!*, or *Potumulod!* 'Come/Go inside!'.

The remaining dynamic verb roots take either the prefix *mog-* or *moN-* in actor voice. The choice between the two is lexically determined. With roots that express actions in which the patient undergoes a severe change of state by means of intentional force, generally *moN-* is used, e.g. *mom-[p]ate* 'kill', *mong-[k]olong* 'cut off', *mong-[k]aan* 'eat'. Otherwise the choice between *mog-* or *moN-* apparently bears little relation to the semantics of the verb root. This can be seen from pairs of verbs belonging to the same

TABLE 22.4: DYNAMIC VERBAL AFFIXES

	Past	Neutral	Imperative	Prohibitive
AV	*no-<um>* *noN-* *nog-*	*mo-<um>* *moN-* *mog-*	*(po-)<um>/Ø* *poN-* *pog-*	*mo-<um>* *moN-* *mog-*
PV	*(n)i-/<in>* *pinoN-* *pinog-*	*-on* *poN- -on* *pog- -on*	*-an* *poN- -an* *pog- -an*	*-e* *poN- -e* *pog- -e*
DV	*(n)i-/<in> -an* *pinoN- -an* *pinog- -an*	*-an* *poN- -an* *pog- -an*	*-e* *poN- -e* *pog- -e*	*-e* *poN- -e* *pog- -e*
IV	*(<in>)* *pinoN-* *pinog-*	*(Ø)* *poN-* *pog-*	*(-an)* *poN- -an* *pog- -an*	*(-e)* *poN- -e* *pog- -e*

semantic class, one of which takes *mog-*, the other *moN-*:

(52) *mog-*   *moN-*
    mo-tegi 'defecate'   *mong-ini* 'urinate'
    mo-botuk 'follow'   *mon-[d]ungan* 'accompany'
    mog-ubi 'carry on back'   *mon-[t]onggili* 'carry child in one's arms'

With verbs beginning with the consonants /l, r, h, s, j, m, n, ŋ/, *mog-* and *moN-* in fact have the same shape, i.e. *mo-* (recall from section 2.6 above, that *mo-* is the general realization of *mog-* before consonants), and thus are practically impossible to tell apart. Note that *mo-* is also the formative for stative patient voice (see 5.2.2 below), but this formative can easily be distinguished from agentive *mo-* by its morphosyntactic properties.

The plural forms of *moN-* and *mog-* are *mongoN-* and *mongog-*, respectively. Their use is not obligatory with plural agents, and they can co-occur with forms not marked for plural in one clause, as in (53).

(53) *Ti   uma   agu   ti   ina...   mongo-bandi   agu   mo-dudogo.*
    PN father and PN mother AV.PL-hoe   and AV-weed
    'Father and Mother.. are hoeing and weeding.'

Verbs in patient or dative voice either take plain voice affixes, *-on* and *-an*, respectively, or they are extended by *pog-* and *poN-*. In patient voice, the use of *pog-* and *poN-* is lexically determined and restricted to a small number of verbs, e.g. *po-gutu-on* 'make'. In dative voice, many verbs can occur both with and without *pog-* and *poN-*, relating to different thematic roles, e.g. *pipi-an* 'wash (clothes)', but *pom-[p]ipi-an* 'wash (clothes) for someone/at some place'. For other verbs, the use of *pog-/poN-* is obligatory in dative voice, e.g. *pong-indu-an* 'ask someone'.

As for instrument voice, the affixes in the first row for instrument voice in Table 22.4 are in parentheses, since they never occur on plain verb roots, but only in combination with other verbal prefixes, such as the stem forming *pog-* and *poN-*, requestive *poki-*, and others.

The past tense marker in the undergoer voices is realized as a prefix *(n)i-* with stems that do not begin with a voiceless stop, e.g. *ni-ala* 'was taken', *ni-dolo* 'was brought', while stems having an initial voiceless stop either can take the prefix *(n)i-* or the infix *<in>*, e.g. *k<in>aan/ni-kaan* 'was eaten'. In combination with prefixes such as *po-*, *poN-*, etc., the infixed variant is preferred.

The paradigm in Table 22.4 displays much homophony, especially regarding the affixes *-e*, *-an*, and *pog-/poN-*. These affixes can however usually be distinguished in context, especially the latter two, since undergoer voice forms in the past and neutral tenses are almost always followed by an agent noun phrase in genitive case, while this is seldom the case with undergoer voice in imperative mood, and never so with actor voice forms.

5.2.2 Stative aspect

Stative aspect occurs in only three voices, since there is no instrument voice form (Table 22.5). There are only two tense/mood categories, past and neutral. An imperative and a prohibitive are not available, since verbs with stative morphology are never used in positive commands, while in negative commands with *nai* 'don't', the neutral form is employed.

The two variant forms in patient voice *mo-* and *moi-* are historically derived from patient and instrument voice forms. However, on the synchronic level in Buol, as in closely related Gorontalo and Bolaang Mongondow, they have become variants of a single voice category, since their distribution does not correlate with patient and instrument voice in dynamic aspect. Use of the two forms in patient voice is in part lexically, and in part semantically, determined: *moi-* is used with most consonant-initial dynamic roots that take *mog-* (realized as *mo-*, see 2.5) in dynamic actor voice. Furthermore, verbs that express a change of location also usually take *moi-*. Otherwise, *mo-* is used.

When stative affixes combine with dynamic verb roots, the focus is shifted from the beginning to the result of the action. The action can be intentional, in which case the focus on the result gives an *abilitative* meaning. If the verb does not refer to intentional actions, stative aspect indicates an *involuntary* meaning. This use of stative aspect corresponds to potentive formations in Tagalog (see HIMMELMANN, TYPOLOGICAL CHARACTERISTICS).

For some intransitive verbs, involuntary and abilitative meaning are formally distinguished by means of voice. With abilitative meaning, the verb is in actor voice, while with an involuntary meaning, the subject is seen as a patient, in which case patient voice is used. Examples are the dynamic roots *polong* 'sleep' and *tulod* 'enter' (cf. *mo-polong* 'go to sleep', *mo-t<um>ulod* 'enter', dynamic actor voice), which can appear in two forms in stative aspect: *moko-polong* 'be able to sleep' vs. *moi-polong* 'fall asleep', *moko-tulod* 'be able to enter' vs. *moi-tulod* 'enter involuntarily'. This is only possible in stative aspect, since in dynamic aspect the subject in different voices always refers to different participants.

For the majority of dynamic verbs (apparently including all transitive verbs) however, involuntary and abilitave meaning are expressed by the same form. The actual meaning can then only be established from context. In example (54), an involuntary interpretation is more likely than an abilitative one, while (55) clearly has an abilitative meaning.

TABLE 22.5: STATIVE VERBAL AFFIXES

	Past	Neutral
AV	*noko-*	*moko-*
PV	*no-*	*mo-*
	noi-	*moi-*
DV	*kino- -an*	*ko- -an*

(54)   *No-bindang-u   bodu-ku.*
       PV.ST.PST-tear-1s.GEN   shirt-1s.GEN
       'I (accidentally) have torn my shirt.'

(55)   *No-ala   no   bali   ti   Dai Bole.*
       PV.ST.PST-take   GEN   enemy   PN.NOM   Dai Bole
       'The enemies captured (or: were able to capture) Dai Bole.'

In the patient and dative voices, most dynamic verb roots take the same voice in dynamic and stative aspect, as can be seen in examples (56) and (57) which are only distinguished by aspect:

(56)   *Nidiotan-io   ulot.*
       DV.PST:step.on-3s.GEN   mat
       'He (intentionally) stepped on the mat.'

(57)   *Kinodiotan-io   ulot.*
       DV.ST.PST:step.on-3s.GEN   mat
       'He (accidentally) stepped on the mat.'

However, occasionally there is some crossover. For instance, the undergoer subject of *butak* 'split, shatter' is marked with dative voice in dynamic aspect, but in stative aspect it is marked with patient voice. Instrument voice in dynamic aspect corresponds to patient voice in stative aspect.

A small group of transitive verb roots which express various kinds of experiences, including perception and cognition, normally occur in stative aspect, e.g. *ondong* 'see', *bou* 'smell', *anduk* 'understand', *tolom* 'remember'. These roots can also occur in dynamic aspect, if the experience is brought about intentionally. For example, the root *ondong* is marked for stative aspect in (58), and therefore expresses uncontrolled perception ('see'), while in (59), the same root appears in dynamic aspect, which indicates controlled perception ('look at').

(58)   *Kinoondongang-u=lon*
       DV.ST.PST:see-1s.GEN=CPL
       'I have already seen it.'

(59)   *Ondonge=lon=ako   tio!*
       DV.IMP:see=CPL=DIR   3s.NOM
       'Just look at him!'

Stative verbs are based on roots that always occur in stative aspect. For most stative verbs, patient voice is the basic voice, with the most affected participant as subject. The largest class of stative verbs are qualitative verbs, which describe an inherent or temporary property of the subject. Qualitative verbs always take the PV prefix *mo-*. In neutral tense, the qualitative verb either describes a state or - in combination with a directional - an expected change of state, e.g. *mo-sehat* 'healthy', but *mo-sehat=agi* 'get better'. The past form always has a resultative meaning, which is illustrated in example (60), where the first verb *mo-giginit* describes the illness as a present state, while the second verb *no-gite(=lon)* indicates the result of a process.

(60)   *Mo-giginit=ai   kuan=ilo,   no-gite=lon=ai   am.*
       PV.ST-ill=RPRT   word=3p.GEN   PV.ST.PST-thin=CPL=RPRT   FAM
       'He is ill, they say, and has become thinner.'

Other stative verbs include those describing events which the subject inherently cannot control such as *moi-dilut* 'slip', *mo-anud* 'drift', *mo-boon* 'sneeze', *moi-tamo* 'arrive'.

Many stative verbs appear in both patient voice and dative voice. When such verbs are marked for dative voice, the patient or theme argument is in genitive case immediately following the verb, while the subject is a noun phrase expressing the location or an experiencer (usually negatively) affected by the event or state expressed by the verb. An example for this is (61), where dative voice relates to the experiencer. The use of the same stative root in patient voice is illustrated in example (62).

(61) *Molavung   taa   kinotutungan   bole.*
     PV.ST:many   NR   DV.ST.PST:burn   house
     'Many people's homes have been consumed by fire.'
     (lit. 'Many are those who have been affected by the burning of (their) houses.')

(62) *Notutung   bole-nilo.*
     PV.ST.PST:burn   house-3p.GEN
     'Their house has been consumed by fire.'

Other examples are *ko-tamo-an* 'arrive at some place/a certain time' (PV: *moi-tamo*), *ko-dovu-an* 'fall on something/someone' (PV: *mo-dovu*), or *kinoilangan doi aku* (DV.ST.PST:be.lost money 1s.NOM) 'I have lost some money' (PV: *mo-ilang*).

A small number of stative verbs only occurs in dative voice and is formed from nouns denoting natural phenomena or times of the day, in which case the subject experiences what is described by the noun, e.g. *ko-ulan-an* 'be caught by the rain' (*ulan* 'rain'), *ko-laung-an* 'to do something until afternoon' (lit. 'to be surprised by the afternoon' *lo-laung* 'afternoon').

In a few cases, stative verbs can also appear in actor voice. Such verbs have a factitive meaning, i.e. the subject has the property of causing the state indicated by the root, as in example (63), where *moko-ugo* 'frightening' is the actor voice counterpart of *mo-ugo* 'afraid'.

(63) *Olo   ku   moko-ugo   kunimu?*
     what   NR   AV.ST:afraid   2s.OBL
     'What are you afraid of?' (lit. 'What is frightening you?')

Other examples include *moko-kiki* 'funny, making laugh' (cf. *mo-kiki* 'laugh'), *moko-ingot* 'irritating' (cf. *mo-ingot* 'angry').

5.2.3 Progressive aspect

Buol verbs fall into two classes with regard to the way progressive aspect is expressed. Verbs of the first group describe actions or events that are extended over a certain stretch of time, e.g. √*kaan* 'eat', √*duti* 'seek', √*digu* 'bathe'. Such verbs can appear in *durative* progressive aspect which is formed by adding proclitic *du=* to the neutral tense form of dynamic aspect forms, which can occur in all voices, as in examples (64) in actor voice and (65) in patient voice.

(64) *Inda   ti   anak   i   Dai Bole   du=mongaano...*
     when   PN   child   PN.GEN   Dai Bole   PRG=AV:eat
     'While the son of Dai Bole was eating...'

(65)   *Olo*   *ku*   *du=dution-um?*
     what   NR   PRG=PV:seek-2s.GEN
     'What are you looking for?'

Verbs of the second group occurring in dynamic or stative aspect express actions or events that occur instantaneously, e.g. √*polong* 'go to/fall asleep', √*dovu* 'drop/fall', √*litu* 'sit down', √*vuko* 'open', √*lobung* 'bury', √*digum* 'grasp', √*potaan* 'put on shoulder'. The proclitic *du=* with such verbs does not express progressive aspect, but marks the very moment of the action or event, e.g. *du=mopolong* 'right now/then going to sleep'. The ongoing resulting state or action is expressed in *resultative* progressive aspect formed by CVCV-reduplication; thus for the above roots one gets: *polo-polong* 'sleeping', *dovu-dovu* 'falling', *litu-litu* 'sitting', *vuko-vuko* 'to be open', *lobu-lobung* 'lie buried', *digu-digum* 'holding/being held in hand', *pota-potaan* 'carrying/being carried on shoulder'. Most of these resultative progressive forms are inherently in patient voice, such as *dovu-dovu* or *lobu-lobung*, but with verbs that express the placing of an undergoer directly on or near to the actor's body, the progressive form is either in actor voice or in patient voice, without explicit marking. In example (66), *dolo-dolo* is employed in actor voice and is followed by an unmarked indefinite undergoer NP. If the progressive form is used in patient voice, common noun agents are in genitive case, e.g. *dolo-dolo n' diuk* (PRG-bring GEN dog) 'brought along by a dog', while personal nouns or pronouns are marked for oblique case, as in example (67).

(66)   *Inda*   *noroe=ako*   *noitamo=lon=agi*   *bunia*   ***dolo-dolo****=agi*
     when   PV.ST.PST:long=DIR   PV.ST.PST:arrive=CPL=DIR   hawk   PRG-bring=DIR
     boyo.
     fish
     'After a while the hawk came bringing fish.'

(67)   *Olo*   *ku*   ***undu-undu***   *kunimu.*
     what   NR   PRG-carry.on.head   2s.OBL
     'What are you carrying on your head?'

There is a special plural form for progressives, which involves the formative *gi- -an* and has the same syntactic properties as the resultative progressive forms just discussed. (68) provides an example.

(68)   *Agu*   *oluo*   *tilo*   *diti*   *molavung*   ***gidoloa(n)***   *manuko…*
     if   EXIST   3p.NOM   small   PV.ST:many   PRG.PL:bring   chicken
     'If there are many boys bringing roosters with them…'

5.3 Causatives

There are two causative-forming prefixes in Buol, *po-* and *poko-*. Both take *mo(g)-* in AV, resulting in *mopo-* and *mopoko-*, while in the undergoer voices, the prefix *po-* is usually preceded by the stem forming prefix *po(g)-*, giving *popo-*. The prefix *poko-* is used with many intransitive verbs, including most stative verbs, but also including some dynamic intransitive verbs. Examples are: *poko-doka* 'enlarge' < *modoka* 'big', *poko-olit* 'put shame on s.o.' < *moolit* 'ashamed', *poko-polong* 'make sleep' < *mopolong* 'sleep'. Most dynamic intransitive and all transitive verbs use the prefix *po-* in deriving causatives, e.g. *po-tulod* 'insert' < *mo-t<um>ulod* 'enter', *po-bulot* 'lend' < *bulot* 'borrow', *po-kaan* 'feed' < *kaan* 'eat'.

With all causative verbs, both the ones derived with *poko-* and the ones with *po-*, the causer is the subject in actor voice. With causative verbs derived by *poko-* the causee is the subject in patient voice, e.g. *poko-polong-on* (CAU-sleep-PV) 'put someone to sleep'. In causative formations from intransitive verbs with *po-*, however, instrument voice is used when the causee is chosen as subject; see (69).

(69)   *Pinopo-lundu=nio=lonọ*   taa   utato.
       IV.PST.CAU-embark=3s.GEN=CPL   NR   sibling
       'She made [her] brother embark.'

In causative derivations from transitive verbs, the causative verb is marked for dative voice in case the causee has to appear in subject function, as in (70).

(70)   *Titai   taa   pinopo-bulot-an-um*   *bodu-ku?*
       who   NR   PST.CAU-borrow-DV-2s.GEN   shirt-1s.GEN
       'To whom have you lent my shirt? (lit. who did you cause/allow to borrow my shirt)'

If the undergoer of the caused action is the subject, such as *tulitọ unggaagi kuni taa bolano* in (71), then the causative verb is marked for instrument voice.

(71)   *Pinopo-ondong   i*   *Perenji   Pombangọ   tulitọ   ungga=agi   kuni*
       IV.PST.CAU-see   PN.GEN   Prince   Pombang   letter   from=DIR   PN.OBL
       taa   bolano   kuni   Muhamadu Taher.
       NR   Dutch   PN.OBL   Muhamadu Taher
       'Prince Pombang showed the letter from the Dutchman to Muhamadu Taher.'

The causee is in oblique case if it is not subject, e.g. *kuni Muhamadu Taher* in (71).

5.4 Requestives

Requestive verbs express that someone requests or orders an action to be performed. They are formed with the prefix *moki-* in actor voice, and the prefix *poki-* in the undergoer voices. The performer of the requested action appears in oblique case if not in subject function, as can be seen in (72). Often the performer is irrelevant and left unexpressed, as in (73) and (74).

(72)   *Agu   ti   taa   madika   moki-dokopọ   boyo   kunimu...*
       if   PN   NR   royal   AV.RQV-catch   fish   2s.OBL
       'If the king orders you to catch fish...'

(73)   *Inda   nong-[k]ambuling=on=agi   a   bole-nio   noki-gutu*
       when   AV.PST-return=CPL=DIR   LOC   house-3s.GEN   AV.PST.RQV-make
       uangu.
       boat
       'Having returned to her house, she ordered to make a boat.'

The undergoer of the requested action is subject in instrument voice, as in (74), while the performer is subject in dative voice, as in (75), where the subject is left unexpressed (but it is known from context).

(74)   *Inda   kodo-too   naa   pinoki-ala=nio*   *ti   Alimuungo.*
       when   like-DIST   PST.go   PV.PST.RQV-get=3s.GEN   PN   Alimuungo
       'Then he had Alimuungo summoned.'

(75) *Inda*   *kodo-too*   *pinoki-gutu-an=on*   *i*   *taa*   *utato̲*   *gokito̲…*
      when   like-DIST   PST.RQV-make-DV=CPL   PN.GEN   NR   sibling   raft
      'Then his sister ordered [him] to make a raft…'

6 NOMINAL DERIVATIONS

As described in 3.3, all verb forms can be used as noun phrases by means of the nominalizers *ku* and *taa*. Apart form this syntactic device, Buol also has morphological derivations of nouns from verb roots.

CV-reduplication, often in combination with the suffix *-an*, is mainly employed to form nouns denoting tools. Nouns formed without the suffix are tools that act directly on the undergoer, e.g. *to-taig* 'comb', *du-dupa* 'hammer', *te-teud* 'scoop', *piipid* 'fan' (< √*pipid*), *duudog* (< √*dudog*) 'weeding tool'. CV-reduplication with the suffix *-an* forms nouns denoting tools that do not directly act on the undergoer, but serve as a receptacle in the widest sense, e.g. *tu-tumbit-an* 'blowpipe' (*tumbit* 'blowpipe arrow'), *gu-gool-an* 'loom' (√*gool* 'weave cloth'), *bu-buti-an* 'grid for roasting' (√*buti* 'roast'), *to-taup-an* 'winnow' (√*taup* 'winnow'). Cf. also the pair *duuduk* 'small pestle' vs. *duuduk-an* 'small mortar', both derived from √*duduk* 'pound'. All these nouns refer to objects that are conventionally employed for the purpose described by the verb root. This contrasts with nominalized verbs in instrument voice, which describe objects that are used as instrument only *ad hoc*, e.g. *ku pinomubog-u kunio* (NR IV.PST:beat-1s.GEN 3s.OBL) 'what I have used for hitting him'.

With some roots, nouns formed by CV-reduplication do not denote tools, but have a more abstract meaning, e.g. *tu-tumul* 'life' (*mo-t<um>umul* 'live, grow' < √*tumul*), *du-dolo* 'character' (√*dolo* 'bring'), *lo-lako* 'reason for going' (√*lako* 'go, walk'), *gu-guman* 'message' (√*guman* 'say').

ACKNOWLEDGEMENTS

I would like to express my thanks to Zakaria Lahamade, Buyung Alitonang (both from Leok) and Ahmad M. Singara (Negeri Lama), who were my primary informants for the Buol language.

REFERENCES

Adriani, N. and Kruyt, A.C. (1914) *De Bare'e sprekende Toradja's van Midden-Celebes*, Part 3:185–192, Batavia: Landsdrukkerij.

Garantjang, A. *et al.* (1984) *Morfologi dan sintaksis bahasa Buol*, Jakarta: Departemen Pendidikan dan Kebudayaan.

——(1986) *Struktur bahasa Buol*, Jakarta: Pusat Pembinaan dan Pengembangan Bahasa.

Grimes, B.F. (ed.) (1996) *Ethnologue* (13th edn), Dallas: Summer Institute of Linguistics.

Jansen, A.J.F. (1855) 'Vergelijkende woordenlijst van talen en dialekten in de Residentie Menado', *Tijdschrift voor Indische Taal-, Land- en Volkenkunde* 4:521–547.

Riedel, J.G.F. (1872) 'Het landschap Boeool', *Tijdschrift voor Indische Taal-, Land- en Volkenkunde* 18:189–208.

Sneddon, J.N. and Usup, H.T. (1986) 'Shared sound changes in the Gorontalic group: implications for subgrouping', *Bijdragen tot de Taal-, Land- en Volkenkunde* 142:407–426.

Stokhof, W.A.L. (ed.) (1983) *Holle lists: vocabularies in languages of Indonesia*, vol. 7/1: *North Sulawesi (Gorontalo group and Tontoli)*, Canberra: Pacific Linguistics.

Usup, H.T. (1986) *Rekonstruksi Protobahasa Gorontalo-Mongondow*, unpublished PhD dissertation, Universitas Indonesia.

van Andel, W.J.D. (1929) 'Boeoolsche adatrechtstermen', *Adatrechtbundels XXXI: Celebes* 15:29–68, 's-Gravenhage: Martinus Nijhoff.

van Wouden, F.A.E. (1941) 'Mythen en maatschappij in Boeol (Noord Celebes)', *Tijdschrift voor Indische Taal-, Land- en Volkenkunde* 81:333–410.

Wurm, S.A. and Hattori, S. (eds) (1983) *Language atlas of the Pacific area*, Canberra: Australian Academy of the Humanities.

CHAPTER TWENTY-THREE

MAKASSAR

Anthony Jukes

1 INTRODUCTION

1.1 Language area and speakers

Makassar (also referred to as Makassarese or Macassarese – the endonym being *basa Mangkásara'*) is one of the larger regional languages of Indonesia, spoken by the Makassarese people of the province of South Sulawesi. The number of speakers is estimated at 1,600,000, making the Makassarese the second largest ethnic group in Sulawesi. The largest are the Bugis with an estimated 3,600,000. Makassar is a member of the South Sulawesi language subgroup which belongs to the (West) Malayo Polynesian branch of the Austronesian language family. Its closest relatives are the nearby languages Konjo and Selayarese, sometimes thought of as dialects of Makassar. More distantly related are the other languages of South Sulawesi such as Bugis, Mandar, and Sa'dan (Toraja); Adelaar (1994; A HISTORICAL PERSPECTIVE) has also proposed a relation between South Sulawesi languages and the Tamanic languages in Borneo. The Makassar languages are the most lexically divergent within the South Sulawesi group, with only 45% lexical similarity to the South Sulawesi group as a whole (Grimes and Grimes 1987:25). This indicates that they split off from proto–South Sulawesi quite early – for discussion of this see Mills (1975a:491ff). The Goa dialect of the Makassar language (see below) is the most divergent (that is to say it has been the most affected by borrowing and innovations), while Konjo and Selayarese relate 5 to 10 percentage points higher to other South Sulawesi languages.

The. Makassarese live in the south–west corner of the peninsula of South Sulawesi. Most of them are concentrated in a fertile coastal plain around the city of Makassar (formerly Ujung Pandang) and to the south; these are the Kabupatens of Goa and Takalar, still considered the heartland of the Makassarese. The Goa dialect (or *Lakiung*) enjoys prestige for cultural and historical reasons, and it is the basis of this description. Space does not permit me to discuss the history of the kingdom of Goa (for which see Andaya 1981), or the voyages of the Makassarese trepangers who regularly visited northern Australia before European colonization, leaving significant cultural and linguistic influences on the Australian Aboriginal inhabitants (see MacKnight 1976 for a general history of this, and Walker and Zorc (1981) or Evans (1992, 1997) for discussion of the linguistic impact).

To the north of Makassar are the Kabupatens of Maros and Pangkajene Kepulauan (Pangkep), which are densely populated with a mixture of Bugis and Makassar speakers, with Bugis becoming more predominant further north from Makassar city. The Kabupatens of Bantaeng and Jeneponto on the south coast are drier and poorer, and their dialects are markedly different from the Goa variety, becoming closer to Konjo, which is spoken in the south–east corner of the peninsula (Kabupaten Bulukumba) and much of the interior. Selayarese is spoken on the island of Selayar to the south. The eastern side of the peninsula is dominated by Bugis speakers.

1.2 Major sources

Makassar has been the subject of study by several linguists from Holland, Indonesia, and elsewhere. The two most significant Dutch authors are B.F. Matthes and A.A. Cense. Matthes (1818–1908) was a Bible translator whose publications include a grammar (1858), a dictionary (1859, revised 1885), and a chrestomathy (1860, revised 1883), as well as a Bible translation and other assorted texts. He also had printing types for the *lontara'* script (see §2.5) cast in the Netherlands, thus allowing mass production of Makassar texts. Cense (1901–77) was government linguist in South Sulawesi from 1930 until 1941, and continued his work after Indonesian independence with the *Koninklijk Instituut voor Taal-, Land- en Volkenkunde* (KITLV) in Leiden. His major publication is the Makassar–Dutch dictionary (Cense 1979), a revision and expansion of Matthes' dictionary, with which he was assisted by Abdurrahim Daeng Mone. Without a doubt the single most useful resource on the Makassar language, this volume of nearly a thousand pages contains a large amount of grammatical and ethnographic information, and a vast number of illustrative sentences. It was Cense's life-work, and was still unfinished at his death – it was prepared for publication by J. Noorduyn and appeared posthumously.

There are several South Sulawesi linguists who have undertaken work on Makassar. Chief among these are Djirong Basang, Abdul Kadir Manyambeang, and Aburaerah Arief, but there have also been many others, because most of the publications on Makassar grammar (for example Manyambeang *et al.* 1979; Syarif *et al.* 1979–80; Mursalin *et al.* 1984) have been compiled by teams of researchers. The major publications are the Makassar–Indonesian dictionary (Aburaereh Arief 1995) and a grammatical description, *Tatabahasa Makassar* (Manyambeang *et al.* 1996).

Little has been written recently by Western linguists about Makassar, though there has been more work on the nearby languages Konjo (Friberg and Friberg 1991a, 1991b; Friberg 1988, 1996) and Selayar (see Mithun and Basri 1987; Basri 1997; Ceria 1993; Finer 1994; Basri, Broselow and Finer 1997; Bhandari 1997; Basri 1999). There is also more general work on the languages of South Sulawesi which includes information on Makassar to a greater or lesser degree. Mills (1975a) is a PhD thesis which makes hypotheses about the order of sound changes from proto-South Sulawesi to the modern languages and also gives a sketch of the phonology and morphology of each of the languages. Mills (1975b) is a summary of the findings. Grimes and Grimes (1987) is a survey of the linguistic situation in South Sulawesi and contains a wordlist for thirty-nine languages, including Makassar.

2 PHONOLOGY

The main things of note in the phonology of Makassar are the preponderance of geminate consonants, and a few interesting morphophonological processes such as Echo-VC (§2.3).

2.1 Phoneme inventory

There are few surprises in the phoneme inventory, with five vowels and seventeen consonants.

The five vowels are /i/, /e/, /a/, /o/, /u/. The main point of interest in the vowel system is the lack of a schwa, and the high frequency of occurrence of /a/ (between 3 and 5 times more common than other vowels). This could indicate that modern /a/ represents

TABLE 23.1: MAKASSAR CONSONANT INVENTORY

	Bilabial	Dental/ alveolar	Palatal	Velar	Glottal
Voiceless stop	p	t	c	k	ʔ<'>
Voiced stop	b	d	ɟ<j>	g	
Nasal	m	n	ɲ<ny>	ŋ<ng>	
Fricative		s			h
Lateral		l			
Trill		r			
Glide			j<y>	w	

the merger of previous phonemes /*a/ and /*ə/. The consonants are given in Table 23.1 (graphemes in parentheses are practical orthographic representations of IPA symbols).

The fricative /h/ only occurs in loan words, while the glottal stop is the realization of a stop in coda position, but cannot be considered phonemic in itself (see §2.2.1).

2.2 Phonotactics

2.2.1 Overview of syllable structure

Basic syllable structure is (C1)V(C2). C1 is largely unrestricted, but C2 is highly constrained. Word-finally only [ʔ] or [ŋ] are possible, while word internally the following possibilities are found:

- any nasal, always homorganic with a following consonant
- any voiceless stop as part of a geminate sequence
- [s], [l] or [r] as part of a geminate sequence
- [ʔ] preceding any voiced consonant or [h].

These restrictions on distribution, along with morphophonemic evidence, indicate that the underlying contrast of C2 is between stop (C) and nasal (N), with phonetic realization determined by assimilation. Thus:

- N is realized as [m] before a labial consonant, [n] before an alveolar consonant, and so forth, and will assimilate to [l] preceding a lateral. Otherwise it will be realized as [ŋ].
- C assimilates to a following voiceless consonant (with the exception of /h/). So C is realized as [p] before /p/, [t] before /t/, [s] before /s/, etc. In all other environments it is realized as [ʔ].

The only sequence not accounted for by the above is [rr], a sequence which only occurs root-internally. It must be considered a 'true' geminate unlike the others which are the result of assimilation (see Goldsmith 1990:80).

2.2.2 Stress

Stress is typically on the penultimate syllable of the word, which may be a reduplicated form (plus affixes) of eight or more syllables. Secondary stress only occurs if the word is a reduplication – in these cases the first element will take secondary stress where primary stress would have been assigned if it were a free-standing word. For example the reduplication *ammekang–mekang* receives stress in the pattern *ammèkang–mékang*.

Suffixes are counted for stress, while enclitics are not. For example: *tedóng–ku* (buffalo–1s.POSS) 'my buffalo' but *tédong=a'* (buffalo=1s.ABS) 'I'm a buffalo'. Thus a word with a suffix will generally retain penultimate stress, while a word with a clitic will have antepenultimate or even pre-antepenultimate stress – the latter occurring when a word hosts a disyllabic clitic combination such as =*mako* (=ma PFV =ko 2s.ABS) in *nái'-mako* 'climb up!'. The suffixes which are counted for stress are the applicatives -*ang* and -*i* (see §5.2); and the possessives -*ku*, -*nu*, -*ta*, and -*na* (see §3.5.2). The clitics which do not affect stress placement are the pronominal enclitics =*a'*, =*ko*, =*ki'*, and =*i* (see §3.2.2) and the aspectuals =*mo*, =*ja*, and =*pa* and variants (see §3.6). The determiner -*a* shows both behaviours, but in different environments as will be discussed below (see §3.5.1). Words may also have deviant stress because of vowel degemination or echo-VC (see §2.3), and there is a small number of words, mostly loans, which have idiosyncratic stress patterns.

2.3 Phonological processes

For the most part Makassarese phonology is straightforward with only five major (morpho)phonological processes which need to be accounted for. These are: nasal substitution, vowel degemination, glottal strengthening, echo-VC, and aphesis of initial /a/.

Nasal substitution refers to the process whereby a stem-initial consonant becomes a homorganic nasal with the addition of the verb prefix *aN(N)-* (§5.1.2). This process is described in detail elsewhere (see HIMMELMANN, TYPOLOGICAL CHARACTERISTICS section 2.1), but the facts specific to Makassarese are these:

- the consonants subject to nasal substitution are *p*, *b*, *t*, *s*, *c*, and *k*. Forms with *s* can result in either alveolar or palatal nasals (*sanggara'* → *annanggara'* or *anynyanggara'* 'fry')
- the result of prefixing and nasal substitution is a geminate rather than single nasal, e.g.: *pekang* 'hook' → *ammekang* 'fish (with a hook)'
- there is also a non-substituting prefix *aN-* (§5.1.3).

Vowel degemination means that sequences of identical vowels are collapsed into a single syllable, resulting in stress on the ultimate syllable. This invariably happens with the applicatives -*ang* and -*i*. For example *jappa* 'walk' + -*ang* → *jappáng* 'walk with...'.

Glottal strengthening (the label is from Friberg and Friberg 1991a) refers to the process whereby a root-final glottal stop is realized as [k] in onset position. This happens when the root hosts a vowel-initial suffix or enclitic, either the applicatives -*i* or -*ang*, the determiner -*a*, or the pronominal clitics =*a'* or =*i*.

(1) *kuparékangi*

ku=	pare'	-ang	=i
1s.ERG=	make	-BEN	=3.ABS

'I made it for him/her.'

(2) *nacinika'*

na=	cini'	=a'
3.ERG=	see	=1s.ABS

'S/he sees me.'

This process only occurs between roots and suffixes or enclitics – it is not seen with the intransitive verbal prefix *aC-*, nor with reduplication or compounding. For example *aC-anrong* → *a'anrong* 'have a mother' (**akanrong*), and reduplicated *ana'* 'child' → *ana'-ana'* 'children' (**anakana'*).

Echo-VC refers to an areal phenomenon in which a large group of three syllable words show antepenultimate stress rather than the usual penultimate stress. These words have a final syllable which begins with /s/, /l/, or /r/; the final vowel is always the same as the penultimate vowel; and they all end in a glottal stop. Examples include *pásara'* 'market', *bótoro'* 'gamble', *lápisi'* 'layer', *bótolo'* 'bottle', and even the ethnonym *Mangkásara'* 'Makassar'.

These final syllables are absent when the roots host the stress-shifting affixes *-i* or *-ang*. For example: *lapís-ang* (layer-NR) 'a layer of ore' and *lapís-i* (layer-TRS) 'cover something with a layer (of something)'. They are, however, present when the roots host pronominal clitics or the determiner (the glottal stop is realized as [k] due to glottal strengthening as described above): *pásaraka'* (market=1s.ABS) 'I (go to) market'; *pásaraka* (market-DET) 'the market'.

It is apparent that /s/, /l/, or /r/, which can be grouped for the sake of convenience into a class of non-nasal continuants, are not allowed in coda position except as the first element of geminates. Unless these consonants can be used as onsets for following syllables within the metrical word (therefore excluding extrametrical clitics), an empty VC slot is appended, which is filled by spreading of the previous vowel and then closed with a glottal stop by default. This VC is extrametrical, resulting in antepenultimate stress. For further discussion of this in Makassarese and Selayarese see Aronoff *et al.* (1987); Mithun and Basri (1987); Goldsmith (1990:131–6); Basri *et al.* (1997); Jukes (1998). For a broader look at final vowels in Sulawesi languages see Sneddon (1993).

Aphesis of initial /a/ refers to the fact that the three verbal prefixes *aC-*, *aN(N)-* and *aN-* (§5.1), as well as the demonstrative set *anne*, *anjo* and *antu*, are all subject to a process of optional deletion which removes the initial vowel in fast speech. This leaves surface forms with initial consonant clusters – *pp*, *tt*, *cc*, *kk*, *mp*, *nt*, *nc*, *ngk*, *'b*, *'d*, *'j*, *'g*, *mb*, *nd*, *nj*, *ngg*, *mm*, *nn*, *nyny*, *ngng*, *ss*, *ns*, *'l*, *ll*, *'r*, *nr* and *'h*. The first consonant of these clusters will liaise with preceding open syllables, as in the following example:

(3) *lanuápaíntu untia*

la-	nu=	apa	=i	antu	unti	-a
FUT-	2s.ERG=	what	=3.ABS	MED	banana	-DET

'What are you going to do with those bananas?'

2.4 Reduplication

Reduplication is a common phenomenon in Makassar, with a range of semantic functions including diminution, non-specificity, and repetition – the semantics are complex and will only be mentioned incidentally here.

For words of two syllables or less, the entire word is copied, and the element produced by reduplication is prefixed to the base (the original element). All normal processes of assimilation take place, and the entire form is treated as one word for the purposes of stress (though in careful speech the penult of the reduplicative prefix can carry secondary stress, as mentioned in §2.2.2). Some examples are: *u'* 'hair' → *u'-u'* 'a kind of sweet'; *ana'* 'child' → *ana'-ana'* 'small child'; *le'leng* 'black' → *le'leng-le'leng* [leʔlellélen] 'blackish'; *bambang* 'hot' → *bambang-bambang* [bambambámban] 'hottish'.

For words of three or more syllables only the first two syllables are copied. The reduplicative prefix will always end in a glottal stop (subject to assimilation), whether the corresponding syllable in the base was open or closed, and even if the original syllable was closed with an acceptable coda consonant such as a nasal. Some examples are: *tettere'* 'fast' → *tette'-tettere'* 'quite fast'; *baine* 'woman' → *bai'-baine* (*bai-baine) 'girl'; *barumbung* 'grey' → *baru'-barumbung* (*barum-barumbung) 'a bit grey'.

When morphologically complex words are reduplicated, generally the root alone forms the base, and the entire reduplicated form then forms the stem for affixation, as in the following examples: *a'-jappa-jappa* (INTR-RDP-walk) 'stroll'; *ka-io–io-ang* (NR-RDP-yes-NR) 'someone who always agrees' (<*io* 'yes'). The exception is a root hosting the nasal substituting verbal prefix *aN(N)-*. In this case it is the nasalized form which is copied, thus: *ammekang-mekang* 'fishing (for fun)' (<*pekang* 'hook').

2.5 Orthography

Makassarese can be written in the local *lontara'* script, or the Roman alphabet. The former (also called the Bugis/Makassar script) is a script shared by the major languages of South Sulawesi, and is still widely understood, if not actively used. It is also referred to locally as *ka-ga-nga*, after the way in which the graphs are ordered. It is a syllabary of Indic origin consisting of 19 graphs representing syllables with the default vowel *a*. The other 4 vowels are shown by diacritics above, below, before, or after the syllable graph.

This script has a major drawback, in that it fails to represent any syllable final consonants. Because of this, it is often called 'defective' (e.g. Noorduyn 1993). As an example, consider the 9 possible pronunciations of the sequence *♪♪♪*: *kaka, kakang, kaka', kangka, kangkang, kangka', kakka, kakkang, kakka'*. As a result of this, even the most fluent reader will often have to work out by context how a word should be read.

Several different conventions for writing Makassar in Roman script have been used, ranging from the rather intricate Dutch based orthography of Matthes (e.g. 1858), to a heavily Indonesianized version which was proposed as a standard in 1975, but is so far used only in academic publications about the language (e.g. Manyambeang *et al.* 1996, Hakim 1991). The main problem with this Indonesian system is the representation of the glottal stop as *k*, which is sometimes confusing, and does not tend to meet native speakers' expectations – representing *a'ana'* [aʔanaʔ] 'have children' as *akanak*, for example.

An informal standard is found in handwritten notes, on the occasional sign, and in the lyrics sheets included with cassettes of popular songs. It is identical to the above 'Indonesian' system except that the glottal stop is either represented by an apostrophe, eg: *cini'* [ciniʔ] 'see', or is omitted altogether – for example *Baji Pamai* (a supermarket),

TABLE 23.2: THE *LONTARA'* SCRIPT

Consonants											Vowels	
♪♪	ka	∿	pa	⌃	ta	∿	ca	∿∿	ya	∿∿	wa	♪♪	ka
∿	ga	⨍	ba	ᵕ	da	⌃	ja	⌃	ra	◇	sa	⁝♪	ki
⋏	nga	ᵕ	ma	⌃	na	∿∿	nya	∿∿	la	∿∿	a	♪⁝	ku
										∞	ha	⟍♪♪	ke
												♪♪⟍	ko

which represents *baji'pa'mai'* 'good character'. Other inconsistencies include the representation of the geminate nasals [ŋŋ] and [ɲɲ] as either *ngng* and *nyny* or *nng* and *nny*, and there is little consensus about the representation of predictable glides between vowels (eg. *rua* or *ruwa* 'two'; *mea* or *meya* 'urine'). Stress is never indicated.

The orthography used here is largely based on this informal standard, with the exception that it has been regularized, predictable glides are not represented, and deviant stress is shown (with an acute accent on the vowel) where this helps to differentiate between words with stress-shifting affixes and those with clitics.

3 BASIC MORPHOSYNTAX

3.1 Morphological units

Makassar has several different types of morphological units, and they show a progression from more lexical to more grammatical. At the lexical end of the scale are lexical roots, then there are non-bound functors, clitics, affixal clitics and affixes. All can be distinguished on both morphosyntactic and phonological criteria.

Roots are minimal non-dependent lexical units, with the ability to host bound units. Note that being *non-dependent* need not mean that they are *independent* – many roots do not occur without derivational morphology. This leads to the practical if inelegant definition that a root is what is left when all identifiable affixal material has been removed. With a few exceptions roots are at least bisyllabic.

Non-bound functors are units which do not necessarily attach phonologically to a host, but carry grammatical rather than lexical meaning, and are not subject to any derivational processes. Some are full phonological words with their own stress contour (such as *tódong* 'also'), which could otherwise be regarded as large clitics – in fact they often have reduced encliticizing allomorphs (in this case =*tong*). Others have some degree of phonological independence (shown by the fact that it is possible to pause before or after uttering them) but are less than the minimal prosodic word and cannot take stress – such as the preposition *ri* (and its allomorph *i*), and the conjunctions *na* and *ka*.

Clitics are used for cross-referencing of arguments, and also for coding a range of tense/aspect and modal meanings. The formal properties of clitics are:

- they are not counted for stress
- they attach to phrases rather than words. For example an adverb or incorporated noun can come between a verb and a cross-referencing clitic, as in:

(4) *naung-todonga'*
naung   todong   =a'
descend   also   =1s.ABS
'I also climbed down.'

(5) *a'jappa-bangkengi*
aC-   jappa   bangkeng   =i
INTR- walk   foot   =3.ABS
'He's going on foot.'

There are proclitics and enclitics: the proclitics are the pronominal set cross-referencing the actor (the 'ergative' clitics), the future tense marker *la*= and the negator *ta*=. The enclitics are the pronominal set cross-referencing the subject of an intransitive clause or the undergoer of a transitive clause (the 'absolute' clitics), and the aspectual/modal markers =*mo*, =*pa*, =*ja* and =*sá*.

There is a small set of units whose behaviour is between that of affixes and clitics. These units are called *affixal clitics*, after Basri, Broselow and Finer (1997). They are the determiners: the definite marker -*a* and the possessive pronouns.

They behave like affixes because:

• They are counted for stress (only after a vowel in the case of -*a*, see §3.5.1).

They behave like clitics because:

• They attach to phrases rather than words. For example in the phrase *balla' lompóa* 'the big house', the determiner attaches to the modifier *lompo* 'big' rather than the head of the NP *balla'* 'house'.
• They attach after echo-VC (§2.3), unlike the true suffixes -*ang* and -*i*. Thus *botol-na* (bottle 3.POSS) → *botolo'na* 'his bottle' (*botolna*).

Affixes are units of derivational morphology – which is to say they affect the base to which they are attached in some way, either by changing its word class or affecting its valence. Affixes have the following properties:

• They attach only to roots or bases formed out of roots and other affixes, i.e. they cannot attach to a word which has already had clitics attached.
• They are counted as part of the prosodic word when stress is assigned. This of course can only be diagnostic for suffixes, not prefixes, because stress is assigned from the end of a word.
• When suffixes -*ang* and -*i* attach to words subject to echo-VC (§2.3) the epenthetic material does not appear.

There are many more prefixes than suffixes (the only true suffixes are the applicatives -*i* and -*ang*). Table 23.3 is a substantially complete list of the monomorphemic affixes, with descriptive labels and abbreviations. Note however that the labels are in some cases only very rough indicators, as some of the affixes appear to have extraordinarily diverse functions – this applies especially to *pa*-, *ka*-, -*ang*, and -*i*.

Affixes can combine in more or less predictable ways – for example *kanre* 'food' takes *pa*- to form a causative verb stem *pakanre* 'to feed', which can then take *ni*- to form a passive causative *nipakanre* 'to be fed' (lit. 'to be caused to eat'). There are also a number of polysyllabic affixes which superficially appear to be constructed out of simpler affixes, but whose grammatical function cannot be considered to be the sum of the apparent parts. For example it is difficult to see how the prefix *maka*- which attaches to numeral stems to denote ordinal numerals could be formed out of the (unproductive)

TABLE 23.3: MONOMORPHEMIC AFFIX FORMS

aC-	INTR	intransitive	*pata*-		without direction
aN(N)-	TR1	transitive (indef. patient)	*taC*-	POT	potentive
aN-	TR2	transitive (focused agent)	*sa*-	DUR	durative
ma-	ST	stative	*si*-	RCP	reciprocal, one
ni-	PASS	passive	*siN*-	RCP	reciprocal
pa-	CAU	causative	*saN*-	RCP	reciprocal
pi-	CAU	causative	*piN*-		multiplier
pa-	NR	nominalizer	-*ang*	BEN	(benefactive) applicative
ka-	NR	nominalizer	-*i*	APP	(locative) applicative

stative prefix *ma-* and the nominalizer *ka-*. There is also evidence of former infixes (such as *-im-* and *-um-*) which are no longer productive.

3.2 Word classes

Lexical roots in Makassar can broadly be divided into a number of word classes, however there is a great deal of overlap and very productive derivation. In this and the following sections, S will be used to represent the single core argument of an intransitive clause, A for the actor-like argument of a transitive clause, and P for the undergoer-like argument of a transitive clause.

3.2.1 Major classes

The major word classes are noun, verb, and adjective; they can be distinguished by some essential distributional differences.

Nouns can be defined syntactically as words with the potential to act as arguments in a clause and be subject to cross-referencing with pronominal clitics. Semantically they tend to refer to entities. Morphologically they have the potential to host the determiner or possessive suffixes – however these elements are attached at phrase level, and are also involved in relativization and subordination so their appearance cannot be taken as diagnostic.

Verbs cannot act as arguments without nominalizing morphology, and they tend to refer to actions or states. The majority of verbs are derived from roots by using a verb prefix (§5.1) – the prefixed form can be considered the citation form of the verb. They also host pronominal clitics referencing S in intransitive or semi-transitive clauses, or A and P in fully transitive clauses, in which case the A (or 'ergative') proclitic replaces the verb prefix. There is a small group of common words with intransitive verb-like meanings which do not require or allow verb prefixes. These include *nia'* 'exist', *mate* 'die', *ero'* 'want', *tinro* 'sleep', *lari* 'run', *naung* 'go down', *nai'* 'go up', *mange* 'go', and *battu* 'come'. Two in particular of these, *ero'* and *mange*, are often involved in serial constructions (such as *ero'a'lampa* 'will go' and *mange assikola* lit. 'go schooling') and could perhaps be considered auxiliaries.

It is unclear whether adjectives should be categorized as a subclass of verb, or as a class on their own. In any case, there are clear distributional differences between certain roots denoting qualities or states, and the vast majority of verbal roots. The main difference is that these roots can function as predicates in intransitive clauses without a verb prefix, e.g.: *bambang=a'* 'I'm hot'; and they require the applicative *-i* (§5.2.1) to make them transitive, e.g.: *bambáng-i* 'heat something'. They can be modified by the comparative suffix *-angngang*, which distinguishes them from nouns and most verbs, though this suffix is also seen on some other word classes. Historically this class was marked by the prefix *(m)a-*. This is now only found in older texts or in conventionalized forms such as *tau ma-lompo* (person st-big) 'governor'.

There are several similarities and overlaps between the major classes. Each of the major classes – nouns, verbs and adjectives – can function as predicates. In addition to this, much of the morphology which is associated with a particular word class may also serve to *derive* that word class from another. For example, most nominal roots with the addition of the verb prefix *aC-* can derive verbs which mean one of 'become-have-use-make NOUN' – this is in addition to the possibility of simply functioning as a nominal predicate without the prefix. To illustrate, *karaeng* 'king' can act as a nominal predicate in *karaeng=a'* (king=1s.ABS) 'I am king' or a verbal predicate in *ak-karaeng=a'* (INTR-king=1s.ABS) 'I became king'. Conversely, roots denoting actions or states such as *lampa*

TABLE 23.4: PARADIGMS OF PRONOMINAL ELEMENTS

	Free pronoun (EMPH)	Proclitic (ERG)	Enclitic (ABS)	Possessive (POSS)
1s	*(i)nakke*	*ku=*	*=a'*	*-ku*
1pi/2p	*(i)katte*	*ki=*	*=ki'*	*-ta*
1pe	*(i)kambe*	*	**=kang*	*-mang*
2s	*(i)kau*	*nu=*	*=ko*	*-nu*
3	*ia*	*na=*	*=i*	*-na*

'go', normally appearing with verb prefixes as in *a'-lampa=i* (INTR-go=3.ABS) 'he left' can also host determiners, as in *lampa-na* (go-3.POSS) 'his departure'.

3.2.2 Pronouns

There are three types of pronominal elements: free pronouns, enclitics marking S and P ('absolutive'), and proclitics marking A ('ergative'). The entire set appears in Table 23.4, along with the related possessive markers.

The first person inclusive also refers to the second person plural, and is in addition the polite form for second person singular. The first person exclusive *kambe* does not have a proclitic counterpart, while the enclitic *=kang* is only found in combinations with modal enclitics and never by itself (see §3.6). The *i* in front of the free pronouns is a personal prefix which also appears before proper names.

The pronominal clitics do most of the work of identifying and tracking referents in discourse, and the free pronouns are rarely used, usually only for strong emphasis. This will be further discussed in §3.3.

3.2.3 Adverbs

There is a small set of modifiers which can be labelled adverbs. They differ from other lexical items because they cannot form the basis of derivations and cannot function as predicates in their own right. These include *dudu* 'very', *todong* 'also' and *sedeng* 'again'. They often encliticize on to preceding elements, and in fact the latter two have reduced clitic forms (*=tong* and *=seng*) as seen in (8).

(6) *lompo**dudu**i tena nakkulle antama ri pattia*
     lompo   dudu   =i   tena   na=   aC-   kulle   aN-   tama
     big   very   =3.ABS   NEG   3.ERG=   INTR- can   TR2-   enter
     ri   patti   -a
     LOC   coffin -DET
     'He was very big (and) he couldn't fit in the coffin.'

(7) *tena nalompo, tena **todong** naca'di*
     tena   na=   lompo   tena   todong   na=   ca'di
     NEG   3.ERG=   big   NEG   also   3.ERG=   small
     'It wasn't big, neither was it small.'

(8) *antekamma**tossengi** i Udin?*
     antekamma=tong   =seng   =i   i   Udin
     how   =also =again   =3.ABS   PN   Udin
     'How also was Udin going?' (i.e. returning to Udin, how was he going?)

3.2.4 Preposition

There is a single preposition, *ri*, which has an allomorph *i*. The form *i* has extremely limited distribution, occurring only before locatives such as *i rate* 'above', and *i lalang* 'inside' (see §4), whereas *ri* is found in all other environments. It marks the following kinds of semantic roles:

• spatial location, source, or goal

(9) *ri Mangkasaraka' ammantang*
    ri   Mangkasar   =a'   aC-   antang
    LOC   Makassar   =1s.ABS   INTR-   stay
    'I live in Makassar.'

(10) *sura' battu ri kakangku*
    sura'   battu   ri   kaka'   -ku
    letter   come   LOC   elder.sibling   -1s.POSS
    'A letter from my elder brother.'

(11) *a'lampa' ri pasaraka*
    aC-   lampa   =a'   ri   pasar   -a
    INTR-   go   =1s.ABS   LOC   market   -DET
    'I go to the market.'

The use of the collocations *mange ri* (go LOC → 'to') and *battu ri* (come LOC → 'from') is understandably common to avoid confusion. In addition to purely spatial reference, *ri* also marks temporal location.

(12) *ri subangngi ammekanga' juku'*
    ri   subangngi   aN(N)-   pekang   =a'   juku'
    LOC   yesterday   TR1-   hook   =1s.ABS   fish
    'Yesterday I was fishing.'

(13) *tette'   sampulo   ri   bari'basa*
    o'clock   ten   LOC   morning
    'Ten o'clock in the morning.'

In passive clauses (those with the prefix *ni-*, see §5.1.4) *ri* marks the (optional) agent.

(14) *nimeái bangkengku (ri kongkong)*
    ni-   mea   -i   bangkeng   -ku   ri   kongkong
    PASS-   urine   -APP   leg   -1s.POSS   by   dog
    'My leg was pissed on (by a dog).'

3.2.5 Conjunctions

There is a substantial set of conjunctions. A non-exhaustive selection is *na* and *siagáng* 'and', *de'* and *iareka* 'or', *ka* and *saba'* 'because', *mingka* 'but', and *punna* 'if/when'. Some examples are given below.

(15) *Nia'mo kugappa a'genna tallungkayu, **na** sikalinna niattommi Antoni **na** Yasuto battu*
    nia'=mo   ku=   gappa   a'geng   -na   tallu   -N-   kayu   na
    EXIST=PRF   1s.ERG=   result   finish   -3.POSS   three   -LK-   CLF   and

si-	kali	-nna	nia'	=tong	=mo	=i	Antoni	na
one-	time	-3.POSS	EXIST	=also	=PRF	=3.ABS	Anthony	and

Yasuto battu
Yasuto come
'I'd already got three (fish), and then Anthony and Yasuto came.'

(16) *lompoangngangi i Udin **na** i Ali*

lompo	-angngang	=i	i	Udin	na	i	Ali
big	-CMPR	=3s.ABS	PN	Udin	and	PN	Ali

'Udin is bigger than Ali.'

The use of *na* to conjoin NPs is somewhat marked, and *siagáng* 'with' tends to be used instead: *Udin **siagáng** Ali* ... 'Udin and Ali...'.

(17) *tena kukkana-kana **ka** tinroi*

tena	ku=	aC-	kana-	kana	ka	tinro	=i
NEG	1s.ERG=	INTR-	RDP-	word	because	sleep	=3.ABS

'I'm not talking because he's asleep.'

(18) *garringi **mingka** mangeji anjama*

garring	=i	mingka	mange	=ja	=i	aN-jama
sick	=3.ABS	but	go	=LIM	=3.ABS	TR-work

'He's sick but he still just works.'

(19) *juku' nitunu **iareka** nisanggara'*

juku'	ni-	tunu	iareka	ni-	sanggara'
fish	PASS-	bake	or	PASS-	fry

'Baked or fried fish.'

(20) *teai ammotere' **punna** tanacini' ana'na i Tanri*

tea	=i	amm-otere'	punna	ta=	na=cini'	ana'
NEG	=3.ABS	INTR-return	if	NEG=	3.ERG=see	child

-na	i	Tanri
-3.POSS	PN	Tanri

'They didn't want to go home if they didn't see Tanri's children.'

3.2.6 Numerals and classifiers

The set of numerals is distinguished because unlike any other class they can host the prefixes *piN-* and *maka-*. Otherwise they are subject to many of the same derivational processes as other roots. Table 23.5 lists the basic numerals.

TABLE 23.5: NUMERALS

1	*se're*	6	*annang*	10	*-pulo*
2	*rua*	7	*tuju*	100	*-bilangngang*
3	*tallu*	8	*sagantuju*	1000	*-sa'bu*
4	*appa'*	9	*salapang*	10000	*-lassa*
5	*lima*	10	*sampulo*		

The word for seven is evidently from Malay *tujuh* whereas most South Sulawesi languages use *pitu*. *Bilangngang* and *salapang* are also Malay loans. The word for eight, *sagantuju*, derives from *si-agáng-tuju* 'one with seven'. All other numerals are formed by combining the above basic numerals, with a few irregularities. 'Ten' is shown by the irregular prefix *saN-*, thus *sampulo*, while larger numbers use the more usual *si-*, thus *sibilangngang* 'one hundred', *sisa'bu* 'one thousand'.

In other complex numbers a nasal linker is inserted between all numerals (with the exceptions of *annang* which already ends with a nasal, and the loans *tuju* and *sagantuju*). In addition to this, in careful speech *-a-* is placed between higher and lower order numerals (i.e. between thousands and hundreds, tens and ones), thus *rua-N-sa'bu* 'two thousand' *-(a)N-lima-N-bilangngang* 'five hundred' *-(a)N-tallu-N-pulo* 'thirty'-*(a)N-rua* 'two' → *ruansa'bu-(a)llimambillangngang-(a)ntallumpulo-(a)nrua* '2532'. As a modifier of a higher order numeral *appa'* 'four' is substituted by *pata*, thus *patassa'bu* '4000'. See Table 23.6 for a few examples.

Numerals and the word *siapa* 'how many'are subject to a number of derivational processes, two of which are unique to this class, others are more general. The prefix *piN-* is used to signify 'X times', thus *pinruang* 'twice', *pissiapa* (piN-siapa) 'how many times'. The nasal after the numeral (*pinruang*) is seen with roots which end in an open syllable, namely *rua*, *tallu*, *lima* and *tuju*. It is not seen in any compounds, including *sagantuju* or in larger numbers, eg. *pimpatampulo* '14 times'. This prefix is not used for 'once' which takes the form *sikali*.

Ordinal numerals are formed with the prefix *maka-*, thus *makarua* 'second', *makatallu* 'third'. In combination with *piN-* it means 'the Xth time', e.g. *makapinruang* 'the second time'.

The classifier system is not extensive, and most classifying elements also function as regular nouns. Table 23.7 shows those I have been able to identify.

Classifiers behave morphophonologically like higher order numerals, thus 'one' takes the bound form *si-* instead of the full form *se're*; and other numerals require insertion of a nasal linker between the numeral and the classifier (again, with the exception of *tuju* and *sagantuju*). In many cases classifiers are optional, e.g. *sitau karaeng, se're karaeng* 'a king' (but **se're tau karaeng, *sikaraeng*). The classifier which is most commonly used is *kayu* for animals including large and small mammals, birds, fish, and insects (interestingly *kayu* itself means 'wood').

TABLE 23.6: HIGHER NUMERALS

10	*sampulo*	20	*ruampulo*
11	*sampulo-(a)sse're*	21	*ruampulo-(a)sse're*
12	*sampulo-(a)nrua*		
13	*sampulo-(a)ntallu*	30	*tallumpulo*
14	*sampulo-(a)ngngappa'*	40	*patampulo*
15	*sampulo-(a)llima*	50	*limampulo*
16	*sampulo-(a)ngngannang*	60	*annampulo*
17	*sampulo-(a)ntuju*	70	*tujupulo*
18	*sampulo-(a)ssagantuju*	80	*sagantujupulo*
19	*sampulo-(a)ssalapang*	90	*salapampulo*
100	*sibilangngang*	1000	*sisa'bu*
200	*ruambilangngang*	2000	*ruassa'bu*
400	*patambilangngang*	4000	*patassa'bu*
700	*tujubilangngang*	7000	*tujusa'bu*

TABLE 23.7: CLASSIFIERS

tau	people	*sitau ana'*	'a child'
kayu	animals	*ruangkayu tedong*	'two buffalo'
bollo	flowers	*tujubollo bunga*	'seven flowers'
lisere'	small round things	*tallullisere'kalereng*	'three marbles'
roko'	packets	*patanroko'te*	'four packets of tea'
lawara'	flat things	*sagantujulawara' baju*	'eight shirts'
batu	other things	*annambatu balla'*	'six houses'
pappa'	rings and cylinders	*ruampappa' ta'bu*	'two pieces of sugarcane'
poko'	trees and branches (also of rivers)	*limampoko' kaluku*	'five coconut palms'

3.3 Basic clause structure

The main division in clause types is between intransitive, semi-transitive and transitive clauses. Predicates in intransitive clauses can be verbal, adjectival or nominal; those in semi-transitive and transitive clauses are verbal. Grammatical relations are marked by pronominal clitics which usually follow an ergative/absolutive pattern, but the appearance and placement of these is conditioned by several factors, some of which will be discussed below.

Word order is fairly free – in the unlikely event of both A and P arguments appearing as full NPs the default order is VAP, but VPA is also possible and ambiguity is not uncommon. There is a pre-predicate focus position which is extensively used for both A and P, thus AVP and PVA are also commonly found.

3.3.1 Intransitive clauses

An intransitive clause usually has an absolutive (ABS) enclitic cross-referencing S, if S is definite (see discussion in §3.3.3), and not in focus (§3.4). An intransitive verb will typically host a verb prefix, usually *aC-* (§5.1.1), but some verb roots, as well as nominal predicates (22) and adjectives (23) do not require these.

(21)   *a'jaranga'*
    ac-   jarang   =a'
    INTR- horse   =1s.ABS
    'I ride a horse.'

(22)   *jaranga'*
    jarang =a'
    horse   =1s.ABS
    'I am a horse.'

(23)   *bambangi alloa*
    bambang =i   allo-a
    hot   =3.ABS day-DET
    'The day is hot.'

In intransitive clauses the absolutive enclitic tends to attach to the first constituent, whatever its category, resulting in the typologically common second position clitic. Example (24) shows an enclitic hosted by a deictic adverb, in (25) the clitic is on an adjective (in the first clause) and a verb (in the second), and (26) it is hosted by a free pronoun.

(24) *anjorengi ri Balanda assikola*
 anjoreng=i   ri   Balanda   aC-sikola
 DIST.ADV=3.ABS   LOC   Holland   INTR-study
 'He studies there in Holland.'

(25) *le'bakki a'je'ne-je'ne naikki ri puloa*
 le'ba'   =ki'   aC-je'ne-je'ne   nai'=ki'   ri   pulo   -a
 finished   =1pi.ABS   INTR-RDP-water   climb=1pi.ABS   LOC   island -DET
 'After we'd swum we landed (went up) on the island.'

(26) *inakkeji*
 inakke   =ja   =i
 1s.EMPH   =LIM   =3.ABS
 'It's only me.'

Apart from the second position constraint on enclitics, constituent order is quite free – for example (24) could also be realized as (27):

(27) *assikolai anjoreng ri Balanda*
 aC-sikola   =i   anjoreng   ri   Balanda
 INTR-study   =3.ABS   DIST.ADV   LOC   Holland

3.3.2 Transitive and ditransitive clauses

In transitive clauses both proclitic and enclitic are canonically on the verb, and there is no verb prefix.

(28) *nakokkoka' miongku*
 na=   kokko'   =a'   miong -ku
 3.ERG=   bite   =1s.ABS   cat   -1s.POSS
 'my cat bit me.'

(29) *lakuarengko Daeng Nakku*
 la=   ku=   areng=ko   Daeng   nakku
 FUT=   1s.ERG=   name=2s.ABS   (title)   yearning
 'I'll call you "Daeng Nakku".'

When both arguments are third person it can sometimes be unclear which pronominal clitic indexes which argument, and the order of free NPs does not help to clarify this, as can be seen in (30). In these situations context or pragmatics must resolve the ambiguity.

(30) *naciniki tedongku i Ali*
 na=   cini'   =i   tedong   -ku
 3.ERG=   see   =3.ABS   buffalo -1s.POSS
 'Ali sees my buffalo/my buffalo sees Ali.'

Exceptions to the normal pattern occur for three main reasons: (1) either A or P may be in focus position (§3.4); (2) there may be two proclitics as a result of clitic movement (§3.3.4); or (3) the clause may have an indefinite Undergoer and therefore be semi-transitive (§3.3.3).

   In ditransitive clauses such as those with the verb *sare* 'give', the absolutive enclitic indexes the recipient, while the theme is not cross-referenced if it is indefinite, e.g. *kusareko bo'bo'* (1s.ERG= give =2s.ABS book) 'I give you a book'. A definite theme can

be licensed by the applicative suffix -*ang*, as in *kusareangko bo'bokku* (1s.ERG=
give-BEN=2s.ABS book -1s.POSS) 'I give you my book'. This pattern is also seen in clauses
with a beneficiary, see §5.2).

3.3.3 Semi-transitive clauses

The term *semi-transitive* refers to clauses which, although clearly describing events
involving two participants, only include a pronominal clitic cross-referencing one of
those participants – the Actor. This is because as a general rule Undergoers must be
definite to be cross-referenced – in other words referred to by name or title (or otherwise
pragmatically salient such as first and second person), or marked with the determiner -*a*
or a possessive suffix. Thus, semi-transitive clauses contain verbs which host only an
absolutive enclitic indexing the Actor, while the Undergoer appears only as an NP and is
not cross-referenced. The verb is marked with a verb prefix, usually *aN(N)-*.

(31)   *angnganrea' taipa*
      aN(N)-   kanre   =a'   taipa
      TR1-   eat   =1s.ABS   mango
      'I eat mangoes.'

3.3.4 Clitic movement

Although clitics are normally patterned according to an ergative system, in several environments an ergative proclitic is found cross-referencing S instead of the expected absolutive enclitic. For example:

(32)   *tena kutinro*
      tena   ku=   tinro
      NEG   1s.ERG= sleep
      'I don't/didn't sleep.'

Compare the normal pattern: *tinroa'* (sleep=1ABS) 'I sleep/slept'. In this case the
'fronting' or procliticization of the clitic pronoun is caused by the presence of the negator
tena, which is one of several preverbal elements which are associated with this
phenomenon; others include discourse connectives such as *apaji* 'what but...' *naia* 'it so
happens...' and the conjunction *na*.

   In transitive clauses where both clitic slots are filled the presence of one of these
preverbal elements can result in two possibilities: either the clitics can stay in their
expected place, or the clitic cross-referencing P can manifest as a proclitic preceding the
A proclitic. Thus both (34) and (35) are possible negations of (33):

(33)   *kuissengi*
      ku=   isseng   =i
      1s.ERG= know   =3.ABS
      'I understand it/I know her.'

(34)   *tena kuissengi*
      tena   ku=   isseng =i
      NEG   1s.ERG= know   =3.ABS
      'I don't understand it/I don't know her.'

(35)   *tena nakuisseng*
      tena   na=   ku=   isseng
      NEG   3.ERG= 1s.ERG= know
      'I don't understand it/I don't know her.'

There is some more discussion of this phenomenon under Negation (§3.3.6).

3.3.5 Existentials

These are formed with the existential verb *nia'*:

(36)   *nia'*   *si-kayu*   *tedong*
      EXIST one-CLF buffalo
      'There was a buffalo.'

(37)   *nia'*   *doe'*   *-nu?*
      EXIST money -2s.POSS
      'Have you money?'

Not only nominals but also states of affairs can be introduced with *nia'*, an example of this was seen in (15) above. *Nia'* does not usually host pronominal clitics because the entity introduced is not yet definite. However, in combination with wh-questions this is possible:

(38)   *angngapai nunia'?*
      angngapa =i   nu=   nia'
      why   =3.ABS 2s.ERG= EXIST
      'Why are you here?'

Nia' is subject to a similar range of derivational possibilities as other verbal roots, for example the nominalizing circumfix *ka- -ang* forms *kaniakkang* 'existence, circumstances'.

3.3.6 Negation

There are three related ways of expressing negation, all based on the clitic *ta=*. Although *ta=* is not the most common negator, it is the most basic (i.e. unambiguously monomorphemic), and the free negators can be seen as lexicalized compounds of it and other elements. In most cases the presence of *ta=* requires the insertion of a stress shifting element *-a* after the host stem and before any enclitics. Although this *-a* has the same form as the determiner *-a*, unlike the latter it is always counted for stress, even after a consonant. Its function is unclear.

(39)   *takuasséngami*
      ta=   ku=   asseng -a   =mo   =i
      NEG= 1s.ERG= know   -?   =PRF =3.ABS
      'I don't know it anymore, I forgot.'

The most common negator is *t(a)ena* – the two variants *taena* and *tena* are distinguished only by level of formality, with *taena* being more formal. It seems likely that *taena* is a grammaticized compound derived from *ta= ia na* (NEG= 3.EMPH COMP), literally 'it's not that…' – the presence of *na* would help to explain why it should cause clitic movement (§3.3.4). This negator does not require epenthetic material – compare the following with (39):

(40) *tena kuássemmi*
      tena   ku=   asseng   =mo   =i
      NEG   1S.ERG=   know   =PRF   =3.ABS
      'I don't know it anymore, I forgot it.'

The combination of *taena* and *ta=* forms a double negative construction. These are quite common, and interestingly, they do not require insertion of *-a-* either.

(41) *baju keboka taena tanamangéi*
      baju   kebo' -a   taena   ta=   na=   mange   -i
      shirt   white -DET   NEG   NEG=   3.ERG=   go   -APP
      'The white shirt goes with everything.' (lit.: 'the white shirt, there's no it not
       going with')

(42) *tenamo tau tampaui*
      tena   =mo   tau   ta=   aN-   pau   =i
      NEG   =PRF   person   NEG=   TR2-   story   =3.ABS
      'Everyone says it.' (lit.: 'there's no longer anyone who doesn't say it')

As the previous example shows, *taena* can host TAM enclitics (§3.6). Its combination with the perfective marker =*mo* means 'no more'. As explained in §3.3.4, the presence of *tenamo* in clause-initial position causes clitic movement:

(43) *tenamo nakkulle accini'*
      tena   =mo   na=   aC-kulle   aC-cini'
      NEG   =PRF   3A=   INTR-can   INTR-see
      'He can't see any more.'

If the clause contains no other elements capable of hosting a pronominal clitic *tenamo* may host it. In the following example the clause consists solely of a prepositional phrase which can not host a pronominal clitic.

(44) *taenami ri barugayya*
      taena   =mo   =i   ri   baruga   -a
      NEG   =PRF   =3.ABS   LOC   baruga   -DET
      'He isn't in the *baruga* (a kind of building) any more.'

The combination of *taena* with the imperfective marker =*pa* means 'not yet' or 'still not…'

(45) *tenapa kuassengi*
      tena   =pa   ku=   asseng   =i
      NEG   =IPF   1S.ERG=   know   =3.ABS
      'I don't know it yet.' (lit. 'I still don't know it')

The third negative element is *tea* (probably derived from *ta= ia* (NEG= 3.EMPH) 'it's not'), which hosts enclitics itself, rather than causing clitic movement.

(46) *tea' angnganre*
      tea   =a'   aN(N)-   kanre
      NEG   =1S.ABS   TR1-   eat
      'I won't eat.'

(47) *teama' nakke naíki ri balla'*

tea	=mo	=a'	nakke	nai'	-i	ri	balla'
NEG	=PRF	=1s.ABS	1s.EMPH	climb-APP		LOC	house

'I won't climb up to the house.'

Speakers tend to explain that *tea* means 'don't want' (*tidak mau*), but it is also used in prohibitives and negative equatives, both of which are illustrated in the following example:

(48) *teako sungkéi andi' punna teai i amma'*

tea	=ko	sungke	-i	andi'	punna	tea	=i	i	amma'
NEG	=2s.ABS	open	-APP	sibling	if	NEG	=3.ABS	PN	mother

'Don't open it (the door), sister, if it's not mother.'

3.4 Focus and Topicalization

Arguments which occur as full NPs directly preceding the predicate are not cross-referenced – for example, compare (49) and (50):

(49) *garringi i Ali*

garring	=i	i	Ali
sick	=3.ABS	PN	Ali

'Ali is sick.'

(50) *i Ali garring*

i	Ali	garring
PN	Ali	sick

'It's Ali that's sick.'

This pre-predicate slot is a focus position, which performs a variety of pragmatic functions such as disambiguating, emphasizing, adding certainty or uncertainty. So while (49) is just a statement of fact, (50) with S in focus can express such meanings as: 'Are you sure it's Ali who is sick?', 'I tell you that Ali is sick', 'I've heard that Ali is sick'. It is also the answer to the question *inai garring?* 'who is sick?' (*wh-* words are always focused). Another example of how focus conveys extended meanings is this:

(51) *ballakku kicini'*

balla'	-ku	ki=	cini'
house	-1s.POSS	2p.ERG=	see

'You see my house.' (in answer to the question: 'what can you give as a guarantee?') (The unmarked way of saying 'you see my house' is *kiciniki ballakku.*)

In transitive clauses either A or P can be in focus (but not both). The following two sentences show A focus and P focus respectively:

(52) *kongkonga ambunoi mionga*

kongkong	-a	aN-	buno	=i	miong	-a
dog	-DET	TR2-	kill	=3.ABS	cat	-DET

'The *dog* killed the cat.'

(53) *mionga nabuno kongkonga*

miong	-a	na=	buno	kongkong	-a
cat	-DET	3.ERG=	kill	dog	-DET

'The dog killed the *cat.*'

Thus, in (52) there is no proclitic cross-referencing *kongkonga* (A), while in (53) *mionga* (P) lacks a corresponding enclitic. In (54) there are no clitics at all, because A is in focus and P is indefinite and thus not cross-referenced. Notice that A is also indefinite – this is no impediment to being focused.

(54)   *miong ammuno kongkong*
　　　miong　　aN(N)-　　buno　　kongkong
　　　cat　　　TR1-　　　kill　　dog
　　　'A cat killed a dog/cats kill dogs.'

Notice also the different verb prefixes in these examples: in (52) the verb is marked with the prefix *aN-* (found in clauses where A is in focus and P is definite, see §5.1.3), (53) has no verb prefix, and (54) has the semi-transitive prefix *aN(N)-* (found when there is an indefinite P, see §5.1.2).

If an argument is topicalized (i.e.: left-dislocated – a clause boundary shown by a clear prosodic break occurs between the argument and the verb), cross-referencing does occur. To my knowledge, only A may be topicalized. This can be seen in both (55) and (56) – in the former both arguments are cross-referenced, in the latter P is focused and A is cross-referenced with a proclitic.

(55)   *kongkonga, nabunoi mionga*
　　　kongkong　-a　　na=　　buno　　=i　　　miong　　-a
　　　dog　　　-DET　3.ERG=　kill　　=3.ABS　cat　　　-DET
　　　'The dog, it killed the cat.'

(56)   *kongkonga, mionga nabuno*
　　　kongkong　-a　　miong　-a　　na=　　buno
　　　dog　　　-DET　cat　　-DET　3.ERG=　kill
　　　'As for the dog, it was the cat that it killed.'

3.5 Noun phrase structure

Nouns in Makassarese are not marked for gender or number, and case is only marked by means of the pronominal clitics. Nouns are subject to morphological marking for definiteness or possession, and may be modified by a number of elements within the NP. The definite and possessive markers can also be affixed to clauses for purposes of relativization and subordination respectively.

Demonstratives generally precede the nouns which they specify, as in *anjo tedong-a* (DIST buffalo-DET) 'that buffalo', though the reverse order, *tedonga anjo*, is also found. Numerals precede the head noun if it is indefinite, as in (57), but follow it if it is definite, in which case the numeral hosts the determiner, as in (58).

(57)   *assibuntulu'ma' rua tau Parancisi'*
　　　aC-　si-　　buntulu'　=ma　　=a'　　　rua　　tau　　　Parancisi'
　　　INTR-　RCP-　meet　　=PRF　　=1S.ABS　two　　person　France
　　　'I met with two French people.'

(58)   *anjo ana'na karaenga tallua*
　　　anjo　ana'　-na　　karaeng　-a　　tallu　-a
　　　DIST　child　-3.POSS　king　　-DET　three　-DET
　　　'Those three children of the king.'

Other elements specifying attributes of the head noun tend to follow it – these may be other nouns as in *kongkong je'ne'* (dog water) 'otter'; adjectives as in *balla' garring* (house sick) 'hospital'; verbs used attributively as in *bembe battu* (goat come) 'a goat which just wandered in'; or relative clauses (see below).

3.5.1 The determiner/nominalizer -a

This affixal clitic (see §3.1) marks definiteness, and is also used to mark relative clauses. Phonologically it behaves like an affix (i.e. it is counted for stress) following a vowel-final base, as in *batúa* 'the stone'; and like a clitic following a consonant-final base, as in *kóngkonga* 'the dog', *júkuka* 'the fish'. A geminate palatal glide *-yy-* is inserted when *-a* is suffixed to bases ending in *a*, as in *matáyya* 'the eye'. As a general rule it marks a noun as being given information, for example after being introduced by the existential *nia'* (§3.3.5). It attaches after most post-head modifiers, as in *tau ruayya* 'the two people', *tedong lompoa* 'the big buffalo', and after the verb in a relative clause (but before any relative clause-internal NPs).

3.5.2 Possessives

The possessive affixal clitics *-ku* (1s.POSS), *-ta* (1pi.POSS), *-nu* (2s.POSS), and *-na* (3.POSS), are attached to the possessed NP. The possessor NP, if present, always follows the possessed NP. Some examples are *ballá'-na* (house-3.POSS) 'his/her/their house', *miong le'léng-ku* (cat black-1s.POSS) 'my black cat', *bone-na guci-a* (contents-3.POSS pot-DEF) 'the pot's contents'. They can also be used directly on adjectives to show possessed attributes, as in *luara'-na* (wide-3.POSS) 'its width'. Each of the possessives has a prenasalized allomorph which appears on some vowel-final roots, for example *lima-ngku* 'my hand' (**lima-ku*). There are also some glottal-final roots which show these prenasalized forms instead of the expected geminate stops, such as *kaka'* → *kakangku* 'my elder sibling' (**kakakku*). No obvious pattern for this has been found (cf. *andi'* → *andikku* 'my younger sibling' (**andingku*)). According to Cense (1979: xi) in some cases both can be used on the same root with different semantics, and gives the example *baine-ngku* (woman-1s.POSS) 'my wife' as opposed to *baine-ku* 'my maid'. However this was not confirmed by modern speakers and it seems likely that the present usage is irregular and conventionalized.

Unlike the determiner *-a*, possessives may be followed by TAM enclitics.

(59) *ri wattunnamo nai' ri biseanga Bruce tepokki anjo tuka'na biseanga*
ri wattu-nna =mo nai' ri biseang -a Bruce tepo' -i
LOC time -3.POSS =PRF climb LOC boat -DET Bruce broken -APP
anjo tuka' -na biseang -a
DIST ladder -3.POSS boat -DEF
'When Bruce climbed back on the boat he broke the boat's ladder.' (lit. 'on his climbing onto the boat time Bruce broke that ship's ladder')

The possessives are also used in a particular kind of subordinate clause (see §3.5.4).

3.5.3 Relative clauses

Relative clauses are constructed like focused clauses (§3.4) in that they always follow the head noun (=focused argument), which is obligatorily gapped (=not cross-referenced).

What marks them as relatives is the addition of the determiner -*a*, which attaches to the relative clause-internal predicate *before* the enclitic cross-referencing the Undergoer, if there is one. (60) and (61) exemplify relatives on the Actor and Undergoer respectively.

(60)   *tau ambunoai tedong ammotere'mi*

tau	aN-	buno	-a	=i	tedong	amm-oter	=mo	=i
person	TR2-	kill	-DET	=3.ABS	buffalo	INTR- return	=PRF	=3.ABS

'The man who killed the buffalo went home.'

(61)   *tedong nabunoa i Baso' lompoi*

tedong	na=	buno	-a	i	Baso'	lompo	=i
buffalo	3.ERG=	kill	-DET	PN	Baso'	big	=3.ABS

'The buffalo that Baso' killed was big.'

A goal may become the head of a relative clause, but the preposition is omitted and the applicative -*i* is used (see 5.2.2). It does not appear possible to relativize on a source.

(62)   *sikola namangéia agangku bajiki*

sikola	na=	mange	-i-a	agang	-ku	baji'	=i
school	3.ERG=	go	-APP-DET	friend	-1s.POSS	good	=3.ABS

'The school my friend goes to is good.'

An instrument may be relativized upon by using an instrumental derivation with the prefix *pa*- (§3.5.5).

(63)   *lading kupammolonga juku' tarangi*

lading	ku=	pa-	aN(N)-	polong	-a	juku'	tarang	=i
knife	1s.ERG=	CAU-	TR1-	cut	-DET	fish	sharp	=3.ABS

'The knife I cut the fish with is sharp.'

Headless relative clauses are not permitted – instead *anu* 'thing', *tau* 'person', or a demonstrative will act as head.

(64)   *anjo/anu kukanrea juku'*

anjo/anu	ku=	kanre	-a	juku'
DIST/thing	1s.ERG=	eat	-DET	fish

'That which I ate was fish.'

3.5.4 Possessed verbs

A possessive suffix can be placed on a verb in place of an enclitic, in which case it forms a subordinate temporal clause. Example (65) shows this on an intransitive clause.

(65)   *antamaku ri balla'na aganna akkuta'nammi Anthony ri aganna angkana '…'*

aN-tama	-ku	ri	balla'	-na	agang	-na	aC-	kuta'nang
TR2- enter	-1s.POSS	LOC	house	-3.POSS	friend	-3.POSS	INTR-	question

=mo	=i	Anthony	ri	agang	-na	aN-	kana
=PRF	=3.ABS	Anthony	LOC	friend	-3.POSS	TR2-	word

'When we entered his friend's house Anthony asked his friend "…"'

And (66) shows it on a transitive clause, in which -*na* is co-referent with the goal Malino.

(66) *kurapi'na Malino sengka angnganre ri warunga*

ku=	rapi' -na	Malino	sengka	aN(N)-	kanre	ri	warung -a
1s.ERG=	reach -3.POSS	Malino	on.the.way	TR1-	eat	LOC	stall -DEF

'When we got to Malino we stopped to eat at the *Warung.*'

If two consecutive clauses show verbs with possessive markers instead of enclitics there is a strong inference that the second clause is a result of the first, as seen in the following examples.

(67) *kucini'na a'lampana*

ku=	cini' -na	aC-	lampa -na
ls.ERG=	see -3.POSS	INTR-	go -3.POSS

'When I looked at him, he left.' (he was afraid of me)

(68) *kucini'na a'lampaku*

ku=	cini' -na	aC-	lampa -ku
1s.ERG=	see -3.POSS	INTR-	go -1s.POSS

'When I saw him, I left.' (I was afraid of him)

3.5.5 Nominal derivations

Makassarese has very productive nominal derivation which mainly involves the prefixes *pa-* and *ka-*, and the suffix *-ang*, either in isolation or in combinations which could be considered circumfixes. A few of the most productive processes are outlined below.

- *pa-* + root X = 'person who does or uses X habitually or as an occupation': *lukka'* 'be stolen' → *palukka'* 'thief'; *inung* 'drink' → *painung* 'drunkard'; *koko* 'field' → *pakoko* 'farmer'.
- *pa-* + prefixed verb X = (usually) 'thing with which X is done': *ande'de'* 'forge metal' → *pande'de'* 'smith's hammer'; *akke'bu'* 'shut door' → *pakke'bu'* 'door'.
- *pa-* + prefixed verb X + *-ang* = 'place (or time) X is done': *a'je'ne'* 'bathe' → *pa'je'nekang* 'bathing place'; *ammekang* 'fish with a hook' → *pammekangang* 'fishing place'; *ammolong* 'cut' → *pammolongang* 'abbatoir'; *appilajara'* 'study' → *appilajarang* 'lesson'.
- *ka-* + adjectival or stative root X + *-ang* = 'the quality of X-ness': *nia'* 'exist' → *kaniakkang* 'existence'; *kalumanynyang* 'rich' → *kakalumanynyangang* 'wealth'.

3.6 Tense, aspect, and mood

This section deals with morphological ways of denoting tense, aspect, mood and modality. These consist of one proclitic: *la=* (FUT future); and four enclitics: *=mo* (PRF perfective), *=pa* (IPF imperfective), *=ja* (LIM limitative), and *=sá* (HORT hortative). The enclitics all behave similarly in that they are typically encliticized onto verb stems, following the applicatives *-i* and *-ang*, and preceding (or merging with) pronominal enclitics. The combinations of TAM and pronominal enclitics are shown in Table 23.8.

As mentioned in §3.2.2 above, the pronominal absolutive clitic *=kang* for the first person plural exclusive occurs only in combination with the TAM enclitics. It should also be pointed out there are numerous lexical ways of denoting TAM related meanings – these are not examined here.

TABLE 23.8: COMBINATIONS OF TAM AND PRONOMINAL ENCLITICS

	1s =a'	1pi/2p =ki'	1pe =kang	2s =ko	3 =i
=mo	→	=ma'	=maki'	=makang	=mako	=mi
=pa	→	=pa'	=paki'	=pakang	=pako	=pi
=ja	→	=ja'	=jaki'	=jakang	=jako	=ji
=sá	→	=sá'	=sáki'	=sákang	=sáko	=sái

3.6.1 Future la=

This is typically attached to a verb stem before all other preposed elements, including the pronominal proclitics. In most cases *la=* is a marker of future tense, in which the time can be left open or specified, ranging from the imminent to the remote or potential.

(69)   *la'lampa'*
       la=   lampa   =a'
       FUT=   go   =1s.ABS
       'I'll go, I'm going.' (time unspecified)

(70)   *lamangea' ri pasaraka ammuko*
       la=   mange   =a'   ri   pasar   -a   ammuko
       FUT=   go   =1s.ABS LOC   market   -DET   tomorrow
       'I'll go to the market tomorrow.'

The meaning of the above sentence can also be expressed with a verb derived from *pasar* 'market' in *lappasaraka' ammuko*.
   La= is also often found on wh-words such as *apa* 'what?' and *kere* 'where?'. Example (70) is the most common greeting formula, although it is usually shortened to *lakeko mae*.

(71)   *lakereko mae*
       la=   kere   =ko   mae
       FUT=   where   =2s.ABS   be
       'Where are you going?' (lit. 'where will you be?')

(72)   *lakuapako*
       la=   ku=   apa   =ko
       FUT=   1s.ERG=   what   =2s.ABS
       'What will I do with you?'

The combination of *la=* and the perfective enclitic *=mo* (see below) means that an action is imminent.

(73)   *tena kuntama ri ballatta ri bangngia ka latinromaki' kucini'*
       tena   ku=   aN-   tama   ri   balla'   -ta   ri   bangngi   -a
       NEG   1s.ERG=   TR2-   enter   LOC   house   -2p.POSS   LOC   night   -DET
       ka   **la**=   tinro   =mo   =ki'   ku=   cini'
       because   FUT=   sleep   =PRF   =2p.ABS   1s.ERG=   see
       'I didn't come in to your house yesterday evening, because I saw that you were about to go to sleep.'

It is also quite common to indicate futurity with *ero'* 'want':

(74) *eroki a'lampa ri Mangkásara'*
    ero' =i aC- lampa ri Mangkasara'
    want =3.ABS INTR- go LOC Makassar
    'He'll go to Makassar.'

3.6.2 Perfective =mo and imperfective =pa

The enclitic =*mo* is an extremely common element with a rather wide range of functions, the main one of which is to mark completion of an action or event, or attainment of a state. In this way it is the most frequent marker of past tense, but is also used for fine aspectual distinctions, as well as some more obviously discourse/mood-related functions such as forming imperatives and expressing certainty. The following examples illustrate the core meaning of completion or attainment.

(75) *angnganrema'*
    aN(N)- kanre =mo =a'
    TR1- eat =PRF =1s.ABS
    'I've already eaten.'

(76) *pirambulammi battanta? sibulamma' taccini' cera'*
    piraN- bulang =mo =i battang -ta
    how.many month =PRF =3.ABS belly -2p.POSS
    si- bulang =mo =a' ta= aC- cini' cera'
    one- month =PRF =1s.ABS NEG =INTR- see blood
    'How many months have you been pregnant?' (lit.: 'how many months your belly?') 'it's already a month since I saw any blood'

In addition, =*mo* is commonly used to form imperatives. This could be viewed as projecting the speaker's certainty that an action will be performed.

(77) *tunrummi*
    tunrung =mo =i
    hit =PRF =3.ABS
    'Go and hit him.'

(78) *mmempomaki'*
    aC- empo =mo =ki'
    INTR- sit =PRF =2p.ABS
    'Please sit yourself down.'

On questions, =*mo* is used when an explicit or certain answer is required. Compare the following:

(79) *kerei mae pammantangannu*
    kere =i mae pa- amm- antang -ang -nu
    where =3.ABS be NR- INTR- live -NR -2s.POSS
    'Where is your home?'

(80) *keremi mae pammantangannu*
    kere =mo =i mae pa- amm- antang -ang -nu
    where =PRF =3.ABS be NR- INTR- live -NR -2s.POSS
    'Where exactly is your home?'

The combination of *tinang* 'never' and *=mo* means 'never again'. This requires the insertion of epenthetic *-a-* before *=mo*.

(81) *tinang niákkamo nasikatinrong karaeng-bainea*

tinang	nia' -a-	=mo	na=	si-	ka-	tinro	-ang
never	EXIST -?-	=PRF	3.ERG=	one-	NR-	sleep	-NR

karaeng	baine	-a
king	woman	-DET

'It never happened again that he slept with the queen.' (lit.: 'there was never again him one-bedding the queen')

The converse of *=mo* is expressed by *=pa* which marks incompletion or remainder.

(82) *mmantampi tallu*

aC-	antang	=pa	=i	tallu
INTR-	stay	=IPF	=3.ABS	three

'There's still three left.'

3.6.3 Limitative =ja and hortative =sá

The enclitic *=ja* means 'only' in the sense 'nothing more than' or 'nothing other than'.

(83) *la'lampaja'*

la=	aC-	lampa	=ja	=a'
FUT=	INTR-	go	=LIM	=1s.ABS

'I'm just going to go.'

(84) *mannantu lompo, lompo bannanji*

manna	antu	lompo	lompo	bannang	=ja	=i
although	MED	big	big	thread	=LIM	=3.ABS

'Even if that's thick, it's only a thick thread.' (i.e. it may be big, but it's only big for a small thing)

(85) *manna le'leng ka i katte angkana buleng, bulenji*

manna	le'leng	ka	i	katte	aN-	kana	buleng	buleng
although	black	because	PN	you	TR2-	word	white	white

=ja	=i
=LIM	=3.ABS

'Although black, since you say "white," it's nothing but white.'

The hortative enclitic *=sá* diverges slightly from the paradigm set by the three previous enclitics. Rather unusually for Makassar, this element defies normal stress rules and always attracts stress. Note though that it does not replace primary stress, but occurs in addition to it, thus there can be two equally stressed peaks in a word:

(86) *parékansá'*

pare'	-ang	=sá	=a'
make	-BEN	=HORT	=1s.ABS

'Make one for me, will you.'

TABLE 23.9: DIRECTIONALS

(i) rate	above	*(i) lau'*	west
(i) rawa	beneath	*(i) timboro'*	south
(i) lalang	inside	*(i) raya*	east
(i) pantara'	outside	*(i) wara'*	north

(87) *mángesáko*
mange =sá =ko
go =HORT =2s.ABS
'go (get a move on)'

4 DEICTICS AND DIRECTIONALS

The deictic and directional systems are not complicated: the deictic system encodes a standard three-way contrast, and although the directionals show both relative and absolute systems neither is pervasive in the language. There is a three way deictic contrast: near speaker, near listener, and remote. This is shown in the demonstrative set: *anne*, *antu*, and *anjo* respectively, and the deictic adverbial set based on them: *anrinni*, *antureng*, and *anjoreng*. Demonstratives function as modifiers as well as as pronouns. They may also be used as emphatic pronouns, as in: *garring=a' anne* (sick=1.ABS PRX) 'me here, I'm sick'.

Formally there are two classes of directionals: those which are preceded by the preposition *ri*, and those which are preceded by its allomorph *i*. If there is a semantic difference between the two classes, it is that the former is more relative, and the latter is more absolute. The first class includes terms such as *boko* 'back, behind', *olo* 'front, before', *dallekang* 'in front of, facing', *kairi* 'left' and *kanang* 'right'. *Boko* and *olo* are also used for units of time, where time before = past, and time behind = future, eg. *bulang ri boko* 'next month'. The second class (given in Table 23.9) has eight members: four general locatives and four compass directions.

Along the south coast of the peninsula the cardinal directions are rotated anti-clockwise, because the sea (*lau'*) lies to the south rather than to the west as in Goa. Thus in Bantaeng *lau'* means 'south', *timboro'* 'east', *raya* 'north' and *wara'* 'west'.

The movement verbs *mange* 'move away, go' and *battu* 'move towards, come' are also important in the directional system. Given the lack of specificity of the single preposition *ri* the collocations *mange ri* 'to' and *battu ri* 'from' are extremely common, and appear to be grammaticizing into prepositions themselves.

5 MAJOR VERBAL ALTERNATIONS

5.1 Verb prefixes marking voice and transitivity

There is a system of verb prefixes and their usc, in combination with the use of pronominal clitics, marks voice and levels of transitivity. There are four major prefixes which can be identified: these are *aC-*, *aN(N)-*, *aN-*, and *ni-*. Most verbs are derived from roots with either *aC-* or *aN(N)-*. These can (roughly) be divided into dynamic intransitive and transitive verbs respectively, and the prefixed forms can be considered citation forms of the verb. There are also a few roots which show both possibilities with different meanings. The prefix *aN*- occurs in particular syntactic circumstances in which it replaces either *aC*- or *aN(N)*-. Any transitive verb can be made passive with the addition of the prefix *ni*-.

There are three less common prefixes: *amm*-, *ta'*-, and *(m)a*-. It has also been mentioned earlier (§3.2.1) that there is a small class of intransitive verbs which do not require a verb prefix.

5.1.1 Prefixes aC- and amm-: Intransitive

The major intransitive prefix *aC*- has the surface forms *a'*-, *ap*-, *at*-, *ak*-, and *as*- (C assimilates to voiceless consonants and has a default glottal realization before voiced segments). Its main function is to derive intransitive verbs from nominal roots, whose meanings cover a wide range, roughly 'have/use/make/seek/go to X' where X is the root noun. A few examples are given in Table 23.10.

There are a few exceptional transitive verbs whose citation form is derived with *aC*-, for example *accini'* 'see', *a'boya* 'search for'. These can function normally in fully transitive clauses, as in *kuciniki* (1s.ERG= see =3.ABS) 'I see him/her/it'.

The prefix form *amm*- appears on certain vowel-initial roots and derives intransitive verbs, such as *ammana'* 'have a child' (← *ana'* 'child'), *ammulu* 'hold head straight' (← *ulu* 'head'). It could thus be said to serve the same function as *aC*-, however the occurrence of *aC*- on other vowel-initial roots (such as *a'anrong* 'have a mother') suggests that there is no simple phonological reason to consider *amm*- an allomorph of *aC*-. Instead it seems likely that forms with *amm*- are words which at one point took an historical pre-/infix *(-)um*-, and were then reanalysed. An example is *ammempo* 'sit', which is cognate with *timpuh* in Malay. Cense (1979:900) hypothesizes an earlier form **tempo*, which then became **t-um-empo* → **m-empo*, and then the initial nasal was assigned to the prefix resulting in *amm-empo*. Similarly *ana'* could hypothetically have followed the progression **um-ana'* → **m-ana'* → *amm-ana'* – a similar process to this seems to have occurred in Bugis (Sirk 1983:36).

5.1.2 Prefix aN(N)-: Transitive

This prefix has surface forms *am(m)*-, *an(n)*-, *any(ny)*-, and *ang(ng)*- (the second nasal is formed by nasal substitution of the initial consonant of the root, if that consonant is a voiceless stop, /s/, or /b/). Nasal-initial roots result in geminate nasals at the original place of articulation, and before vowels the form is *angng*-. With /s/-initial roots the nasal may be alveolar or palatal in seemingly free variation (§2.3). Voiced stops other than /b/ are not subject to nasal substitution – in which case the allomorph *aN*- appears.

TABLE 23.10: VERBS DERIVED WITH *aC*-

Root	Root gloss		Verb form	Verb meaning
tedong	buffalo	→	*attedong*	keep buffalo
sapatu	shoe	→	*assapatu*	wear shoes
jarang	horse	→	*a'jarang*	ride a horse
ingkong	tail	→	*a'ingkong*	have a tail
oto	car	→	*a'oto*	drive a car
búburu'	rice porridge	→	*a'búburu'*	make rice porridge
juku'	fish	→	*a'juku'*	go fishing
pasara'	market	→	*appasara'*	go to market
Bantaeng	name of a town	→	*a'Bantaeng*	go to Bantaeng

TABLE 23.11: VERBS DERIVED WITH *aN(N)-*

Root	Root gloss		Verb form	Verb meaning
pekang	hook	→	*ammekang*	fish with a hook
balli	price	→	*ammalli*	buy
cokko	secret	→	*anynyokko*	hide (something)
kanre	rice/food	→	*angnganre*	eat
sanggara'	fried	→	*anynyanggara'/* *annangara'*	fry
(nekkere')	(drill)		*annekkere'*	drill
(inung)	(drink)	→	*angnginung*	drink
(gappa)	(find)	→	*anggappa*	find

TABLE 23.12: VERBS DERIVED WITH BOTH *aC-* AND *aN(N)-*

Root	Root gloss		Verb form	Verb meaning
baji'	good	→	*a'baji'*	get better
		→	*ammaji'*	fix something
bise	oar	→	*a'biséang*	sail around
		→	*ammise*	row a boat
kokkoro'	crumbling	→	*akkokkoro'*	tumble down
			angngokkoro'	knock down
cokko	secret	→	*accokko*	hide (self)
		→	*anynyokko*	hide (something)

The main function of this prefix is to derive the citation form of transitive verbs, thus in discourse it is mostly seen in semi-transitive clauses (i.e. those with indefinite Undergoers), because the verb in a fully transitive clause will host an ergative proclitic, and proclitics and verb prefixes rarely co-occur. Table 23.11 gives some examples of verbs with *aN(N)-*. Notice that some of the roots (those in parentheses) do not occur independently. This is far more common with *aN(N)-* roots than with *aC-* roots.

A small number of roots can be derived with either *aC-* or *aN(N)-* with intransitive or transitive readings respectively. Some examples are given in Table 23.12.

5.1.3 Prefix aN-: Transitive with Actor Focus

This prefix is usually found in a particular syntactic circumstance – basically when a transitive verb (with a definite Undergoer) appears without an ergative proclitic due to Actor focus (see §3.4). With few exceptions (notably *antama* 'enter'), this prefix does not derive citation forms of verbs, but instead replaces *aN(N)-* (or more rarely *aC-*) in this restricted environment. It is identical in form to *aN(N)-*, with the difference that it does not cause nasal substitution, for example *ambuno* 'kill' (cf. *ammuno*), *ampekang* 'hook' (cf. *ammekang*). It can be noted here that in many environments the distinction between *aN(N)-* and *aN-* is neutralized: on stems with initial voiced stops other than /b/; with nasal-initial stems, and with vowel-initial stems. A few examples follow.

(88)   *inai angkanrei untiku?*
   i-   nai   aN-   kanre   =i   unti   -ku
   DET-   who   TR2-   eat   =3.ABS   banana   -1s.POSS
   'Who ate my banana?' (cf. *inai angnganre unti* 'who ate bananas?')

(89) *kongkong ambunoi miongku*

kongkong	aN-	buno	=i	miong	-ku
dog	TR2-	kill	=3.ABS	cat	-1s.POSS

'A dog killed my cat.' (compare (52), (53) and (54) earlier)

(90) *Pung Tedong mange amboyangi kanre ana'na*

pung	tedong	mange	aN-	boya	-ang	=i	kanre	ana'	-na
lady	buffalo	go	TR2-	search	-BEN	=3.ABS	food	child	-3.POSS

'Lady Buffalo went looking for food for her children.' (*boya* is normally derived with *aC*-)

5.1.4 Prefix ni-: Passive

The prefix *ni-* replaces the ergative proclitic in a transitive clause, and results in the Undergoer (marked with an absolutive enclitic) becoming the only core argument. The Actor may optionally be expressed as an oblique marked by the preposition *ri* – this must follow the verb.

(91) *niempóia' (ri Ali)*

ni-	empo	-i	=a'	ri	Ali
PASS-	sit	-APP	=1s.ABS	by	Ali

'I was sat on (by Ali).'

(92) *mionga nibunoi (ri kongkonga)*

miong	-a	ni-	buno	=i	ri	kongkong	-a
cat	-DET	PASS-	kill	=3.ABS	by	dog	-DET

'The cat was killed (by the dog).'

(93) *Nilangngere'mi ri ataya*

ni-	langnger	=mo	=i	ri	ata	-a
PASS-	listen	=PRF	=3.ABS	by	servant	-DET

'She was heard by the servant.'

5.1.5 Potentive and stative prefixes taC- and (m)a-

The prefix *taC*- (comparable with Malay *ter-*, and appearing on vowel-initial roots as *tar-*) is a marker of non-agentivity or non-volitionality which is conventionally associated with certain roots, such as: *mea* 'urine' → *ta'mea* 'urinate'; *do'do'* (no underived meaning, but seen in *a'do'do'* 'walk slowly') → *ta'do'do'* 'be tired'; and *kijang* (also no underived meaning) → *takkijang* 'startled'. It also sometimes has an abilitative reading, as in *taralle* 'easy to get'.

(94) *punna nia' pulisi' taralle ngasenginjo pabotoroka*

punna	nia'	pulis	taC-	alle	ngaseng	=i	(a)njo
if	EXIST	police	POT-	take	all	=3.ABS	DIST

pa-	botor	-a
CAU-	gamble	-DET

'When the police come, all those gamblers will get caught.' (lit. 'those gamblers are all easy to get if there are police')

The prefix *(m)a-*, now unproductive, historically functioned as an adjective marker (Cense 1979). In the modern language it remains only in some stereotypical constructions – particularly in nicknames, for example *Daeng Makulle* (TITLE ADJ-can) 'Mr Capability' and other attribute based labels such as *tu-malompo* (person-ADJ-big) 'governor' and *tu-matinroa* (person-ADJ-sleep-DET) 'the sleeping one'.

5.2 Applicatives

There are two suffix forms which are used pervasively in Makassarese – these are *-ang* and *-i*. They serve many different functions, but for convenience they have been provisionally labelled applicatives.

5.2.1 *Applicative* -ang

The suffix *-ang* is used widely for many purposes – as an indication it is given nine distinct senses in the dictionary (Cense 1979). However, one of its most regular functions is as a valence increasing suffix. For example, in three-participant constructions such as those with *sare* 'give', *-ang* licenses a theme while the absolutive enclitic indexes the recipient:

(95) *lakusaréangko bo'bokku*

la=	ku=	sare	-ang	=ko	bo'bo'	-ku
FUT=	1s.ERG=	give	-APP	=2s.ABS	book	-1s.POSS

'I'll give you my book.'

It is also used to add a benefactive meaning to transitive clauses, in which case the beneficiary is the absolutive argument.

(96) *kuballiangi baju anakku*

ku=	balli	-ang	=i	baju	ana'	-ku
1s.ERG=	buy	-BEN	=3.ABS	shirt	child	-1s.POSS

'I bought a shirt for my child.'

(97) *naboyánga' anjo pa'ballea*

na=	boya	-ang	=a'	anjo	pa'balle	-a
3.ERG=	search	-BEN	=1s.ABS	DIST	medicine	-DET

'He looks for that medicine for me.'

In many other cases the nature of the additional participant is less clear. For example *mangeang* (go-APP) means 'go with', but only in the sense of going with a choice, such as *apa numangeang* (what 2s.ERG= go-APP) 'which card will you play?'

5.2.2 *Applicative* -i

This suffix also serves a variety of purposes, but two central related functions can be identified. The first is licensing a goal argument in clauses such as the following:

(98) *nabattúia' pongoro'*

na=	battu	-i	=a'	pongor'
3.ERG=	come	-APP	=1s.ABS	madness

'Madness came over me.'

(99)   *naempóia' i Ali*

na=	empo	-i	=a'	i	Ali
3.ERG=	sit	-APP	=1s.ABS	PN	Ali

'Ali sat on me.'

This could be seen as promoting an NP out of a PP into the clause nucleus (here to avoid the use of the free pronoun *nakke*), as it is also the kind of construction seen when focusing a goal, as in *tappere' kuempói* (mat 1s.ERG=sit-APP) 'I sit on a mat' or relativizing on one, as in *tappere' kuempoía* (mat 1s.ERG=sit-APP-DEF) 'the mat I sit on' (see §3.5.3).

The other main function of *-i* is to transitivize adjectival roots:

(100)   *kubambángi je'neka*

ku=	bambang	-i	je'ne' -a
1s.ERG=	hot	-APP	water-DET

'I heated the water.'

(101)   *nalompói pa'maikku*

na=	lompo	=i	pa'mai'	-ku
3.ERG=	big	=3.ABS	heart	-1s.POSS

'He encourages me.'

In some rare examples *-i* indicates habituality or iterativity – this is perhaps similar to the 'plural marking' on verbs described for Selayarese in Basri (1997).

(102)   *lakusaréiko bunga-bunga sollanna nuga'ga'*

la=	ku=	sare	-i	=ko	bunga-	bunga	sollanna
FUT=	1s.ERG=	give	-APP	=2s.ABS	RDP-	flower	so.that

nu=	ga'ga'
2s.ERG=	pretty

'I'll keep you provided with flowers so that you're beautiful.'

REFERENCES

Adelaar, K.A. (1994) 'The classification of Tamanic languages (West Kalimantan)', in T. Dutton and D. Tryon (eds) *Language contact and language change in the Austronesian world*, Trends in Linguistics. Studies and Monographs. Berlin: Mouton de Gruyter. 1–41.

Andaya, L. (1981) *The heritage of Arung Palakka*, The Hague: Martinus Nijhoff.

Aburaerah Arief (1995) *Kamus Makassar – Indonesia*, Ujung Pandang: Yayasan Perguruan Islam Kapita DDI.

Aronoff, M., Azhar Arsyad, Hasan Basri and Broselow, E. (1987) 'Tier configuration in Makassarese reduplication', in B. Need *et al.* (eds) *Papers from the 23rd Annual Regional Meeting of the Chicago Linguistic Society*, Chicago: Chicago Linguistic Society. 1–15

Basri, Hasan (1997) 'Number marking in Selayarese'. Paper from the fourth meeting of the Austronesian Formal Linguistics Association, University of California Los Angeles. [http://semlab2.sbs.sunysb.edu/Users/dfiner/sel.html]

—— (1999) *Phonological and syntactic reflections of the morphological structure of Selayarese*. PhD dissertation, State University of New York, Stony Brook.

Basri, Hasan, Broselow, E. and Finer, D. (1997) 'Clitics and crisp edges in Makassarese'. Paper from the fourth meeting of the Austronesian Formal Linguistics Association, University of California Los Angeles. [http://semlab2.sbs.sunysb.edu/Users/dfiner/ sel.html]

Bhandari, R. (1997) 'Alignment and nasal substitution strategies in Austronesian languages'. Paper from the fourth meeting of the Austronesian Formal Linguistics Association, University of California Los Angeles. [http://semlab2.sbs.sunysb.edu/ sers/dfiner/sel.html]

Cense, A.A. in samenwerking met Abdoerrahim. (1979) *Makassar–Nederlands Woordenboek*. 's-Gravenhage: Martinus Nijhoff.

Ceria, V. (1993) 'Verb morphology and valence change in Selayarese', *University of Pittsburgh Working Papers in Linguistics* (1993) II. 76–185.

Evans, N. (1992) 'Macassan loanwords in Top End languages', *Australian Journal of Linguistics* 12/1: 45–91.

——(1997) 'Macassan loans and linguistic stratigraphy in western Arnhem Land', in Patrick McConvell and Nicholas Evans (eds) *Understanding Ancient Australia*, Melbourne: Oxford University Press.

Finer, D. (1994) 'On the nature of two A' positions in Selayarese', in Corver and van Riemsdijk (eds) *Studies on scrambling*, Berlin: Mouton de Gruyter: 153–183.

——(1996) 'Covert movement in Selayarese and the distribution of the absolutive marker'. [http://semlab2.sbs.sunysb.edu/Users/dfiner/sel.html]

——(1997) 'V to D raising in Sulawesi relatives', Paper from the fourth meeting of the Austronesian Formal Linguistics Association, University of California Los Angeles. [http://semlab2.sbs.sunysb.edu/Users/dfiner/sel.html]

Friberg, B. (1988) 'Ergativity, focus and verb morphology in several South Sulawesi languages', in R. Harlow and R. Clark (eds) *VICAL 2: Western Austronesian and contact languages: papers from the Fifth International Conference on Austronesian Linguistics*, Auckland: Linguistic Society of New Zealand, 103–130.

——(1996) 'Konjo's peripatetic person markers', in H. Steinhauer (ed.) *Papers in Austronesian Linguistics No. 3*, Canberra: Pacific Linguistics A-84, 137–171.

Friberg, T. and Friberg, B. (1991a) 'Notes on Konjo phonology'. *NUSA* 33, 71–115.

——(1991b) 'Excerpts from the complete do-it-yourself Konjo generation kit: a statement of Konjo morphology', Paper presented at the Sixth International Conference on Austronesian Linguistics, May 1991.

Goldsmith, J. (1990) *Autosegmental & metrical phonology*, Oxford: Blackwell.

Grimes, C and Grimes, B. (1987) *Languages of South Sulawesi*, Canberra: Pacific Linguistics D-78.

Hakim, Zainuddin (1991) *Rupama (cerita rakyat Makassar)*, Jakarta: Departemen Pendidikan dan Kebudayaan.

Jukes, A. (1998) *The phonology and verbal morphology of Makassar*, MA thesis, The University of Melbourne.

MacKnight, C. (1976) *The Voyage to Marege'; Macassan trepangers in northern Australia*, Melbourne: Melbourne University Press.

Manyambeang, A. Kadir, Abdul Azis Syarif, Abdul Rahim Hamid, Djirong Basang and Aburaerah Arief (1979) *Morfologi dan sintaksis bahasa Makassar*, Jakarta: Pusat Bahasa.

Manyambeang, A. Kadir, Abdul Kadir Mulya and Nasruddin (1996) *Tatabahasa Makassar*, Jakarta: Pusat Bahasa.

Matthes, B.F. (1858) *Makassaarsche Spraakkunst*, Amsterdam: Frederik Muller.

——(1883) *Makassaarsche Chrestomathie*, 2nd edn. 's-Gravenhage: Martinus Nijhoff.

——(1885) *Makassaarsche–Hollandsch Woordenboek*, 2nd edn. 's-Gravenhage: Martinus Nijhoff.

Mills, R. (1975a) *Proto-South Sulawesi and proto-Austronesian phonology*, PhD thesis, University of Michigan.

——(1975b) 'The reconstruction of proto-South Sulawesi', *Archipel* 10:205–81.

Mithun, M. and Hasan Basri (1987) 'The phonology of Selayarese', *Oceanic Linguistics* 25:210–54.

Mursalin, Said, Djirong Basang, Sugira Wahid, Abdullah Azis Syarif, Abdullah Hamid Rasjid and Ramli Sannang (1984) *Sistem perulangan bahasa Makassar*, Jakarta: Pusat Bahasa.

Noorduyn, J. (1993) 'Variation in the Bugis/Makasarese script', *Bijdragen tot de Taal-, Land- en Volkenkunde* 149:533–70.

Sirk, Ü. (1983) *The Buginese Language*, Moscow: Nauka.

Sneddon, J.N. (1993), 'The drift towards final open syllables in Sulawesi languages', *Oceanic Linguistics* 32:1–44.

Syarif, Abdul Azis, Djirong Basang, A.M. Junus, Alimuddin, Rasdina, Aburaerah Arief and Arah Suyuthi. (1979–80) *Sistem morfologi kata kerja bahasa Makassar*, Ujung Pandang: Proyek Penelitian Bahasa dan Sastra Indonesia dan Daerah Sulawesi Selatan.

Walker, A. and Zorc, D. (1981) 'Austronesian loanwords in Yolngu-Matha of northeast Arnhem Land, *Aboriginal History* 5:109–134.

CHAPTER TWENTY-FOUR

MORI BAWAH

David Mead

1 INTRODUCTION

1.1 Language area and speakers

The Mori Bawah language area is located on the eastern coast of Sulawesi (Sneddon 1983), in the region where the southeastern and eastern peninsulas intersect to form the Tomori Bay. In 1988, the number of Mori Bawah speakers was estimated at between 12,000 and 18,000. Mori Bawah isolects are related through complex chaining, but following Esser (1927:4–5), five dialects may be recognized as principal: Tinompo, Tiu, Moiki, Watu and Karunsi'e. Tinompo was the variety spoken by the Mori royalty, and consequently was also promoted as a standard by the Dutch. Today Tinompo remains the prestige dialect, and is the subject of the present study.

Although Mori Bawah is better known in the literature simply as 'Mori', the latter is a broader term which is meant to include the neighboring languages (often considered simply dialects) of Padoe and Mori Atas. As has recently been demonstrated (Mead 1998), however, there is no genetic basis for grouping these languages closely together. Mori Bawah along with Bungku, Wawonii, Kulisusu and Moronene compose the eastern branch of the Bungku-Tolaki family, while Padoe and Mori Atas along with Tolaki belong to the western branch thereof. Intriguingly, even the Watu and Karunsi'e dialects of Mori Bawah exhibit a demonstrable Tolaki substratum, from which we may surmise that in prehistory there must have been a migration of (proto)-Tolaki speakers to the Mori Bawah area. The apparent close relationship which the various Mori isolects share must to a significant degree be the result of convergence.

1.2 Major sources

The earliest linguistic description of Mori Bawah – at that time called Petasia – is contained in a brief treatise written by the Dutch linguist N. Adriani (1900), in which he also described aspects of the Bungku and Mori Atas languages. Some of his same data on Mori Bawah appeared again in the third volume of *De Bare'e-sprekende Toradja's van Midden-Celebes* (Adriani and Kruyt 1914:89–90, 217 ff). Other works of the Dutch period include a collection of five Mori Bawah stories with free translation and grammar notes by Van Eelen and Ritsema (1918–1919) and a description of Mori Bawah numerals by J. Kruyt (1919); the latter author's ethnographic article, 'De Moriërs van Tinompo' (Kruyt 1924) also contains some songs and proverbs with Dutch translation. For grammatical analysis, however, all these works were superseded by S.J. Esser's two-volume and thoroughly researched *Klank- en Vormleer van het Morisch* (Esser 1927, 1933), which remains the principle work on Mori Bawah to date. It is in fact this grammar which forms the basis of the present chapter, though I myself take responsibility for the selection of data and the analysis presented herein. Two Holle wordlists of

Mori Bawah – the second of lesser quality and mislabelled as 'To Padoé' – also survived and are published in Stokhof (1985:43–58, 95–112).

The second principle work on Mori Bawah – and the only description to appear in English – is Barsel's 1994 description of verb morphology in the Tinompo dialect (the publication of her 1984 dissertation). Most other linguistic descriptions in the post-war period have been prepared by Indonesian authors, including various theses (reviewed in Noorduyn 1991), two basic descriptions of Mori Bawah grammar (Garantjang *et al.* 1981; Inghuong *et al.* 1986), and a collection of ten Mori Bawah stories with Indonesian free translation (Saro, Kadir and Hamid 1993). Lexicostatistic approaches to the Mori dialect situation are presented in Karhunen and Vuorinen (1991) as well as Mead (1999). Finally, much additional Mori Bawah data – presented from a comparative perspective – may be found in Mead (1998). For linguistic works regarding other Bungku-Tolaki languages, the reader is referred to Noorduyn's important annotated bibliography (1991:107–119); a rather more comprehensive list of published works – not limited to linguistic treatises – is contained in Mead (1999:80–92).

2 PHONOLOGY

Mori Bawah is an open syllable language, the only allowable syllable patterns being V and CV. Stress is non-phonemic, occurring on the penultimate syllable of the word. Mori Bawah has a typical five vowel system /i, e, a, o, u/, and there are twenty-two consonants (sequences of nasal plus homorganic obstruent are analyzed as unit phonemes). Notable in Table 24.1 is the absence of any palatals, affricates or semivowels.

The phoneme /ŋk/ is represented orthographically as *ngk*, /ŋg/ as *ngg*, /ŋ/ as *ng*, and /β/ as *w*, while an apostrophe is used to represent glottal stop. Word initially, glottal stop does not contrast with null and is not written, e.g. *ate* /ʔate/ 'liver', *uwoi* /ʔuβoi/ 'water'.

Only two morphophonemic processes need be noted for Mori Bawah. The first is vowel contraction, and where it has taken place within examples presented below, I adopt the convention of representing the underlying form between slashes following the word, e.g. *laki* /lako + i/ 'go to', *nahu* /nahi + u/ 'you did not', etc.

The only other significant morphophonemic process found in Mori Bawah is nasal assimilation, the potential for which is represented by *N*. This morphophoneme by itself serves as a ligature between compounded elements, e.g. *wiwi ntahi* 'seashore' (< *wiwi* 'edge' + *N* + *tahi* 'sea') and it also occurs as the coda of certain verbal prefixes, e.g. *mompuai* 'dry something in the sun' (< *moN-* + stem *puai*). In most cases, the

TABLE 24.1: MORI BAWAH CONSONANT INVENTORY

	Bilabial	Alveolar	Velar	Glottal
Prenas vl stop	/mp/	/nt/	/ŋk/	
Vd stop	/mb/	/nd/	/ŋg/	
Fricative		/ns/		
Vl stops	/p/	/t/	/k/	/ʔ/
Vd stops	/b/	/d/	/g/	
Fricatives	/β/	/s/		/h/
Nasals	/m/	/n/	/ŋ/	
Lateral		/l/		
Trill/flap		/r/		

morphophoneme *N* results in the prenasalization of a following *p*, *t*, *k* or *s*, while preceding other consonants it has a zero realization, including those cases where the stem begins with a glottal stop, e.g *mo'inu* 'drink something' (< *moN-* + stem *inu* /ʔinu/). The morphophoneme *N* sometimes has a zero realization even preceding *p*, *t*, *k* and *s* when the following syllable already contains a prenasalized stop, e.g. *mopingko* 'finish something off' (< *moN-* + stem *pingko*).

3 BASIC MORPHOSYNTAX

3.1 Word classes

The major, open word classes are verbs and nouns. Adjectives and most adverbs may be considered a subclass of stative verbs. Minor classes include pronouns, prepositions, numerals, and various series of deictic elements. Although Mori Bawah has a number of elements which could be considered conjunctions, they do not form a homogeneous class, and are treated below only incidentally.

3.1.1 Verbs and nouns

In Mori Bawah, verbs may be defined morphologically as those stems which have the potential to take the plural subject prefix *(me)N-* and/or stems which have the potential to be marked with a nominative, future or absolutive pronoun. As such, they contrast with nouns which never take *(me)N-* and are inflected with possessive pronouns.

There is also a distributional difference between nouns and verbs. At this point, suffice it to say that when a verb appears in non-predicate position it must assume a nominalized form. Compare (1) where *ponako* 'steal' occupies the predicate position, versus (2) where it does not.

(1) *Manu-do*   *do=m-ponako=o*   *mia.*
     chicken-3p.POSS   3p.NOM=PL-steal=3s.ABS   person
     'Their chickens had been stolen by some people.'

(2) *Aku*   *h<um>uku-akomu*   *ponako-mu.*
     1s.FUT   PART:punish-APP: 2s.ABS   steal-2s.POSS
     'I shall punish you on account of your thievery.'

3.1.2 Prepositions

There are three prepositions in Mori Bawah, *ndi*, *i* and *a*. This last preposition – which can also be articulated as *ia* – has the peculiarity that it is followed by the same nasal ligature *N* as occurs in compounds. The preposition *ndi* occurs only with pronouns, personal names, and sometimes also with kinship terms (*ndi ongkue* 'at, on, to, etc. me', *ndi Lagiwa* 'with Deer', *ndi ana-ku* 'to my child'), while *i* and *a* occur elsewhere. In contexts where the two prepositions *i* and *a* contrast, in general the preposition *i* is likely to have either the more figurative or broader reading, *a* the more literal or narrower reading, e.g. *i raha* 'at home' next to *a raha* 'in the house, on the house', but also meaning 'at home'; *i wita andio* (at ground PRX) 'in this land' next to *a wita andio* 'in this place, on this spot'; *sangka i koroi-ku* (adornment at body-1s.POSS) 'my own adornments' next to *sangka a ng-koroi-ku* 'the adornments on my body'.

All three forms are prepositions of a very general nature, with specific interpretation usually dependent on context. Where required, greater specificity in direction can be achieved by using a verb with a directional component preceding the preposition:

(3) *inso*   *i*   *Dale*   *hawe*   *i*   *Tinompo*
     be.from   at   Dale   arrive   at   Tinompo
     'from Dale to Tinompo'

Similarly, greater specificity in location can be achieved by using a part–whole construction (either a compound or genitive construction) following the preposition, e.g. *ia hori wuwu*, literally 'at the side (*hori*) of the fish trap (*wuwu*)', but idiomatically 'beside the fish trap', similarly *i laro-no burua* (at interior-3s.poss bureau) 'inside the bureau', *a n-toto ng-kompo-no* (at LK-space.below LK-belly-3s.poss) 'under his belly'.

3.1.3 Pronouns

The six sets of Mori Bawah pronouns are presented in Table 24.2. Across all pronoun sets, second and third person plural forms may be used as polite singular forms. First person plural inclusive forms, on the other hand, sometimes have a generic reading, e.g. *ba=to mo'ipi*…(if=1pi.NOM dream) 'if we/you/one/someone dream(s)…'. In general but not exclusively, plural marking is reserved for humans or personified referents, the third person singular being used in most cases for animals, plants and inanimate objects regardless of referential number.

Technically, the pronoun sets in the first two columns of Table 24.2 are *both* nominative, i.e. used to index both transitive and intransitive subjects. Because pronouns of the second set are used only in future contexts, however, I adopt the label FUTURE as an unambiguous shorthand; conversely I henceforth use the term NOMINATIVE to refer only to the first set of pronouns. The third person singular ABSOLUTIVE enclitic, regularly *o*, has the allomorph *no* following the stem *kaa* 'eat' as well as the suffixes *-Cako* and *-ako* described in §5.5.

ADDITIVE pronouns, which can be used in conjunction with independent pronouns, imply that the referent(s) identified by the pronoun shares some similarity with another or others, and can usually be translated as '(pronoun) also'.

(4) *Anu=mo*   *k<in>aa-miu,*   *onae=mo*   *ngkuda*.
     REL=PFV   PASS:eat-2p.POSS   3s=PFV   1s.ADDITIVE
     ku=pong-kaa.
     1s.NOM=APASS-eat
     'That which is eaten by you, that I will also eat of.'

TABLE 24.2: MORI BAWAH PRONOUN SETS

	Nominative	Future	Absolutive	Possessive	Independent	Additive
1s	*ku*	*(a)ku*	*aku*	*ku*	*(o)ngkue*	*ngkuda('a)*
2s	*u*	*(i)ko*	*ko*	*mu*	*(o)mue*	*muda('a)*
3s	*i*	*ta*	*o*	*no*	*(o)nae*	*nada('a)*
1pi	*to*	*kita*	*kita*	*to*	*(o)tae*	*ntada('a)*
1pe	*ki*	*kami*	*kami*	*mami*	*(o)mami*	*mamida('a)*
2p	*i*	*(i)komiu*	*komiu*	*miu*	*(o)miu*	*mida('a)*
3p	*do*	*ira*	*ira*	*do*	*(o)ndae*	*ndada('a)*

TABLE 24.3: MORI BAWAH NUMERALS

	Independent	Bound
1	*(a)asa*	*asa, ho-*
2	*orua*	*rua*
3	*otolu*	*tolu*
4	*opaa*	*pato*
5	*olima*	*lima*
6	*onoo*	*nomo*
7	*opitu*	*pitu*
8	*hoalu*	*halu*
9	*osio*	*sio*
How many?	*opia*	*pia*

3.1.4 Numerals

As shown in Table 24.3, numerals from one through nine occur in two sets. The prefix *ho-* 'one' is a special bound form which occurs only preceding *pulu* 'ten'; *asa* is the ordinary bound form.

Independent numerals can modify nouns directly, while bound numerals – in order to modify a noun – must occur in compound construction with a following classifier or measure word.

(5) *ambau   opaa*
    carabao   four
    'four carabaos'

(6) *wunta   rua   lewe*
    paper   two   flat.flexible.object
    'two sheets of paper'

Bound forms also occur preceding powers of ten *pulu* 'ten', *etu* 'hundred', *sowu* 'thousand' and *riwu* 'ten thousand', as in the numeric expression *asa'etu ka nomopulu ka opitu* 'one hundred sixty-seven'.

3.2 Basic clause structure

3.2.1 Clause types

The predicate of a Mori Bawah clause will either be verbal or non-verbal. The only clauses which regularly allow non-verbal predicates are those which encode identification (including material composition), and which consist simply of two juxtaposed nominal elements; see example (7). As shown by example (8), one of the juxtaposed elements may be a headless relative clause. On rare occasions one of the elements can be a deictic adverb or a prepositional phrase, in which case the structure encodes location.

(7) *Nee-no   torukuno   atuu | Lagisa.*
    name-3s.POSS   mountain   DIST | Lagisa
    'The name of that mountain is Lagisa.'

(8) *Mia   otolu* | *anu   me-laki*   /me + lako + i/   *Dale.*
    person   three | REL   PL-go:to   Dale
    'It was three people who went to Dale.'

There is no copular element except in the negative, where *ia* may optionally follow the negator *nahi*. As emerges below, *nahi* is the standard negator used with all clause types; it has the allomorph *na* when immediately followed by the perfective marker *mo*, the incompletive marker *po*, or the existential verb *hina*.

(9) *Ba   nahia* /nahi + ia/   *ongkue   um-engomi=ko...*
    if   NEG:COP   1s   PART-protect=2s.ABS
    'If I am not the one who protects you...'

(10) *Sine   tawatawa   atuu   nahi   komba   ia   linili.*
    but   gong   DIST   NEG   by.any.means   COP   brass
    'But that gong was by no means brass.'

All other clauses have verbal predicates. The verb used to predicate existence, *hina*, has the peculiarity that it can only be indexed with a third person singular pronoun.

(11) *Hina=o   orua='ira   mia   anu   l<um>ako*
    exist=3s.ABS   two=3p.ABS   person REL   PART:go
    mesantu...
    PART:play.k.o.musical.instrument
    'There were two people who went thrumming on the *santu*...'

Compare in the negative: *nahi ta hina hawe* (NEG 3s.FUT exist come) 'there will not be one (anyone) who comes', *na-hina mia anu t<um>o'ori=o* (NEG-exist person REL PART:know=3s.ABS) 'there is not a person who knows it'.

Location is usually predicated using one of the locational verbs discussed in §4.1. Compare here:

(12) *Ndio=o=mo   ia   uwoi   api.*
    be.here=3s.ABS=PFV   at   water   fire
    'The fire was in the water.'

(13) *Na=mi/* na + mo + i/   *tahu   i   dunsi.*
    NEG=PFV: 3s.NOM   be.up.there   at   attic
    'She was no longer up in the attic.'

When numerals are used predicatively, they are treated as stative intransitive stems:

(14) *...ranta   ka=do   me-'opitu   ana-no.*
    until   and=3s.NOM   PL-seven   child-3s.POSS
    '...until her children were seven, until she had seven children.'

The same is also true of nouns which predicate class membership, compare *men-sorodadu= 'ira aka-ku* (PL-soldier=3p.ABS older.sibling-1s.POSS) 'my older brothers are soldiers', *nahi ku=mokole* (NEG 1s.NOM=k.o.nobility) 'I am no *mokole*!'.

Mori Bawah has no separate means to predicate possession. A common circumlocution is to use the existential verb *hina* followed by a possessed noun as subject, e.g. *ba hina=o totoka-do ue-to...* (if exist=3s.ABS guest-3p.POSS lord-1pi.POSS) thus literally 'if our lord's guests exist...' but idiomatically 'if our lord has guests...'. See also example (14).

3.2.2 Pronominal indexing of core arguments

Table 24.4 summarizes the Mori Bawah agreement system. Only absolutive pronouns can index transitive undergoers (O), and in fact this indexing is obligatory on transitive verbs. On the other hand two sets are available for indexing transitive actors (A), while three sets are available for indexing the single core argument of intransitive verbs (S).

S and A core arguments are not only similar with regard to pronominal indexing but are treated alike in other areas of the grammar as well, such as in plural marking for human referents (see §5.4) and the ability to be relativized on (see §3.4). The term SUBJECT is thus used here as a cover term for both S and A arguments, TRANSITIVE SUBJECT then referring to A arguments and INTRANSITIVE SUBJECT to S arguments. O arguments are referred to as OBJECTS.

I begin with transitive verbs. In both (15) and (16), we find the verb preceded by a nominative pronoun which indexes the transitive subject, and followed by an (obligatory) absolutive pronoun which indexes the object. Although Mori Bawah has what might be termed flexible word order, clauses are predominantly verb-initial in narrative discourse.

(15)   *I=pe'ata='ira=mo*   *i*   *Ana*   *Wulaa*   *mia*
       3s.NOM=enslave=3p.ABS=PFV   PN   Child   Gold   person
       atuu-do.
       DIST-3p.POSS
       'Gold Child took those people as slaves.'

(16)   *Tedoa*   *ntu'u*   *u='uraga='aku*   *ongkue.*
       very   truly   2s.NOM=cheat=1s.ABS   1s
       'You have really and truly taken me in.'

As is illustrated in these two examples, in most cases nominative pronouns are proclitics which attach to the verb. Following a limited number of preclausal particles, however, these pronouns act as enclitics.

(17)   *Inehe-mu*   *ba=ku*   *kutui=ko?*
       desire-2s.POSS   if=1s.NOM   delouse=2s.ABS
       'Is your desire that I delouse you?'

(18)   *Ka=do*   *me-'ungke=o*   *i*   *Nggasi,*
       and=3p.NOM   PL-seek=3s.ABS   PN   Tarsier
       do=me-hawe=o   *a*   *ng-karadali.*
       3p.NOM=PL-encounter=3s.ABS   at   LK-tree.recess
       'Then they sought Tarsier (kind of monkey), they found him in the recess of a tree.'

Alternatively, transitive subjects can be indexed with future pronouns. Future pronouns may indicate future absolutely, that is with respect to the utterance time as in example (19), or relatively, that is with respect to some other event (in narrative, usually the story time established up to that point) as in example (20).

TABLE 24.4: PRONOMINAL INDEXING OF CORE ARGUMENTS

A	S	O
NOM	NOM	–
FUT	FUT	–
–	ABS	ABS

(19)   *Po'ia'ia*=*mo*   *indi'ai*,   **aku**=*po*   *t<um>aloi*=**ko**.
       stay=PFV   here   1s.FUT=INCPL   PART:defend=2s.ABS
       'Stay here, I will still defend you.'

(20)   *Onae*=*mo*   *ka*=*do*   *m-pekule*,
       3s=PFV   and=3p.NOM   PL-return
       ira   *m-pepate*=**o**   *i*   *Re'a*
       3p.FUT   PL-kill=3s.ABS   PN   Turtle
       'Thereupon they returned, they were going to kill Turtle.'

Another, formal difference between the use of nominative and future pronouns is found in the form of the verb which follows. When a nominative pronoun is used, the following verb never occurs with the so-called participle marker -*um*-, but this is not true of future pronouns – compare particularly example (17) with example (19). In using the term 'participle' I follow Esser who referred to these forms with the Dutch word *deelword*. It should be noted, however, that the term is inadequate for characterizing these forms in all aspects of their distribution. In essence when a verb is transitive (or antipassive, or active intransitive; in a word, DYNAMIC), there are only three conditions under which the participle marker is omitted: either the verb is preceded by a nominative pronoun, the verb is prefixed by the plural subject marker *(me)N*-; and/or the verb is used imperatively. Regarding dynamic verbs and the participle marker -*um*- with its allomorphs, see further in §5.2; regarding plural subject marking, see further §5.4.

Turning now to intransitive verbs, we find that all three pronoun sets – nominative, future *and* absolute – can be used to index intransitive subjects. In Mori Bawah, this choice is determined by syntactic and discursive contexts. Nominative indexing, for example, is required in imperative mood, e.g.:

(21)   **I**=*lako*=*mo*   *mo'ia*   *ira'ai*.
       2p.NOM=go=PFV   PART:reside   there
       'You two go stay there!'

Included herewith are hortatives and prohibitions, compare respectively *ndo*='*aiwa*=*mo*, *kami m-petitidu* (3p.NOM=come=PFV 1pe.FUT PL-box) 'let them come, we will box together', *si to*=*hori me'u'ua* (don't 1pi.NOM=ever PART:quarrel) 'let's never quarrel'. Frequently, however, reference to an understood 'you' is omitted altogether, e.g.: *lako ungke*=*o!* (go seek= 3s.ABS) 'go look for it!' *pewangu, si m-poturi!* (arise don't PL-sleep) 'get up, don't sleep!'.

Except in future contexts, nominative indexing of intransitive subjects is also required in negated clauses as in (22), and clauses introduced by the consecutive linking particle *ka* 'and, so that' as in (23).

(22)   *Ongkue*   *nahi*   **ku**=*momee*.
       1s   NEG   1s.NOM=afraid
       'Me, I'm not afraid.'

(23)   *Sio*   *n-ta'u*   *mbo'u*   *ka*=**do**   *men-saki*   *i*
       nine   LK-year   again   and=3p.NOM   PL-crossed.over   at
       wita-do.
       earth-3p.POSS
       'Again nine years, and they were crossed over into their land.'

Compare with future reading:

(24)   *Nahi*   *komba*   **aku**   *tekuda*.
       NEG   by.any.means   1s.FUT   angry
       'By no means will I be angry.'

(25) *Onae=mo* *pu'u-no*   *ka*   **ta**   *l<um>ako.*
   3s=PFV base-3s.POSS and 3s.FUT PART:go
   'That's the reason that he shall go.'

Nominative indexing of subjects also occurs with some frequency in quote formulas preceding the verb *potae* 'say', as well as in certain kinds of subordinate clauses, including those introduced by the subordinators *da iaopo* 'as soon as, with that' (literally 'it was still that'), *rau* 'then' (literally 'be over there'), *meronga* 'at the moment that' (literally 'together'), and *maupo* 'even though'.

(26) **Do**=*m-potae:*   *opia*   *ke,*   *Nggasi,*   *oli-no?*
   3p.NOM=PL-say how.many Q Tarsier buy-3s.POSS
   'They said: how much, Tarsier (kind of monkey), is the price?'

(27) *Tehine=o=mo*   **ku**=*mahaki.*
   long.time=3s.ABS=PFV 1s.NOM=sick
   'It's been a long time that I've been sick.'

(28) *Maupo*   **to**=*m-pe'ula*   *a*   *bangka…*
   even.though 1pi.NOM=PL-get.on at boat
   'Even should we board a boat…'

Absolutive indexing of intransitive subjects, on the other hand, can be regarded as the elsewhere case of the Mori Bawah fluid-S system; compare example (29) as well as numerous other examples throughout this chapter.

(29) *Mawongko=**o**=mo*   *aroa-do*   *nde*
   pleased=3s.ABS=PFV inside-3p.POSS because
   *m-po-hawe=**'ira**=mo*   *kinaa-do*
   PL-APASS-encounter=3p.ABS=PFV food-3p.POSS
   'Their hearts became glad because they had found some food for themselves.'

Just as a pronoun which indexes the object is obligatory following transitive verbs, so also a pronoun which indexes the subject is obligatory in most clauses. There are, however, important exceptions, not all of which can be mentioned here. Imperatives were already cited above as one context where subject indexing may lapse. It is sometimes also omitted in quote formulas, e.g. *s<um>angki i Re'a:…*(PART:reply PN Turtle) 'replied Turtle:…'. Occasionally one even finds lengthening of two-syllable stems in lieu of an expected third person singular pronoun, e.g. *saaba wuku-no i Lagiwa* (appear bone-3s.POSS PN Deer) 'Deer's bones were visible' (<*saba* 'appear, emerge'); confer the short forms of locational verbs discussed in §4.1 which present a somewhat similar case. Finally, note that gapping of subjects in relative clauses (§3.4) usually entails the omission of any subject-indexing pronoun.

3.3 Serial verbs

Examples (30) and (31) illustrate what I term SERIAL VERB CHAINS in Mori Bawah.

(30) *Mewangu=o=mo*   *lako* *k<um>ita=o*   *wuwu-no.*
   PART:arise=3s.ABS=PFV go PART:see=3s.ABS fish.trap-3s.POSS
   'He arose and went and looked at his fish traps.'

(31) *Ondae   i   Weho   me-'aiwa='ira   m-pesinggeraha   hieno.*
      3p   PN   Weho   PL-come=3p.ABS   PL-stop.by   near.past
      'Weho and those with her just now came and stopped in.'

Criteria which establish verb chains as coherent structures include: (a) the verbs of
a chain are related by coreference, namely the subject of a following verb must be
the same as the subject of the preceding verb; (b) this subject is indexed only once
per verb chain; (c) the locus of subject indexing is the first verb (the locus of object
indexing, on the other hand, is the transitive verb regardless of its position in the verb
chain); (d) the verbs of a verb chain may not be separately negated; and (e) the verbs of
a serial verb chain may not be separated by a conjunction. Conjunctions in fact introduce new clauses/verb chains and almost always require the subject thereof to be
indexed again.

3.4 Noun phrase structure

Nouns in Mori Bawah are unmarked for plurality, case or gender. Elements which may
occur as modifiers of a head noun within the scope of a noun phrase include (occurring
roughly in the order given):

(a) the particles *i* and *io*. The marker *i* precedes names of persons and personified referents (or any expression serving as a personal name), and is obligatory in all contexts
except the vocative, where it is absent. Compare *ama-no i Wakuka* (father-3s.POSS PN
Wakuka) 'Wakuka's father' and *i=lulu= 'aku i Tantadu* (3s.NOM=chase=1s.ABS PN
Caterpillar) 'Caterpillar is chasing me', versus in the vocative:

(32) *Tenangi=ko=mo,   Bange,   moturi=ko=mo.*
      defeated=2s.ABS=PFV   Monkey   PART:sleep=2s.ABS=PFV
      'You have been defeated, Monkey, already you sleep.'

The particle *io* also precedes nouns, but does not collocate with personal names. The
purpose of this particle can be described as more or less focusing attention on the noun
which follows, though admittedly this function sometimes devolves into *io* being nothing more than a filler while a speaker searches for the exact word or term he or she
wishes to use. Compare:

(33) *Io   bange   koa   anu   hawe   k<um>aa=no.*
      EMPH monkey   just   REL   arrive PART:eat=3s.ABS
      It was a monkey that came and ate it.'

(34) *L<um>ako='ira   s<um>owi=o   io   lere-do.*
      PART:go=3p.ABS   PART:harvest=3s.ABS EMPH   dry.field-3p.POSS
      'They went to harvest their dry rice field.'

The only context where *io* is syntactically required is in answer to questions such as:

(35) *Hapa   ke   arau?   Io   bange.*
      what   Q   DIST.LEVEL EMPH   monkey
      'What is that yonder? (It is) a monkey'

(b) numerals or numeral compounds, e.g. *asa-bawaa io bange* (one-herd EMPH
monkey) 'a troop of monkeys'. When the enumerated entities are conceived of individually,

the numeral may be followed by an absolutive pronoun, for example *mia otolu*= '*ira andio* (person three=3p.ABS PRX) 'these three people', *opaa*= '*ira ambau* (four=3p.ABS carabao) 'four carabao'.

Aligning with numerals are various quantifiers, among others *hadio* 'many', *tedei* 'few' and *sompo* 'every' – compare *tedoa hadio mia mate* (very many people dead) 'very many dead people'. Numerals, numeral compounds and quantifiers may either precede or follow the head noun which they modify (see also examples (5) and (6) above). Other modifiers described below always follow.

(c) possessors. Possessors must be indexed on the head noun, and – when expressed nominally – immediately follow it. Nesting of possessive constructions is possible.

(36) *ue-do*   *ana-ni*/ ana + no + i/   *Sinongi*
       grandparent-3p.POSS   child-3s.POSS:PN   Sinongi
       'the grandfather of Sinongi's children'

(d) prepositional phrases (including the deictic adverbs described in §4.1), e.g. *mia i Tinompo* 'people in Tinompo, people of Tinompo'.

(e) relative clauses. Relative clauses are optionally introduced by the relative marker *anu*. Mori Bawah follows a pattern common to other Austronesian languages in that generally only subjects and possessors can be relativized.

(37) *mia*   *anu*   *wela*   *m-ponakopi*= '*aku*   *andio*
       person REL   repeatedly   PL-rob=1s.ABS   PRX
       'these people who keep stealing from me'

(38) *mia*   *anu*   *na*=*mi* /na + mo + i/   *mengkaa*   *lara-no*
       person   REL   NEG=PFV: 3s.NOM   visible   scar-3s.POSS
       subi-do
       vaccinate-3p.POSS
       'people whose vaccination scars are no longer visible'

As in example (37), a relativized subject is ordinarily gapped in the relative clause. An exception occurs in future contexts, where – because in Mori Bawah future tense is expressed using future pronouns – a pronoun retention strategy must be used.

(39) *ambau*   *anu*   *ta*   *t*<*um*>*andu*=*ko*
       carabao   REL   3s.FUT   PART:horn=2s.ABS
       'a carabao which will gore you'

Regarding the pseudo-relativization of patients, instruments and locations using nominalized clauses, see §6. On rare occasions, relativized patients are encountered without nominalization, that is to say, the predicates of such relative clauses are clearly verbal, e.g.:

(40) *watu*   *anu*   *do*=*wela*   *mem-palu*=*o*   *mia*
       rock   REL   3p.NOM=repeatedly   PL-hammer=3s.ABS   person
       'a boulder which the people had hammered time and again'

(f) demonstratives. Demonstratives are listed in Table 24.5, §4.1. The third person plural possessive pronoun -*do* may be added to a demonstrative to indicate that a plural (usually somewhat large) number is being spoken of, as in *mia anu me-mate alou-do* (person REL PL-dead DIST.DOWN-3p.POSS) 'those (many) people who are dead down there'.

Demonstratives always occur last in the noun phrase, except in rare cases where they are fronted to avoid ambiguity of reference, for example:

(41) *mia*   *anu*   *k<um>aa=no*   *andio*   *ana-no*
      person   REL   PART:eat=3s.ABS   this   child-3s.POSS
      'these people who had eaten her child'

Demonstratives and relative clauses can be used independently–that is, without any head noun – in the same syntactic positions ordinarily filled by noun phrases, for example *nahi ku=to'ori=o atuu* (NEG 1s.NOM=know=3s.ABS DIST) 'I don't know that', *dei-dei= 'ira=mo koa anu m-pekule* (RDP-few=3p.ABS=PFV just REL PL-return) 'the ones who returned were only a few'.

In cases such as *raha ngara* 'horse stall' and *mia mota'u* 'parent, elder' the modifiers – respectively the noun *ngara* 'horse' and the stative verb *mota'u* 'old' – do not occupy any noun phrase position but rather stand in compound relationship with the preceding noun. Compounding in Mori Bawah always occurs inner with respect to any possessive marking – compare *mia mota'u-do* (person old-3p.POSS) 'their parents' – and in some cases may be further indicated by the presence of nasal ligature, e.g. *rombia ng-korui* 'thorny sago' (<*rombia* 'sago' plus *korui* 'having thorns'), or, particularly in the case of stative verbs, by clipping of the derivational prefix, e.g. *kotuo lea* 'variety of betel plant' (<*kotuo* 'betel' plus *molea* 'spicy, hot').

3.5 Aspect

The aspectual particles *mo* (perfective) and *po* (incompletive) are wide ranging in both their function and distribution, so that only a cursory description can be offered here. Both are enclitic second position particles which occur after the first element of the structure which they modify, whether verb phrase or noun phrase.

In broad scope, the incompletive marker *po* has three related functions: (a) to indicate that an action or state of affairs has some future realization, e.g. *ndi=aku=po mate…* (be.here=1s.ABS=INCPL dead) 'later when I am here dead…, not until I am dead…'; (b) to indicate that an action or state of affairs continues from the past, perhaps even against expectation (roughly translatable as 'yet, still'), e.g. *ba=u behe=po* (if=2s.NOM be.willing=INCPL) 'if you are still willing'; and (c) to indicate some continuation or connection with what has preceded or been previously mentioned (roughly translatable as 'again, likewise, also'), e.g.:

(42) *Tehine*   *me'ana=o=mo*   *i*   *Elu-Elu,*   *nggapu;*
      long.time   PART:give.birth=3s.ABS=PFV PN   Orphan   cat
      tehine   *mbo'u,*   *me'ana=o=**po**,*   *nggapu=**po**.*
      long.time   again   PART:give.birth=3s.ABS=INCPL   cat=INCPL
      'After some time Orphan gave birth, to a cat; some time later she gave birth again, again a cat.'

The particle *mo* ranges in meaning from clearly indicating perfectivity (compare with negator *na=mo* 'no longer, not any more' versus *na=po* 'not yet') to simply focusing attention on certain predications or nominal constituents. With stative verbs, the perfective sense of *mo* usually implies a change of state, e.g. *me-momee= 'ira=mo* (PL-afraid=3p.ABS=PFV) 'they became afraid', while *mo* following a future pronoun increases the sense of immediacy or certainty, e.g. *ta=mo mate uai-ku* (3s.FUT=PFV dead younger.sibling-1s.POSS) 'my younger brother is about to die'. The particle *mo* is also widely used in imperatives, either to strengthen the force of the imperative or to indicate that the time for action has come, e.g. *lako=mo!* 'go!, go now!' (compare *lako=po!* which is also imperative, but means 'go again!'). The particle *mo* also occurs as an element in various more or less fixed expressions, e.g. *ongkue-ku=mo koa ngkuda* (1s-1s.POSS=PFV just 1s.ADDITIVE) 'I myself'.

4 DEIXIS

4.1 Static deictics

Mori Bawah has a person-oriented system of spatial deixis, with terms for 'near speaker' and 'near addressee', and three terms (depending on elevation) for something relatively remote from either the speaker or addressee. Static deictics occur in three sets, shown in Table 24.5.

The primary function of the demonstratives is as noun modifiers. Derivationally related to the demonstratives are the adverbs *kanandio* 'like this', *kanatuu* 'like that (there by you)', *kanarau* 'like that yonder', *kanalou* 'like that down there' and *kanatahu* 'like that up there' (compare *kana* 'like').

(43) *Tewala   kanatuu   kami   mem-pongu=ko.*
      when   like.that   1pe.FUT   PL-tie=2s.ABS
      'If it's like that (if that's the case), we shall tie you up.'

Locational verbs predicate location in a particular sphere. As with other verbs, they may be marked with the plural prefix *(me)N-*, and/or indexed for person and number of the subject.

(44) *Nahi   do=me-ndio,   me-lako= 'ira=mo   m-pom-paho.*
      NEG   3p.NOM=PL-be.here   PL-go=3p.ABS=PFV   PL-APASS-plant
      'They are not here, they have gone out to plant.'

(45) *Da   men-tuu=komiu   m-pong-kaa?*
      still   PL-be.there=2p.ABS   PL-APASS-eat
      'Are you still there eating?'

(46) *Ka=i   pensiro,   da   lou=o   mbo'u.*
      and=3s.NOM   look.down   still   be.down.there =3s.ABS   again
      'And he looked down, again it was still down there.'

TABLE 24.5: MORI BAWAH STATIC DEICTICS

	Demonstratives	Locational verbs	Deictic adverbs
Near speaker	*andio*	*ndio*	*indi'ai*
Near hearer	*atuu*	*tuu*	*itu'ai*
Remote, level	*arau*	*rau*	*ira'ai*
Remote, higher	*atahu*	*tahu*	*itahai*
Remote, lower	*alou*	*lou*	*ilo'ai*

When followed by an absolutive pronoun, the locational verbs have alternate short forms which omit the final vowel of the locational verb, compare short forms *ndi= 'aku* (be.here=1s.ABS), *tu=ko* (be.there=2s.ABS), *ra= 'ira* (be.over.there=3p.ABS), *lo= 'ira* (be.down.there=3p.ABS), *tah=ira* (be.up.there=3p.ABS). In the third person singular, however, it is the absolutive pronoun *-o* which is omitted, in other words in the third person singular, short forms are identical to the stem forms of the locational verbs (whether the short form *ndio* omits the final syllable or the pronoun is moot). Unlike long forms, short forms are only rarely marked for plural subject, and semantically short forms are used to present, compare *ndio=mo* 'here it is!', versus long form *ndio=o=mo* 'it is already here'. Examples of short forms in context are:

(47) *Ndi= 'ira=mo*   *mia*   *hawe*   *w<in>awa-ku.*
be.here=3p.ABS=PFV person   arrive   PASS:bring-1s.POSS
'Here are the people I have come bringing.'

(48) *Rau*   *wela*   *mo-binti*   *watu.*
be.over.there   repeatedly   PART:APASS-heave   stone
'There he is yonder heaving stones.'

(49) *Tahu=mo*   *i*   *Wula,*   *menggenanggena=kami.*
be.up.there=PFV PN   Moon   PART:be.alike = 1pe.ABS
'Up there is Moon, we are like unto each other.'

In some contexts short forms have developed discourse uses somewhat removed from their literal meanings. The following are illustrative:

(50) *Tuu=mo,*   *Tandungkokabo,*   *ko=mo*   *l<um>ako...*
be.there=PFV   Tandungkokabo   2s.FUT=PFV   PART:go
'Now (lit. There it is), Tandungkokabo, you are about to go away...'

(51) *Ndi= 'ira*   *me-'olai*   *i=booli= 'ira=mo*   *i*   *Re'a.*
be.here=3p.ABS   PL-far   3s.NOM=call=3p.ABS=PFV   PN   Turtle
'When they were far away (lit. Here they were far), Turtle called out to them.'

(52) *Rau=mo*   *ira'ai*   *ka=do*   *m-pepate=o.*
be.over.there=PFV   over.there   and=3p.NOM   PL-kill=3s.ABS
'Then and there they killed her.'

When a Mori Bawah speaker uses a demonstrative or a locational verb to refer to an entity present in the utterance situation, usually that entity must be visible. Deictic adverbs, on the other hand, are used to indicate the general location of a person or thing without implying that it is visible, compare for example *Ndio=mo!* (be.here=PFV) 'Here it is!', said of an object which is in the speaker's hand or visible in the speaker's immediate vicinity, versus *indi'ai i=po'ia* (here 3s.NOM=reside) 'It's here', said of an object which the speaker knows to be near him or her, but which is not immediately visible. A similar contrast exists between, say, *i Alipa atahu* 'Alipa up there' (typically Alipa himself is visible, but also used when the speaker can see the house where Alipa is, or the speaker is very familiar with Alipa's house and garden, etc.) versus *i Alipa itahai* 'Alipa up there' (somewhere upstream). Compare also:

(53) *Polai*   *itu'ai!*
flee   there
'Get away from there!'

(54) *Mo'ia=aku*   *ilo'ai*   *i*   *Sampalowo*   *indi'upua.*
      PART:live=2s.ABS   down.there   at   Sampalowo   former.time
      'Formerly I lived down there in Sampalowo.'

4.2 Directional deictics

In addition to the static deictics discussed in the preceding section, Mori Bawah has five directional deictics which imply motion in a particular direction. These are listed in Table 24.6.

TABLE 24.6: MORI BAWAH DIRECTIONAL DEICTICS

	Directionals
Toward here	*ramai, tamahi*
Toward there, level	*raane*
Toward there, higher	*tahane*
Toward there, lower	*loane*

Although the forms *ramai* and *tamahi* are used synonymously in the Tinompo dialect, in closely related isolects *tamahi* means specifically 'toward here from a higher elevation'. There is thus evidence that the present system of five directionals developed from an earlier system in which the locative roots *ra*, *tah* and possibly also *lo* combined with the directional components respectively *mai* 'come toward speaker' or *ane* 'go away from speaker'. Directionals distribute similarly to intransitive verbs of motion.

(55) *Me-ramai='ira=mo*   *i*   *Laengko.*
      PL-hither=3p.ABS=PFV   PN   Laengko
      'Laengko and those with him are already coming.'

(56) *Loane=o=mo*   *i*   *Kalamboro*
      thither.downward=3s.ABS=PFV   PN   People.eater

      l<um>ulu=o   *i*   *Padalara.*
      PART:chase=3s.ABS   PN   Padalara
      'People Eater set off downstream chasing Padalara.'

The prefix *ngkoN-* can also be supplied to directionals, resulting in the formations *ngkoramai*, *(ng)kontamahi*, *ngkoraane*, *ngkoloane* and *(ng)kontahane*. These forms differ from the standard set in that they appear to emphasize direction as against actual movement, compare *sala anu ngkontahane i koana* (path REL thither.upward at right) 'the path which runs in an upward direction on the right hand side'.

5 MAJOR VERBAL ALTERNATIONS

5.1 Verb types

Based on their role structure and associated morphosyntactic properties, Mori Bawah verbs fall into four major types: transitive, antipassive, passive and intransitive. I prefer the term type rather than class or subclass, as these four categories combine the traditional notions of voice and parts-of-speech.

Transitive verbs are two-place predicates, and are the only verbs which allow the pronominal indexing of both a transitive subject (A) and an object (O), illustrated in example (57).

(57) *Isua*   *u=hawe=o*   *ama-mu?*
      where   2s.NOM=encounter=3s.ABS   father-2s.POSS
      'Where did you meet your father?'

Pronominal indexing of the object is in fact obligatory, regardless of whether the patient is referred to elsewhere in the clause.

Antipassive verbs take the prefix *poN-* (participle form *moN-*, see §5.2), which marks the pragmatic and syntactic demotion of the patient. Unlike with corresponding transitive verbs, with antipassives the patient is indefinite and/or nonspecific and receives no agreement marking on the verb, though it may appear elsewhere in the clause as a NP without oblique marking. Compare example (58), which is transitive, with example (59), which is antipassive.

(58) *…ka=i*   *pepate='ira* *ana-no.*
      and=3s.NOM   kill=3p.ABS   child-3s.POSS
      '…and she killed her children.'

(59) *…ka=i*   *pom-pepate* *singa.*
      and=3s.NOM   APASS-kill   lion
      '…and he killed a lion.'

With respect to case marking, antipassive verbs are treated entirely like intransitive verbs, namely only one argument – the subject (S) – can be indexed pronominally on the verb.

Passive verbs take the infix *-in-*. Passive verbs allow the expression of only one argument, the derived subject; in this respect they also align with ordinary intransitives, with the proviso that in this case the surface S-argument is the underlying patient.

(60) *Ta*   *p<in>epate.*
      3s.FUT   PASS:kill
      'He will/shall/must be killed.'

(61) *Onae=mo* *ka=do*   *mem-p<in>oboi* *me-laki* *Dale.*
      3s=PFV   and=3p.NOM   PL-PASS:call   PL-go:to   Dale
      'That is why they were called to go to Dale.' (lit. 'It was that and…')

As these examples illustrate, passives in Mori Bawah are agent-deleting, that is, when the verb is passive no agent can be expressed – not even as an oblique. Where other languages might employ a passive clause with oblique agent, a similar pragmatic function can be achieved in Mori Bawah by fronting the object NP of a regular transitive construction; see example (1) above.

As may be observed in examples (58) through (60), the same stem (in this particular case, *pepate* 'kill') which has the potential for being indexed for its object may in other contexts be marked with the antipassive prefix *poN-* or the passive infix *-in-*. All stems with this marking potential are here designated TRANSITIVE VERB BASES. Some transitive verb bases may elsewhere in the language function as other parts of speech, for example as a transitive verb base the stem *hawe* means 'encounter' (compare *hawe'ira* 'encounter them', *mohawe* 'encounter something' *hinawe* 'encountered'), but the stem *hawe* by itself also serves as an intransitive verb meaning 'arrive'. In point of fact, a number of stems which are nouns may be used without further derivation as transitive verb bases. Although such stems could be regarded as cases of zero-derivation, in context transitive verb bases do not appear alone, but must occur with some accompanying morpheme – namely the prefix *poN-*, the infix *-in-*, or an object-indexing pronoun – and it is this marking which makes clear when a stem is serving as a transitive verb base. For consistency, I use the antipassive participle as the CITATION FORM when citing transitive verb bases, thus:

(62)   a.   *horo* 'floor'   *mohoro* 'supply (e.g. a house) with a floor'
       b.   *kansai* 'lance'   *mo(ng)kansai* 'throw at with a lance'
       c.   *dopi* 'plank'   *modopi* 'make planks out of, cut into planks'

5.2 Dynamic verbs and participle forms thereof

In addition to its transitivity type, any Mori Bawah verb can also be classed as either DYNAMIC or STATIVE. Formally, dynamic verbs are those stems which – in the appropriate contexts – take the participle marker *-um-* or one of its allomorphs, while stative verbs are stems which are never so marked. According to this criterion, all transitive and antipassive verbs are dynamic, while all passive verbs are stative. Some intransitive verbs are dynamic while other intransitive verbs are stative.

Example (63) shows a sample of dynamic verbs in their PRIMARY and PARTICIPLE forms (transitive verbs are cited with absolutive pronoun). The participle marker has three allomorphs: the infix *-um-* placed after the first stem consonant (other than a bilabial), a zero allomorph when the underived stem begins with a bilabial consonant, and – in the particular case of *p*-initial prefixes – replacement of *p* by *m*.

		PRIMARY	PARTICIPLE	
(63)	a.	*somba*	*s<um>omba*	'sail'
	b.	*nahu=o*	*n<um>ahu=o*	'cook it'
	c.	*bongo='aku*	*b<Ø>ongo='aku*	'thrash me'
	d.	*pae=o*	*p<Ø>ae=o*	'drag it'
	e.	*pepate-'ira*	*mepate-'ira*	'kill them'
	f.	*pompepate*	*mompepate*	'kill (something)'
	g.	*po'ia*	*mo'ia*	'stay, reside'
	h.	*pekule*	*mekule*	'return'

Primary and participle forms are in complementary distribution. The so-called participle form is used when a dynamic verb modifies a noun as in relative clauses, see example (11); when a dynamic verb occurs as the second or subsequent verb of a chain, see example (56); and when a dynamic verb occurs as the first (or sole) verb of a clause, indexed for its subject with an absolutive or future pronoun, see among others examples (25) and (54). (Note that the verb *lako* 'go' is exceptional in that even though it does have a participle form *lumako*, nonetheless the primary form is sometimes used in contexts where the participle would be expected.) The participle form is also the form usually given when a verb is elicited or uttered out of context.

The primary form, on the other hand, must be used whenever a dynamic verb is immediately preceded by a nominative pronoun, see examples (58) and (59). Primary forms are also used in imperative mood – see example (53) – and as one might expect, they serve as input to derivational processes. Another, important use of primary forms is as nominalizations; see §6.

Several prefixes are associated with deriving dynamic intransitive verbs in Mori Bawah, the most frequently encountered of which is the middle marker *pe-* (participle form *me-*). Added to transitive verb bases, *pe-* derives dynamic intransitive verbs with middle semantics, compare *mesikori* 'wait' versus *monsikori* 'await, wait for'; *mewuni* 'hide oneself' versus *mowuni* 'hide (something)'; and *me'ula* 'board, get on' versus *mo'ula* 'load (cargo)'. Added to noun stems, *pe-* derives dynamic intransitive verbs which variously mean to have, use, seek, etc. that which is denoted by the base, compare *mehawu* 'wear a sarong (*hawu*)' and *melere* 'set out a dry rice field (*lere*), work, farm in a dry rice field'. In other cases such as *mebee* 'cry' and *melempa* 'go, walk', the root is not separately encountered.

5.3 Stative verbs

Unlike dynamic verbs, stative verbs do not have separate participle forms. Instead, the same, invariant form is used in all contexts. Verbs which are formally stative in this sense include all passive verbs as well as many intransitive verbs. Typically, stative verbs encode properties and states, or if actions, ones which are not controlled by the subject (e.g. *mo'ipi* 'dream', *mo'ai* 'be burning, be consumed with flames'). The verbs *aiwa* 'come', *hawe* 'arrive' and the five directionals discussed under §4.2 are also formally treated by the grammar as stative. There are furthermore a handful of intransitive verbs which apparently contain *-um-* as a frozen element, including *umari* 'finish', *umolo* 'suffer hunger', and *rumodi* 'nubby' (said of immature maize). Because the *-um-* in these forms is fixed and never deletes, these stems are likewise classed as stative.

Several prefixes are associated with deriving stative intransitive stems in Mori Bawah, including the regular stative prefix *mo-* as in *mota'u* 'old', *mokula* 'hot', *motu'i* 'dry', and *molori* 'slick, smooth', and the so-called non-agentive prefix *te-* as in *tewuni* 'hidden', *tetadi* 'gotten away, missing, disappeared, lost', and *tegoo* 'belch'.

5.4 The plural subject prefix *(me)N-*

Any verb stem, dynamic or stative, may take the plural subject prefix *(me)N-*. When present, this prefix signals that the subject is plural, specifically 'three or more' (dual forms are addressed below). The plural prefix has two allomorphs, *N-* and *meN-*. In general but not exclusively, dynamic stems which take the nasal replacement allomorph of the participle marker – see example (63e–h) – also take the *N-* allomorph of the plural prefix, e.g. *pekule* 'return' (primary), *mekule* (participle), *mpekule* (plural). An important aspect of plural subject marking is that the *primary/participle distinction* described in §5.2 *is neutralized with plural verb forms*. In other words, any dynamic verb has only one plural form which is used in all environments.

Because the plural subject prefix *(me)N-* refers to three or more, while a plural pronoun refers to two or more (in polite speech it can also refer to the singular), in effect the grammar can distinguish between singular, dual and plural subjects, for example *ka=i pekule* (and=3s.NOM return) 'and he/she/it returned' (singular) versus *ka=do pekule* (and=3p.NOM return) 'and they returned' (dual) versus *ka=do m-pekule* (and=3p.NOM PL-return) 'and they returned' (three or more). By and large plural subject marking is grammatically required whenever the subject argument refers to three or more human or personified referents; as throughout the grammar, non-humans are almost always treated as singular regardless of referential number. In the case of verb chains or, rarely, two verbs in closely linked clauses, plural marking may be omitted from one of the verbs.

5.5 Applicative suffixes

Mori Bawah has four verbal derivational suffixes, all of which can be considered applicative suffixes in that they introduce a new argument into the role structure of the predicate, at least in some of their uses. These are *-Ci*, *-Cari*, *-Cako* and *-ako*. Capital *C* indicates that the suffix is often preceded by an inserted consonant, compare *t*, *s* and *m* in respectively *moberiti* 'tear (*moberi*) into small pieces', *mo'alasi* 'take (*mo'ala*) many things', and *moreremi* 'supply with a wall (*rere*)' – though in some cases no consonant is inserted, as in *mogolai* 'sweeten, add sugar (*gola*) to'. A capital *C* is used when citing the general forms of these suffixes, because the value of the inserted consonants depends on the stem to which the suffix attaches.

A concern regarding applicative suffixes is, to what extent is the newly introduced argument treated like a core argument? For *-Ci*, *-Cari* and *-Cako*, the answer is straightforward: in general, these suffixes derive two place predicates which behave almost completely like ordinary transitive bases, the newly introduced argument clearly being treated as a transitive object. Note that in many but not all of their truly applicative uses, these suffixes are added to intransitive stems. The use of *-ako*, on the other hand, is one of the most intricate areas of Mori Bawah grammar. The account given below, though detailed, must necessarily remain incomplete in a work of this scope.

5.5.1 The suffix -Ci

The suffix *-Ci* has five primary functions. However, in only three of these functions (the first three discussed below) can *-Ci* be considered a true applicative suffix which introduces a new argument into the role structure of the predicate.

When added to dynamic intransitive stems, *-Ci* introduces the goal toward which an action is directed. (The derived transitive verb bases in the second column are cited in their antipassive participle form, thus prefixed with *moN-*.)

(64) a. *mekuu* 'dive'   *mompekuumi* 'dive or stoop toward, dive for'
      b. *mekule* 'return'   *mompekuleti* 'return to'
      c. *mebee* 'cry'   *mompebeeki* 'mourn for'

When added to stative stems, *-Ci* implies external agency. Any stative prefix present on the base (§5.3) is usually omitted in the transitive derivation.

(65) a. *buke* 'full'   *mobuketi* 'fill'
      b. *mowuwu* 'turbid'   *mowuwui* 'make turbid'
      c. *masola* 'have misfortune'   *monsolangi* 'subject to, bring into misfortune'
      d. *tedonta* 'fall'   *modontai* 'let fall, drop'

When *-Ci* is added to a noun stem, the resulting verb means to bring that which is denoted by the base onto or over (or away from) something.

(66) a. *pakuli* 'medicine'   *mompakulisi* 'medicate, treat with medicine'
      b. *kutu* 'louse'   *mongkutui* 'delouse'
      c. *sau* 'umbrella'   *monsaumi* 'hold an umbrella over'
      d. *pabawa* 'power'   *mompabawai* 'rule over'

Another, extremely common use of -*Ci* is to indicate that an action is performed with added force, repeatedly, over an extended period of time, and/or over an extensive area. The base may be transitive or intransitive, with no change in valency.

(67) a. *mo'ungke* 'seek'   *mo'ungkesi* 'seek well, thoroughly, everywhere'
      b. *mongkara* 'bite'   *mongkarasi* 'bite repeatedly or powerfully'
      c. *mebee* 'cry'   *mebeeli* 'cry protractedly'

Finally there are certain instances where -*Ci* is added to transitive verb bases, which are united in that semantically the -*Ci* form indicates that the patient is less affected, that the action is less thoroughly carried out, and/or that the action is otherwise performed in some non-prototypical manner. Included hereunder are *monseumi* 'sew on, stick into' next to *monseu* 'sew' (a shirt, for example); *mongkabesi* 'partially draw near to oneself' (as with a flower or plant) next to *mongkabe* 'take near to oneself, receive' (as with something that is passed); and *mo'onsoi* 'obstruct someone's way, hold someone back on the way' next to *mo'onso* 'close off with a stopper or plug (*onso*), obstruct a watercourse'.

5.5.2 The suffix -Cari

When added to intransitive and antipassive verb bases, the suffix -*Cari* introduces the location at, in, on, or toward which the action is performed.

(68) a. *melere* 'have a dry field'   *mompelereari* 'prepare a dry rice field on'
      b. *mo'ia* 'stay, reside'   *mompo'iangari* 'reside at, settle'
      c. *mongkaa* 'eat'   *mompongkaangari* 'eat out of'
      d. *mompaho* 'plant'   *mompompahoari* 'plant in' (a field, etc.)
      e. *monaa* 'place, store'   *momponaapari* 'lay, place, set in'

The forms cited in the second column of (68) are antipassive participles. In context, however, usually the transitive form (with object indexing) is employed.

(69) ...*nde   i   Bungku   anu   lako   mo'ia-ngari=o.*
      because PN   Bungku   REL   go   PART:settle-LOC=3s.ABS
      '...because Bungku was the one who went and settled it (that area)'

When the base to which -*Cari* is added itself expresses a transitive concept as in (68c–e), the resulting verb has two undergoers. However, the theme (the thing eaten, planted, etc.) is treated as indefinite, while the location (what one eats out of, where one plants, etc.) may be definite or indefinite, in other words only the location can be indexed pronominally.

(70) *Aku   mom-paho-ari=o   osole   bonde.*
      1s.FUT   PART:APASS-plant-LOC=3s.ABS   corn   garden
      'I will plant the garden with corn.'

Furthermore it is the location, not the theme, which becomes the derived subject in corresponding passive forms, e.g.:

(71) *sa'u   anu   p<in>o-naa-pari   inisa*
      k.o.basket REL   PASS:APASS-store-LOC   pestled.rice
      'a basket which pestled rice is stored in'

5.5.3 The suffix -Cako

The suffix -*Cako* has two primary functions in Mori Bawah. Added to both intransitives and transitive verb bases, -*Cako* may indicate the action is performed in a more intense or haphazard manner (without any change in valency of the predicate).

(72) a. *mentoro* 'sit down'   *mentoropako* 'sit down suddenly'
     b. *me'ini* 'hold oneself on' *me'iniako* 'hold oneself on tightly or strongly'
     c. *morawo* 'sow, scatter'   *morawosako* 'scatter in a rough manner, strew'

In some cases the -*Cako* form indicates the activity is performed by a large number of people, compare *metonda* 'go one after another' (said of two or more people) versus *metondarako* 'go one after another' (of a great number of people). In other cases the two forms are nearly synonymous, e.g. *mobangku*, *mobangkuako* 'knock over, topple something', *medontai*, *medontaihako* 'let oneself fall'.

In its other primary function, -*Cako* is added to certain intransitive verbs of motion, adjectives and nouns. In the resulting predicate, which is transitive, the agent is a causer who effects movement by physically carrying, manipulating or escorting the patient.

(73) a. *molai* 'flee'   *mompolaisako* 'flee with, be on the run with'
     c. *saki* 'crossed over'   *monsakiako* 'take across, take over'
     d. *asi* 'crack' (noun)   *mo'asipako* 'stick or stuff into a crack'

Compare in context:

(74) *Do='ala=o*   *koroi-no*   *ka=do*   *polaisako=no.*
      3p.NOM=take=3s.ABS   body-3s.POSS   and=3p.NOM   flee.with=3s.ABS
      'They took his body and fled with it.'

Nevertheless, there are a few transitive verb bases derived with -*Cako* which appear not to fit under either of the above categories, including *mo'iangako* 'guard, look after' (compare *mo'ia* 'stay, reside'), *mongkorahako* 'carry through with, attempt to carry through with' (said of intentions or desires) (compare *mokora* 'strong').

5.5.4 The suffix -ako

The applicative suffix -*ako* is used to introduce a wide range of arguments into the role structure of the predicate, including beneficiaries, instruments, and causes (the latter category including the stimuli of psychological events). As a result of phonological coalescence and certain analogical extensions, the absolutive pronouns which historically followed -*ako* usually no longer have their ordinary forms (see Table 24.7).

In many instances the pronoun which follows -*ako* (and has merged with it) also indexes the argument introduced by -*ako*. This is the case whenever -*ako* introduces a beneficiary. In fact following transitive verbs pronominal indexing of the beneficiary supersedes pronominal indexing of the object, which is otherwise required; compare example (75) with example (58) above.

(75) *...tembio   ka=u   lako   mepate-akita*
      why   and=2s.NOM   go   PART:kill-APP: 1pi.ABS
      ana-no   dahu-to?
      child-3s.POSS   dog-1pi.POSS
      '...why did you go kill our puppies for us?'

TABLE 24.7: FUSION OF -*AKO* WITH ABSOLUTIVE PRONOUNS

	Absolutive	*ako* + absolutive
1s	*aku*	*akune*
2s	*ko*	*akomu*
3s	*o*	*akono*
1pi	*kita*	*akita*
1pe	*kami*	*akami*
2p	*komiu*	*akomiu*
3p	*ira*	*ako'ira*

On the other hand, when the stem is transitive and -*ako* introduces an instrument or cause, it is still the object of the non-applicative form which is indexed following -*ako*, *not* the argument which -*ako* introduces.

(76) *Aku   h<um>uku-akomu   ponako-mu.*
      1s.FUT   PART:punish-APP: 2s.ABS   steal-2s.POSS
      'I will punish you on account of your thievery.'

(77) *Lauro   andio   te'ingka   ku='oho-akomiu.*
      rattan PRX   near.future 1s.NOM=bind-APP: 2p.ABS
      'In a moment I (will) bind you with this rattan.'

A cause (or rarely an instrument) can be indexed pronominally only when -*ako* follows an *intransitive* stem, and even then indexing is often optional as in (78), or omitted as in (79).

(78) *Api-no   i   Elu-Elu   ku=momee-ako(no)*
      fire-3s.POSS   PN   Orphan   1s.NOM=afraid-APP:(3s.ABS)
      'I was afraid of Orphan's fire.'

(79) *io   ambau-no   kalamboro   anu*
      EMPH   carabao-3s.POSS people.eater REL
      menee-ako   i   Tandungkokabo
      PART:have.name-APP   PN   Tandungkokabo
      'the people eater's carabao, who has the name of (who is named with) Tandungkokabo'

With transitive verb bases, the antipassive marker *poN-* signals the indefiniteness of the object of the non-applicative form, whether -*ako* introduces a beneficiary, cause or instrument.

(80) *Aku   mon-tena*
      1s.FUT   PART:APASS-command
      mo-wawa-akomiu   inahu   eu.
      PART:APASS-bring-APP: 2p.ABS vegetable spinach
      'I will send someone to bring you spinach.'

(81) *Onae   ku=po-'ungke-ako   kaanga.*
      3s   1s.NOM=APASS-seek-APP   things.to.eat
      'That's how I seek sustenance.' (lit. With that, by means of that I seek food.)

Only when *-ako* follows an intransitive stem can *poN-* be used to signal the indefiniteness of a cause or instrument, and even then its presence is usually optional, e.g. *(mo)-lingkau-ako onitu* (PART:APASS-afraid-APP spirit) 'afraid of ghosts', *(mon)-teta'i-ako rea* (PART:APASS-defecate-APP blood) 'pass blood'. It is also only when the original stem is intransitive that one finds passive forms involving causes and instruments, compare for example the passive nominalizations *m<in>o'ipiako* 'that which one has dreamt of' (*<mo'ipi* 'dream'), *p<in>eneeako* 'that which one has as a name, that which one is named with' (*<menee* 'have a name, be named').

When *-ako* introduces a beneficiary, however, the presence of *-in-* signals the promotion of the beneficiary to subject position, regardless of the transitivity of the base. When the patient is indefinite and the beneficiary occurs as surface subject, the verb will then occur with both the antipassive marker *poN-* and the passive marker *-in-*.

(82)   *Mem-p<in>o-'isa-ako=kami   inisa.*
       PL-PASS:APASS-pestle-APP=1pe.ABS   pestled.rice
       'We were pestled some rice (rice was pestled for us).'

Note also from this example that absolutive pronouns which index *subjects* do not exhibit phonological coalescence with *-ako* (viz. not *mempino'isaakami*).

6 NOMINALIZATIONS AND NOMINAL MORPHOLOGY

In general, a Mori Bawah verb stem requires no further derivation to be used as a noun. Although this may lead to ambiguity when considering stems *in the abstract*, in most cases the grammar distinguishes *in context* whether a stem is being used as a noun or a verb. In particular, the following differences between verbs and corresponding nominalizations may be cited: (a) a nominalization may be marked only with a possessive pronoun, the corresponding verb usually only with a future, nominative, and/or absolutive pronoun (two exceptions are mentioned below); (b) although under the appropriate circumstances dynamic verbs take *-um-*, this prefix is obligatorily absent from all nominalizations; and (c) unlike verbs, nominalizations are never marked with the plural subject prefix *(me)N-*. According to these criteria, *pepau* in (83) may be identified as a verb; conversely the same form in (84) is a nominalization.

(83)   *Kongkono   koa   do=m-pepau   kanandio.*
       always   just   3p.NOM=PL-speak   like.this
       'They always speak like this.'

(84)   *Maka'ali=o=mo   pepau-do.*
       excited=3s.ABS=PFV   speak-3s.POSS
       'Their speech became animated.'

What is made clear by morphology is generally supported by distribution: the predicate slot is filled by stems taking verbal morphology, while argument slots must be filled by stems taking nominal morphology. This statement can only be made, however, with the understanding that in Mori Bawah nominalized clauses are sometimes used where other languages would most naturally employ verbal forms: compare the following sentence which literally means 'the cooking of these vegetables is not good'.

(85)   *Nahi/ nahi + i/   moiko   nahu-no   inehu   andio.*
       NEG: 3s.NOM   good   cook-3s.POSS   vegetable   PRX
       'These vegetables aren't cooked well.'

The above notwithstanding, there is one affix in Mori Bawah which derives nominalizations from verbal stems: the locative nominalizer -*Ca*. Formally, a stem which has been suffixed with -*Ca* is explicitly marked as a noun stem, and thus never appears with verbal marking. The suffix -*Ca* derives nouns which indicate the location or time of an event, or – if the stem expresses a stative concept – the place where an attribute or quality holds forth, for example *pelerea* 'site for farming' (<*melere* 'set out a dry rice field'), *lakoa* 'destination', also 'time of departure' (<*lumako* 'go'), *pe'iwalia* 'wartime, war' (<*me'iwali* 'conduct warfare'), *molusaa* 'soft spot, soft part' (<*molusa* 'soft, yielding'). In rare cases -*Ca* nominalizations may profile the referent in patient role, as in *tunua* 'firewood' (cf. *montunu* 'burn').

Nominalizations without the suffix -*Ca*, on the other hand, typically profile the performance of an action, the manner in which an action is performed, the instrument with which it is performed, and/or the action or state considered as an abstract, compare *ponako* 'thieving, thievery' (<*monako* 'steal'): *pelempa* 'walking, manner of walking' (<*melempa* 'go, walk'); *powemba* 'lance with one barbed hook' (<*mowemba* 'hunt'); *mokula* 'heat, hotness' (<*mokula* 'hot'; recall from §5.3 that stative verb stems remain unchanged in all of their uses, including nominalizations). Such forms can also be used to profile the person who performs an action, but only if such a person does the activity on behalf of another (thus more or less still conceived of as an instrument), for example *polombo* 'clothes washing, clothes washer' (<*molombo* 'wash (clothes)').

As illustrated in (86) through (88), nominalizations both with and without -*Ca* can be used as noun modifiers. In this use they are often the functional equivalents of relative clauses (in which the location or, respectively, the instrument has been relativized), and may even optionally be preceded by the relative clause marker *anu*. Nonetheless, they are still nominalizations according to the formal criteria set forth above.

(86) *togo*   *lako-a-do*
      island   go-NR-3p.POSS
      'the island to which they are going'

(87) *mia*   *anu*   *pesikeno-a-ku*   *indiawi*
      person   REL   inquire-NR-1p.POSS   yesterday
      'the person to whom I made inquiries yesterday'

(88) *pena*   *po-buri-ku*   *wunta*   *andio*
      pen   GER-write-1s.POSS   letter   PRX
      'the pen with which I wrote this letter'

There are special considerations when transitive verbs are nominalized. As may be recalled from §5.1, a transitive verb base will appear in context either prefixed with the antipassive marker *poN-*, indexed for its object with an absolutive pronoun, or infixed with the passive marker -*in-*. However, when nominalized the *poN-* form can be used whether the patient is definite or indefinite, compare example (88) where the nominalized form is prefixed with *poN-*, even though *wunta andio* 'this letter' is definite. In fact with a fair number of transitive verb bases, the *poN-* form serves as something akin to an active gerund, while the base itself serves as the corresponding passive gerund, compare *pohoru-no* 'her weaving, her way of weaving' versus *horu-no* 'its weaving, it's way of being woven'; *ponahu-no* 'his cooking, his way of cooking' versus *nahu-no* 'its way of being cooked' (which distinction also carries over into -*Ca* nominalizations, e.g. *po-nahua-no* 'his place of cooking', *nahua-no* 'its place of being cooked, the thing in which it is cooked'). The nominalized versions of passive -in- verbs, on the other hand, serve only to profile the referent in patient role, and are not known to be further derived with -Ca. Nominalizations with -in- are widely used in pseudo-relativization of patients (in example (89) the head noun *kinaa* also happens to be a patient nominalization, from the transitive verb base *kaa* 'eat').

(89)   *kinaa*   *anu*   *n<in>ahu-no*
       food   REL   PASS:cook-3s.POSS
       'the food (cooked rice) which was cooked by him'

The above criteria for disambiguating verbs from nominalizations fail in two areas of the grammar. The first case concerns stative verbs which allow an evaluator to be indexed on the verb with a possessive pronoun, as in *moiko-ku* (good-1s.POSS) 'I find it good, I esteem it good, it's good by me, it is good in my opinion' (*'I am good'). Although such constructions have the form of nominalizations, they regularly occur in predicate position, for example:

(90)   *To-lako-mo*   *ari*   *me'uho,*   *ba*
       1p.NOM-go-PFV   only   PART:seek.periwinkle   if
       mo'ahi-mu   *koa*   *muda*   *uho.*
       delicious-2p.POSS   just   2s.ADDITIVE   periwinkle
       'Let's go seek periwinkles, if you also find periwinkles delicious.'

The second case concerns preposed temporal clauses. Historically such clauses must have been nominalized, as seen for example in that subjects of such clauses are still marked by possessive pronouns, and dynamic verbs still appear in their primary forms (example (92) actually contains two such clauses, in correlative construction):

(91)   *Hawe-do*   *ira'ai*   *mentoa='ira=mo*
       arrive-3p.POSS   over.there   PART:jump.down=3p.ABS=PFV
       ana-do   *mokole*   *andio*   *a*   *ng-korono.*
       child-3p.POSS   k.o.nobility   PRX   at   LK-river
       'Their having arrived there, the *mokole*'s sons jumped into the river.' (here indexing of the *mokole* with a plural pronoun indicates respect)

(92)   *Petii-ku*   *a*   *uwoi,*   *pekuu-ku=mo.*
       descend-1s.POSS   at   water   dive-1s.POSS=PFV
       'No sooner had I gone into the water, than in I dived.'

However, preposed temporal clauses are now atypical of nominalizations in that the verb may be marked with the plural subject prefix *(me)N-*, compare *me-lako-do andio...*(PL-go-3p.POSS PRX) 'when they had gone...'. Such clauses may also contain verb chains, in which case the second verb is treated as verbal, compare *sa-'umari-no me'ula...* (when-finish-3s.POSS PART:get.on) 'when she had finished getting in...'. A further peculiarity yet is that the subordinator *sa-* 'when' may itself attract the possessive pronoun, compare example (93) which also illustrates the use of future pronouns in preposed temporal clauses.

(93)   *Sa-do*   *ira*   *m-pon-siwu,...*
       when-3p.POSS   3p.FUT   PL-APASS-make.sago.porridge.of
       'When they were going to make sago porridge...'

708 THE AUSTRONESIAN LANGUAGES

REFERENCES

Adriani, N. (1900) 'De talen der To Boengkoe en To Mori', *Mededeelingen van wege het Nederlandsche Zendelinggenootschap* 44:249–318.

Adriani, N. and Kruyt, A.C. (1914) *De Bare'e-sprekende Toradja's van Midden-Celebes*, vol. 3: *Taal- en letterkundige schets der Bare'e-taal en overzicht van het taalgebied Celebes–Zuid-Halmahera*, Batavia: Landsdrukkerij.

Barsel, L.A. (1994) *The verb morphology of Mori, Sulawesi*, Canberra: Pacific Linguistics.

Esser, S.J. (1927) *Klank- en vormleer van het Morisch*, part 1. Leiden: Vros.

——(1933) *Klank- en vormleer van het Morisch*, part 2. Bandoeng: Nix.

——(in progress) *Phonology and morphology of Mori*, translated by D. Mead.

Garantjang, A., Kadir, A., Wumbu, I. and Mustafa, D. (1981) *Struktur Bahasa Mori*, Jakarta: Pusat Pembinaan dan Pengembangan Bahasa.

Inghuong, S., Wumbu, I., Rahim, A.A. and Baso, N. (1986) *Morfologi dan sintaksis Bahasa Mori*, Jakarta: Pusat Pembinaan dan Pengembangan Bahasa.

Karhunen, M. and Vuorinen, P. (1991) 'Sociolinguistic survey: Mori and Padoe area', in T. Friberg (ed.) *UNHAS-SIL: more Sulawesi sociolinguistic surveys*, 35–53. Ujung Pandang: Summer Institute of Linguistics.

Kruyt, J. (1919) 'De telwoorden in het Oost-Morisch', *Mededeelingen van wege het Nederlandsche Zendelinggenootschap* 63:328–346.

——(1924) 'De Moriërs van Tinompo', *Bijdragen tot de Taal-, Land- en Volkenkunde van Nederlandsch-Indië* 80:33–217.

Mead, D. (1998) *Proto–Bungku-Tolaki: reconstruction of its phonology and aspects of its morphosyntax*, Ph.D. dissertation, Houston: Rice University.

——(1999) *The Bungku-Tolaki languages of south-eastern Sulawesi, Indonesia*, Canberra: Pacific Linguistics.

Noorduyn, J. (1991) *A critical survey of studies on the languages of Sulawesi*, Leiden: KITLV Press.

Saro, A., Kadir, A. and Hamid, I.A. (1993) *Struktur sastra lisan Mori*, Jakarta: Pusat Pembinaan dan Pengembangan Bahasa.

Sneddon, J.N. (1983) 'Southern Celebes (Sulawesi)', in S.A. Wurm and S. Hattori (eds) *Language atlas of the Pacific area*, part 2: *Japan area, Taiwan (Formosa), Philippines, mainland and insular South-east Asia*, map 44, Canberra: Pacific Linguistics.

Stokhof, W.A.L. (1985) *Holle lists: vocabularies in languages of Indonesia*, vol. 7/4: *South-east Sulawesi and neighboring islands, west and north-east Sulawesi*, Canberra: Pacific Linguistics.

Van Eelen, H.G. and Ritsema, J. (1918–1919) 'Morische verhalen', *Mededeelingen van wege het Nederlandsche Zendelinggenootschap* 62:211–229, 276–295; 63:312–327.

CHAPTER TWENTY-FIVE

KAMBERA

Marian Klamer

1 INTRODUCTION

Kambera is spoken by approximately 150,000 speakers in the eastern region of the island of Sumba (province Nusa Tenggara Timur) in Eastern Indonesia. It is classified as belonging to the Central-Malayo-Polynesian subgroup (see Blust 1993). Several other indigenous languages (or 'dialects', Onvlee 1984) are spoken on Sumba, including Weyewa (75,000), Kodi (40,000), Lamboya (15,000), Wanukaka (10,000), Anakalang (14,000) and Mamboru (16,000) (Wurm 1994). Of those, Weyewa and Kodi in particular appear to be unintelligible to speakers of Kambera. For that reason, at least the latter three varieties may be considered separate languages rather than dialects. It is as yet unclear whether the remaining varieties should be classified as dialects or languages.

The oldest publication in which a language of Sumba is mentioned is Heymering (1846), which contains a brief word list of the dialect of Mangili. Other word lists are given by Roos (1872), De Roo van Alderwerelt (1891), Vermast (1895), Pos (1901), and Wielenga (1917). Van der Velden (1900) is a brief description of the language of the Laura district in western Sumba. Wielenga (1909), Onvlee (1925) and Kapita (1983) are short grammars of Kambera. Klamer (1998a) is a recent grammar. The two Kambera dictionaries are Kambera–Indonesian (Kapita 1982) and Kambera–Dutch (Onvlee 1984). Kambera texts with Dutch translations are Wielenga (1913) and Onvlee (1925). Kambera traditional ritual speech, songs, stories and sayings are documented by Kapita (1977, 1979, 1986, 1987). These four publications, together with the Kambera New Testament (*'Na Paràndingu Bidi'*, 1961) and Hymn book (*'Ludu Pamalangu'*, 1979), make up the Kambera written literature. Kambera ritual speech is discussed in Forth (1981) and Fox (1988), while Kuipers (1998) deals with aspects of ritual speech in Weyewa. Forth (1985) is an anthropological study of the Kambera-speaking community of Rindi.

2 PHONOLOGY AND ORTHOGRAPHY

2.1 Segment inventory, syllable structure and stress

Table 25.1 presents the nineteen consonant segments of Kambera, with their orthography in brackets. Kambera has no plain voiced stops. The three plain voiceless stops all have a prenasalised counterpart. The language has eight complex consonants: two implosive stops (labial and alveolar), one affricate and five prenasalised segments.

Kambera has only one fricative, /h/. At the end of the nineteenth century, Kambera still had an /s/, but a rapid consonant shift occurred between 1872 and 1909 which changed all /s/s into /h/s. For example, *sai* 'comb', *pa-usi* 'gather', *bunggas* 'to open X' in Roos (1872) have become *hai, pa-uhi* and *bunggah* by the time of Wielenga (1909) (cf. Klamer 1998a:12). Kambera has a non-phonemic glottal stop as the default realization of an

TABLE 25.1: KAMBERA CONSONANT PHONEMES

	Labial	Alveolar	Velar	Glottal
Voiceless plain stop	p	t	k	
Voiced implosive stop	ɓ(b)	ɗ (d)		
Voiced affricate		ʤ (j)		
Nasal	m	n	ŋ (ng)	
Prenasalized stop	mb	nd	ŋg (ngg)	
Prenasalized affricate		nʤ (nj)		
Fricative				h
Lateral liquid		l		
Rhotic liquid		r		
Glide	w	j (y)		
Prenasalised glide		nj (ny)		

TABLE 25.2: KAMBERA VOWELS AND DIPHTHONGS

	Front	Central	Back
High	i (ì)		u (u)
	i: (i)		u: (ú)
Low	e	a (à)	o
	ai	a: (a)	au

empty onset in root-initial syllables (*angu* [ʔáŋu] 'friend'). Main stress is always on the root-initial syllable (see below).

The Kambera vowels are given in Table 25.2, with their orthographic representations in brackets. All the vowels can occur in the initial, stressed, syllable of the root, but in unstressed contexts we only find the cardinal vowels /i, a, u/. Of all the logically possible VV combinations, only /ea/ and /oa/ do not occur. The contrast between /u/ and /u:/ is clearly quantitative, but the contrast between /a, i/ and /a:, i:/ may also be realised qualitatively as a lax/tense distinction. That is, /a/ is phonetically either [a] or [ɑ], /i/ as [i] or [ɪ], while /a:/ may be realized as [a:] or [a], and /i:/ as [i:] or [i]. One allophone is thus shared between the tense and the lax phonemes (i.e. [a] and [i]). The three Kambera vowels that only occur in the specific semantic domain of ideophonic roots (/ɛ/, /ɔ/ and very short /ù/) are not represented in this table.

The sequences /ai/ and /au/ are analysed as diphthongs because phonotactically, they behave like the long counterparts of the short mid vowels /e,o/: they only occur in a heavy syllable, like the other long vowels and unlike the short vowels. Also, their feature composition resembles that of the short mid-vowels. And third, some of the words now containing a diphthong are historically related to forms with a plain vowel.

Kambera has three syllable types: CVV (where VV is a long vowel, a diphthong or a vowel sequence), CV, and CVC. Kambera does not allow closed syllables at the surface, i.e. CVC syllables are only found lexically. Roots are disyllabic and main stress is without exception on the root-initial syllable. Only CVV and CV syllables can bear stress, CVC syllables are never stressed. Prefixes, suffixes and almost all clitics are unstressed. The smallest lexical items are CVV – the absence of CV roots in Kambera indicates a constraint on the shape of lexical roots, which states that a root should be minimally bimoraic.

(1) presents a summary of the possible Kambera root types. Identical subscripts indicate identical vowel slots.

(1) a. CV CV
        nomu 'six'

    b. CV$_j$V$_k$
        wài 'water'

    c. CV$_k$V$_k$
        yú [ju:] 'tongue'

    d. CV$_j$V$_k$ CV
        paita 'bitter'

    e. CV$_k$V$_k$ CV
        hili [hi:li] 'again'

    f. CV CVC(V)
        danggang(u) 'sell X'

    g. CV$_j$V$_k$ CVC(V)
        wàindal(u) 'sway arm'

In a sample of approximately 1000 items (roots and derived forms) the root types (a,e) make up 50% of the forms, while the structure in (f) represents 30% of the items, (b,c) 15%, and (d,g) 5%.

2.2 Orthography

Kambera orthography in the Kambera New Testament and Hymn Book is based on Indonesian orthography and basically follows Kapita (1982, 1983) and Onvlee (1984). The orthographic conventions in these sources and the present chapter differ only in the marking of vowel quality and clitics. Here, I maintain the proposal of Klamer (1998a) to mark the long-short (tense-lax) distinction of the vowels more consistently: contrastive short (lax) vowels /a/ and /i/ are represented with a grave accent (*à* and *ì*), just like the short, low vowels of ideophones (*è, ò, ù*). A plain *a, i, e,* or *o* therefore represents either a long (tense) vowel, or a vowel unspecified for length or tenseness. The vowels /u/ and /u:/ differ in length (not tenseness), but, in contrast to long /i:/ and /a:/, /u/ is specified for length only very rarely. Therefore, only the contrastively long /u:/ is marked as such, with an acute accent (*ú*). See also the information on vowel length given in section 2.1.

2.3 Phonological alternations

Kambera has a phonological process of umlaut that applies to the mid vowels /e, o/ when they are followed by a syllable containing the low vowel /a/. Umlaut of /e, o/ yields the lowered allophones [ɛ, ɔ] and/or results in the broken vowels [jɛ, wɔ]. The domain of the umlaut process is a prosodic constituent: the foot. The foot is isomorphic to a morphological constituent, the root (section 2.1). The vowels /e, o/ do not change under influence of a following /i, u/, and neither does /a/ trigger umlaut on /i, u/.

(2) *rengga* [rjéŋga] 'hurry, be quick', *bera* [bjéra] 'to split, break', *podah* [pɔ́dahu] 'wipe X (clean)', *mbola* [mbwɔ́la] 'basket', *toma* [tɔ́ma] 'arrive'. Compare e.g.: *mbeni* [mbéni] be fierce/angry'.

The non-lexical, default vowel in Kambera is /u/ (default vowels are also referred to as 'paragogic' vowels in Austronesian studies, cf. Sneddon 1993). This vowel is the result of a phonetic process which applies to roots with a final CVC syllable. As Kambera does not allow closed syllables at the surface, the paragogic vowel is added so that the root-final consonant can surface as the onset of a CV syllable. The root-final position, i.e. preceding the paragogic [u], can only be filled by the consonants /l, r, h, t, k, ŋ/:

(3) *akat* > *akat[u]* 'be bad', *bànjal* > *bànjal[u]* 'put X', *padang* > *padang[u]* 'field', *kikir* > *kikir[u]* 'shave', *mbunggah* > *mbunggah[u]* 'open X', *kotak* > *kotak[u]* 'village'.

The result of the phonetic rule of paragogic vowel addition is that at the surface, Kambera has trisyllabic roots, of which the third syllable contains a default vowel. Note that the fact that Kambera lacks roots with a lexical vowel in the third syllable, such as *rimuna, *obali, or *puita, shows that it does not generally allow trisyllabic roots. It is also evidence that existing root forms with vowel sequences such as *paita* 'bitter' and *ka-lauki* are not underlyingly trisyllabic, but are disyllabic: [páj-ta], [ka-láw-ki].

The default vowel /u/ also plays a role in borrowings: as Kambera lacks CVC roots, loan words such as *tep* 'tape' or *cet* 'paint' are adapted to Kambera phonotactics by adding the default vowel, resulting in e.g. *tepu* '(to) tape, a taperecorder' and *cetu* '(to) paint'.

2.4 Reduplication

From a formal point of view, there are three kinds of reduplication processes in Kambera: CV reduplication, foot reduplication, and reduplication of a prosodic word (= a foot plus possible affixes). In the regular case, the same word may undergo syllable, foot or word reduplication. There is no robust contrast in the semantics of the three reduplications.

The base of a reduplication can be a noun, verb, adverb, question word, or a measure word. The reduplication of nouns derives a collective or distributive meaning ('a group of Ns, various Ns'), while the reduplication of non-nominals derives either an intensive meaning (including notions of iteration, excessive degree, continuity, emphasis) or various non-intensive meanings, including diminutive, indifference, or an activity done for fun/pleasure.

CV reduplication copies the first consonant and vowel of the root: *palu* 'hit' > *pa-palu* 'hit (iterative, intensive)'. As Kambera syllables may be larger than just CV, CV reduplication is not identical to syllable reduplication: *haila* 'saddle' is reduplicated as *ha-haila* 'various saddles', not as *hai-haila*. In case the reduplicated vowel is a low/broken vowel as a result of undergoing umlaut, the entire vowel is reduplicated, with the result that it appears as if the process of umlaut has 'overapplied' in reduplicated forms: *pena* 'pencil' is reduplicated as *pjɛ-pjɛna* 'various pencils', not as *pi-pjena* or *pe-pjena*. CV reduplication treats vowel sequences as bivocalic structures, reduplicating only the first vowel. When long vowels are reduplicated, the vowel length is not transferred to the reduplicative prefix (*wútu* 'be fat' > *wu-wútu* 'be very fat', compare *wú-wútu*).

Foot reduplication copies the stress foot of the base: *ài* > *ài-ài* 'wood'. The reduplicated element is a foot. The foot often coincides with the lexical root, but need not do so: *wunang(u)* 'priest' > *wuna-wunang(u)* 'various priests', *wunang-wunang(u)*. The foot is minimally bimoraic, but two morae or vowels do not always form a foot: *kaunda* 'stalk away' > *kaunda-kaunda* 'stalk away (intensive)', cf. *kau-kaunda*.

Full reduplication is the reduplication of the prosodic word, i.e. a root plus possible affixes: *ha-atu* 'one' > *haatu-haatu* 'each and every one', *pa-peka-ng* 'story' > *papekang-papekang* 'all kinds of stories', *ta-mbumba* 'pound' > *tambumba-tambumba* 'continuous pounding, clatter of hoofs'.

3 BASIC MORPHOSYNTAX

3.1 Word classes

The major distinction within the Kambera lexicon is between content words and function words. Kambera content words are minimally bimoraic, can occur as independent words (prosodic and grammatical), have an independent meaning, and are members of an open class. Content words belong to the word classes verb, noun and adverb. Function words, on the other hand, are generally smaller than content words – often consisting of only one monomoraic syllable – express grammatical meanings, and form closed classes. They include conjunctions, prepositions, articles and negations. Strictly speaking, these items – as well as the markers of embedded clauses and the markers of mood, aspect and pronominal reference – are clitics in Kambera. Clitics differ from words because they do not need to be bimoraic, and cannot be stressed, i.e. they need a phonological host and do not form independent prosodic words. They differ from affixes in that they do not have selectional restrictions for a specific morphological base. Though syntactically attaching to the edge of a syntactic phrase, prosodically they attach to the element that happens linearly to precede them (enclitics) or follow them (proclitics).

Following common practice, conjunctions, prepositions, articles and negations are orthographically represented as independent words. The syntactic attachment of the clitics marking embedded (relativized, controlled) clauses and the markers of mood, pronominal reference and aspect is indicated by an equal sign (=), while the morphological attachment of affixes is indicated by a hyphen (-) when this is required for expository reasons.

There are no structural arguments to distinguish a separate lexical category of adjectives in Kambera. The morphosyntactic properties of words expressing typical adjectival notions (size, colour, dimension, shape) correspond to those of the class of intransitive verbs such as *meti* 'die', *laku* 'go', or *lai* 'run', i.e. Kambera adjectival notions are expressed by stative intransitive verbs. On the other hand, the language does have a category of adverbs (section 3.1.2).

3.1.1 Verbs and nouns

Compared to many other Austronesian languages, the morphosyntactic differences between the major categories of verbs and nouns are relatively clear in Kambera. A root form can be classified as unambiguously nominal if (i) it can be preceded by an article marking definiteness and number, (ii) it can be modified by an emphatic or demonstrative pronoun (section 4), and (iii) it can be quantified by a numeral phrase or by the quantifier *mbu ndàba* 'all', a nominal constituent that is 'possessed' by the NP it quantifies:

(4) *Da=munju   da   kokur   mbú ndàba=da*
     3p.NOM=fall.off ART   coconut   all=3p.GEN
     'The coconuts all fell off (the tree).'

Typical verbal properties include (i) the possibility of having a nominative subject, and (ii) the possibility of being modified by an adverb, e.g. *lalu* 'too (much)':

(5) *Lalu   mbana=na   na   lodu*
     too.much   be.hot=3s.GEN   ART   sun
     'It's too hot.' (lit. 'The sun is too hot.')

Kambera does have exclusively verbal derivational morphology: items derived with the prefixes *pa-* and *ta-*, the suffix *-ng* and the circumfix *ka–k* are always verbal (see section 5). The other Kambera derivational morphemes (*la-*, *ma-*, *ha-*) are unproductive and occur in both nominal and verbal forms.

Verbs and nouns are similar in that both may occur as (heads of) either predicates or nominal constituents that express verbal arguments. An illustration of the latter is (6), where the verbs *rambang* 'snatch' and *ribang* 'steal' are part of a nominal constituent functioning as the argument of *pa-laku*, and are cross-referenced on that verb by the enclitic *=ya*:

(6) *Na=juju=ta*   *pa=pa-laku=ya*   *na*   *rambang*   *na*   *ribang*
    3s.NOM=incite=1p.ACC   SR=CAU-go=3s.ACC   ART snatch   ART rob
    'He (i.e. the devil) incites us to steal and rob.'

Both nouns and verbs may also function as modifiers in verbal and nominal constituents (Klamer 1998a:96–109), compare the NPs in (7) and (8):

(7) *tau*   *wàu*   *wàu*   *tau*
    person to.smell   to.smell person
    'Smelly person'   'Smell like a human, have human scent'

(8) *iyang* *tau*   *wàu*   *iyang* *wàu*   *tau*
    fish   person to.smell   fish   to.smell person
    'Fish of smelly person'   'Fish smelling of people'

In Kambera there are also so-called 'multifunctional' roots, and derived words that function both nominally and verbally without having an overt morpheme relating these two categories derivationally. Examples include:

(9) *bàndil*   'rifle'; 'to shoot, to shoot X'
    hilu   'language (exchange of words); 'to (ex)change X'
    ludu   'song'; 'to emit sound, to sing'
    ka-ninu   'mirror'; 'to investigate X (poetical)'
    ha-yandal 'comfort'; 'to live in comfort'
    ma-nganga 'theft'; 'to steal (X)'

Nouns borrowed from Indonesian can often be used verbally as well, e.g., *karenja* (< *gereja*) 'church', 'to go to church'; *pareta* (< *pe(me)rintah*) 'government', 'to govern, reign'.

3.1.2 Adverbs

Kambera has a separate lexical category of adverbs. They may precede or follow the verb. Occurring directly adjacent to the verb, they modify it for aspect, mood, quantity, degree, or manner. Adverbs are independent prosodic words and separate lexical items, and constitute a phrasal constituent with the adjacent verb. (10) and (11) illustrate the preverbal adverb *tika* 'almost' and the postverbal adverb *lia* 'maybe':

(10) *Da=tika*   *pakoja=du=ya*   *nyuna*
     3p.NOM=almost   stab=EMPH=3s.ACC he
     'They almost stabbed him to death.'

(11) *Laku lia=nanya=ka*   *una*
     go maybe=3s.CONT=PFV EMPH.3s
     'He may be going.'

Unlike nouns and verbs, adverbs cannot undergo productive derivation with the affixes *pa-* or *-ng*. The following derivations have plausible semantics, yet they are not possible words, suggesting that the morphological restriction is structurally, rather than semantically, motivated:

(12) *lalu* 'too much' **pa-lalu* Intended reading 'cause to be too much'
      lia 'maybe'   **pa-lia*   Intended reading 'cause to be uncertain'

Adverbs also differ from verbs and nouns in not being able to project a separate, independent phrase: they are always part of a verbal predicate phrase (see section 3.2).

3.1.3 Prepositions

Kambera prepositions form a closed class of only four items (viz. *la*, *lai*, *hu* and *dàngu*). They are formally distinct from verbs and nouns because they cannot host clitics. *La* is a general preposition that is used to express locations and directions in both space and time. It governs nouns, verbs, deverbal nominals, and nominal deictics. It forms complex prepositions with locational nouns (front, back, cover, side, top, etc.), some of which still function as independent nouns. Examples are: *la lumbu* (LOC cover) 'underneath', *la pinu* (LOC top) 'on (top of)', *la hangga* (LOC front) 'before, in front of'. Complex prepositions have the same distribution as simple prepositions:

(13) a. *Ka-tuda [la   topu]*   b. *Ka-tuda   [la   lumbu [topu]]*
         sleep   LOC   mat   sleep   LOC under   mat
         'Sleep on a mat.'   'Sleep under a mat.'

La is also used in temporal expressions:

(14) a. *La   mbaru*   b. *Na   lodu   mbaru*
         LOC   early.morning   ART day   early.morning
         'In the morning (6–10 a.m.).'   'The (early) morning.'

(15) *La   maling*
      LOC   late afternoon-early evening
      'In the afternoon/evening (4–7 p.m.)'

The second preposition is *lai*. This preposition functions to express spatial location at (a) person(s). As such, it can govern proper names, personal and demonstrative pronouns, as illustrated in (16). Historically, it is probably a merged form of *la* and the proper article *i*.

(16) *lai   nyudas/Ama/Miri/Windi/nuna*
      LOC   they/father/Lord/Windi/DIST.3s
      'To/for/at them/father/the Lord/Windi/that one'

Lai is distinct from the general preposition *la* in that it does *not* combine with locational nouns to form complex prepositions. To express locations, it combines with deictic elements:

(17) *lai   nú/wawa/dita/luru/dia*
      LOC   DIST/down/up/downstream/upstream
      'Over there/down there/up there/downstream/upstream'

The third preposition is *hu*. This is a directional preposition that combines with deictics. It only indicates directions, never locations:

(18) *Ku=ngàndi=ya   duku   hu   wawa*
      1s.NOM=take=3s.ACC   EMPH.1s   DIR   down
      'I'll take it down.'

Finally, Kambera has a comitative preposition *dàngu* which relates nominals to each other and forms a prepositional phrase (PP) with one of them:

(19) *Kopi*   *[dàngu   nggula]*PP
      coffee   with   sugar

(20) *Na=riki*   *[dàngu   nyungga]*PP
      3s.NOM=laugh   with   I
      'He laughed and (so did) I'

Dàngu also functions to derive verbal compounds with a comitative reading (see section 5.4).

3.1.4 Pronouns

The paradigms of pronouns and pronominal clitics in Kambera are given in Table 25.3. The pronominal clitics mark person (1/2/3), in/exclusiveness, number (sg/pl), as well as case. They are optionally doubled by NPs which are not case-marked (see also section 3.2). Observe that – except for the third person plural forms – the genitive paradigm consists of prenasalized nominatives and the dative clitics are prenasalized accusatives. But contrary to what a superficial look at the data might suggest, all paradigms are synchronically separate paradigms and not the result of regular phonological assimilation of a nasal morpheme with the nominative or accusative paradigms (for extensive argumentation see Klamer 1998a:214–222).

The demonstrative pronouns are discussed in section 4. There is also a group of emphatic pronouns that consist of the nominative pronominal paradigm preceded by the emphatic morpheme *du*. Some of the forms have onsetless variants.

(21) *du=ku, du=mu, (d)u=na, (d)u=ta, du=ma, di=mi, (d)u=da*

Observe that the direction of attachment of the nominative morpheme in emphatic pronouns is special: instead of *pro*cliticizing like regular nominative clitics, the nominative morphemes are *en*clitics here. Unlike demonstrative pronouns, emphatic pronouns are never used independently, and only function as nominal modifiers, as illustrated in (22). In this example, it functions to emphasize the preceding NP.

(22) *[[[Na   mbola]   nuna]   (d)una]*
      ART   basket   DIST.3s EMPH.3s
      'THAT basket'

The emphatic morpheme *du* also occurs in the clitic cluster attached to the predicate phrase (section 3.2) where it functions to emphasize the predicate.

TABLE 25.3: KAMBERA PRONOUNS AND PRONOMINAL CLITICS

	Pronoun	NOM	GEN	ACC	DAT
1s	nyungga	ku=	=nggu	=ka	=ngga
2s	nyumu	(m)u=	=mu	=kau	=nggau
3s	nyuna	na=	=na	=ya	=nya
1p incl	nyuta	ta=	=nda	=ta	=nda
1p excl	nyuma	ma=	=ma	=kama	=nggama
2p	nyimi	(m)i=	=mi	=ka(m)i	=ngga(m)i
3p	nyuda	da=	=da	=ha	=nja

3.1.5 Classifiers

A classifier is used when quantified items are presented as individual, countable entities. Kambera basically has the four nominal classifiers that are given in (23). Each of them has a plain and a prenasalized form. The classifier *wua* is related to the noun *wua* 'fruit'. Of the remaining forms, none is presently in use as an independent noun.

(23) *wua/mbua*   classifier for spherical objects
       pungu/mbungu   classifier for oblong objects
       wàla/mbàla   classifier for flat, thin objects
       iu/ngiu   classifier for animals

In addition to these four classifiers, we also find the merged forms *hau*, *dàmbu* and *heu*. In (24), the merged classifier forms are printed in bold:

(24)

hau	*kajawa*	**dàmbu**	*kajawa*	*tailu*	*mbua*	*kajawa*
one:CLF	papaya	two:CLF	papaya	three	CLF	papaya
ha-pungu	*pena*	*dua*	*mbungu*	*pena*	*tailu*	*mbungu*	*pena*
ha-CLF	pen	two	CLF	pen	three	CLF	pen
ha-wàla	*kapambal*	*dua*	*mbàla*	*kapambal*	*tailu*	*mbàla*	*kapambal*
ha-CLF	plank	two	CLF	plank	three	CLF	plank
heu	*kamambi*	*dua*	*ngiu*	*kamambi*	*tailu*	*ngiu*	*kamambi*
one:CLF	goat	two	CLF	goat	three	CLF	goat

In the merged forms *hau*, *dàmbu* and *heu*, the quantitative prefix *ha-* 'one' (cognate to Malay *se*, PAn *isa), which also occurs in *ha-pungu* and *ha-wàla*, is merged with the root form of the classifier: *hau* derives from *ha-wua* 'one-CLF (spherical objects)', and *heu* derives from *ha-iu* 'one-CLF (animals)'. Similarly, the merged form *dàmbu* can be analysed as a contraction of *dua mbua* 'two CLF (spherical objects)'.

Observe that there is no classifier for humans. The quantification of human beings differs from that of animals and objects. 'One person' is translated as *ha-atu tau*, and *ha-atu* 'one' is the only context where the root *atu* occurs. Larger quantities are expressed with postnominal relative clauses, as in (25). (Relative clauses are further discussed in section 3.3).

(25) *tau*   **ma**=*dua*
       person   REL=two
       'two people/persons'

3.1.6 Numerals

Numbers used for counting are given in (26).The numeral '1' *diha* is derived from a verb meaning 'to count', as in (27), and is only used in counting.

(26)   1 *diha*, 2 *dua*, 3 *tailu*, 4 *patu*, 5 *lima*, 6 *nomu*,
        7 *pitu*, 8 *walu*, 9 *hiwa*, 10 *ha-kambulu*

(27) *Diha=ha*   *da*   *hapi!*
       count=3p.ACC   ART   cow
       'Count the cows!'

To indicate a quantity of one, either the prefix *ha-* is affixed to the noun, or the classifiers *heu*, *hau*, *ha-pungu*, or *ha-wàla* are used, or the form *ha-atu* (see above). Kambera thus formally distinguishes between counting and quantification. 'Tens' are counted with *ka-mbulu*:

(28)   *kambulu* 'tens':
    10 *ha-kambulu* (*ha-* < PAn **isa*),
    11 *ha-kambulu hau* (**ha-kambulu diha*),
    12 *ha-ka-mbulu dambu* (**ha-ka-mbulu dua*)
    13/14/15/16 etc. *ha-ka-mbulu tailu/patu/lima/nomu* etc.
    20 *dua ka-mbulu*, 30 *tailu ka-mbulu*
    21/22/23/24 etc. *dua ka-mbulu hau/dàmbu/tailu/patu* etc.

'Hundreds' are *ngahu*, a form that is homophonous with *ngahu* 'breath, soul, spirit'. 'Thousands' are *riu*, and millions are *njuta* (from Indonesian *jutah*). Onvlee (1984:443) lists *riu* as 'ten thousand' but in the area under study it was never used as such.

(29)   100 *ha-ngahu*, 200 *dua ngahu*, 300 *tailu ngahu*, etc.
    1000 *ha-riu*, 2000 *dua riu*, 3000 *tailu riu*, etc.
    10.000 *ha-ka-mbulu riu*, 100.000 *ha-ngahu riu*, etc.
    1.000.000 *hau njuta*, 2.000.000 *dua njuta*, etc.
    3.242 *tailu riu dua ngahu patu ka-mbulu dàmbu*

Combinations of numerals and nouns normally occur with a classifier, but high numbers such as 10, 50, 60, 1000, especially when they combine with temporal nouns like *wula(ng)* 'month' or *ndau(ng)* 'year', do not select a classifier: *hakambulu ndaung* 'ten years' (compare **hakambulu mbua ndaung*). With smaller numbers of months or years, classifiers are obligatory: *hau ndaung/wulang* 'one year/month', *patu mbua wula* 'four months'. The explanation for this difference may be that a short period is conceived of as a set of individual, countable months or years, while longer stretches of time are not.

3.2 Basic clause structure

The grammatical relations that are assumed for Kambera are intransitive subject (S), transitive subject (A), and transitive object (O) (Dixon 1994). Kambera has two types of objects: primary (direct) objects (semantic Patients or Themes), and secondary (indirect) objects (semantic Recipients, Benefactives, Goals or Locations). All these grammatical relations can be cross-referenced on the verb. For a structural motivation of the relations, see Klamer (1998a, 1998b).

The preferred word order in a Kambera transitive declarative clause is AVO, while the preferred order for intransitive clauses is VS. This description is typologically of limited value for the following reasons. First, word (= NP) order in Kambera is rather free, so that the orders given above are no more than *preferred* orders, and word order changes have no syntactic function. Second, while A, S and O represent the nominal constituents (NPs) in the sentence, Kambera verbal arguments are normally expressed by pronominal *clitics*, rather than by NPs. If we represent the clitics marking {S, A, O} as {s, a, o} attached to a predicate phrase (PredP, see below), the following orders are attested: a=PredP=o, PredP=a=o, s=PredP, and PredP=s.

The pronominal clitics are the obligatory encodings of (definite) verbal arguments, while the NPs function as optional adjuncts and are coreferent with the pronominal arguments. The NPs function to disambiguate or emphasize the referent, or to make it more salient/contrastive in discourse. This implies that in running texts, where the subject is often the discourse topic and (therefore) known from the context, subject clitics are usually not doubled by an NP. In other words, in natural speech most clauses do not contain an NP expressing the A/S relation. The cross-reference of objects depends on their grammatical definiteness (i.e., whether or not they have a (definite) article): definite objects are cross-referenced on the predicate and optionally doubled, indefinite objects are not cross-referenced but rather expressed by bare (indefinite) NPs.

A Kambera sentence shows a mix of 'configurational' and 'non-configurational' properties. It is build on the basis of a 'nuclear' (or 'minimal') clause which consists of both the Predicate Phrase and a clitic cluster attached to that PredP. In the diagram in (30), the nuclear clause is everything that is dominated by the lowest S node. The diagram shows that the two lowest S's are 'flat', non-configurational structures, while the structure higher up the tree is clearly more configurational.

(30)

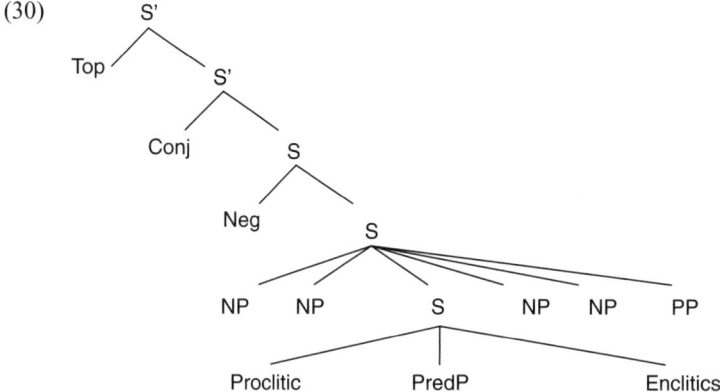

The cluster of enclitics contains up to nine clitics that mark pronominal reference as well as aspect (perfective/imperfective) and mood (emphasis, etc.). In a sentence, the clitic cluster attaches to the right edge of the PredP (30). The nominative proclitic is the only clitic that attaches to the left of the PredP. The internal structure of the clitic cluster is complicated, and is discussed elsewhere (see Klamer 1997, 1998a, 1998b, Klamer and Spencer 2000).

Adjoined to S, we find the optional NPs. Maximally two NPs may precede the nuclear clause, and maximally two may follow it. Postpredicate NPs may be followed by locational or directional PPs, which are non-obligatory constituents, or by other adjuncts. The NPs and PPs are within the scope of the negation ('Neg') and conjunction ('Conj') constituent. Their position is distinct from that of topicalized or left-dislocated constituents: such constituents are clause-external – they can only occur preceding the conjunction and occupy the position referred to as 'Top' in the diagram.

Kambera has two distinct basic clause types: clauses with a verbal predicate, and clauses with a non-verbal predicate. The head of a verbal predicate is a verb, the head of a non-verbal predicate is either nominal or prepositional, as illustrated in 3.2.2.

3.2.1 Verbal predicates

In a declarative, transitive clause the A is canonically nominative, and the O accusative (primary object) or dative (secondary object). Example (31) illustrates the marking of A and (primary) O, with a nominative proclitic and an accusative enclitic, respectively.

(31) *(Na tau   wútu)   **na**=palu=**ka**   (nyungga)*
      ART person   be.fat   3s.NOM=hit=1s.ACC   I
      'The big man hit me.'

The sentences in (32) illustrate how objects are marked. In case of a ditransitive verb, the secondary object is always cross-referenced (32a). In addition, the primary object (Patient, Theme) may be cross-referenced if it is definite. In this case, it follows the clitic marking the secondary object and must be dative as well (32b, see also section 5.2).

(32) a. *I   Ama   na=kei=**nja**   ri*
          ART   father   3s.NOM=buy.for=3p.DAT   vegetable
          'Father buys them vegetables.' (indefinite Patient)

      b. *(I   Ama)   na=kei=**ngga**=**nya***
          ART   father   3s.NOM=buy.for=1s.DAT=3s.DAT
          'Father buys it for me.' (definite Patient)

The subject of an intransitive verb is also canonically nominative.

(33) *Na   ài   **na**=tambuta   dàngu   amung*
      ART   wood   3s.NOM=drop.out   with   root
      'That tree is uprooted.'

Another very common strategy is to mark the subject of a verbal predicate with a genitive clitic. These clauses will be referred to as 'nominal clauses'.

(34) *Palu=**nggu**=nya*
      hit=1s.GEN=3s.DAT
      'I hit him.'

(35) *Mbàda   laku=**na**=ka*
      already   go=3s.GEN=PFV
      'He's already gone.'

Nominal clauses have the external syntax of possessed NPs: they can be specified for definiteness, and if they are definite, they can be cross-referenced as an argument of the main verb. They can also be clefted and compared. Though syntactically independent, nominal clauses have a dependent status in discourse – they express a circumstance of the main clause, with recent perfective aspect. This function is comparable to the English gerund in *Running away, he shouted 'don't shoot!'*. Note however that, in contrast to English, Kambera nominal clauses contain an overt subject (genitive), and are syntactically independent (for further discussion cf. Klamer 1998a:96–105).

3.2.2 Non-verbal predicates

Clauses with non-verbal predicates express proper inclusion, equation, attribution, and location. Two illustrations are (36) and (37). Kambera has no copular verb.

(36) *[Tau   hàmu]=ya*
      person   be.good=3s.ACC
      'He's a good person.'

(37) *[Mbapa=nggu   nyungga]=ya*
      husband=1s.GEN   I=3s.ACC
      'He's my husband.'

Note that the clitic that encodes the S is accusative. This is the common way to express the argument of a non-verbal predicate. In this respect, non-verbal clauses are fundamentally distinct from verbal ones: in verbal clauses, the marking of S is generally nominative or genitive (or continuative aspect, cf. below).

A non-verbal predicate can be a nominal phrase, with a noun as its head (38)–(39), including deictic nouns (40), and nominal question words (41). It may also be a prepositional phrase (42). In all these instances, the S is marked accusative.

(38) *[Tau   mini]*_{NP}*=ya*
      person   male=3s.ACC
      'It's a man.'

(39) *[Potu=na   [na   apu=nggu   la   Humba]]*_{NP}*=ya*
      photo=3s.GEN   ART   granny=1s.GEN   LOC   Sumba=3s.ACC
      'It's a picture of my Sumbanese granny.'

(40) *Nú=ya   nú*
      DIST=3s.ACC   DIST
      'Thus it is.'

(41) *Ka   nggi=kau?*
      CNJ   where=2s.ACC
      'Where are you?'

(42) *[Lai   nú]*_{PP}*=ya*
      LOC   DIST=3s.ACC
      'He/she/it (is) there.'

Though accusative S's mainly occur in non-verbal predicate contexts, we also find them in a limited set of contexts with verbal predicates. This is discussed in the next section.

3.2.3 More on the marking of S

So far we have seen that the standard marking of the S of verbal predicates is either nominative or genitive, while the S of non-verbal predicates is standardly marked accusative. However, accusative Ss also appear with verbal predicates in a limited set of grammatical contexts. In this section we discuss them briefly.

The accusative S appears with verbs when the predicate is emphasized, and S is subsequently 'backgrounded'. Typically, this is the case in imperatives. In imperatives, emphasis is on the activity to be carried out, rather than on the addressee. It is thus not surprising that S's in imperative clauses are marked with an accusative:

(43) *Katuda=**kau**   nàhu!*
      sleep=2s.ACC   now
      'Go to sleep now!'

In transitive imperatives, the accusative is used to mark the O rather than the A, the addressee:

(44) *Kinju=**ha**!*
      examine=3p.ACC
      'Examine them!'

Thus, in imperatives, the morphological marking of S follows an absolutive-ergative pattern – it patterns with O rather than A.

Another context where we find accusative S is when predicates are emphasized or 'foregrounded' by repetition and left-dislocation of the verb, as in (45).

(45)   *Tembang,   nda   tembang=a=ya=pa*   *[i   Windi]*
       be.stupid   NEG   be.stupid=MOD=3s.ACC=IPF   ART   Windi
       '(As for) being stupid, Windi is no longer stupid.'

Third, in clauses where the verb is modified for (excessive) degree, as in (46), we also find an accusative S. Obviously; the predicate in such clauses also carries an additional degree of emphasis:

(46)   *Dira   mayila   ai lulu=**kama***
       extremely   be.needy   very=1pe.ACC
       'We are so very, very poor.'

And finally, an S with a generic or impersonal referent, as in (47), is also marked accusatively. In such clauses, the emphasis is again on the predicate, not on the argument, which remains underspecified:

(47)   *Jàka   nda   nyumu,   ti=**ya**=ka   làti*
       CNJ   NEG   you   die=3s.ACC=PFV   in.fact
       'Without you, one would die/have died.'

In all these grammatical contexts the accusative marking of S is obligatory, and their common denominator is that they emphasize the predicate more than the argument.

In addition to these markings where S is obligatorily accusative, there are also contexts where the choice for an accusative S is optional, and determined pragmatically.

(48)   a.   *Hí=ma=a=**ya**=ka*   *i   Umbu   Mada   una*
            cry=EMPH=MOD=3s.ACC=PFV   ART   Sir   Mada   EMPH.3s
            'Sir Mada just cried and cried.' (i.e. could do nothing else)

       b.   *Hí=ma=a=**nanya**=ka*   *i   Umbu Mada   una*
            cry=EMPH=MOD=3s.CONT=PFV   ART   Sir Mada   EMPH.3s
            'Sir Mada was crying.' (but could have chosen not to)

In (48a,b) the contrast between the accusative clitic=*ya* and the marker=*nanya* third singular continuative aspect' (cf. below) reflects a semantic distinction: an accusative S is *less active* than the canonical meaning of the verb would lead us to expect. The argument of an intransitive verb can thus be presented as a less active participant in the situation or activity expressed by the verb by marking it accusative.

To make the picture complete, we should briefly mention that there are yet two more ways to morphologically encode S. The first is illustrated in (48b), where the S is expressed by a combination of a genitive and dative morpheme. The genitive clitic marks the person and number features of S, while the second, dative clitic is always third person singular, regardless of the actual person and number of the S. Though its form is identical to the '3s.DAT' clitic, it is referentially empty, and therefore not glossed as such. A clitic cluster with a combination of genitive and dative clitics marking one referent, the S, has special aspectual properties: the situation expressed by the intransitive verb continues or endures, i.e. marks 'continuative aspect' (glossed as 'CONT'). (Klamer 2000b presents a synchronic and diachronic analysis of this construction.)

Finally, S can also be marked by a combination of a nominative and an accusative clitic, as in (49). This marking of S is used to express certainty or obligation, is normally restricted to poetic and religious register, and is considered slightly archaic.

(49) *Jàka   nda   nyumu,   **da**=meti=**ha**=ka*   *làti*
      if   NEG   you   3p.NOM=die=3s.ACC=PFV   in.fact
      'Without you, they would die/have died for sure.'

In sum, the marking of S in Kambera combines information from morphology, syntax, semantics and pragmatics. In addition, it shows a mix of nominative-accusative and absolutive-ergative properties.

3.2.4 Negation

Kambera has various negative markers. The general negation is *ndia* 'no' (50), and predicate negators are *nda* 'negative' or *ndedi* 'not yet', (50)–(51).

(50) **Ndia,   nda**   *ku=puli=ya*
      no   NEG   1s.NOM=let.go=3s.ACC
      'No, I won't let it go.'

(51) **Ndedi**   *na=pí=a=nya*   *Nipong   ma=tobu=nja*
      NEG.IPF   3s.NOM=know=MOD=3s.DAT   Japan   REL=slaughter=3p.DAT
      'The Japanese didn't know yet (who) slaughtered them.'

To emphasize the negation, an emphatic second negator *ndoku* can be used:

(52) **Nda**   *na=pí=a=nya*   **ndoku**   *Nipong   ma=tobu=nja*
      NEG   3s.NOM=know=MOD=3s.DAT   NEG.EMPH   Japan   REL=slaughter=3p.DAT
      'The Japanese didn't know [at all] (who) slaughtered them.'

The negation of nominal predicates is identical to that of verbal predicates, as illustrated in (53).

(53) *Nina*   **nda**   *tustel=a=ya,*   *senteru=ya*
      PRX.3s   NEG   camera=MOD=3s.ACC   torch=3s.ACC
      'That's not a camera, it's a torch.'

The irrealis negation *àmbu* is used to express future negation, as illustrated in (54), and negation in imperatives, as in (55).

(54) *Bita=nja*   *da   mata=na*
      cover=3p.DAT   ART   eye=3s.GEN

      *ka   **àmbu**   peku   ita=na=nja*   *da   ana=na*
      CNJ   NEG.IRR   be.able   see=3s.GEN=3p.DAT   ART   child=3s.GEN
      'Cover her eyes so she won't be able to see her children.'

(55) **Àmbu**   *katuda=kau   nàhu!*
      NEG.IRR   sleep=2s.ACC   now
      'Don't go to sleep now!'

3.2.5 Existentials

The deictic verb *ni(ngu)* 'be (here)' (see also section 4) expresses existence, location and possession (section 4). (56) illustrates existence:

(56) *Ningu*   *uma*   *lai*   *nú*
      PRX.APP   house   LOC   DIST
      'There is a house over there.'/ 'There are houses over there.'

The existential or locational argument of *ni(ngu)* is cross-referenced on the verb when it is definite. This is done with a dative clitic, as illustrated in (57):

(57) *Ni=nya*   *na*   *tau*   *na*   *tamu=na*   *Landu   Niki*
      PRX.APP=3s.DAT   ART   person   ART   name=3s.GEN   Landu   Niki
      'There is/was this person named Landu Niki.'

Clauses of this type have a single argument (here an existential argument). This argument can only be marked with the dative, i.e. it can only surface as an object, not as a subject. Note also that the cross-referencing dative clitic causes the final syllable of the verb (*ngu*) to disappear. Location is expressed in the same way as existence:

(58) *Ni=nya*   *la*   *uma*
      PRX.APP=3s.DAT   LOC   house
      'He's at home.'

A construction with *ningu* can also express possession. In such a context, the genitive enclitic marks the possessor. The possessee cannot be cross-referenced on the verb, compare (59a,b):

(59) a.   *Ningu*   *uma=nggu*
           PRX.APP   house=1s.GEN
           'I have a house.'

      b.   **Ni=nya*   *na*   *uma=nggu*
           PRX.APP=3s.DAT   ART   house=1s.GEN
           'I have a house.'

Another way to express identity and existence is by using a cleft-construction with the the clause-external marker *jia*. In such constructions, the existential argument is encoded as an accusative clitic attached to *jia*, as in (60) and (61).

(60) *Jia=ya*   *na*   *mbapa=nggu*
      EXIST=3s.ACC   ART   husband=1s.GEN
      'It's my husband.'

(61) *Na   Umbu-na*   *i*   *Ranji,*   *hi*   *jia=ha*   *da*   *bidi   mini,...*
      ART   lord-3s.GEN   ART   Ranji   CONJ   EXIST=3p.ACC   ART   new   male
      'The master of Ranji, and there were also some young men,...'

The exact nature of the marker *jia* is unclear. Onvlee (1984:115) assumes that it developed out of a third person pronoun and translates it as a demonstrative pronoun or article. In my data, it only appears in the existential cleft construction.

3.3 Noun phrase structure

Kambera NPs are not marked for case. There are three articles, *na* 'definite singular', *da* 'definite plural', and *i* 'proper name'. The absence of an article marks an NP as indefinite. Articles, numerals and classifiers precede the head noun, while modifiers and possessors follow it. The head of an NP may be a proper or common noun, a personal pronoun, or a demonstrative pronoun.

Nouns can be modified by nouns and verbs (cf. section 3.1.1), and, of course, by relative clauses. NPs consisting of a noun and a (N/V) modifier are structurally identical to nominal compounds. Both constructs have the same stress pattern, both are head-initial, and neither of them has special morphology. The decision whether nominal constituents like the following are compounds or NPs can only be based on their semantics: a nominal phrase which has developed a meaning that is not a sum total of its parts, is considered a compound. On this analysis, (62a–b) are clearly compounds, but the forms (62c–d) show that the distinction between a phrase or a compound is not always clear-cut.

(62) a. *tàda*   *ngaru*   b. *tàda*   *ài*
          skin/bark   mouth 'lip'   skin/bark   wood   'medicine'

      c. *tau*   *mini*   d. *bidi mini*
          person   male 'man'   new male   'young man'

Possession is expressed by genitive enclitics marking the possessor on the possessee NP, as illustrated in (63a,b). The genitive enclitic is obligatory, the possessor NP may be absent. (63c) shows that the genitive clitic attaches to a syntactic phrase (the possessee NP) rather than a word.

(63) a. *Na   uma=nggu (nyungga)*
          ART house=1s.GEN
          'My house.'

      b. *Na   uma=na   na   ama=nggu*
          ART house=3s.GEN ART   father=1s.GEN
          'My father's house.'

      c. *Na   uma   bidi=nggu*
          ART house new=1s.GEN
          'My new house.'

Possessive expressions can be indefinite: by omitting the article *na* in (63c), the phrase *uma bidi=nggu* becomes indefinite, 'a new house of mine'.

Kambera relativizations are always restrictive, compare (64a,b), and may be headed or headless, as in (64c,d). Relative clauses have the same distributional properties as ordinary nouns, and they may be marked for definiteness with an article, as in (64c). A definite relative clause agrees in number with its head by using either a singular or a plural article (compare (65) and (66)).

(64) a. *pau   rara*
          mango   be.red
          'A ripe mango.'

      b. *pau   ma=rara*
          mango   REL=be.red
          'A ripe (rather than unripe) mango.'

      c. *na   pau   na   ma=rara*
          ART   mango   ART   REL=be.red
          'The mango that is ripe.'

      d. *ningu   ma=rara*
          PRX.APP REL=be.red
          'There are ripe ones.'

Kambera has two relativization strategies: one for 'subjects' (S/A) and possessors, and one for objects (direct and indirect). Subject and possessor head nouns are relativized by a clause with the marker *ma=*, objects are relativized with a clause marked with *pa=*. This is illustrated for an A subject in (65).

(65)   *Na=meti=ka*
       3s.NOM=die=PFV
       *[na   tau   na   **ma=**piti=ya   na   kabela=nggu]*
       ART person   ART   REL=take=3s.ACC   ART   sword=1s.GEN
       '[The person that took my sword] (he has) died already.'

An S subject is relativized in (66):

(66)   *Da=meti=ka*   *[da   tau   da   **ma=**hidu]*
       3s.NOM=die=PFV   ART   person   ART   REL=be.ill
       '[The people who were sick] (have) died.'

Possessor head nouns are also relativised by a clause with *ma=*:

(67)   *Nyuna   na   ma=ràbih   karàha   kalai=na*
       he   ART   REL=trickle   side   left=3s.GEN
       'He whose left side trickles.' (= lets water through)

Object relativizations (direct and indirect) are illustrated in (68) and (69). Note that the A, if overtly expressed, has to be expressed by a genitive clitic:

(68)   *Na   kabela   na   **pa=**piti=na   na   tau   nuna,   na=ruhak*
       ART SWORD   ART   REL=take=3s.GEN   ART   person   DIST.3s   3s.NOM=be.broken
       '[The sword that was taken by that man] (it) is broken.'

(69)   *Na   tau   na   pa=ngàndi=nggu   nggula*
       ART person   ART   REL=take=1s.GEN   sugar
       'The person whom I brought (some) sugar.'

Relative structures are widely used, not only as nominal modifiers but also as (deverbal) nouns (see section 5.3) and in questions. In questions, the interrogative pronoun is followed by a subject or object relative clause:

(70)   *Nggamu   na   ma=ita=nggau?*
       who   ART   REL=see=2s.DAT
       'Who saw you?'

(71)   *Nggamu   na   pa-ita-mu?*
       Who   ART   REL=see=2s.GEN
       'Who did you see?'

Apart from the relative clause markers, there is very little nominal morphology in Kambera. There is no other productive nominal derivation.

4 DEICTICS AND DIRECTIONALS

The four major deictic elements in Kambera are *ni* 'at/near speaker (PRX)', *na* 'at hearer (MID)', *nu* 'remote from both speaker and hearer (DIST)' and *nai* 'near speaker (further away than *ni*)'. Demonstrative pronouns consist of one of these deictics plus a third person marker: singular *na* or plural *da*. Demonstrative pronouns can function as independent NPs, as in (72), and as nominal modifiers, as in (73).

(72) *Nuna   atau   nina?*
      DIST.3s   or   PRX.3s
      'That one or this one?'

(73) *Ngandi=ya   na   mbola   nuna*
      take=3s.ACC   ART   basket   DIST.3s
      'Take that basket.'

In these formations, the vowel of the deictics is short. But the basic deictic elements can also appear as unbound morphemes, i.e. independent words. As such they must meet the minimal word requirement that roots should be bimoraic (section 2.1), hence their vowel is lengthened, as in the following examples which illustrate spatial (74a–b), (75b), temporal (75a–b), and discourse deictic (76a–b) uses.

(74) a. *Nina   ná*   b. *Lai   ní*
          PRX.3s   mid   LOC   PRX
          'This one (near you)'   'Over here'

(75) a. *La   njam   ní*   b. *Nú   nú*
          LOC   hour   PRX   DIST   DIST
          'At this moment'   'Then (and) there'

(76) a. *Ndia   ná!*   b. *Nú=du=ya=ka*
          No   MID   DIST=EMPH=3s.ACC=PFV
          'No!' (not like that)   'Yes indeed' (lit.: 'Thus it is')

As independent words they mostly function as nominal modifiers, as in (74a), (75a). But, as (76b) shows, they can be used as predicates too (section 3.2.2). They can be governed by prepositions, as illustrated in (74b).

In order to function as a verb, the deictic morphemes must be derived with the verbalizing suffix *-ng* (section 5.2), plus a paragogic vowel *u*. Deictic verbs include *ni-ng(u)* 'be (at speaker), exist' and *na-ng(u)* 'come towards you'. Unlike *ni* and *na*, the deictics *nu* and *nai* cannot form the base of derived deictic verbs. Deictic verbs are always intransitive (see section 3.2.5).

5 MAJOR VERBAL ALTERNATIONS

The two most pervasive derivational processes are prefixation with *pa-* and suffixation with *-ng*. *Pa-* derives verbs with, among other things, a causative interpretation (section 5.1), while *-ng* derives verbs that are mostly applicative (section 5.2). The other three productive affixes are *ta-*, *ma-*, and *ka-k* (section 5.3). Verbal compounding is another productive morphological derivation (section 5.4).

5.1 Prefix *pa-*: causative and related interpretations

The prefix *pa-* derives verbs from nominal or verbal bases. The base may be a root or a morphologically complex form. When attached to a verbal base, the interpretation of the derived verb is causative, manipulative ('make X do something'), directive ('let X do something'), intensive, habitual, or reciprocal.

The majority of causatives are derived from stative intransitive verbs, whose base argument becomes the object of the derived verb:

(77)   *Da=rara*   *hàmu*   *da*   *pàu*
      3p.NOM=be.red   be.good   ART   mango
      'The mangoes are nice and ripe.'

(78)   *Pa-rara=ya*   *na*   *pàu*
      CAU-be.red=3s.ACC   ART   mango
      'Let the mango ripen.'

Other examples include: *ànga* 'be foolish/useless' > *pa-ànga* 'confuse, cheat X', *ka-tuda* 'sleep' > *pa-ka-tuda*, 'put to sleep', *ka-baba* 'be brief/short' > *pa-ka-baba* 'shorten X'. There are also causatives of active intransitive bases: *laku* 'go' > *pa-laku* 'let X go, carry out X', *hadang* 'stand up' > *pa-hadang* 'wake up X, make X stand up'.

Denominal verbs with *pa-* are also very frequent. They express concepts like possession ('have N'), (ascribed) identity ('be N', 'call someone N', 'treat someone as N'), location ('be at/in N'), instrument ('use as N') etc. Examples are *ana* 'child' > *pa-ana* 'have children', *ihi* 'content'> *pa-ihi* '(cause to) have content', *lunggi* 'hair' > *pa-lunggi* '(cause to) have hair/ be hairy', *aya* 'older sibling' > *pa-aya* 'call X *aya*', *tau* 'person' > *pa-tau* 'honour X; consider X human'. As the examples show, the derived verbs may be either transitive (causative) or intransitive. That is, prefixation of *pa-* to nouns increases the valency of the base with one or two arguments, and often both options are allowed in the same derivation, cf. *pa-ihi* and *pa-lunggi*.

While there are not many of them, *pa-*forms with transitive verbal bases do exist. Sentence (79) contains the transitive root verb *rongu* 'hear X', (80) illustrates the derived form.

(79)   *Na*   *tau*   *na*   *ma=kawanga*   *nda na=rongu=a*
      ART   person   ART   REL=be.deaf   NEG 3s.NOM=hear=MOD
      'The deaf don't hear.'

(80)   *Na tau*   *na*   *ma=kawanga*   *na=pa-rongu=ya*
      ART person   ART   REL=be.deaf   3s.NOM=CAU-hear=3s.ACC
      'He heals the deaf.'

Bases from minor categories include the locational nouns *dita* 'up' > *pa-dita* 'hoist/lift up X' and *wawa* 'down' > *pa-wawa* 'humiliate X/look down on X', the numeral *dua* 'two' > *pa-dua* 'divide X (in two or more portions)', the existential marker *jia* > *pa-jia* 'agree with X, profess faith', and the negation *ndia* 'no'> *pa-ndia* 'deny X'

Note that not all derivations with *pa-* are causative. In other words, the semantic change caused by prefixing *pa-* does not always result in a valency change: some derivations of intransitive and transitive verbs only change their reading into more intensive, habitual or reciprocal, while retaining their original valency:

(81)   *torung*   'endure, not give up'   > *pa-torung*   X' 'persevere, stand up to X'
      palu   'hit X'   > *pa-palu*   'hit X (habitually)'
      tabi   'greet X'   > *pa-tabi*   'greet (each other)'

(82)   *Na=tila=ya*   *na*   *tau*
      3s.NOM=kick=3s.ACC   ART   person
      'He kicked the person/people.'

(83)   *Rimang,   na=pa-tila   na   njara*
       be.careful   3s.NOM=pa-kick   ART   horse
       'Be careful, the horse kicks.' (i.e. it's his character)

(84)   *Da=pa-tila   da   njara*
       3p.NOM=pa-kick   ART   horse
       'The horses kick (each other).'

5.2 Suffix -*ng*: applicative and aspectual interpretation

The suffix -*ng* has many different functions. Its major function is to derive verbs. When
-*ng* is suffixed to verbal or nominal bases, the result is an applicative verb, with an additional non-Agent argument. But this suffix is not simply an applicative morpheme: when
it is suffixed to deictic elements, quantifiers and locational nouns it has a general
verbalising function.

Formally, the suffix -*ng* has two different manifestations. It is simply -*ng* when no
pronominal clitics are added (which means that the added O – if there is one – is indefinite
or implicit), cf. *wua-ng* in (85a).

(85)   a.   *Jàka   ngga-nggamu=bia,   nda   na=wua-**ng**=a*
            if   RDP-who=MOD   NEG   3s.NOM=give-APP=MOD
            'He doesn't give it to just anyone.'

       b.   *Na=wua=ngga   na   njara*
            3s.NOM=give:APP=1s.DAT   ART   horse
            'He gives me the horse.'

However, in actual discourse, the majority of applicative verbs have at least one cliticized
object, as in (85b), usually the added (applicative) object. This object is marked with the
dative clitic (Table 25.3). In such cases, the final -*ng* disappears. We could say that the
formative -*ng* and the dative clitic are in complementary distribution. Arguments why
the disappearance of -*ng* is not a phonologically conditioned process are presented in
Klamer (1998a:197–234).

When the base is a transitive verb, suffixing with -*ng* increases the valency of the verb
by one, adding a Goal/Recipient/Benefactive/Location argument: *bunggah(u)* 'open X' >
bunggahung 'open (X) for Y'; *tú* 'put X' > *tú-ng* 'put (X) in Y' The additional argument
is implied when no object cross-referencing occurs on the verb, as in (86a). Here the
argument is also expressed as part of a locative PP, but this constituent is optional. The
sentences (86b, c) show how the verb's objects are cross-referenced: in (86b) the (one)
object (Patient/Theme) of the verb is cross-referenced on the verb with the accusative
clitic =*ya*. In (86c) the verb is applicative, and its secondary object (Goal/Recipient etc.)
is marked with the dative clitic =*nya*. The shape of the clitic (accusative vs. dative) is
thus the clue to the valency of the verb (monotransitive vs. ditransitive).

(86)   a.   *Da=ngàndi-ng   uhu   (lai   Ama)*
            3p.NOM=take-APP   rice   LOC   father
            'They bring rice (to father).'

       b.   *Da=ngàndi=ya   na   uhu*
            3p.NOM=take=3s.ACC   ART   rice
            'They take/bring the rice.'

    c. *Da=ngàndi=nya*   *na*   *uhu* *i*   *Ama*
       3p.NOM=take:APP=3s.DAT   ART rice ART father
       'They bring father the rice.'

When the base verb is an intransitive verb, suffixing with -*ng* also adds a Goal/Recipient/Benefactive/Source/Location argument: *hei* 'climb' > *hei-ng* 'climb X', *riki* 'laugh' > *riki-ng* 'laugh at/about X', *katuda* 'sleep' > *katuda-ng* 'sleep on X', *luhu* 'go out, exit' > *luhu-ng* 'leave X'. There is a semantic difference between a locative adjunct and the argument added by applicative derivation. The latter is usually more affected. In (87) the location/source is expressed as an adjunct PP, the verb *luhu* is intransitive, and *luhu weling la X* translates as 'come out of X'. In (87) the location/source is expressed as an argument of the derived applicative verb *luhu-ng* 'leave X', and is cross-referenced with =*nya*.

(87) *Na=luhu=ka*   *weling*   *la*   *omang*
      3s.NOM=exit=PFV move.from LOC forest
      'He came out of the forest.'

(88) *Na=luhu=nya=ka*   *na*   *omang*
      3s.NOM=exit:APP=3s.DAT=PFV ART forest
      'He had left the forest.'

The suffix -*ng* also derives denominal verbs. In that case it adds a Theme/Patient/Location argument. The nouns that can be the base for this suffix mainly refer to family relations (*ana* 'child' > *ana-ng* 'be child of X'), locations (*tana* 'land' > *tana-ng* 'have/possess land X'), or instruments (*kataka* 'axe' > *kataka-ng* 'have/use X as an axe'). Derivations often have an 'open semantics', with various possible interpretations:

(89) *Na=tilu-ng*   *watu*
      3s.NOM=egg-APP stone
      'She lays pebbles as (if they were) eggs'

(90) *Na=tilu=nya=ka*   *na*   *watu*
      3s.NOM=egg:APP=3s.DAT=PFV ART stone
      'She laid the stone as if it were an egg' or 'She laid eggs on the rock'

The suffix -*ng* also has a more general verbalising function. As already discussed in section 4, it attaches to deictic elements. It also attaches to quantifiers: *hakudu* 'a little bit' > *hakudu-ng* 'be a small amount', and to locational nouns such as *wawa* 'down' > *wawa-ng* 'sit on/occupy lower part of X', *papa* 'yonder' > *papa-ng* 'to live yonder'. The derived verb is not obligatorily transitive, cf. *hakudu-ng* and *papa-ng*, which are intransitive. Thus, the semantic change induced by suffixing -*ng* often implies an increase in valency, but not necessarily so.

It should be noted that, apart from its derivational function, the suffix -*ng* has a secondary function as inflectional suffix marking non-delimited, durative aspect: *nyaba* 'swallow X' > *nyaba-ng* 'continue swallow X, swallow X again and again', *tàka* 'arrive' > *tàka-ng* 'to be arriving, to be approaching'. In this case, -*ng* does not change the valency of the base verb: (91a–b) show that *tàka* and *tàka-ng* are both intransitive, with the goal argument part of an adjunct PP.

(91) a. *Mareni* *tàka=da*   *la*   *uma*
        near   arrive=3p.GEN LOC house
        'They were almost at home.'

b. *Mareni tàka-ng=da   la   uma*
near   arrive-DUR=3p.GEN   LOC   house
'They were almost approaching home.'

Despite the different functions of *-ng*, I assume that there is only one, polysemous, suffix *-ng*, rather than two homophonous ones. A possible explanation of the polysemy of *-ng* is given in Klamer (1998a:222–227).

5.3 Other productive verbal derivations

The prefix *ta-* derives non-intentional, accidental, sudden or unexpected intransitive achievement verbs from transitive or intransitive verbal forms: *binu* 'peel X' > *ta-binu* 'be (unexpectedly, suddenly, etc.) peeled', *bunggah* 'open X' > *ta-bunggah* 'be (unexpectedly, etc.) open(ed)', *mbutuh* 'slip off' > *ta-mbutuh* 'slip off unexpectedly, etc.)'. The subject of *ta-* derivations is an undergoer, and there is also no implied agent: compare *ta-binu* with *pa-binu* 'be peeled (by someone)', and *ta-bunggah* with *pa-bunggah* 'be opened (by someone). The subject of *ta-* derivations is never an agent: it is always a non-volitional, and (therefore) canonically an inanimate, entity.

The prefix *ma-* as it occurs in verbs (*ma-yila* 'be poor/sad', *ma-ngàdat* 'be afraid', *ma-nandang* 'be beautiful') and nouns (*ma-nila* 'peanut', *ma-ràmba* 'king') is generally unproductive. However, in some forms the Kambera subject relative clause marker *ma-* (section 3.3) acts as a nominalising prefix: *rapu* 'something hidden/unknown' > *ma-rapu* 'spirits of ancestors', *ka-weda* 'be old' > *ma-ka-weda* 'old woman', *rara* '(be) red/ripe' > *ma-rara* 'gold'.

Kambera has one circumfix, *ka-k*. This morpheme is used to derive verbs from ideophonic roots. Kambera ideophones are lexical root forms that directly refer to sounds, motions and sights (Klamer 1998a, 2002b). In order to be used as verbs, ideophonic roots must be either reduplicated, or circumfixed with *ka–k*: *mbùtu* 'thud' (sound) > *ka-mbùtu-k* '(fall) with a thud', *ngidi* 'shiver (of cold) (motion)' > *ka-ngidi-k* 'to shiver of cold', *jila* 'flicker, flash' (sight) > *ka-jila-k* 'to flicker, flash'.

5.4 Serial verbs or verbal compounds

Kambera makes extensive use of serial verbs: combinations of two verbs that jointly constitute a single predicate. Some serial verb constructions contain two more or less homonymic verbs – these are often used in ritual language (Fox 1988, Kapita 1987).

In non-ritual, everyday language, the first verb in a serial construction is the semantic head, while the second functions as the modifier.

Kambera serial verbs are analysed as verbal compounds, and they are structurally analogous to the nominal compounds (section 3.3). Kambera compounds are syntactically left-headed, and prosodically right-headed (the second element has word stress). In verbal compounds, both verbs operate as one unit and cannot be separated by an object. Their shared argument(s) are expressed only once by clitics attached at the edge of the predicate phrase. In this respect, serial verbs contrast with biclausal structures; compare (92) with (93). Negations and adverbial words also occur only once and have scope over both verbs.

(92) *[Na=[palài wàru]ᵥ=ma=a=nja]ₛ*
3s.NOM=run   dispose.of=EMPH=MOD=3p.DAT
'He ran leaving them behind.'

(93)   *[Na=palài=ma=a]*ₛ   *[na=wàru hàla=ma=a=nja]*ₛ
       3s.NOM=run=EMPH=MOD   3s.NOM=dispose.of complete=EMPH=MOD=3p.DAT
       'He just ran (and) he just left them all behind.'

A Kambera serial verb consists of two verbs, transitive or intransitive, in any combination. Two intransitives: *hei puru* 'climb and descend: go up and down', intransitive and transitive: *hei toma* 'go up and reach X: go up towards X', transitive and intransitive: *hema ha-danggit* 'answer X and be out of breath: answer curtly to X', transitive and transitive: *palu pa-meti* 'hit X and kill X: hit dead X'. The resulting combination is transitive, but when it involves two intransitive verbs the combination is also intransitive.

Verbal compounding also functions to add new arguments to the verb. When the second element of the compound is the instrumental verb *wà(ngu)* 'use', an instrumental argument is added. Combining a verb with the preposition *dà(ngu)* 'with' adds a comitative argument. In (94) and (95) the applicative suffixation of *riki* and *pabanjar* is contrasted with both instrumental and comitative compounding.

(94)   *riki*   'laugh'
       riki-ng   'laugh at/about X'
       riki wà (ngu)   'laugh about/because of X'
       riki dà (ngu)   'laugh together with X'

(95)   *pabanjar*   'talk'
       pabanjaru-ng   'talk about X'
       pabanjar wà (ngu) 'talk using (language) X', 'talk with X', 'talk about X'
       pabanjar dà (ngu) 'talk with X'

Note that the final syllable *-ngu* of *wàngu* and *dàngu* only surfaces when the object is indefinite or implied; it is lost when the (definite) object clitic attaches to the verbal compound. Compare the indefinite (implied) object in (96a) with the definite one in (96b):

(96)   a.   *[Riki   dàngu]*ᵥ
            Laugh   with
            'Laugh with someone.'

       b.   *Na=[riki dà]*ᵥ*=ngga*   *nyungga*
            3s.NOM=laugh with=1s.DAT   I
            'He laughed with me.'

When the base verb is transitive, like *banjal* in (97), the comitative argument is 'promoted' to become the object that is crossreferenced on the compound verb and is expressed with a dative enclitic (cf. Klamer 1998a:295–301).

(97)   a.   *Ku=banjal=ya*   *na*   *uhu* *lai*   *Windi*
            1s.NOM=put=3s.ACC   ART   rice   LOC   Windi
            'I store the rice at Windi's.'

       b.   *Ku=banjal   dà=nya*   *i*   *Windi*   *na*   *uhu*
            1s.NOM=put   with=3s.DAT   ART   Windi   ART   rice
            'I put down the rice with Windi.' ('I help Windi to put down the rice.')

Sentences (98) and (99) illustrate the instrumental compound. The added instruments are *Hilu Humba* 'Sumbanese' and the NP translated as 'who owned it':

(98)   *Ba*   *[pabanjar wàngu]=nanya*   *hilu*   *Humba=du=ka*
       CNJ   talk   use   =3s.CONT   language   Sumba=EMPH=PFV
       'Because she was talking (in) Sumbanese.'

(99)   *Da=[pabànjar wà]=nya*   *nggamu=ya na*   *ma=mangu=ya*
       3p.NOM=talk use=3s.DAT   who=3s.ACC ART   REL=own=3s.ACC
       'They talked about who owned it.'

These two example sentences show again that the cliticization of the objects of compound verbs depends on their definiteness: an indefinite O is not marked on the verb, (98), a definite O is, (99).

ACKNOWLEDGEMENTS

I wish to thank the editors of this volume for their valuable suggestions. This chapter was written with a Fellowship of the Royal Netherlands Academy of Arts and Sciences (KNAW).

REFERENCES

Blust, R.A. (1993) 'Central and Central-Eastern Malayo Polynesian', *Oceanic Linguistics* 32:241–293.
De Roo van Alderwerelt, J. (1891) 'Soembaneesch-Hollandsche woordenlijst met een schets eener grammatika', *Tijdschrift voor Indische Taal-, Land- en Volkenkunde* 34:234–282.
Dixon, R.M.W. (1994) *Ergativity*, Cambridge: Cambridge University Press.
Forth, G. (1981) *Rindi: an ethnographic study of traditional domain in Eastern Sumba*, The Hague: Martinus Nijhoff.
——(1985) 'The language of number and numerical ability in Eastern Sumba', *Centre for South-East Asian Studies, Occasional Paper no. 9*. The University of Hull.
Fox, J.J. (ed.) (1988) *To speak in pairs: essays on the ritual languages of Eastern Indonesia*, Cambridge: Cambridge University Press.
Heymering, G. (1846) 'Bijdrage tot de kennis van de taal der Z.W. Eilanden, benevens een proeve van vergelijking derzelve met acht andere inlandsche talen', *Tijdschrift voor Nederlandsch-Indië* 8/3:1–81.
Kapita, Oe. H. (1976) *Sumba di dalam jankauan jaman*, Waingapu: Gereja Kristen Sumba.
——(1977) *Ludu Humba: Pakangutuna*, Waingapu: Gereja Kristen Sumba.
——(1979) *Lii Ndai: Rukuda da Kabihu dangu la Pahunga Lodu (Sejara Suku-suku di Sumba Timur)*, Waingapu: Gereja Kristen Sumba.
——(1982) *Kamus Sumba/Kambera-Indonesia*, Waingapu: Gereja Kristen Sumba.
——(1983) *Tatabahasa Sumba Timur dalam dialek Kambera*, Ende: Arnoldus.
——(1986) *Pamangu ndewa (Perjamuan dewa)*, Ende: Arnoldus.
——(1987) *Lawiti luluku Humba (Pola peribahasa Sumba)*, Ende: Arnoldus.
Klamer, M. (1994) 'Applicatives in Kambera', in P. Ackema and M. Schoorlemmer (eds) *Proceedings of Console 1*, 135–151, The Hague: Holland Academic Graphics.
——(1996) 'Kambera has no passive', in M. Klamer (ed.) *Voice in Austronesian [Nusa 39]*, Jakarta: Universitas Atma Jaya.

——(1997) 'Spelling out clitics in Kambera', *Linguistics* 35:895–927.

——(1998a) *A grammar of Kambera*, Berlin/New York: Mouton de Gruyter.

——(1998b) 'Kambera intransitive argument linking', *Studia Linguistica* 52/2:77–111.

Klamer, M. (2000a) 'How report verbs become quote markers and complementisers', *Lingua* 110:69–98.

——(2000b) 'Continuative aspect and the dative clitic in Kambera', in I. Paul, V. Phillips and L.Travis (eds) *Formal issues in Austronesian Linguistics*, 49–63, Dordrecht: Kluwer Academic Publishers.

——(2001) 'Expressives and iconicity in the lexicon', in F.K.E. Voeltz and Ch. Kilian-Hatz (eds) *Ideophones*, 165–181, Amsterdam: Benjamins.

——(2002a) 'Report constructions in Kambera (Austronesian)', in T. Güldemann and M. von Rucador (eds) *Reported discourse*, 323–340, Amsterdam: Benjamins.

——(2002b) 'Semantically motivated lexical patterns: a study of Dutch and Kambera expressives', *Language* 78/2:258–286.

Klamer, M. and Spencer, A. (2000) 'A Paradigm Function Analysis of Kambera Clitics.' Paper presented at the 9th International Morphology Meeting, Vienna, 25–27 February, 2000.

Kuipers, J.C. (1998) *Language, identity and marginality in Indonesia: the changing nature of ritual speech on the island of Sumba*, Cambridge: Cambridge University Press.

Kambera Hymn Book [*'Ludu Pamalangu'*], (1979) Ende: Percetakan Offset Arnoldus.

Kambera New Testament [*'Na Paràndingu Bidi'*], (1961) Ende: Percetakan Offset Arnoldus.

Onvlee, L. (1925) *Eenige Sumbasche Vertellingen*, Leiden: Brill.

——(1984) *Kamberaas (Oost-Soembaas)–Nederlands Woordenboek*, Dordrecht: Foris.

Pos, W. (1901) 'Sumbaneesche woordenlijst', *Bijdragen tot de Taal-, Land- en Volkenkunde van Nederlandsch-Indië* 58:184–284.

Roos, S. (1872) 'Bijdrage tot de kennis van taal, land en volk op het eiland Sumba', *Verhandelingen van het Bataviaasch Genootschap van Kunsten en Wetenschappen* 36:1–125.

Sneddon, J.N. (1993) 'The drift towards final open syllables in Sulawesi languages', *Oceanic Linguistics* 32:1–44.

Van der Hulst, H. and Klamer, M. (1996) 'The uneven trochee and the structure of Kambera roots', in M. Nespor and N. Smith (eds) *Dam Phonology*, 39–57, The Hague: Holland Academic Graphics.

——(1997) 'The prosodic structure of Kambera roots and words', in C. Odé and W. Stokhof (eds) *Proceedings of the Seventh International Conference on Austronesian Linguistics*, 105–123, Amsterdam: Rodopi.

Van der Velden, A.J.H. (1900) 'Proeve eener spraakleer van de Laoraneesche taal', *Tijdschrift voor Indische Taal-, Land- en Volkenkunde* 42:57–101.

Vermast, A.M. (1895) 'Lijst van Soembaneesche woorden en uitdrukkingen, alphabetisch gerangschikt', *Veeartsenijkundige Bladen voor Nederlandsch-Indië* 9:122–142.

Wielenga, D.K. (1909) *Schets van een Soembaneesche spraakkunst (naar 't dialect van Kambera)*, Batavia: Landsdrukkerij.

——(1913) 'Soembaneesche verhalen in het dialect van Kambera, met vertaling en aan-teekeningen', *Bijdragen tot de Taal-, Land- en Volkenkunde van Nederlandsch Indië* 68:1–287.

——(1917) 'Vergelijkende woordenlijst der verschillende dialecten op het eiland Sumba en eenige Soembaneesche spreekwijzen', *Verhandelingen van het Bataviaasch Genootschap van Kunsten en Wetenschappen* 61:1–96.

Wurm, S. (1994) 'Australasia and the Pacific', in C. Moseley (ed.) *Atlas of the world's languages*, London: Routledge.

CHAPTER TWENTY-SIX

TETUN AND LETI

Aone van Engelenhoven and Catharina Williams-van Klinken

1 INTRODUCTION

1.1 Location and dialects

Tetun and Leti are native to the neighboring islands of Timor and Leti respectively (Wurm and Hattori 1981:map 40). Although traditionally classified as a single language, Tetun (alternatively spelled 'Tetum') has two main varieties, Dili Tetun and Tetun Terik, which are virtually mutually unintelligible. In addition to large differences in vocabulary, there are grammatical differences in such basic areas as subject marking, possessives, aspect, negation, and prefixes. Between them, the two Tetuns have about 300,000 to 400,000 native speakers, with as many again being conversant with Tetun at some level.

Dili Tetun (or 'Tetun Dili', formerly known as 'Tetun Prasa'), is spoken as a first language in Dili, and as a lingua franca throughout most of East Timor. It is a creole with large-scale borrowing from Portuguese.

The second variety, Tetun Terik (a cover term used by Dili Tetun speakers), is spoken in two unconnected areas of Timor. Its East Tetun dialect is spoken around Soibada, in the south of East Timor. The North and South Tetun dialects are spoken in the north and south respectively of a strip crossing central Timor from the north to the south coast. This strip is situated mostly on the western side of the East Timor–West Timor border, in the regency (*kabupaten*) of Belu, but also covers some neighboring portions of East Timor. The description of Tetun in this chapter is based on the conservative South Tetun (or 'Fehan') dialect, as it is spoken in and around the town of Betun in West Timor.

Leti is spoken in five of the seven villages on the island of Leti in Southwest Maluku, off the tip of East Timor. While approximately 4600 speakers live on the island, the majority of Leti speakers live outside the region in migrant communities in Jakarta, Kupang (West Timor), Ambon (Central Maluku), and, up to 1999, in Dili (East Timor).

Leti has little dialect differentiation. The indigenous classification is based on the word for 'cassava' and distinguishes an *anïama*-group (Tutukei, Batumiau and Tutuwaru) and a *nammalai*-group (Tomra and Nuwewang). The latter, together with the Batumiau communalect, feature many loans and calques from Malay. The Tutukei communalect distinguishes two sociolects: a conservative one spoken in the original village on Tutukei cape, on which the description in this chapter is based, and a variant heavily influenced by Tomra, spoken on the beach.

Speakers of both Tetun and Leti use parallelism in literary style, and allow this to be sung. Both have a taboo language associated with fishing, which is differentiated by vocabulary rather than phonology or grammar (van Klinken 1999:8f). Leti also appears to have a secret language (van Engelenhoven 1999:99f), while Tetun has a register used for talking with nobles (Therik 1995:40; van Klinken 1999:7f).

736 THE AUSTRONESIAN LANGUAGES

1.2 Subgrouping

A close genetic relationship between the Austronesian languages of Timor and of Southwest Maluku has long been proposed, based on various criteria. For instance, Brandes (1884) classed Tetun and Leti together on the basis of having a 'reversed genitive construction', in which the possessor noun precedes the possessed noun. Jonker noted shared phonological innovations (1932) as well as two morphological similarities: pronominal subject agreement and derivation by means of consonantal suffixes (1911). Several of these suffixes are retained in Tetun, albeit unproductively; in Leti, however, the suffixes are no longer functional, having become an intrinsic part of the root morpheme.

According to van Engelenhoven (1995b), Leti and all other Austronesian languages of Southwest Maluku (excluding Wetar and West-Damar) form a subgroup, while Tetun and many other Timorese languages make up a separate, closely related, subgroup.

1.3 Language history

In West Timor, the Tetun-speaking areas were relatively isolated until the twentieth century. West Timor has been part of Indonesia since its independence from the Netherlands, and Tetun in that region has used Indonesian (or rather the West Timorese variety of it) as its main source of borrowings. East Timor, in contrast, was a Portuguese colony for over 400 years prior to the Indonesian takeover in 1975, and was subsequently under Indonesian rule until it opted for independence in 1999. This history is reflected in its lingua franca, Dili Tetun, with numerous borrowings from Portuguese (even for such everyday concepts as *agora* 'now', *ajuda* 'help' and *kanta* 'sing'), superimposed by more recent borrowings from Indonesian. The history of Dili Tetun is discussed in some detail by Thomaz (1981) and Hull (1994).

Leti, like other Southwest Malukan languages, has few loans from other languages. This is largely due to its remote location and low economic attractiveness to outsiders (van Engelenhoven 1999). Malay became the lingua franca in Southwest Maluku around the beginning of the twentieth century. According to Southwest Malukan tradition, the previous contact language used in the islands is preserved as a special register in the Austronesian languages of the region.

1.4 Major sources

A sizable amount of literature has been published in Tetun, from the late nineteenth century onwards. Most is religious, with a range of translated liturgies and Bible portions being available. Some publications are bilingual, making Tetun texts accessible to non-Tetun speakers. Those available in English include folktales from the northern dialect (Bartkowiak 1979), and stories from East Timor (Langker 1996; Morris 1984a). The Sydney-based Mary McKillop Institute of East Timorese Studies is currently further promoting the publication of texts, particularly in Dili Tetun, both with and without English translation.

A significant quantity of material has been written about Tetun. Most of these works are dictionaries, some with grammatical sketches. These include sizeable dictionaries in English (Hull 1999; Morris 1984b), Portuguese (das Dores 1907; Mendes and Laranjeira 1935), Dutch (Mathijsen 1906), and Indonesian (Monteiro 1985; Serantes and Doko 1976).

The major grammatical work on Tetun is van Klinken's (1999) grammar of the southern Fehan dialect. Hull and Eccles (2001) and Williams-van Klinken *et al.* (2002) provide descriptions of Dili Tetun. Troeboes *et al.* (1987) present a shorter grammar of the dialect of northern Belu. The most comprehensive Tetun-teaching books are Fernandes (1937) in Portuguese and Hull (1996) and Peace Corps East Timor (2003) in English.

Leti has been the subject of far less literary and linguistic interest than Tetun. The earliest note on Leti is a small list of numerals at the end of Barchewitz's (1730) itinerary. The first fuller attempts to write in Leti occurred during the Christianization campaign of the Dutch Missionary Society (1828–1841). Leading missionaries differed on whether Leti should be used as a vehicle of instruction and public worship. Nevertheless, Luijke (1834) produced a small catechism, which, despite being heavily corrupted by Dutch calques, is clearly an attempt to represent the Batumiau communalect. Around this time, Heijmering (1846) produced a grammatical sketch of Leti. As the main advocate for the use of Leti in sermons, he was also the first to stress the importance of lexical parallelism in discourse. Such parallelism is further discussed in van Engelenhoven (1997). Except for a few prayers (Riedel 1886) and a standard wordlist, the so-called Holle list produced by L.Ch.A. Moorrees in 1895 (Stokhof 1981:19–31), no language material was produced for many decades after the Society's withdrawal from the region in 1841.

Until recently, the most extensive work on Leti was Jonker's posthumously published wordlist and grammatical notes (1932). This was the basis for the first English article on Leti, namely Mills and Grima's (1980) diachronic analysis of metathesis. Van Engelenhoven's (1995a) comprehensive description of Leti phonology and grammar has since become the major source for this language.

Only a few other Austronesian languages in the Timor region have been comprehensively described, including Rotinese (Jonker 1915) and 'Dawan' (or 'Atoni' or 'Uab Meto') (Middelkoop 1950) on West-Timor, and Iliun (Wetar) and Wetan in Southwest Maluku (de Josselin de Jong 1947, 1987).

2 PHONOLOGY

2.1 Segment inventory

Tetun and Leti have similar consonant inventories, shown in Table 26.1. Both are relatively simple.

Tetun has no significant allophonic variation for consonants. In Leti, the alveodental nasal /n/ has a velar nasal allophone [ŋ] before velar plosives, there is a non-phonemic

TABLE 26.1: ORIGINAL CONSONANT INVENTORY (IN IPA)

		Bilabial	Labio dental	Alveo dental	Velar	Glottal
Stop	voiceless	(p)		t	k	<ʔ>
	voiced	<b>		d		
Nasal		m		n		
Fricative	voiceless		<f>	s		<h>
	voiced	(β)				
Lateral				l		
Trill				r		
Glide		<w>				

Note
Consonants in angle brackets are confined to Tetun, while those in round brackets are confined to Leti.

glottal stop before word initial vowels, and [h] is an optional realization of /s/ in the deictics *sai* and *so* (see section 3.6.2). Leti also features some very salient sandhi phenomena, of which the most frequently occurring are the progressive homorganic partial assimilation of the nasal /n/ to [m] before /p/ and to [ŋ] before /k/, the progressive full assimilation of /d/ to [n] (e.g. *kun-ne* 'his horse', from *kuda* 'horse' + ne 'his') and the regressive full assimilation of /n/ to [l] within morphemes (e.g. *vulla* as the metathesized form of *vulan* 'moon').

Both Tetun and Leti have five vowels: /i, e, a, o, u/. Leti distinguishes long and short phonemes for all five vowels. Tetun too has long vowels, but these are analyzed as sequences of two short vowels rather than as separate phonemes. Pretonic short high vowels in Leti have glide allophones preceding mid and low vowels.

In both languages the mid vowel phonemes have high and low variants, respectively [e, o] and [ε, ɔ]. In Tetun the low variants are confined to unstressed (i.e. final or antepenultimate) syllables, and to stressed syllables if the following unstressed syllable also contains /e/ or /o/ (e.g. *bele* [bélε] 'can, able to', *feto* [fétɔ] 'woman'). Otherwise the high allophones are used (e.g. *keta* [kéta] 'don't', *hosi* [hósi] 'from').

In Leti morphemes the mid-vowels are confined to the penultimate syllable of the free form. The low variant is used if the ultimate syllable either contains an /a/ (e.g. *lèra* [léra] 'sun,' *pòka* [pɔ́ka] 'gun') or is an onsetless syllable with the vowel /i/ (e.g. *mmèi* [mːέi] 'table', *lòi* [lɔ́i] 'type of canoe'). Otherwise the high counterpart is used (e.g. *peli* [péli] 'cotton', *toku* [tóku] 'shop', *rou* [róu] 'motive'). However in Leti the high allophones are developing into separate phonemes and in some lexemes occur where the low variants are expected (e.g. /tera/ [téra] 'bamboo spear' instead of the expected *[tέra], and /ioa/ [ʔjóa] 'corral' instead of the expected *[ʔjɔ́a]).

2.2 Orthography

Tetun has always been written in the Latin script, using spelling systems based on Portuguese, Dutch, and Indonesian. A summary of the main differences between these systems is presented in Table 26.2, where alternative representations for the same sound are separated by commas. The orthography in this chapter basically follows Monteiro (1985).

Leti does not have a writing tradition, with its speakers preferring to write in Indonesian. Table 26.3 lists the main differences between the various orthographies that have been used by Dutch missionaries and academics. The orthography in this chapter is largely phonemic, but does indicate glide allophones.

TABLE 26.2: TETUN ORTHOGRAPHIES

Phoneme/Allophone	Portuguese (das Dores 1907)	Portuguese (Fernandes 1937)	Dutch (Mathijsen 1906)	Indonesian (Monteiro 1985)
Long vowel ([aː])	aa, á	á	aa, á	aa
High allophone of /o/	ô	ô	o	o
/u/	u, o (finally)	u	oe	u
/k/	k	k, c	k, kk	k
/s/	s, ss	s, ç, c	s	s
/w/	u	u	w	w
/e'e/	eé	e'e	eë	e'e

TABLE 26.3: LETI ORTHOGRAPHIES

Phoneme/Allophone	Luijke (1834)	Heijmering (1846)	Jonker (1932)	This chapter
Long vowel ([aː])	a	aa	ā	a:
Stressed vowel (/a/)	a	A	a	a
/i/	i, ij	i, I	i	i
/u/	u	oe, OE	u	u
/β/ (labial fricative)	w	w	w	v
/w/ (labial glide)	w	w	~w	ü
/y/ (palatal glide)	j	j	j	ï
Low allophone of /o/	o	o	o	ò
Low allophone of /e/	e	e	e	è

2.3 Syllable and word structure

The syllable structure in both languages is (C)V(C). Lexical words have at least two syllables, but both languages have some function words that are monosyllabic. In the Tutukei dialect of Leti, all such monosyllabic words have a disyllabic allomorph in sentence-initial position (e.g. sentence-medial *po* vs. sentence-initial *apo* 'then').

In both Tetun and Leti, stress falls on the penultimate syllable, with secondary stress on the fourth-last syllable.

Underived lexical morphemes in Tetun have from two to four syllables. As in Leti, most lexical morphemes are disyllabic. Unstressed (hence ultimate and antepenultimate) syllables may be closed, while stressed syllables are always open. The coda of ante-penultimate syllables is always /k/ (e.g. *haklelek* 'speak abuse'). The word-final coda can be any of the consonants /k, t, s, r, n/ (e.g. *inur* 'nose').

Tetun words of two or three syllables may begin with a consonant cluster, of which the first member is always /k/. This extrasyllabic consonant can combine with any consonant except the glottals (e.g. *kfui* 'flute', *ktodan* 'heavy', *klalaras* 'average'). Consonant gem-inates do not occur in Tetun, and consonant clusters other than those beginning in /k/ are found only as a result of omitting vowels in contractions (e.g. *man-tolun* 'bird egg', from *manu-tolun*).

Underived lexical morphemes in Leti have two or three syllables. In citation form and in phrase-final position, they all end on a vowel but many also have consonant-final forms in other environments. There are strong restrictions against having the same phoneme occur both as morpheme-final consonant and as the onset of the ultimate or penultimate syllable of that morpheme (e.g. **sètas*, **tèsas*). In particular, /m/ is the only consonant that occurs within the same morpheme both as the final consonant and as the onset of the penultimate syllable (e.g. *mètam* 'black' (citation form *mètma*)). Only /n/ is found in both the onset and coda slots in the final syllable of a lexical morpheme (e.g. *anin* 'wind' (citation form *anni*)). If the morpheme-final consonant is either /l/ or /r/, then the onset of the final syllable is never /n/, /l/ or /r/. Similarly, if the morpheme-final consonant is a labial, then the onset of the final syllable is never a labial.

Consonant clusters are a salient feature in Leti phonotactics. The possibilities are displayed in Table 26.4. As can be seen from the table, all consonants except the labial fricative occur as geminates, in which case they are confined to morpheme-initial posi-tion. Geminate /d/ is phonetically realized as a voiceless retroflex occlusive geminate, for example *ddalu* [ʈalu] 'bull' vs. *dila* [díla] 'kind of plant'.

TABLE 26.4: CONSONANT CLUSTERS IN UNDERIVED LETI LEXICAL MORPHEMES

C2 *C1*	p	m	v	t	n	s	d	l	r	k
p	pp			pt	pn	ps	pd	pl	pr	pk
m		mm		mt	mn	ms		ml	mr	mk
v				vt	vn	vs		vl	vr	
t	tp	tm		tt	tn			tl	tr	tk
n		nm	nv	nt	nn	ns				
s	sp	sm			sn	ss		sl	sr	sk
d		dm	dv				dd			
l	lp	lm	lv	lt		ls		ll		lk
r		rm	rv	rt	rn	rs			rr	
k	kp	km	kv	kt	kn	ks	kd	kl	kr	kk

Note
Shaded clusters are confined to onsets of the initial syllables of lexical morphemes.

Both Tetun and Leti have initial syllables beginning with a full vowel (e.g. Tetun *ina* 'mother', Leti *ama* 'father').

Tetun allows all sequences of two vowels, except for a high vowel followed by a mid-vowel, or the sequence */ao/. All sequences of vowels are disyllabic, with long vowels being vowel geminates. Since vowel sequences only occur within a metrical foot, they necessarily carry (primary or secondary) stress (e.g. *haree* [haré:] 'see' vs. *hare* [háre] 'rice').

Leti allows all sequences of two vowels, except that it disallows final mid-vowels in lexical morphemes (e.g. Tetun *malae* 'non-native' corresponds to Leti *Malai* 'Timorese'). Morpheme-final vowel sequences are disyllabic. Leti also has initial syllables that are sequences of a high vowel and a stress-bearing non-high vowel; in this case the initial high vowel is realized as a preglottalized glide allophone that functions as onset (e.g. *üèra* [ʔwéra] 'water', *ïaklu* [ʔjáklu] 'play-top'). Such glide allophones may be preceded by a consonant or consonant cluster (e.g. *düòna* 'basil', *kdïeli* 'ring'). Long vowels are confined to the penultimate syllable of free form morphemes and require an onset in the ultimate syllable (e.g. *vu:ra* [βú:ra] 'mountain' vs. *vura* [βúra] 'oil'). In contrast to Tetun, such long vowels head single heavy syllables.

2.4 Apocope and metathesis in Leti

As mentioned above, Leti lexical morphemes all end in a vowel in their citation form and in phrase-final position in most types of phrases. However, four morphonological processes conspire to make some morphemes consonant-final phrase-internally. These processes are internal and external metathesis, apocope, and devocalization of the final vowel; together they are referred to in this chapter as 'A&M' or 'apocope and metathesis'. They permeate the entire Leti language, and occur whenever morphemes which are linked within certain constructions also satisfy particular phonological conditions. The result of these processes is that the left morpheme in a construction of two morphemes is only vowel-final if the following morpheme begins with a consonant cluster or a consonant followed by a glide, or if the left morpheme ends in a sequence of two vowels. Tables 26.5a and 26.5b give examples of all types of A&M.

Internal metathesis occurs when the initial morpheme ends in either VCCV or V:CV, and the following morpheme starts with a single consonant or glide. In internal metathesis, the

TABLE 26.5A: LETI APOCOPE AND DEVOCALIZATION

End of morpheme		Beginning of morpheme		
		#CC 'bowels' *tnïèi*	**#V[+high]** 'skin' *ulti*	**#V[−high]** 'baby' *a:na*
VV#				
'garfish'	srui	srui-tnïèi	sru-ulti	sruĭ-a:na
'civet'	lau	lau-tnïè	la-ulti	laü-a:na
'snake'	nia	nia-tnïèi	ni-ulti	ni-a:na
VCV#				
'goat'	pipi	pipi-tnïèi	pip-ulti	pipĭ-a:na
'dog'	asu	asu-tnïèi	as-ulti	asü-a:na
'cat'	kusa	kusa-tnïèi	kus-ulti	kus-a:na
V:CV#				
'dugong'	ru:ni	ru:ni-tnïèi	ru:n-ulti	ru:nĭ-a:na
'bird'	ma:nu	ma:nu-tnïèi	ma:n-ulti	ma:nü-a:na
'fish'	i:na	i:na-tnïèi	i:n-ulti	i:n-a:na
VCCV#				
'donni snake'	donni	donni-tnïèi	donn-ulti	donnï-a:na
'forest pigeon'	varnu	varnu-tnïèi	varn-ulti	varnü-a:na
'heron'	samra	samra-tnïèi	samr-ulti	samr-a:na

Note
Dark shading indicates apocope; light shading indicates devocalization of final vowel.

TABLE 26.5B: LETI APOCOPE AND METATHESIS

End of morpheme		Beginning of morpheme		
		#GV 'face' *üòa*	**#CV[+high]** 'bone' *ruri*	**#CV[−high]** 'eye' *mata*
VV#				
'garfish'	srui	sru-üòa	sru-ruri	sru~mïata
'civet'	lau	la-üòa	la-ruri	as~müata
'snake'	nia	ni-üòa	ni-ruri	ni-mata
VCV#				
'goat'	pipi	pip-üòa	pip-ruri	pip~mïata
'dog'	asu	as-üòa	as-ruri	as~müata
'cat'	kusa	kus-üòa	kus-ruri	kus-mata
V:CV#				
'dugong'	ru:ni	ruin-üòa	ruin-ruri	ruin-mata
'bird'	ma:nu	maun-üòa	maun-ruri	maun-mata
'fish'	i:na	ian-üòa	ian-ruri	ian-mata
VCCV#				
'donni snake'	donni	donin-üòa	donin-ruri	donin-mata
'forest pigeon'	varnu	varun-üòa	varun-ruri	varun-mata
'heron'	samra	samar-üòa	samar-ruri	samar-mata

Note
Dark shading indicates apocope; light shading indicates internal or external metathesis; '#G' stands for an initial glide.

final CV of a morpheme is inverted to become VC (e.g. *llarna* 'fly' + *mòta* 'be blue/green' results in *llaran-mòta* 'house-fly'), with the long vowel being shortened (e.g. *vu:ra* 'mountain' + *lali* 'sulphur' results in *vuar-lali* 'volcano').

In external metathesis, the final high vowel of the first morpheme is inverted with the initial consonant of the following morpheme, and is realized as a glide allophone (e.g. *asu* 'dog' + *davdavra* 'greedy' results in *asdüavdavra* 'praying mantis (kind of insect)'). This occurs when the initial morpheme ends in V(C)V, and the following morpheme starts with CV, with the vowel being non-high.

In apocope, the final vowel of the initial morpheme is omitted. If there is no metathesis, and the following morpheme does not begin with CC, then final /a/ is always deleted in morpheme concatenations (e.g. *kus-nisa* 'cat's tooth', from *kusa* 'cat' + *nisa* 'tooth'). Final high vowels are deleted if the next syllable has a high vowel nucleus or a glide onset (e.g. *lau* 'civet' + *irnu* 'nose' results in *la-irnu* 'civet's nose').

In devocalization, the final high vowel of the initial morpheme is expressed by a glide allophone. This occurs when the vowel immediately precedes a stressed non-high vowel (e.g. *müania:na* [mwanjá:na] 'Tiny Man (clan)' from *müani* [mwáni] 'man' + *a:na* [ʔá:na] 'child'; *tultulüenu* [tultulwénu] 'sunhat' from *tul-tulu* [tultúlu] (RDP-high) 'hat' + *enu* [ʔénu] 'turtle').

At the phrase level, A&M connects heads and modifiers in a link we label 'adhesion', as in (1). On the clause level it combines verbs and complement arguments in a link we label 'cohesion', as exemplified in (2). Cohesion is complementarily distributed with the indexer clitic that occurs in phrase-final position (see section 3.2).

(1)　　*aslüalavansai*
Leti　asu=lalavan=sai
　　　dog=big=PRX.ATD
　　　'this big dog'

(2)　　*Mèsre*　　　*nvalvïatlua*　　　*serio.*
Leti　Mèsr=e　　　nvali=vatu=la　　seri=o.
　　　teacher=IDX　3s-turn=stone=DIR　side=IND
　　　'The teacher turns a stone aside.'

Leti has a set of pronominal prefixes which are attached to the verb as subject agreement markers, as illustrated in (2). For most verbs, A&M applies just as one would expect on the basis of the phonology of the prefix and of the verb. That is, some verbs occur with A&M affixation, others with full prefixation, as illustrated in Table 26.6. For some other verbs, A&M does not apply even though it would be expected to on phonological grounds (i.e. the requirement for full prefixation is lexically conditioned). For a few lexemes, the use of full pronominal prefixes (i.e. not applying A&M) is a morphological device to create causative verbs (see also section 3.4).

Leti also has a set of pronominal suffixes of the form CV (listed in Table 26.12 in section 3.3.1). These are appended to the vowel-final form of possessed nouns. The A&M rules for these suffixes are somewhat different to the general A&M rules specified above. Nouns ending in /a:CV/ undergo internal metathesis (e.g. *paun-ku* 'my umbrella' from *pa:nu-ku*, and *laar-mu* 'your sirikaya-tree' from *la:ra-mu*). In all other cases the final vowel of the noun is deleted (e.g. *rur-ku* 'my bone' from *ruri* 'bone'). Having deleted the final vowel, nouns ending in VCCV have an /a/ inserted between the two consonants, thus preventing a sequence of three consonants (e.g. *masan-ku* 'my meat' from *masni-ku*). Nouns ending in V:CV similarly require the insertion of /a/ before the consonant, as well

TABLE 26.6: PRONOMINAL PREFIXATION ON LETI VERBS

A&M PREFIXATION

		kernu 'descend'	*suri* 'pour'	*emnu* 'drink'
'1s'	u-	küernu	suri	ü-emnu
'2s'	mu-	mküernu	m-suri	mü-emnu
'3s'	na-	n-kernu	n-suri	n-emnu
'1pi'	ta-	t-kernu	t-suri	t-emnu
'1pe'	ma-	m-kernu	m-suri	m-emnu
'2p'	mi-	mkïernu	m-suri	
'3p'	ra-	r-kernu	r-suri	r-emnu

FULL PREFIXATION

		Phonotactically conditioned	Lexically conditioned		Causatives	
		mmali 'laugh'	*va:ti* 'wait'	*uli* 'praise'	*kernu* 'lower'	
'1s'	u-	u-mmali	u-va:ti	u-uli	u-kernu
'2s'	mu-	mu-mmali	mu-va:ti	mu-uli	mu-kernu
'3s'	na-	na-mmali	na-va:ti	na-uli	na-kernu
'1pi'	ta-	ta-mmali	ta-va:ti	ta-uli	ta-kernu
'1pe'	ma-	ma-mmali	ma-va:ti	ma-uli	ma-kernu
'2p'	mi-	mi-mmali	mi-va:ti	mi-uli	mi-kernu
'3p'	ra-	ra-mmali	ra-va:ti	ra-uli	ra-kernu

as the shortening of the long vowel (thus preventing a closed syllable featuring a long vowel nucleus) (e.g. *nuan-mu* 'your banyan' from *nu:nu-mu*). Nouns ending in VV compensatorily lengthen their remaining (first) vowel (e.g. *vu:-ku* 'my necklace' from *vui-ku*).

Whereas the suffixes for first person singular and for second person singular and plural have fixed vowels, the vowel of third person and first person plural suffixes is determined by the final vowel of the citation form of the noun. In particular, the suffix is *-ne* where the noun ends in /a/ (e.g. *òr-ne* 'his/her bamboo' from *òra-nV*), but otherwise it is a copy of the final vowel (e.g. *rat-ni* 'his/her grave' from *rati-nV*, *motar-nu* 'his/her motor boat' from *motru-nV*).

2.5 Reduplication

Reduplication is a productive morphological process in both Tetun and Leti. Reduplication is either partial, in which case it copies part of the penultimate syllable of the morpheme, or full, in which case it copies the final two syllables. This also holds for trisyllabic morphemes (see below). In neither language is a root-final consonant or the first member of an initial consonant cluster involved in reduplication.

Tetun partial reduplication productively derives abstract, instrument and undergoer nouns from verbs. Where the root ends in a vowel, a *-k* or *-n* suffix is added, with no apparent synchronic basis for the choice between them. As illustrated in Table 26.7, partial reduplication involves the copying of the onset of the penultimate syllable followed by /a/; as vowel-initial verbs are rare, it is unknown how onsetless syllables would be reduplicated. An antepenultimate syllable is deleted except for its coda.

One function of full reduplication in Tetun is to derive adverbs, usually from adjectives. Reduplication of numerals usually indicates that the specified number of items are being

TABLE 26.7: PARTIAL REDUPLICATION IN TETUN

Template	Base	Gloss	Reduplication	Gloss
CVV	hoo	'have'	ha-hoo-k	'possessions'
CVCVC	sukat	'measure'	sa-sukat	'measuring tool'
CCVCVC	krakat	'angry'	k-ra-rakat	'anger'
Trisyllabic	hakees	'talk'	ka-kees	'talking'

TABLE 26.8: FULL REDUPLICATION IN TETUN

Template	Base	Gloss	Reduplication	Gloss
CVV	baa	'go'	ba-baa-(n)	'go for no reason'
VVC	aat	'bad'	a-'aat	'variously bad'
CVCVC	di'ak	'good'	di('a)-di'ak	'well'
CCVCVC	kmetis	'tight'	k-me(ti)-metis	'tightly'
Trisyllabic	haklelek	'abuse'	k-le-lelek	'abuse for no reason'

TABLE 26.9: PARTIAL REDUPLICATION IN LETI

Template	Base	Gloss	Pre-glide shift	Reduplication	Gloss
VV	(see Table 26.10)				
CVV	rèi	'pull'		(n-)rè-rèi	'which he pulls'
CVVC	vail	'pelt'		(n-)va-vail	'which he pelts'
…GVCV	vèïata	'destroy'		(n-)vè-ïa-ïata	'which he destroys'
CVCV	pòka	'shoot'		(m-)pò-pòka	'which he shoots'
CGVCV	tüòna	'ask'	tò-tüòna	(na-)tüò-tòna	'which he asks'
CCVVC	kriat	'be slow'		k-ri-riat	'slow'
$C_1C_1V…$	ppèrat	'be heavy'		pè-ppèrat	'heavy'

Note
The prefixes in brackets are compulsory subject marking prefixes.

considered together. Reduplicated verbs in combination with a preceding *na'i* and an (apparently optional) suffix *-n* show that the action referred to is being done aimlessly, or heedless of the prescribed rules. While full reduplication of some adjectives derives adverbs, full reduplication of others signifies that the referents being described are plural, and usually also varied. In full reduplication, the final (C)CVCV is copied, with any antepenultimate syllable being deleted except for the coda. A glottal stop is inserted between the base and the reduplicative affix if the penultimate syllable lacks an onset. The bisyllabic reduplicative affix is optionally shortened to the initial (C)V, as in *di-di'ak* 'well'. Tetun full reduplication is illustrated in Table 26.8.

In Leti, verbs in object relative clauses are partially reduplicated. The onset (whether this be a consonant or a glide allophone) and vowel of the penultimate syllable are copied. If the penultimate syllable does not have an onset, full reduplication is used instead. Glides in consonant-glide clusters are not copied, but are instead shifted into the reduplicative affix. Inasmuch as the phonological conditions detailed in section 2.4 are met, A&M occurs between reduplicative affix and base. Leti partial reduplication is illustrated in Table 26.9.

Leti full reduplication, illustrated in Table 26.10, derives adjectives from nouns, and instrument nouns, adjectives and adverbs from verbs. Full reduplication of

TABLE 26.10: FULL REDUPLICATION IN LETI

Template	Base	Gloss	Pre-A&M	Post-A&M	Gloss
VV	ou	'blow'		oü-ou	'blowpipe'
…VCV	vaili	'choose'	va-ili-ili	(n-)va-il-ili	'which he chooses'
…VCVC	nautun	'be a lot'	na-utu-utun	na-ut-utun	'many'
CVV	kòi	'scrape'	kòi-kòi	kòkïòi	'coconut-scraper'
CVVC	dous	'suck'	dou-dous	dodüous	'pipette'
CVCV	kòra	'rattle'	kòra-kòra	kòr-kòra	'type of drum'
CVCVC	petuk	'jump'	petu-petuk	petpüetuk	'hop'
CCGVCV	tmüèla	'darken'	*t-mèla-müèla*	t-müèl-mèla	'dark'
C_1C_1V…	(see Table 26.9)				

verbs is also used to mark atelic aktionsart. As in partial reduplication, glide members in initial consonant-glide clusters are shifted into the reduplicative affix. A&M combines the reduplicative affix and the base. If the base has an initial geminate onset, partial reduplication is used instead.

3 BASIC MORPHOSYNTAX

3.1 Word and morpheme classes

Tetun and Leti have similar word classes. In both, nouns and pronouns are the only classes of words that can head complete noun phrases, that can function as possessor within a noun phrase, and that can be modified by the full range of determiners (section 3.6.2). Verbs head verb phrases, and take subject marking (although in Tetun this depends on the phonology of the verb). They may be transitive or intransitive, and are further classifiable according to the types of oblique objects they can take, if any. Other word classes include adjective, numeral/quantifier, adverb, preposition, connector (to join clauses), interjection, tag, and determiner. Classes unique to Tetun are numeral classifier, auxiliary (the corresponding lexemes in Leti being adverbs), and prepositional verb (combining characteristics of verbs and of prepositions).

A major difference between Tetun and Leti concerns the relationship between verbs and the other classes. In Tetun, there is very little overlap between the classes, and the means of deriving nouns from verbs and vice versa are not highly productive. Tetun predicates can be headed by a range of word classes, including transitive and intransitive verbs, adjectives, prepositions, numerals and nouns. In contrast, Leti allows all non-human nouns to be turned into verbs by adding a subject marking prefix; this is also possible for adjectives and some numerals. Except in equational clauses, all predicates must be headed by a verb.

The distinction between affixes and clitics is the same in both languages. Derivational affixes are distinguished by applying to only some members of a word class; they usually change meaning and word class or verb transitivity. In contrast to derivational affixes, clitics can apply to any member of a word class (e.g. Tetun *la*= 'not' and genitive =n, Leti subject clitics and indicative =o).

3.2 The Letinese indexer clitic

Leti has one clitic which is so pervasive, multifunctional and typologically unusual that it warrants special attention. This 'indexer' ('IDX') is found on noun phrases, verb phrases and conjunctions.

It has two manifestations. First, if the citation form of the final word of the indexed phrase ends in /a/, this /a/ is replaced by /e/ (e.g. *lar*=*e* (sail=IDX) from *lara* 'sail'). Otherwise there is no phonological segment that can be glossed as the indexer (e.g. *spou* 'boat' or 'boat:IDX'). The second manifestation is that indexing prevents the word to which the indexer is attached from cohering with what follows. Thus, in constructions in which A&M is otherwise required, lack of A&M indicates that the phrase is indexed; conversely, the presence of the expected A&M indicates that there is no indexer. However, if the phrase does not end in =*e*, and there is no possibility for A&M to apply, the phrase is inherently ambiguous with regard to indexing.

The functions of the indexer are difficult to state precisely. On noun phrases, the indexer cannot co-occur with spatial, time of reference or attitudinal deictics, nor with possessive suffixes. When these are absent, an indexer indicates that the noun phrase appropriately designates the referent, while the lack of an indexer indicates that the noun phrase need not necessarily appropriately designate the referent. The latter may be because the speaker cannot readily find the right expression, or because the use of a correct designation does not matter (among other things, lack of indexing is common in certain backgrounded clauses). For instance, *rum*=*lalavn*=*e* (house=big=IDX) is used if the speaker intends to correctly designate a big house, while unindexed *rum*=*lalavna* could be used to refer to something which looked like a big house, but which the speaker acknowledges may have in fact been something else. For place names, this greater specificity of indexed phrases results in indexed place names being translatable as 'on/at X' or 'on/at a particular place in X', while unindexed place names are better translated as 'somewhere on/at X'. For proper nouns referring to people, the lack of an indexer indicates that only the named person is referred to, while the presence of an indexer gives a more inclusive interpretation of 'this person and everything/everyone that belongs to her'.

On verb phrases, the indexer has several functions. One is much like its function on noun phrases, in that the presence of an indexer indicates that the verb phrase appropriately designates the action or state referred to, while the absence of an indexer indicates that the designation need not necessarily be appropriate. Thus, for instance, *m-pòpr*=*e* (3s-shiver=IDX) means that someone shivered, while unindexed *m-pòpr*>*a* means that the person under discussion looked like he or she was shivering, but may in fact have been doing something else. A second function of the indexer on verb phrases is to mark an unemphatic third person object (e.g. *n-takr*=*e* (3s-see=IDX) 'she sees him'); this usage reflects its presumed diachronic source as a third person pronoun. Also reflecting this source is the third use of the indexer on verb phrases, namely to mark the fact that an object has been omitted or topicalized.

(3)	*Tantakrauo.*		*Adue*	*tantakre.*
Leti	Ta=n-takra=au=o.		Au=de	ta=n-takra=e.
	NEG=3s-see=1s=IND		1s=REM	NEG=3s-see=IDX
	'He did not see me.'		'Me he did not see.'	

On the predicate of a nominalized complement clause, the indexer encodes evidential mood; that is, it indicates that the speaker identifies the proposition expressed in the complement as a fact within his or her frame of reference. This is illustrated by the contrast between the indexed complement of (4) and the unindexed complement of (5).

(4)	*A*=*ü-atu*	*[lo*=*utan*=*tipru*	*r-sòpl*=*e*=*la*	*Eul]*.
Leti	1s=1s-know:IDX	LOC=rain=east:IDX	3p-sail=IDX=DIR	Eul:IND
	'I know they (usually) sail to Eul during the east monsoon.'			

(5) *A=ü-atu*   *[lo=utan=tipru*   *r-sòpal=la*   *Eul]*.
Leti 1s=1s-know:IDX   LOC=rain=east:IDX   3p-sail=DIR   Eul:IND
      'I know they (may) sail to Eul during the east monsoon.'

Finally, on conjunctions (e.g. *mèna* 'but'), the indexer is used if the speaker knows what to say after the conjunction, while lack of an indexer signals hesitation.

3.3 Basic clause structure

3.3.1 Verbal clauses

Verbal clauses in both Tetun and Leti have basic subject–verb–object word order, with subject marking on the verb. In both languages, the subject noun phrase is clearly identified by its preverbal position, by the fact that the subject marking prefix on the verb agrees with it, and by its omission in certain coordinate constructions which require same-subject deletion.

(6) *Ha'u   k-atene   nia*.
Tetun 1s   1s-know   3s
       'I know her.'

(7) *Atüoli*   *kaptè:ne*.
Leti   A=u-toli   kaptè:na=e
       1s=1s-see:IDX   captain=IDX
       'I see the captain.'

Since a core feature of many clauses are the subject agreement prefixes, it will be useful briefly to review the pronominal system before proceeding to other aspects of the structure of verbal clauses. Tetun and Leti have the same system of personal pronouns, with the exception that Tetun uses the 1pi form (*ita*) as a polite form for 'you', while Leti does not. Tetun personal pronouns and subject prefixes are listed in Table 26.11. The genitive clitics are further discussed in section 3.7.

The full form of Tetun pronouns is always used in writing. In speaking, the full form can be used in all contexts allowing pronouns, while the phonologically reduced forms (which tend to be proclitics) are used only for subjects and preposed possessors (see section 3.7), and even then only if the pronoun is not emphasized or modified. Since there is a strong tendency for Tetun subjects to refer to something which has already been

TABLE 26.11: TETUN PERSONAL PRONOUNS

Full pronoun	Reduced form	Subject marking prefix	Genitive clitic	Description
ha'u	ha, h	k-	=n	I (1s)
ita	it	–	=n, =r	we, excluding addressee (1pe)
ami	am	–	=n, =r	we, including addressee (1pi)
oo	o, a	m-	=n	you singular (2s)
ita	–	–	=n	you singular respectful (2s)
emi	em	–	=n, =r	you plural (2p)
nia	ni, na	n-	=n	he, she (3s)
sia, sira	si, sa	r-, n-	=n, =r	they (3p)

mentioned, such reduced forms are common for subjects; alternatively, the subject is relatively often omitted if understood from context.

In Tetun, only verbs beginning in /h/ take the full range of subject marking prefixes, with the prefixed consonant replacing the /h/, as in the verbs *halai* 'run', *hola* 'go.via' and *hikar* '(go) back' in (8).

(8)   *Sia   r-alai   r-ola   r-ikar   loro-sa'e=n   baa.*
Tetun   3p   3p-run   3p-go.via   3p-back   sun-ascend=GEN   DIST
        'They ran away further to the east.'

Verbs beginning in other consonants take subject marking only for 1s subjects, with the prefix *k-* preceding the root (e.g. *k-bolu* '1s-call'). This restriction to 1s *k-* prefixes is consistent with the fact that all consonant clusters in the Fehan dialect of Tetun begin with /k/. Since Tetun disallows geminate consonants, *k-* is not applied to verbs beginning with /k/. Inflection of non-/h/-initial verbs is inconsistently applied in speaking, and usually not done in writing, which tends to follow the northern dialect where non-/h/-initial verbs are not inflected. Vowel-initial verbs, which are rare, do not take subject marking; nor do adjectives, numerals or prepositions. There is no subject marking at all in Dili Tetun.

Leti pronouns and subject agreement prefixes are shown in Table 26.12.

In Leti, the subject may be a noun phrase or a full pronoun plus one or more modifiers; for pronominal subjects without modifiers, the clitic form of the pronoun is used. Such subject clitics are usually optional, being used to emphasize the subject. However they are obligatory in certain circumstances involving first person subjects, namely: (1) When the subject is first person singular; (2) When a first person exclusive plural subject is used in a context where A&M applies to it; (3) When a first person inclusive plural subject is used in a context where A&M applies to it and the verb begins in /t/. Subject marking is obligatory on all verbs, with A&M applying to the subject prefixes under conditions discussed in section 2.4.

(9)   *T-nèm=e.*   *I=t-nèm=e.*
Leti   1pi-fly=IDX   1pi=1pi-fly=IDX
       'We fly.'   'We fly.'

Nominal subjects in Leti verbal clauses cannot be marked for plurality. If the subject is plural, this is indicated exclusively by the subject marking prefix.

(10)   *Kus=e   na-mdudu.*   *Kus=e   ra-mdudu.*
Leti   cat=IDX   3s-sleep:IDX   cat=IDX   3p-sleep:IDX
        'The cat sleeps.'   'The cats sleep.'

TABLE 26.12: LETI PERSONAL PRONOUNS

Full pronoun	Subject clitic	Subject marking prefix	Possessive suffix	Description
au	a=	u-	-ku	I (1s)
ami		ma-	-nV	we, excluding addressee (1pe)
ita	i=	ta-		we, including addressee (1pi)
oa	o=	mu-	-mu	you singular (2s)
mia	mi=	mi-	-mi	you plural (2p)
ea	e=	na-	-nV	he, she, it (3s)
ira	i=	ra-		they (3p)

The full form of Leti pronouns is used in most object noun phrases, in topics and oblique arguments, and in preposed possessors (see section 3.7). Possessive suffixes indicate the possessor within noun phrases, and are also used for nominalizing stative verbs (see section 4).

Turning now to other aspects of basic verbal clause structure, the default position for object noun phrases in both languages is immediately following a transitive verb. In Tetun, object noun phrases can be headed by either nouns or pronouns; objects are however frequently omitted if they can be understood from context (as in example (11), where '(S)' and '(O)' indicate omitted subjects and objects).

(11)   *Ami   hodi   kuda   baa,   (S)   sai,   (S)   baa   kesi   (O)   iha   hae.*
Tetun 1pe   bring   horse   go   exit   go   tie   LOC   grass
'We will take the horses, go out, and go and tie (them) up in the grass.'

In Leti, pronominal objects are obligatorily attached to the verb by A&M (see section 2.4). Most person–number combinations allow only full pronouns as objects, but the clitic =*o* represents unemphatic 2s objects, as in (12), and the indexer clitic =*e* is used for unemphatic 3s and 3p. A nominal object is only attached to the verb (in 'cohesion') if the verb is unindexed.

(12)   *N-takr=oa?*   *N-takr=o?*
Leti   3s-see=2s   3s-see=2s
'Does he see yóu?'   'Does he see you?'

Oblique objects follow the direct object noun phrase. In Tetun oblique objects are introduced by the general locative preposition *iha*, or by the prepositional verb *baa*. Although this *baa* (often shortened to *ba*) is presumably historically derived from the verb *baa* 'go (away from speaker)', it is used to introduce recipients and addressees regardless of whether or not they refer to the speaker, as shown in (13). Oblique objects in Leti are, as in (14), introduced by any of the three directional prepositions *ma*, *ti*, and *la*, which are further described in section 3.3.6.

(13)   *Oo   foo   saa   baa   ha'u?*
Tetun 2s   give   what   DIR   1s
'What will you give me?'

(14)   *Ra-natu   surt=e=ma   ïau=o.*
Leti   3p-send:IDX   letter=IDX=DIR   1s=IND
'They send the letter to me.'

In Leti, pronominal recipients can, without any introductory preposition, precede an attitudinal deictic (see section 3.6.2) functioning as direct object.

(15)   *Ranatüasüaio.*
Leti   ra-natu=au=sai=o
3p-send=1s=PRX.ATD=IND
'They send me this.'

Object noun phrases can be topicalized by fronting them to before the subject, as in (16). In Leti, the predicate must then be marked by an indexer, indicated in (17) by the absence of cohesion. Leti allows oblique objects introduced by *la* to be topicalized in the same way as direct objects; in Tetun, some oblique objects introduced by the prepositional verb *baa* 'DIR' can be fronted, while those introduced by 'true' prepositions can not.

(16)   *Oa   ne'e   oo   m-atene   lale?*
Tetun   child   PRX   2s   2s-know   no
        'This child – do you know (him) or not?'

(17)   *Vètra=e=di,   a=u-olu=la   Sin=e.*
Leti   maize=IDX=NOW   1s=1s-sell:IDX=DIR   China=IDX
        'That is the maize that I am to sell to the Chinese.'

Tetun allows a subject–object–verb constituent order in irrealis clauses (such as negative clauses or questions), if the object noun phrase is non-referential. This constituent
order is required for the inherently negative verb *lalek* 'lack', illustrated in (18), but
optional in other irrealis clauses, such as (19).

(18)   *Nia   ina=n   lalek,   ama=n   lalek.*
Tetun   3s   mother=GEN   lack   father=GEN   lack
        'She has no mother, and has no father.'

(19)   *Mais   ami   malae   la=hatene,   hakerek   la=hatene.*
Tetun   but   1pe   non-native   NEG=know   write   NEG=know
        'But we don't know Indonesian, and don't know (how to) write.'

3.3.2 *Existential and possessive clauses*

Existential clauses in Tetun make use of *iha* 'be present' (e.g. *Ina la=iha* 'Mother (is)
not=present'; *iha* is also the general locative preposition), or *noo* 'exist'. Where an existential clause using *noo* introduces a new participant, the existent noun phrase follows the
predicate, as illustrated in (20). In all other instances it precedes the predicate, as in (21);
this is just as one would expect of a Tetun subject.

(20)   *Ei!   Noo   feto   ida.   Noo   feto   ida   noo   oa!*
Tetun   INTJ   EXIST woman   one   EXIST woman   one   and   child
        'Ei! There is a woman! There is a woman and child!' (Said by a man who
        suddenly observed them on a remote island.)

(21)   *Aikanoik   nee   hori   rai   moris   noo   kedas.*
Tetun   story   this   since   earth   born   EXIST   immediately
        'This story has existed since the beginning of the world.'

Leti existentials use *la*, literally 'go', with a preceding subject.

(22)   *Kupn=e   e=la=e.*   *Kupn=e   ta=la=e.*
Leti   money=IDX   3s=EXIST=IDX   money=IDX   NEG=EXIST=IDX
        'There is money.'   'There is no money.'

A common means of expressing clausal possession (and in fact the only means of
negating possession in Leti clauses) is to express the possessor as an initial topic noun
phrase, and the possessed entity as the argument of a following existential clause, as in
(23) and (24).

(23)   *Lale.   Ha'u   buat   e'e   sia   noo.*
Tetun   no   1s   thing   PRX   PL   EXIST
        'No. I have these things.' (So there is no need for you to give them to me.)

(24)   *Au   kupn=e   ta=la=e.*
Leti   1s   money=IDX   NEG=DIR=IDX
    'I don't have the money.'

An alternative in Tetun is to use the transitive verb *hoo* 'have', illustrated in (25). An alternative in Leti is to verbalize the noun that refers to the possessed entity, by adding a subject marker that agrees with the possessor, as in (26).

(25)   *Oo   m-oo   ama.*
Tetun   2s   2s-have   father
    'You have a father.'

(26)   *Mu-kupn=e.*
Leti   2s-money=IDX
    'You have money.'

3.3.3 Other clause types

In both Tetun and Leti, nominal predicates are usually simply juxtaposed to the subject, without an intervening copula, as in (27). Possessor predicates follow the same pattern, as shown by (28).

(27)   *Buku   Lasak   e'e   ata.*
Tetun   Buku   Lasak   PRX   slave
    'This Buku Lasak was a slave.'

(28)   *Rum=e   o=e.*
Leti   house=IDX   2s=IDX
    'The house is yours.'

Unlike Leti, Tetun has an optional copula *nii*; it indicates a relationship of unique identity, in which the referent of the second noun phrase is presented as uniquely satisfying the description given in the initial noun phrase.

(29)   *Lale.   Tais   oo=k   nii   nia.*
Tetun   no   cloth   2s=POSS   be   3s
    'No. That is your sarong.' (None of the others are yours.)

Leti has a predicate type in which a stative verb is nominalized by a possessive suffix which agrees with the preceding noun phrase. The verb specifies a characteristic which is perceived to be an intrinsic and unchanging feature of the referent being described.

(30)   *Vuar=dí   tul-lu   vali=o.*
Leti   mountain=PRX   high-3.POSS   also=IND
    'This mountain is high too.'

Other predicate types in Tetun include adjective phrases (e.g. *Ha'u di'ak* 'I (am) good') and numeral phrases such as in (31).

(31)   *Nia=kan   ulu=n   aa   hitu.*
Tetun   3s=POSS   head=GEN   DEF   seven
    'It (this snake) has seven heads.' (Literally 'Its heads are seven.')

In Leti, adjectives and numerals must be verbalized by the addition of a subject marking prefix if they are to be used predicatively (e.g. *n-kèrna* (3s-dry) 'it is dry', *a=m-rua* (1pe=1pe-two) 'we are two').

Both Tetun and Leti have prepositional phrase predicates (e.g. Tetun *Ha'u iha uma* 'I (am) in (the) house'). Although these do not take subject marking prefixes, in Leti the preposition obligatorily takes a third person subject clitic.

(32)   *Pana:ru   e=ma   lèt=e.*
Leti   altar:IDX   3s=DIR   village=IDX
'The altar is in the village.'

Another predicate type in Tetun is frequently used to express character, emotions and physical attributes. It usually consists of a single noun denoting a body part or other characteristic (e.g. *naran* 'name') followed by a single-word intransitive verb or adjective. Such predicates often constitute standardized expressions (e.g. *isin di'ak* (body good) 'well', *folin ktodan* (price heavy) 'expensive'); however they can also be creative (e.g. *raan midar* (blood sweet) 'has sweet-tasting blood'). Although Leti has some standardized expressions of this form, they are not common.

(33)   *Ida   matan   aat,   ida   tilun   diuk.*
Tetun   one   eye   bad   one   ear   deaf
'One was blind, and one was deaf.'

3.3.4 Negation

Tetun has a pre-predicate negative clitic, *la=* (e.g. *la=di'ak* 'not good'). Alternatives for negating a predicate are the slightly more emphatic post-verbal negator *ha'i* (e.g. *di'ak ha'i*), or an emphatic combination of both (*la=di'ak ha'i* 'definitely not good'). Nominal clauses can be negated by *ha'i*, as in (34), but not by *la=*. A wide range of constituents can be negated by the contrastive negator *lahoos*, illustrated in (35).

(34)   *Oo!   Buat   e'e   Bei   Beur   ha'i!*
Tetun   oh   thing   PRX   Mr   deceive   not
'Oh! This thing (actually a person) isn't Mr Trickster!'

(35)   *Ne'e   lahoos   ema   lian.   Manu   lian.*
Tetun   PRX   indeed.not   person   voice   bird   voice
'This isn't a person's voice. (It's) a bird's voice.'

In Leti, a verbal or pronominal predicate is negated by procliticizing *ta=* 'not' to it, as shown in (36). Nominal predicates cannot be negated; instead a topic-comment construction is used in which the predicate is a negated pronoun, as in (37).

(36)   *Müani   ta=na-natu   surt=e.*
Leti   man:IDX   NEG=3s-send:IDX   letter=IDX
'The man did not send the letter.'

(37)   *Kokkodie,   ata   tahaio.*
Leti   Kòkkòi=de,   ata   ta=hai=o.
child=REM   slave   NEG=PRX.ATD=IND
'The child is not a slave.'

3.3.5 Mood

Leti marks declarative clauses by an indicative clitic =*o* on the final word in the sentence; this triggers internal metathesis. Although the indicative enclitic is found on all clause types, it is only applicable if the final word does not have the indexer or a mono-syllabic deictic or pronoun. Tetun has no such marker of declarative clauses.

(38)	*Kude*	*ntikilo.*	*Kude*	*ntiklio.*
Leti	kuda=e	n-tikli=o.	kuda=e	n-tikli=o.
	horse=IDX	3s-kick=IND	horse=IDX	3s-kick=2s
	'The horse kicked.'		'The horse kicked you.'	

Neither Tetun nor Leti has imperative mood. Rather, most commands are recognized as such from context and the use of a second person subject in a declarative clause.

(39)	*Msüòlka*	*püòrse.*
Leti	mu-sòlka	püòrsa=e
	2s-shut	door=IDX
	'Shut the door.'	

In Tetun, commands or invitations for the addressee to do something without the speaker can be indicated by final *baa* (literally 'go'), as in *Haa baa* 'You eat (without me)', while invitations to do something with the speaker can be preceded by *Mai ita* (literally 'come 1pi') 'let's' (e.g. *Mai ita hamulak* 'Let us pray'). Leti invitations are semantically similar. They consist of two clauses joined by *po* '(and) then', of which the first features the verb 'come', and the second has a verb inflected for first person plural inclusive. In careful speech the 'come' of the first clause is inflected for second person singular or plural. In fast speech, however, it may occur uninflected.

(40)	*Mmüapo*	*tamtïètano.*
Leti	mu-ma=po	ta-mtïètna=o.
	2s-come=then	1pi-sit=IND
	'Let's sit down.'	

The Tetun auxiliary *keta* 'do not' is commonly used in prohibitions (e.g. *Keta baa!* 'Don't go!'). The comparable form in Leti is *ïa*, which is the monosyllabic allomorph of the negative optative marker *ïena* 'may (he/she) not'.

(41)	*Ïammüatio!*	*Ïena*	*nmatio!*
Leti	ïa=mu-mati=o!	ïena	n-mati=o!
	may.not2s-die=IND	may.not	3s-die=IND
	'Don't die!'	'May he not die!'	

Both Tetun and Leti form information interrogatives by placing an interrogative word in the same slot as the questioned constituent (see also section 3.6.3).

(42)	*Katuas*	*m-aa*	*saa?*
Tetun	mature.man	2s-eat	what
	'What are you (old man) eating?'		

(43)	*Muveni*	*mü-o:ru*	*Apnu?*
Leti	when	2s-travel:IDX	Ambon.
	'When do you travel to Ambon?'		

Disjunctive and yes–no interrogatives are very similar in the two languages. In disjunctive interrogatives, the alternatives are usually separated by *ka* 'or', although in Tetun they can be simply juxtaposed.

(44)   *Kapl=e   Sin=e=ka   Ïapa:n=e=ka?*
Leti   ship=IDX   China=IDX=or   Japan=IDX=or
     'Is the ship Chinese or Japanese?'

For yes–no questions, it is more common in both languages for the alternative to be shortened to 'or not' (e.g. Tetun *Di'ak ka lale?* '(Is it) good or not?'), further truncated to 'not' (e.g. Tetun *Di'ak lale?*), or be left open by a final 'or' (e.g. Tetun *Di'ak ka?*). Alternatively, final rising intonation alone can signal that an utterance is a question (e.g. Tetun *Bele?* 'Can (we)?').

3.3.6 Prepositional phrase

Prepositional phrases in both Tetun and Leti consist of a preposition followed by a noun phrase (e.g. Tetun *iha Betun* 'in Betun', *hori lale'an* 'down.from heaven', *to'o sasawan* 'until morning'). While Tetun has over a dozen prepositions, Leti has only four, namely the general locative preposition *lo* and three directional ones, which derive from verbs. The locative preposition *lo* 'at' and the directional *ma* 'at/to X (where X is related to the speaker)' and *la* 'at/to X (where X is not related to speaker or hearer)' are enclitics to the preceding verb phrase (if any), while directional *ti* 'at/to X (where X is related to the hearer)' cliticizes to the following noun phrase.

Tetun and Leti both have a single commonly used preposition to introduce location. In Tetun, exact location is indicated by this preposition together with an inalienably possessed location noun, e.g. *iha uma laran* (LOC house inside) 'inside the house', *iha uma kotuk* (LOC house back) ('behind the house'). Leti uses a similar construction for exact location, but distinguishes between two classes of location nouns, one taking a possessive suffix in careful speech (e.g. *lo=rume nain-ne* (LOC=house inside-3.POSS) 'inside the house'), and the other taking no possessive suffix. There is no apparent semantic distinction between these two classes; for instance *vavna* 'top' and *rïarma* 'inside' take a possessive suffix, while *sïanni* 'top' and *ra:m* 'inside' do not.

3.3.7 Auxiliaries and other tense/aspect markers

In both Tetun and Leti, marking of tense and aspect is not obligatory, with these notions being largely implicit. Thus, for instance, Tetun *Nia baa* (3s go) can be interpreted according to context as 'She went', 'She is going' or 'She will go'. Nevertheless, temporal relationships can be made explicit through words and phrases which refer to situation-external time (e.g. Tetun *kala-kalan* 'nightly', Leti *ka:ti* 'soon') and through aspectual adverbs which are slotted in somewhere after the verb. The common Tetun temporal and aspectual adverbs are *ti'an* 'already' (perfective aspect), *ti'a* 'and after that', *kedan* 'immediately', *onan* (sometimes cliticized as *=n* on the final word of the clause) 'imminent' (marking the event specified by the clause as imminent and inevitable), and *lai* 'first, beforehand' (indicating that the event in the clause must happen before some other, often unspecified, event takes place). Leti aspectual adverbs include *ma:ta* 'still' and *sala/salmèka* 'already'.

Tetun also has preverbal aspectual auxiliaries, namely progressive *ho'i*, *foin* 'only just', *sei* 'still', *sei dauk* 'not yet', and *atu* 'about to, want to, intend to, in order to'. Leti has no aspectual auxiliaries, instead using nominalization to optionally mark two aspects. Resultative aspect is encoded by means of the nominalizing affixes discussed in section 4 plus full subject agreement (e.g. *na-l-ï-òkra* 'he has sworn' from *lòkra*). Placing a nominalized verb in the object slot of the verb *èla* 'be (temporarily) at' signals progressive aspect (e.g. *r-èla knïakri* (3p-be.at NR:cry) 'they are crying').

Both languages allow a verb (including its subject marker) to be repeated to indicate continuation of the action (e.g. Leti *r-nèma r-nèma* (3p-fly 3p-fly) 'they keep on flying').

3.4 Major verbal alternations

Neither Tetun nor Leti have a system of voice.

Causative verbs in both languages are derived by the addition of a prefix to an adjective or intransitive verb. In Tetun this prefix is *ha-* (e.g. *ha-sa'e* 'raise' from *sa'e* 'ascend', *ha-metan* 'blacken' from *metan* 'black'), while Leti uses a subject marking prefix which is not subject to A&M to derive transitive causative verbs from intransitive verbs (see Table 26.6 above). These prefixes can also be added to many nouns (in Leti to all non-human nouns) to derive a verb which indicates an act or state which is indissolubly connected with that which is expressed by the root noun (e.g. Tetun *ha-tolu* 'lay egg' from *tolun* 'egg', Leti *na-ara* 'he makes war' from *ara* 'war').

Reciprocals in Tetun use the free lexeme *malu* in the postverbal slot (e.g. *Sira haklelek malu* 'They verbally abuse each other'). Some reciprocal verbs in Tetun are derived from transitive verb bases by the addition of the circumfix *hak- -k* (e.g. *hak-tuda-k* 'throw spears at each other' from *tuda* 'throw spear at'); most of these verbs refer to methods of fighting. In Leti, reciprocity is encoded by having *ida* 'one' as both subject and object. Additionally, the reciprocal enclitic *=mma* is attached to the subject *ida*.

(45)   *Ida=mm=e*   *m-pòk=id=o.*
Leti   one=RCP=IDX   3s-shoot=one=IND
    'They shot one another.'

Leti also has an unproductive prefix *va-* which derives reciprocal verbs from some transitive verbs (e.g. *r-va-su:ti* 'they butt against each other', from *su:ti* 'butt against').

Reflexives in Tetun are marked by *aan* in the postverbal slot (e.g. *hakraik aan* 'humble oneself'), or by the inflected postverbal adverb *hika(r)* 'back, return to earlier location, state or activity' in conjunction with either an object pronoun, as in (46), or reflexive *aan*.

(46)   *Ni=la'en*   *aa*   *sona*   *n-o'o*   *n-ika*   *nia.*
Tetun   3s=husband   DEF   pierce   3s-kill   3s-back   3s
    'Her husband stabbed and killed himself.'

Leti has no special marker of reflexives, simply using the appropriate personal pronoun in the object slot.

(47)   *Mtüorio.*
Leti   Mu-tori=o
    2s-shave=2s
    'You shave yourself.'

3.5 Serial verbs

Tetun has a range of common serial verb constructions, while Leti does not. The shared features of Tetun serial verb constructions are similar to those noted in other languages: no verb is subordinate to the other, or modifies the other. The verbs fall under a single intonation contour. There are no syntactic or phonological indications of a clause boundary between the verbs, and no intervening peripheral constituents (such as time or location phrases). The subject of the second verb is interpreted as being identical to either the subject or the object of the preceding verb, depending on the type of serialization. The verbs share negation, aspect and auxiliaries.

In one type of serialization, two consecutive verbs may be used to describe a situation in which the action specified by the initial, transitive, verb has a result described by the second, intransitive, verb. The object of the first verb follows the second verb, and functions semantically as its subject. Only the first verb takes subject marking.

(48) *Oo   mai,   **m-aa   siit**   nuu   kain   ne'e   lai.*
Tetun 2s   come   2s-eat be.cut.off coconut stalk PRX   first
      'You come, and chew through this coconut stalk now.'

The second type of serialization similarly involves a final intransitively used verb, but the first verb may be either transitive or intransitive, and the two verbs share the subject. Only the first verb takes subject marking. Commonly the initial verb specifies manner of motion, while the second specifies direction (*sa'e* 'ascend', *tuun* 'descend', *tama* 'enter' or *sai* 'exit'), as in *halai sai* 'run outside'. Alternatively there is an initial verb of motion followed by *liu* 'go further, go past' (shown in (49)), or a verb (not necessarily of motion) followed by *uluk* 'go first, go ahead' (e.g. *mate uluk* 'die first (before someone else dies)').

(49) *Tudik   e'e   la=**tama   liu**   laran   baa.*
Tetun knife   PRX   NEG=enter go.further interior DIST
      'The knife didn't enter right into the inside' (of the body).

A third type of serialization involves two consecutive transitive verbs which share both the subject and the object. The second verb slot appears to be reserved for a closed class of verbs, of which by far the most common is *hola* 'take, fetch, hold'; others include *ho'o* 'kill' and *hela* 'leave'. Both verbs take subject marking.

(50) *Nia   **kawen   n-ola**   Feto   Ikun.*
Tetun 3s   marry   3s-take woman   tail
      'He married Youngest Sister.'

(51) *Hori.fonin   ha'u   **k-sona**   **k-o'o**   ti'an   fahi   inan   ida.*
Tetun last.night   1s   1s-spear   1s-kill already pig   female   one
      'Last night I speared to death a sow.'

A fourth type of Tetun serialization involves an intransitive verb of motion followed by a non-stative verb, which can be either transitive or intransitive. This construction is particularly common for the motion verbs *baa* 'go' and *mai* 'come', but also occurs with other verbs, including *la'o* 'walk, go, travel' and *tone* 'go (usually towards addressee)'. The unmarked interpretation is that the verbs represent two events that follow each other, with the first (the moving) usually being done in order to do the second. As illustrated in (52), both verbs take subject marking, and the verbs can be separated by an adverb, or by the negator *ha'i* 'not'.

(52) *Nia   **k-tone   k-aa**.   Lale   ha'u   **k-tone**   ha'i   **k-aa**.*
Tetun then   1s-go   1s-eat   else   1s   1s-go   not   1s-eat
      'Then (if you do as I ask) I'll go and eat. Otherwise I won't go and eat.'

In the remaining types of Tetun serial verb construction, one verb in the series introduces an argument role which has oblique status for the other, in particular source or goal location, instrument, or co-actor. Both verbs take subject marking.

Source location is introduced by the verb *hosi* 'from', while goal location may be introduced by a range of verbs including *baa* 'go, DIR', *mai* 'come' (usually followed by the locative preposition iha), *hatutuk* 'directly to (without detour or delay)', *ho'i* 'to (reaching destination)', and *to'o* 'reach, arrive at'. Source and goal location may follow a verb of motion (e.g. *halai mai uma* (run come home) 'run here to home') or a transitive verb such as *tau* 'put' or *solok* 'send', which specifies that the referent of the object noun phrase is moved (e.g. *solok surat baa Australia* 'send letter to Australia').

The Tetun verb *hodi* (which basically means 'bring, take' when used as a sole verb), is commonly used in construction with a preceding or following verb to mean 'use', thus introducing an instrument noun phrase. Where the instrument precedes the other verb, as in (53), *hodi* is fully verbal, readily allowing omission of its object noun phrase if it can be understood from context, and allowing its object to be fronted as topic noun phrase.

(53)   *Nia*   ***n-odi***   *tudik*   *e'e*   ***ko'a***   ***siit***   *ti'a,...*
Tetun   3s   3s-use   knife   PRX   cut   be.cut.off   already
       'Having cut through (the umbilical cord) with the knife, ...'

Where the instrument follows the other verb, in contrast, *hodi* is still verbal in that it takes subject marking, as in (54). However it is like a preposition in that its object cannot be omitted or fronted. Furthermore, the instrument in such cases is nearly always non-specific. *Hodi* is here analyzed as a prepositional verb rather than a full verb in serialization.

(54)   *..., dadi*   *at*   ***n-aroun***   *odan*   ***n-odi***   *saa?*
Tetun   so   OPT   3s-lower   ladder   3s-use   what
       '(Her legs and arms were firmly tied,) so what could (she) lower
       the ladder with?'

The verb *hoo* 'accompany' introduces co-actors. Like *hodi*, it is fully verbal when it precedes the other verb in the construction, as in (55), but like a preposition (except that it takes subject marking) when it follows the verb, as in (56).

(55)   *Oo*   ***m-oo***   *na'i*   *sia*   *ruas*   ***fila***   *m-ika*   *onan.*
Tetun   2s   2s-accompany   darling   PL   two   return   2s-back   now
       'You return (home) now with the two children.'

(56)   *Ha'u*   ***baa***   ***k-oo***   *loos*   *Ama*   *Bo'uk*   *dei.*
Tetun   1s   go   1s-accompany   just   father   Bo'uk   only
       'I will go with only Ama Bo'uk.' (i.e. No-one else will go.)

As mentioned above, Leti has no verb serialization. Like Tetun, it uses a verb (*odi* 'carry' or *ela* 'take') to introduce an instrument for a subsequent verb, as shown in (57). However, unlike Tetun, the verbs head separate clauses which are joined by *po* 'and then', are independently marked for aspect, and can be independently negated. Co-actors are similarly introduced in the first of two clauses, although these are not separated by a conjunction, as illustrated in (58).

(57)   ***R-odi***   *spou=po*   ***r-sòpl=e=la***   *Ralïavn=e.*
Leti   3p-carry:IDX   boat:IDX=and.then   3p-sail=IDX=DIR   Timor=IDX
       'They carry the boat, and then sail (with it) to a certain place on Timor.'

(58)   *E=**n-òra**   müani   **r-sòpl**=e=la   Ralïavan=o.*
Leti   3s=3s-be.with   man:IDX   3p-sail=IDX=DIR   Timor=IND
       'He is with the man, and they sail to somewhere on Timor.'

3.6 Noun phrase

3.6.1 Basic noun phrase structure

The word order for simple adjectivally modified noun phrases is the same in both Tetun and Leti, namely: Noun (Adjective Phrase) (Determiner). In Leti, a 'simple' noun phrase like this has adhesion between all the constituents (see section 2.4).

(59)   *illïalavandí*
Leti   ili-lalavna=dí
       hill-big=PRX
       'this big hill (here)'

It is also possible in Leti to have a noun phrase with two heads, as in (60), or two modifiers as in (61), in which case there is no adhesion between the heads or the modifiers.

(60)   *koni*   *ma:nu*   *vevïeindavre.*
Leti   koni   ma:nu   vei-ve:ni=davra=e
       grasshopper   bird   RDP-beautiful=very=IDX
       'the very beautiful grasshopper and very beautiful bird'

(61)   *kusmèmètma*   *vòrue*
Leti   kusa=mè-mètma   vòrua=e
       cat=RDP-black   two=IDX
       'the two black cats'

Tetun readily allows two non-determiner modifiers within a noun phrase, with more than two being rare. Where more than one modifier occurs, the relative order is as follows (where 'NUMP' numeral phrase (section 3.8), 'ADJP' adjective phrase, 'RELCL' relative clause (section 3.6.4), and 'DET' determiner or plural marker (section 3.6.2)).

(Possessor) Noun   (*ida* 'one') (ADJP)   (DET) (PP) (RELCL) (DET)
                   (ADJP) (NUMP)

Note that interrogative and indefinite determiners (e.g. *saa* 'what, anything' and *ida* 'one, a') precede prepositional phrases and relative clauses, while *ne'e* 'PRX' and *sia* 'PL' (included as a determiner for the purpose of this formula) usually follow them.

(62)   *Nia la=n-atene,   lia   saa   mak   nia   atu   n-akees.*
Tetun   3s   NEG=3s-know   word   what   REL   3s   OPT   3s-say
       'He doesn't know what he is going to say.'

(63)   *feto   kawa'ik   na'in   neen   ne'e*
Tetun   woman   older   CLF.HUM   six   PRX
       'these six older women'

(64)   *feto   ida   ki'ik   aa*
Tetun   woman   one   small   DEF
       'the youngest woman'

(65)   *ai.fuan*   *oi'oik*   *mak=siin*
Tetun   fruit   various   REL=sour
        'various fruits which are sour'

Tetun, but not Leti, allows a limited range of premodifiers within a noun phrase. These are *ohin* 'aforementioned', *sura* 'every' (also a transitive verb meaning 'count'), and a limited class of restrictive relative clauses (discussed in section 3.6.4).

Both Tetun and Leti have adjective phrases consisting of an adjective followed by an intensifying adverb (e.g. Leti *mèmètam=davra* (black very) 'very black'). Tetun also has two premodifying adverbs, *laduun* 'not very' (e.g. *laduun boot* 'not.very big') and *mesa* 'solely' (e.g. *ema mesa boot* (person solely big) 'only big people').

3.6.2 Demonstratives, determiners and plural marking

Tetun and Leti differ significantly in their system of demonstratives. Tetun has a two-way distance distinction (*ne'e* 'PRX' vs. *nia* 'DIST'), and also uses the two basic spatial terms anaphorically. Leti makes a three-way distinction for spatial deixis, as shown in Table 26.13. There is a phonologically related set of clitics for distinguishing how long ago the referent was last mentioned in the discourse ("time of reference deixis"). The Tetun demonstratives can all be used either as noun phrase head or as noun phrase modifier, while the Leti ones function only as noun phrase modifiers.

In addition to spatial and time of reference deictics, Leti has a set of 'attitudinal' deictics, listed in Table 26.14, which signal whether the speaker can see the referent, and whether the speaker knows or likes that referent. They may be used as either noun phrase heads or noun phrase modifiers (e.g. *polias=sai* 'this policeman whom I can see and like/know'). The attitudinal determiners have human plural forms ending in *=ra*; the corresponding subject clitics, however, are not marked for human plurality.

Apart from the deictics just mentioned, both Tetun and Leti allow other elements to function as determiners. Tetun has definite *aa*, indefinite *ida*, plural *sia* and interrogatives, while in Leti the indexer clitic is the primary alternative to deictic determiners.

A Tetun noun phrase can be marked as definite by one of the demonstratives (usually proximal *ne'e*) or by *aa*. The latter marker of definiteness is however used in only a very restricted geographical area (the south of West Timor), and even there is avoided by some

TABLE 26.13: LETI DEMONSTRATIVES

Spatial deictic		Time of reference deictic	
dí	'PRX' (within reach of speaker)	di	'NOW' (discussed now)
dó	'MED' (within call of speaker, but not in reach)	do	'RCT' (discussed then)
dé	'DIST'	de	'REM' (discussed once)

TABLE 26.14: LETI ATTITUDINAL DEICTICS

Deictic	Subject clitic	Description
sai/hai	ha=	PRX.ATD (that I see and like/know)
so/ho	ho=	MED.ATD (that I see but don't like/know)
se	se=	DIST.ATD (that I cannot see, but know of)

people. In addition it is restricted phonologically, in that it is always the final element in a phonological phrase (and so not used, for instance, on preposed possessor noun phrases), and tends to be stressed and uttered slowly. There is no corresponding term in Leti.

(66)   ...   *Tama   alas   laran   aa   maa   manu   kokoreek.*
Tetun   enter   forest   interior   DEF   and.the   bird   crow
(They reached a forest.) 'They entered the middle of the forest, and then a cock crowed.'

In Tetun, a noun phrase without a determiner can be interpreted as generic, as in (67). However, in some cases it is definite; for instance, if a story is about a man and a woman, it is common after the initial introductions to refer to the man simply as *mane* 'man' and the woman as *feto* 'woman', without any determiner, as illustrated in (68). A definite interpretation is encouraged if the noun phrase has a possessor (e.g. *uma nia=k* (house 3s=POSS) 'his house').

(67)   *Dadi ema   feto   mii   la=kdook.*   *Ema   mane   mii,   kdook.*
Tetun   so   person woman   urinate   NEG=far   person   male   urinate   far
'So, women don't urinate far.'   '(When) men urinate, (it goes) far.'

(68)   *N-osi   mane   monu,   mane   tate   ta=baa   feto   ti'an.*
Tetun   3s-from   man   fall   man   pay.fine   already=DIR   woman   already
'The man's (side in the dispute) lost, and the man paid the woman a fine.'

Leti allows a sequence of an attitudinal deictic or spatial deictic followed by a determiner indicating time of reference, e.g. *pòtal=sai=do* (bottle=PRX.ATD=RCT), meaning 'this bottle here, which I discussed just now'.

Leti time of reference deictics are often used to nominalize clauses functioning as topics. A common result is a 'fake stack' of two or more determiners in combinations which are not permitted within a simple noun phrase. So, for instance, the verb of a nominalized clause may be marked by the indexer but still be followed immediately by a time of reference deictic, as in (69), or it may be nominalized by a time of reference deictic and also be followed by another time deictic modifying the nominalized clause as a whole, as in (70).

(69)   *Nòramm=e   [l-lòl=e]   de,*
Leti   thereupon=IDX   3s-pass=IDX   REM
'Then when he paddled in it,'

üèr=e   l-lòl=e   turtur-ne.
water=IDX   3s-pass=IDX   knee-3.POSS
'the water flowed around his knees.'

(70)   *Kai   [msüòplela   Ralïavande]   de*
Leti   Kai   [mu-sòpla=e=la   Ralïavna=de]   de
perhaps   2s-sail=IDX=DIR   Timor=REM   REM
'Your aforementioned (planned) sailing trip to Timor'

prèatne   tanresi   [msüòpalla   Apnu]
prèèta-ne   ta=n-resi   [mu-sòpla=la   Apnu]
long-3.POSS   NEG=3s-win:IDX   2s-sail=DIR   Ambon:IDX
'presumably won't take as long as a sailing trip to Ambon would.'

In Tetun, plural marking is syntactically optional, and takes the form *sia* regardless of whether the noun is human (*maun sia* 'older brothers') or non-human (*rate sia* 'graves'). Note however that *sia* as personal pronoun 'they' can only refer to humans. In Tetun it is usual to have at most one indication of plurality. As such, *sia* is not usually used in conjunction with a numeral (e.g. *asu rua* (dog two) 'two dogs'), quantifying adjective (e.g. *wa'in* 'many'), plural pronoun head (e.g. *emi* '2p') or coordination. Another means of indicating plurality is by full reduplication of the head noun or the modifying adjective (not reduplication of their combination as in Leti); this is usually interpreted to mean that the multiple referents are also varied in some way.

(71)   *Uma   malae   n-oo   ke'an ke'an.*
Tetun house non-native 3-have room   room
        'Non-native houses have many and varied rooms' (e.g. for sleeping, cooking).

(72)   *Nia la=baa   iha   uma   se-seluk.*
Tetun 3s   NEG=go LOC house RDP-other
        'She didn't go to other houses.'

Plural marking in Leti distinguishes between human and non-human referents and signals variety, rather than sheer plurality. For human referents, plurality is marked only on definite noun phrases, where it is obligatorily indicated by the plural form of a determiner; this form corresponds to the singular form plus a final =*ra*.

(73)   *nakòddódi*   *nakòddódira*
Leti   nakòda=dó=di   nakòda=dó=di=ra
        skipper=MED=NOW   skipper=MED=NOW=PL
        'that skipper (there now)'   'those skippers (there now)'

Noun phrases with non-human referents, both definite and indefinite, optionally encode plurality by repeating the head and adjective slots. The determiner is not repeated, remaining in final position within the noun phrase.

(74)   *nuskèrna   nus=kèran=de*
Leti   REPETITION island=dry=REM
        'the dry islands (discussed at some stage)'

3.6.3 Interrogative pronouns

Tetun and Leti have similar sets of interrogative pronouns, distinguishing persons (Tetun *see*, Leti *sèi* 'who'), places (Tetun *nabee*, Leti *mèa* 'where') and objects (Tetun *saa*, Leti *sïaa* 'what'). The interrogative pronouns in Tetun are also used for unknown entities, in non-interrogative contexts. For instance, *see* means 'who' in interrogatives, and elsewhere means 'someone, anyone, whoever'. The Tetun interrogative pronouns can all also be used as noun phrase modifiers (e.g. *ema see* (person who) 'which person'). In Leti, only *sïaa* 'what' can modify a noun phrase; in this case it takes the form *sïa* and is a proclitic within the noun phrase (e.g. *sïa=kud=e* (what=horse=IDX) 'which horse'). This form *sïa* is also the subject clitic form for 'what'; the remaining Leti interrogatives, in contrast, have an invariant form.

3.6.4 Relative clause

Relative clauses follow the noun phrase head in both Tetun and Leti, with the exception of a small class of premodifying clauses in Tetun.

In Tetun, most relative clauses begin with the relative clause marker *mak=* (sometimes *ma'ak*); this is however optional. Where relativization is on the subject or object, the subject or object slot within the relative clause is simply left empty, as shown in (75) and (76) respectively. Where relativization is on the object of a preposition, a pronoun (*ne'e* 'PRX' or *nia* '3s, DIST') is retained in that object of preposition slot, as in (77).

(75) *bei*   *mak=mate*   *kleur*   *ti'an*
Tetun ancestor   REL=die   long.time   already
       'ancestor(s) who died long ago'

(76) *sala*   *mak=sia*   *foo*   *baa*   *ha'u*
Tetun fine   REL-3p   give   DIR   1s
       'the fine which they gave (i.e. imposed on) me'

(77) *tasi* *ida* *mak=sia* *atu* *n-akdiuk* *iha* *ne'e*
Tetun sea   one   REL=3p   OPT   3-play   LOC   PRX
       'a (part of the) sea in which they would play'

Tetun has a class of premodifying relative clauses. These are found only with the head noun *fatik* (sometimes *fatin*) 'place', and are syntactically restricted to 'minimal clauses' consisting of a single verb (e.g. *toba fatin* (sleep place) 'bed'), a subject plus verb (e.g. *roo-semo tuur fatik* (boat-fly sit place) 'airport') or verb plus object (e.g. *fasi dai fatik* (wash net place) 'place for washing nets'). Although there is no phonological evidence of compounding in such constructions, the resulting noun phrase has the semantic character of a compound, in that it represents a conventional name.

Leti relative clauses behave differently according to whether relativization is on the subject or on some other constituent. Subject relative clauses, illustrated in (78), are restricted to human subjects; they use the relative clause subject clitic *ma=* (*mak=* before the negative clitic *ta=*) and the relative clause subject agreement prefix *ka-/k-*. When relativization is on the object or oblique object, in contrast, normal subject clitics and subject marking are used, the verb within the relative clause is partially reduplicated, and the predicate of the relative clause obligatorily has the same indexer status as the predicate of the main clause. Example (79) illustrates this for relativization on the direct object.

(78) *püat=e*   *ma=k-pasi*   *spòl=e*
Leti   woman=IDX   REL=REL-wash:IDX   trousers=IDX
       'the woman who washed the trousers'

(79) *vètra=e*   *kòkkòi*   *ra-kdïo-dori=la*   *pnïëpan-ku*
Leti   maize=IDX   child:IDX   3p-RDP-steal:IDX=DIR   garden-1s.POSS
       'the maize which the children stole from my garden'

3.7 Possession

In Leti, pronominal possession is indicated by a suffix on the possessed noun (e.g. *kus-ku* (cat-1s.POSS) 'my cat'). The suffix distinguishes 1s (*-ku*), 2s (*-mu*) and 2p (*-mi*), with all other person-number combinations being represented by *-nV*. (See section 2.4 for the morphophonemics of V in *-nV*, and see Table 26.12 for a full listing of Leti pronoun forms.) If the identity of the possessor is to be made more explicit in the latter case, the possessum is preceded by the appropriate full pronoun (e.g. *ira kus-ne* (3p cat-POSS) 'their cat'). Possessive suffixes do not adhere to any following modifiers.

(80)   *ri:-ku*   *rururi   ida*
Leti   brother.in.law-1s.poss   strong   one
      'a strong brother-in-law of mine'

In Tetun, the person-number enclitics have for some speakers been reduced to a single generalized =*n* (glossed 'GEN' for 'genitive'), which can be used for all person-number combinations (see Table 26.11 in section 3.3.1). An alternative clitic, =*r*, is used by some speakers for plural (particularly third person plural) possessors. The person and number of the possessor are shown by a preceding pronoun, which is optionally marked as possessive by =*kan* (e.g. *ami(=kan) ama*=*n* (1pe(=POSS) father=GEN) 'my father').

Both Tetun and Leti distinguish between inalienable and alienable nouns; in Tetun there are also two intermediate classes. Inalienable nouns include all nouns referring to indissolubly connected parts of entities (e.g. Leti *ulti* 'skin') and relative location nouns (e.g. Tetun *laran* 'inside'). Inalienable nouns in Leti also include kin terms, except when these are used as terms of address. In both languages, inalienable nouns in most contexts are obligatorily marked for possession, by a possessive suffix (in Leti) or genitive clitic (in Tetun). So, for instance, all Tetun body parts and location nouns take a final =*n* (unless they already end in another consonant), and a Leti person cannot refer to *ali* 'man's brother', without adding a suffix to indicate whose brother it is (e.g. *al-mu* 'your brother'). In Tetun, kin terms are not quite like inalienable nouns. They do obligatorily carry genitive marking if there is a preceding possessor (e.g. *ni ina*=*n* (3s mother=GEN) 'his/her mother'), but this is optional if no possessor is specified (e.g. *Ina(n) baa…* 'The mother went…'), and, as in Leti, inapplicable if the word is used as a term of address. Tetun has the further phonological restriction that genitive clitics (like all consonantal suffixes and enclitics) apply only to vowel-final words.

Alienable nouns (e.g. nouns referring to personal possessions) are marked as possessed only if one wants to mention the fact of possession. In Leti, this means they only take a suffix if they are possessed (e.g. *kud-ku* (horse-1s.POSS) 'my horse', but *kuda* '(a) horse'), while in Tetun, alienable nouns never take a genitive clitic, even when they are possessed (e.g. *nia faru* 'his/her clothes', not **nia faru*=*n*). Two Tetun nouns, *rai* 'land' and *uma* 'house', are like inalienable nouns in that they take genitive marking when preceded by a possessor (e.g. *ha'u*=*kan rai*=*n* 'my land'), but like alienable ones in that they otherwise cannot have such a clitic (e.g. *iha rai seluk ne'e* (at land other PRX) 'in this other land', not **iha rai*=*n seluk ne'e*).

Tetun has an alternative word order which is not shared by Leti, in which a pronominal possessor follows the possessed noun. There is then no genitive clitic, and the possessor pronoun is marked by =*k* (e.g. *uma ita*=*k* (house 1pi=POSS) 'our house'). Postposed possessors are not possible for body parts and location terms (which in any case require a genitive clitic), but are possible for kin terms (e.g. *ina ha'u*=*k* (mother 1s=POSS) 'my mother') and alienably possessed nouns (e.g. *to'os nia*=*k* (garden 3s=POSS) 'his/her garden').

In Leti, non-pronominal possessors are simply juxtaposed to the following possessed noun phrase (e.g. *püat*=*e lavar-ne* (woman=IDX sarong-3.POSS) 'the woman's sarong'). Such juxtaposition of noun phrases is also possible in Tetun (e.g. *Na'in Lakuleik rai*=*n* ('noble Lakuleik land=GEN) 'the noble Lakuleik's land') except for fully alienable possession (e.g. **ema batar* 'person's maize'). However it is far more common to use an intervening third person possessive pronoun, which indicates the number of the possessor (e.g. *tamukun nia*=*kan fee*=*n* (village.head 3s=POSS wife=GEN) '(the) village head's wife', *feto sia*=*kan uma*=*n* (woman 3p=POSS house=GEN) '(the) women's house'). Non-pronominal possessors can also follow the possessed noun phrase in Tetun; in this case a following possessive pronoun is required (e.g. *inan-aman feto nia=k* (mother-father woman 3s=POSS) 'parents of the girl').

3.8 Numeral phrase

Both Tetun and Leti use a decimal numeral system, with the formula for complex numerals being similar for both. Numerals are illustrated in Table 26.15.

In both languages, the numeral 10 is idiosyncratic, being *sanulu* in Tetun, and *sanunu* in Leti. In Leti, thousands and hundreds are not modified by *ida* 'one' unless it is a simple numeral (e.g. *ras-ida* '100', but *rasu ida* '101'). Leti numerals from 2 to 9 are obligatorily prefixed by *vò-*, even when they occur within a complex numeral. They never display adhesion (e.g. *pipi vòrua* (goat two) 'two goats'). In Tetun it is impolite to say *tolu* 'three' (as it is homophonous with *tolu* 'egg, testicles'); the common avoidance term is *kabau* (literally 'buffalo'), and *tolu* is obligatorily shortened to *to-* in *to-nulu* '30'.

Malay is used for larger numbers; in Tetun it is normally used for a million or more, while in Leti it is used for complex numbers over 110 (e.g. 112), and for simple numbers from 10,000 onward (e.g. 100,000).

Tetun has no ordinal numbers in common use. Malay loans are usually used instead, although some speakers say that the (presumably Malay) ordinal prefix *ka-* can be added to Tetun numbers (e.g. to derive *ka-lima* 'fifth' from *lima* 'five'). In Leti, 'first' is represented by the ordinal noun *nïaulu*. Ordinal numbers from 2 to 10 are adjectives, which are derived from numerals by means of partial reduplication (see section 2.5), e.g. *vò-li-lima* 'fifth' from *vò-lima* 'five'. There are no larger ordinal numbers.

TABLE 26.15: NUMERALS

	1000s	100s	10s	Linker for	Digits
Tetun	rihun	atus	-nulu	resin	
Leti	rivnu	rasu	vïèl/vïèr-	vò-	
Tetun examples			haat-nulu	resin lima	'45'
		atus rua		resin tolu	'203'
	rihun ida	atus ida	sanulu		'1110'
	rihun neen	atus hitu	walu-nulu	resin siwi	'6789'
Leti examples			vïèl-ata	vò-lima	'45'
		rasü-ò-rua		vò-telu	'203'
	rivnu	rasu	sanunu		'1110'
	rivun-vò-nema	rasü-ò-itu	vïèl-ava	vò-sia	'6789'

TABLE 26.16: TETUN NUMERAL CLASSIFIERS

Classifier	Noun meaning	Classifier for
na'in	noble, owner	persons
matan	eye, source	buffalo, pigs
lolon	trunk	long cylindrical objects, e.g. fish, candles, ribs
tahan	leaf	thin flat objects, e.g. paper, books, clothing
fuan	fruit, heart	whole roundish objects, e.g. coconuts, eggs
musan	seed	very small round objects, e.g. tablets

In contrast to Leti, which does not have numeral classifiers, numerals in Tetun are preceded by numeral classifiers when certain types of entities are enumerated. For instance, when enumerating humans, it is strongly preferred for the numeral to be preceded by the classifier *na'in* (e.g. *feto na'in rua* (woman CLF two) 'two women', *sira na'in haat* (they CLF four) 'the four of them'). The set of classifiers is limited, with Table 26.16 presenting a reasonably full list of those in common use. Other entities (e.g. animals other than the large traditional animals buffalo and pigs) are enumerated without a classifier (e.g. *bibi rua* (goat two) 'two goats').

4 NOMINAL MORPHOLOGY

Tetun and Leti both have little derivational morphology, with reduplication being the most productive means of deverbal nominalization in both languages (section 2.5).

In Tetun, instrument, undergoer and result nouns are mostly derived by partial reduplication (in combination with a suffix -*n* or -*k* if the root is vowel-final) or the prefix *k(a)*- (sometimes in combination with a suffix -*k*). The suffixes -*k* and -*n* on their own have a similar function, but are uncommon. Table 26.17 lists examples of each.

Tetun abstract nouns are derived from verbs and adjectives by partial reduplication, in combination with a suffix -*k* or -*n* if the root is vowel-final. Such derivations nearly always occur as possessed nouns (e.g. *nia=kan ha-halo-k* (3s=POSS RDP-do-k) 'his behavior').

Leti has three means of deriving nouns from verbs: full reduplication, nominal affixation, and possessive suffixation. Full reduplication derives instrument nouns from both transitive and intransitive verbs (e.g. *sòr-sòra* 'needle' from *sòra* 'sew', *pal~pïali* 'raft' from *pali* 'float'). It is confined to verbs that also accept one of the nominalizing affixes -*ï*-, -*n*-, or -*nï*-.

Nonstative verbs in Leti can be nominalized by prefixation or infixation, both of which are illustrated in Table 26.18. Most resulting nouns refer to the verbal act or to the result of that activity. In a few instances, the meaning of the resulting noun is lexicalized (e.g. *l-i-èta* 'custom' from *lèta* 'found a village', *t-n-utu* 'hammer' from *tutu* 'pound'). Nominalizing affixation is also used to encode progressive and resultative aspect (section 3.3.7). There are seven nominalizing affixes, with the choice between them being primarily determined by the phonology of the initial syllable of the verb.

All verbs that take full subject agreement markers (i.e. those not exhibiting A&M, see section 2.4) take the *nïa*- prefix. Verbal stems with an initial non-high vowel have either an *ï*- prefix or a *nï*- prefix or both. For those verbs that take both these prefixes, one derives result nouns and the other derives nouns referring to acts. The infix -*ï*- is inserted

TABLE 26.17: TETUN DERIVATION OF NON-ABSTRACT NOUNS FROM VERBS

Affix	Root	Gloss	Noun	Gloss
Partial RDP	fo'at	'catch in noose'	fa-fo'at	'lasso'
	kodo	'filter (sago)'	ka-kodo-k	'filter for sago'
	simu	'receive'	sa-simu-n	'that which is received'
k(a)-	feur	'rotate'	ka-feur	'spinning top (toy)'
k(a)- -k	lele	'float'	k-lele-k	'boat' (sea taboo term)
-k	hada	'build flooring'	hada-k	'floor (of split palm)'
-n	futu	'tie up'	futu-n	'bundle'

TABLE 26.18: LETI NOMINALIZING AFFIXATION

Affix	Root	Gloss	Noun	Gloss
nïa-	ltïeri	'speak'	nïa-ltïeri	'act of speaking, speech'
	olu	'sell'	nïa-olu	'act of selling, sale'
	keni	'place'	nïa-keni	'act of placing'
ï-, nï-	odi	'carry'	ï-odi	'load, act of carrying'
	osri	'follow'	ï-osri	'act of following'
	osri	'follow'	nï-osri	'public, audience'
	atu	'know'	ï-atu	'knowledge'
	atu	'know'	nï-atu	'act of knowing'
-ï-	mai	'come'	m-ï-ai	'act of coming'
	lòi	'dance'	l-ï-òi	'act of dancing'
i- -ï-	na:ru	'chew betel'	i-n-ï-a:ru	'act of betel-chewing'
-n-	virna	'peel'	v-n-irna	'act of peeling'
	tu:ni	'fall'	t-n-u:ni	'act of falling'
-nï-	pèpna	'fence'	p-nï-èpna	'fence, act of fencing'
	vaka	'ask'	v-nï-aka	'act of asking'

into initial syllables that have a nasal or alveolar onset and a non-high nucleus. A few such verbs take a prefix *i-* in addition to the infix. When the initial syllable has an onset which is neither nasal nor alveolar, the infix *-n-* is inserted if the nucleus is a high vowel, while the infix *-nï-* is used if the vowel is non-high. Verbs which either begin with an alveolar consonant onset or lack an onset, and which have a high vowel nucleus in the initial syllable, are nominalized without any change in form.

Stative verbs are nominalized by possessive suffixation (e.g. *mèr-ne* (red-3.poss) '(its) redness'). Such derived nouns are inalienable, and signal an inherent and unchanging state.

ACKNOWLEDGEMENTS

Catharina expresses thanks to Ama Bo'uk, Pak Hendrikus and many others in Betun for their generous assistance. Aone expresses thanks to the clans of Tilupun-Slaupun and of Wurwole for their help.

REFERENCES

Barchewitz, E.C. (1730) *Allerneueste und wahrhaffte Ost-Indianische Reise-Beschreibung*, Chemnitz: Johann Christoph & Johann David Stösseln.
Bartkowiak, T. (1979) *Gems from the island of Timor*, Ende, Flores: Nusa Indah.
Brandes, J.L.A. (1884) *Bijdrage tot de vergelijkende klankleer der westersche afdeeling van de Maleisch-Polynesische taalfamilie*, PhD Utrecht University.
das Dores, R. (1907) Diccionario Teto-Português, Lisbon: Imprensa Nacional.
de Josselin de Jong, J.P.B. (1947) *Studies in Indonesian Culture II: The community of Erai (Wetar)*, Amsterdam: Verhandelingen der Koninklijke Akademie van Wetenschappen afd. Letterkunde, nieuwe reeks 20/2.
——(1987) *Wetan Fieldnotes, some eastern Indonesian texts with linguistic notes and and a vocabulary*, Verhandelingen van het Koninklijk Instituut voor Taal-, Land- en Volkenkunde 30, Dordrecht: Foris.
Fernandes, A.J. (1937) *Método prático para aprender o Tétum*, Macao: Escola Tipográfica do Orfanato de Macau.

Heijmering, G. (1846) 'Bijdrage tot de kennis van de taal der Z.W. Eilanden, benevens eene proeve van vergelijking derzelve met acht andere inlandsche talen', *Tijdschrift voor Nederlandsch-Indië* 8/3:1–81.

Hull, G. (1994) 'A national language for East Timor', in I. Fodor and C. Hagège (eds) *Language reform: History and future*, volume 6, 347–366, Hamburg: Helmut Buske Verlag.

——(1996) *Mai kolia Tetun: a beginner's course in Tetum-Praça: the lingua franca of East Timor* (second edition), North Sydney: Australian Catholic Relief and the Australian Catholic Social Justice Council.

——(1999) *Standard Tetum–English dictionary*, Sydney: Allen & Unwin.

——and Eccles, L. (2001) *Tetum reference grammar*, Winston Hills: Sebastião Aparício da Silva Project in conjunction with Instituto Nacional de Linguística, Universidade de Timor Lorosa'e.

Jonker, J.C.G. (1911) 'Over de "vervoegde" werkwoordsvormen in de maleisch-polynesische talen', *Bijdragen tot de Taal-, Land-, en Volkenkunde* 65:266–333.

——(1915) *Rottineesche Spraakkunst*, Leiden: E.J. Brill.

——(1932) *Lettineesche taalstudien*, Verhandelingen van het Bataviaasch Genootschap 70, Bandoeng: A.C. Nix & Co.

Langker, B. (1996) *Tanuku the baby crocodile. Lafaek-oan ida naran Tanuku*, Sydney: Mary McKillop Institute of East Timorese Studies.

Luijke, W. (1834) *Wenijatutu makakapurij ida, ponawatutu rije makawajowe poksaranij*, Batavia.

Mathijsen, A. (1906) *Tettum-Hollandsche woordenlijst met beknopte spraakkunst*, Batavia: Albrecht & Co.

Mendes, M.P. and Laranjeira, M.M. (1935) *Dicionário Tetum-Português*, Macao: Tipografia Mercantil de N.T. Fernandes & Filhos.

Middelkoop, P. (1950) 'Proeve van een Timorese grammatica', *Bijdragen tot de Taal-, Land- en Volkenkunde* 106:375–517.

Mills, R.F. and Grima, J. (1980) 'Historical developments in Lettinese', in P.B. Naylor (ed.) *Austronesian studies. Papers from the second eastern conference on Austronesian languages*, 273–283, Michigan: Ann Arbor.

Monteiro, F. (1985) *Kamus Tetun-Indonesia*, Jakarta: Pusat Pembinaan dan Pengembangan Bahasa.

Morris, C. (1984a) *Ai knananuk ho ai knanoik nousi Rai Timur: rai nousi lafaek dukur. Verse and legends from Timor the land of the sleeping crocodile, book 1*, Frankston, Victoria: H.C. Morris.

——(1984b) *Tetun–English dictionary*, Canberra: Pacific Linguistics.

Peace Corps East Timor (2003) Peace Corps East Timor Tetun Language Manual, Dili: Peace Corps East Timor.

Riedel, J.G.F. (1886) *De sluik- en kroesharige rassen tusschen Selebes en Papua*, The Hague: Martinus Nijhoff.

Serantes, P.J. and Doko, I.H. (1976) *Kamus kecil Indonesia – Tetun – Belu Tetun Dili*, Bandung: Penerbit Ganaco NV.

Stokhof, W.A.L. (ed.) (1981) *Holle lists: vocabularies in languages of Indonesia, volume 3/1: Southern Moluccas; Central Moluccas: Seram (1)*, Canberra: Pacific Linguistics.

Therik, G.T. (1995) *Wehali: the four corner land: the cosmology and traditions of a Timorese ritual centre*, PhD thesis, Research School of Pacific and Asian Studies, The Australian National University.

Thomaz, L.F.F.R. (1981) 'The formation of Tetun-Praça, vehicular language of East Timor', in N. Phillips and A. Khaidir (eds) *Papers on Indonesian languages and literatures*, 54–83, Paris: Cahier d'Archipel 13.

Troeboes *et al.* (1987) *Struktur Bahasa Tetum*, Jakarta: Departement Pendidikan dan Kebudayaan.

van Engelenhoven, A. (1995a) *A Description of the Leti Language (as spoken in Tukutei)*, PhD Leiden University.
van Engelenhoven, A. (1995b) 'Van Proto-Malayo-Polynesisch naar Proto-Luangisch-Kisarisch', in C. Baak, M. Bakker and D. van der Meij (eds) *Tales from a concave world: Liber amicorum Bert Voorhoeve*, 246–264, Leiden: Department of Languages and Cultures of Southeast Asia and Oceania.
——(1997) 'Words and expressions: notes on parallelism in Leti (East-Indonesia)', *Cakalele Maluku Research Journal* 8:1–25.
——(1999) 'Epítetos e Epítomes: uso e perda do conhecimento narrativo no sudoeste das Molucas (Leste da Indonésia)', *Econtros de divulgação e debate em estudos sociais* 4:99–107.
van Klinken, C.L. (1999) *A grammar of the Fehan dialect of Tetun, an Austronesian language of West Timor*, Canberra: Pacific Linguistics.
Williams-van Klinken, C.L., Hajek, J. and Nordlinger, R. (2002) *Tetun Dili: a grammar of an East Timorese language*, Canberra: Pacific Linguistics.
Wurm, S. and Hattori, S. (1981) *Language atlas of the Pacific area*, Canberra: Pacific Linguistics.

CHAPTER TWENTY-SEVEN

TABA

John Bowden

1 INTRODUCTION

Taba is a South Halmahera Austronesian language spoken by around 30,000 people on Makian island, Kayoa island, and nearby parts of Moti and southern Halmahera as well as in Ternate city and a local transmigration area near Kao in the northern part of Halmahera. Taba is also known as Makian Dalam in Indonesian and sometimes as East Makian in English. The eastern side of Makian island is the traditional home of Taba. On the western half of Makian a non-Austronesian language is spoken: this language is known as Makian Luar in Indonesian, West Makian in English, Taba Lik ('Outer Taba') in Taba, and as Moi by its own speakers.

Makian is a volcano with a long history of devastating eruptions which have brought about periodic mass migrations from the island. In the early 1980s, government seismological reports suggested that Makian island was due for an imminent eruption and a government-sponsored transmigration scheme designed to move the Makianese at danger was implemented. Under this scheme, a large number of Makianese moved to a transmigration area at Malifut, near Kao on Halmahera island. The rest of the Makianese left the island after an eruption took place in 1987, but most of these people have since returned. The language is still used vigorously on Makian island, but it is not so widely used in places like Malifut where young people are not generally learning the language as fluent speakers any more.

Lucardie (1983) discusses aspects of traditional Makianese migration, in the periods before migration to Malifut was instituted. These early waves of migration also often came about as a result of volcanic activity, and often involved large numbers of people. There have been reports of Makianese communities in various parts of North Maluku which supposedly migrated after earlier eruptions. In some of these communities it appears that Taba remains the preferred language. I can verify the existence of a Taba-speaking village on Bacan island, but I have been unable to confirm any other reports. Such issues make it impossible to give an accurate number of speakers for the language today. The total number of Taba-speakers today is probably somewhere between 20,000 and 40,000.

There is minor dialectal variation between all of the villages in which Taba is spoken. A major split between a southern dialect (which retains historical *a as /a/, e.g. *mta* 'eye' < *mata*) and a northern dialect (which often reflects *a as /o/, e.g. *mto* 'eye' < *mata*) is found. This article is based on my fieldwork amongst speakers of the northern dialect in Ngofakiaha village.

Taba has for a long time been subject to the influences of other languages, both Austronesian and non-Austronesian. Makian island is one of a group of four small islands in the region to which cloves are indigenous, and Taba has long been influenced by the role of trade in the region. Early 'Arab' traders brought Islam and Malay (as well as traces of Arabic) to the region. (The earliest Malay documents found in Ternate, the regional metropolitan center, date from the fifteenth century.) European colonizers brought influences from Spanish, Portuguese, and most notably Dutch to the area from the beginning of the sixteenth century. Ternatan, the metropolitan language, which was once used as a lingua franca in the area, is a West Papuan language and its influence has been quite profound, most notably for its role in supplying much of Taba's *alus* (high speech level) vocabulary. Ternatan also probably provided a model for parts of Taba's grammatical typology, particularly the possessor–possessed ordering in possessive noun phrases. Contemporary Taba is being increasingly affected by North Moluccan Malay, which is having quite drastic effects on the characteristic discourse structures found in Taba. Some of these noteworthy effects are the borrowing of conjunctions (§3.1.5) and prepositions (§3.5). More details are provided in Bowden (2002).

The earliest source on Taba is Adriani and Kruijt (1914), which provides brief grammatical notes and comparative remarks on Taba and nearby Austronesian languages. Collins (1982) gives a wordlist and further brief grammatical notes. Bowden (2001), a reference grammar, is the most comprehensive source on the language to have appeared so far.

2 PHONOLOGY

Taba segmental phonology is unexceptional. However, the language has a wide variety of initial geminates and consonant clusters which can be realized in a variety of ways, and there is also productive metathesis.

2.1 Segment inventory

Contemporary Taba has an inventory of five vowels and nineteen consonants, four of which have been borrowed and are nativized to varying degrees. Vowels are listed in Table 27.1, and consonants (with loans in parentheses) are shown in Table 27.2. Loan phonemes vary widely in their degree of nativization, from /f/ which occurs in a large number of words from sources as diverse as English, Dutch, Ternatan, and Arabic, etc. through /tʃ/ and /dʒ/ to /ʔ/ which is highly marginal, and occurs in only a few words, all ultimately of Arabic origin.

TABLE 27.1: TABA VOWEL PHONEMES

	Front (unrounded)	Central (unrounded)	Back (rounded)
High	i		u
Mid	e		o
Low		a	

TABLE 27.2: TABA CONSONANT PHONEMES

	Labial	Apico-alveolar	Lamino-palatal	Dorso-velar	Glottal
Voiced stops	b	d		g	(ʔ)
Voiceless stops	p	t		k	
Nasals (voiced)	m	n		ŋ	
Voiced affricate			(dʒ)		
Voiceless affricate			(tʃ)		
Fricatives	(f)	s			h
Trill		r			
Lateral		l			
Approximants	w		j		

Generally speaking, there are no long vowels in Taba. However, there are a few marginal exceptions to this generalization. A few monosyllabic words have expressive long vowels, although none of these contrast with short vowels, e.g. *kii* 'vagina', *sii* 'penis'. A contrast in length does exist between the negator *te* and the discourse connector *tee* 'if not'. This contrast, however, is probably better attributed to intonation, since the negator *te* always occurs at the end of the constituent it negates (§3.2.12) while the discourse connector *tee* (§3.1.5) always occurs in the preclausal fronted position.

2.2 Syllable structure and stress

Post-initial syllables in Taba are of the form (C)V(C), but initial syllables may begin with consonant clusters: (C)(C)V(C). Syllable peaks consist of a single vowel: there are no diphthongs in Taba, and apart from a few marginal exceptions, there are no long vowels either.

Most initial clusters occur in words which were either historically multimorphemic or which remain multimorphemic in contemporary Taba. The most common examples occur at the beginning of consonant-initial roots which have been prefixed by pronominal cross-referencing affixes, e.g. *t=ngongano* '1pi=hope', or as a result of post-nasal apocope, e.g. *mto* < **mata* 'eye' or *mnihis* < **ma-nipis* 'ST-thin'. Some synchronic initial geminates came about as a result of the reduction of reduplications (see §2.5), e.g. *ddoba* 'earth' < **daddoba* < **dab-doba* 'RDP-garden'.

Phonological clusters can be realized in a variety of ways, depending on the nature of the segments involved and the nature of surrounding segments. Resyllabification so that initial consonants occur as the coda of a preceding syllable is frequent, the insertion of epenthetic *e* occurs when an initial cluster follows a consonant coda from a preceding syllable, but many clusters which violate so-called sonority constraints remain when they occur utterance initially and the above processes cannot operate. These are dealt with phonetically in a variety of ways. Coarticulation of adjacent heterorganic stops is frequent (e.g. *k=poas* (1s=row) 'I row' may be realized as [k͡poas]). Other clusters are produced as phonetic clusters in spite of sonority mismatches, e.g. *n=luklik* '3s=roll something' is produced as a genuine cluster with no syllabification of the initial nasal. (See Bowden 2001:chapter 2 and Bowden and Hajek 1999 for more details.)

Stress is indicated by higher pitch, longer duration and greater intensity and generally falls on the penultimate syllable of multisyllabic words or on the only syllable of monosyllables. Stress is unaffected by affixation. A few exceptions, where stress occurs on the final syllable of multisyllabic words, are also found. This most notably affects words which were historically multimorphemic, e.g. *makót* 'be red', which was presumably formed with the no longer productive **ma-* stative prefix, and forms which end in nasals synchronically, since many of these have undergone historical deletion of post-nasal vowels, e.g. *mapín* 'woman' < **ma-binay*. Some recent multisyllabic loanwords also receive final stress, e.g. *masín* 'engine'. In spite of minor variation in stress placement, there do not appear to be any minimal pairs based on stress assignment.

2.3 Orthography

Taba is not widely used for writing and there is no standard orthography. Most Taba speakers tend to use Indonesian for written communication. However, Taba is written on occasion, perhaps when a child is living away from North Maluku for study and writes to his or her parents. In such cases, a kind of de facto written standard has emerged, based on Indonesian orthography. In this de facto standard, the affricates /ʤ/ and /tʃ/ are written as 'j' and 'c' respectively; the glottal stop is either written with an apostrophe or not at all, the palatal approximant /j/ is written 'y' and the velar nasal is written as a digraph: 'ng'. In this article, any occurrences of the glottal stop will be represented by an apostrophe, and if stress occurs anywhere other than the penultimate syllable it will be marked by an acute accent.

2.4 Major phonological alternations

/s/ is always realized as [tʃ] after alveolars, e.g. *n=sobal* (3s=sail) is realized as [ntʃóbal]. /e/ is raised towards [i] before velars, e.g. *yak e k=han* (1s FOC 1s=go) is realized as [yak i khan]. /h/ is deleted if it occurs in the onset of an unstressed syllable anywhere but in word-initial position: *n=ha-mót* (3s=CAU-die) is realized as [namót]. Phonemically geminate vowels are realized phonetically as short vowels. Unstressed /h/ deletion is ordered before vowel degemination so that, for example, *a=ha-pon* (1pe=ACT-whistle) occurs as [apón]. Unstressed vowel deletion often occurs with applicative suffixation. Productive metathesis also occurs with applicativization.

Taba has two applicative suffixes, *-o*, which allows locations to occur as arguments of a verb and *-Vk*, which most commonly allows instruments to occur as arguments, but also occasionally licenses a recipient or theme (§5.2). Suffixation with *-o* triggers deletion of any unstressed vowel occurring in the final syllable of the root, whether the root ends in an open or closed syllable, (e.g. *halusa* 'to say', *haluso* 'to tell someone'; *lekat* 'be bad', *lekto* 'go rotten'). Roots ending in stressed vowels, whether mono- or multisyllabic are unaffected by the rule (e.g. *battalón* 'to sit', *battalóno* 'to sit on something').

The most common form of the *-Vk* applicative suffix is *-ak*. This form of the suffix occurs on all but a few forms with stressed final syllables (*sung* 'to enter', *sungak* 'to enter with something'). In a few exceptional cases *-ik* occurs on stressed final syllables, presumably because an historical final vowel /i/ has been lost from the stem (e.g. *wet* 'to hit', *wetik* 'to hit with an instrument'). If a verb root ends in a vowel, the suffix occurs simply as *-k*, e.g. *sagu* 'to shoot, spear (intr.)', *saguk* 'to throw a spear (tr.)'. When *-Vk* suffixation applies to stems with unstressed closed syllables, metathesis is triggered (e.g. *bulay* 'to spin around', *bulyak* 'to twist something'; *baling* 'to wrap something up'; *balngik* 'to wrap something with something').

2.5 Reduplication

Taba has three kinds of reduplication. Full reduplication is not very common. It usually serves to create intensive forms but sometimes reduplicated forms have quite lexicalized meanings too. In full reduplication, stress is maintained on both parts of the reduplicated form, e.g. *ngán-ngán* 'often/every day' < *ngán* 'sun, day'; *misilí-misilí* 'little by little' < *misilí* 'a little'.

CVC partial reduplication is very productive and works by taking a copy of the initial CVC sequence of a root in which V is replaced by /a/ and prefixing it to the root. (With vowel initial roots, the initial VC sequence serves as the template, but the C in this sequence occurs both before and after the vowel to create a CVC prefix.) This process derives nouns describing instruments used to bring about an action referred to by the root, e.g. *balbulay* 'device used to coil rope or cord onto' < *bal-bulay* 'RDP-wind/coil'; *taktek* 'water scoop' < *tak-tek* 'RDP-scoop water'. These derived forms are often subject to assimilation, either partial as in *pampón* 'nocturnal bird believed to make its call as the instrument of malignant spirits' < *pan-pon* 'RDP-whistle', or complete as in *pappít* 'snare/trap (n.)' < *pat-pit* 'RDP-snare/trap (v.)'. Assimilation is often variable. Whether or not it occurs in a particular form depends on both ease of articulation and the frequency of particular derived forms: for example, frequently occurring reduplications are more likely to undergo assimilation than are new coinings.

The final type of reduplication is used to derive 'plurality of action' verbs. In this process, a template is formed by taking the first syllable of a stem which refers to an activity, plus the onset and nucleus of the second syllable if it has one, replacing any vowels with /a/, and prefixing the whole form to the stem.

(1) a. *K=sung   um*
         1s=enter   house
         'I entered the house.'

     b. *K=sang-sung   um*
         1s=RDP-enter   house
         'I kept on entering the house(s).'

(2) a. *N=ot-ik   si   yan*
         3s=take-APP[give]   3p   fish
         'He gave them fish.'

     b. *N=ata-ot-ik   si   yan   lloci*
         3s=RDP-take-APP[RDP-give]   3p   fish many
         'He kept giving them loads of fish.'

3 BASIC MORPHOSYNTAX

3.1 Morphological units and word classes

It is useful to be able to make a distinction between 'words', 'particles', 'affixes' and 'clitics' in Taba, based on the degree of (in)dependence these units exhibit in terms of their phonological and syntactic characteristics. Words attract primary stress and may occur on their own as free forms. Words are typically nouns, verbs, or members of a variety of minor classes discussed further below. Particles also attract primary stress but they cannot occur on their own, unless supported by a word. For example, the word *n-han* (3s-go) '(s)he has gone/is going, etc.', consisting of the cross-referencing proclitic *n-* '3s' and the verbal stem *han* 'go', could be uttered on its own in response to a question such as 'what has (s)he done?'. However, the stressed realis-marking particle *do* can only be used if it is supported by a predicate of some kind, e.g. *nhan do* '(s)he has gone'. Neither affixes nor clitics attract stress and both are bound to phonological hosts. They differ in that affixes are attached to words while clitics are attached to phrases. The applicative suffixes are both true affixes, because they always attach themselves to verbal stems, e.g. *wet* 'to hit (TR)' can be suffixed by the instrumental applicative *-Vk*, producing the ditransitive form *wetik* 'to hit something with something'. Cross-referencing markers, on the other hand, are proclitics, because they are prefixed to phrases consisting of an active verb plus any particle that may precede the verb, e.g. *l=wet* (3p=hit) 'they hit (something)', but *l=maka wet* (3p=RCP hit) 'they hit each other'.

Taba has two major open word classes: nouns and verbs. There are a variety of minor classes including demonstratives, directionals, adpositions, quantifiers, interrogatives, pronouns, conjunctions and discourse connectors. Strictly speaking, Taba has no class of possessive pronouns but it does have a set of possessive 'ligatures' which are discussed along with pronouns in §3.1.2.

There is no adjective class. Words describing properties or attributes usually occur as Undergoer-oriented intransitive verbs in Taba (see §3.2.2). Demonstratives, directionals and adpositions are discussed in later sections of this article. The other minor word classes will be discussed below.

3.1.1 Nouns and verbs

Nouns and verbs are readily distinguished morphosyntactically, but distinguishing between word classes on lexical grounds is generally not possible: the same roots often occur either as nouns or as verbs. Nouns may be identified as such because they occur as arguments, are qualified by demonstratives, or because they are quantified, etc. Verbs may be thus identified because they are found with causative or applicative morphology, or because they are cross-referenced by Actor marking proclitics, etc. However, it is not usually possible to distinguish roots as either nouns or verbs: the same root may often appear in either morphosyntactic class. For example, *poas* occurs as a noun in the phrase *poas ne* (oar PRX) 'this oar', but a verb in *n=poas* (3s=row) '(s)he's rowing'. A number of derived forms do have unambiguous class membership though: to give a few examples, causativized (§5.1) or applicativized (§5.2) stems are verbs; instrumental reduplications (§2.5) are nouns.

The major subclasses of verbs (discussed further in §3.2) are Actor-oriented and Undergoer-oriented intransitives (unergatives and unaccusatives), canonical transitives, semi-transitives, and two types of ditransitive verbs which are labeled 'close' and 'remote' ditransitives, as well as a class labeled non-Actor bivalent verbs. There is also a small class of verbs referring to acts of excretion which have some peculiarities of their own and which must be treated as a separate class. These are identified according to the number and types of arguments that may co-occur with them, and according to whether and how these arguments are cross-referenced.

Subclasses of nouns include pronouns (§3.1.2), quantifiers (§3.1.3) and some derived directionals (§4).

3.1.2 Pronouns

The Taba independent pronouns and pronominal proclitics are listed in Table 27.3.

Plural number is reserved for humans; the 2nd and 3rd person plural forms are also used for polite address and reference respectively. In general, polite forms are used for addressees or referents that are older than the speaker.

TABLE 27.3: TABA PRONOUNS

	Independent pronoun	Clitic form		Independent pronoun	Clitic form
1s	*yak*	*k=*	1pi	*tit*	*t=*
			1pe	*am*	*a=*
2s	*au*	*m=*	2p	*meu*	*h=*
3s	*i*	*n=*	3p	*si*	*l=*

TABLE 27.4: TABA POSSESSIVE LIGATURES

1s	*nik*	1pi	*nit*
		1pe	*amam*
2s	*nim*	2p	*memeu*
3s	*ni*	3p	*nidi*

Pronominal reference with the independent pronouns can only be made to animates. Demonstrative pronouns (introduced in §4) can, however, be used to refer to inanimates. The independent pronouns can be used in virtually any syntactic context in which a full noun phrase referring to an animate can be used. The clitic forms obligatorily cross-reference the Actors of Actor intransitive verbs, as well as those of the different types of transitive and ditransitive verbs discussed in §3.2.

Taba has no real possessive pronouns, but it does have a set of possessive 'ligatures' which intervene between a noun referring to a possessor and another noun referring to something that is possessed. Most, but not all of the possessive forms are created by taking the base *ni* and adding a suffix that cross references the possessor to it. Because possessor NPs are often ellipsed, the ligatures frequently look like possessive pronouns. Compare, for example *yak nik mapin* (1s 1s.POSS wife) 'my wife' with *nik mapin* (1s.POSS wife), also 'my wife'. The forms of the possessive ligatures are presented in Table 27.4.

3.1.3 Quantifiers

Quantifiers occur as the heads of measure phrases and are of two types: independent quantifiers such as *lloci* 'many', *misili* 'a little', and classifier-numeral collocations. The basic numeral roots from one to nine are listed in (3). Note that these roots never occur on their own unless they are supported by classifiers. In (3), they co-occur with the default classifier *p-* which can be used (amongst other things) to count pieces of fruit.

(3)	1	*p-so*	*niwi pso*	'one coconut'
	2	*p-lu*	*niwi plu*	'two coconuts'
	3	*p-tol*	*niwi ptol*	'three coconuts'
	4	*p-hot*	*niwi phot*	'four coconuts'
	5	*p-lim*	*niwi plim*	'five coconuts'
	6	*p-oenam*	*niwi poenam*	'six coconuts'
	7	*p-hit*	*niwi phit*	'seven coconuts'
	8	*p-wal*	*niwi pwal*	'eight coconuts'
	9	*p-sio*	*niwi psio*	'nine coconuts'

Taba has at least 20 classifiers. The less common classifiers take the form of independent words, e.g. *ising* 'hand (of bananas)', *ai* 'tree', *luklik* 'long thin things which are rolled up'. The more commonly occurring classifiers are often proclitics, e.g. *ha=* used for counting measurements or intervals which are not classifiers themselves, *mat=* used for humans and *sis=* used for counting animals. The default classifier shown in (3) is a simple prefix, *p-*. The clitic classifiers precede quantifier phrases while the prefix precedes a numeral root. Compare *ha=lu pa tol* (CLF-two or three) 'two or three (times, etc.)' with *p-lu pa p-tol* (CLF-two or CLF-three) 'two or three (fruit, etc.)'.

TABLE 27.5: TABA INTERROGATIVES

Form	Word class	Interrogative meaning	Indefinite meaning
lo	locative noun	'where'	'somewhere'
alho	noun	'who'	'someone'
hapu	verb	'how, why'	'somehow'
CLF-*i-so*	quantifier	'how many'	'some number'
poiso	temporal adverb	'when'	'sometime'
pu	noun	'what'	'something'

The forms which refer to multiples of a hundred, and a thousand are themselves formally classifiers: *utin* 'hundred' [< -*utin* 'to gather'], *calan* 'thousand' [independent form unattested].

3.1.4 Interrogatives

Interrogatives are a mixed class, most of them being nouns, but some belong to other major word classes. They share the property of being used to question the nature of a participant or event, etc. and all of them can also be used as indefinite nouns. The complete list of Taba interrogatives is given in Table 27.5.

Questions using interrogative words and statements using indefinites are distinguished solely on the basis of intonation. The example shown in (4) could function as either a statement or a question: with a rising final intonation it will be a question; with falling final intonation a statement.

(4)   *Alho   n=wom*
    who   3s=come
    'Who came?' [or 'Someone came.']

3.1.5 Conjunctions and discourse connectors

Taba has a fairly small set of conjunctions, some of which are used for conjoining noun phrases and others of which may conjoin clauses. Those which can be used to conjoin noun phrases are listed in (5).

(5)   *lo*   'and'
    ada   'and/with'
    pa   'or'

Taba discourse is generally characterized by loose paratactic bonds between clauses where the meaningful relationships between clauses must be interpreted pragmatically; overtly conjoined clauses are relatively rare. A listing of conjunctions which conjoin clauses is given in (6).

(6)   *lo*   'and'   coordinating
    ada   'and/with'   coordinating   (also occurs as instrumental
                                                              preposition)
    ma/mai/me   'then/but'   coordinating
    pa   'or'   coordinating
    turus   'immediately'   coordinating   (< Malay *turus* 'then'; also
                                                              occurs as discourse connector)

tapi	'but'	coordinating	(< Malay *tapi* 'but')
malai	'then'	coordinating	(< Malay *mulai* 'begin'?; also occurs as discourse connector)
de	'in order that'	subordinating	
polo	'if'	subordinating	
tutik(ma)	'until'	subordinating	(also occurs as discourse connector)
ndadi	'so/thus'	subordinating	(< Malay *jadi*; also occurs as discourse connector)
karna	'because'	subordinating	(< Malay *karena*; also occurs as discourse connector
sabab	'because'	subordinating	(< Malay *sebab*; also occurs as discourse connector)

It is noteworthy that many of the Taba conjunctions have been borrowed from Malay. It appears that Taba discourse patterns are undergoing a rather drastic remodeling in the direction of Malay with less parataxis being employed as more overt conjunctions are borrowed from Malay (see Bowden 2002 for more details of this).

Discourse connectors occur at the beginning of the clause in which they appear and they are distinguished from conjunctions on two grounds. First, there is a looser intonational bond between a clause with a discourse connector and its preceding clause than is the case with conjoined clauses. Second, the semantic connection formed by a conjunction is one between what is expressed in two adjacent clauses, while the semantic connection between a clause containing a discourse connector is with a whole preceding chunk of discourse rather than with just one clause. Some forms (listed above) can occur with both functions. A few more discourse connectors, which never occur as conjunctions, are listed in (7).

(7)   *odo*   'on the other hand'
       pu pu ma   'but what if…'
       tee   'if not'

3.2 Basic clause structure

In classifying different clause types in Taba, it is useful to make distinctions according to the kinds of predicates that are involved, as well as according to the number, and kinds of arguments that may occur in clauses of each variety. Three basic kinds of predicates may be involved: verb phrases, noun phrases, and (very occasionally) adpositional phrases. While nominal predicates and adpositional predicates may take no more than a single argument, verbal predicates may have as many as three arguments. Ellipsis of readily retrievable arguments is common in Taba, and cross-referencing only affects a subset of argument types. Since the actual occurrence of an NP is optional, it is the potential for co-occurrence without any adpositional or other marking with particular predicate types that is taken as defining the subtypes of predicates presented here.

Taba can be broadly classified as having a mixed nominative-accusative and split-S system for the representation of arguments in intransitive and basic transitive clauses. Taba also has a split in O marking which will be discussed in the following sections (see also Bowden 2000a for more details).

3.2.1 Clauses with no arguments (ambient clauses)

Clauses with no arguments (ambient clauses) are usually used to describe meteorological states. Such clauses may occur with either verbal or nominal predicates, as illustrated in (8) and (9) respectively.

(8)   *Midin   kwat*
      cold   EMPH
      'It's cold.'

(9)   *Ulan*
      rain
      'It's raining.'

Taba has no indigenous existential verb (but the Malay form *ada* is often used for this purpose). Indigenous existential constructions in Taba are formed by using a predicate that consists of just an NP referring to whatever's existence is being asserted as in (10). These can be classified as ambient clauses.

(10) *Ssu!*
      earthquake
      'There's an earthquake!'

3.2.2 Intransitive nominal clauses

The arguments of nominal clauses may be distinguished from predicates from the fact that arguments are often referential and trackable in discourse while predicates are not. In nominal clauses with arguments which are full NPs (including demonstratives), the full NP argument precedes the predicating NP, as in (11), while pronominal arguments follow their predicating NPs as in (12).

(11) *Ni   sso   lahar   midin*
      3s.POSS   name   lava   cold
      'Its name is "cold lava".'

(12) *Mapin   i*
      female   3s
      'It's a female.'

Different types of nominal clauses can be identified on the basis of the different kinds of semantic relationships between NPs which are encoded. In identity clauses, the predicator encodes some new information about the identity of an argument, which is given information. Examples (11) and (12) were both examples of identity clauses as is (13).

(13) *Idia   Irianti   ni   kobit*
      i-dia   Irianti   ni   kobit
      DEM-DIST   girl's.name   3s.POSS knife
      'That's Irianti's knife.'

In quantifier clauses, the argument refers to some entity which the predicator quantifies. The predicating quantifiers may be either classifier numeral collocations as in (14) or independent quantifiers as in (15). (See §3.1.3 for more on quantifiers.)

(14) *Mapinci   mathit*
      mapin=si   mat=hit
      woman=PL   CLF=seven
      'There are seven women.'

(15) *Hamasik   ne   lloci*
      rice   PRX   much
      'There is a lot of rice here.'

In (13), above, there is a possessive NP which functions as predicate of a nominal clause. Taba also has what can be called possessive nominal clauses, in which something that is possessed by someone or something functions as an argument, while a possessor and an inflected possessive ligature (§3.1.2) function as a predicate.

(16) *Kabin   da   si   nidi*
      goat   DIST   3p   3p.POSS
      'That goat is theirs.'

In locational nominal clauses an argument refers to something that is in a location which is expressed by a predicating NP. Quite complex conditions determine how these may be used idiomatically (see §4 below on 'independent and dependent locatives' and also Bowden 1997b for more details). The simplest kinds of locative clauses consist of just an argument and an independent locative, as in (17).

(17) *Nim   capeyo   noge*
      nim   capeyo   no-ge
      2s.POSS   hat   there-ESS
      'Your hat is there.'

Greater precision in the specification of location can be obtained by adding a dependent locative after an independent one as in (18).

(18) *Nim   capeyo   noge   kurusi   li*
      nim   capeyo   no-ge   kurusi   li
      2s.POSS   hat   there-ESS   chair   LOC
      'Your hat is there on the chair.'

3.2.3 Intransitive adpositional clauses

Taba adpositional clauses occur rather infrequently. In (19) the adposition *ada* 'with' expresses accompaniment, or possession.

(19) *Karna   yak   ada   nik   motor*
      because   1s   with   1s.POSS   boat
      'because I had my boat [lit. I was with my boat].'

Locative postpositional clauses are occasionally encountered too. These are quite rare because postpositional locative phrases are dependent locatives which normally require the support of an independent locative. Occasionally, if an independent locative can be retrieved either anaphorically or exophorically, postpositional locative phrases can function as predicates in their own right (§4). Contrast the postpositional locative clause in (20) with the referentially equivalent nominal clauses in (17) and (18) above.

(20) *Nim   capeyo   kurusi   li*
      nim   capeyo   kurusi   li
      2s.POSS   hat   chair   LOC
      'Your hat is (there) on the chair.'

3.2.4 *Intransitive verbal predicates*

Taba has a split intransitive system, whereby 'Actor-oriented' verbs (or unergatives) occur with cross-referencing of their single arguments while 'Undergoer-oriented' verbs (or unaccusatives) have no cross-referencing. Example (21) shows an Actor-oriented verb. The sole argument 'Mina' is cross-referenced with the third singular proclitic $n=$.

(21) *Mina   nhan   do*
      Mina   n=han   do
      Mina   3s=go   RLS
      'Mina has gone.'

Example (22) shows an Undergoer-oriented verb. In this case there is no cross-referencing of the argument *niwi ni sapo da* 'the coconut fruit'.

(22) *Niwi   ni   sapo   da   mtat   do*
      coconut   3s.POSS   fruit   DIST   fall   RLS
      'The coconut fell.'

Whether an intransitive verb is Actor-oriented, or Undergoer-oriented depends on whether its argument refers to a human or not, and on whether or not the argument is an 'effector'. (An effector is defined, following Van Valin and Wilkins (1996:289), as 'the dynamic participant doing something in an event'.) If a human argument is involved, then it almost invariably occurs with an Actor-oriented intransitive verb no matter what the semantic role of the argument. (A few marginal exceptions, where the behavior of a human argument is seen as less than human in some way occur. In such cases a human can occur as an Undergoer. See §5.3 for an example.) If a non-human referring NP is the argument, then it occurs as a cross-referenced Actor if it is an effector, but as an Undergoer if it is not an effector.

(23) **Non-human effector = Actor**
      Motor   nhan   do
      motor   n=han   do
      boat   3s=go   RLS
      'The boat has gone.'

(24) **Non-human non-effector = Undergoer**
      Ubang   da   mlongan
      fence   DIST   be.long
      'The fence is long.'

(25) **Human effector=Actor**
      Iswan   ncopang   do
      Iswan   n=sopang   do
      man's.name   3s=come.down   RLS
      'Iswan has come down.'

(26) **Human non-effector = Actor**
    Mado   *namtat*
    Mado   n=ha-mtat
    man's.name   3s=ACT-fall
    'Mado fell over.'

Undergoer-oriented intransitive clauses are similar to nominal clauses in that neither take pronominal cross-referencing. In both cases full NP arguments occur preverbally while pronominal arguments occur postverbally.

3.2.5 Transitive verbal predicates

Transitive clauses take both an Actor and an Undergoer argument. The Actor is cross-referenced on the verb by a proclitic while the Undergoer is not cross-referenced. Neither argument needs to be expressed overtly (except that an Actor must be cross-referenced on the verb). Example (27) shows a transitive clause with pronominal arguments and (28) shows one with full NP arguments.

(27) *I*   *n=wet*   *yak*
    3s   3s=hit   1s
    'He hit me.'

(28) *Banda*   *nposak*   *wog*
    Banda   n=poas-Vk   wog
    Banda   3s=row-APP   canoe
    'Banda rowed the canoe.'

3.2.6 Semitransitive verbal predicates

Semitransitive verbal predicates are distinguished by the fact that they take an Actor argument as well as what I will call a 'remote' Undergoer. Remote Undergoers are labeled thus because they may optionally occur with a supporting adposition. Remote Undergoers are thus not neatly classifiable as either good arguments or adjuncts, but rather sit in an intermediate position on a scale between the core and the periphery of the clause (see Bowden 2000a for details). Underived semitransitive clauses always involve verbs of motion with locative remote Undergoers as illustrated in (29). Derived semi-transitives occur with applicativized stems and may include either comitatives/instruments or locations as remote Undergoers. A concomitant remote Undergoer in a derived semitransitive is illustrated in (30).

(29) *Yanti*   *ncung*   *um*   *(li)*
    yanti   n=sung   um   (li)
    Yanti   3s=enter   house   (LOC)
    'Yanti entered the house.'

(30) *Iswan*   *nhanak*   *(ada)*   *Nou*
    Iswan   n=han-Vk   (ada)   Nou
    Iswan   3s=go-APP   (with)   Nou
    'Iswan went with Nou.'

3.2.7 Ditransitive verbal predicates

There are no underived ditransitive verbs in Taba, nor are there any causative derived ditransitives: all of them are derived by applicativization. There are two types of ditransitive clauses: close ditransitives and remote ditransitives.

Close ditransitives involve just verbs of transfer with an animate recipient and a theme in addition to a cross-referenced Actor. The non-Actor arguments involved in close ditransitives are never marked adpositionally. The recipient (or 'Primary Undergoer') occurs immediately postverbally while the theme (or 'Secondary Undergoer') occurs after that, as illustrated in (31).

(31) *Banda   notik*   *Ahmad   yan   lloci*
      Banda   n=ot-Vk   Ahmad   yan   lloci
      Banda   3s=get-APP [give]   Ahmad   fish   many
      'Banda gave Ahmad a lot of fish.'

Remote ditransitives also take an Actor and a Primary Undergoer, but the second occurring Undergoer in a remote ditransitive clause is a remote Undergoer like those discussed in §3.2.6 since it is optionally marked by an adposition. The remote Undergoers in remote ditransitives, just like those of semitransitive verbs, are always either instruments/concomitants or locations. An instrumental remote ditransitive is illustrated in (32) and a locative remote ditransitive is shown in (33).

(32) *Npunak   kolay   da   (ada)   peda*
      n=pun-Vk   kolay   da   (ada)   peda
      3s=kill-APP   snake   DIST   (with)   machete
      'He killed the snake with a machete.'

(33) *Mina   nggono   kartas   ni   ggowo   (li)*
      Mina   n=gon-o   kartas   ni   ggowo   (li)
      Mina   3s=put-APP   paper   POSS   place   (LOC)
      'Mina put the papers in their place.'

3.2.8 Non-Actor bivalent verbal predicates

Non-Actor bivalent verbs are generally derived from Undergoer intransitives by applicativization. These verbs take two Undergoers, the first of which is a primary 'direct' Undergoer, and the second of which is a secondary 'remote' Undergoer. Such clauses usually refer to situations whereby the direct Undergoer has been affected by the instrumentality of the remote Undergoer in some way as in (34) or they involve posture verbs where the location of the direct Undergoer is described with respect to the remote Undergoer occur as in (35).

(34) *Loka   da   posak*   *(ada)   niwi*
      loka   da   posa-Vk   (ada)   niwi
      banana   DIST   be.boiled-APP   (with)   coconut
      'The banana was boiled with coconut.'

(35) *Nonas   da   kaóp-o*   *nonas   maleo   (li)*
      coconut.shell   DIST   be.brought.into.contact-APP   coconut.shell   other   (LOC)
      'That coconut shell has been brought into contact with the other coconut shell.'

3.2.9 Overview of verbal predicates

The Taba verbal predicates just discussed are distinguished according to the number and types of arguments they take. Arguments are either Actors or Undergoers, and Undergoers subdivide further into either direct or remote Undergoers. Direct Undergoers may not co-occur with an adposition while remote Undergoers may be optionally marked by an adposition. Virtually any combination of these three types of argument may occur in a clause, except that clauses with just a remote Undergoer are not found. Table 27.6 shows schematically each verbal clause type found in Taba, along with a classification of the kinds of arguments found with them.

3.2.10 Excretion verbs

In addition to the clause types outlined above, Taba has a small class of verbs referring to excretion which have some morphosyntactic irregularities in that the sole referent of them is cross-referenced twice, by both a prefix and a suffix. The verbs involved are *sio* 'shit', *mio* 'piss', *sito* 'fart' and *hantolo* 'lay eggs'. A complete paradigm of the verb *sio* 'shit' is provided in Table 27.7, where prefixes and suffixes are given in bold.

These verb forms, although only having one referent, must be viewed as formally transitive. The evidence for this claim comes from applicativization and detransitivization and is presented in §5.2 and §5.3. See Bowden (1997c and 2001) for more discussion.

3.2.11 The possessive verb

The Taba possessive verb also has some peculiarities which warrant separate discussion. All of the forms of this verb except those for 1pe and for 2p are made by causativizing the possessive ligatures discussed in §3.1.2. The derived form is then cross-referenced with the pronominal clitic appropriate to the Actor possessor. The possessive verbs are formally transitive and the possessor occurs as Actor while the thing possessed occurs as Undergoer. The forms of the verb are illustrated in Table 27.8.

TABLE 27.6: OVERVIEW OF TABA VERBAL CLAUSE TYPES

Actor	Direct Undergoer	Remote Undergoer	Clause type
1	0	0	Actor intransitive
0	1	0	Undergoer intransitive
0	0	1	(Doesn't occur)
1	1	0	Normal transitive
1	0	1	Semitransitive
1	2	0	Close ditransitive
1	1	1	Remote ditransitive
0	1	1	Non-Actor bivalent

TABLE 27.7: CONJUGATION OF EXCRETION VERBS

1s	*yak ksiok/yak ksioyak*	'I shit'	1pi	*tit tciotit (t-sio-tit)*	'we (incl.) shit'
			1pe	*am asioam*	'we (excl.) shit'
2s	*au msioau*	'you (sg) shit'	2p	*meu hsiomeu*	'you (pl.) shit'
3s	*i ncioi (n-sio-i)*	's/he shits'	3p	*si lciosi (l-sio-si)*	'they shit'

TABLE 27.8: TABA POSSESSIVE VERB

1s	yak kanik (k-ha-nik)	'I have'	1pi	tit tanit (t-ha-nit)	'we (incl.) have'
			1pe	am amam	'we (excl.) have'
2s	au manim (m-ha-nim)	'you (sg) have'	2p	meu memeu	'you (pl.) have'
3s	i nani (n-ha-ni)	's/he has'	3p	si lanidi (l-ha-nidi)	'they have'

3.2.12 Negation

Negation is expressed in Taba by adding the negative particle *te* at the end of the constituent which is negated. The constituents which can be negated are either noun phrases or clauses, as illustrated in (36) and (37) respectively.

(36)   *Idia   te*
       DIST   NEG
       'Not that one.'

(37)   *Nhan   te*
       n=han   NEG
       'S/he didn't go.'

The negative particle can also occur in derived forms including TAM markers (§3.4).

3.3 NP-structure

A basic outline of Taba NP structure is in (38).

(38)   (Poss) $\begin{Bmatrix} N \\ NP \end{Bmatrix}$ (-PL) (Attribute) (Quantifier) (Demonstrative) (Directional) (*do*)

Most of the elements of the NP are discussed elsewhere, but 'attributes' and the reflexive particle *do* are introduced here.

All attributes are classified as relative clauses, whether verbal or nominal. There is a strong preference in discourse for a relativized argument to occur as either S_A or S_O. S_O is most preferred, since all attributive uses of Undergoer verbs occur with this relation. Relative clauses are generally unmarked by any overt relativizer, but *yang* 'REL' borrowed from Malay is occasionally used to mark a relative clause, and occurs directly before the relative clause. In (39), the relativized noun occurs in the prefronted position of the matrix clause containing the verb *lewit* and has the O role in it. It is also S_O of the relative clause which contains the Undergoer-oriented intransitive verb *bakan* 'be big'.

(39)   *Yan   bakan,   mat=lu   l=lewit*
       fish   be.big,   CLF=two   3p=carry on shoulders with pole
       'A huge fish, two people (were needed to) carry it on a pole.'

All of the arguments of semi-transitive verbs, of ditransitives, and of non-Actor bivalent verbs can be relativized. While adpositional marking of remote Undergoers is generally optional with these verbs, if a remote Undergoer occurs as the head of a relative clause, it must be marked adpositionally.

(40)   *Mado   n=yat   peda   n=pun-ak   kolay   ada*
       Mado   3s=carry   machete   3s=kill-APP   snake   with
       'Mado is carrying the machete he killed the snake with.'

Example (41) shows a relativized adjunct.

(41)   L=tala   ai   mamatuo=si   l=tagil   ada
       3p=find   stick old.people=PL 3p=walk   with
       'They found a stick that old people walk with.'

'Headless' relative clauses or nominalizations are discussed in §6.

Taba has no strongly grammaticalized means for marking reflexive clauses. However, the particle *do* (which also occurs as an independent noun meaning 'self') can be used to mark a NP as reflexive Actor. Clauses which contain NPs marked in this way are all inherently ambiguous.

(42)   *Acan   do   n=wet   i*
       Acan   RFL/self   3s=hit 3s
       'Acan_i hit himself_i' or 'Acan_i himself hit her/him_j'.

3.4 TAM marking

Taba has two clausal particles which are used for tense-aspect-mood (TAM) marking, *do* 'realis' and *hu* 'continuative'. Neither of these is obligatory and both appear at the end of the clause they occur in.

(43)   *Ncobal   akla   do*
       n=sobal   ak-la   do
       3s=sail   to-sea   RLS
       'He has sailed seawards' or 'He is sailing seawards'.

(44)   *L=wom   hu*
       3p=come   CONT
       'They are coming' or 'they were coming', etc.

Occasionally, both TAM markers are found in the same clause. In this case the realis particle always precedes the continuative particle.

(45)   *N=han   do   hu*
       3s=go   RLS   CONT
       'He's going at the moment.'

When they occur in negative clauses, the TAM particles are suffixed to the negative particle *te* (§3.2.12).

(46)   *N=han   te-hu*
       3s=go   NEG-CONT
       'It isn't working.'

There is also one other modality marking suffix that occurs with the negator *te* but which does not occur on its own. This is *su* POT 'potential' which marks an expectation that although there is a negative state of affairs at the time referred to in the utterance, a positive state of affairs will eventuate at some later time.

(47)   *N=tagil   te-su*
       3s=walk   NEG-POT
       'She's not walking yet.' [said of a young baby who is expected to learn to walk later]

3.5 Prepositional phrases

Taba has both prepositions and a postposition. The adpositions found in Taba are:

li	postposition	locative
ada	preposition	comitative/instrumental
lo	preposition	similative
tutik	preposition	'until'
pake	preposition	instrumental
untuk	preposition	benefactive

The first four are indigenous forms while the last two are borrowed from North Moluccan Malay. Only the postposition *li* and the preposition *untuk* occur just as adpositions; the other forms also occur as conjunctions (*ada* and *lo*), discourse connector (*tutik*) or serial verb (*pake*).

Adpositional phrases most commonly occur at the end of the clause they belong to as in (48), but they are also found in the fronted preclausal focus position as in (49).

(48) *Kwom   appo   ada   nik   mapin*
      k=wom   ap-po   ada   nik   mapin
      1s=come   ALL-down   with   1s.POSS   wife
      'I came down with my wife.'

(49) *Pake   senter,   hwet   i   lo*
      pake   senter   h=wet   i   lo
      with   torch   2p=hit   3s   IMP
      'With the torch, hit him!'

Taba is somewhat unusual typologically in allowing, like English, 'stranded prepositions' to occur, as in (50), where the postposition *li* 'LOC' indexes *kurusi* 'chair', an argument which is head of the relative clause *ntua lai mo* 'he bought (the chair) recently'. Such adpositional stranding only occurs with the adpositions *li* 'LOC' and *ada* 'with'.

(50) *Nbattalono   kurusi   ntua   lai   mo   li*
      n=battalon-o   kurusi   n=tua   lai   mo   li
      3s=sit-APP   chair   3s=buy   just   come   LOC
      'He's sitting on the chair he just bought.'

3.6 Serial verbs

A fairly wide variety of serial verb constructions (SVCs) are found in Taba. Except in adverbial serialization, there is a requirement that the individual verbs in a SVC must share at least one argument. If the verbs in a SVC share a common Actor argument, cross-referencing of the Actor on the second verb is optional (as illustrated in (51) below, without cross-referencing, and in (52), with cross-referencing). Serialization in Taba only ever involves two verbs at a time. Four types of serialization are introduced here: motion serialization, causative serialization, instrumental serialization, and adverbial serialization.

The most commonly encountered SVCs involve motion serialization. These constructions involve a verb describing an action along with a motion verb which may either precede or follow the semantically primary action verb (illustrated in (51) and (52) respectively). Some of these combinations are quite lexicalized.

(51)   N=han   ait   do
       3s=go   ascend   RLS
       'She's gone up.' [usually with lexicalized sense 'she's gone up (to work in the
       gardens)']

(52)   Ncopang   nmul   tesu
       n=sopang   n=mul   te-su
       3s=descend   3s=return   NEG-CONT
       'He hasn't come down yet.' [usually with lexicalized sense of returning from
       work in the gardens]

Causative serialization involves an initial verb expressing a cause which brings about
a result described by the second verb. The initial verb in these constructions is always
transitive and the Undergoer of the initial verb is always an argument of the second verb.

(53)   Nyo   da   n=babas   welik   n=mot
       dog   DIST   3s=bite   pig   3s=die
       'The dog bit the pig dead.'

In instrumental serialization the first verb describes an action, while the second verb
is *pake* 'use'. The Actors of both verbs are always coreferential in these structures.

(54)   N=pun   bobay   n=pake   sandal
       3s=kill   mosquito   3s=use   sandal
       'She killed a mosquito with a sandal.'

Adverbial serialization might be further subdivided into three types: manner, modal,
and aspectual serialization. The second verb in a manner SVC describes the manner in
which whatever referred to by the first verb was carried out.

(55)   Sagala   bum   dumik
       stuff   be.lost   be.exhausted
       'The stuff was totally lost.'

In modal serialization, the second verb provides a modal evaluation of ability to carry
out whatever is described by the first verb.

(56)   K=pe   k=ahate
       1s=do   1s=be.unable
       'I can't do it.'

Aspectual serialization involves a semantically main verb with another verb providing
aspectual information. The aspectual verb may either precede or follow the main verb,
depending on the aspectual meaning involved.

(57)   K=yoa   k=han
       1s=search(almost)   1s=go
       'I've almost gone.'

(58)   L=ahon   okik   do
       3p=eat   be.finished   RLS
       'They've finished eating.'

4 DEICTICS AND DIRECTIONALS

Paradigms of demonstratives and directionals are introduced in this section. Taba, like other languages from North Maluku, whether the languages are Austronesian or non-Austronesian, has a relatively complex set of directionals. The Taba demonstratives are listed in Table 27.9.

The root forms listed in the table are used attributively with nouns (and may also co-occur with pronouns). Demonstrative pronouns may fill a complete noun phrase on their own. Although they are transparently derived from the third person singular and plural pronouns to which the demonstrative roots have been suffixed, they must be treated as a separate form class. The major reason for this is that although normal pronouns cannot be used for inanimate reference (§3.1.2), the demonstrative pronouns are often used to refer to inanimates. The locative nouns translate roughly to English 'here' and 'there', and they may occur in the same syntactic slots as other independent locative nouns (including the nominal directionals outlined below). Similative nouns can be translated as 'like this', 'like that', (cf. Malay *begini/begitu*) or sometimes like French *voila!* Demonstrative pronouns and the deictic locative nouns in the table here are often used anaphorically for already topical referents: the proximal forms can only be used for referents first mentioned in the previous intonation unit while the distal forms are used for any previously mentioned referent. The similative forms may be used cataphorically. If the derived forms are used to express relative physical location, they are almost invariably accompanied by a gesture (see Bowden 2000b for more details).

The distal demonstrative root has two forms: a stressed variant *dia* and an unstressed form *da*. The unstressed form is used most often; the stressed form is reserved for instances when a speaker wishes to give stronger emphasis for some reason. 'Proximal' and 'distal' prototypically refer to relative location, but they can also be used with temporal and other affective notions of distance in mind. The recognitional encodes an expectation on the part of the speaker that the addressee should have some knowledge of the referent involved, and might be translated as 'you know the one'. It is used to establish a referent as topical on its first mention, and is generally never used for any subsequent mentions of the referent. Since it is never used anaphorically or cataphorically there are no forms derived from it as with the other demonstratives (see Bowden 2000b for more extensive discussion of this).

A complete listing of the Taba directionals is given in Table 27.10.

ESSIVE directionals are locative nouns (cf. locative nominal demonstratives discussed above). The ALLATIVE and VENITIVE forms refer to direction towards a goal that is either 'seawards', 'landwards', etc. away from some presumed deictic center, or motion towards

TABLE 27.9: TABA DEMONSTRATIVES

	Proximal	Distal	Recognitional
Root form	*ne*	*da/dia*	*ya*
Pronouns	*ine* (sg)	*idia* (sg)	–
	sine (pl)	*sidia* (pl)	
Locative nouns	*ane*	*adia*	–
Similative forms	*tane* (*biasa* register)	*tadia* (*biasa* register)	–
	tadine (*alus* register)	*taddia* (*alus* register)	
	hatadine (*alus* register)	*hatadia* (*alus* register)	
	dodine (*kasar* register)	*dodia* (*kasar* register)	

TABLE 27.10: TABA DIRECTIONALS

Root	*ya* (up)	*po* (down)	*la* (sea)	*le* (land)	*no* (there)
ESSIVE	*yase*	*pope*	*lawe*	*lewe*	*noge*
ALLATIVE	*attia*	*appo*	*akla*	*akle*	*akno*
VENITIVE	*yama*	*poma*	*lama*	*lema*	*noma*
NOMINALIZED	*tattubo*	*umpo*	*kla*	*kle*	*kno*

a presumed deictic centre respectively. The nominalized forms refer to parts of things that are oriented in a particular direction and are obligatorily possessed by a noun referring to the entity of which they constitute a part.

Taba directionals are used extensively in Taba discourse, occurring in around 30% of all narrative clauses. Extensive discussion of them is found in Bowden (1997b).

5 MAJOR VERBAL ALTERNATIONS

The major verbal alternations in Taba are more like those of the Oceanic languages discussed in Lynch *et al.* (2002) than those of the majority of western Malayo-Polynesian languages discussed elsewhere in this volume. There is no real system of verbal voice operating in Taba, but there are a variety of valence affecting affixation processes including causativization, applicativization, and detransitivization, as well as the alternation between Actor-oriented and Undergoer-oriented intransitive verbs discussed in §3.2.2 above.

5.1 Causatives and derivation of Actor-oriented intransitives from other classes

The Taba causative prefix is *ha-*. When used with its causativizing function it derives transitive verbs from Actor-oriented intransitives. (Ditransitives are always derived by applicativization (§5.2) and never by causativization.) Causative *ha-* is illustrated in (59).

(59) a. *Paramalam   n=mot*
          lamp   3s=die
          'The lamp went out.'

      b. *Ahmad   namot   paramalam*
          Ahmad   n=ha-mot   paramalam
          Ahmad   3s=CAU-die   lamp
          'Ahmad turned the lamp out.'

The *ha-* prefix is also very productively used to create Actor intransitive verbs (§3.2.2) from Undergoer intransitives and roots of just about any other form class. Its productivity with this function can be gauged from (60) which was used to describe the actions of a small boy walking along a path repeating the nonsense sound [ɛ̃].

(60) *Acan   na-[ɛ̃].*
       Acan   n=ha-[ɛ̃]
       Acan   3s=CAU-[ɛ̃]
       'Acan is making [ɛ̃] noises.'

5.2 Applicatives

Taba has two applicative suffixes: -*Vk* usually licenses an instrument (but may also license a theme or a recipient) to occur as an Undergoer, and -*o* normally licenses a location. The applicative suffixes may be added to Undergoer-oriented intransitive verbs, Actor-oriented intransitives or canonical transitives deriving non-Actor bivalent verbs, semi-transitives or ditransitives respectively. Extensive exemplification of all the most common types of applicativization has been given in §3 and will not be repeated here. Applicativization of excretion verbs has not been discussed so far, and it provides evidence for the claim that the excretion roots themselves are formally transitive although there is only one referent involved (see §3.2.10). Example (61) illustrates this process. In (61b) the cross-referencing suffix -*k* has been displaced by the applicative -*Vk*, but the Undergoer-referring argument *yak* still occurs following the applicative suffix. The applied theme (in this case *niwi* 'coconut') occurs after the Primary Undergoer *yak*. The resultant form is a close ditransitive (§3.2.7).

(61) a. *Yak   k=sio-k   do*
          1s   1s=shit-1s   RLS
          'I've already shitted.'

      b. *Yak   ksiak   yak   niwi*
          yak   k=sio-Vk   yak   niwi
          1s   1s=shit-APP   1s   coconut
          'I'm shitting coconut.'

5.3 Detransitivization

The Taba detransitivizing prefix is *ta-*. Its function is to eliminate an underlying Actor from the argument structure of the verb to which it is attached. It can be prefixed to ditransitive roots or canonical transitive roots, deriving non-Actor bivalent verbs and Undergoer-oriented intransitives respectively. It is illustrated with these functions in (62) and (63) respectively. Example (62) involves the ditransitive applicativized excretion verb *sio* as the stem. When *ta-* is prefixed to this form, a non-Actor bivalent verb is derived, having the excretor as Primary Undergoer, and the theme *niwi* 'coconut' as secondary Undergoer. (The derived form shown in (62b) is one of the exceptional cases in which human arguments are not treated as Actors of a clause (§3.2.4). The exceptional grammatical behavior shown here presumably comes about because uncontrollable shitting is seen as something less than human.)

(62) a. *Yak   ksiak   yak   niwi*
          yak   k=sio-Vk   yak   niwi
          1s   1s=shit-APP   1s   coconut
          'I'm shitting coconut.'

      b. *Tasiak   yak   niwi*
          ta-sio-Vk   yak   niwi
          DTR-shit-APP   1s   coconut
          'I'm uncontrollably shitting coconut.' [as when someone has diarrhea]

(63) a. *Male   tcakal   boa*
          male   t=sakal   boa
          necessary 1pi=smash   door
          'We had to smash down the doors.'

b. *Boa   ta-sakal*
door   DTR-smash
'The door was smashed down.'

Many derived forms occur with the detransitivizing suffix although there is no independent attestation of the roots involved. Such derived forms are all Undergoer intransitive verbs referring to states of disrepair of some kind.

(64) *Masin   ni   reng   ta-dopas*
engine   3s.POSS   seal   DTR-perish
'The engine's seal has perished.'

6 NOMINALIZATIONS AND NOMINAL MORPHOLOGY

Taba has both morphological and syntactic nominalization. Morphological nominalization derives instruments from verbal roots by means of partial reduplication (see §2.5 for morphophonological details). This process is quite productive and is often used to coin new words, e.g. *kakkokodok* (*kak-kokodok*) 'rooster's beak' or literally 'thing used to crow with' < RDP-crow.

Syntactic nominalization is very frequent, but it is unmarked in any way. Syntactic nominalizations may be analyzed as headless relative clauses (cf. §3.3). Nominalized clauses are readily identified as such because they serve as the arguments of verbs. Sometimes these may occur so frequently that they have lexicalized nominal meanings, as does *lagah* 'thief' in (65).

(65) *Lagah   lhan   Mado   li*
l=ha-gah   l=han   Mado   li
3p-CAU-steal [thieves]   3p=go   Mado   LOC
'Thieves have been to Mado's place.'

ACKNOWLEDGEMENTS

I would like to thank above all the Makianese people who made my studies of their language possible, especially *nik mama lo babasi Taba* Ahmad Hamaya and Mina Hamaya, and *nik wang lomo* Banda Tais.

REFERENCES

Adriani, N. and Kruijt, A.C. (1914) *De Bare'e sprekende Toradja's van Midden Celebes*, vol. 3. Batavia: Landsdrukkerij.
Bowden, J. (1997a) *Taba (Makian Dalam): description of an Austronesian language from eastern Indonesia*, PhD thesis, University of Melbourne.
——(1997b) 'The meanings of directionals in Taba', in Gunter Senft (ed.) *Referring to space: studies in Austronesian and Papuan languages*, Oxford: Clarendon Press.
——(1997c) *Double agreement with verbs of excretion in Taba*. Paper presented to The First Victorian Southeast Asian Linguistics Symposium. University of Melbourne, July 1997.
——(2000a) 'Taba as a "split-O" language: applicatives in a Split-S system', *RSPAS Online Working Papers in Linguistics*, No. 2. <http://rspas.anu.edu.au/linguistics/WP/Bowden2.html>
——(2000b) *Pointing to Taba demonstratives and figuring out what they point to*, MS Australian National University.

Bowden, J.(2001) *Taba: description of a South Halmahera language*, Canberra: Pacific Linguistics.

——(2002) 'The impact of Malay on Taba: a type of incipient language death or the incipient death of a language type?', in D. and M. Bradley (eds) *Language endangerment and language maintenance*, 114–143, London: Routledge Curzon.

Bowden, J. and J. Hajek (1999) 'Taba and Roma: clusters and germinates in two Austronesian languages', *Proceedings of the XIVth International Congress of Phonetic Sciences* 1033–1036.

Collins, J.T. (1982) 'A short vocabulary of East Makian', in C.L. Voorhoeve (ed.) *The Makian languages and their neighbours*, 99–128, Canberra: Pacific Linguistics.

Lucardie, G.R.E. (1983) 'The geographical mobility of the Makianese: migratory traditions and resettlement problems', in E.K.M. Masinambouw (ed.) *Halmahera dan Raja Ampat sebagai kesatuan majemuk: studi-studi terhadap suatu daerah transisi*, 333–345. Jakarta: LEKNAS-LIPI.

Lynch, J., Ross, M.D., and Crowley, T. (eds) (2002) *The Oceanic Languages*, London: Curzon Press.

Van Valin, R.D. and Wilkins, D.P. (1996) 'The case for "effector": Case roles, agents, and agentivity revisited', in M. Shibatani and S.A. Thompson (eds) *Grammatical constructions: their form and meaning*, 289–322, Oxford: Clarendon Press.

CHAPTER TWENTY-EIGHT

BIAK

Hein Steinhauer

1 INTRODUCTION

The Biak language is a continuum of closely related dialects, spoken on the islands north and northwest of the Bird's Head peninsula of West New Guinea, notably on the major Schouten Islands (Biak, Supiori and Numfor) and on West Waigeo, Salawati, and further on smaller islands in the Dore Bay and the Raja Ampat archipelago. Sizable numbers of Biak speakers are found today in the cities of Sorong and Merauke and in small villages along the north coast of the Bird's Head.

For centuries Schouten Islanders have been the intermediaries between the peoples from the west and the population of the Bird's Head's interior. This was not always to the benefit of the latter: up to the end of the nineteenth century the people from Biak were feared for their raids on the West New Guinea coasts and on Moluccan Islands, which provided them with slaves whom they traded with the north Moluccan sultanate of Tidore. These raids became an indirect mode of colonial control used by the Dutch. In more recent days the people from Biak became the intermediaries for other western values. Already in the second half of the nineteenth century German and subsequently Dutch Protestant missionaries started their efforts to convert the Biak-speaking population. Words for 'clothes', 'school' and other cultural innovations they introduced in many Bird's Head languages were borrowed from Biak.

The first descriptions of Biak were based on the Numfor dialect (also called Mafor and Nufor in those early days) of the Dore Bay area. In this area the first missionary posts were established, dating from the second half of the nineteenth century (J.L. van Hasselt 1868, 1876, Ottow 1862). Kern (1885) identified Biak as an Austronesian language because of its similarities with Fijian. A concise grammar of the Numfor dialect, remarkable for its time because of its lack of European biases, was written by the son of J.L. van Hasselt some twenty-five years later (F.J.F. van Hasselt 1905). Around the same time a collection of texts with Dutch translation was published (J.L. van Hasselt 1908), most of them again in Numfor, but some evidently from Biak or Supiori. A Numfor–Dutch dictionary was published posthumously after the Second World War (Hasselt and Hasselt 1947). This dictionary was the basis for a Biak–Indonesian dictionary (Soeparno 1977). Both dictionaries contain items from other dialects. Patz (1978) uses J.L. van Hasselt (1905) to draw some speculative conclusions about the structure of Biak. Finally, Steinhauer (1985) discusses the grammaticalization of number in the Biak dialect of Sawias on Supiori.

On Supiori Island, in Korido village, the missionaries established their first regular elementary school. Here pupils from all over the Schouten islands met, while many of them lived in the school's boarding house throughout the year, to return to their villages only for the holidays. The language of instruction was Malay, but Biak was used in reading edifying texts such as those produced by the missionaries W.L. Jens (1883) and I.S. Kijne (1950). The combined effect of these prestigious texts, prepared by foreigners, and the mixture of dialects at the school in a village which had its own dialect, may have created some tolerance towards hybridized forms of the language. However, the situation did not result in a Biak koine, although the language of the missionaries remained influential.

As Biak speakers were among the first Papuans under Dutch colonial rule who received schooling and became christianized, they were employed by the Dutch in local administration and as (assistant) preachers, in their own areas as well as elsewhere in West New Guinea. Trained in Malay as they were, and living outside the Biak-speaking area, they had to use another language, usually Malay. This situation continued under Indonesian rule (i.e. since 1962). With the rise of mass education the influence of Malay (in its standardized form of Indonesian) grew. Increased mobility and interethnic contacts heightened the pressure on the regional languages. The main international airport of West New Guinea has always been near the town of Biak on the island of the same name. In this capital of the district the intensity of contacts with the outside world has caused a shift of Biak to Malay. In the villages, however, the various dialects of Biak are still in vigorous use. The number of speakers today is estimated to exceed 50,000.

Biak belongs to the South Halmahera–West New Guinea (SHWNG) branch of the Eastern Malayo-Polynesian language group (Blust 1978). This branch is characterized by a number of 'distinctive linguistic innovations...[which] spread more-or-less uniformly through the SHWNG dialect chain in opposing directions' (Blust 1993:244). The exact relationships among the forty to forty-five languages allegedly belonging to the SHWNG subgroup is still largely unknown, which is mainly due to the lack of descriptive data on most of them.

The description of the Biak language below will be based on the dialect of Sowek ([sówɛk] or [sowk]) spoken some 25 kilometers west of Korido town on the south coast of Supiori, which is the mother tongue of my main informant, Zacharias Sawor.

2 PHONOLOGY

2.1 Segment inventory

The Biak language of Sowek has a simple five vowel system: /i, u, e, o, a/, and two semivowels: /y/ (written as *j* by the missionaries) and /w/. The mid-vowels are realized relatively low in closed syllables, relatively high in open ones. The missionaries used double vs. single vowels or diacritic signs to indicate these non-phonemic differences.

The inventory of Biak consonants is presented in Table 28.1.

The phonemes /g/ and /t/ only occur in borrowings and are adapted as /k/ and /s/ respectively: *guru* or *kuru* 'teacher', *oto* or *oso* 'car'. They never occur at the end of a syllable; neither do /b/ and /d/. All other phonemes occur in all positions.

TABLE 28.1: BIAK CONSONANTS

		Stop	Continuant		
			Fricative	Nasal	Trill
Labial	voiceless	*p*	*f*		
	voiced	*b*	*v*	*m*	
Dental	voiceless	(*t*)	*s*		
	voiced	*d*		*n*	*r*
Velar	voiceless	*k*			
	voiced	(*g*)			

Within a morpheme, /k/ is usually realised as [g] (in the traditional spelling written as *g*) when it is preceded by a nasal, e.g. *mka* [mga] 'eye' and (with a petrified prefix) *-m-kak* [mgak] 'be afraid' (cf. *-fa-kak* 'frighten').

/n/ before a velar or labial stop is optionally assimilated as [ŋ] and [m] respectively. The sequence /mr/ is always realized as [mbr].

/i/ and /y/ are in opposition between a consonant and a vowel, such as in the clause medial forms *bin-ya* 'the woman' vs. *bin-ia* 'that woman'.

/v/ and /f/ are bilabial ([β,Φ]); /w/ is bilabial and unrounded.

In the spelling tradition introduced by the missionaries and their followers both /b/ and /v/ were written as *b* in all positions, and they were pronounced likewise from the pulpit. As a consequence, pronouncing both phonemes as [b] has become a sign of solemnity and culture, also among native speakers.

Consonant clusters are various and frequent, e.g. *mka-si* (eye-1s/3s.INAL) 'my/his/her/its eye(s)', *n-paysem* (3p.INAN.SBJ-black) 'they are black', *kpu* '(classificatory) grandchild or grandparent', *in kbor* 'young (initiated) woman'. Geminates of /n/, /k/ and /s/ are the result of morphological processes:

(1) *bon=na* [bón:a] (mountain=3p.INAN.DEF) 'the mountains'
　　 n-na-nyar [n:aɲár] (3p.INAN.SBJ-RDP-yellow) 'they are yellow'
　　 y-ak-kanes [y-ák:anɛs] (1s.SBJ-too-cry) 'I also cry (=join in crying)'
　　 s-so [s:o] (3p.AN.SBJ-throw) 'they throw'
　　 insos=si [insós:i] (adolescent.girl=3p.AN.DEF) 'the adolescent girls'

The sonorants (/m, n, r/) may become syllabic through the loss of preceding /e/:

(2) *i-kenem* (3s.SBJ-live) 'he/she/it lives'
　　 i-kenm va [ikénm̩ba] (3s.SBJ-live NEG) 'he/she/it does not live'

　　 noken 'string bag'
　　 nokn di suru [nókn̩disuru] (string.bag-LK-two) 'two string bags'
　　 nokn=na [nókn̩na] (string.bag=3p.INAN.DEF) 'the string bags'

　　 ro vavn-di [roβáβn̩di] (LOC underside-1s/3s.INAL) 'under me/him/her/it'
　　 ro vavn-m-ri [roβáβn̩mbri] (LOC underside-2-SG.INAL) 'under you (SG)'

　　 d-oper (3s.SBJ-jump) 'he/she/it jumps'
　　 d-opr ro war ve-ki [dópr̩owárβeki] (3s.SBJ-jump LOC water REL-flow)
　　 'he/she/it jumps into the river'
　　 d-opr ve (a)ya [dópr̩βe(a)yá] (3s.SBJ-jump DIR 1s) 'he/she/it jumps
　　 towards me'

Stress seems to be marginally phonemic. In isolation most polysyllabic roots ending in *a*CV(C) have end stress. For other patterns penultimate stress seems to be the rule. Minimal pairs appear to be rare, and in the few cases I came across they were always related to morphological processes. An example is *y-anan* [yánan] (1s.SBJ-stamp) 'I stamp' vs. *y-an-an* [yanán] (1s.SBJ-RDP-eat) 'I am eating'. In context stress often shifts to enclitics according to rules which are still insufficiently understood. But variation appears to be frequent. To what extent stress is a perceptual reality to native speakers should therefore be subject to further research. Pending such research and given the observed variability I refrain from indicating stress in the phonemic spelling below.

In the examples throughout this chapter morpheme boundaries are indicated everywhere, except in names. These retain their conventionalized, non-phonemic spelling.

2.2 Morphophonemics

/v/ after a nasal is replaced by a stop (/b/) across morpheme and word boundaries. Compare: *mnu ve-ba* (village REL-big) [mnuβebá] 'a big village' vs. *rum ve-ba* [rumbebá] 'a big house'. In such a position /n/ tends to be assimilated as [m] in allegro speech, even across word boundaries: *in ve-ba* [inbebá, imbebá] 'a big fish'. Below I shall write *v* at the beginning of a word, but *b* after a morpheme boundary within a word. Constituents of compounds are written as separate words.

Many polysyllabic roots which end in VCeC# when occurring in isolation or before a pause drop this /e/ in normal and allegro speech when they are followed by an enclitic or another word in the same phrase (some examples are presented in (2) above). There may be some lexical exceptions to this rule, but a complicating factor in verifying this is that here too the missionaries have put their imprint on language use. They propagated consistency in spelling by consistently writing *e* and pronouncing the words accordingly. As with the pronunciation [b] for /v/, this pulpit pronunciation became a characteristic of elevated speech, also with native speakers. Below I shall write such a floating *e* in parentheses when quoting a word in isolation.

Biak has complicated patterns of reduplication not all details of which can be presented here. There are two basic patterns, depending on the shape of the added segment: Ca- or (C)aC-. In both patterns the added segment immediately precedes the segment of which it is a copy. The vowel of the copy is always -*a*-. If the segment subject to reduplication begins with a consonant cluster, this cluster may be broken up by insertion of -*a*- before reduplication is applied. The resulting patterns are presented in Table 28.2. The copied syllables in Table 28.2 are the last syllable of the word form which is subject to reduplication. Those ending in a consonant, however, may still be followed by the sequence -(*e*)C# (in which (*e*) is a 'floating e'). In (3) and (4) some examples are given of deverbal nouns, respectively with open and closed syllable reduplication.

(3)	*-pok*	'able, strong'	*pa-pok*	'strength'
	-mun	'kill'	*ma-mun*	'murder'
	-masi	'bathe'	*ma-sa-si*	'bathing (n.)'
	-kandor	'be shocked'	*ka-na-ndor*	'shock'
	-vye	'be good'	*va-vye*	'goodness'
	-fnak	'play'	*fa-fnak*	'game'
	-frur	'make, do'	*fa-ra-rur*	'deed, action'
	-msor	'be angry'	*ma-sa-sor*	'anger'
	-myawum	'echo'	*mya-wa-wum*	'echo (n.)'
	-vor(e)s	'row'	*va-vor(e)s*	'(distant) rowing trip'
	-rmom(e)n	'revenge'	*ra-rmom(e)n*	'revenge (n.)'

(4)	*-an*	'eat'	*an-an*	'eating (n.)'
	-sun	'wear'	*san-sun*	'cloths'
	-karaw	'steal'	*ka-raw-raw*	'theft'
	-mrif	'laugh'	*ma-raf-rif*	'laughter'
	-sren	'be clean'	*sa-ran-den*	'cleanliness'
			(with r>d after the nasal)	
	-fuk(e)n	'ask'	*fak-fuk(e)n*	'questioning'
	-ar(e)m	'betroth'	*ar-ar(e)m*	'brideprice'
	-fnov(e)k	'help'	*fa-nav-nov(e)k*	'help, assistence'

TABLE 28.2: PATTERNS OF REDUPLICATION

Copied segment		Added segment	
		Ca-	CaC-
C_1V		C_1a–C_1V	–
C_1VC_2		C_1a–C_1VC_2	C_1aC_2–C_1VC_2
			(C_1 may be zero)
$C_1C_2VC_3$	C_1C_2 preserved	C_1a–$C_1C_2VC_3$	–
		(C_3 may be zero)	
	$C_1 > C_1a$	C_1a–C_2a–C_2VC_3	C_1a–C_2aC_3–C_2VC_3
		(C_3 may be zero)	

Other examples and some deviating patterns will be discussed in sections 5 and 6 on verbal and nominal morphology.

3 BASIC MORPHOSYNTAX

3.1 Word classes

Personal pronominal forms appear to be omnipresent in Biak syntax, in both noun and verb phrases. They are discussed in 3.1.1. Major word classes in Biak are nouns and verbs (discussed in 3.1.2 and 3.1.3). Biak has a well-developed decimal numeral system (described in 3.1.4). Possessive pronominal forms are dealt with in relation to NP-structure (see 3.3.2). To the minor word classes belong adverbs, prepositions, conjunctions and various particles; they will not be discussed separately.

3.1.1 Personal pronouns and the pronominal articles

Personal pronominal forms are differentiated for person (first, second, third), number (singular, dual, trial and plural), and gender ('animate' and 'inanimate'). A separate trial form only exists for the third person. For the first person dual and plural (covering a number of three or more), exclusive and inclusive forms are distinguished. Gender opposition only applies to the third person plural.

Personal pronouns in Biak may be bound or free. The free forms occur in syntactic isolation, or as an object of a verb or preposition in a non-embedded clause. The third person pronouns function as markers of definiteness at the end of noun phrases which are not otherwise marked for definiteness (such as inalienable nouns). These pronominal articles are analysed as enclitics: they are phonologically bound, but not to a particular word class. The pronouns appear in a 'clause-final' and a 'clause-medial' form. In the clause-final form the dual and trial third person pronouns require an additional -i when they function as pronominal articles. The exact distribution of the clause-medial and clause-final variants remains unclear and needs further investigation. For instance, the clause-final forms may still be followed by positional and directional formatives or by the topic marker ma; on the other hand, the clause-medial forms may occasionally be found in clause-final position.

Finally, personal pronominal forms may appear in the shape of prefixes, infixes and – in the case of the zero prefix – modification of the first root consonant (v- > b-); see Table 28.3. These bound forms are typical of verbal inflection and of the possessive pronominal system. With verbal stems they refer to person, number and gender of the

TABLE 28.3: PERSONAL PRONOUNS, FREE AND BOUND

	Free pronoun	Article Clause-final	Article Clause-medial	Subject agreement marker Vocalic	Non-vocalic	Mixed
1s	*(a)ya*[1]			*ya-*	*y-*	*ya-*
2s	*aw*			*wa-*	*w-*	*-w-/0*[3]
3s	*i*	*=i*[4]	*=ya*[4]	*i-*	*d-*	*-y-*
1di	*ku*			*ku-*	*kuy-*	*ku-*
1de	*nu*			*nu-*	*nuy-*	*nu-*
2d	*mu*			*mu-*	*muy-*	*mu*
3d	*su*	*=sui*	*=suya*	*su-*	*suy-*	*su-*
3t	*sko*	*=skoi*	*=skoya*	*sko-*	*sk-*	*sko-*
1pi	*ko*			*ko-*	*k-*	*ko-*
1pe	*(i)nko*[2]			*(i)nko-*[2]	*(i)nk-*[2]	*(i)nko-*[2]
2p	*mko*			*mko-*	*mk-*	*mko-*
3p anim	*si*	*=si*	*=sya*	*si-*	*s-*	*s-*
3p inan	*na*	*=na*	*=na*	*na-*	*n-*	*n-*

Notes
1 The short form occurs in allegro speech after a preposition ending in a vowel.
2 The forms with initial *i-* occur in careful speech only.
3 The zero prefix is used with stems beginning with a labial consonant: /p, f, m, v/; stem-initial /v/ changes into /b/ in this form.
4 There exist variants with a preceding *d*; these will be discussed below.

agent of the action, or the experiencer of the process or state indicated by the verbal stem. They will consequently be called (subject) agreement markers.

Based on the shape of subject agreement marking on various verbs, three inflectional subsets of pronouns are distinguished: a vocalic type (in which all prefixes end in a vowel), a non-vocalic type (with all prefixes ending in a consonant), and a mixed one. The distribution of these patterns will be discussed in the section on the verb (3.1.3). A survey of all possible personal pronominal forms is presented in Table 28.3.

The third person pronominal forms in their function as articles may be preceded by the formative *an-*, which explicitly indicates that the referent has been discussed previously (to be glossed as OLD (old information)). So alongside *rum=i* 'the house', *rum=sui* 'the two houses', *rum=skoi* 'the three houses', *rum=na* 'the (PL) houses', one has *rum=an-i* 'the mentioned house', *rum=an-na* 'the (PL) mentioned houses', etc. Likewise, *rum=an-ya* 'the house', *rum=an-suya* 'the two houses' and *rum=an-skoya* 'the three houses' are used for the clause-medial forms. Compare the following sentences:

(5) *bin=an-suya   su-fan   snon=an-i*
     woman=OLD-3d.DEF   3d.SBJ-feed   man=OLD-3s.DEF
     'The two women feed the man.'

(6) *snon=an-ya   f-y-an   bin=an-sui*
     man=OLD-3d.DEF -3s.SBJ-feed   woman=OLD-3d.DEF
     'The man feeds the two women.'

3.1.2 Nouns

Nouns refer to entities and are the head of a noun phrase. A noun phrase consists at least of a noun, which may be followed by one or more attributes. Moreover, it may be (and usually is) closed by a marker of definiteness (pronominal article, see Tables 28.3 and 28.10). The exact semantic nature of 'definiteness' in Biak has to be subject to further research (see also 3.3.1).

Biak nouns are either alienable or inalienable. With alienable nouns, possession is expressed by means of independent possessive pronominal forms. Number (singular, dual, trial and plural), and - only in the plural – grammatical gender ('animate' and 'inanimate') are covert categories becoming apparent only from demonstratives, the pronominal articles, (subject) agreement inflection on the verb or other types of pronominal (co-)reference (see Table 28.3).

For semantic and formal reasons alienable nouns are subdivided into names, mass nouns and common nouns. Mass nouns have limited possibilities of being combined with number categories. With plural pronominal reference a mass noun X has to be interpreted as 'a large amount of X'.

Some nouns are inherently plural or dual: *kawasa* '(mass of) people' and *ro fan-fan* (thing RDP-feed) 'cattle' are only plural; the compound *in ve-swa* [ímbeswa] (entity.with.feminine.features REL-spouse) 'husband and wife, couple' is inherently dual.

Names are inherently definite. They do not have separate clause-medial forms of the singular marker for definiteness. Compare the dual forms in (7) and the singular forms in (8):

(7) *ya-mam*   *bin=**sui***   *bin=**suya***   *su-ra-ma*
     1s.SBJ-see   woman=3d.DEF   woman=3d.DEF   3d.SBJ-go-VEN
     'I saw the two women; the two women came.'

     ya-mam   *Maria=**sui**;*   *Maria=**suya***   *su-ra-ma*
     1s.SBJ-see   Mary=3d.DEF   Mary=3d.DEF   3d.SBJ-go-VEN
     'I saw the two Maries; the two Maries came.'

(8) *ya-mam*   *bin=**i**;*   *bin=**ya***   *r-y-a-ma*
     1s.SBJ-see   woman=3s.DEF   woman=3s.DEF   -3s.SBJ-go-VEN
     'I saw the woman; the woman came.'

     ya-mam   *Maria=**i***   *Maria=**i***   *r-y-a-ma*
     1s.SBJ-see   Mary=3s.DEF   Mary=3s.DEF   -3s.SBJ-go-VEN
     'I saw Mary; Mary came.'

Personal names are animate, geographical names inanimate:

(9) *John=i,*   *Petrus=i,*   *Markus=i*   *ma*   *Jack=i*
     J.=3s.DEF   P.=3s.DEF,   M.=3s.DEF   and   J.=3s.DEF
     s-ra-ma
     3p.AN.SBJ-go-VEN
     'John, Petrus, Markus and Jack came.'

(10) *sup*   *Vyak=i,*   *Mansinam=i,*   *Meoswar=i*   *ma*
     land   Biak=3s.DEF   Mansinam=3s.DEF   Meoswar=3s.DEF   and
     sup   *Yapn=i*   *meos*   ***na**-iri*
     land   Yapen=3s.DEF   island   3p.INAN.SBJ-COP
     'Biak, Mansinam, Meoswar and Yapen are islands.'

For other alienable nouns the allocation of gender is less transparent. Most nouns denoting other entities than animals and human beings are inanimate. But a number of nouns denoting entities which in the common European perception would be inanimate are nonetheless grammatically animate in Biak. Examples are *ankray* 'lemon', *asyok* 'spoon', *ben* 'plate', *braw(e)n* 'gold', *fas* 'rice', *katela* 'maize', *kraf* '(piece of) meat', *mak* 'star', *mankok* 'cup', *imbyef* 'banana', *mor* 'seed', *pipi* 'money', *sir(e)f* 'drum', *sus* 'woman's breast', *vrampin* 'finger', *wewur* 'footprint'. A noun like *rar(e)s* 'root' is inanimate when it refers to the root of an inedible plant or tree (e.g. *kor rars=na* 'mangrove roots', *asar rars=na* 'banyan tree roots'), but may be both animate and inanimate *rars=na/rars=si* when it is the root of a *timur* 'cassava', *dyapan* 'taro', *(i)mbyef* 'banana tree' or *baryam* 'sago palm'. It could be that 'animateness' in the early Biak perception of the world comprised also things indispensable for one's livelihood, but this remains to be tested.

Inalienable nouns are subdivided into kinship terms and nouns indicating parts of wholes (including nouns such as *sno-* 'name'). They have obligatory affixes for the 'possessor' (i.e. for kin: the ego, for parts: the whole), for number (singular, dual, trial or plural) and – in the plural – also for grammatical gender (kin belong to the 'animate' nouns, parts of wholes are 'inanimate'). Inalienable nouns are inherently definite.

The different possessive constructions which justify the differentiaton between the alienable and inalienable subclasses of nouns are discussed in section 3.3.2.

3.1.3 Verbs

Verbs typically function as heads of predicates. As such they show the person, number, and gender inflection set out in Table 28.3. The vocalic subset is obligatory for verb stems beginning with a consonant cluster, such as *-frur* 'do', *-mkak* 'fear', *-mran* 'walk', *-kfo* 'shoot with bow and arrow'. Also stems beginning with a *d-* or a semi-vowel require the vocalic subset; examples are *-dis(e)n* 'sing', *-war(e)k* 'hold off'. The non-vocalic affixes are obligatory for verb stems beginning with a vowel, such as *-an* 'eat', *-en(e)f* 'sleep', *-or* 'call', *-un* 'take', *-in(e)m* 'drink'. For stems with a single initial consonant other than *d-* or a semi-vowel the pattern of inflection is unpredictable: *-kaki* 'be high' and *-so* 'follow' have vocalic prefixes, *-kapu* 'defecate' and *-so* 'throw' follow the mixed pattern. Some of those verbs may have forms from both paradigms, apparently without a semantic difference, e.g. *i-kapar* and *k-y-apar* 'she gives birth'. The three patterns are illustrated in Table 28.4: *-kfo* 'shoot' and *-bis(e)r* 'be hungry' illustrate the vocalic pattern, *-an* 'eat' the non-vocalic, and *-ra* 'go' and *-vov* 'sell' the two variants of the mixed pattern.

Most equivalents of English adjectives are verbs in Biak, i.e. they are inflected for subject agreement when they are used predicatively, and they have to be preceded by the prefix *ve-*, glossed as REL ('relative clause marker') when they are used attributively, with only very few exceptions. One of these is *kasun* 'small', as in *snaw kasun* 'small branch', *kavray kasun* 'thin rope'; another one *babo* 'new' in the sense of 'recently acquired/arrived'. In the sense of 'recently produced', however, it requires *ve-* if used attributively:

(11)   *rum=i-wa*   *b-y-abo*
       house=3s-DIST   -3s.SBJ-new
       'That house there is new.'

(12)   *ya-mam*   *rum*   *ve-babo=i*
       1s.SBJ-see house REL-new=3s.DEF
       'I see the new(ly built) house.'

TABLE 28.4: PATTERNS OF VERBAL INFLECTION (SUBJECT AGREEMENT)

	'shoot'	'be hungry'	'eat'	'go'	'sell'
1s	ya-kfo	ya-bis(e)r	y-an	ya-ra	ya-vov
2s	wa-kfo	wa-bis(e)r	w-an	r-w-a	bov²
3s	i-kfo	i-bis(e)r	d-an	r-y-a	v-y-ov
1di	ku-kfo	ku-bis(e)r	kuy-an	ku-ra	ku-vov
1de	nu-kfo	nu-bis(e)r	nuy-an	nu-ra	nu-vov
2d	mu-kfo	mu-bis(e)r	muy-an	mu-ra	mu-vov
3d	su-kfo	su-bis(e)r	suy-an	su-ra	su-vov
3t	sko-kfo	sko-bis(e)r	sk-an	sko-ra	sko-vov
1pi	ko-kfo	ko-bis(e)r	k-an	ko-ra	ko-vov
1pe	nko-kfo	nko-bis(e)r	nk-an	nko-ra	nko-vov
2p	mko-kfo	mko-bis(e)r	mk-an	mko-ra	mko-vov
3p.AN	si-kfo	si-bis(e)r	s-an	s-ra	s-vov
3p.INAN	na-kfo	na-bis(e)r	n-an	n-da¹	n-bov²

Notes
1 After *n-*, the initial /r/ of the verbal stem is replaced by /d/.
2 /v/ is replaced by /b/ in this form, and – because of the preceding nasal – also in the third person plural inanimate.

(13)   *ya-mam*   *rum*   *babo=i*
       1s.SBJ-see   house   new=3s.DEF
       'I saw the new (= recently moved into) house.'

Finally, mention should be made of the existence of transposition, i.e. cases of the use of a nominal root as a verb root by adding the subject agreement affixation. A few examples are: *dom(e)s* 'sweat (n.)', *i-dom(e)s* 's/he sweats'; *asis* 'comb (n.)', *d-asis (vru-ri)* 's/he combs (his/her/its "head")'; *kapu* 'faeces', *k-y-apu* 's/he defecates'; *rum(e)k* 'k.o. seaweed', *r-y-um(e)k* 'he/she/it is green', *rik* 'blood', *i-rik* 1. 'he/she/it bleeds', 2. 'he/she/it is red'; *vos* 'bundle', *v-y-os* 'he/she/it bundles'.

3.1.4 Numerals

Biak has a decimal numeral system. The simple cardinal numerals from 1–9 are *oser* (in allegro speech *eser*), *suru, kyor, fyak, rim, won(e)m, fik, war* and *siw*. Compound numerals are formed with multiples of 1000 *(syaran (oser))*, 100 *(utin (oser))* and/or 10 *(samfur)*, in that order. The numbers 2–9 are always preceded by the linker *di* if the entity counted is mentioned: *samfur di suru* '20 (two tens)', *rum di siw* 'nine houses'. Other numerals, whether simple or complex, follow the entity counted directly: *syaran oser* '1000', *syaran samfur* '10,000', *rum oser* 'one house', *rum utin di siw* '900 houses', *rum syaran di suru* '2000 houses'.

Final simple numerals in complex numerals are preceded by the particle *sesr: samfur sesr oser* '11', *samfur di suru sesr oser* '21', *syaran (oser) sesr samfur* '1010', and with *oser* disambiguating 1011 from 10,001 and 11,000: *syaran oser samfur sesr oser* '1011', *syaran samfur oser sesr oser* '10,001', *syaran samfur sesr oser* '11,000'.

The final unit numbers 2–9 in complex numerals require again the linker *di*, in which case *sesr* may be replaced by *sesn: samfur sesr/sesn di suru* '12', *utin di rim samfur di wonem sesr/sesn di kyor* '563'.

With the exception again of *oser* all cardinal numerals can be prefixed with *ve-* (glossed as QUA 'qualify as, function as, become'), resulting in a verbal stem with the meaning 'become X, functioning as X', which is inflected for subject concord according to the mixed pattern of Table 28.3 (example 14). This stem can be used adverbially in the meaning 'X times' (example 15). With the relativizing prefix *ve-* (see 3.3.4), which is homonymous to *ve-* (QUA), this stem acquires the meaning of an ordinal numeral: 'X-th' (example 16).

(14) *sra=ya*   *i-kpef*   *ra*   *v-y-e-suru*
      coconut=3s.DEF   3s.SBJ-crack   so.that   -3s.SBJ-QUA-two
      'The coconut cracked into two.'

(15) *i-duf*   *ve-suru*   *kwar*
      3s.SBJ-ill   QUA-two   PFV
      'S/he has been ill twice.'

(16) *rum*   *ve-ve-suru*
      house   REL-QUA-two
      'second home'

3.2 Basic clause structure

Biak clauses can be verbal or nominal. Verbal clauses may consist of a single inflected verb, i.e. a verb with subject agreement marking, e.g. *wa-bur* 'you (SG) go away', *sko-bur* 'the three of them go away'.

As indicated above, the subject agreement marker indicates the agent of the action or the experiencer of the process or state indicated by the verbal stem. Its referent will be called the subject of the verb. The term subject (of a given verb form with *third* person agreement marking) will also be used for the referent of a noun phrase, which (1) is coreferent with that subject agreement marker, (2) immediately precedes the verb, and (3) is not intonationally separated from it. Subjects cannot be expressed by independent pronouns. Subject NPs are nearly always definite.

Verbs with a second person subject agreement marker may also be used as imperatives: *wa-bur* 'go away (SG)!', *mu-bur* 'go away you two!'

Verbs may be intransitive, such as *-bur* 'go away', or transitive, such as *-fnap* 'cook' or *-mam* 'see'. A transitive verb is usually followed by an expression for the patient, either a free personal pronoun or a noun phrase. With verbs such as *-mam* 'see' the patient may be a clause itself (as in (19) and (20)).

(17) *ben=ya*   *m-y-am*   *aya*
      pig=3s.DEF   -3s.SBJ-see   1s
      'The pig sees me.'

(18) *ya-mam*   *ben=i*
      1s.SBJ-see   pig=3s.DEF
      'I see the pig.'

(19) *ya-mam*   *ben=ya*   *d-enef*
      1s.SBJ-see   pig=3s.DEF   3s.SBJ-sleep
      'I see that the pig sleeps.'

(20) *ya-mam*   *d-enef*
      1s.SBJ-see   3s.SBJ-sleep
      'I see that s/he sleeps.'

(21) *bin=ya*   *i-fnap*   *ben*   *kraf*
      woman=3s.DEF   3s.SBJ-cook   pig   meat/flesh
      'The woman cooks pork.'

(22) *bin=sya*   *si-fnap*   *ben*   *kraf*
      woman=3p.AN.DEF   3p.AN.SBJ-cook   pig   meat/flesh
      'The women cook pork.'

The order (Subject NP) + Verb + Patient NP is the neutral word order for transitive clauses. It is also possible, however, to topicalize the patient. In that case the patient NP precedes (the Subject NP +) the inflected verb but is still represented by a coreferential independent pronoun in postverbal position, such as in the following examples:

(23) *ben=i-wa*   *ya-mam*   *i*
      pig=3s.DEF-DIST   1s.SBJ-see   3s
      'That pig over there, I see it.'

(24) *ben=an-suya*   *ya-mam*   *su*
      pig=OLD-3d.DEF   1s.SBJ-see   3d
      'The two (mentioned) pigs, I see them.'

(25) *rum=na-wa*   *ya-mam*   *na*
      house=3p.INAN.DEL-DIST   1s.SBJ-see   3p.INAN
      'Those houses over there, I see them.'

Question words are clause-initial. Therefore, if a question concerns the identification of a patient the construction is parallel to the one of the examples (23)–(25): [Patient-NP]$_i$ ± [Subject-NP]$_j$ + [Pron]$_j$-Verb + [Personal Pronoun]$_i$, e.g.:

(26) *man-say*   *O-mam*   *si*
      man-Q   2s.SBJ-see   3p.AN
      'Whom (PL) do you see?'

(27) *ro-say*   *mko-fnap*   *i*
      thing-Q   2p.SBJ-cook   3s
      'What do you (PL) cook?'

Transitive clauses may also convey reflexive and reciprocal meanings simply by using the appropriate pronominal form both in subject and object function:

(28) *ya-mam*   *aya*
      1s.SBJ-see   1s
      'I see myself.'

(29) *si-mam*   *si*
      3p.AN.SBJ-see   3p.AN
      1. 'They$_i$ (PL) see them$_j$ (PL).'
      2   'They (PL) see themselves.'
      3. 'They (PL) see each other.'

(30) *bin=suya*   *su-mam*   *su*
      woman=3d.DEF   3d.SBJ-see   3d
      1. 'The two women see the two of them.'
      2. 'The two women see themselves.'
      3. 'The two women see each other.'

Disambiguation is possible in the preceding examples by means of the marker *yaye* indicating intended reciprocality, and by the stem *mankun-* (*mankund-* before a vowel) '(one)self' for reflexivity. Both forms are followed by the appropriate personal pronouns:

(31) *si-mam*   *yaye*   *si*
      3p.AN.SBJ-see   RCP   3p.AN
      'They (PL) look at each other.'

(32) *ya-mam*   *mankund-aya,*   *mko-mam*   *mankun-mko*
      1s.SBJ-see   self-1s   2p-see   self-2p
      'I see myself, you (PL) see yourselves.'

(33) *bin=suya*   *su-mam*   *mankun-su*
      woman=3d.DEF   3d.SBJ-see   self-3d
      'The two women see themselves.'

Nominal clauses have a nominal predicate which is formed by a nominal stem plus two clitics, the clause-final form of the article (with *-ri-di* for the singular, however), plus a copula which is formally identical to the free pronoun forms (with *s* preceding the 1s and 2s forms, and with *-(i)ri* for the third person). In Table 28.5 the paradigm for 'I am a teacher' – 'they are teachers' is presented. For the third person the forms for 'it is a house' etc. are added in order to provide an instance of an inanimate noun. Note the differences in the expression of number with a third and non-third person subject of the equation.

The forms in the bottom row of Table 28.5 can be preceded by a noun phrase representing the subject of the equation:

(34) *bin=sui-wa*   *kuru=sui=ri*
      woman=3d.DEF-DIST   teacher=3d.DEF=3.COP
      'Those two women are teachers.'

(35) *mov=na-ya*   *rum=na=iri*
      place=3p.INAN.DEF-MED   house-3p.INAN.DEF=3.COP
      'Those spots are houses.'

The copula can also be used after independent personal pronouns and after noun phrases which are already definite, such as an inalienable noun or a noun followed by a possessive pronoun, e.g. *aya=**iri*** 'it's me', *i=**ri*** 'it's him/her', *mam-i=**s-aw*** 'you (SG) are my father', *rum b-e=di=**ri*** 'it is your (SG) house'.

TABLE 28.5: INFLECTION OF NOMINAL PREDICATES (e.g. 'be a teacher')

Person	SG	DU	TR	PL
1 IN		*kuru=si=ku*	*kuru=si=ko*	
1 EX	*kuru=*ri=saya	*kuru=si=nu*	*kuru=si=nko*	
2	*kuru=*ri=saw	*kuru=si=mu*	*kuru=si=mko*	
3 AN	*kuru=*ri=ri	*kuru=sui=ri*	*kuru=skoi=ri*	*kuru=si=ri*
3 INAN	*rum=di=ri*[1]	*rum=sui=ri*	*rum=skoi=*ri	*rum=na=iri*[2]

Notes

1 After *r, y* or a nasal *-ri-* is replaced by *-di-*. The exact phonetic conditions for the variation should be further investigated.

2 Given the form *=iri* after *=na*, it is likely that the final *=ri* in the other forms derives from *=iri*.

There are two more equative constructions. One pattern is juxtaposition which is less frequent and perhaps restricted to constructions involving a name such as *sno-ri Vien* 'her name is Vien', *aya Hein=i* 'I am Hein'. The other pattern employs the copula *iso* (*so* after *-i*). It is said to emphasize the equation and is typical of cleft sentences, in which case it is followed by a relative clause, e.g.

(36) *snon=i-wa*   *iso*   *ve-duf-i*
       man=3s.DEF-DIST   COP.EMPH   REF-ill-3s.DEF
       'That man over there is the one who is ill.'

Both verbal and nominal clauses allow adjuncts which include temporal expressions such as *ras=i-ne* 'this day', *rov-rov* 'every night', *arwo-arwo* 'every morning', adverbials such as *fasaw* 'quickly', *na-bor* (ADV-much) 'profusely', prepositional phrases (see 3.4), and, with equivalents of gradable adjectives, expressions for degree, such as in the following set:

(37) *rum=ya*   *i-ba*   *(kaku)*
       house=3s.DEF   3s.SBJ-big   (real)
       'The house is (very) big.'

(38) *rum=suya*   *su-ba*   *su-mnis*
       house=3d.DEF   3d.SBJ-big   3d.SBJ-be.alike
       'The two houses are equally big.'

(39) *rum=i-wa*   *i-ba*   *syadi*   *(rum=i-ne)*
       house=3s.DEF-DIST   3s.SBJ-big   more   house=3s.DEF-PRX
       'That house is bigger (than this).'

(40) *rum=i-wa*   *i-ba*   *syadi*   *wer*
       house=3s.DEF-DIST   3s.SBJ-big   more   again
       'That house is the biggest.'

Negation is postpositional: *y-enf va* 'I do not sleep', *y-enf vaim* 'I do not sleep yet', *w-enf awer* 'do not sleep!'. Also with transitive verbs:

(41) *d-an*   *(i)mbyef=ya*   *va*
       3s.SBJ-eat   banana=3s.DEF   NEG
       'S/he does not eat the banana.'

(42) *rum=i-ne*   *i-ba*   *va*   *kaku*
       house=3s.DEF-PRX   3s.SBJ-big   NEG   real
       'This house is not big at all.'

With a non-core argument the position of the negation defines its scope:

(43) *d-enf*   *ro*   *di-ne*   *va*
       3s.SG-sleep   LOC   3s.DEF-PRX   NEG
       'He does not sleep here' (but somewhere else).

(44) *d-enf*   *va*   *ro*   *di-ne*
       3s.SG-sleep   NEG   LOC   3s.DEF-PRX
       'He does not sleep here' (but does something else here).

Yes/no questions are marked by intonation and an optional sentence final question marker *ke*, e.g.: *mam aya (ke)?* (2s:see 1s Q) 'do you (SG) see me?'.

Finally I should mention the existence of the sentence final suffix *-e* in dialects other than Sowek. Its distribution is subject to various as yet unclear phonemic and perhaps lexical constraints. Its pragmatic function also needs further investigation. Interestingly, in the dialect of Sowek this suffix has become an infix (occurring also only in the last word of a sentence) through a process of metathesis: *i-du(-e-)f* 's/he is ill' (in other dialects *i-duf-e*).

3.3 NP-structure

3.3.1 Definiteness

Noun phrases in Biak are either generic, indefinite or definite (and specific). Generic NPs lack any formal marker, as illustrated by the bolded expressions in (45) and (46).

(45)   **padamara**   *v-y-uk*   **sananay**
       lamp   -3s.SBJ-give   light
       'Lamps gives light.'

(46)   *padamara=ya*   *v-y-uk*   **sananay**
       lamp=3s.DEF   -3s.SBJ-give   light
       'The lamp gives light.'

Another type of NP that may occur without any marker are unique referents, in spite of their being definite and specific:

(47)   *ya-ra*   *ve*   **swan**
       1s.SBJ-go   DIR   sea
       'I go to the sea (i.e. to fish).'

(48)   *k-y-apu*   *ro*   **rum**   *akyek*
       -3s.SBJ-defecate   LOC   house   toilet
       'He defecates in the toilet.'

Indefinite NPs are marked by *o* 'a (certain)':

(49)   **snon   o**   *sno-ri*   *(i)so*   *Zacharias*
       man   INDEF.SG   name-3s.INAL   COP.EMPH   Zacharias
       Man-so-ben
       Man-spear-pig.
       '(Once upon a time there was) a man whose name was Zacharias Pighunter.'

The following categories of noun phrases are definite: (1) noun phrases ending in a pronominal article (see Table 28.3, and examples throughout this chapter); (2) noun phrases ending in a deictic expression (to be discussed in section 4 below); (3) inalienable nouns (whether or not preceded by a nominal expression for the possessor), e.g. *ben=i-wa vru-ri* (pig=3s.DEF-DIST head-3s.INAL) 'that pig's head' (see 3.1 and the discussion in 3.3.2 hereafter); and (4) noun phrases ending in a possessive pronoun, e.g. *snon=i-wa rum v-y-e=di* (man=3s.DEF-DIST house -3s-POSS-NOLD=3s.DEF) 'that man's house' (for which see 3.3.2).

3.3.2 Possessive constructions

Alienable and inalienable nouns have different types of possessive construction. With inalienable nouns the non-singular agreement marking prefixes of Table 28.3 are used to

TABLE 28.6: INALIENABLE INFLECTION FOR PAIRED BODY
PARTS (e.g. ears)

Person of the possessor	Number of possessor		
	SG		Non-SG
	Number of possessum implicit	Dual number of possessum stressed	
1 and 3	-s-i	-s-su	-s-na
2	-m-s-i	-m-s-su	-m-s-na

indicate person and non-singular number (and for the plural: gender) of the possessor (those of the vocalic pattern if the root begins with a consonant, otherwise those of the consonantal pattern). Absence of a prefix implies singularity of the possessor. A suffix -*m* immediately after the root indicates a second person possessor. Further suffixes mark number (and gender) of the possessum.

There are two types of inalienable nouns: parts of the body and kinship terms. Terms for parts of the body which come in pairs (e.g. ears, eyes, legs) obtain a suffix -*s*. Their endings are given in Table 28.6. Examples are, apart from *mka-s-i* 'my eye(s), his/her/its eye(s)': *knani-m-s-i* 'your (SG) ear(s)', *we-m-s-na* 'your (PL) legs/feet', *vra-s-i* 'my arm(s)/hand(s), his/her/its arm(s)/leg(s)', while also *snoni-s-i* 'my nose, his/her/its nose' follows this pattern.

With paired parts of the body number of the possessum is usually not made explicit. A single possessor has a singular blind eye, even if both his eyes do not function. Only when that latter fact has to be emphasized may a speaker use suffixation for duality of the possessum. Two or more possessors can again only have eyes in plurality. Compare the following sentences/constructions:

(50) *mka-si*   *i-praf*
  eye-SG.INAL   3s.SBJ-blind
  'My/his/her/its eye(s) is/are blind.'

(51) *mka-ssu*   *su-praf*
  eye-DU.INAL   3d.SBJ-blind
  'Both my/his/her/its eyes are blind.'

(52) *su-mka-sna*   *na-praf*
  3d-eye-PL.INAL   3p.INAN.SBJ-blind
  'Their (DU) eyes are blind.'

(53) *si-mka-sna*   *na-praf*
  3p.AN-eye-PL.INAL   3p.INAN.SBJ-blind
  'Their (PL) eyes are blind.'

For single parts of the body the endings for SG and non-SG possession are less predictable. If the root does not contain any *r* the endings are as given in Table 28.7. Examples following this pattern are *sne-ri* 'my/his/her/its belly', *sno-ri* 'my/his/her/its name', *mko-sva-m-na* 'your (PL) mouths', *sasu-ri* 'my/his/her/its throat', *fi-m-ri* 'your (SG) vagina', *su-si-s-na* 'their (DU) penises'.

**TABLE 28.7: INALIENABLE INFLECTION
FOR (SOME) SINGLE PARTS OF THE BODY**

Person of the possessor	Number of the possessum	
	SG	non-SG
1 and 3	-ri	-s-na
2	-m-ri	-m-na

TABLE 28.8: INALIENABLE INFLECTION (SINGLE PARTS OF WHOLES)

Possessor	'belly'	'head'	'back'
1s, 3s	sne-ri	vru-ri	kru-ri
2s	sne-**m-ri**	vru-**m-di**	kru-**m-di**
2d	mu-sne-**m-na**	mu-vru-**m-na**	mu-kru-**m-s-na**
2p	mko-sne-**m-na**	mko-vru-**m-na**	mko-kru-**m-s-na**
1di	ku-sne-s-na	ku-vru-s-na	ku-kru-s-na
1de	nu-sne-s-na	nu-vru-s-na	nu-kru-s-na
1pi	ko-sne-s-na	ko-vru-s-na	ko-kru-s-na
1pe	nko-sne-s-na	nko-vru-s-na	nko-kru-s-na
3d	su-sne-s-na	su-vru-s-na	su-kru-s-na
3t	sko-sne-s-na	sko-vru-s-na	sko-kru-s-na
3p.INAN	si-sne-s-na	si-vru-s-na	si-kru-s-na

However, if the root contains *r* the ending of the second person singular possessor becomes -*m-di* instead of -*m-ri*. For a non-singular second person possessor the ending is unpredictable. It may be -*m-s-na* or -*m-na*. See Table 28.8, in which the paradigms are given for *sne-* 'belly', *vru-* 'head' and *kru-* 'back'. Also for single parts of wholes the subject concord marker is *na-* for non-SG numbers. Compare the following two sentences:

(54)   *sno-ri*   *(i)so*   *Maria*
       name-3s.INAL   COP.EMPH   Maria
       'Her name is Maria.'

(55)   *su-sno-sna*   *na-iso*   *Maria ma Ria*
       3d-name-3p.INAL   3p.INAN.SBJ-COP.EMPH   Maria and Ria
       'Their (DU) names are Maria and Ria.'

For kinship terms there are no constraints on the number of referents which can be 'possessed' by any number of egos: the three of us obviously may have one, two, three or many (classificatory) parents or grandchildren. Person and non-singular number of the 'possessor' (the ego) is again expressed by the agreement marking prefixes of Table 28.3. Absence of a prefix indicates a single ego. The suffix -*m-* immediately after the stem is again the marker of a second person 'possessor'. The final suffixes -*su*, -*sko* and -*si* mark respectively dual, trial and plural number of the possessum (i.e. the kin indicated by the root); for example, for a third person ego with the roots *kpu-* '(classificatory) grandparent/grandchild': *kpu-su*, *kpu-sko*, *kpu-si* 'his/her two/three/more than three (classificatory) grandparents/grandchildren'. For a single kin the suffix is -*i* or -*di* if the root ends in a consonant, -*ri*

TABLE 28.9: PARTIAL PARADIGMS FOR SOME KINSHIP TERMS WITH A SINGULAR EGO

Kin Ego		Classificatory Mother	Classificatory Father	Classificatory Grandparent	Spouse	Sibling of opposite sex
SG	1s	*awin-i*	*(ka)mam-i*	*apus-i*	*swa ye=di*	*srar (y)e=di*
	2s	*sna-m-i*	*kma-m-i*	*kpu-m-i*	*swa-m-ri*	*srar-m-di*
	3s	*sna-ri*	*kma-ri*	*kpu-ri*	*swa-ri*	*srar-di*
DU	1s	*awin-su*	*(ka)mam(i)-su*	*apus-su*	*swa ye=sui*	*srar (y)e=sui*
	2s	*sna-m-su*	*kmam(i)-su*	*kpu-m-su*	*swa-m-su*	*srar-m-su*
	3s	*sna-su*	*kma- su*	*kpu- su*	*swa- su*	*srar- su*

if it ends in a vowel: *srar-di* 'his/her sibling of opposite gender', *kpu-ri* 'his/her grand-child/grandparent'.

The forms for first person possessors show deviating stems and even suppletion (Table 28.9 includes examples in the columns for classificatory mother, father and grandparent), or are replaced by a parallel analytic construction with the independent possessive pronoun (on which see below; Table 28.9 includes examples in the columns for 'spouse' and 'sibling of opposite sex'). Especially the paradigm of classificatory father is irregular, and subject to individual and dialectal variation. In Table 28.9 the paradigms are given for one and two classificatory mothers, classificatory fathers, classificatory grandparents, spouses and siblings of opposite sex of a singular ego.

In contrast to inalienable nouns, alienable nouns need independent pronominal expressions to indicate that what they refer to is the possessum in a possessive construction. These pronominal expressions are built around a root which expresses possession and has a basic shape -*v*- (for the alternants of which see Table 28.10). The expressions furthermore indicate:

- person, number and gender of the possessor (expressed by prefixes, infixes in the inflectional stem, and/or root modification);
- the possessum being presented as old information or not, expressed by the suffixes -*an* (OLD [=old information]), and -*e* (NLOD [=non-old information]), with the usual understanding that for NLOD the referent of the possessum is merely not presented as old information, although it may well be so);
- number and gender of the possessum expressed by the 'pronominal articles' (of Table 28.3) which are marked for clause-final or clause-medial position. The clause final forms of the article may be followed by a string of one to three 'positional' formatives. These include demonstrative and directional formatives and will be discussed in section 4. Table 28.10 illustrates the structure of the possessive pronouns.

The following two sentences are examples of possessive pronouns in clause-final and clause-medial position:

(56) *ya-mam*   *rum*   *mko-v-an=sui*
     1s.SBJ-see   house   2p-POSS-OLD=3d.DEF
     'I see your (PL) two (mentioned) houses.'

(57) *rum*   *b-an=suya*   *su-ba*
     house   2s.POSS-OLD=3d.DEF   3d.SBJ-big
     'Your (SG) two (mentioned) houses are big.'

Table 28.10: STRUCTURE OF THE POSSESSIVE PRONOUNS INCLUDING THE ARTICLES

Possessor (number person, gender)	Possessor + Root -v-	Old information (OLD)	Not old (NOLD)	Possessum (number, gender)	Definiteness marker (article)	
					Clause-final[3]	Clause-medial[3]
1s	(y)-[1]					
2s	b-			SG	=(d)i[2]	=(d)ya[2]
3s	v-y-					
1di	ku-v-					
1de	nu-v-	+	+	DU	=sui	=suya
2d	mu-v-	-an	-e			
3d	su-v-					
3t	sko-v-			TR	=skoi	=skoya
1pi	ko-v-					
1pe	(i)nko-v-[1]			PL.AN	=si	=sya
2p	mko-v-					
3p.AN	s-			PL.INAN	=na	=na
3p.INAN	n(-b)-					

Notes

1 The phonemes in parentheses are only pronounced in careful speech; if the possessum ends in a vowel, y- for the first person SG possessor is obligatory, however.

2 The variants with d- are used after -e NOLD.

3 The difference between 'clause medial' and 'clause final' has been discussed in 3.1.1 and will not be indicated in the glosses of the examples below.

The most common order of a possessive construction in which the possessor is expressed by a noun phrase is *Possessor + Possessum + Possessive Pronominal form*:

(58)   (ya-mam)   snon=ya   rum   v-y-e=di
       1s.SBJ-see   man-3s.DEF   house   -3s-POSS-NOLD-3s.DEF
       '(I see) the house of the man.'

However, the construction *Possessum + Possessor + Possessive Pronoun* also occurs, presumably when the expression for the possessor is not too long, e.g. *rum snon=ya v-y-e=di* 'the man's house'.

In Table 28.9 a partial paradigm was given for some kinship terms. Not all forms are equally likely: 'the three classificatory fathers of the two of you' may not be a daily topic of discourse. For such more complex notions the analytical 'alienable' expressions are preferred: *kma mu-v-e=skoi*, etc.

For all inalienable nouns such analytical alternatives are in fact available: the possessum may be expressed by the inalienable root (which thus is not necessarily a bound form), a morphologically related stem or a (not always transparent) compound, e.g. *srar* alongside *srar-* 'sibling of opposite sex', *snon-snon* alongside *sno-* 'name', *we kor* (leg bone) alongside *we-s-* 'leg(s)', *knani kor* (ear bone) alongside *kani-s-* 'ear(s)', *sne war* (belly water?) alongside *sne-* 'belly', and *vu kor* (head? bone) alongside *vru-* 'head'.

The alienable alternatives have to be used for all inalienables when specification with a demonstrative suffix (59) or another attribute (60) is required:

(59)   vu   kor   b-e=di-**ne**
       head?   bone   2s.POSS-NOLD=3s.DEF-PRX
       'this head of yours (SG)'

(60)   *vu*   *kor*   **ve-ba**   *b-e=di*
        head?   bone   REL-big   2s.POSS-NOLD=3s.DEF
        'your (SG) big head'

In case of parts of wholes the analytic (=alienable) construction has also to be used when
the possessor is some other entity than the whole to which the part belongs (61):

(61)   *vu*   *kor*   *sko-v-e=di*
        head?   bone   3t-POSS-NOLD=3s.DEF
        'their (TR) head (cut off from some animal)'

In other instances of a specific whole both constructions are possible. The analytic construction (62) seems to be possible in all instances, but it is prefered to (63) when the
pig's head is cut off:

(62)   *ben=ya*   *vu*   *kor*   *v-y-e=di*
        pig=3s.DEF   head?   bone   -3s-POSS-NOLD=3s.DEF
        'the pig its head, the head of the pig'

(63)   *ben=ya*   *vru-ri*
        pig=3s.DEF   head-SG.INAL
        'the pig's head' (= the head of the pig).

However, when the whole is not specific 'possession' is not morphologically expressed.
Instead a compound-like construction N + N is used:

(64)   *ben*   *vu*   *kor=i*
        pig   head?   bone=3s.DEF
        'the pig's head' (= the head of a pig)

For parts of wholes only singular and non-singular possessions are distinguished: in (65)
three pigs' heads are discussed, but in the analytical construction the plural clitic =*na* is
used instead of *=*skoi* (see also example (55) above):

(65)   *ben=skoya*   *vu*   *kor*   *sko-v-e=na*
        pig=3t.DEF   head?   bone   3t-POSS-NOLD=3p.INAN.DEF
        'the heads of the three pigs'.

3.3.3 *Relative clauses*

The subject of an intransitive clause can be made the antecedent of a relative clause
with the aid of the relative marker *ve-* according to the following formula:
Noun=DEF + SBJ-Verb$_{intr}$ (+ Adjunct) → Noun + *ve*-Verb$_{intr}$ (+ Adjunct)=DEF, e.g.:

(66)   *rum=ya*   *i-kaki*   →   *rum*   *ve-kaki=i*
        house=3s.DEF   3s.SBJ-high   house   REL-high=3s.DEF
        'The house is high.'   →   'the high house'

(67)   *naf=sya*   *si-mar*   *ro*   *rum=i-ne*
        dog=3p.AN.DEF   3p.AN.SBJ-die   LOC   house=3s.DEF-PRX
        'The dogs died in this house.'

        →   *naf*   *ve-mar*   *ro*   *rum=i-ne=si*
            dog   REL-die   LOC   house=3s.DEF-PRX=3p.AN.DEF
            'the dogs which died in this house'

Similarly with a subject of a transitive clause: Noun=DEF + SBJ-Verb$_{tr}$ + NP$_{patient}$ (+ Adjunct) → Noun + ve-Verb$_{tr}$ + NP$_{patient}$ (+ Adjunct)=DEF. If the patient NP is definite while the adjunct slot is empty, a stack of two DEF markers is the result. In such cases the final definite marker is often preceded by a linker *n-*, the appearance of which seems to be subject to morphological constraints which are still insufficiently understood. Examples in full sentences:

(68)   *naf   su-v-e=dya*   *d-an*   *in*   *ve-paysm=i*
        dog$_i$ 3d-POSS-NOLD=3s.DEF$_i$ 3s.SBJ$_i$-eat   fish$_j$ REL-black=3s.DEF$_j$
        'Their (DU) dog ate the black fish.'

   →   *naf   su-v-e   ve-an   in*
        dog$_i$ 3d-POSS-NOLD   REL-eat   fish$_j$
        ve-paysm=ya=n-ya   *i-mar*   *kwar*
        REL-black=3s.DEF$_j$=LK-3s.DEF$_i$ 3s.SBJ$_i$-die   PFV
        'Their (DU) dog who ate the black fish is already dead.'

(69)   *pankun=ya   r-y-o   nokn=ya   do-ri*
        packet$_i$=3s.DEF$_i$ -3s.SBJ$_i$-LOC   bag$_j$=3s.DEF$_j$ inside-3s.INAL$_j$
        'The packet is inside the bag.'
   →   *pankun   ve-ro   nokn=ya*
        packet$_i$ REL-LOC   bag$_j$=3s.DEF$_j$
        do-ri=n-ya   *i-paysem*
        inside-3s.INAL$_j$=LK-3s.DEF$_i$ 3s.SBJ$_i$-black
        'The packet which is inside the bag is black.'

These examples clearly show the phrase final character of the definiteness marker.

It is possible to leave out the antecedent if the situation or context is sufficiently informative:

(70)   *ve-ark   aya=n-ya   i-mar   kwar*
        REL-bite   1s=LK-3s.DEF   3s.SBJ-die   PFV
        'The one that bit me is already dead.'

Relative clauses with an antecedent other than the subject follow the antecedent paratactically, in which case a DEF marker fills the original position of the antecedent. It corresponds with the antecedent in number and gender and is marked again for clause-medial and clause-final position. The following full sentences are examples of such relative clauses in context.

(71)   *y-an   in   bin=i-wa*   *i-ʃnap=si*
        1s.SG-eat   fish   woman=3s.DEF-DIST   3s.SBJ-cook=3p.AN.DEF
        'I eat the fish (PL) which that woman over there cooked.'

(72)   *in   y-an=ya*   *i-mafen*
        fish   1s.SBJ-eat=3s.DEF   3s.SBJ-tasty
        'The fish I eat is tasty.'

(73)   *ya-mam   rum   mam-i   d-enf   ro=i*
        1s.SBJ-see   house   father-1s.INAL   3s.SBJ-sleep   LOC=3s.DEF
        'I see the house in which my father sleeps.'

(74)   rum   mam-i   d-enf   ro=ya   i-kaki
       house   father-1s.INAL 3s.SBJ-sleep   LOC=3s.DEF 3s.SBJ-high
       'The house in which my father sleeps is high.'

3.4 Prepositional phrases

Noun phrases may be preceded by prepositions. Biak has a limited set of prepositions, the core of which is formed by the comitative-instrumental *kukr*, the locative prepositions *ve* and *ro*, and derivations of the latter, *ma-ro* and *fa-ro*.

Kukr 'with' can be instrumental and comitative:

(75)   r-y-a   ve   yaf   kukr   aya/swa-ri
       -3s.SBJ-go   DIR   garden   with   1s/spouse-3s.INAL
       'He goes to the garden with me/his wife.'

(76)   si-fes   aya   kukr   kavray
       3p.AN.SBJ-bind   1s   with   rope
       'They bound me with a rope.'

Ve indicates that its object (i.e. the following nominal expression) is an intended goal. It is glossed as DIR and translated as 'to, towards, (turning/made) into, (intended) as' and the like.

(77)   ya-ra   ve   sup   vyak=i
       1s.SBJ-go   DIR   land   Biak=3s.DEF
       'I go to Biak.'

(78)   s-y-o   keru=i-ne   ve   (a)ya
       -3s.SBJ-throw   stone=3s.DEF-PRX   DIR   1s
       'He threw this stone at me.'

(79)   d-un   keru=ya   ve   afyak
       3s.SBJ-take   stone=3s.DEF   DIR   cushion
       'He took the stone as a cushion.'

The latter interpretation of *ve* seems to approach the meaning of the verbalizing prefix *ve-* QUA ('qualifying as, function as, become') introduced above (3.1.4). The directional *ve* also seems to be related to the verb *-ve* 'be about to'. But note that while there appear to be semantic links, these three formatives of the shape *ve* have different grammatical properties. *Ve-* QUA is combined with a nominal or numeral stem and is inflected according to the mixed pattern of inflection with – optionally – the particularities of the inflection of the possessive *-v-e* (see Table 28.3 and Table 28.10), whereas *-ve* 'be about to' is inflected according to the vocalic pattern and has to be followed by another inflected verb. Compare (80) and (81):

(80)   v-y-e-man-sar   kwar
       -3s.SBJ-QUA-man-wrong   PFV
       'He has become an old man (already).' (*man-sar* is a compound, see §6)

(81)   man-say   i-ve   v-y-uk   i
       man-Q   3s.SBJ-be.about.to   -3s.SBJ-marry   3s
       'Whom is s/he going to marry?'

Note also that there is yet another formative of the same shape, the passive prefix *ve-*, which is treated in section 5.

Movement away from some entity, as well as being at or in a certain location in space or time is indicated by the preposition *ro*. It is glossed as LOC and translated as 'from, at, in, on'. Its use also covers topics of discourse: 'on, about'.

(82)   *rik=na*   *na-bor*   *na-daf*   *ro*
       blood=3p.INAN.DEF   3p.INAN-many   3p.INAN.SBJ-flush   LOC
       par   *v-y-e=sui*
       wound   -3s-POSS=3d.DEF
       'A lot of blood flushed from his two wounds.'

(83)   *k-y-ain*   *ro*   *saprop*
       -3s.SBJ-sit   LOC   ground
       'He sits on the ground.'

(84)   *k-y-ain*   *ro*   *sup*   *vyak=i*
       -3s.SBJ-sit   LOC   land   Biak=3s.DEF
       'He lives on Biak.'

(85)   *f-y-ar*   *ro*   *ma-ra-ran*   *v-y-e=na*
       -3s.SBJ-tell   LOC   -RDP-walk   -3s-POSS=3p.INAN.DEF
       'He told about his journeys.'

Ma-ro and *fa-ro* are formed from the directional formatives *ma* 'towards the speaker' and *fa* 'away from the speaker/towards the hearer' (see the next section for a more detailed discussion). *Ma-ro* indicates moreover that the object of the preposition is the speaker or some entity near him, whereas *fa-ro* indicates the opposite.

(86)   *su-wos*   *ma-ro*   *aya*
       3d.SBJ-speak   VEN-LOC   1s
       'The two of them spoke to me.'

(87)   *ya-vuk*   *pipi=sya*   *si-bor*   *fa-ro*   *rum*
       1s.SBJ-give   money=PL.AN.DEF   3p.AN-many   AND-LOC   house
       farkor=i-wa
       learn/teach=3s.DEF-DIST
       'I gave a lot of money to that school.'

4 DEMONSTRATIVES AND DIRECTIONALS

Biak demonstrative and directional formatives occur in a wide variety of constructions: adnominal and adverbial, nominal and verbal. Adnominally used demonstrative and directional constructions are combinations of the following formatives, of which (i) and (iii) are obligatory:

(i)   The personal pronouns for the third person (namely the articles of Table 28.3 in their clause final shape), which indicate number, gender and definiteness of the entity whose location is to be specified.

(ii)   Those expressing relative position with respect to the position of the speaker (S): 'in front of S' (*-pon*) ~ 'behind S' (*-pur*); 'above S' (*-yas*) ~ 'below S' (*-vav*), or relative to the position of the speaker and some area of orientation: 'between S and the sea'

(-ra; after -n-: -da) ~ 'between S and the inland' (-re/-de) ~ 'outside the place where S is' (-ri/-di);

(iii) Formatives expressing relative distance from the speaker: 'here (PRX)' (-ne), 'there (MED)' (-i, clause medially -ya), and 'yonder (DIST)' (-wa). The distance for an entity to be qualified as PRX etc. depends on its volume. A distance of 5 meters would qualify a house as being PRX, but a scorpion as DIST.

(iv) Formatives which indicate the direction in which the entity is moving with regard to the position of the speech partners, with the possible values 'towards the speaker (VEN)' (-ma), 'away from the speaker/towards the hearer (AND)' (-fa), and 'not related to the speech situation (GO)' (-ra).

The following combinations occur: (i) + (iii), (i) + (ii) + (iii), (i) + (iii) + (iv). In Table 28.11 the forms are given for all possible combinations for a single entity using the third person singular marker i-. For non-singular numbers the formative i- has to be replaced by sui- (DU), skoi- (TR), and si- (PL.AN) or na- (PL.INAN). Compare: rum=i-ra-ine (house=3s.DEF-seawards-PRX) 'the house here on the sea side', rum=sui-re-wa (house=3d.DEF-landwards-DIST) 'those two houses over there towards the inland', naf=i-wa-ma (dog=3s.DEF-DIST-VEN) 'that dog over there coming towards me', naf=si-ya-fa (dog=3p.AN-MED-AND) 'those dogs (PL) coming in your direction'.

The forms of Table 28.11 for an entity which is not indicated to be moving can be made into the object of a preposition (ro 'in, at', ve 'to') resulting in deictic (place) adverbials, in which case initial i- is preceded by d-, e.g.: ro di-ne 'here', ro di-ra-i 'there towards the sea', ve di-yas-wa 'to yonder place up there'. With the exception of the forms for 'behind S' and 'in front of S' the adverbials indicating a location relative to the position of the speaker may occur without indication of relative distance from the speaker: ro di-yas 'above', ro di-vav 'below', ro di-ra 'between here and the sea', ro di-re 'between here and the inland', ro di-ri 'outside'. The constructions with ro can be made into the head of a clause, in which case ro is inflected like a verb (with the mixed pattern of

TABLE 28.11: ADNOMINALLY USED DEMONSTRATIVES FOR A SINGULAR ENTITY

		Relative distance from the speaker (S)		
		PRX	MED[1]	DIST
Entity is	in the area of S	i-ne	i-i	i-wa
at rest	in front of S	i-pon-ne	i-pon-i	i-pon-wa
	behind S	i-pur-ne	i-pur-i	i-pur-wa
	above S	i-yas-ne	i-yas-i	i-yas-wa
	below S	i-vav-ne	i-vav-i	i-vav-wa
	seawards from S	i-ra-ine	i-ra-i	i-ra-wa
	inland from S	i-re-ine	i-re-i	i-re-wa
	outside where S is	i-ri-ine	i-ri-i	i-ri-wa
moving	towards S (VEN)	i-ne-ma	i-ya-ma	i-wa-ma
	away from S (AND)[2]	i-ne-fa	i-ya-fa	i-wa-fa
	elsewhere (GO)	i-ne-ra	i-ya-ra	i-wa-ra[3]

Notes
1 The forms in this column are clause final forms; in the clause medial forms–i is replaced by–ya.
2 More often than not the implication is 'towards the hearer'.
3 This form also has temporal meaning: ro fyor i-wa-ra (LOC time 3s.DEF-DIST-GO) 'some time ago'.

inflection), e.g. *r-y-o di-ne* (-3s.SBJ-LOC 3s.DEF-PRX) 'he/she/it is here', *s-ro di-pon-wa* 3p.AN.SBJ-LOC 3s.DEF-front-DIST) 'they are over there in front of me', and with the relativizing prefix *ve-*: *rum ve-ro di-pur-wa=na* (house REF-LOC 3s.DEF-back-DIST=3p.INAN.DEF) 'the houses (PL) which are over there behind me'.

Parallel to the deictic forms which adnominally indicate the relative location of an entity with respect to the speaker, Biak has a series of relational space nouns. Three forms are monomorphemic: *do(n)* 'inside (n.)', *bo(n)* 'top, area above', *vav(n)* 'area below'. The other forms are prefixed with *var-/van-* (also *vor-/von-*): *var-pon* 'front', *var-pur* 'backside', *van-da* 'seaside', *van-de* 'landside', *van-di* 'outside (n.)', and also *van-dum* 'inside (of a house and the like)'. They may be preceded by a preposition: *ro do* 'in it, in the middle' (of a given space, e.g. a plate), *ve bo* 'upwards', *ro van-da* 'on the seaside'. These constructions do *not* have to relate to the position of the speaker, which distinguish them from constructions like *ve di-yas* 'upwards from here' and *ro di-ra* 'between here and the sea' which have a purely deictic meaning. The forms with the prefix *var-/van-* can also be combined with the verb *-ra* 'go', *-ra var-X* meaning 'go/walk on the X-side'.

If the entity with regard to which a location has to be specified is mentioned explicitly, a possessive construction is used, based on the relational nouns just discussed. Constructions with a possessive pronoun are possible, e.g. *ro var-pur(y)-e=di* (LOC side-back 1s.POSS-NOLD=3s.DEF) 'at my backside, behind me', *ro van-da mko-v-e=di* (LOC side-seawards 2p-POSS-NOLD-3s.DEF) 'on your (PL) seaside', but with a 'third person' orientation point inalienable alternatives are common (compare 3.3.2). In Table 28.12 the forms for such a third person possessor are given. My data also contain forms such as *bo-m-ri* 'space above you (SG), top of you (SG)' and *vavn-m-ri* 'space under you (SG)', in which *-m-* refers to a second person possessor (see Tables 28.6–28.8) but to what extent complete paradigms are extant has to be subject to further research. Three examples of the use of these inalienable location nouns suffice:

(88)   *rum=ya*   *d-ors*   *ro*   *bon-ya*   *bo-ri*
     house=3s.DEF   3s.SBJ-stand   LOC   mountain-3s.DEF   top-3s.INAL.
     'The house stands on the (top of the) mountain.'

TABLE 28.12: RELATIONAL NOUNS WITH INALIENABLE PRONOMINAL SUFFIXES INDICATING POSITION WITH RESPECT TO A THIRD PERSON ORIENTATION POINT

'the space …	3s	3d	3t	3p.AN	3p.INAN
inside'	*do-ri*	*don-su*	*don-sko*	*don-si*	*don-na*
above' ('the top of')	*bo-ri*	*bon-su*	*bon-sko*	*bon-si*	*bon-na*
below'	*vavn-di*	*vavn-su*	*vavn-sko*	*vavn-si*	*vavn-na*
in front of' na	*var-pon-(d)i*	*var-pon-su*	*var-pon-sko*	*var-pon-si*	*var-pon-*
behind'	*var-pur-i*	*var-pur-su*	*var-pur-sko*	*var-pur-si*	*var-pur-na*
at the seaside of'	*van-da-ri*	*van-da-su*	*van-da-sko*	*van-da-si*	*van-da-na*
at the landside of'	*van-de-ri*	*van-de-su*	*van-de-sko*	*van-de-si*	*van-de-na*
outside'	*van-di-ri*	*van-di-su*	*van-di-sko*	*van-di-si*	*van-di-na*

(89) *rum   ve-ro   bon=suya   bon-su=skoya   sko-ba*
     house   REL-LOC   mountain=3d.DEF   top-3d.INAL=3t.DEF   3t.SBJ-big
     'The three houses on top of the two mountains are big.'

(90) *man   koko=sya   s-kain   ro   rum=ya*
     bird   cuckle=3p.AN.DEF   3p.AN.SBJ-sit   LOC   house=3s.DEF
     vavn-di
     space.below-3s.INAL
     'The chickens stay under the house.'

The set of directional verbs is formed (1) on the basis of the root *-ra* 'go (in an unspec-ified direction)', which is inflected according to the mixed pattern of inflection (see Table 28.3), and (2) on the basis of the root *-(i)s-* 'EXIST, be there (on one's way to/from…)'. With the latter root the relative distance from the speaker has to be expressed, resulting in the derived stems *-(i)s-ne* 'EXIST-PRX', *-(i)s-ya* 'EXIST-MED', and *-(i)s-wa* 'EXIST-DIST'. These verbs have a deviating pattern of subject agreement marking: *a-is-*'1s-EXIST', *aw-s-* '2s-EXIST', *i-s-* '3s-EXIST', *ku-/nu-/mu-/su-is-* '1di-/1de-/2d-/3d-EXIST', *ko-/nko-/mko-/sko-/na-is-* '1pi-/1pe-/2p-/3t-/3p.INAN-EXIST', *si-s-* '3p.AN-EXIST'. In the directional verbs the direction of the movement vis-à-vis the speaker and vis-à-vis another orientation point or area is indicated by the suffixes *-ma* or *-m-* VEN, *-fa* or *-f-* AND, and *-r-* or *-n-* GO (direction not related to the speech situation). The suffixes for the secondary orientation point or area are the already familiar ones, with the addition of *-rum* (after *-n-*: *-dum*) for 'inside (the house)' (cf. the noun *rum* 'house'). (91a–c) are examples of such directional verbs.

(91a) *ya-ra-f-rum*
     1s.SBJ-go-AND-house
     'I go into the house (where you are).'

(91b) *aw-s-wa-n-da*
     2s.SBJ-EXIST-DIST-GO-seawards
     'You (SG) were over there on your way in the direction of the sea (where you and I are not).'

(91c) *mko-is-ya-m-ra*
     2p-EXIST-MED-VEN-seawards
     'You (PL) are on your way towards the sea (where I am).'

All the suffixes and suffix combinations of the directional verbs may be preceded by the formative *mu-*, resulting in directional adjuncts. *Mu-* evokes a picture of duration and a trajectory and is consequently obligatory if the place from where the movement started is mentioned explicitly; below it will be glossed as PATH. In Table 28.13 the relevant forms are listed. (92)–(95) are examples of adjuncts with *mu-*:

(92) *r-y-a   mu-m-rum*
     -3s.SBJ-go   PATH-VEN-house:
     'S/he comes (from somewhere) into the house.'

TABLE 28.13: SPECIFICATION OF DIRECTION WITH -ra- 'GO'

'go'	'towards the speaker' (VEN)	'away from the speaker' (AND)	'in a direction not related to the speech situation' (GO)
unspecified as to secondary orientation	(mu)-ma	(mu)-fa	– [zero]
'up'	(mu)-m-yas	(mu)-f-yas	(mu)-r-yas
'down'	(mu)-m-bav	(mu)-f-vav	(mu)-r-vav
'to the front'	(mu)-m-pon	(mu)-f-pon	(mu)-r-pon
'to the back'	(mu)-m-pur	(mu)-f-pur	(mu)-r-pur
'seawards'	(mu)-m-ra	(mu)-f-ra	(mu)-n-da
'landwards'	(mu)-m-re	(mu)-f-re	(mu)-n-de
'outside'	(mu)-m-ri	(mu)-f-ri	(mu)-n-di
'inside'	(mu)-m-rum	(mu)-f-rum	(mu)-n-dum

(93) r-y-o   pasar=ya   mu-f-re
      -3s.SBJ-LOC   market=3s.DEF   PATH-AND-landwards
      'S/he went from the market inland to you.'

(94) d-ek   mu-r-yas
      3s.SBJ-climb   PATH-GO-above
      'S/he climbs (all the way) to the place up there.'

(95) ya-ra   mu-f-rum
      1s.SBJ-go   PATH-AND-house
      'I go (from where I am) to you (who are) inside the house.'

5 MAJOR VERBAL DERIVATIONS

Many transitive and intransitive verb roots can be prefixed with the prefix -ak- 'also be X-ing, join in X-ing'. Some examples are:

(96) y-an   'I eat'   y-ak-an   'I join in eating'
      y-en(e)f   'I sleep'   y-ak-en(e)f   'I sleep too'
      y-in(e)m   'I drink'   y-ak-in(e)m   'I join in drinking'
      ya-fnak   'I play'   y-ak-fnak   'I join in a/the game'
      ya-mrif   'I laugh'   y-ak-mrif   'I join in the laughter'
      ya-kan(e)s   'I cry'   y-ak-kan(e)s   'I cry too'
      ya-prer   'I hit'   y-ak-prer   'I also hit'

Suffixation of -ep(e)n derives transitive verbs with the implication of increased effort (often from an already transitive root). The process does not seem to be productive. Some examples are:

(97) -fas   'write'   -fas-ep(e)n   'note down'
      -kar   'break, cut down' -kar-ep(e)n   'clear (garden)'
      -kin   'hold'   -kin-ep(e)n   'squeeze'
      -mam   'see, look at'   -mam-ep(e)n   'not lose sight of'
      -swar   'think'   -swar-ep(e)n   'remember'
      -var(e)k   'lie down'   -vark-ep(e)n   'hatch'

More conspicuous are the complex patterns of partial reduplication. Verb stems are subject to the patterns of partial reduplication discussed in 2.2. The same patterns derive other verb stems and nouns. With action verbs the derived nouns tend to be action nouns, with stative verbs the derived nouns usually denote the abstract quality ('X-ness, the being X'). In 2.2 some examples have been presented; in (98) more examples of such derivations are given. The derived verbs have a durative meaning (seen in the examples in (99)).

(98)

-duf	'be ill'	*daf-duf*	'illness'
-mar	'die'	*mar-mar*	'death'
-bis(e)r	'be hungry'	*bas-bis(e)r*	'hunger, famine'
-kun	'burn'	*kan-kun*	'burning' (n.)
-fas	'write'	*fas-fas*	'writing' (n.)
-an	'eat'	*an-an*	'eating' (n.)
-op(e)r	'jump'	*ap-op(e)r*	'jumping' (n.)
-sar	'be wrong'	*sa-sar*	'mistake, sin'
-mkak	'be afraid'	*ma-ka-kak*	'fear'
-faryor	'ask'	*fa-ra-ryor*	'request'
-pyum	'be beautiful'	*pa-yam-yum*	'beauty'
-myar(e)n	'be diligent'	*ma-yar-yar(e)n*	'diligence'

(99)

-an	'eat'	*-an-an*	'have a meal, be eating'
-duf	'be ill'	*-daf-duf*	'be ill all the time'
-fas	'write'	*-fas-fas*	'be writing'
-op(e)r	'jump'	*-ap-op(e)r*	'jump up and down'
-mun	'kill'	*-ma-mun*	'go on a head-hunting raid'
-masi	'bathe'	*-ma-sa-si*	'be bathing'
-vor(e)s	'row'	*-va-vor(e)s*	'go on a distant rowing trip'
-frur	'make, do'	*-fa-ra-rur*	'work'

So far it is not clear whether there are semantic correlates for the various patterns of reduplication. More than one pattern may occur with the same stem. From *-mran* 'walk' for instance the following reduplicated forms are found: *ma-ra-ran* 'journey', and (with $r > d$ after *n*) *ma-ran-dan* 'walk' (n.).

The patterns discussed in 2.2 are not exhaustive. There appear to be various lexically conditioned deviations, such as

(100)

-fakfo	'disappointed'	*fa-fakfo*	'disappointment'
-faya	'tell'	*fa-faya*	'story'
-ankar	'deceive'	*an-kar-kar*	'deceit'
-vak	'pay'	*va-v-y-ak*	'payment'
-var	'twine'	*va-v-y-ar*	'twining'

Reduplicated verbs from transitive verb stems are detransitivized (compare 101a and 101b):

(101a)   *ya-kun   ben   kraf*
         1s.SBJ-burn   pig   meat/flesh
         'I burn pork.'

(101b)   *ya-kan-kun*
         1s.SBJ-RDP-burn
         'I cook food, I do the cooking.'

However, whereas the durative verb is detransitivized by the reduplication, the corresponding reduplicated action noun can still be followed by the patient NP:

(102) *an-an*   *ben*   *kraf*   *i-vye*   *va*
       RDP-eat   pig   meat/flesh   3s.SBJ-good   NEG
       'Eating pork is bad.'

(103) *fak-fukn*   *ar-arem*   *fa-ro*   *bin=i-ne*   *i-ba*
       RDP-ask   RDP-betroth AND-LOC   woman=3s.DEF-PRX   3s.SBJ-big
       kaku
       real
       'The brideprice asking for this woman is very high.'

Biak has an agentless passive, formed with the double prefix *ve-ve-*. The single prefix *ve-* is found with a passive meaning in some compounds, such as *ro ve-an* (thing PASS-eat) 'food'. The outer prefix *ve-* is inflected for subject agreement in the same way as the inflectional stem of the possessive pronoun *v-e-* (see Table 28.10), with the exception of the first person singular (which is *ya-ve-*), and with more regular alternatives for the 3p forms (*s-ve-*, *n-be-* alongside *s-e-* and *n-e-*):

(104) *inari*   *ben=sya*   *s-(v)eve-an*
       FUT   pig=3p.AN.DEF   3p.AN.SBJ-PASS-eat
       'The pigs will be eaten.'

(105) *war=ya*   *v-y-eve-inm*   *kwar*
       water=3s.DEF   -3s.SBJ-PASS-drink   PFV
       'The water has already been drunk.'

(106) *san-sun*   *b-e-na*   *n-(b)eve-pap*
       RDP-wear   2s.POSS-OLD-3p.INAN   3p.INAN.SBJ-PASS-wash
       'Your (SG) clothes (PL) are washed.'

This outer prefix *ve-* is probably related to the prefix *ve-* QUA discussed in 3.1.4. and 3.4: *si-pyoper* (3s.AN.SBJ-white) 'they are white', *s-(v)e-pyoper* (3s.AN.SBJ-QUA-white) 'they become white'. Some examples with nominal stems are:

(107) *ya-ve-pandeta*
       1s.SBJ-QUA-minister
       'I function as a minister, I am a minister.'

(108) *ino=ya*   *v-y-e-rik*
       knife-3s.DEF   -3s.SBJ-QUA-blood
       'The knife is stained with blood.'

(109) *ayar=ya*   *v-y-e-syos*
       fence=3s.DEF   -3s.SBJ-QUA-layer/generation
       'The fence is double.'

Apart from the patterns of derivation discussed so far, there are some remnants of petrified forms.

One example has already been mentioned: *-m-kak* 'fear, be afraid' vs. *-fa-kak* 'frighten' with a petrified causative prefix. I have not come across other cases of morphologically derived causatives. The usual way to form causatives is with the aid of the verb *-frur* 'do, make'. Compare *ya-kan(e)s* 'I cry' and *kan-kan(e)s* 'crying' (n.) with:

(110)   *i-frur*   *fa*   *ya-kan(e)s*
        3s.SBJ-do   in.order.to   1s.SBJ-cry
        'S/he makes me cry.'

(111)   *i-frur*   *kan-kan(e)s*
        3s.SBJ-do   RDP-cry
        'S/he causes crying', 'S/he is pitiful.'

(112)   *i-frur*   *kan-kans*   *aya*
        3s.SBJ-do   RDP-cry   1s
        'S/he made me feel sorry.'

Another example concerns the unproductive 'joint action' prefix *far-*, found in *-far-vuk* 'marry each other' (presumably from *-vuk* 'give') and *far-vak-vuk* 'marriage'.

6 COMPOUNDING

Nominal compounds may consist of a sequence of two nouns, or of a noun and a verbal stem; in some cases the components are linked by the relative clause marker *ve-*.

There are three basic types of semantic relations between the constituent nouns ($N_1 + N_2$) of a Noun-Noun compound:

1 'N_2 part of N_1', e.g. *ben kraf* (pig meat/flesh) 'pork', *ay knam* (tree trunk) 'tree trunk';
2 'N_1 originating from N_2', e.g. *wos vyak* (word/language Biak) 'the Biak language', *ro war* (thing water) 'eel', or 'N_1 made of N_2', e.g. *korwar braw(e)n* (ancestor.statue gold) 'golden ancestor statue'; and
3 'N_1 of the N_2 type', e.g. *ben bin* (pig woman) 'sow', *kuru bin* (teacher woman) 'female teacher', *naf snon* (dog man) 'male dog'.

Many compound nouns consist of a noun followed by a verbal stem (N + V), in which the noun acts as an argument of the verb and can be actor/instrument, experiencer, location or patient or, in the case of a verbal stem indicating a quality, that quality. Examples: *ay* 'tree, wood' + *-kara* 'measure' → *ay kara* 'ruler'; *ro* 'thing' + *-ma-mun* 'killing' → *ro ma-mun* 'weapon'; *romawa* 'boy' + *-farkor* 'teach, learn' → *romawa farkor* 'schoolboy'; *ay* 'tree, wood' + *-kun* 'burn' → *ay kun* 'smoldering log'; *rwa* 'arm, hand' + *-sar* 'wrong' → *rwa sar* 'left hand'; *bin* 'woman' + *-sar* 'wrong' → *bin sar* 'old woman'; *rum* 'house' + *-kan-kun* 'cook food' → *rum kan-kun* 'kitchen'; *rum* + *-farkor* 'teach, learn' → *rum farkor* 'school'; *ro* 'thing' + *-fan* 'feed' → *ro fan* 'domestic animal, dog'; *ro* 'thing' + *-ka-k(e)r* 'planting' → *ro ka-k(e)r* '(planted) plant/tree'.

If the verbal stem of the compound is transitive the compound may even be extended with a noun indicating the patient of the verb:

(113)   *man* 'bird, entity with male features' + *-kar* 'cut down' + *wa* 'proa'
            →   *man kar wa* 'pick axe, hoe'
        man + *-kaw-ep(e)n* 'clasp' + *san-sun* 'clothes'
            →   *man kaw-epn san-sun* 'clothes-peg'

Nominal compounds may also consist of a noun followed by a verb stem with the relative clause marker *ve-*. Some examples are:

(114) *man* + *ve-* + *-sak* 'flame'   → *man ve-sak* [mambesák] 'yellow bird of paradise'

    in 'fish, entity with female features' + *ve-* + *-ris* → *in ve-ris* [imberís] 'make frightening noises as ghosts do'   'k.o. mollusc'

    war 'water' + *ve-* + *-ki* 'flow' → *war ve-ki* 'river'

    ro 'thing' + *ve-* + *-rok* 'make noise' → *ro ve-rok* 'k.o. drum'

    ro + *ve-* + *-frar* 'run' → *ro ve-frar* 'mouse'

As was discussed in the previous section, *ve-* may form a passive stem when prefixed to a transitive verbal base. This derived stem appears in nominal compounds, in which the nominal head is the patient of the action indicated by the verb, such as in:

(115) *in* + *ve-kin* 'be-seized' → *in ve-kin* 'daughter-in-law'

    man + *ve-kin* 'be-seized' → *man ve-kin* 'son-in-law'

    ro + *ve-an* 'be-eaten' → *ro ve-an* 'food'

    ro + *ve-na* 'be-owned' → *ro ve-na* 'possession'

A final type of compound is formed on the basis of *man* and *in* and the root of a kinship term prefixed with *ve-*. The kinship term denotes a symmetric family relationship, the compound two people having such a relationship, e.g.

(116) *in* + *ve-* + *-kpu* 'kin two generations up or down'
    → *in ve-kpu* 'grandmother and grandchild'

(117) *man* + *ve-* + *-kpu* 'kin two generations up or down'
    → *man ve-kpu* 'grandfather and grandchild'

(118) *in* + *ve-* + *-swa* 'spouse'
    → *in ve-swa* 'couple, man and wife'
    (a parallel form with *man* does not occur)

Compounds with *ro* 'thing', and with *man* 'entity with male features, bird' and *in* 'entity with female features, fish' are rather frequent. Those with *ro* refer to things, plants and some animals. Those with *man* and *in* may also refer to entities other than birds, fish or human individuals. This suggests a rudimentary gender system, which may have emerged through contact with certain West Papuan Phylum languages which have a fully fledged gender system along comparable lines.

ACKNOWLEDGEMENTS

I am grateful to my informant Zacharias Sawor for his always cheerful and enthusiastic help, and also to Vien Sawor, Ellen Paardekooper, Michael Cysouw, and Dries van den Elzen, without whose active participation in the Biak fieldwork course at Nijmegen University (1999–2000) this chapter could not have been written. Needless to say, the responsibility for the formulation and interpretation of our findings are mine. I also wish to thank the editors of this volume for their detailed and useful comments on an earlier version of this chapter.

REFERENCES

Blust, R.A. (1978) 'Eastern-Malayo-Polynesian: a subgrouping argument', in S.A. Wurm and L. Carrington (eds) *Second International Conference on Austronesian Linguistics, Proceedings, Fascicle I. Western Austronesian*, 181–234, Canberra: Pacific Linguistics.

——(1993) 'Central and Central-Eastern Malayo-Polynesian', *Oceanic Linguistics* 32/2:241–293.

Hasselt, F.J.F. van (1905) *Spraakkunst der Nufoorsche Taal*, Den Haag: Martinus Nijhoff.

Hasselt, J.L. van (1868) *Allereerste beginselen van de Papoesch-Mafoorsche taal*, Utrecht: Kemink & Zoon.

——(1876) *Beknopte spraakkunst der Nufoorsche taal*, Utrecht: Kemink & Zoon

——(1876/1893) *Hollandsch-Noefoorsch en Noefoorsch-Hollandsch woordenboek*, Utrecht: Kemink & Zoon.

——(1908) 'Numfoorsche fabelen en vertellingen', *Bijdragen tot de Taal-, Land- en Volkenkunde van Nederlandsch-Indië* LXI:477–588.

Hasselt, J.L. van, and Hasselt, F.J.F van (1947) *Noemfoorsch Woordenboek uitgegeven onder auspiciën van Het Nieuw-Guinea Studie-Comité en het Koninklijk Instituut voor de Taal-, Land- en Volkenkunde te 's-Gravenhage*, Amsterdam: De Bussy.

Jens, W.L. (1883) *Soerat FarkoorWasja faro romawa farkoor ro Soep Papoewa*, Utrecht: Kemink & Zoon.

Kern, H. (1885) 'Over de verhouding van het Nufoorsch tot de Maleisch-Polynesische talen', *Verspreide Geschriften* 6:35–76, 's-Gravenhage: Nijhoff.

Kijne, I.S. (1950) *Surat Wasja: kitab batjaan bahasa Biak*, 2nd edn, Groningen: Wolters.

Ottow, W. (1862) 'Woordenlijst der te Doreh en omstreken gesproken wordende Myfoorsche (Noemfoorsch, Mafoorsch, Nufoorsch etc.) taal', *Nieuw-Guinea 1862*: 201–233, Amsterdam: Fred Muller.

Patz, F. (1978) 'The case marking and role coding system of Numfoor Biak', *Oceanic Linguistics* 7/2:141–161.

Soeparno (1977) *Kamus bahasa Biak-Indonesia*, Jakarta: Pusat Pembinaan dan Pengembangan Bahasa.

Steinhauer, H. (1985) 'Number in Biak: counter-evidence to two alleged language universals', *Bijdragen tot de Taal-, Land- en Volkenkunde* 141:462–485.

LANGUAGE INDEX

This index includes names of languages and dialects. For dialects, the language they belong to is given in parentheses.

SUBJECT INDEX

The numbers in *italics* refer to the illustrations.